PEÑÍNGUIDE
TO
SPANISH
WINE

www.guiapenin.com

© PI&ERRE

All rights reserved. No part of this publication may be reproduced, stored in a retrieval system, or transmitted, in any form or by any means, without the prior permission in writing of PI&ERRE.

Team:

Director: Carlos González
Editor in Chief: Javier Luengo
Tasting team: Carlos González, Javier Luengo and Pablo Vecilla
Texts: Javier Luengo and Carlos González
Database manager: Erika Laymuns
Advertising: Mª Carmen Hernández
Cover design, layout and desktop publishing: Raul Salgado and Luis Salgado
Supervising editor: José Peñín

PUBLISHED BY: PI&ERRE
Santa Leonor, 65 - Edificio A - Bajo A
28037 – MADRID
SPAIN
Tel.: 0034 914 119 464 - Fax: 0034 915 159 499
comunicacion@guiapenin.com
www.guiapenin.com

ISBN: 978-84-95203-96-0
Copyright library: M-23139-2013
Printed by: Gamacolor
Translation: John Mullen Connelly

DISTRIBUTED BY: GRUPO COMERCIAL ANAYA
Juan Ignacio Luca de Tena, 15
Tel: 0034 913 938 800
28027 MADRID
SPAIN

DISTRIBUTED BY: ACC PUBLISHING GROUP
Antique Collector's Club Ltd.
Sandy Jane, Old Martlesham
Woodbridge, Suffolk
IP12 45D, United Kingdom

...CS DEL PENEDÈS (DO PENEDÈS)   MILMANDA (DO CONCA DE BARBERÀ)   PRIORAT (DOQ PRIORAT)

DELIGHT IN A DAY *of experiences*
DISCOVER BODEGAS TORRES.

For more information:
Tel. 93 817 75 68 / 93 817 74 87
reservas@torres.es

TORRES

1870

www.clubtorres.com
www.facebook.com/bodegastorres

Reaching the
10.000 mark

You are Reading the twenty-fourth edition of the most complete guide to Spanish wines in the world as regards the number of wineries and brands referred to and, more importantly, the wines tasted. We never give up repeating that this guide is not intended to create dogma, our intention is to offer a consulting tool for professionals and consumers and, that the points are not a decisive factor but rather an aid to choose a brand.

Again our team of tasters (page 6) packed their suitcases and travelled throughout Spain in order to taste the wines in context and together with other similar wines so as to present the wine growing novelties coming onto the market in 2014. The work was hard but exciting and involved approximately 1,300 brands.

For the first time the Guía Peñín went beyond the barrier of 10,000 wines tasted, a genuine landmark for this firm and is a response to the adaptation of the wineries to the increase in exports, to the crisis and stagnation of consumption by the domestic market, and, we should also point out that it is due to the increased confidence of the wine producers in the evaluation system of the Guía Peñín and its increased relevance in international markets.

Moreover, the well-known development of winery technology and the perfecting of the production systems, which have enabled generalized improvement of Spanish wine over the last five years. We have now fully entered the era of the vineyard. We have verified how the producers have improved their interpretation of the grape maturing processes. Thus, the decline of the personality of the variety due to delaying the grape harvest in search of colour, maturity and alcoholic level, as was done by the Spanish wineries until now, is prevented. This personality which is transferred by the vine, the climate and the soil is the grand value of the wine.

The inevitable evolution/revolution which was begun some time ago by those who are the best Spanish winery owners today (see The Podium of this year) and little by little is affecting a growing number of wineries with a domino effect. The coming years will be splendid for the profession and for the consumer, who will be able to experience this evolution through the wine. We can assert that that never in the history of Spain have the wines had the quality and diversity that they have today.

The spectacular decision to decide for the native varieties in all the production areas contributes to enriching the extensive stylistic range of Spanish wines. It should be said that this interest in native strains did not mean that important winery owners and wine producers gave up the rich legacy of foreign varieties which have fused with the terrain over the years.

Finally, there are a few recommendations. Before comparing the scores of the wines from each area, it is very important to read the comments and the classification of the harvests in the text of each Denominación de Origen, which will enable the reader to better understand the evaluations of the wines. The relation of the wine with its with its price-quality must also be taken into account as this is a tool which makes it possible to enjoy superb wines at inexpensive prices (this is available in the Spanish version as it is difficult to specify the sale price in third countries).

TEAM

Carlos González Sáez (Director)
cgonzalez@guiapenin.com

Born in Avila in 1979, Carlos Gonzalez is an Agricultural Engineer (University of Salamanca), with Masters in Enology and Viticulture (Torras and Associates) and a Masters in Wine Business Management (IE Business School). After practicing as a winemaker and vineyard technician, he undertook work as technical director for The Vintages of Spain. For the last seven years he has headed the Technical Department of the Peñin Guide, responsible for the coordination of staff assignments and development of wine tastings that appear in the various guides under the Peñin group.

Javier Luengo (Editor in Chief and taster)
jluengo@guiapenin.com

Born in Castellón de la Plana in 1976, Javier Luengo graduated with a degree in Journalism from the Universidad Complutense of Madrid and is also qualified in Integral Communications, University Francisco de Vitoria. After working as a journalist in different media agencies and publications, he joined the communication department of IP & ERRE as account director. Javier has been a professional taster for the Peñin team for five years, both wines and distillates. He is currently responsible for the different editorial publishing products covered by the Peñin Guide.

Pablo Vecilla (Taster)
pvecilla@guiapenin.com

Born in Madrid in 1985, Pablo studies agricultural technical engineering at the Polytechnic University of Madrid. He has been head of the Cultural Association of La Carrasca, an entity that promotes wine culture in the university, which was also under his responsibility during 2008 and 2009. Pablo joined the Peñin tasting team in 2010. He currently operates the tasting courses organized by the Peñin Tasting School.

ACKNOWLEDGMENTS

To all the **Consejos Reguladores** that have so readily collaborated with the Guide, providing their buildings and professional staff to make the tastings possible. In other cases it was not their fault but problems on our part that did not make them happen in the end. We have to thank also –and very especially– **José Matás** from **Enoteca Casa Bernal**, in El Palmar (Murcia); **Juan Luis Pérez de Eulate** from **La Vinoteca**, a wine shop in Palma de Mallorca; Quim Vila from **Vila Viniteca**, a wine shop in Barcelona; **Casa del Vino La Baranda** from El Sauzal, and particularly **José Alfonso González Lorente**, as well as the **Casa del Vino of Gran Canaria; the Parque Tecnológico del Vino (VITEC)**, in Falset (Tarragona), and **Vinatería Pámpano** in Almendralejo (Badajoz).

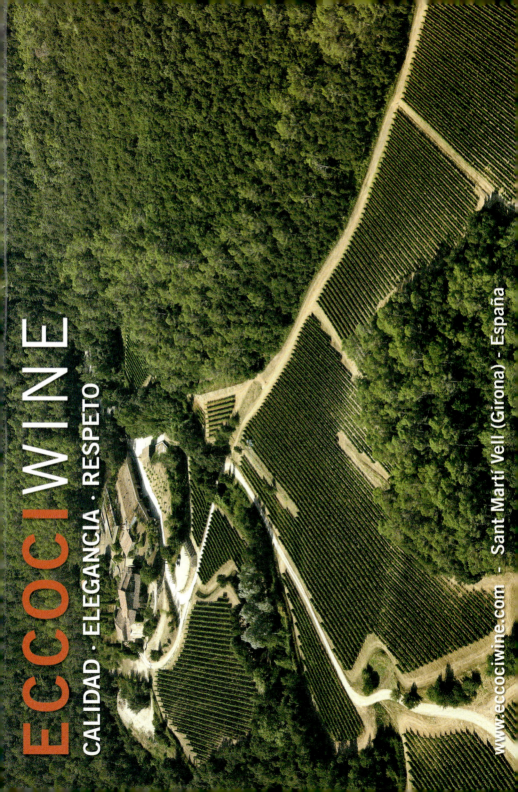

ECCOCI WINE

CALIDAD · ELEGANCIA · RESPETO

www.eccociwine.com - Sant Martí Vell (Girona) - España

SUMMARY

EXCEPTIONAL WINES

Each year, the tasting of more than 10,000 wines provides us with a select group of brands which, due to their high scores, become part of the "exceptional wines" (Page 22) of the Guía Peñín. These are the wines which achieve 95 points and more, which come near to sensorial perfection and become essential references for those seeking wines throughout the world. Each one of these wines can be considered to be the portrait of a specific moment in time, from a particular soil, just like enclosing a moment in time in a bottle in order to enjoy it years later.

The approximately 200 highest scoring wines on this Podium have passed a double "exam" each year. One was the tasting of the wine carried out by each Regulating Board together with similar wines. The other process is the so-called Second Tasting of the Guía Peñín. This second tasting is now a ritual in this firm and is repeated annually in the month of July as a failsafe counter-analysis. I is carried out behind closed doors and our tasters hone the scoring of the wines, which, above 94 points, becomes a task involving millimetres.

The wines are positioned by score, style, variety, harvest and zones over a number of month. Each one of these wines has its glass in front so that after an organoleptic examination and a comparison with wines which have a similar style and scoring, it is possible determine whether the wine in question may rise, keep its initial score or drop if its quality does not settle at the level of the others. The possible improvement of the wine is the result of it improving over the possible tables, 94, 95, 96, 97, 98 in order to guarantee its splendid qualities as regards wines with higher scores so that it it finally perfectly fits one of these tables and obtains a definitive score. This is the fairest and most analytic way for a wine to achieve a high score.

Therefore, we invite you to let yourself be seduced by this exquisite world of grand Spanish wines, a podium which shows what a grand wine can achieve in each of its types.

The triumph of the soil and the vine over technological wines. The knowledge transmitted from grandparents to parents and from those to their children and so on.

EXCEPTIONAL WINES (SWEET WINES AND GENEROSOS)

POINTS	WINE
98	Alvear PX 1830 PX Reserva
98	La Bota de Palo Cortado nº 41 "Bota NO" PC
97	Casta Diva Reserva Real 2002 B Reserva
97	Gonzalez Byass Añada 1982 PC
97	Molino Real 2009 B
97	Osborne Solera BC 200 OL
97	Venerable VORS PX
96	Allende Dulce 2009 B
96	Colección Roberto Amillo Palo Cortado PC
96	Don Gonzalo VOS OL
96	Jorge Ordóñez & Co. Nº3 Viñas Viejas 2008 B
96	La Bota de Manzanilla (Bota nª 42) MZ
96	La Cañada PX
96	Oloroso Tradición VORS OL
96	Osborne AOS AM
96	PX Navazos Gran Solera. Saca Mayo 2013 PX
96	Recóndita Armonía 1987 Fondillón
96	Reliquia AM
96	Reliquia PX
96	Solera Su Majestad VORS OL
96	Tostado de Costeira 2007 B
95	Advent Samso Dulce Natural 2010 RD
95	Amontillado del Duque VORS AM
95	Barbadillo Amontillado VORS AM
95	Casa del Inca 2011 PX
95	Casta Diva Esencial 2012 B
95	Chivite Colección 125 2010 BFB
95	Chivite Colección 125 Vendimia Tardía 2009 B
95	Colección Roberto Amillo Amontillado AM
95	Colección Roberto Amillo Oloroso OL
95	Colección Roberto Amillo Pedro Ximénez PX
95	De Muller Garnacha Solera 1926 Solera
95	El Grifo Canari Dulce de Licor B

EXCEPTIONAL WINES (SWEET WINES AND GENEROSOS)

TYPE	D.O.	PAGE
GENEROSO	Montilla-Moriles	333
GENEROSO	Jerez	252
BLANCO DULCE	Alicante	38
GENEROSO	Jerez	253
BLANCO DULCE	Málaga y Sierras de Málaga	308
GENEROSO	Jerez	249
GENEROSO	Jerez	249
BLANCO DULCE	Rioja	663
GENEROSO	Jerez	253
GENEROSO	Jerez	256
BLANCO DULCE	Málaga y Sierras de Málaga	309
GENEROSO	Jerez	252
GENEROSO	Montilla-Moriles	338
GENEROSO	Jerez	250
GENEROSO	Jerez	248
GENEROSO	Jerez	252
GENEROSO	Alicante	38
GENEROSO	Jerez	245
GENEROSO	Jerez	245
GENEROSO	Jerez	256
BLANCO DULCE	Ribeiro	491
ROSADO	Penedès	401
GENEROSO	Jerez	253
GENEROSO	Jerez	244
GENEROSO	Montilla-Moriles	336
BLANCO DULCE	Alicante	38
BLANCO DULCE	Navarra	378
BLANCO DULCE	Navarra	378
GENEROSO	Jerez	252
GENEROSO	Jerez	253
GENEROSO	Jerez	253
GENEROSO	Tarragona	754
BLANCO DULCE	Lanzarote	300

EXCEPTIONAL WINES (SWEET WINES AND GENEROSOS)

POINTS	WINE
95	El Tresillo 1874 Amontillado Viejo AM
95	Humboldt 16 años Barrica 1997 B
95	Humboldt 1997 Blanco dulce
95	Jorge Ordóñez & Co Nº 2 Victoria 2012 Blanco dulce
95	La Bota de Oloroso nº46 OL
95	La Ina Fl
95	Pajarete Solera 1851 Rancio
95	Reliquia OL
95	Reliquia PC
95	Sacristía AB MZ
95	San León Reserva de Familia MZ
95	Sibarita V.O.R.S. OL
95	Solear en Rama MZ
95	Teneguía Malvasía Dulce 2006 B Reserva
95	Teneguía Malvasía Dulce Estelar 1996 B Reserva
95	Tío Pepe en Rama Fl
95	Viñaredo Tostado 2011 B

EXCEPTIONAL WINES (SWEET WINES AND GENEROSOS)

TYPE	D.O.	PAGE
GENEROSO	Jerez	254
BLANCO DULCE	Tacoronte-Acentejo	746
BLANCO DULCE	Tacoronte-Acentejo	746
BLANCO DULCE	Málaga y Sierras de Málaga	309
GENEROSO	Montilla-Moriles	336
GENEROSO	Jerez	251
RANCIO	Tarragona	754
GENEROSO	Jerez	245
GENEROSO	Jerez	245
GENEROSO	Jerez	255
GENEROSO	Jerez	254
GENEROSO	Jerez	249
GENEROSO	Jerez	245
BLANCO DULCE	La Palma	296
BLANCO DULCE	La Palma	296
GENEROSO	Jerez	253
BLANCO DULCE	Valdeorras	827

EXCEPTIONAL WINES (RED WINES)

POINTS	WINE
98	Artadi El Carretil 2011
97	Artadi La Poza de Ballesteros 2011
97	Artadi Viña El Pisón 2011
97	Avrvs 2010
97	Contador 2011
97	Dominio de Atauta Llanos del Almendro 2009
97	Finca El Bosque 2010
97	L'Ermita 2011 TC
97	La Faraona 2010
97	La Faraona 2011
97	Pingus 2011
97	San Vicente 2010
97	Vega Sicilia Reserva Especial 94/95/00
97	Vega Sicilia Único 2004
97	Victorino 2011
97	Viña Sastre Pesus 2010
96	Alabaster 2011
96	Amancio 2010
96	Artadi Valdeginés 2011
96	Artuke K4 2011
96	Calvario 2010
96	Castillo Ygay 2004 TGR
96	Cirsion 2010
96	Dalmau 2007 TR
96	Dominio de Atauta Valdegatiles 2009
96	Dominio do Bibei B 2010
96	El Nido 2010
96	El Puntido 2009
96	El Puntido 2010
96	Espectacle 2010
96	Ferratus Sensaciones Décimo 2003
96	Finca El Bosque 2011
96	Gran Vino de Arínzano 2008
96	La Cueva del Contador 2011
96	La Nieta 2010
96	La Viña de Andrés Romeo 2011

	D.O.	PAGE
	Rioja	*650*
	Rioja	*650*
	Rioja	*650*
	Rioja	*663*
	Rioja	*586*
	Ribera del Duero	*545*
	Rioja	*693*
	Priorat	*427*
	Bierzo	*70*
	Bierzo	*70*
	Ribera del Duero	*546*
	Rioja	*681*
	Ribera del Duero	*530*
	Ribera del Duero	*530*
	Toro	*801*
	Ribera del Duero	*516*
	Toro	*800*
	Rioja	*692*
	Rioja	*650*
	Rioja	*582*
	Rioja	*663*
	Rioja	*673*
	Rioja	*638*
	Rioja	*673*
	Ribera del Duero	*545*
	Ribeira Sacra	*475*
	Jumilla	*263*
	Rioja	*691*
	Rioja	*691*
	Montsant	*353*
	Ribera del Duero	*511*
	Rioja	*693*
	Pago Señorío de Arinzano	*884*
	Rioja	*586*
	Rioja	*691*
	Rioja	*586*

EXCEPTIONAL WINES (RED WINES)

POINTS	WINE
96	Macán 2010
96	Numanthia 2010
96	Pago de Carraovejas "Cuesta de las Liebres" Vendimia Seleccionada 2009 TR
96	Pegaso "Granito" 2010
96	Quest 2011
96	Quincha Corral 2011
96	Regina Vides 2010
96	Sierra Cantabria Colección Privada 2011
96	Somni Magnum 2010
96	Termanthia 2010
96	Toga XL 2011
96	Victorino 2010
95	Abadía da Cova de Autor Magnum 2012
95	Abadía Retuerta Petit Verdot PV
95	Abel Mendoza Tempranillo Grano a Grano 2010
95	Alabaster 2010
95	Alión 2010
95	Alto Moncayo 2010
95	Altos de Lanzaga 2009
95	Amancio 2009
95	Aquilón 2010
95	Aro 2009
95	Artadi Pagos Viejos 2011
95	Artuke Finca de los Locos 2011
95	As Caborcas 2010
95	Bernabeleva "Carril del Rey" 2011
95	Bosque de Matasnos Selección Privada 2009
95	Casa Cisca 2011
95	Castillo Ygay 2005 TGR
95	Celsus 2011
95	Clos Mogador 2010
95	Colección Vivanco 4 Varietales Dulce de Invierno 2010
95	Corteo 2010
95	Cortijo Los Aguilares Tadeo 2010
95	Dalmau 2009 TR
95	Dominio de Atauta La Mala 2009 TC

D.O.	PAGE
Rioja	*593*
Toro	*785*
Ribera del Duero	*553*
VT CastyLe	*942*
Costers del Segre	*206*
Vino de Pago El Terrerazo	*882*
Ribera del Duero	*516*
Rioja	*693*
Priorat	*437*
Toro	*785*
Ribera del Duero	*550*
Toro	*800*
Ribeira Sacra	*472*
VT CastyLe	*933*
Rioja	*586*
Toro	*800*
Ribera del Duero	*532*
Campo de Borja	*104*
Rioja	*657*
Rioja	*692*
Campo de Borja	*104*
Rioja	*624*
Rioja	*650*
Rioja	*583*
Valdeorras	*825*
Vinos de Madrid	*861*
Ribera del Duero	*539*
Yecla	*875*
Rioja	*673*
Toro	*793*
Priorat	*438*
Rioja	*603*
Jumilla	*263*
Málaga y Sierras de Málaga	*308*
Rioja	*673*
Ribera del Duero	*545*

EXCEPTIONAL WINES (RED WINES)

POINTS	WINE
95	Dominio de Es 2011
95	Don Miguel Comenge 2009
95	El Cf de Chozas Carrascal 2012
95	El Titán del Bendito 2009
95	Finca La Emperatriz Parcela nº 1 2011
95	Finca La Emperatriz Terruño 2010
95	Finca Sandoval Cuvee TNS Magnum 2009
95	Finca Villacreces Nebro 2011 TC
95	Flor de Pingus 2011
95	Gaudium Gran Vino 2008 TR
95	Irius Premium 2009
95	La Basseta 2010
95	La Carrerada 2011
95	La Nieta 2011
95	Las Lamas 2010
95	Las Lamas 2011
95	Macán Clásico 2010
95	Malpuesto 2011
95	Mentor Roberto Torretta 2010
95	Moncerbal 2011
95	Pago de Carraovejas 2010 TR
95	Pago de Carraovejas El Anejón de la Cuesta de las Liebres 2009
95	Parada de Atauta 2010
95	Rejón 2011
95	San Román 2010
95	San Vicente 2009
95	Sierra Cantabria 2004 TGR
95	Sierra Cantabria Colección Privada 2010
95	Sierra Cantabria Garnacha 2010
95	Sietejuntos Syrah 2011
95	Sot Lefriec 2007
95	Termes 2011
95	Terreus 2010
95	Thalarn 2011
95	Tinta Amarela 2012
95	Valbuena 5º 2009

D.O.	PAGE
Ribera del Duero	546
Ribera del Duero	542
Vino de Pago Chozas Carrascal	881
Toro	795
Rioja	613
Rioja	613
Manchuela	316
Ribera del Duero	547
Ribera del Duero	546
Rioja	618
Somontano	736
Priorat	429
Montsant	352
Rioja	691
Bierzo	70
Bierzo	70
Rioja	593
Rioja	628
Rioja	622
Bierzo	70
Ribera del Duero	553
Ribera del Duero	554
Ribera del Duero	546
VT CastyLe	939
Toro	793
Rioja	681
Rioja	682
Rioja	693
Rioja	682
VT CastyLe	936
Penedès	387
Toro	785
VT CastyLe	938
Costers del Segre	206
Vino de Mesa/Vino	979
Ribera del Duero	530

EXCEPTIONAL WINES (WHITE WINES)

POINTS	WINE
98	Chivite Colección 125 2004 BFB
97	Sorte O Soro 2011
96	Mártires 2012
96	Remelluri 2010
95	As Sortes 2011
95	Belondrade y Lurton 2011
95	La Bota de Florpower nº 44 2010
95	La Comtesse 2010
95	Naiades 2010
95	Nora da Neve 2010
95	Pazo de Piñeiro 2010
95	Pazo Señorans Selección de Añada 2006
95	Qué Bonito Cacareaba 2012

EXCEPTIONAL WINES (SPARKLING WINES)

POINTS	WINE
97	Gramona Celler Batlle 2001 BR Gran Reserva
96	Raventós i Blanc Gran Reserva Personal M.R.N. 1998 BN
95	Gramona Enoteca Finca Celler Batlle 2000 BR Gran Reserva
95	Raventós i Blanc Gran Reserva Personal M.R.N. 2000 BN Gran Reserv
95	Recaredo Reserva Particular 2003 BN Gran Reserva

EXCEPTIONAL WINES (WHITE WINES)

D.O.	PAGE
Navarra	377
Valdeorras	827
Rioja	663
Rioja	666
Valdeorras	827
Rueda	699
Vino de Mesa/Vino	979
Rias Baixas	465
Rueda	710
Rias Baixas	470
Rias Baixas	448
Rias Baixas	466
Rioja	586

EXCEPTIONAL WINES (SPARKLING WINES)

D.O.	PAGE
Cava	152
Vinos Espumosos	987
Cava	152
Vinos Espumosos	987
Cava	175

WINERIES and the TASTING of the WINES by DESIGNATION of ORIGIN

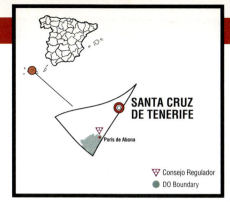

Consejo Regulador
DO Boundary

SANTA CRUZ DE TENERIFE
Porís de Abona

DO ABONA/D.O.P.

LOCATION:

In the southern area of the island of Tenerife, with vineyards which occupy the slopes of the Teide down to the coast. It covers the municipal districts of Adeje, Arona, Vilaflor, San Miguel de Abona, Granadilla de Abona, Arico and Fasnia.

CLIMATE:

Mediterranean on the coastal belt, and gradually cools down inland as a result of the trade winds. Rainfall varies between 350 mm per year on the coast and 550 mm inland. In the highest region, Vilaflor, the vineyards do not benefit from these winds as they face slightly west. Nevertheless, the more than 200 Ha of this small plateau produce wines with an acidity of 8 g/l due to the altitude, but with an alcohol content of 13%, as this area of the island has the longest hours of sunshine.

SOIL:

Distinction can be made between the sandy and calcareous soil inland and the more clayey, well drained soil of the higher regions, seeing as they are volcanic. The so-called 'Jable' soil is very typical, and is simply a very fine whitish volcanic sand, used by the local winegrower to cover the vineyards in order to retain humidity in the ground and to prevent weeds from growing. The vineyards are located at altitudes which range between 300 and 1,750 m (the better quality grapes are grown in the higher regions), which determines different grape harvesting dates in a period spanning the beginning of August up to October.

GRAPE VARIETIES:

WHITE: albillo, marmajuelo, forastera blanca, güal, malvasía, moscatel alejandría, sabro, verdello, vijariego, baboso blanco, listán blanco, pedro ximénez and torrontés.
RED: castellana negra, listán negro, malvasía rosada, negramoll, tintilla, baboso negro, cabernet sauvignon, listán prieto, merlot, moscatel negro, pinot noir, ruby cabernet, syrah, tempranillo and vijariego negro.

FIGURES:

Vineyard surface: 1.032,95 – **Wine-Growers:** 1,236 – **Wineries:** 18 – **2012 Harvest rating:** Very Good – **Production 12:** 675.000 litres – **Market percentages:** 100% domestic

VINTAGE RATING PEÑÍNGUIDE				
2008	2009	2010	2011	2012
VERY GOOD	GOOD	EXCELLENT	VERY GOOD	VERY GOOD

CONSEJO REGULADOR
Martín Rodríguez, 9 - 38588 Porís de Abona - Arico (Santa Cruz de Tenerife)
☎: +34 922 164 241 - Fax: +34 922 164 135 vinosdeabona@vinosdeabona.com www.vinosdeabona.com

BODEGA REVERÓN

Ctra. Gral. Vilaflor, Los Quemados, 8
38620 Vilaflor (Santa Cruz de Tenerife)
☎: +34 922 725 044 - Fax: +34 922 725 044
www.bodegasreveron.com
bodegasreveron@bodegasreveron.com

LOS QUEMADOS 2012 B
albillo

85 Colour: bright straw. Nose: medium intensity, fresh fruit, floral. Palate: fruity, easy to drink, good finish.

LOS QUEMADOS 2012 BFB
albillo

87 Colour: bright straw. Nose: sweet spices, creamy oak, ripe fruit. Palate: flavourful, toasty, good acidity, ripe fruit.

LOS QUEMADOS 2012 T
syrah

87 Colour: black cherry, purple rim. Nose: ripe fruit, sweet spices, warm. Palate: flavourful, good structure, ripe fruit.

PAGO REVERÓN 2011 T
listán negro, ruby, cabernet sauvignon, tempranillo

84

PAGOS REVERÓN 2011 T BARRICA
listán negro, ruby, cabernet sauvignon, tempranillo

86 Colour: cherry, garnet rim. Nose: toasty, spicy, ripe fruit. Palate: fruity, flavourful, round tannins.

PAGOS REVERÓN 2012 B
listán blanco

85 Colour: bright straw. Nose: fresh fruit, faded flowers. Palate: balanced, correct, good acidity, long.

PAGOS REVERÓN 2012 RD
listán negro, tempranillo

85 Colour: rose, purple rim. Nose: red berry notes, ripe fruit, powerfull. Palate: sweet, fruity, flavourful, easy to drink.

PAGOS REVERÓN AFRUTADO 2012 B
listán blanco

85 Colour: bright straw. Nose: fresh, fresh fruit, white flowers. Palate: flavourful, fruity, good acidity, balanced, sweet.

PAGOS REVERÓN NATURALMENTE DULCE 2011 B
listán blanco

88 Colour: bright golden. Nose: candied fruit, honeyed notes, powerfull. Palate: flavourful, fruity, long, sweet.

PAGOS REVERÓN NATURALMENTE DULCE 2011 T
listán negro, tempranillo, syrah

85 Colour: very deep cherry. Nose: grassy, ripe fruit. Palate: flavourful, fruity, sweet, balsamic, good acidity.

BODEGA SAN MIGUEL

Ctra. General del Sur, 5
38620 San Miguel de Abona (Santa Cruz de Tenerife)
☎: +34 922 700 300 - Fax: +34 922 700 301
www.sanmiguelappis.com
bodega@casanmiguel.com

CHASNERO 2012 T
listán negro, listán prieto

84

CHASNERO ACACIA 2012 B

86 Colour: bright straw. Nose: medium intensity, fresh fruit, floral. Palate: flavourful, fruity, fine bitter notes, good acidity.

CHASNERO LISTÁN PRIETO 2012 T
listán prieto

85 Colour: cherry, garnet rim. Nose: ripe fruit, waxy notes, spicy. Palate: light-bodied, fruity, easy to drink.

MARQUÉS DE FUENTE 2012 B
albillo, gual, malvasía, marmajuelo

85 Colour: bright straw. Nose: medium intensity, jasmine, white flowers. Palate: fruity, flavourful, easy to drink.

MARQUÉS DE FUENTE 2012 T BARRICA
baboso negro, vijariego negro, castellana

82

MARQUÉS DE FUENTE SEMIDULCE 2010 T
baboso negro

86 Colour: light cherry, brick rim edge. Nose: faded flowers, sweet spices, overripe fruit. Palate: fruity, fine bitter notes.

CUMBRES DE ABONA

Bajada El Vizo, s/n
38580 Arico (Santa Cruz de Tenerife)
☎: +34 922 768 604 - Fax: +34 922 768 234
www.cumbresabona.com
bodega@cumbresdeabona.es

CUMBRES DE ABONA 2012 RD
100% listán negro

81

CUMBRES DE ABONA 2012 T
100% listán negro

88 Colour: cherry, purple rim. Nose: fruit expression, violet drops, balanced. Palate: fruity, good acidity, round tannins.

FLOR DE CHASNA 2011 T
100% listán negro

90 Colour: cherry, garnet rim. Nose: ripe fruit, spicy, wild herbs. Palate: balanced, ripe fruit, spicy, round tannins.

FLOR DE CHASNA 2012 B
100% listán blanco

87 Colour: bright straw. Nose: ripe fruit, tropical fruit, powerfull. Palate: fruity, flavourful, long.

FLOR DE CHASNA 2012 RD

84

FLOR DE CHASNA 2012 T MACERACIÓN CARBÓNICA
100% listán negro

88 Colour: cherry, garnet rim. Nose: red berry notes, ripe fruit, medium intensity, violcts. Palate: flavourful, balanced, good acidity.

FLOR DE CHASNA AFRUTADO 2012 B
100% listán blanco

84

FLOR DE CHASNA NATURALMENTE DULCE S/C B
100% listán blanco

91 Colour: old gold. Nose: ripe fruit, expressive, faded flowers, honeyed notes, acetaldehyde. Palate: flavourful, balanced, long.

FLOR DE CHASNA NATURALMENTE DULCE S/C T

83

FLOR DE CHASNA SENSACIÓN 2012 B
100% listán blanco

85 Colour: bright straw, greenish rim. Nose: fresh, scrubland, dried flowers. Palate: fruity, sweetness, correct.

FLOR DE CHASNA VARIETAL 2012 T
30% listán negro, 40% ruby cabernet, 30% tempranillo

88 Colour: deep cherry, purple rim. Nose: medium intensity, red berry notes, ripe fruit, balanced. Palate: fruity, flavourful, round tannins.

TESTAMENTO MALVASÍA 2012 BFB
100% malvasía

90 Colour: bright yellow. Nose: balanced, ripe fruit, faded flowers, honeyed notes, elegant. Palate: fruity, spicy.

TESTAMENTO MALVASÍA DRY 2012 B
100% malvasía

87 Colour: yellow. Nose: white flowers, faded flowers, medium intensity. Palate: fruity, good acidity, flavourful.

TESTAMENTO MALVASÍA DULCE 2012 BLANCO DULCE
100% malvasía

86 Colour: bright yellow. Nose: white flowers, jasmine, ripe fruit. Palate: flavourful, fruity, sweet, good acidity.

TESTAMENTO MALVASÍA ESENCIA 2008 B
malvasía

89 Colour: bright golden. Nose: balanced, faded flowers, honeyed notes. Palate: flavourful, sweet, creamy, long.

FRONTOS

Lomo Grande, 1- Los Blanquitos
38612 Granadilla de Abona (Santa Cruz de Tenerife)
☎: +34 922 777 253 - Fax: +34 922 777 246
www.tierradefrontos.com
bodega@frontos.es

FRONTOS 2011 T
100% baboso negro

86 Colour: cherry, garnet rim. Nose: dried herbs, ripe fruit. Palate: light-bodied, fruity, good finish.

FRONTOS 2012 B
verdello, marmajuelo, albillo, malvasía

86 Colour: bright straw. Nose: fresh fruit, white flowers, medium intensity. Palate: flavourful, fruity, good acidity, correct, spicy.

DO ABONA / D.O.P.

FRONTOS 2012 RD
100% listán prieto

80

FRONTOS BLANCO SECO ECOLÓGICO 2012 B
100% listán blanco

87 Colour: bright straw. Nose: floral, fresh, balanced, ripe fruit. Palate: fruity, flavourful, correct, fine bitter notes.

FRONTOS SEMISECO 2012 B
100% listán blanco

84

FRONTOS TINTO TIERRA 2011 T
75% syrah, 25% listán prieto

88 Colour: cherry, garnet rim. Nose: ripe fruit, spicy, toasty, complex, balsamic herbs. Palate: flavourful, round tannins, fine bitter notes.

MENCEY CHASNA

Marta, 3 Chimiche
38594 Granadilla de Abona (Santa Cruz de Tenerife)
☎: +34 922 777 285 - Fax: +34 922 777 259
www.menceychasna.es
ventas@menceychasna.com

LOS TABLEROS 2012 T BARRICA
listán negro, tempranillo, syrah

85 Colour: bright cherry. Nose: ripe fruit, sweet spices, medium intensity. Palate: flavourful, fruity, round tannins.

LOS TABLEROS AFRUTADO 2012 B
listán blanco

85 Colour: bright straw. Nose: white flowers, fresh fruit, tropical fruit, fragrant herbs. Palate: correct, light-bodied, easy to drink.

LOS TABLEROS ECOLÓGICO 2012 B
listán blanco

85 Colour: bright straw. Nose: wild herbs, fresh fruit, balanced. Palate: fruity, astringent, easy to drink.

MENCEY DE CHASNA 2012 B
listán blanco

87 Colour: bright straw. Nose: medium intensity, white flowers, fresh, balanced. Palate: flavourful, fruity, fine bitter notes, good acidity.

MENCEY DE CHASNA 2012 T
listán negro, tempranillo, ruby

86 Colour: cherry, purple rim. Nose: medium intensity, red berry notes, balanced, violets, balsamic herbs. Palate: easy to drink, good finish.

MENCEY DE CHASNA AFRUTADO 2012 B
listán blanco

86 Colour: bright straw. Nose: medium intensity, fresh fruit, citrus fruit. Palate: fruity, flavourful, balanced, sweet.

MENCEY DE CHASNA VIJARIEGO NEGRO 2012 T
vijariego negro

82

PEDRO HERNÁNDEZ TEJERA

Ctra. Archifira, s/n
38570 Fasnia (Tenerife)
☎: +34 616 920 832

VIÑA ARESE 2012 T BARRICA

88 Colour: bright cherry, purple rim. Nose: ripe fruit, sweet spices, violet drops. Palate: good structure, round tannins, long.

VIÑA ARESE 2012 T

86 Colour: bright cherry, purple rim. Nose: violet drops, ripe fruit. Palate: fruity, flavourful, easy to drink, balanced.

Consejo Regulador
DO Boundary

BARCELONA

LOCATION:

It extends over the regions of El Maresme and el Vallès in Barcelona. It covers the municipal districts of Alella, Argentona, Cabrils, El Masnou, La Roca del Vallès, Martorelles, Montornès del Vallès, Montgat, Orrius, Premià de Dalt, Premià de Mar, Santa Mª de Martorelles, Sant Fost de Campsentelles, Teià, Tiana, Vallromanes, Vilanova del Vallès and Vilasar de Salt. The main feature of this region is the urban environment which surrounds this small stretch of vineyards; in fact, one of the smallest DO's in Spain.

CLIMATE:

A typically Mediterranean microclimate with mild winters and hot dry summers. The coastal hills play an important role, as they protect the vines from cold winds and condense the humidity from the sea.

SOIL:

Distinction can be made between the clayey soils of the interior slope of the coastal mountain range and the soil situated along the coastline. The latter, known as Sauló, is the most typical. Almost white in colour, it is renowned for it high permeability and great capacity to retain sunlight, which makes for a better ripening of the grapes.

GRAPE VARIETIES:

WHITE: *Pansa Blanca* (similar to the *Xarel·lo* from other regions in Catalonia), *Garnatxa Blanca, Pansa Rosada, Picapoll, Malvasía, Macabeo, Parellada, Chardonnay, Sauvignon Blanc* and *Chenin Blanc.*
RED (MINORITY): *Garnatxa Negra, Ull de Llebre (Tempranillo), Merlot, Pinot Noir, Syrah, Monastrell, Cabernet Sauvignon, Sumoll* and *Mataró.*

FIGURES:

Vineyard surface: 287,84 – **Wine-Growers:** 68 – **Wineries:** 8 – **2012 Harvest rating:** Very Good – **Production :** 711.503 litres – **Market percentages:** 86% domestic. 14% export

VINTAGE RATING **PEÑÍN**GUIDE

2008	2009	2010	2011	2012
VERY GOOD	GOOD	VERY GOOD	VERY GOOD	VERY GOOD

CONSEJO REGULADOR
Avda. San Mateu, 2 - Masía Can Magarola - 08328 Alella (Barcelona) ☎: +34 935 559 153 - Fax: +34 935 405 249
doalella@doalella.org www.doalella.org

ALELLA VINÍCOLA

Angel Guimerà, 62
8328 Alella (Barcelona)
☎: +34 935 403 842 - Fax: +34 935 401 648
www.alellavinicola.com
xavi@alellavinicola.com

COSTA DEL MARESME 2008 T
garnacha

89 Colour: cherry, garnet rim. Nose: ripe fruit, damp earth, wild herbs, creamy oak, fine reductive notes. Palate: powerful, flavourful, long.

IVORI 2012 B
garnacha blanca, pansa blanca

87 Colour: bright straw. Nose: fresh, fresh fruit, white flowers, expressive. Palate: flavourful, fruity, good acidity, balanced.

IVORI NEGRE 2008 T
garnacha, syrah, cabernet sauvignon

90 Colour: cherry, garnet rim. Nose: ripe fruit, spicy, creamy oak, toasty, fine reductive notes. Palate: powerful, flavourful, toasty, round tannins.

MARFIL 2008 TC
garnacha

86 Colour: cherry, garnet rim. Nose: red berry notes, ripe fruit, cocoa bean, toasty, waxy notes, tobacco. Palate: powerful, flavourful, toasty, correct.

MARFIL 2010 BN
pansa blanca, chardonnay

87 Colour: bright straw. Nose: medium intensity, fresh fruit, dried herbs, fine lees, floral. Palate: fresh, fruity, flavourful, good acidity, fine bitter notes.

MARFIL 2010 TC
garnacha, cabernet sauvignon, syrah

85 Colour: cherry, garnet rim. Nose: ripe fruit, fruit preserve, balsamic herbs, toasty. Palate: powerful, flavourful, long.

MARFIL BLANC DE NOIRS 2010 BR
garnacha

88 Colour: bright straw. Nose: fine lees, dry nuts, fragrant herbs, complex. Palate: powerful, flavourful, good acidity, fine bead, fine bitter notes.

MARFIL BLANCO SECO 2012 B
pansa blanca

84

MARFIL CLÀSSIC 2012 B
pansa blanca

85 Colour: bright straw. Nose: white flowers, fragrant herbs, ripe fruit. Palate: rich, fruity, flavourful.

MARFIL GENEROSO SEC B
pansa blanca

90 Colour: bright yellow. Nose: powerfull, complex, elegant, dry nuts, toasty. Palate: rich, fine bitter notes, fine solera notes, long, spicy.

MARFIL GENEROSO SEMI B
pansa blanca

91 Colour: bright golden. Nose: acetaldehyde, varnish, spicy, creamy oak, expressive. Palate: powerful, flavourful, sweetness, balanced. Personality.

MARFIL MOLT DOLÇ B
pansa blanca

93 Colour: golden. Nose: powerfull, floral, honeyed notes, candied fruit, fragrant herbs. Palate: flavourful, sweet, fresh, fruity, good acidity, long, fine solera notes, elegant.

MARFIL MOSCATEL 2010 ESP
moscatel

90 Colour: bright straw. Nose: fresh fruit, fine lees, white flowers, wild herbs, lactic notes. Palate: fresh, fruity, flavourful, good acidity, sweetness, balanced. Personality.

MARFIL ROSADO 2010 BR
garnacha

87 Colour: light cherry. Nose: ripe fruit, lactic notes, wild herbs. Palate: rich, good acidity, powerful, flavourful.

MARFIL ROSAT 2012 RD
merlot

86 Colour: rose, purple rim. Nose: powerfull, ripe fruit, red berry notes, floral. Palate: powerful, fruity, fresh.

MARFIL VI NEGRE 2012 T
tempranillo, merlot

88 Colour: cherry, purple rim. Nose: ripe fruit, scrubland, earthy notes. Palate: flavourful, correct, easy to drink.

MARFIL VIOLETA T
garnacha

92 Colour: cherry, garnet rim. Nose: ripe fruit, fruit preserve, acetaldehyde, sweet spices, cocoa bean, dark chocolate, toasty. Palate: rich, powerful, fruity, flavourful, balanced.

MAYLA ROSADO DE AGUJA NATURAL 2012 RD
syrah, garnacha blanca

84

VALLMORA MAGNUM 2008 T
garnacha

87 Colour: cherry, garnet rim. Nose: fruit preserve, balsamic herbs, earthy notes, fine reductive notes, aged wood nuances. Palate: flavourful, spicy, balanced.

ALTA ALELLA

Camí Baix de Tiana s/n
8328 Alella (Barcelona)
☎: +34 934 693 720 - Fax: +34 934 691 343
www.altaalella.cat
altaalella@altaalella.cat

ALTA ALELLA BLANC DE NEU 2011 BFB
pansa blanca, otras

90 Colour: golden. Nose: powerfull, floral, honeyed notes, candied fruit, fragrant herbs. Palate: flavourful, sweet, fresh, fruity, good acidity, long.

ALTA ALELLA DOLÇ MATARÓ 2011 TINTO DULCE
mataró

91 Colour: cherry, garnet rim. Nose: ripe fruit, sweet spices, aromatic coffee, toasty. Palate: powerful, flavourful, sweet.

ALTA ALELLA EXEO 2012 BFB
chardonnay, viognier

89 Colour: bright yellow. Nose: ripe fruit, sweet spices, creamy oak, fragrant herbs, citrus fruit. Palate: rich, flavourful, fresh, good acidity.

ALTA ALELLA LANIUS 2012 BFB
pansa blanca, otras

91 Colour: bright straw. Nose: fresh, fresh fruit, white flowers, wild herbs. Palate: flavourful, fruity, good acidity.

ALTA ALELLA ORBUS 2011 T
syrah

89 Colour: very deep cherry, purple rim. Nose: powerfull, expressive, aromatic coffee, sweet spices. Palate: good structure, full, round tannins.

ALTA ALELLA PARVUS CHARDONNAY 2012 B
chardonnay

87 Colour: bright straw. Nose: citrus fruit, ripe fruit, spicy, dried herbs. Palate: powerful, flavourful, spicy, easy to drink.

ALTA ALELLA PARVUS ROSÉ 2012 RD
cabernet sauvignon, syrah

86 Colour: rose. Nose: powerfull, ripe fruit, red berry notes, floral, expressive. Palate: powerful, fruity, fresh.

ALTA ALELLA PARVUS SYRAH 2011 T
syrah

86 Colour: cherry, garnet rim. Nose: sweet spices, creamy oak, ripe fruit, fruit liqueur notes. Palate: flavourful, fruity, toasty.

ALTA ALELLA PRIVAT PANSA BLANCA 2012 B
pansa blanca

87 Colour: bright straw. Nose: floral, dried herbs, fruit expression, spicy. Palate: fresh, fruity, powerful, flavourful.

ALTA ALELLA SYRAH DOLÇ 2006 T
syrah

91 Colour: dark-red cherry. Nose: ripe fruit, acetaldehyde, spicy, varnish, aromatic coffee, toasty. Palate: powerful, flavourful, spicy, long.

BODEGAS CASTILLO DE SAJAZARRA

Del Río, s/n
26212 Sajazarra (La Rioja)
☎: +34 941 320 066 - Fax: +34 941 320 251
www.castillodesajazarra.com
bodega@castillodesajazarra.com

IN VITA 2012 B
40% sauvignon blanc, 60% pansa blanca

90 Colour: bright straw. Nose: fresh, fresh fruit, white flowers, fragrant herbs. Palate: flavourful, fruity, good acidity, balanced.

IN VITA 2011 B
40% sauvignon blanc, 60% pansa blanca

91 Colour: bright straw. Nose: floral, dried herbs, mineral, citrus fruit, fresh fruit. Palate: elegant, flavourful, fresh, fruity, balanced.

BODEGAS ROURA - JUAN ANTONIO PÉREZ ROURA

Valls de Rials s/n
8328 Alella (Barcelona)
☎: +34 933 527 456 - Fax: +34 933 524 339
www.roura.es
roura@roura.es

ROURA COUPAGE 2009 T
50% merlot, 30% garnacha, 20% cabernet sauvignon

87 Colour: cherry, garnet rim. Nose: red berry notes, ripe fruit, sweet spices, creamy oak. Palate: spicy, balsamic, long.

ROURA CRIANZA TRES CEPS 2009 TC
50% cabernet sauvignon, 20% syrah, 30% merlot

87 Colour: cherry, garnet rim. Nose: ripe fruit, spicy, creamy oak, wild herbs. Palate: powerful, flavourful, toasty, spicy.

ROURA MERLOT 2007 T
100% merlot

85 Colour: pale ruby, brick rim edge. Nose: spicy, fine reductive notes, wet leather, aged wood nuances, fragrant herbs. Palate: spicy, toasty, flavourful.

ROURA MERLOT 2012 RD
100% merlot

83

ROURA SAUVIGNON BLANC 2012 B
100% sauvignon blanc

86 Colour: bright straw. Nose: tropical fruit, fresh fruit, dried herbs. Palate: fresh, fruity, flavourful.

ROURA XAREL.LO PANSA BLANCA 2012 B
xarel.lo, pansa blanca

87 Colour: bright straw. Nose: fresh, fresh fruit, white flowers, expressive. Palate: flavourful, fruity, good acidity, balanced.

BOUQUET D'ALELLA S.L.

Sant Josep de Calassanç, 8
8328 Alella (Barcelona)
bouquetda@bouquetdalella.com

BOUQUET D'A BLANC + 2012 BFB
pansa blanca, garnacha blanca

92 Colour: bright yellow. Nose: ripe fruit, sweet spices, creamy oak, fragrant herbs. Palate: rich, flavourful, fresh, balanced.

BOUQUET D'A BLANC 2012 B
pansa blanca, garnacha blanca

86 Colour: bright straw. Nose: floral, dried herbs, spicy, medium intensity. Palate: light-bodied, fresh, easy to drink.

GALACTICA 2010 B
pansa blanca

92 Colour: bright yellow. Nose: powerfull, ripe fruit, sweet spices, creamy oak, fragrant herbs. Palate: rich, smoky aftertaste, flavourful, fresh, good acidity.

MARQUÉS DE ALELLA ALLIER 2010 BFB
chardonnay

91 Colour: bright yellow. Nose: powerfull, ripe fruit, sweet spices, creamy oak, fragrant herbs. Palate: rich, flavourful, fresh, good acidity.

MARQUÉS DE ALELLA PANSA BLANCA 2012 B
pansa blanca

89 Colour: bright straw. Nose: fresh, fresh fruit, white flowers, tropical fruit. Palate: flavourful, fruity, good acidity, balanced.

MARQUÉS DE ALELLA PANSA BLANCA SENSE SULFITS 2012 B
pansa blanca

86 Colour: bright straw. Nose: floral, dried herbs, ripe fruit. Palate: correct, powerful, slightly evolved.

PERFUM DE PANSA BLANCA 2010 B
pansa blanca

89 Colour: bright golden. Nose: ripe fruit, dry nuts, powerfull, toasty, aged wood nuances. Palate: flavourful, fruity, spicy, toasty, long.

SEPO 2012 B
pansa blanca

86 Colour: bright straw. Nose: ripe fruit, faded flowers, wild herbs. Palate: correct, light-bodied, fresh, fruity.

SAPIENS THE GAME SCP

Carrer dels Roures, 3
8348 Cabrils (Barcelona)
☎: +34 679 448 722
www.testuan.com
info@testuan.com

2 DE TESTUAN 2012 B
90% pansa blanca, 10% macabeo

87 Colour: bright straw. Nose: ripe fruit, white flowers, fragrant herbs. Palate: fresh, fruity, easy to drink.

DO ALICANTE / D.O.P.

Consejo Regulador
DO Boundary

LOCATION:

In the province of Alicante (covering 51 municipal districts), and a small part of the province of Murcia. The vineyards extend over areas close to the coast (in the surroundings of the capital city of Alicante, and especially in the area of La Marina, a traditional producer of Moscatel), as well as in the interior of the province.

CLIMATE:

Distinction must be made between the vineyards situated closer to the coastline, where the climate is clearly Mediterranean and somewhat more humid, and those inland, which receive continental influences and have a lower level of rainfall.

SOIL:

In general, the majority of the soils in the region are of a dun limestone type, with little clay and hardly any organic matter.

GRAPE VARIETIES:

WHITE: *Merseguera, Moscatel de Alejandría, Macabeo, Planta Fina, Verdil, Airén, Chardonnay* and *Sauvignon Blanc.*
RED: *Monastrell, Garnacha Tinta* (*Alicante* or *Giró*), *Garnacha Tintorera, Bobal, Tempranillo, Cabernet Sauvignon, Merlot, Pinot Noir, Syrah* and *Petit Verdot.*

FIGURES:

Vineyard surface: 9.166 – **Wine-Growers:** 2,500 – **Wineries:** 56 – **2012 Harvest rating:** Very Good – **Production:** 12.186.200 litres – **Market percentages:** 77,12% domestic. 22,88% export

VINTAGE RATING **PEÑÍN**GUIDE

2008	2009	2010	2011	2012
EXCELLENT	VERY GOOD	VERY GOOD	VERY GOOD	VERY GOOD

CONSEJO REGULADOR
Monjas, 6 - 03002 Alicante - ☎: +34 965 984 478 - Fax: +34 965 229 295
crdo.alicante@crdo-alicante.org   www.crdo-alicante.org

BODEGA COOP, DE ALGUEÑA COOP. V.

Ctra. Rodriguillo, s/n
3668 Algueña (Alicante)
☎: +34 965 476 113 - Fax: +34 965 476 229
www.vinosdealguenya.com
bodega@vinosdealguenya.es

ALHENIA 2009 T
monastrell

83

CASA JIMÉNEZ 2010 TC
monastrell

85 Colour: cherry, garnet rim. Nose: toasty, aromatic coffee. Palate: fine bitter notes, good acidity.

DOMINIO DE TORREVIÑAS 2012 RD
monastrell, syrah

86 Colour: rose, purple rim. Nose: powerfull, ripe fruit, red berry notes, floral. Palate: powerful, fruity, fresh.

DOMINIO DE TORREVIÑAS DOBLE PASTA 2012 T
monastrell

87 Colour: cherry, purple rim. Nose: red berry notes, floral, balsamic herbs. Palate: fine bitter notes, powerful, flavourful.

FONDILLÓN 1980 FONDILLÓN
monastrell

89 Colour: dark mahogany. Nose: varnish, aged wood nuances, sweet spices, creamy oak, expressive, acetaldehyde. Palate: fine bitter notes, powerful, flavourful.

FONDONET 2010 T
monastrell

87 Colour: cherry, garnet rim. Nose: ripe fruit, spicy, creamy oak, toasty, fruit preserve. Palate: powerful, flavourful, toasty.

BODEGA NUESTRA SEÑORA DE LAS VIRTUDES COOP. V.

Ctra. de Yecla, 9
3400 Villena (Alicante)
☎: +34 965 802 187
www.coopvillena.com
coopvillena@coopvillena.com

VINALOPÓ 2009 TC
50% monastrell, 50% cabernet sauvignon

86 Colour: cherry, garnet rim. Nose: ripe fruit, spicy, creamy oak, toasty, complex. Palate: powerful, flavourful, toasty, round tannins.

VINALOPÓ 2012 T
50% monastrell, 50% merlot

88 Colour: cherry, purple rim. Nose: red berry notes, ripe fruit, sweet spices. Palate: powerful, flavourful, fine bitter notes, good acidity.

VINALOPÓ ESENCIA DEL MEDITERRÁNEO 2012 B
50% moscatel, 50% sauvignon blanc

88 Colour: bright straw. Nose: fresh, fresh fruit, white flowers, expressive. Palate: flavourful, fruity, good acidity, balanced.

VINALOPÓ MONASTRELL 2011 T
100% monastrell

84

VINALOPÓ PETIT VERDOT 2010 T ROBLE
100% petit verdot

87 Colour: bright cherry. Nose: ripe fruit, sweet spices, creamy oak, expressive. Palate: flavourful, fruity, toasty, round tannins.

VINALOPÓ SELECCIÓN 2011 T
50% monastrell, 50% syrah

84

BODEGA VINESSENS

Ctra. de Caudete, Km. 1
3400 Villena (Alicante)
☎: +34 965 800 265 - Fax: +34 965 800 265
www.vinessens.es
comercial@vinessens.es

EL TELAR 2010 TC
90% monastrell, 10% cabernet sauvignon

92 Colour: cherry, garnet rim. Nose: ripe fruit, spicy, creamy oak, toasty. Palate: powerful, flavourful, toasty, round tannins.

ESSENS 2012 BFB
100% chardonnay

90 Colour: bright yellow. Nose: powerfull, ripe fruit, sweet spices, creamy oak, fragrant herbs. Palate: rich, flavourful, fresh, good acidity.

SEIN 2010 TC
60% monastrell, 40% syrah

92 Colour: cherry, garnet rim. Nose: ripe fruit, spicy, creamy oak, toasty, complex, mineral. Palate: powerful, flavourful, toasty, round tannins.

BODEGAS ALEJANDRO PÉREZ MARTÍNEZ

El Mañán, HJ10
3640 Monóvar (Alicante)
☎: +34 966 960 291
bodegasalejandro@gmail.com

VEGA CUYAR 2010 TC
tempranillo, cabernet sauvignon

90 Colour: cherry, garnet rim. Nose: characterful, powerfull, overripe fruit, raspberry. Palate: powerful, sweetness, round tannins.

VEGA CUYAR 2012 B
merseguera

86 Colour: bright straw. Nose: fresh, white flowers, expressive. Palate: flavourful, fruity, good acidity, balanced.

VEGA CUYAR 2012 T
monastrell

87 Colour: cherry, purple rim. Nose: expressive, fresh fruit, red berry notes, floral. Palate: flavourful, fruity, good acidity, round tannins.

BODEGAS BERNABÉ NAVARRO

Ctra. Villena-Cañada, Km. 3
3400 Villena (Alicante)
☎: +34 966 770 353 - Fax: +34 966 770 353
www.bodegasbernabenavarro.com
info@bodegasbernabenavarro.com

BERYNA 2011 TC
80% monastrell, 10% tempranillo, 10% garnacha

92 Colour: cherry, garnet rim. Nose: ripe fruit, spicy, creamy oak, dark chocolate, cocoa bean. Palate: powerful, flavourful, toasty, round tannins.

CASA BALAGUER 2009 T
70% monastrell, 10% syrah, 10% merlot, 5% tempranillo, 5% cabernet sauvignon

93 Colour: cherry, garnet rim. Nose: spicy, creamy oak, toasty, complex, candied fruit, fruit expression. Palate: powerful, flavourful, toasty, round tannins.

BODEGAS BOCOPA

Paraje Les Pedreres, Autovía A-31, km. 200 - 201
3610 Petrer (Alicante)
☎: +34 966 950 489 - Fax: +34 966 950 406
www.bocopa.com
info@bocopa.com

ALCANTA 2009 TC
monastrell, tempranillo

85 Colour: cherry, garnet rim. Nose: medium intensity, ripe fruit, balsamic herbs. Palate: correct, flavourful, spicy.

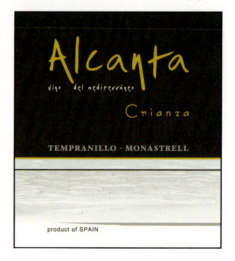

ALCANTA MONASTRELL 2012 T
monastrell

88 Colour: deep cherry. Nose: ripe fruit, spicy. Palate: fine bitter notes, good acidity.

FONDILLÓN ALONE FONDILLÓN
monastrell

90 Colour: pale ruby, brick rim edge. Nose: candied fruit, fruit liqueur notes, toasty, aged wood nuances. Palate: flavourful, powerful, fine bitter notes, good acidity.

LAUDUM 2008 TC
cabernet sauvignon, monastrell, merlot

83

LAUDUM CABERNET SAUVIGNON 2008 T
cabernet sauvignon

84

LAUDUM CHARDONNAY 2011 BFB
chardonnay

85 Colour: bright yellow. Nose: powerfull, ripe fruit, sweet spices, creamy oak. Palate: rich, flavourful, fresh, good acidity.

LAUDUM NATURE 2011 T
tempranillo, monastrell, cabernet sauvignon

88 Colour: cherry, garnet rim. Nose: powerfull, fruit liqueur notes, spicy, dark chocolate. Palate: powerful, fine bitter notes, round tannins.

MARINA ALTA 2012 B
moscatel de alejandría

88 Colour: bright straw. Nose: fresh, fresh fruit, white flowers, expressive, candied fruit. Palate: flavourful, fruity, good acidity, balanced.

MARINA ESPUMANTE B
moscatel de alejandría

87 Colour: golden. Nose: powerfull, floral, honeyed notes, candied fruit. Palate: flavourful, sweet, fresh, fruity, good acidity.

MARINA ESPUMANTE RD
monastrell

85 Colour: brilliant rose. Nose: ripe fruit, candied fruit, floral. Palate: fresh, fruity, powerful, flavourful.

LAUDUM PETIT VERDOT 2008 T
petit verdot

84

SOL DE ALICANTE DULCENEGRA T
monastrell

87 Colour: bright cherry. Nose: ripe fruit, sweet spices, creamy oak, expressive. Palate: flavourful, fruity, toasty, round tannins, sweet.

SOL DE ALICANTE MOSCATEL B
moscatel

88 Colour: golden. Nose: powerfull, floral, honeyed notes, candied fruit. Palate: flavourful, sweet, fresh, fruity, good acidity, long.

BODEGAS E. MENDOZA

Partida El Romeral, s/n
3580 Alfaz del Pi (Alicante)
☎: +34 965 888 639 - Fax: +34 965 889 232
www.bodegasmendoza.com
bodegas-mendoza@bodegasmendoza.com

ENRIQUE MENDOZA CABERNET - SHIRAZ 2009 TR
50% cabernet sauvignon, 50% syrah

91 Colour: cherry, garnet rim. Nose: ripe fruit, spicy, creamy oak, toasty, complex. Palate: powerful, flavourful, toasty, round tannins.

ENRIQUE MENDOZA CABERNET MONASTRELL 2009 T
50% cabernet sauvignon, 50% monastrell

89 Colour: cherry, garnet rim. Nose: spicy, creamy oak, toasty. Palate: powerful, flavourful, toasty, round tannins.

ENRIQUE MENDOZA DOLÇ DE MENDOZA 2008 T
100% monastrell

90 Colour: cherry, garnet rim. Nose: candied fruit, ripe fruit, dried herbs, sweet spices, aged wood nuances. Palate: powerful, flavourful, complex, balanced.

ENRIQUE MENDOZA MERLOT MONASTRELL 2009 T
50% merlot, 50% monastrell

89 Colour: very deep cherry. Nose: powerfull, ripe fruit, sweet spices. Palate: powerful, fine bitter notes, round tannins.

ENRIQUE MENDOZA SANTA ROSA 2008 TR
70% cabernet sauvignon, 15% merlot, 15% syrah

93 Colour: cherry, garnet rim. Nose: spicy, creamy oak, toasty, complex. Palate: powerful, flavourful, toasty, round tannins.

ENRIQUE MENDOZA SHIRAZ 2010 TC
100% syrah

92 Colour: bright cherry. Nose: ripe fruit, sweet spices, creamy oak, expressive. Palate: flavourful, fruity, toasty, round tannins.

ESTRECHO MONASTRELL 2008 T
100% monastrell

93 Colour: cherry, garnet rim. Nose: ripe fruit, balsamic herbs, earthy notes, expressive, elegant. Palate: flavourful, spicy, toasty, round tannins, elegant.

LAS QUEBRADAS 2010 T
100% monastrell

94 Colour: cherry, garnet rim. Nose: ripe fruit, spicy, toasty, complex, earthy notes, dark chocolate. Palate: powerful, flavourful, toasty, round tannins.

BODEGAS FAELO

Partida de Matola, Pol. 3 Nº 18
3296 Elche (Alicante)
☎: +34 655 856 898
www.vinosladama.com
info@vinosladama.com

L'ALBA DE FAELO 2012 RD
syrah

88 Colour: rose, purple rim. Nose: powerfull, ripe fruit, red berry notes, floral. Palate: powerful, fruity, fresh.

L'ALBA DEL MAR 2012 B
chardonnay

84

LA DAMA 2010 TC
60% cabernet sauvignon, 30% monastrell, 10% petit verdot

89 Colour: cherry, garnet rim. Nose: ripe fruit, spicy, creamy oak, toasty, characterful. Palate: powerful, flavourful, toasty, round tannins.

PALMA BLANCA 2012 B
moscatel

87 Colour: golden. Nose: powerfull, floral, honeyed notes, candied fruit, fragrant herbs. Palate: flavourful, sweet, fresh, fruity, good acidity, long.

BODEGAS FRANCISCO GÓMEZ

Ctra. Villena - Pinoso, Km. 8,8
3400 Villena (Alicante)
☎: +34 965 979 195 - Fax: +34 965 979 196
www.bodegasfranciscogomez.es
info@bodegasfranciscogomez.es

BOCA NEGRA 2008 TC
monastrell

89 Colour: cherry, garnet rim. Nose: ripe fruit, spicy, toasty, balsamic herbs. Palate: powerful, flavourful, toasty, balanced.

FRUTO NOBLE 2008 TC
cabernet franc, monastrell, syrah

85 Colour: pale ruby, brick rim edge. Nose: spicy, fine reductive notes, wet leather, aged wood nuances, fruit liqueur notes. Palate: spicy, long.

FRUTO NOBLE 2011 T ROBLE
monastrell, syrah

86 Colour: deep cherry. Nose: roasted coffee, varnish, dark chocolate. Palate: fine bitter notes, spicy.

FRUTO NOBLE 2012 B
sauvignon blanc

88 Colour: bright straw. Nose: fresh, white flowers, citrus fruit, tropical fruit. Palate: flavourful, fruity, good acidity, balanced.

FRUTO NOBLE 2012 RD
monastrell, syrah

89 Colour: onion pink. Nose: elegant, candied fruit, dried flowers, fragrant herbs, red berry notes. Palate: light-bodied, flavourful, good acidity, long, spicy.

FRUTO NOBLE 2012 T
monastrell, syrah

89 Colour: cherry, purple rim. Nose: expressive, fresh fruit, red berry notes, floral. Palate: flavourful, fruity, good acidity, round tannins.

MORATILLAS 2008 TC
monastrell, merlot, syrah

85 Colour: cherry, garnet rim. Nose: ripe fruit, spicy, creamy oak, toasty, fine reductive notes. Palate: powerful, flavourful, spicy.

SERRATA 2008 TR
merlot, petit verdot, cabernet sauvignon, monastrell

87 Colour: cherry, garnet rim. Nose: ripe fruit, spicy, toasty, aged wood nuances. Palate: powerful, flavourful, toasty, harsh oak tannins.

BODEGAS GUTIÉRREZ DE LA VEGA

Les Quintanes, 1
3792 Parcent (Alicante)
☎: +34 966 403 871 - Fax: +34 966 405 257
www.castadiva.es
info@castadiva.es

CABALETTA 2011 ESP
moscatel

85 Colour: bright yellow. Nose: dried flowers, fragrant herbs, citrus fruit, spicy, sulphur notes, candied fruit. Palate: powerful, flavourful, spicy, long, balsamic.

CASTA DIVA CAVATINA 2012 MOSCATEL ESPUMOSO DULCE
moscatel

90 Colour: bright straw. Nose: floral, citrus fruit, candied fruit, honeyed notes, pattiserie. Palate: good acidity, fruity, flavourful, balanced.

CASTA DIVA COSECHA MIEL 2011 B
moscatel

93 Colour: golden. Nose: powerfull, floral, honeyed notes, candied fruit, fragrant herbs, complex, citrus fruit. Palate: flavourful, sweet, fresh, fruity, long, balanced.

CASTA DIVA ESENCIAL 2012 B
moscatel

95 Colour: old gold, amber rim. Nose: toasty, pattiserie, ripe fruit, dried herbs, complex. Palate: rich, powerful, flavourful, fruity, long.

CASTA DIVA RESERVA REAL 2002 B RESERVA
moscatel

97 Colour: iodine, amber rim. Nose: caramel, sweet spices, honeyed notes, dark chocolate, cocoa bean, acetaldehyde. Palate: powerful, rich, spicy, long, fine solera notes, balanced.

FURTIVA LÁGRIMA 2012 B
moscatel

92 Colour: golden. Nose: powerfull, floral, honeyed notes, candied fruit, fragrant herbs. Palate: flavourful, sweet, fresh, fruity, good acidity.

LA DIVA 2011 B
moscatel

93 Colour: bright yellow. Nose: candied fruit, citrus fruit, floral, wild herbs, sweet spices. Palate: powerful, flavourful, spicy, long.

PRÍNCIPE DE SALINAS 2010 TC
monastrell

89 Colour: cherry, garnet rim. Nose: medium intensity, ripe fruit, wild herbs, spicy. Palate: fruity, flavourful.

RECÓNDITA ARMONÍA 1987 FONDILLÓN
monastrell

96 Colour: very deep cherry. Nose: powerfull, characterful, warm, fruit preserve, sweet spices, aromatic coffee, dark chocolate. Palate: spirituous, powerful, spirituous.

RECÓNDITA ARMONÍA 2001 FONDILLÓN

94 Colour: black cherry. Nose: spicy, aromatic coffee, dark chocolate, overripe fruit, fruit liqueur notes. Palate: spirituous, sweet, concentrated, powerful.

RECÓNDITA ARMONÍA 2010 T
monastrell

93 Colour: cherry, garnet rim. Nose: fruit preserve, dark chocolate, spicy, toasty, balanced. Palate: powerful, flavourful, spicy, rich, balanced.

VIÑA ULISES 2010 TC
monastrell

87 Colour: cherry, garnet rim. Nose: ripe fruit, spicy, dried herbs. Palate: balanced, ripe fruit, round tannins.

BODEGAS MURVIEDRO

Ampliación Pol. El Romeral, s/n
46340 Requena (Valencia)
☎: +34 962 329 003 - Fax: +34 962 329 002
www.bodegasmurviedro.es
murviedro@murviedro.es

CUEVA DEL PERDÓN 2010 TR
60% monastrell, 40% syrah

91 Colour: cherry, garnet rim. Nose: ripe fruit, spicy, creamy oak, mineral, expressive. Palate: powerful, flavourful, long, balanced, unctuous.

DULCE DE MURVIEDRO B
100% moscatel de alejandría

85 Colour: golden. Nose: powerfull, floral, honeyed notes, candied fruit, fragrant herbs. Palate: flavourful, sweet, fresh, fruity.

BODEGAS PARCENT

Avda. Denia, 15
3792 Parcent (Alicante)
☎: +34 636 536 693 - Fax: +34 966 405 173
www.bodegasparcent.com
armando@bodegasparcent.com

COMTAT DE PARCENT 2011 TC
cabernet sauvignon, merlot

84

DOLÇ D'ART 2012 B
moscatel

88 Colour: bright straw. Nose: powerfull, floral, honeyed notes, candied fruit. Palate: flavourful, sweet, fresh, fruity, good acidity, long.

FRUIT D'AUTOR 2012 VINO DE LICOR

85 Colour: brilliant rose. Nose: red berry notes, ripe fruit, dried flowers. Palate: powerful, flavourful, fruity.

GRÀ D'OR BLANCO SECO 2012 B
moscatel

83

ROSAT 2012 RD
syrah

85 Colour: rose, purple rim. Nose: ripe fruit, dried flowers, balsamic herbs. Palate: easy to drink, flavourful.

BODEGAS SIERRA DE CABRERAS

La Molineta, 27
3638 Salinas (Alicante)
☎: +34 647 515 590
www.carabibas.com
info@carabibas.com

CARABIBAS VS 2011 T
cabernet sauvignon, merlot, monastrell

91 Colour: cherry, garnet rim. Nose: ripe fruit, spicy, creamy oak, toasty, complex. Palate: powerful, flavourful, toasty, round tannins.

BODEGAS SIERRA SALINAS

Paraje del Puerto, s/n (Ctra. Villena-Pinoso, km. 16)
30400 Villena (Alicante)
☎: +34 968 791 271 - Fax: +34 968 791 900
www.sierrasalinas.com
office@sierrasalinas.com

MIRA SALINAS 2010 T
50% monastrell, 20% cabernet sauvignon, 20% garnacha tintorera, 10% petit verdot

93 Colour: cherry, garnet rim. Nose: ripe fruit, spicy, creamy oak, toasty, characterful. Palate: powerful, flavourful, toasty, round tannins.

MO SALINAS MONASTRELL 2011 T
85% monastrell, 10% cabernet sauvignon, 5% garnacha tintorera

90 Colour: cherry, purple rim. Nose: powerfull, red berry notes, sweet spices. Palate: flavourful, ripe fruit.

MO SALINAS MONASTRELL 2012 RD
90% monastrell, 5% cabernet sauvignon, 5% garnacha tintorera

89 Colour: rose, purple rim. Nose: powerfull, ripe fruit, red berry notes, floral, expressive. Palate: powerful, fruity, fresh.

PUERTO SALINAS 2010 T
65% monastrell, 20% cabernet sauvignon, 15% garnacha tintorera

91 Colour: bright cherry. Nose: ripe fruit, sweet spices, creamy oak, red berry notes. Palate: flavourful, fruity, toasty, round tannins.

SALINAS 1237 2008 T
40% garnacha tintorera, 40% cabernet sauvignon, 20% monastrell

93 Colour: cherry, garnet rim. Nose: overripe fruit, powerfull, characterful, toasty, dark chocolate. Palate: fine bitter notes, powerful, ripe fruit.

BODEGAS VICENTE GANDÍA

Ctra. Cheste a Godelleta, s/n
46370 Chiva (Valencia)
☎: +34 962 524 242 - Fax: +34 962 524 243
www.vicentegandia.es
info@vicentegandia.com

EL MIRACLE ART 2009 T
25% monastrell, 20% pinot noir, 20% syrah, 20% merlot, 15% tempranillo

88 Colour: cherry, garnet rim. Nose: ripe fruit, spicy, creamy oak, toasty, fine reductive notes. Palate: powerful, flavourful, toasty.

EL MIRACLE FUSIÓN 2012 B
70% chardonnay, 20% sauvignon blanc, 10% moscatel

85 Colour: bright straw. Nose: dried flowers, ripe fruit, balsamic herbs. Palate: powerful, flavourful, spicy.

EL MIRACLE MUSIC 2012 RD
syrah, garnacha

86 Colour: rose. Nose: red berry notes, ripe fruit, floral, lactic notes, balanced. Palate: powerful, fruity, flavourful, balanced.

EL MIRACLE PLANET ORGANIC WINE 2011 T
100% monastrell

83

PUERTO ALICANTE CHARDONNAY 2012 B
100% chardonnay

87 Colour: bright yellow. Nose: floral, fragrant herbs, ripe fruit. Palate: powerful, rich, flavourful.

PUERTO ALICANTE SYRAH 2011 T
100% syrah

87 Colour: cherry, purple rim. Nose: red berry notes, ripe fruit, floral. Palate: flavourful, fruity, thin.

BODEGAS VOLVER

Pza. de Grecia, 1 Local 1B
45005 Toledo (Toledo)
☎: +34 925 167 493 - Fax: +34 925 167 059
www.bodegasvolver.com
export@bodegasvolver.com

TARIMA 2012 B
merseguera, macabeo

88 Colour: bright straw. Nose: fresh, fresh fruit, white flowers. Palate: flavourful, fruity, good acidity, balanced.

TARIMA HILL 2011 T
100% monastrell

93 Colour: cherry, garnet rim. Nose: spicy, toasty, overripe fruit, mineral. Palate: powerful, flavourful, toasty, round tannins.

TARIMA MONASTREL 2012 T
100% monastrell

90 Colour: bright cherry. Nose: ripe fruit, sweet spices, creamy oak, roasted coffee. Palate: flavourful, fruity, toasty, round tannins.

BODEGAS XALÓ

Ctra. Xaló Alcalali, s/n
3727 Xaló (Alicante)
☎: +34 966 480 034 - Fax: +34 966 480 808
www.bodegasxalo.com
comercial@bodegasxalo.com

BAHÍA DE DENIA 2012 B JOVEN
moscatel

90 Colour: bright straw. Nose: fresh, fresh fruit, white flowers, expressive. Palate: flavourful, fruity, good acidity, balanced.

BAHÍA DE DENIA BRUT NATURE 2011 ESP
moscatel

83

CASTELL D'AIXA 2010 TC
garnacha, tempranillo

84

PLACER VALL DE POP 2012 B
moscatel

86 Colour: bright straw. Nose: fresh, white flowers. Palate: flavourful, fruity, good acidity, balanced.

PLACER VALL DE POP 2012 T
garnacha

86 Colour: cherry, garnet rim. Nose: candied fruit, fruit liqueur notes, sweet spices, dark chocolate. Palate: fine bitter notes, spicy, grainy tannins.

RIU RAU 2011 B
moscatel

90 Colour: golden. Nose: powerfull, floral, honeyed notes, candied fruit, fragrant herbs. Palate: flavourful, sweet, fresh, fruity, good acidity, long.

SERRA DE BERNIA 2011 T ROBLE
garnacha, cabernet sauvignon

87 Colour: cherry, garnet rim. Nose: powerfull, ripe fruit, spicy. Palate: flavourful, sweetness.

VALL DE XALÓ 2012 B
moscatel

85 Colour: bright straw. Nose: fresh, fresh fruit, white flowers, expressive. Palate: flavourful, good acidity, balanced.

VALL DE XALÓ 2012 MISTELA
moscatel

87 Colour: bright straw. Nose: candied fruit, white flowers, fragrant herbs, honeyed notes. Palate: rich, flavourful, long.

VALL DE XALÓ 2012 RD
garnacha

85 Colour: rose, purple rim. Nose: powerfull, ripe fruit, red berry notes, floral, balsamic herbs. Palate: powerful, fruity, fresh.

VALL DE XALÓN VINO DE LICOR 2012 T
garnacha

89 Colour: bright cherry. Nose: sweet spices, creamy oak, candied fruit, overripe fruit. Palate: flavourful, toasty, round tannins.

BODEGAS Y VIÑEDOS EL SEQUÉ

El Sequé, 59
3650 (Alicante)
☎: +34 945 600 119 - Fax: +34 945 600 850
elseque@artadi.com

EL SEQUÉ 2011 T
100% monastrell

94 Colour: bright cherry. Nose: sweet spices, creamy oak, ripe fruit, balsamic herbs. Palate: flavourful, fruity, toasty, powerful tannins, good acidity.

EL SEQUÉ DULCE 2011 T
100% monastrell

93 Colour: cherry, garnet rim. Nose: powerfull, overripe fruit, fruit preserve. Palate: powerful, flavourful, good acidity, sweet.

COMERCIAL GRUPO FREIXENET S.A.

Joan Sala, 2
8770 Sant Sadurní D'Anoia (Barcelona)
☎: +34 938 917 000 - Fax: +34 938 183 095
www.freixenet.es
freixenet@freixenet.es

NAUTA 2009 TC
monastrell

88 Colour: cherry, garnet rim. Nose: ripe fruit, spicy, creamy oak, toasty. Palate: powerful, flavourful, toasty.

FINCA COLLADO

Ctra. de Salinas a Villena, s/n
3638 Salinas (Alicante)
☎: +34 607 510 710 - Fax: +34 962 878 818
www.fincacollado.com
info@fincacollado.com

FINCA COLLADO 2010 T
cabernet sauvignon, merlot

88 Colour: cherry, garnet rim. Nose: spicy, creamy oak, toasty, characterful. Palate: powerful, flavourful, toasty, round tannins.

FINCA COLLADO MERLOT 2010 T
merlot

87 Colour: bright cherry. Nose: sweet spices, creamy oak, fruit liqueur notes. Palate: flavourful, fruity, toasty, round tannins.

IBERICA BRUNO PRATS

CV 830, km. 3,2
3640 Monovar (Alicante)
☎: +34 645 963 122
www.fideliswines.com
stephanepoint@hotmail.com

ALFYNAL 2010 T
monastrell

90 Colour: cherry, garnet rim. Nose: ripe fruit, spicy, creamy oak, toasty. Palate: powerful, flavourful, toasty, round tannins.

MOSYCA 2010 T
monastrell, syrah, cabernet sauvignon, petit verdot

90 Colour: cherry, garnet rim. Nose: ripe fruit, spicy, creamy oak, toasty, complex, balsamic herbs. Palate: powerful, flavourful, toasty, round tannins.

LA BODEGA DE PINOSO

Paseo de la Constitución, 82
3650 Pinoso (Alicante)
☎: +34 965 477 040 - Fax: +34 966 970 149
www.labodegadepinoso.com
dptocomercial@labodegadepinoso.com

PONTOS 1932 2008 TC
monastrell

86 Colour: cherry, garnet rim. Nose: ripe fruit, toasty, aged wood nuances, fine reductive notes. Palate: powerful, flavourful, toasty.

PONTOS CEPA 50 2011 T
monastrell

87 Colour: bright cherry. Nose: ripe fruit, sweet spices, creamy oak, mineral. Palate: flavourful, fruity, toasty, round tannins.

PONTOS CLASIC 09 2006 TC
monastrell, merlot, cabernet sauvignon

84

TORRE DEL RELOJ 2012 B
airén, macabeo

86 Colour: bright straw. Nose: fresh fruit, white flowers. Palate: flavourful, fruity, good acidity, balanced.

TORRE DEL RELOJ 2012 RD
monastrell, tempranillo, syrah

84

TORRE DEL RELOJ MONASTRELL 2011 T
monastrell

84

VERGEL 2011 T
alicante bouschet, merlot, monastrell

89 Colour: bright cherry. Nose: ripe fruit, balsamic herbs, spicy. Palate: flavourful, fruity, round tannins, easy to drink.

VERGEL SELECCIÓN BARRICAS 2009 T
monastrell, syrah, merlot

89 Colour: bright cherry. Nose: ripe fruit, sweet spices, creamy oak, aged wood nuances. Palate: flavourful, fruity, toasty, round tannins.

VERMADOR 2011 T
monastrell

84

VERMADOR 2011 T BARRICA
monastrell, syrah

84

VERMADOR 2012 B
airén, macabeo

88 Colour: bright straw. Nose: fresh, fresh fruit, white flowers. Palate: flavourful, fruity, good acidity, balanced.

VERMADOR 2012 RD
monastrell

87 Colour: rose, purple rim. Nose: powerfull, red berry notes, floral. Palate: powerful, fruity, fresh.

PRIMITIVO QUILES

Mayor, 4
3640 Monóvar (Alicante)
☎: +34 965 470 099 - Fax: +34 966 960 235
www.primitivoquiles.com
info@primitivoquiles.com

GRAN IMPERIAL GE
moscatel

92 Colour: dark mahogany. Nose: dry nuts, varnish, spicy, creamy oak, toasty, balanced, expressive, acetaldehyde. Palate: elegant, round, powerful, flavourful.

PRIMITIVO QUILES FONDILLÓN 1948 FONDILLÓN
monastrell

91 Colour: iodine, amber rim. Nose: powerfull, complex, elegant, dry nuts, toasty. Palate: rich, fine bitter notes, fine solera notes, long, spicy.

PRIMITIVO QUILES MONASTRELL-MERLOT 2010 T ROBLE
60% monastrell, 40% merlot

84

PRIMITIVO QUILES MOSCATEL EXTRA S/C VINO DE LICOR
moscatel

88 Colour: dark mahogany. Nose: acetaldehyde, ripe fruit, caramel, sweet spices, toasty. Palate: powerful, flavourful, spicy, balanced.

PRIMITIVO QUILES MOSCATEL LAUREL B
moscatel

88 Colour: golden. Nose: powerfull, floral, honeyed notes, candied fruit, fragrant herbs. Palate: flavourful, sweet, fresh, fruity, good acidity, long.

RASPAY 2006 TR
monastrell

83

VINS DEL COMTAT

Turballos, 1
3820 Cocentaina (Alicante)
☎: +34 667 669 287 - Fax: +34 965 593 194
www.vinsdelcomtat.com
vinsdelcomtat@gmail.com

CRISTALÍ 2012 B
100% moscatel de alejandría

91 Colour: golden. Nose: powerfull, floral, honeyed notes, candied fruit, fragrant herbs. Palate: flavourful, sweet, fresh, fruity, good acidity, long.

MAIGMÓ 2010 TR
100% monastrell

86 Colour: cherry, garnet rim. Nose: ripe fruit, fruit preserve, scrubland, sweet spices. Palate: powerful, flavourful, rich, complex.

MONTCABRER 2006 TR
100% cabernet sauvignon

85 Colour: pale ruby, brick rim edge. Nose: spicy, fine reductive notes, wet leather, aged wood nuances, fruit liqueur notes. Palate: spicy, fine tannins, long.

PENYA CADIELLA SELECCIÓ 2008 T
20% monastrell, 20% cabernet sauvignon, 15% merlot, 15% syrah, 15% tempranillo, 20% giró

89 Colour: cherry, garnet rim. Nose: creamy oak, toasty, complex, overripe fruit, fruit liqueur notes, wet leather. Palate: powerful, flavourful, toasty, round tannins.

PEÑA CADIELLA 2008 TC
25% monastrell, 25% cabernet sauvignon, 15% merlot, 15% tempranillo, 20% giró

85 Colour: cherry, purple rim. Nose: ripe fruit, aged wood nuances, spicy, old leather. Palate: spirituous, correct.

SANTA BÁRBARA 2010 T ROBLE
50% monastrell, 50% cabernet sauvignon

86 Colour: bright cherry. Nose: ripe fruit, sweet spices, creamy oak. Palate: flavourful, fruity, toasty, slightly dry, soft tannins.

SERRELLA 2007 T
33% monastrell, 33% petit verdot, 33% pinot noir

86 Colour: very deep cherry. Nose: powerfull, overripe fruit, toasty, sweet spices. Palate: fine bitter notes, spicy, ripe fruit.

VERDEVAL 2012 B
60% moscatel de alejandría, 20% macabeo, 10% chardonnay

85 Colour: bright straw. Nose: fresh, fresh fruit, white flowers, balsamic herbs. Palate: flavourful, fruity, good acidity.

VIÑEDO Y BODEGA HERETAT DE CESILIA

Paraje Alcaydias, 4
3660 Novelda (Alicante)
☎: +34 965 605 385 - Fax: +34 965 604 763
www.heretatdecesilia.com
administracion@heretatdecesilia.com

AD 2011 T

88 Colour: bright cherry. Nose: ripe fruit, sweet spices, creamy oak, expressive. Palate: flavourful, fruity, toasty, round tannins.

CESILIA BLANC 2012 B
moscatel, malvasía

89 Colour: bright straw. Nose: fresh, white flowers, candied fruit. Palate: flavourful, fruity, good acidity, balanced.

CESILIA ROSÉ 2012 RD
merlot, monastrell, syrah

88 Colour: salmon. Nose: elegant, medium intensity, floral. Palate: spicy, ripe fruit, long.

VIÑEDOS CULTURALES

Plaza Constitución, 8 - 1º
3380 Bigastro (Alicante)
☎: +34 966 770 353 - Fax: +34 966 770 353
vinedosculturales.blogspot.com.es
vinedosculturales@gmail.com

BENIMAQUIA MOSCATEL 2012 B
moscatel

90 Colour: golden. Nose: powerfull, floral, honeyed notes, candied fruit, fragrant herbs. Palate: flavourful, fresh, fruity, good acidity, long, fine bitter notes. Personality.

BENIMAQUIA TINAJAS 2012 B
moscatel

92 Colour: bright golden. Nose: expressive, varietal, characterful, earthy notes. Palate: good acidity, fine bitter notes, long. Personality.

EL MORRÓN 2012 T
100% garnacha

90 Colour: cherry, garnet rim. Nose: fruit liqueur notes. Palate: ripe fruit, good acidity, fine bitter notes.

KULIN 2012 T
monastrell

88 Colour: deep cherry. Nose: overripe fruit, balsamic herbs, acetaldehyde, complex. Palate: fine bitter notes, powerful, flavourful, spirituous.

LA AMISTAD 2012 RD
rojal

86 Colour: rose. Nose: raspberry, fruit preserve, characterful, powerfull. Palate: fine bitter notes, sweetness.

LOS CIPRESES DE USALDÓN 2012 T
100% garnacha peluda

93 Colour: light cherry. Nose: fresh fruit, fruit expression, floral, scrubland, elegant. Palate: good acidity, fine bitter notes, easy to drink, fine tannins.

MUSIKANTO 2012 RD
100% garnacha peluda

88 Colour: onion pink. Nose: elegant, dried flowers, fragrant herbs, overripe fruit. Palate: light-bodied, good acidity, long, spicy.

RAMBLIS DEL ARCO 2012 T
forcayat

89 Colour: cherry, garnet rim. Nose: medium intensity, violet drops. Palate: fresh, light-bodied.

RAMBLIS GIRÓ 2012 T
100% giró

91 Colour: cherry, purple rim. Nose: expressive, fresh fruit, red berry notes, floral. Palate: flavourful, fruity, good acidity, round tannins.

RAMBLIS MONASTRELL 2012 T
100% monastrell

92 Colour: light cherry. Nose: candied fruit, scrubland, spicy. Palate: flavourful, good acidity, elegant.

TRAGOLARGO 2012 T
100% monastrell

89 Colour: cherry, purple rim. Nose: fresh fruit, red berry notes, violet drops. Palate: flavourful, good acidity, round tannins.

Consejo Regulador
DO Boundary

LOCATION:

In the South East region of the province of Albacete. It covers the municipal areas of Almansa, Alpera, Bonete, Corral Rubio, Higueruela, Hoya Gonzalo, Pétrola and the municipal district of El Villar de Chinchilla.

CLIMATE:

Of a continental type, somewhat less extreme than the climate of La Mancha, although the summers are very hot, with temperatures which easily reach 40 °C. Rainfall, on the other hand, is scant, an average of about 350 mm a year. The majority of the vineyards are situated on the plains, although there are a few situated on the slopes.

SOIL:

The soil is limy, poor in organic matter and with some clayey areas. The vineyards are situated at an altitude of about 700 m.

GRAPE VARIETIES:

WHITE: *Chardonnay, moscatel de grano menudo, Verdejo* and *Sauvignon Blanc.*
RED: *Garnacha Tintorera (most popular), Cencibel (Tempranillo), Monastrell (second most popular), Syrah, cabernet sauvignon, merlot, granacha, petit verdot and pinot noir.*

FIGURES:

Vineyard surface: 7,400 – **Wine-Growers:** 760 – **Wineries:** 12 – **2012 Harvest rating:** Very Good – **Production:** 5.478.300 litres – **Market percentages:** 20% domestic. 80% export

VINTAGE RATING PEÑÍNGUIDE				
2008	**2009**	**2010**	**2011**	**2012**
VERY GOOD	GOOD	VERY GOOD	VERY GOOD	VERY GOOD

CONSEJO REGULADOR
Avda. Carlos III (Apdo. 158) - 02640 Almansa (Albacete) ☎: +34 967 340 258. Fax: +34 967 310 842
info@vinosdealmansa.com   www.vinosdealmansa.com

BODEGA SANTA CRUZ DE ALPERA

Cooperativa, s/n
2690 Alpera (Albacete)
☎: +34 967 330 108 - Fax: +34 967 330 903
www.bodegasantacruz.com
comercial@bodegasantacruz.com

RUPESTRE DE ALPERA 2009 T BARRICA
garnacha tintorera

90 Colour: cherry, garnet rim. Nose: ripe fruit, spicy, creamy oak, toasty, complex. Palate: powerful, flavourful, toasty, round tannins.

SANTA CRUZ DE ALPERA 2012 B
verdejo

86 Colour: bright yellow. Nose: candied fruit, fragrant herbs, floral, citrus fruit. Palate: powerful, flavourful, fruity.

SANTA CRUZ DE ALPERA 2012 RD
syrah

85 Colour: rose. Nose: floral, red berry notes, candied fruit, balsamic herbs, violet drops. Palate: fresh, light-bodied, easy to drink.

SANTA CRUZ DE ALPERA 2012 T MACERACIÓN CARBÓNICA
garnacha tintorera

90 Colour: cherry, purple rim. Nose: fresh fruit, red berry notes, floral, violet drops. Palate: flavourful, fruity, good acidity, round tannins.

SANTA CRUZ DE ALPERA MOSTO PARCIALMENTE FERMENTADO 2012 B
verdejo

82

SANTA CRUZ DE ALPERA MOSTO PARCIALMENTE FERMENTADO 2012 RD
syrah

85 Colour: rose, purple rim. Nose: powerfull, ripe fruit, red berry notes, floral. Palate: powerful, fruity, fresh, sweetness.

BODEGAS ALMANSEÑAS

Ctra. de Alpera, CM 3201 Km. 98,6
2640 Almansa (Albacete)
☎: +34 967 098 116 - Fax: +34 967 098 121
www.ventalavega.com
adaras@ventalavega.com

ADARAS 2008 T
garnacha tintorera

91 Colour: cherry, garnet rim. Nose: ripe fruit, spicy, creamy oak, toasty, complex. Palate: powerful, flavourful, toasty, round tannins, balanced, elegant.

ALDEA DE ADARAS 2012 T
monastrell

89 Colour: cherry, purple rim. Nose: fresh fruit, red berry notes, floral. Palate: flavourful, fruity, good acidity, round tannins.

CALIZO DE ADARAS 2012 T
garnacha tintorera, monastrell, syrah

90 Colour: cherry, purple rim. Nose: red berry notes, wild herbs, floral, mineral. Palate: fresh, fruity, flavourful, balanced.

LA HUELLA DE ADARAS 2011 T
garnacha tintorera, monastrell, syrah

89 Colour: cherry, purple rim. Nose: red berry notes, ripe fruit, balsamic herbs, spicy. Palate: powerful, fruity, balanced.

LA HUELLA DE ADARAS 2012 B
sauvignon blanc, verdejo

86 Colour: bright yellow. Nose: powerfull, ripe fruit, sweet spices, creamy oak, fragrant herbs. Palate: rich, smoky aftertaste, flavourful, fresh.

VENTA LA VEGA OLD VINE 2010 T
garnacha tintorera, monastrell

89 Colour: cherry, garnet rim. Nose: red berry notes, ripe fruit, balsamic herbs, creamy oak. Palate: powerful, flavourful, correct, balanced.

VENTA LA VEGA VINTAGE 2012 T
garnacha tintorera, monastrell, syrah

86 Colour: cherry, purple rim. Nose: expressive, fresh fruit, red berry notes, floral. Palate: flavourful, fruity, good acidity, round tannins.

BODEGAS ATALAYA

Ctra. Almansa - Ayora, Km. 1
2640 Almansa (Albacete)
☎: +34 968 435 022 - Fax: +34 968 716 051
www.orowines.com
info@orowines.com

ALAYA 2010 T
100% garnacha tintorera

92 Colour: very deep cherry. Nose: powerfull, toasty, creamy oak, cocoa bean, ripe fruit. Palate: fruity, powerful, smoky aftertaste, sweet tannins.

ALAYA 2011 T
100% garnacha tintorera

91 Colour: cherry, garnet rim. Nose: creamy oak, toasty, complex, dried fruit, overripe fruit. Palate: powerful, flavourful, toasty, round tannins, sweetness.

LA ATALAYA 2011 T
85% garnacha tintorera, 15% monastrell

92 Colour: cherry, garnet rim. Nose: ripe fruit, spicy, creamy oak, toasty, characterful. Palate: powerful, flavourful, toasty, round tannins.

LAYA 2012 T
70% garnacha, 30% monastrell

91 Colour: bright cherry. Nose: sweet spices, creamy oak, expressive, fruit expression. Palate: flavourful, fruity, toasty, round tannins.

BODEGAS CASA ROJO

Sánchez Picazo, 53
30332 Balsapintada (Murcia)
☎: +34 968 151 520 - Fax: +34 968 151 690
www.casarojo.com
info@casarojo.com

CAVALLS 2010 TC
100% garnacha tintorera

88 Colour: cherry, garnet rim. Nose: ripe fruit, sweet spices, creamy oak, spicy. Palate: long, toasty, flavourful.

BODEGAS PIQUERAS

Zapateros, 11
2640 Almansa (Albacete)
☎: +34 967 341 482 - Fax: +34 967 345 480
www.bodegaspiqueras.es
info@bodegaspiqueras.es

CASTILLO DE ALMANSA SAUVIGNON VERDEJO 2012 B
verdejo, sauvignon blanc

85 Colour: bright straw. Nose: white flowers, tropical fruit, fragrant herbs. Palate: fresh, fruity, easy to drink.

CASTILLO DE ALMANSA 2010 TR
monastrell, syrah, tempranillo

88 Colour: cherry, garnet rim. Nose: ripe fruit, creamy oak, toasty, dark chocolate. Palate: powerful, flavourful, toasty.

CASTILLO DE ALMANSA 2011 TC
monastrell, tempranillo, cabernet sauvignon

86 Colour: cherry, garnet rim. Nose: red berry notes, ripe fruit, aged wood nuances, dry stone. Palate: powerful, flavourful, correct.

CASTILLO DE ALMANSA 2012 T
garnacha tintorera

88 Colour: cherry, purple rim. Nose: expressive, fresh fruit, red berry notes, floral. Palate: flavourful, fruity, round tannins, balanced.

CASTILLO DE ALMANSA SELECCIÓN 2008 T
monastrell, syrah, garnacha tintorera, tempranillo

89 Colour: cherry, garnet rim. Nose: ripe fruit, spicy, balsamic herbs, aged wood nuances. Palate: powerful, spicy, long, toasty.

PIQUERAS BLACK LABEL 2011 T
syrah, monastrell

89 Colour: cherry, purple rim. Nose: toasty, aromatic coffee, balsamic herbs, ripe fruit, earthy notes. Palate: powerful, flavourful, toasty.

VALCANTO 2011 T
monastrell

87 Colour: bright cherry. Nose: ripe fruit, sweet spices, creamy oak, toasty. Palate: flavourful, fruity, toasty, round tannins.

VALCANTO SYRAH 2011 T
syrah

85 Colour: cherry, garnet rim. Nose: ripe fruit, spicy, creamy oak. Palate: powerful, flavourful, toasty.

SOC. COOP. AGRARIA CLM SANTA QUITERIA

Baltasar González Sáez, 34
2694 Higueruela (Albacete)
☎: +34 967 287 012 - Fax: +34 967 287 031
www.tintoralba.com
direccion@tintoralba.com

TINTORALBA 2012 B
sauvignon blanc, verdejo

85 Colour: bright straw. Nose: fresh, fresh fruit, white flowers. Palate: flavourful, fruity, good acidity, balanced.

TINTORALBA 2012 T
garnacha tintorera

89 Colour: cherry, purple rim. Nose: expressive, red berry notes, floral, fragrant herbs. Palate: flavourful, fruity, powerful, easy to drink.

TINTORALBA ECOLÓGICO 2012 T
100% garnacha tintorera

88 Colour: bright cherry. Nose: ripe fruit, sweet spices, creamy oak. Palate: flavourful, toasty, balanced.

Amurrio

VITORIA-GASTEIZ

▽ Consejo Regulador
● DO Boundary

DO ARABAKO TXAKOLINA / D.O.P.

LOCATION:

It covers the region of Aiara (Ayala), situated in the north west of the province of Alava on the banks of the Nervion river basin. Specifically, it is made up of the municipalities of Amurrio, Artziniega, Aiara (Ayala), Laudio (Llodio) and Okondo.

CLIMATE:

Similar to that of the DO Bizkaiko Txakolina, determined by the influence of the Bay of Biscay, although somewhat less humid and slightly drier and fresher. In fact, the greatest risk in the region stems from frost in the spring. However, it should not be forgotten that part of its vineyards borders on the innermost plantations of the DO Bizkaiko Txakolina.

SOIL:

A great variety of formations are found, ranging from clayey to fundamentally stony, precisely those which to date are producing the best results and where fairly stable grape ripening is achieved.

GRAPE VARIETIES:

MAIN: *Hondarrabi Zuri* (80%).
AUTHORIZED: *Petit Manseng, Petit Corbu* and *Gross Manseng*.

FIGURES:

Vineyard surface: 100,58 – **Wine-Growers:** 45 – **Wineries:** 8 – **2012 Harvest rating:** Excellent – **Production:** 385.722 litres – **Market percentages:** 80% domestic. 20% export

2008	2009	2010	2011	2012
VERY GOOD	N/A	N/A	N/A	EXCELLENT

CONSEJO REGULADOR
Dionisio Aldama, 7- 1ºD Apdo. 36 - 01470 Amurrio (Álava) ☎: +34 656 789 372 - Fax: +34 945 891 211
merino@txakolidealava.com   www.txakolidealava.com

ARABAKO TXAKOLINA

Avda. Maskuribai s/n
1470 Amurrio (Álava)
☎: +34 945 891 211
www.xarmant.net
arabakotxakolinaeuskalnet.net

XARMANT 2012 B
hondarrabi zuri, petit corbu, gros manseng

86 Colour: bright yellow. Nose: floral, citrus fruit, candied fruit, wild herbs. Palate: fresh, fruity, flavourful.

ARTOMAÑA TXAKOLINA

Masalarreina, s/n
1468 Amurrio (Alava)
☎: +34 945 891 211 - Fax: +34 945 891 211
www.eukeni.net
artomanatxakolina@euskalnet.net

EUKENI 2012 B
80% hondarrabi zuri, 10% petit corbu, 10% gros manseng

87 Colour: bright straw. Nose: fresh, fresh fruit, white flowers, citrus fruit. Palate: flavourful, fruity, balsamic.

BODEGA SEÑORÍO DE ASTOBIZA

Barrio Jandiola, 16 (Caserío Aretxabala)
1409 Okondo (Bizkaia)
☎: +34 945 898 516 - Fax: +34 945 898 447
www.senoriodeastobiza.com
comercial@senoriodeastobiza.com

MALKOA TXAKOLI EDICIÓN LIMITADA 2012 B
100% hondarrabi zuri

89 Colour: bright straw. Nose: dried flowers, ripe fruit, citrus fruit, balsamic herbs. Palate: fresh, fruity, balanced, elegant.

SEÑORÍO DE ASTOBIZA 2012 B
70% hondarrabi zuri, 15% gros manseng, 15% petit corbu

88 Colour: bright straw. Nose: faded flowers, wild herbs, fruit expression. Palate: correct, fresh, fruity.

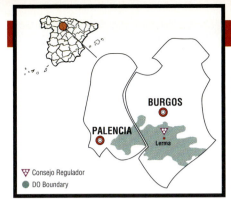

Consejo Regulador
DO Boundary

BURGOS

PALENCIA
Lerma

LOCATION:

With the medieval city of Lerma at the core of the region, Arlanza occupies the central and southern part of the province of Burgos, on the river valleys of the Arlanza and its subsidiaries, all the way westwards through 13 municipal districts of the province of Palencia until the Pisuerga River is reached.

CLIMATE:

The climate of this wine region is said to be one of the harshest within Castilla y León, with lower temperatures towards the western areas and rainfall higher on the eastern parts, in the highlands of the province of Soria.

SOIL:

Soil in the region is not particularly deep, with soft rocks underneath and good humidity levels. The landscape is one of rolling hills where vines are planted on varied soils, from limestone to calcareous, with abundant granite on certain areas.

GRAPE VARIETIES:

RED: *Tempranillo, Garnacha* and *Mencía*.
WHITE: *Albillo* and *Viura*.

FIGURES:

Vineyard surface: 430 – **Wine-Growers**: 80– **Wineries:** 16 – **2012 Harvest rating:** Very Good – **Production:** 750.000 litres – **Market percentages:** 87% domestic. 13% export

VINTAGE RATING	PEÑÍNGUIDE			
2008	2009	2010	2011	2012
GOOD	GOOD	VERY GOOD	VERY GOOD	VERY GOOD

CONSEJO REGULADOR
Ronda de la Cárcel, 4 - Edif. Arco de la Cárcel - 09340 Lerma (Burgos) ☎: +34 947 171 046 - Fax: +34 947 171 046
info@arlanza.org   www.arlanza.org

BODEGA Y VIÑEDOS GARMENDIA

Finca Santa Rosalia, s/n
34260 Vizmalo (Burgos)
☎: +34 947 166 171 - Fax: +34 947 166 147
www.bodegasgarmendia.com
maria@bodegasgarmendia.com

GARMENDIA 2009 TC
80% tempranillo, 20% garnacha

91 Colour: cherry, garnet rim. Nose: powerfull, ripe fruit, fruit expression, spicy. Palate: powerful, toasty, mineral.

GARMENDIA 2009 TGR
100% tempranillo

92 Colour: deep cherry. Nose: powerfull, roasted coffee, aromatic coffee, new oak. Palate: powerful, fine bitter notes, good acidity.

GARMENDIA 2009 TR
90% tempranillo, 10% merlot

90 Colour: very deep cherry. Nose: ripe fruit, toasty, dark chocolate. Palate: powerful, spicy, ripe fruit, fine bitter notes.

WINE FROM SPAIN

GARMENDIA

Tempranillo / Merlot

RESERVA 2009

VINO DE UVAS DE AGRICULTURA ECOLÓGICA
WINE FROM ORGANIC GRAPES

BODEGAS ARLANZA

Ctra. Madrid-Irún km 203,800
9390 Villalmanzo (Burgos)
☎: +34 947 172 070 - Fax: +34 947 170 259
www.bodegasarlanza.com
comercial@bodegasarlanza.com

DOMINIO DE MANCILES 2005 TR
100% tempranillo

88 Colour: pale ruby, brick rim edge. Nose: ripe fruit, spicy, creamy oak, fine reductive notes. Palate: powerful, balsamic, spicy, toasty.

DOMINIO DE MANCILES 2009 TC
100% tempranillo

85 Colour: cherry, garnet rim. Nose: ripe fruit, creamy oak, toasty, fine reductive notes. Palate: powerful, flavourful, toasty.

DOMINIO DE MANCILES 2012 B
50% albillo, 50% viura

85 Colour: bright straw. Nose: white flowers, fragrant herbs, fresh fruit. Palate: light-bodied, fresh, fruity, easy to drink.

DOMINIO DE MANCILES 2012 RD
70% tempranillo, 30% garnacha

88 Colour: rose, purple rim. Nose: floral, fragrant herbs, red berry notes, candied fruit, lactic notes. Palate: rich, fruity, powerful, flavourful.

DOMINIO DE MANCILES 2012 RD BARRICA
70% tempranillo, 30% garnacha

89 Colour: rose. Nose: creamy oak, toasty, ripe fruit, fragrant herbs, dried flowers. Palate: powerful, flavourful, spicy, toasty.

DOMINIO DE MANCILES 2012 T
80% tempranillo, 15% cabernet sauvignon, 5% mencía

86 Colour: cherry, purple rim. Nose: fruit liqueur notes, balsamic herbs, ripe fruit. Palate: powerful, flavourful, correct.

DOMINIO DE MANCILES 2012 T BARRICA
80% tempranillo, 15% cabernet sauvignon, 5% mencía

84

DOMINIO DE MANCILES SELECCIÓN 2007 TC
100% tempranillo

87 Colour: bright cherry. Nose: ripe fruit, sweet spices, creamy oak, expressive. Palate: flavourful, fruity, toasty, round tannins.

BODEGAS ARLESE

Pol. Ind. de Villamanzo Parcela 109
9390 Villalmanzo (Burgos)
☎: +34 947 172 866 - Fax: +34 947 172 866
www.bodegasarlese.com
info@bodegasarlese.com

ALMANAQUE 2010 TC
tempranillo

88 Colour: cherry, garnet rim. Nose: ripe fruit, spicy, creamy oak, toasty, cocoa bean. Palate: powerful, flavourful, toasty.

ALMANAQUE 2011 T ROBLE
100% tempranillo

86 Colour: bright cherry. Nose: ripe fruit, sweet spices, creamy oak, expressive. Palate: flavourful, fruity, toasty.

ALMANAQUE 2012 RD
100% tempranillo

87 Colour: rose, purple rim. Nose: powerfull, ripe fruit, red berry notes, floral, expressive. Palate: powerful, fruity, fresh.

SEÑORÍO DE ALDAVIÑA 2010 TC
100% tempranillo

88 Colour: cherry, garnet rim. Nose: ripe fruit, scrubland, spicy, toasty. Palate: powerful, flavourful, toasty.

BODEGAS LERMA

Ctra. Madrid-Irún, Km. 202,5
9340 Lerma (Burgos)
☎: +34 947 177 030 - Fax: +34 947 177 004
www.tintolerma.com
info@tintolerma.com

LERMA SELECCIÓN 2009 TR
tempranillo

90 Colour: bright cherry. Nose: ripe fruit, sweet spices, creamy oak, dark chocolate, toasty. Palate: flavourful, fruity, toasty.

RISCO 2012 RD
tempranillo, garnacha, viura

85 Colour: rose, purple rim. Nose: powerfull, ripe fruit, red berry notes, floral. Palate: powerful, fruity, fresh.

BODEGAS MONTE AMÁN

Ctra. Santo Domingo de Silos, s/n
9348 Castrillo de Solarana (Burgos)
☎: +34 947 173 304 - Fax: +34 947 173 308
www.monteaman.com
bodegas@monteaman.com

MONTE AMÁN 2004 TR
100% tempranillo

87 Colour: pale ruby, brick rim edge. Nose: ripe fruit, scrubland, fruit liqueur notes, aged wood nuances, fine reductive notes, spicy. Palate: powerful, flavourful.

MONTE AMÁN 2007 TC
100% tempranillo

85 Colour: bright cherry. Nose: ripe fruit, sweet spices, creamy oak, aged wood nuances. Palate: flavourful, fruity, toasty.

MONTE AMÁN 2012 RD
100% tempranillo

84

MONTE AMÁN 2012 T
100% tempranillo

88 Colour: cherry, purple rim. Nose: red berry notes, fruit liqueur notes, balsamic herbs. Palate: flavourful, fruity, good acidity.

MONTE AMÁN 5 MESES DE BARRICA 2011 T ROBLE
100% tempranillo

85 Colour: cherry, garnet rim. Nose: ripe fruit, fruit preserve, balsamic herbs, toasty. Palate: powerful, flavourful, spicy.

MONTE AMÁN PAGO DE VALDEÁGUEDA VIÑAS VIEJAS 2004 T
100% tempranillo

89 Colour: pale ruby, brick rim edge. Nose: elegant, spicy, fine reductive notes, wet leather, aged wood nuances, fruit liqueur notes. Palate: spicy, fine tannins, elegant, long.

BODEGAS SIERRA

Ctra. Madrid-Irún km 203,7
9390 Villalmanzo (Burgos)
☎: +34 947 170 083
www.bodegassierra.com
info@bodegassierra.com

CASCAJUELO 2009 T ROBLE
tempranillo

88 Colour: cherry, garnet rim. Nose: ripe fruit, fragrant herbs, creamy oak. Palate: powerful, flavourful, spicy.

CASCAJUELO 2011 RD
tempranillo

84

CASCAJUELO 2011 T
tempranillo

84

CASTILLO DE URA 2004 TR
tempranillo

87 Colour: pale ruby, brick rim edge. Nose: spicy, fine reductive notes, wet leather, aged wood nuances, fruit liqueur notes. Palate: spicy, elegant, long.

CASTILLO DE URA 2007 TC
tempranillo

88 Colour: cherry, garnet rim. Nose: ripe fruit, spicy, toasty. Palate: powerful, flavourful, toasty, balanced.

SUEÑOS DEL DUQUE 2004 TR
tempranillo

89 Colour: pale ruby, brick rim edge. Nose: spicy, fine reductive notes, wet leather, aged wood nuances, fruit liqueur notes. Palate: spicy, fine tannins, elegant, long.

BUEZO

Paraje Valdeazadón, s/n
9342 Mahamud (Burgos)
☎: +34 947 616 899 - Fax: +34 947 616 885
www.buezo.com

BUEZO NATTAN 2005 TR
tempranillo

92 Colour: ruby red, orangey edge. Nose: ripe fruit, spicy, creamy oak, toasty, earthy notes. Palate: powerful, flavourful, toasty, round tannins, balanced.

BUEZO PETIT VERDOT TEMPRANILLO 2005 TR
50% petit verdot, 50% tempranillo

91 Colour: dark-red cherry, orangey edge. Nose: ripe fruit, balsamic herbs, wild herbs, spicy, creamy oak. Palate: powerful, flavourful, spicy, balsamic.

BUEZO TEMPRANILLO 2006 TC
100% tempranillo

88 Colour: cherry, garnet rim. Nose: ripe fruit, scrubland, spicy, creamy oak, fine reductive notes. Palate: powerful, flavourful, fine tannins, long.

BUEZO VARIETALES 2005 TR
50% tempranillo, 25% merlot, 25% cabernet sauvignon

88 Colour: pale ruby, brick rim edge. Nose: spicy, fine reductive notes, wet leather, aged wood nuances, fruit liqueur notes. Palate: spicy, fine tannins, long.

OLIVIER RIVIÈRE VINOS

Pepe Blanco, 6 1C
26140 Lardero (La Rioja)
☎: +34 690 733 541 - Fax: +34 941 452 476
olive_riviere@yahoo.fr

BASQUEVANAS 2010 B BARRICA
albillo

92 Colour: bright yellow. Nose: citrus fruit, ripe fruit, wild herbs, mineral, sweet spices, creamy oak. Palate: powerful, rich, flavourful, spicy, long, balanced, elegant.

EL QUEMADO 2010 T
tempranillo, garnacha

92 Colour: bright cherry. Nose: ripe fruit, sweet spices, creamy oak, expressive, balsamic herbs, scrubland. Palate: flavourful, fruity, toasty, round tannins.

VIÑAS DEL CADASTRO 2010 T
tempranillo, garnacha

94 Colour: cherry, garnet rim. Nose: ripe fruit, spicy, creamy oak, toasty, complex, floral, scrubland, balsamic herbs. Palate: powerful, flavourful, toasty, round tannins.

PAGOS DE NEGREDO VIÑEDOS

Avda. Casado del Alisal, 26
34001 Palencia (Palencia)
☎: +34 979 700 450 - Fax: +34 979 702 171
www.pagosdenegredo.com
administracion@pagosdenegredo.com

PAGOS DE NEGREDO 2010 TC
tinto fino

89 Colour: cherry, garnet rim. Nose: ripe fruit, creamy oak, toasty, expressive. Palate: powerful, flavourful, toasty, round tannins.

PAGOS DE NEGREDO 2012 T ROBLE
tinto fino

88 Colour: bright cherry. Nose: ripe fruit, sweet spices, creamy oak, fragrant herbs. Palate: flavourful, fruity, toasty.

SABINARES Y VIÑAS

Vista Alegre, 21
9340 Lerma (Burgos)
☎: +34 983 406 212
www.vinoval.es
info@sabinares.com

EL CONFIN 2011 T
tempranillo, garnacha, mencía, otras

93 Colour: cherry, garnet rim. Nose: red berry notes, ripe fruit, balsamic herbs, damp earth, spicy, creamy oak. Palate: powerful, flavourful, rich, spicy, long.

EL TEMIDO 2011 T
tempranillo, garnacha, mencía, otras

92 Colour: bright cherry. Nose: ripe fruit, sweet spices, creamy oak, wild herbs. Palate: flavourful, fruity, toasty, balanced.

SABINARES 2011 B
viura, verdejo, otras

87 Colour: bright yellow. Nose: floral, ripe fruit, fragrant herbs, spicy, slightly evolved. Palate: powerful, flavourful, spicy, long.

SEÑORÍO DE VALDESNEROS

Avda. La Paz, 4
34230 Torquemada (Palencia)
☎: ı34 979 800 545 - Fax: +34 979 800 545
www.bodegasvaldesneros.com
sv@bodegasvaldesneros.com

ERUELO 2007 TC
tempranillo

85 Colour: pale ruby, brick rim edge. Nose: ripe fruit, wet leather, tobacco, waxy notes, spicy, creamy oak. Palate: correct, powerful, spicy.

SEÑORÍO DE VALDESNEROS 2008 TC
tempranillo

86 Colour: cherry, garnet rim. Nose: ripe fruit, spicy, creamy oak, toasty, fine reductive notes. Palate: powerful, flavourful, spicy.

SEÑORÍO DE VALDESNEROS 2009 T ROBLE
tempranillo

85 Colour: bright cherry. Nose: ripe fruit, sweet spices, creamy oak, expressive. Palate: flavourful, fruity, toasty.

SEÑORÍO DE VALDESNEROS 2012 RD
tempranillo

88 Colour: rose, purple rim. Nose: powerfull, ripe fruit, red berry notes, floral, lactic notes. Palate: fruity, fresh, correct, balanced.

DO ARRIBES / D.O.P.

LOCATION:

In Las Arribes National Park, it comprises a narrow stretch of land along the southwest of Zamora and northeast of Salamanca. The vineyards occupy the valleys and steep terraces along the river Duero. Just a single municipal district, Fermoselle, has up to 90% of the total vineyard surface.

CLIMATE:

This wine region has a strong Mediterranean influence, given the prominent decrease in altitude that the territory features from the flat lands of the Sáyago area along the Duero valley until the river reaches Fermoselle, still in the province of Zamora. Rainfall is low all through the year, even during the averagely hot summer.

SOIL:

The region has shallow sandy soils with abundant quartz and stones, even some granite found in the area of Fermoselle. In the territory which is part of the province of Salamanca it is quite noticeable the presence of slate, the kind of rock also featured on the Portuguese part along the Duero, called Douro the other side of the border. The slate subsoil works a splendid thermal regulator capable of accumulating the heat from the sunshine during the day and to slowly release it during the night time.

GRAPE VARIETIES:

WHITE: *Malvasía, Verdejo* and *Albillo.*
RED: *Juan García, Rufete, Tempranillo* (preferential); *Mencía, Garnacha* (authorized).

FIGURES:

Vineyard surface:- – **Wine-Growers:** – **Wineries:** - – **2012 Harvest rating:** Excellent – **Production:** -litres – **Market percentages:** -% domestic. -% export

2008	2009	2010	2011	2012
VERY GOOD	VERY GOOD	VERY GOOD	VERY GOOD	VERY GOOD

CONSEJO REGULADOR
La Almofea, 95 - 37175 Pereña de la Ribera (Salamanca) ☎: +34 923 573 413 - Fax: +34 923 573 209
info@doarribes.es   www.vinoarribesduero.com

ALMAROJA

Las Fontanicas, 35
49220 Fermoselle (Zamora)
☎: +34 691 916 260
www.almaroja.com
info@almaroja.com

CHARLOTTE ALLEN 2009 TC
juan garcía, rufete, bruñal, tempranillo

88 Colour: dark-red cherry. Nose: powerfull, slightly evolved, sweet spices. Palate: flavourful, powerful, fine bitter notes.

PIRITA 2009 TC
juan garcía

84

PIRITA 2012 B
malvasía, albillo, godello, puesta en cruz

87 Colour: bright straw. Nose: ripe fruit, earthy notes. Palate: flavourful, fine bitter notes.

BODEGA ARRIBES DEL DUERO, S. COOP

Ctra. Masueco, s/n
37251 Corporario - Aldeadavila (Salamanca)
☎: +34 923 169 195 - Fax: +34 923 169 195
www.bodegasarribesdelduero.com
secretaria@bodegasarribesdelduero.com

ARRIBES DE VETTONIA 2006 TR
juan garcía

89 Colour: cherry, garnet rim. Nose: ripe fruit, spicy, creamy oak, toasty. Palate: powerful, flavourful, toasty, round tannins.

ARRIBES DE VETTONIA 2007 BFB
malvasía

90 Colour: old gold, amber rim. Nose: candied fruit, citrus fruit, honeyed notes. Palate: fine bitter notes, good acidity, flavourful.

ARRIBES DE VETTONIA 2010 TC
juan garcía

87 Colour: dark-red cherry. Nose: medium intensity, ripe fruit. Palate: flavourful, fruity, spicy.

ARRIBES DE VETTONIA 2012 B
malvasía

87 Colour: bright straw. Nose: fresh, fresh fruit, white flowers. Palate: flavourful, fruity, good acidity, balanced.

ARRIBES DE VETTONIA 2012 RD
juan garcía

82

ARRIBES DE VETTONIA VENDIMIA SELECIONADA 2007 T ROBLE
bruñal

90 Colour: very deep cherry. Nose: powerfull, mineral, spicy, cocoa bean. Palate: flavourful, spicy, ripe fruit.

HECHANZA REAL 2010 TC
juan garcía

86 Colour: dark-red cherry, orangey edge. Nose: medium intensity, balanced, spicy, ripe fruit. Palate: flavourful, fruity.

SECRETO DEL VETTON 2009 T
bruñal

92 Colour: cherry, garnet rim. Nose: expressive, ripe fruit, spicy, earthy notes, balsamic herbs. Palate: flavourful, fine bitter notes, good acidity, fine tannins.

BODEGA COOP. VIRGEN DE LA BANDERA

Avda. General Franco, 24
49220 Fermoselle (Zamora)
☎: +34 980 613 023 - Fax: +34 980 613 023
www.vinosborbon.com
vinosborbon@vinosborbon.com

VIÑA BORBON 2010 TC
juan garcía

85 Colour: dark-red cherry. Nose: ripe fruit, undergrowth, cocoa bean. Palate: flavourful, powerful, fruity.

VIÑA BORBON 2012 T
juan garcía

84

VIÑA BORBON MALVASIA 2012 B
100% malvasía

85 Colour: straw. Nose: macerated fruit, wild herbs. Palate: fruity, flavourful.

BODEGA DESCORCHANDO

La Colina, 9 N 417
29620 Torremolinos (Málaga)
☎: +34 634 676 868
www.descorchando.com
jgarcia@descorchando.com

JG 2008 T
juan garcía

88 Colour: bright cherry. Nose: sweet spices, creamy oak, expressive, scrubland. Palate: flavourful, fruity, toasty, round tannins.

BODEGA QUINTA LAS VELAS

Humilladero, 44
37248 Ahigal de los Aceiteros (Salamanca)
☎: +34 619 955 735
www.quintalasvelas.com
quintalasvelas@esla.com

QUINTA LAS VELAS 2010 TC
tempranillo

88 Colour: bright cherry. Nose: sweet spices, creamy oak, ripe fruit. Palate: flavourful, fruity, toasty, round tannins.

BODEGA VIÑA ROMANA

Pereña, 11
37160 Villarino de los Aires (Salamanca)
☎: +34 629 756 328
www.vinaromana.com
joseluis@vinaromana.com

HEREDAD DEL VIEJO IMPERIO 2009 T
juan garcía

90 Colour: cherry, garnet rim. Nose: ripe fruit, spicy, creamy oak, roasted coffee, balsamic herbs. Palate: powerful, flavourful, toasty, round tannins.

HEREDAD DEL VIEJO IMPERIO HOMENAJE SELECCIÓN 2010 T
bruñal

91 Colour: cherry, garnet rim. Nose: creamy oak, toasty, scrubland. Palate: powerful, flavourful, toasty, round tannins.

BODEGAS LAS GAVIAS

Avda. Constitución, 2
37175 Pereña de la Ribera (Salamanca)
☎: +34 902 108 031 - Fax: +34 987 218 751
www.bodegaslasgavias.com
info@bodegaslasgavias.com

ALDANA 2011 T ROBLE
juan garcía

83

BODEGAS PASTRANA

Toro, 9
49018 (Zamora)
☎: +34 664 546 131
www.bodegaspastrana.es

PARAJE BANCALES 2010 T
100% juan garcía

89 Colour: dark-red cherry. Nose: ripe fruit, medium intensity, spicy. Palate: powerful, flavourful, fruity, good structure, ripe fruit.

BODEGAS RIBERA DE PELAZAS

Camino de la Ermita, s/n
37175 Pereña de la Ribera (Salamanca)
☎: +34 902 108 031 - Fax: +34 987 218 751
www.bodegasriberadepelazas.com
bodega@bodegasriberadepelazas.com

ABADENGO 2004 TR
juan garcía

86 Colour: cherry, garnet rim. Nose: medium intensity, ripe fruit. Palate: flavourful, powerful, fruity, spirituous.

ABADENGO 2008 TC
juan garcía

87 Colour: cherry, garnet rim. Nose: short, neat, balanced. Palate: flavourful, fruity, easy to drink.

ABADENGO 2011 T ROBLE
juan garcía

84

ABADENGO MALVASIA 2012 B
100% malvasía

85 Colour: pale. Nose: fresh fruit, neat, fresh, burnt matches. Palate: correct, balanced, light-bodied, flavourful, dry.

BRUÑAL 2007 T
bruñal

88 Colour: dark-red cherry. Nose: dry stone, ripe fruit, creamy oak. Palate: correct, balanced, flavourful, fruity.

GRAN ABADENGO 2006 TR
juan garcía

90 Colour: cherry, garnet rim. Nose: toasty, spicy. Palate: flavourful, fine bitter notes, good acidity.

GALLO VISCAY

Avda. San Amaro, 52
37160 Villarino de los Aires (Salamanca)
☎: +34 659 159 218
www.galloviscay.com
galloviscay@gmail.com

EIGHTEEN 18 2010 T
juan garcía, rufete

90 Colour: deep cherry. Nose: ripe fruit, creamy oak, toasty, scrubland. Palate: flavourful, fine bitter notes, good acidity.

HACIENDA ZORITA NATURAL RESERVE

Ctra. Zamora - fermoselle, km. 58
49220 Fermoselle (Zamora)
☎: +34 980 613 163 - Fax: +34 980 613 163
www.the-haciendas.com
agarcia@the-haciendas.com

HACIENDA ZORITA 2010 TC
100% tempranillo

89 Colour: dark-red cherry. Nose: varietal, balanced, ripe fruit, creamy oak, balsamic herbs, spicy. Palate: correct, balanced, flavourful.

LA CASITA DEL VIÑADOR

Plaza, 5
37220 La Fregeneda (Salamanca)
☎: +34 636 529 130
www.lacasita-wine.com
chus@lacasita-wine.com

AREALES 2008 TC
rufete, juan garcía, tempranillo

86 Colour: dark-red cherry. Nose: neat, fresh, ripe fruit, spicy. Palate: flavourful, ripe fruit, spicy.

CRUZ DE SAN PEDRO 2007 TC
60% juan garcía, 25% rufete, 15% tempranillo

88 Colour: bright cherry. Nose: ripe fruit, sweet spices, creamy oak. Palate: flavourful, fruity, toasty, round tannins, good acidity.

DONALOBA 2008 TC
60% juan garcía, 20% rufete, 20% tempranillo

89 Colour: cherry, garnet rim. Nose: ripe fruit, spicy, creamy oak, toasty, characterful, wet leather. Palate: powerful, flavourful, toasty, round tannins.

LA SETERA

Calzada, 7
49232 Fornillos de Fermoselle (Zamora)
☎: +34 980 612 925 - Fax: +34 980 612 925
www.lasetera.com
lasetera@lasetera.com

LA SETERA 2010 T ROBLE
mencía

88 Colour: bright cherry. Nose: sweet spices, creamy oak, overripe fruit. Palate: flavourful, fruity, toasty, round tannins.

LA SETERA 2011 T
juan garcía

84

LA SETERA 2012 B
100% malvasía

84

LA SETERA SELECCIÓN ESPECIAL 2010 T ROBLE
touriga nacional

90 Colour: dark-red cherry. Nose: medium intensity, neat, expressive. Palate: correct, balanced, round, powerful, flavourful.

LA SETERA TINAJA 2011 T ROBLE
juan garcía, bruñal, rufete, bastardillo, mencía

93 Colour: cherry, garnet rim. Nose: ripe fruit, spicy, toasty, complex, fruit expression, damp earth. Palate: powerful, flavourful, toasty, round tannins.

OCELLUM DURII

San Juan 56 - 57
49220 Fermoselle (Zamora)
☎: +34 983 390 606
ocellumdurii@hotmail.com

CONDADO DE FERMOSEL 2011 T
juan garcía, tempranillo, garnacha

91 Colour: cherry, garnet rim. Nose: ripe fruit, spicy, creamy oak, toasty, complex, balsamic herbs, mineral. Palate: powerful, flavourful, toasty, round tannins.

CONDADO DE FERMOSEL 2012 T
juan garcía, tempranillo, bruñal, rufete

92 Colour: cherry, garnet rim. Nose: red berry notes, ripe fruit, balsamic herbs, sweet spices, creamy oak. Palate: powerful, flavourful, fruity, toasty.

OCILA TRANSITIUM DURII 2006 T
juan garcía, tempranillo, rufete, bruñal

89 Colour: cherry, garnet rim. Nose: ripe fruit, fruit liqueur notes, scrubland, spicy, earthy notes, fine reductive notes. Palate: flavourful, spicy, long, balanced, balsamic, mineral. Personality.

TRANSITIUM DURII 2007 T
juan garcía, tempranillo, bruñal

91 Colour: dark-red cherry, orangey edge. Nose: red berry notes, ripe fruit, wild herbs, spicy, creamy oak. Palate: powerful, flavourful, long, balsamic, balanced, elegant.

TRANSITIUM DURII 2008 T
juan garcía, tempranillo, bruñal

90 Colour: dark-red cherry, orangey edge. Nose: scrubland, dry stone, ripe fruit, spicy, creamy oak. Palate: spicy, long, flavourful, mineral, balanced.

TERRAZGO BODEGAS DE CRIANZA S.L.

Portugal, 7
49232 Fornillos de Fermoselle (Zamora)
☎: +34 663 069 035
www.terrazgo.com
terrazgobc@yahoo.es

TERRAZGO 2008 T
juan garcía, rufete, tempranillo

91 Colour: cherry, garnet rim. Nose: earthy notes, spicy, ripe fruit. Palate: spicy, balsamic, good acidity, elegant.

Consejo Regulador
DO Boundary

LOCATION:

In the north west of the province of León. It covers 23 municipal areas and occupies several valleys in mountainous terrain and a flat plain at a lower altitude than the plateau of León, with higher temperatures accompanied by more rainfall. It may be considered an area of transition between Galicia, León and Asturias.

CLIMATE:

Quite mild and benign, with a certain degree of humidity due to Galician influence, although somewhat dry like Castilla. Thanks to the low altitude, late frost is avoided quite successfully and the grapes are usually harvested one month before the rest of Castilla. The average rainfall per year is 721 mm.

SOIL:

In the mountain regions, it is made up of a mixture of fine elements, quartzite and slate. In general, the soil of the DO is humid, dun and slightly acidic. The greater quality indices are associated with the slightly sloped terraces close to the rivers, the half - terraced or steep slopes situated at an altitude of between 450 and 1,000 m.

GRAPE VARIETIES:

WHITE: *Godello, Palomino, Dona Blanca* and *Malvasia.*
RED: *Mencía* or *Negra* and *Garnacha Tintorera.*

FIGURES:

Vineyard surface: 3.033 – **Wine-Growers:** 2.555 – **Wineries:** 70 – **2012 Harvest rating:** Excellent – **Production:** 9.642.800 litres – **Market percentages:** 72% domestic. 28% export

2008	2009	2010	2011	2012
AVERAGE	GOOD	EXCELLENT	GOOD	VERY GOOD

CONSEJO REGULADOR
Mencía, 1 - 24540 Cacabelos (León) ☎: +34 987 549 408 - Fax: +34 987 547 077
info@crdobierzo.es   www.crdobierzo.es

AKILIA

Ctra. LE-142, PK. 54,7
24401 Ponferrada (León)
☎: +34 902 848 127
www.akiliawines.com
info@akiliawines.com

AKILIA 2012 T
100% mencía

92 Colour: dark-red cherry. Nose: fruit expression, red berry notes, complex, fresh. Palate: creamy, balsamic, spicy.

ÁLVAREZ DE TOLEDO VIÑEDOS Y GRUPO BODEGAS

Río Selmo, 8
24560 Toral de los Vados (León)
☎: +34 981 563 551 - Fax: +34 987 563 532
www.bodegasalvarezdetoledo.com
admon@bodegasalvarezdetoledo.com

ÁLVAREZ DE TOLEDO 2010 T ROBLE
mencía

87 Colour: cherry, garnet rim. Nose: ripe fruit, wild herbs, creamy oak. Palate: powerful, flavourful, toasty.

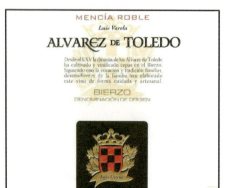

ÁLVAREZ DE TOLEDO 2011 T ROBLE
mencía

89 Colour: bright cherry. Nose: ripe fruit, sweet spices, creamy oak, expressive. Palate: flavourful, fruity, toasty, round tannins.

ÁLVAREZ DE TOLEDO GODELLO 2012 B
godello

86 Colour: bright straw. Nose: fresh, fresh fruit, white flowers. Palate: flavourful, fruity, good acidity.

ARTURO GARCÍA VIÑEDOS Y BODEGAS

La Escuela, 3
24516 Perandones (León)
☎: +34 987 553 000 - Fax: +34 987 553 001
www.bodegarturo.com
info@bodegarturo.com

HACIENDA SAEL GODELLO 2012 B
100% godello

88 Colour: bright yellow. Nose: jasmine, tropical fruit, ripe fruit, scrubland. Palate: powerful, rich, fruity.

HACIENDA SAEL MENCÍA 2012 T
100% mencía

89 Colour: cherry, purple rim. Nose: red berry notes, ripe fruit, fragrant herbs, expressive. Palate: fresh, fruity, flavourful.

SOLAR DE SAEL 2009 TC
100% mencía

90 Colour: cherry, garnet rim. Nose: ripe fruit, spicy, creamy oak, toasty. Palate: powerful, flavourful, toasty, round tannins.

AURELIO FEO VITICULTOR

El Oteiro, 7 San Andrés de Montejos
27791 Ponferrada (León)
☎: +34 987 401 865 - Fax: +34 987 401 865
www.bodegafeo.es
bodega@bodegafeo.es

BUENCOMIEZO 2011 T
mencía

88 Colour: cherry, garnet rim. Nose: powerfull, warm, overripe fruit, toasty. Palate: fine bitter notes, sweetness.

CRUZ DE SAN ANDRES 2011 B
palomino, dona blanca, godello

84

CRUZ DE SAN ANDRES 2011 T
mencía

87 Colour: cherry, garnet rim. Nose: powerfull, earthy notes. Palate: fine bitter notes, good acidity, spicy.

AXIAL

Pla-za Calle Castillo de Capua, 10 Nave 7
50197 (Zaragoza)
☎: +34 976 780 136 - Fax: +34 976 303 035
www.axialvinos.com
info@axialvinos.com

LA MANO MENCÍA 2011 T ROBLE
100% mencía

84

BODEGA ALBERTO LEDO

Estación, 6
24500 Villafranca del Bierzo (León)
☎: +34 636 023 676
www.albertoledo.com
aallrs@msn.com

LEDO CLUB DE BARRICAS 2007 T
100% mencía

90 Colour: dark-red cherry. Nose: damp earth, fresh fruit, neat, complex, varietal, cocoa bean. Palate: round, powerful, fruity.

LEDO GODELLO 2011 B
100% godello

87 Colour: bright straw. Nose: fresh, white flowers, ripe fruit. Palate: flavourful, fruity, good acidity, balanced.

LEDO MENCÍA 2011 T
100% mencía

88 Colour: cherry, garnet rim. Nose: powerfull, ripe fruit, earthy notes, toasty, spicy. Palate: flavourful, spicy, ripe fruit.

LEDO SELECCIÓN 2007 T
100% mencía

88 Colour: deep cherry. Nose: cocoa bean, expressive, fresh, neat. Palate: round, correct, flavourful, fruity.

LEDO. 8 2008 T
100% mencía

89 Colour: cherry, garnet rim. Nose: neat, complex, damp earth, spicy, creamy oak. Palate: ripe fruit, flavourful, powerful, full.

BODEGA DEL ABAD

Ctra. N-VI, km. 396
24549 Carracedelo (León)
☎: +34 987 562 417 - Fax: +34 987 562 428
www.bodegadelabad.com
vinos@bodegadelabad.com

ABAD DOM BUENO GODELLO 2012 B
godello

89 Colour: bright straw. Nose: fresh, fresh fruit, white flowers, expressive. Palate: flavourful, fruity, good acidity, balanced.

ABAD DOM BUENO SEÑORÍO DE VALCARCE 2011 T ROBLE
mencía

90 Colour: cherry, garnet rim. Nose: powerfull, characterful, mineral. Palate: fine bitter notes, good acidity, spicy.

CARRACEDO 2010 TC
mencía

90 Colour: deep cherry. Nose: ripe fruit, balanced. Palate: spicy, ripe fruit, creamy.

GOTÍN DEL RISC ESSENCIA 2007 TC
mencía

90 Colour: deep cherry. Nose: roasted coffee, ripe fruit, neat. Palate: creamy, ripe fruit, powerful, flavourful.

GOTÍN DEL RISC GODELLO LÍAS 2008 B
godello

92 Colour: bright golden. Nose: ripe fruit, dry nuts, powerfull, toasty, aged wood nuances. Palate: flavourful, fruity, spicy, toasty, long.

BODEGA LUZDIVINA AMIGO

Ctra. Villafranca, 10
24516 Parandones (León)
☎: +34 987 544 826 - Fax: +34 987 544 826
www.bodegaluz.com
info@bodegaluz.com

BALOIRO 2009 TR
mencía

88 Colour: cherry, garnet rim. Nose: spicy, creamy oak, toasty, warm. Palate: powerful, flavourful, toasty, round tannins.

BALOIRO 2012 B
godello, dona blanca, palomino

88 Colour: bright straw. Nose: dry stone, ripe fruit, grassy. Palate: fresh, fruity, flavourful.

BODEGA MARTÍNEZ YEBRA

San Pedro, 96
24530 Villadecanes (León)
☎: +34 987 562 082 - Fax: +34 987 562 082
www.bodegamartinezyebra.es
info@bodegamartinezyebra.es

CANES 2011 B
godello

86 Colour: bright straw. Nose: faded flowers, medium intensity. Palate: light-bodied, fine bitter notes, good acidity.

VIÑADECANES 2009 TC
mencía

87 Colour: cherry, garnet rim. Nose: roasted coffee, aged wood nuances, ripe fruit. Palate: ripe fruit, spicy, round tannins.

VIÑADECANES TRES RACIMOS 2009 T
mencía

88 Colour: cherry, garnet rim. Nose: spicy, creamy oak, toasty, expressive. Palate: powerful, flavourful, toasty, round tannins.

BODEGA Y VIÑEDOS LUNA BEBERIDE

Ant. Ctra. Madrid - Coruña, Km. 402
24540 Cacabelos (León)
☎: +34 987 549 002 - Fax: +34 987 549 214
www.lunabeberide.es
info@lunabeberide.es

ART LUNA BEBERIDE 2010 T
mencía

90 Colour: deep cherry. Nose: aromatic coffee, ripe fruit, complex. Palate: flavourful, fresh, fruity, creamy, soft tannins.

FINCA LA CUESTA LUNA BEBERIDE 2010 T ROBLE
mencía

90 Colour: cherry, garnet rim. Nose: varietal, fresh, neat, aromatic coffee. Palate: flavourful, full, good structure.

GODELLO LUNA BEBERIDE 2012 B
godello

90 Colour: bright straw. Nose: powerfull, ripe fruit, citrus fruit. Palate: flavourful, fruity, fresh.

MENCÍA LUNA BEBERIDE 2012 T
mencía

88 Colour: dark-red cherry. Nose: fruit expression, varietal, neat, fresh. Palate: flavourful, full, fruity, fresh.

BODEGA Y VIÑEDOS MAS ASTURIAS

Fueros de Leon nº 1
24400 Ponferrada (León)
☎: +34 650 654 492
www.bodegamasasturias.com
jose_mas_asturias@hotmail.com

MASSURIA 2009 T
mencía

91 Colour: bright cherry. Nose: ripe fruit, sweet spices, creamy oak. Palate: flavourful, fruity, toasty, round tannins.

BODEGAS ADRIÁ

Antigua Ctra. Madrid - Coruña, Km. 408
24500 Villafranca del Bierzo (León)
☎: +34 987 540 907 - Fax: +34 987 540 347
www.bodegasadria.com
info@bodegasadria.com

VEGA MONTÁN ADRIÁ 2010 T
mencía

89 Colour: bright cherry. Nose: ripe fruit, sweet spices, creamy oak, earthy notes, varietal. Palate: flavourful, fruity, toasty, round tannins.

VEGA MONTÁN GODELLO 2012 B
godello

89 Colour: bright straw. Nose: fruit expression, fragrant herbs.

VEGA MONTÁN SILK 2010 T
mencía

88 Colour: dark-red cherry. Nose: medium intensity, neat, fresh, ripe fruit. Palate: round, correct, creamy, flavourful.

BODEGAS ALMÁZCARA MAJARA

Las Eras, 5
24398 Almázcara (León)
☎: +34 659 954 908 - Fax: +34 987 418 544
www.almazcaramajara.com
javier.alvarez@es.coimgroup.com

ALMÁZCARA MAJARA 2009 T
100% mencía

87 Colour: bright cherry. Nose: sweet spices, creamy oak, overripe fruit. Palate: flavourful, fruity, toasty, round tannins.

COBIJA DEL POBRE 2011 B
100% godello

90 Colour: bright straw. Nose: ripe fruit, powerfull, mineral. Palate: flavourful, powerful, full.

DEMASIADO CORAZÓN 2010 B
100% godello

90 Colour: bright yellow. Nose: wild herbs, sweet spices. Palate: fruity, powerful, flavourful.

JARABE DE ALMÁZCARA 2010 T
100% mencía

88 Colour: cherry, garnet rim. Nose: fresh fruit, fruit expression. Palate: good acidity, round, fruity, flavourful.

BODEGAS BERNARDO ÁLVAREZ

San Pedro, 75
24530 Villadecanes (León)
☎: +34 987 562 129 - Fax: +34 987 562 129
www.bodegasbernardoalvarez.com
vinos@bodegasbernardoalvarez.com

CAMPO REDONDO 2011 T ROBLE
mencía

91 Colour: deep cherry. Nose: cocoa bean, aromatic coffee, elegant, complex. Palate: powerful, flavourful, fruity, concentrated.

CAMPO REDONDO GODELLO 2012 B
godello

89 Colour: bright straw. Nose: dried herbs, ripe fruit, citrus fruit. Palate: flavourful, fruity.

VIÑA MIGARRÓN 2008 TC
mencía

87 Colour: cherry, garnet rim. Nose: ripe fruit, spicy, creamy oak, toasty, characterful. Palate: powerful, flavourful, toasty, round tannins.

VIÑA MIGARRÓN 2011 T
100% mencía

88 Colour: cherry, garnet rim. Nose: ripe fruit, spicy, earthy notes. Palate: fine bitter notes, good acidity, round tannins.

VIÑA MIGARRÓN 2012 B
godello, dona blanca, palomino

89 Colour: bright straw. Nose: fresh fruit, white flowers. Palate: flavourful, fruity, good acidity, balanced.

VIÑA MIGARRÓN 2012 RD
mencía

87 Colour: rose. Nose: powerfull, ripe fruit, fruit expression. Palate: flavourful, easy to drink.

BODEGAS CUATRO PASOS

Santa María, 43
24540 Cacabelos (León)
☎: +34 987 548 089 - Fax: +34 986 526 901
www.cuatropasos.es
bierzo@martincodax.com

CUATRO PASOS 2011 T
100% mencía

90 Colour: cherry, garnet rim. Nose: sweet spices, ripe fruit, red berry notes. Palate: flavourful, fruity, fresh.

CUATRO PASOS 2012 RD
100% mencía

88 Colour: rose, purple rim. Nose: red berry notes, ripe fruit. Palate: flavourful, fruity, fresh.

MARTÍN SARMIENTO 2010 T
100% mencía

92 Colour: deep cherry. Nose: neat, fresh, varietal, sweet spices. Palate: good structure, fruity, powerful, flavourful, varietal.

PIZARRAS DE OTERO 2012 T
100% mencía

90 Colour: cherry, purple rim. Nose: fresh fruit, red berry notes, floral, varietal. Palate: flavourful, fruity, good acidity, round tannins.

BODEGAS GODELIA

Antigua Ctra. N-VI, Pieros Cacabelos, Km. 403,5
24547 Cacabelos (León)
☎: +34 987 546 279 - Fax: +34 987 548 026
www.godelia.es
info@godelia.es

GODELIA 2010 T ROBLE
100% mencía

90 Colour: cherry, garnet rim. Nose: ripe fruit, spicy, sweet spices, dark chocolate, mineral. Palate: powerful, flavourful, toasty.

GODELIA 2011 T
100% mencía

91 Colour: bright cherry. Nose: ripe fruit, sweet spices, creamy oak. Palate: flavourful, fruity, toasty, round tannins.

GODELIA 2012 B
80% godello, 20% dona blanca

88 Colour: bright straw. Nose: floral, wild herbs, mineral, citrus fruit, fruit expression. Palate: rich, powerful, flavourful, spicy.

GODELIA BLANCO SELECCIÓN 2011 B
100% godello

90 Colour: bright yellow. Nose: ripe fruit, sweet spices, creamy oak, fragrant herbs. Palate: rich, flavourful, fresh, good acidity.

VIERNES 2012 T
100% mencía

89 Colour: cherry, purple rim. Nose: red berry notes, ripe fruit, balsamic herbs, powerfull. Palate: spicy, fresh, fruity.

VIERNES ROSÉ 2012 RD
100% mencía

87 Colour: rose, purple rim. Nose: powerfull, ripe fruit, red berry notes, floral, dried herbs. Palate: powerful, fruity, fresh.

BODEGAS PEIQUE

El Bierzo, s/n
24530 Valtuille de Abajo (León)
☎: +34 987 562 044 - Fax: +34 987 562 044
www.bodegaspeique.com
bodega@bodegaspeique.com

PEIQUE 2012 RD
mencía

87 Colour: brilliant rose. Nose: fresh, fruit expression, raspberry. Palate: fruity, light-bodied.

PEIQUE GODELLO 2012 B
godello

89 Colour: bright straw. Nose: mineral, fruit expression, neat, fresh. Palate: powerful, flavourful, fresh.

PEIQUE SELECCIÓN FAMILIAR 2007 T
mencía

92 Colour: cherry, garnet rim. Nose: toasty, spicy, ripe fruit, warm. Palate: flavourful, powerful, sweetness, long.

PEIQUE TINTO MENCÍA 2012 T
mencía

90 Colour: deep cherry. Nose: fruit expression, fresh fruit, neat, fresh. Palate: full, powerful.

PEIQUE VIÑEDOS VIEJOS 2008 T ROBLE
mencía

92 Colour: cherry, garnet rim. Nose: ripe fruit, spicy, creamy oak, toasty, earthy notes. Palate: powerful, flavourful, toasty, round tannins.

RAMÓN VALLE 2010 T
mencía

88 Colour: dark-red cherry. Nose: neat, fresh, short. Palate: flavourful, fruity, sweetness.

BODEGAS Y VIÑEDOS AMAYA

San Pedro, 49-53
24530 Villadecanes (León)
☎: +34 644 162 550
www.bodegasyvinedosamaya.es
byvamontuno@gmail.com

MONTUNO 2012 T
100% mencía

88 Colour: cherry, purple rim. Nose: powerfull, characterful, ripe fruit, spicy, dried herbs, varietal. Palate: flavourful, powerful, round.

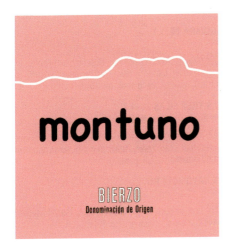

BODEGAS Y VIÑEDOS BERGIDENSES

Antigua N-VI Km. 400. Apdo. Correos, 62
24540 Cacabelos (León)
☎: +34 987 546 725 - Fax: +34 987 546 725
bergidenses@tegula.e.telefonica.net

TÉGULA 2010 T

87 Colour: cherry, garnet rim. Nose: toasty, ripe fruit, balanced. Palate: spicy, toasty, ripe fruit.

VEGA DEL CÚA 2011 T

84

VIÑA GARNELO 2012 B

88 Colour: bright straw. Nose: medium intensity, ripe fruit, citrus fruit. Palate: flavourful, fruity.

BODEGAS Y VIÑEDOS CASTRO VENTOSA

Finca El Barredo, s/n
24530 Valtuille de Abajo (León)
☎: +34 987 562 148 - Fax: +34 987 562 103
www.castroventosa.com
info@castroventosa.com

CASTRO VENTOSA "VINTAGE" 2008 T
mencía

89 Colour: dark-red cherry. Nose: medium intensity, fresh, ripe fruit. Palate: flavourful, ripe fruit, fine tannins.

CASTRO VENTOSA 2012 T
mencía

90 Colour: cherry, purple rim. Nose: fresh fruit, red berry notes, floral, varietal. Palate: flavourful, fruity, good acidity, round tannins.

EL CASTRO DE VALTUILLE 2008 T
mencía

92 Colour: cherry, garnet rim. Nose: ripe fruit, spicy, creamy oak, toasty, scrubland. Palate: powerful, flavourful, toasty, round tannins.

EL CASTRO DE VALTUILLE JOVEN 2012 T
mencía

87 Colour: cherry, garnet rim. Nose: powerfull, warm, overripe fruit. Palate: sweetness, warm, powerful.

VALTUILLE 2008 T BARRICA
mencía

94 Colour: cherry, garnet rim. Nose: ripe fruit, spicy, creamy oak, toasty, complex, dry stone, wild herbs. Palate: powerful, flavourful, toasty, round tannins, elegant.

BODEGAS Y VIÑEDOS GANCEDO

Vistalegre, s/n
24548 Quilós (León)
☎: +34 987 134 980 - Fax: +34 987 563 278
www.bodegasgancedo.com
info@bodegasgancedo.com

GANCEDO 2011 T
mencía

92 Colour: cherry, garnet rim. Nose: spicy, creamy oak, toasty, complex, characterful, mineral. Palate: powerful, flavourful, toasty, round tannins.

VAL DE PAXARIÑAS CAPRICHO 2012 B
godello, dona blanca

93 Colour: bright straw. Nose: fresh, fresh fruit, white flowers, fine lees, mineral. Palate: flavourful, fruity, good acidity, balanced.

BODEGAS Y VIÑEDOS MENGOBA

Avda. del Parque, 7
24544 San Juan de Carracedo (León)
☎: +34 649 940 800
www.mengoba.com
gregory@mengoba.com

BREZO 2012 RD

88 Colour: rose, purple rim. Nose: powerfull, ripe fruit, red berry notes, floral, expressive. Palate: powerful, fruity, fresh.

BREZO 2012 T
mencía, garnacha tintorera

88 Colour: dark-red cherry. Nose: fresh fruit, ripe fruit, red berry notes. Palate: fresh, fruity, flavourful.

BREZO GODELLO Y DOÑA BLANCA 2012 B
godello, dona blanca

90 Colour: bright straw. Nose: powerfull, expressive, ripe fruit. Palate: flavourful, good acidity, fine bitter notes.

FLOR DE BREZO 2011 T
mencía, garnacha tintorera

91 Colour: dark-red cherry. Nose: fruit expression, characterful, varietal, balanced. Palate: powerful, flavourful, fresh, fruity, complex.

MENGOBA GODELLO SOBRE LÍAS 2011 B
godello

94 Colour: bright yellow. Nose: powerfull, ripe fruit, sweet spices, creamy oak. Palate: rich, smoky aftertaste, flavourful, fresh, good acidity.

MENGOBA MENCÍA DE ESPANILLO 2010 T
mencía, garnacha tintorera

93 Colour: cherry, garnet rim. Nose: ripe fruit, spicy, creamy oak, toasty, complex, expressive, varietal. Palate: powerful, flavourful, toasty, round tannins.

BODEGAS Y VIÑEDOS MERAYO

Ctra. de la Espina, km. 6 Finca Miralmonte. San Andrés de Montejos
24491 Ponferrada (León)
☎: +34 987 057 925
www.bodegasmerayo.com
info@byvmerayo.com

AQUIANA 2011 T
100% mencía

92 Colour: cherry, garnet rim. Nose: red berry notes, fruit liqueur notes, balsamic herbs, earthy notes, creamy oak. Palate: flavourful, spicy, long, balanced.

LAS TRES FILAS 2011 T
mencía

91 Colour: cherry, garnet rim. Nose: ripe fruit, spicy, creamy oak, characterful. Palate: powerful, flavourful, toasty, round tannins.

MERAYO 2012 RD
mencía

89 Colour: rose. Nose: fresh, varietal. Palate: flavourful, varietal, mineral.

MERAYO GODELLO 2012 B
godello

90 Colour: bright straw. Nose: ripe fruit, citrus fruit, dried herbs. Palate: flavourful, fruity, good acidity.

MERAYO MENCÍA 2012 T
mencía

91 Colour: cherry, purple rim. Nose: fresh fruit, red berry notes, floral. Palate: flavourful, fruity, good acidity, round tannins.

BODEGAS Y VIÑEDOS PAIXAR

Ribadeo, 56
24500 Villafranca del Bierzo (León)
☎: +34 987 549 002 - Fax: +34 987 549 214
info@lunabeberide.es

PAIXAR MENCÍA 2009 T
mencía

92 Colour: cherry, garnet rim. Nose: ripe fruit, spicy, creamy oak, toasty, characterful. Palate: powerful, flavourful, toasty, round tannins.

CASAR DE BURBIA

Travesía la Constitución, s/n
24459 Carracedelo (León)
☎: +34 987 562 910 - Fax: +34 987 562 850
www.casardeburbia.com
info@casardeburbia.com

CASAR DE BURBIA 2011 T
97% mencía, 3% garnacha

91 Colour: bright cherry. Nose: ripe fruit, sweet spices, expressive, earthy notes. Palate: flavourful, fruity, toasty.

CASAR GODELLO 2011 B
100% godello

88 Colour: bright yellow. Nose: white flowers, fragrant herbs, fruit expression, dry stone, spicy. Palate: flavourful, rich, spicy, long.

CASAR GODELLO 2012 B
100% godello

91 Colour: bright straw. Nose: citrus fruit, fragrant herbs, dry stone, sweet spices. Palate: rich, fresh, fruity, spicy, long.

HOMBROS 2011 T
100% mencía

93 Colour: cherry, garnet rim. Nose: ripe fruit, spicy, creamy oak, toasty, complex. Palate: powerful, flavourful, toasty, round tannins.

TEBAIDA 2011 T
100% mencía

93 Colour: cherry, garnet rim. Nose: sweet spices, red berry notes, ripe fruit, mineral, expressive. Palate: powerful, flavourful, spicy, balanced.

TEBAIDA NEMESIO 2010 T
100% mencía

92 Colour: bright cherry. Nose: sweet spices, creamy oak, red berry notes, ripe fruit, balsamic herbs. Palate: flavourful, fruity, toasty.

CEPAS DEL BIERZO

Ctra. de Sanabria, 111
24401 Ponferrada (León)
☎: +34 987 412 333 - Fax: +34 987 412 912
coocebier@coocebier.e.telefonica.net

DON OSMUNDO 2008 T BARRICA
mencía

85 Colour: cherry, garnet rim. Nose: medium intensity, candied fruit, spicy. Palate: fine bitter notes, spicy.

DON OSMUNDO 2010 T
mencía

90 Colour: deep cherry. Nose: neat, toasty, medium intensity. Palate: round, flavourful, ripe fruit, soft tannins.

FANEIRO 2012 T
mencía

87 Colour: cherry, purple rim. Nose: ripe fruit, red berry notes. Palate: flavourful, fruity.

COBERTIZO DE VIÑA RAMIRO

Promadelo Pol. 33 Parcela 407
24530 Valtuille de Abajo (León)
☎: +34 987 562 157 - Fax: +34 987 562 157
www.bodegacobertizo.com
vinos@bodegacobertizo.com

COBERTIZO 2008 T ROBLE

80

COBERTIZO 2012 T
100% mencía

85 Colour: bright cherry. Nose: short, fresh, macerated fruit. Palate: correct, good acidity, short.

COBERTIZO SELECCIÓN 2008 T ROBLE
100% mencía

81

COMPAÑÍA SANTA TRINIDAD XXI

Travesía Fernández Luaña, 1 1ªA
24402 Ponferrada (León)
☎: +34 987 418 595 - Fax: +34 987 418 540
asesores@asofi.es

CORRO DAS XANAS 2010 T
mencía

87 Colour: deep cherry. Nose: powerfull, overripe fruit, warm, toasty, spicy. Palate: flavourful, fine bitter notes, good acidity.

CORRO DAS XANAS 2011 T
mencía

89 Colour: bright cherry. Nose: ripe fruit, sweet spices, creamy oak. Palate: flavourful, fruity, toasty, round tannins.

DESCENDIENTES DE J. PALACIOS

Avda. Calvo Sotelo, 6
24500 Villafranca del Bierzo (León)
☎: +34 987 540 821 - Fax: +34 987 540 851
info@djpalacios.com

LA FARAONA 2010 T
mencía

97 Colour: very deep cherry. Nose: scrubland, balsamic herbs, ripe fruit, spicy. Palate: good acidity, elegant, round, spicy.

LA FARAONA 2011 T
mencía

97 Colour: bright cherry, garnet rim. Nose: expressive, complex, elegant, fruit expression, spicy, scrubland. Palate: full, varietal, elegant, round, fine tannins.

LAS LAMAS 2010 T
mencía

95 Colour: very deep cherry. Nose: powerfull, ripe fruit, fruit expression, spicy. Palate: flavourful, fruity, spicy, ripe fruit, fine tannins.

LAS LAMAS 2011 T
mencía

95 Colour: very deep cherry. Nose: floral, expressive, characterful, complex, earthy notes. Palate: fruity, good acidity, elegant, fine tannins.

MONCERBAL 2010 T
mencía

94 Colour: bright cherry. Nose: ripe fruit, sweet spices, creamy oak, balsamic herbs. Palate: flavourful, fruity, toasty, round tannins.

MONCERBAL 2011 T
mencía

95 Colour: deep cherry. Nose: fruit expression, red berry notes, floral, balsamic herbs. Palate: fruity, fresh, spicy.

PÉTALOS DEL BIERZO 2011 T
95% mencía, 3% uva blanca, alicante bouschet, otras

93 Colour: bright cherry. Nose: sweet spices, creamy oak, balsamic herbs, scrubland. Palate: flavourful, fruity, round tannins.

PÉTALOS DEL BIERZO 2012 T
mencía

92 Colour: bright cherry, purple rim. Nose: red berry notes, ripe fruit, balsamic herbs, spicy. Palate: round tannins, long, balanced.

VILLA DE CORULLÓN 2010 T
mencía

94 Colour: cherry, garnet rim. Nose: ripe fruit, spicy, complex, earthy notes. Palate: flavourful, toasty, round tannins, ripe fruit, balanced.

VILLA DE CORULLÓN 2011 T
mencía

94 Colour: deep cherry. Nose: floral, fresh fruit, fruit expression, balsamic herbs, scrubland, toasty. Palate: light-bodied, fruity, spicy, ripe fruit.

ESTEFANÍA

Ctra. de Dehesas - Posada del Bierzo, s/n
24390 Ponferrada (León)
☎: +34 987 420 015 - Fax: +34 987 420 015
www.tilenus.com
info@tilenus.com

TILENUS 2006 TC
100% mencía

92 Colour: cherry, garnet rim. Nose: ripe fruit, spicy, creamy oak, toasty, complex. Palate: powerful, flavourful, toasty, round tannins.

TILENUS 2010 T ROBLE
100% mencía

88 Colour: dark-red cherry. Nose: balanced, medium intensity, neat. Palate: flavourful, fruity, fresh, correct.

TILENUS 2012 T
100% mencía

87 Colour: deep cherry. Nose: powerfull, varietal, ripe fruit, sweet spices. Palate: flavourful, powerful, fine bitter notes.

TILENUS PAGOS DE POSADA 2004 T
100% mencía

90 Colour: pale ruby, brick rim edge. Nose: powerfull, complex, spicy, toasty. Palate: aged character, spicy, toasty.

TILENUS PIEROS 2004 T
100% mencía

90 Colour: orangey edge. Nose: neat, fresh, fruit expression, aromatic coffee. Palate: creamy, ripe fruit, flavourful, full.

JORGE VEGA GARCÍA

Ctra. NV, Km. 404
24516 Parandones (León)
☎: +34 609 134 798
www.bodegaspuertadelviento.com
bodegaspuertadelviento@gmail.com

PUERTA DEL VIENTO 2010 T
mencía

90 Colour: bright cherry, garnet rim. Nose: sweet spices, creamy oak, expressive, red berry notes, ripe fruit. Palate: flavourful, fruity, toasty, round tannins.

JOSE ANTONIO GARCÍA GARCÍA

El Puente s/n
24530 Valtuille de Abajo (León)
☎: +34 648 070 581 - Fax: +34 987 562 223
jose.viticultor@gmail.com

AIRES DE VENDIMIA 2011 T
mencía

90 Colour: cherry, garnet rim. Nose: spicy, creamy oak, toasty, characterful, mineral, warm. Palate: powerful, flavourful, toasty, round tannins.

JOSÉ BUITRON GARCÍA

Crucero, 10
24491 San Andrés de Montejos - Ponferrada (León)
☎: +34 675 912 709
sendakyrios3@hotmail.com

KYKEON 2011 T
mencía

88 Colour: bright cherry. Nose: ripe fruit, sweet spices, creamy oak. Palate: flavourful, fruity, toasty, round tannins.

LA VIZCAINA DE VINOS

Bulevar Rey Juan Carlos 1º Rey de España, 11 B
24400 Ponferrada (León)
☎: +34 679 230 480
www.raulperezbodegas.es
raulperez@raulperezbodegas.es

EL RAPOLAO 2011 T
mencía, bastardo negro, alicante bouché

93 Colour: cherry, purple rim. Nose: expressive, balanced, mineral, spicy, ripe fruit. Palate: good structure, rich, round tannins, balsamic.

LA GALBANA 2011 T
mencía, bastardo negro, alicante bouche

93 Colour: bright cherry. Nose: ripe fruit, sweet spices, expressive, scrubland. Palate: flavourful, fruity, toasty, round tannins.

LA VITORIANA 2011 T
mencía, bastardo negro, alicante bouché

93 Colour: very deep cherry. Nose: expressive, elegant, ripe fruit, spicy, balsamic herbs, toasty. Palate: good structure, full, good acidity, balanced.

LS DEL VIVO 2011 B
100% dona blanca

88 Colour: bright yellow. Nose: ripe fruit, faded flowers, dry nuts, slightly evolved. Palate: rich, long, flavourful, fine bitter notes, good acidity.

LOSADA VINOS DE FINCA

Ctra. a Villafranca LE-713, Km. 12
24540 Cacabelos (León)
☎: +34 987 548 053 - Fax: +34 987 548 069
www.losadavinosdefinca.com
bodega@losadavinosdefinca.com

5 ROSAS 2012 RD
100% mencía

87 Colour: rose, purple rim. Nose: powerfull, ripe fruit, red berry notes, floral. Palate: powerful, fruity, fresh.

ALTOS DE LOSADA 2009 T
100% mencía

92 Colour: deep cherry. Nose: powerfull, varietal, fresh, undergrowth. Palate: flavourful, powerful, full, rich.

LA BIENQUERIDA 2009 T
95% mencía, 5% otras

93 Colour: cherry, garnet rim. Nose: creamy oak, spicy, earthy notes, mineral. Palate: fine bitter notes, good acidity, balanced, long.

LOSADA 2010 T
100% mencía

92 Colour: deep cherry. Nose: medium intensity, fresh. Palate: powerful, flavourful, complex.

OTERO SANTÍN

Ortega y Gasset, 10
24402 Ponferrada (León)
☎: +34 987 410 101 - Fax: +34 987 418 544
oterobenito@gmail.com

OTERO SANTÍN 2007 TC
100% mencía

87 Colour: deep cherry. Nose: ripe fruit, neat, fresh, medium intensity. Palate: good acidity, fresh, fruity.

OTERO SANTÍN 2012 B
100% godello

91 Colour: bright straw. Nose: fresh, white flowers, varietal. Palate: flavourful, fruity, good acidity, balanced.

OTERO SANTÍN 2012 RD
mencía, godello

86 Colour: rose, purple rim. Nose: powerfull, ripe fruit, red berry notes, floral. Palate: powerful, fruity, fresh, easy to drink.

VALDECAMPO 2012 T
100% mencía

87 Colour: cherry, purple rim. Nose: red berry notes, floral, ripe fruit. Palate: flavourful, fruity, good acidity, round tannins.

PÉREZ CARAMÉS

Peña Picón, s/n
24500 Villafranca del Bierzo (León)
☎: +34 987 540 197 - Fax: +34 987 540 314
www.perezcarames.com
enoturismo@perezcarames.com

VALDAIGA X 2012 T
100% mencía

88 Colour: cherry, purple rim. Nose: medium intensity, ripe fruit, red berry notes. Palate: powerful, ripe fruit.

PRADA A TOPE

La Iglesia, s/n
24546 Canedo (León)
☎: +34 987 563 366 - Fax: +34 987 567 000
www.pradaatope.es
info@pradaatope.es

LEGADO DE CANEDO 2009 T
mencía

87 Colour: light cherry. Nose: short, powerfull. Palate: flavourful, powerful, fruity, sweetness.

PALACIO DE CANEDO 2006 TC
mencía

86 Colour: cherry, garnet rim. Nose: spicy, toasty. Palate: spicy, ripe fruit, fine bitter notes.

PALACIO DE CANEDO 2006 TR
mencía

87 Colour: cherry, garnet rim. Nose: medium intensity, fruit liqueur notes, toasty, spicy. Palate: fine bitter notes, toasty.

PICANTAL 2010 T
mencía

90 Colour: very deep cherry. Nose: short, medium intensity, neat, fresh.

PRADA 2012 RD
godello, mencía

88 Colour: rose. Nose: fresh fruit, characterful, scrubland. Palate: flavourful, good acidity.

PRADA A TOPE 2012 T MACERACIÓN CARBÓNICA
mencía

88 Colour: deep cherry. Nose: ripe fruit, maceration notes, balanced. Palate: sweetness, flavourful, ripe fruit, round, lacks expression.

PRADA FINCA VALETÍN 2010 T ROBLE
mencía

87 Colour: deep cherry. Nose: medium intensity, neat, ripe fruit, varietal. Palate: flavourful, ripe fruit.

PRADA GODELLO 2012 B
godello

91 Colour: bright straw. Nose: fragrant herbs, fresh fruit, fruit expression. Palate: fruity, powerful, complex.

RIBAS DEL CÚA

Finca Robledo, Apdo. Correos 83
24540 Cacabelos (León)
☎: +34 987 971 017 - Fax: +34 987 971 016
www.ribasdelcua.com
bodega@ribasdelcua.com

RIBAS DEL CÚA 2012 T
100% mencía

87 Colour: cherry, garnet rim. Nose: medium intensity, varietal, red berry notes, ripe fruit. Palate: flavourful, round, fruity, easy to drink.

RODRÍGUEZ SANZO

Manuel Azaña, 9
47014 (Valladolid)
☎: +34 983 150 150 - Fax: +34 983 150 151
www.rodriguezsanzo.com
comunicacion@valsanzo.com

TERRAS DE JAVIER RODRÍGUEZ BIERZO 2010 T
100% mencía

91 Colour: cherry, garnet rim. Nose: creamy oak, toasty, complex, overripe fruit. Palate: powerful, flavourful, toasty, round tannins.

SILVA BROCO

Bodega Silva Broco
24516 Lg. Parandones - Toral Vados (León)
☎: +34 987 553 043 - Fax: +34 987 553 043
antoniosilvabroco@hotmail.com

LAGAR DE CAXÁN 2011 T
mencía

89 Colour: cherry, garnet rim. Nose: fruit expression, fresh fruit, red berry notes. Palate: fruity, powerful, fresh.

VIÑA BROCO 2012 T
mencía

89 Colour: bright cherry. Nose: sweet spices, red berry notes. Palate: flavourful, fruity, toasty, round tannins.

SOTO DEL VICARIO

Ctra. Cacabelos- San Clemente, Pol. Ind. 908
Parcela 155
24547 San Clemente (León)
☎: +34 670 983 534 - Fax: +34 926 666 029
www.sotodelvicario.com
sandra.luque@pagodelvicario.com

GO DE GODELLO 2011 BFB
100% godello

91 Colour: bright straw. Nose: fresh fruit, white flowers. Palate: flavourful, fruity, good acidity, fine bitter notes.

SOTO DEL VICARIO MEN 2009 T
100% mencía

90 Colour: deep cherry. Nose: powerfull, overripe fruit, warm, toasty, spicy. Palate: fine bitter notes, good acidity, long.

SOTO DEL VICARIO MEN SELECCIÓN 2009 T
100% mencía

92 Colour: dark-red cherry. Nose: candied fruit, overripe fruit, toasty, spicy. Palate: powerful, fine bitter notes, good acidity, round.

TENOIRA GAYOSO BODEGA Y VIÑEDOS

Doctor Aren, 8
24500 Villafranca del Bierzo (León)
☎: +34 987 540 307
www.tenoiragayoso.com
info@tenoiragayoso.com

TENOIRA 2009 T ROBLE
mencía

88 Colour: dark-red cherry. Nose: mineral, creamy oak, fresh fruit. Palate: good structure, powerful, flavourful, fruity.

TENOIRA 2011 T
mencía

87 Colour: dark-red cherry. Nose: varietal, expressive, neat, fresh. Palate: fruity, flavourful, fresh.

TENOIRA 2012 B
godello

86 Colour: bright straw. Nose: floral, fruit expression, fresh, expressive. Palate: astringent, fruity, fresh.

TENOIRA 2012 T
mencía

90 Colour: cherry, purple rim. Nose: red berry notes, floral, ripe fruit. Palate: flavourful, fruity, good acidity, round tannins.

VINNICO

Muela, 16
3730 Jávea (Alicante)
☎: +34 965 791 967 - Fax: +34 966 461 471
www.vinnico.com
info@vinnico.com

VIÑA ALTAMAR 2012 T
mencía

88 Colour: cherry, purple rim. Nose: red berry notes, ripe fruit, balsamic herbs, sweet spices. Palate: flavourful, fruity, balanced.

VIÑA ALTAMAR MENCÍA BARREL SELECT 2011 T
mencía

89 Colour: cherry, garnet rim. Nose: red berry notes, ripe fruit, balsamic herbs, earthy notes. Palate: powerful, flavourful, fruity, balanced.

VINOS DE ARGANZA

Río Ancares
24560 Toral de los Vados (León)
☎: +34 987 544 831 - Fax: +34 987 563 532
www.vinosdearganza.com
admon@vinosdearganza.com

FLAVIUM PREMIUM 2009 T
mencía

87 Colour: dark-red cherry, garnet rim. Nose: ripe fruit, spicy, balsamic herbs, creamy oak. Palate: powerful, flavourful, spicy.

FLAVIUM PREMIUM 2010 T
mencía

89 Colour: cherry, garnet rim. Nose: red berry notes, ripe fruit, sweet spices, fragrant herbs. Palate: fruity, balsamic, flavourful.

SÉCULO 2010 T
mencía

87 Colour: cherry, garnet rim. Nose: ripe fruit, spicy, creamy oak, toasty. Palate: powerful, flavourful, toasty.

SÉCULO 2011 T ROBLE
mencía

88 Colour: cherry, garnet rim. Nose: ripe fruit, creamy oak, balsamic herbs. Palate: flavourful, fruity, toasty.

ENCANTO CHARM 2010 T
mencía

88 Colour: cherry, garnet rim. Nose: red berry notes, ripe fruit, balsamic herbs, creamy oak. Palate: flavourful, toasty, correct.

ENCANTO CHARM SELECCIÓN 2008 T
mencía

89 Colour: cherry, garnet rim. Nose: ripe fruit, spicy, balsamic herbs, creamy oak. Palate: balanced, powerful, flavourful.

ENCANTO VINTAGE 2009 T
mencía

90 Colour: cherry, garnet rim. Nose: spicy, creamy oak, ripe fruit, fruit preserve. Palate: powerful, flavourful, toasty, round tannins.

FLAVIUM GODELLO 2012 B
godello

83

VINOS DEL BIERZO S. COOP.

Avda. Constitución, 106
24540 Cacabelos (León)
☎: +34 987 546 150 - Fax: +34 987 549 236
www.vinosdelbierzo.com
info@vinosdelbierzo.com

ARMAS DE GUERRA 2012 B
dona blanca, jerez

87 Colour: bright straw. Nose: medium intensity, citrus fruit, fragrant herbs. Palate: flavourful, fruity, rich.

ARMAS DE GUERRA 2012 RD
mencía

87 Colour: light cherry. Nose: powerfull, red berry notes, ripe fruit, lactic notes, violets. Palate: flavourful, fruity, fruity aftestaste.

ARMAS DE GUERRA GODELLO 2012 B
godello

90 Colour: bright straw. Nose: fresh, varietal, citrus fruit, fresh fruit. Palate: flavourful, balanced, good acidity, fine bitter notes.

ARMAS DE GUERRA MENCÍA 2012 T
mencía

87 Colour: cherry, purple rim. Nose: balanced, wild herbs, ripe fruit, varietal. Palate: fruity, round tannins.

ARMAS DE GUERRA MENCÍA 2012 T ROBLE
mencía

87 Colour: cherry, purple rim. Nose: sweet spices, ripe fruit, dried herbs. Palate: flavourful, balanced.

ARMAS DE GUERRA MENCÍA 9 MESES 2011 T
mencía

89 Colour: deep cherry, garnet rim. Nose: medium intensity, ripe fruit, balsamic herbs, mineral. Palate: flavourful, fruity, round tannins, long.

BLISS 2012 B

85 Colour: bright straw. Nose: floral, citrus fruit, medium intensity. Palate: good acidity, easy to drink, sweet, balanced.

GUERRA 2008 TC
mencía

86 Colour: dark-red cherry, garnet rim. Nose: ripe fruit, spicy, wild herbs. Palate: flavourful, round tannins, spicy.

GUERRA 2012 T
mencía

83

SEÑORÍO DEL BIERZO 2008 TR
mencía

87 Colour: cherry, garnet rim. Nose: ripe fruit, spicy, toasty, complex. Palate: flavourful, round tannins, balsamic.

SEÑORÍO DEL BIERZO 2012 B
godello

89 Colour: bright straw. Nose: medium intensity, ripe fruit, floral. Palate: rich, flavourful, long, spicy,

VINICIO GODELLO 2012 B

86 Colour: bright straw. Nose: fragrant herbs, ripe fruit, faded flowers. Palate: flavourful, long, fine bitter notes.

VIÑA ORO 2012 B
dona blanca, jerez

85 Colour: bright straw. Nose: fresh, grassy, citrus fruit. Palate: fruity, easy to drink, good finish.

VINOS VALTUILLE

Promacelo, s/n
24530 Valtuille de Abajo (León)
☎: +34 987 562 165 - Fax: +34 987 549 425
www.vinosvaltuille.com
info@vinosvaltuille.com

PAGO DE VALDONEJE 2012 T
100% mencía

88 Colour: bright cherry. Nose: sweet spices, creamy oak. Palate: flavourful, fruity, toasty, round tannins.

PAGO DE VALDONEJE VIÑAS VIEJAS 2009 TC
100% mencía

90 Colour: bright cherry. Nose: sweet spices, expressive, roasted coffee. Palate: flavourful, fruity, toasty, round tannins.

VIÑA ALBARES

Camino Real, s/n
24310 Albares de la Ribera (León)
☎: +34 635 600 449
www.vinaalbareswine.com
info@vinaalbareswine.com

TIERRAS DE ALBARES 2009 TC
mencía

88 Colour: dark-red cherry. Nose: closed, balanced, medium intensity, varietal. Palate: spicy, flavourful.

TIERRAS DE ALBARES 2011 T
mencía

87 Colour: deep cherry. Nose: grassy, fresh fruit. Palate: flavourful, fine bitter notes, good acidity.

VIÑAS DEL BIERZO

Ctra. Ponferrada a Cacabelos, s/n
24410 Camponaraya (León)
☎: +34 987 463 009 - Fax: +34 987 450 323
www.granbierzo.com
vdelbierzo@granbierzo.com

FUNDACIÓN 1963 2006 TR
mencía

85 Colour: cherry, garnet rim. Nose: toasty, sweet spices, ripe fruit. Palate: fine bitter notes, good acidity.

GRAN BIERZO 2006 TR
mencía

83

GRAN BIERZO 2007 TC
mencía

85 Colour: cherry, garnet rim. Nose: toasty, spicy, dark chocolate, ripe fruit. Palate: flavourful, powerful, fine bitter notes.

MARQUÉS DE CORNATEL 2012 B
godello

85 Colour: bright straw. Nose: faded flowers, candied fruit, citrus fruit, spicy. Palate: flavourful, fine bitter notes.

MARQUÉS DE CORNATEL 2012 RD
mencía

87 Colour: rose, purple rim. Nose: powerfull, ripe fruit, red berry notes, floral, lactic notes. Palate: powerful, fruity, fresh.

MARQUÉS DE CORNATEL 2012 T ROBLE
mencía

90 Colour: bright cherry. Nose: sweet spices, creamy oak, red berry notes, ripe fruit. Palate: flavourful, fruity, toasty, round tannins.

VALMAGAZ MENCÍA 2012 T
mencía

87 Colour: cherry, purple rim. Nose: fresh fruit, red berry notes, floral. Palate: flavourful, fruity, good acidity, round tannins.

VIÑEDOS SINGULARES

Cuzco, 26 - 28, Nave 8
8030 (Barcelona)
☎: +34 609 168 191 - Fax: +34 934 807 076
www.vinedossingulares.com
info@vinedossingulares.com

CORRAL DEL OBISPO 2012 T
mencía

91 Colour: deep cherry. Nose: medium intensity, balsamic herbs, ripe fruit, balanced. Palate: balanced, flavourful, round tannins.

VIÑEDOS Y BODEGAS DOMINIO DE TARES

P.I. Bierzo Alto, Los Barredos, 4
24318 San Román de Bembibre (León)
☎: +34 987 514 550 - Fax: +34 987 514 570
www.dominiodetares.com
info@dominiodetares.com

BALTOS 2011 T
100% mencía

89 Nose: medium intensity, fresh, neat, varietal. Palate: round, powerful, flavourful, fruity, fine tannins.

BEMBIBRE 2008 T
100% mencía

91 Colour: cherry, garnet rim. Nose: spicy, creamy oak, toasty, complex, earthy notes, mineral, characterful. Palate: powerful, flavourful, toasty, round tannins.

DOMINIO DE TARES CEPAS VIEJAS 2009 TC
100% mencía

91 Colour: cherry, garnet rim. Nose: ripe fruit, spicy, creamy oak, toasty, characterful. Palate: powerful, flavourful, toasty, round tannins.

DOMINIO DE TARES GODELLO 2012 BFB
100% godello

93 Colour: bright straw. Nose: floral, elegant, fresh, powerfull, varietal, dry stone. Palate: creamy, light-bodied, powerful, fruity.

TARES P. 3 2008 T ROBLE
mencía

93 Colour: deep cherry. Nose: cocoa bean, spicy, damp earth, ripe fruit, expressive, aromatic coffee. Palate: spicy, powerful, flavourful, full, good structure.

VIÑEDOS Y BODEGAS PITTACUM

De la Iglesia, 11
24546 Arganza (León)
☎: +34 987 548 054 - Fax: +34 987 548 028
www.pittacum.com
pittacum@pittacum.com

LA PROHIBICIÓN 2009 T
100% garnacha tintorera

94 Colour: bright cherry, garnet rim. Nose: ripe fruit, sweet spices, creamy oak, dry stone. Palate: flavourful, fruity, toasty, round tannins, rich, balanced, elegant. Personality.

PITTACUM 2008 T BARRICA
100% mencía

92 Colour: cherry, garnet rim. Nose: ripe fruit, spicy, creamy oak, toasty, complex, mineral. Palate: powerful, flavourful, toasty, round tannins.

PITTACUM AUREA 2008 TC
100% mencía

93 Colour: dark-red cherry. Nose: fresh fruit, damp earth, roasted coffee. Palate: creamy, balsamic, good finish, ripe fruit, spicy.

TRES OBISPOS 2012 RD
100% mencía

84

DO BINISSALEM MALLORCA / D.O.P.

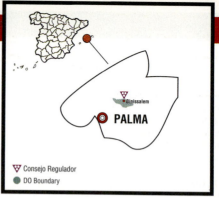

LOCATION:

In the central region on the island of Majorca. It covers the municipal areas of Santa María del Camí, Binissalem, Sencelles, Consell and Santa Eugenia.

CLIMATE:

Mild Mediterranean, with dry, hot summers and short winters. The average rainfall per year is around 450 mm. The production region is protected from the northerly winds by the Sierra de Tramuntana and the Sierra de Alfabia mountain ranges.

SOIL:

The soil is of a brownish - grey or dun limey type, with limestone crusts on occasions. The slopes are quite gentle, and the vineyards are situated at an altitude ranging from 75 to 200 m.

GRAPE VARIETIES:

WHITE: *Moll* or *Prensal Blanc* (46 Ha), *Macabeo, Parellada, Moscatel* and *Chardonnay.*
RED: *Manto Negro, Callet, Tempranillo, Syrah, Monastrell, Cabernet Sauvignon, Gorgollassa, Giró Ros* and *Merlot.*

FIGURES:

Vineyard surface: 601,06 – **Wine-Growers:** 126– **Wineries:** 15 – **2012 Harvest rating:** - – **Production:** 1.704.014 litres – **Market percentages:** 89% domestic. 11% export

2008	2009	2010	2011	2012
GOOD	VERY GOOD	VERY GOOD	VERY GOOD	VERY GOOD

CONSEJO REGULADOR
Celler de Rei, 9-1º - 07350 Binissalem (Mallorca) ☎: +34 971 512 191 - Fax: +34 971 512 191
info@binissalemdo.com   www.binissalemdo.com

ANTONIO NADAL

Finca Son Roig. Camino Son Roig, s/n
7350 Binissalem (Illes Balears)
☎: +34 971 451 146
www.bodegasantonionadal.es
info@bodegasantonionadal.es

BLANC DE MOLL 2012 B
moll, macabeo

83

FRESC 2012 B
moll, macabeo

84

ROS 2012 RD
manto negro, macabeo

82

BODEGA BINIAGUAL

Llogaret de Biniagual, Cami de Muro s/n
7350 Binissalem (Mallorca)
☎: +34 678 079 148 - Fax: +34 971 886 108
www.bodegabiniagual.com
info@bodegabiniagual.com

BLANC VERÁN 2012 B
65% prensal, 19% moscatel de alejandría, 16% chardonnay

87 Colour: bright straw. Nose: fresh fruit, medium intensity, balanced, neat. Palate: fresh, fruity, light-bodied, powerful, flavourful.

GRAN VERÁN SELECCIONADO 2009 T
67% manto negro, 33% syrah

91 Colour: cherry, garnet rim. Nose: scrubland, earthy notes, damp earth. Palate: flavourful, powerful, good acidity.

VERÁN ROSAT 2012 RD
100% manto negro

88 Colour: salmon. Nose: fresh fruit, powerfull, fresh, raspberry. Palate: light-bodied, flavourful, powerful.

BODEGAS JOSÉ LUIS FERRER

Conquistador, 103
7350 Binissalem (Illes Balears)
☎: +34 971 511 050 - Fax: +34 971 870 084
www.vinosferrer.com
secretaria@vinosferrer.com

JOSÉ L. FERRER BRUT VERITAS 2011 ESP
moll, moscatel, parellada

84

JOSÉ L. FERRER PEDRA DE BINISSALEM 2010 T
manto negro, cabernet sauvignon

89 Colour: bright cherry. Nose: ripe fruit, sweet spices, creamy oak, expressive. Palate: flavourful, fruity, toasty, round tannins.

JOSÉ L. FERRER PEDRA DE BINISSALEM 2012 B
100% moll

87 Colour: bright straw. Nose: closed, short, fresh. Palate: fresh, fruity, light-bodied, flavourful.

JOSÉ L. FERRER PEDRA DE BINISSALEM ROSAT 2012 RD
manto negro, cabernet sauvignon

83

JOSÉ L. FERRER VERITAS 2005 TC
manto negro, cabernet sauvignon, tempranillo, callet

86 Colour: light cherry, orangey edge. Nose: medium intensity, short, neat, spicy. Palate: correct, spirituous, sweetness, lacks expression, spicy.

JOSÉ L. FERRER VERITAS 2012 B
moll, chardonnay

87 Colour: bright straw. Nose: fresh, fresh fruit, white flowers. Palate: flavourful, fruity, good acidity, balanced.

JOSÉ L. FERRER VERITAS DOLÇ 2011 MOSCATEL
moscatel

88 Colour: bright straw. Nose: candied fruit, expressive, varietal. Palate: elegant, sweet, fruity, full, powerful, flavourful.

JOSÉ L. FERRER VERITAS DOLÇ SELECCIÓN BARRICA 2010 B
moscatel

88 Colour: golden. Nose: aged wood nuances, candied fruit, wild herbs. Palate: concentrated, sweet, good structure, powerful.

JOSÉ L. FERRER VERITAS VIÑES VELLES 2009 T
manto negro, cabernet sauvignon, callet

87 Colour: cherry, garnet rim. Nose: powerfull, warm, roasted coffee. Palate: fine bitter notes, powerful, sweetness.

JOSÉ LUIS FERRER 2008 TR
manto negro, cabernet sauvignon, callet

88 Colour: dark-red cherry. Nose: closed, short, neat, ripe fruit, spicy, toasty. Palate: powerful, full, flavourful, creamy, ripe fruit.

JOSÉ LUIS FERRER 2010 TC
manto negro, cabernet sauvignon, tempranillo, callet, syrah

90 Colour: bright cherry. Nose: sweet spices, creamy oak. Palate: flavourful, fruity, toasty, round tannins.

JOSÉ LUIS FERRER 2012 RD
manto negro, callet, tempranillo, cabernet sauvignon, syrah

87 Colour: light cherry. Nose: powerfull, ripe fruit, red berry notes, floral, expressive. Palate: powerful, fruity, fresh.

JOSÉ LUIS FERRER BLANC DE BLANCS 2012 B
moll, chardonnay, moscatel

86 Colour: bright straw. Nose: fresh, fresh fruit, white flowers. Palate: flavourful, fruity, good acidity, balanced.

JOSÉ LUIS FERRER CAPROIG 2012 RD
manto negro, callet, syrah

87 Colour: raspberry rose. Nose: fresh fruit, short, neat, fresh. Palate: fresh, fruity, good acidity.

JOSÉ LUIS FERRER MANTO DOLÇ 2011 T
manto negro

89 Colour: dark-red cherry. Nose: candied fruit, fresh, powerfull. Palate: sweet, spirituous, fruity, powerful, flavourful, full.

JOSÉ LUIS FERRER RESERVA ESPECIAL 2005 T
manto negro, cabernet sauvignon, callet

88 Colour: cherry, garnet rim. Nose: ripe fruit, medium intensity, spicy. Palate: flavourful, spirituous, ripe fruit.

BODEGUES MACIÀ BATLE

Camí Coanegra, s/n
7320 Santa María del Camí (Illes Balears)
☎: +34 971 140 014 - Fax: +34 971 140 086
www.maciabatle.com
correo@maciabatle.com

DOS MARIAS 2010 T ROBLE
manto negro, cabernet sauvignon, merlot, syrah

88 Colour: cherry, garnet rim. Nose: ripe fruit, spicy, toasty. Palate: powerful, flavourful, toasty, round tannins.

LLUM 2012 B
prensal, chardonnay

91 Colour: bright yellow. Nose: powerfull, ripe fruit, creamy oak, fragrant herbs. Palate: rich, smoky aftertaste, flavourful, fresh, good acidity.

MACIÀ BATLE 2010 TC
manto negro, cabernet sauvignon, merlot, syrah

88 Colour: light cherry, garnet rim. Nose: closed, balanced, dry stone. Palate: soft tannins, light-bodied, flavourful, fruity.

MACIÀ BATLE 2012 RD
manto negro, cabernet sauvignon, merlot, syrah

88 Colour: onion pink. Nose: neat, fresh, varietal, fresh fruit. Palate: flavourful, powerful, fruity, sweetness.

MACIÀ BATLE 2012 T MACERACIÓN CARBÓNICA
manto negro

90 Colour: cherry, purple rim. Nose: fresh fruit, red berry notes, floral. Palate: flavourful, fruity, good acidity, round tannins.

MACIÀ BATLE BLANC DE BLANCS 2012 B
prensal, chardonnay

88 Colour: bright yellow. Nose: medium intensity, neat, fresh, fresh fruit. Palate: fresh, fruity, light-bodied, powerful, flavourful.

MACIÀ BATLE BLANC DOLÇ 2009 B
prensal

90 Colour: golden. Nose: powerfull, honeyed notes, candied fruit, fragrant herbs. Palate: flavourful, sweet, fresh, fruity, good acidity, long.

MACIÀ BATLE BLANC MARGARITA LLOMPART 2012 B

90 Colour: straw. Nose: floral, fruit expression, expressive, complex. Palate: complex, full, flavourful, powerful.

MACIÀ BATLE BLANC UNIC 2012 B
prensal, chardonnay

91 Colour: pale. Nose: fruit expression, powerfull, neat, fresh. Palate: fruity, powerful, full, complex, rich.

MACIÀ BATLE GUILLEM CRESPÍ 2010 TC
manto negro, cabernet sauvignon, merlot, syrah

90 Colour: deep cherry. Nose: powerfull, ripe fruit, creamy oak. Palate: fine bitter notes, good acidity, spicy.

MACIÀ BATLE RESERVA PRIVADA 2009 TR
manto negro, cabernet sauvignon, merlot, syrah

89 Colour: cherry, garnet rim. Nose: spicy, ripe fruit. Palate: powerful, flavourful, fruity, smoky aftertaste, lacks expression.

P. DE MARÌA 2010 T
manto negro, cabernet sauvignon, merlot, syrah

92 Colour: cherry, garnet rim. Nose: ripe fruit, spicy, creamy oak, complex, new oak. Palate: powerful, flavourful, toasty, round tannins.

PIEDRA PAPEL TIJERA 2012 B
prensal, chardonnay

88 Colour: bright straw. Nose: fresh, fresh fruit, white flowers, expressive. Palate: flavourful, fruity, good acidity, balanced.

CELLER TIANNA NEGRE

Camí des Mitjans. Desvio a la izquierda en el km. 1,5 de la Ctra. Binissalem-Inca
7350 Binissalem (Illes Baleares)
☎: +34 971 886 826 - Fax: +34 971 226 201
www.tiannanegre.com
info@tiannanegre.com

SES NINES BLANC 2012 B
prensal, chardonnay, moscatel de frontignan

84

SES NINES NEGRE 2011 T
manto negro, cabernet sauvignon, callet, syrah, merlot

91 Colour: cherry, garnet rim. Nose: characterful, expressive, spicy, fruit liqueur notes. Palate: flavourful, ripe fruit, fine bitter notes.

VÉLOROSÉ 2012 RD
manto negro

88 Colour: raspberry rose. Nose: balanced, expressive, varietal. Palate: correct, sweetness, flavourful, powerful.

SES NINES SELECCIO 2011 T
manto negro, cabernet sauvignon, callet, syrah, merlot

90 Colour: cherry, garnet rim. Nose: powerfull, characterful, toasty, earthy notes. Palate: flavourful, powerful, fine bitter notes.

TIANNA BOCCHORIS NEGRE 2011 T
manto negro, cabernet sauvignon, callet, syrah, merlot

93 Colour: cherry, garnet rim. Nose: spicy, creamy oak, toasty, complex, earthy notes, ripe fruit. Palate: powerful, flavourful, toasty, round tannins.

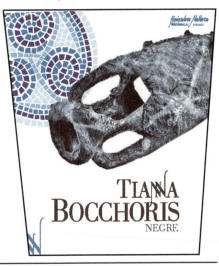

DO BINISSALEM MALLORCA / D.O.P.

TIANNA NEGRE 2011 T
manto negro, cabernet sauvignon, callet, syrah, merlot

92 Colour: cherry, garnet rim. Nose: ripe fruit, spicy, creamy oak, toasty, complex, earthy notes. Palate: powerful, flavourful, toasty, round tannins.

JAUME DE PUNTIRÓ

Pza. Nova 23
7320 Santa María del Camí (Illes Balears)
☎: +34 971 620 023
www.vinsjaumedepuntiro.com
pere@vinsjaumedepuntiro.com

BUC 2009 TC
manto negro, cabernet sauvignon

88 Colour: pale ruby, brick rim edge. Nose: medium intensity, wet leather, toasty. Palate: spicy, good acidity, round tannins.

J.P. 2007 TR

90 Colour: cherry, garnet rim. Nose: fresh, spicy, ripe fruit. Palate: powerful, flavourful, sweetness, spirituous.

JAUME DE PUNTIRÓ BLANC 2012 B
prensal

87 Colour: bright straw. Nose: fresh, white flowers, candied fruit. Palate: flavourful, fruity, good acidity, balanced.

JAUME DE PUNTIRÓ CARMESÍ 2010 T
manto negro, cabernet sauvignon, syrah, callet

90 Colour: bright cherry. Nose: sweet spices, creamy oak, overripe fruit. Palate: flavourful, fruity, toasty, round tannins.

JAUME DE PUNTIRÓ MOSCATEL DOLÇ 2012 B
moscatel

87 Colour: bright golden. Nose: closed, neat, fresh, fresh fruit. Palate: slightly acidic, correct, fruity, fresh, flavourful.

VINS NADAL

Ramón Llull, 2
7350 Binissalem (Illes Balears)
☎: +34 971 511 058 - Fax: +34 971 870 150
www.vinsnadal.com
albaflor@vinsnadal.com

ALBAFLOR 2009 TC
manto negro, cabernet sauvignon, merlot

89 Colour: cherry, garnet rim. Nose: spicy, creamy oak, toasty, expressive, characterful. Palate: powerful, flavourful, toasty, round tannins.

ALBAFLOR 2012 B
prensal

82

ALBAFLOR 2012 RD
43% manto negro, 37% merlot, 19% cabernet sauvignon, 1% syrah

88 Colour: rose, purple rim. Nose: powerfull, ripe fruit, red berry notes, floral, expressive. Palate: powerful, fruity, fresh.

VINYA TAUJANA

Balanguera, 40
7142 Santa Eugenia (Illes Balears)
☎: +34 971 144 494 - Fax: +34 971 144 494
www.vinyataujana.es
vinyataujana@gmail.com

TORRENT FALS 2010 TC
manto negro, cabernet sauvignon, syrah

88 Colour: bright cherry. Nose: ripe fruit, sweet spices, creamy oak, expressive. Palate: flavourful, fruity, toasty, round tannins.

VINYA TAUJANA BLANC DE BLANC 2012 B
100% prensal

88 Colour: bright straw. Nose: fresh, fresh fruit, white flowers. Palate: flavourful, fruity, good acidity, balanced.

VINYA TAUJANA ROSAT 2012 RD
100% manto negro

82

VINYES I VINS CA SA PADRINA

Camí dels Horts, s/n
7140 Sencelles (Illes Balears)
☎: +34 660 211 939 - Fax: +34 971 874 370
cellermantonegro@gmail.com

MOLLET SUÑER BIBILONI 2011 B JOVEN
prensal, chardonnay

90 Colour: bright straw. Nose: white flowers, fragrant herbs, fresh fruit. Palate: elegant, good acidity, balanced, powerful, flavourful.

MONTENEGRO 2012 T ROBLE
manto negro, merlot, cabernet sauvignon, callet

90 Colour: light cherry, garnet rim. Nose: short, medium intensity, neat, balanced. Palate: full, flavourful, light-bodied.

ROSAT DE CA SA PADRINA 2012 RD
manto negro, merlot

82

Consejo Regulador
● DO Boundary

LOCATION:

In the province of Vizcaya. The production region covers both coastal areas and other areas inland.

CLIMATE:

Quite humid and mild due to the influence of the Bay of Biscay which tempers the temperatures. Fairly abundant rainfall, with an average of 1,000 to 1,300 mm per year.

SOIL:

Mainly clayey, although slightly acidic on occasions, with a fairly high organic matter content.

GRAPE VARIETIES:

WHITE: *Hondarrabi Zuri, Folle Blanche.*
RED: *Hondarrabi Beltza.*

FIGURES:

Vineyard surface: 371 – **Wine-Growers:** 223 – **Wineries:** 50 – **2012 Harvest rating:** S/C – **Production:** 1.647.673 litres – **Market percentages:** 97,28% domestic. 2,72% export

VINTAGE RATING PEÑÍNGUIDE				
2008	2009	2010	2011	2012
VERY GOOD	EXCELLENT	EXCELLENT	EXCELLENT	EXCELLENT

CONSEJO REGULADOR
Bº Mendibile, 42 - 48940 Leioa (Bizkaia) ☎: +34 946 076 071 - Fax: +34 946 076 072
info@bizkaikotxacolina.org   www.bizkaikotxakolina.org

ABIO TXAKOLINA

Barrio Elexalde, 5 Caserío Basigo
48130 Bakio (Bizkaia)
☎: +34 657 794 754
www.abiotxakolina.com

ABIO TXAKOLINA 2012 B
90% hondarrabi zuri, 10% folle blanch

88 Colour: bright straw. Nose: white flowers, ripe fruit, medium intensity. Palate: fruity, fresh, balanced.

AMEZKETAKO TXAKOLINA

Santa Marina, 4
48215 Iurreta
☎: +34 946 813 800

AMEZKETA 2012 B
84

AXPE (JOSE A. BILBAO)

Bº Atxondoa, Cº Axpe, 13
48300 Markina - Xemein (Bizkaia)
☎: +34 946 168 285 - Fax: +34 946 168 285
www.axpesagardotegia.com

AXPE 2012 B

87 Colour: bright straw. Nose: fresh fruit, fragrant herbs, dry stone, expressive. Palate: fresh, fruity, flavourful.

BASALBEITIKO TXAKOLINA

Barrio Goitioltza, 37 Caserío Basalbeiti
48196 Lezama
☎: +34 944 556 146

BASALBEITIKO 2012 B
80% hondarrabi zuri, 20% folle blanch

84

BIKANDI TXAKOLINA

Eguzkitza, 6A
48200 Durango (Bizkaia)
☎: +34 616 292 436 - Fax: +34 946 816 519
www.bikanditxakolina.com
miren@bikanditxakolina.com

BIKANDI TXAKOLINA 2012 B
riesling, hondarrabi zuri

86 Colour: bright straw. Nose: faded flowers, dried herbs, ripe fruit, fruit preserve. Palate: powerful, flavourful, spicy.

MIKELDI TXAKOLINA 2012 B
hondarrabi zuri, riesling, grosse mansenl, folle blanch

88 Colour: bright straw. Nose: ripe fruit, white flowers, fragrant herbs. Palate: powerful, flavourful, fresh, fruity.

BODEGA ADOS BASARTE

Bº Urkitzaurrealde, 4
48130 Bakio (Bizkaia)
☎: +34 605 026 115
www.basarte.net
basarte@basarte.net

ADOS 2012 B
100% hondarrabi zuri

87 Colour: bright straw. Nose: fresh, fresh fruit, white flowers, medium intensity. Palate: flavourful, fruity, good acidity, balanced.

BODEGA AMUNATEGI

San Bartolomé, 57
48350 Busturia (Bizkaia)
☎: +34 685 737 398
www.amunategi.eu
info@amunategi.eu

AMUNATEGI 2012 B

89 Colour: bright straw. Nose: fresh, fresh fruit, white flowers, mineral. Palate: flavourful, fruity, good acidity, balanced.

BODEGA BERROJA

48008 Bilbao (Bizkaia)
☎: +34 944 106 254 - Fax: +34 946 309 390
www.bodegaberroja.com
txakoli@bodegaberroja.com

TXAKOLI AGUIRREBEKO 2012 B
85% hondarrabi zuri, 10% riesling, 5% folle blanch

88 Colour: bright straw. Nose: citrus fruit, candied fruit, balsamic herbs, floral. Palate: light-bodied, fresh, fruity, easy to drink.

TXAKOLI BERROJA 2011 B
80% hondarrabi zuri, 20% riesling

90 Colour: bright yellow. Nose: powerfull, ripe fruit, sweet spices, fragrant herbs, fine lees. Palate: rich, smoky aftertaste, flavourful, fresh.

TXAKOLI BERROJA 2012 B
80% hondarrabi zuri, 20% riesling

89 Colour: bright straw. Nose: fresh, fresh fruit, white flowers, citrus fruit, wild herbs. Palate: flavourful, fruity, balanced.

BODEGA ELIZALDE

Barrio Mendraka, 1
48230 Elorrio (Bizkaia)
☎: +34 946 820 000 - Fax: +34 946 820 000
kerixa@gmail.com

MENDRAKA 2012 B
hondarrabi zuri zerratia

90 Colour: bright straw, greenish rim. Nose: expressive, balanced, white flowers, fresh. Palate: fruity, flavourful, long, good acidity.

BODEGA HARIZPE

Eguidazu Kaia, 19
48700 Ondarroa (Bizkaia)
☎: +34 615 730 615 - Fax: +34 946 830 807
www.harizpe.com
txakoliharizpe@gmail.com

HARIZPE 2012 B
hondarrabi zuri, hondarrabi zuri zarratia

89 Colour: bright straw. Nose: fresh, fresh fruit, white flowers, mineral. Palate: flavourful, fruity, good acidity.

BODEGA JON ANDER REKALDE

San Roke Bekoa, 11 (Artxanda)
48150 Sondika
☎: +34 944 458 631

ARTXANDA 2012 B
85% hondarrabi zuri, 5% mune mahatsa, 10% otras

88 Colour: bright straw. Nose: fresh fruit, floral, medium intensity, balanced. Palate: fruity, fresh, good acidity, correct.

BODEGA ULIBARRI

Barrio Zaldu, 1 Caserío Isuskiza Handi
48192 Gordexola
☎: +34 665 725 735
ulibarriartzaiak@gmail.com

ARTZAI 2010 BFB
hondarrabi zuri

90 Colour: bright yellow. Nose: medium intensity, petrol notes, ripe fruit, faded flowers. Palate: fruity, ripe fruit, fine bitter notes, rich.

ARTZAI 2011 B BARRICA
hondarrabi zuri

88 Colour: bright yellow. Nose: ripe fruit, spicy, dried flowers, faded flowers. Palate: fruity, fine bitter notes, spicy.

ULIBARRI 2012 B
hondarrabi zuri

87 Colour: bright straw. Nose: medium intensity, balanced, ripe fruit, floral. Palate: fruity, flavourful, correct.

BODEGAS DE GALDAMES S.L.

El Bentorro, 4
48191 Galdames (Bizkaia)
☎: +34 627 992 063 - Fax: +34 946 100 107
www.vinasulibarria.com
info@vinasulibarria.com

TORRE DE LOIZAGA BIGARREN 2012 B
hondarrabi zuri, hondarrabi zuri zerratia

85 Colour: bright straw. Nose: ripe fruit, faded flowers, dried herbs. Palate: powerful, flavourful, spicy.

ARETXONDO 2012 B
50% hondarrabi zuri, 45% hondarrabi zerratia, 5% mune mahatsa

89 Colour: bright straw, greenish rim. Nose: medium intensity, elegant, white flowers, ripe fruit. Palate: flavourful, fruity, long, good acidity.

ARIMA DE GORKA IZAGIRRE VENDIMIA TARDÍA 2010 B
hondarrabi zerratia

90 Colour: old gold. Nose: candied fruit, honeyed notes, balanced, expressive, toasty, spicy, dry nuts. Palate: rich, flavourful, good acidity.

E-GALA 2012 B
67% hondarrabi zuri, 33% hondarrabi zerratia

87 Colour: bright straw. Nose: fresh, white flowers, jasmine, expressive. Palate: fresh, good acidity, easy to drink.

G22 DE GORKA IZAGIRRE 2011 B
hondarrabi zerratia

91 Colour: bright yellow. Nose: complex, ripe fruit, faded flowers, balanced. Palate: full, flavourful, fine bitter notes, rich.

GORKA IZAGIRRE 2012 B
50% hondarrabi zuri, 50% hondarrabi zerratia

90 Colour: yellow, greenish rim. Nose: balanced, white flowers, ripe fruit, neat, dry stone. Palate: flavourful, fruity, long.

MUNETABERRI 2012 B

88 Colour: bright straw. Nose: fruit expression, floral, balsamic herbs, dried herbs. Palate: fine bitter notes, powerful, flavourful, spicy, long.

SARATSU 2012 B
hondarrabi zerratia

90 Colour: bright straw. Nose: ripe fruit, balsamic herbs, dried herbs, floral, balanced, expressive, fine lees. Palate: powerful, flavourful, rich, elegant.

TORREKO 2012 B
50% hondarrabi zuri, 45% hondarrabi zerratia, 5% mune mahatsa

88 Colour: bright straw. Nose: ripe fruit, balanced, citrus fruit. Palate: fruity, good acidity, fine bitter notes.

UIXAR 2012 B
hondarrabi zerratia

89 Colour: yellow, greenish rim. Nose: ripe fruit, dried herbs, dried flowers. Palate: fruity, correct, balanced, fine bitter notes.

BODEGAS GURRUTXAGA

Baurdo Auzoa, s/n
48289 Mendexa
☎: +34 946 844 937
www.bodegasgurrutxaga.com

GURRUTXAGA 2012 B
84

DONIENE GORRONDONA TXAKOLINA

Gibelorratzagako San Pelaio, 1
48130 Bakio (Bizkaia)
☎: +34 946 194 795 - Fax: +34 946 195 831
www.donienegorrondona.com
gorrondona@donienegorrondona.com

DONIENE 2011 BFB
100% hondarrabi zuri

91 Colour: bright yellow. Nose: powerfull, ripe fruit, sweet spices, fragrant herbs, faded flowers. Palate: rich, smoky aftertaste, flavourful, good acidity.

DONIENE 2012 B
hondarrabi zuri

89 Colour: bright straw. Nose: fresh, fresh fruit, white flowers, expressive. Palate: flavourful, fruity, good acidity, balanced.

DONIENE 2012 BFB
hondarrabi zuri

90 Colour: bright straw. Nose: sweet spices, creamy oak, white flowers, ripe fruit. Palate: fruity, flavourful, balanced.

DONIENE APARDUNE 2011 ESP
80% hondarrabi zuri, 20% mune mahatsa

86 Colour: bright straw. Nose: medium intensity, fresh fruit, dried herbs, fine lees, faded flowers. Palate: fresh, fruity, flavourful, good acidity.

GORRONDONA 2012 B
85% hondarrabi zuri, 5% mune mahatsa, 5% hondarrabi beltza, 5% otras

88 Colour: greenish rim. Nose: medium intensity, fresh fruit, white flowers. Palate: balanced, fine bitter notes, easy to drink, fruity.

GORRONDONA 2012 T
100% hondarrabi beltza

87 Colour: cherry, purple rim. Nose: balsamic herbs, red berry notes, medium intensity, expressive. Palate: flavourful, fruity, slightly dry, soft tannins.

ERDIKOETXE LANDETXEA

Goitioltza, 38
48196 Lezama (Bizkaia)
☎: +34 944 573 285 - Fax: +34 944 573 285
erdikoetxelandetxea@hotmail.com

ERDIKOETXE 2012 B
hondarrabi zuri, gros manseng

86 Colour: bright straw, greenish rim. Nose: fresh fruit, scrubland, balanced. Palate: flavourful, correct, fine bitter notes.

ERDIKOETXE 2012 T
hondarrabi beltza

84

GARKALDE TXAKOLINA

Barrio Goitioltza, 8 - Caserio Garkalde
48196 Lezama
☎: +34 944 556 412
garkaldetxakolina@hotmail.com

GARKALDE TXAKOLINA 2012 B
hondarrabi zuri

87 Nose: fresh fruit, white flowers, medium intensity. Palate: fruity, fresh, good acidity, balanced, fine bitter notes.

ITSASMENDI

Barrio Arane, 3
48300 Gernika (Bizkaia)
☎: +34 946 270 316 - Fax: +34 946 251 032
www.bodegasitsasmendi.com
info@bodegasitsasmendi.com

EKLIPSE ITSAS MENDI 2011 T
50% pinot noir, 50% hondarrabi beltza

92 Colour: light cherry, garnet rim. Nose: expressive, ripe fruit, wild herbs, balanced. Palate: fruity, flavourful, balanced, spicy.

ITSAS ARTIZAR 2011 B
100% hondarrabi zuri

88 Colour: bright yellow. Nose: ripe fruit, creamy oak, fragrant herbs, faded flowers. Palate: rich, flavourful, fresh.

ITSAS MENDI UREZTI 2009 B
100% hondarrabi zuri

93 Colour: bright golden. Nose: acetaldehyde, ripe fruit, dry nuts, balsamic herbs, creamy oak, sweet spices, faded flowers. Palate: powerful, flavourful, rich, balanced, elegant.

ITSASMENDI 2012 B
50% hondarrabi zuri, 50% hondarrabi zuri zerratia

86 Colour: bright straw. Nose: fresh, fresh fruit, white flowers, dried herbs. Palate: flavourful, fruity, good acidity.

ITSASMENDI Nº 7 2011 B
80% hondarrabi zuri, 20% riesling

91 Colour: bright straw. Nose: white flowers, expressive, ripe fruit, faded flowers. Palate: flavourful, fruity, good acidity, balanced, rich.

JOSÉ ETXEBARRÍA URRUTIA

Txonebarri-C. Igartua, s/n
48110 Gatika (Bizkaia)
☎: +34 946 742 010

TXAKOLI ETXEBARRÍA 2012 B

85 Colour: bright straw. Nose: medium intensity, floral, wild herbs. Palate: correct, good acidity, fresh.

MAGALARTE LEZAMA

B. Garaioltza, 92 B
48196 Lezama (Bizkaia)
☎: +34 636 621 455 - Fax: +34 944 556 508
www.magalartelezamatxakolina.com

MAGALARTE IÑAKI ARETXABALETA 2012 BFB
hondarrabi zuri

89 Colour: bright yellow. Nose: powerfull, ripe fruit, sweet spices, creamy oak, fragrant herbs. Palate: rich, smoky aftertaste, flavourful, fresh, good acidity.

MAGALARTE IÑAKI ARETXABALETA 2012 B
hondarrabi zuri

89 Colour: bright straw. Nose: medium intensity, ripe fruit, faded flowers. Palate: flavourful, full, ripe fruit, long.

SAGASTIBELTZA KARRANTZA 2012 B
hondarrabi zuri

88 Colour: bright straw. Nose: fresh, fresh fruit, white flowers, expressive. Palate: flavourful, fruity, good acidity, balanced.

MAGALARTE ZAMUDIO

Arteaga Auzoa, 107
48170 Zamudio (Bizkaia)
☎: +34 944 521 431 - Fax: +34 944 521 431
magalarte@hotmail.com

MAGALARTE ZAMUDIO 2012 B
hondarrabi zuri, petit manseng, hondarrabi zuri zerratia, riesling, mune mahatsa

89 Colour: bright straw. Nose: dried flowers, dried herbs, mineral, balanced, citrus fruit. Palate: powerful, flavourful, fresh.

ZABALONDO 2012 B
hondarrabi zuri, hondarrabi zuri zerratia, petit manseng, riesling

88 Colour: bright straw. Nose: floral, fresh fruit, tropical fruit, fragrant herbs. Palate: light-bodied, fresh, fruity, flavourful.

MAISU C.B.

Barrio Ibazurra, 1
48460 Urduña/Orduña (Bizkaia)
☎: +34 945 384 126 - Fax: +34 945 384 126
www.gureahaleginak.com
maitedurana@gureahaleginak.com

FILOXERA 2011 T
hondarrabi zuri

84

GURE AHALEGINAK 2012 B
hondarrabi zuri

85 Colour: bright straw, greenish rim. Nose: medium intensity, dried flowers, dried herbs. Palate: correct, easy to drink.

MERRUTXU

Caserío Merrutxu, Arboliz 15
48311 Ibarrangelu (Bizkaia)
☎: +34 946 276 435
www.txakolibizkaia.com
info@merrutxu.com

MERRUTXU 2012 B
hondarrabi zuri, chardonnay

87 Colour: bright straw, greenish rim. Nose: medium intensity, white flowers, balanced. Palate: flavourful, fresh, good acidity.

OTXANDURI TXAKOLINA

Torrezar Auzoa, 10
48410 Bengoetxea (Bizkaia)
☎: +34 946 481 769
otxanduri@euskalnet.net

EGIAENEA MAHASTIA 2012 B
100% hondarrabi zuri zerratia

88 Colour: bright straw. Nose: floral, fruit expression, dried herbs, mineral, spicy. Palate: fresh, fruity, balanced, rich.

MARKO 2012 B
100% hondarrabi zuri zerratia

91 Colour: bright straw. Nose: floral, fresh fruit, fragrant herbs, fresh, elegant. Palate: balanced, flavourful, spicy, long, round.

MENDIOLAGAN 2012 B
100% hondarrabi zuri

89 Colour: bright straw. Nose: fresh, fresh fruit, white flowers, balanced. Palate: flavourful, fruity, good acidity, balanced.

OTXANDURI 2012 B
88% hondarrabi zuri, 12% riesling

90 Colour: bright straw. Nose: fresh fruit, floral, fragrant herbs, mineral, expressive. Palate: flavourful, fresh, fruity, balanced, elegant.

OXINBALTZA

Barrio Magunas, 27
48391 Muxika (Bizkaia)
☎: +34 686 345 131
www.oxinbaltza.com
oxinbaltza@oxinbaltza.com

MAIORA 2012 B
90% hondarrabi zuri, 10% riesling

88 Colour: bright yellow. Nose: balanced, faded flowers, ripe fruit, citrus fruit. Palate: rich, flavourful, fine bitter notes.

TALLERI

Barrio Erroteta s/n
48115 Morga (Bizkaia)
☎: +34 944 651 689 - Fax: +34 944 651 689
www.bodegatalleri.com

BITXIA 2012 B

86 Colour: bright straw. Nose: medium intensity, white flowers, ripe fruit. Palate: fruity, easy to drink, correct, fine bitter notes.

BITXIA SELECCIÓN 2012 B

88 Colour: bright yellow. Nose: ripe fruit, fragrant herbs, earthy notes, expressive. Palate: rich, powerful, flavourful.

TXAKOLI KERIXENE

Barrio Orueta, 6
48314 Gautegiz-Arteaga
☎: +34 946 256 861

TXAKOLI KERIXENE 2012 B

85 Colour: bright straw. Nose: dried flowers, dried herbs, ripe fruit, earthy notes. Palate: flavourful, fresh, ripe fruit.

TXAKOLI LARRABE

Barrio Garaioltza, 103 - Caserío Usategi
48196 Lezama
☎: +34 944 556 491

TXAKOLI LARRABE 2012 B

85 Colour: bright straw. Nose: medium intensity, dried flowers. Palate: ripe fruit, good finish, correct.

TXAKOLI SASINES

Barrio Bersonaga, 33 - Caserio Sasines
48195 Larrabetzu
☎: +34 944 558 196

SASINE 2012 B

89 Colour: bright straw, greenish rim. Nose: fresh, fresh fruit, white flowers, expressive. Palate: flavourful, fruity, good acidity, balanced.

TXAKOLI TXABARRI

Muñeron, 17
48850 Zalla (Bizkaia)
☎: +34 946 390 947 - Fax: +34 946 390 947
www.txakolitxabarri.com
itxasa@yahoo.es

TXABARRI 2012 B
hondarrabi zuri

87 Colour: bright straw. Nose: citrus fruit, ripe fruit, balsamic herbs, dried flowers. Palate: rich, fruity, flavourful, correct.

TXABARRI 2012 RD
95% hondarrabi beltza, 5% hondarrabi zuri

80

TXABARRI 2012 T
hondarrabi beltza

84

TXOÑE

Iguatua, 25
48110 Gatika
☎: +34 646 514 154
kepa@larrabeiti.com

BUTROI 2012 B

87 Colour: bright yellow. Nose: faded flowers, ripe fruit, dried herbs. Palate: flavourful, fruity, rich, spicy.

URIONDO

Barrio Urriondo, 2
48480 Zaratamo (Bizkaia)
☎: +34 946 711 870
uriondo.txakoli@gmail.com

URIONDO 2012 B
hondarrabi zuri, mune mahatsa

87 Colour: bright straw. Nose: fragrant herbs, medium intensity, citrus fruit. Palate: fresh, fruity, easy to drink.

URIONDO CUVÉE 2011 BFB

87 Colour: bright yellow. Nose: powerfull, ripe fruit, sweet spices, creamy oak. Palate: rich, smoky aftertaste, flavourful, fresh.

VIRGEN DE LOREA

Barrio de Lorea
48860 Otxaran-Zalla (Bizkaia)
☎: +34 944 242 680 - Fax: +34 946 670 521
www.bodegasvirgendelorea.com
virgendelorea@spankor.com

ARETXAGA 2012 B
80% hondarrabi zuri, 20% folle blanch

89 Colour: bright straw. Nose: fresh, fresh fruit, white flowers, expressive. Palate: flavourful, fruity, good acidity.

SEÑORÍO DE OTXARAN 2012 B
hondarrabi zuri, folle blanch

90 Colour: bright straw. Nose: ripe fruit, citrus fruit, floral, wild herbs, powerfull, expressive. Palate: rich, flavourful, spicy, long, elegant.

DO BULLAS / D.O.P.

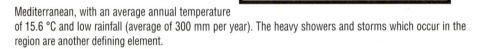

LOCATION:

In the province of Murcia. It covers the municipal areas of Bullas, Cehegín, Mula and Ricote, and several vineyards in the vicinity of Calasparra, Moratalla and Lorca.

CLIMATE:

Mediterranean, with an average annual temperature of 15.6 °C and low rainfall (average of 300 mm per year). The heavy showers and storms which occur in the region are another defining element.

SOIL:

Brownish - grey limey soil, with limestone crusts, and alluvial. The terrain is rugged and determined by the layout of the little valleys, each with their own microclimate. Distinction can be made between 3 areas: one to the north north - east with an altitude of 400 – 500 m; another in the central region, situated at an altitude of 500 – 600 m; and the third in the western and north - western region, with the highest altitude (500 – 810 m), the highest concentration of vineyards and the best potential for quality.

GRAPE VARIETIES:

WHITE: *Macabeo* (main), *Airén, Chardonnay, Malvasía, Moscatel de Grano Menudo* and *Sauvignon Blanc.*
RED: *Monastrell* (main), *Petit Verdot, Tempranillo, Cabernet Sauvignon, Syrah, Merlot* and *Garnacha.*

FIGURES:

Vineyard surface: 2,137– **Wine-Growers:** 345 – **Wineries:** 12 – **2012 Harvest rating:** Very Good – **Production:** 1.847.340 litres – **Market percentages:** 59% domestic.41% export

BODEGA "SAN ISIDRO" BULLAS

Pol. Ind. Marimingo, Altiplano, s/n
30180 Bullas (Murcia)
☎: +34 968 654 991 - Fax: +34 968 652 160
nicolas@bodegasanisidrobullas.com

CEPAS DEL ZORRO 2011 T
100% monastrell

88 Colour: cherry, purple rim. Nose: fresh fruit, red berry notes, floral. Palate: flavourful, fruity, good acidity, round tannins.

CEPAS DEL ZORRO 2012 RD
80% monastrell, 20% garnacha

88 Colour: rose, purple rim. Nose: expressive, raspberry, ripe fruit. Palate: flavourful, fruity, fresh.

CEPAS DEL ZORRO 2012 T
85% monastrell, 15% syrah

88 Colour: cherry, purple rim. Nose: powerfull, ripe fruit, red berry notes. Palate: good acidity, flavourful.

CEPAS DEL ZORRO MACABEO 2012 B
100% macabeo

87 Colour: bright straw. Nose: powerfull, ripe fruit, white flowers. Palate: flavourful, fruity, fresh.

BODEGA BALCONA

Ctra. Bullas-Avilés, Km. 12 Valle del Aceniche
30180 Bullas (Murcia)
☎: +34 968 652 891
www.partal-vinos.com
info@partal-vinos.com

37 BARRICAS DE PARTAL 2006 TC
60% monastrell, 20% syrah, 10% tempranillo, 10% cabernet sauvignon

88 Colour: cherry, garnet rim. Nose: ripe fruit, spicy, creamy oak, toasty, warm. Palate: powerful, flavourful, toasty, round tannins.

PARTAL 2006 T
50% monastrell, 25% syrah, 15% merlot, 10% cabernet sauvignon

88 Colour: cherry, garnet rim. Nose: overripe fruit, fruit liqueur notes, toasty, smoky. Palate: fine bitter notes, spicy, round tannins.

BODEGA HEREDAD MAYBRI

Cañada Siscar s/n
30180 Bullas (Murcia)
☎: +34 607 861 329
www.heredadmaybri.es
pedroolivares@heredadmaybri.es

MAYBRI 2009 T
100% monastrell

88 Colour: cherry, garnet rim. Nose: spicy, creamy oak, toasty, overripe fruit. Palate: powerful, flavourful, toasty, round tannins.

MAYBRI 2011 T BARRICA
100% monastrell

87 Colour: cherry, garnet rim. Nose: powerfull, warm, overripe fruit. Palate: flavourful, powerful, sweetness.

MAYBRI CUVÉE 2012 T
100% monastrell

80

MAYBRI LOS PECHOS 2011 T
100% monastrell

91 Colour: bright cherry. Nose: ripe fruit, sweet spices, creamy oak, balsamic herbs. Palate: flavourful, fruity, toasty, round tannins.

MAYBRI OJO DE PERDIZ 2012 RD
100% monastrell

83

BODEGA MONASTRELL

Ctra. Bullas-Avilés, km. 9,3
30180 Bullas (Murcia)
☎: +34 648 702 412 - Fax: +34 968 653 708
www.bodegamonastrell.com
info@bodegamonastrell.com

ALMUDÍ 2010 T
90% monastrell, 5% tempranillo, petit verdot

90 Colour: cherry, garnet rim. Nose: ripe fruit, creamy oak, toasty, complex, balsamic herbs. Palate: powerful, flavourful, toasty, round tannins.

CHAVEO 2010 TC
100% monastrell

88 Colour: cherry, garnet rim. Nose: spicy, creamy oak, toasty, candied fruit. Palate: powerful, flavourful, toasty, round tannins.

VALCHE 2007 TC
100% monastrell

90 Colour: cherry, garnet rim. Nose: ripe fruit, spicy, creamy oak, toasty, smoky. Palate: powerful, flavourful, toasty, round tannins, roasted-coffee aftertaste.

BODEGA TERCIA DE ULEA

Tercia de Ulea, s/n Ctra. B35, km. 3,5
30440 Moratalla (Murcia)
☎: +34 968 433 213 - Fax: +34 968 433 965
www.terciadeulea.com
info@terciadeulea.com

ADIVINAD 2011 RD
62% monastrell, 38% syrah

78

TERCIA DE ULEA 2009 TC
63% monastrell, 23% syrah, 14% tempranillo

87 Colour: cherry, garnet rim. Nose: dark chocolate, overripe fruit, dried fruit. Palate: fine bitter notes, ripe fruit, spicy.

VIÑA BOTIAL 2011 T ROBLE
67% monastrell, 33% syrah

84

BODEGAS MERCADER-QUESADA

Paraje de Balamonte (C/Herrera)
30180 Bullas (Murcia)
☎: +34 609 121 647 - Fax: +34 968 654 205
www.mundoenologico.com
pilarquesadagil@yahoo.es

MERCADER QUESADA 2010 TC
syrah

88 Colour: cherry, garnet rim. Nose: powerfull, creamy oak, sweet spices, ripe fruit. Palate: powerful, fine bitter notes, grainy tannins.

MERCADER QUESADA 2012 T
monastrell

87 Colour: cherry, purple rim. Nose: red berry notes, floral, candied fruit. Palate: flavourful, fruity, good acidity, round tannins.

CARRASCALEJO

Finca El Carrascalejo, s/n
30180 Bullas (Murcia)
☎: +34 968 652 003 - Fax: +34 968 652 003
www.carrascalejo.com
carrascalejo@carrascalejo.com

CARRASCALEJO 2009 TC
60% monastrell, 20% syrah, 20% cabernet sauvignon

82

CARRASCALEJO 2011 T
100% monastrell

86 Colour: cherry, garnet rim. Nose: powerfull, ripe fruit. Palate: flavourful, fine bitter notes.

CARRASCALEJO 2012 RD
100% monastrell

85 Colour: rose, purple rim. Nose: powerfull, ripe fruit, red berry notes. Palate: good acidity, fine bitter notes.

COOP. AGROVINÍCOLA NTRA. SRA. DEL ROSARIO

Avda. de la Libertad, s/n
30180 Bullas (Murcia)
☎: +34 968 652 075 - Fax: +34 968 653 765
www.bodegasdelrosario.com
info@bodegasdelrosario.com

3000 AÑOS 2009 T
50% monastrell, 50% syrah

92 Colour: cherry, garnet rim. Nose: ripe fruit, spicy, creamy oak, toasty, characterful, powerfull, smoky. Palate: powerful, flavourful, toasty, round tannins.

LAS REÑAS 2012 T
80% monastrell, 20% tempranillo

89 Colour: cherry, purple rim. Nose: expressive, fresh fruit, red berry notes. Palate: flavourful, fruity, good acidity, round tannins.

LAS REÑAS BARRICA 2011 T
70% monastrell, 15% syrah, 15% tempranillo

85 Colour: bright cherry. Nose: sweet spices, creamy oak, overripe fruit. Palate: flavourful, fruity, toasty, round tannins.

LAS REÑAS DULCE MONASTRELL 2011 T
100% monastrell

87 Colour: bright cherry. Nose: ripe fruit, sweet spices, creamy oak, expressive. Palate: flavourful, fruity, toasty, sweet.

LAS REÑAS MACABEO 2012 B
85% macabeo, 15% malvasía

87 Colour: bright straw. Nose: fresh, white flowers. Palate: flavourful, fruity, good acidity, balanced.

LAS REÑAS MONASTRELL - SHIRAZ 2010 TC
70% monastrell, 30% syrah

87 Colour: cherry, garnet rim. Nose: powerfull, warm, overripe fruit, dark chocolate. Palate: spicy, ripe fruit.

LAS REÑAS MONASTRELL 2012 RD
100% monastrell

85 Colour: rose, purple rim. Nose: raspberry, red berry notes. Palate: flavourful, fruity, fresh.

LAS REÑAS SELECCIÓN 2010 TC
60% monastrell, 40% syrah

89 Colour: cherry, garnet rim. Nose: ripe fruit, spicy, creamy oak, toasty, complex. Palate: powerful, flavourful, toasty, round tannins.

LORCA SELECCIÓN 2011 T
100% monastrell

91 Colour: bright cherry. Nose: ripe fruit, sweet spices, creamy oak, expressive. Palate: flavourful, fruity, toasty, round tannins.

LORCA SYRAH 2011 T
100% syrah

88 Colour: bright cherry. Nose: sweet spices, creamy oak, overripe fruit. Palate: flavourful, fruity, toasty, round tannins.

SEÑORÍO DE BULLAS 2009 TR
70% monastrell, 30% syrah

86 Colour: cherry, garnet rim. Nose: candied fruit, roasted coffee, dark chocolate. Palate: fine bitter notes, powerful, round tannins.

DOMINIO DE ANTARGU

Ronda de Atocha, 16
28012 (Madrid)
☎: +34 915 275 244
www.dominio de antargu.es
dominiodeantargu@gmail.com

DA 2010 T
monastrell

87 Colour: cherry, garnet rim. Nose: ripe fruit, spicy, toasty, fine reductive notes. Palate: powerful, flavourful, toasty, warm.

FERNANDO CARREÑO PEÑALVER

Ginés de Paco, 22
30430 Cehegín (Murcia)
☎: +34 968 740 004 - Fax: +34 968 740 004
www.bodegascarreno.com
carrenobodegas@terra.es

MARMALLEJO 2010 TC
60% monastrell, 40% petit verdot

86 Colour: cherry, garnet rim. Nose: ripe fruit, spicy, toasty. Palate: powerful, flavourful, toasty.

VIÑA AZENICHE 2011 T ROBLE
50% monastrell, 30% petit verdot, 13% cabernet sauvignon, 7% syrah

85 Colour: cherry, garnet rim. Nose: dried herbs, ripe fruit, mineral, expressive, spicy, creamy oak. Palate: correct, powerful, flavourful.

VIÑA AZENICHE 2012 RD
monastrell

84

MOLINO Y LAGARES DE BULLAS

Paraje Venta del Pino, s/n - Parcela 38
30180 Bullas (Murcia)
☎: +34 638 046 694 - Fax: +34 968 654 494
www.bodegaslavia.com
lavia@bodegaslavia.com

LAVIA MONASTRELL SYRAH 2009 TC
70% monastrell, 30% syrah

93 Colour: bright cherry. Nose: ripe fruit, sweet spices, creamy oak, expressive, balsamic herbs. Palate: flavourful, fruity, toasty, round tannins, long.

LAVIA+ 2007 TC
100% monastrell

90 Colour: cherry, garnet rim. Nose: candied fruit, scrubland, dried herbs, aromatic coffee. Palate: flavourful, sweetness, fine bitter notes.

DO CALATAYUD / D.O.P.

LOCATION:

It is situated in the western region of the province of Zaragoza, along the foothills of the Sistema Ibérico, outlined by the network of rivers woven by the different tributaries of the Ebro: Jalón, Jiloca, Manubles, Mesa, Piedra and Ribota, and covers 46 municipal areas of the Ebro Valley.

CLIMATE:

Semi - arid and dry, although somewhat cooler than Cariñena and Borja, with cold winters, an average annual temperature which ranges between 12 and 14 °C, and a period of frost of between 5 and 7 months which greatly affects the production. The average rainfall ranges between 300 – 550 mm per year, with great day/night temperature contrasts during the ripening season.

SOIL:

In general, the soil has a high limestone content. It is formed by rugged stony materials from the nearby mountain ranges and is on many occasions accompanied by reddish clay. The region is the most rugged in Aragón, and the vineyards are situated at an altitude of between 550 and 880 m.

GRAPE VARIETIES:

WHITE: PREFERRED: *Macabeo* (25%) and *Malvasía*.
AUTHORIZED: *Moscatel de Alejandría, Garnacha Blanca, Sauvignon Blanc, Gewurztraiminer* and *Chardonnay*.
RED: PREFERRED: *Garnacha Tinta* (61.9%), *Tempranillo* (10%) and *Mazuela*.
AUTHORIZED: *Monastrell, Cabernet Sauvignon, Merlot, Bobal* and *Syrah*.

FIGURES:

Vineyard surface: 3,200 – **Wine-Growers:** 900– **Wineries:** 16 – **2012 Harvest rating:** Very Good – **Production:** 6.400.000 litres – **Market percentages:** 15% domestic. 85% export

VINTAGE RATING PEÑÍNGUIDE				
2008	**2009**	**2010**	**2011**	**2012**
VERY GOOD	**VERY GOOD**	**VERY GOOD**	**VERY GOOD**	**VERY GOOD**

ONSEJO REGULADOR
Ctra. de Valencia, 8 - 50300 Calatayud (Zaragoza) ☎: +34 976 884 260 - Fax: +34 976 885 912
administracion@docalatayud.com   www.docalatayud.com

AGUSTÍN UBERO

La Charluca, s/n
50300 Calatayud (Zaragoza)
☎: +34 976 886 606
www.bodegascubero.com
calatayud@bodegascubero.com

STYLO 2011 T
100% garnacha

90 Colour: bright cherry. Nose: ripe fruit, sweet spices, creamy oak, roasted coffee. Palate: flavourful, fruity, toasty, round tannins.

STYLO 2012 T
garnacha

89 Colour: cherry, garnet rim. Nose: red berry notes, ripe fruit, balsamic herbs, aromatic coffee, roasted coffee. Palate: rich, powerful, flavourful.

UNUS 2012 B
macabeo

87 Colour: bright straw. Nose: fresh, fresh fruit, white flowers, fragrant herbs. Palate: flavourful, fruity, correct.

ALIANZA DE GARAPITEROS

Plaza España, 6 Planta 1ª
50001 (Zaragoza)
☎: +34 976 094 033 - Fax: +34 976 094 033
www.alianzadegarapiteros.es
info@alianzadegarapiteros.es

ALQUÉZ GARNACHA VIÑAS VIEJAS 2010 T

89 Colour: cherry, garnet rim. Nose: roasted coffee, ripe fruit, aromatic coffee. Palate: powerful, flavourful, long, toasty.

ALQUÉZ GARNACHA VIÑAS VIEJAS 2011 T

90 Colour: deep cherry, garnet rim. Nose: powerfull, ripe fruit, sweet spices, creamy oak, cocoa bean. Palate: balanced, round tannins.

LAMIN 2010 T

90 Colour: bright cherry. Nose: ripe fruit, sweet spices, creamy oak, expressive, roasted coffee. Palate: flavourful, fruity, toasty, balanced.

NIETRO GARNACHA VIÑAS VIEJAS 2012 T
100% garnacha

91 Colour: cherry, purple rim. Nose: expressive, fresh fruit, red berry notes, floral. Palate: flavourful, fruity, good acidity, round tannins.

NIETRO MACABEO VIÑAS VIEJAS 2012 B
100% macabeo

87 Colour: bright straw. Nose: citrus fruit, faded flowers. Palate: flavourful, fruity, fine bitter notes.

AXIAL

Pla-za Calle Castillo de Capua, 10 Nave 7
50197 (Zaragoza)
☎: +34 976 780 136 - Fax: +34 976 303 035
www.axialvinos.com
info@axialvinos.com

MARQUÉS DE MONTAÑANA
SELECCIÓN ESPECIAL 2011 T
100% garnacha

85 Colour: cherry, garnet rim. Nose: fruit preserve, balsamic herbs, wild herbs, mineral, creamy oak. Palate: powerful, flavourful, spicy.

BODEGA ASTILLO DE MALUENDA

Avda. José Antonio, 61
50340 Maluenda (Zaragoza)
☎: +34 976 893 017 - Fax: +34 976 546 969
www.castillodemaluenda.com
info@castillodemaluenda.com

ALTO LAS PIZARRAS 2010 T
100% garnacha

90 Colour: bright cherry, garnet rim. Nose: ripe fruit, spicy, powerfull, mineral. Palate: full, round tannins, good acidity.

ASTILLO DE MALUENDA 2009 T
70% tempranillo, 30% garnacha

84

ASTILLO DE MALUENDA 2012 RD
100% garnacha

80

ASTILLO DE MALUENDA 2012 T
60% tempranillo, 40% syrah

84

LARAVAL 2010 T
70% garnacha, 15% tempranillo, 10% syrah, 5% cabernet sauvignon

89 Colour: cherry, garnet rim. Nose: expressive, ripe fruit, dried herbs, mineral. Palate: balanced, long, round tannins.

LAS PIZARRAS 2010 T
100% garnacha

90 Colour: cherry, garnet rim. Nose: ripe fruit, spicy, toasty, mineral. Palate: powerful, flavourful, toasty, balanced.

LAS PIZARRAS OLLECTION SIOSY 2012 T
100% syrah

87 Colour: cherry, garnet rim. Nose: ripe fruit, balanced. Palate: balsamic, round tannins.

LAS PIZARRAS OLLECTION VOLCÁN 2012 T
100% tempranillo

88 Colour: cherry, garnet rim. Nose: ripe fruit, sweet spices, balanced. Palate: flavourful, ripe fruit.

TEOREMA 2010 T ROBLE
100% garnacha

89 Colour: cherry, garnet rim. Nose: medium intensity, ripe fruit, scrubland. Palate: flavourful, fruity, round tannins.

VIÑA ALARBA 2007 TR
40% tempranillo, 30% syrah, 30% garnacha

85 Colour: cherry, garnet rim. Nose: medium intensity, spicy, old leather. Palate: powerful, slightly dry, soft tannins.

VIÑA ALARBA 2012 B
100% macabeo

80

BODEGA OOP. VIRGEN DE LA SIERRA

Avda. de la Cooperativa, 21-23
50310 Villarroya de la Sierra (Zaragoza)
☎: +34 976 899 015 - Fax: +34 976 899 132
www.bodegavirgendelasierra.com
oficina@bodegavirgendelasierra.com

ALBADA 2011 T
garnacha

90 Colour: cherry, garnet rim. Nose: mineral, scrubland, ripe fruit. Palate: spicy, round tannins, ripe fruit.

ALBADA 2012 B
macabeo

87 Colour: bright straw. Nose: balanced, ripe fruit, citrus fruit, tropical fruit. Palate: flavourful, fruity, good acidity.

RUZ DE PIEDRA 2012 B
macabeo

85 Colour: bright straw. Nose: floral, citrus fruit, fragrant herbs. Palate: light-bodied, fresh, fruity.

RUZ DE PIEDRA 2012 RD
garnacha

86 Colour: rose, purple rim. Nose: powerfull, ripe fruit, red berry notes, floral. Palate: powerful, fruity, flavourful.

RUZ DE PIEDRA 2012 T
garnacha

88 Colour: cherry, garnet rim. Nose: ripe fruit, spicy, creamy oak. Palate: powerful, flavourful, toasty.

RUZ DE PIEDRA APRICHO 2009 T
garnacha

89 Colour: deep cherry, garnet rim. Nose: medium intensity, balanced, ripe fruit, spicy. Palate: flavourful, round tannins.

RUZ DE PIEDRA SELECCIÓN ESPECIAL 2011 T
garnacha

90 Colour: cherry, garnet rim. Nose: ripe fruit, spicy, toasty, dark chocolate. Palate: powerful, flavourful, toasty.

BODEGA SAN GREGORIO

Ctra. Villalengua, s/n
50312 Cervera de la Cañada (Zaragoza)
☎: +34 976 899 206 - Fax: +34 976 896 240
www.bodegasangregorio.com
tresojos@bodegasangregorio.com

ARMANTES 2008 TR
70% garnacha, 22% tempranillo, 8% syrah, merlot, cabernet sauvignon

88 Colour: cherry, garnet rim. Nose: ripe fruit, balsamic herbs, spicy, toasty. Palate: powerful, flavourful, toasty.

ARMANTES 2010 T
42% tempranillo, 35% merlot, 23% syrah

87 Colour: cherry, garnet rim. Nose: ripe fruit, spicy, creamy oak, toasty. Palate: powerful, flavourful, toasty.

ARMANTES 2012 B
macabeo

84

ARMANTES 2012 BFB
macabeo

89 Colour: bright straw. Nose: ripe fruit, floral, sweet spices. Palate: good acidity, spicy, fruity, easy to drink.

ARMANTES 2012 RD
50% garnacha, 50% tempranillo

86 Colour: rose, purple rim. Nose: powerfull, red berry notes, floral, lactic notes. Palate: powerful, fruity, fresh.

ARMANTES 2012 T
50% garnacha, 50% tempranillo

89 Colour: cherry, purple rim. Nose: expressive, fresh fruit, red berry notes, floral. Palate: flavourful, fruity, good acidity, round tannins.

ARMANTES VENDIMIA SELECCIONADA 2010 T
60% garnacha, 22% tempranillo, 6% merlot, 6% syrah, 6% cabernet sauvignon

92 Colour: cherry, garnet rim. Nose: expressive, balanced, ripe fruit, wild herbs, mineral. Palate: good structure, fruity.

ARMANTES VENDIMIA SELECCIONADA 2011 T
60% garnacha, 22% tempranillo, 6% merlot, 6% syrah, 6% cabernet sauvignon

90 Colour: bright cherry. Nose: ripe fruit, sweet spices, creamy oak, expressive, dry stone. Palate: flavourful, fruity, toasty.

TRES OJOS GARNACHA 2011 T
garnacha

87 Colour: bright cherry. Nose: ripe fruit, sweet spices, creamy oak, toasty. Palate: flavourful, fruity, toasty.

TRES OJOS GARNACHA 2012 T
garnacha

86 Colour: light cherry. Nose: red berry notes, ripe fruit, fragrant herbs, floral. Palate: powerful, flavourful, spicy.

TRES OJOS TEMPRANILLO 2011 T
tempranillo

87 Colour: cherry, garnet rim. Nose: medium intensity, ripe fruit, balsamic herbs. Palate: flavourful, fruity, easy to drink, correct.

BODEGA VIRGEN DEL MAR Y DE LA UESTA

Ctra. Monasterio de la Piedra, s/n
50219 Munebrega (Zaragoza)
☎: +34 976 895 071 - Fax: +34 976 895 071
bodegamunebrega@hotmail.com

MUZARES 2012 B
100% macabeo

83

MUZARES 2012 RD
100% garnacha

86 Colour: light cherry, bright. Nose: balanced, red berry notes, ripe fruit, dried herbs. Palate: fruity, correct, easy to drink.

MUZARES 2012 T
85% garnacha, 15% tempranillo

87 Colour: cherry, garnet rim. Nose: ripe fruit, warm. Palate: flavourful, fruity, long.

BODEGAS ATECA

Ctra. N-II, s/n
50200 Ateca (Zaragoza)
☎: +34 968 435 022 - Fax: +34 968 716 051
www.orowines.com
info@orowines.com

ATTECA 2011 T
100% garnacha

93 Colour: cherry, garnet rim. Nose: spicy, creamy oak, toasty, characterful. Palate: powerful, flavourful, toasty, round tannins.

ATTECA ARMAS 2009 T
garnacha

93 Colour: deep cherry, garnet rim. Nose: complex, balanced, mineral, sweet spices. Palate: flavourful, fruity, round tannins.

ATTECA ARMAS 2010 T
100% garnacha

92 Colour: cherry, garnet rim. Nose: fruit liqueur notes, powerfull, sweet spices, new oak, roasted coffee. Palate: powerful, fine bitter notes, good acidity, spicy.

HONORO VERA GARNACHA 2012 T
100% garnacha

89 Colour: deep cherry. Nose: spicy, ripe fruit, toasty, scrubland. Palate: spicy, ripe fruit, flavourful.

BODEGAS BRECA

Ctra. Monasterio de Piedra
50219 Munebrega (Zaragoza)
☎: +34 952 504 706
www.grupojorgeordonez.com
info@jorgeordonez.es

BRECA 2010 T
100% garnacha

93 Colour: cherry, garnet rim. Nose: powerfull, creamy oak, ripe fruit, toasty, balsamic herbs. Palate: flavourful, full.

GARNACHA DE FUEGO 2012 T
garnacha

87 Colour: bright cherry. Nose: medium intensity, wild herbs, balanced. Palate: ripe fruit, round tannins.

BODEGAS LANGA

Ctra. Nacional II, Km. 241,700
50300 Calatayud (Zaragoza)
☎: +34 976 881 818 - Fax: +34 976 884 463
www.bodegas-langa.com
info@bodegas-langa.com

LANGA EMOCIÓN 2011 T
cabernet sauvignon, syrah

89 Colour: bright cherry. Nose: ripe fruit, sweet spices, creamy oak, roasted coffee. Palate: flavourful, fruity, toasty.

LANGA MERLOT 2011 T
merlot

88 Colour: cherry, garnet rim. Nose: ripe fruit, fragrant herbs, spicy, mineral, sweet spices. Palate: flavourful, fresh, balsamic.

LANGA TRADICIÓN 2011 T
garnacha

88 Colour: bright cherry. Nose: ripe fruit, sweet spices, creamy oak, roasted coffee. Palate: flavourful, fruity, toasty.

REAL DE ARAGÓN 2010 T
garnacha

92 Colour: cherry, garnet rim. Nose: balanced, balsamic herbs, ripe fruit, mineral. Palate: good structure, flavourful, spicy, long.

REYES DE ARAGÓN 2008 TR
garnacha, merlot

88 Colour: cherry, garnet rim. Nose: sweet spices, cocoa bean, ripe fruit. Palate: good structure, flavourful, round tannins.

REYES DE ARAGÓN GARNACHA ABERNET 2010 T
garnacha, cabernet sauvignon

88 Colour: cherry, garnet rim. Nose: ripe fruit, scrubland. Palate: balanced.

BODEGAS SAN ALEJANDRO

Ctra. Calatayud - Cariñena, Km. 16
50330 Miedes de Aragón (Zaragoza)
☎: +34 976 892 205 - Fax: +34 976 890 540
www.san-alejandro.com
contacto@san-alejandro.com

BALTASAR GRACIÁN 2009 T
70% garnacha, 20% tempranillo, 10% syrah

91 Colour: cherry, garnet rim. Nose: ripe fruit, spicy, creamy oak, toasty, dry stone. Palate: powerful, flavourful, toasty.

BALTASAR GRACIÁN 2008 TR
70% garnacha, 20% tempranillo, 10% cabernet sauvignon

91 Colour: cherry, garnet rim. Nose: medium intensity, balanced, wild herbs, ripe fruit. Palate: good structure, round tannins, long.

BALTASAR GRACIÁN GARNACHA 2012 RD
100% garnacha

88 Colour: light cherry, bright. Nose: red berry notes, wild herbs, balanced. Palate: flavourful, fruity, good acidity.

BALTASAR GRACIÁN GARNACHA 2012 T
100% garnacha

90 Colour: cherry, purple rim. Nose: balanced, mineral, scrubland. Palate: balanced, ripe fruit, round tannins.

BALTASAR GRACIÁN GARNACHA VIÑAS VIEJAS 2011 T
100% garnacha

90 Colour: deep cherry, garnet rim. Nose: cocoa bean, ripe fruit, balanced, fruit preserve. Palate: flavourful, full, good acidity.

BALTASAR GRACIÁN MACABEO 2012 B
100% macabeo

87 Colour: bright straw. Nose: fresh fruit, white flowers, expressive. Palate: flavourful, fruity, good acidity, balanced.

EVODIA 2011 T
100% garnacha

89 Colour: cherry, garnet rim. Nose: balanced, ripe fruit, spicy, cocoa bean, mineral. Palate: fruity, easy to drink, balanced.

LAS ROCAS GARNACHA 2011 T
100% garnacha

92 Colour: cherry, garnet rim. Nose: varietal, red berry notes, ripe fruit, balsamic herbs. Palate: flavourful, balanced, long.

LAS ROCAS GARNACHA VIÑAS VIEJAS 2011 T
100% garnacha

93 Colour: cherry, garnet rim. Nose: red berry notes, ripe fruit, balsamic herbs, spicy, toasty, dry stone. Palate: powerful, flavourful, long, spicy.

OLAS VITICULTORES

Calle Lanuza 28
50230 Alhama de Aragón (Zaragoza)
☎: +34 976 840 062
colasviticultores@gmail.com

ROQUE OLÁS 2010 T
tempranillo, cabernet sauvignon, garnacha, merlot

90 Colour: cherry, garnet rim. Nose: ripe fruit, spicy, creamy oak, toasty, complex. Palate: powerful, flavourful, toasty, round tannins.

EL ESCOCÉS VOLANTE

Barrio La Rosa Bajo, 16
50300 Calatayud (Zaragoza)
☎: +34 637 511 133
www.escocesvolante.es
info@escocesvolante.es

ES LO QUE HAY 2011 T
100% garnacha

94 Colour: cherry, garnet rim. Nose: red berry notes, ripe fruit, balsamic herbs, sweet spices, mineral, earthy notes. Palate: flavourful, fresh, fruity, round tannins.

LA MULTA GARNACHA VIÑAS VIEJAS 2011 T
100% garnacha

89 Colour: bright cherry, garnet rim. Nose: balanced, ripe fruit, wild herbs. Palate: flavourful, round tannins, balsamic.

MANGA DEL BRUJO 2011 T
70% garnacha, 15% syrah, 10% tempranillo, 5% mazuelo

93 Colour: bright cherry. Nose: ripe fruit, sweet spices, creamy oak, expressive. Palate: flavourful, fruity, toasty, harsh oak tannins.

FLORIS LEGERE

Ecuador, 5 2º 1ª
50012 (Zaragoza)
☎: +34 608 974 809
ludoswines.blogspot.com.es
vano.ludovic@gmail.com

ALAVIANA 2011 T
80% garnacha, 20% syrah

90 Colour: cherry, garnet rim. Nose: red berry notes, ripe fruit, fragrant herbs, mineral. Palate: spicy, balsamic, balanced.

ATRACTYLIS 2011 T
syrah

93 Colour: cherry, garnet rim. Nose: ripe fruit, sweet spices, creamy oak, balsamic herbs, dry stone. Palate: flavourful, fruity, toasty, round tannins, elegant.

NIÑO JESÚS

Las Tablas, s/n
50313 Aniñón (Zaragoza)
☎: +34 976 899 150 - Fax: +34 976 896 160
www.satninojesus.com
administracion@satninojesus.com

ESTECILLO 2011 BFB
macabeo

87 Colour: bright yellow. Nose: powerfull, ripe fruit, sweet spices, creamy oak, fragrant herbs. Palate: rich, flavourful, good acidity.

ESTECILLO 2012 B
macabeo

86 Colour: bright straw. Nose: fresh, fresh fruit, white flowers. Palate: flavourful, fruity, good acidity, correct.

ESTECILLO 2012 T
garnacha, tempranillo

86 Colour: cherry, purple rim, cherry, garnet rim. Nose: medium intensity, ripe fruit. Palate: flavourful, ripe fruit, long.

ESTECILLO GARNACHA 2012 T
garnacha

84

ESTECILLO LEGADO GARNACHA & SYRAH 2012 T
garnacha, syrah

86 Colour: bright cherry, garnet rim. Nose: balanced, ripe fruit, dried herbs. Palate: flavourful, fruity, long.

PAGOS ALTOS DE ACERED

Avda. Río Jalón, 62
50300 Calatayud (Zaragoza)
☎: +34 976 887 496
www.lajas.es
manuel@lajas.es

LAJAS 2007 T
garnacha

93 Colour: deep cherry, orangey edge. Nose: balanced, expressive, ripe fruit, wild herbs, warm. Palate: flavourful, good structure, round tannins.

LAJAS 2008 T
garnacha

92 Colour: cherry, garnet rim. Nose: mineral, powerfull, cocoa bean, sweet spices. Palate: flavourful, powerful, long.

LAJAS 2010 T
garnacha

93 Colour: cherry, garnet rim. Nose: medium intensity, ripe fruit, mineral. Palate: powerful, full, flavourful, long, good acidity.

LAJAS FINCA EL PEÑISCAL 2009 T
garnacha

94 Colour: bright cherry, garnet rim. Nose: expressive, balanced, complex, mineral, ripe fruit. Palate: good structure, complex, flavourful, round tannins.

RESERVA Y CATA

Conde de Xiquena, 13
28004 (Madrid)
☎: +34 913 190 401 - Fax: +34 913 190 401
www.reservaycata.com
info@reservaycata.com

PAGOS MISTICOS 2011 T
60% garnacha, 22% tempranillo, 6% cabernet sauvignon, 6% syrah, 6% merlot

88 Colour: cherry, garnet rim. Nose: ripe fruit, spicy, creamy oak, toasty, complex. Palate: powerful, flavourful, toasty.

Consejo Regulador
DO Boundary

ZARAGOZA

DO CAMPO DE BORJA / D.O.P.

LOCATION:

The DO Campo de Borja is made up of 16 municipal areas, situated in the north west of the province of Zaragoza and 60 km from the capital city, in an area of transition between the mountains of the Sistema Ibérico (at the foot of the Moncayo) and the Ebro Valley: Agón, Ainzón, Alberite, Albeta, Ambel, Bisimbre, Borja, Bulbuente, Burueta, El Buste, Fuendejalón, Magallón, Malejan, Pozuelo de Aragón, Tabuenca and Vera del Moncayo.

CLIMATE:

A rather extreme continental climate, with cold winters and dry, hot summers. One of its main characteristics is the influence of the 'Cierzo', a cold and dry north - westerly wind. Rainfall is rather scarce, with an average of between 350 and 450 mm per year.

SOIL:

The most abundant are brownish - grey limey soils, terrace soils and clayey ferrous soils. The vineyards are situated at an altitude of between 350 and 700 m on small slightly rolling hillsides, on terraces of the Huecha river and the Llanos de Plasencia, making up the Somontano del Moncayo.

GRAPE VARIETIES:

WHITE: *Macabeo, Garnacha Blanca, Moscatel, Chardonnay, Sauvignon Blanc* and *Verdejo.*
RED: *Garnacha* (majority with 75%), *Tempranillo, Mazuela, Cabernet Sauvignon, Merlot* and *Syrah.*

FIGURES:

Vineyard surface: 6.815– **Wine-Growers:** 1.485 – **Wineries.** 17 – **2012 Harvest rating:** Very Good – **Production.** 17.340.413 litres – **Market percentages:** 33% domestic. 67% export

VINTAGE RATING PEÑÍNGUIDE				
2008	2009	2010	2011	2012
VERY GOOD	VERY GOOD	VERY GOOD	VERY GOOD	VERY GOOD

CONSEJO REGULADOR
Subida de San Andrés, 6 - 50570 Ainzón (Zaragoza) ☎: +34 976 852 122 - Fax: +34 976 868 806
vinos@docampodeborja.com   www.docampodeborja.com

AXIAL

Pla-za Calle Castillo de Capua, 10 Nave 7
50197 (Zaragoza)
☎ +34 976 780 136 - Fax: +34 976 303 035
www.axialvinos.com
info@axialvinos.com

PENÉLOPE SÁNCHEZ 2011 T
85% garnacha, 15% syrah

90 Colour: bright cherry. Nose: ripe fruit, sweet spices, creamy oak, balsamic herbs, mineral. Palate: flavourful, fruity, toasty, round tannins.

BODEGA PICOS

Ctra. Nacional 122, Km. 55'400
50520 Magallón (Zaragoza)
☎: +34 976 863 006
www.bodegapicos.com
info@bodegapicos.com

GREGORIANO BLANCO DE HIELO 2012 B
moscatel, macabeo

85 Colour: bright straw. Nose: faded flowers, dried herbs, candied fruit. Palate: fresh, fruity, flavourful.

LOTETA 2010 T
garnacha, tempranillo, cabernet sauvignon

84

BODEGAS ALTO MONCAYO

Ctra. CV-606 Borja - El Buste, Km. 1,700
50540 Borja (Zaragoza)
☎: +34 976 868 098 - Fax: +34 976 868 147
www.bodegasaltomoncayo.com
info@bodegasaltomoncayo.com

ALTO MONCAYO 2010 T
100% garnacha

95 Colour: cherry, garnet rim. Nose: red berry notes, ripe fruit, spicy, sweet spices, creamy oak, balsamic herbs, balanced, elegant. Palate: rich, powerful, flavourful, long, fresh, elegant.

ALTO MONCAYO VERATÓN 2010 T
100% garnacha

93 Colour: deep cherry, garnet rim. Nose: powerfull, cocoa bean, sweet spices, creamy oak, ripe fruit. Palate: flavourful, balanced, round tannins.

AQUILÓN 2010 T
100% garnacha

95 Colour: deep cherry, garnet rim. Nose: medium intensity, balanced, ripe fruit, cocoa bean, spicy, balsamic herbs. Palate: good structure, round tannins, long, full.

BODEGAS ARAGONESAS

Ctra. Magallón, s/n
50529 Fuendejalón (Zaragoza)
☎: +34 976 862 153 - Fax: +34 976 862 363
www.bodegasaragonesas.com
info@bodegasaragonesas.com

ARAGONIA SELECCIÓN ESPECIAL 2010 T
100% garnacha

91 Colour: cherry, garnet rim. Nose: complex, expressive, ripe fruit, dark chocolate, creamy oak. Palate: flavourful, good structure, round tannins, powerful.

ARAGUS 2012 T
85% garnacha, 15% cabernet sauvignon

89 Colour: bright cherry, purple rim. Nose: medium intensity, balanced, ripe fruit. Palate: fruity, ripe fruit, easy to drink.

ARAGUS ECOLÓGICO 2012 T
100% garnacha

88 Colour: cherry, purple rim. Nose: wild herbs, red berry notes, ripe fruit. Palate: powerful, flavourful, spicy.

COTO DE HAYAS 2009 TR
100% garnacha

90 Colour: cherry, garnet rim. Nose: ripe fruit, spicy, dark chocolate. Palate: flavourful, balanced, round tannins.

COTO DE HAYAS 2010 TC
60% garnacha, 40% tempranillo

88 Colour: cherry, garnet rim. Nose: spicy, creamy oak, toasty, red berry notes, ripe fruit. Palate: powerful, flavourful, toasty, slightly dry, soft tannins.

COTO DE HAYAS 2011 BFB
80% chardonnay, 3% moscatel, 17% macabeo

88 Colour: bright yellow. Nose: powerfull, ripe fruit, sweet spices, creamy oak, fragrant herbs. Palate: rich, smoky aftertaste, flavourful, fresh, good acidity.

COTO DE HAYAS 2012 RD
90% garnacha, 10% cabernet sauvignon

86 Colour: rose, purple rim. Nose: ripe fruit, red berry notes, floral, dried herbs. Palate: powerful, fruity, fresh.

COTO DE HAYAS CHARDONNAY 2012 B
100% chardonnay

85 Colour: bright straw. Nose: citrus fruit, ripe fruit, floral, dried herbs. Palate: powerful, flavourful, balsamic.

COTO DE HAYAS GARNACHA CENTENARIA 2012 T
100% garnacha

92 Colour: deep cherry, purple rim. Nose: balanced, expressive, red berry notes, ripe fruit. Palate: flavourful, balanced, long.

COTO DE HAYAS GARNACHA SYRAH 2012 T
85% garnacha, 15% syrah

89 Colour: bright cherry, purple rim. Nose: balanced, ripe fruit, violet drops. Palate: fruity, flavourful.

COTO DE HAYAS MISTELA 2012
VINO DULCE NATURAL
100% garnacha

90 Colour: cherry, garnet rim. Nose: acetaldehyde, ripe fruit, varnish, aged wood nuances, toasty. Palate: fine bitter notes, powerful, flavourful, spicy.

COTO DE HAYAS MOSCATEL 2012 B
100% moscatel grano menudo

86 Colour: golden. Nose: powerfull, floral, honeyed notes, candied fruit. Palate: flavourful, sweet, fresh, fruity, good acidity, long.

COTO DE HAYAS SOLO 10 2012 T
100% syrah

90 Colour: cherry, purple rim. Nose: red berry notes, violet drops, wild herbs, sweet spices, toasty. Palate: powerful, flavourful, correct, balanced.

COTO DE HAYAS TEMPRANILLO
CABERNET 2012 T ROBLE
70% tempranillo, 30% cabernet sauvignon

88 Colour: deep cherry, purple rim. Nose: medium intensity, toasty, sweet spices, ripe fruit. Palate: spicy, ripe fruit.

DON RAMÓN 2011 T BARRICA
75% garnacha, 25% tempranillo

87 Colour: cherry, garnet rim. Nose: dark chocolate, sweet spices, ripe fruit. Palate: correct, balanced, slightly dry, soft tannins.

ECCE HOMO 2012 T
100% garnacha

86 Colour: bright cherry, purple rim. Nose: medium intensity, ripe fruit. Palate: fruity, easy to drink, correct.

ECCE HOMO SELECCIÓN 2009 T
100% garnacha

88 Colour: cherry, garnet rim. Nose: balanced, ripe fruit, sweet spices. Palate: flavourful, round tannins, reductive nuances.

FAGUS DE COTO DE HAYAS 2011 T
100% garnacha

92 Colour: very deep cherry, garnet rim. Nose: powerfull, creamy oak, dark chocolate, ripe fruit, fruit preserve. Palate: flavourful.

OXIA 2010 TC
100% garnacha

92 Colour: cherry, garnet rim. Nose: dark chocolate, sweet spices, creamy oak, ripe fruit. Palate: flavourful, fruity, round tannins.

SOLO TIÓLICO 2012 B
100% moscatel de alejandría

88 Colour: bright straw. Nose: fresh, fresh fruit, white flowers, mineral. Palate: flavourful, fruity, good acidity, balanced.

BODEGAS BORDEJÉ

Ctra. Borja a Rueda, Km. 3
50570 Ainzón (Zaragoza)
☎: +34 976 868 080 - Fax: +34 976 868 989
www.bodegasbordeje.com
ainzon@bodegasbordeje.com

ABUELO NICOLÁS 2011 T
100% merlot

85 Colour: bright cherry. Nose: ripe fruit, sweet spices, creamy oak, fragrant herbs. Palate: flavourful, fruity, toasty.

BORDEJÉ 2006 TR
50% tempranillo, 50% garnacha

88 Colour: pale ruby, brick rim edge. Nose: spicy, fine reductive notes, wet leather, aged wood nuances, fruit liqueur notes. Palate: spicy, long, round tannins.

BORDEJÉ DON PABLO 2008 TR
50% tempranillo, 50% garnacha

86 Colour: light cherry, orangey edge. Nose: spicy, creamy oak, ripe fruit, balsamic herbs. Palate: flavourful, spicy, long.

FINCA ROMEROSO·2008 TR
100% tempranillo

89 Colour: cherry, garnet rim. Nose: ripe fruit, mineral, sweet spices, creamy oak, balanced. Palate: powerful, flavourful, toasty, long.

LELES DE BORDEJE 2010 TR
100% garnacha

87 Colour: cherry, garnet rim. Nose: ripe fruit, spicy, creamy oak, toasty. Palate: powerful, flavourful, toasty.

LIDIA 2010 B

88 Colour: bright straw. Nose: citrus fruit, ripe fruit, dried flowers, dried herbs, creamy oak. Palate: rich, flavourful, long, balanced.

BODEGAS BORSAO

Ctra. N- 122, Km. 63
50540 Borja (Zaragoza)
☎: +34 976 867 116 - Fax: +34 976 867 752
www.bodegasborsao.com
info@bodegasborsao.com

BORSAO BEROLA 2009 T
80% garnacha, 20% syrah

92 Colour: cherry, garnet rim. Nose: complex, balanced, expressive, ripe fruit, wild herbs, mineral. Palate: flavourful, full, round tannins.

BORSAO BOLE 2010 T
70% garnacha, 30% syrah

89 Colour: cherry, garnet rim. Nose: ripe fruit, spicy, creamy oak, balsamic herbs. Palate: powerful, flavourful, fruity, toasty.

BORSAO SELECCIÓN 2010 TC
60% garnacha, 20% tempranillo, 20% merlot

88 Colour: cherry, garnet rim. Nose: medium intensity, ripe fruit. Palate: fruity, correct, good finish.

BORSAO SELECCIÓN 2012 RD
100% garnacha

87 Colour: onion pink. Nose: elegant, candied fruit, dried flowers, fragrant herbs, red berry notes. Palate: light-bodied, flavourful, good acidity, spicy.

BORSAO SELECCIÓN 2012 T
70% garnacha, 20% syrah, 10% tempranillo

89 Colour: cherry, purple rim. Nose: red berry notes, ripe fruit, balsamic herbs, mineral. Palate: powerful, flavourful, fruity, rich.

BORSAO TRES PICOS 2011 T
100% garnacha

93 Colour: cherry, purple rim. Nose: red berry notes, ripe fruit, balsamic herbs, sweet spices, toasty, expressive. Palate: powerful, flavourful, spicy, balsamic, long, balanced.

BODEGAS CARLOS VALERO

Castillo de Capúa, 10 Nave 1
50197 (Zaragoza)
☎: +34 976 180 634 - Fax: +34 976 186 326
www.bodegasvalero.com
info@bodegasvalero.com

HEREDAD H CARLOS VALERO 2011 T
100% garnacha

89 Colour: cherry, garnet rim. Nose: ripe fruit, spicy, toasty, balsamic herbs. Palate: flavourful, spicy, correct, round tannins.

BODEGAS ROMÁN S.C.

Ctra. Gallur - Agreda
50546 Balbuente (Zaragoza)
☎: +34 976 852 936 - Fax: +34 976 852 936
www.bodegasroman.es
info@bodegasroman.es

PORTAL DE MONCAYO 2012 T
100% garnacha

89 Colour: cherry, purple rim. Nose: red berry notes, balsamic herbs, powerfull, balanced. Palate: correct, flavourful, fruity, good acidity.

PORTAL DEL MONCAYO 2011 T ROBLE
100% garnacha

89 Colour: bright cherry. Nose: ripe fruit, creamy oak. Palate: flavourful, toasty, good structure, long.

ROMÁN 2010 T
100% garnacha

89 Colour: cherry, garnet rim. Nose: ripe fruit, spicy, creamy oak, toasty. Palate: powerful, flavourful, toasty.

BODEGAS SANTO CRISTO

Ctra. Tabuenca, s/n
50540 Ainzón (Zaragoza)
☎: +34 976 869 696 - Fax: +34 976 868 097
www.bodegas-santo-cristo.com
bodegas@bodegas-santo-cristo.com

CAYUS SELECCIÓN 2011 T ROBLE
100% garnacha

92 Colour: bright cherry. Nose: ripe fruit, sweet spices, creamy oak, balsamic herbs, expressive. Palate: flavourful, fruity, toasty, complex.

MOSCATEL AINZÓN 2012 B
100% moscatel grano menudo

87 Colour: golden. Nose: powerfull, honeyed notes, candied fruit, fragrant herbs, dried flowers. Palate: flavourful, sweet, fresh, fruity, good acidity, long.

MOSCATEL AINZÓN 90 DÍAS 2012 B BARRICA
100% moscatel grano menudo

92 Colour: bright golden. Nose: ripe fruit, powerfull, toasty, aged wood nuances, honeyed notes, citrus fruit. Palate: flavourful, fruity, spicy, toasty, long.

PEÑAZUELA SELECCIÓN 2011 T ROBLE
100% garnacha

86 Colour: bright cherry. Nose: ripe fruit, creamy oak, wild herbs. Palate: flavourful, fruity, toasty.

SANTO CRISTO 2012 T ROBLE
60% tempranillo, 30% cabernet sauvignon, 10% garnacha

87 Colour: deep cherry, purple rim. Nose: balanced, ripe fruit, dried herbs. Palate: fruity, flavourful, long.

TERRAZAS DEL MONCAYO GARNACHA 2009 T ROBLE
100% garnacha

91 Colour: bright cherry, garnet rim. Nose: expressive, ripe fruit, dark chocolate, sweet spices, creamy oak. Palate: full, flavourful, good structure, round tannins.

VIÑA AINZÓN 2008 TR
70% garnacha, 30% tempranillo

87 Colour: cherry, garnet rim. Nose: medium intensity, ripe fruit, balsamic herbs, spicy. Palate: flavourful, ripe fruit.

VIÑA AINZÓN 2010 TC
70% garnacha, 30% tempranillo

90 Colour: deep cherry, garnet rim. Nose: balanced, expressive, complex, balsamic herbs, ripe fruit. Palate: flavourful, ripe fruit, good acidity.

VIÑA AINZÓN PREMIUM 2009 TR
100% garnacha

88 Colour: cherry, garnet rim. Nose: medium intensity, spicy, dried herbs, ripe fruit. Palate: good structure, flavourful, long.

VIÑA COLLADO 2012 B
100% macabeo

84

VIÑA COLLADO 2012 RD
100% garnacha

85 Colour: rose, purple rim. Nose: powerfull, ripe fruit, red berry notes, floral. Palate: powerful, fruity, fresh.

VIÑA COLLADO 2012 T
100% garnacha

87 Colour: cherry, purple rim. Nose: red berry notes, wild herbs, mineral, powerfull. Palate: flavourful, balsamic, rich.

PAGOS DEL MONCAYO

Ctra. Z-372, Km. 1,6
50580 Vera de Moncayo (Zaragoza)
☎: +34 976 900 256
www.pagosdelmoncayo.com
info@pagosdelmoncayo.com

PAGOS DEL MONCAYO GARNACHA 2011 T
100% garnacha

90 Colour: very deep cherry, garnet rim. Nose: powerfull, scrubland, wild herbs, ripe fruit, mineral. Palate: flavourful, good structure, slightly dry, soft tannins.

PAGOS DEL MONCAYO GARNACHA SYRAH 2012 T
65% garnacha, 35% syrah

89 Colour: bright cherry, purple rim. Nose: powerfull, toasty, spicy, ripe fruit. Palate: fruity, flavourful, easy to drink.

PAGOS DEL MONCAYO PRADOS 2011 T
85% syrah, 15% garnacha

90 Colour: very deep cherry, purple rim. Nose: powerfull, balanced, sweet spices, cocoa bean. Palate: flavourful, good structure, spicy.

PAGOS DEL MONCAYO SYRAH 2011 T
100% syrah

91 Colour: bright cherry. Nose: sweet spices, creamy oak, violet drops, toasty. Palate: flavourful, fruity, toasty, round tannins.

RUBERTE HERMANOS

Tenor Fleta, s/n
50520 Magallón (Zaragoza)
☎: +34 976 858 106 - Fax: +34 976 858 475
www.bodegasruberte.com
info@bodegasruberte.com

ALIANA CARÁCTER 2012 T
syrah

88 Colour: deep cherry, purple rim. Nose: ripe fruit, violet drops, expressive. Palate: fruity, flavourful, balanced.

RUBERTE 2004 TR
garnacha

88 Colour: deep cherry, orangey edge. Nose: old leather, cigar, balsamic herbs. Palate: flavourful, spicy, long.

RUBERTE 2012 T JOVEN
garnacha

86 Colour: cherry, purple rim. Nose: ripe fruit, medium intensity. Palate: fruity, easy to drink.

RUBERTE SYRAH 2010 T
syrah

86 Colour: bright cherry. Nose: ripe fruit, sweet spices, creamy oak. Palate: flavourful, fruity, toasty.

LOCATION:

In the province of Zaragoza, and occupies the Ebro valley covering 14 municipal areas: Aguarón, Aladrén, Alfamén, Almonacid de la Sierra, Alpartir, Cariñena, Cosuenda, Encinacorba, Longares, Mezalocha, Muel, Paniza, Tosos and Villanueva de Huerva.

CLIMATE:

A continental climate, with cold winters, hot summers and low rainfall. The viticulture is also influenced by the effect of the 'Cierzo'.

SOIL:

Mainly poor; either brownish - grey limey soil, or reddish dun soil settled on rocky deposits, or brownish - grey soil settled on alluvial deposits. The vineyards are situated at an altitude of between 400 and 800 m.

GRAPE VARIETIES:

WHITE: PREFERRED: *Macabeo* (majority 20%).
AUTHORIZED: *Garnacha Blanca, Moscatel Romano, Parellada* and *Chardonnay*.
RED: PREFERRED: *Garnacha Tinta* (majority 55%), *Tempranillo, Mazuela* (or *Cariñena*).
AUTHORIZED: *Juan Ibáñez, Cabernet Sauvignon, Syrah, Monastrell, Vidadillo* and *Merlot.*

FIGURES:

Vineyard surface: 14.388– **Wine-Growers:** 1.540– **Wineries:** 30 – **2012 Harvest rating:** Very Good– **Production:** 55.048.324 litres – **Market percentages:** 28,78% domestic. 71,22% export

VINTAGE RATING PEÑINGUIDE				
2008	**2009**	**2010**	**2011**	**2012**
GOOD	VERY GOOD	VERY GOOD	GOOD	GOOD

CONSEJO REGULADOR
Camino de la Platera, 7 - 50400 Cariñena (Zaragoza) ☎: +34 976 793 143 / +34 976 793 031 - Fax: +34 976 621 107
consejoregulador@docarinena.com   www.docarinena.com

AXIAL

Pla-za Calle Castillo de Capua, 10 Nave 7
50197 (Zaragoza)
☎: +34 976 780 136 - Fax: +34 976 303 035
www.axialvinos.com
info@axialvinos.com

LA GRANJA 360 GARNACHA 2012 RD
100% garnacha

85 Colour: light cherry. Nose: floral, red berry notes, ripe fruit, dried herbs. Palate: light-bodied, fresh, easy to drink.

LA GRANJA 360 GARNACHA SYRAH 2012 T
50% garnacha, 50% syrah

86 Colour: bright cherry. Nose: ripe fruit, creamy oak, expressive. Palate: flavourful, fruity, toasty, spicy.

LA GRANJA 360 TEMPRANILLO 2012 T
100% tempranillo

85 Colour: cherry, purple rim. Nose: red berry notes, ripe fruit, wild herbs. Palate: powerful, flavourful, easy to drink.

LA GRANJA 360 TEMPRANILLO GARNACHA 2012 T
50% garnacha, 50% tempranillo

84

BIOENOS

Mayor, 88
50400 Cariñena (Zaragoza)
☎: +34 976 620 045 - Fax: +34 976 622 082
www.bioenos.com
bioenos@bioenos.com

GORYS CRESPIELLO 2007 T
vidadilo, crespiello

92 Colour: cherry, garnet rim. Nose: ripe fruit, spicy, creamy oak, toasty, fine reductive notes. Palate: powerful, flavourful, toasty, slightly dry, soft tannins.

GORYS CRESPIELLO 2008 T
vidadilo, crespiello

90 Colour: cherry, garnet rim. Nose: ripe fruit, balsamic herbs, spicy, creamy oak. Palate: correct, powerful, flavourful, harsh oak tannins.

GORYS CRESPIELLO 2009 T
vidadilo, crespiello

89 Colour: cherry, garnet rim. Nose: balsamic herbs, spicy, creamy oak, fruit preserve. Palate: flavourful, concentrated, long.

BODEGA PAGO AYLÉS

Finca Aylés. Ctra. A-1101, Km. 24
50152 Mezalocha (Zaragoza)
☎: +34 976 140 473 - Fax: +34 976 140 268
www.pagoayles.com
pagoayles@pagoayles.com

ALDEYA DE AYLÉS GARNACHA 2012 T
garnacha

89 Colour: cherry, purple rim. Nose: red berry notes, ripe fruit, balsamic herbs, spicy. Palate: powerful, flavourful, rich.

ALDEYA DE AYLÉS ROSADO 2012 RD
garnacha, syrah

87 Colour: rose, purple rim. Nose: powerfull, ripe fruit, red berry notes, floral, expressive. Palate: powerful, fruity, fresh.

ALDEYA DE AYLÉS TINTO 2012 T
syrah, tempranillo, merlot, cabernet sauvignon

86 Colour: cherry, purple rim. Nose: red berry notes, balsamic herbs, medium intensity. Palate: flavourful, fruity, good acidity.

ALDEYA DE AYLÉS TINTO BARRICA 2009 T
tempranillo, syrah, merlot

87 Colour: cherry, garnet rim. Nose: powerfull, ripe fruit, spicy, creamy oak, fine reductive notes. Palate: powerful, flavourful, spicy.

DORONDÓN CHARDONNAY DE AYLÉS 2012 B
chardonnay

87 Colour: bright yellow. Nose: ripe fruit, floral, fragrant herbs. Palate: powerful, flavourful, fruity.

SERENDIPIA CHARDONNAY DE AYLÉS 2012 B
chardonnay

90 Colour: bright yellow. Nose: floral, dried herbs, citrus fruit, ripe fruit, expressive. Palate: balanced, powerful, flavourful, complex.

SERENDIPIA GARNACHA DE AYLÉS 2009 T
garnacha

90 Colour: cherry, garnet rim. Nose: ripe fruit, scrubland, fine reductive notes, spicy, creamy oak. Palate: powerful, flavourful, spicy, long.

BODEGAS AÑADAS

Ctra. Aguarón km 47,100
50400 Cariñena (Zaragoza)
☎: +34 976 793 016 - Fax: +34 976 620 448
www.carewines.com
bodega@carewines.com

CARE 2010 TC
tempranillo, merlot

88 Colour: cherry, garnet rim. Nose: ripe fruit, sweet spices, cocoa bean. Palate: flavourful, fruity, correct.

CARE 2012 RD
tempranillo, cabernet sauvignon

87 Colour: rose, bright. Nose: medium intensity, ripe fruit, faded flowers. Palate: flavourful, easy to drink, fine bitter notes.

CARE 2012 T ROBLE
garnacha, syrah

88 Colour: bright cherry. Nose: ripe fruit, sweet spices, creamy oak, roasted coffee. Palate: flavourful, fruity, toasty.

CARE CHARDONNAY 2012 B
chardonnay

89 Colour: bright yellow. Nose: floral, ripe fruit, balanced. Palate: fruity, flavourful, good acidity.

CARE FINCA BANCALES 2009 TR
garnacha

92 Colour: cherry, garnet rim. Nose: ripe fruit, spicy, creamy oak, toasty, complex. Palate: powerful, flavourful, toasty, round tannins.

CARE XCLNT 2009 T
garnacha, syrah, cabernet sauvignon

90 Colour: cherry, garnet rim. Nose: ripe fruit, spicy, creamy oak, toasty, fine reductive notes. Palate: powerful, flavourful, toasty, round tannins.

BODEGAS CARLOS VALERO

Castillo de Capúa, 10 Nave 1
50197 (Zaragoza)
☎: +34 976 180 634 - Fax: +34 976 186 326
www.bodegasvalero.com
info@bodegasvalero.com

HEREDAD X CARLOS VALERO 2012 T
100% garnacha

91 Colour: cherry, garnet rim. Nose: red berry notes, ripe fruit, balsamic herbs, sweet spices, cocoa bean, toasty. Palate: powerful, flavourful, spicy, long.

BODEGAS ESTEBAN MARTÍN

Camino Virgen de Lagunas, s/n
50461 Alfamén (Zaragoza)
☎: +34 976 628 490 - Fax: +34 976 628 488
www.estebanmartin.com
carlosarnal@estebanmartin.es

ESTEBAN MARTÍN 2008 TR
garnacha, cabernet sauvignon

85 Colour: cherry, garnet rim. Nose: ripe fruit, spicy, creamy oak, toasty, complex. Palate: powerful, flavourful, toasty, round tannins.

ESTEBAN MARTÍN 2010 TC
garnacha, syrah

85 Colour: pale ruby, brick rim edge. Nose: scrubland, spicy, creamy oak. Palate: powerful, flavourful, slightly evolved.

ESTEBAN MARTÍN 2012 B
chardonnay, macabeo

84

ESTEBAN MARTÍN 2012 RD
garnacha, syrah

84

ESTEBAN MARTÍN 2012 T
garnacha, syrah

85 Colour: cherry, purple rim. Nose: red berry notes, ripe fruit, floral, balsamic herbs. Palate: flavourful, rich.

BARÓN DE LAJOYOSA 2006 TGR
garnacha, tempranillo, cariñena

86 Colour: very deep cherry, garnet rim. Nose: dark chocolate, sweet spices, tobacco, candied fruit.

BODEGAS IGNACIO MARÍN

San Valero, 1
50400 Cariñena (Zaragoza)
☎: +34 976 621 129 - Fax: +34 976 621 031
www.ignaciomarin.com
comercial@ignaciomarin.com

BARÓN DE LAJOYOSA MOSCATEL 2011 MISTELA
moscatel

89 Colour: bright golden. Nose: candied fruit, sweet spices, pattiserie, faded flowers. Palate: flavourful, rich, long.

DUQUE DE MEDINA 2012 T
garnacha, tempranillo, cariñena

84

MARÍN CABERNET 2010 T
cabernet sauvignon

89 Colour: deep cherry, garnet rim. Nose: balanced, ripe fruit, cocoa bean, sweet spices. Palate: flavourful, good structure, good acidity.

MARÍN GARNACHA 2010 T
garnacha

88 Colour: cherry, garnet rim. Nose: balanced, ripe fruit, candied fruit, sweet spices, dark chocolate. Palate: flavourful, easy to drink.

BODEGAS PANIZA

Ctra. Valencia, Km. 53
50480 Paniza (Zaragoza)
☎: +34 976 622 515 - Fax: +34 976 622 958
www.bodegasvirgenaguila.com
info@bodegaspaniza.com

ARTIGAZO 2007 T
garnacha, cabernet sauvignon, syrah

89 Colour: cherry, garnet rim. Nose: dry stone, ripe fruit, cocoa bean. Palate: good structure, flavourful, balanced, long.

JABALÍ GARNACHA-CABERNET 2012 RD
garnacha, cabernet sauvignon

86 Colour: rose, purple rim. Nose: powerfull, ripe fruit, red berry notes, lactic notes. Palate: powerful, fruity, fresh.

JABALÍ GARNACHA-SYRAH 2012 T
garnacha, syrah

89 Colour: cherry, purple rim. Nose: expressive, fresh fruit, red berry notes, floral. Palate: flavourful, fruity, good acidity, round tannins.

JABALÍ TEMPRANILLO - CABERNET 2012 T
tempranillo, cabernet sauvignon

88 Colour: cherry, garnet rim. Nose: red berry notes, scrubland, floral. Palate: powerful, flavourful, long, balsamic.

JABALÍ VIURA & CHARDONNAY 2012 B
viura, chardonnay

86 Colour: bright straw. Nose: medium intensity, ripe fruit, floral. Palate: fruity, balanced, correct, easy to drink.

LOS ROYALES 2009 TR
tempranillo

87 Colour: cherry, garnet rim. Nose: ripe fruit, spicy, creamy oak, toasty, complex. Palate: powerful, flavourful, toasty, round tannins.

LOS ROYALES 2010 TR
tempranillo

88 Colour: cherry, garnet rim. Nose: roasted coffee, spicy, ripe fruit. Palate: good structure, good acidity, long.

PANIZA 2007 TGR
tempranillo, garnacha, cabernet sauvignon

88 Colour: very deep cherry, garnet rim. Nose: toasty, spicy. Palate: good structure, fruity, smoky aftertaste, round tannins.

PANIZA 2008 TR
tempranillo, garnacha, cabernet sauvignon

87 Colour: deep cherry, garnet rim. Nose: spicy, medium intensity, ripe fruit. Palate: correct, ripe fruit.

PANIZA 2009 TC
tempranillo, garnacha, cabernet sauvignon

89 Colour: cherry, garnet rim. Nose: ripe fruit, spicy, creamy oak, toasty, complex. Palate: powerful, flavourful, toasty, round tannins.

SEÑORIO DE GAYAN 2008 TGR
tempranillo, garnacha

88 Colour: cherry, garnet rim. Nose: ripe fruit, spicy, creamy oak, toasty, complex. Palate: powerful, flavourful, toasty, round tannins.

VAL DE PANIZA 2012 B
macabeo, chardonnay

86 Colour: yellow, pale. Nose: balanced, tropical fruit, jasmine. Palate: correct, easy to drink.

VAL DE PANIZA 2012 RD
garnacha

88 Colour: rose, bright. Nose: red berry notes, ripe fruit, floral, balanced. Palate: flavourful, fruity, ripe fruit, easy to drink.

VAL DE PANIZA 2012 T
tempranillo, garnacha, syrah

88 Colour: cherry, purple rim. Nose: expressive, fresh fruit, red berry notes, floral. Palate: flavourful, fruity, good acidity.

BODEGAS PRINUR

Ctra. N-330, Km. 449
50400 Cariñena (Zaragoza)
☎: +34 976 621 039 - Fax: +34 976 620 714
www.bodegasprinur.com
info@bodegasprinur.com

PRINUR BLUE JEANS 2012 T
garnacha, cabernet sauvignon, syrah

87 Colour: cherry, purple rim. Nose: ripe fruit, violet drops. Palate: flavourful, fruity, balanced.

PRINUR CHARDONNAY 2012 B
chardonnay

85 Colour: bright yellow. Nose: ripe fruit, tropical fruit, balsamic herbs. Palate: flavourful, rich, fruity.

PRINUR MACABEO MOUNTAIN 2012 B
macabeo

84

PRINUR RED PASSION 2012 RD
syrah

87 Colour: rose, purple rim. Nose: expressive, ripe fruit, red berry notes, rose petals. Palate: flavourful, fruity, long.

PRINUR VIÑAS VIEJAS 2006 T
syrah, cabernet sauvignon

92 Colour: deep cherry, garnet rim. Nose: balanced, cocoa bean, wild herbs, ripe fruit, dry stone. Palate: flavourful, good structure, good acidity.

BODEGAS SAN VALERO

Ctra. Nacional 330, Km. 450
50400 Cariñena (Zaragoza)
☎: +34 976 620 400 - Fax: +34 976 620 398
www.sanvalero.com
bsv@sanvalero.com

CARINVS 2011 T ROBLE
tempranillo, garnacha, cabernet sauvignon, merlot, syrah

84

CARINVS CHARDONNAY 2012 B
100% chardonnay

85 Colour: bright straw. Nose: floral, dried herbs, ripe fruit. Palate: correct, fresh, balsamic.

CARINVS MUSCAT 2012 B
100% moscatel

86 Colour: bright straw. Nose: fresh, fresh fruit, white flowers, expressive. Palate: flavourful, fruity, balanced.

CASTILLO DUCAY 2012 RD
garnacha, cabernet sauvignon

85 Colour: rose, purple rim. Nose: balanced, red berry notes, powerfull. Palate: flavourful, fruity.

CASTILLO DUCAY 2012 B
macabeo, chardonnay

84

CASTILLO DUCAY 2012 T
garnacha, tempranillo, cabernet sauvignon

88 Colour: cherry, purple rim. Nose: red berry notes, candied fruit, floral, balsamic herbs. Palate: powerful, flavourful, fruity.

MARQUÉS DE TOSOS 2006 TR
tempranillo, garnacha, cabernet sauvignon

87 Colour: cherry, garnet rim. Nose: ripe fruit, spicy, creamy oak, toasty. Palate: powerful, flavourful, toasty.

MARQUÉS DE TOSOS 2009 TC
tempranillo, garnacha, cabernet sauvignon

87 Colour: cherry, garnet rim. Nose: ripe fruit, creamy oak, toasty. Palate: powerful, flavourful, toasty.

MONTE DUCAY 2012 RD
garnacha, cabernet sauvignon

88 Colour: rose, purple rim. Nose: ripe fruit, red berry notes, floral, expressive. Palate: powerful, fruity, fresh.

MONTE DUCAY 2004 TGR
tempranillo, cabernet sauvignon, garnacha

87 Colour: pale ruby, brick rim edge. Nose: spicy, fine reductive notes, wet leather, aged wood nuances, fruit liqueur notes, balanced. Palate: spicy, fine tannins, long.

MONTE DUCAY 2010 TC
merlot, syrah, garnacha

85 Colour: cherry, garnet rim. Nose: ripe fruit, creamy oak, toasty. Palate: powerful, toasty, harsh oak tannins.

MONTE DUCAY 2012 B

85 Colour: pale. Nose: medium intensity, fresh. Palate: fruity, light-bodied, easy to drink.

SIERRA DE VIENTO GARNACHA 2009 TR
100% garnacha

90 Colour: cherry, garnet rim. Nose: spicy, fine reductive notes, wet leather, aged wood nuances, fruit liqueur notes. Palate: spicy, elegant, long.

SIERRA DE VIENTO MOSCATEL VENDIMIA TARDÍA 2011 B
moscatel de alejandría

92 Colour: old gold. Nose: expressive, candied fruit, honeyed notes. Palate: flavourful, good acidity, unctuous, sweet, long.

SIERRA DE VIENTO OLD VINES GARNACHA 2010 T ROBLE
garnacha

87 Colour: deep cherry, garnet rim. Nose: spicy, toasty, ripe fruit, dried herbs. Palate: fruity, round tannins.

SIERRA DE VIENTO TEMPRANILLO 2012 T
100% tempranillo

86 Colour: very deep cherry. Nose: overripe fruit, powerfull. Palate: flavourful, fruity, good finish, correct, round tannins.

CAMPOS DE LUZ

Avda. Diagonal, 590, 5° - 1
8021 (Barcelona)
☎: +34 660 445 464
www.vinergia.com
info@vinergia.com

CAMPOS DE LUZ 2010 TC
100% garnacha

89 Colour: cherry, garnet rim. Nose: medium intensity, ripe fruit, spicy, dried herbs. Palate: fruity, round tannins.

CAMPOS DE LUZ 2012 B
viura, chardonnay, moscatel

84

CAMPOS DE LUZ 2012 RD
100% garnacha

85 Colour: light cherry, bright. Nose: red berry notes, ripe fruit, dried herbs, faded flowers. Palate: fruity, flavourful.

CAMPOS DE LUZ GARNACHA 2009 TR
100% garnacha

88 Colour: cherry, garnet rim. Nose: ripe fruit, spicy, creamy oak, toasty, balsamic herbs. Palate: powerful, flavourful, toasty.

CAMPOS DE LUZ GARNACHA 2012 T
100% garnacha

86 Colour: cherry, purple rim. Nose: red berry notes, ripe fruit, dry stone, balsamic herbs. Palate: powerful, flavourful, balanced.

CARREFOUR

Campezo, 16
28022 Madrid (Madrid)
☎: +34 902 202 000
www.carrefour.es

RÍO MAYOR 2009 TR
tempranillo, garnacha, cariñena, mazuelo

86 Colour: cherry, garnet rim. Nose: ripe fruit, spicy, toasty. Palate: powerful, flavourful, toasty, round tannins.

RÍO MAYOR 2010 TC
tempranillo, garnacha, cariñena, mazuelo

86 Colour: cherry, garnet rim. Nose: spicy, ripe fruit. Palate: fruity, easy to drink, correct, round tannins.

RÍO MAYOR 2012 T
tempranillo, garnacha, cariñena, mazuelo

83

COVINCA (COMPAÑÍA VITIVINÍCOLA)

Ctra, Valencia, s/n
50460 Longares (Zaragoza)
☎: +34 976 142 653 - Fax: +34 976 142 402
www.covinca.es
info@covinca.es

TERRAI 2011 T
cariñena

87 Colour: cherry, garnet rim. Nose: ripe fruit, grassy, spicy. Palate: powerful, flavourful, correct.

TORRELONGARES LICOR DE GARNACHA S/C VINO DE LICOR
garnacha

90 Colour: cherry, garnet rim. Nose: fruit liqueur notes, varnish, powerfull, balsamic herbs. Palate: sweet, rich, spirituous, balanced.

TORRELONGARES MICRO RELATOS 2012 B

84

TORRELONGARES MICRO RELATOS 2012 RD
garnacha, tempranillo

84

TORRELONGARES MICRO RELATOS 2012 T
garnacha

83

GRANDES VINOS Y VIÑEDOS

Ctra. Valencia Km 45,700
50400 Cariñena (Zaragoza)
☎: +34 976 621 261 - Fax: +34 976 621 253
www.grandesvinos.com
info@grandesvinos.com

ANAYÓN CARIÑENA 2011 T
cariñena

91 Colour: black cherry, purple rim. Nose: powerfull, ripe fruit, candied fruit, dark chocolate, creamy oak. Palate: flavourful, good structure, good acidity.

ANAYÓN CHARDONNAY 2011 B BARRICA
chardonnay

89 Colour: bright yellow. Nose: ripe fruit, sweet spices, creamy oak, medium intensity. Palate: rich, flavourful, spicy.

ANAYÓN GARNACHA SELECCIÓN 2008 T
garnacha

91 Colour: cherry, garnet rim. Nose: ripe fruit, scrubland, spicy, creamy oak, fine reductive notes. Palate: correct, powerful, flavourful, complex.

ANAYÓN SELECCIÓN 2011 T BARRICA
cariñena

89 Colour: black cherry, garnet rim. Nose: creamy oak, sweet spices, dark chocolate. Palate: flavourful, spicy, round tannins.

BESO DE VINO GARNACHA 2012 RD
garnacha

85 Colour: rose, purple rim. Nose: powerfull, red berry notes, floral, expressive. Palate: fruity, fresh, easy to drink.

BESO DE VINO MACABEO 2012 B
macabeo

82

BESO DE VINO OLD VINE GARNACHA 2011 T
garnacha

87 Colour: cherry, garnet rim. Nose: ripe fruit, dried herbs, spicy. Palate: correct, ripe fruit.

BESO DE VINO SELECCIÓN 2011 T
syrah, garnacha

88 Colour: deep cherry, garnet rim. Nose: medium intensity, ripe fruit, spicy. Palate: flavourful, fruity, round tannins.

CORONA DE ARAGÓN 2009 TC
tempranillo, cabernet sauvignon, garnacha, cariñena

89 Colour: cherry, garnet rim. Nose: ripe fruit, spicy, creamy oak, toasty, fine reductive notes. Palate: powerful, flavourful, toasty.

CORONA DE ARAGÓN 2004 TGR
tempranillo, cabernet sauvignon, cariñena, garnacha

88 Colour: cherry, garnet rim. Nose: ripe fruit, wet leather, cigar, balsamic herbs, fruit liqueur notes, aged wood nuances. Palate: powerful, flavourful, spirituous, fine tannins.

CORONA DE ARAGÓN 2006 TR
tempranillo, cabernet sauvignon, cariñena, garnacha

88 Colour: cherry, garnet rim. Nose: ripe fruit, spicy, old leather, tobacco. Palate: flavourful, fine tannins.

CORONA DE ARAGÓN DISPARATES CARIÑENA 2010 T
cariñena

90 Colour: very deep cherry, garnet rim. Nose: toasty, spicy, ripe fruit. Palate: flavourful, fruity, good acidity, spicy.

CORONA DE ARAGÓN GARNACHA 2012 T
garnacha

85 Colour: deep cherry, purple rim. Nose: medium intensity, ripe fruit. Palate: fruity, correct.

CORONA DE ARAGÓN GARNACHA SYRAH 2012 RD
garnacha, syrah

84

CORONA DE ARAGÓN MACABEO CHARDONNAY 2012 B
chardonnay, macabeo

84

CORONA DE ARAGÓN MOSCATEL S/C B
moscatel de alejandría

86 Colour: bright yellow. Nose: white flowers, ripe fruit, varietal. Palate: flavourful, rich, sweet.

CORONA DE ARAGÓN OLD VINE GARNACHA 2009 T
garnacha

87 Colour: cherry, garnet rim. Nose: ripe fruit, spicy, creamy oak, toasty. Palate: powerful, flavourful, toasty, round tannins.

CORONA DE ARAGÓN SPECIAL SELECTION 2011 T
garnacha, cariñena

88 Colour: bright cherry. Nose: ripe fruit, creamy oak, spicy. Palate: flavourful, fruity, toasty.

EL CIRCO GARNACHA 2012 RD
garnacha

85 Colour: rose, purple rim. Nose: powerfull, ripe fruit, red berry notes, floral, expressive. Palate: powerful, fruity, fresh.

EL CIRCO GARNACHA 2012 T
garnacha

87 Colour: deep cherry, purple rim. Nose: medium intensity, ripe fruit, balanced, dried herbs. Palate: fruity, ripe fruit.

EL CIRCO MACABEO 2012 B
macabeo

84

EL CIRCO TEMPRANILLO 2011 T
tempranillo

84

MONASTERIO DE LAS VIÑAS 2008 TC
garnacha, tempranillo, syrah

83

MONASTERIO DE LAS VIÑAS 2012 B
macabeo

84

MONASTERIO DE LAS VIÑAS 2005 TGR
garnacha, tempranillo, cariñena

86 Colour: pale ruby, brick rim edge. Nose: spicy, fine reductive notes, wet leather, aged wood nuances, fruit liqueur notes. Palate: spicy, fine tannins, long.

MONASTERIO DE LAS VIÑAS 2006 TR
garnacha, tempranillo, cariñena

85 Colour: cherry, garnet rim. Nose: old leather, tobacco, spicy, ripe fruit. Palate: correct, fruity, good finish.

MONASTERIO DE LAS VIÑAS 2012 RD
garnacha

87 Colour: light cherry, bright. Nose: balanced, red berry notes, ripe fruit, wild herbs, floral. Palate: flavourful, fruity.

MONASTERIO DE LAS VIÑAS GARNACHA TEMPRANILLO 2012 T
garnacha, tempranillo

84

HACIENDA MOLLEDA

Ctra. Belchite, km 29,3
50154 Tosos (Zaragoza)
☎: +34 976 620 702 - Fax: +34 976 620 102
www.haciendamolleda.com
hm@haciendamolleda.com

GHM GRAN HACIENDA MOLLEDA 2009 T ROBLE
mazuelo

90 Colour: cherry, garnet rim. Nose: ripe fruit, spicy, balanced. Palate: fruity, good acidity, long.

GHM GRAN HACIENDA MOLLEDA 2011 T ROBLE
garnacha, mazuelo

87 Colour: bright cherry. Nose: ripe fruit, sweet spices, creamy oak. Palate: flavourful, fruity, toasty.

GHM HACIENDA MOLLEDA 2008 T ROBLE
garnacha

88 Colour: bright cherry. Nose: ripe fruit, creamy oak, balsamic herbs. Palate: flavourful, fruity, toasty.

HACIENDA MOLLEDA 2011 T
garnacha, tempranillo

85 Colour: cherry, garnet rim. Nose: ripe fruit, scrubland, spicy. Palate: powerful, flavourful, balsamic.

HACIENDA MOLLEDA 2012 B
macabeo

83

HACIENDA MOLLEDA 2012 RD
garnacha

84

HACIENDA MOLLEDA 2012 T
garnacha, tempranillo

85 Colour: cherry, purple rim. Nose: medium intensity, ripe fruit, red berry notes. Palate: light-bodied, easy to drink, correct.

HACIENDA MOLLEDA GARNACHA 2009 T ROBLE
garnacha

90 Colour: cherry, garnet rim. Nose: balanced, expressive, ripe fruit, wild herbs. Palate: flavourful, balanced, ripe fruit.

LLEDA COUPAGE 2012 T
tempranillo, garnacha, cabernet sauvignon, syrah

84

HEREDAD ANSÓN

Camino Eras Altas, s/n
50450 Muel (Zaragoza)
☎: +34 976 141 133 - Fax: +34 976 141 133
www.bodegasheredadanson.com
info@bodegasheredadanson.com

HEREDAD DE ANSÓN 2007 TC
80% garnacha, 10% tempranillo, 10% syrah

80

HEREDAD DE ANSÓN 2012 B
macabeo

83

HEREDAD DE ANSÓN 2012 RD
garnacha

84

HEREDAD DE ANSÓN MERLOT SYRAH 2012 T
50% merlot, 50% syrah

86 Colour: cherry, garnet rim. Nose: ripe fruit, balanced, wild herbs. Palate: fruity, correct, easy to drink.

HEREDAD DE ANSÓN VENDIMIA SELECCIONADA 2008 T
85% garnacha, 15% syrah

81

LEGUM 2007 T
garnacha

88 Colour: dark-red cherry, orangey edge. Nose: candied fruit, fruit liqueur notes, spicy, dark chocolate, fine reductive notes. Palate: flavourful, good acidity.

LIASON GARNACHA 2012 T
garnacha

82

JORDÁN DE ASSO

Cariñena, 55
50408 Aguarón (Zaragoza)
☎: +34 976 620 291 - Fax: +34 976 230 270
www.jordandeasso.com
info@jordandeasso.com

JORDÁN DE ASSO 2007 TC
garnacha, cariñena, cabernet sauvignon

86 Colour: cherry, garnet rim. Nose: fruit preserve, balsamic herbs, spicy, old leather. Palate: powerful, flavourful, spicy.

JORDÁN DE ASSO 2007 TR
tempranillo, cabernet sauvignon, syrah

85 Colour: black cherry, garnet rim. Nose: tobacco, fruit preserve, spicy. Palate: flavourful, round tannins.

JORDÁN DE ASSO 2008 TC
garnacha, cariñena, cabernet sauvignon

85 Colour: cherry, garnet rim. Nose: ripe fruit, creamy oak, toasty, fine reductive notes. Palate: powerful, flavourful, toasty.

JORDÁN DE ASSO GARNACHA 2012 T
garnacha

84

JORDÁN DE ASSO TEMPRANILLO 2012 T
tempranillo

85 Colour: deep cherry, garnet rim. Nose: medium intensity, ripe fruit, fruit preserve. Palate: correct, fruity.

LONG WINES

Avda. del Puente Cultural, 8 Bloque B Bajo 7
28702 San Sebastián de los Reyes (Madrid)
☎: +34 916 221 305 - Fax: +34 916 220 029
www.longwines.com
adm@longwines.com

PLEYADES 2007 TR
65% tempranillo, 20% syrah, 15% garnacha

87 Colour: cherry, garnet rim. Nose: ripe fruit, balsamic herbs, sweet spices. Palate: powerful, flavourful, spicy.

PLEYADES GARNACHA VENDIMIA SELECCIONADA 2012 T
100% garnacha

86 Colour: cherry, garnet rim. Nose: powerfull, ripe fruit, fruit preserve, wild herbs. Palate: ripe fruit, long.

PLEYADES SYRAH 2012 T
100% syrah

86 Colour: black cherry, purple rim. Nose: fruit preserve, powerfull. Palate: flavourful, fruity, good structure.

MANUEL MONEVA E HIJOS

Avda. Zaragoza, 10
50108 Almonacid de la Sierra (Zaragoza)
☎: +34 976 627 020 - Fax: +34 976 627 334
www.bodegasmanuelmoneva.com
info@bodegasmanuelmoneva.com

VIÑA VADINA GARNACHA 2012 T
100% garnacha

83

VIÑA VADINA TEMPRANILLO GARNACHA 2012 T
tempranillo, garnacha

84

NAVASCUÉS ENOLOGÍA

Alfonso Xel Sabio 4, principal oficina B
50006 Zaragoza (Zaragoza)
☎: +34 651 845 176
www.cutio.es

CUTIO 2012 T

92 Colour: bright cherry. Nose: sweet spices, creamy oak, expressive, mineral, red berry notes, ripe fruit. Palate: flavourful, fruity, ripe fruit, long.

CUTIO GARNACHA 2011 T
garnacha

89 Colour: bright cherry. Nose: sweet spices, creamy oak, fruit expression. Palate: flavourful, fruity, toasty.

SOLAR DE URBEZO

San Valero, 14
50400 Cariñena (Zaragoza)
☎: +34 976 621 968 - Fax: +34 976 620 549
www.solardeurbezo.es
info@solardeurbezo.es

ALTIUS 2010 TC
merlot, cabernet sauvignon, syrah

90 Colour: cherry, garnet rim. Nose: ripe fruit, spicy, creamy oak, toasty, complex. Palate: powerful, flavourful, toasty.

ALTIUS MERLOT 2012 RD
merlot

87 Colour: rose, purple rim. Nose: powerfull, ripe fruit, red berry notes, floral, lactic notes. Palate: powerful, fruity, fresh.

ALTIUS VENDIMIA SELECCIONADA 2012 T
garnacha, cabernet sauvignon, merlot

90 Colour: cherry, garnet rim. Nose: balanced, fruit expression, powerfull. Palate: good structure, flavourful, round tannins.

DANCE DEL MAR 2012 T
tempranillo, merlot

87 Colour: cherry, purple rim. Nose: red berry notes, ripe fruit, fragrant herbs, balsamic herbs. Palate: powerful, flavourful, warm.

URBEZO 2007 TGR
garnacha, cabernet sauvignon

87 Colour: pale ruby, brick rim edge. Nose: fruit liqueur notes, balsamic herbs, spicy, old leather, tobacco. Palate: powerful, flavourful, spicy, toasty.

URBEZO 2008 TR
cabernet sauvignon, merlot, syrah

84

URBEZO 2010 TC
syrah, merlot, cabernet sauvignon

90 Colour: cherry, garnet rim. Nose: ripe fruit, spicy, creamy oak, dried herbs. Palate: powerful, flavourful, round tannins.

URBEZO CHARDONNAY 2012 B
100% chardonnay

89 Colour: bright yellow. Nose: balanced, white flowers, ripe fruit, tropical fruit. Palate: flavourful, rich, long.

URBEZO GARNACHA 2012 T
100% garnacha

88 Colour: cherry, garnet rim. Nose: red berry notes, ripe fruit, floral, fragrant herbs. Palate: powerful, flavourful, concentrated.

URBEZO MERLOT 2012 RD
100% merlot

87 Colour: light cherry, bright. Nose: red berry notes, ripe fruit, floral, rose petals. Palate: flavourful, full, long, ripe fruit.

URBEZO VENDIMIA SELECCIONADA 2007 T
garnacha, cabernet sauvignon, cariñena, syrah

86 Colour: dark-red cherry, orangey edge. Nose: old leather, cigar, fruit liqueur notes. Palate: correct, easy to drink, good finish.

VIÑA URBEZO 2012 T MACERACIÓN CARBÓNICA
garnacha, tempranillo, syrah

89 Colour: cherry, purple rim. Nose: expressive, fresh fruit, red berry notes, floral. Palate: flavourful, fruity, good acidity.

YSIEGAS 2007 TGR
garnacha, cabernet sauvignon

87 Colour: pale ruby, brick rim edge. Nose: spicy, fine reductive notes, wet leather, aged wood nuances, fruit liqueur notes. Palate: long, spicy, correct.

YSIEGAS 2008 TR
cabernet sauvignon, merlot, syrah

84

YSIEGAS 2010 TC
syrah, merlot, cabernet sauvignon

90 Colour: cherry, garnet rim. Nose: ripe fruit, spicy, creamy oak, toasty, fragrant herbs. Palate: flavourful, long, spicy.

YSIEGAS 2012 T
garnacha, tempranillo, syrah

85 Colour: cherry, garnet rim. Nose: ripe fruit, fruit liqueur notes, balsamic herbs. Palate: flavourful, correct, easy to drink.

YSIEGAS CHARDONNAY 2012 B
chardonnay

89 Colour: bright straw. Nose: fresh, fresh fruit, white flowers, fragrant herbs. Palate: flavourful, fruity, good acidity, balanced.

YSIEGAS GARNACHA 2012 T
garnacha

88 Colour: bright cherry. Nose: ripe fruit, sweet spices, creamy oak, expressive. Palate: flavourful, fruity, toasty.

YSIEGAS MERLOT 2012 RD
merlot

87 Colour: rose, purple rim. Nose: powerfull, ripe fruit, red berry notes, floral, lactic notes. Palate: powerful, fruity, fresh.

YSIEGAS TEMPRANILLO MERLOT 2012 T
tempranillo, merlot

86 Colour: cherry, garnet rim. Nose: ripe fruit, spicy, creamy oak. Palate: powerful, flavourful, toasty.

SUCESORES DE MANUEL PIQUER

Ctra. de Valencia Pol. Ind. Las Norias
50450 Muel (Zaragoza)
☎: +34 976 141 156 - Fax: +34 976 141 156
www.bodegaspiquer.com
bodegaspiquer@bodegaspiquer.com

VALDETOMÉ 2012 RD
garnacha

84

VALDETOMÉ 2012 T
tempranillo

84

VALDETOMÉ 2012 T
garnacha

87 Colour: cherry, purple rim. Nose: red berry notes, ripe fruit, balsamic herbs, characterful. Palate: rich, flavourful, fruity.

VINNICO

Muela, 16
3730 Jávea (Alicante)
☎: +34 965 791 967 - Fax: +34 966 461 471
www.vinnico.com
info@vinnico.com

CAPA GARNACHA 2011 T
garnacha

83

CASTILLO DEL ROCÍO OLD VINES GARNACHA 2012 T

84

EL TOCADOR 2012 T
tempranillo

85 Colour: dark-red cherry, purple rim. Nose: ripe fruit, balsamic herbs, powerfull, creamy oak. Palate: rich, balsamic, flavourful.

VIÑAS DE ALADREN

Via Universitas, 15
50009 (Zaragoza)
☎: +34 637 809 441
www.viñasdealadren.com
info@viasdaladren.com

SOLANILLO 2012 T
merlot, syrah

84

VIÑEDOS Y BODEGAS PABLO

Avda. Zaragoza, 16
50108 Almonacid de la Sierra (Zaragoza)
☎: +34 976 627 037 - Fax: +34 976 627 102
www.granviu.com
granviu@granviu.com

GRAN VÍU GARNACHA DEL TERRENO 2010 T
garnacha

92 Colour: black cherry, garnet rim. Nose: expressive, ripe fruit, cocoa bean, creamy oak, dry stone. Palate: flavourful, fruity, round tannins, long.

GRAN VÍU SELECCIÓN 2009 T
garnacha, tempranillo, cabernet sauvignon, syrah

89 Colour: cherry, garnet rim. Nose: ripe fruit, spicy, creamy oak, balsamic herbs. Palate: powerful, flavourful, spicy, long.

MENGUANTE GARNACHA 2012 T
garnacha

86 Colour: deep cherry, purple rim. Nose: medium intensity, ripe fruit, dried herbs. Palate: fruity, flavourful, balanced.

MENGUANTE GARNACHA BLANCA 2012 B
garnacha blanca

89 Colour: bright straw. Nose: dried flowers, fragrant herbs, ripe fruit, expressive. Palate: rich, balsamic, balanced.

MENGUANTE SELECCIÓN GARNACHA 2011 T
garnacha

90 Colour: bright cherry. Nose: ripe fruit, sweet spices, creamy oak, expressive. Palate: flavourful, fruity, toasty, round tannins.

MENGUANTE TEMPRANILLO 2012 T ROBLE
tempranillo

86 Colour: very deep cherry, purple rim. Nose: ripe fruit, fruit preserve, warm, toasty. Palate: flavourful, ripe fruit.

MENGUANTE VIDADILLO 2010 T
vidadilo

89 Colour: deep cherry, garnet rim. Nose: fruit preserve, toasty, wild herbs. Palate: ripe fruit, round tannins.

LOCATION:

The production area covers the traditional vine - growing Catalonian regions, and practically coincides with the current DOs present in Catalonia plus a few municipal areas with vine - growing vocation.

CLIMATE AND SOIL:

Depending on the location of the vineyard, the same as those of the Catalonian DO's, whose characteristics are defined in this guide. See Alella, Empordà, Conca de Barberà, Costers del Segre, Montsant, Penedès, Pla de Bages, Priorat, Tarragona and Terra Alta.

GRAPE VARIETIES:

WHITE:
RECOMMENDED: *Chardonnay, Garnacha Blanca, Macabeo, Moscatel de Alejandría, Moscatel de Grano Menudo, Parellada, Riesling, Sauvignon Blanc* and *Xarel·lo.*
AUTHORIZED: *Gewürztraminer, Subirat Parent (Malvasía), Malvasía de Sitges, Picapoll, Pedro Ximénez, Chenin, Riesling* and *Sauvignon Blanc*
RED:
RECOMMENDED: *Cabernet Franc, Cabernet Sauvignon, Garnacha, Garnacha Peluda, Merlot, Monastrell, Pinot Noir, Samsó (Cariñena), Trepat, Sumoll* and *Ull de Llebre (Tempranillo).*
AUTHORIZED: *Garnacha Tintorera* and *Syrah.*

FIGURES:

Vineyard surface: 48.145 – **Wine-Growers:** 9.097 – **Wineries:** 200 – **2012 Harvest rating:** Very Good – **Production:** 53.000.026 litres – **Market percentages:** 45,52% domestic. 59.13% export

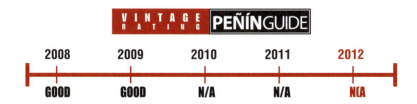

2008	2009	2010	2011	2012
GOOD	GOOD	N/A	N/A	N/A

CONSEJO REGULADOR
Edifici de l'Estació Enológica - Passeig Sunyer, 4-6 1º - 43202 Reus (Tarragona) ☎ +34 977 328 103 - Fax: +34 977 321 357
info@do-catalunya.com   www.do-catalunya.com

1898 RAMÓN ROQUETA

Ctra. de Vic, 81
8241 Manresa (Barcelona)
☎: +34 938 743 511 - Fax: +34 938 737 204
www.1898ramonroqueta.com
info@1898ramonroqueta.com

RAMÓN ROQUETA TEMPRANILLO 2012 T
100% tempranillo

88 Colour: cherry, purple rim. Nose: expressive, fresh fruit, red berry notes, floral. Palate: flavourful, fruity, good acidity, round tannins.

SYNERA 2009 TC
60% cabernet sauvignon, 20% merlot, 20% tempranillo

86 Colour: cherry, garnet rim. Nose: spicy, toasty, ripe fruit, balsamic herbs. Palate: powerful, flavourful, spicy.

SYNERA 2012 B
85% macabeo, 15% moscatel

84

SYNERA 2012 RD
50% tempranillo, 50% garnacha

86 Colour: rose, purple rim. Nose: floral, red berry notes, candied fruit, lactic notes. Palate: correct, powerful, fresh, fruity.

SYNERA 2012 T
75% tempranillo, 25% cabernet sauvignon

85 Colour: bright cherry. Nose: ripe fruit, creamy oak, spicy. Palate: flavourful, fruity, toasty.

VINYA NOSTRA 2012 B
xarel.lo

87 Colour: bright straw. Nose: fresh, fresh fruit, white flowers, expressive. Palate: flavourful, fruity, good acidity, balanced.

ALBET I NOYA

Camí Can Vendrell de la Codina, s/n
8739 Sant Pau D'Ordal (Barcelona)
☎: +34 938 994 812 - Fax: +34 938 994 930
www.albetinoya.cat
albetinoya@albetinoya.cat

ALBET I NOYA PETIT ALBET NEGRE 2011 T
cabernet sauvignon, tempranillo, garnacha

86 Colour: cherry, garnet rim. Nose: fruit liqueur notes, balsamic herbs, sweet spices. Palate: powerful, flavourful, spicy.

ALBET I NOYA VINYA LAIA 2010 T
garnacha, syrah, cabernet sauvignon

88 Colour: cherry, garnet rim. Nose: ripe fruit, creamy oak, toasty. Palate: powerful, flavourful, toasty.

ALBET I NOYA VINYA LAIA 2011 B
garnacha blanca, parellada

87 Colour: bright straw. Nose: white flowers, dried herbs, candied fruit, ripe fruit. Palate: fresh, fruity, flavourful.

BODEGA EL GRIAL S.L.

Ctra. Perelló-Rasquera Km. 6
43519 El Perelló (Tarragona)
☎: +34 977 475 351
www.bodegaselgrial.com
b.elgrial@yahoo.es

EL GRIAL NEGRE 2011 T
50% cabernet franc, 30% syrah, 20% merlot

85 Colour: cherry, garnet rim. Nose: ripe fruit, spicy, earthy notes, balsamic herbs, creamy oak. Palate: rich, flavourful, complex.

SAFRANER 2012 B
50% sauvignon blanc, 50% gewürztraminer

85 Colour: bright yellow. Nose: ripe fruit, citrus fruit, dried flowers, balsamic herbs. Palate: powerful, flavourful, slightly evolved.

BODEGAS PINORD

Doctor Pasteur, 6
8720 Vilafranca del Penedès (Barcelona)
☎: +34 938 903 066 - Fax: +34 938 170 979
www.pinord.com
visites@pinord.com

MIREIA 2012 B
66% moscatel, 18% gewürztraminer, 16% sauvignon blanc

88 Colour: bright straw. Nose: expressive, floral, powerfull, citrus fruit. Palate: fruity, flavourful, easy to drink.

BODEGAS PUIGGRÒS

Ctra. de Manresa, Km. 13
8711 Odena (Barcelona)
☎: +34 629 853 587
www.bodegaspuiggros.com
bodegaspuiggros@telefonica.net

MESTRE VILA VELL VINYES VELLES 2011 T
100% sumoll

90 Colour: cherry, garnet rim. Nose: wild herbs, ripe fruit, spicy. Palate: good structure, flavourful, round tannins.

SENTITS BLANCS 2012 B
100% garnacha blanca

91 Colour: bright yellow. Nose: powerfull, ripe fruit, sweet spices, fragrant herbs. Palate: rich, flavourful, fresh, good acidity.

SENTITS NEGRES 2011 T
100% garnacha

93 Colour: deep cherry, purple rim. Nose: expressive, ripe fruit, wild herbs, cocoa bean. Palate: good structure, full, good acidity.

SIGNES 2011 T
80% sumoll, 20% garnacha

90 Colour: cherry, garnet rim. Nose: ripe fruit, smoky, toasty, dried herbs. Palate: fruity, round tannins, good acidity.

CA N'ESTRUC

Ctra. C-1414, Km. 1,05
8292 Esparreguera (Barcelona)
☎: +34 937 777 017 - Fax: +34 937 771 108
www.canestruc.com
canestruc@vilaviniteca.es

CA N'ESTRUC 2012 T

90 Colour: cherry, purple rim. Nose: expressive, fresh fruit, red berry notes, floral, sweet spices. Palate: flavourful, fruity, good acidity, round tannins.

CA N'ESTRUC BLANC 2012 B
xarel.lo, moscatel, garnacha blanca, macabeo, chardonnay

88 Colour: bright straw. Nose: ripe fruit, citrus fruit, white flowers. Palate: flavourful, ripe fruit, fine bitter notes.

CA N'ESTRUC XAREL.LO 2012 B
100% xarel.lo

90 Colour: bright straw. Nose: fresh, fresh fruit, white flowers. Palate: flavourful, fruity, good acidity, balanced.

IDOIA 2011 T
syrah, garnacha, cariñena

89 Colour: deep cherry, purple rim. Nose: powerfull, sweet spices, ripe fruit. Palate: flavourful, round tannins.

IDOIA BLANC 2012 BFB
xarel.lo, garnacha blanca, chardonnay, macabeo

92 Colour: bright straw. Nose: ripe fruit, candied fruit, citrus fruit, scrubland. Palate: flavourful, fruity, fresh, good acidity.

L'EQUILIBRISTA 2010 T
syrah, garnacha, cariñena

92 Colour: deep cherry, garnet rim. Nose: powerfull, ripe fruit, cocoa bean, balsamic herbs. Palate: good structure, flavourful, fine tannins, good acidity.

L'EQUILIBRISTA 2011 B
100% xarel.lo

93 Colour: bright straw, greenish rim. Nose: expressive, ripe fruit, sweet spices, faded flowers. Palate: full, rich, fine bitter notes, complex.

L'EQUILIBRISTA GARNATXA 2010 T
100% garnacha

92 Colour: cherry, garnet rim. Nose: powerfull, ripe fruit, cocoa bean. Palate: good structure, flavourful, balsamic, fine tannins, good acidity.

CAN GRAU VELL

Can Grau Vell, s/n
8781 Hostalets de Pierola (Barcelona)
☎: +34 676 586 933 - Fax: +34 932 684 965
www.grauvell.cat
info@grauvell.cat

ALCOR 2009 T
syrah, garnacha, monastrell, marcelan, cabernet sauvignon

93 Colour: cherry, garnet rim. Nose: spicy, creamy oak, toasty, fruit expression. Palate: powerful, flavourful, toasty, round tannins.

QUIKE 2012 RD
100% garnacha

90 Colour: brilliant rose. Nose: elegant, candied fruit, dried flowers, fragrant herbs, red berry notes. Palate: light-bodied, flavourful, good acidity, long, spicy.

CASTELL D'OR

Mare Rafols, 3- 1º 4º
8720 Vilafranca del Penedès (Barcelona)
☎: +34 938 905 446 - Fax: +34 938 905 446
www.castelldor.com
castelldor@castelldor.com

FLAMA D'OR 2006 TR
40% cabernet sauvignon, 40% tempranillo

85 Colour: pale ruby, brick rim edge. Nose: spicy, fine reductive notes, wet leather, aged wood nuances, fruit liqueur notes. Palate: spicy, long, flavourful.

FLAMA D'OR 2012 B
60% macabeo, 40% xarel.lo

83

FLAMA D'OR 2012 RD
100% tempranillo

84

PUIG DE SOLIVELLA 2011 B
80% macabeo, 20% parellada

81

PUIG DE SOLIVELLA 2012 T
75% tempranillo, 25% garnacha

83

CAVAS BOHIGAS

Finca Can Maciá s/n
8711 Ódena (Barcelona)
☎: +34 938 048 100 - Fax: +34 938 032 366
www.bohigas.es
comercial@bohigas.es

FERMÍ DE FERMÍ BOHIGAS 2009 TR
syrah

90 Colour: cherry, garnet rim. Nose: ripe fruit, spicy, creamy oak, fine reductive notes, earthy notes. Palate: powerful, flavourful, toasty.

UDINA DE FERMÍ BOHIGAS 2012 B
xarel.lo, garnacha blanca, chenin blanc

88 Colour: bright straw. Nose: ripe fruit, dried herbs, floral. Palate: fine bitter notes, powerful, flavourful.

BOHIGAS BLANC DE BLANCS 2012 B
xarel.lo

90 Colour: bright straw. Nose: fresh, fresh fruit, white flowers, expressive. Palate: flavourful, fruity, good acidity, balanced, elegant.

BOHIGAS CABERNET SAUVIGNON 2010 TC
cabernet sauvignon, garnacha

88 Colour: cherry, garnet rim. Nose: red berry notes, ripe fruit, balsamic herbs, spicy, creamy oak. Palate: powerful, flavourful, spicy, correct.

CAVAS DEL AMPURDÁN

Pza. del Carme, 1
17491 Perelada (Girona)
☎: +34 972 538 011 - Fax: +34 972 538 277
www.blancpescador.com
perelada@castilloperelada.com

MASIA DONADEU 2011 T
30% ull de llebre, 70% garnacha

82

MASIA DONADEU 2012 B
59% macabeo, 41% garnacha

84

MASIA DONADEU 2012 RD
66% ull de llebre, 34% garnacha

84

CAVES CONDE DE CARALT S.A.

Ctra. Sant Sadurní-Sant Pere de Riudebitlles, Km. 5
8775 Torrelavit (Barcelona)
☎: +34 938 917 070 - Fax: +34 938 996 006
www.condedecaralt.com
condedecaralt@condedecaralt.com

CONDE DE CARALT 2012 RD
tempranillo, merlot, monastrell

82

CONDE DE CARALT BLANC DE BLANCS 2012 B
macabeo, xarel.lo, parellada

84

CELLER DE CAPÇANES

Llebaria, 4
43776 Capçanes (Tarragona)
☎: +34 977 178 319 - Fax: +34 977 178 319
www.cellercapcanes.com
cellercapcanes@cellercapcanes.com

6/X PINOT NOIR DE CAPÇANES 2011 T
100% pinot noir

90 Colour: cherry, garnet rim. Nose: ripe fruit, spicy, creamy oak, toasty, fragrant herbs. Palate: powerful, flavourful, toasty, round tannins, elegant.

CLOS D'AGON

Afores, s/n
17251 Calonge (Girona)
☎: +34 972 661 486 - Fax: +34 972 661 462
www.closdagon.com
info@closdagon.com

CLOS D'AGON 2010 T
45% cabernet franc, 30% syrah, 10% merlot, 10% petit verdot, 5% cabernet sauvignon

94 Colour: bright cherry. Nose: ripe fruit, sweet spices, creamy oak, expressive, mineral. Palate: flavourful, fruity, toasty, round tannins, balanced, elegant.

CLOS D'AGON 2011 B
39% viognier, 22% marsenne, 39% roussanne

93 Colour: bright yellow. Nose: floral, fragrant herbs, spicy, creamy oak, expressive. Palate: balanced, elegant, flavourful, spicy, complex.

**CLOS MONTBLANC CASTELL
MACABEO CHARDONNAY B**
macabeo, chardonnay

86 Colour: bright straw. Nose: fresh, white flowers, ripe fruit, balsamic herbs. Palate: flavourful, fruity, fine bitter notes.

**CLOS MONTBLANC CASTELL
TEMPRANILLO 2012 T**
tempranillo, cabernet sauvignon

87 Colour: cherry, garnet rim. Nose: ripe fruit, balsamic herbs, sweet spices. Palate: powerful, flavourful, spicy.

CLOS MONTBLANC CHARDONNAY 2012 BFB
100% chardonnay

86 Colour: bright yellow. Nose: powerfull, ripe fruit, sweet spices, fragrant herbs, roasted coffee. Palate: rich, smoky aftertaste, flavourful.

CLOS MONTBLANC XIPELLA TC
monastrell, garnacha, samsó, syrah

88 Colour: cherry, garnet rim. Nose: ripe fruit, spicy, toasty, fine reductive notes. Palate: powerful, flavourful, toasty.

JAUME GRAU - VINS GRAU S.L.

Ctra. C-37, Km. 75,5
8255 Maians (Barcelona)
☎: +34 938 356 002 - Fax: +34 938 356 812
www.vinsgrau.com
info@vinsgrau.com

CLOS DEL RECÓ 2012 B
macabeo, xarel.lo, parellada

84

CLOS DEL RECÓ 2012 RD
merlot

86 Colour: rose, purple rim. Nose: powerfull, ripe fruit, red berry notes, floral, expressive. Palate: powerful, fruity, fresh.

CLOS DEL RECÓ 2012 T
tempranillo

84

JAUME SERRA
(J. GARCÍA CARRIÓN)

Ctra. de Vilanova, Km. 2,5
8800 Vilanova i la Geltru (Barcelona)
☎: +34 938 936 404 - Fax: +34 938 147 482
www.garciacarrion.es
jaumeserra@jgc.es

VINYA DEL MAR SECO 2012 B
40% macabeo, 40% xarel.lo, 20% parellada

82

VIÑA DEL MAR 2012 RD
80% tempranillo, 20% mazuelo

82

VIÑA DEL MAR 2012 T
80% tempranillo, 20% mazuelo

80

VIÑA DEL MAR SEMIDULCE 2012 B
60% macabeo, 40% xarel.lo

80

MASET DEL LLEÓ

C-244, Km. 32,5
8792 La Granada del Penedès (Barcelona)
☎: +34 902 200 250 - Fax: +34 938 921 333
www.maset.com
info@maset.com

MASET DEL LLEÓ GRAN ROBLE 2009 TR
tempranillo

91 Colour: cherry, garnet rim. Nose: red berry notes, ripe fruit, dark chocolate, sweet spices, toasty. Palate: spicy, long, powerful, flavourful.

MASET DEL LLEÓ ROBLE 2010 T ROBLE
tempranillo

89 Colour: bright cherry. Nose: ripe fruit, sweet spices, creamy oak, expressive. Palate: flavourful, fruity, toasty, round tannins.

MASET DEL LLEÓ SYRAH 2009 TR
syrah

92 Colour: cherry, garnet rim. Nose: ripe fruit, fruit liqueur notes, floral, balsamic herbs, sweet spices, creamy oak. Palate: powerful, flavourful, long, spicy.

MASIA BACH

Ctra. Martorell Capellades, km. 20,5
8635 Sant Esteve Sesrovires (Barcelona)
☎: +34 937 714 052
www.grupocodorniu.com
codinfo@codorniu.es

BACH MOSCATO FRIZZANTE B
100% moscato

87 Colour: bright straw. Nose: fresh, white flowers, candied fruit. Palate: flavourful, fruity, good acidity, balanced.

MIGUEL TORRES S.A.

Miguel Torres i Carbó, 6
8720 Vilafranca del Penedès (Barcelona)
☎: +34 938 177 400 - Fax: +34 938 177 444
www.torres.es
mailadmin@torres.es

DECASTA 2012 RD
65% garnacha, 35% cariñena

86 Colour: rose, purple rim. Nose: powerfull, ripe fruit, red berry notes, floral. Palate: powerful, fruity, fresh.

HABITAT 2012 B
garnacha, xarel.lo

89 Colour: bright straw. Nose: white flowers, dried herbs, candied fruit, balanced. Palate: fresh, fruity, flavourful.

SAN VALENTÍN 2012 B
100% parellada

85 Colour: bright straw. Nose: white flowers, candied fruit, fragrant herbs. Palate: fresh, fruity, flavourful, easy to drink.

SANGRE DE TORO 2011 T
65% garnacha, 35% cariñena

87 Colour: cherry, garnet rim. Nose: ripe fruit, spicy, creamy oak, toasty. Palate: powerful, flavourful, toasty.

VIÑA ESMERALDA 2012 B
85% moscatel, 15% gewürztraminer

87 Colour: bright straw. Nose: fresh, fresh fruit, white flowers, expressive. Palate: flavourful, fruity, good acidity, balanced.

VIÑA SOL 2012 B
parellada, garnacha blanca

87 Colour: bright straw. Nose: ripe fruit, floral, dried herbs, powerfull. Palate: flavourful, rich, easy to drink.

PONS TRADICIÓ S.L.U.

Ctra. LV-7011, km. 4,5
25155 L'Albagés (Lleida)
☎: +34 973 070 737
www.clospons.com
clospons@grup-pons.com

ALONIA 2011 T
garnacha, syrah

85 Colour: cherry, garnet rim. Nose: ripe fruit, spicy, aged wood nuances. Palate: powerful, flavourful, toasty.

RENÉ BARBIER

Ctra. Sant Sadurní a St. Pere Riudebitlles, km. 5
8775 Torrelavit (Barcelona)
☎: +34 938 917 070 - Fax: +34 938 996 006
www.renebarbier.com
renebarbier@renebarbier.es

RENÉ BARBIER KRALINER 2012 B
macabeo, xarel.lo, parellada

85 Colour: bright straw. Nose: fresh, fresh fruit, white flowers. Palate: flavourful, fruity, good acidity, balanced.

RENÉ BARBIER ROSADO TRADICIÓN 2012 RD
tempranillo, merlot, monastrell

84

RENÉ BARBIER VIÑA AUGUSTA 2012 B
macabeo, xarel.lo, parellada, moscatel

85 Colour: bright straw. Nose: white flowers, candied fruit, lactic notes, fresh. Palate: easy to drink, light-bodied, fresh, fruity.

ROCAMAR

Major, 80
8755 Castellbisbal (Barcelona)
☎: +34 937 720 900 - Fax: +34 937 721 495
www.rocamar.net
info@rocamar.net

BLANC DE PALANGRE B
macabeo, parellada

78

MASIA RIBOT 2012 B
macabeo, parellada

81

MASIA RIBOT 2012 T
tempranillo, garnacha

80

ROSAT DE PALANGRE RD
trepat

82

SPIRITUS BARCELONA

Domenech Soberano, 9
43203 Reus (Tarragona)
☎: +34 609 750 184
www.spiritusbarcelona.com
customer@spiritusbarcelona.com

GRAND VINAFOC CABERNET SAUVIGNON 2009 T
cabernet sauvignon

86 Colour: very deep cherry, garnet rim. Nose: wild herbs, ripe fruit. Palate: correct, round tannins.

GRAND VINAFOC MERLOT 2009 T
merlot

87 Colour: deep cherry, garnet rim. Nose: sweet spices, toasty, ripe fruit, fruit preserve. Palate: correct, fine bitter notes.

GRAND VINAFOC SYRAH 2009 T
syrah

88 Colour: deep cherry, garnet rim. Nose: balanced, ripe fruit, violet drops. Palate: fruity, easy to drink.

TOMÁS CUSINÉ

Plaça Sant Sebastià, 13
25457 El Vilosell (Lleida)
☎: +34 973 176 029 - Fax: +34 973 175 945
www.tomascusine.com
info@tomascusine.com

DRAC MÀGIC 2011 T

86 Colour: bright cherry. Nose: ripe fruit, sweet spices, creamy oak, expressive. Palate: flavourful, fruity, toasty, round tannins.

DRAC MÀGIC 2012 B

87 Colour: bright straw. Nose: fresh, fresh fruit, white flowers, tropical fruit. Palate: flavourful, fruity, good acidity, balanced.

VALLFORMOSA

La Sala, 45
8735 Vilobi del Penedès (Barcelona)
☎: +34 938 978 286 - Fax: +34 938 978 355
www.vallformosa.com
vallformosa@vallformosa.es

LAVIÑA 2012 B
macabeo, garnacha
83

LAVIÑA 2012 RD
tempranillo, merlot
83

LAVIÑA SEMI DULCE 2012 B
macabeo, garnacha
83

VALLPLATA 2012 B
macabeo, garnacha
83

VALLPLATA 2012 RD
tempranillo, merlot
84

VALLPLATA 2012 T
merlot, tempranillo
84

VINS DEL MASSIS

Ctra. de Gava - Avimyonet, Km. 18,7
8795 Olesa de Bonesvails (Barcelona)
☎: +34 655 931 286
vinsdelmassis@yahoo.com

CELLER MASSIS 2011 B
55% xarel.lo, 45% garnacha blanca

89 Colour: bright yellow. Nose: powerfull, ripe fruit, sweet spices, creamy oak. Palate: rich, smoky aftertaste, flavourful, fresh, good acidity.

MACIZO 2011 B
60% garnacha blanca, 40% xarel.lo

91 Colour: bright yellow. Nose: ripe fruit, spicy, creamy oak, sweet spices, balsamic herbs, expressive. Palate: long, powerful, flavourful, complex, toasty, balanced.

DO CAVA / D.O.P.

LOCATION:

The defined Cava region covers the sparkling wines produced according to the traditional method of a second fermentation in the bottle of 63 municipalities in the province of Barcelona, 52 in Tarragona, 12 in Lleida and 5 in Girona, as well as those of the municipal areas of Laguardia, Moreda de Álava and Oyón in Álava, Almendralejo in Badajoz, Mendavia and Viana in Navarra, Requena in Valencia, Ainzón and Cariñena in Zaragoza, and a further 18 municipalities of La Rioja.

CLIMATE:

That of each producing region stated in the previous epigraph. Nevertheless, the region in which the largest part of the production is concentrated (Penedès) has a Mediterranean climate, with some production areas being cooler and situated at a higher altitude.

SOIL:

This also depends on each producing region.

GRAPE VARIETIES:

WHITE: *Macabeo* (*Viura*), *Xarel.lo, Parellada, Subirat* (*Malvasía Riojana*) and *Chardonnay*.
RED: *Garnacha Tinta, Monastrell, Trepat* and *Pinot Noir.*

FIGURES:

Vineyard surface: 32.355– **Wine-Growers:** 6.561 – **Wineries:** 253 – **2012 Harvest rating:** Very Good – **Production:** 182.424.000litres – **Market percentages:** 33,6% domestic 66,4% export

This denomination of origin, due to the wine-making process, does not make available single-year wines indicated by vintage, so the following evaluation refers to the overall quality of the wines that were tasted this year.

CONSEJO REGULADOR
Avinguda Tarragona, 24 - 08720 Vilafranca del Penedès (Barcelona) ☎: +34 938 903 104 - Fax: +34 938 901 567
consejo@crcava.es   www.crcava.es

1 + 1 = 3

Masía Navinés
8736 Guardiola de Font-Rubí (Barcelona)
☎: +34 938 974 069 - Fax: +34 938 974 724
www.umesufan3.com
umesu@umesufan3.com

1 + 1 = 3 BN
parellada, xarel.lo, macabeo

89 Colour: bright straw. Nose: medium intensity, fresh fruit, dried herbs, fine lees, floral. Palate: fresh, fruity, flavourful, good acidity.

1 + 1 = 3 BR
macabeo, xarel.lo, parellada

89 Colour: bright straw. Nose: fresh fruit, dried herbs, fine lees, floral. Palate: fresh, fruity, flavourful, good acidity.

**1 + 1 = 3 GRAN RESERVA ESPECIAL
2007 BN GRAN RESERVA**
xarel.lo, pinot noir

92 Colour: bright golden. Nose: fine lees, dry nuts, fragrant herbs, complex. Palate: powerful, flavourful, good acidity, fine bead, fine bitter notes.

1 + 1 = 3 PINOT NOIR BN
pinot noir

87 Colour: rose. Nose: powerfull, characterful, candied fruit, red berry notes. Palate: good acidity, ripe fruit.

CYGNUS 1 + 1 = 3 BN RESERVA
macabeo, xarel.lo, parellada

90 Colour: bright straw. Nose: medium intensity, dried herbs, fine lees, floral, citrus fruit, fresh fruit. Palate: fresh, fruity, flavourful, good acidity.

CYGNUS 1 + 1 = 3 BR
parellada, xarel.lo, macabeo

88 Colour: bright straw. Nose: medium intensity, fresh fruit, dried herbs, fine lees. Palate: fresh, fruity, flavourful, good acidity.

AGRÍCOLA DE BARBERÀ

Carrer Comerç, 40
43422 Barberà de la Conca (Tarragona)
☎: +34 977 887 035 - Fax: +34 977 887 035
www.coop-barbera.com
cobarbera@doconcadebarbera.com

CASTELL DE LA COMANDA BR
50% macabeo, 50% parellada

86 Colour: bright straw. Nose: medium intensity, fresh fruit, dried herbs, fine lees, dried flowers. Palate: fresh, fruity, flavourful, good acidity.

**CASTELL DE LA COMANDA
2008 BN GRAN RESERVA**
macabeo, parellada

88 Colour: bright golden. Nose: fine lees, dry nuts, fragrant herbs, complex. Palate: powerful, flavourful, good acidity, fine bead, fine bitter notes.

**CASTELL DE LA COMANDA
2008 BR GRAN RESERVA**
macabeo, parellada

86 Colour: bright straw. Nose: fresh fruit, dry nuts, medium intensity. Palate: correct, good acidity.

AGUSTÍ TORELLÓ MATA

La Serra, s/n (Camí de Ribalta)
8770 Sant Sadurní D'Anoia (Barcelona)
☎: +34 938 911 173 - Fax: +34 938 912 616
www.agustitorellomata.com
comunicacio@agustitorellomata.com

AGUSTÍ TORELLÓ MATA 2008 BN GRAN RESERVA
38% macabeo, 28% xarel.lo, 34% parellada

91 Colour: bright straw. Nose: expressive, neat, candied fruit, spicy. Palate: fine bitter notes, balanced, fine bead.

AGUSTÍ TORELLÓ MATA 2009 BR RESERVA
44% macabeo, 24% xarel.lo, 32% parellada

89 Colour: bright straw. Nose: dried herbs, fine lees, floral, ripe fruit. Palate: fresh, fruity, flavourful, good acidity.

**AGUSTÍ TORELLÓ MATA GRAN
RESERVA BARRICA 2008 BN**
100% macabeo

91 Colour: bright straw. Nose: toasty, ripe fruit. Palate: flavourful, powerful, ripe fruit.

AGUSTÍ TORELLÓ MATA MAGNUM 2006 BN GRAN RESERVA
45% macabeo, 25% xarel.lo, 30% parellada

92 Colour: bright golden. Nose: dry nuts, fragrant herbs, complex, fine lees, spicy, petrol notes. Palate: powerful, flavourful, good acidity, fine bead, fine bitter notes.

AGUSTÍ TORELLÓ MATA ROSAT TREPAT 2010 BR RESERVA
100% trepat

89 Colour: salmon. Nose: powerfull, raspberry, fruit liqueur notes. Palate: sweetness, fruity.

BAYANUS 375ML 2008 BN GRAN RESERVA
40% macabeo, 30% xarel.lo, 30% parellada

91 Colour: bright straw. Nose: candied fruit, faded flowers, spicy. Palate: fine bitter notes, good acidity, spicy.

BAYANUS ROSAT 375 2009 BR RESERVA
100% trepat

87 Colour: coppery red. Nose: faded flowers, candied fruit, fruit liqueur notes. Palate: spicy, ripe fruit, fine bitter notes.

KRIPTA 2007 BN GRAN RESERVA
45% macabeo, 20% xarel.lo, 35% parellada

92 Colour: bright straw. Nose: expressive, candied fruit, spicy. Palate: spicy, ripe fruit, good acidity, fine bead.

ALBET I NOYA

Camí Can Vendrell de la Codina, s/n
8739 Sant Pau D'Ordal (Barcelona)
☎: +34 938 994 812 - Fax: +34 938 994 930
www.albetinoya.cat
albetinoya@albetinoya.cat

ALBET I NOYA BR RESERVA
macabeo, xarel.lo, parellada, chardonnay

86 Colour: bright straw. Nose: medium intensity, fresh fruit, dried herbs, fine lees, floral. Palate: fresh, fruity, flavourful, good acidity.

ALBET I NOYA BRUT 21 BARRICA 2006 BR
pinot noir, chardonnay

92 Colour: bright golden. Nose: candied fruit, pattiserie, sweet spices, jasmine. Palate: flavourful, good acidity, fine bitter notes.

ALBET I NOYA BRUT 21 BR
chardonnay, parellada

91 Colour: bright golden. Nose: fine lees, dry nuts, fragrant herbs, complex. Palate: powerful, flavourful, good acidity, fine bead, fine bitter notes.

ALBET I NOYA BRUT ROSAT PINOT NOIR BR
pinot noir

88 Colour: rose. Nose: ripe fruit, red berry notes, floral. Palate: flavourful, fruity.

ALBET I NOYA DOLÇ DE POSTRES RESERVA
xarel.lo, parellada, chardonnay

88 Colour: bright straw. Nose: floral, fragrant herbs, fine lees, medium intensity, spicy. Palate: correct, powerful, flavourful.

ALBET I NOYA MILLÉSSIME 2009 BN GRAN RESERVA
xarel.lo, chardonnay, macabeo, parellada

90 Colour: bright golden. Nose: fine lees, dry nuts, fragrant herbs, white flowers, faded flowers. Palate: flavourful, good acidity, fine bead, fine bitter notes.

ALBET I NOYA PETIT ALBET BRUT BR
macabeo, xarel.lo, parellada

89 Colour: bright straw. Nose: dried herbs, fine lees, floral, ripe fruit. Palate: fresh, fruity, flavourful, good acidity.

ALSINA SARDÁ

8770 Pla del Penedès (Barcelona)
☎: +34 938 988 132 - Fax: +34 938 988 671
www.alsinasarda.com
alsina@alsinasarda.com

ALSINA & SARDÁ BR RESERVA
macabeo, xarel.lo, parellada

87 Colour: bright straw. Nose: medium intensity, fresh fruit, floral. Palate: fresh, fruity, flavourful, good acidity, easy to drink.

ALSINA & SARDÁ 2010 BN RESERVA
macabeo, xarel.lo, parellada

87 Colour: bright straw. Nose: medium intensity, fresh fruit, dried herbs. Palate: fresh, fruity, flavourful, good acidity.

ALSINA & SARDÁ GRAN CUVÉE VESTIGIS 2007 BN GRAN RESERVA
macabeo, xarel.lo, parellada, pinot noir, chardonnay

90 Colour: bright golden. Nose: fine lees, dry nuts, fragrant herbs, citrus fruit. Palate: powerful, flavourful, good acidity, fine bead, fine bitter notes.

ALSINA & SARDÁ GRAN RESERVA ESPECIAL 2008 BN GRAN RESERVA
chardonnay, xarel.lo

89 Colour: bright golden. Nose: fine lees, dry nuts, fragrant herbs, complex, toasty. Palate: powerful, flavourful, good acidity, fine bead, fine bitter notes.

ALSINA & SARDÁ MAS D'ALSINA BN RESERVA
chardonnay, macabeo, xarel.lo, parellada

88 Colour: bright straw. Nose: medium intensity, dried herbs, ripe fruit, dried flowers. Palate: fresh, fruity, flavourful, good acidity.

ALSINA & SARDA PINOT NOIR BN
pinot noir

88 Colour: coppery red. Nose: ripe fruit, floral, fragrant herbs, sweet spices. Palate: powerful, flavourful, ripe fruit, fine bead.

ALSINA & SARDÁ SELLO 2009 BN GRAN RESERVA
xarel.lo, macabeo, parellada

86 Colour: bright golden. Nose: fine lees, dry nuts, fragrant herbs, sweet spices. Palate: powerful, flavourful, good acidity, fine bead.

ALTA ALELLA

Camí Baix de Tiana s/n
8328 Alella (Barcelona)
☎: +34 934 693 720 - Fax: +34 934 691 343
www.altaalella.cat
altaalella@altaalella.cat

ALTA ALELLA MIRGIN 2008 BN GRAN RESERVA
chardonnay, pinot noir

89 Colour: bright yellow. Nose: balanced, sweet spices, dry nuts. Palate: fruity, flavourful, fine bitter notes, good acidity.

ALTA ALELLA MIRGIN ROSÉ 2008 BN
pinot noir

87 Colour: raspberry rose. Nose: balanced, medium intensity, dried flowers. Palate: fruity, fine bitter notes, good acidity.

PRIVAT 2010 BN
pansa blanca, macabeo, parellada

87 Colour: bright straw. Nose: medium intensity, fresh fruit, dried herbs, fine lees, floral. Palate: fresh, fruity, flavourful, good acidity.

PRIVAT BR
pansa blanca, macabeo, parellada

86 Colour: bright straw. Nose: fresh, floral, balanced. Palate: correct, balanced, good acidity, easy to drink.

PRIVAT EVOLUCIÓ CHARDONNAY BN RESERVA
chardonnay

88 Colour: bright straw. Nose: dried herbs, fine lees, floral, candied fruit. Palate: fresh, fruity, flavourful, good acidity.

PRIVAT LAIETÀ 2010 BN RESERVA
chardonnay, pinot noir

88 Colour: bright yellow. Nose: medium intensity, balanced, dried flowers. Palate: good acidity, fresh, balanced.

PRIVAT LAIETÀ ILURO BN
mataró

89 Colour: coppery red, bright. Nose: scrubland, expressive, slightly evolved, dry nuts. Palate: flavourful, fruity, long, good acidity.

PRIVAT NU 2011 BN
pansa blanca

88 Colour: bright straw. Nose: white flowers, ripe fruit. Palate: flavourful, fruity.

PRIVAT OPUS EVOLUTIUM BN GRAN RESERVA
chardonnay, pinot noir

91 Colour: bright yellow. Nose: floral, fine lees, candied fruit, balanced, complex. Palate: good structure, flavourful, fine bitter notes, good acidity.

PRIVAT ROSÉ 2010 BN
pinot noir, mataró

87 Colour: salmon. Nose: raspberry, red berry notes. Palate: flavourful, fruity, fresh.

AVINYÓ CAVAS

Masia Can Fontanals
8793 Avinyonet del Penedès (Barcelona)
☎: +34 938 970 055 - Fax: +34 938 970 691
www.avinyo.com
avinyo@avinyo.com

AVINYÓ BLANC DE NOIRS BN RESERVA
pinot noir

86 Colour: bright straw. Nose: medium intensity, fresh fruit, dried herbs, fine lees, floral. Palate: fresh, fruity, flavourful, good acidity.

AVINYÓ BN RESERVA
macabeo, xarel.lo, parellada

87 Colour: bright straw. Nose: dried herbs, fine lees, floral, ripe fruit. Palate: fresh, fruity, flavourful, good acidity.

AVINYÓ BR RESERVA
macabeo, xarel.lo, parellada

88 Colour: bright straw. Nose: fresh, dry nuts, fine lees, faded flowers. Palate: correct, fine bitter notes, good acidity, fresh.

AVINYÓ ROSÉ SUBLIM BR RESERVA
100% pinot noir

88 Colour: coppery red. Nose: fresh fruit, dried herbs, fine lees, floral. Palate: fresh, fruity, flavourful, good acidity, balanced.

AVINYÓ SELECCIÓ LA TICOTA
2007 BN GRAN RESERVA
macabeo, xarel.lo

89 Colour: bright yellow. Nose: fine lees, dry nuts, fragrant herbs, complex, sweet spices. Palate: powerful, flavourful, good acidity, fine bead, fine bitter notes.

BLANCHER-CAPDEVILA PUJOL

Plaça Pont Romà, Edificio Blancher
8770 Sant Sadurní D'Anoia (Barcelona)
☎: +34 938 183 286 - Fax: +34 938 911 961
www.blancher.es
blancher@blancher.es

BLANCHER 2008 BN RESERVA
xarel.lo, macabeo, parellada

87 Colour: bright straw. Nose: medium intensity, dried herbs, fine lees, floral. Palate: fresh, fruity, flavourful, good acidity.

BLANCHER ROSAT 2009 BR RESERVA
pinot noir, trepat, garnacha

84

CAPDEVILA PUJOL 2009 BN RESERVA
xarel.lo, macabeo, parellada

87 Colour: bright yellow. Nose: ripe fruit, citrus fruit, faded flowers, powerfull. Palate: fine bitter notes, fine bead, correct.

TERESA BLANCHER DE LA TIETA
2007 BN GRAN RESERVA
xarel.lo, macabeo, parellada

90 Colour: bright golden. Nose: expressive, candied fruit, ripe fruit. Palate: good acidity, fine bitter notes, fine bead.

BODEGA SANSTRAVÉ

De la Conca, 10
43412 Solivella (Tarragona)
☎: +34 977 892 165 - Fax: +34 977 892 073
www.sanstrave.com
bodega@sanstrave.com

SANSTRAVÉ 2009 BN GRAN RESERVA
macabeo, parellada, xarel.lo, chardonnay

87 Colour: bright golden. Nose: fine lees, dry nuts, fragrant herbs. Palate: powerful, flavourful, good acidity, fine bead.

SANSTRAVÉ ROSÉ 2011 BN GRAN RESERVA
trepat

89 Colour: onion pink. Nose: candied fruit, dried flowers, fragrant herbs, red berry notes. Palate: light-bodied, flavourful, good acidity, long, spicy.

BODEGA SEBIRAN

Pérez Galdos, 1
46352 Campo Arcis - Requena (Valencia)
☎: +34 962 303 321 - Fax: +34 962 301 560
www.sebiran.es
info@sebiran.es

COTO D'ARCIS BN
macabeo

87 Colour: bright yellow. Nose: dry nuts, fragrant herbs, complex. Palate: powerful, flavourful, good acidity, fine bead, fine bitter notes.

COTO D'ARCIS ESPECIAL BR
macabeo

86 Colour: bright straw. Nose: medium intensity, dried herbs, floral, candied fruit, fruit preserve, lees reduction notes. Palate: fresh, fruity, flavourful, good acidity.

BODEGAS ABANICO

Pol. Ind Ca l'Avellanet - Susany, 6
8553 Seva (Barcelona)
☎: +34 938 125 676 - Fax: +34 938 123 213
www.bodegasabanico.com
info@exportiberia.com

RENAIXENÇA BN
macabeo, parellada, xarel.lo

86 Colour: bright straw. Nose: candied fruit, spicy. Palate: flavourful, good acidity, fine bitter notes.

RENAIXENÇA BR
macabeo, parellada, xarel.lo

87 Colour: bright straw. Nose: dried herbs, fine lees, floral, dry nuts. Palate: fresh, fruity, flavourful, good acidity.

RENAIXENÇA DELUXE GRAN CUVÉE BR
macabeo, parellada, xarel.lo

88 Colour: bright yellow. Nose: expressive, balanced, faded flowers, fresh. Palate: flavourful, easy to drink.

BODEGAS ARRAEZ

Arcediano Ros, 35
46630 La Font de la Figuera (Valencia)
☎: +34 962 290 031 - Fax: +34 962 290 339
www.bodegasarraez.com
julian@bodegasarraez.com

A-2 BR RESERVA
80% macabeo, 20% chardonnay

85 Colour: bright straw. Nose: medium intensity, dried herbs, fine lees, floral, ripe fruit. Palate: fresh, flavourful, fine bitter notes.

BODEGAS BORDEJÉ

Ctra. Borja a Rueda, Km. 3
50570 Ainzón (Zaragoza)
☎: +34 976 868 080 - Fax: +34 976 868 989
www.bodegasbordeje.com
ainzon@bodegasbordeje.com

CAVA BORDEJÉ CHARDONNAY BN
chardonnay

84

CAVA BORDEJÉ MACABEO ESP
macabeo

84

CAVA BORDEJÉ ROSADO DE GARNACHA BN
garnacha

84

BODEGAS CA N'ESTELLA

Masia Ca N'Estella, s/n
8635 Sant Esteve Sesrovires (Barcelona)
☎: +34 934 161 387 - Fax: +34 934 161 620
www.fincacanestella.com
a.vidal@fincacanestella.com

RABETLLAT I VIDAL BRUT ROSADO
trepat

86 Colour: rose. Nose: ripe fruit, red berry notes, faded flowers. Palate: good acidity, fine bitter notes.

RABETLLAT I VIDAL 2010 BN
80% chardonnay, 20% macabeo

88 Colour: bright straw. Nose: dried herbs, fine lees, floral, fruit expression. Palate: fresh, fruity, flavourful, good acidity.

RABETLLAT I VIDAL BRUT CA N'ESTELLA 2011 BR
60% macabeo, 40% xarel.lo

86 Colour: bright straw. Nose: dried flowers, dried herbs, ripe fruit, fine lees. Palate: flavourful, fresh, fruity.

RABETLLAT I VIDAL GRAN RESERVA DE LA FINCA 2007 EXTRA BRUT
80% chardonnay, 20% macabeo

87 Colour: bright straw. Nose: spicy, toasty, candied fruit. Palate: sweetness, fine bitter notes.

BODEGAS CAPITÀ VIDAL

Ctra. Villafranca-Igualada, Km. 21
8733 Pla del Penedès (Barcelona)
☎: +34 938 988 630 - Fax: +34 938 988 625
www.capitavidal.com
capitavidal@capitavidal.com

FUCHS DE VIDAL BN GRAN RESERVA
50% xarel.lo, 30% macabeo, 20% parellada

90 Colour: bright golden. Nose: fine lees, dry nuts, fragrant herbs, complex, candied fruit. Palate: powerful, flavourful, good acidity, fine bead, fine bitter notes.

FUCHS DE VIDAL CINCO BR
40% xarel.lo, 35% macabeo, 25% parellada

86 Colour: bright straw. Nose: medium intensity, dried herbs, fine lees, floral. Palate: fresh, fruity, flavourful, good acidity.

FUCHS DE VIDAL CUVÉE BN RESERVA
40% xarel.lo, 35% macabeo, 25% parellada

90 Colour: bright straw. Nose: medium intensity, fresh fruit, dried herbs, fine lees. Palate: fresh, fruity, flavourful, good acidity.

FUCHS DE VIDAL ROSÉ PINOT NOIR BN
100% pinot noir

84

FUCHS DE VIDAL UNIC BN
35% pinot noir, 50% chardonnay, 15% macabeo, xarel.lo, parellada

88 Colour: bright straw. Nose: dried herbs, fine lees, floral, candied fruit. Palate: fresh, fruity, flavourful, balanced.

GRAN FUCHS DE VIDAL BN
40% xarel.lo, 35% macabeo, 25% parellada

89 Colour: bright straw. Nose: medium intensity, fresh fruit, dried herbs, fine lees, floral. Palate: fresh, fruity, flavourful, good acidity.

PALAU SOLÁ BN
40% xarel.lo, 35% macabeo, 25% parellada

84

BODEGAS COVIÑAS

Avda. Rafael Duyos, s/n
46340 Requena (Valencia)
☎: +34 962 300 680 - Fax: +34 962 302 651
www.covinas.com
covinas@covinas.com

ENTERIZO BN
macabeo, xarel.lo, parellada

83

ENTERIZO BR
macabeo, xarel.lo, parellada

87 Colour: bright straw. Nose: medium intensity, fresh fruit, dried herbs, fine lees, floral. Palate: fruity, flavourful, good acidity, sweetness.

MARQUÉS DE PLATA BN
macabeo, xarel.lo, parellada

85 Colour: bright yellow. Nose: faded flowers, dry nuts, dried herbs. Palate: fine bitter notes, flavourful, powerful.

MARQUÉS DE PLATA BR
macabeo, xarel.lo, parellada

83

BODEGAS ESCUDERO

Ctra. de Arnedo, s/n
26587 Grávalos (La Rioja)
☎: +34 941 398 008 - Fax: +34 941 398 070
www.familiaescudero.com
info@familiaescudero.com

BENITO ESCUDERO BN
100% viura

86 Colour: bright straw. Nose: dried herbs, floral, candied fruit. Palate: fresh, fruity, flavourful, good acidity.

BENITO ESCUDERO BR
100% viura

87 Colour: bright straw. Nose: dried flowers, fragrant herbs, candied fruit, balanced. Palate: light-bodied, fresh, fruity, good acidity.

DIORO BACO BR
50% viura, 50% chardonnay

86 Colour: bright straw. Nose: medium intensity, dried herbs, fine lees, floral, dry nuts. Palate: fresh, fruity, flavourful.

DIORO BACO EXTRA BRUT
100% chardonnay

84

DIORO BACO ROSADO BR
100% pinot noir

85 Colour: brilliant rose. Nose: candied fruit, fragrant herbs, floral, medium intensity. Palate: fresh, fruity, flavourful.

BODEGAS FAUSTINO

Ctra. de Logroño, s/n
1320 Oyón (Álava)
☎: +34 945 622 500 - Fax: +34 945 622 511
www.bodegasfaustino.es
info@bodegasfaustino.es

CAVA FAUSTINO BR RESERVA
viura, chardonnay

84

DO CAVA / D.O.P.

BODEGAS HISPANO SUIZAS

Ctra. N-322, Km. 451,7 El Pontón
46357 Requena (Valencia)
☎: +34 661 894 200
www.bodegashispanosuizas.com
info@bodegashispanosuizas.com

**TANTUM ERGO CHARDONNAY
PINOT NOIR 2010 BN**
chardonnay, pinot noir

92 Colour: bright straw. Nose: medium intensity, fresh fruit, dried herbs, fine lees, floral. Palate: fresh, fruity, flavourful, good acidity.

TANTUM ERGO PINOT NOIR ROSÉ 2011 BN
pinot noir

91 Colour: salmon. Nose: candied fruit, raspberry, medium intensity. Palate: good acidity, fine bitter notes.

TANTUM ERGO VINTAGE 2008 BN
chardonnay, pinot noir

90 Colour: bright golden. Nose: candied fruit, fruit liqueur notes, toasty. Palate: fine bitter notes, good acidity, correct, roasted-coffee aftertaste.

BODEGAS MARCELINO DÍAZ

Mecánica, s/n
6200 Almendralejo (Badajoz)
☎: +34 924 677 548 - Fax: +34 924 660 977
www.madiaz.com
bodega@madiaz.com

PUERTA PALMA BR
macabeo

85 Colour: bright straw. Nose: fresh fruit, fine lees, floral. Palate: fresh, fruity, flavourful, good acidity.

BODEGAS MUGA

Barrio de la Estación, s/n
26200 Haro (La Rioja)
☎: +34 941 311 825
www.bodegasmuga.com
juan@bodegasmuga.com

CONDE DE HARO MAGNUM BR
viura, malvasía

90 Colour: bright straw. Nose: fresh fruit, dried herbs, fine lees, floral, citrus fruit. Palate: fresh, fruity, flavourful, good acidity, balanced.

BODEGAS MUR BARCELONA

Rambla de la Generalitat, 1-9
8720 Sant Sadurni D'Anoia (Barcelona)
☎: +34 938 911 551 - Fax: +34 938 911 662
www.mur-barcelona.com
info@mur-barcelona.com

GRAN MONTESQUIUS 2010 BN RESERVA
xarel.lo, macabeo, parellada

86 Colour: bright straw. Nose: dry nuts, ripe fruit, dried herbs. Palate: fresh, fruity, flavourful, thin.

ROBERT J. MUR ESPECIAL MILLESIMÉE 2009 BN
xarel.lo, parellada, macabeo, chardonnay

89 Colour: bright yellow. Nose: fragrant herbs, floral, candied fruit, pattiserie, sweet spices. Palate: fresh, fruity, flavourful.

**ROBERT J. MUR ESPECIAL TRADICIÓ
2010 BN RESERVA**
xarel.lo, parellada, macabeo

88 Colour: bright straw. Nose: medium intensity, fresh fruit, dried herbs, fine lees, floral. Palate: fresh, fruity, flavourful, good acidity.

**ROBERT J. MUR ESPECIAL TRADICIÓ
ROSÉ 2010 BN RESERVA**
monastrell, garnacha, pinot noir, trepat

88 Colour: onion pink. Nose: fine lees, dry nuts, fragrant herbs, dried flowers. Palate: powerful, flavourful, good acidity, fine bead, fine bitter notes.

BODEGAS MURVIEDRO

Ampliación Pol. El Romeral, s/n
46340 Requena (Valencia)
☎: +34 962 329 003 - Fax: +34 962 329 002
www.bodegasmurviedro.es
murviedro@murviedro.es

COROLILLA CHARDONNAY BR
100% chardonnay

85 Colour: bright golden. Nose: complex, lees reduction notes, dry nuts. Palate: powerful, flavourful, good acidity, fine bead.

EXPRESIÓN SOLIDARITY CUVÉE CHARDONNAY BN
100% chardonnay

88 Colour: bright straw. Nose: dried herbs, fine lees, ripe fruit, tropical fruit. Palate: fresh, fruity, flavourful, good acidity.

LUNA DE MURVIEDRO BR
100% macabeo

88 Colour: bright straw. Nose: medium intensity, fresh fruit, dried herbs. Palate: fresh, fruity, flavourful, good acidity.

LUNA DE MURVIEDRO ROSÉ BR
100% garnacha

85 Colour: rose. Nose: expressive, ripe fruit, red berry notes. Palate: sweetness, ripe fruit, spicy.

BODEGAS OLARRA

Avda. de Mendavia, 30
26009 Logroño (La Rioja)
☎: +34 941 235 299 - Fax: +34 941 253 703
www.bodegasolarra.es
bodegasolarra@bodegasolarra.es

AÑARES BN
100% viura

84

AÑARES BR
100% viura

85 Colour: bright yellow. Nose: floral, wild herbs. Palate: fresh, flavourful, good finish, easy to drink.

BODEGAS ONDARRE

Ctra. de Aras, s/n
31230 Viana (Navarra)
☎: +34 948 645 300 - Fax: +34 948 646 002
www.bodegasondarre.es
bodegasondarre@bodegasondarre.es

ONDARRE BN
100% viura

84

ONDARRE BR
100% viura

85 Colour: bright straw. Nose: dried herbs, fine lees, dried flowers. Palate: fresh, fruity, flavourful, good acidity.

BODEGAS PINORD

Doctor Pasteur, 6
8720 Vilafranca del Penedès (Barcelona)
☎: +34 938 903 066 - Fax: +34 938 170 979
www.pinord.com
visites@pinord.com

DIBON 2010 BR RESERVA
macabeo, xarel.lo, parellada

87 Colour: bright straw. Nose: candied fruit, citrus fruit, medium intensity. Palate: easy to drink, ripe fruit.

MARRUGAT 2007 BN GRAN RESERVA
xarel.lo, macabeo, parellada

86 Colour: bright golden. Nose: ripe fruit, dried flowers, medium intensity. Palate: fresh, fine bitter notes, flavourful.

MARRUGAT CHARDONNAY 2006 BR RESERVA
chardonnay

82

MARRUGAT RIMA 32 2007 BN RESERVA
pinot noir, chardonnay

90 Colour: bright yellow. Nose: medium intensity, fresh fruit, dried herbs, fine lees, floral. Palate: fresh, fruity, flavourful, good acidity.

MARRUGAT ROSADO 2009 BR RESERVA
garnacha

87 Colour: bright straw. Nose: medium intensity, fine lees, floral. Palate: fresh, fruity, flavourful, good acidity.

MARRUGAT SUSPIRUM 2007 BN
xarel.lo, macabeo, parellada, chardonnay

85 Colour: bright yellow. Nose: candied fruit, faded flowers, powerfull. Palate: flavourful, correct.

BODEGAS ROMALE

Pol. Ind. Parc. 6, Manz. D
6200 Almendralejo (Badajoz)
☎: +34 924 667 255 - Fax: +34 924 665 877
www.romale.com
romale@romale.com

PRIVILEGIO DE ROMALE 2009 BN
macabeo, parellada

84

BODEGAS ROURA - JUAN ANTONIO PÉREZ ROURA

Valls de Rials s/n
8328 Alella (Barcelona)
☎: +34 933 527 456 - Fax: +34 933 524 339
www.roura.es
roura@roura.es

ROURA 5 * BN
50% xarel.lo, 50% chardonnay

87 Colour: bright straw. Nose: medium intensity, fresh fruit, dried herbs, fine lees, floral. Palate: fresh, fruity, flavourful.

ROURA BN
70% xarel.lo, 30% chardonnay

85 Colour: bright straw. Nose: fresh fruit, fine lees, floral, medium intensity, fragrant herbs. Palate: fresh, fruity, flavourful.

ROURA BR
75% xarel.lo, 25% chardonnay

84

ROURA ROSAT BN
100% trepat

85 Colour: rose. Nose: medium intensity, fresh fruit, fine lees, floral. Palate: fresh, fruity, easy to drink.

BODEGAS TROBAT

Castelló, 10
17780 Garriguella (Girona)
☎: +34 972 530 092 - Fax: +34 972 552 530
www.bodegastrobat.com
bodegas.trobat@bmark.es

CELLER TROBAT 2008 BN GRAN RESERVA
macabeo, xarel.lo, parellada, chardonnay

86 Colour: bright golden. Nose: dry nuts, fragrant herbs, lees reduction notes. Palate: powerful, flavourful, good acidity, fine bead, fine bitter notes.

CELLER TROBAT 2009 BN RESERVA
macabeo, xarel.lo, parellada, chardonnay

88 Colour: bright golden. Nose: fine lees, dry nuts, fragrant herbs, lees reduction notes. Palate: powerful, flavourful, good acidity.

CELLER TROBAT 2012 SS
macabeo, xarel.lo, parellada

86 Colour: bright straw. Nose: candied fruit, citrus fruit, ripe fruit. Palate: flavourful, ripe fruit, good acidity.

CELLER TROBAT ROSAT 2011 BR
garnacha, monastrell

83

CELLER TROBAT VINTAGE 2012 BR
macabeo, xarel.lo, parellada

88 Colour: bright straw. Nose: medium intensity, fresh fruit, dried herbs, floral. Palate: fresh, fruity, flavourful, good acidity.

GRAN AMAT 2012 BN
macabeo, xarel.lo, parellada

86 Colour: bright straw. Nose: medium intensity, dried herbs, floral, candied fruit. Palate: fresh, fruity, flavourful, good acidity.

BODEGAS VEGAMAR

Garcesa, s/n
46175 Calles (Valencia)
☎: +34 962 109 813
www.bodegasvegamar.com
info@bodegasvegamar.com

DOMINIO DE CALLES 2011 BN
macabeo, chardonnay

85 Colour: bright straw. Nose: floral, candied fruit, fragrant herbs. Palate: correct, light-bodied, fruity.

DOMINIO DE CALLES ROSE 2011 BN
macabeo, chardonnay

84

PRIVÉE 18 2010 BN RESERVA
macabeo, chardonnay

86 Colour: bright straw. Nose: medium intensity, fresh fruit, dried herbs, fine lees, floral. Palate: fresh, good acidity, easy to drink.

BODEGAS VICENTE GANDÍA

Ctra. Cheste a Godelleta, s/n
46370 Chiva (Valencia)
☎: +34 962 524 242 - Fax: +34 962 524 243
www.vicentegandia.es
info@vicentegandia.com

EL MIRACLE BR
macabeo, chardonnay

86 Colour: bright straw. Nose: candied fruit, dried herbs, floral. Palate: fresh, fruity, flavourful, easy to drink.

HOYA DE CADENAS BN
100% macabeo

87 Colour: bright straw. Nose: citrus fruit, faded flowers, dried herbs, fine lees. Palate: powerful, fresh, flavourful, good acidity.

HOYA DE CADENAS BR
macabeo, chardonnay

86 Colour: bright straw. Nose: fine lees, dried flowers, dried herbs. Palate: fresh, fruity, flavourful, easy to drink.

HOYA DE CADENAS ROSADO BR
garnacha

83

VICENTE GANDÍA BN
macabeo

87 Colour: bright straw. Nose: medium intensity, fresh fruit, dried herbs, fine lees, floral. Palate: fresh, fruity, flavourful, good acidity.

VICENTE GANDÍA BR
macabeo, chardonnay

85 Colour: bright straw. Nose: medium intensity, dried herbs, fine lees, floral, citrus fruit. Palate: fresh, fruity, flavourful.

VICENTE GANDÍA ROSADO BR
garnacha

84

BODEGUES SUMARROCA

El Rebato, s/n
8739 Subirats (Barcelona)
☎: +34 938 911 092 - Fax: +34 938 911 778
www.sumarroca.es
info@sumarroca.es

CAVA SUMARROCA ROSAT GRAN BRUT BRUT ROSADO
100% pinot noir

87 Colour: light cherry. Nose: complex, red berry notes. Palate: fine bitter notes, ripe fruit.

NÚRIA CLAVEROL BR GRAN RESERVA
xarel.lo

94 Colour: bright straw. Nose: powerfull, ripe fruit, fruit expression, fragrant herbs. Palate: fruity, flavourful, fine bead.

SUMARROCA 2009 BN GRAN RESERVA
parellada, xarel.lo, macabeo, chardonnay

90 Colour: bright golden. Nose: fine lees, dry nuts, fragrant herbs. Palate: powerful, flavourful, good acidity, fine bead, fine bitter notes.

SUMARROCA 2009 BR RESERVA
parellada, xarel.lo, macabeo, chardonnay

89 Colour: bright straw. Nose: fresh fruit, dried herbs, fine lees, floral. Palate: fresh, fruity, flavourful, good acidity.

SUMARROCA ALLIER BR GRAN RESERVA
chardonnay, pinot noir, parellada

93 Colour: bright golden. Nose: fine lees, dry nuts, fragrant herbs. Palate: powerful, flavourful, good acidity, fine bead, fine bitter notes.

SUMARROCA CUVÉE BN GRAN RESERVA
parellada, chardonnay

90 Colour: bright golden. Nose: dry nuts, fragrant herbs. Palate: powerful, flavourful, good acidity, fine bead, fine bitter notes.

SUMARROCA GRAN BRUT 2008 BR RESERVA
chardonnay, pinot noir blanc de noirs, parellada

92 Colour: bright straw. Nose: ripe fruit, citrus fruit, spicy. Palate: flavourful, full, powerful, fine bead.

SUMARROCA INSITU EXTRA BRUT RESERVA
macabeo, xarel.lo, parellada

88 Colour: bright straw. Nose: ripe fruit, citrus fruit, white flowers. Palate: flavourful, ripe fruit, good acidity.

SUMARROCA ROSÉ PINOT NOIR BRUT BR RESERVA
pinot noir

90 Colour: salmon. Nose: expressive, candied fruit, red berry notes. Palate: flavourful, fruity, fine bitter notes, good acidity.

BOLET VINS I CAVES

Finca Mas Lluet, s/n
8732 Castellvi de la Marca (Barcelona)
☎: +34 938 918 153
www.cavasbolet.com
cavasbolet@cavasbolet.com

BOLET PINOT NOIR 2012 RD
pinot noir

86 Colour: rose, purple rim. Nose: powerfull, ripe fruit, red berry notes, floral, expressive. Palate: powerful, fruity, fresh.

CAN DESCREGUT

Masia Can Descregut, s/n
8735 Vilobi del Penedès (Barcelona)
☎: +34 938 978 273
www.descregut.com
info@descregut.com

MEMÒRIA 2007 BN GRAN RESERVA
50% xarel.lo, 50% chardonnay

87 Colour: bright golden. Nose: dry nuts, fragrant herbs, complex, sweet spices. Palate: powerful, flavourful, good acidity, fine bead, fine bitter notes.

MONT D'ARAC 2010 BN RESERVA
xarel.lo, macabeo, parellada, chardonnay

85 Colour: bright golden. Nose: dry nuts, fragrant herbs, complex, sweet spices. Palate: powerful, flavourful, good acidity, fine bead, fine bitter notes.

MONT D'ARAC ROSAT 2009 BN RESERVA
pinot noir

84

CANALS & MUNNÉ

Plaza Pau Casals, 6
8770 Sant Sadurní D'Anoia (Barcelona)
☎: +34 938 910 318 - Fax: +34 938 911 945
www.canalsimunne.com
info@canalsimunne.com

CANALS & MUNNÉ "1915 BY C Y M" 2009 BN GRAN RESERVA
40% pinot noir, 30% chardonnay, 20% xarel.lo, 15% macabeo

87 Colour: bright yellow. Nose: dry nuts, dried herbs. Palate: powerful, flavourful, good acidity, fine bead.

CANALS & MUNNÉ 2009 BN GRAN RESERVA
40% macabeo, 30% chardonnay, 30% parellada

89 Colour: bright yellow. Nose: faded flowers, ripe fruit, dry nuts, fragrant herbs. Palate: good acidity, fine bead, flavourful.

CANALS & MUNNÉ 2009 BR GRAN RESERVA
30% macabeo, 50% xarel.lo, 20% parellada

90 Colour: bright golden. Nose: fine lees, fragrant herbs, characterful, ripe fruit. Palate: powerful, flavourful, good acidity, fine bead, fine bitter notes.

CANALS & MUNNÉ GRAN DUC 2008 BN GRAN RESERVA
60% chardonnay, 25% xarel.lo, 15% macabeo

90 Colour: bright yellow. Nose: floral, balanced, fine lees, candied fruit. Palate: flavourful, spicy, fine bitter notes, good acidity.

CANALS & MUNNÉ INSUPERABLE 2010 BR RESERVA
40% macabeo, 30% xarel.lo, 30% parellada

89 Colour: bright straw. Nose: medium intensity, fresh fruit, dried herbs, fine lees, floral. Palate: fresh, fruity, flavourful, good acidity.

CANALS & MUNNÉ RESERVA DE L'AVI 2009 BN GRAN RESERVA
50% chardonnay, 15% macabeo, 20% xarel.lo, 15% parellada

90 Colour: bright yellow. Nose: dried flowers, ripe fruit, fragrant herbs, complex. Palate: fine bitter notes, powerful, flavourful, fine bead.

CANALS & MUNNÉ RESERVA DE L'AVI JEROBOAM (3 LITROS) 2009 RESERVA
50% chardonnay, 15% macabeo, 20% xarel.lo, 15% parellada

90 Colour: bright yellow. Nose: fresh, balanced, fragrant herbs. Palate: fruity, good acidity, balanced, fine bitter notes.

CANALS & MUNNÉ ROSÉ 2010 BR RESERVA
100% pinot noir

87 Colour: rose. Nose: expressive, fresh, red berry notes. Palate: flavourful, fruity, fresh.

DIONYSUS ECO 2009 BN RESERVA
60% xarel.lo, 30% chardonnay, 10% macabeo

87 Colour: bright straw. Nose: fresh fruit, dried herbs, medium intensity, fine lees. Palate: flavourful, fine bitter notes, good acidity.

CANALS & NUBIOLA S.A.

Avda. Casetes Mir, 2
8770 Sant Sadurní D'Anoia (Barcelona)
☎: +34 938 917 025 - Fax: +34 938 910 126
www.canalsnubiola.com
canalsnubiola@canalsnubiola.es

CANALS & NUBIOLA GRAPA BRUT 2011 BR
30% parellada, 30% macabeo, 40% xarel.lo

86 Colour: bright straw. Nose: expressive, ripe fruit. Palate: flavourful, ripe fruit.

CANALS & NUBIOLA GRAPA NATURE 2010 BN RESERVA
33% parellada, 33% macabeo, 33% xarel.lo

86 Colour: bright straw. Nose: ripe fruit, dried flowers, dried herbs. Palate: powerful, flavourful, easy to drink.

CANALS & NUBIOLA PLATA BRUT 2011 BR
40% parellada, 50% macabeo, 10% xarel.lo

84

CANALS CANALS CAVA

Avda. Mare de Deu Montserrat, 9
8769 Castellví de Rosanes (Barcelona)
☎: +34 937 755 446 - Fax: +34 937 741 719
www.canalscanals.com
cava@canalscanals.com

CANALS CANALS CLÀSSIC 2011 BN
xarel.lo, macabeo, parellada

88 Colour: bright straw. Nose: dried herbs, fine lees, floral, ripe fruit. Palate: fresh, fruity, flavourful, good acidity.

CANALS CANALS CLÀSSIC 2011 BR
xarel.lo, macabeo, parellada

87 Colour: bright straw. Nose: medium intensity, dried herbs, fine lees, candied fruit. Palate: fresh, fruity, flavourful, good acidity.

CANALS CANALS RESERVA NUMERADA 2010 BN
xarel.lo, macabeo, parellada

90 Colour: bright golden. Nose: fine lees, fragrant herbs. Palate: powerful, flavourful, good acidity, fine bead, fine bitter notes.

MARTA 2009 BN RESERVA
xarel.lo, macabeo, parellada

86 Colour: bright straw. Nose: medium intensity, dried herbs, fine lees, floral, candied fruit. Palate: fresh, fruity, flavourful, good acidity.

MARTA DELUXE BN GRAN RESERVA
xarel.lo, macabeo, parellada

89 Colour: bright straw. Nose: dried herbs, fine lees, floral, ripe fruit. Palate: fresh, fruity, flavourful, good acidity.

MARTA MAGNUM 2007 BN GRAN RESERVA
xarel.lo, macabeo, parellada

90 Colour: bright golden. Nose: fine lees, dry nuts, fragrant herbs, complex, sweet spices. Palate: powerful, flavourful, good acidity, fine bead, fine bitter notes, balanced.

RAMÓN CANALS GRAN RESERVA LIMITADA 2008 BN GRAN RESERVA
xarel.lo, macabeo, parellada

89 Colour: bright golden. Nose: fine lees, dry nuts, fragrant herbs. Palate: powerful, flavourful, good acidity, fine bead, fine bitter notes.

CANALS NADAL

Ponent, 2
0733 El Pla del Penedès (Barcelona)
☎: +34 938 988 081 - Fax: +34 938 989 050
www.canalsnadal.com
cava@canalsnadal.com

ANTONI CANALS NADAL CUPADA SELECCIÓ 2009 BR RESERVA
50% macabeo, 40% xarel.lo, 10% parellada

91 Colour: bright yellow. Nose: floral, fresh fruit, citrus fruit, balsamic herbs, sweet spices. Palate: powerful, flavourful, fresh, fruity, balanced, elegant.

CANALS NADAL 2008 BN GRAN RESERVA
50% macabeo, 40% xarel.lo, 10% parellada

89 Colour: bright golden. Nose: fine lees, dry nuts, fragrant herbs, complex. Palate: powerful, flavourful, good acidity, fine bead, fine bitter notes.

CANALS NADAL 2009 BN RESERVA
45% macabeo, 40% xarel.lo, 15% parellada

88 Colour: bright straw. Nose: fresh, medium intensity, dried flowers. Palate: fresh, good acidity, correct.

CANALS NADAL 2009 BR RESERVA
45% macabeo, 40% xarel.lo, 15% parellada

89 Colour: bright yellow. Nose: balanced, medium intensity, dried flowers, dried herbs. Palate: flavourful, fruity, easy to drink, good acidity.

CANALS NADAL 2011 BR
40% macabeo, 40% xarel.lo, 20% parellada

85 Colour: bright straw. Nose: medium intensity, fresh fruit, dried herbs. Palate: fresh, fruity, flavourful, good acidity.

CANALS NADAL GRAN VINTAGE 2009 BR RESERVA
40% chardonnay, 30% macabeo, 20% xarel.lo

90 Colour: bright yellow. Nose: balanced, expressive, ripe fruit, floral. Palate: long, fresh, good acidity, fine bitter notes.

CANALS NADAL MAGNUM 2008 BN GRAN RESERVA
45% macabeo, 40% xarel.lo, 15% parellada

90 Colour: bright golden. Nose: fine lees, fragrant herbs. Palate: powerful, flavourful, good acidity, fine bead, fine bitter notes.

CANALS NADAL MAGNUM 2010 BN
50% macabeo, 40% xarel.lo, 10% parellada

90 Colour: bright straw. Nose: medium intensity, fresh fruit, dried herbs, fine lees, floral. Palate: fresh, fruity, flavourful, good acidity.

CANALS NADAL ROSÉ 2011 BR RESERVA
100% trepat

88 Colour: bright straw. Nose: fine lees, ripe fruit, grassy, dried flowers. Palate: fresh, fruity, flavourful, good acidity.

CARREFOUR

Campezo, 16
28022 Madrid (Madrid)
☎: +34 902 202 000
www.carrefour.es

CASTELL DEL LLAC ARTESANO BN
macabeo, xarel.lo, parellada

87 Colour: bright straw. Nose: fresh fruit, dried herbs, floral, lees reduction notes. Palate: fresh, fruity, flavourful, good acidity.

CAVA CASTELL DEL LLAC 20 CL. BR
macabeo, xarel.lo, parellada

85 Colour: bright straw. Nose: candied fruit, citrus fruit, dried herbs. Palate: fine bitter notes, good acidity.

CAVA CASTELL DEL LLAC BN
macabeo, xarel.lo, parellada

88 Colour: bright straw. Nose: fresh fruit, dried herbs, fine lees, floral. Palate: fresh, fruity, flavourful, good acidity.

CAVA CASTELL DEL LLAC BR
macabeo, xarel.lo, parellada

87 Colour: bright straw. Nose: medium intensity, fresh fruit, dried herbs, fine lees. Palate: fresh, fruity, flavourful, good acidity.

CAVA CASTELL DEL LLAC DULCE RD
trepat, garnacha

84

CAVA CASTELL DEL LLAC ROSADO 20 CL. BR
trepat, garnacha

85 Colour: coppery red. Nose: red berry notes, candied fruit, faded flowers. Palate: flavourful, sweet.

CAVA CASTELL DEL LLAC SS
macabeo, xarel.lo, parellada

85 Colour: bright straw. Nose: medium intensity, fresh fruit, dried herbs, fine lees. Palate: fresh, good acidity, sweetness.

CAVA CASTELL DEL LLAC XXI BR RESERVA
macabeo, xarel.lo, parellada

91 Colour: bright golden. Nose: fine lees, dry nuts, fragrant herbs, complex. Palate: powerful, flavourful, good acidity, fine bead, fine bitter notes.

CASTELL D'AGE

Ctra.de Martorell a Capellades, 6-8
8782 La Beguda Baixa (Barcelona)
☎: +34 937 725 181 - Fax: +34 937 727 061
www.castelldage.com
info@castelldage.com

CASTELL D'AGE ANNE MARIE 2010 RESERVA
xarel.lo, macabeo, parellada

87 Colour: bright straw. Nose: fine lees, white flowers, fragrant herbs, balanced. Palate: flavourful, fresh, fruity, fine bitter notes.

CASTELL D'AGE AURÈLIA 2009 GRAN RESERVA
xarel.lo, macabeo, parellada, chardonnay

89 Colour: bright golden. Nose: fine lees, dry nuts, fragrant herbs, complex. Palate: powerful, flavourful, good acidity, fine bead, fine bitter notes.

CASTELL D'AGE OLIVIA 2009 RESERVA
chardonnay

85 Colour: bright yellow. Nose: balanced, white flowers, medium intensity. Palate: flavourful, fruity, good acidity, fresh, fine bitter notes.

CASTELL D'AGE ROSAT 2011
pinot noir

86 Colour: rose. Nose: powerfull, ripe fruit. Palate: powerful, sweetness, flavourful.

POCULUM BONI GENI 2006 GRAN RESERVA
chardonnay, pinot noir

89 Colour: bright golden. Nose: fine lees, dry nuts, fragrant herbs, complex. Palate: powerful, flavourful, good acidity, fine bead, fine bitter notes.

CASTELL D'OR

Mare Rafols, 3- 1º 4º
8720 Vilafranca del Penedès (Barcelona)
☎: +34 938 905 446 - Fax: +34 938 905 446
www.castelldor.com
castelldor@castelldor.com

COSSETÀNIA BN
50% xarel.lo, 30% macabeo, 20% parellada

86 Colour: bright straw. Nose: fresh fruit, dried herbs, fine lees, floral. Palate: fresh, fruity, flavourful, good acidity.

COSSETÀNIA BR RESERVA
50% xarel.lo, 30% macabeo, 20% parellada

88 Colour: bright straw. Nose: dried flowers, ripe fruit, spicy. Palate: flavourful, good acidity.

COSSETÀNIA ROSADO BR
100% trepat

86 Colour: rose. Nose: red berry notes, powerfull. Palate: ripe fruit, correct.

FLAMA D'OR BN
40% xarel.lo, 35% macabeo, 25% parellada

85 Colour: bright straw. Nose: medium intensity, fresh fruit, dried herbs, faded flowers. Palate: fresh, fruity, flavourful.

FLAMA D'OR BRUT ROSAT BR
100% trepat

87 Colour: rose. Nose: ripe fruit, floral. Palate: flavourful, fine bitter notes.

FLAMA D'OR SS
30% xarel.lo, 50% macabeo, 20% parellada

86 Colour: bright straw. Nose: medium intensity, fresh fruit, dried herbs, fine lees, floral. Palate: fresh, fruity, sweetness.

FRANCOLI BN
50% macabeo, 50% parellada

85 Colour: bright straw. Nose: medium intensity, fresh fruit, dried herbs. Palate: fruity, flavourful, good acidity.

FRANCOLÍ BR RESERVA
50% macabeo, 50% parellada

86 Colour: bright golden. Nose: faded flowers, fragrant herbs, ripe fruit. Palate: powerful, flavourful, fine bead.

FRANCOLI ROSAT BR
100% trepat

85 Colour: rose. Nose: floral, red berry notes, ripe fruit, fragrant herbs. Palate: powerful, flavourful, easy to drink.

PUIG SOLIVELLA BN
60% macabeo, 40% parellada

84

PUIG SOLIVELLA BR
60% macabeo, 40% parellada

85 Colour: bright straw. Nose: medium intensity, fresh fruit, dried herbs, floral. Palate: fresh, fruity, flavourful.

CASTELL SANT ANTONI

Passeig del Parc, 13
8770 Sant Sadurní D'Anoia (Barcelona)
☎: +34 938 183 099 - Fax: +34 938 184 451
www.castellsantantoni.com
cava@castellsantantoni.com

CASTELL SANT ANTONI 37.5 BRUT BR
macabeo, xarel.lo, parellada, chardonnay

91 Colour: bright yellow. Nose: balanced, white flowers, faded flowers, medium intensity. Palate: flavourful, good acidity.

CASTELL SANT ANTONI 37.5 BRUT NATURE BN
macabeo, xarel.lo, parellada, chardonnay

90 Colour: bright straw. Nose: medium intensity, fresh fruit, dried herbs, fine lees, floral. Palate: fresh, fruity, flavourful, good acidity.

CASTELL SANT ANTONI BRUT DE POSTRE BR
macabeo, xarel.lo, parellada, chardonnay

89 Colour: bright straw. Nose: medium intensity, fresh fruit, dried herbs, floral. Palate: fresh, fruity, flavourful, sweetness.

CASTELL SANT ANTONI CAMÍ DEL SOT BN RESERVA
macabeo, xarel.lo, parellada

91 Colour: bright straw. Nose: dried herbs, fine lees, white flowers, fruit expression. Palate: fresh, fruity, flavourful, good acidity, balanced.

CASTELL SANT ANTONI CAMÍ DEL SOT MAGNUM BN RESERVA
macabeo, xarel.lo, parellada, chardonnay

91 Colour: bright yellow. Nose: dried flowers, fine lees, ripe fruit, fragrant herbs, spicy. Palate: powerful, flavourful, complex, spicy, balanced.

CASTELL SANT ANTONI GRAN BARRICA BN GRAN RESERVA
macabeo, xarel.lo, parellada, chardonnay

91 Colour: bright straw. Nose: spicy, toasty, ripe fruit. Palate: flavourful, ripe fruit, good acidity.

CASTELL SANT ANTONI GRAN BRUT BR GRAN RESERVA
macabeo, xarel.lo, parellada, chardonnay

89 Colour: bright golden. Nose: fine lees, dry nuts, fragrant herbs, complex. Palate: powerful, flavourful, good acidity, fine bead.

CASTELL SANT ANTONI GRAN BRUT MAGNUM BR GRAN RESERVA
macabeo, xarel.lo, parellada, chardonnay

91 Colour: bright straw. Nose: medium intensity, fresh fruit, dried herbs. Palate: fresh, fruity, flavourful, good acidity.

CASTELL SANT ANTONI GRAN RESERVA MAGNUM BN
macabeo, xarel.lo, parellada, chardonnay

94 Colour: bright golden. Nose: fine lees, dry nuts, fragrant herbs. Palate: powerful, flavourful, good acidity, fine bead, fine bitter notes.

CASTELL SANT ANTONI GRAN RESERVA 2005 BN GRAN RESERVA
macabeo, xarel.lo, parellada, chardonnay

92 Colour: bright straw. Nose: dried herbs, fine lees, floral, ripe fruit, fragrant herbs. Palate: fresh, fruity, flavourful, good acidity.

CASTELL SANT ANTONI GRAN ROSAT PINOT NOIR BN
pinot noir

87 Colour: light cherry. Nose: ripe fruit, fruit liqueur notes, balsamic herbs, sweet spices. Palate: powerful, flavourful, fine bitter notes.

CASTELL SANT ANTONI TORRE DE L'HOMENATGE 1999 BN
xarel.lo, macabeo, parellada

92 Colour: bright golden. Nose: dry nuts, fragrant herbs, complex, toasty, spicy. Palate: powerful, flavourful, good acidity, fine bead, fine bitter notes.

CASTELL SANT ANTONI TORRE DE L'HOMENATGE 2003 BN GRAN RESERVA
xarel.lo, macabeo, parellada

94 Colour: bright golden. Nose: fine lees, dry nuts, fragrant herbs, complex, toasty. Palate: powerful, flavourful, good acidity, fine bead, fine bitter notes.

CASTELLBLANCH

Avda. Casetes Mir, 2
8770 Sant Sadurní D'Anoia (Barcelona)
☎: +34 938 917 025 - Fax: +34 938 910 126
www.castellblanch.com
castellblanch@castellblanch.es

CASTELLBLANCH BRUT ZERO 2009 BR RESERVA
60% parellada, 30% macabeo, 10% xarel.lo

87 Colour: bright yellow. Nose: medium intensity, fresh fruit, dried herbs, dried flowers, varnish. Palate: fresh, flavourful, good acidity.

CASTELLBLANCH DOS LUSTROS
2008 BN RESERVA
40% macabeo, 20% xarel.lo, 40% parellada

90 Colour: bright yellow. Nose: medium intensity, fresh fruit, dried herbs, fine lees, floral, petrol notes. Palate: fresh, fruity, flavourful, good acidity.

CASTELLBLANCH GRAN CUVEÉ 2008 BN RESERVA
40% parellada, 30% macabeo, 30% xarel.lo

90 Colour: bright golden. Nose: fine lees, dry nuts, fragrant herbs, characterful. Palate: powerful, flavourful, good acidity, fine bead, fine bitter notes.

CASTELLBLANCH ROSADO 2011 RD
70% trepat, 30% garnacha

85 Colour: coppery red. Nose: floral, jasmine, fragrant herbs, candied fruit. Palate: fresh, fruity, sweet.

CASTELLROIG - FINCA SABATÉ I COCA

Ctra. Sant Sadurní d'Anoia a Vilafranca del Penedès, Km. 1
8739 Subirats (Barcelona)
☎: +34 938 911 927 - Fax: +34 938 914 055
www.castellroig.com
info@castellroig.com

CASTELLROIG 2007 BN GRAN RESERVA
xarel.lo, macabeo

89 Colour: bright golden. Nose: fine lees, dry nuts, fragrant herbs, spicy. Palate: good acidity, fine bead, fine bitter notes, flavourful.

CASTELLROIG 2009 BN GRAN RESERVA
xarel.lo, macabeo

85 Colour: bright golden. Nose: fine lees, dry nuts, fragrant herbs. Palate: powerful, flavourful, fine bead, fine bitter notes.

CASTELLROIG 2010 BN RESERVA
xarel.lo, macabeo, parellada

88 Colour: bright straw. Nose: dried herbs, fine lees, floral, ripe fruit. Palate: fresh, fruity, flavourful, good acidity.

CASTELLROIG 2011 BN
macabeo, xarel.lo, parellada

88 Colour: bright straw. Nose: fresh fruit, dried herbs, fine lees, floral. Palate: fresh, fruity, flavourful, good acidity.

SABATÉ I COCA RESERVA FAMILIAR
2009 BN RESERVA
xarel.lo

91 Colour: bright straw. Nose: dried herbs, fine lees, floral, candied fruit. Palate: fresh, fruity, flavourful, good acidity.

CASTILLO PERELADA VINOS Y CAVAS

Avda. Barcelona, 78
8720 Vilafranca del Penedès (Barcelona)
☎: +34 938 180 676 - Fax: +34 938 180 926
www.castilloperelada.com
perelada@castilloperelada.com

CASTILLO PERELADA 2010 BN
45% parellada, 30% xarel.lo, 25% macabeo

88 Colour: bright straw. Nose: medium intensity, fresh fruit, dried herbs, fine lees, floral. Palate: fresh, fruity, flavourful, good acidity.

CASTILLO PERELADA BR RESERVA
40% macabeo, 30% xarel.lo, 30% parellada

88 Colour: bright yellow. Nose: white flowers, fresh fruit. Palate: fresh, good acidity, fruity, easy to drink.

CASTILLO PERELADA BRUT NATURE CUVÉE ESPECIAL 2011 BN
macabeo, parellada, xarel.lo, chardonnay

90 Colour: bright straw. Nose: medium intensity, fresh fruit, fine lees, floral. Palate: fresh, fruity, flavourful, good acidity.

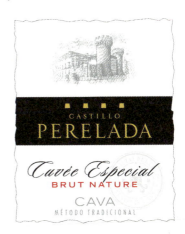

CASTILLO PERELADA BRUT ROSADO
trepat, monastrell, pinot noir

88 Colour: light cherry, bright. Nose: floral, rose petals, red berry notes, balanced. Palate: flavourful, fruity, long.

CASTILLO PERELADA CHARDONNAY 2009 BN
chardonnay

87 Colour: bright straw. Nose: balanced, floral, fresh fruit. Palate: correct, good acidity, flavourful.

CASTILLO PERELADA CUVÉE ESPECIAL ROSADO 2009 BR
trepat

88 Colour: raspberry rose. Nose: fresh, floral, dried herbs, fine lees. Palate: balanced, fine bitter notes, good acidity.

GRAN CLAUSTRO CUVÉE ESPECIAL DE CASTILLO PERELADA 2008 BN GRAN RESERVA
chardonnay, pinot noir, parellada, xarel.lo, macabeo

90 Colour: bright golden. Nose: fine lees, dry nuts, fragrant herbs, sweet spices. Palate: powerful, flavourful, good acidity, fine bead.

GRAN CLAUSTRO DE CASTILLO PERELADA 2010 BN RESERVA
chardonnay, pinot noir, parellada, macabeo

89 Colour: bright straw. Nose: dried herbs, balanced, fine lees, fresh. Palate: fruity, fresh, good acidity, fine bitter notes.

STARS 2010 BN
parellada, xarel.lo, macabeo

87 Colour: bright straw. Nose: balanced, dried flowers, candied fruit. Palate: flavourful, fruity, good acidity, easy to drink.

TORRE GALATEA BR
pinot noir, trepat, monastrell

84

CAVA & HOTEL MAS TINELL

Ctra. de Vilafranca a St. Martí Sarroca, Km. 0,5
8720 Vilafranca del Penedès (Barcelona)
☎: +34 938 170 586 - Fax: +34 938 170 500
www.mastinell.com
info@mastinell.com

MAS TINELL BRUT REAL 2007 BR RESERVA
macabeo, xarel.lo, parellada

88 Colour: bright yellow. Nose: medium intensity, dried flowers, fresh. Palate: good acidity, fine bitter notes, easy to drink.

MAS TINELL BRUT ROSÉ 2008 BR RESERVA
trepat

90 Colour: coppery red, bright. Nose: medium intensity, rose petals, red berry notes. Palate: correct, fine bitter notes, good acidity, fresh.

MAS TINELL CARPE DIEM RESERVA ESPECIAL 2006 BN
xarel.lo, parellada, chardonnay

90 Colour: bright yellow. Nose: balanced, fragrant herbs, fresh fruit, balsamic herbs. Palate: balanced, fine bitter notes, good acidity.

MAS TINELL CRISTINA 2006 EXTRA BRUT GRAN RESERVA
macabeo, xarel.lo, parellada, chardonnay

89 Colour: bright golden. Nose: fine lees, dry nuts, balsamic herbs, expressive. Palate: flavourful, good acidity, fine bitter notes.

MAS TINELL NATURE REAL 2005 BN GRAN RESERVA
macabeo, xarel.lo, parellada, chardonnay

86 Colour: bright straw. Nose: medium intensity, dried herbs, floral, lees reduction notes. Palate: fruity, flavourful, good acidity.

CAVA BERDIÉ

Les Conilleres (La Conillera Gran)
8732 Castellví de la Marca (Barcelona)
☎: +34 902 800 229 - Fax: +34 938 919 735
www.cavaberdie.com
info@cavaberdie.com

BERDIÉ AMOR 2010 BR RESERVA
macabeo, xarel.lo, parellada, garnacha

87 Colour: bright straw. Nose: medium intensity, fine lees, floral, candied fruit. Palate: fresh, fruity, flavourful, good acidity.

BERDIÉ GRAN ANYADA 2004 EXTRA BRUT GRAN RESERVA

87 Colour: bright golden. Nose: dry nuts, fragrant herbs, sweet spices, toasty, lees reduction notes. Palate: powerful, flavourful, fine bead, fine bitter notes.

BERDIÉ GRAN ANYADA 2005 EXTRA BRUT
macabeo, xarel.lo, parellada

87 Colour: bright yellow. Nose: faded flowers, candied fruit, dry nuts. Palate: flavourful, fine bitter notes, ripe fruit.

BERDIÉ GRAN NATURE 2009 BN GRAN RESERVA
macabeo, xarel.lo, parellada

88 Colour: bright golden. Nose: fine lees, dry nuts, fragrant herbs. Palate: powerful, flavourful, fine bitter notes.

BERDIÉ GRAN RUPESTRE 2007 EXTRA BRUT GRAN RESERVA
macabeo, xarel.lo, parellada

89 Colour: bright yellow. Nose: dry nuts, candied fruit, fine lees. Palate: balanced, fine bitter notes, good acidity.

BERDIÉ NATURE BN RESERVA
macabeo, xarel.lo, parellada

87 Colour: bright straw. Nose: medium intensity, fresh fruit, dried herbs. Palate: fresh, fruity, flavourful, good acidity.

BERDIÉ ROSA 2010 BR RESERVA
monastrell, garnacha

84

BERDIÉ RUPESTRE 2010 BR RESERVA
macabeo, xarel.lo, parellada

87 Colour: bright straw. Nose: medium intensity, faded flowers, dry nuts. Palate: flavourful, fine bitter notes, good acidity.

CAVA CONDE DE VALICOURT

Sant Antoni, 33-35
8770 Sant Sadurní D'Anoia (Barcelona)
☎: +34 938 910 036
www.condedevalicourt.com
cavas@condedevalicourt.com

COUPAGE DE ALICIA 2010 BN GRAN RESERVA
macabeo, parellada, xarel.lo

80

COUPAGE DE ALICIA 2011 BR RESERVA
macabeo, parellada, xarel.lo

84

MAJESTUOSO 2009 BN GRAN RESERVA
macabeo, parellada, xarel.lo

88 Colour: bright golden. Nose: dry nuts, fragrant herbs, complex, sweet spices. Palate: powerful, flavourful, good acidity, fine bead, fine bitter notes.

PAS DE SUCRE 2009 BN GRAN RESERVA
macabeo, parellada, xarel.lo

86 Colour: bright straw. Nose: candied fruit, citrus fruit, slightly evolved. Palate: good acidity, correct.

PERMONT'S 2012 BN RESERVA
macabeo, parellada, xarel.lo

85 Colour: bright straw. Nose: medium intensity, fresh fruit, dried herbs, fine lees, floral. Palate: fresh, fruity, flavourful, good acidity.

ROSÉ DE VALICOURT 2011 BR RESERVA
100% garnacha

80

CAVA CRISTINA COLOMER BERNAT

Diputació, 58-60
8770 Sant Sadurní D'Anoia (Barcelona)
☎: +34 938 910 804 - Fax: +34 938 913 034
www.cavescolomer.com
info@cavescolomer.com

COLOMER "ER" MAGNUM 2008 BN GRAN RESERVA
xarel.lo, macabeo, parellada, chardonnay, pinot noir

90 Colour: bright yellow. Nose: fine lees, candied fruit, fragrant herbs, spicy, expressive, dried flowers. Palate: fresh, fruity, flavourful, balanced.

**COLOMER BRUT D'AUTOR
2010 BR GRAN RESERVA**
xarel.lo, macabeo, parellada, chardonnay

90 Colour: bright straw. Nose: fresh fruit, dried herbs, fine lees, floral. Palate: fresh, fruity, flavourful, good acidity, balanced.

COLOMER COSTA 1907 CUPATGE BN RESERVA
xarel.lo, macabeo, parellada

90 Colour: bright yellow. Nose: white flowers, balanced, expressive. Palate: flavourful, fruity, fine bitter notes, fine bead.

COLOMER COSTA 2011 BN RESERVA
xarel.lo, macabeo, parellada

90 Colour: bright straw. Nose: medium intensity, fresh fruit, dried herbs, fine lees, floral. Palate: fresh, fruity, flavourful, good acidity.

COLOMER COSTA MAGNUM 2008 BN RESERVA
xarel.lo, macabeo, parellada

89 Colour: bright straw. Nose: fine lees, fresh fruit, ripe fruit, dried herbs, white flowers. Palate: fine bitter notes, flavourful, fruity, good acidity.

**COLOMER HOMENATGE A GAUDÍ PINOT
NOIR ROSÉ 2011 BR RESERVA**
100% pinot noir

84

**COLOMER PRESTIGE DE DALI
2008 BN GRAN RESERVA**
xarel.lo, macabeo, parellada, chardonnay, pinot noir

91 Colour: bright golden. Nose: dry nuts, fragrant herbs, complex, sweet spices. Palate: powerful, flavourful, good acidity, fine bead, fine bitter notes.

CAVA JOSEP M. FERRET GUASCH

Barri L'Alzinar, 68
8798 Font-Rubí (Barcelona)
☎: +34 938 979 037 - Fax: +34 938 979 414
www.ferretguasch.com
ferretguasch@ferretguasch.com

**JOSEP M. FERRET GUASCH
2004 BN GRAN RESERVA**
20% macabeo, 60% xarel.lo, 20% parellada

87 Colour: bright golden. Nose: fine lees, dry nuts, fragrant herbs. Palate: powerful, flavourful, fine bead, fine bitter notes.

**JOSEP M. FERRET GUASCH
79 AU 2006 BR RESERVA**
15% macabeo, 60% xarel.lo, 25% parellada

87 Colour: bright straw. Nose: medium intensity, ripe fruit. Palate: flavourful, fruity, fresh, sweetness.

**JOSEP M. FERRET GUASCH ROSAT
2007 BN GRAN RESERVA**
60% garnacha, 20% pinot noir, 20% trepat

84

CAVA M. BOSHC

Ctra. San Martí Sarroca s/n
8737 Torroella de Foix (Barcelona)
☎: +34 938 405 488 - Fax: +34 938 403 026
www.cavesmbosch.com
info@grupombosch.com

M. BOSCH RESERVA FAMILIAR 2010 BN RESERVA
macabeo, xarel.lo, parellada

85 Colour: bright straw. Nose: medium intensity, dried herbs, fine lees, fruit preserve. Palate: fresh, fruity, flavourful, good acidity.

CAVA MARTÍN SOLER

Finca La Serra de Sabanell, s/n
8739 Font-Rubí (Barcelona)
☎: +34 938 988 220 - Fax: +34 938 988 681
www.cavamartinsoler.com
marketing@cavamartinsoler.com

**MARTIN SOLER "MARGARITA DE
SOLER" 2010 BN GRAN RESERVA**
macabeo, xarel.lo, parellada

87 Colour: bright golden. Nose: dry nuts, fragrant herbs, sweet spices, pattiserie. Palate: powerful, flavourful, good acidity, fine bead, fine bitter notes.

MARTIN SOLER 2010 BN RESERVA
macabeo, xarel.lo, parellada

85 Colour: bright straw. Nose: dried herbs, fine lees, floral, ripe fruit. Palate: fresh, fruity, flavourful.

MARTIN SOLER ROSADO 2011 BR
trepat

86 Colour: ochre. Nose: dried flowers, fragrant herbs, red berry notes, fruit preserve. Palate: correct, powerful, flavourful.

CAVA MESTRES

Plaça Ajuntament, 8
8770 Sant Sadurní D'Anoia (Barcelona)
☎: +34 938 910 043 - Fax: +34 938 911 611
www.mestres.es
cava@mestres.es

MESTRE CLOS NOSTRE SENYOR 2002 BN GRAN RESERVA
20% macabeo, 60% xarel.lo, 20% parellada

92 Colour: bright golden. Nose: dry nuts, fragrant herbs, complex, sweet spices, toasty, cocoa bean. Palate: flavourful, good acidity, fine bead, fine bitter notes, balanced.

MESTRES CUPAGE 50 AÑOS DE "CAVA" 2007 BR GRAN RESERVA
25% macabeo, 50% xarel.lo, 25% parellada

90 Colour: bright yellow. Nose: spicy, floral, ripe fruit, fragrant herbs, sweet spices. Palate: powerful, flavourful, rich, balanced.

MESTRES CUPAGE 80 ANIVERSARIO 2006 BR GRAN RESERVA
25% macabeo, 60% xarel.lo, 15% parellada

91 Colour: bright golden. Nose: fine lees, dry nuts, fragrant herbs, smoky. Palate: powerful, flavourful, good acidity, fine bead, fine bitter notes, balanced.

MESTRES CUPAGE BARCELONA RESERVA ESPECIAL 2008 BR GRAN RESERVA
40% macabeo, 30% xarel.lo, 30% parellada

91 Colour: bright golden. Nose: fine lees, fragrant herbs, complex, dried flowers, sweet spices. Palate: powerful, flavourful, fine bead.

MESTRES CUPAGE MADRID RESERVA ESPECIAL 2008 BN
40% macabeo, 30% xarel.lo, 30% parellada

90 Colour: bright yellow. Nose: dried flowers, fragrant herbs, candied fruit, spicy. Palate: correct, fine bead, good acidity, flavourful.

MESTRES MAS VÍA 2000 BR GRAN RESERVA
15% macabeo, 75% xarel.lo, 10% parellada

90 Colour: bright golden. Nose: fine lees, dry nuts, fragrant herbs, complex, toasty, sweet spices. Palate: powerful, flavourful, good acidity, fine bead, fine bitter notes.

CAVA OLIVÉ BATLLORI

Barri Els Casots
8739 Subirats (Barcelona)
☎: +34 938 993 103
www.olivebatllori.com
info@olivebatllori.com

GRAN BRUT OLIVE BATLLORI 2010 BN
macabeo, xarel.lo, parellada, pinot noir, chardonnay

90 Colour: bright golden. Nose: fine lees, dry nuts, fragrant herbs, complex. Palate: powerful, flavourful, good acidity, fine bead, fine bitter notes.

OLIVE BATLLORI 2010 BN
macabeo, xarel.lo, parellada

85 Colour: bright straw. Nose: medium intensity, fresh, dried flowers. Palate: light-bodied, good acidity.

OLIVE BATLLORI 2011 BR
pinot noir

88 Colour: salmon. Nose: medium intensity, floral, fresh. Palate: fruity, fine bitter notes, balanced, good acidity.

CAVA REVERTÉ

Paseo Tomás García Rebull, 4
43885 Salomó (Tarragona)
☎: +34 977 629 246 - Fax: +34 977 629 246
www.cavareverte.com
enricreverte@terra.es

CAVA REVERTÉ "ELECTE" 2009 BN
40% xarel.lo, 20% macabeo, 20% parellada, 20% chardonnay

89 Colour: bright straw. Nose: fine lees, floral, fragrant herbs, dry nuts. Palate: fresh, fruity, flavourful, good acidity.

CAVA REVERTÉ 2009 BN
60% xarel.lo, 20% macabeo, 20% parellada

88 Colour: bright straw. Nose: fresh fruit, dried herbs, fine lees, floral, citrus fruit. Palate: fresh, fruity, flavourful, fine bead.

CAVA VIDAL I FERRÉ

Nou, 6
43815 Les Pobles (Tarragona)
☎: +34 977 638 554 - Fax: +34 977 638 554
www.vidaliferre.com
vidaliferre@terra.es

VIDAL I FERRÉ 2006 BN GRAN RESERVA
macabeo, xarel.lo, parellada

90 Colour: bright straw. Nose: ripe fruit, citrus fruit, spicy.
Palate: good acidity, fine bead.

VIDAL I FERRÉ 2010 BN RESERVA
macabeo, xarel.lo, parellada

87 Colour: bright straw. Nose: medium intensity, fresh
fruit, dried herbs, fine lees, floral. Palate: fresh, good acidity.

VIDAL I FERRÉ 2010 BR RESERVA
macabeo, xarel.lo, parellada

88 Colour: bright straw. Nose: dried herbs, fine lees, floral.
Palate: fresh, fruity, flavourful, good acidity.

VIDAL I FERRÉ 2010 SS
macabeo, xarel.lo, parellada

87 Colour: bright straw. Nose: balanced, fresh, dried
herbs, medium intensity. Palate: flavourful, correct, balanced.

CAVAS BOHIGAS

Finca Can Maciá s/n
8711 Ódena (Barcelona)
☎: +34 938 048 100 - Fax: +34 938 032 366
www.bohigas.es
comercial@bohigas.es

BOHIGAS BN RESERVA
macabeo, xarel.lo, parellada

88 Colour: bright straw. Nose: medium intensity, balanced,
floral, fresh. Palate: correct, good acidity, easy to drink.

NOA DE BOHIGAS 2009 BN
pinot noir, xarel.lo

88 Colour: bright yellow. Nose: fresh, floral, dried herbs,
fine lees. Palate: correct, balanced, good acidity.

CAVAS FERRET

Avda. de Catalunya, 36
8736 Guardiola de Font-Rubí (Barcelona)
☎: +34 938 979 148 - Fax: +34 938 979 285
www.cavasferret.com
ferret@cavasferret.com

CELIA DE FERRET ROSADO BN GRAN RESERVA

83

EZEQUIEL FERRET BN GRAN RESERVA

89 Colour: bright golden. Nose: dry nuts, fragrant herbs,
complex. Palate: powerful, flavourful, good acidity, fine
bead, fine bitter notes.

FERRET BN GRAN RESERVA

91 Colour: bright golden. Nose: dry nuts, fragrant herbs.
Palate: powerful, flavourful, good acidity, fine bead, fine bitter notes.

FERRET BN RESERVA

90 Colour: bright straw. Nose: dried herbs, fine lees, floral.
Palate: fresh, fruity, flavourful, good acidity.

FERRET BR RESERVA

90 Colour: bright straw. Nose: fresh fruit, dried herbs, fine
lees. Palate: fresh, fruity, flavourful, good acidity.

FERRET BARRICA BN GRAN RESERVA

87 Colour: bright golden. Nose: dry nuts, fragrant herbs, lees reduction notes, toasty. Palate: powerful, flavourful, good acidity, fine bead, fine bitter notes.

FERRET ROSADO BR RESERVA

89 Colour: coppery red, bright. Nose: fresh fruit, red berry notes, floral, balanced. Palate: balanced, fine bitter notes, good acidity.

FERRET ROSADO RD GRAN RESERVA

87 Colour: rose. Nose: powerfull, ripe fruit, red berry notes. Palate: fine bitter notes, good acidity.

CAVAS HILL

Bonavista, 2
8734 Moja (Barcelona)
☎: +34 938 900 588 - Fax: +34 938 170 246
www.cavashill.com
cavashill@cavashill.com

CAVA 1887 BR
macabeo, xarel.lo, parellada

88 Colour: bright straw. Nose: medium intensity, fresh fruit, dried herbs, fine lees, floral. Palate: fresh, fruity, flavourful, good acidity.

CAVAS HILL ARTESANÍA BN
macabeo, xarel.lo, parellada, chardonnay

84

CAVAS HILL BRUT DE BRUT
ARTESANÍA BR RESERVA
macabeo, xarel.lo, parellada, chardonnay

86 Colour: bright straw. Nose: medium intensity, fresh fruit, dried herbs, fine lees, floral. Palate: fresh, fruity, flavourful, good acidity.

CAVAS HILL VINTAGE 2008 BN GRAN RESERVA
macabeo, xarel.lo, parellada, chardonnay

89 Colour: bright yellow. Nose: fine lees, dry nuts, fragrant herbs. Palate: powerful, flavourful, good acidity, fine bead, fine bitter notes.

CAVES CONDE DE CARALT S.A.

Ctra. Sant Sadurní-Sant Pere de Riudebitlles, Km. 5
8775 Torrelavit (Barcelona)
☎: +34 938 917 070 - Fax: +34 938 996 006
www.condedecaralt.com
condedecaralt@condedecaralt.com

CONDE DE CARALT BLANC DE BLANCS BR
macabeo, xarel.lo, parellada

90 Colour: bright straw. Nose: medium intensity, fresh, dried flowers. Palate: correct, good acidity, easy to drink, balanced, fine bitter notes.

CONDE DE CARALT BR
macabeo, xarel.lo, parellada

87 Colour: bright straw. Nose: medium intensity, fresh, dried herbs. Palate: fresh, easy to drink, good acidity.

CAVES EL MAS FERRER

Caves El Mas Ferrer
8739 Subirats (Barcelona)
☎: +34 938 988 292 - Fax: +34 938 988 545
www.elmasferrer.com
info@elmasferrer.com

EL MAS FERRER 2011 BR

89 Colour: bright straw. Nose: fresh fruit, dried herbs, fine lees, floral. Palate: fresh, fruity, flavourful, good acidity.

EL MAS FERRER 2010 BN RESERVA
34% macabeo, 28% xarel.lo, 38% parellada

88 Colour: bright straw. Nose: dried herbs, fine lees, floral, fruit expression. Palate: fresh, fruity, flavourful, fine bead.

EL MAS FERRER 2010 BR RESERVA
34% macabeo, 28% xarel.lo, 38% parellada

87 Colour: bright straw. Nose: fine lees, dried flowers, candied fruit, fragrant herbs. Palate: powerful, flavourful, fresh.

EL MAS FERRER FAMILIAR
2007 BN GRAN RESERVA
32% macabeo, 35% xarel.lo, 33% parellada

89 Colour: bright yellow. Nose: dry nuts, dried flowers, balanced, fine lees. Palate: fresh, good acidity, fine bitter notes.

EL MAS FERRER ROSAT 2010 BR RESERVA
20% pinot noir, 80% garnacha

86 Colour: rose. Nose: ripe fruit, red berry notes, dried flowers. Palate: correct, powerful, flavourful.

EL MAS FERRER SEGLE XXI 2007 EXTRA BRUT GRAN RESERVA
32% macabeo, 38% xarel.lo, 30% parellada

89 Colour: bright golden. Nose: dry nuts, fragrant herbs, toasty, sweet spices. Palate: powerful, flavourful, fine bitter notes.

CAVES GRAMONA

Industria, 34-36
8770 Sant Sadurní D'Anoia (Barcelona)
☎: +34 938 910 113 - Fax: +34 938 183 284
www.gramona.com
comunicacion@gramona.com

GRAMONA ARGENT 2008 BR RESERVA
100% chardonnay

93 Colour: bright straw. Nose: dried herbs, fine lees, floral, expressive, neat, ripe fruit. Palate: fresh, fruity, flavourful, good acidity.

GRAMONA ARGENT ROSÉ 2009 RD GRAN RESERVA
100% pinot noir

91 Colour: salmon. Nose: lactic notes, fine lees, ripe fruit, red berry notes. Palate: good acidity, fine bitter notes.

GRAMONA CELLER BATLLE 2001 BR GRAN RESERVA
70% xarel.lo, 30% macabeo

97 Colour: old gold, amber rim. Nose: macerated fruit, pattiserie, sweet spices, roasted almonds, dry nuts. Palate: elegant, balanced, fine bead, long, creamy.

GRAMONA CELLER BATLLE 2002 BR GRAN RESERVA
70% xarel.lo, 30% macabeo

93 Colour: bright golden. Nose: dry nuts, fragrant herbs, complex, lactic notes. Palate: powerful, flavourful, good acidity, fine bead, fine bitter notes.

GRAMONA COLECCIÓN DE ARTE MAGNUM BR GRAN RESERVA
100% chardonnay

94 Colour: bright golden. Nose: dry nuts, fragrant herbs, complex, smoky, toasty, lees reduction notes. Palate: powerful, flavourful, good acidity, fine bead, fine bitter notes, balanced, elegant, smoky aftertaste.

GRAMONA ENOTECA FINCA CELLER BATLLE BN
70% xarel.lo, 30% parellada

93 Colour: bright golden. Nose: dry nuts, fragrant herbs, complex, lees reduction notes, pungent. Palate: powerful, flavourful, good acidity, fine bead, fine bitter notes.

GRAMONA ENOTECA FINCA CELLER BATLLE 2000 BR GRAN RESERVA
70% xarel.lo, 30% macabeo

95 Colour: bright straw. Nose: expressive, elegant, ripe fruit, sweet spices. Palate: flavourful, good acidity, fine bitter notes, long.

GRAMONA III LUSTROS 2004 BN GRAN RESERVA
70% xarel.lo, 30% macabeo

94 Colour: bright straw. Nose: fragrant herbs, toasty, spicy, candied fruit. Palate: round, good acidity, fine bead.

GRAMONA III LUSTROS 2005 BN GRAN RESERVA
70% xarel.lo, 30% macabeo

92 Colour: bright straw. Nose: white flowers, candied fruit, spicy, toasty. Palate: flavourful, long, spicy, fine bitter notes.

GRAMONA IMPERIAL 2007 BR GRAN RESERVA
50% xarel.lo, 40% macabeo, 10% chardonnay

92 Colour: bright straw. Nose: fresh fruit, fine lees, floral, fragrant herbs. Palate: fresh, fruity, flavourful, good acidity.

GRAMONA IMPERIAL 2009 BR GRAN RESERVA

93 Colour: bright straw. Nose: medium intensity, fresh fruit, dried herbs, fine lees, floral. Palate: fresh, fruity, flavourful, good acidity.

CAVES NAVERÁN

Can Parellada Torrelavit
8735 Torrelavit (Barcelona)
☎: +34 938 988 274 - Fax: +34 938 989 027
www.naveran.com
naveran@naveran.com

NAVERAN MILLESIME 2010 BN
chardonnay, parellada, macabeo, xarel.lo

91 Colour: bright yellow. Nose: citrus fruit, ripe fruit, fine lees, floral, dried herbs. Palate: fine bitter notes, flavourful, fresh, fruity, elegant.

NAVERAN PERLES BLANQUES 2010 BR
pinot noir, chardonnay

92 Colour: bright golden. Nose: fine lees, dry nuts, fragrant herbs, complex. Palate: powerful, flavourful, good acidity, fine bead, fine bitter notes.

NAVERÁN PERLES ROSES PINOT NOIR 2010 BR
pinot noir

90 Colour: raspberry rose. Nose: floral, candied fruit, fragrant herbs, balanced, expressive. Palate: powerful, flavourful, correct, fine bitter notes.

ODISEA NAVERÁN BN
chardonnay, parellada

91 Colour: bright straw. Nose: fresh fruit, dried herbs, fine lees, floral, sweet spices. Palate: fresh, fruity, flavourful, good acidity.

CELLER CARLES ANDREU

Sant Sebastià, 19
43423 Pira (Tarragona)
☎: +34 977 887 404 - Fax: +34 977 887 427
www.cavandreu.com
celler@cavandreu.com

CAVA BRUT CARLES ANDREU BR
parellada, macabeo

89 Colour: bright straw. Nose: medium intensity, dried herbs, fine lees, floral, ripe fruit. Palate: fruity, flavourful, good acidity.

CAVA BRUT NATURE CARLES ANDREU BN
parellada, macabeo

87 Colour: bright straw. Nose: fresh fruit, dried herbs, fine lees. Palate: fresh, fruity, flavourful, good acidity.

CAVA RESERVA BARRICA BRUT NATURE CARLES ANDREU BN RESERVA
parellada, macabeo, chardonnay

88 Colour: bright yellow. Nose: toasty, creamy oak, dry nuts. Palate: flavourful, spicy, good acidity.

CAVA RESERVA BRUT NATURE CARLES ANDREU 2009 BN
parellada, macabeo, chardonnay

88 Colour: bright yellow. Nose: medium intensity, fresh, dried herbs, dried flowers. Palate: fresh, easy to drink, good acidity.

CAVA ROSADO TREPAT BRUT CARLES ANDREU BR
100% trepat

88 Colour: rose. Nose: raspberry, ripe fruit, floral. Palate: flavourful, ripe fruit.

CAVA ROSADO TREPAT RESERVA BARRICA BRUT CARLES ANDREU BR
100% trepat

91 Colour: raspberry rose, bright. Nose: balanced, red berry notes, floral. Palate: spicy, good acidity, fine bitter notes.

CELLER DE CAN SURIOL DEL CASTELL

Castell de Grabuac
8736 Grabuac (Barcelona)
☎: +34 938 978 426 - Fax: +34 938 978 426
www.suriol.com
cansuriol@suriol.com

CASTELL DE GRABUAC 2007 BN FERMENTADO EN BARRICA
macabeo, xarel.lo

84

CASTELL DE GRABUAC MILLESIME BN
macabeo, xarel.lo, parellada

86 Colour: bright straw. Nose: fruit preserve, toasty, lees reduction notes. Palate: fine bitter notes, good acidity.

SURIOL 2011 BN
macabeo, xarel.lo, parellada

85 Colour: bright straw. Nose: medium intensity, ripe fruit. Palate: good acidity, correct.

SURIOL 2010 BRUT ROSÉ

83

CELLER DEL RAVAL

Vinyals, 161
8223 Terrassa (Barcelona)
☎: +34 937 330 695 - Fax: +34 937 333 605
www.angelcava.com
jcernuda@asociadis.com

ANGEL BRUT DE BRUTS 2011 BR RESERVA
xarel.lo, macabeo, parellada

87 Colour: bright yellow. Nose: floral, balanced, medium intensity. Palate: good acidity, correct, good finish.

ANGEL CUPATGE 2011 BN RESERVA
chardonnay, xarel.lo, macabeo, parellada

86 Colour: bright yellow. Nose: candied fruit, dry nuts, faded flowers. Palate: fine bitter notes, good acidity, correct.

ANGEL NOIR 2010
pinot noir, garnacha, trepat

86 Colour: light cherry. Nose: powerfull, ripe fruit, red berry notes, faded flowers. Palate: flavourful, ripe fruit, long, fine bitter notes.

CELLER JORDI LLUCH

Barrio Les Casetes, s/n
8777 Sant Quinti de Mediona (Barcelona)
☎: +34 938 988 138 - Fax: +34 938 988 138
www.vinyaescude.com
vinyaescude@vinyaescude.com

VINYA ESCUDÉ 523 EXTRA BRUT RESERVA
macabeo, xarel.lo, parellada

86 Colour: bright straw. Nose: fresh, citrus fruit, medium intensity. Palate: correct, balanced.

VINYA ESCUDÉ ROSAT PINOT NOIR BN
pinot noir

83

CELLER MARIOL

Rosselló, 442
8025 (Barcelona)
☎: +34 934 367 628 - Fax: +34 934 500 281
www.casamariol.com
celler@cellermariol.es

CASA MARIOL BN RESERVA
macabeo, xarel.lo, parellada

86 Colour: bright golden. Nose: fine lees, dry nuts, fragrant herbs, complex. Palate: powerful, flavourful, good acidity, fine bead, fine bitter notes.

CASA MARIOL BN RESERVA
macabeo, xarel.lo, parellada

87 Colour: bright straw. Nose: fresh fruit, dried herbs, fine lees, floral. Palate: fresh, fruity, flavourful, good acidity.

CASA MARIOL ARTESANAL SS
macabeo, xarel.lo, parellada

85 Colour: bright straw. Nose: balanced, floral, fresh fruit, medium intensity. Palate: flavourful, fruity, good acidity, correct.

CASA MARIOL TREPAT BR RESERVA
macabeo, xarel.lo, parellada, trepat

85 Colour: rose. Nose: ripe fruit, faded flowers, balsamic herbs. Palate: correct, fine bitter notes, good acidity.

CELLER VELL

Partida Mas Solanes, s/n
8770 Sant Sadurní D'Anoia (Barcelona)
☎: +34 938 910 290 - Fax: +34 938 183 246
www.cellervell.com
info@cellervell.com

CELLER VELL 2009 BN RESERVA
xarel.lo, macabeo, parellada

89 Colour: bright straw. Nose: medium intensity, fresh fruit, dried herbs, fine lees, dried flowers. Palate: fresh, fruity, flavourful, good acidity.

CELLER VELL CUVÈE LES SOLANES 2008 BN RESERVA
xarel.lo, chardonnay, pinot noir

89 Colour: bright yellow. Nose: dried flowers, lees reduction notes, sweet spices, dried herbs. Palate: fine bitter notes, good acidity, fine bead.

CELLER VELL EXTRA BRUT 2009 GRAN RESERVA
xarel.lo, macabeo, parellada, chardonnay

88 Colour: straw. Nose: fine lees, dried flowers, fragrant herbs, sweet spices. Palate: good acidity, fine bead, easy to drink.

CELLERS CAROL VALLÈS

Can Parellada, s/n - Corral del Mestre
8739 Subirats (Barcelona)
☎: +34 938 989 078 - Fax: +34 938 988 413
www.cellerscarol.com
info@cellerscarol.com

GUILLEM CAROL 2008 BN GRAN RESERVA
20% chardonnay, 40% parellada, 40% xarel.lo

89 Colour: bright golden. Nose: fine lees, dry nuts, complex. Palate: powerful, flavourful, good acidity, fine bead, fine bitter notes.

GUILLEM CAROL 2008 EXTRA BRUT GRAN RESERVA
40% parellada, 40% xarel.lo, 20% chardonnay

84

GUILLEM CAROL CHARDONNAY PINOT NOIR 2007 BR RESERVA
60% chardonnay, 40% pinot noir

86 Colour: bright yellow. Nose: powerfull, candied fruit, faded flowers, slightly evolved. Palate: good structure, full, flavourful, good acidity.

GUILLEM CAROL MILLENIUM 2005 BR GRAN RESERVA
35% parellada, 30% xarel.lo, 20% macabeo, 15% chardonnay

87 Colour: bright golden. Nose: fine lees, dry nuts, fragrant herbs, slightly evolved. Palate: powerful, flavourful, good acidity, fine bead.

GUILLEM CAROL PINOT NOIR ROSAT 2010 BN RESERVA
100% pinot noir

82

PARELLADA I FAURA 2010 BN RESERVA
40% parellada, 30% macabeo, 30% xarel.lo

87 Colour: bright straw. Nose: fine lees, ripe fruit. Palate: good acidity, fine bitter notes.

PARELLADA I FAURA MILLENIUM 2009 BN RESERVA
30% parellada, 40% macabeo, 30% xarel.lo

88 Colour: bright yellow. Nose: candied fruit, spicy, faded flowers. Palate: flavourful, good acidity, balanced.

CELLERS GRAU DORIA

Plaza Eliseo Oliver, s/n
8811 Canyelles (Barcelona)
☎: +34 938 973 263
www.graudoria.com
info@graudoria.com

BRUT DE GRAU DORIA 2011 BR
viura, xarel.lo, parellada

85 Colour: bright straw. Nose: medium intensity, fresh fruit, fine lees, floral. Palate: fresh, fruity, flavourful, good acidity.

BRUT NATURE DE GRAU DORIA 2010 BN
xarel.lo, parellada, viura

88 Colour: bright straw. Nose: balanced, floral, dry nuts, fine lees, medium intensity. Palate: fresh, fine bitter notes, good acidity.

MERCÈ GRAU DORIA 2004 BN GRAN RESERVA
xarel.lo, viura, parellada, chardonnay, pinot noir

91 Colour: bright golden. Nose: fine lees, dry nuts, fragrant herbs, complex. Palate: powerful, flavourful, good acidity, fine bead, fine bitter notes, balanced.

MERCÈ GRAU DORIA 2007 BN GRAN RESERVA
xarel.lo, viura, parellada, chardonnay, pinot noir

89 Colour: bright golden. Nose: fine lees, dry nuts, fragrant herbs, complex. Palate: powerful, flavourful, good acidity, fine bead, fine bitter notes.

NATURE RESERVA DE GRAU DORIA 2007 BN RESERVA
xarel.lo, parellada, chardonnay

87 Colour: bright straw. Nose: medium intensity, fresh fruit, dried herbs, fine lees, floral. Palate: fresh, fruity, slightly acidic.

NATURE RESERVA DE GRAU DORIA 2008 BN RESERVA
xarel.lo, parellada, chardonnay

89 Colour: bright straw. Nose: fresh fruit, dried herbs, fine lees. Palate: fresh, fruity, flavourful, good acidity.

CELLERS PLANAS ALBAREDA

Ctra. Guardiola, Km. 3
8735 Vilobí del Penedès (Barcelona)
☎: +34 938 922 143 - Fax: +34 938 922 143
www.planasalbareda.com
planasalbareda@yahoo.es

PLANAS ALBAREDA 2009 BN RESERVA
macabeo, xarel.lo, parellada

86 Colour: bright straw. Nose: medium intensity, dried herbs, floral. Palate: fresh, fruity, good acidity.

PLANAS ALBAREDA 2010 BN
macabeo, xarel.lo, parellada

84

PLANAS ALBAREDA RESERVA DE L'AVI 2008 BN RESERVA
macabeo, xarel.lo, parellada, chardonnay

84

PLANAS ALBAREDA ROSAT 2011 BR

84

CHOZAS CARRASCAL

Vereda Real de San Antonio s/n
46390 San Antonio de Requena (Valencia)
☎: +34 963 410 395
www.chozascarrascal.es
chozas@chozascarrascal.es

EL CAVA DE CHOZAS CARRASCAL 2010 BN RESERVA
chardonnay, macabeo

93 Colour: bright yellow. Nose: ripe fruit, fine lees, balanced, dried herbs. Palate: good acidity, flavourful, ripe fruit, long.

CODORNÍU

Avda. Jaume Codorníu, s/n
8770 Sant Sadurní D'Anoia (Barcelona)
☎: +34 938 183 232
www.codorniu.com
codinfo@codorniu.com

ANNA DE CODORNÍU BLANC DE NOIRS BR
100% pinot noir

88 Colour: bright straw. Nose: expressive, ripe fruit, toasty, spicy. Palate: fine bitter notes, good acidity.

GRAN CODORNÍU CHARDONNAY BR RESERVA
100% chardonnay

89 Colour: bright straw. Nose: powerfull, candied fruit, spicy. Palate: flavourfull, fine bitter notes.

GRAN CODORNÍU CHARDONNAY 2007 BN GRAN RESERVA
100% chardonnay

93 Colour: bright straw. Nose: dried herbs, fine lees, floral, candied fruit, sweet spices. Palate: fresh, fruity, flavourful, good acidity.

GRAN CODORNÍU PINOT NOIR 2007 BR GRAN RESERVA
100% pinot noir

92 Colour: bright straw. Nose: dried herbs, fine lees, floral, characterful, complex, ripe fruit. Palate: fresh, fruity, flavourful, good acidity.

GRAN CODORNÍU PINOT NOIR VINTAGE 2007 BR
100% pinot noir

90 Colour: salmon. Nose: candied fruit, red berry notes, fragrant herbs. Palate: flavourful, good acidity, fine bead.

GRAN CODORNÍU XAREL.LO 2007 BR GRAN RESERVA
100% xarel.lo

93 Colour: bright golden. Nose: fine lees, dry nuts, fragrant herbs, complex. Palate: powerful, flavourful, good acidity, fine bead, fine bitter notes.

JAUME CODORNÍU 2008 BR GRAN RESERVA
pinot noir, chardonnay

92 Colour: bright golden. Nose: fine lees, dry nuts, fragrant herbs. Palate: powerful, flavourful, good acidity, fine bead, fine bitter notes.

**REINA Mª CRISTINA BLANC DE
NOIRS VINTAGE 2010 BR RESERVA**
pinot noir

91 Colour: bright straw. Nose: powerfull, characterful, varietal, ripe fruit. Palate: fine bitter notes, good acidity, long.

COVIDES VIÑEDOS BODEGAS

Rambla Nostra Senyora, 45 - 1er
8720 Vilafranca del Penedès (Barcelona)
☎: +34 938 172 552 - Fax: +34 938 171 798
www.covides.com
covides@covides.com

DUC DE FOIX BR RESERVA ESPECIAL
macabeo, xarel.lo, chardonnay

89 Colour: bright straw. Nose: fresh fruit, dried herbs, fine lees, floral. Palate: fresh, fruity, flavourful, good acidity.

CUM LAUDE

Sant Sadurní D'Anoia (Barcelona)
☎: +34 941 454 050 - Fax: +34 941 452 929
www.bodegasriojanas.com
rrpp@bodegasriojanas.com

CUM LAUDE 2011 BN RESERVA
40% xarel.lo, 30% macabeo, 30% parellada

86 Colour: bright yellow. Nose: balanced, faded flowers, fresh. Palate: fruity, easy to drink, correct.

DOMINIO DE LA VEGA

Ctra. Madrid - Valencia, N-III Km. 270,6
46390 Requena (Valencia)
☎: +34 962 320 570 - Fax: +34 962 320 330
www.dominiodelavega.com
dv@dominiodelavega.com

ARTEMAYOR IV CAVA BN
macabeo, chardonnay

92 Colour: bright straw. Nose: dried herbs, fine lees, floral, characterful, candied fruit, toasty. Palate: fresh, fruity, flavourful, good acidity.

DOMINIO DE LA VEGA 2010 BN RESERVA
macabeo, chardonnay

90 Colour: bright yellow. Nose: dry nuts, dried flowers, candied fruit. Palate: good acidity, balanced, fine bitter notes, toasty.

DOMINIO DE LA VEGA BN
100% macabeo

88 Colour: bright straw. Nose: medium intensity, fresh fruit, dried herbs. Palate: fresh, fruity, flavourful, good acidity, fine bitter notes.

DOMINIO DE LA VEGA BR
100% garnacha

86 Colour: bright straw. Nose: fresh fruit, dried herbs, fine lees, floral. Palate: fresh, fruity, flavourful, good acidity.

DOMINIO DE LA VEGA BR
100% macabeo

87 Colour: bright straw. Nose: medium intensity, fresh fruit, dried herbs, fine lees, floral. Palate: fresh, fruity, flavourful, good acidity.

DOMINIO DE LA VEGA PINOT NOIR BR
100% pinot noir

86 Colour: rose. Nose: ripe fruit, faded flowers, dried herbs. Palate: powerful, flavourful, easy to drink.

**DOMINIO DE LA VEGA RESERVA
ESPECIAL 2010 BR RESERVA**
macabeo, chardonnay

89 Colour: bright yellow. Nose: balanced, ripe fruit, dried flowers. Palate: spicy, ripe fruit, fine bitter notes, balanced.

EL XAMFRÀ - F. DOMÍNGUEZ

Lavernó, 25-27
8770 Sant Sadurní D'Anoia (Barcelona)
☎: +34 938 910 182 - Fax: +34 938 910 176
www.elxamfra.com
info@elxamfra.com

EL XAMFRÀ 2008 BN RESERVA
macabeo, xarel.lo, parellada

85 Colour: bright yellow. Nose: fine lees, dry nuts, fragrant herbs. Palate: powerful, flavourful, good acidity, fine bead, fine bitter notes.

EL XAMFRÀ BN RESERVA
macabeo, xarel.lo, parellada

87 Colour: bright straw. Nose: citrus fruit, ripe fruit, dried flowers, fragrant herbs. Palate: good acidity, light-bodied, fresh, fruity.

EL XAMFRÀ BR
trepat

86 Colour: rose. Nose: medium intensity, fresh fruit, dried herbs, fine lees, floral. Palate: fresh, fruity, flavourful.

EL XAMFRÀ BR GRAN RESERVA
macabeo, xarel.lo

86 Colour: bright golden. Nose: dry nuts, fragrant herbs, honeyed notes. Palate: powerful, flavourful, good acidity, fine bead, fine bitter notes.

MERCAT BN
macabeo, xarel.lo, parellada

83

MERCAT BR
macabeo, xarel.lo, parellada

85 Colour: rose. Nose: candied fruit, dried herbs, fine lees, floral. Palate: powerful, fresh, fruity, good acidity.

ELVIWINES

Antoni Caballé, 8
8197 Valldoreix- St Cugat del Vallès (Tarragona)
☎: +34 935 343 026 - Fax: +34 936 750 316
www.elviwines.com
moises@elviwines.com

ADAR CAVA 2010 BR
macabeo, xarel.lo

86 Colour: bright yellow. Nose: medium intensity, dried herbs. Palate: balanced, good acidity, easy to drink.

CAVA ELVIWINES 2009 BR
parellada, macabeo, xarel.lo

87 Colour: bright straw. Nose: medium intensity, fine lees, floral, ripe fruit. Palate: fresh, fruity, flavourful, good acidity.

EMENDIS

Barrio de Sant Marçal, 67
8732 Castellet i La Gornal (Barcelona)
☎: +34 938 186 119 - Fax: +34 938 918 169
www.emendis.es
avalles@emendis.es

EMENDIS BN GRAN RESERVA
macabeo, xarel.lo, parellada, chardonnay, pinot noir

91 Colour: bright golden. Nose: fine lees, fragrant herbs, complex. Palate: powerful, flavourful, good acidity, fine bead, fine bitter notes, balanced.

EMENDIS BR
xarel.lo, macabeo, parellada

88 Colour: bright straw. Nose: medium intensity, fresh fruit, fine lees, citrus fruit, white flowers. Palate: fresh, fruity, flavourful, good acidity.

EMENDIS IMUM BN RESERVA
xarel.lo, macabeo, parellada

89 Colour: bright straw. Nose: dried herbs, fine lees, floral, candied fruit. Palate: fresh, fruity, flavourful, good acidity.

EMENDIS IMUM MAGNUM BN RESERVA

90 Colour: bright yellow. Nose: ripe fruit, fine lees, spicy, dried flowers. Palate: correct, fine bitter notes, powerful, flavourful.

EMENDIS MAGNUM BN GRAN RESERVA
xarel.lo, macabeo, parellada, chardonnay

89 Colour: bright golden. Nose: fine lees, dry nuts, fragrant herbs. Palate: powerful, flavourful, good acidity, fine bead, fine bitter notes.

EMENDIS ROSÉ
trepat

87 Colour: raspberry rose. Nose: candied fruit, floral, fragrant herbs, expressive. Palate: powerful, flavourful, fresh, fruity.

FERRE I CATASUS

Masía Gustems s/n Ctra. Sant Sadurní, Km. 8
8792 La Granada (Barcelona)
☎: +34 647 806 896 - Fax: +34 938 974 758
www.ferreicatasus.com
maracalvo@ferreicatasus.com

CELLER BALLBE 2009 BN
macabeo, xarel.lo, parellada

89 Colour: bright straw. Nose: fresh fruit, dried herbs, fine lees, floral. Palate: fresh, fruity, flavourful, good acidity.

FERRÉ I CATASÚS 2008 BN RESERVA
macabeo, xarel.lo, parellada

91 Colour: bright straw. Nose: fresh fruit, dried herbs, fine lees, floral, fruit preserve. Palate: fresh, fruity, flavourful, good acidity.

FERRÉ I CATASÚS 2008 BR RESERVA
macabeo, xarel.lo, parellada

85 Colour: bright golden. Nose: powerfull, ripe fruit, citrus fruit, slightly evolved. Palate: fine bitter notes, spicy, ripe fruit.

FERRÉ I CATASÚS ROSÉ 2008 BR
pinot noir

85 Colour: rose. Nose: powerfull, characterful, fruit preserve. Palate: fine bitter notes, good acidity.

MAS SUAU 2009 BN CRIANZA
macabeo, xarel.lo, parellada

87 Colour: bright yellow. Nose: fresh fruit, dried flowers, medium intensity. Palate: correct, fine bitter notes, easy to drink.

MAS SUAU ROSE 2009 BR
trepat, monastrell

78

FINCA TORREMILANOS

Finca Torremilanos, s/n
9400 Aranda de Duero (Burgos)
☎: +34 947 510 377 - Fax: +34 947 508 044
www.torremilanos.com
torremilanos@torremilanos.com

PEÑALBA-LÓPEZ BN
90% viura, 10% chardonnay

85 Colour: bright straw. Nose: medium intensity, dried herbs, faded flowers. Palate: fresh, fruity, good acidity.

FINCA VALLDOSERA

Masia Les Garrigues, Urb. Can Trabal
8734 Olèrdola (Barcelona)
☎: +34 938 143 047 - Fax: +34 938 935 590
www.fincavalldosera.com
general@fincavalldosera.com

CAVA SUBIRAT PARENT 2009 BN
100% subirat parent

89 Colour: bright yellow. Nose: dried flowers, citrus fruit, fruit liqueur notes, fragrant herbs. Palate: fine bitter notes, powerful, flavourful, fine bead.

CAVA VALLDOSERA 2009 BN
45% xarel.lo, 30% macabeo, 10% parellada, 10% chardonnay, 5% subirat parent

88 Colour: bright golden. Nose: dry nuts, fragrant herbs. Palate: powerful, flavourful, fine bead, fine bitter notes.

MS 4.7 2008 BN
35% xarel.lo, 30% macabeo, 20% parellada, 10% chardonnay, 5% subirat parent

89 Colour: bright straw. Nose: fresh fruit, dried herbs, fine lees, dried flowers, spicy. Palate: fresh, fruity, flavourful, good acidity.

FREIXA RIGAU

Santa Llucía, 15
17750 Capmany (Girona)
☎: +34 972 549 012 - Fax: +34 972 549 106
www.grupoliveda.com
comercial@grupoliveda.com

FAMILIA OLIVEDA BR
50% macabeo, 30% xarel.lo, 20% parellada

86 Colour: bright straw. Nose: medium intensity, fresh fruit, floral. Palate: fresh, fruity, flavourful, good acidity, fine bitter notes.

FREIXA RIGAU BN RESERVA
60% macabeo, 40% xarel.lo

86 Colour: bright straw. Nose: medium intensity, fresh fruit, dried herbs, fine lees. Palate: fresh, fruity, flavourful, good acidity.

FREIXA RIGAU NATURE MIL.LÈSSIMA RESERVA FAMILIAR 2009 BN
40% macabeo, 30% xarel.lo, 30% parellada

87 Colour: bright straw. Nose: white flowers, ripe fruit, toasty, spicy. Palate: flavourful, fine bitter notes, good acidity.

GRAN RIGAU 2009 BN RESERVA
40% macabeo, 30% xarel.lo, 30% parellada

85 Colour: bright yellow. Nose: medium intensity, faded flowers. Palate: flavourful, good finish, fine bitter notes, correct.

GRAN RIGAU CHARDONNAY 2009 BN
100% chardonnay

86 Colour: bright straw. Nose: faded flowers, fresh fruit, scrubland. Palate: correct, balanced, good acidity.

GRAN RIGAU PINOT NOIR 2009 BN
100% pinot noir

82

FREIXENET

Joan Sala, 2
8770 Sant Sadurní D'Anoia (Barcelona)
☎: +34 938 917 000 - Fax: +34 938 183 095
www.freixenet.es
freixenet@freixenet.es

CORDÓN NEGRO BR RESERVA
parellada, macabeo, xarel.lo

86 Colour: bright straw. Nose: balanced, medium intensity, dried flowers. Palate: balanced, good acidity, easy to drink.

CUVÉE D.S. 2007 BR GRAN RESERVA
macabeo, xarel.lo, parellada

88 Colour: bright straw. Nose: dried herbs, fine lees, floral, grassy. Palate: fresh, fruity, flavourful, good acidity.

ELYSSIA GRAN CUVÉE BR RESERVA
chardonnay, macabeo, parellada, pinot noir

88 Colour: bright golden. Nose: dry nuts, fragrant herbs. Palate: powerful, flavourful, good acidity, fine bead, fine bitter notes.

ELYSSIA PINOT NOIR ROSÉ BR RESERVA
pinot noir

89 Colour: brilliant rose. Nose: candied fruit, fruit preserve. Palate: fine bitter notes, good acidity.

FREIXENET 2007 BN GRAN RESERVA
macabeo, xarel.lo, parellada

87 Colour: bright straw. Nose: fresh fruit, dried herbs, fine lees, white flowers. Palate: fresh, fruity, good acidity, fine bitter notes.

FREIXENET CARTA NEVADA BR RESERVA
macabeo, xarel.lo, parellada

88 Colour: bright straw. Nose: fragrant herbs, white flowers. Palate: flavourful, fruity, fresh.

FREIXENET MALVASÍA 2001 B GRAN RESERVA
malvasía

85 Colour: bright golden. Nose: dry nuts, fragrant herbs, lees reduction notes. Palate: powerful, flavourful, fine bitter notes, spirituous.

FREIXENET MONASTRELL XAREL.LO 2009 BR
monastrell, xarel.lo

89 Colour: bright golden. Nose: fine lees, dry nuts, fragrant herbs. Palate: powerful, flavourful, good acidity, fine bead, fine bitter notes.

MERITUM 2007 BR GRAN RESERVA
xarel.lo, macabeo, parellada

92 Colour: bright golden. Nose: fine lees, dry nuts, fragrant herbs, complex. Palate: powerful, flavourful, good acidity, fine bead, fine bitter notes.

RESERVA REAL BR GRAN RESERVA
macabeo, xarel.lo, parellada

94 Colour: bright straw. Nose: dried herbs, fine lees, floral, ripe fruit, spicy. Palate: fruity, flavourful, good acidity, full.

TREPAT 2011 BR
trepat

90 Colour: salmon. Nose: ripe fruit, candied fruit, floral. Palate: flavourful, fruity, fresh.

GASTÓN COTY S.A.

Avernó, 28-30
8770 Sant Sadurní D'Anoia (Barcelona)
☎: +34 938 183 602 - Fax: +34 938 913 461
www.lorigancava.com
lorigan@lorigancava.com

AIRE DE L'O DE L'ORIGAN 2009 BN
macabeo, xarel.lo, parellada, chardonnay

91 Colour: bright straw. Nose: fine lees, dry nuts, dried flowers. Palate: powerful, flavourful, good acidity, fine bead, fine bitter notes.

L'ORIGAN BN
macabeo, xarel.lo, chardonnay

90 Colour: bright golden. Nose: dry nuts, fragrant herbs. Palate: powerful, flavourful, good acidity, fine bead, fine bitter notes.

L'ORIGAN ROSAT BN
pinot noir, chardonnay

87 Colour: old gold. Nose: toasty, ripe fruit, waxy notes. Palate: fine bitter notes, good acidity.

GIRÓ DEL GORNER

Finca Giró del Gorner, s/n
8797 Puigdálber (Barcelona)
☎: +34 938 988 032
www.girodelgorner.com
gorner@girodelgorner.com

GIRÓ DEL GORNER 2006 BN GRAN RESERVA
macabeo, xarel.lo, parellada

87 Colour: bright straw. Nose: dried herbs, fine lees, floral, ripe fruit. Palate: fresh, fruity, flavourful, good acidity.

GIRÓ DEL GORNER 2006 BR GRAN RESERVA
macabeo, xarel.lo, parellada

88 Colour: bright golden. Nose: fine lees, fragrant herbs, characterful. Palate: powerful, flavourful, good acidity, fine bead, fine bitter notes.

GIRÓ DEL GORNER 2008 BN RESERVA
macabeo, xarel.lo, parellada

87 Colour: bright straw. Nose: dried herbs, fine lees, floral, characterful. Palate: fresh, fruity, flavourful, good acidity.

GIRÓ DEL GORNER 2009 BR RESERVA
macabeo, xarel.lo, parellada

88 Colour: bright straw. Nose: medium intensity, fresh fruit, dried herbs, fine lees, floral. Palate: fresh, fruity, flavourful, good acidity.

GIRÓ DEL GORNER 2012 BR
100% pinot noir

88 Colour: rose. Nose: red berry notes, ripe fruit, floral. Palate: flavourful, fruity.

GIRÓ RIBOT, S.L.

Finca El Pont, s/n
8792 Santa Fe del Penedès (Barcelona)
☎: +34 938 974 050 - Fax: +34 938 974 311
www.giroribot.es
giroribot@giroribot.es

EXCELSUS 100 MAGNUM
50% xarel.lo, 30% macabeo, 20% parellada

93 Colour: bright yellow. Nose: sweet spices, pattiserie, fine lees, fragrant herbs, floral, ripe fruit, dry nuts. Palate: fresh, flavourful, good acidity, fine bead, balanced, elegant.

GIRÓ RIBOT AB ORIGINE BR RESERVA
50% macabeo, 30% xarel.lo, 10% parellada, 10% chardonnay

87 Colour: bright straw. Nose: fresh fruit, dried herbs, fine lees, floral, candied fruit. Palate: fresh, fruity, flavourful, good acidity.

GIRÓ RIBOT AB ORIGINE BRUT ROSADO
85% trepat, 15% pinot noir

89 Colour: rose. Nose: floral, red berry notes, ripe fruit, fragrant herbs, expressive. Palate: powerful, balanced, flavourful.

GIRÓ RIBOT AB ORIGINE 2007 BN GRAN RESERVA
50% macabeo, 30% xarel.lo, 10% parellada, 10% chardonnay

87 Colour: bright golden. Nose: fine lees, fragrant herbs, complex. Palate: powerful, flavourful, fine bead, fine bitter notes.

GIRÓ RIBOT AVANT BR RESERVA
45% xarel.lo, 40% chardonnay, 15% macabeo

93 Colour: bright golden. Nose: ripe fruit, dried flowers, dried herbs, sweet spices, creamy oak. Palate: good acidity, fine bead, flavourful, rich.

GIRÓ RIBOT DIVINIS MAGNUM BN RESERVA
90% chardonnay, 10% parellada

93 Colour: bright yellow. Nose: dried flowers, fragrant herbs, fine lees, candied fruit. Palate: fine bitter notes, powerful, flavourful, balanced.

GIRÓ RIBOT MARE 2007 BN GRAN RESERVA
50% xarel.lo, 30% macabeo, 20% parellada

92 Colour: bright golden. Nose: fine lees, dry nuts, fragrant herbs, complex, elegant. Palate: powerful, flavourful, good acidity, fine bead, fine bitter notes.

GIRÓ RIBOT MARE MAGNUM 2006 BN GRAN RESERVA
50% xarel.lo, 30% macabeo, 20% parellada

91 Colour: bright yellow. Nose: balanced, candied fruit, fragrant herbs. Palate: flavourful, good acidity, fine bitter notes.

GIRÓ RIBOT TENDENCIAS EXTRA BRUT
40% macabeo, 30% xarel.lo, 15% parellada, 15% chardonnay

87 Colour: bright straw. Nose: medium intensity, fresh fruit, dried herbs, fine lees, floral. Palate: fresh, fruity, flavourful, good acidity.

GIRÓ RIBOT UNPLUGGED BR BARRICA
pinot noir

91 Colour: coppery red. Nose: fine lees, dry nuts, fragrant herbs, complex, sweet spices. Palate: powerful, flavourful, good acidity, fine bead, fine bitter notes, elegant.

PAUL CHENEAU BLANC DE BLANCS BR RESERVA
45% macabeo, 40% xarel.lo, 10% chardonnay, 10% parellada

88 Colour: bright straw. Nose: medium intensity, dried herbs, fine lees, citrus fruit, sweet spices, dried flowers. Palate: fresh, fruity, flavourful, good acidity.

GRAN DUCAY BODEGAS

Ctra. N-330, Km. 450
50400 Cariñena (Zaragoza)
☎: +34 976 620 400 - Fax: +34 976 620 398
www.sanvalero.com
bsv@sanvalero.com

GRAN DUCAY BN
macabeo, parellada, xarel.lo

85 Colour: bright straw. Nose: medium intensity, dried herbs, fine lees. Palate: fresh, fruity, flavourful, good acidity.

GRIMAU DE PUJADES

Barri Sant Sepulcre s/n
8734 Olerdola (Barcelona)
☎: +34 938 918 031
www.grimau.com
grimau@grimau.com

GRIMAU BN
xarel.lo, macabeo, parellada

89 Colour: bright straw. Nose: dried flowers, dried herbs, ripe fruit, fine lees. Palate: powerful, flavourful, fine bitter notes.

GRIMAU BR
xarel.lo, macabeo, parellada

88 Colour: bright straw. Nose: medium intensity, fresh fruit, dried herbs, fine lees, floral. Palate: fresh, fruity, flavourful, good acidity.

GRIMAU RESERVA FAMILIAR BN
chardonnay, xarel.lo, macabeo, parellada

89 Colour: bright golden. Nose: fine lees, dry nuts, fragrant herbs, complex. Palate: powerful, flavourful, good acidity, fine bead, fine bitter notes.

GRIMAU SS
xarel.lo, macabeo, parellada

83

TRENCADÍS BN
xarel.lo, macabeo, parellada, chardonnay

88 Colour: bright straw. Nose: fresh fruit, dried herbs, fine lees. Palate: fresh, fruity, flavourful, good acidity.

TRENCADÍS ROSAT BN
pinot noir, garnacha

85 Colour: rose. Nose: ripe fruit, fine lees, fragrant herbs. Palate: fresh, fruity, flavourful, correct.

JANÉ VENTURA

Ctra. Calafell, 2
43700 El Vendrell (Tarragona)
☎: +34 977 660 118 - Fax: +34 977 661 239
www.janeventura.com
janeventura@janeventura.com

JANÉ VENTURA DE L'ORGUE 2006 BN GRAN RESERVA
32% macabeo, 40% xarel.lo, 28% parellada

92 Colour: bright golden. Nose: fine lees, dry nuts, fragrant herbs, complex. Palate: powerful, flavourful, good acidity, fine bead, fine bitter notes.

JANÉ VENTURA RESERVA DE LA MÚSICA 2010 BN RESERVA
39% xarel.lo, 32% macabeo, 29% parellada

90 Colour: bright straw. Nose: fresh fruit, dried herbs, fine lees, floral. Palate: fresh, fruity, flavourful, good acidity.

JANÉ VENTURA RESERVA DE LA MÚSICA 2010 BR
39% xarel.lo, 32% macabeo, 29% parellada

89 Colour: bright straw. Nose: fresh fruit, dried herbs, fine lees, floral. Palate: fresh, fruity, flavourful, good acidity.

**JANÉ VENTURA ROSÉ RESERVA
DE LA MÚSICA 2010 BR RESERVA**
100% garnacha

88 Colour: rose. Nose: powerfull, ripe fruit, red berry notes. Palate: flavourful, fruity.

**JANÉ VENTURA VINTAGE DO
2008 BN GRAN RESERVA**
26% macabeo, 60% xarel.lo, 14% parellada

91 Colour: bright golden. Nose: fine lees, fragrant herbs, characterful. Palate: powerful, flavourful, good acidity, fine bead, fine bitter notes.

JANÉ VENTURA VINTAGE DO 2009 BN
26% macabeo, 60% xarel.lo, 14% parellada

90 Colour: bright straw. Nose: fine lees, floral, expressive, dried herbs, jasmine. Palate: fresh, fruity, flavourful, good acidity.

JAUME GIRÓ I GIRÓ

Montaner i Oller, 5
8770 Sant Sadurní D'Anoia (Barcelona)
☎: +34 938 910 165 - Fax: +34 938 911 271
www.cavagiro.com
cavagiro@cavagiro.com

JAUME GIRÓ I GIRÓ BR RESERVA
30% xarel.lo, 40% parellada, 10% chardonnay, 20% macabeo

87 Colour: bright straw. Nose: dried herbs, fine lees, floral, candied fruit. Palate: fresh, fruity, flavourful, good acidity.

JAUME GIRÓ I GIRÓ 2005 BN GRAN RESERVA
40% parellada, 40% xarel.lo, 20% chardonnay

87 Colour: bright golden. Nose: fine lees, dry nuts, fragrant herbs, sweet spices. Palate: powerful, flavourful, good acidity, fine bead, fine bitter notes.

**JAUME GIRÓ I GIRÓ BOMBONETTA
2008 BR GRAN RESERVA**
37% macabeo, 29% xarel.lo, 19% parellada

89 Colour: bright straw. Nose: ripe fruit, spicy, faded flowers. Palate: good acidity, fine bitter notes.

JAUME GIRÓ I GIRÓ DE CAL REI ROSAT 2011 BR
100% trepat

86 Colour: rose. Nose: powerfull, ripe fruit, red berry notes, floral. Palate: powerful, fruity, fresh.

**JAUME GIRÓ I GIRÓ ELABORACIÓN
ARTESANA 2010 BN RESERVA**
45% xarel.lo, 20% parellada, 20% macabeo, 15% chardonnay

86 Colour: bright straw. Nose: medium intensity, fresh fruit, dried herbs. Palate: fresh, fruity, flavourful, good acidity.

**JAUME GIRÓ I GIRÓ GRANDALLA
2007 BR GRAN RESERVA**
40% parellada, 33% xarel.lo, 5% chardonnay, 22% macabeo

90 Colour: bright golden. Nose: fine lees, dry nuts, fragrant herbs, complex. Palate: powerful, flavourful, good acidity, fine bead, fine bitter notes.

**JAUME GIRÓ I GIRÓ GRANDALLA
DE LUXE 2004 BR GRAN RESERVA**
40% parellada, 45% xarel.lo, 15% chardonnay

89 Colour: bright yellow. Nose: candied fruit, faded flowers, fine lees. Palate: spicy, ripe fruit, good acidity, fine bitter notes.

**JAUME GIRÓ I GIRÓ MONTANER
2008 BR GRAN RESERVA**
40% parellada, 30% xarel.lo, 10% chardonnay, 20% macabeo

87 Colour: bright straw. Nose: fresh fruit, dried herbs, fine lees, floral, neat. Palate: fresh, fruity, flavourful, good acidity.

**JAUME GIRÓ I GIRÓ SELECTE
2007 BN GRAN RESERVA**
37,5% parellada, 30% xarel.lo, 25% macabeo, 5% chardonnay, 2,5% pinot noir

91 Colour: bright golden. Nose: dry nuts, fragrant herbs, complex. Palate: powerful, flavourful, good acidity, fine bead, fine bitter notes.

JAUME LLOPART ALEMANY

Font Rubí, 9
8736 Font-Rubí (Barcelona)
☎: +34 938 979 133 - Fax: +34 938 979 133
www.jaumellopartalemany.com
info@jaumellopartalemany.com

JAUME LLOPART ALEMANY 2008 BN RESERVA
macabeo, xarel.lo, parellada

87 Colour: bright straw. Nose: medium intensity, fresh fruit, dried herbs, fine lees, floral. Palate: fresh, fruity, flavourful, good acidity.

**JAUME LLOPART ALEMANY
2008 BN GRAN RESERVA**
macabeo, parellada, xarel.lo

90 Colour: bright straw. Nose: expressive, ripe fruit, candied fruit, spicy. Palate: flavourful, powerful, spicy.

JAUME LLOPART ALEMANY 2008 BR RESERVA
macabeo, parellada, xarel.lo

88 Colour: bright straw. Nose: medium intensity, fresh fruit, dried herbs, fine lees, floral. Palate: fresh, fruity, flavourful, good acidity.

JAUME LLOPART ALEMANY AINA ROSADO 2010 BR RESERVA
100% pinot noir

85 Colour: rose. Nose: expressive, ripe fruit, raspberry. Palate: powerful, flavourful.

JAUME LLOPART ALEMANY VINYA D'EN FERRAN 2007 BN GRAN RESERVA
pinot noir, chardonnay

92 Colour: bright golden. Nose: fine lees, dry nuts, fragrant herbs, complex. Palate: powerful, flavourful, good acidity, fine bead, fine bitter notes.

JAUME SERRA (J. GARCÍA CARRIÓN S.A.)

Ctra. de Vilanova, Km. 2,5
8800 Vilanova i la Geltrú (Barcelona)
☎: +34 938 936 404 - Fax: +34 938 147 482
www.garciacarrion.es
jaumeserra@jgc.es

CRISTALINO JAUME SERRA BR
50% macabeo, 35% parellada, 15% xarel.lo

85 Colour: bright straw. Nose: candied fruit, faded flowers. Palate: flavourful, fruity.

CRISTALINO JAUME SERRA SS
parellada, macabeo, xarel.lo

84

JAUME SERRA BN
macabeo, parellada

84

JAUME SERRA BN RESERVA
45% macabeo, 25% parellada, 15% xarel.lo, 15% chardonnay

85 Colour: bright straw. Nose: fresh fruit, dried herbs. Palate: fresh, fruity, flavourful, good acidity.

JAUME SERRA BR
50% macabeo, 35% parellada, 15% xarel.lo

84

JAUME SERRA ROSADO BR
80% trepat, 20% pinot noir

82

JAUME SERRA SS
50% macabeo, 25% xarel.lo, 25% parellada

82

JAUME SERRA VINTAGE 2009 BR RESERVA
30% macabeo, 25% parellada, 15% xarel.lo, 30% chardonnay

80

JOAN RAVENTÓS ROSELL

Ctra. Sant Sadurní a Masquefa, Km. 6,5
8783 Masquefa (Barcelona)
☎: +34 937 725 251 - Fax: +34 937 727 191
www.raventosrosell.com
raventosrosell@raventosrosell.com

HERETAT VALL-VENTÓS GRAN HERETAT BR
chardonnay, macabeo, parellada, pinot noir

85 Colour: bright golden. Nose: dry nuts, fragrant herbs. Palate: powerful, flavourful, good acidity, fine bead, fine bitter notes.

JOAN RAVENTÓS ROSELL BN
chardonnay, macabeo, parellada, xarel.lo

85 Colour: bright straw. Nose: candied fruit, white flowers. Palate: flavourful, powerful.

JOAN RAVENTÓS ROSELL BR
chardonnay, macabeo, parellada, xarel.lo

85 Colour: bright straw. Nose: medium intensity, dried herbs, fine lees, candied fruit. Palate: fresh, fruity, flavourful, good acidity.

JOAN RAVENTÒS ROSELL HERETAT BR
chardonnay, macabeo, parellada

83

MARIEN BN
chardonnay, macabeo, parellada, xarel.lo

88 Colour: bright straw. Nose: candied fruit, sweet spices, toasty. Palate: fine bitter notes, good acidity.

MARIEN BR
chardonnay, macabeo, parellada, xarel.lo

85 Colour: bright straw. Nose: candied fruit, citrus fruit, toasty, spicy. Palate: good acidity, fine bitter notes.

MARIEN BR RESERVA
chardonnay, macabeo, parellada

88 Colour: bright golden. Nose: powerfull, lees reduction notes, candied fruit, reduction notes. Palate: powerful, sweetness, fine bitter notes.

JOAN SARDÀ

Ctra. Vilafranca a St. Jaume dels Domenys, Km. 8,1
8732 Castellvi de la Marca (Barcelona)
☎: +34 937 720 900 - Fax: +34 937 721 495
www.joansarda.com
joansarda@joansarda.com

JOAN SARDÀ BN RESERVA
macabeo, xarel.lo, parellada

89 Colour: bright straw. Nose: fresh fruit, dried herbs, fine lees, floral, fresh. Palate: fresh, fruity, flavourful, good acidity.

JOAN SARDÀ BR RESERVA
macabeo, xarel.lo, parellada

88 Colour: bright straw. Nose: balanced, expressive, fresh, dried flowers, dried herbs. Palate: fruity, flavourful, good acidity.

JOAN SARDÀ MILLENIUM BN GRAN RESERVA
macabeo, xarel.lo, parellada

87 Colour: bright straw. Nose: faded flowers, dried herbs, dry nuts. Palate: flavourful, fresh, ripe fruit.

JOAN SARDÁ ROSÉ BR RESERVA
monastrell, garnacha

86 Colour: rose. Nose: red berry notes, ripe fruit, expressive. Palate: flavourful, sweetness, ripe fruit.

JUVÉ Y CAMPS

Sant Venat, 1
8770 Sant Sadurní D'Anoia (Barcelona)
☎: +34 938 911 000 - Fax: +34 938 912 100
www.juveycamps.com
juveycamps@juveycamps.com

GRAN JUVÉ CAMPS 2009 BR GRAN RESERVA
26% macabeo, 40% xarel.lo, 9% parellada, 25% chardonnay

93 Colour: bright golden. Nose: fine lees, dry nuts, fragrant herbs, complex, ripe fruit. Palate: powerful, flavourful, good acidity, fine bead, fine bitter notes.

JUVÉ & CAMPS BLANC DE NOIRS 2011 BR RESERVA
90% pinot noir, 10% xarel.lo

88 Colour: bright straw. Nose: dried herbs, candied fruit, faded flowers. Palate: flavourful, fine bead, ripe fruit.

JUVÉ & CAMPS CINTA PÚRPURA BR RESERVA
33% macabeo, 53% xarel.lo, 14% parellada

89 Colour: bright straw. Nose: medium intensity, fresh fruit, dried herbs, floral. Palate: fresh, fruity, flavourful, fine bead.

JUVÉ & CAMPS MILESIMÉ CHARDONNAY 2010 BR RESERVA
100% chardonnay

91 Colour: bright straw. Nose: fine lees, floral, expressive, varietal, ripe fruit. Palate: fresh, fruity, flavourful, good acidity.

JUVÉ & CAMPS MILESIMÉ MAGNUM 2009 BR RESERVA
100% chardonnay

93 Colour: bright straw. Nose: dried herbs, fine lees, floral, characterful, expressive, fresh fruit. Palate: fresh, fruity, flavourful, good acidity.

JUVÉ & CAMPS RESERVA DE LA FAMILIA 2009 BN GRAN RESERVA
30% macabeo, 50% xarel.lo, parellada, 10% chardonnay

92 Colour: bright straw. Nose: dried herbs, fine lees, floral, powerfull, ripe fruit. Palate: fresh, fruity, flavourful, good acidity.

JUVÉ & CAMPS RESERVA DE LA FAMILIA MAGNUM 2009 BN GRAN RESERVA
30% macabeo, 50% xarel.lo, 10% parellada, 10% chardonnay

91 Colour: bright straw. Nose: medium intensity, fresh fruit, dried herbs, fine lees. Palate: fresh, fruity, flavourful, good acidity.

JUVÉ & CAMPS ROSÉ BR
100% pinot noir

88 Colour: rose. Nose: lactic notes, red berry notes, ripe fruit, floral. Palate: flavourful, fresh, fruity, correct.

JUVÉ CAMPS SWEET RESERVA
33% macabeo, 53% xarel.lo, 14% parellada

88 Colour: bright straw. Nose: candied fruit, citrus fruit, spicy. Palate: flavourful, balanced, sweet.

LATIDOS DE VINO (EPILENSE DE VINOS Y VIÑEDOS)

La Quimera del oro, 30 - 3ºD
50019 (Zaragoza)
☎: +34 669 148 771
www.latidosdevino.com
fmora@latidosdevino.com

LATIDOS DE VINO "FRENESI" BN
macabeo, chardonnay

87 Colour: bright straw. Nose: grassy, medium intensity. Palate: flavourful, fresh, fruity.

LLOPART

Ctra. de Sant Sadurni - Ordal, Km. 4
8739 Subirats (Els Casots) (Barcelona)
☎: +34 938 993 125 - Fax: +34 938 993 038
www.llopart.com
llopart@llopart.com

LLOPART 2010 BN RESERVA
30% macabeo, 40% xarel.lo, 20% parellada, 10% chardonnay

89 Colour: bright straw. Nose: fresh fruit, dried herbs, floral, lees reduction notes. Palate: fresh, fruity, flavourful, good acidity.

LLOPART EX-VITE 2006 BR GRAN RESERVA
60% xarel.lo, 40% macabeo

91 Colour: bright yellow. Nose: fine lees, petrol notes, dry nuts, fragrant herbs. Palate: long, spicy, flavourful, balanced.

LLOPART IMPERIAL 2009 BR GRAN RESERVA
40% macabeo, 50% xarel.lo, 10% parellada

89 Colour: bright golden. Nose: fine lees, dry nuts, fragrant herbs. Palate: powerful, flavourful, good acidity, fine bead, fine bitter notes.

LLOPART INTEGRAL (375 ML) 2011 BN RESERVA
40% chardonnay, 40% parellada, 20% xarel.lo

87 Colour: bright straw. Nose: medium intensity, dried herbs, fine lees, floral. Palate: fresh, fruity, flavourful, good acidity.

LLOPART INTEGRAL 2011 BN RESERVA
40% parellada, 40% chardonnay, 20% xarel.lo

88 Colour: bright straw. Nose: fresh fruit, dried herbs, fine lees, floral. Palate: fresh, fruity, flavourful, good acidity, correct.

LLOPART LEOPARDI 2008 BN GRAN RESERVA
40% macabeo, 40% parellada, 10% parellada, 10% chardonnay

92 Colour: bright yellow. Nose: fresh, medium intensity, white flowers, fragrant herbs. Palate: fresh, good acidity, fine bitter notes.

LLOPART MAGNUM IMPERIAL 2009 BR GRAN RESERVA
50% xarel.lo, 40% macabeo, 10% parellada

91 Colour: bright yellow. Nose: balanced, fresh, white flowers, dried flowers, fragrant herbs. Palate: flavourful, fruity, fine bitter notes.

LLOPART MICROCOSMOS ROSÉ 2009 BN RESERVA
85% pinot noir, 15% monastrell

89 Colour: rose, purple rim. Nose: powerfull, ripe fruit, red berry notes, floral, expressive. Palate: powerful, fruity, fresh, balanced.

LLOPART NÉCTAR TERRENAL 2010 SEMIDULCE RESERVA
70% xarel.lo, 30% parellada

86 Colour: bright yellow. Nose: white flowers, fresh. Palate: fruity, flavourful, sweet, good acidity, easy to drink.

LLOPART ORIGINAL 1887 2007 BN GRAN RESERVA
50% parellada, 25% xarel.lo, 25% macabeo

93 Colour: bright golden. Nose: fine lees, dry nuts, fragrant herbs. Palate: powerful, flavourful, good acidity, fine bitter notes, spicy.

LLOPART ROSÉ (375 ML) 2010 BR RESERVA
60% monastrell, 20% garnacha, 20% pinot noir

89 Colour: onion pink. Nose: candied fruit, dried flowers, fragrant herbs, red berry notes. Palate: light-bodied, flavourful, good acidity, long, spicy.

LLOPART ROSÉ 2010 BR RESERVA
60% monastrell, 20% garnacha, 20% pinot noir

89 Colour: onion pink. Nose: candied fruit, dried flowers, fragrant herbs, red berry notes. Palate: light-bodied, flavourful, good acidity, long, spicy.

LONG WINES

Avda. del Puente Cultural, 8 Bloque B Bajo 7
28702 San Sebastián de los Reyes (Madrid)
☎: +34 916 221 305 - Fax: +34 916 220 029
www.longwines.com
adm@longwines.com

ESCAPADA BR
55% macabeo, 40% parellada, 5% chardonnay

87 Colour: bright straw. Nose: faded flowers, fresh, citrus fruit, candied fruit. Palate: flavourful, correct, good acidity.

MARÍA CASANOVAS

Ctra. BV-2242, km. 7,5
8160 Sant Jaume Sesoliveres (Barcelona)
☎: +34 938 910 812
www.mariacasanovas.com
mariacasanovas@brutnature.com

MARÍA CASANOVAS 2010 BN GRAN RESERVA
38% pinot noir, 42% chardonnay, 20% xarel.lo, macabeo, parellada

93 Colour: bright straw. Nose: fresh fruit, dried herbs, fine lees, floral, characterful. Palate: fresh, fruity, flavourful, good acidity.

MARÍA CASANOVAS GLAÇ
ROSE 2011 BN RESERVA
pinot noir, otras

86 Colour: brilliant rose. Nose: floral, ripe fruit, balsamic herbs, sweet spices. Palate: powerful, flavourful, fine bitter notes.

MARQUÉS DE GELIDA - L'ALZINAR

Can Llopart de Les Alzines
8770 Sant Sadurní D'Anoia (Barcelona)
☎: +34 938 912 353 - Fax: +34 038 183 956
www.vinselcep.com
crami@vinselcep.com

L'ALZINAR 2007 BN GRAN RESERVA
macabeo, xarel.lo, parellada, chardonnay

88 Colour: bright golden. Nose: fine lees, fragrant herbs, complex. Palate: powerful, flavourful, good acidity, fine bead, fine bitter notes.

L'ALZINAR 2009 BN RESERVA
macabeo, xarel.lo, parellada, chardonnay

88 Colour: bright straw. Nose: fresh fruit, dried herbs, fine lees, floral. Palate: fresh, fruity, flavourful, good acidity.

L'ALZINAR 2010 BR RESERVA
macabeo, xarel.lo, parellada, chardonnay

86 Colour: bright straw. Nose: fresh fruit, dried herbs, fine lees, floral. Palate: fresh, fruity, flavourful, good acidity.

MARQUÉS DE GELIDA 2008 BN GRAN RESERVA
macabeo, xarel.lo, parellada, chardonnay

85 Colour: bright straw. Nose: ripe fruit, faded flowers, grassy, spicy. Palate: powerful, flavourful, ripe fruit.

MARQUÉS DE GELIDA BRUT
ECOLÒGIC 2009 BR RESERVA
macabeo, xarel.lo, parellada, chardonnay

88 Colour: bright yellow. Nose: medium intensity, candied fruit, white flowers. Palate: flavourful, fresh, fruity, good acidity.

MARQUÉS DE GELIDA BRUT
EXCLUSIVE 2009 BR RESERVA
macabeo, xarel.lo, parellada, chardonnay

88 Colour: bright straw. Nose: medium intensity, fresh fruit, dried herbs, fine lees, floral. Palate: fresh, fruity, flavourful, good acidity.

MARQUÉS DE GELIDA CLAROR
2008 BN GRAN RESERVA
macabeo, xarel.lo, parellada

86 Colour: bright yellow. Nose: faded flowers, dried herbs, ripe fruit. Palate: powerful, flavourful, good acidity, ripe fruit.

MARQUÉS DE GELIDA GRAN SELECCIÓ
2007 BN GRAN RESERVA
macabeo, xarel.lo, parellada, chardonnay

90 Colour: bright yellow. Nose: medium intensity, faded flowers, citrus fruit, balanced. Palate: flavourful, good acidity, fine bitter notes.

MARQUÉS DE GELIDA PINOT
NOIR 2010 BR RESERVA
pinot noir

86 Colour: raspberry rose. Nose: candied fruit, floral, fragrant herbs. Palate: fresh, fruity, light-bodied, easy to drink.

MARQUÉS DE LA CONCORDIA

Monistrol D'Anoia, s/n
8770 Sant Sadurní D'Anoia (Barcelona)
☎: +34 914 365 900
www.haciendas-espana.com

MM PREMIUM CUVÉE MILLESIME (MARQUÉS DE LA CONCORDIA FAMILY OF WINES) 2008 BN
chardonnay, macabeo, parellada, xarel.lo

91 Colour: bright yellow. Nose: fine lees, dry nuts, fragrant herbs, fruit expression. Palate: powerful, flavourful, good acidity, fine bead, fine bitter notes.

MM RESERVA DE LA FAMILIA BRUT MILLESIME ROSÉ 2009 BR
70% pinot noir, 30% monastrell

89 Colour: light cherry. Nose: medium intensity, fresh fruit, dried herbs, fine lees, floral. Palate: fresh, fruity, flavourful, good acidity.

MARQUÉS DE MONISTROL

Monistrol d'Anoia s/n
8770 Sant Sadurní D'Anoia (Barcelona)
☎: +34 914 365 924
www.haciendas-espana.com

CLOS DE MONISTROL 2010 BN
25% chardonnay, 20% macabeo, 35% xarel.lo, 20% parellada

87 Colour: bright straw. Nose: dried herbs, fine lees, floral, dry nuts. Palate: fresh, fruity, flavourful, good acidity.

MONISTROL PREMIUM CUVÉE 2009 BN
25% chardonnay, 30% macabeo, 15% xarel.lo, 30% parellada

86 Colour: bright yellow. Nose: ripe fruit, fine lees, dry nuts, faded flowers. Palate: powerful, flavourful, correct.

MONISTROL PREMIUM CUVÉE 2010 BRUT ROSÉ
pinot noir, 30% monastrell

87 Colour: light cherry. Nose: floral, red berry notes, fruit expression, fragrant herbs. Palate: correct, good acidity, easy to drink.

MONISTROL SELECCIÓN ESPECIAL S/C BR

84

MONISTROL SELECCIÓN ESPECIAL S/C BR
25% chardonnay, 30% macabeo, 15% xarel.lo, 30% parellada

85 Colour: bright yellow. Nose: medium intensity, dried flowers, dried herbs, citrus fruit, ripe fruit. Palate: fresh, fruity, correct.

MONISTROL WINEMAKERS SELECT 2010 BN
25% chardonnay, 30% macabeo, 15% xarel.lo, 30% parellada

86 Colour: bright straw. Nose: floral, fragrant herbs, spicy, fine lees, dry nuts. Palate: fresh, fruity, flavourful.

MARTÍ SERDÀ

Camí Mas del Pont s/n
8792 Santa Fe del Penedès (Barcelona)
☎: +34 938 974 411 - Fax: +34 938 974 405
www.martiserda.com
info@martiserda.com

MARTÍ SERDÀ 2007 BN GRAN RESERVA
15% macabeo, 30% xarel.lo, 25% chardonnay, 30% vino reserva

87 Colour: bright yellow. Nose: fine lees, dry nuts, fragrant herbs, complex. Palate: powerful, flavourful, good acidity, fine bead, fine bitter notes.

MARTÍ SERDÀ BN RESERVA
35% macabeo, 40% xarel.lo, 25% parellada

85 Colour: bright yellow. Nose: faded flowers, balsamic herbs, ripe fruit. Palate: fine bitter notes, powerful, flavourful.

MARTÍ SERDÀ BR
35% macabeo, 30% xarel.lo, 35% parellada

88 Colour: bright straw. Nose: white flowers, ripe fruit. Palate: flavourful, fruity, fresh.

MARTÍ SERDÀ BRUT ROSÉ
30% trepat, 35% pinot noir, 35% garnacha

86 Colour: rose. Nose: red berry notes, ripe fruit, dried flowers, dried herbs. Palate: fine bitter notes, powerful, flavourful.

MARTÍ SERDÀ CHARDONNAY BR
100% chardonnay

87 Colour: bright straw. Nose: expressive, fresh fruit, grassy. Palate: flavourful, fruity, fresh.

MARTÍ SERDÀ CUVÉE REAL 2006 BN GRAN RESERVA
50% macabeo, 25% xarel.lo, 25% vino reserva

90 Colour: bright golden. Nose: candied fruit, spicy, toasty, dried herbs. Palate: fine bitter notes, good acidity.

MARTÍ SERDÀ SS
20% macabeo, 35% xarel.lo, 45% parellada

87 Colour: bright straw. Nose: floral, fresh fruit. Palate: flavourful, fruity, fresh, sweetness.

MASÍA D'OR BN
30% macabeo, 45% xarel.lo, 25% parellada

87 Colour: bright straw. Nose: medium intensity, fresh fruit, dried herbs, fine lees. Palate: fresh, fruity, flavourful, good acidity.

MASÍA D'OR BR
20% macabeo, 35% parellada, 35% xarel.lo

84

MAS CODINA

Barri El Gorner, s/n - Mas Codina
8797 Puigdalber (Barcelona)
☎: +34 938 988 166 - Fax: +34 938 988 166
www.mascodina.com
info@mascodina.com

MAS CODINA 2008 BN GRAN RESERVA
chardonnay, xarel.lo, macabeo, pinot noir

89 Colour: bright yellow. Nose: fine lees, dry nuts, fragrant herbs, complex. Palate: powerful, flavourful, good acidity, fine bead, fine bitter notes.

MAS CODINA 2009 BN RESERVA
chardonnay, xarel.lo, macabeo, pinot noir

89 Colour: bright straw. Nose: medium intensity, fresh fruit, dried herbs, fine lees, floral. Palate: fresh, fruity, flavourful, good acidity.

MAS CODINA 2009 BR RESERVA
chardonnay, xarel.lo, macabeo, pinot noir

85 Colour: bright straw. Nose: medium intensity, fresh fruit, dried herbs, floral. Palate: fresh, fruity, flavourful, good acidity.

MAS CODINA ROSÉ 2010 BR
pinot noir

85 Colour: brilliant rose. Nose: candied fruit, raspberry, spicy. Palate: fine bitter notes, good acidity.

MASCARÓ

Casal, 9
8720 Vilafranca del Penedès (Barcelona)
☎: +34 938 901 628 - Fax: +34 938 901 358
www.mascaro.es
mascaro@mascaro.es

CUVÉE ANTONIO MASCARÓ 2008 BN GRAN RESERVA
50% parellada, 35% macabeo, 15% chardonnay

90 Colour: bright golden. Nose: fine lees, dry nuts, fragrant herbs, complex. Palate: powerful, flavourful, good acidity, fine bead, fine bitter notes.

MASCARÓ "AMBROSIA" 2010 SS RESERVA
60% parellada, 30% macabeo, 10% xarel.lo

87 Colour: bright straw. Nose: white flowers, candied fruit, fragrant herbs. Palate: light-bodied, fresh, fruity.

MASCARÓ NIGRUM 2010 BR RESERVA
60% parellada, 30% macabeo, 10% xarel.lo

87 Colour: bright straw. Nose: medium intensity, fresh fruit, dried herbs, fine lees, floral. Palate: fresh, fruity, flavourful, good acidity.

MASCARÓ PURE 2010 BN RESERVA
80% parellada, 20% macabeo

90 Colour: bright straw. Nose: medium intensity, fresh fruit, dried herbs, fine lees, floral. Palate: fresh, fruity, flavourful, good acidity.

MASCARÓ ROSADO "RUBOR AURORAE" 2011 BR
100% garnacha

88 Colour: raspberry rose. Nose: floral, dried flowers, fragrant herbs, fresh fruit. Palate: light-bodied, fresh, fruity, fine bead.

MASET DEL LLEÓ

C-244, Km. 32,5
8792 La Granada del Penedès (Barcelona)
☎: +34 902 200 250 - Fax: +34 938 921 333
www.maset.com
info@maset.com

MASET DEL LLEÓ AURUM BN RESERVA
xarel.lo, parellada

87 Colour: bright straw. Nose: fresh fruit, fine lees, floral, fresh. Palate: fresh, fruity, flavourful, good acidity, fine bitter notes.

MASET DEL LLEÓ BN RESERVA
macabeo, xarel.lo, parellada

84

MASET DEL LLEÓ BR
macabeo, xarel.lo, parellada

85 Colour: bright straw. Nose: faded flowers, fine lees, fragrant herbs. Palate: light-bodied, fresh, fruity.

MASET DEL LLEÓ BR RESERVA
macabeo, xarel.lo, parellada

88 Colour: bright straw. Nose: medium intensity, fresh fruit, dried herbs, fine lees, floral. Palate: fresh, fruity, flavourful, good acidity.

MASET DEL LLEÓ L'AVI PAU BN RESERVA
macabeo, xarel.lo, parellada, chardonnay

88 Colour: bright straw. Nose: medium intensity, fresh fruit, dried herbs, fine lees. Palate: fresh, fruity, flavourful, good acidity.

MASET DEL LLEÓ ROSÉ BR
garnacha, trepat

85 Colour: coppery red, bright. Nose: medium intensity, dried herbs, dried flowers. Palate: fruity, fresh, easy to drink, good acidity.

MASET DEL LLEÓ VINTAGE BN RESERVA
macabeo, xarel.lo, parellada

85 Colour: bright straw. Nose: medium intensity, dried herbs, fine lees, floral, citrus fruit. Palate: fresh, fruity, flavourful, good acidity.

MATA I COLOMA

Montserrat, 73
8770 Sant Sadurní D'Anoia (Barcelona)
☎: +34 938 183 968
www.matacoloma.com
info@matacoloma.com

PERE MATA 2009 BR RESERVA
macabeo, xarel.lo, parellada

87 Colour: bright straw. Nose: balanced, medium intensity, fresh fruit. Palate: correct, balanced, good acidity.

PERE MATA CUPADA Nº 8 2009 BN RESERVA
macabeo, xarel.lo, parellada

86 Colour: bright straw. Nose: dried flowers, medium intensity, balanced. Palate: correct, fine bitter notes, good acidity.

PERE MATA L'ENSAMBLATGE 2007 BN GRAN RESERVA
macabeo, xarel.lo, parellada

87 Colour: bright golden. Nose: fine lees, dry nuts, fragrant herbs, complex. Palate: powerful, flavourful, good acidity, fine bead, fine bitter notes.

PERE MATA RESERVA FAMILIA 2007 BN GRAN RESERVA
macabeo, xarel.lo, parellada

88 Colour: bright golden. Nose: dry nuts, fragrant herbs, complex, sweet spices. Palate: flavourful, fine bead, fine bitter notes, sweetness.

MIQUEL PONS

Baix Llobregat, 5
8792 La Granada (Barcelona)
☎: +34 938 974 541 - Fax: +34 938 974 710
www.cavamiquelpons.com
miquelpons@cavamiquelpons.com

EULÀLIA DE PONS 2010 BR RESERVA
macabeo, xarel.lo, parellada

87 Colour: bright straw. Nose: medium intensity, fresh fruit, dried herbs, fine lees, floral. Palate: fresh, fruity, flavourful, good acidity.

EULÀLIA DE PONS ROSÉ 2011 BN
trepat

86 Colour: rose. Nose: candied fruit, raspberry. Palate: fine bitter notes, good acidity, correct.

MIQUEL PONS 2008 BN GRAN RESERVA
macabeo, xarel.lo, parellada

91 Colour: bright golden. Nose: fine lees, fragrant herbs, expressive, characterful. Palate: powerful, flavourful, good acidity, fine bead, fine bitter notes.

MIQUEL PONS 2010 BN RESERVA
macabeo, xarel.lo, parellada

88 Colour: bright straw. Nose: medium intensity, dried herbs, fine lees, floral, ripe fruit. Palate: fresh, fruity, flavourful, good acidity.

MIQUEL PONS 2010 BR RESERVA
macabeo, xarel.lo, parellada

86 Colour: bright golden. Nose: ripe fruit, faded flowers, dry nuts, sweet spices. Palate: powerful, ripe fruit.

MIQUEL PONS MONTARGULL 2010 BN
chardonnay, macabeo, xarel.lo, parellada

88 Colour: bright yellow. Nose: white flowers, candied fruit, fragrant herbs, expressive. Palate: balanced, fine bitter notes, fruity.

MONT MARÇAL

Finca Manlleu
8732 Castellví de la Marca (Barcelona)
☎: +34 938 918 281 - Fax: +34 938 919 045
www.mont-marcal.com
mrivas@mont-marcal.com

AUREUM DE MONT MARÇAL BN GRAN RESERVA
50% xarel.lo, 30% chardonnay, 10% pinot noir, 10% parellada

91 Colour: bright golden. Nose: fine lees, dry nuts, fragrant herbs, characterful. Palate: powerful, flavourful, good acidity, fine bead, fine bitter notes.

MONT MARÇAL BRUT ROSADO
100% trepat

85 Colour: rose. Nose: powerfull, ripe fruit. Palate: flavourful, fine bitter notes, correct.

MONT MARÇAL EXTREMARIUM BR
35% xarel.lo, 25% macabeo, 20% parellada, 20% chardonnay

88 Colour: bright straw. Nose: dried herbs, fine lees, floral, ripe fruit. Palate: fresh, fruity, flavourful, good acidity.

MONT MARÇAL EXTREMARIUM ROSADO BN
100% pinot noir

90 Colour: brilliant rose. Nose: rose petals, red berry notes. Palate: long, fruity, fresh.

MONT MARÇAL GRAN CUVÉE BR RESERVA
40% xarel.lo, 25% macabeo, 15% parellada, 20% chardonnay

86 Colour: bright straw. Nose: dried herbs, fine lees, floral, candied fruit. Palate: fresh, fruity, flavourful, good acidity.

MONT MARÇAL BR
40% xarel.lo, 30% macabeo, 20% parellada, 10% chardonnay

87 Colour: bright straw. Nose: dried herbs, fine lees, floral, powerfull. Palate: fresh, fruity, flavourful, good acidity.

MONT-FERRANT

Abat Escarré, 1
17300 Blanes (Girona)
☎: +34 934 191 000 - Fax: +34 934 193 170
www.montferrant.com
jcivit@montferrant.com

**AGUSTÍ VILARET 2007 EXTRA
BRUT GRAN RESERVA**
70% chardonnay, 10% macabeo, 10% parellada, 10% xarel.lo

90 Colour: bright straw. Nose: medium intensity, fresh fruit, dried herbs, fine lees, white flowers. Palate: fresh, flavourful, good acidity.

BERTA BOUZY 2008 BR RESERVA
36% xarel.lo, 25% parellada, 24% macabeo, 15% chardonnay

91 Colour: bright straw. Nose: fresh fruit, dried herbs, fine lees. Palate: fresh, fruity, flavourful, good acidity.

BLANES NATURE 2007 BN GRAN RESERVA
29% macabeo, 40% xarel.lo, 26% parellada, 5% chardonnay

88 Colour: bright straw. Nose: dried herbs, fine lees, floral, ripe fruit. Palate: fresh, fruity, flavourful, good acidity.

L´AMERICANO 2007 BN GRAN RESERVA
29% macabeo, 40% xarel.lo, 26% parellada, 5% chardonnay

89 Colour: bright straw. Nose: ripe fruit, citrus fruit, spicy, toasty. Palate: fine bitter notes, good acidity.

L´AMERICANO 2008 BR RESERVA
30% macabeo, 40% xarel.lo, 25% parellada, 5% chardonnay

90 Colour: bright straw. Nose: white flowers, expressive, neat. Palate: good acidity, fine bead.

MONT FERRANT EXTRA BRUT GRAN RESERVA

89 Colour: bright golden. Nose: fine lees, dry nuts, fragrant herbs. Palate: powerful, flavourful, good acidity, fine bead, fine bitter notes.

MONT FERRANT TRADICIÓ 2008 BR RESERVA
35% macabeo, 25% xarel.lo, 30% parellada, 10% chardonnay

87 Colour: bright straw. Nose: medium intensity, fresh fruit, dried herbs, fine lees, white flowers. Palate: fresh, fruity, flavourful, good acidity.

MOST DORÉ

Rambla de la Generalitat, 8
8770 Sant Sadurní d'Anoia (Barcelona)
☎: +34 938 183 641
www.objetodedeseo.eu
lodeseo@objetodedeseo.eu

MOST - DORÉ "OBJETO DE DESEO 2010 EXTRA BRUT RESERVA
monastrell, pinot noir

88 Colour: onion pink. Nose: dried flowers, fragrant herbs, spicy, fine lees, red berry notes, ripe fruit. Palate: fresh, fruity, good acidity, easy to drink.

MOST - DORÉ OBJETO DE DESEO 2010 EXTRA BRUT RESERVA
xarel.lo, parellada, macabeo

90 Colour: bright straw. Nose: fresh fruit, dried herbs, fine lees, floral. Palate: fresh, fruity, good acidity, fine bead.

MUNGUST S.L.

San Josep, 10-12 (Sant Jaume Sesoliveres)
8784 Piera (Barcelona)
☎: +34 937 763 016
www.cavesmungust.com
info@cavesmungust.com

MUNGUST 2006 BN RESERVA
xarel.lo, macabeo, parellada

82

MUNGUST 2007 BR RESERVA
xarel.lo, macabeo, parellada

85 Colour: bright straw. Nose: medium intensity, fresh fruit, dried herbs, faded flowers. Palate: fresh, fruity, good acidity.

PERE MUNNÉ DURÁN 2007 BN RESERVA
xarel.lo, macabeo, parellada

85 Colour: bright yellow. Nose: medium intensity, dried herbs, dry nuts, slightly evolved. Palate: fruity, good acidity.

PERE MUNNÉ DURÁN 2011 BN
xarel.lo, macabeo, parellada

84

PERE MUNNÉ DURÁN 2011 BR
xarel.lo, macabeo, parellada

85 Colour: bright yellow. Nose: medium intensity, dried herbs, fine lees. Palate: correct, fine bitter notes, easy to drink.

NADAL

Finca Nadal de la Boadella, s/n
8775 El Pla del Penedès (Barcelona)
☎: +34 938 988 011 - Fax: +34 938 988 443
www.nadal.com
comercial@nadal.com

NADAL 2007 BN GRAN RESERVA
51% parellada, 28% macabeo, 21% xarel.lo

90 Colour: bright golden. Nose: fine lees, fragrant herbs, expressive. Palate: powerful, flavourful, good acidity, fine bead, fine bitter notes.

RAMÓN NADAL GIRÓ 2004 BR GRAN RESERVA
62% xarel.lo, 32% parellada

84

SALVATGE 2007 BR GRAN RESERVA
18% xarel.lo, 60% macabeo, 22% parellada

88 Colour: bright yellow. Nose: dried flowers, ripe fruit, dry nuts. Palate: fine bitter notes, good acidity, fine bead.

SALVATGE ROSÉ 2010 RD RESERVA
100% pinot noir

89 Colour: salmon. Nose: candied fruit, red berry notes, fragrant herbs. Palate: fine bitter notes, good acidity.

ORIOL ROSSELL

Propietat Can Cassanyes, s/n
8732 St. Marçal (Barcelona)
☎: +34 977 670 207 - Fax: +34 977 670 207
www.oriolrossell.com
oriolrossell@oriolrossell.com

ORIOL ROSSELL 2009 BN GRAN RESERVA
xarel.lo, macabeo

89 Colour: bright golden. Nose: fine lees, dry nuts, fragrant herbs, toasty. Palate: powerful, flavourful, good acidity, fine bead.

ORIOL ROSSELL 2010 BN RESERVA
xarel.lo, macabeo, parellada

86 Colour: bright yellow. Nose: balanced, powerfull, white flowers. Palate: flavourful, fine bitter notes, good acidity.

ORIOL ROSSELL 2011 BRUT ROSÉ
trepat

88 Colour: light cherry, bright. Nose: red berry notes, floral, balanced. Palate: flavourful, fruity, good acidity.

ORIOL ROSSELL RESERVA DE LA PROPIETAT 2008 BN GRAN RESERVA
xarel.lo, macabeo, parellada

91 Colour: bright yellow. Nose: dry nuts, toasty, sweet spices, balanced. Palate: correct, flavourful, good acidity, fine bitter notes.

PAGO DE THARSYS

Ctra. Nacional III, km. 274
46340 Requena (Valencia)
☎: +34 962 303 354 - Fax: +34 962 329 000
www.pagodetharsys.com
pagodetharsys@pagodetharsys.com

PAGO DE THARSYS 2008 BN GRAN RESERVA
macabeo, parellada

87 Colour: bright golden. Nose: dry nuts, fragrant herbs, complex, lees reduction notes. Palate: powerful, flavourful, good acidity, fine bitter notes.

PAGO DE THARSYS 2010 BN
macabeo, chardonnay

86 Colour: bright straw. Nose: dried herbs, fine lees, candied fruit. Palate: fresh, fruity, flavourful, good acidity.

PAGO DE THARSYS BRUT ROSADO 2011 BR
garnacha

87 Colour: rose. Nose: candied fruit, lactic notes, fine lees, floral. Palate: powerful, flavourful, easy to drink.

PAGO DE THARSYS MILLÉSIME CHARDONNAY 2011 BN
chardonnay

88 Colour: bright straw. Nose: candied fruit, citrus fruit, faded flowers. Palate: powerful, fine bitter notes.

PARATÓ

Can Respall de Renardes
8733 El Pla del Penedès (Barcelona)
☎: ı34 938 988 ı82 - Fax: +34 938 988 510
www.parato.es
info@parato.es

ÁTICA 2009 EXTRA BRUT GRAN RESERVA
macabeo, xarel.lo, parellada, chardonnay

89 Colour: bright golden. Nose: fine lees, dry nuts, complex, candied fruit. Palate: powerful, flavourful, good acidity, fine bead, fine bitter notes.

ÁTICA PINOT NOIR 2010 RD
pinot noir

85 Colour: rose. Nose: ripe fruit, wild herbs, faded flowers. Palate: powerful, flavourful, spicy, ripe fruit.

ELIAS I TERNS 2005 BN GRAN RESERVA
xarel.lo, macabeo, chardonnay, parellada

90 Colour: bright golden. Nose: fine lees, dry nuts, fragrant herbs, sweet spices. Palate: powerful, flavourful, good acidity, fine bead, fine bitter notes.

PARATÓ 2009 BN RESERVA
macabeo, xarel.lo, parellada, chardonnay

87 Colour: bright yellow. Nose: dried flowers, fine lees, fruit expression, dried herbs. Palate: flavourful, fresh, spicy.

PARATÓ 2010 BR
macabeo, xarel.lo, parellada, chardonnay

88 Colour: bright straw. Nose: medium intensity, fresh fruit, dried herbs, floral. Palate: fresh, fruity, good acidity, easy to drink.

RENARDES 2011 BN
macabeo, xarel.lo, parellada, chardonnay

86 Colour: bright straw. Nose: medium intensity, fresh fruit, dried herbs, fine lees, dried flowers. Palate: fresh, fruity, flavourful, good acidity.

PARÉS BALTÀ

Masía Can Baltá, s/n
8796 Pacs del Penedès (Barcelona)
☎: +34 938 901 399 - Fax: +34 938 901 143
www.paresbalta.com
paresbalta@paresbalta.com

BLANCA CUSINÉ 2009 BR
chardonnay, pinot noir

93 Colour: bright golden. Nose: dry nuts, fragrant herbs, complex, faded flowers. Palate: powerful, flavourful, good acidity, fine bead, fine bitter notes.

PARÉS BALTÀ BN
macabeo, xarel.lo, parellada

88 Colour: bright straw. Nose: dried herbs, fine lees, floral, ripe fruit, citrus fruit. Palate: fresh, fruity, flavourful, good acidity.

PARÉS BALTÀ SELECTIO BR
macabeo, xarel.lo, parellada, chardonnay

91 Colour: bright straw. Nose: dried herbs, fine lees, floral, neat, ripe fruit. Palate: fresh, fruity, flavourful, good acidity.

ROSA CUSINE ROSADO 2009 BR
garnacha

91 Colour: coppery red. Nose: fragrant herbs, candied fruit, faded flowers. Palate: flavourful, sweetness, good acidity.

PARXET

Torrent, 38
8391 Tiana (Barcelona)
☎: +34 933 950 811
www.parxet.es
info@parxet.es

GRAN RESERVA MARÍA CABANE 2009 EXTRA BRUT GRAN RESERVA
pansa blanca, macabeo, parellada

91 Colour: bright golden. Nose: fine lees, dry nuts, fragrant herbs. Palate: powerful, flavourful, good acidity, fine bead, fine bitter notes.

PARXET 2010 BN
pansa blanca, macabeo, parellada

87 Colour: bright straw. Nose: fine lees, floral, candied fruit, fragrant herbs. Palate: fresh, fruity, flavourful, good acidity.

PARXET 2010 BR RESERVA
pansa blanca, macabeo, parellada

90 Colour: bright straw. Nose: fine lees, grassy, spicy. Palate: fine bitter notes, good acidity, ripe fruit.

PARXET ANIVERSARI 92 BN
chardonnay, pinot noir

93 Colour: bright yellow. Nose: candied fruit, floral, fragrant herbs, sweet spices. Palate: balanced, flavourful, fresh, fruity.

PARXET BR
pansa blanca, macabeo, parellada

90 Colour: bright straw. Nose: fresh fruit, dried herbs, fine lees, floral. Palate: fresh, fruity, flavourful, good acidity.

PARXET CUVÉE 21 BR
pansa blanca, macabeo, parellada

90 Colour: bright straw. Nose: dried herbs, fine lees, ripe fruit. Palate: fresh, fruity, flavourful, good acidity.

PARXET CUVÉE DESSERT 375 ML. RD
pinot noir

86 Nose: powerfull, ripe fruit, red berry notes, floral, expressive. Palate: powerful, fruity, fresh.

PARXET ROSÉ BR
pinot noir

88 Colour: brilliant rose. Nose: ripe fruit, red berry notes, floral, fragrant herbs. Palate: rich, flavourful, fresh, fruity.

PARXET SS RESERVA
pansa blanca, macabeo, parellada

88 Colour: bright straw. Nose: fresh fruit, dried herbs, fine lees, floral. Palate: fresh, flavourful, good acidity, sweetness.

RECAREDO

Tamarit, 10 Apartado 15
8770 Sant Sadurní D'Anoia (Barcelona)
☎: +34 938 910 214 - Fax: +34 938 911 697
www.recaredo.es
cava@recaredo.es

RECAREDO BRUT DE BRUT 2004 BN GRAN RESERVA
67% macabeo, 33% xarel.lo

92 Colour: bright yellow. Nose: fragrant herbs, fresh, balanced, faded flowers. Palate: fruity, fine bitter notes, good acidity.

RECAREDO BRUT NATURE 2008 BN GRAN RESERVA
46% xarel.lo, 40% macabeo, 14% parellada

93 Colour: bright yellow. Nose: complex, petrol notes, expressive, dried flowers. Palate: flavourful, good acidity, fine bead, fine bitter notes.

RECAREDO INTENS ROSAT 2009 BN GRAN RESERVA
77% pinot noir, 23% monastrell

88 Colour: light cherry, bright. Nose: red berry notes, floral, expressive. Palate: fruity, flavourful, good acidity, fine bitter notes.

RECAREDO RESERVA PARTICULAR 2003 BN GRAN RESERVA
64% macabeo, 36% xarel.lo

95 Colour: bright golden. Nose: dry nuts, fragrant herbs, complex, fine lees, macerated fruit. Palate: powerful, flavourful, good acidity, fine bead, fine bitter notes.

RECAREDO SUBTIL 2007 BN GRAN RESERVA
62% xarel.lo, 8% macabeo, 30% chardonnay

91 Colour: bright yellow. Nose: medium intensity, balanced, fresh, dried herbs. Palate: flavourful, good acidity, fine bitter notes.

TURO D'EN MOTA 2001 BN RESERVA
100% xarel.lo

92 Colour: bright yellow. Nose: complex, petrol notes, slightly evolved, toasty, sweet spices. Palate: good structure, full, fine bitter notes. Personality.

REXACH BAQUES

Santa María, 12
8736 Guardiola de Font-Rubí (Barcelona)
☎: +34 938 979 170
www.rexachbaques.com
info@rexachbaques.com

P. BAQUÉS 100 ANIVERSARI 2006 BR GRAN RESERVA
xarel.lo, macabeo, parellada, pinot noir

89 Colour: bright yellow. Nose: floral, balanced, medium intensity, fine lees. Palate: fine bitter notes, good acidity, flavourful.

REXACH BAQUES 2008 BN GRAN RESERVA
xarel.lo, macabeo, parellada

89 Colour: bright golden. Nose: fine lees, dry nuts, fragrant herbs, complex. Palate: powerful, flavourful, good acidity, fine bead, fine bitter notes.

REXACH BAQUES BRUT IMPERIAL 2009 BR RESERVA
xarel.lo, macabeo, parellada

89 Colour: bright straw. Nose: medium intensity, fresh fruit, dried herbs, floral. Palate: fresh, fruity, flavourful, good acidity.

REXACH BAQUES GRAN CARTA 2010 BR RESERVA
xarel.lo, macabeo, parellada

87 Colour: bright straw. Nose: medium intensity, fresh fruit, dried herbs. Palate: fresh, fruity, flavourful, good acidity.

RIMARTS

Avda. Cal Mir, 44
8770 Sant Sadurní D'Anoia (Barcelona)
☎: +34 938 912 775 - Fax: +34 938 912 775
www.rimarts.net
rimarts@rimarts.net

RIMARTS BR RESERVA
xarel.lo, macabeo, parellada

89 Colour: bright straw. Nose: dried herbs, fine lees, floral, ripe fruit, neat. Palate: fresh, fruity, flavourful, good acidity.

RIMARTS 24 BN GRAN RESERVA

92 Colour: bright golden. Nose: dry nuts, complex, grassy. Palate: powerful, flavourful, good acidity, fine bead, fine bitter notes.

RIMARTS 40 2009 BN GRAN RESERVA
xarel.lo, macabeo, parellada, chardonnay

93 Colour: bright golden. Nose: fine lees, dry nuts, fragrant herbs, complex, toasty, spicy, ripe fruit. Palate: powerful, flavourful, good acidity, fine bead, fine bitter notes.

RIMARTS CHARDONNAY BN RESERVA ESPECIAL
chardonnay

93 Colour: bright golden. Nose: dry nuts, fragrant herbs, complex, toasty, spicy, fine lees. Palate: powerful, flavourful, good acidity, fine bead, fine bitter notes.

RIMARTS UVAE 2006 BN GRAN RESERVA
xarel.lo, chardonnay

88 Colour: bright straw. Nose: candied fruit, white flowers. Palate: good acidity, correct.

ROCAMAR

Major, 80
8755 Castellbisbal (Barcelona)
☎: +34 937 720 900 - Fax: +34 937 721 495
www.rocamar.net
info@rocamar.net

CASTELL DE RIBES BR
macabeo, xarel.lo, parellada

87 Colour: bright straw. Nose: candied fruit, citrus fruit, spicy. Palate: flavourful, ripe fruit.

ROGER GOULART

Major, s/n
8635 Sant Esteve Sesrovires (Barcelona)
☎: +34 934 191 000 - Fax: +34 934 193 170
www.rogergoulart.com
jcivit@montferrant.com

ROGER GOULART 2007 BN RESERVA
40% xarel.lo, 30% macabeo, 25% parellada, 5% chardonnay

90 Colour: bright straw. Nose: floral, fresh fruit, fine lees, balanced. Palate: powerful, flavourful, good structure, fine bitter notes.

ROGER GOULART ROSÉ 2007 BR
60% garnacha, 40% monastrell

86 Colour: light cherry. Nose: powerfull, ripe fruit, raspberry. Palate: flavourful, powerful, fruity.

ROSELL & FORMOSA

Rambla de la Generalitat, 14
8770 Sant Sadurní D'Anoia (Barcelona)
☎: +34 938 911 013 - Fax: +34 938 911 967
www.roselliformosa.com
rformosa@roselliformosa.com

DAURAT "BRUT DE BRUTS" 2007 BN GRAN RESERVA
35% macabeo, 40% xarel.lo, 25% parellada

88 Colour: bright golden. Nose: fine lees, dry nuts, fragrant herbs. Palate: powerful, flavourful, good acidity, fine bitter notes.

ROSELL I FORMOSA 2008 BN GRAN RESERVA
30% macabeo, 40% xarel.lo, 30% parellada

87 Colour: bright yellow. Nose: medium intensity, dry nuts, faded flowers, fine lees. Palate: flavourful, correct, fine bitter notes.

ROSELL I FORMOSA 2009 BR RESERVA
35% macabeo, 40% xarel.lo, 25% parellada

86 Colour: bright yellow. Nose: faded flowers, candied fruit, powerfull. Palate: powerful, flavourful, fruity, easy to drink, good acidity.

ROSELL I FORMOSA ROSAT 2009 BR
60% garnacha, 40% monastrell

85 Colour: rose, bright. Nose: powerfull, ripe fruit, rose petals. Palate: flavourful, full.

ROSELL GALLART

Montserrat, 56
8770 Sant Sadurní D'Anoia (Barcelona)
☎: +34 938 912 073 - Fax: +34 938 183 539
www.rosellgallart.com
info@rosellgallart.com

ROSELL GALLART 2008 BN RESERVA
xarel.lo, macabeo, parellada, chardonnay

88 Colour: bright yellow. Nose: candied fruit, faded flowers, spicy. Palate: flavourful, correct, fine bitter notes.

ROSELL RAVENTÓS CRISTAL 2005 BN RESERVA
xarel.lo, macabeo, parellada, chardonnay

84

TERESA MATA GARRIGA 2009 BN RESERVA
xarel.lo, macabeo, parellada, chardonnay

87 Colour: bright straw. Nose: medium intensity, fresh fruit, faded flowers. Palate: light-bodied, easy to drink, fine bitter notes.

ROVELLATS

Finca Rovellats - Bº La Bleda
8731 Sant Marti Sarroca (Barcelona)
☎: +34 934 880 575 - Fax: +34 934 880 819
www.cavasrovellats.com
rovellats@cavasrovellats.com

ROVELLATS 2011 BR
macabeo, xarel.lo, parellada

84

ROVELLATS COL.LECCIÓ 2007 EXTRA BRUT
xarel.lo, parellada

90 Colour: bright yellow. Nose: dried flowers, fragrant herbs, candied fruit. Palate: powerful, flavourful, correct, fine bitter notes, balanced.

ROVELLATS GRAN RESERVA 2007 BN GRAN RESERVA
macabeo, xarel.lo, parellada

87 Colour: bright yellow. Nose: medium intensity, balanced, dried flowers. Palate: flavourful, correct, easy to drink, good acidity.

ROVELLATS IMPERIAL 2010 BR
macabeo, xarel.lo, parellada

87 Colour: bright straw. Nose: medium intensity, fresh fruit, fine lees, floral. Palate: fresh, fruity, flavourful, fine bead.

ROVELLATS IMPERIAL ROSÉ 2010 BR
garnacha, monastrell

86 Colour: rose. Nose: red berry notes, ripe fruit, floral, dried herbs. Palate: good acidity, powerful, flavourful.

ROVELLATS MAGNUM 2007 BN
macabeo, xarel.lo, parellada

91 Colour: bright straw. Nose: fragrant herbs, ripe fruit, fruit expression, fine lees. Palate: flavourful, fruity, fresh, fine bead.

ROVELLATS MASIA S. XV MILLESIMEE 2005 BN GRAN RESERVA
macabeo, xarel.lo, parellada, chardonnay

87 Colour: bright straw. Nose: medium intensity, dried herbs, fine lees, floral. Palate: fresh, fruity, good acidity, spicy.

ROVELLATS PREMIER 2011 BN
macabeo, parellada

85 Colour: bright straw. Nose: medium intensity, dried herbs, floral, reduction notes. Palate: fresh, fruity, flavourful, good acidity.

ROVELLATS PREMIER BRUT 2011 BR
macabeo, parellada

83

SEGURA VIUDAS

Ctra. Sant Sadurní a St. Pere de Riudebitlles, Km. 5
8775 Torrelavit (Barcelona)
☎: +34 938 917 070 - Fax: +34 938 996 006
www.seguraviudas.com
seguraviudas@seguraviudas.es

ARIA BN
macabeo, xarel.lo, parellada

86 Colour: bright straw. Nose: medium intensity, dried herbs, fine lees, floral. Palate: fresh, fruity, flavourful.

LAVIT BN
macabeo, parellada

88 Colour: bright straw. Nose: fresh fruit, dried herbs, fine lees, white flowers. Palate: fresh, flavourful, fine bead, fine bitter notes.

LAVIT ROSADO BR
trepat, monastrell, garnacha

89 Colour: coppery red. Nose: candied fruit, floral, fragrant herbs, fine lees. Palate: powerful, flavourful, balanced, fine bitter notes.

SEGURA VIUDAS BR RESERVA
macabeo, xarel.lo, parellada

88 Colour: bright straw. Nose: fresh fruit, dried herbs, fine lees, floral, candied fruit. Palate: fresh, fruity, flavourful, good acidity.

SEGURA VIUDAS BRUT VINTAGE 2008 BN GRAN RESERVA
macabeo, parellada

88 Colour: bright golden. Nose: fine lees, fragrant herbs, ripe fruit. Palate: powerful, flavourful, good acidity, fine bitter notes.

SEGURA VIUDAS RESERVA HEREDAD 2008 BR GRAN RESERVA
macabeo, parellada

92 Colour: bright golden. Nose: fine lees, dry nuts, fragrant herbs, complex. Palate: powerful, flavourful, good acidity, fine bead, balanced.

SIGNAT

Torrent 38
8391 Tiana (Barcelona)
☎: +34 935 403 400
info@signatcava.com

SIGNAT 5 ESTRELLAS BR RESERVA
xarel.lo, macabeo, parellada

89 Colour: bright straw. Nose: candied fruit, fragrant herbs, faded flowers. Palate: correct, ripe fruit.

SIGNAT BN
xarel.lo, macabeo, parellada

88 Colour: bright straw. Nose: expressive, ripe fruit, citrus fruit. Palate: flavourful, fruity, good acidity.

SIGNAT BR
xarel.lo, macabeo, parellada

87 Colour: bright straw. Nose: sweet spices, ripe fruit. Palate: flavourful, fruity, fresh.

SIGNAT MAGENTA ROSÉ BR
xarel.lo, macabeo, parellada

90 Colour: rose. Nose: red berry notes, ripe fruit, dried herbs, floral. Palate: powerful, flavourful, easy to drink, balanced.

SIMÓ DE PALAU

Ctra. N-240, Km. 39,5
43440 L'Esplugá de Francoli (Tarragona)
☎: +34 977 862 599 - Fax: +34 977 875 039
www.cavasimodepalau.com
caves@simodepalau.com

SIMÓ DE PALAU 2004 BN GRAN RESERVA
macabeo, xarel.lo, parellada

89 Colour: bright golden. Nose: candied fruit, citrus fruit, spicy. Palate: flavourful, powerful.

SIMÓ DE PALAU 2010 BN RESERVA
macabeo, xarel.lo, parellada

89 Colour: bright straw. Nose: dried herbs, fine lees, white flowers, citrus fruit. Palate: fresh, fruity, flavourful, good acidity.

SIMÓ DE PALAU ROSAT 2011 BR
trepat

85 Colour: light cherry. Nose: slightly evolved, candied fruit, red berry notes. Palate: fine bitter notes, spicy.

SOGAS MASCARÓ

Amalia Soler, 35
8720 Vilafranca del Penedès (Barcelona)
☎: +34 650 370 691
info@sogasmascaro.com

SOGAS MASCARÓ 2008 BN RESERVA
macabeo, xarel.lo, parellada

86 Colour: bright yellow. Nose: medium intensity, dried flowers. Palate: correct, fine bitter notes, easy to drink.

SOGAS MASCARÓ BN
macabeo, xarel.lo, parellada

86 Colour: bright straw. Nose: medium intensity, faded flowers, candied fruit. Palate: fresh, fruity, flavourful, good acidity.

TITIANA

Torrente, 38
8391 Tiana (Barcelona)
☎: +34 933 950 811
info@parxet.es

TITIANA PANSA BLANCA 2010 BR
pansa blanca

90 Colour: bright straw. Nose: medium intensity, fresh fruit, dried herbs, fine lees, floral, citrus fruit. Palate: fresh, fruity, flavourful, good acidity.

TITIANA PINOT NOIR ROSÉ 2010 BR
pinot noir

88 Colour: rose. Nose: expressive, ripe fruit, red berry notes. Palate: sweetness, fruity.

TITIANA VINTAGE 2010 BN
chardonnay

89 Colour: bright straw. Nose: medium intensity, dried herbs, fine lees, floral. Palate: fresh, fruity, flavourful, good acidity.

TORELLÓ

Can Martí de Baix (Apartado Correos nº8)
8770 Sant Sadurní D'Anoia (Barcelona)
☎: +34 938 910 793 - Fax: +34 938 910 877
www.torello.com
torello@torello.es

GRAN TORELLÓ 2008 BN GRAN RESERVA
macabeo, xarel.lo, parellada

92 Colour: bright straw. Nose: powerfull, candied fruit, lees reduction notes. Palate: powerful, ripe fruit, flavourful.

GRAN TORELLÓ MAGNUM 2008 BN GRAN RESERVA
macabeo, xarel.lo, parellada

93 Colour: bright straw. Nose: medium intensity, fresh fruit, dried herbs, fine lees, floral, powerfull. Palate: fresh, fruity, flavourful, good acidity.

JEROBOAM TORELLÓ 2008 BN GRAN RESERVA
macabeo, xarel.lo, parellada

94 Colour: bright golden. Nose: fine lees, dry nuts, fragrant herbs, complex. Palate: powerful, flavourful, good acidity, fine bead, fine bitter notes.

JEROBOAM TORELLÓ 2009 BN GRAN RESERVA

93 Colour: bright golden. Nose: fine lees, fragrant herbs, complex, fruit expression. Palate: powerful, flavourful, good acidity, fine bead, fine bitter notes.

TORELLÓ 2009 BN GRAN RESERVA
macabeo, xarel.lo, parellada

90 Colour: bright yellow. Nose: fine lees, dried herbs, floral, citrus fruit, ripe fruit, spicy. Palate: balanced, flavourful, spicy, powerful.

TORELLO 2009 BR RESERVA
macabeo, xarel.lo, parellada

87 Colour: bright straw. Nose: candied fruit, medium intensity, fragrant herbs. Palate: fine bitter notes, spicy, flavourful.

TORELLÓ 225 2009 BN GRAN RESERVA
macabeo, xarel.lo, parellada

93 Colour: bright straw. Nose: powerfull, ripe fruit, sweet spices, cocoa bean. Palate: good acidity, powerful, fine bitter notes.

TORELLÓ BY CUSTO 3D 2008 BR GRAN RESERVA
macabeo, xarel.lo

91 Colour: bright yellow. Nose: fine lees, dry nuts, fragrant herbs, floral, sweet spices, complex. Palate: powerful, flavourful, good acidity, fine bead, fine bitter notes, elegant.

TORELLÓ MAGNUM 2009 BN GRAN RESERVA
macabeo, xarel.lo, parellada

89 Colour: bright straw. Nose: candied fruit, powerfull, fruit liqueur notes. Palate: powerful, fruity, spicy.

TORELLÓ ROSÉ 2010 BR RESERVA
monastrell, garnacha

88 Colour: rose. Nose: ripe fruit, floral. Palate: fruity, fresh, good acidity.

TORRENS MOLINER

Ctra Sant Sadurni - Piera BV-2242, km 10,5
8784 La Fortesa (Barcelona)
☎: +34 938 911 033 - Fax: +34 938 911 761
www.torrensmoliner.com
tormol@torrensmoliner.com

TORRENS & MOLINER BN RESERVA
xarel.lo, macabeo, parellada

87 Colour: bright straw. Nose: medium intensity, dried herbs, floral, sweet spices, candied fruit. Palate: fresh, fruity, flavourful.

TRIAS BATLLE

Pere El Gran, 21
8720 Vilafranca del Penedès (Barcelona)
☎: +34 677 497 892
www.triasbatlle.com
peptrias@triasbatlle.com

TRIAS BATLLE 2007 BN GRAN RESERVA
40% xarel.lo, 30% macabeo, 20% parellada, 10% chardonnay

90 Colour: bright yellow. Nose: fine lees, dry nuts, fragrant herbs, complex. Palate: powerful, flavourful, good acidity, fine bead, fine bitter notes, balanced.

TRIAS BATLLE BN RESERVA
45% macabeo, 30% xarel.lo, 25% parellada

89 Colour: bright straw. Nose: medium intensity, fresh fruit, dried herbs, fine lees, floral. Palate: fresh, fruity, flavourful, good acidity, easy to drink.

TRIAS BATLLE BR RESERVA
45% macabeo, 30% xarel.lo, 25% parellada

87 Colour: bright yellow. Nose: citrus fruit, ripe fruit, dry nuts, dried herbs. Palate: fresh, fruity, spicy.

TRIAS BATLLE ROSADO 2010 BR
100% trepat

84

UNIÓN VINÍCOLA DEL ESTE

Pl. Ind. El Romeral- Construcción, 74
46340 Requena (Valencia)
☎: +34 962 323 343 - Fax: +34 962 349 413
www.uveste.es
cava@uveste.es

NASOL DE RECHENNA BN
90% macabeo, 10% chardonnay

84

NASOL DE RECHENNA BR
90% macabeo, chardonnay

84

VEGA MEDIEN BN
50% chardonnay, 50% macabeo

86 Colour: bright straw. Nose: candied fruit, spicy, faded flowers. Palate: fine bitter notes, good acidity.

VEGA MEDIEN BR
50% chardonnay, 50% macabeo

84

VALLDOLINA

Plaça de la Creu, 1
8795 Olesa de Bonesvalls (Barcelona)
☎: +34 938 984 181 - Fax: +34 938 984 181
www.valldolina.com
info@valldolina.com

TUTUSAUS ECO 2009 BN GRAN RESERVA
macabeo, xarel.lo, parellada

87 Colour: bright straw. Nose: medium intensity, faded flowers, balanced, candied fruit. Palate: correct, fine bitter notes.

VALLDOLINA ECO 2008 BR GRAN RESERVA
macabeo, xarel.lo, parellada, chardonnay

90 Colour: bright golden. Nose: fine lees, dry nuts, fragrant herbs, complex, ripe fruit. Palate: flavourful, good acidity, fine bitter notes, fine bead.

VALLDOLINA ECO 2010 BN RESERVA
macabeo, xarel.lo, parellada, chardonnay

91 Colour: bright straw. Nose: fresh fruit, dried herbs, fine lees, floral. Palate: fresh, fruity, flavourful, good acidity, balanced.

VALLFORMOSA

La Sala, 45
8735 Vilobi del Penedès (Barcelona)
☎: +34 938 978 286 - Fax: +34 938 978 355
www.vallformosa.com
vallformosa@vallformosa.es

ORIGEN 2010 BN
macabeo, xarel.lo, parellada

87 Colour: bright yellow. Nose: balanced, candied fruit, dried flowers. Palate: correct, fine bitter notes, good acidity.

ORIGEN 2010 BR
macabeo, xarel.lo, parellada

86 Colour: bright yellow. Nose: dry nuts, dried flowers, balanced. Palate: flavourful, good acidity.

ORIGEN 2010 SC CRIANZA
macabeo, xarel.lo, parellada

86 Colour: bright yellow. Nose: dried flowers, dried herbs, ripe fruit, fine lees. Palate: powerful, flavourful, fine bitter notes.

ORIGEN 2010 SS CRIANZA
macabeo, xarel.lo, parellada

88 Colour: bright yellow. Nose: medium intensity, dried herbs, floral, citrus fruit. Palate: fruity, flavourful, good acidity, correct.

ORIGEN ROSADO 2011 BR
garnacha, monastrell

90 Colour: coppery red, bright. Nose: dried flowers, red berry notes, sweet spices, neat. Palate: fruity, flavourful, balanced, fine bitter notes.

VALLFORMOSA COL.LECCIÓ 2010 BN RESERVA
macabeo, xarel.lo, parellada, chardonnay

88 Colour: bright straw. Nose: candied fruit, dried flowers, dried herbs, fine lees. Palate: powerful, flavourful, correct, fine bitter notes.

VALLFORMOSA COL.LECCIÓ 2010 BR RESERVA
macabeo, xarel.lo, parellada, chardonnay

87 Colour: bright straw. Nose: medium intensity, dried herbs, fine lees, floral. Palate: fresh, fruity, flavourful, good acidity.

VALLFORMOSA COL.LECCIÓ PINOT NOIR 2011
pinot noir

89 Colour: raspberry rose. Nose: floral, red berry notes, expressive. Palate: fruity, flavourful, fine bitter notes.

VÍA DE LA PLATA

Zugasti, 9
6200 Almendralejo (Badajoz)
☎: +34 924 661 155 - Fax: +34 924 661 155
www.bodegasviadelaplata.com
cava@bodegasviadelaplata.com

VÍA DE LA PLATA BR

83

VÍA DE LA PLATA BR

85 Colour: bright straw. Nose: dried herbs, fine lees, floral, citrus fruit. Palate: fresh, fruity, flavourful, good acidity.

VÍA DE LA PLATA CHARDONNAY BN RESERVA

87 Colour: bright yellow. Nose: candied fruit, floral, fragrant herbs. Palate: fresh, fruity, light-bodied, good acidity.

VÍA DE LA PLATA NATURE BN GRAN RESERVA

87 Colour: bright golden. Nose: fine lees, dry nuts, fragrant herbs, complex. Palate: powerful, flavourful, good acidity, fine bead, fine bitter notes.

VÍA DE LA PLATA SS

84

VILARNAU

Ctra. d'Espiells, Km. 1,4 Finca "Can Petit"
8770 Sant Sadurní D'Anoia (Barcelona)
☎: +34 938 912 361 - Fax: +34 938 912 913
www.vilarnau.es
vilarnau@vilarnau.es

ALBERT DE VILARNAU CHARDONNAY PINOT NOIR 2009 BN GRAN RESERVA
50% chardonnay, 50% pinot noir

91 Colour: bright straw. Nose: fresh fruit, dried herbs, fine lees, white flowers. Palate: fresh, fruity, flavourful, good acidity.

ALBERT DE VILARNAU FERMENTADO EN BARRICA 2008 BN GRAN RESERVA
40% chardonnay, 20% macabeo, 20% parellada, 20% chardonnay

93 Colour: bright straw. Nose: ripe fruit, spicy, fine lees, citrus fruit. Palate: flavourful, good acidity, fine bitter notes.

VILARNAU 2010 BN RESERVA
50% macabeo, 35% parellada, 15% chardonnay

87 Colour: bright straw. Nose: candied fruit, spicy, white flowers. Palate: fine bitter notes, ripe fruit, good acidity.

VILARNAU BR

88 Colour: bright straw. Nose: fresh fruit, dried herbs, fine lees. Palate: fresh, fruity, flavourful, good acidity.

VILARNAU BRUT ROSÉ BRUT ROSADO
85% trepat, 15% pinot noir

88 Colour: rose. Nose: ripe fruit, raspberry, rose petals. Palate: flavourful, ripe fruit, fine bitter notes.

VILARNAU VINTAGE BN GRAN RESERVA
35% macabeo, 30% parellada, 30% chardonnay, 5% pinot noir

91 Colour: bright golden. Nose: fine lees, fragrant herbs, characterful. Palate: powerful, flavourful, good acidity, fine bead, fine bitter notes.

VINÍCOLA DE NULLES S.C.C.L.

Estació, s/n
43887 Nulles (Tarragona)
☎: +34 977 602 622 - Fax: +34 977 602 622
www.vinicoladenulles.com
botiga@vinicoladenulles.com

ADERNATS BR RESERVA
50% macabeo, 25% xarel.lo, 25% parellada

89 Colour: bright straw. Nose: fresh fruit, dried herbs, fine lees, floral. Palate: fresh, fruity, flavourful, good acidity.

ADERNATS 2008 BN GRAN RESERVA
40% macabeo, 30% xarel.lo, 30% chardonnay

89 Colour: bright yellow. Nose: citrus fruit, ripe fruit, dried flowers, fragrant herbs, fine lees. Palate: flavourful, light-bodied, fine bitter notes.

ADERNATS 2008 BR GRAN RESERVA
40% macabeo, 30% xarel.lo, 30% chardonnay

89 Colour: bright golden. Nose: ripe fruit, dry nuts, floral, dried herbs. Palate: correct, fine bitter notes, powerful, flavourful.

ADERNATS DOLÇ 2010
50% macabeo, 25% xarel.lo, 25% parellada

86 Colour: bright straw. Nose: ripe fruit, candied fruit, dried flowers. Palate: fresh, fruity, easy to drink.

ADERNATS RESERVA BN RESERVA
50% macabeo, 25% xarel.lo, 25% parellada

89 Colour: bright straw. Nose: floral, dried herbs, ripe fruit, dried flowers, fine lees. Palate: flavourful, fresh, easy to drink.

ADERNATS ROSAT 2011 BR
100% trepat

85 Colour: onion pink. Nose: floral, ripe fruit, fragrant herbs. Palate: flavourful, light-bodied, fruity, slightly evolved.

ADERNATS XC 2006 BN
100% xarel.lo

91 Colour: bright yellow. Nose: candied fruit, faded flowers, dry nuts, balanced, fine lees. Palate: long, flavourful, fine bitter notes, good acidity.

VINÍCOLA DE SARRAL Í SELECCIÓ DE CREDIT

Avinguda de la Conca, 33
43424 Sarral (Tarragona)
☎: +34 977 890 031 - Fax: +34 977 890 136
www.cava-portell.com
cavaportell@covisal.es

PORTELL 2010 BN
70% macabeo, 30% parellada

86 Colour: bright straw. Nose: fruit liqueur notes, candied fruit, citrus fruit. Palate: good acidity, fine bitter notes.

PORTELL 2011 BR
70% macabeo, 30% parellada

88 Colour: bright straw. Nose: fresh fruit, dried herbs, fine lees. Palate: fresh, fruity, flavourful, good acidity.

PORTELL PETRIGNANO 2009 BN GRAN RESERVA
85% macabeo, 15% parellada

86 Colour: bright golden. Nose: fine lees, dry nuts, fragrant herbs. Palate: powerful, flavourful, fine bead, fine bitter notes.

PORTELL ROSAT 2011 BR
100% trepat

84

PORTELL SUBLIM ROSADO 2010 BN
100% trepat

88 Colour: bright straw. Nose: fresh fruit, dried herbs, fine lees, floral. Palate: fresh, fruity, flavourful, good acidity.

PORTELL VINTAGE 2009 BN
80% macabeo, 20% parellada

88 Colour: bright straw. Nose: fruit preserve, fruit liqueur notes, spicy. Palate: fine bitter notes, good acidity.

VINS I CAVES ARTIUM

Cr. Rocafort, 44
8271 Artés (Barcelona)
☎: +34 938 305 325 - Fax: +34 938 306 289
www.cavesartium.com
artium@cavesartium.com

ARTIUM 2004 BR GRAN RESERVA
macabeo, xarel.lo, parellada

83

ARTIUM 2011 BN RESERVA
macabeo, xarel.lo, parellada

86 Colour: bright yellow. Nose: medium intensity, dried flowers, fresh. Palate: correct, good acidity, easy to drink.

ARTIUM 2011 BR RESERVA
macabeo, xarel.lo, parellada

85 Colour: bright straw. Nose: dried flowers, dried herbs, ripe fruit. Palate: fine bitter notes, fine bead, good acidity.

ARTIUM ROSAT 2011 BR RESERVA
trepat

85 Colour: raspberry rose. Nose: medium intensity, fresh fruit, dried herbs, floral. Palate: fresh, fruity, flavourful.

VINS I CAVES CUSCÓ BERGA

Esplugues, 7
8793 Avinyonet del Penedès (Barcelona)
☎: +34 930 970 164
www.cuscoberga.com
cuscoberga@cuscoberga.com

CUSCÓ BERGA 2010 BN RESERVA
30% macabeo, 50% xarel.lo, 20% parellada

84

CUSCÓ BERGA 2008 BR GRAN RESERVA
30% macabeo, 50% xarel.lo, 20% parellada

88 Colour: bright golden. Nose: dry nuts, fragrant herbs, complex. Palate: powerful, flavourful, good acidity, fine bead, fine bitter notes.

CUSCÓ BERGA 2010 BR
30% macabeo, 50% xarel.lo, 20% parellada

83

CUSCÓ BERGA ROSÉ 2010 BR
100% trepat

85 Colour: coppery red. Nose: ripe fruit, fruit liqueur notes, dried flowers, balsamic herbs. Palate: powerful, flavourful, fruity, easy to drink.

VINYA NATURA

Herrero, 32- Sº 12
12005 Castellón (Castellón)
☎: +34 670 056 497
www.vinyanatura.com
info@vinyanatura.com

BABEL DE VINYA NATURA 2011 BR
100% macabeo

90 Colour: bright straw. Nose: fresh, medium intensity, dried herbs, fine lees. Palate: balanced, fine bitter notes, good acidity, fine bead.

VIVES AMBRÒS

Mayor, 39
43812 Montferri (Tarragona)
☎: +34 639 521 652 - Fax: +34 977 606 579
www.vivesambros.com
covives@tinet.org

VIVES AMBRÒS 200 / BN GRAN RESERVA
40% xarel.lo, 35% macabeo, 25% chardonnay

87 Colour: bright golden. Nose: fine lees, fragrant herbs. Palate: powerful, flavourful, good acidity, fine bead, fine bitter notes.

VIVES AMBRÒS 2009 BR RESERVA
40% xarel.lo, 35% macabeo, 25% parellada

88 Colour: bright straw. Nose: dried herbs, fine lees, floral. Palate: fresh, fruity, flavourful, good acidity.

VIVES AMBRÒS JUJOL 2009 BN GRAN RESERVA
100% xarel.lo

91 Colour: bright golden. Nose: fine lees, dry nuts, fragrant herbs, complex, expressive. Palate: powerful, flavourful, good acidity, fine bead, fine bitter notes.

VIVES AMBRÒS SALVATGE 2007 GRAN RESERVA
60% xarel.lo, 40% macabeo

86 Colour: bright golden. Nose: ripe fruit, fruit preserve, faded flowers, sweet spices. Palate: powerful, flavourful, long.

**VIVES AMBRÒS SALVATGE MAGNUM
2007 BN GRAN RESERVA**
60% xarel.lo, 40% macabeo

90 Colour: bright straw. Nose: fresh fruit, dried herbs, fine lees, floral, characterful, lactic notes. Palate: fresh, fruity, flavourful, good acidity.

Consejo Regulador

DO Boundary

LOCATION:

The region stretches to the north of the Duero depression and on both sides of the Pisuerga, bordered by the Cérvalos and the Torozos hills. The vineyards are situated at an altitude of 750 m; the DO extends from part of the municipal area of Valladolid (the wine estate known as 'El Berrocal') to the municipality of Dueñas in Palencia, also including Cabezón de Pisuerga, Cigales, Corcos del Valle, Cubillas de Santa Marte, Fuensaldaña, Mucientes, Quintanilla de Trigueros, San Martín de Valvení, Santovenia de Pisuerga, Trigueros del Valle and Valoria la Buena.

CLIMATE:

The climate is continental with Atlantic influences, and is marked by great contrasts in temperature, both yearly and day/night. The summers are extremely dry; the winters are harsh and prolonged, with frequent frost and fog; rainfall is irregular.

SOIL:

The soil is sandy and limy with clay loam which is settled on clay and marl. It has an extremely variable limestone content which, depending on the different regions, ranges between 1% and 35%.

TYPES OF WINE:

ROSÉS: Cigales Nuevo. Produced with at least 60% of the *Tinta del País* variety and at least 20% of white varieties. The vintage must be displayed on the label. Cigales. Produced with at least 60% of the *Tinta del País* variety and at least 20% of white varieties. Marketed from 31st December of the following year. **REDS:** Produced with at least 85% of the Tinta del País and the *Garnacha Tinta* varieties.

GRAPE VARIETIES:

WHITE: *Verdejo, Albillo, Sauvignon Blanc* and *Viura*. **RED:** *Tinta del País* (*Tempranillo*), *Garnacha Tinta, Garnacha Gris, Merlot, Syrah* and *Cabernet Sauvignon*.

FIGURES:

Vineyard surface: 2.100 – **Wine-Growers:** 480– **Wineries:** 35 – **2012 Harvest rating:** Very Good– **Production:** 5.670.000 litres – **Market percentages:** 80% domestic. 20% export

VINTAGE RATING PEÑÍNGUIDE				
2008	2009	2010	2011	2012
GOOD	GOOD	EXCELLENT	EXCELLENT	VERY GOOD

CONSEJO REGULADOR

Corro Vaca, 5 - 47270 Cigales (Valladolid) ☎: +34 983 580 074 - Fax: +34 983 586 590
consejo@do-cigales.es   www.do-cigales.es

AURELIO PINACHO

Ronda Las Huertas, 17
47194 Mucientes (Valladolid)
☎: +34 983 587 859 - Fax: +34 983 586 954
lpigo@hotmail.com

PINACHO 2012 RD
80% tempranillo, 20% albillo, viura

84

AVELINO VEGAS

Real del Pino, 36
40460 Santiuste (Segovia)
☎: +34 921 596 002 - Fax: +34 921 596 035
www.avelinovegas.com
ana@avelinovegas.com

ZARZALES 2012 RD
tempranillo, garnacha, albillo, verdejo

87 Colour: rose, purple rim. Nose: ripe fruit, red berry notes, floral. Palate: powerful, fruity, fresh.

BODEGA CÉSAR PRÍNCIPE

Ctra. Fuensaldaña-Mucientes, s/n
47194 Fuensaldaña (Valladolid)
☎: +34 983 663 123
www.cesarprincipe.es
cesarprincipe@cesarprincipe.es

CÉSAR PRÍNCIPE 2010 TC
100% tempranillo

94 Colour: cherry, garnet rim. Nose: ripe fruit, spicy, complex, sweet spices, aromatic coffee. Palate: powerful, flavourful, toasty, round tannins.

BODEGA COOPERATIVA DE CIGALES

Las Bodegas, s/n
47270 Cigales (Valladolid)
☎: +34 983 580 135 - Fax: +34 983 580 682
www.bodegacooperativacigales.com
bcc@bodegacooperativacigales.com

TORONDOS 2012 RD
tempranillo, garnacha, verdejo, albillo

88 Colour: rose, purple rim. Nose: powerfull, ripe fruit, red berry notes. Palate: powerful, fruity, fresh.

BODEGA HIRIART

Avda. Los Cortijos, 38
47270 Cigales (Valladolid)
☎: +34 983 580 094 - Fax: +34 983 100 701
www.bodegahiriart.es
info@bodegahiriart.es

HIRIART 2010 T ROBLE
tinta del país

87 Colour: cherry, garnet rim. Nose: ripe fruit, sweet spices, toasty. Palate: ripe fruit, spicy.

HIRIART 2010 TC
tinta del país

90 Colour: cherry, garnet rim. Nose: toasty, spicy. Palate: flavourful, good acidity.

HIRIART 2012 RD FERMENTADO EN BARRICA
tinta del país, garnacha, verdejo

88 Colour: rose, purple rim. Nose: powerfull, ripe fruit, floral, sweet spices. Palate: powerful, fruity, fresh.

HIRIART ÉLITE 2012 RD
tinta del país, garnacha, verdejo

90 Colour: rose, purple rim. Nose: ripe fruit, red berry notes, floral, expressive. Palate: powerful, fruity, fresh.

HIRIART LÁGRIMA 2012 RD
tinta del país, garnacha, verdejo

89 Colour: rose, purple rim. Nose: powerfull, ripe fruit, red berry notes, floral. Palate: powerful, fruity, fresh.

BODEGA VALDELOSFRAILES

Camino de Cubillas, s/n
47290 Cubillas de Santa Marta (Valladolid)
☎: +34 983 485 028 - Fax: +34 983 485 024
www.valdelosfrailes.es
valdelosfrailes@matarromera.es

SELECCIÓN PERSONAL CARLOS MORO VALDELOSFRAILES RESERVA ESPECIAL 2006 T
tempranillo

90 Colour: cherry, garnet rim. Nose: ripe fruit, spicy, creamy oak, roasted coffee. Palate: powerful, toasty, round tannins.

VALDELOSFRAILES 2012 RD
80% tempranillo, 20% verdejo

90 Colour: rose, purple rim. Nose: powerfull, ripe fruit, red berry notes, floral, varietal. Palate: powerful, fruity, fresh.

VALDELOSFRAILES PAGO DE LAS COSTANAS 2005 T
100% tempranillo

88 Colour: cherry, garnet rim. Nose: ripe fruit, spicy, creamy oak, roasted coffee. Palate: powerful, flavourful, toasty, round tannins.

VALDELOSFRAILES PRESTIGIO 2006 TR
100% tempranillo

90 Colour: pale ruby, brick rim edge. Nose: spicy, fine reductive notes, wet leather, aged wood nuances, fruit liqueur notes. Palate: spicy, fine tannins, elegant, long.

VALDELOSFRAILES TEMPRANILLO 2011 T
100% tempranillo

87 Colour: bright cherry. Nose: ripe fruit, sweet spices. Palate: flavourful, fruity, round tannins.

VALDELOSFRAILES VENDIMIA SELECCIONADA 2006 TC
100% tempranillo

88 Colour: cherry, garnet rim. Nose: fruit liqueur notes, warm, toasty, spicy. Palate: spicy, ripe fruit, toasty.

BODEGAS FERNÁNDEZ CAMARERO

Don Alvaro de Bazán, 1 4ºB
28003 Madrid (Madrid)
☎: +34 677 682 426
www.balvinar.com
javier.fernandez@balvinar.com

BALVINAR PAGOS SELECCIONADOS 2007 TC
100% tempranillo

90 Colour: cherry, garnet rim. Nose: ripe fruit, spicy, creamy oak, toasty, characterful, wet leather. Palate: powerful, flavourful, toasty, round tannins.

BODEGAS HIJOS DE FÉLIX SALAS

Corrales, s/n
47280 Corcos del Valle (Valladolid)
☎: +34 983 580 378 - Fax: +34 983 580 262
www.bodegasfelixsalas.com
bodega@bodegasfelixsalas.com

VIÑA PICOTA 2012 RD

86 Colour: rose, purple rim. Nose: powerfull, expressive. Palate: powerful, fruity, fresh.

BODEGAS LEZCANO-LACALLE

Ctra. de Valoria, s/n
47282 Trigueros del Valle (Valladolid)
☎: +34 629 280 515
www.lezcano-lacalle.com
info@lezcano-lacalle.com

DOCETAÑIDOS 2012 RD
tempranillo, albillo, verdejo, sauvignon blanc

86 Colour: light cherry. Nose: candied fruit, medium intensity. Palate: good acidity, correct.

LEZCANO-LACALLE DÚ 2006 T
tempranillo, merlot, cabernet sauvignon

90 Colour: cherry, garnet rim. Nose: ripe fruit, spicy, creamy oak, toasty, characterful, wet leather. Palate: powerful, flavourful, toasty, round tannins.

MAUDES 2010 TC
tempranillo, merlot, cabernet sauvignon

86 Colour: cherry, garnet rim. Nose: ripe fruit, spicy, roasted coffee, warm. Palate: powerful, flavourful, toasty, round tannins.

BODEGAS SANTA RUFINA

Pago Fuente La Teja. Pol. Ind. 3 - Parcela 102
47290 Cubillas de Santa Marta (Valladolid)
☎: +34 983 585 202 - Fax: +34 983 585 202
www.bodegassantarufina.com
info@bodegassantarufina.com

A SOLAS 2012 B
100% verdejo

82

VIÑA RUFINA 2006 TR
100% tempranillo

87 Colour: deep cherry. Nose: powerfull, warm, roasted coffee, aromatic coffee. Palate: fine bitter notes, toasty.

VIÑA RUFINA 2010 TC
100% tempranillo

87 Colour: cherry, garnet rim. Nose: ripe fruit, roasted coffee. Palate: fine bitter notes, good acidity, correct.

BODEGAS Y VIÑEDOS ALFREDO SANTAMARÍA

Poniente, 18
47290 Cubillas de Santa Marta (Valladolid)
☎: +34 983 585 006 - Fax: +34 983 440 770
www.bodega-santamaria.com
info@bodega-santamaria.com

ALFREDO SANTAMARÍA 2008 TC
tempranillo

89 Colour: cherry, garnet rim. Nose: ripe fruit, spicy, creamy oak, toasty, complex. Palate: powerful, flavourful, toasty, round tannins.

TRASCASAS 2007 TR
tempranillo

88 Colour: cherry, garnet rim. Nose: spicy, toasty, ripe fruit. Palate: ripe fruit, easy to drink, elegant.

VALVINOSO 2012 B
verdejo

85 Colour: bright straw. Nose: fresh fruit, white flowers. Palate: flavourful, fruity, good acidity, balanced.

VALVINOSO 2012 RD
80% tempranillo, 10% albillo, 10% verdejo

86 Colour: light cherry. Nose: red berry notes, floral. Palate: light-bodied, flavourful.

BODEGAS Y VIÑEDOS ROSAN

Santa María, 6
47270 Cigales (Valladolid)
☎: +34 983 580 006 - Fax: +34 983 580 006
rodriguezsanz@telefonica.net

ALBÉITAR 2011 T
tinto fino

88 Colour: bright cherry. Nose: sweet spices, creamy oak, fruit expression. Palate: flavourful, fruity, toasty, round tannins.

ROSAN 2012 RD
tinto fino, verdejo

86 Colour: light cherry. Nose: elegant, dried flowers, fragrant herbs, red berry notes. Palate: light-bodied, flavourful, good acidity.

BODEGAS Y VIÑEDOS SINFORIANO

San Pedro, 12
47194 Mucientes (Valladolid)
☎: +34 983 663 008 - Fax: +34 983 660 465
www.sinforianobodegas.com
sinfo@sinforianobodegas.com

50 VENDIMIAS DE SINFORIANO 2012 RD
tempranillo, verdejo, albillo

89 Colour: rose, purple rim. Nose: powerfull, ripe fruit, red berry notes, floral. Palate: powerful, fruity, fresh.

SINFO 2011 T ROBLE
tempranillo

86 Colour: bright cherry. Nose: sweet spices, creamy oak, warm, overripe fruit. Palate: flavourful, fruity, toasty, round tannins.

SINFORIANO 2008 TR
tempranillo

89 Colour: cherry, garnet rim. Nose: characterful, powerfull, toasty, aromatic coffee. Palate: fine bitter notes, round tannins.

SINFORIANO 2009 TC
100% tempranillo

91 Colour: cherry, garnet rim. Nose: spicy, creamy oak, toasty, complex, mineral, fruit expression. Palate: powerful, flavourful, toasty, round tannins.

SINFORIANO 2010 TC
100% tempranillo

89 Colour: cherry, garnet rim. Nose: spicy, creamy oak, toasty, powerfull, warm. Palate: powerful, toasty, round tannins.

C.H. VINOS DE CUBILLAS

Paseo Fuente la Teja, 31
47290 Cubillas de Santa Marta (Valladolid)
☎: +34 983 585 203 - Fax: +34 983 585 203
www.bodegaschvinosdecubillas.com
info@bodegaschvinosdecubillas.com

SELECCIÓN VIÑEDOS VIEJOS VALDECABADO 2006 TR
100% tempranillo

88 Colour: cherry, garnet rim. Nose: ripe fruit, spicy, creamy oak, toasty. Palate: powerful, flavourful, toasty, round tannins.

VALDECABADO 2012 RD
60% tempranillo, 40% albillo, garnacha

87 Colour: light cherry. Nose: medium intensity, red berry notes. Palate: flavourful, fruity.

COMPAÑÍA DE VINOS MIGUEL MARTÍN

Ctra. Burgos - Portugal, Km. 101
47290 Cubillas de Santa María (Valladolid)
☎: +34 983 250 319 - Fax: +34 983 250 329
www.ciadevinos.com
exportacion@ciadevinos.com

CASA CASTILLA 2012 RD
tempranillo, garnacha

86 Colour: rose, purple rim. Nose: red berry notes, ripe fruit, floral, fragrant herbs. Palate: fresh, fruity, flavourful, easy to drink.

VIÑA GOY 2012 RD
tempranillo, garnacha

87 Colour: rose, purple rim. Nose: lactic notes, red berry notes, ripe fruit, balsamic herbs. Palate: powerful, flavourful, fresh, fruity.

CONCEJO BODEGAS

Ctra. Valoria, Km. 3.6
47200 Valoria La Buena (Valladolid)
☎: +34 983 502 263 - Fax: +34 983 502 253
www.concejobodegas.com
info@concejobodegas.com

CARREDUEÑAS 2012 RD
tempranillo

89 Colour: rose, purple rim. Nose: powerfull, ripe fruit, red berry notes, floral. Palate: powerful, fruity, fresh.

CARREDUEÑAS 2012 RD FERMENTADO EN BARRICA
tempranillo

91 Colour: rose, purple rim. Nose: powerfull, ripe fruit, expressive, creamy oak, sweet spices. Palate: powerful, fruity, fresh.

CARREDUEÑAS DOLCE 2012 RD
tempranillo

88 Colour: deep cherry. Nose: powerfull, candied fruit, fruit preserve. Palate: sweet, good acidity.

VIÑA CONCEJO 2010 T

91 Colour: bright cherry. Nose: ripe fruit, sweet spices, creamy oak, fruit expression. Palate: flavourful, fruity, toasty, round tannins.

FINCA MUSEUM

Ctra. Cigales - Corcos, Km. 3
47270 Cigales (Valladolid)
☎: +34 983 581 029 - Fax: +34 983 581 030
www.bodegasmuseum.com
info@bodegasmuseum.com

MUSEUM 2010 TR
tempranillo

91 Colour: cherry, garnet rim. Nose: spicy, creamy oak, toasty, complex, fruit expression. Palate: powerful, flavourful, toasty, round tannins.

VINEA 2010 TC
tempranillo

91 Colour: bright cherry. Nose: ripe fruit, sweet spices, creamy oak. Palate: flavourful, fruity, toasty, round tannins.

FRUTOS VILLAR

Camino Los Barreros, s/n
47270 Cigales (Valladolid)
☎: +34 983 586 868 - Fax: +34 983 580 180
www.bodegasfrutosvillar.com
bodegasfrutosvillar@bodegasfrutosvillar.com

CALDERONA 2011 T
100% tempranillo

88 Colour: cherry, purple rim. Nose: fresh fruit, red berry notes, floral. Palate: flavourful, fruity, good acidity, round tannins.

CALDERONA 2007 TR
100% tempranillo

84

CONDE ANSÚREZ 2008 TC
100% tempranillo

88 Colour: cherry, garnet rim. Nose: ripe fruit, spicy, creamy oak, toasty. Palate: powerful, flavourful, toasty, round tannins.

CONDE ANSÚREZ 2011 T
100% tempranillo

87 Colour: very deep cherry. Nose: ripe fruit, red berry notes. Palate: flavourful, good structure.

CONDE ANSÚREZ 2012 RD
100% tempranillo

84

VIÑA CALDERONA 2012 RD
tempranillo

85 Colour: light cherry. Nose: ripe fruit, medium intensity. Palate: easy to drink, light-bodied.

GONZÁLEZ LARA S.A.

Ctra. Fuensaldaña s/n
47194 Mucientes (Valladolid)
☎: +34 983 587 881 - Fax: +34 983 587 881
www.bodegasgonzalezlara.com
gonzalezlara@bodegasgonzalezlara.com

FUENTE DEL CONDE 2012 RD
tinta del país, verdejo, garnacha

85 Colour: light cherry. Nose: candied fruit, overripe fruit. Palate: fine bitter notes, sweetness.

HIJOS DE MARCOS GÓMEZ S.L.

San Vicente, 39
47194 Mucientes (Valladolid)
☎: +34 625 115 619 - Fax: +34 983 587 764
www.salvueros.com
bodegas@salvueros.com

SALVUEROS 2012 RD
80% tempranillo, 20% verdejo, albillo

89 Colour: rose, purple rim. Nose: ripe fruit, red berry notes, floral, expressive, characterful. Palate: powerful, fruity, fresh.

CARRATRAVIESA 2012 RD
80% tempranillo, 20% garnacha, albillo, verdejo

89 Colour: rose, purple rim. Nose: powerfull, ripe fruit, red berry notes, floral, expressive. Palate: powerful, fruity, fresh.

LA LEGUA

Ctra. Cigales, km. 1
47194 Fuensaldaña (Valladolid)
☎: +34 983 583 244 - Fax: +34 983 583 172
www.lalegua.com
lalegua@lalegua.com

LA LEGUA 2009 TR
tempranillo

86 Colour: cherry, garnet rim. Nose: characterful, warm, toasty. Palate: spicy, ripe fruit.

LA LEGUA 2010 TC
tempranillo

87 Colour: deep cherry. Nose: overripe fruit, roasted coffee, aromatic coffee. Palate: fine bitter notes, balanced, harsh oak tannins.

LA LEGUA 2011 T ROBLE
tempranillo

87 Colour: deep cherry. Nose: overripe fruit, warm, toasty. Palate: spicy, fine bitter notes, correct.

LA LEGUA 2012 T
95% tempranillo, 5% garnacha

83

LA LEGUA CAPRICHO 2009 T
tempranillo

90 Colour: cherry, garnet rim. Nose: ripe fruit, spicy, complex, roasted coffee. Palate: powerful, flavourful, toasty, round tannins.

OVIDIO GARCÍA

Malpique, s/n
47270 Cigales (Valladolid)
☎: +34 628 509 475
www.ovidiogarcia.com
info@ovidiogarcia.com

OVIDIO GARCÍA 2007 TR
100% tempranillo

89 Colour: cherry, garnet rim. Nose: spicy, creamy oak, roasted coffee. Palate: powerful, flavourful, toasty, round tannins.

OVIDIO GARCÍA ESENCIA 2009 TC
100% tempranillo

90 Colour: cherry, garnet rim. Nose: ripe fruit, spicy, creamy oak, toasty, complex. Palate: powerful, flavourful, toasty, round tannins.

TRASLANZAS

Barrio de las Bodegas, s/n
47194 Mucientes (Valladolid)
☎: +34 639 641 123
www.traslanzas.com
traslanzas@traslanzas.com

TRASLANZAS 2009 T
tempranillo

90 Colour: cherry, garnet rim. Nose: ripe fruit, spicy, toasty, complex, aromatic coffee. Palate: powerful, flavourful, toasty, round tannins.

DO CONCA DE BARBERÀ / D.O.P.

LOCATION:

In the north of the province of Tarragona with a production area covering 14 municipalities, to which two new ones have recently been added: Savallà del Comtat and Vilanova de Prades.

CLIMATE:

Mediterranean and continental influences, as the vineyards occupy a river valley surrounded by mountain ranges without direct contact with the sea.

SOIL:

The soil is mainly brownish-grey and limy. The vines are cultivated on slopes protected by woodland. An important aspect is the altitude which gives the wines a fresh, light character.

GRAPE VARIETIES:

WHITE: *Macabeo, Parellada* (majority 3,300 Ha) *Chardonnay, Sauvignon Blanc* and *Viognier.*
RED: *Trepat, Ull de Llebre* (*Tempranillo*), *Garnatxa, Cabernet Sauvignon, Merlot, Syrah* and *Pinot Noir.*

FIGURES:

Vineyard surface: 3.599,6 – **Wine-Growers:** 857– **Wineries:** 21 – **2012 Harvest rating:** Very Good – **Production:** 1.419.000 litres – **Market percentages:** 74,9% domestic. 25,1% export

VINTAGE RATING PEÑÍNGUIDE				
2008	**2009**	**2010**	**2011**	**2012**
VERY GOOD	**GOOD**	**GOOD**	**GOOD**	**VERY GOOD**

CONSEJO REGULADOR
Torre del Portal de Sant Antoni - De la Volta, 2 - 43400 Montblanc ☎: +34 977 926 905 - Fax: +34 977 926 906
cr@doconcadebarbera.com   www.doconcadebarbera.com

ABADÍA DE POBLET

Passeig de l'Abat Conill, 6
43448 Poblet (Tarragona)
☎: +34 977 870 358
www.grupocodorniu.com
info@abadiadepoblet.es

ABADÍA DE POBLET 2009 T
100% pinot noir

84

INTRAMURS 2011 T
tempranillo, merlot, cabernet sauvignon

87 Colour: deep cherry. Nose: fruit preserve, dried herbs, spicy. Palate: good structure, round tannins.

LES MASIES DE POBLET 2010 T
100% pinot noir

85 Colour: light cherry. Nose: fruit preserve, wild herbs, spicy, waxy notes, wet leather. Palate: powerful, warm, spicy.

AGRÍCOLA DE BARBERÀ

Carrer Comerç, 40
43422 Barberà de la Conca (Tarragona)
☎: +34 977 887 035 - Fax: +34 977 887 035
www.coop-barbera.com
cobarbera@doconcadebarbera.com

CABANAL TREPAT 2011 T
100% trepat

86 Colour: cherry, purple rim. Nose: red berry notes, fruit liqueur notes, balsamic herbs. Palate: spicy, flavourful, easy to drink.

BODEGA SANSTRAVÉ

De la Conca, 10
43412 Solivella (Tarragona)
☎: +34 977 892 165 - Fax: +34 977 892 073
www.sanstrave.com
bodega@sanstrave.com

**SANSTRAVÉ FINCA GASSET
CHARDONNAY 2011 BFB**
chardonnay

88 Colour: bright yellow. Nose: powerfull, ripe fruit, sweet spices, creamy oak, fragrant herbs. Palate: rich, flavourful, fresh, good acidity.

**SANSTRAVÉ FINCA GASSET TEMPRANILLO
CABERNET 2002 TGR**
tempranillo, cabernet sauvignon

89 Colour: pale ruby, brick rim edge. Nose: elegant, spicy, fine reductive notes, wet leather, aged wood nuances, fruit liqueur notes. Palate: spicy, fine tannins, elegant, long.

SANSTRAVÉ PARTIDA DELS JUEUS 2009 TC
merlot, garnacha, trepat, tempranillo, cabernet sauvignon

90 Colour: cherry, garnet rim. Nose: ripe fruit, spicy, creamy oak, toasty, complex. Palate: powerful, flavourful, toasty, round tannins.

BODEGAS BELLOD

Avda. Mare de Déu de Montserrat, 6
8970 Sant Joan Despí (Barcelona)
☎: +34 933 731 151 - Fax: +34 933 731 354
www.bodegasbellod.com
bodegasbellod@bodegasbellod.com

MAS DEL NEN VAILET 2012 B
moscatel

85 Colour: golden. Nose: powerfull, floral, candied fruit, fragrant herbs. Palate: flavourful, fresh, fruity, good acidity.

MAS DEL NEN VALL ROJA 2010 T
46% cabernet sauvignon, 20% garnacha, 20% merlot, 14% syrah

88 Colour: cherry, garnet rim. Nose: red berry notes, ripe fruit, roasted coffee, creamy oak. Palate: powerful, flavourful, toasty.

PRINCIPAT 2012 RD
garnacha

85 Colour: rose, purple rim. Nose: powerfull, ripe fruit, red berry notes, floral. Palate: powerful, fruity, fresh.

CASTELL D'OR

Mare Rafols, 3- 1º 4º
8720 Vilafranca del Penedès (Barcelona)
☎: +34 938 905 446 - Fax: +34 938 905 446
www.castelldor.com
castelldor@castelldor.com

CASTELL DE LA COMANDA 2006 T
100% tempranillo

84

CASTELL DE LA COMANDA 2008 TR
100% cabernet sauvignon

87 Colour: cherry, garnet rim. Nose: ripe fruit, spicy, toasty, balsamic herbs. Palate: powerful, flavourful, long.

CASTELL DE LA COMANDA 2011 T
100% tempranillo

86 Colour: bright cherry. Nose: ripe fruit, sweet spices, balsamic herbs, roasted coffee. Palate: flavourful, fruity, toasty.

CASTELL DE LA COMANDA 2012 B
20% parellada, 80% macabeo

82

CASTELL DE LA COMANDA 2012 RD
100% trepat

85 Colour: light cherry. Nose: candied fruit, fragrant herbs, red berry notes. Palate: light-bodied, flavourful, easy to drink.

FRANCOLI 2006 TR
60% cabernet sauvignon, 40% tempranillo

85 Colour: bright cherry. Nose: ripe fruit, sweet spices, creamy oak. Palate: flavourful, fruity, toasty.

FRANCOLI 2008 TC
60% cabernet sauvignon, 40% tempranillo

85 Colour: cherry, garnet rim. Nose: ripe fruit, scrubland, creamy oak. Palate: powerful, flavourful, spicy.

FRANCOLI 2011 T
50% trepat, 50% tempranillo

86 Colour: bright cherry. Nose: ripe fruit, sweet spices, creamy oak. Palate: flavourful, fruity, correct.

FRANCOLI 2012 B
20% parellada, 80% macabeo

82

FRANCOLI 2012 RD
100% trepat

84

CELLER CARLES ANDREU

Sant Sebastià, 19
43423 Pira (Tarragona)
☎: +34 977 887 404 - Fax: +34 977 887 427
www.cavandreu.com
celler@cavandreu.com

PARELLADA CARLES ANDREU 2012 B
100% parellada

87 Colour: bright yellow. Nose: powerfull, ripe fruit, sweet spices, citrus fruit. Palate: rich, smoky aftertaste, flavourful, fresh, good acidity.

VINO TINTO TREPAT CARLES ANDREU 2011 T
100% trepat

90 Colour: bright cherry. Nose: creamy oak, red berry notes, ripe fruit, floral, earthy notes. Palate: flavourful, fruity, toasty, round tannins.

CELLER GUSPÍ

Avda. Arnau de Ponç, 10
43423 Pira (Tarragona)
☎: +34 636 816 724
www.guspi.com
viguspi@gmail.com

GUSPI BLANCTRESC 2011 B
60% macabeo, 30% chardonnay, 10% sauvignon blanc

84

GUSPI EMBIGATS DE LA MARÍA 2009 T
100% tempranillo

88 Colour: cherry, garnet rim. Nose: ripe fruit, spicy, creamy oak, toasty, balsamic herbs. Palate: powerful, flavourful, toasty.

GUSPI PINETELL 2010 T
100% merlot

87 Colour: light cherry. Nose: red berry notes, ripe fruit, grassy, creamy oak. Palate: flavourful, spicy, balsamic.

GUSPI TREPAT 2012 T
100% trepat

87 Colour: cherry, purple rim. Nose: red berry notes, ripe fruit, floral. Palate: powerful, flavourful, easy to drink.

CELLER MAS FORASTER

Camino Ermita de Sant Josep, s/n
43400 Montblanc (Tarragona)
☎: +34 977 860 229 - Fax: +34 977 875 037
www.josepforaster.com
info@josepforaster.com

JOSEP FORASTER 2010 TC
40% cabernet sauvignon, 25% tempranillo, 25% syrah, 10% trepat

86 Colour: cherry, garnet rim. Nose: ripe fruit, spicy, toasty, aromatic coffee, balsamic herbs, fine reductive notes. Palate: powerful, flavourful, toasty.

JOSEP FORASTER BLANC DEL COSTER 2012 B
90% macabeo, 10% garnacha blanca

84

JOSEP FORASTER BLANC SELECCIÓ 2011 BFB
50% garnacha blanca, 40% macabeo, 10% chardonnay

86 Colour: bright yellow. Nose: fruit preserve, dried herbs, roasted coffee. Palate: powerful, flavourful, spicy, toasty.

JOSEP FORASTER COLLITA 2012 T
90% tempranillo, 10% cabernet sauvignon

88 Colour: cherry, purple rim. Nose: expressive, fresh fruit, red berry notes, floral, lactic notes. Palate: flavourful, fruity, good acidity.

JOSEP FORASTER SELECCIÓ 2007 TR
90% cabernet sauvignon, 10% tempranillo

89 Colour: cherry, garnet rim. Nose: ripe fruit, spicy, creamy oak, toasty, fine reductive notes. Palate: powerful, flavourful, toasty, balanced.

JOSEP FORASTER TREPAT 2011 T
100% trepat

88 Colour: light cherry. Nose: fresh fruit, red berry notes, floral, sweet spices. Palate: flavourful, fruity, good acidity.

CELLER MOLÍ DELS CAPELLANS

Celler de Viveristes de Barberà de la Conca
43422 Barberà de la Conca (Tarragona)
☎: +34 651 034 221
www.molidelscapellans.com
info@molidelscapellans.com

MOLÍ DELS CAPELLANS 2011 BFB
100% chardonnay

87 Colour: bright yellow. Nose: powerfull, ripe fruit, sweet spices, creamy oak, fragrant herbs. Palate: rich, smoky aftertaste, flavourful, fresh, good acidity.

MOLÍ DELS CAPELLANS 2011 T
100% trepat

89 Colour: bright cherry. Nose: ripe fruit, sweet spices, creamy oak, fragrant herbs, earthy notes. Palate: flavourful, fruity, spicy.

MOLÍ DELS CAPELLANS SELECCIÓ 2010 T
syrah, cabernet sauvignon, ull de llebre

87 Colour: cherry, garnet rim. Nose: red berry notes, ripe fruit, balsamic herbs, spicy. Palate: powerful, flavourful, toasty.

CELLER VEGA AIXALÁ

De la Font, 11
43439 Vilanova de Prades (Tarragona)
☎: +34 636 519 821 - Fax: +34 977 869 019
www.vegaaixala.com
info@vegaaixala.com

VEGA AIXALÁ 2012 T
tempranillo, garnacha, syrah

89 Colour: cherry, purple rim. Nose: expressive, fresh fruit, red berry notes, floral, lactic notes. Palate: flavourful, fruity, good acidity.

VEGA AIXALÁ AVENC 2012 B
garnacha blanca, chardonnay

84

VEGA AIXALÁ VIERN 2009 TC
cabernet sauvignon, garnacha, syrah, merlot, tempranillo

86 Colour: cherry, garnet rim. Nose: ripe fruit, spicy, grassy, wet leather, cigar. Palate: powerful, flavourful, toasty.

CELLER VIDBERTUS

Anselm Clavé, 13
43440 L'Espluga de Francolí (Tarragona)
☎: +34 626 330 511
www.vidbertus.com
info@vidbertus.com

996 2010 T
garnacha, merlot, monastrell

89 Colour: bright cherry. Nose: ripe fruit, sweet spices, creamy oak, expressive. Palate: flavourful, fruity, toasty.

CLOS MONTBLANC

Ctra. Montblanc-Barbera, s/n
43422 Barberà de la Conca (Tarragona)
☎: +34 977 887 030 - Fax: +34 977 887 032
www.closmontblanc.com
club@closmontblanc.com

CLOS MONTBLANC MASÍA LES COMES 2007 TR
cabernet sauvignon, merlot

89 Colour: pale ruby, brick rim edge. Nose: elegant, spicy, fine reductive notes, wet leather, aged wood nuances. Palate: spicy, elegant, long.

CLOS MONTBLANC MERLOT 2009 TC
100% merlot

87 Colour: cherry, garnet rim. Nose: ripe fruit, spicy, grassy, fine reductive notes. Palate: powerful, flavourful, toasty.

CLOS MONTBLANC PINOT NOIR 2011 TC
100% pinot noir

88 Colour: light cherry. Nose: red berry notes, fruit liqueur notes, spicy, balsamic herbs. Palate: flavourful, spicy, long.

CLOS MONTBLANC SAUVIGNON BLANC 2012 B
100% sauvignon blanc

86 Colour: bright straw. Nose: ripe fruit, floral, fragrant herbs, tropical fruit. Palate: fresh, fruity, flavourful.

CLOS MONTBLANC SYRAH 2010 T
100% syrah

87 Colour: cherry, garnet rim. Nose: ripe fruit, balsamic herbs, spicy. Palate: flavourful, correct, balanced.

CLOS MONTBLANC XIPELLA BLANC 2012 B
macabeo, parellada, sauvignon blanc

88 Colour: bright straw. Nose: fresh, fresh fruit, white flowers, citrus fruit. Palate: flavourful, fruity, good acidity, balanced.

GRAN CLOS MONTBLANC UNIC TREPAT 2010
trepat

89 Colour: light cherry. Nose: red berry notes, ripe fruit, balsamic herbs, earthy notes, spicy. Palate: powerful, flavourful, spicy.

GATZARA VINS

Josep M. Tossas, 47. 1º-2º
43400 Montblanc (Tarragona)
☎: +34 977 861 175 - Fax: +34 977 861 175
viverdecelleristes.concadebarbera.cat
info@gatzaravins.com

GATZARA 2010 TC
68% merlot, 32% ull de llebre

87 Colour: cherry, garnet rim. Nose: ripe fruit, spicy, toasty, complex, balsamic herbs, scrubland. Palate: powerful, flavourful, toasty, round tannins.

GATZARA 2012 T
100% trepat

92 Colour: deep cherry. Nose: mineral, expressive, scrubland. Palate: spicy, long, balsamic.

GATZARA BLANC 2012 B
65% macabeo, chardonnay

90 Colour: bright yellow. Nose: ripe fruit, sweet spices, creamy oak, fragrant herbs. Palate: rich, flavourful, fresh, good acidity.

MIGUEL TORRES S.A.

Miguel Torres i Carbó, 6
8720 Vilafranca del Penedès (Barcelona)
☎: +34 938 177 400 - Fax: +34 938 177 444
www.torres.es
mailadmin@torres.es

GRANS MURALLES 2010 TR
monastrell, garnacha, garró, samsó, cariñena

94 Colour: very deep cherry. Nose: expressive, characterful, complex, powerfull, dark chocolate. Palate: spicy, long, balanced, powerful tannins, ripe fruit.

MILMANDA 2010 B
chardonnay

91 Colour: bright golden. Nose: ripe fruit, powerfull, toasty, aged wood nuances, citrus fruit, dried flowers. Palate: flavourful, fruity, spicy, toasty, long, balanced, elegant.

RENDÉ MASDÉU

Avda. Catalunya, 44
43440 L'Espluga de Francolí (Tarragona)
☎: +34 977 871 361 - Fax: +34 977 871 361
www.rendemasdeu.cat
celler@rendemasdeu.cat

RENDÉ MASDEU 2012 RD
syrah

88 Colour: light cherry. Nose: powerfull, ripe fruit, red berry notes, floral, expressive. Palate: powerful, fruity, fresh.

RENDÉ MASDEU ARNAU 2010 T
syrah

89 Colour: bright cherry. Nose: ripe fruit, sweet spices, creamy oak, expressive. Palate: flavourful, fruity, toasty, round tannins.

RENDÉ MASDÉU MANUELA VENTOSA 2009 T
70% cabernet sauvignon, 30% syrah

90 Colour: cherry, garnet rim. Nose: ripe fruit, spicy, creamy oak, toasty, complex. Palate: powerful, flavourful, toasty, round tannins.

RENDÉ MASDÉU TREPAT DEL JORDIET 2012 T
trepat

89 Colour: light cherry. Nose: floral, fragrant herbs, red berry notes, mineral. Palate: light-bodied, fresh, fruity, flavourful.

ROSA MARÍA TORRES

Avda. Anguera, 2
43424 Sarral (Tarragona)
☎: +34 977 890 013 - Fax: +34 977 890 173
www.rosamariatorres.com
info@rosamariatorres.com

RD ROURE 2011 T
cabernet sauvignon, merlot

85 Colour: cherry, garnet rim. Nose: ripe fruit, floral, balsamic herbs, creamy oak. Palate: flavourful, spicy, correct.

SUSEL 2012 T
cabernet sauvignon

86 Colour: cherry, purple rim. Nose: red berry notes, balsamic herbs, fragrant herbs. Palate: flavourful, fresh, balsamic.

SUSEL VIOGNIER 2012 B
viognier

85 Colour: bright straw. Nose: fresh, fresh fruit, white flowers, candied fruit. Palate: flavourful, fruity, easy to drink.

VINYA PLANS 2011 TC
cabernet franc, cabernet sauvignon, syrah

88 Colour: cherry, garnet rim. Nose: ripe fruit, spicy, creamy oak, toasty, grassy. Palate: powerful, flavourful, toasty, balsamic.

VIOGNIER 2010 BFB
viognier

88 Colour: bright yellow. Nose: powerfull, ripe fruit, sweet spices, fragrant herbs. Palate: rich, flavourful, fresh, good acidity.

SUCCÉS VINÍCOLA

Vinyols, 3
43400 Montblanc (Tarragona)
☎: +34 677 144 629
www.succesvinicola.com
succesvinicola@gmail.com

SUCCÉS EL MENTIDER 2011 T
100% trepat

90 Colour: bright cherry, garnet rim. Nose: ripe fruit, sweet spices, creamy oak, mineral, balsamic herbs. Palate: flavourful, fruity, toasty, balanced, elegant.

SUCCÉS LA CUCA DE LLUM 2012 T
100% trepat

89 Colour: cherry, garnet rim. Nose: mineral, red berry notes, ripe fruit, expressive. Palate: powerful, flavourful, spicy, balsamic, balanced.

TINTORÉ DE VIMBODÍ I POBLET

Copèrnic, 44
8021 (Barcelona)
☎: +34 932 096 101 - Fax: +34 934 145 236
oriol@tinto-re.com

RE 2010 TC
garnacha, cariñena, cabernet sauvignon

91 Colour: cherry, garnet rim. Nose: ripe fruit, spicy, creamy oak, toasty, earthy notes. Palate: powerful, flavourful, toasty, long.

VINÍCOLA DE SARRAL Í SELECCIÓ DE CREDIT

Avinguda de la Conca, 33
43424 Sarral (Tarragona)
☎: +34 977 890 031 - Fax: +34 977 890 136
www.cava-portell.com
cavaportell@covisal.es

PORTELL 2006 TR
50% merlot, 40% cabernet sauvignon, 10% tempranillo

87 Colour: cherry, garnet rim. Nose: ripe fruit, spicy, creamy oak, toasty. Palate: powerful, flavourful, toasty, round tannins.

PORTELL 2012 BLANCO DE AGUJA
55% macabeo, 45% parellada

83

PORTELL BLANC DE BLANCS 2012 B
85% macabeo, 15% parellada

85 Colour: bright straw. Nose: fresh, fresh fruit, white flowers, expressive. Palate: flavourful, fruity, good acidity.

PORTELL SELECCIÓ 2º ANY 2011 T
70% ull de llebre, 15% cabernet sauvignon, 15% merlot

85 Colour: cherry, garnet rim. Nose: ripe fruit, spicy, balsamic herbs, fine reductive notes. Palate: powerful, flavourful, spicy.

PORTELL TREPAT 2012 RD
100% trepat

87 Colour: rose, purple rim. Nose: powerfull, ripe fruit, red berry notes, floral. Palate: powerful, fruity, fresh, easy to drink.

PORTELL TREPAT 2012 ROSADO DE AGUJA
100% trepat

85 Colour: light cherry. Nose: candied fruit, floral, lactic notes. Palate: fresh, fruity, easy to drink.

VINS DE PEDRA

Ctra. de Montblanc a Rojals s/n
43400 Montblanc (Tarragona)
☎: +34 630 405 118
celler@vinsdepedra.es

L'ORNI 2012 B
chardonnay

89 Colour: bright yellow. Nose: white flowers, fragrant herbs, ripe fruit, mineral. Palate: elegant, powerful, flavourful, complex.

LA MUSA 2011 T
merlot, cabernet sauvignon

88 Colour: cherry, garnet rim. Nose: fruit preserve, floral, earthy notes, spicy. Palate: powerful, flavourful, balanced.

Consejo Regulador
DO Boundary

HUELVA

LOCATION:

In the south east of Huelva. It occupies the plain of Bajo Guadalquivir. The production area covers the municipal areas of Almonte, Beas, Bollullos Par del Condado, Bonares, Chucena, Gibraleón, Hinojos, La Palma del Condado, Lucena del Puerto, Manzanilla, Moguer, Niebla, Palos de la Frontera, Rociana del Condado, San Juan del Puerto, Villalba del Alcor, Villarrasa and Trigueros.

CLIMATE:

Mediterranean in nature, with certain Atlantic influences. The winters and springs are fairly mild, with long hot summers. The average annual temperature is 18 °C, and the average rainfall per year is around 550 mm, with a relative humidity of between 60% and 80%.

SOIL:

In general, flat and slightly rolling terrain, with fairly neutral soils of medium fertility. The soil is mainly reddish, brownish-grey with alluvium areas in the proximity of the Guadalquivir.

GRAPE VARIETIES:

WHITE: *Zalema* (majority with 86% of vineyards), *Palomino, Listán de Huelva, Garrido Fino, Moscatel de Alejandría* and *Pedro Ximénez*.
RED: *Merlot, Syrah, Tempranillo, Cabernet Sauvignon* and *Cabernet Franc*.

FIGURES:

Vineyard surface: 2.413 – **Wine-Growers:** 1.512 – **Wineries:** 30 – **2012 Harvest rating:** Excellent – **Production:** 19.548.124 litres – **Market percentages:** 90% domestic. 10% export

2008	2009	2010	2011	2012
VERY GOOD	GOOD	GOOD	GOOD	VERY GOOD

CONSEJO REGULADOR
Plaza Ildefonso Pinto, s/n. - 21710 Bollullos Par del Condado (Huelva) ☎: +34 959 410 322 - Fax: +34 959 413 859
cr@condadodehuelva.es   www.condadodehuelva.es

AGROALIMENTARIA VIRGEN DEL ROCÍO

Avda. de Cabezudos, s/n
21730 Almonte (Huelva)
☎: +34 959 406 146 - Fax: +34 959 407 052
www.raigal.com
administracion@raigal.com

RAIGAL 2012 B
100% zalema

86 Colour: bright straw. Nose: fresh, balanced, wild herbs. Palate: balanced, fruity, good acidity.

TEJARES CONDADO DULCE GE
100% zalema

82

TEJARES CONDADO PÁLIDO FI
100% zalema

86 Colour: bright yellow. Nose: faded flowers, dry nuts, pungent. Palate: flavourful, balanced, fine bitter notes.

TEJARES CONDADO VIEJO VINO DE LICOR
100% zalema

86 Colour: light mahogany. Nose: balanced, candied fruit, sweet spices, pattiserie. Palate: flavourful, balanced, fine bitter notes.

BODEGAS ANDRADE

Avda. Coronación, 35
21710 Bollullos del Condado (Huelva)
☎: +34 959 410 106 - Fax: +34 959 410 305
www.bodegasandrade.es
informacion@bodegasandrade.es

ANDRADE PEDRO XIMÉNEZ 1985 GE RESERVA
100% pedro ximénez

87 Colour: mahogany. Nose: pattiserie, cocoa bean, sweet spices, dried fruit, honeyed notes. Palate: spicy, correct, sweet.

ANDRADE VINO NARANJA GE
moscatel de alejandría

88 Colour: mahogany. Nose: candied fruit, pattiserie, citrus fruit. Palate: spicy, fruity, flavourful, sweet.

DOCEAÑERO CR
pedro ximénez, zalema

88 Colour: light mahogany. Nose: dried fruit, pattiserie, balanced. Palate: good structure, fine bitter notes, spicy.

DOCEAÑERO OLOROSO CONDADO VIEJO
zalema

87 Colour: light mahogany. Nose: powerfull, sweet spices, dry nuts, candied fruit. Palate: full, good structure, balanced, fine bitter notes.

BODEGAS CONTRERAS RUIZ

Almonte, 5
21720 Rociana del Condado (Huelva)
☎: +34 959 416 426 - Fax: +34 959 416 744
www.bodegascontreras.com
contreras@bodegascontreras.com

VIÑA BARREDERO 2012 B
100% zalema

87 Colour: bright yellow. Nose: floral, fruit expression, dried herbs, balanced. Palate: flavourful, good acidity, balanced.

BODEGAS DEL DIEZMO NUEVO

Sor Ángela de la Cruz, 56
21800 Moguer (Huelva)
☎: +34 959 370 004 - Fax: +34 959 370 004
www.bodegadiezmonuevo.com
info@bodegadiezmonuevo.com

MELQUÍADES SÁENZ B

86 Colour: dark mahogany. Nose: powerfull, pattiserie, dark chocolate, candied fruit. Palate: ripe fruit, spicy, long.

VIÑA EL PATRIARCA S/C B
zalema

82

BODEGAS DÍAZ

Pol. Ind. El Lirio Toneleros, 6
21710 Bollullos del Condado (Huelva)
☎: +34 959 410 340 - Fax: +34 959 408 095
www.bodegasdiaz.com
diaz@bodegasdiaz.com

1955 CONDADO PÁLIDO CONDADO PÁLIDO
palomino

86 Colour: bright straw. Nose: medium intensity, dry nuts. Palate: flavourful, fine bitter notes, good acidity, spicy.

1955 CONDADO VIEJO
zalema, listán blanco

86 Colour: mahogany. Nose: cocoa bean, pattiserie, candied fruit, balanced. Palate: fine bitter notes, long, spicy.

DAIZ S/C T
tempranillo, syrah

84

GRAN ONUBIS PEDRO XIMÉNEZ VIEJO PX
pedro ximénez

88 Colour: mahogany. Nose: fruit liqueur notes, dried fruit, pattiserie, toasty. Palate: sweet, rich, unctuous, powerful.

NARANJA DE ORO VINO NARANJA
zalema

86 Colour: mahogany. Nose: candied fruit, citrus fruit, faded flowers. Palate: flavourful, fruity, spicy, sweet.

ONUBIS GE
moscatel de alejandría

86 Colour: dark mahogany. Nose: cocoa bean, sweet spices, pattiserie. Palate: sweet, fruity, balanced.

VADO DEL QUEMA S/C B
100% zalema

86 Colour: bright straw. Nose: ripe fruit, floral, balanced. Palate: easy to drink, balanced, good acidity.

BODEGAS IGLESIAS

Teniente Merchante, 2
21710 Bollullos del Condado (Huelva)
☎: +34 959 410 439 - Fax: +34 959 410 463
www.bodegasiglesias.com
bodegasiglesias@bodegasiglesias.com

LETRADO SOLERA 1992 GE SOLERA
100% zalema

83

PAR VINO NARANJA VINO DE LICOR
85% zalema, 15% pedro ximénez

88 Colour: mahogany. Nose: fresh, citrus fruit, floral, fruit liqueur notes. Palate: flavourful, balanced, good acidity, sweet.

RICAHEMBRA SOLERA 1980 GE
85% zalema, 15% pedro ximénez

86 Colour: dark mahogany. Nose: powerfull, fruit liqueur notes, spicy, fruit liqueur notes. Palate: flavourful, sweet, unctuous, long.

UZ CIEN X CIEN UVA ZALEMA 2012 B JOVEN
100% zalema

86 Colour: bright straw. Nose: fresh fruit, wild herbs, citrus fruit, floral. Palate: fresh, balanced, fine bitter notes, good acidity.

UZT TARDÍA 2012 B
100% zalema

85 Colour: bright yellow. Nose: floral, medium intensity, balanced, tropical fruit. Palate: correct, good acidity, easy to drink.

BODEGAS OLIVEROS

Rábida, 12
21710 Bollullos Par del Condado (Huelva)
☎: +34 959 410 057 - Fax: +34 959 410 057
www.bodegasoliveros.com
oliveros@bodegasoliveros.com

JUAN JAIME 2012 B
100% zalema

88 Colour: bright straw. Nose: medium intensity, fresh fruit, dried flowers, balanced. Palate: fruity, fine bitter notes, good acidity.

OLIVEROS 2010 TC
70% tempranillo, 30% syrah

85 Colour: cherry, garnet rim. Nose: fruit preserve, balanced, sweet spices. Palate: flavourful, correct, fruity.

OLIVEROS OLOROSO OL
zalema, palomino, garrido

82

OLIVEROS PEDRO XIMÉNEZ PX
pedro ximénez

90 Colour: dark mahogany. Nose: complex, dried fruit, pattiserie, varietal, dark chocolate. Palate: sweet, rich, unctuous, powerful, long.

OLIVEROS VINO NARANJA B
zalema, pedro ximénez

85 Colour: mahogany. Nose: fruit liqueur notes, wild herbs, spicy, citrus fruit. Palate: sweet, good finish.

BODEGAS RAPOSO
(JOSÉ ANTONIO RAPOSO)

Miguel Hernández, 31
21710 Bollullos Par del Condado (Huelva)
☎: +34 959 410 565 - Fax: +34 959 413 821
bodegas-raposo@terra.es

AVELLANERO CREAM GE
zalema, palomino, garrido fino

85 Colour: dark mahogany. Nose: candied fruit, sweet spices, fruit liqueur notes, cocoa bean. Palate: flavourful, sweet, correct.

AVELLANERO OLOROSO
CONDADO VIEJO CRIANZA
palomino, garrido, zalema

84

M.F. LA NUEZ CONDADO PÁLIDO
listán, garrido, palomino

86 Colour: bright straw. Nose: faded flowers, fresh, dry nuts. Palate: fine bitter notes, correct, balanced.

RAPOSO MOSCATEL PASAS GE
moscatel de alejandría, zalema

84

BODEGAS SAUCI

Doctor Fleming, 1
21710 Bollullos del Condado (Huelva)
☎: +34 959 410 524 - Fax: +34 959 410 331
www.bodegassauci.es
sauci@bodegassauci.es

ESPINAPURA CONDADO PÁLIDO
100% palomino

87 Colour: bright straw. Nose: fresh fruit, medium intensity, saline. Palate: flavourful, fine bitter notes, balanced, fresh.

RIODIEL SOLERA 1980 CONDÁDO VIEJO
palomino

85 Colour: light mahogany. Nose: powerfull, balanced, candied fruit, varnish, sweet spices. Palate: balanced, fine bitter notes, long.

S' NARANJA VINO DE LICOR
80% pedro ximénez, 20% palomino

88 Colour: mahogany. Nose: faded flowers, medium intensity, candied fruit, pattiserie. Palate: fruity, flavourful, ripe fruit.

S' PX DULCE NATURAL VINO DE LICOR
100% pedro ximénez

89 Colour: mahogany. Nose: candied fruit, aromatic coffee, dark chocolate. Palate: flavourful, sweet, balanced, unctuous, concentrated.

S' PX SOLERA 1989 PX
100% pedro ximénez

91 Colour: dark mahogany. Nose: complex, fruit liqueur notes, dried fruit, pattiserie, toasty. Palate: sweet, rich, unctuous, powerful, concentrated.

SAUCI 2012 B JOVEN
100% zalema

86 Colour: bright straw. Nose: wild herbs, fresh fruit, white flowers, medium intensity. Palate: balanced, good acidity, easy to drink.

SAUCI CREAM SOLERA 1980 CR
75% palomino, 25% pedro ximénez

85 Colour: mahogany. Nose: pattiserie, sweet spices, cocoa bean, candied fruit. Palate: powerful, flavourful, balanced.

SAUCI VENDIMIA TARDÍA 2012 B JOVEN
100% zalema

84

CONVENTO DE MORAÑINA

Avda. de la Paz, 43
21710 Bollullos Par del Condado (Huelva)
☎: +34 959 412 250
www.bodegasconvento.com
bodega@bodegasconvento.com

CONVENTO DE MORAÑINA 2011 T ROBLE
syrah, tempranillo

85 Colour: cherry, garnet rim. Nose: ripe fruit, sweet spices, toasty. Palate: fruity, correct, balanced.

CONVENTO DE MORAÑINA 2012 B
100% zalema

86 Colour: bright straw. Nose: wild herbs, fresh fruit, medium intensity. Palate: correct, good acidity, fine bitter notes.

CONVENTO NARANJA 2008 SEMIDULCE
100% zalema

89 Colour: mahogany. Nose: expressive, characterful, fruit liqueur notes, citrus fruit, pattiserie, cocoa bean. Palate: flavourful, fruity, sweet, long.

CONVENTO PX RESERVA
100% pedro ximénez

90 Colour: dark mahogany. Nose: varietal, expressive, powerfull, dried fruit, sweet spices. Palate: unctuous, sweet, full, flavourful, long.

SECRETO DEL CONVENTO 1960 CR
palomino, listán blanco, pedro ximénez

90 Colour: mahogany. Nose: balanced, expressive, acetaldehyde, candied fruit, cocoa bean. Palate: flavourful, good structure, full, long.

MARQUÉS DE VILLALÚA

Ctra. A-472, Km. 25,2
21860 Villalba del Alcor (Huelva)
☎: +34 959 420 905 - Fax: +34 959 421 141
www.marquesdevillalua.com
santiago@marquesdevillalua.com

AGUADULCE DE VILLALÚA 2012 SEMIDULCE
zalema, moscatel

83

MARQUÉS DE VILLALÚA 2012 B
zalema, moscatel

87 Colour: bright straw. Nose: medium intensity, wild herbs, floral. Palate: correct, good acidity, good finish.

MARQUÉS DE VILLALÚA COLECCIÓN 1000 S/C B
zalema, moscatel, sauvignon blanc

87 Colour: bright yellow. Nose: medium intensity, citrus fruit, floral. Palate: fruity, good acidity, balanced.

SANTA AGUEDA VINO NARANJA
zalema, moscatel

86 Colour: light mahogany. Nose: expressive, citrus fruit, fruit liqueur notes, sweet spices. Palate: balanced, easy to drink.

NUESTRA SEÑORA DEL SOCORRO

Carril de los Moriscos, 72
21720 Rociana del Condado (Huelva)
☎: +34 959 416 108 - Fax: +34 959 416 108
jl63@nuestrasenoradelsocorro.com

DON FREDE 2008 TC
tempranillo, syrah

86 Colour: deep cherry, garnet rim. Nose: fruit preserve, powerfull, sweet spices. Palate: flavourful, good structure.

DON FREDE 2012 RD
tempranillo

81

DON FREDE 2012 T
70% tempranillo, 30% syrah

84

VIÑAGAMO SECO 2012 B
zalema

85 Colour: bright straw. Nose: fresh, citrus fruit, wild herbs. Palate: flavourful, fruity, good acidity.

VIÑAGAMO SEMIDULCE 2012 B

81

PRIMER CONSORCIO DE BODEGUEROS ESPAÑOLES

Torno, 27
11500 El Puerto de Santa María (Cádiz)
☎: +34 956 056 642 - Fax: +34 956 056 641
www.vinodenaranja.com
admin@emc3.es

ORANGE TREE (VINO NARANJA) 2012
zalema

87 Colour: light mahogany. Nose: balanced, floral, citrus fruit, ripe fruit. Palate: sweet, flavourful, rich, balanced.

VINÍCOLA DEL CONDADO S. COOP. AND.

San José, ?
21710 Bollullos del Condado (Huelva)
☎: +34 959 410 261 - Fax: +34 959 410 171
www.vinicoladelcondado.com
comercial@vinicoladelcondado.com

LANTERO ROBLE SYRAH 2009 T ROBLE
syrah

83

MIORO 2012 B
zalema

84

MIORO GRAN SELECCIÓN 2012 B
75% zalema, 25% moscatel

86 Colour: bright straw. Nose: fresh fruit, white flowers, wild herbs, medium intensity. Palate: balanced, good acidity.

MISTERIO DULCE GE
zalema

84

MISTERIO OLOROSO SECO OL
zalema

87 Colour: light mahogany. Nose: medium intensity, dry nuts, balanced. Palate: fine bitter notes, long, spicy.

VDM ORANGE
50% zalema, 50% moscatel

88 Colour: old gold. Nose: candied fruit, pattiserie, sweet spices, balanced, expressive, citrus fruit. Palate: rich, flavourful, long.

LOCATION:

In the southern regions of Lleida, and a few municipal areas of Tarragona. It covers the sub-regions of: Artesa de Segre, Garrigues, Pallars Jussà, Raimat, Segrià and Valls del Riu Corb.

CLIMATE:

Rather dry continental climate in all the sub-regions, with minimum temperatures often dropping below zero in winter, summers with maximum temperatures in excess of 35° on occasions, and fairly low rainfall figures: 385 mm/year in Lleida and 450 mm/year in the remaining regions.

SOIL:

The soil is mainly calcareous and granitic in nature. Most of the vineyards are situated on soils with a poor organic matter content, brownish-grey limestone, with a high percentage of limestone and very little clay.

GRAPE VARIETIES:

WHITE: PREFERRED: *Macabeo, Xarel·lo, Parellada, Chardonnay, Garnacha Blanca, Moscatel de Grano Menudo, Malvasía, Gewürtztraminer, Albariño, Riesling* and *Sauvignon Blanc.*
RED: PREFERRED: *Garnacha Negra, Ull de Llebre* (*Tempranillo*), *Cabernet Sauvignon, Merlot, Monastrell, Trepat, Samsó, Pinot Noir* and *Syrah.*

SUB-REGIONS:

Artesa de Segre: Located on the foothills of the Sierra de Montsec, just north of the Noguera region, it has mainly limestone soils. **Urgell:** Located in the central part of the province of Lleida, at an average altitude of 350 meters, its climate is a mix of mediterranean and continental features. **Garrigues:** To the southeast of the province of Lleida, it is a region with a complex topography and marl soils. Its higher altitude is near 700 meters. **Pallars Jussà:** Located in the Pyrenees, it is the northernmost sub-zone. Soils are predominantly limestone and its type of climate mediterranean with strong continental influence. **Raimat:** Located in the province of Lleida and with predominantly limestone soils, it has a mediterranean climate with continental features, with predominantly cold winters and very hot summers. **Segrià:** Is the central sub-zone of the DO, with limestone soils. **Valls del Riu Corb:** Located in the southeast of the DO, its climate is primarily mediterranean-continental softened by both the beneficial effect of the sea breezes (called marinada in the region) and "el Seré", a dry sea-bound inland wind.

FIGURES:

Vineyard surface: 4.535 – **Wine-Growers:** 601 – **Wineries:** 41 – **2012 Harvest rating:** Excellent– **Production:** 9.013.300 litres – **Market percentages:** 60% domestic. 40% export

VINTAGE RATING PEÑÍNGUIDE				
2008	2009	2010	2011	2012
VERY GOOD	AVERAGE	GOOD	VERY GOOD	VERY GOOD

CONSEJO REGULADOR
Complex de la Caparrella, 97 - 25192 Lleida ☎ +34 973 264 583 - Fax: +34 973 264 583
secretari@costersdelsegre.es   www.costersdelsegre.es

BODEGAS COSTERS DEL SIÓ

Ctra. de Agramunt, Km. 4,2
25600 Balaguer (Lleida)
☎: +34 973 424 062 - Fax: +34 973 424 112
www.costersio.com
administracio@costersio.com

ALTO SIÓS 2009 T
60% syrah, 30% tempranillo, 10% garnacha

91 Colour: cherry, garnet rim. Nose: powerfull, ripe fruit, dark chocolate, sweet spices, toasty. Palate: powerful, rich, spicy, long.

FINCA SIÓS 2010 T
35% cabernet sauvignon, 30% syrah, 20% tempranillo, 15% garnacha

91 Colour: bright cherry. Nose: ripe fruit, sweet spices, creamy oak, mineral. Palate: flavourful, fruity, toasty, round tannins.

PETIT SIÓS 2012 B
45% sauvignon blanc, 40% chardonnay, 15% moscatel grano menudo

89 Colour: bright straw. Nose: fresh, fresh fruit, white flowers, expressive. Palate: flavourful, fruity, good acidity, balanced.

SIÓS CAU DEL GAT 2011 T
85% syrah, 15% garnacha

90 Colour: bright cherry. Nose: sweet spices, creamy oak, expressive, red berry notes, ripe fruit. Palate: flavourful, fruity, toasty, round tannins.

SIÓS LES CREUS 2010 T
85% tempranillo, 15% garnacha

88 Colour: cherry, garnet rim. Nose: ripe fruit, spicy, creamy oak, fragrant herbs. Palate: powerful, flavourful, toasty.

SIÓS VIOLES VELLES 2012 RD
85% garnacha, 15% syrah

88 Colour: onion pink. Nose: elegant, candied fruit, dried flowers, fragrant herbs, red berry notes, lactic notes. Palate: light-bodied, flavourful, long.

CASTELL D'ENCUS

Ctra. Tremp a Santa Engracia, Km. 5
25630 Talarn (Lleida)
☎: +34 973 252 974
www.encus.org
rbobet@encus.org

ACUSP 2011 T
pinot noir

93 Colour: cherry, garnet rim. Nose: balsamic herbs, scrubland, ripe fruit, fruit liqueur notes, sweet spices, dry stone. Palate: round, mineral, balsamic, spicy, balanced.

EKAM 2012 B
riesling, albariño

90 Colour: bright straw. Nose: white flowers, fragrant herbs, citrus fruit, fruit expression. Palate: rich, flavourful, fresh, fruity.

QUEST 2011 T
cabernet sauvignon, cabernet franc

96 Colour: cherry, garnet rim. Nose: red berry notes, ripe fruit, spicy, mineral, cocoa bean, dark chocolate, creamy oak. Palate: powerful, rich, flavourful, fruity, long, balanced.

TALEIA 2012 B
sauvignon blanc, semillón

94 Colour: bright yellow. Nose: powerfull, ripe fruit, sweet spices, creamy oak. Palate: rich, flavourful, fresh, good acidity.

THALARN 2011 T
syrah

95 Colour: cherry, garnet rim. Nose: spicy, creamy oak, toasty, complex, fragrant herbs, fruit expression. Palate: powerful, flavourful, toasty, round tannins.

CASTELL DEL REMEI

Finca Castell del Remei
25333 Castell del Remei (Lleida)
☎: +34 973 580 200 - Fax: +34 973 718 312
www.castelldelremei.com
info@castelldelremei.com

CASTELL DEL REMEI 1780 2007 T
50% cabernet sauvignon, 15% tempranillo, 15% garnacha, 10% merlot, 10% syrah

91 Colour: cherry, garnet rim. Nose: spicy, creamy oak, toasty, complex, earthy notes. Palate: powerful, flavourful, toasty, round tannins.

CASTELL DEL REMEI BLANC PLANELL 2012 B
55% sauvignon blanc, 45% macabeo

88 Colour: bright straw, greenish rim. Nose: balanced, floral, fruit liqueur notes. Palate: balanced, good acidity, fine bitter notes, long.

CASTELL DEL REMEI GOTIM BRU 2011 T
35% tempranillo, 20% garnacha, 20% cabernet sauvignon, 20% merlot, 5% syrah

90 Colour: very deep cherry. Nose: sweet spices, candied fruit, ripe fruit. Palate: fine bitter notes, good acidity, balsamic.

CASTELL DEL REMEI ODA 2009 T
55% merlot, 20% cabernet sauvignon, 20% tempranillo, 5% garnacha

89 Colour: bright cherry, orangey edge. Nose: balanced, spicy, wild herbs. Palate: fruity, round tannins, good acidity.

CASTELL DEL REMEI ODA BLANC 2012 BFB
53% macabeo, 47% chardonnay

90 Colour: bright straw. Nose: ripe fruit, sweet spices, creamy oak, powerfull. Palate: rich, flavourful, correct, toasty.

CASTELL DEL REMEI SÍCORIS 2010 T
35% garnacha, 30% cabernet sauvignon, 20% tempranillo, 10% syrah, 5% merlot

87 Colour: cherry, garnet rim. Nose: dried herbs, varnish, fruit liqueur notes, sweet spices. Palate: flavourful, round tannins.

CELLER ANALEC

Ctra. a Nalec, s/n
25341 Nalec (Lleida)
☎: +34 973 303 190
www.analec.net
info@analec.net

ANALEC 2010 BN
50% macabeo, 50% parellada

85 Colour: bright straw. Nose: medium intensity, fresh fruit, dried herbs, floral. Palate: fresh, fruity, flavourful.

ANALEC BRUT ROSAT 2010 ESP
100% trepat

84

ANALEC CINÈRIA 2009 B
100% macabeo

85 Colour: golden. Nose: powerfull, candied fruit, fragrant herbs, acetaldehyde, varnish. Palate: flavourful, sweet, fresh, fruity, long.

ANALEC GUALECH RESERVA ESPECIAL 2009 ESP
40% macabeo, 40% parellada, 20% chardonnay

89 Colour: bright straw. Nose: medium intensity, fresh fruit, dried herbs, fine lees, floral. Palate: fresh, fruity, flavourful.

ANALEC SORT ABRIL 2008 ESP RESERVA
50% macabeo, 50% parellada

84

LA CREU BLANC 2011 B
50% macabeo, 50% chardonnay

88 Colour: bright yellow. Nose: powerfull, ripe fruit, sweet spices, creamy oak, fragrant herbs. Palate: flavourful, fresh, roasted-coffee aftertaste, rich.

LA CREU NEGRO 2010 T
100% tempranillo

85 Colour: light cherry. Nose: ripe fruit, spicy, toasty. Palate: long, balsamic, spicy.

LA ROMIGUERA 2010 T
50% tempranillo, 30% cabernet sauvignon, 20% syrah

87 Colour: bright cherry. Nose: ripe fruit, sweet spices, creamy oak, roasted coffee. Palate: flavourful, fruity, toasty.

CELLER CASA PATAU

Costa del Senyor, s/n
25139 Menarguens (Lleida)
☎: +34 973 180 367
www.casapatau.com
info@casapatau.com

L'ERAL DE CASA PATAU 2012 B
macabeo

86 Colour: bright straw. Nose: white flowers, ripe fruit, dried herbs. Palate: flavourful, fruity, good acidity, easy to drink.

L'ERAL DE CASA PATAU 2012 RD
merlot

83

PATAU 2010 TC
cabernet sauvignon, garnacha, ull de llebre

84

CELLER CERCAVINS

Ctra. LV-2101, km. 0,500
25340 Verdú (Lleida)
☎: +34 646 558 515 - Fax: +34 973 348 114
www.cellercercavins.com
jsoleroca@cellercercavins.com

BRU DE VERDÚ 14 2008 T
syrah, tempranillo, merlot

87 Colour: cherry, garnet rim. Nose: ripe fruit, toasty, tobacco, old leather. Palate: powerful, flavourful, round tannins, spicy.

BRU DE VERDÚ 2010 T
tempranillo, syrah, merlot

86 Colour: cherry, garnet rim. Nose: ripe fruit, spicy, toasty, cocoa bean. Palate: powerful, flavourful, long.

GUILLA 2011 BFB
macabeo, sauvignon blanc

87 Colour: bright yellow. Nose: ripe fruit, sweet spices, fragrant herbs, medium intensity. Palate: flavourful, fresh, good acidity, spicy.

GUILLAMINA 2012 B
sauvignon blanc, garnacha blanca, gewürztraminer, chardonnay

85 Colour: bright straw. Nose: dried flowers, fragrant herbs, ripe fruit. Palate: flavourful, spicy, balsamic.

LO VIROL 2012 RD
syrah

87 Colour: rose, purple rim. Nose: powerfull, ripe fruit, red berry notes, floral, lactic notes. Palate: powerful, fruity, fresh.

LO VIROL 2012 T
tempranillo, syrah, merlot

88 Colour: cherry, purple rim. Nose: expressive, red berry notes, floral. Palate: flavourful, fruity, good acidity, round tannins.

CELLER VILA CORONA

Camí els Nerets, s/n
25654 Vilamitjana (Lleida)
☎: +34 973 652 638 - Fax: +34 973 652 638
www.vilacorona.cat
vila-corona@avired.com

LLABUSTES CABERNET SAUVIGNON 2008 TC
cabernet sauvignon

86 Colour: pale ruby, brick rim edge. Nose: spicy, fine reductive notes, wet leather, aged wood nuances, fruit liqueur notes. Palate: spicy, fine tannins, long.

LLABUSTES CHARDONNAY 2011 B
chardonnay

84

LLABUSTES MERLOT 2010 T
85% merlot, 15% ull de llebre

88 Colour: pale ruby, brick rim edge. Nose: ripe fruit, sweet spices, fragrant herbs, mineral. Palate: spicy, long, balanced.

LLABUSTES RIESLING 2012 B
riesling

87 Colour: bright yellow. Nose: ripe fruit, floral, dried herbs, spicy. Palate: powerful, flavourful, ripe fruit.

LLABUSTES ULL DE LLEBRE 2010 T
ull de llebre

86 Colour: bright cherry. Nose: ripe fruit, sweet spices, creamy oak, fragrant herbs. Palate: flavourful, fruity, toasty.

TU RAI 2011 T
monastrell, ull de llebre, garnacha

87 Colour: bright cherry. Nose: ripe fruit, creamy oak, expressive. Palate: flavourful, fruity, toasty, round tannins.

CÉRVOLES CELLER

Avda. Les Garrigues, 26
25471 La Pobla de Cèrvoles (Lleida)
☎: +34 973 175 101 - Fax: +34 973 718 312
www.cervoles.com
info@cervolesceller.com

CÉRVOLES 2012 BFB
55% macabeo, 45% chardonnay

91 Colour: bright yellow. Nose: powerfull, ripe fruit, sweet spices, fragrant herbs. Palate: rich, flavourful, fresh, good acidity.

CÉRVOLES COLORS 2012 B
75% macabeo, 25% chardonnay

88 Colour: bright yellow. Nose: powerfull, citrus fruit, candied fruit. Palate: flavourful, sweetness, spicy.

CÉRVOLES ESTRATS 2006 T
42% cabernet sauvignon, 36% tempranillo, 17% garnacha, 5% merlot

94 Colour: cherry, garnet rim. Nose: spicy, creamy oak, toasty, complex, earthy notes, mineral. Palate: powerful, flavourful, toasty, round tannins.

CÉRVOLES NEGRE 2007 T
44% cabernet sauvignon, 32% tempranillo, 16% garnacha, 8% merlot

90 Colour: bright cherry, garnet rim. Nose: balanced, wild herbs, spicy. Palate: flavourful, rich, fine tannins.

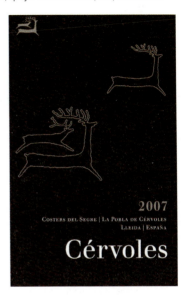

CLOS PONS

Ctra. LV-7011, km. 4,5
25155 L'Albagés (Lleida)
☎: +34 973 070 737 - Fax: 34 973 070 738
www.clospons.com
clospons@grup-pons.com

CLOS PONS 809 2009 T
marcelan

88 Colour: cherry, garnet rim. Nose: ripe fruit, spicy, old leather, balsamic herbs. Palate: powerful, flavourful, toasty.

CLOS PONS 810 2010 T
marcelan

93 Colour: dark-red cherry, garnet rim. Nose: ripe fruit, fragrant herbs, cocoa bean, sweet spices, creamy oak, mineral, expressive. Palate: powerful, flavourful, rich, long, spicy. Personality.

CLOS PONS ALGES 2010 TC
garnacha, syrah, tempranillo

89 Colour: dark-red cherry. Nose: aged wood nuances, creamy oak, roasted coffee, ripe fruit, balsamic herbs, earthy notes. Palate: powerful, flavourful, spicy, rich.

CLOS PONS ROC DE FOC 2011 B
macabeo

91 Colour: bright yellow. Nose: ripe fruit, powerfull, toasty, aged wood nuances. Palate: flavourful, fruity, spicy, toasty, long.

CLOS PONS ROC NU 2010 TC
garnacha, tempranillo, cabernet sauvignon

91 Colour: dark-red cherry. Nose: ripe fruit, spicy, creamy oak, balsamic herbs, fine reductive notes. Palate: flavourful, spicy, toasty.

CLOS PONS SISQUELLA 2011 B
garnacha blanca, albariño, moscatel de alejandría

90 Colour: bright yellow. Nose: ripe fruit, dried herbs, sweet spices, creamy oak. Palate: spicy, long, powerful, flavourful.

L'OLIVERA SCCL

La Plana, s/n
25268 Vallbona de les Monges (Lleida)
☎: +34 973 330 276 - Fax: +34 973 330 276
www.olivera.org
olivera@olivera.org

AGALIU 2011 BFB
macabeo

88 Colour: bright yellow. Nose: powerfull, ripe fruit, creamy oak, dried herbs. Palate: flavourful, fresh, spicy.

BLANC DE MARGES 2010 BFB
parellada, moscatel, sauvignon blanc

88 Colour: bright yellow. Nose: powerfull, sweet spices, creamy oak, fragrant herbs, citrus fruit, tropical fruit. Palate: rich, flavourful, fresh, good acidity.

BLANC DE ROURE 2011 B
macabeo, parellada, chardonnay

88 Colour: bright yellow. Nose: powerfull, ripe fruit, sweet spices, creamy oak, dried flowers. Palate: flavourful, fresh, good acidity.

BLANC DE SERÈ 2012 B
macabeo, parellada, chardonnay

87 Colour: bright straw. Nose: fresh, fresh fruit, white flowers, fragrant herbs. Palate: flavourful, fruity, good acidity.

EIXADERS 2010 BFB
chardonnay

91 Colour: bright yellow. Nose: ripe fruit, powerfull, toasty, aged wood nuances, sweet spices. Palate: flavourful, fruity, spicy, toasty, long, balanced.

L'OLIVERA 2009 BN
macabeo, parellada, chardonnay

87 Colour: bright straw. Nose: medium intensity, fresh fruit, dried herbs, fine lees, floral. Palate: fresh, fruity, flavourful, good acidity.

L'OLIVERA GRAN RESERVA 2008 BN
macabeo, parellada, chardonnay

88 Colour: bright golden. Nose: fine lees, dry nuts, fragrant herbs, complex, sweet spices. Palate: powerful, flavourful, good acidity, fine bead, fine bitter notes, elegant.

MISSENYORA 2011 BFB
macabeo

90 Colour: bright straw. Nose: fruit expression, floral, dried herbs, sweet spices. Palate: flavourful, fresh, fruity, balanced.

NALTRES 2011 T
cabernet sauvignon, garnacha, trepat

88 Colour: cherry, garnet rim. Nose: ripe fruit, spicy, creamy oak, toasty, damp earth. Palate: powerful, flavourful, toasty, round tannins.

RASIM VI PANSIT 2012 B
garnacha blanca, malvasía, xarel.lo

90 Colour: bright golden. Nose: citrus fruit, honeyed notes, ripe fruit, sweet spices, dried herbs, floral. Palate: powerful, flavourful, rich, complex.

RASIM VIMADUR 2011 T BARRICA
garnacha

89 Colour: cherry, garnet rim. Nose: candied fruit, fruit liqueur notes, aromatic coffee, balsamic herbs, creamy oak. Palate: powerful, flavourful, rich.

VALLISBONA 89 2010 BFB
chardonnay

92 Colour: bright yellow. Nose: floral, citrus fruit, ripe fruit, fragrant herbs, sweet spices, creamy oak, elegant. Palate: powerful, rich, flavourful, balanced.

LAGRAVERA

Ctra. de Tamarite, 9
25120 Alfarrás (Lleida)
☎: +34 973 761 374 - Fax: +34 973 760 218
www.lagravera.com
info@lagravera.com

CREA BLANC 2012 B
garnacha blanca, xarel.lo

88 Colour: bright yellow. Nose: dried flowers, dried herbs, ripe fruit, spicy. Palate: powerful, flavourful, long.

CREA NEGRE 2012 T
garnacha, monastrell, trobat, mandó

90 Colour: cherry, purple rim. Nose: expressive, fresh fruit, red berry notes, floral, mineral, spicy. Palate: flavourful, fruity, good acidity, round tannins.

LALTRE 2012 T
monastrell, garnacha, merlot

86 Colour: cherry, purple rim. Nose: floral, red berry notes, ripe fruit, balsamic herbs. Palate: flavourful, fruity, good acidity.

ÒNRA BLANC 2012 B
garnacha blanca, chenin blanc, sauvignon blanc

87 Colour: bright straw. Nose: white flowers, dry stone, ripe fruit, fragrant herbs. Palate: flavourful, fruity, good acidity, balanced.

ÓNRA MOLTA HONRA BLANC 2012 B
garnacha blanca, sauvignon blanc

89 Colour: bright yellow. Nose: powerfull, ripe fruit, sweet spices, creamy oak, fragrant herbs. Palate: rich, smoky aftertaste, flavourful, fresh, good acidity.

ÓNRA MOLTA HONRA NEGRE 2011 T
garnacha, cabernet sauvignon

91 Colour: cherry, garnet rim. Nose: damp earth, ripe fruit, sweet spices, creamy oak. Palate: powerful, flavourful, spicy, long.

ÒNRA NEGRE 2011 T
garnacha, merlot, cabernet sauvignon

90 Colour: cherry, garnet rim. Nose: mineral, red berry notes, ripe fruit, sweet spices, balsamic herbs. Palate: powerful, flavourful, spicy, long.

ÒNRA VI DE PEDRA 2009 SOLERA
garnacha blanca

93 Colour: bright golden. Nose: ripe fruit, dry nuts, dried flowers, fragrant herbs, mineral, dry stone, varnish, sweet spices. Palate: powerful, flavourful, long, toasty.

MAS BLANCH I JOVÉ

Paratge Llinars. Pol. Ind. 9- Parc. 129
25471 La Pobla de Cérvoles (Lleida)
☎: +34 973 050 018 - Fax: +34 973 391 151
www.masblanchijove.com
sara@masblanchijove.com

PETIT SAÓ 2010 T
tempranillo, garnacha, cabernet sauvignon

86 Colour: cherry, garnet rim. Nose: ripe fruit, balsamic herbs, spicy, creamy oak. Palate: powerful, flavourful, spicy.

SAÓ ABRIVAT 2009 T
garnacha, cabernet sauvignon, merlot, tempranillo

90 Colour: cherry, garnet rim. Nose: ripe fruit, balsamic herbs, spicy, creamy oak, mineral. Palate: powerful, flavourful, spicy, long.

SAÓ BLANC 2012 B
macabeo

90 Colour: bright yellow. Nose: powerfull, ripe fruit, sweet spices, creamy oak. Palate: flavourful, fresh, balanced.

SAÓ EXPRESSIU 2008 T
garnacha, tempranillo, cabernet sauvignon

91 Colour: cherry, garnet rim. Nose: ripe fruit, spicy, creamy oak, toasty, complex. Palate: powerful, flavourful, toasty, round tannins, balanced.

SAÓ ROSAT 2012 RD
garnacha, syrah

85 Colour: rose. Nose: ripe fruit, fruit preserve, scrubland, jasmine. Palate: flavourful, powerful, long, easy to drink.

RAIMAT

Ctra. Lleida, s/n
25111 Raimat (Lleida)
☎: +34 973 724 000
www.grupocodorniu.com
info@raimat.es

CASTELL DE RAIMAT CABERNET SAUVIGNON 2008 TC
100% cabernet sauvignon

87 Colour: cherry, garnet rim. Nose: ripe fruit, spicy, creamy oak, toasty. Palate: powerful, flavourful, toasty.

CASTELL DE RAIMAT CHARDONNAY 2012 B
100% chardonnay

90 Colour: bright straw. Nose: white flowers, fragrant herbs, ripe fruit. Palate: flavourful, fruity, good acidity, balanced.

CASTELL DE RAIMAT XAREL.LO CHARDONNAY 2011 B
50% xarel.lo, 50% chardonnay

90 Colour: bright yellow. Nose: floral, fragrant herbs, citrus fruit, ripe fruit. Palate: powerful, flavourful, spicy, long.

RAIMAT ABADÍA 2010 TC
cabernet sauvignon, tempranillo

84

RAIMAT TERRA CHARDONNAY 2012 B
100% chardonnay

89 Colour: bright straw. Nose: fresh, fresh fruit, white flowers, dried herbs. Palate: flavourful, fruity, good acidity.

RAIMAT VALLCORBA 2010 T
70% cabernet sauvignon, 30% syrah

90 Colour: deep cherry, garnet rim. Nose: balanced, expressive, wild herbs. Palate: full, round tannins, spicy.

TOMÁS CUSINÉ

Plaça Sant Sebastià, 13
25457 El Vilosell (Lleida)
☎: +34 973 176 029 - Fax: +34 973 175 945
www.tomascusine.com
info@tomascusine.com

AUZELLS 2012 B
macabeo, sauvignon blanc, chardonnay, riesling, albariño, moscatel, muller thurgau

93 Colour: bright straw. Nose: ripe fruit, fragrant herbs, dried flowers, dry stone, complex. Palate: flavourful, fruity, good acidity, balanced.

CARA NORD 2012 B
macabeo, chardonnay

90 Colour: bright straw. Nose: ripe fruit, citrus fruit, fruit expression. Palate: flavourful, fruity, fresh.

FINCA COMABARRA 2009 T
50% cabernet sauvignon, 25% syrah, 25% garnacha

91 Colour: cherry, garnet rim. Nose: spicy, creamy oak, mineral, fruit liqueur notes. Palate: powerful, flavourful, toasty, round tannins, balanced.

FINCA LA SERRA 2012 B
chardonnay

93 Colour: yellow. Nose: complex, floral, balanced. Palate: spicy, fruity, full, long, balanced, fine bitter notes, rich.

GEOL 2009 T
merlot, cabernet sauvignon, cabernet franc, garnacha, cariñena, marselan.

94 Colour: cherry, garnet rim. Nose: ripe fruit, spicy, creamy oak, toasty, complex, earthy notes. Palate: powerful, flavourful, toasty, round tannins, elegant.

LLEBRE 2011 T
tempranillo, merlot, cabernet sauvignon, garnacha, cariñena, syrah.

87 Colour: bright cherry. Nose: ripe fruit, sweet spices, creamy oak, balsamic herbs. Palate: flavourful, fruity, toasty.

MACABEU FINCA RACONS 2012 B
100% macabeo

94 Colour: bright yellow. Nose: ripe fruit, sweet spices, creamy oak, fragrant herbs. Palate: rich, smoky aftertaste, flavourful, fresh, good acidity, spicy.

VILOSELL 2010 T
tempranillo, syrah, merlot, cabernet sauvignon, cariñena

91 Colour: cherry, garnet rim. Nose: ripe fruit, spicy, creamy oak, complex, roasted coffee. Palate: powerful, flavourful, toasty, round tannins.

VALL DE BALDOMAR

Ctra. de Alós de Balaguer, s/n
25737 Baldomar (Lleida)
☎: +34 973 402 205
www.cristiari.com
administracion@cristiari.com

BALDOMÀ SELECCIÓ 2011 T
merlot, cabernet sauvignon, tempranillo

84

CRISTIARI 2010 T
merlot

85 Colour: cherry, garnet rim. Nose: fruit preserve, floral, balsamic herbs, spicy. Palate: spicy, easy to drink, flavourful.

CRISTIARI 2012 B
riesling

87 Colour: bright straw. Nose: fresh fruit, white flowers, expressive. Palate: flavourful, fruity, good acidity, balanced.

CRISTIARI 2012 RD
merlot, cabernet sauvignon

85 Colour: rose, purple rim. Nose: powerfull, ripe fruit, red berry notes, floral. Palate: powerful, fruity, fresh.

CRISTIARI D'ALÒS MERLOT 2011 T ROBLE
merlot

84

PETIT BALDOMA 2012 T
merlot, cabernet sauvignon

82

VINYA ELS VILARS

Camí de Puiggrós, s/n
25140 Arbeca (Lleida)
☎: +34 973 149 144 - Fax: +34 973 160 719
www.vinyaelsvilars.com
vinyaelsvilars@vinyaelsvilars.com

LEIX 2009 T
syrah

89 Colour: light cherry. Nose: ripe fruit, fragrant herbs, spicy. Palate: powerful, flavourful, long, toasty.

TALLAT DE LLUNA 2009 T
syrah

89 Colour: cherry, garnet rim. Nose: fruit preserve, spicy, creamy oak, cocoa bean. Palate: long, spicy, powerful, flavourful, toasty.

VILARS 2009 T ROBLE
merlot, syrah

86 Colour: cherry, garnet rim. Nose: ripe fruit, spicy, fine reductive notes. Palate: powerful, flavourful, toasty.

VILARS 2009 T
merlot, syrah

87 Colour: cherry, garnet rim. Nose: ripe fruit, spicy, aged wood nuances, earthy notes. Palate: powerful, flavourful, toasty.

VILARS GERAR 2009 T
merlot

86 Colour: light cherry. Nose: ripe fruit, fragrant herbs, creamy oak. Palate: flavourful, long, spicy.

VINYA L'HEREU DE SERÓ

Molí, s/n
25739 Sero - Artesa de Segre (Lleida)
☎: +34 973 400 472 - Fax: +34 973 400 472
www.vinyalhereu.com
vinyalhereu@vinyalhereu.com

FLOR DE GREALÓ 2009 T
merlot, syrah, cabernet sauvignon

89 Colour: cherry, garnet rim. Nose: fruit preserve, balsamic herbs, sweet spices, creamy oak, fine reductive notes. Palate: powerful, flavourful, long, spicy.

PETIT GREALÓ 2010 T
syrah, merlot, cabernet sauvignon

88 Colour: cherry, garnet rim. Nose: balsamic herbs, damp earth, spicy. Palate: powerful, flavourful, spicy.

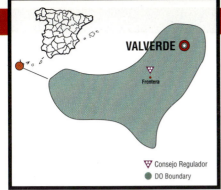

DO EL HIERRO / D.O.P.

LOCATION:

On the island of El Hierro, part of the Canary Islands. The production area covers the whole island, although the main growing regions are Valle del Golfo, Sabinosa, El Pinar and Echedo.

CLIMATE:

Fairly mild in general, although higher levels of humidity are recorded in high mountainous regions. Rainfall is relatively low.

SOIL:

Volcanic in origin, with a good water retention and storage capacity. Although the vineyards were traditionally cultivated in the higher regions, at present most of them are found at low altitudes, resulting in an early ripening of the grapes.

GRAPE VARIETIES:

WHITE: *Verijadiego* (majority with 50% of all white varieties), *Listán Blanca, Bremajuelo, Uval* (*Gual*), *Pedro Ximénez, Baboso* and *Moscatel*.
RED: *Listán Negro, Negramoll, Baboso Negro* and *Verijadiego Negro*.

FIGURES:

Vineyard surface: 192 – **Wine-Growers:** 256 – **Wineries:** 8 – **2012 Harvest rating:** N/A – **Production:** 90,000 litres – **Market percentages:** 99% domestic. 1% export

2008	2009	2010	2011	2012
GOOD	GOOD	VERY GOOD	N/A	N/A

CONSEJO REGULADOR
Oficina de Agricultura. El Matorral, s/n - 38911 Frontera (El Hierro). ☎: +34 922 556 064 / +34 922 559 744 - Fax: +34 922 559 691
doelhierro@hotmail.com   www.elhierro.tv

SDAD. COOPERATIVA DEL CAMPO "FRONTERA" VINÍCOLA INSULAR

El Matorral, s/n
38911 Frontera - El Hierro (Tenerife)
☎: +34 922 556 016 - Fax: +34 922 556 042
www.cooperativafrontera.com
coopfrontera@cooperativafrontera.com

VIÑA FRONTERA 2012 T MACERACIÓN CARBÓNICA
100% listán negro

87 Colour: light cherry. Nose: medium intensity, red berry notes, ripe fruit, balanced, balsamic herbs. Palate: flavourful, fruity.

VIÑA FRONTERA AFRUTADO 2012 B
60% verijadiego, 30% listán blanco, 10% vidueño

83

VIÑA FRONTERA BABOSO 2011 T
100% baboso negro

83

VIÑA FRONTERA VERIJADIEGO 2010 T
100% verijadiego

84

DO EMPORDÀ / D.O.P.

Consejo Regulador
DO Boundary

LOCATION:

In the far north west of Catalonia, in the province of Girona. The production area covers 40 municipal areas and is situated the slopes of the Rodes and Alberes mountain ranges forming an arch which leads from Cape Creus to what is known as the Garrotxa d'Empordà.

CLIMATE:

The climatology is conditioned by the 'Tramontana', a strong north wind which affects the vineyards. Furthermore, the winters are mild, with hardly any frost, and the summers hot, although somewhat tempered by the sea breezes. The average rainfall is around 600 mm.

SOIL:

The soil is in general poor, of a granitic nature in the mountainous areas, alluvial in the plains and slaty on the coastal belt.

GRAPE VARIETIES:

WHITE:
PREFERRED: *Garnacha Blanca, Macabeo (Viura)* and *Moscatel de Alejandría.*
AUTHORIZED: *Xarel.lo, Chardonnay, Gewürztraminer, Malvasía, Moscatel de Gra Petit, Picapoll Blanc* and *Sauvignon Blanc.*
RED:
PREFERRED: *Cariñena* and *Garnacha Tinta.*
AUTHORIZED: *Cabernet Sauvignon, Cabernet Franc, Merlot, Monastrell, Tempranillo, Syrah, Garnacha Roja (lledoner roig)* and *Garnacha Peluda.*

FIGURES:

Vineyard surface: 1.777– **Wine-Growers:** 332 – **Wineries:** 50 – **2012 Harvest rating:** Very Good – **Production:** 5.248.000 litres – **Market percentages:** 80% domestic. 20% export

VINTAGE RATING **PEÑÍN**GUIDE

2008	2009	2010	2011	2012
GOOD	GOOD	VERY GOOD	VERY GOOD	GOOD

CONSEJO REGULADOR
Avda. Marignane, 2 - 17600 Figueres (Girona) ☎: +34 972 507 513 - Fax: +34 972 510 058
info@doemporda.cat   www.doemporda.cat

AGRÍCOLA DE GARRIGUELLA

Ctra. de Roses, s/n
17780 Garriguella (Girona)
☎: +34 972 530 002 - Fax: +34 972 531 747
www.cooperativagarriguella.com
info@cooperativagarriguella.com

DINARELLS BLANC 2012 B
70% macabeo, 30% garnacha blanca

83

DINARELLS NEGRE 2012 T
28% cariñena, 27% merlot, 25% garnacha, 20% cabernet sauvignon

83

DINARELLS ROSAT 2012 RD
62% cariñena, 26% garnacha, 12% tempranillo

85 Colour: raspberry rose. Nose: balsamic herbs, dried flowers, red berry notes, ripe fruit. Palate: powerful, flavourful.

DOLÇ DE GERISENA 2005 VINO DE LICOR
75% garnacha, 25% cariñena

91 Colour: pale ruby, brick rim edge. Nose: acetaldehyde, varnish, spicy, creamy oak, candied fruit. Palate: spicy, long, powerful, flavourful.

ESSENCIA DE GERISENA 2012 B
moscatel de alejandría

90 Colour: golden. Nose: powerfull, floral, honeyed notes, candied fruit, fragrant herbs. Palate: flavourful, sweet, fresh, fruity, good acidity, long.

GARRIGUELLA 2010 TC
50% cariñena, 40% cabernet sauvignon, 10% garnacha

86 Colour: cherry, garnet rim. Nose: ripe fruit, spicy, creamy oak. Palate: powerful, flavourful, toasty.

GARRIGUELLA GARNATXA D'EMPORDÁ NEGRA 2007 T
100% garnacha

85 Colour: dark-red cherry. Nose: fruit preserve, dry nuts, spicy, aromatic coffee. Palate: powerful, flavourful, spirituous.

GARRIGUELLA GARNATXA D'EMPORDÁ ROJA VINO DEL LICOR
100% garnacha roja

84

GARRIGUELLA MOSCATEL D'EMPORDÁ 2012 B
100% moscatel de alejandría

85 Colour: golden. Nose: powerfull, floral, candied fruit, fragrant herbs. Palate: flavourful, sweet, fresh, fruity, good acidity, long.

GARRIGUELLA NOVELL 2012 T
50% syrah, 30% garnacha, 20% cariñena

87 Colour: cherry, purple rim. Nose: expressive, fresh fruit, red berry notes, floral. Palate: flavourful, fruity, good acidity.

GERISENA SEL.LECCIÓ 2012 T
50% cabernet sauvignon, 30% garnacha, 20% merlot

87 Colour: cherry, garnet rim. Nose: red berry notes, ripe fruit, balsamic herbs. Palate: powerful, flavourful, spicy, balsamic.

PUNTILS BLANC 2012 B
73% garnacha blanca, 27% moscatel

83

PUNTILS NEGRE 2012 T
40% cabernet sauvignon, 35% garnacha, 25% cariñena

85 Colour: cherry, purple rim. Nose: floral, balsamic herbs, ripe fruit. Palate: flavourful, fruity, good acidity.

PUNTILS ROSAT 2012 RD
40% tempranillo, 37% garnacha, 23% merlot

83

AV BODEGUERS

Sant Baldiri, 23
17781 Vilamaniscle (Girona)
☎: +34 676 231 199
www.avbodeguers.com
info@avbodeguers.com

NEREUS 2009 T BARRICA
merlot, syrah, garnacha

86 Colour: cherry, garnet rim. Nose: ripe fruit, spicy, creamy oak, grassy. Palate: powerful, flavourful, toasty.

NEREUS GARNACHA NEGRA 2010 T
garnacha

87 Colour: cherry, garnet rim. Nose: ripe fruit, mineral, wild herbs. Palate: spicy, long, balanced.

SUNEUS 2011 T
garnacha, syrah

85 Colour: bright cherry. Nose: ripe fruit, balsamic herbs, spicy. Palate: flavourful, fruity, toasty.

SUNEUS 2012 B
garnacha blanca

86 Colour: bright straw. Nose: powerfull, ripe fruit, sweet spices, fragrant herbs. Palate: rich, flavourful, good acidity.

SUNEUS 2012 RD
merlot

82

BODEGAS MAS VIDA

Afuera, 24
17741 Cistella (Girona)
☎: +34 932 045 598 - Fax: +34 932 037 541
www.bodegasmasvida.com
info@bodegasmasvida.com

MAS VIDA 17 2012 B
chardonnay

84

MAS VIDA 23 2010 T
merlot, cabernet sauvignon, tempranillo

83

MAS VIDA 32 2010 T ROBLE
merlot

84

BODEGAS TROBAT

Castelló, 10
17780 Garriguella (Girona)
☎: +34 972 530 092 - Fax: +34 972 552 530
www.bodegastrobat.com
bodegas.trobat@bmark.es

AMAT BLANC 2012 B
xarel.lo

86 Colour: bright straw. Nose: white flowers, ripe fruit, dried herbs. Palate: flavourful, fruity, good acidity, balanced.

AMAT NEGRE 2009 TC
samsó, merlot, syrah

88 Colour: cherry, garnet rim. Nose: ripe fruit, spicy, balsamic herbs, creamy oak. Palate: correct, flavourful, spicy, long.

AMAT NEGRE 2012 T
merlot, syrah, garnacha

81

AMAT SAUVIGNON BLANC 2012 B
sauvignon blanc

86 Colour: bright straw. Nose: floral, citrus fruit, fresh fruit, balsamic herbs. Palate: fresh, fruity, flavourful, balanced.

NOBLE CHARDONNAY 2012 B
chardonnay

85 Colour: bright straw. Nose: fragrant herbs, citrus fruit, ripe fruit. Palate: flavourful, fruity, good acidity.

NOBLE NEGRE 2010 T
cabernet sauvignon, syrah, samsó, garnacha

87 Colour: bright cherry. Nose: ripe fruit, sweet spices, creamy oak, expressive. Palate: flavourful, fruity, toasty.

CASTILLO PERELADA
VINOS Y CAVAS

Pl. del Carmen, 1
17491 Perelada (Girona)
☎: +34 972 538 011 - Fax: +34 972 538 277
www.castilloperelada.com
perelada@castilloperelada.com

CASTILLO DE PERELADA 3 FINCAS 2010 TC
35% garnacha, 35% samsó, 15% cabernet sauvignon, 15% merlot

85 Colour: cherry, garnet rim. Nose: ripe fruit, spicy, creamy oak, toasty, wild herbs. Palate: powerful, flavourful, toasty.

CASTILLO DE PERELADA 5 FINCAS 2008 TR
26% merlot, 9% cabernet sauvignon, 39% garnacha, 26% syrah

90 Colour: cherry, garnet rim. Nose: ripe fruit, balsamic herbs, spicy, creamy oak. Palate: powerful, flavourful, long, spicy.

CASTILLO DE PERELADA EX EX 10 2011 T
100% cabernet franc

93 Colour: cherry, garnet rim. Nose: dry stone, ripe fruit, spicy, creamy oak. Palate: powerful, flavourful, fine bitter notes, balanced.

CASTILLO PERELADA 2012 RD
37% garnacha, 35% merlot, 38% ull de llebre

87 Colour: rose, purple rim. Nose: powerfull, ripe fruit, red berry notes, floral, expressive. Palate: powerful, fruity, fresh.

CASTILLO PERELADA BLANC DE BLANCS 2012 B
53% macabeo, 31% chardonnay, 16% sauvignon blanc

86 Colour: bright straw. Nose: white flowers, candied fruit, dried herbs. Palate: powerful, flavourful, balanced.

CASTILLO PERELADA CABERNET SAUVIGNON 2012 RD
86% cabernet sauvignon, 14% merlot

88 Colour: rose, purple rim. Nose: powerfull, ripe fruit, red berry notes, lactic notes, wild herbs. Palate: powerful, fruity, flavourful.

CASTILLO PERELADA CHARDONNAY 2012 B
100% chardonnay

89 Colour: bright straw. Nose: floral, fragrant herbs, candied fruit. Palate: fresh, fruity, balanced, easy to drink.

CASTILLO PERELADA FINCA ESPOLLA 2010 T
31% monastrell, 31% cabernet sauvignon, 19% syrah, 19% garnacha

93 Colour: bright cherry. Nose: ripe fruit, sweet spices, creamy oak, mineral. Palate: flavourful, fruity, toasty, round tannins.

CASTILLO PERELADA FINCA MALAVEÏNA 2009 T
40% merlot, 30% cabernet sauvignon, 20% syrah, 10% garnacha

90 Colour: cherry, garnet rim. Nose: ripe fruit, spicy, creamy oak, toasty, complex. Palate: powerful, flavourful, toasty, round tannins.

CASTILLO PERELADA FINCA MALAVEÏNA 2010 T
30% merlot, 25% cabernet sauvignon, 20% cabernet franc, 15% syrah, 10% garnacha

89 Colour: cherry, garnet rim. Nose: red berry notes, fruit liqueur notes, dry stone, sweet spices, creamy oak. Palate: powerful, flavourful, spicy, long.

CASTILLO PERELADA GARNATXA BLANCA 2012 B
100% garnacha blanca

88 Colour: bright straw. Nose: ripe fruit, citrus fruit, floral, balsamic herbs. Palate: correct, fine bitter notes, powerful, flavourful.

CASTILLO PERELADA GARNATXA DE L'EMPORDÀ B
80% garnacha roja, 20% garnacha blanca

92 Colour: light mahogany. Nose: varnish, acetaldehyde, aged wood nuances, sweet spices, elegant, roasted almonds. Palate: aged character, powerful, flavourful, spicy, long.

CASTILLO PERELADA GRAN CLAUSTRO 2006 T
40% cabernet sauvignon, 20% merlot, 20% garnacha, 20% samsó

91 Colour: pale ruby, brick rim edge. Nose: elegant, spicy, fine reductive notes, aged wood nuances, fruit liqueur notes. Palate: spicy, fine tannins, elegant, long.

CASTILLO PERELADA JARDINS BLANC 2012 B
55% macabeo, 45% sauvignon blanc

86 Colour: bright straw. Nose: fresh fruit, white flowers, wild herbs. Palate: flavourful, fruity, balanced.

CASTILLO PERELADA JARDINS ROSÉ 2012 RD
62% garnacha, 38% merlot

86 Colour: rose. Nose: powerfull, ripe fruit, red berry notes, floral, jasmine, balsamic herbs. Palate: powerful, fruity, fresh.

CASTILLO PERELADA LA GARRIGA 2010 T
100% samsó

88 Colour: cherry, garnet rim. Nose: ripe fruit, sweet spices, smoky, balsamic herbs. Palate: round, balanced, flavourful.

CASTILLO PERELADA LA GARRIGA 2011 B
40% cariñena blanca, 40% chardonnay, 20% sauvignon blanc

92 Colour: bright yellow. Nose: powerfull, ripe fruit, sweet spices, creamy oak, fragrant herbs. Palate: rich, smoky aftertaste, flavourful, fresh, good acidity.

CASTILLO PERELADA SAUVIGNON BLANC 2012 B
100% sauvignon blanc

85 Colour: bright straw. Nose: balsamic herbs, faded flowers, ripe fruit. Palate: flavourful, fruity, good acidity, rich.

CIGONYES 2011 T
90% garnacha, 10% syrah

89 Colour: cherry, garnet rim. Nose: ripe fruit, spicy, fragrant herbs, creamy oak. Palate: flavourful, good structure, correct.

CIGONYES 2012 B
100% macabeo

88 Colour: bright straw. Nose: fresh, expressive, floral, citrus fruit. Palate: flavourful, fruity, balanced.

CIGONYES 2012 RD
86% garnacha, 8% samsó, 6% merlot

86 Colour: onion pink. Nose: elegant, candied fruit, dried flowers, fragrant herbs, citrus fruit. Palate: light-bodied, flavourful, good acidity.

FINCA GARBET 2006 T
90% syrah, 10% cabernet sauvignon

91 Colour: dark-red cherry, orangey edge. Nose: fruit preserve, fine reductive notes, spicy, creamy oak. Palate: powerful, ripe fruit, long, balanced, round.

FINCA GARBET 2007 T
100% syrah

93 Colour: cherry, garnet rim. Nose: ripe fruit, spicy, creamy oak, toasty, complex, expressive. Palate: powerful, flavourful, toasty, balanced, elegant.

CELLER ARCHÉ PAGÈS

Sant Climent, 31
17750 Capmany (Girona)
☎: +34 626 647 251 - Fax: +34 972 549 229
www.cellerarchepages.com
bonfill@capmany.com

BONFILL 2008 T
garnacha, cariñena

89 Colour: cherry, garnet rim. Nose: ripe fruit, spicy, fragrant herbs, aged wood nuances. Palate: powerful, flavourful, long.

CARTESIUS 2007 T
garnacha, merlot, cabernet sauvignon

87 Colour: pale ruby, brick rim edge. Nose: spicy, wet leather, aged wood nuances, fruit liqueur notes. Palate: spicy, long, flavourful.

SÀTIRS BLANC 2012 B
macabeo

83

ULL DE SERP 2010 T
garnacha

86 Colour: cherry, garnet rim. Nose: ripe fruit, spicy, creamy oak, toasty. Palate: powerful, flavourful, toasty, round tannins.

CELLER BELL-LLOC

Finca Bell-Lloc, s/n
17230 Palamós (Girona)
☎: +34 972 316 203
www.fincabell-lloc.com
info@brugarol.com

BELL-LLOC 2009 TC
38% cabernet franc, 34% cabernet sauvignon, 21% lladoner, 7% samsó

89 Colour: pale ruby, brick rim edge. Nose: elegant, spicy, fine reductive notes, wet leather, aged wood nuances, earthy notes. Palate: spicy, fine tannins, elegant, long.

CELLER CAN SAIS

Raval de Dalt, 10
17253 Vall-Llobrega (Girona)
☎: +34 647 443 873
www.cellercansais.com
correu@cellercansais.com

CAN SAIS EXPRESSIÓ ZERO SULFITS 2012 T
garnacha

86 Colour: bright cherry. Nose: expressive, spicy, ripe fruit, medium intensity. Palate: flavourful, fruity, long.

CAN SAIS GREGAL 2012 RD
garnacha, merlot, syrah

84

CAN SAIS MESTRAL 2012 B
malvasía, xarel.lo, garnacha, macabeo

83

CAN SAIS MIGJORN 2012 T
merlot, cabernet franc, garnacha, cariñena, ull de llebre

85 Colour: bright cherry. Nose: ripe fruit, sweet spices. Palate: flavourful, fruity, spicy.

CAN SAIS SELECCIÓ 2010 T
merlot, garnacha, ull de llebre

86 Colour: pale ruby, brick rim edge. Nose: ripe fruit, dried herbs, faded flowers, damp earth. Palate: long, flavourful.

CELLER COOPERATIU D'ESPOLLA

Ctra. Roses, s/n
17753 Espolla (Girona)
☎: +34 972 563 049 - Fax: +34 972 563 178
www.cellerespolla.com
info@cellerespolla.com

BABALÀ VI BLANC SIMPÀTIC 2012 B
70% cariñena blanca, 30% moscatel de alejandría

85 Colour: bright straw. Nose: expressive, dried flowers, ripe fruit. Palate: flavourful, fruity, easy to drink.

CASTELL DE PANISSARS 2010 TC
45% cariñena, 30% lladoner, 25% merlot

86 Colour: cherry, garnet rim. Nose: ripe fruit, spicy, toasty. Palate: powerful, flavourful, toasty.

CASTELL DE PANISSARS 2012 B
55% lladoner blanco, 35% macabeo, 10% moscatel

84

CASTELL DE PANISSARS 2012 RD
60% merlot, 40% lladoner

86 Colour: rose, purple rim. Nose: ripe fruit, red berry notes, floral, lactic notes. Palate: powerful, fruity, fresh.

CLOS DE LES DÒMINES 2009 TR
45% merlot, 30% cabernet sauvignon, 25% cariñena

86 Colour: cherry, garnet rim. Nose: ripe fruit, spicy, creamy oak, balsamic herbs. Palate: powerful, flavourful, spicy.

CLOS DE LES DÒMINES 2011 BFB
40% lladoner blanco, 40% cariñena, 20% moscatel de alejandría

86 Colour: bright yellow. Nose: ripe fruit, powerfull, toasty, aged wood nuances, honeyed notes. Palate: flavourful, fruity, spicy, toasty, long.

GARNATXA D'EMPORDÀ NATURALMENTE DULCE
65% lladoner blanco, 35% lladoner

90 Colour: iodine, amber rim. Nose: powerfull, dry nuts, toasty, varnish, acetaldehyde, fruit liqueur notes. Palate: rich, fine bitter notes, fine solera notes, long, spicy.

MUSCAT D'EMPORDÀ ESPOLLA B
moscatel de alejandría

82

NEGRE JOVE 2012 T
45% lladoner negre, 45% lladoner roig, 10% merlot

85 Colour: cherry, purple rim. Nose: fresh fruit, red berry notes, floral. Palate: flavourful, fruity, good acidity, round tannins.

SOLISERENA GARNATXA D'EMPORDÀ DULCE NATURAL
65% lladoner blanco, 35% lladoner

90 Colour: light mahogany. Nose: sweet spices, caramel, creamy oak, dry nuts. Palate: powerful, flavourful, sweet, balanced.

CELLER LA VINYETA

Ctra. de Mollet de Peralada a Masarac, s/n
17752 Mollet de Peralada (Girona)
☎: +34 647 748 809
www.lavinyeta.es
celler@lavinyeta.es

HEUS BLANC 2012 B
macabeo, garnacha blanca, xarel.lo, moscatel, malvasía

83

HEUS NEGRE 2012 T
cariñena, syrah, garnacha, merlot

89 Colour: cherry, purple rim. Nose: fresh fruit, red berry notes, floral. Palate: flavourful, fruity, good acidity, round tannins.

HEUS ROSAT 2012 RD
garnacha, cariñena, merlot, syrah

85 Colour: coppery red. Nose: powerfull, ripe fruit, red berry notes, floral. Palate: powerful, fruity, fresh.

LLAVORS 2011 T
cariñena, merlot, cabernet sauvignon, cabernet franc

85 Colour: cherry, garnet rim. Nose: ripe fruit, balsamic herbs, spicy. Palate: long, oaky, flavourful.

MICROVINS BLANC MACABEU BARRICA 2012 B
100% macabeo

87 Colour: bright yellow. Nose: ripe fruit, creamy oak, fragrant herbs, dried flowers. Palate: rich, flavourful, fresh, good acidity.

MICROVINS BLANC MACABEU LÍAS 2012 B
100% macabeo

85 Colour: bright straw. Nose: dried flowers, wild herbs, ripe fruit, candied fruit. Palate: spicy, flavourful, rich.

PUNTIAPART 2010 T
cabernet sauvignon, cariñena

89 Colour: cherry, garnet rim. Nose: ripe fruit, spicy, creamy oak. Palate: powerful, flavourful, toasty, round tannins.

SOLS* 2010 DULCE
garnacha blanca, garnacha roja

85 Colour: light mahogany. Nose: creamy oak, toasty, candied fruit, dry nuts. Palate: spirituous, powerful, flavourful.

CELLER MARIÀ PAGÈS

Pujada, 6
17750 Capmany (Girona)
☎: +34 972 549 160 - Fax: +34 972 549 160
www.cellermpages.com
info@cellermpages.com

CELLER MARÍÀ PAGÈS GARNACHA 2011 B

90 Colour: light mahogany. Nose: candied fruit, honeyed notes, caramel, creamy oak. Palate: correct, powerful, flavourful.

CELLER MARÍÀ PAGÈS MOSCAT 2011 B
moscatel de alejandría

89 Colour: golden. Nose: powerfull, floral, honeyed notes, candied fruit, fragrant herbs. Palate: flavourful, sweet, fruity, good acidity, long, unctuous.

MARÍÀ PAGÈS GARNATXA 2011 B RESERVA
garnacha blanca, garnacha

86 Colour: iodine, amber rim. Nose: powerfull, honeyed notes, candied fruit, fragrant herbs. Palate: flavourful, sweet, fresh, fruity, good acidity, long.

SERRASAGUÉ 2007 TC
garnacha, merlot, cabernet sauvignon

85 Colour: dark-red cherry. Nose: fruit preserve, scrubland, spicy, fine reductive notes. Palate: powerful, flavourful, spirituous.

SERRASAGUÉ 2012 T
garnacha, merlot, cabernet sauvignon

87 Colour: cherry, purple rim. Nose: balsamic herbs, red berry notes, ripe fruit, smoky. Palate: powerful, flavourful, complex.

SERRASAGUÉ ROSA - T 2012 RD
garnacha, merlot

87 Colour: rose, purple rim. Nose: powerfull, ripe fruit, red berry notes, floral. Palate: powerful, fruity.

SERRASAGUÉ TACA NEGRE 2010 T
garnacha, merlot, cabernet franc

84

SERRASAGUÉ VINYA DE HORT 2012 B
garnacha blanca, chardonnay, moscatel

83

CELLER MARTÍ FABRA

Barrio Vic, 26
17751 Sant Climent Sescebes (Girona)
☎: +34 972 563 011 - Fax: +34 972 563 867
info@cellermartifabra.com

FLOR D'ALBERA 2011 BFB
100% moscatel

89 Colour: bright straw. Nose: fresh, fresh fruit, white flowers, expressive. Palate: flavourful, fruity, good acidity, balanced.

L'ORATORI 2010 T
50% garnacha, 30% cabernet sauvignon, 20% cariñena

85 Colour: cherry, garnet rim. Nose: ripe fruit, spicy, creamy oak, grassy. Palate: powerful, flavourful, spicy.

LLADONER 2012 RD
100% garnacha

87 Colour: rose, purple rim. Nose: powerfull, ripe fruit, red berry notes, floral, lactic notes. Palate: powerful, fruity, fresh.

MARTÍ FABRA SELECCIÓ VINYES VELLES 2009 T ROBLE
60% garnacha, 25% cariñena, 8% syrah, 5% cabernet sauvignon, 2% tempranillo

89 Colour: cherry, garnet rim. Nose: ripe fruit, spicy, creamy oak, toasty. Palate: powerful, flavourful, toasty.

MASÍA CARRERAS BLANC 2011 BFB
40% cariñena blanca, 30% cariñena rosada, 10% garnacha blanca, 10% garnacha rosada, 10% picapoll

91 Colour: bright yellow. Nose: floral, fragrant herbs, dry stone, spicy, expressive. Palate: rich, flavourful, spicy, long.

MASÍA CARRERAS NEGRE 2008 T
90% cariñena, 10% merlot

88 Colour: cherry, garnet rim. Nose: fruit preserve, balsamic herbs, toasty, fine reductive notes. Palate: long, spicy, flavourful.

MASÍA PAIRAL CAN CARRERAS GARNATXA DE L'EMPORDÀ B
garnacha blanca, garnacha rosada

88 Colour: dark mahogany. Nose: complex, fruit liqueur notes, dried fruit, pattiserie, toasty. Palate: sweet, rich, unctuous, powerful.

MASÍA PAIRAL CAN CARRERAS MOSCAT 2010 B
100% moscatel

90 Colour: golden. Nose: powerfull, floral, honeyed notes, candied fruit, fragrant herbs. Palate: flavourful, sweet, fresh, fruity, good acidity, long.

VERD ALBERA 2012 B
65% garnacha blanca, 20% moscatel, 10% garnacha rosada, 5% chardonnay

87 Colour: bright yellow. Nose: ripe fruit, balsamic herbs, floral. Palate: fresh, fruity, spicy, easy to drink.

CELLER MAS PATIRÀS

Jardins de l'Empordà
17110 Fonteta (Girona)
☎: +34 972 642 687
www.jardinsemporda.com
info@jardinsemporda.com

BLAU DE TRAMUNTANA 2008 T
garnacha, syrah, samsó

79

CELLER MAS ROMEU

Gregal, 1
17495 Palau-Saverdera (Girona)
☎: +34 687 744 056 - Fax: +34 934 368 572
www.cellermasromeu.com
info@cellermasromeu.cat

BLANC FITÓ 2011 B
chardonnay, moscatel

80

FINCA MALESA 2007 TR
garnacha, merlot

85 Colour: pale ruby, brick rim edge. Nose: medium intensity, spicy, fine reductive notes. Palate: flavourful, spicy, ripe fruit.

FITÓ 2007 TR
cabernet sauvignon, syrah

86 Colour: pale ruby, brick rim edge. Nose: wet leather, cigar, spicy, creamy oak. Palate: powerful, flavourful, spicy.

CELLERS D'EN GUILLA

Camí de Perelada nº 1, Delfià
17754 Rabós d'Empordà (Girona)
☎: +34 660 001 622
www.cellersdenguilla.com
info@cellersdenguilla.com

MAGENC 2012 B
garnacha blanca, macabeo, moscatel

88 Colour: bright straw. Nose: citrus fruit, fresh fruit, wild herbs. Palate: flavourful, fresh, fruity, easy to drink.

REC DE BRAU 2011 T
cariñena, garnacha

86 Colour: cherry, garnet rim. Nose: wild herbs, ripe fruit, spicy. Palate: powerful, long.

VINYA DEL METGE 2012 RD
garnacha roja, garnacha negra

88 Colour: light cherry. Nose: floral, rose petals, fragrant herbs, candied fruit. Palate: balanced, elegant, easy to drink.

CELLERS SANTAMARÍA

Pza. Mayor, 6
17750 Capmany (Girona)
☎: +34 972 549 033 - Fax: +34 972 549 022
www.granrecosind.com
info@granrecosind.com

GRAN RECOSIND 2005 TR
100% merlot

86 Colour: pale ruby, brick rim edge. Nose: cigar, waxy notes, aged wood nuances, spicy, fragrant herbs. Palate: flavourful, spirituous, long.

GRAN RECOSIND 2006 TC
garnacha, syrah, tempranillo, cabernet sauvignon, merlot

83

GRAN RECOSIND 2008 BC
50% macabeo, 50% chardonnay

82

GRAN RECOSIND CABERNET SAUVIGNON MERLOT 2004 TR
50% cabernet sauvignon, 50% merlot

84

CLOS D'AGON

Afores, s/n
17251 Calonge (Girona)
☎: +34 972 661 486 - Fax: +34 972 661 462
www.closdagon.com
info@closdagon.com

AMIC DE CLOS D'AGON 2011 B
garnacha blanca

88 Colour: bright straw. Nose: floral, ripe fruit, dried herbs, petrol notes. Palate: powerful, flavourful, balanced.

AMIC DE CLOS D'AGON 2011 T
66% garnacha, 21% cabernet sauvignon, 9% merlot, 4% syrah

90 Colour: bright cherry. Nose: ripe fruit, creamy oak, expressive. Palate: flavourful, fruity, toasty, round tannins.

COCA I FITÓ & ROIG PARALS

Garriguella, 8
17752 Mollet de Peralada (Girona)
☎: +34 972 634 320 - Fax: +34 935 457 092
www.tocatdelala.cat
info@cocaifito.cat

TOCAT DE L'ALA 2011 TC
60% garnacha, 40% cariñena

90 Colour: cherry, garnet rim. Nose: earthy notes, ripe fruit, balsamic herbs, characterful. Palate: round, flavourful, spicy.

COLL DE ROSES

Ctra. de les Arenes, s/n
17480 Roses (Girona)
☎: +3 497 256 465 - Fax: +34 972 531 741
www.collderoses.es
info@collderoses.es

COLL DE ROSES 2012 B
macabeo, chardonnay

86 Colour: bright straw. Nose: fresh fruit, white flowers, dried herbs. Palate: flavourful, fruity, good acidity.

COLL DE ROSES 2012 T
garnacha, tempranillo

88 Colour: cherry, purple rim. Nose: red berry notes, ripe fruit, balsamic herbs, floral, earthy notes. Palate: powerful, flavourful, spicy, long.

COLL DE ROSES FINCA DEL MAR 2011 T
garnacha, cabernet sauvignon

90 Colour: bright cherry, garnet rim. Nose: ripe fruit, creamy oak, wild herbs, mineral, complex. Palate: flavourful, fruity, round tannins.

EMPORDÀLIA

Ctra. de Roses, s/n
17494 Pau (Girona)
☎: +34 972 530 140 - Fax: +34 972 530 528
www.empordalia.com
info@empordalia.com

SINOLS 2008 TR
cariñena, garnacha, cabernet sauvignon

85 Colour: cherry, garnet rim. Nose: spicy, creamy oak, balsamic herbs. Palate: long, spicy, flavourful.

SINOLS 2010 TC
cariñena, garnacha, cabernet sauvignon, syrah, merlot

87 Colour: cherry, garnet rim. Nose: earthy notes, balsamic herbs, ripe fruit, spicy. Palate: powerful, flavourful, balanced.

SINOLS NEGRE 2012 T
cariñena, garnacha, syrah

85 Colour: cherry, purple rim. Nose: red berry notes, ripe fruit, fragrant herbs, floral. Palate: spicy, powerful, flavourful.

SINOLS ROSAT 2012 RD
cariñena, garnacha

84

ESPELT VITICULTORS

Mas Espelt s/n
17493 Vilajuiga (Girona)
☎: +34 972 531 727 - Fax: +34 972 531 741
www.espeltviticultors.com
info@espeltviticultors.com

ESPELT COMABRUNA 2010 T
100% cariñena

92 Colour: cherry, garnet rim. Nose: ripe fruit, spicy, creamy oak, toasty, complex, elegant. Palate: powerful, flavourful, toasty, round tannins, balanced.

ESPELT CORALI 2012 RD
garnacha

85 Colour: onion pink. Nose: dried flowers, fragrant herbs, candied fruit. Palate: fresh, fruity, easy to drink.

ESPELT GARNACHA AIRAM B
garnacha, garnacha gris

87 Colour: iodine, amber rim. Nose: powerfull, complex, dry nuts, toasty. Palate: rich, fine bitter notes, long, spicy.

ESPELT LLEDONER 2012 RD
lledoner

87 Colour: light cherry. Nose: elegant, candied fruit, dried flowers, fragrant herbs, red berry notes. Palate: light-bodied, flavourful, good acidity, spicy.

ESPELT MARENY 2012 B
70% sauvignon blanc, 30% moscatel

85 Colour: bright straw. Nose: fresh, fresh fruit, white flowers, expressive. Palate: flavourful, fruity, good acidity, balanced.

ESPELT QUINZE ROURES 2011 BFB
garnacha gris, garnacha blanca

90 Colour: bright yellow. Nose: powerfull, ripe fruit, creamy oak, scrubland. Palate: rich, flavourful, fresh, good acidity.

ESPELT SAULÓ 2012 T
garnacha, cariñena

87 Colour: cherry, purple rim. Nose: expressive, fresh fruit, red berry notes, floral. Palate: flavourful, fruity, good acidity, round tannins.

ESPELT TERRES NEGRES 2011 T
80% cariñena, 20% garnacha

89 Colour: cherry, garnet rim. Nose: ripe fruit, mineral, fragrant herbs, creamy oak. Palate: powerful, flavourful, long, balanced.

ESPELT VAILET 2012 B
50% garnacha blanca, 50% macabeo

83

ESPELT VIDIVÍ 2011 T
garnacha, merlot

85 Colour: cherry, garnet rim. Nose: ripe fruit, grassy, toasty. Palate: correct, flavourful, spicy.

JOAN SARDÀ

Ctra. Vilafranca a St. Jaume dels Domenys, Km. 8,1
8732 Castellvi de la Marca (Barcelona)
☎: +34 937 720 900 - Fax: +34 937 721 495
www.joansarda.com
joansarda@joansarda.com

CAP DE CREUS CORALL 2011 T
lladoner, samsó

83

CAP DE CREUS NACRE 2011 B
lladoner, lladoner blanco

82

LORDINA

Ctra. de Roses, Km. 9,5
17493 Vilajuiga (Girona)
☎: +34 629 578 001
www.lordina.net
lordina@lordina.es

LORDINA "AMPHORA" 2010 T
70% syrah, 30% garnacha

88 Colour: cherry, garnet rim. Nose: ripe fruit, spicy, complex, balsamic herbs. Palate: powerful, flavourful, toasty.

LORDINA MESSAGE 2011 T
cariñena, garnacha, syrah

85 Colour: cherry, garnet rim. Nose: candied fruit, fragrant herbs, dried flowers. Palate: powerful, flavourful, fruity.

LORDINA MESSAGE 2012 B
sauvignon blanc, moscatel

86 Colour: bright straw. Nose: white flowers, candied fruit, dried herbs. Palate: flavourful, fruity, fine bitter notes, balanced.

LORDINA MESSAGE 2012 RD
garnacha

85 Colour: light cherry. Nose: floral, fragrant herbs, red berry notes, ripe fruit. Palate: fine bitter notes, flavourful, fruity.

MALAJAMBOTA

Urb. La Mora s/n
17489 El Port de la Selva (Girona)
☎: +33 676 664 531
didierwollenschlaeger@yahoo.fr

MALAJAMBOTA 2012 RD
garnacha, cabernet sauvignon

79

MALAJAMBOTA 2009 T ROBLE
syrah, cabernet sauvignon, garnacha

84

MALAJAMBOTA MUSCAT 2009 B
moscatel de alejandría

84

MALAJAMBOTA MUSCAT 2011 B
moscatel de alejandría

80

MAS ESTELA

Mas Estela
17489 Selva de Mar (Girona)
☎: +34 972 126 176 - Fax: +34 972 388 011
www.masestela.com
masestela@hotmail.com

ESPIRITU 2008 TC
80% garnacha, 10% syrah, 10% samsó

85 Colour: cherry, garnet rim. Nose: spicy, creamy oak, fine reductive notes. Palate: powerful, flavourful, round tannins.

MAS LLUNES

Ctra. de Vilajuiga, s/n
17780 Garriguella (Girona)
☎: +34 972 552 684 - Fax: +34 972 530 112
www.masllunes.es
masllunes@masllunes.es

CERCIUM 2011 T
33% samsó, 28% garnacha, 21% syrah, 18% cabernet sauvignon

88 Colour: cherry, garnet rim. Nose: ripe fruit, fragrant herbs, spicy, red berry notes. Palate: powerful, flavourful, balanced.

EMPÓRION 2007 T
86% cabernet sauvignon, 14% syrah

86 Colour: deep cherry. Nose: fruit preserve, balsamic herbs, spicy, creamy oak. Palate: flavourful, reductive nuances.

MARAGDA 2012 B
74% garnacha blanca, 17% garnacha roja, 9% macabeo

84

MARAGDA ROSA 2012 RD
72% garnacha, 28% syrah

85 Colour: rose, purple rim. Nose: powerfull, ripe fruit, red berry notes, floral. Palate: powerful, fruity, fresh.

MAS LLUNES GARNATXA D'EMPORDA SOLERES B SOLERA
100% garnacha roja

91 Colour: iodine, amber rim. Nose: powerfull, complex, elegant, dry nuts, toasty. Palate: rich, fine bitter notes, fine solera notes, long, spicy.

NIVIA 2011 BFB
69% garnacha blanca, 31% samsó blanc

89 Colour: bright yellow. Nose: powerfull, ripe fruit, sweet spices, creamy oak, fragrant herbs. Palate: rich, flavourful, good acidity, balanced.

RHODES 2008 T
72% samsó, 28% syrah

90 Colour: pale ruby, brick rim edge. Nose: ripe fruit, balsamic herbs, fine reductive notes, spicy, creamy oak. Palate: flavourful, rich, spicy, long.

MAS OLLER

Ctra. GI-652, Km. 0,23
17123 Torrent (Girona)
☎: +34 972 300 001 - Fax: +34 972 300 001
www.masoller.es
info@masoller.es

MAS OLLER MAR 2012 B
picapoll, malvasía

91 Colour: bright straw. Nose: fruit preserve, candied fruit, citrus fruit. Palate: fine bitter notes, good acidity.

MAS OLLER PLUS 2011 T
syrah, garnacha

92 Colour: very deep cherry. Nose: powerfull, candied fruit, ripe fruit, warm. Palate: powerful, fine bitter notes, good acidity.

MAS OLLER PUR 2012 T
syrah, garnacha, cabernet sauvignon

92 Colour: cherry, garnet rim. Nose: spicy, creamy oak, toasty, characterful. Palate: powerful, flavourful, toasty, round tannins.

MASIA SERRA

Dels Solés, 20
17708 Cantallops (Girona)
☎: +34 689 703 687
www.masiaserra.com
masiaserra@masiaserra.com

AROA 2008 T
100% garnacha

89 Colour: cherry, garnet rim. Nose: ripe fruit, smoky, spicy, wild herbs. Palate: good structure, round tannins.

IO MASIA SERRA 2009 T
70% garnacha, 20% cabernet franc, 10% merlot

91 Colour: cherry, garnet rim. Nose: ripe fruit, spicy, creamy oak, toasty. Palate: powerful, flavourful, toasty, round tannins.

OLIVEDA S.A.

La Roca, 3
17750 Capmany (Girona)
☎: +34 972 549 012 - Fax: +34 972 549 106
www.grupoliveda.com
comercial@grupoliveda.com

FINCA FUROT 2006 TR
10% cabernet sauvignon, 80% garnacha, 10% merlot

85 Colour: dark-red cherry, orangey edge. Nose: fruit preserve, grassy, tobacco, waxy notes. Palate: spicy, long.

MASIA OLIVEDA BLANC DE BLANCS 2012 B
60% macabeo, 40% chardonnay

86 Colour: bright straw. Nose: floral, candied fruit, fragrant herbs. Palate: flavourful, fresh, fruity, balanced.

MASIA OLIVEDA NEGRE JOVE 2012 T
40% samsó, 60% cabernet sauvignon

83

MASIA OLIVEDA ROSAT FLOR 2012 RD
20% samsó, 50% garnacha, 30% cabernet sauvignon

87 Colour: rose, purple rim. Nose: powerfull, ripe fruit, red berry notes, floral, lactic notes. Palate: powerful, fruity, fresh.

OLIVER CONTI

Puignau, s/n
17550 Capmany (Girona)
☎: +34 972 193 161 - Fax: +34 972 193 040
www.oliverconti.com
oliverconti@oliverconti.com

OLIVER CONTI ARA 2010 T
garnacha, cabernet sauvignon

89 Colour: cherry, garnet rim. Nose: ripe fruit, spicy, creamy oak, balsamic herbs. Palate: powerful, flavourful, toasty, spicy.

OLIVER CONTI CARLOTA 2010 T
cabernet franc

90 Colour: cherry, garnet rim. Nose: ripe fruit, spicy, creamy oak, earthy notes. Palate: powerful, flavourful, toasty, round tannins, elegant.

OLIVER CONTI ETIQUETA NEGRA 2010 B BARRICA
gewürztraminer, macabeo, moscatel

90 Colour: bright straw. Nose: white flowers, candied fruit, fragrant herbs, sweet spices, creamy oak. Palate: powerful, flavourful, spicy. Personality.

OLIVER CONTI ETIQUETA NEGRA 2010 T
cabernet sauvignon, merlot

87 Colour: cherry, garnet rim. Nose: fruit preserve, fragrant herbs, creamy oak. Palate: spicy, long, flavourful.

OLIVER CONTI TREYU 2012 B
gewürztraminer, macabeo

87 Colour: bright straw. Nose: ripe fruit, white flowers, jasmine, fragrant herbs. Palate: long, rich, flavourful.

OLIVER CONTI TURÓ NEGRE 2010 T
cabernet sauvignon, merlot, cabernet franc

90 Colour: bright cherry. Nose: ripe fruit, sweet spices, creamy oak, balsamic herbs. Palate: flavourful, fruity, toasty, round tannins.

PERE GUARDIOLA

Ctra. GI-602, Km. 2,9
17750 Capmany (Girona)
☎: +34 972 549 096 - Fax: +34 972 549 097
www.pereguardiola.com
vins@pereguardiola.com

ANHEL D'EMPORDÀ 2012 B
70% xarel.lo, 30% garnacha blanca

86 Colour: bright straw. Nose: citrus fruit, ripe fruit, fragrant herbs, spicy. Palate: balsamic, spicy, easy to drink.

ANHEL D'EMPORDÀ 2012 RD
garnacha

85 Colour: light cherry. Nose: floral, candied fruit, fragrant herbs, balanced. Palate: fresh, fruity, flavourful.

CLOS FLORESTA 2005 TR
garnacha, syrah, cabernet sauvignon

88 Colour: light cherry. Nose: ripe fruit, spicy, creamy oak, toasty, fine reductive notes. Palate: powerful, flavourful, toasty.

FLORESTA 2008 TC
merlot, syrah, cabernet sauvignon, samsó

88 Colour: cherry, garnet rim. Nose: ripe fruit, spicy, creamy oak, balsamic herbs. Palate: powerful, flavourful, toasty.

FLORESTA 2012 B
macabeo, sauvignon blanc, xarel.lo, garnacha blanca, chardonnay

85 Colour: bright straw. Nose: white flowers, fragrant herbs, citrus fruit. Palate: flavourful, fruity, good acidity, balanced.

FLORESTA 2012 RD
garnacha, merlot, cabernet sauvignon, samsó

85 Colour: rose, purple rim. Nose: ripe fruit, floral, balsamic herbs. Palate: easy to drink, powerful, flavourful.

FLORESTA 3B8 2007 T
merlot, garnacha, samsó

84

JONCÀRIA MOSCAT BARRICA 2010 BFB
moscatel de alejandría

88 Colour: bright yellow. Nose: candied fruit, floral, honeyed notes, creamy oak. Palate: creamy, long, powerful, flavourful.

TORRE DE ÇAPMANY GARNATXA D'EMPORDÀ B GRAN RESERVA

88 Colour: light mahogany. Nose: powerfull, floral, honeyed notes, candied fruit, fragrant herbs, sweet spices. Palate: flavourful, sweet, good acidity, long.

ROIG PARALS

Garriguella, 8
17752 Mollet de Peralada (Girona)
☎: +34 972 634 320
www.roigparals.cat
info@roigparals.cat

CAMÍ DE CORMES 2008 T
100% samsó

88 Colour: pale ruby, brick rim edge. Nose: fruit preserve, sweet spices, creamy oak, fine reductive notes. Palate: long, spicy, balsamic.

FINCA PLA DEL MOLÍ 2008 T
50% cabernet sauvignon, 50% merlot

87 Colour: pale ruby, brick rim edge. Nose: spicy, fine reductive notes, wet leather, aged wood nuances, fruit liqueur notes. Palate: spicy, long.

LA BOTERA 2010 T
80% samsó, 20% cabernet sauvignon

83

ROIG PARALS 2011 T
samsó, garnacha

88 Colour: cherry, garnet rim. Nose: ripe fruit, spicy, creamy oak, toasty, complex. Palate: powerful, flavourful, toasty, round tannins.

SETZEVINS CELLER

Relliquer, 11 Baixos
17753 Espolla (Girona)
☎: +34 639 264 313
www.setzevins.cat
setzevins@gmail.com

NÉSTOR DE SETZEVINS 2010 T
garnacha, cariñena, syrah

85 Colour: dark-red cherry, orangey edge. Nose: damp earth, fruit preserve, grassy. Palate: powerful, flavourful.

OCTUBRE DE SETZEVINS 2007 T
cariñena, garnacha, syrah

85 Colour: pale ruby, brick rim edge. Nose: fruit preserve, fragrant herbs, creamy oak. Palate: flavourful, spicy.

OCTUBRE DE SETZEVINS 2009 T
garnacha, syrah, cariñena

82

SOTA ELS ÀNGELS

Apdo. Correos 27
17100 La Bisbal (Girona)
☎: +34 872 006 976
www.sotaelsangels.com
info@sotaelsangels.com

DESEA 2009 TR
syrah, samsó, carmènère, merlot, cabernet sauvignon

88 Colour: cherry, garnet rim. Nose: ripe fruit, balsamic herbs, spicy, creamy oak. Palate: spicy, long, balsamic.

SOTA ELS ÀNGELS 2007 TR
syrah, samsó, merlot, cabernet sauvignon, carménère

89 Colour: deep cherry. Nose: ripe fruit, fragrant herbs, spicy, creamy oak, fine reductive notes. Palate: powerful, unctuous, spicy.

SOTA ELS ÀNGELS 2008 TR
cabernet sauvignon, samsó, carménère

90 Colour: deep cherry. Nose: ripe fruit, fragrant herbs, spicy, creamy oak, fine reductive notes. Palate: powerful, flavourful, spicy.

SOTA ELS ÀNGELS 2011 BFB
picapoll, viognier

90 Colour: bright yellow. Nose: powerfull, ripe fruit, sweet spices, creamy oak, fragrant herbs. Palate: rich, flavourful, fresh, good acidity, elegant.

VINÍCOLA DEL NORDEST

Empolla, 9
17752 Mollet de Peralada (Girona)
☎: +34 972 563 150 - Fax: +34 972 545 134
www.vinicoladelnordest.com
vinicola@vinicoladelnordest.com

ANUBIS GARNATXA DE L'EMPORDÀ DULCE NATURAL GRAN RESERVA
100% garnacha roja

89 Colour: iodine, amber rim. Nose: dry nuts, fruit liqueur notes, caramel, creamy oak, varnish, acetaldehyde. Palate: long, spicy, powerful, flavourful.

COVEST 2012 RD
samsó, garnacha

79

COVEST BLANC 2012 B
macabeo, chardonnay, sauvignon blanc, garnacha blanca, moscatel de alejandría

82

COVEST GARNATXA DE L'EMPORDA B RESERVA
100% garnacha roja

87 Colour: light mahogany. Nose: candied fruit, dry nuts, acetaldehyde, sweet spices. Palate: powerful, flavourful, spicy.

COVEST MOSCATEL DE L'EMPORDA B
moscatel de alejandría

88 Colour: golden. Nose: powerfull, floral, honeyed notes, candied fruit, fragrant herbs. Palate: flavourful, sweet, fresh, fruity, good acidity, long.

GARRIGAL 2009 TC
80% garnacha, 20% samsó

82

VINOS JOC - JORDI OLIVER CONTI

Mas Marti
17467 Sant Mori (Girona)
☎: +34 607 222 002
www.vinojoc.com
info@vinojoc.com

JOC BLANC EMPORDÀ 2012 B
60% garnacha, 40% macabeo

87 Colour: bright straw. Nose: floral, candied fruit, fragrant herbs. Palate: balanced, good acidity, easy to drink.

JOC NEGRE EMPORDÀ 2011 T
65% garnacha, 15% syrah, 10% cabernet sauvignon, 10% cabernet franc

84

VINYES D'OLIVARDOTS

Paratge Olivadots, s/n
17750 Capmany (Girona)
☎: +34 650 395 627
www.olivardots.com
vdo@olivardots.com

BLANC DE GRESA 2011 B
garnacha blanca, garnacha rosada, cariñena blanca

89 Colour: bright yellow. Nose: ripe fruit, creamy oak, fragrant herbs, aged wood nuances. Palate: rich, flavourful, fresh, good acidity.

FINCA OLIVARDOTS 2011 T
70% syrah, 20% garnacha, 10% cariñena

90 Colour: cherry, purple rim. Nose: floral, red berry notes, ripe fruit, creamy oak. Palate: flavourful, long, spicy, elegant.

GRESA 2008 T
30% garnacha, 30% cariñena, 30% syrah, 10% cabernet sauvignon

92 Colour: cherry, garnet rim. Nose: ripe fruit, spicy, creamy oak, toasty, balanced, mineral. Palate: powerful, flavourful, toasty, balanced, elegant.

VD'O 1.09 2009 T
100% cariñena

92 Colour: cherry, garnet rim. Nose: ripe fruit, fragrant herbs, dry stone, spicy, creamy oak, balanced. Palate: powerful, flavourful, complex, spicy, balanced.

VD'O 2.09 2009 T
100% cariñena

92 Colour: cherry, garnet rim. Nose: ripe fruit, balsamic herbs, sweet spices, creamy oak, earthy notes. Palate: flavourful, balanced, long, spicy, elegant.

VD'O 4.09 2009 T
100% cabernet sauvignon

91 Colour: cherry, garnet rim. Nose: earthy notes, ripe fruit, balsamic herbs, sweet spices, creamy oak. Palate: round tannins, flavourful, balanced, elegant.

VD'O 5.10 2010 T
100% garnacha

91 Colour: cherry, garnet rim. Nose: ripe fruit, spicy, creamy oak, toasty, fragrant herbs. Palate: powerful, flavourful, toasty, round tannins, elegant.

VINYES DELS ASPRES

Requesens, 7
17708 Cantallops (Girona)
☎: +34 619 741 442 - Fax: +34 972 420 662
www.vinyesdelsaspres.cat
vinyesdelsaspres@vinyesdelsaspres.cat

BAC DE LES GINESTERES VINO DULCE NATURAL 2004 DULCE
garnacha roja

86 Colour: old gold, amber rim. Nose: acetaldehyde, varnish, aromatic coffee, candied fruit. Palate: correct, long, spicy.

BLANC DELS ASPRES 2011 BFB
100% garnacha blanca

85 Colour: bright yellow. Nose: ripe fruit, powerfull, toasty, aged wood nuances. Palate: flavourful, fruity, spicy, toasty, long.

NEGRE DELS ASPRES 2009 TC
garnacha, cariñena, merlot, cabernet sauvignon

89 Colour: cherry, garnet rim. Nose: ripe fruit, spicy, creamy oak, toasty, complex. Palate: powerful, flavourful, toasty, round tannins.

ORIOL DELS ASPRES 2012 T
54% cariñena, 39% garnacha, 7% cabernet sauvignon

87 Colour: cherry, purple rim. Nose: expressive, red berry notes, floral, spicy, balsamic herbs. Palate: flavourful, fruity, good acidity.

S'ALOU 2009 TC
50% garnacha, 25% syrah, 25% cabernet sauvignon

90 Colour: cherry, garnet rim. Nose: ripe fruit, spicy, creamy oak, toasty, complex. Palate: powerful, flavourful, toasty, round tannins.

VI DE PANSES DELS ASPRES 2006 B
garnacha roja

85 Colour: old gold. Nose: dried fruit, sweet spices, honeyed notes, toasty. Palate: powerful, flavourful, spirituous.

DO GETARIAKO TXAKOLINA / D.O.P.

SAN SEBASTIÁN

GUIPÚZCOA

▽ Consejo Regulador
● DO Boundary

LOCATION:

Mainly on the coastal belt of the province of Guipuzcoa, covering the vineyards situated in the municipal areas of Aia, Getaria and Zarauz, at a distance of about 25 km from San Sebastián.

CLIMATE:

Fairly mild, thanks to the influence of the Bay of Biscay.
The average annual temperature is 13°C, and the rainfall is plentiful with an average of 1,600 mm per year.

SOIL:

The vineyards are situated in small valleys and gradual hillsides at altitudes of up to 200 m. They are found on humid brownish-grey limy soil, which are rich in organic matter.

GRAPE VARIETIES:

WHITE: : *hondarrabi zuri, gros manseng, riesling, chardonnay y petit courbu.*
RED: *Hondarrabi Beltza.*

FIGURES:

Vineyard surface: 402 – **Wine-Growers:** 96 – **Wineries:** 27 – **2012 Harvest rating:** Excellent– **Production:** 2.268.700 litres – **Market percentages:** 93% domestic. 7% export

VINTAGE RATING **PEÑÍN**GUIDE

2008	2009	2010	2011	2012
VERY GOOD	VERY GOOD	VERY GOOD	VERY GOOD	EXCELLENT

CONSEJO REGULADOR
Parque Aldamar, 4 bajo - 20808 Getaria (Gipuzkoa) ☎: +34 943 140 383 - Fax: +34 943 896 030
info@getariakotxakolina.com   www.getariakotxakolina.com

ADUR

Paseo De Zubiaurre N° 30 1°lzq
20013 Donostia (Gipuzkoa)
☎: +34 617 216 617
www.adurtxakolina.com
info@adurtxakolina.com

ADUR 2012 B
100% hondarrabi zuri

89 Colour: bright straw. Nose: fresh, fresh fruit, white flowers, citrus fruit, balsamic herbs. Palate: flavourful, fruity, spicy.

AGERRE

Agerre Baserria - B° Askizu
20808 Getaria (Gipuzkoa)
☎: +34 943 140 446 - Fax: +34 943 140 446
www.agerretxakolina.com
agerre@agerretxakolina.com

AGERRE 2012 B
hondarrabi zuri

86 Colour: bright straw. Nose: fresh, white flowers, medium intensity. Palate: correct, easy to drink, balsamic, fruity.

AIZPURUA

Ctra. de Meagas
20808 Getaria (Gipuzkoa)
☎: +34 943 140 696
www.txakoliaizpurua.com
aizpuruaaialle@yahoo.es

AIZPURUA. B 2012 B
hondarrabi zuri

88 Colour: bright straw. Nose: white flowers, jasmine, fruit expression, balsamic herbs. Palate: balanced, flavourful, fruity.

ARREGI

Talaimendi, 727- Bajo
20800 Zarautz (Gipuzkoa)
☎: +34 943 580 835
www.txakoliarregi.com
info@txakoliarregi.com

ARREGI 2012 B
hondarrabi zuri

87 Colour: bright straw. Nose: candied fruit, dried flowers, fragrant herbs. Palate: flavourful, fresh, fruity.

ARREGI 2012 RD
hondarrabi beltza

86 Colour: raspberry rose. Nose: medium intensity, fresh fruit, balanced, scrubland. Palate: fruity, fresh.

BODEGA REZABAL

Itsas Begi Etxea, 628
20800 Zarautz (Gipuzkoa)
☎: +34 943 580 899 - Fax: +34 943 580 775
www.txakolirezabal.com
info@txakolirezabal.com

TXAKOLI REZABAL 2012 B
100% hondarrabi zuri

90 Colour: bright straw. Nose: floral, citrus fruit, ripe fruit, fragrant herbs, expressive. Palate: fresh, fruity, flavourful, spicy, long.

TXAKOLI REZABAL 2012 RD
100% hondarrabi beltza

87 Colour: raspberry rose. Nose: balanced, expressive, red berry notes, balsamic herbs, faded flowers. Palate: fruity, flavourful, fresh, long.

BODEGAS SANTARBA

Santa Bárbara, 7
20800 Zarautz (Gipuzkoa)
☎: +34 943 140 452
santarba-txakolindegia@hotmail.es

SANTARBA 2012 B
hondarrabi zuri

86 Colour: bright straw. Nose: fresh, balanced, fresh fruit, citrus fruit, scrubland. Palate: fruity, flavourful, balanced, good acidity.

GAÑETA

Agerre Goikoa Baserria
20808 Getaria (Gipuzkoa)
☎: +34 943 140 174 - Fax: +34 943 140 174
gainetatxakolina@gmail.com

GAÑETA 2012 B
hondarrabi zuri

86 Colour: bright yellow. Nose: dried herbs, ripe fruit, fragrant herbs. Palate: powerful, flavourful, ripe fruit.

GAÑETA BEREZIA 2011 B
hondarrabi zuri

88 Colour: bright straw. Nose: floral, ripe fruit, fragrant herbs, expressive. Palate: flavourful, good structure, balanced, elegant.

GAÑETA ROSÉ 2012 RD
hondarrabi beltza

85 Colour: raspberry rose. Nose: fresh, balanced, red berry notes, scrubland. Palate: fruity, flavourful, good finish.

GOROSTI

Bio. Elorriaga
20820 Deba (Gipuzkoa)
☎: +34 670 408 439
gorostibodega@hotmail.com

FLYSCH 2012 B
hondarrabi zuri, petit corbo

89 Colour: bright straw. Nose: fresh, white flowers, citrus fruit, ripe fruit. Palate: flavourful, fruity, good acidity.

HIRUZTA

Barrio Jaizubia, 266
20280 Hondarribia (Gipuzkoa)
☎: +34 943 646 689 - Fax: +34 943 260 801
www.hiruzta.com
info@hiruzta.com

HIRUZTA BEREZIA 2012 B
95% hondarrabi zuri, 5% gros manseng

92 Colour: bright straw. Nose: floral, dried herbs, fragrant herbs, candied fruit, balanced, expressive. Palate: powerful, spicy, long, balanced, elegant.

HIRUZTA TXAKOLINA 2012 B
95% hondarrabi zuri, 5% gros manseng

89 Colour: bright straw, greenish rim. Nose: scrubland, fresh fruit, balanced. Palate: flavourful, good acidity, balanced.

JAVIER ARREGUI

Xaserio Egi-Handi Bº Musakola
20500 Arrasate (Gipuskoa)
☎: +34 943 771 913 - Fax: +34 943 770 621
arregui.her@telefonica.net

KATAIDE 2012 B
hondarrabi zuri, petit corbu

82

JOSEBA IÑAKI ETXEBERRIA ZUBIZARRETA Y OTRO

Bengoetxe Baserria
20212 Olaberria (Gipuzkoa)
☎: +34 943 884 955 - Fax: +34 943 884 955
www.txakolibengoetxe.com
inakietxeberria@hotmail.es

BENGOETXE 2012 B
hondarrabi zuri, gros manseng

86 Colour: bright yellow. Nose: dried flowers, citrus fruit, fragrant herbs, fruit expression. Palate: light-bodied, fresh, fruity.

BENGOETXE BEREZIA 2011 B
hondarrabi zuri, gros manseng

87 Colour: bright yellow. Nose: expressive, ripe fruit, faded flowers, dry stone. Palate: flavourful, correct, balanced.

JUAN CELAYA

Upaingoa-Barrio Zañartuko
20560 Oñati (Gipuzkoa)
☎: +34 948 782 255 - Fax: +34 948 401 182
www.upain.es
administracion@naparralde.com

UPAINGOA 2009 B
hondarrabi zuri, riesling

86 Colour: bright yellow. Nose: ripe fruit, faded flowers, fragrant herbs, undergrowth. Palate: flavourful, fruity, long.

UPAINGOA 2010 B
hondarrabi zuri, riesling

85 Colour: bright yellow. Nose: dry nuts, faded flowers, wild herbs. Palate: flavourful, fine bitter notes.

UPAINGOA 2011 B
hondarrabi zuri, riesling

86 Colour: bright straw, greenish rim. Nose: faded flowers, ripe fruit, balanced. Palate: rich, fruity, correct.

UPAINGOA 2012 B
hondarrabi zuri, riesling

87 Colour: bright straw. Nose: floral, fresh fruit, expressive. Palate: fruity, fresh, good acidity, correct.

K5

Apdo. Correos 258
20800 Zarautz (Gipuzkoa)
☎: +34 943 240 005
www.txakolina-k5.com
bodega@txakolina-k5.com

K5 2012 B
100% hondarrabi zuri

89 Colour: bright yellow. Nose: warm, ripe fruit, balsamic herbs, dried herbs. Palate: powerful, flavourful, long, balanced.

SAGARMIÑA

Sagarmiña Baserria
20830 Mitriku (Gipuzcoa)
☎: +34 943 603 225
www.txakolisagarmina.com
txakolisagarmina@live.com

SAGARMIÑA 2012 B
hondarrabi zuri

87 Colour: bright straw. Nose: fresh fruit, white flowers, medium intensity, expressive. Palate: fruity, good acidity, fine bitter notes.

TALAI BERRI

Talaimendi, 728
20800 Zarautz (Gipuzkoa)
☎: +34 943 132 750 - Fax: +34 943 132 750
www.talaiberri.com
info@talaiberri.com

TXAKOLI FINCA JAKUE 2012 B
hondarrabi zuri

87 Colour: bright straw. Nose: dried flowers, citrus fruit, ripe fruit, dried herbs, expressive. Palate: flavourful, balsamic, spicy.

TXAKOLI TALAI BERRI 2012 B
90% hondarrabi zuri, hondarrabi beltza

87 Colour: bright straw. Nose: medium intensity, fresh fruit, fragrant herbs, floral. Palate: fresh, fruity, easy to drink.

TXAKOLI TALAI BERRI 2012 T
100% hondarrabi beltza

84

TXAKOLI AKARREGI TXIKI

Caserío Akarregi Txiki
20808 Guetaria (Gipuzkoa)
☎: +34 689 035 789
www.akarregitxiki.com
lasaldeelkartea@hotmail.com

AKARREGI TXIKI 2012 B
hondarrabi zuri, hondarrabi beltza

87 Colour: bright straw. Nose: medium intensity, scrubland, white flowers. Palate: flavourful, fruity, correct, good acidity.

TXAKOLI AMEZTOI

Eitzaga Auzoa, 10
20808 Getaria (Gipuzkoa)
☎: +34 943 140 918 - Fax: +34 943 140 169
www.txakoliameztoi.com
ameztoi@txakoliameztoi.com

AMEZTOI 2012 B
hondarrabi zuri

89 Colour: bright straw. Nose: white flowers, citrus fruit, fresh fruit, expressive. Palate: good acidity, long, fruity, fresh.

AMEZTOI PRIMUS 2012 B
hondarrabi zuri

90 Colour: bright straw. Nose: ripe fruit, expressive, floral, tropical fruit. Palate: fruity, flavourful, long, good acidity, fresh.

AMEZTOI RUBENTIS 2012 RD
hondarrabi zuri, hondarrabi beltza

88 Colour: raspberry rose. Nose: balanced, floral, red berry notes, expressive. Palate: fresh, fruity, easy to drink.

TXAKOLI ELKANO

Barrio de Eitzaga Nº24
20808 Getaria (Gipuzkoa)
☎: +34 600 800 259
www.txakolielkano.com
txakolielkano@hotmail.com

TXAKOLI ELKANO 2012 B
hondarrabi zuri, hondarrabi beltza

89 Colour: bright straw. Nose: fresh, fresh fruit, white flowers, expressive. Palate: flavourful, fruity, good acidity, balanced, elegant.

TXAKOLI GAINTZA S.L.

Caserío Gaintza
20808 Getaria (Gipuzkoa)
☎: +34 943 140 032
www.gaintza.com
info@txakoligaintza.com

AITAKO CEPAS CENTENARIAS 2011 B
hondarrabi zuri, hondarrabi beltza, chardonnay

85 Colour: bright straw. Nose: faded flowers, wild herbs, medium intensity. Palate: fruity, good acidity, correct, fine bitter notes.

GAINTZA 2012 B
hondarrabi zuri, hondarrabi beltza, gros manseng

89 Colour: bright straw. Nose: white flowers, fragrant herbs, mineral, balanced. Palate: powerful, flavourful, fresh, fruity.

TXAKOLI ULACIA

Ctra. Meagas
20808 Getaria (Gipuzkoa)
☎: +34 943 140 893 - Fax: +34 943 140 893
nicolasulacia@euskalnet.net

TXAKOLI ULACIA 2012 B
hondarrabi zuri, hondarrabi beltza

86 Colour: bright straw. Nose: wild herbs, fresh fruit, citrus fruit, floral. Palate: flavourful, fruity, balanced, fine bitter notes.

TXOMIN ETXANIZ

Txomin Etxaniz Barrio Eitzaiga, 13
20808 Getaria (Gipuzkoa)
☎: +34 943 140 702 - Fax: +34 943 140 462
www.txominetxaniz.com
txakoli@txominetxaniz.com

EUGENIA TXOMÍN ETXANÍZ 2012 ESP
100% hondarrabi zuri

87 Colour: bright straw. Nose: fresh fruit, dried herbs, fine lees, floral. Palate: fresh, fruity, flavourful.

TXOMÍN ETXANÍZ GORRIA 2012 RD
40% hondarrabi zuri, 60% hondarrabi beltza

88 Colour: light cherry, bright. Nose: balanced, red berry notes, scrubland. Palate: flavourful, fruity, good acidity, balanced.

TXOMÍN ETXANÍZ 2012 B
100% hondarrabi zuri

90 Colour: bright straw. Nose: fresh, fresh fruit, white flowers, fragrant herbs, expressive. Palate: flavourful, fruity, good acidity, balanced.

TXOMÍN ETXANÍZ BEREZIA 2012 B
90% hondarrabi zuri, 10% hondarrabibeltza

91 Colour: bright straw. Nose: citrus fruit, ripe fruit, dried flowers, fragrant herbs, mineral. Palate: balanced, elegant, flavourful, fruity, long.

TXOMÍN ETXANÍZ UYDI 2012 B
100% hondarrabi zuri

88 Colour: bright straw. Nose: powerfull, floral, candied fruit, fragrant herbs. Palate: flavourful, sweet, fresh, fruity, good acidity, long.

TXOMÍN ETXANÍZ WHITE 2012 B
80% hondarrabi zuri, 20% chardonnay

88 Colour: bright straw. Nose: fragrant herbs, ripe fruit, tropical fruit. Palate: powerful, flavourful, ripe fruit.

ZUDUGARAI

Ctra. Zarautz - Aia Bº Laurgain
20809 Aia (Gipuzkoa)
☎: +34 943 830 386 - Fax: +34 943 835 952
www.txakolizudugarai.com
txakolizudugarai@euskalnet.net

AMATS 2012 B
100% hondarrabi zuri

85 Colour: bright yellow. Nose: balanced, floral, citrus fruit, fresh fruit. Palate: fruity, flavourful, easy to drink, good acidity.

ANTXIOLA 2012 B
100% hondarrabi zuri

84

ZUDUGARAI 2012 B
100% hondarrabi zuri

85 Colour: bright straw. Nose: ripe fruit, floral, dried herbs, spicy. Palate: fresh, fruity, easy to drink.

ZUDUGARAI 2012 RD
100% hondarrabi beltza

84

DO GRAN CANARIA / D.O.P.

LAS PALMAS DE GRAN CANARIA

▼ Consejo Regulador
● DO Boundary

LOCATION:

The production region covers 99% of the island of Gran Canaria, as the climate and the conditions of the terrain allow for the cultivation of grapes at altitudes close to sea level up to the highest mountain tops. The DO incorporates all the municipal areas of the island, except for the Tafira Protected Landscape which falls under an independent DO, Monte de Lentiscal, also fully covered in this Guide.

CLIMATE:

As with the other islands of the archipelago, the differences in altitude give rise to several microclimates which create specific characteristics for the cultivation of the vine. Nevertheless, the climate is conditioned by the influence of the trade winds which blow from the east and whose effect is more evident in the higher-lying areas.

SOIL:

The vineyards are found both in coastal areas and on higher grounds at altitudes of up to 1500 m, resulting in a varied range of soils.

GRAPE VARIETIES:

WHITE:
PREFERRED: *Malvasía, Güal, Marmajuelo* (*Bermejuela*), *Vijariego, Albillo* and *Moscatel.*
AUTHORIZED: *Listán Blanco, Burrablanca, Torrontés, Pedro Ximénez, Brebal* and *Bastardo Blanco.*
RED:
PREFERRED: *Listán Negro, Negramoll, Tintilla, Malvasía Rosada.*
AUTHORIZED: *Moscatel Negra, Bastardo Negro, Listán Prieto, Vijariego Negro, Bastardo Negro, Listón Prieto* und *Vijariego Negro.*

FIGURES:

Vineyard surface: 240– **Wine-Growers:** 348 – **Wineries:** 39 – **2012 Harvest rating:** Very Good – **Production:** 262.343 litres – **Market percentages:** 99% domestic. 1% export

2008	2009	2010	2011	2012
AVERAGE	N/A	VERY GOOD	VERY GOOD	VERY GOOD

CONSEJO REGULADOR
Calvo Sotelo, 26 - 35300 Santa Brígida (Las Palmas) ☎: +34 928 640 462 - Fax: +34 928 640 982
crdogc@yahoo.es   www.vinosdegrancanaria.es

BENTAYGA

El Alberconcillo, s/n
35360 Tejeda (Las Palmas)
☎: +34 928 426 047 - Fax: +34 928 418 795
www.bodegasbentayga.com
info@bodegasbentayga.com

AGALA 2012 T
listán negro, tintilla

86 Colour: black cherry, purple rim. Nose: spicy, ripe fruit. Palate: ripe fruit, spicy, round tannins, good acidity.

AGALA 2012 T BARRICA
baboso negro, vijariego negro, tintilla

87 Colour: cherry, purple rim. Nose: fruit expression, red berry notes, balanced, expressive. Palate: fruity, flavourful, good acidity, balanced.

AGALA AFRUTADO 2012 B
moscatel de alejandría, albillo, vijariego blanco

87 Colour: bright yellow. Nose: fresh fruit, white flowers, honeyed notes, balanced. Palate: correct, balanced, good acidity, easy to drink.

AGALA SECO 2012 B
vijariego blanco, albillo

88 Colour: bright yellow. Nose: floral, citrus fruit, medium intensity, expressive, fresh fruit. Palate: good acidity, flavourful, fruity, full.

BODEGA LOS BERRAZALES

Subida de los Romeros s/n
35480 Agaete (Las Palmas)
☎: +34 628 922 588 - Fax: +34 928 898 154
www.bodegalosberrazales.com
lugojorge3@hotmail.com

LOS BERRAZALES 2011 T ROBLE
listán negro, tintilla

84

LOS BERRAZALES 2012 T
listán negro, tintilla

82

LOS BERRAZALES 2012 T
listán negro, tintilla

86 Colour: very deep cherry, cherry, purple rim. Nose: powerfull, expressive, ripe fruit, toasty, spicy. Palate: good structure, flavourful, fruity.

LOS BERRAZALES DULCE VENDIMIA NOCTURNA 2010 B
90% moscatel, 10% malvasía

91 Colour: golden. Nose: powerfull, floral, honeyed notes, varietal, jasmine. Palate: flavourful, sweet, fruity, good acidity, long.

LOS BERRAZALES SECO 2010 BFB
60% malvasía, 40% moscatel

87 Colour: bright straw. Nose: fresh, fresh fruit, white flowers, expressive. Palate: flavourful, fruity, good acidity, balanced.

LOS BERRAZALES SECO VENDIMIA NOCTURNA 2012 B
60% malvasía, 40% moscatel

87 Colour: bright yellow. Nose: white flowers, faded flowers, ripe fruit, expressive, honeyed notes. Palate: flavourful, fruity, powerful.

LOS BERRAZALES SEMISECO VENDIMIA NOCTURNA 2012 B
60% moscatel, 40% malvasía

90 Colour: bright yellow. Nose: floral, fresh fruit, citrus fruit, tropical fruit. Palate: balanced, good acidity, long, flavourful.

BODEGA VEGA DE GÁLDAR

Camino de La Longuera - La Vega de Gáldar
35460 Gáldar (Las Palmas)
☎: +34 605 043 047
vinoamable@gmail.com

CONVENTO 2011 T
listán negro, castellana

84

EL CONVENTO DE LA VEGA 2010 T
listán negro, castellana

83

NUBIA 2012 B
50% listán blanco, 50% malvasía

87 Colour: bright straw. Nose: fresh, fresh fruit, white flowers, expressive. Palate: flavourful, fruity, balanced.

NUBIA GUAL/ALBILLO 2012 B
gual, albillo

84

VIÑA AMABLE 2011 T
70% listán negro, 30% castellana

88 Colour: cherry, garnet rim. Nose: ripe fruit, spicy, toasty, cocoa bean. Palate: powerful, flavourful, toasty, round tannins.

VIÑA AMABLE 2012 T
60% listán negro, 40% castellana

91 Colour: cherry, garnet rim. Nose: complex, balanced, expressive, ripe fruit, creamy oak. Palate: good structure, flavourful, good acidity, long.

LA HIGUERA MAYOR

El Palmital Ctra. de Telde a Santa Brígida GC 80,P.K., 7,5
35218 Telde (Las Palmas)
☎: +34 630 285 454
www.lahigueramayor.com
lahigueramayor@gmail.com

LA HIGUERA MAYOR 2011 T
tintilla, castellana, negramoll, listán negro

83

LA SAVIA ECOLÓGICA

Soront Semidan, 3 Bajo
35460 Galdar (Las Palmas)
☎: +34 617 455 863
ondina@ondinasurf.com

CALETÓN 2009 T BARRICA
listán negro, castellana

83

CALETÓN DULCE 2010 T
listán negro, castellana

88 Colour: cherry, garnet rim. Nose: candied fruit, pattiserie, sweet spices, cocoa bean, balsamic herbs. Palate: flavourful, long, good acidity.

LAUREANO ROCA DE ARMAS

Cuesta del Reventón 52
35310 Santa Brígida (Palmas de Gran Canaria)
☎: +34 607 528 868

MONTE ROCA 2012 T BARRICA

87 Colour: bright cherry. Nose: ripe fruit, sweet spices, creamy oak, expressive. Palate: flavourful, fruity, toasty, round tannins.

MONDALÓN PICACHOS S.L.

Cuesta del Mondalón, 6
35017 Palmas de Gran Canaria
(Palmas de Gran Canaria)
☎: +34 928 356 066

MONDALON 2012 B

87 Colour: bright yellow. Nose: medium intensity, white flowers, expressive. Palate: correct, balanced, good acidity.

MONDALON 2012 T

86 Colour: cherry, purple rim. Nose: medium intensity, ripe fruit, dried herbs. Palate: correct, flavourful, round tannins.

MONDALON SEMIDULCE 2012 B

88 Colour: bright straw. Nose: white flowers, expressive, elegant. Palate: fresh, fruity, flavourful, good acidity.

VIÑEDOS Y BODEGAS AGUERE

38280 Tegueste (Santa Cruz de Tenerife)
☎: +34 637 372 458
www.vinosblessed.com
bodega@vinosblesses.com

BLESSED 2011 B
100% forastera gomera

87 Colour: yellow. Nose: medium intensity, balanced, fresh fruit. Palate: fruity, fresh, good acidity, fine bitter notes.

BLESSED 2011 T
syrah, merlot, tintilla, baboso negro

86 Colour: cherry, garnet rim. Nose: macerated fruit, ripe fruit, scrubland, waxy notes. Palate: fruity, flavourful.

BLESSED VERDELLO 2011 B
verdello

86 Colour: bright yellow. Nose: ripe fruit, white flowers. Palate: flavourful, fruity, rich, good acidity.

DO JEREZ-XÉRÈS-SHERRY-MANZANILLA DE SANLÚCAR DE BARRAMEDA / D.O.P.

LOCATION:

In the province of Cádiz. The production area covers the municipal districts of Jerez de la Frontera, El Puerto de Santa María, Chipiona, Trebujena, Rota, Puerto Real, Chiclana de la Frontera and some estates in Lebrija.

CLIMATE:

Warm with Atlantic influences. The west winds play an important role, as they provide humidity and help to temper the conditions. The average annual temperature is 17.5°C, with an average rainfall of 600 mm per year.

SOIL:

The so-called 'Albariza' soil is a key factor regarding quality. This type of soil is practically white and is rich in calcium carbonate, clay and silica. It is excellent for retaining humidity and storing winter rainfall for the dry summer months. Moreover, this soil determines the so-called 'Jerez superior'. It is found in Jerez de la Frontera, Puerto de Santa María, Sanlúcar de Barrameda and certain areas of Trebujena. The remaining soil, known as 'Zona', is muddy and sandy.arenas.

GRAPE VARIETIES:

WHITE: *Palomino* (90%), *Pedro Ximénez*, *Moscatel*, *Palomino Fino* and *Palomino de Jerez*.

FIGURES:

Vineyard surface:6.281 – **Wine-Growers:** 1.721 – **Wineries:** 88 – **2012 Harvest rating:** N/A – **Production:** 25.696.243 litres – **Market percentages:** 28% domestic. 72% export

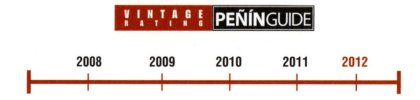

This denomination of origin, due to the wine-making process, does not make available single-year wines indicated by vintage, so the following evaluation refers to the overall quality of the wines that were tasted this year.

CONSEJO REGULADOR
Avda. Álvaro Domecq, 2 - 11405 Jerez de la Frontera (Cádiz) ☎: +34 956 332 050 - Fax: +34 956 338 908
vinjerez@sherry.org   www.sherry.org

AECOVI-JEREZ

Urb. Pie de Rey, 3- Local Izquierda
11407 Jerez de la Frontera (Cádiz)
☎: +34 956 180 873 - Fax: +34 956 180 301
www.aecovi-jerez.com
crecio@aecovi-jerez.com

ALEXANDRO MZ
palomino

88 Colour: bright straw. Nose: dried flowers, flor yeasts, pungent, saline. Palate: light-bodied, fresh, spicy.

ALEXANDRO OL
palomino

85 Colour: iodine, amber rim. Nose: dry nuts, toasty, medium intensity. Palate: rich, long, spicy.

ALEXANDRO PC
palomino

88 Colour: old gold, amber rim. Nose: ripe fruit, dry nuts, sweet spices, creamy oak. Palate: spicy, toasty, powerful, flavourful.

ALEXANDRO PX
pedro ximénez

87 Colour: mahogany. Nose: dried fruit, candied fruit, dark chocolate, sweet spices. Palate: rich, spicy, long, creamy.

ALVARO DOMECQ

Madre de Dios s/n
11401 Jerez de la Frontera (Cádiz)
☎: +34 956 339 634 - Fax: +34 956 340 402
www.alvarodomecq.com
alvarodomecqsl@alvarodomecq.com

1730 VORS OL
100% palomino

93 Colour: iodine, amber rim. Nose: powerfull, complex, elegant, dry nuts, toasty, pungent, acetaldehyde. Palate: rich, long, fine solera notes, spicy.

ALBUREJO OL
100% palomino

90 Colour: dark mahogany. Nose: powerfull, complex, elegant, dry nuts, toasty. Palate: rich, long, fine solera notes, spicy.

ARANDA CREAM CR
palomino, pedro ximénez

87 Colour: iodine, amber rim. Nose: dried fruit, toasty, sweet spices. Palate: sweetness, fine bitter notes.

LA JACA MZ
100% palomino

88 Colour: bright yellow. Nose: complex, saline, flor yeasts, faded flowers. Palate: rich, powerful, flavourful.

LA JANDA FI
100% palomino

91 Colour: bright yellow. Nose: expressive, pungent, saline, dried flowers. Palate: rich, powerful, fine bitter notes.

PEDRO XIMÉNEZ 1730 PX
100% pedro ximénez

92 Colour: dark mahogany. Nose: complex, fruit liqueur notes, dried fruit, dark chocolate, aromatic coffee. Palate: sweet, rich, unctuous, powerful, fine solera notes.

BEAM SPAIN, S.L.

San Ildefonso, 3
11403 Jerez de la Frontera (Cádiz)
☎: +34 956 151 500 - Fax: +34 956 338 674
www.bodegasharveys.com
bodegasdejerez@beamglobal.com

HARVEYS BRISTOL CREAM CR
palomino, pedro ximénez

85 Colour: mahogany. Nose: caramel, toasty, creamy oak, dry nuts, dried fruit. Palate: sweet, flavourful, correct.

HARVEYS FI
100% palomino

92 Colour: bright yellow. Nose: complex, expressive, pungent, saline, dried herbs. Palate: rich, powerful, fresh, fine bitter notes.

HARVEYS FINE OLD VORS AM

92 Colour: iodine, amber rim. Nose: powerfull, toasty, aged wood nuances, creamy oak, roasted almonds. Palate: rich, fine bitter notes, fine solera notes, long, spicy.

HARVEYS VORS PC
100% palomino

93 Colour: light mahogany. Nose: acetaldehyde, pattiserie, spicy, aged wood nuances, expressive. Palate: fine solera notes, powerful, flavourful, complex, balanced, elegant.

HARVEYS VORS PX
100% pedro ximénez

90 Colour: dark mahogany. Nose: complex, fruit liqueur notes, dried fruit, pattiserie, toasty. Palate: sweet, rich, unctuous, spicy.

HARVEYS VORS RICH OLD OL
90% palomino, 10% pedro ximénez

94 Colour: iodine, amber rim. Nose: complex, elegant, dry nuts, toasty, acetaldehyde, varnish. Palate: rich, long, fine solera notes, spicy, balanced.

TERRY AMONTILLADO AM
100% palomino

90 Colour: iodine, amber rim. Nose: acetaldehyde, aged wood nuances, sweet spices. Palate: powerful, flavourful, dry.

TERRY FINO FI
100% palomino

90 Colour: bright yellow. Nose: complex, expressive, pungent, sweet spices. Palate: rich, powerful, fresh, sweetness.

TERRY OLOROSO OL
100% palomino

90 Colour: iodine, amber rim. Nose: powerfull, complex, dry nuts, toasty. Palate: rich, long, fine solera notes, spicy.

TERRY PEDRO XIMÉNEZ PX
100% pedro ximénez

91 Colour: dark mahogany. Nose: complex, fruit liqueur notes, dried fruit, pattiserie, toasty. Palate: sweet, rich, unctuous, powerful.

BODEGA CÉSAR FLORIDO

Padre Lerchundi, 35-37
11550 Chipiona (Cádiz)
☎: +34 956 371 285 - Fax: +34 956 370 222
www.bodegasflorido.com
florido@bodegasflorido.com

CÉSAR FLORIDO MOSCATEL DORADO MOSCATEL
moscatel

89 Colour: iodine, amber rim. Nose: honeyed notes, sweet spices, pattiserie, creamy oak. Palate: round, rich, powerful, flavourful.

CÉSAR FLORIDO MOSCATEL ESPECIAL MOSCATEL
100% moscatel

91 Colour: dark mahogany. Nose: citrus fruit, aromatic coffee, dark chocolate, creamy oak, acetaldehyde. Palate: spirituous, powerful, flavourful.

CÉSAR FLORIDO MOSCATEL PASAS MOSCATEL
moscatel

88 Colour: iodine, amber rim. Nose: spicy, candied fruit, dried fruit. Palate: spirituous, powerful, sweet.

CRUZ DEL MAR CR
75% moscatel, 25% palomino

85 Colour: dark mahogany. Nose: cocoa bean, toasty, powerfull, sweet spices. Palate: sweetness, spirituous, burning notes.

CRUZ DEL MAR OL
100% palomino

87 Colour: iodine, amber rim. Nose: varnish, aged wood nuances, spicy, medium intensity. Palate: correct, fine bitter notes, toasty.

FINO CÉSAR FLORIDO FI
100% palomino

90 Colour: bright straw. Nose: spicy, floral, saline. Palate: flavourful, dry, long.

PALO CORTADO RESERVA DE FAMILIA "PEÑA DEL ÁGUILA" PC
100% palomino

90 Colour: iodine, amber rim. Nose: varnish, aged wood nuances, spicy, toasty. Palate: spirituous, fine bitter notes, powerful, flavourful.

BODEGAS BARBADILLO

Luis de Eguilaz, 11
11540 Sanlúcar de Barrameda (Cádiz)
☎: +34 956 385 500 - Fax: +34 956 385 501
www.barbadillo.com
barbadillo@barbadillo.com

BARBADILLO AMONTILLADO VORS AM
palomino

95 Colour: iodine, amber rim. Nose: powerfull, complex, elegant, dry nuts, toasty, acetaldehyde. Palate: rich, fine bitter notes, fine solera notes, long, spicy.

BARBADILLO OLOROSO DULCE VORS OL
pedro ximénez, palomino

91 Colour: iodine, amber rim. Nose: powerfull, complex, dry nuts, toasty. Palate: rich, long, fine solera notes, spicy, sweet.

BARBADILLO OLOROSO SECO VORS OL
palomino

92 Colour: iodine, amber rim. Nose: powerfull, complex, elegant, dry nuts, toasty. Palate: rich, long, fine solera notes, spicy.

BARBADILLO PALO CORTADO VORS PC
palomino

93 Colour: iodine, amber rim. Nose: pattiserie, spicy, varnish, dry nuts, toasty, pungent. Palate: good acidity, flavourful, fine bitter notes, spicy.

CUCO OLOROSO SECO OL
palomino

91 Colour: iodine, amber rim. Nose: powerfull, dry nuts, toasty, acetaldehyde. Palate: rich, long, fine solera notes, spicy.

EVA CREAM CR
pedro ximénez, palomino

90 Colour: iodine, amber rim. Nose: toasty, spicy. Palate: flavourful, fine bitter notes, sweetness.

LA CILLA PX
pedro ximénez

89 Colour: dark mahogany. Nose: complex, fruit liqueur notes, dried fruit, sweet spices. Palate: sweet, rich, unctuous, powerful, flavourful.

LAURA MOSCATEL
moscatel

88 Colour: iodine, amber rim. Nose: overripe fruit, honeyed notes, spicy, sweet spices. Palate: flavourful, sweet.

MUYFINA MZ
palomino

89 Colour: bright yellow. Nose: expressive, pungent, saline. Palate: rich, powerful, fresh, fine bitter notes.

OBISPO GASCÓN PC
palomino

93 Colour: iodine, amber rim. Nose: candied fruit, toasty, sweet spices, pungent. Palate: long, fine solera notes, fine bitter notes.

PRÍNCIPE AM
palomino

91 Colour: iodine, amber rim. Nose: powerfull, complex, elegant, dry nuts, pungent. Palate: rich, fine bitter notes, fine solera notes, long, spicy.

RELIQUIA AM
palomino

96 Colour: iodine, amber rim. Nose: powerfull, complex, elegant, dry nuts, toasty, acetaldehyde, pungent. Palate: rich, fine bitter notes, fine solera notes, long, spicy.

RELIQUIA OL
palomino

95 Colour: iodine, amber rim. Nose: powerfull, complex, elegant, dry nuts, toasty. Palate: rich, long, fine solera notes, spicy.

RELIQUIA PC
palomino

95 Colour: iodine, amber rim. Nose: acetaldehyde, pungent, spicy, varnish, creamy oak, dry nuts. Palate: flavourful, powerful, fine solera notes, long.

RELIQUIA PX
pedro ximénez

96 Colour: dark mahogany. Nose: complex, fruit liqueur notes, dried fruit, pattiserie, toasty, aged wood nuances, acetaldehyde. Palate: sweet, rich, unctuous, powerful.

SAN RAFAEL OL
pedro ximénez, palomino

88 Colour: iodine, amber rim. Nose: powerfull, dry nuts, toasty. Palate: rich, long, spicy, sweetness.

SOLEAR EN RAMA MZ
palomino

95 Colour: bright golden. Nose: complex, expressive, pungent, saline, acetaldehyde, powerfull. Palate: rich, powerful, fresh, fine bitter notes, complex.

SOLEAR MZ
palomino

92 Colour: bright yellow. Nose: pungent, saline, faded flowers, flor yeasts. Palate: fresh, flavourful, complex, elegant.

BODEGAS BARÓN

Molinillo 2a 2 y 3
11540 Sanlúcar de Barrameda (Cádiz)
☎: +34 956 360 796 - Fax: +34 956 363 256
www.bodegasbaron.net
baron.as@terra.es

BARÓN AM GRAN RESERVA
palomino

90 Colour: iodine, amber rim. Nose: powerfull, complex, elegant, dry nuts, toasty, varnish. Palate: rich, fine bitter notes, fine solera notes, long, spicy.

BARÓN MOSCATEL RESERVA
palomino

87 Colour: light mahogany. Nose: dried fruit, sweet spices, fruit liqueur notes. Palate: powerful, fine bitter notes, long.

MANZANILLA FINA BARÓN MZ
palomino

89 Colour: pale. Nose: pungent, saline, floral. Palate: rich, powerful, fresh, fine bitter notes.

MANZANILLA PASADA BARÓN MZ
palomino

92 Colour: bright yellow. Nose: complex, expressive, pungent, saline. Palate: rich, powerful, fresh, fine bitter notes, elegant.

P.X. BARÓN VIEJO PX
pedro ximénez

92 Colour: dark mahogany. Nose: complex, fruit liqueur notes, dried fruit, pattiserie, toasty. Palate: sweet, rich, unctuous, powerful.

BODEGAS DIOS BACO

Tecnología, A-14
11407 Jerez de la Frontera (Cádiz)
☎: +34 956 333 337 - Fax: +34 956 333 825
www.bodegasdiosbaco.com
info@bodegasdiosbaco.com

BACO DE ÉLITE MEDIUM AM
99,5% palomino, pedro ximénez

89 Colour: light mahogany. Nose: dried fruit, sweet spices, creamy oak. Palate: flavourful, powerful, sweetness.

BACO DE ÉLITE MEDIUM OL
99,5% palomino, pedro ximénez

90 Colour: iodine, amber rim. Nose: powerfull, complex, sweet spices. Palate: rich, long, fine solera notes, spicy, sweetness.

BACO IMPERIAL 30 AÑOS VORS PC
100% palomino

92 Colour: iodine, amber rim. Nose: powerfull, complex, elegant, dry nuts, toasty. Palate: rich, fine bitter notes, fine solera notes, long, spicy.

BULERÍA FI
100% palomino

88 Colour: bright yellow. Nose: expressive, pungent, sweet spices. Palate: rich, powerful, fresh, fine bitter notes.

DIOS BACO CR
85% palomino, 15% pedro ximénez

89 Colour: iodine, amber rim. Nose: fruit liqueur notes, aged wood nuances, sweet spices, varnish. Palate: spicy, long, sweetness, flavourful.

DIOS BACO OL
100% palomino

92 Colour: iodine, amber rim. Nose: powerfull, complex, elegant, dry nuts, toasty. Palate: rich, long, fine solera notes, spicy, dry.

ESNOBISTA MOSCATEL PASA MOSCATEL
moscatel

89 Colour: light mahogany. Nose: smoky, dark chocolate, aged wood nuances. Palate: spicy, long, concentrated.

OXFORD 1970 PX
100% pedro ximénez

90 Colour: dark mahogany. Nose: complex, fruit liqueur notes, dried fruit, pattiserie, toasty. Palate: sweet, rich, unctuous, powerful.

RIÁ PITÁ MZ
100% palomino

87 Colour: pale. Nose: saline, flor yeasts, dried herbs. Palate: light-bodied, fresh, flavourful.

BODEGAS GUTIÉRREZ COLOSÍA

Avda. Bajamar, 40
11500 El Puerto de Santa María (Cádiz)
☎: +34 956 852 852 - Fax: +34 956 542 936
www.gutierrezcolosia.com
info@gutierrezcolosia.com

CAMPO DE GUÍA FI
palomino

88 Colour: bright yellow. Nose: complex, expressive, pungent, saline. Palate: rich, powerful, fresh, fine bitter notes.

GUTIÉRREZ COLOSÍA AM
palomino

90 Colour: iodine, amber rim. Nose: elegant, dry nuts, toasty, aged wood nuances. Palate: rich, fine bitter notes, fine solera notes, long, spicy, dry.

GUTIÉRREZ COLOSÍA CR
palomino, pedro ximénez

87 Colour: dark mahogany. Nose: sweet spices, aged wood nuances, varnish, dark chocolate. Palate: fine bitter notes, toasty, long.

GUTIÉRREZ COLOSÍA FI
palomino

92 Colour: bright yellow. Nose: saline, dried flowers, balanced, elegant. Palate: rich, powerful, fresh, fine bitter notes, round.

GUTIÉRREZ COLOSÍA FINO EN RAMA FI
palomino

88 Colour: bright golden. Nose: acetaldehyde, iodine notes, sweet spices. Palate: correct, powerful, flavourful.

GUTIÉRREZ COLOSÍA MOSCATEL
SOLEADO MOSCATEL
moscatel

88 Colour: iodine, amber rim. Nose: dried fruit, candied fruit, sweet spices, pattiserie. Palate: concentrated, sweetness, powerful.

GUTIÉRREZ COLOSÍA OL
palomino

89 Colour: iodine, amber rim. Nose: powerfull, complex, dry nuts, caramel, sweet spices. Palate: rich, long, fine solera notes, spicy.

GUTIÉRREZ COLOSÍA PX
pedro ximénez

88 Colour: dark mahogany. Nose: fruit liqueur notes, dried fruit, pattiserie, toasty, dark chocolate. Palate: sweet, rich, unctuous, flavourful.

GUTIÉRREZ COLOSÍA SOLERA FAMILIAR AM
palomino

89 Colour: dark mahogany. Nose: smoky, aged wood nuances, slightly evolved, iodine notes. Palate: spirituous, spicy, oaky.

GUTIÉRREZ COLOSÍA SOLERA FAMILIAR OL
palomino

92 Colour: old gold, amber rim. Nose: smoky, toasty, acetaldehyde. Palate: fine bitter notes, powerful, fine solera notes.

GUTIÉRREZ COLOSÍA SOLERA FAMILIAR PC
palomino

90 Colour: iodine, amber rim. Nose: powerfull, characterful, candied fruit, toasty, pungent. Palate: powerful, fine bitter notes, good acidity.

GUTIÉRREZ COLOSÍA SOLERA FAMILIAR PX
pedro ximénez

91 Colour: dark mahogany. Nose: complex, fruit liqueur notes, roasted coffee, aromatic coffee. Palate: sweet, rich, unctuous, powerful, complex.

MARI PEPA CR
palomino, pedro ximénez

87 Colour: dark mahogany. Nose: aged wood nuances, sweet spices, caramel, creamy oak. Palate: spirituous, sweetness, toasty.

SANGRE Y TRABAJADERO OL
palomino

88 Colour: light mahogany. Nose: caramel, varnish, dried fruit, dry nuts. Palate: powerful, flavourful, dry.

BODEGAS HIDALGO-LA GITANA

Banda de Playa, 42
11540 Sanlúcar de Barrameda (Cádiz)
☎: +34 956 385 304 - Fax: +34 956 363 844
www.lagitana.es
bodegashidalgo@lagitana.es

ALAMEDA CR
75% palomino, 25% pedro ximénez

87 Colour: iodine, amber rim. Nose: toasty, sweet spices, dried fruit. Palate: sweetness, fine bitter notes.

FARAÓN 30 AÑOS VORS 50 CL. OL
100% palomino

90 Colour: iodine, amber rim. Nose: dry nuts, toasty, acetaldehyde, rancio notes. Palate: rich, fine solera notes, spicy.

FARAÓN OL
100% palomino

88 Colour: iodine, amber rim. Nose: powerfull, elegant, dry nuts, toasty. Palate: rich, long, fine solera notes, spicy.

LA GITANA EN RAMA (SACA DE INVIERNO) MZ
100% palomino

92 Colour: bright golden. Nose: complex, expressive, pungent, saline, spicy. Palate: rich, powerful, fresh, fine bitter notes, fine solera notes.

LA GITANA MZ
100% palomino

90 Colour: bright straw. Nose: complex, expressive, pungent, saline. Palate: rich, powerful, fresh, fine bitter notes.

NAPOLEÓN 30 AÑOS VORS 50 CL. AM
100% palomino

93 Colour: iodine, amber rim. Nose: spicy, creamy oak, roasted almonds, varnish, expressive. Palate: balanced, powerful, flavourful, spicy, long.

NAPOLEÓN AM
100% palomino

88 Colour: iodine, amber rim. Nose: dry nuts, toasty, dried fruit, powerfull. Palate: rich, fine bitter notes, fine solera notes, long, spicy, sweetness.

PASTRANA MANZANILLA PASADA MZ
100% palomino

94 Colour: bright golden. Nose: expressive, powerfull, spicy, toasty, acetaldehyde, pungent. Palate: powerful, fine bitter notes, spicy, long.

TRIANA 30 AÑOS VORS PX
100% pedro ximénez

92 Colour: dark mahogany. Nose: fruit liqueur notes, dried fruit, toasty, aromatic coffee, acetaldehyde. Palate: sweet, rich, unctuous, powerful.

TRIANA PX
100% pedro ximénez

90 Colour: dark mahogany. Nose: complex, fruit liqueur notes, dried fruit, pattisserie, toasty. Palate: sweet, rich, unctuous, powerful.

WELLINGTON 30 AÑOS VORS PC
100% palomino

91 Colour: light mahogany. Nose: powerfull, complex, elegant, dry nuts, toasty, acetaldehyde. Palate: rich, fine bitter notes, fine solera notes, long, spicy.

WELLINGTON JEREZ CORTADO 20 AÑOS VOS PC
100% palomino

90 Colour: iodine, amber rim. Nose: aged wood nuances, spicy, creamy oak, pattisserie. Palate: powerful, complex, fine solera notes, balanced.

BODEGAS LA CIGARRERA

Pza. Madre de Dios, s/n
11540 Sanlúcar de Barrameda (Cádiz)
☎: +34 956 381 285 - Fax: +34 956 383 824
www.bodegaslacigarrera.com
lacigarrera@bodegaslacigarrera.com

LA CIGARRERA 2012 AM
100% palomino

90 Colour: iodine, amber rim. Nose: powerfull, dry nuts, toasty. Palate: rich, fine bitter notes, fine solera notes, long, spicy.

LA CIGARRERA 2012 MOSCATEL
100% moscatel

92 Colour: light mahogany. Nose: sweet spices, pattisserie, dark chocolate, varnish. Palate: sweet, concentrated, powerful.

LA CIGARRERA 2012 MZ
100% palomino

86 Colour: bright yellow. Nose: pungent, saline, slightly evolved. Palate: rich, fresh, fine bitter notes.

LA CIGARRERA 2012 OL
palomino

86 Colour: old gold, amber rim. Nose: fruit preserve, grapey, slightly evolved. Palate: spicy, oaky, fine bitter notes.

LA CIGARRERA 2012 PX
100% pedro ximénez

89 Colour: dark mahogany. Nose: complex, fruit liqueur notes, toasty, aged wood nuances, dried fruit, fruit preserve. Palate: sweet, rich, unctuous.

BODEGAS OSBORNE

Fernán Caballero, 7
11500 El Puerto de Santa María (Cádiz)
☎: +34 956 869 000 - Fax: +34 925 869 026
www.osborne.es
carolina.cerrato@osborne.es

10 RF OL
palomino, pedro ximénez

88 Colour: iodine, amber rim. Nose: powerfull, complex, dry nuts, toasty. Palate: rich, long, fine solera notes, spicy.

AMONTILLADO 51-1ª V.O.R.S AM
100% palomino

93 Colour: iodine, amber rim. Nose: powerfull, complex, elegant, dry nuts, toasty, pungent. Palate: rich, fine bitter notes, fine solera notes, long, spicy.

BAILÉN OL
100% palomino

88 Colour: iodine, amber rim. Nose: powerfull, elegant, dry nuts, toasty. Palate: rich, long, fine solera notes, spicy.

CAPUCHINO V.O.R.S PC
100% palomino

94 Colour: iodine, amber rim. Nose: powerfull, complex, elegant, dry nuts, toasty. Palate: rich, fine bitter notes, fine solera notes, long, spicy, sweetness.

COQUINERO FI
100% palomino

93 Colour: bright golden. Nose: complex, expressive, pungent, saline. Palate: rich, powerful, fine bitter notes, sweetness.

FINO QUINTA FI
100% palomino

94 Colour: bright yellow. Nose: complex, expressive, pungent, saline. Palate: rich, powerful, fresh, fine bitter notes.

OSBORNE AOS AM
palomino

96 Colour: iodine, amber rim. Nose: powerfull, complex, elegant, dry nuts, toasty, acetaldehyde, saline, pungent. Palate: rich, fine bitter notes, fine solera notes, long, spicy.

OSBORNE PEDRO XIMÉNEZ 1827 PX
100% pedro ximénez

91 Colour: dark mahogany. Nose: complex, fruit liqueur notes, dried fruit, pattiserie, toasty. Palate: sweet, rich, unctuous, powerful, spicy, long.

OSBORNE RARE SHERRY PX VORS PX
100% pedro ximénez

93 Colour: dark mahogany. Nose: complex, fruit liqueur notes, dried fruit, dark chocolate, aromatic coffee. Palate: sweet, rich, unctuous, fine solera notes, balanced, elegant.

OSBORNE SOLERA BC 200 OL
pedro ximénez, palomino

97 Colour: iodine, amber rim. Nose: powerfull, complex, elegant, dry nuts, toasty, acetaldehyde, iodine notes. Palate: rich, long, fine solera notes, spicy.

OSBORNE SOLERA INDIA OL
pedro ximénez, palomino

94 Colour: iodine, amber rim. Nose: powerfull, complex, dry nuts, toasty. Palate: rich, long, fine solera notes, spicy, sweetness.

OSBORNE SOLERA PAP PC
pedro ximénez, palomino

94 Colour: iodine, amber rim. Nose: acetaldehyde, pungent, varnish, sweet spices. Palate: fine bitter notes, long, fine solera notes.

SANTA MARÍA CREAM CR
pedro ximénez, palomino

87 Colour: dark mahogany. Nose: caramel, sweet spices, dried fruit. Palate: spicy, sweetness, flavourful

SIBARITA V.O.R.S. OL
98% palomino, 2% pedro ximénez

95 Colour: iodine, amber rim. Nose: acetaldehyde, expressive, elegant, cocoa bean, sweet spices, varnish. Palate: round, flavourful, spicy, long, balanced.

VENERABLE VORS PX
pedro ximénez

97 Colour: dark mahogany. Nose: aromatic coffee, dark chocolate, spicy, acetaldehyde, elegant. Palate: powerful, flavourful, complex, toasty, long, fine solera notes. Personality.

BODEGAS PEDRO ROMERO

Trasbolsa, 84
11540 Sanlúcar de Barrameda (Cádiz)
☎: +34 956 360 736 - Fax: +34 956 361 027
www.pedroromero.es
pedroromero@pedroromero.es

AURORA EN RAMA MZ
palomino

90 Colour: bright golden. Nose: faded flowers, pungent, saline, acetaldehyde. Palate: powerful, flavourful, long, fine bitter notes.

TRES ÁLAMOS EDICIÓN ESPECIAL PX
pedro ximénez

90 Colour: dark mahogany. Nose: complex, fruit liqueur notes, dried fruit, pattiserie, toasty. Palate: sweet, rich, unctuous, powerful.

BODEGAS REY FERNANDO DE CASTILLA

San Fco. Javier, 3
11404 Jerez de la Frontera (Cádiz)
☎: +34 956 182 454 - Fax: +34 956 182 222
www.fernandodecastilla.com
bodegas@fernandodecastilla.com

FERNANDO DE CASTILLA "AMONTILLADO ANTIQUE" AM

94 Colour: iodine, amber rim. Nose: powerfull, complex, elegant, dry nuts, aged wood nuances. Palate: rich, fine bitter notes, fine solera notes, long, spicy, elegant.

FERNANDO DE CASTILLA "FINO ANTIQUE" FI
palomino

92 Colour: bright yellow. Nose: complex, pungent, saline, medium intensity, elegant. Palate: rich, powerful, fresh, fine bitter notes.

FERNANDO DE CASTILLA "OLOROSO ANTIQUE" OL

92 Colour: iodine, amber rim. Nose: powerfull, complex, dry nuts, toasty. Palate: rich, long, fine solera notes, spicy.

FERNANDO DE CASTILLA "P.X. ANTIQUE" PX

94 Colour: dark mahogany. Nose: complex, dried fruit, toasty, expressive, dark chocolate, cocoa bean. Palate: sweet, rich, unctuous, powerful, balanced, elegant. Personality.

FERNANDO DE CASTILLA "PALO CORTADO ANTIQUE" PC

94 Colour: iodine, amber rim. Nose: acetaldehyde, saline, sweet spices. Palate: spicy, fine solera notes.

FERNANDO DE CASTILLA "PX CLASSIC" PX

91 Colour: dark mahogany. Nose: fruit liqueur notes, dried fruit, pattiserie, toasty, dark chocolate. Palate: sweet, rich, unctuous, powerful, balanced.

FERNANDO DE CASTILLA FINO CLASSIC FI

90 Colour: bright yellow. Nose: complex, expressive, pungent, saline. Palate: rich, powerful, fresh, fine bitter notes.

BODEGAS TRADICIÓN

Cordobeses, 3
11408 Jerez de la Frontera (Cádiz)
☎: +34 956 168 628 - Fax: +34 956 331 963
www.bodegastradicion.com
visitas@bodegastradicion.com

AMONTILLADO TRADICIÓN VORS AM
palomino

93 Colour: iodine, amber rim. Nose: acetaldehyde, saline, aged wood nuances, dry nuts, spicy. Palate: powerful, flavourful, fine solera notes, spicy, balanced.

OLOROSO TRADICIÓN VORS OL
palomino

96 Colour: iodine, amber rim. Nose: powerfull, complex, elegant, dry nuts, toasty, smoky, varnish, acetaldehyde. Palate: rich, long, fine solera notes, spicy.

PALO CORTADO TRADICIÓN VORS PC
palomino

92 Colour: iodine, amber rim. Nose: powerfull, complex, elegant, dry nuts, toasty. Palate: rich, fine bitter notes, fine solera notes, long, spicy.

PEDRO XIMÉNEZ TRADICIÓN VOS PX
pedro ximénez

92 Colour: dark mahogany. Nose: complex, fruit liqueur notes, dried fruit, roasted coffee, acetaldehyde. Palate: sweet, rich, unctuous, powerful.

CARREFOUR

Campezo, 16
28022 Madrid (Madrid)
☎: +34 902 202 000
www.carrefour.es

LOS JARALES MZ
palomino

88 Colour: bright straw. Nose: dry nuts, saline, pungent. Palate: correct, fine bitter notes, long.

DELGADO ZULETA

Avda. Rocío Jurado, s/n
11540 Sanlúcar de Barrameda (Cádiz)
☎: +34 956 360 133 - Fax: +34 956 360 780
www.delgadozuleta.com
direccioncomercial@delgadozuleta.com

BARBIANA MZ
100% palomino

86 Colour: bright yellow. Nose: saline, faded flowers, slightly evolved. Palate: oaky, powerful.

LA GOYA MZ
100% palomino

91 Colour: bright yellow. Nose: complex, expressive, pungent, saline. Palate: rich, powerful, fresh, fine bitter notes.

MONTEAGUDO AM
100% palomino

90 Colour: light mahogany. Nose: sweet spices, varnish, pungent, iodine notes. Palate: fine solera notes, long, flavourful, dry.

MONTEAGUDO CR
palomino, moscatel, pedro ximénez

86 Colour: dark mahogany. Nose: creamy oak, dark chocolate, sweet spices. Palate: spirituous, powerful, toasty.

MONTEAGUDO PEDRO XIMÉNEZ PX
pedro ximénez

87 Colour: dark mahogany. Nose: acetaldehyde, fruit preserve, aromatic coffee, sweet spices. Palate: powerful, flavourful, rich.

QUO VADIS AM
100% palomino

92 Colour: iodine, amber rim. Nose: powerfull, complex, elegant, dry nuts, dark chocolate, sweet spices. Palate: rich, fine bitter notes, fine solera notes, long.

DIEZ - MÉRITO

Ctra. Morabita, Km. 2
11407 Jerez de la Frontera (Cádiz)
☎: +34 956 186 112 - Fax: +34 956 303 500
www.diezmerito.com
info@diezmerito.com

FINO IMPERIAL 30 AÑOS VORS AM
palomino

92 Colour: iodine, amber rim. Nose: elegant, dry nuts, toasty, aged wood nuances, varnish, acetaldehyde. Palate: rich, fine bitter notes, fine solera notes, long, flavourful.

PEMARTÍN AM

92 Colour: iodine, amber rim. Nose: powerfull, complex, dry nuts, toasty, sweet spices. Palate: rich, fine bitter notes, fine solera notes, long, spicy.

PEMARTÍN CR
palomino

85 Colour: dark mahogany. Nose: caramel, sweet spices, fruit liqueur notes, creamy oak. Palate: powerful, sweetness, flavourful.

PEMARTÍN FI
palomino

86 Colour: bright yellow. Nose: pungent, saline, dried herbs. Palate: rich, fresh, fine bitter notes.

PEMARTÍN OL
palomino

87 Colour: iodine, amber rim. Nose: elegant, dry nuts, toasty. Palate: rich, long, fine solera notes, fine bitter notes.

PEMARTÍN PX
pedro ximénez

88 Colour: dark mahogany. Nose: fruit liqueur notes, dried fruit, pattiserie, toasty. Palate: sweet, unctuous, powerful, balanced.

VICTORIA REGINA VORS OL
palomino

92 Colour: iodine, amber rim. Nose: powerfull, complex, elegant, dry nuts, toasty. Palate: rich, long, fine solera notes, spicy, balanced.

VIEJA SOLERA 30 AÑOS PX
pedro ximénez

92 Colour: dark mahogany. Nose: complex, fruit liqueur notes, pattiserie, aromatic coffee, dark chocolate. Palate: sweet, rich, unctuous, powerful, balanced.

EMILIO LUSTAU

Arcos, 53
11402 Jerez de la Frontera (Cádiz)
☎: +34 956 341 597 - Fax: +34 956 859 204
www.lustau.es
lustau@lustau.es

CANDELA CR
palomino, pedro ximénez

85 Colour: light mahogany. Nose: aged wood nuances, creamy oak, powerfull, sweet spices. Palate: powerful, flavourful, sweetness, long.

LA INA FI
palomino

95 Colour: bright yellow. Nose: complex, expressive, saline, pungent, powerfull. Palate: rich, powerful, fresh, fine bitter notes, long, good acidity.

LUSTAU ALMACENISTA PALO CORTADO VIDES PC
palomino

89 Colour: iodine, amber rim. Nose: powerfull, complex, elegant, dry nuts, toasty. Palate: rich, fine bitter notes, fine solera notes, long, spicy.

LUSTAU AÑADA 1997 OLOROSO DULCE OL
palomino

92 Colour: iodine, amber rim. Nose: powerfull, complex, elegant, toasty, sweet spices. Palate: rich, long, fine solera notes, spicy, sweet.

LUSTAU EAST INDIA CR
palomino, pedro ximénez

91 Colour: dark mahogany. Nose: acetaldehyde, caramel, sweet spices, varnish. Palate: spicy, powerful, flavourful, sweetness.

LUSTAU EMILÍN MOSCATEL
moscatel

91 Colour: dark mahogany. Nose: honeyed notes, sweet spices, toasty, creamy oak. Palate: long, spicy, flavourful, rich.

LUSTAU EMPERATRIZ EUGENIA OL
palomino

89 Colour: iodine, amber rim. Nose: powerfull, complex, dry nuts, toasty, dried fruit. Palate: rich, long, fine solera notes, spicy.

LUSTAU ESCUADRILLA AM
palomino

91 Colour: iodine, amber rim. Nose: powerfull, complex, elegant, dry nuts, toasty, sweet spices. Palate: rich, fine bitter notes, fine solera notes, long, spicy.

LUSTAU JARANA FI
palomino

93 Colour: bright yellow. Nose: complex, expressive, pungent, saline. Palate: rich, powerful, fresh, fine bitter notes.

LUSTAU PAPIRUSA MZ SOLERA
palomino

94 Colour: bright yellow. Nose: complex, expressive, pungent, saline, flor yeasts, spicy. Palate: rich, powerful, fresh, fine bitter notes.

LUSTAU PUERTO FINO FI
palomino

94 Colour: bright yellow. Nose: expressive, pungent, saline, powerfull, floral. Palate: rich, powerful, fresh, fine bitter notes.

LUSTAU SAN EMILIO PX
pedro ximénez

93 Colour: dark mahogany. Nose: complex, fruit liqueur notes, dried fruit, pattiserie, toasty, aromatic coffee, cocoa bean. Palate: sweet, rich, unctuous, powerful, elegant.

LUSTAU VORS AM
palomino

90 Colour: iodine, amber rim. Nose: dry nuts, toasty, sweet spices, pattiserie. Palate: rich, fine bitter notes, fine solera notes, long, spicy.

LUSTAU VORS PX
pedro ximénez

92 Colour: dark mahogany. Nose: complex, fruit liqueur notes, dried fruit, toasty, aromatic coffee. Palate: sweet, rich, unctuous, powerful, long.

MACARENA MZ
palomino

90 Colour: yellow, greenish rim. Nose: pungent, flor yeasts, faded flowers, saline. Palate: fresh, flavourful, long.

RÍO VIEJO OL
palomino

93 Colour: iodine, amber rim. Nose: powerfull, complex, dry nuts, toasty. Palate: rich, long, fine solera notes, spicy.

VIÑA 25 PX
pedro ximénez

89 Colour: dark mahogany. Nose: fruit liqueur notes, dried fruit, pattiserie, toasty, powerfull, acetaldehyde. Palate: sweet, unctuous, powerful, flavourful.

EQUIPO NAVAZOS

Cartuja, 1 - módulo 6
11401 Jerez de la Frontera (Cádiz)
www.equiponavazos.com
equipo@navazos.com

FINO NAVAZOS. SACA JULIO 2013 FI
palomino

94 Colour: bright golden. Nose: expressive, powerfull, lees reduction notes, iodine notes. Palate: fine bitter notes, good acidity, fine bitter notes.

LA BOTA DE MANZANILLA (BOTA Nª 42) MZ
palomino

96 Colour: bright golden. Nose: complex, expressive, pungent, saline, powerfull. Palate: rich, powerful, fresh, fine bitter notes.

LA BOTA DE PALO CORTADO Nº 41 "BOTA NO" PC
palomino

98 Colour: iodine, amber rim. Nose: powerfull, complex, elegant, dry nuts, toasty, pungent, expressive. Palate: rich, long, fine solera notes, spicy, fine bitter notes, good acidity.

MANZANILLA I THINK. SACA FEBRERO 2013 MZ

94 Colour: bright yellow. Nose: lees reduction notes, saline. Palate: rich, powerful, fine bitter notes, good acidity.

PX NAVAZOS GRAN SOLERA. SACA MAYO 2013 PX
pedro ximénez

96 Colour: dark mahogany. Nose: powerfull, characterful, dried fruit, candied fruit, aromatic coffee, dark chocolate, fruit liqueur notes. Palate: powerful, sweet, concentrated, long.

ESPÍRITUS DE JEREZ

Pza. Cocheras, 3
11403 Jerez de la Frontera (Cádiz)
☎: +34 649 456 990
direccion@espiritusdejerez.com

COLECCIÓN ROBERTO AMILLO AMONTILLADO AM
palomino

95 Colour: iodine, amber rim. Nose: elegant, dry nuts, toasty, powerfull, characterful, saline, iodine notes. Palate: rich, fine bitter notes, fine solera notes, long, spicy.

COLECCIÓN ROBERTO AMILLO OLOROSO OL
palomino

95 Colour: iodine, amber rim. Nose: powerfull, complex, elegant, dry nuts, toasty. Palate: rich, long, fine solera notes, spicy.

COLECCIÓN ROBERTO AMILLO PALO CORTADO PC
palomino

96 Colour: light mahogany. Nose: pungent, saline, fruit liqueur notes, acetaldehyde. Palate: spicy, long, good acidity, fine bitter notes.

COLECCIÓN ROBERTO AMILLO PEDRO XIMÉNEZ PX
pedro ximénez

95 Colour: dark mahogany. Nose: fruit liqueur notes, dried fruit, pattiserie, toasty, powerfull. Palate: sweet, rich, unctuous, powerful.

GONZÁLEZ BYASS JEREZ

Manuel María González, 12
11403 Jerez de la Frontera (Cádiz)
☎: +34 956 357 000 - Fax: +34 956 357 043
www.gonzalezbyass.es
elrincondegb@gonzalezbyass.es

ALFONSO OL
100% palomino

90 Colour: iodine, amber rim. Nose: powerfull, complex, elegant, dry nuts, toasty. Palate: rich, long, fine solera notes, spicy, dry.

AMONTILLADO DEL DUQUE VORS AM
100% palomino

95 Colour: iodine, amber rim. Nose: powerfull, complex, elegant, dry nuts, toasty, acetaldehyde. Palate: rich, fine bitter notes, fine solera notes, long, spicy, balanced, elegant.

APÓSTOLES VORS PC
90% palomino, 10% pedro ximénez

92 Colour: light mahogany. Nose: sweet spices, creamy oak, pattiserie. Palate: powerful, flavourful, fine solera notes, balanced.

GONZALEZ BYASS AÑADA 1982 PC
100% palomino

97 Colour: iodine, amber rim. Nose: acetaldehyde, pungent, fruit liqueur notes, roasted almonds, pattiserie, spicy, complex. Palate: flavourful, spirituous, full, fine solera notes.

LEONOR PC
100% palomino

92 Colour: iodine, amber rim. Nose: spicy, aged wood nuances, sweet spices, cocoa bean. Palate: long, powerful, flavourful, balanced, elegant.

MATUSALEM VORS OL
75% palomino, 25% pedro ximénez

92 Colour: iodine, amber rim. Nose: powerfull, complex, dry nuts, toasty, acetaldehyde. Palate: rich, long, fine solera notes, spicy, confected.

NÉCTAR PX
100% pedro ximénez

90 Colour: dark mahogany. Nose: fruit liqueur notes, dried fruit, pattiserie, aromatic coffee. Palate: sweet, unctuous, flavourful, balanced.

NOÉ VORS PX
pedro ximénez

94 Colour: dark mahogany. Nose: complex, fruit liqueur notes, dried fruit, aromatic coffee, dark chocolate, acetaldehyde. Palate: sweet, rich, unctuous, powerful, balanced, elegant.

SOLERA 1847 CR
palomino, pedro ximénez

87 Colour: light mahogany. Nose: fruit liqueur notes, varnish, creamy oak, sweet spices. Palate: complex, powerful, flavourful, long.

TÍO PEPE EN RAMA FI
100% palomino

95 Colour: bright yellow. Nose: powerfull, complex, fine lees, pungent, saline. Palate: powerful, spicy, good acidity, long.

TÍO PEPE FI
100% palomino

94 Colour: bright yellow. Nose: complex, expressive, pungent, saline. Palate: rich, powerful, fresh, fine bitter notes.

VIÑA AB AM
100% palomino

91 Colour: iodine, amber rim. Nose: elegant, dry nuts, toasty, saline, pungent. Palate: rich, fine bitter notes, fine solera notes, long, spicy.

HEREDEROS DE ARGÜESO S.A.

Mar, 8
11540 Sanlúcar de Barrameda (Cádiz)
☎: +34 956 385 116 - Fax: +34 956 368 169
www.argueso.es
argueso@argueso.es

ARGÜESO AM

89 Colour: iodine, amber rim. Nose: dry nuts, toasty. Palate: rich, fine bitter notes, fine solera notes, long, spicy.

ARGÜESO AMONTILLADO VIEJO AM
palomino

93 Colour: iodine, amber rim. Nose: powerfull, complex, elegant, dry nuts, toasty, saline. Palate: rich, fine bitter notes, fine solera notes, long, spicy.

ARGÜESO CREAM CR
palomino, pedro ximénez

85 Colour: iodine, amber rim. Nose: varnish, dried fruit, sweet spices. Palate: sweetness, spicy, ripe fruit.

ARGÜESO OL
palomino

85 Colour: iodine, amber rim. Nose: dry nuts, toasty, sweet spices. Palate: rich, fine solera notes, spicy, sweetness.

ARGÜESO PX
pedro ximénez

85 Colour: dark mahogany. Nose: dried fruit, pattiserie, toasty. Palate: sweet, rich, unctuous.

LAS MEDALLAS DE ARGÜESO MZ
palomino

92 Colour: bright yellow. Nose: complex, expressive, pungent, saline. Palate: rich, powerful, fresh, fine bitter notes.

SAN LEÓN "CLÁSICA" MZ
100% palomino

93 Colour: bright yellow. Nose: complex, pungent, saline, characterful, floral. Palate: rich, powerful, fresh, fine bitter notes.

SAN LEÓN RESERVA DE FAMILIA MZ
palomino

95 Colour: bright golden. Nose: powerfull, characterful, flor yeasts, saline, spicy. Palate: powerful, fine bitter notes, good acidity, round.

HIDALGO

Clavel, 29
11402 Jerez de la Frontera (Cádiz)
☎: +34 956 341 078 - Fax: +34 956 320 922
www.hidalgo.com
emiliohidalgo@emiliohidalgo.es

EL TRESILLO 1874 AMONTILLADO VIEJO AM
palomino

95 Colour: iodine, amber rim. Nose: powerfull, complex, elegant, dry nuts, toasty. Palate: rich, fine bitter notes, fine solera notes, long, spicy.

EL TRESILLO AMONTILLADO FINO AM

93 Colour: iodine, amber rim. Nose: powerfull, complex, elegant, dry nuts, toasty, pungent. Palate: rich, fine bitter notes, fine solera notes, long.

LA PANESA ESPECIAL FINO FI
palomino

94 Colour: bright yellow. Nose: complex, expressive, pungent, saline, dried flowers. Palate: rich, powerful, fresh, fine bitter notes, balanced, elegant.

VILLAPANÉS OL
palomino

94 Colour: iodine, amber rim. Nose: powerfull, complex, elegant, dry nuts, sweet spices. Palate: rich, long, fine solera notes, spicy, elegant.

HIJOS DE RAINERA PÉREZ MARÍN

Ctra. Nacional IV, Km. 640
11408 Jerez de la Frontera (Cádiz)
☎: +34 956 321 004 - Fax: +34 956 340 216
www.grupoestevez.com
info@grupoestevez.com

LA GUITA MZ
100% palomino

90 Colour: bright yellow. Nose: complex, expressive, pungent, saline. Palate: rich, powerful, fresh, fine bitter notes.

LUIS CABALLERO

San Francisco, 32
11500 El Puerto de Santa María (Cádiz)
☎: +34 956 851 751 - Fax: +34 956 859 204
www.caballero.es
marketing@caballero.es

PAVÓN PUERTO FINO FI SOLERA
palomino

94 Colour: bright yellow. Nose: complex, expressive, pungent, saline, varnish, roasted almonds. Palate: rich, powerful, fresh, fine bitter notes, elegant.

MARQUÉS DEL REAL TESORO

Ctra. Nacional IV, Km. 640
11408 Jerez de la Frontera (Cádiz)
☎: +34 956 321 004 - Fax: +34 956 340 216
www.grupoestevez.es
info@grupoestevez.com

DEL PRÍNCIPE AM
100% palomino

93 Colour: iodine, amber rim. Nose: powerfull, complex, elegant, dry nuts, toasty, pungent, candied fruit. Palate: rich, fine bitter notes, fine solera notes, long, spicy.

TÍO MATEO FI
100% palomino

93 Colour: bright yellow. Nose: complex, expressive, pungent, saline, powerfull. Palate: rich, powerfull, fresh, fine bitter notes.

SACRISTÍA AB

Sevilla, 2 1º Izq.
11540 Sanlúcar de Barrameda (Cádiz)
☎: +34 607 920 337
www.sacristiaab.com

SACRISTÍA AB MZ
palomino

95 Colour: bright golden. Nose: spicy, toasty, acetaldehyde, petrol notes. Palate: fine bitter notes, good acidity, fine solera notes.

SÁNCHEZ ROMATE

Lealas, 26
11404 Jerez de la Frontera (Cádiz)
☎: +34 956 182 212 - Fax: +34 956 185 276
www.romate.com
romate@romate.com

CARDENAL CISNEROS PX
100% pedro ximénez

91 Colour: dark mahogany. Nose: complex, fruit liqueur notes, dried fruit, pattiserie, toasty. Palate: sweet, unctuous, powerful, balanced, elegant.

DON JOSÉ OL
100% palomino

91 Colour: iodine, amber rim. Nose: powerfull, elegant, dry nuts, toasty, dried fruit. Palate: rich, long, fine solera notes, spicy.

DUQUESA PX
100% pedro ximénez

90 Colour: dark mahogany. Nose: aromatic coffee, sweet spices, creamy oak, varnish. Palate: spirituous, powerful, flavourful, rich.

IBERIA CR
70% palomino, 30% pedro ximénez

89 Colour: dark mahogany. Nose: caramel, sweet spices, creamy oak. Palate: sweetness, powerful, flavourful, toasty.

MARISMEÑO FI
100% palomino

90 Colour: bright yellow. Nose: complex, expressive, pungent, saline. Palate: rich, powerful, fresh, fine bitter notes.

NPU AM
100% palomino

93 Colour: iodine, amber rim. Nose: complex, elegant, dry nuts, toasty. Palate: rich, fine bitter notes, fine solera notes, long, spicy, dry, elegant.

OLD & PLUS AMONTILLADO VORS AM
100% palomino

92 Colour: iodine, amber rim. Nose: powerfull, complex, elegant, dry nuts, toasty. Palate: rich, fine bitter notes, fine solera notes, long, spicy.

OLD & PLUS OLOROSO OL
100% palomino

93 Colour: iodine, amber rim. Nose: powerfull, dry nuts, spicy, acetaldehyde. Palate: rich, long, fine solera notes, spicy.

OLD & PLUS P.X. PX
pedro ximénez

93 Colour: dark mahogany. Nose: dried fruit, aromatic coffee, dark chocolate, powerfull, expressive. Palate: flavourful, complex, long, toasty, balanced.

REGENTE PC
100% palomino

92 Colour: iodine, amber rim. Nose: powerfull, complex, elegant, dry nuts, toasty. Palate: rich, fine bitter notes, fine solera notes, long, spicy.

SANDEMAN JEREZ

Porrera, 3 of. 8 y 11
11403 Jerez de la Frontera (Cádiz)
☎: +34 956 151 700 - Fax: +34 956 300 007
www.sandeman.eu
jose.moreno@sogrape.pt

SANDEMAN ROYAL AMBROSANTE VOS PX
pedro ximénez

92 Colour: dark mahogany. Nose: complex, fruit liqueur notes, dried fruit, pattiserie, toasty, fruit preserve. Palate: sweet, rich, unctuous, powerful, fine solera notes.

SANDEMAN ROYAL CORREGIDOR MEDIUM SWEET VOS OL
palomino, pedro ximénez

91 Colour: iodine, amber rim. Nose: powerfull, complex, dry nuts, toasty, dried fruit. Palate: rich, long, fine solera notes, spicy.

SANDEMAN ROYAL ESMERALDA VOS AM
palomino

93 Colour: iodine, amber rim. Nose: aged wood nuances, woody, varnish, acetaldehyde, expressive. Palate: powerful, flavourful, spicy, fine solera notes, balanced.

VALDESPINO

Ctra. Nacional IV, Km.640
11408 Jerez de la Frontera (Cádiz)
☎: +34 956 321 004 - Fax: +34 956 340 216
www.grupoestevez.es
visitas@grupoestevez.com

DON GONZALO VOS OL
100% palomino

96 Colour: iodine, amber rim. Nose: powerfull, complex, elegant, dry nuts, toasty, acetaldehyde. Palate: rich, long, fine solera notes, spicy.

EL CANDADO PX
100% pedro ximénez

90 Colour: dark mahogany. Nose: complex, fruit liqueur notes, dried fruit, pattiserie, caramel. Palate: sweet, unctuous, powerful, flavourful.

MOSCATEL PROMESA MOSCATEL
moscatel

93 Colour: iodine, amber rim. Nose: citrus fruit, caramel, sweet spices, creamy oak. Palate: powerful, flavourful, rich, complex, elegant.

SOLERA 1842 VOS OL
100% palomino

94 Colour: iodine, amber rim. Nose: powerfull, complex, elegant, dry nuts, toasty, smoky, fruit liqueur notes. Palate: rich, long, fine solera notes, spicy, sweetness.

SOLERA SU MAJESTAD VORS OL
100% palomino

96 Colour: iodine, amber rim. Nose: powerfull, complex, elegant, dry nuts, toasty, acetaldehyde, pungent. Palate: rich, long, fine solera notes, spicy.

TÍO DIEGO AM
100% palomino

91 Colour: iodine, amber rim. Nose: powerfull, complex, elegant, dry nuts, toasty, pungent. Palate: rich, fine bitter notes, fine solera notes, long, spicy.

YNOCENTE FI
100% palomino

93 Colour: bright yellow. Nose: complex, expressive, pungent, saline, flor yeasts. Palate: rich, powerful, fresh, fine bitter notes.

WILLIAMS & HUMBERT S.A.

Ctra. N-IV, Km. 641,75
11408 Jerez de la Frontera (Cádiz)
☎: +34 956 353 401 - Fax: +34 956 353 412
www.williams-humbert.com
secretaria@williams-humbert.com

CANASTA CR
palomino, pedro ximénez

87 Colour: mahogany. Nose: powerfull, complex, dry nuts, toasty. Palate: rich, fine solera notes, long, spicy.

DON GUIDO SOLERA ESPECIAL 20 AÑOS VOS PX
pedro ximénez

93 Colour: dark mahogany. Nose: fruit liqueur notes, dried fruit, pattiserie, toasty, aromatic coffee, dark chocolate, complex. Palate: sweet, rich, unctuous, powerful, balanced, long.

DOS CORTADOS PC
palomino

93 Colour: light mahogany. Nose: aged wood nuances, sweet spices, creamy oak, dry nuts, ripe fruit. Palate: long, powerful, spicy, fine solera notes, roasted-coffee aftertaste.

DRY SACK "SOLERA ESPECIAL" 15 AÑOS OL
palomino, pedro ximénez

91 Colour: mahogany. Nose: spicy, creamy oak, sweet spices, dry nuts, acetaldehyde. Palate: powerful, rich, spicy, long, balanced.

DRY SACK FINO FI
palomino

90 Colour: bright yellow. Nose: pungent, saline, aged wood nuances, spicy, flor yeasts. Palate: rich, powerful, fresh, fine bitter notes.

DRY SACK MEDIUM DRY CR
palomino, pedro ximénez

88 Colour: old gold, amber rim. Nose: ripe fruit, sweet spices, pattiserie, creamy oak. Palate: sweetness, spicy, balanced.

JALIFA VORS "30 YEARS" AM

93 Colour: iodine, amber rim. Nose: powerfull, complex, elegant, dry nuts, toasty, sweet spices. Palate: rich, fine bitter notes, fine solera notes, long, spicy.

LA PEPA 2012 CR

90 Colour: light mahogany. Nose: spicy, varnish, aged wood nuances, ripe fruit, expressive. Palate: sweetness, complex, spicy, long, toasty.

LA PEPA 2012 MZ

91 Colour: bright yellow. Nose: complex, expressive, pungent, saline, flor yeasts. Palate: rich, powerful, fresh, fine bitter notes.

LA PEPA 2012 PX

92 Colour: dark mahogany. Nose: fruit liqueur notes, pattiserie, toasty, fruit preserve. Palate: sweet, rich, unctuous, powerful, balanced, elegant.

DO JUMILLA / D.O.P.

LOCATION:

Midway between the provinces of Murcia and Albacete, this DO spreads over a large region in the southeast of Spain and covers the municipal areas of Jumilla (Murcia) and Fuente Álamo, Albatana, Ontur, Hellín, Tobarra and Montealegre del Castillo (Albacete).

CLIMATE:

Continental in nature with Mediterranean influences. It is characterized by its aridity and low rainfall (270 mm) which is mainly concentrated in spring and autumn. The winters are cold and the summers dry and quite hot.

SOIL:

The soil is mainly brownish-grey, brownish-grey limestone and limy. In general, it is poor in organic matter, with great water retention capacity and medium permeability.

GRAPE VARIETIES:

RED: *Monastrell* (main 35,373 Ha), *Garnacha Tinta, Garnacha Tintorera, Cencibel* (*Tempranillo*), *Cabernet Sauvignon, Merlot, Petit Verdot* and *Syrah*.
WHITE: *Airén* (3,751 Ha), *Macabeo, Malvasía, Pedro Ximénez, Chardonnay, Sauvignon Blanc* and *Moscatel de Grano Menudo*.

FIGURES:

Vineyard surface: 25.500– **Wine-Growers:** 2.100 – **Wineries:** 43 – **2012 Harvest rating:** Very Good – **Production:** 25.552.635 litres – **Market percentages:** 55% domestic. 45% export

CONSEJO REGULADOR
San Roque, 15 - 30520 Jumilla (Murcia) ☎: +34 968 781 761 - Fax: +34 968 781 900
info@vinosdejumilla.org   www.vinosdejumilla.org

ALCEÑO WINES

Barrio Iglesias, 55
30520 Jumilla (Murcia)
☎: +34 968 780 142 - Fax: +34 968 716 256
www.alceno.com
plmsa@alceno.com

ALCEÑO 2012 B
sauvignon blanc, airén

86 Colour: bright straw. Nose: fresh, fresh fruit, white flowers, expressive. Palate: flavourful, fruity, good acidity, balanced.

ALCEÑO 2012 RD
monastrell, syrah

87 Colour: rose, purple rim. Nose: powerfull, ripe fruit, red berry notes, floral, balsamic herbs. Palate: powerful, fruity, fresh.

ALCEÑO 12 MESES 2011 T
monastrell, syrah

92 Colour: cherry, garnet rim. Nose: spicy, creamy oak, complex, overripe fruit, sweet spices. Palate: powerful, flavourful, toasty, round tannins.

ALCEÑO 2011 T
monastrell, syrah, garnacha

89 Colour: bright cherry. Nose: ripe fruit, sweet spices, creamy oak, expressive, toasty, roasted coffee. Palate: flavourful, fruity, toasty, round tannins.

ALCEÑO 2012 T
monastrell, syrah, tempranillo, garnacha

90 Colour: cherry, purple rim. Nose: expressive, fresh fruit, red berry notes, floral. Palate: flavourful, fruity, good acidity, round tannins.

ALCEÑO DULCE 2012 T
monastrell

91 Colour: cherry, garnet rim. Nose: complex, fruit liqueur notes, dried fruit, pattiserie, toasty, acetaldehyde. Palate: sweet, rich, unctuous, powerful.

ALCEÑO PREMIUM 2012 T
syrah, monastrell

92 Colour: cherry, garnet rim. Nose: ripe fruit, spicy, creamy oak, toasty, complex, raspberry, red berry notes. Palate: powerful, flavourful, toasty, round tannins.

ALCEÑO SELECCIÓN 2009 TC
monastrell, syrah, tempranillo

88 Colour: cherry, garnet rim. Nose: ripe fruit, warm, spicy, toasty. Palate: spicy, ripe fruit, good acidity.

ARTIGA FUSTEL

Progres, 21 Bajos
8720 Vilafranca del Penedès (Barcelona)
☎: +34 938 182 317 - Fax: +34 938 924 499
www.artiga-fustel.com
info@artiga-fustel.com

EL CAMPEADOR 2008 TR
90% monastrell, 10% tempranillo

88 Colour: pale ruby, brick rim edge. Nose: spicy, fine reductive notes, wet leather, aged wood nuances, fruit liqueur notes. Palate: spicy, fine tannins, long.

EL CAMPEADOR 2012 T
70% syrah, 25% monastrell, 5% petit verdot

87 Colour: cherry, purple rim. Nose: fresh fruit, red berry notes, floral. Palate: flavourful, fruity, good acidity, round tannins.

ASENSIO CARCELÉN N.C.R.

Ctra. RM-714, km. 8
30520 Jumilla (Murcia)
☎: +34 968 435 543 - Fax: +34 968 435 542
www.facebook.com/AsensioCarcelen
bodegascarcelen@terra.es

100 X 100 MONASTRELL 2011 T ROBLE
100% monastrell

80

PURA SANGRE 2006 TR
100% monastrell

84

BARÓN DEL SOLAR

Paraje El Jurado s/n
30520 Jumilla (Murcia)
☎: +34 968 117 204
www.barondelsolar.com
info@barondelsolar.com

BARÓN DEL SOLAR 2011 T
monastrell

87 Colour: bright cherry. Nose: ripe fruit, sweet spices, creamy oak, expressive. Palate: flavourful, fruity, toasty, round tannins.

BARÓN DEL SOLAR COLECCIÓN PRIVADA 2010 T
monastrell

90 Colour: cherry, garnet rim. Nose: ripe fruit, spicy, varnish, cocoa bean, creamy oak. Palate: powerful, flavourful, long, spicy.

COLMENERO 2011 T
monastrell

83

BODEGA ARTESANAL VIÑA CAMPANERO

Ctra. de Murcia, s/n- Apdo. 346
30520 Jumilla (Murcia)
☎: +34 968 780 754 - Fax: +34 968 780 754
www.vinacampanero.com
bodegas@vinacampanero.com

VEGARDAL CUCO DEL ARDAL 2009 TC
100% monastrell

85 Colour: pale ruby, brick rim edge. Nose: ripe fruit, balsamic herbs, fine reductive notes, spicy. Palate: powerful, flavourful, correct.

VEGARDAL CUCO DEL ARDAL EDICIÓN ESPECIAL 2010 T
100% monastrell

83

VEGARDAL MONASTRELL CEPAS NUEVAS 2012 T
100% monastrell

85 Colour: cherry, purple rim. Nose: fresh fruit, red berry notes, floral. Palate: flavourful, fruity, good acidity.

VEGARDAL MONASTRELL CEPAS VIEJAS 2011 T
100% monastrell

85 Colour: cherry, purple rim. Nose: red berry notes, floral, ripe fruit. Palate: flavourful, fruity, good acidity, round tannins.

VEGARDAL MONASTRELL CEPAS VIEJAS 2012 T
100% monastrell

88 Colour: cherry, purple rim. Nose: expressive, fresh fruit, red berry notes, floral, lactic notes. Palate: flavourful, fruity, good acidity, round tannins.

VEGARDAL ORGÁNIC 2011 T
monastrell, syrah

85 Colour: cherry, garnet rim. Nose: ripe fruit, floral, fragrant herbs. Palate: powerful, flavourful, correct.

BODEGA TORRECASTILLO

Ctra. de Bonete, s/n
2650 Montealegre del Castillo (Albacete)
☎: +34 967 582 188 - Fax: +34 967 582 339
www.torrecastillo.com
bodega@torrecastillo.com

TORRECASTILLO 2012 B
sauvignon blanc

86 Colour: bright straw. Nose: fresh, fresh fruit, dried flowers. Palate: flavourful, fruity, good acidity, balanced.

TORRECASTILLO 2012 RD
monastrell

84

TORRECASTILLO 2012 T ROBLE
monastrell

88 Colour: bright cherry. Nose: ripe fruit, sweet spices, creamy oak. Palate: flavourful, fruity, toasty, round tannins.

TORRECASTILLO EL TOBAR 2010 TC
monastrell

89 Colour: cherry, garnet rim. Nose: ripe fruit, spicy, creamy oak, toasty, complex. Palate: powerful, flavourful, toasty, round tannins.

BODEGA VIÑA ELENA S.L.

Estrecho Marín, s/n
30520 Jumilla (Murcia)
☎: +34 968 781 340
www.vinaelena.com
info@vinaelena.com

FAMILIA PACHECO 2011 T ROBLE
monastrell, cabernet sauvignon, syrah

85 Colour: bright cherry. Nose: ripe fruit, sweet spices, balsamic herbs. Palate: flavourful, fruity, toasty.

FAMILIA PACHECO ORGÁNICO 2011 T
monastrell, syrah

87 Colour: bright cherry. Nose: ripe fruit, sweet spices, creamy oak. Palate: flavourful, fruity, toasty.

FAMILIA PACHECO SELECCIÓN 2009 T
monastrell, cabernet sauvignon, syrah

89 Colour: cherry, garnet rim. Nose: ripe fruit, spicy, creamy oak, toasty, complex. Palate: powerful, flavourful, toasty, round tannins.

LOS CUCOS DE LA ALBERQUILLA 2011 T
cabernet sauvignon

86 Colour: bright cherry. Nose: ripe fruit, sweet spices, creamy oak, balsamic herbs. Palate: flavourful, fruity, toasty.

BODEGAS AGRUPADAS PONTE

Eduardo Pondal, 3 Entpa B
36001 (Pontevedra)
☎: +34 986 840 064 - Fax: +34 986 710 230
www.bodegasagrupadasponte.com
info@bodegasagrupadasponte.com

LA ELECCIÓN DE CARMEN 2009 TC
90% monastrell, 10% tempranillo

87 Colour: cherry, garnet rim. Nose: creamy oak, roasted coffee, fruit preserve. Palate: powerful, flavourful, toasty.

BODEGAS ARLOREN

Ctra. del Puerto s/n Cañada del Trigo
30520 Jumilla (Murcia)
☎: +34 968 821 096
www.arloren.es
bodegas.arloren@arloren.com

MIRIAR - AMBAR 2010 T
monastrell

84

MIRIAR - CUARZO 2009 T
monastrell, syrah, cabernet sauvignon

87 Colour: cherry, garnet rim. Nose: ripe fruit, spicy, toasty. Palate: powerful, flavourful, toasty, balanced.

MIRIAR - RUBÍ 2008 T
monastrell, syrah, merlot

85 Colour: cherry, garnet rim. Nose: toasty, ripe fruit, fruit preserve. Palate: powerful, flavourful, toasty, warm.

VEGACAÑADA 2009 T
monastrell, merlot, tempranillo, syrah

81

VEGACAÑADA 2010 T
monastrell

80

BODEGAS BLEDA

Ctra. Jumilla - Ontur, Km. 2.
30520 Jumilla (Murcia)
☎: +34 968 780 012 - Fax: +34 968 782 699
www.bodegasbleda.com
vinos@bodegasbleda.com

CASTILLO DE JUMILLA 2007 TR
90% monastrell, 10% tempranillo

86 Colour: cherry, garnet rim. Nose: ripe fruit, toasty, aromatic coffee. Palate: spicy, ripe fruit.

CASTILLO DE JUMILLA 2010 TC
90% monastrell, 10% tempranillo

85 Colour: cherry, garnet rim. Nose: powerfull, warm, spicy, varnish, overripe fruit. Palate: good structure, flavourful, round tannins.

CASTILLO DE JUMILLA 2012 RD
monastrell

86 Colour: rose, purple rim. Nose: powerfull, ripe fruit, red berry notes, floral, expressive. Palate: powerful, fruity, fresh.

CASTILLO DE JUMILLA MONASTRELL - TEMPRANILLO 2012 T
monastrell, tempranillo

88 Colour: cherry, purple rim. Nose: fresh fruit, red berry notes, floral. Palate: flavourful, fruity, good acidity, round tannins.

CASTILLO DE JUMILLA MONASTRELL 2012 T
monastrell

88 Colour: cherry, purple rim. Nose: fresh fruit, red berry notes, floral. Palate: flavourful, fruity, good acidity, round tannins.

DIVUS 2011 T
monastrell

90 Colour: cherry, garnet rim. Nose: sweet spices, toasty, ripe fruit, woody, balsamic herbs. Palate: good structure, round tannins.

PINODONCEL 2012 T
monastrell, syrah, merlot

87 Colour: cherry, purple rim. Nose: expressive, red berry notes, balsamic herbs. Palate: flavourful, fruity, round tannins.

PINODONCEL CINCO MESES 2012 T
monastrell, syrah, petit verdot

88 Colour: deep cherry, purple rim. Nose: powerfull, warm, ripe fruit, cocoa bean. Palate: flavourful, good structure, full, long.

BODEGAS CARCHELO

Casas de la Hoya, s/n
30520 Jumilla (Murcia)
☎: +34 968 435 137 - Fax: +34 968 435 200
www.carchelo.com
comex@carchelo.com

ALTICO SYRAH 2011 T
100% syrah

89 Colour: cherry, garnet rim. Nose: ripe fruit, sweet spices, creamy oak, expressive. Palate: powerful, flavourful, long, balanced.

CANALIZO 2008 TC
40% monastrell, 40% syrah, 20% tempranillo

90 Colour: bright cherry. Nose: sweet spices, creamy oak, characterful, overripe fruit. Palate: flavourful, fruity, toasty, round tannins.

CARCHELO 2011 T
40% monastrell, 40% tempranillo, 20% cabernet sauvignon

88 Colour: bright cherry. Nose: ripe fruit, sweet spices, creamy oak, expressive. Palate: flavourful, fruity, toasty, round tannins.

SIERVA 2010 T
monastrell, syrah, tempranillo

91 Colour: cherry, garnet rim. Nose: ripe fruit, spicy, creamy oak, toasty, complex. Palate: powerful, flavourful, toasty, round tannins.

VEDRÉ 2010 T
50% monastrell, 25% syrah, 25% tempranillo

89 Colour: cherry, garnet rim. Nose: spicy, creamy oak, toasty, overripe fruit. Palate: powerful, flavourful, toasty, round tannins.

BODEGAS CASA ROJO

Sánchez Picazo, 53
30332 Balsapintada (Murcia)
☎: +34 968 151 520 - Fax: +34 968 151 690
www.casarojo.com
info@casarojo.com

CASA DEL ROJO 2007 T
100% monastrell

87 Colour: cherry, garnet rim. Nose: ripe fruit, fragrant herbs, cocoa bean, sweet spices, creamy oak. Palate: rich, powerful, flavourful, balanced.

BODEGAS EL NIDO

Ctra. de Fuentealamo - Paraje de la Aragona
30520 Jumilla (Murcia)
☎: +34 968 435 022 - Fax: +34 968 435 653
www.orowines.com
info@bodegaselnido.com

CLÍO 2010 T
70% monastrell, 30% cabernet sauvignon

93 Colour: cherry, garnet rim. Nose: spicy, creamy oak, toasty, complex, overripe fruit, earthy notes. Palate: powerful, flavourful, toasty, round tannins.

CORTEO 2010 T
100% syrah

95 Colour: cherry, garnet rim. Nose: powerfull, characterful, ripe fruit, sweet spices, toasty. Palate: powerful, concentrated, ripe fruit, round tannins.

EL NIDO 2010 T
70% cabernet sauvignon, 30% monastrell

96 Colour: cherry, garnet rim. Nose: ripe fruit, spicy, creamy oak, complex, earthy notes, roasted coffee. Palate: powerful, flavourful, toasty, round tannins, fine bitter notes.

BODEGAS HACIENDA DEL CARCHE

Ctra. del Carche, Km. 8,3- Apdo. Correos 257
30520 Jumilla (Murcia)
☎: +34 968 108 248 - Fax: +34 968 975 935
www.haciendadelcarche.com
info@haciendadelcarche.com

HACIENDA DEL CARCHE 2012 B
sauvignon blanc, airén, macabeo

86 Colour: bright straw. Nose: dried flowers, dried herbs, ripe fruit. Palate: flavourful, fruity, powerful.

HACIENDA DEL CARCHE CEPAS VIEJAS 2009 TC
monastrell, cabernet sauvignon

87 Colour: cherry, garnet rim. Nose: ripe fruit, spicy, creamy oak, toasty, fine reductive notes. Palate: powerful, flavourful, toasty.

TAVS SELECCIÓN 2011 T
monastrell, syrah, cabernet sauvignon

89 Colour: cherry, garnet rim. Nose: fruit preserve, balsamic herbs, earthy notes, spicy, aged wood nuances. Palate: ripe fruit, powerful, flavourful.

TAVS 2012 T
monastrell, syrah, garnacha

90 Colour: cherry, garnet rim. Nose: ripe fruit, balsamic herbs, floral, fragrant herbs. Palate: powerful, flavourful, long.

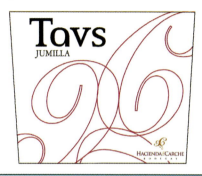

BODEGAS JUAN GIL

Ctra. Fuentealamo - Paraje de la Aragona
30520 Jumilla (Murcia)
☎: +34 968 435 022 - Fax: +34 968 716 051
www.juangil.es
info@juangil.es

HONORO VERA ORGANIC 2012 T
100% monastrell

89 Colour: very deep cherry. Nose: ripe fruit, complex, dried herbs. Palate: fruity, fine bitter notes, good acidity.

JUAN GIL 12 MESES 2010 T
100% monastrell

92 Colour: cherry, garnet rim. Nose: spicy, creamy oak, toasty, warm, overripe fruit. Palate: powerful, flavourful, toasty, round tannins.

JUAN GIL 18 MESES 2010 T
60% monastrell, 30% cabernet sauvignon, 10% syrah

91 Colour: cherry, garnet rim. Nose: sweet spices, creamy oak, toasty, overripe fruit. Palate: fine bitter, ripe fruit, spicy, round tannins.

JUAN GIL 4 MESES 2012 T
100% monastrell

90 Colour: very deep cherry. Nose: powerfull, warm, spicy, ripe fruit. Palate: powerful, sweetness, fine bitter notes.

JUAN GIL MOSCATEL 2012 B
100% moscatel

89 Colour: bright straw. Nose: fresh, white flowers, expressive, candied fruit. Palate: flavourful, fruity, good acidity, balanced.

· BODEGAS LUZÓN

Ctra. Jumilla-Calasparra, Km. 3,1
30520 Jumilla (Murcia)
☎: +34 968 784 135 - Fax: +34 968 781 911
www.bodegasluzon.com
info@bodegasluzon.com

ALTOS DE LUZÓN 2009 T
50% monastrell, 25% tempranillo, 25% cabernet sauvignon

92 Colour: cherry, garnet rim. Nose: ripe fruit, spicy, creamy oak, toasty, characterful, roasted coffee. Palate: powerful, flavourful, toasty, round tannins.

CASTILLO DE LUZÓN 2010 TC
50% monastrell, 20% tempranillo, 20% cabernet sauvignon, 10% merlot

90 Colour: cherry, garnet rim. Nose: overripe fruit, roasted coffee, dark chocolate. Palate: flavourful, powerful, fine bitter notes, good acidity.

LUZÓN 2011 T ROBLE
100% monastrell

88 Colour: bright cherry. Nose: ripe fruit, sweet spices, creamy oak. Palate: flavourful, fruity, toasty, round tannins.

LUZÓN 2012 B
macabeo, airén

85 Colour: bright straw. Nose: fresh, expressive, lactic notes, tropical fruit. Palate: flavourful, fruity, good acidity.

LUZÓN 2012 T
70% monastrell, 30% syrah

92 Colour: cherry, garnet rim. Nose: ripe fruit, spicy, creamy oak, toasty, characterful. Palate: powerful, flavourful, toasty, round tannins.

LUZÓN VERDE ORGANIC 2012 T
100% monastrell

92 Colour: cherry, garnet rim. Nose: ripe fruit, spicy, creamy oak, toasty, raspberry. Palate: powerful, flavourful, toasty, round tannins.

BODEGAS MADROÑO

Ctra., Jumilla-Ontur, km. 16
30520 Jumilla (Murcia)
☎: +34 662 380 985
gmartinez@vinocrapula.com

MADROÑO 2011 T
monastrell, syrah

89 Colour: bright cherry. Nose: sweet spices, creamy oak, expressive, fruit preserve. Palate: flavourful, fruity, toasty, round tannins.

MADROÑO T ROBLE
100% syrah

90 Colour: bright cherry. Nose: ripe fruit, sweet spices, creamy oak, expressive, elegant. Palate: flavourful, fruity, toasty, balanced.

BODEGAS MONTEREBRO

Barrio Iglesias, 55
30520 Jumilla (Murcia)
☎: +34 669 359 647
www.monterebro.com
info@monterebro.com

MONTEREBRO 2010 TC
85% monastrell, 15% syrah

89 Colour: cherry, garnet rim. Nose: ripe fruit, spicy, creamy oak, balsamic herbs, dark chocolate, cocoa bean. Palate: powerful, flavourful, long, spicy.

MONTEREBRO 2011 B
100% sauvignon blanc

86 Colour: bright straw. Nose: ripe fruit, tropical fruit, floral, dried herbs. Palate: powerful, flavourful, rich.

MONTEREBRO 2011 T
85% monastrell, 15% syrah

88 Colour: cherry, purple rim. Nose: ripe fruit, balsamic herbs, floral, powerfull. Palate: powerful, flavourful, long, ripe fruit, balanced.

MONTEREBRO 2011 T BARRICA
85% monastrell, 15% syrah

86 Colour: bright cherry. Nose: ripe fruit, creamy oak, aged wood nuances. Palate: flavourful, fruity, toasty, powerful.

MONTEREBRO 2011 TC
85% monastrell, 15% syrah

88 Colour: cherry, garnet rim. Nose: ripe fruit, spicy, creamy oak, toasty, complex. Palate: flavourful, balanced, toasty.

MONTEREBRO 2012 RD
60% monastrell, 40% syrah

85 Colour: rose, purple rim. Nose: powerfull, ripe fruit, red berry notes, floral. Palate: powerful, fruity, fresh.

MONTEREBRO 2012 T
85% monastrell, 15% syrah

87 Colour: cherry, purple rim. Nose: violet drops, fruit preserve, balsamic herbs. Palate: powerful, rich, fruity.

MONTEREBRO 2012 T BARRICA
85% monastrell, 15% syrah

87 Colour: cherry, garnet rim. Nose: spicy, creamy oak, ripe fruit. Palate: balsamic, long, spicy, toasty.

MONTEREBRO SELECCIÓN 2011 T
85% syrah, 15% monastrell

90 Colour: cherry, garnet rim. Nose: ripe fruit, spicy, creamy oak, toasty, complex. Palate: powerful, flavourful, toasty, round tannins, balanced.

MONTEREBRO SELECCIÓN 2012 T
85% syrah, 15% monastrell

89 Colour: cherry, purple rim. Nose: ripe fruit, sweet spices, creamy oak, expressive. Palate: flavourful, fruity, toasty, round tannins.

BODEGAS OLIVARES

Vereda Real, s/n
30520 Jumilla (Murcia)
☎: +34 968 780 180 - Fax: +34 968 756 474
www.bodegasolivares.com
correo@bodegasolivares.com

ALTOS DE LA HOYA 2011 T
100% monastrell

88 Colour: bright cherry. Nose: ripe fruit, sweet spices, creamy oak, expressive. Palate: flavourful, fruity, toasty, round tannins.

OLIVARES 2012 RD
70% monastrell, 30% syrah

83

OLIVARES 2012 T
75% monastrell, 15% garnacha, 10% syrah

85 Colour: cherry, purple rim. Nose: fruit preserve, floral, balsamic herbs. Palate: powerful, flavourful, long.

OLIVARES DULCE MONASTRELL 2010 T
100% monastrell

92 Colour: cherry, garnet rim. Nose: ripe fruit, fruit preserve, balsamic herbs, acetaldehyde, pattiserie, creamy oak, toasty. Palate: spicy, long, rich. Personality.

BODEGAS PÍO DEL RAMO

Ctra. Almanza, s/n
2652 Ontur (Albacete)
☎: +34 967 323 230
www.piodelramo.com
info@piodelramo.com

PÍO DEL RAMO 2009 TC
syrah, monastrell, cabernet sauvignon, petit verdot

89 Colour: cherry, garnet rim. Nose: ripe fruit, scrubland, sweet spices. Palate: powerful, flavourful, long, toasty.

PÍO DEL RAMO ECOLÓGICO 2011 T
monastrell

87 Colour: bright cherry. Nose: ripe fruit, sweet spices, creamy oak, expressive. Palate: flavourful, fruity, toasty.

BODEGAS SAN DIONISIO, S. COOP

Ctra. Higuera, s/n
2651 Fuenteálamo (Albacete)
☎: +34 967 543 032 - Fax: +34 967 543 136
www.bodegassandinisio.es
sandionisio@bodegassandionisio.es

SEÑORÍO DE FUENTEÁLAMO
MONASTRELL SYRAH 2009 TC
60% monastrell, 40% syrah

86 Colour: cherry, garnet rim. Nose: ripe fruit, spicy, creamy oak, toasty, complex, fine reductive notes. Palate: powerful, flavourful, toasty.

MAINETES PETIT VERDOT 2010 T ROBLE
100% petit verdot

85 Colour: bright cherry. Nose: ripe fruit, sweet spices, premature reduction notes. Palate: flavourful, toasty.

MAINETES SAUVIGNON BLANC 2012 B
100% sauvignon blanc

85 Colour: bright straw. Nose: ripe fruit, fragrant herbs, tropical fruit. Palate: correct, fine bitter notes, easy to drink.

MAINETES SELECCIÓN 2009 T BARRICA
33% monastrell, 33% syrah, 33% merlot

86 Colour: cherry, garnet rim. Nose: ripe fruit, sweet spices, creamy oak, expressive. Palate: flavourful, fruity, toasty.

SEÑORÍO DE FUENTEÁLAMO SELECCIÓN 2009 T
100% monastrell

88 Colour: ruby red. Nose: ripe fruit, spicy, creamy oak, toasty, complex. Palate: powerful, flavourful, toasty, round tannins.

SEÑORÍO DE FUENTEÁLAMO SYRAH 2012 RD
100% syrah

88 Colour: rose, purple rim. Nose: powerfull, ripe fruit, red berry notes, floral, expressive. Palate: powerful, fruity, fresh.

BODEGAS SILVANO GARCÍA S.L.

Avda. de Murcia, 29
30520 Jumilla (Murcia)
☎: +34 968 780 767 - Fax: +34 968 716 125
www.silvanogarcia.com
bodegas@silvanogarcia.com

SILVANO GARCÍA DULCE MONASTRELL 2011 T
100% monastrell

90 Colour: dark mahogany. Nose: complex, fruit liqueur notes, dried fruit, pattiserie, toasty. Palate: sweet, rich, unctuous, powerful.

SILVANO GARCÍA MOSCATEL 2011 B
100% moscatel

91 Colour: golden. Nose: floral, honeyed notes, candied fruit, fragrant herbs. Palate: flavourful, sweet, fresh, fruity, good acidity, long.

VIÑAHONDA 2012 B
100% macabeo

86 Colour: bright straw. Nose: fresh, fresh fruit, white flowers, balsamic herbs. Palate: flavourful, fruity, good acidity, balanced.

VIÑAHONDA 2012 RD
100% monastrell

86 Colour: rose, purple rim. Nose: lactic notes, red berry notes, ripe fruit, floral. Palate: fresh, fruity, powerful.

VIÑAHONDA ALLIER FINESSE 2011 T
60% monastrell, 30% tempranillo, 10% syrah

90 Colour: cherry, garnet rim. Nose: ripe fruit, spicy, creamy oak, toasty, complex. Palate: powerful, flavourful, toasty, round tannins.

BODEGAS SIMÓN

Madrid, 15
2653 Albatana (Albacete)
☎: +34 967 323 340 - Fax: +34 967 323 340
www.bodegassimon.com
info@bodegassimon.com

GALÁN DEL SIGLO PETIT VERDOT 2008 T

86 Colour: pale ruby, brick rim edge. Nose: spicy, fine reductive notes, wet leather, aged wood nuances, fruit liqueur notes. Palate: spicy, long, flavourful.

GALÁN DEL SIGLO TRADICIÓN FAMILIAR 2009 T

84

BODEGAS VOLVER

Pza. de Grecia, 1 Local 1B
45005 Toledo (Toledo)
☎: +34 925 167 493 - Fax: +34 925 167 059
www.bodegasvolver.com
export@bodegasvolver.com

WRONGO DONGO 2012 T
monastrell

92 Colour: bright cherry. Nose: ripe fruit, sweet spices, creamy oak, expressive, wild herbs. Palate: flavourful, fruity, toasty, round tannins.

BODEGAS Y VIÑEDOS CASA DE LA ERMITA

Ctra. El Carche, Km. 11,5
30520 Jumilla (Murcia)
☎: +34 968 783 035 - Fax: +34 968 716 063
www.casadelaermita.com
bodega@casadelaermita.com

ALTOS DEL CUCO 2012 T
60% monastrell, 20% syrah, 20% tempranillo

87 Colour: cherry, purple rim. Nose: ripe fruit, red berry notes. Palate: flavourful, powerful, sweetness.

ALTOS DEL CUCO GARNACHA 2012 T
80% garnacha, 20% monastrell

88 Colour: bright cherry. Nose: sweet spices, creamy oak, overripe fruit. Palate: flavourful, fruity, toasty, round tannins.

ALTOS DEL CUCO MONASTRELL ECOLÓGICO 2012 T
100% monastrell

86 Colour: cherry, purple rim. Nose: expressive, red berry notes, warm, overripe fruit. Palate: flavourful, fruity, good acidity, round tannins.

CARACOL SERRANO 2012 T
60% monastrell, 20% syrah, 15% cabernet sauvignon, 5% petit verdot

86 Colour: bright cherry. Nose: sweet spices, creamy oak, fruit preserve, overripe fruit. Palate: flavourful, fruity, toasty, round tannins.

CASA DE LA ERMITA 2009 TC
60% monastrell, 25% tempranillo, 25% cabernet sauvignon

88 Colour: cherry, garnet rim. Nose: spicy, creamy oak, toasty, characterful, overripe fruit. Palate: powerful, flavourful, toasty, round tannins.

CASA DE LA ERMITA 2011 T ROBLE
80% monastrell, 20% petit verdot

89 Colour: bright cherry. Nose: ripe fruit, sweet spices, creamy oak, expressive. Palate: flavourful, fruity, toasty, round tannins.

CASA DE LA ERMITA 2012 B

88 Colour: bright straw. Nose: fresh, white flowers, expressive, wild herbs, lactic notes. Palate: flavourful, fruity, good acidity, balanced.

CASA DE LA ERMITA 2012 T
60% monastrell, 40% syrah

87 Colour: cherry, purple rim. Nose: expressive, fresh fruit, red berry notes, floral, balanced. Palate: flavourful, fruity, good acidity, round tannins.

CASA DE LA ERMITA CRIANZA ECOLÓGICO 2009 TC
100% monastrell

89 Colour: cherry, garnet rim. Nose: ripe fruit, spicy, creamy oak, toasty. Palate: powerful, flavourful, toasty, round tannins.

CASA DE LA ERMITA DULCE 2012 B
83

CASA DE LA ERMITA DULCE MONASTRELL 2010 T
100% monastrell

85 Colour: cherry, garnet rim. Nose: ripe fruit, fruit preserve, spicy, toasty, aged wood nuances. Palate: powerful, flavourful, sweetness.

CASA DE LA ERMITA ECOLÓGICO MONASTRELL 2012 T
100% monastrell

90 Colour: bright cherry. Nose: ripe fruit, sweet spices, creamy oak, red berry notes. Palate: flavourful, fruity, toasty, round tannins.

CASA DE LA ERMITA IDÍLICO 2008 TC
65% petit verdot, 35% monastrell

89 Colour: cherry, garnet rim. Nose: spicy, creamy oak, toasty, overripe fruit. Palate: powerful, flavourful, toasty, round tannins.

CASA DE LA ERMITA PETIT VERDOT 2009 T
100% petit verdot

87 Colour: cherry, garnet rim. Nose: toasty, dark chocolate, overripe fruit. Palate: fine bitter notes, powerful, grainy tannins.

MONASTERIO DE SANTA ANA MONASTRELL 2011 T
100% monastrell

88 Colour: bright cherry. Nose: sweet spices, creamy oak, ripe fruit. Palate: flavourful, fruity, toasty, round tannins.

MONASTERIO DE SANTA ANA TEMPRANILLO MONASTRELL ECOLÓGICO 2011 T
50% tempranillo, 50% monastrell

84

BSI BODEGAS SAN ISIDRO

Ctra. Murcia, s/n
30520 Jumilla (Murcia)
☎: +34 968 780 700 - Fax: +34 968 782 351
www.bsi.es
bsi@bsi.es

GÉMINA MONASTRELL 2010 T
100% monastrell

85 Colour: cherry, garnet rim. Nose: ripe fruit, spicy, toasty, aged wood nuances. Palate: powerful, flavourful, toasty.

GÉMINA PREMIUM 2006 TR
100% monastrell

87 Colour: cherry, garnet rim. Nose: ripe fruit, balsamic herbs, spicy, creamy oak. Palate: powerful, flavourful, spicy.

GENUS 2011 T ROBLE
monastrell

83

GENUS MONASTRELL SYRAH 2010 T
monastrell, syrah

86 Colour: cherry, garnet rim. Nose: ripe fruit, spicy, creamy oak, toasty, complex. Palate: powerful, flavourful, toasty.

LACRIMA CHRISTI T
monastrell

89 Colour: light mahogany. Nose: powerfull, elegant, dry nuts, toasty, acetaldehyde. Palate: rich, fine solera notes, long, spicy.

GÉMINA CUVÉE SELECCIÓN 2010 T
100% monastrell

86 Colour: cherry, garnet rim. Nose: ripe fruit, spicy, creamy oak, toasty. Palate: powerful, flavourful, toasty.

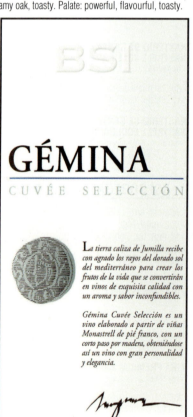

GÉMINA

CUVÉE SELECCIÓN

La tierra caliza de Jumilla recibe con agrado los rayos del dorado sol del mediterráneo para crear los frutos de la vida que se convertirán en vinos de exquisita calidad con un aroma y sabor inconfundibles.

Gémina Cuvée Selección es un vino elaborado a partir de viñas Monastrell de pié franco, con un corto paso por madera, obteniéndose así un vino con gran personalidad y elegancia.

BODEGAS SAN ISIDRO

SABATACHA 2009 TC
monastrell

85 Colour: cherry, garnet rim. Nose: ripe fruit, spicy, creamy oak, toasty, complex. Palate: powerful, flavourful, toasty, round tannins.

SABATACHA PETIT VERDOT 2009 T
petit verdot

84

SABATACHA SYRAH 2012 T
100% syrah

88 Colour: cherry, purple rim. Nose: expressive, fresh fruit, red berry notes, floral. Palate: flavourful, fruity, good acidity, round tannins.

SABATACHA 2007 TR
monastrell

85 Colour: cherry, garnet rim. Nose: ripe fruit, spicy, creamy oak, toasty, fine reductive notes. Palate: powerful, flavourful, toasty.

SABATACHA MONASTRELL 2012 T
100% monastrell

89 Colour: cherry, purple rim. Nose: expressive, fresh fruit, red berry notes, floral. Palate: flavourful, fruity, good acidity, round tannins.

CAMPOS DE RISCA

Avda. Diagonal, 590, 5 1
8021 (Barcelona)
☎: +34 660 445 464
www.vinergia.com
vinergia@vinergia.com

CAMPOS DE RISCA 2012 T
90% monastrell, 10% syrah

85 Colour: bright cherry. Nose: ripe fruit, sweet spices, creamy oak. Palate: flavourful, fruity, toasty.

CARREFOUR

Campezo, 16
28022 Madrid (Madrid)
☎: +34 902 202 000
www.carrefour.es

PEÑARRUBIA 2010 TC
81

PEÑARRUBIA 2012 T

85 Colour: cherry, purple rim. Nose: ripe fruit, balanced, medium intensity, warm. Palate: fruity, correct, easy to drink, good finish.

PEÑARRUBIA 2012 T ROBLE
100% monastrell

82

CRAPULA WINES, S.L.

Avda. de la Asunción, 42 2D
30520 Jumilla (Murcia)
☎: +34 968 781 855
gmartinez@vinocrapula.com

CÁRMINE 2010 T
monastrell, syrah

91 Colour: cherry, garnet rim. Nose: fruit preserve, candied fruit, toasty. Palate: spicy, ripe fruit, round tannins.

CÁRMINE 3 MESES 2010 T
monastrell

90 Colour: cherry, purple rim. Nose: ripe fruit, toasty, sweet spices. Palate: fine bitter notes, warm.

CELEBRE 2009 TC
monastrell, syrah

90 Colour: cherry, garnet rim. Nose: fruit preserve, candied fruit, toasty. Palate: fine bitter notes, powerful, round tannins.

CELEBRE 2011 T ROBLE
monastrell, syrah

91 Colour: cherry, garnet rim. Nose: ripe fruit, fruit expression, sweet spices, creamy oak. Palate: flavourful, powerful, concentrated.

CRÁPULA 2010 T
85% monastrell, 15% otras

90 Colour: cherry, garnet rim. Nose: toasty, spicy, fruit preserve, sweet spices, dark chocolate. Palate: powerful, concentrated, sweetness.

CRÁPULA SOUL 2009 T
monastrell, petit verdot, cabernet sauvignon, syrah

93 Colour: cherry, garnet rim. Nose: ripe fruit, spicy, creamy oak, toasty, complex, characterful. Palate: powerful, flavourful, toasty, round tannins.

DULCE CRÁPULA 2010 T
monastrell

88 Colour: cherry, garnet rim. Nose: candied fruit, fruit preserve, fragrant herbs, sweet spices, toasty. Palate: powerful, flavourful, long.

G WINE 2009 T
monastrell, syrah

91 Colour: cherry, garnet rim. Nose: ripe fruit, floral, balsamic herbs, fragrant herbs, spicy, creamy oak. Palate: round, flavourful, complex.

NDQ (NACIDO DEL QUORUM) 2011 T
monastrell

91 Colour: bright cherry. Nose: ripe fruit, sweet spices, creamy oak, expressive. Palate: flavourful, fruity, toasty, round tannins.

NDQ (NACIDO DEL QUORUM) SELECCIÓN 2010 T
monastrell, syrah, cabernet sauvignon

93 Colour: cherry, garnet rim. Nose: ripe fruit, spicy, creamy oak, toasty, complex, mineral. Palate: powerful, flavourful, toasty, round tannins.

EGO BODEGAS

Plaza Santa Gertrudis, Nº 1, Entresuelo A
30001 (Murcia)
☎: +34 968 964 326 - Fax: +34 968 964 326
www.egobodegas.com
ioana.paunescu@egobodegas.com

CLOS ALAYA 2009 TC
monastrell, petit verdot

87 Colour: cherry, garnet rim. Nose: ripe fruit, spicy, complex, balsamic herbs, cigar, tobacco. Palate: powerful, flavourful, toasty.

CLOS ALAYA 2011 T
monastrell, syrah

88 Colour: bright cherry. Nose: ripe fruit, sweet spices, creamy oak, expressive. Palate: flavourful, fruity, toasty, round tannins.

ORO WINES

Ctra. de Fuentealamo - Paraje de la Aragona
30520 Jumilla (Murcia)
☎: +34 968 435 022 - Fax: +34 968 716 051
www.orowines.com
info@orowines.com

COMOLOCO 2012 T
100% monastrell

85 Colour: deep cherry. Nose: powerfull, dried fruit, warm. Palate: fruity, sweetness.

PROPIEDAD VITÍCOLA CASA CASTILLO

Ctra. Jumilla - Hellín, RM-428, Km. 8
30520 Jumilla (Murcia)
☎: +34 968 781 691 - Fax: +34 968 716 238
www.casacastillo.es
info@casacastillo.es

CASA CASTILLO MONASTRELL 2012 T
100% monastrell

90 Colour: cherry, purple rim. Nose: red berry notes, ripe fruit. Palate: flavourful, fruity, good acidity, round tannins.

CASA CASTILLO PIE FRANCO 2010 T
100% monastrell

94 Colour: cherry, garnet rim. Nose: spicy, creamy oak, toasty, characterful, varietal, mineral. Palate: powerful, flavourful, toasty, round tannins.

EL MOLAR 2011 T
100% garnacha

93 Colour: bright cherry. Nose: ripe fruit, sweet spices, creamy oak, balsamic herbs, characterful. Palate: flavourful, fruity, toasty, round tannins.

LAS GRAVAS 2010 T
70% monastrell, 10% garnacha, 20% syrah

94 Colour: cherry, garnet rim. Nose: spicy, creamy oak, toasty, ripe fruit, characterful. Palate: powerful, toasty, round tannins.

VALTOSCA 2011 T
100% syrah

92 Colour: cherry, garnet rim. Nose: spicy, creamy oak, toasty, complex, earthy notes. Palate: powerful, flavourful, toasty, round tannins.

RED BOTTLE INTERNATIONAL

Rosales, 6
9400 Aranda de Duero (Burgos)
☎: +34 947 515 884 - Fax: +34 947 515 886
www.redbottleint.com
rbi@redbottleint.com

CASPER 2011 T ROBLE
100% monastrell

88 Colour: cherry, garnet rim. Nose: varietal, fruit preserve, dried fruit, toasty. Palate: powerful, sweetness, concentrated.

SOC. COOP. DE CLM SAN JOSÉ

Camino de Hellín, s/n
2652 Ontur (Albacete)
☎: +34 967 324 212 - Fax: +34 967 324 186
www.bodegasanjose.com
comercial@bodegasanjose.com

DOMINIO DE ONTUR MERLOT 2012 T
merlot

86 Colour: cherry, purple rim. Nose: ripe fruit, balsamic herbs, fragrant herbs, powerfull. Palate: correct, flavourful.

DOMINIO DE ONTUR MONASTRELL 2012 T
monastrell

82

DOMINIO DE ONTUR SELECCIÓN 2010 T
syrah, monastrell

88 Colour: bright cherry. Nose: ripe fruit, sweet spices, creamy oak, expressive. Palate: flavourful, fruity, toasty, round tannins.

DOMINIO DE ONTUR SYRAH 2012 T
syrah

86 Colour: cherry, purple rim. Nose: floral, ripe fruit, fragrant herbs. Palate: flavourful, fresh, fruity.

PATRE 2010 T
monastrell, syrah

86 Colour: cherry, garnet rim. Nose: ripe fruit, spicy, mineral, fine reductive notes. Palate: powerful, flavourful, toasty, round tannins.

RAVEN & BULL 2010 T
monastrell

85 Colour: cherry, garnet rim. Nose: ripe fruit, spicy, creamy oak, toasty, balsamic herbs. Palate: powerful, flavourful, toasty.

VILLA DE ONTUR 2012 B
verdejo

85 Colour: bright straw. Nose: ripe fruit, faded flowers, dried herbs. Palate: powerful, flavourful, easy to drink.

VILLA DE ONTUR 2012 RD
syrah

84

DO LA GOMERA / D.O.P.

LOCATION:

SAN SEBASTIÁN DE LA GOMERA

Vallehermoso

▽ Consejo Regulador
● DO Boundary

The majority of the vineyards are found in the north of the island, in the vicinity of the towns of Vallehermoso (some 385 Ha) and Hermigua. The remaining vineyards are spread out over Agulo, Valle Gran Rey – near the capital city of La Gomera, San Sebastián– and Alajeró, on the slopes of the Garajonay peak.

CLIMATE:

The island benefits from a subtropical climate together with, as one approaches the higher altitudes of the Garajonay peak, a phenomenon of permanent humidity known as 'mar de nubes' (sea of clouds) caused by the trade winds. This humid air from the north collides with the mountain range, thereby creating a kind of horizontal rain resulting in a specific ecosystem made up of luxuriant valleys. The average temperature is 20°C all year round.

SOIL:

The most common soil in the higher mountain regions is deep and clayey, while, as one approaches lower altitudes towards the scrubland, the soil is more Mediterranean with a good many stones and terraces similar to those of the Priorat.

GRAPE VARIETIES:

WHITE: *Forastera* (90%), *Gomera Blanca, Listán Blanca, Marmajuelo, Malvasía* and *Pedro Ximenez.*
RED: *Listán Negra* (5%), *Negramoll* (2%); **Experimental:** *Tintilla Castellana, Cabernet Sauvignon* and *Rubí Cabernet.*

FIGURES:

Vineyard surface: 125 – **Wine-Growers:** 230 – **Wineries:** 15 – **2012 Harvest rating:** Very Good – **Production:** 70.000 litres – **Market percentages:** 100% domestic

VINTAGE RATING PEÑÍNGUIDE

2008	2009	2010	2011	2012
N/A	N/A	N/A	N/A	N/A

CONSEJO REGULADOR
Avda. Guillermo Ascanio,16 - 38840 Vallehermoso (La Gomera) ☎: +34 922 800 801 - Fax: +34 922 801 146
crdolagomera@922800801.e.telefonica.net   www.vinosdelagomera.es

DO LA MANCHA / D.O.P.

LOCATION:

On the southern plateau in the provinces of Albacete, Ciudad Real, Cuenca and Toledo. It is the largest wine-growing region in Spain and in the world.

CLIMATE:

Extreme continental, with temperatures ranging between 40/45°C in summer and −10/12°C in winter. Rather low rainfall, with an average of about 375 mm per year.

SOIL:

The terrain is flat and the vineyards are situated at an altitude of about 700 m above sea level. The soil is generally sandy, limy and clayey.

GRAPE VARIETIES:

WHITE: *Airén* (majority), *Macabeo, Pardilla, Chardonnay, Sauvignon Blanc, Verdejo, Moscatel de Grano Menudo, Gewürztraminer, Parellada, Pero Ximénez, Riesling* and *Torrontés*.
RED: *Cencibel* (majority amongst red varieties), *Garnacha, Moravia, Cabernet Sauvignon, Merlot, Syrah, Cabernet Franc, Graciano, Malbec, Mencía, Monastrell, Pinot Noir, Petit Verdot* and *Bobal*.

FIGURES:

Vineyard surface: 163.686– **Wine-Growers:** 16.795 – **Wineries:** 264 – **2012 Harvest rating:** Excellent – **Production:** 145.919.211 litres – **Market percentages:** 41% domestic. 59% export

CONSEJO REGULADOR
Avda. de Criptana, 73 - 13600 Alcázar de San Juan (Ciudad Real) ☎: +34 926 541 523 - Fax: +34 926 588 040
consejo@lamanchawines.com   www.lamanchawines.com

¡EA! VINOS MANUEL MANZANEQUE SUÁREZ VITICULTOR Y ENÓLOGO

Avda. Jose prat 14 Esc 3. 1° D1
2008 (Albacete)
☎: +34 967 278 578 - Fax: +34 967 278 578
www.eavinos.com
info@eavinos.com

¡EA! 2011 T
cencibel

89 Colour: cherry, garnet rim. Nose: red berry notes, fruit liqueur notes, wild herbs, spicy, creamy oak. Palate: powerful, flavourful, spicy, long.

¡EA! 2012 T
cencibel

88 Colour: cherry, purple rim. Nose: red berry notes, ripe fruit, floral, balsamic herbs, sweet spices. Palate: powerful, flavourful, spicy.

AMANCIO MENCHERO MÁRQUEZ

Legión, 27
13260 Bolaños de Calatrava (Ciudad Real)
☎: +34 926 870 076 - Fax: +34 926 871 558
www.vinos-menchero.com
amanciomenchero@hotmail.com

FINCA MORIANA 2008 TC
tempranillo

84

FINCA MORIANA 2012 B
airén

80

BODEGA CENTRO ESPAÑOLAS

Ctra. Alcázar, s/n
13700 Tomelloso (Ciudad Real)
☎: +34 926 505 654 - Fax: +34 926 505 652
www.allozo.com
allozo@allozo.com

ALLOZO 2008 TC
100% tempranillo

86 Colour: cherry, garnet rim. Nose: ripe fruit, spicy, creamy oak, balsamic herbs. Palate: powerful, flavourful, toasty.

ALLOZO 2005 TGR
100% tempranillo

87 Colour: pale ruby, brick rim edge. Nose: spicy, fine reductive notes, wet leather, aged wood nuances, fruit liqueur notes. Palate: spicy, long.

ALLOZO 2006 TR
100% tempranillo

87 Colour: cherry, garnet rim. Nose: ripe fruit, spicy, creamy oak, toasty. Palate: powerful, flavourful, toasty, round tannins.

ALLOZO 927 2010 T
tempranillo, merlot, syrah

87 Colour: bright cherry. Nose: ripe fruit, creamy oak, violet drops. Palate: flavourful, fruity, toasty.

ALLOZO GARNACHA 2012 T
100% garnacha

87 Colour: cherry, purple rim. Nose: medium intensity, ripe fruit, raspberry. Palate: flavourful, spicy, ripe fruit.

ALLOZO MERLOT 2012 T
100% merlot

81

ALLOZO MERLOT DE FINCA LOMA DE LOS FRAILES 2012 T
100% merlot

81

ALLOZO TEMPRANILLO 2012 T
100% tempranillo

84

ALLOZO VERDEJO 2012 B

85 Colour: bright straw. Nose: fresh, fresh fruit, white flowers. Palate: flavourful, fruity, good acidity, balanced.

FINCA TEMPRANAL 2012 T
100% tempranillo

80

FUENTE DEL RITMO 2006 TR
100% tempranillo

87 Colour: cherry, garnet rim. Nose: ripe fruit, spicy, creamy oak, toasty. Palate: powerful, flavourful, toasty, round tannins.

FUENTE DEL RITMO 2012 B
airén

85 Colour: bright straw. Nose: ripe fruit, spicy, sweet spices. Palate: good acidity, fine bitter notes, ripe fruit.

FUENTE DEL RITMO 2012 T
100% tempranillo

82

BODEGA LA TERCIA-ORGANIC WINES

Pl. Santa Quiteria, 12
13600 Alcázar de San Juan (Ciudad Real)
☎: +34 926 550 104 - Fax: +34 926 550 104
www.bodegalatercia.com
bodegalatercia@gmail.com

YEMANUEVA AIRÉN ECOLÓGICO 2012 B
airén

83

YEMANUEVA TEMPRANILLO ECOLÓGICO 2011 T
tempranillo

85 Colour: garnet rim. Nose: ripe fruit, spicy, balsamic herbs, powerfull. Palate: flavourful, spicy, correct.

YEMASERENA TEMPRANILLO SELECCIÓN LIMITADA 2008 T
tempranillo

86 Colour: cherry, garnet rim. Nose: ripe fruit, spicy, creamy oak, toasty. Palate: powerful, flavourful, toasty.

BODEGA Y VIÑAS ALDOBA S.A.

Ctra. Alcázar, s/n
13700 Tomelloso (Ciudad Real)
☎: +34 926 505 653 - Fax: +34 926 505 652
aldoba@allozo.com

ALDOBA 2008 TC
100% tempranillo

83

ALDOBA 2012 B
100% macabeo

82

ALDOBA 2006 TR
100% tempranillo

89 Colour: cherry, garnet rim. Nose: ripe fruit, spicy, creamy oak, toasty, complex, red berry notes. Palate: powerful, flavourful, toasty, round tannins.

ALDOBA SELECCIÓN 2012 T
100% tempranillo

85 Colour: deep cherry, purple rim. Nose: medium intensity, ripe fruit, red berry notes. Palate: flavourful, fruity, fresh.

BODEGAS AGROCALAVERON

Cno. Sisante S/N Apdo. 341
2600 Villarrobledo (Albacete)
☎: +34 659 744 374
www.marycristivineyards.com
comercial@marycristivineyards.com

VIÑA MARY-CRISTI 2009 TC
100% tempranillo

88 Colour: cherry, garnet rim. Nose: spicy, creamy oak, toasty. Palate: powerful, flavourful, toasty, round tannins.

VIÑA MARY-CRISTI 2009 TR
100% tempranillo

90 Colour: cherry, garnet rim. Nose: ripe fruit, spicy, creamy oak, toasty, complex. Palate: powerful, flavourful, toasty, slightly dry, soft tannins.

BODEGAS ALCARDET

Mayor, 130
45810 Villanueva de Alcardete (Toledo)
☎: +34 925 166 375 - Fax: +34 925 166 611
www.alcardet.com
alcardet@alcardet.com

ALCARDET NATURA RED 2012 T
tempranillo, petit verdot

85 Colour: cherry, purple rim. Nose: red berry notes, ripe fruit, floral, balsamic herbs. Palate: fresh, fruity, easy to drink.

ALCARDET NATURA WHITE 2012 B
airén, chardonnay

84

ALCARDET SOMMELIER 2009 TC
tempranillo, petit verdot

86 Colour: cherry, garnet rim. Nose: ripe fruit, spicy, creamy oak, toasty, complex. Palate: powerful, flavourful, toasty.

ALCARDET SOMMELIER 2012 B
sauvignon blanc, airén, verdejo

84

ALCARDET SOMMELIER 2012 RD
tempranillo, syrah, garnacha

83

GRUMIER 2008 TC

84

BODEGAS AYUSO

Miguel Caro, 6
2600 Villarrobledo (Albacete)
☎: +34 967 140 458 - Fax: +34 967 144 925
www.bodegasayuso.es
export@bodegasayuso.es

CASTILLO DE BENIZAR CABERNET SAUVIGNON 2012 RD
100% cabernet sauvignon

83

CASTILLO DE BENIZAR MACABEO 2012 B
100% macabeo

83

ESTOLA 2004 TGR
65% tempranillo, 35% cabernet sauvignon

86 Colour: cherry, garnet rim. Nose: ripe fruit, spicy, creamy oak, toasty. Palate: powerful, flavourful, toasty, round tannins.

ESTOLA 2008 TR
75% tempranillo, 25% cabernet sauvignon

85 Colour: cherry, garnet rim. Nose: spicy, fruit liqueur notes, wet leather. Palate: flavourful, fine bitter notes, spicy.

ESTOLA 2009 TC
100% tempranillo

85 Colour: bright cherry. Nose: ripe fruit, sweet spices, creamy oak. Palate: flavourful, fruity, toasty, round tannins.

ESTOLA 2011 BFB
80% airén, 20% chardonnay

86 Colour: bright yellow. Nose: powerfull, ripe fruit, sweet spices, creamy oak, fragrant herbs. Palate: rich, smoky aftertaste, flavourful.

ESTOLA VERDEJO 2012 B
100% verdejo

86 Colour: bright straw. Nose: fresh, fresh fruit, white flowers. Palate: flavourful, fruity, good acidity, balanced.

FINCA LOS AZARES 2007 T
50% cabernet sauvignon, 50% merlot

85 Colour: deep cherry, orangey edge. Nose: ripe fruit, spicy, balsamic herbs, wet leather. Palate: powerful, flavourful, spirituous.

FINCA LOS AZARES PETIT VERDOT 2009 T
100% petit verdot

85 Colour: cherry, garnet rim. Nose: ripe fruit, fruit preserve, balsamic herbs, powerfull. Palate: spicy, flavourful, correct.

FINCA LOS AZARES SAUVIGNON BLANC 2012 B
100% sauvignon blanc

85 Colour: bright straw. Nose: ripe fruit, floral, fragrant herbs. Palate: correct, flavourful, fresh, fruity.

BODEGAS CAMPOS REALES

Castilla La Mancha, 4
16670 El Provencio (Cuenca)
☎: +34 967 166 066 - Fax: +34 967 165 032
www.bodegascamposreales.com
info@bodegascamposreales.com

CÁNFORA 2009 TR
tempranillo

90 Colour: pale ruby, brick rim edge. Nose: spicy, fine reductive notes, wet leather, aged wood nuances, fruit liqueur notes. Palate: spicy, fine tannins, elegant, long.

CANFORRALES 2009 TC
cabernet sauvignon

87 Colour: cherry, garnet rim. Nose: ripe fruit, spicy, creamy oak, toasty, characterful. Palate: powerful, flavourful, toasty, round tannins.

CANFORRALES CLÁSICO TEMPRANILLO 2012 T
tempranillo

86 Colour: very deep cherry. Nose: ripe fruit, fruit preserve, powerfull. Palate: flavourful, powerful, fine bitter notes.

CANFORRALES GARNACHA 2012 RD
garnacha

84

CANFORRALES LUCÍA 2012 B
airén

82

CANFORRALES SAUVIGNON BLANC 2011 B
sauvignon blanc

86 Colour: bright straw. Nose: ripe fruit, grassy. Palate: flavourful, fruity.

CANFORRALES SELECCIÓN 2011 T
tempranillo

86 Colour: garnet rim. Nose: ripe fruit, creamy oak, sweet spices. Palate: powerful, flavourful, spicy.

CANFORRALES SYRAH 2011 T ROBLE
syrah

88 Colour: bright cherry. Nose: ripe fruit, sweet spices, creamy oak, expressive. Palate: flavourful, fruity, toasty.

GLADIUM TEMPRANILLO 2012 T
tempranillo

86 Colour: cherry, purple rim. Nose: expressive, red berry notes, ripe fruit, raspberry. Palate: flavourful, fruity, good acidity, round tannins.

GLADIUM VIÑAS VIEJAS 2009 TC
tempranillo

91 Colour: cherry, garnet rim. Nose: ripe fruit, spicy, creamy oak, toasty, complex. Palate: powerful, flavourful, toasty, round tannins.

BODEGAS CASA ANTONETE

Barrio San José, s/n
2100 Tarazona de la Mancha (Albacete)
☎: +34 967 480 074 - Fax: +34 967 480 294
www.casaantonete.com
launion@casaantonete.com

CASA ANTONETE 2005 TR
tempranillo

79

CASA ANTONETE 2008 TC
tempranillo

83

CASA ANTONETE 2012 RD
tempranillo

83

CASA ANTONETE MACABEO 2012 B
macabeo

85 Colour: bright straw. Nose: fresh fruit, white flowers, wild herbs. Palate: flavourful, fruity, good acidity.

CASA ANTONETE TEMPRANILLO 2012 T
tempranillo

82

NÉGORA CABERNET 2010 T
cabernet sauvignon

84

NÉGORA CHARDONNAY 2012 B
chardonnay

85 Colour: bright straw. Nose: fresh, fresh fruit, white flowers, expressive. Palate: flavourful, fruity, good acidity, balanced.

NÉGORA MERLOT 2010 T
merlot

80

NÉGORA SYRAH 2010 T
syrah

84

NÉGORA VERDEJO 2012 B
verdejo

85 Colour: bright straw. Nose: fresh fruit, expressive. Palate: flavourful, light-bodied.

BODEGAS CRISTO DE LA VEGA

General Goded, 6
13630 Socuéllamos (Ciudad Real)
☎: +34 926 530 388 - Fax: +34 926 530 024
www.bodegascrisve.com
info@bodegascrisve.com

EL YUGO 2012 RD
garnacha, tempranillo

87 Colour: rose, purple rim. Nose: lactic notes, floral, red berry notes. Palate: easy to drink, light-bodied, flavourful.

EL YUGO 2012 T
tempranillo, syrah, merlot

88 Colour: cherry, purple rim. Nose: lactic notes, red berry notes, scrubland. Palate: good acidity, flavourful, fine bitter notes.

EL YUGO AIRÉN 2012 B
100% airén

87 Colour: bright straw. Nose: tropical fruit, candied fruit, lactic notes. Palate: light-bodied, easy to drink, flavourful.

BODEGAS DEL SAZ

Maestro Manzanares, 57
13610 Campo de Criptana (Ciudad Real)
☎: +34 926 562 424 - Fax: +34 926 562 659
www.bodegasdelsaz.com
bodegasdelsaz@bodegasdelsaz.com

VIDAL DEL SAZ 2009 TC
tempranillo

85 Colour: cherry, garnet rim. Nose: ripe fruit, spicy, toasty. Palate: powerful, flavourful, toasty, round tannins.

VIDAL DEL SAZ 2010 T ROBLE
tempranillo

86 Colour: bright cherry. Nose: sweet spices, creamy oak, overripe fruit. Palate: flavourful, fruity, toasty, round tannins.

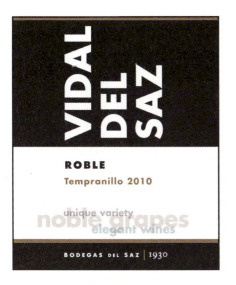

VIDAL DEL SAZ SELECCIÓN ROSÉ 2012 RD
syrah, merlot

80

VIDAL DEL SAZ SELECCIÓN WHITE 2012 B
macabeo, sauvignon blanc, verdejo

85 Colour: bright straw. Nose: ripe fruit, fragrant herbs, dried flowers. Palate: powerful, flavourful, fruity.

BODEGAS EL PROGRESO

Avda. de la Virgen, 89
13670 Villarubia de los Ojos (Ciudad Real)
☎: +34 926 896 135 - Fax: +34 926 896 135
www.bodegaselprogreso.com
laboratorio@bodegaselprogreso.com

OJOS DEL GUADIANA BR
100% airén

84

OJOS DEL GUADIANA 2004 TGR
100% tempranillo

86 Colour: cherry, garnet rim. Nose: ripe fruit, spicy, creamy oak, toasty, wet leather. Palate: powerful, flavourful, toasty, round tannins.

OJOS DEL GUADIANA 2008 TC
100% tempranillo

84

OJOS DEL GUADIANA 2008 TR
100% tempranillo

87 Colour: cherry, garnet rim. Nose: ripe fruit, spicy, creamy oak, expressive. Palate: powerful, flavourful, balsamic.

OJOS DEL GUADIANA AIRÉN 2012 B
100% airén

84

OJOS DEL GUADIANA CHARDONNAY 2012 B
100% chardonnay

85 Colour: bright straw. Nose: powerfull, ripe fruit, faded flowers. Palate: flavourful, powerful, ripe fruit.

OJOS DEL GUADIANA SELECCIÓN 2010 T
syrah, merlot, cabernet sauvignon

85 Colour: cherry, garnet rim. Nose: powerfull, ripe fruit, spicy. Palate: flavourful, good acidity.

OJOS DEL GUADIANA SYRAH 2011 T ROBLE
syrah

87 Colour: bright cherry. Nose: ripe fruit, expressive, spicy, floral, balsamic herbs. Palate: flavourful, fruity, toasty, round tannins.

OJOS DEL GUADIANA TEMPRANILLO 2012 T
100% tempranillo

88 Colour: cherry, purple rim. Nose: expressive, fresh fruit, red berry notes, floral, maceration notes. Palate: flavourful, fruity, good acidity, round tannins.

OJOS DEL GUADIANA VERDEJO 2012 B
100% verdejo

83

BODEGAS ENTREMONTES (NUESTRA SEÑORA DE LA PIEDAD)

Ctra. Circunvalación, s/n
45800 Quintanar de la Orden (Toledo)
☎: +34 925 180 237 - Fax: +34 925 560 092
comercial@bodegasentremontes.com

CLAVELITO 2012 RD
100% tempranillo

80

CLAVELITO AIRÉN 2012 B
100% airén

83

CLAVELITO MACABEO 2012 B
100% macabeo

80

CLAVELITO SAUVIGNON BLANC 2012 B
100% sauvignon blanc

76

CLAVELITO VERDEJO 2012 B
100% verdejo

81

ENTREMONTES 2002 TGR
100% tempranillo

87 Colour: pale ruby, brick rim edge. Nose: elegant, spicy, fine reductive notes, wet leather, aged wood nuances, fruit liqueur notes. Palate: spicy, fine tannins, elegant, long.

ENTREMONTES 2003 TR
100% tempranillo

84

ENTREMONTES 2005 TC
100% tempranillo

81

ENTREMONTES 2009 T ROBLE
100% tempranillo

85 Colour: bright cherry. Nose: sweet spices, creamy oak, ripe fruit. Palate: flavourful, fruity, toasty, round tannins.

ENTREMONTES BN
60% macabeo, 40% verdejo

82

ENTREMONTES CABERNET SAUVIGNON 2012 T
100% cabernet sauvignon

83

ENTREMONTES GARNACHA 2011 T
100% garnacha

84

ENTREMONTES SS
airén

82

ENTREMONTES SYRAH 2012 T
100% syrah

87 Colour: cherry, purple rim. Nose: expressive, red berry notes, floral, ripe fruit. Palate: flavourful, fruity, good acidity, round tannins.

ENTREMONTES TEMPRANILLO 2011 T
100% tempranillo

81

BODEGAS ISLA

Nuestra Señora de la Paz, 9
13210 Villarta San Juan (Ciudad Real)
☎: +34 926 640 004 - Fax: +34 926 640 004
www.bodegasisla.com
b.isla@terra.es

ISLA ORO AIRÉN 2012 B
100% airén

78

ISLA ORO GARNACHA 2012 RD
garnacha

75

ISLA ORO TEMPRANILLO 2009 TC
tempranillo

79

ISLA ORO TEMPRANILLO 2012 T
100% tempranillo

75

ISLA ORO TEMPRANILLO SYRAH MERLOT 2012 T
33% tempranillo, 33% syrah, 33% merlot

76

BODEGAS LA ESTACIÓN

Avda Castilla la Mancha, 38
45370 Santa Cruz de la Zarza (Toledo)
☎: +34 925 143 234 - Fax: +34 925 125 154
www.bodegaslaestacion.es
enologia@bodegaslaestacion.es

VIÑAS DE RIBOCHE RD
tempranillo

82

BODEGAS LA REMEDIADORA

Alfredo Atieza, 149-151
2630 l a Roda (Albacete)
☎: +34 967 440 600 - Fax: +34 967 441 465
www.laremediadora.com
info@laremediadora.com

LA VILLA REAL 2008 TC
merlot, cabernet sauvignon

90 Colour: cherry, garnet rim. Nose: ripe fruit, spicy, creamy oak, toasty, complex. Palate: powerful, flavourful, toasty, round tannins.

LA VILLA REAL 2008 TR
merlot, cabernet sauvignon

85 Colour: pale ruby, brick rim edge. Nose: fruit liqueur notes, spicy, fragrant herbs. Palate: powerful, flavourful, spicy.

LA VILLA REAL 2012 RD
tempranillo

87 Colour: brilliant rose. Nose: candied fruit, red berry notes, floral. Palate: light-bodied, good acidity.

LA VILLA REAL MACABEO 2012 B
100% macabeo

84

LA VILLA REAL MOSCATEL 2011 B
moscatel grano menudo

83

LA VILLA REAL VENDIMIA SELECCIONADA 2011 T
tempranillo, syrah

84

BODEGAS LAHOZ

Ctra. N-310, km. 108,5
13630 Socuéllamos (Ciudad Real)
☎: +34 926 699 083 - Fax: +34 926 514 929
www.bodegaslahoz.com
info@bodegaslahoz.com

LAHOZ TEMPRANILLO 2008 T ROBLE
tempranillo

88 Colour: bright cherry. Nose: sweet spices, creamy oak, ripe fruit. Palate: flavourful, fruity, toasty, round tannins.

VEGA CÓRCOLES 2012 RD
tempranillo

86 Colour: rose, purple rim. Nose: powerfull, ripe fruit, red berry notes, floral, expressive. Palate: powerful, fruity, fresh.

VEGA CÓRCOLES AIRÉN 2012 B
airén

85 Colour: pale. Nose: white flowers, fresh fruit. Palate: fruity, fresh, flavourful.

VEGA CÓRCOLES SAUVIGNON BLANC 2012 B
sauvignon blanc

85 Colour: bright straw. Nose: tropical fruit, wild herbs, white flowers. Palate: correct, good acidity.

VEGA CÓRCOLES TEMPRANILLO 2008 T ROBLE
tempranillo

88 Colour: bright cherry. Nose: ripe fruit, sweet spices, creamy oak, expressive. Palate: flavourful, fruity, toasty, balanced.

BODEGAS LATÚE

Camino Esperilla, s/n
45810 Villanueva de Alcardete (Toledo)
☎: +34 925 166 350 - Fax: +34 925 166 673
www.latue.com
info@latue.com

LATÚE 2012 RD
tempranillo

85 Colour: rose, purple rim. Nose: powerfull, ripe fruit, red berry notes, floral. Palate: powerful, fruity, fresh, easy to drink.

LATÚE AIRÉN 2012 B
airén

84

LATÚE BRUT NATURE 2011 ESP
airén

88 Colour: bright straw. Nose: dried herbs, fine lees, floral, complex, candied fruit. Palate: fresh, fruity, flavourful, fine bead.

LATÚE CABERNET SAUVIGNON & SYRAH 2010 T
cabernet sauvignon, syrah

89 Colour: bright cherry. Nose: ripe fruit, sweet spices, creamy oak, expressive. Palate: flavourful, fruity, toasty, round tannins.

LATÚE TEMPRANILLO 2012 T
tempranillo

86 Colour: cherry, purple rim. Nose: powerfull, ripe fruit, spicy. Palate: flavourful, powerful, fine bitter notes, round tannins.

PINGOROTE 2008 TR
tempranillo

86 Colour: cherry, garnet rim. Nose: ripe fruit, spicy, creamy oak, toasty, characterful. Palate: powerful, flavourful, toasty, round tannins.

PINGOROTE 2009 TC
tempranillo

88 Colour: cherry, garnet rim. Nose: ripe fruit, spicy, creamy oak, toasty, complex. Palate: powerful, flavourful, toasty, round tannins.

PINGOROTE CHARDONNAY 2011 B
chardonnay

82

PINGOROTE SAUVIGNON BLANC 2012 B
sauvignon blanc

86 Colour: pale. Nose: floral, fresh fruit. Palate: flavourful, light-bodied, fruity.

BODEGAS LOZANO

Avda. Reyes Católicos, 156
2600 Villarrobledo (Albacete)
☎: +34 967 141 907 - Fax: +34 967 138 087
www.bodegas-lozano.com
p.delacruz@bodegas-lozano.com

AÑORANZA 2012 RD
100% tempranillo

85 Colour: rose, purple rim. Nose: powerfull, ripe fruit, red berry notes, floral. Palate: powerful, fruity, fresh, correct.

AÑORANZA CABERNET SHIRAZ 2012 T
60% cabernet sauvignon, 40% syrah

87 Colour: cherry, purple rim. Nose: red berry notes, ripe fruit, balsamic herbs, violet drops. Palate: rich, fruity, easy to drink.

AÑORANZA SAUVIGNON BLANC 2012 B
sauvignon blanc

84

AÑORANZA TEMPRANILLO 2012 T
tempranillo

85 Colour: cherry, purple rim. Nose: fresh fruit, red berry notes, floral, lactic notes. Palate: flavourful, fruity, good acidity.

GRAN ORISTÁN 2007 TGR
65% tempranillo, 35% cabernet sauvignon

89 Colour: pale ruby, brick rim edge. Nose: elegant, spicy, fine reductive notes, wet leather, aged wood nuances, fruit liqueur notes. Palate: spicy, fine tannins, elegant, long.

ORISTÁN 2009 TR
65% tempranillo, 35% cabernet sauvignon

87 Colour: cherry, garnet rim. Nose: ripe fruit, creamy oak, fine reductive notes. Palate: powerful, flavourful, toasty.

ORISTÁN BRONZE 2010 TC
40% tempranillo, 30% syrah, 30% cabernet sauvignon

88 Colour: cherry, garnet rim. Nose: ripe fruit, spicy, creamy oak, toasty. Palate: powerful, flavourful, toasty, round tannins.

BODEGAS MARTÍNEZ SÁEZ

6200 Villarrobledo (Albacete)
☎: +34 967 443 088 - Fax: +34 967 440 204
www.bodegasmartinezsaez.es
bodegas@lapina.es

VIÑA ESCAMEL ESP
83

VIÑA ORCE 2008 TC
60% tempranillo, 40% cabernet sauvignon

85 Colour: bright cherry. Nose: ripe fruit, sweet spices, creamy oak. Palate: flavourful, fruity, toasty, round tannins.

VIÑA ORCE 2011 T ROBLE
tempranillo

83

VIÑA ORCE 2012 RD
merlot

86 Colour: rose, purple rim. Nose: powerfull, ripe fruit, red berry notes, floral, expressive. Palate: powerful, fruity, fresh.

VIÑA ORCE MACABEO 2012 B
macabeo

83

VIÑA ORCE SYRAH 2011 T
syrah

78

BODEGAS QUIÑÓN DE ROSALES

Avda. Castilla - La Mancha, 6
45820 El Toboso (Toledo)
☎: +34 925 197 043 - Fax: +34 925 197 043
www.vinosdeltoboso.com
info@vinosdeltoboso.com

GALÁN DE DULCINEA 2012 B
100% sauvignon blanc

83

QUIÑÓN DE ROSALES AIRÉN 2012 B
100% airén

85 Colour: bright straw. Nose: fresh, fresh fruit, white flowers. Palate: flavourful, fruity, good acidity.

QUIÑÓN DE ROSALES TEMPRANILLO 2007 TR
100% tempranillo

85 Colour: cherry, garnet rim. Nose: ripe fruit, spicy, creamy oak, toasty. Palate: powerful, flavourful, toasty, round tannins.

QUIÑÓN DE ROSALES TEMPRANILLO 2008 TC
100% tempranillo

85 Colour: cherry, garnet rim. Nose: ripe fruit, spicy, creamy oak, toasty. Palate: powerful, flavourful, toasty.

QUIÑÓN DE ROSALES TEMPRANILLO 2011 T
100% tempranillo

87 Colour: cherry, purple rim. Nose: powerfull, ripe fruit, raspberry. Palate: flavourful, powerful.

BODEGAS ROMERO DE ÁVILA SALCEDO

Avda. Constitución, 4
13200 La Solana (Ciudad Real)
☎: +34 926 631 426
www.bodegasromerodeavila.com
administracion@bodegasromerodeavila.com

PORTENTO 2008 TC
tempranillo, cabernet sauvignon

79

PORTENTO SYRAH 2011 T
syrah

86 Colour: cherry, garnet rim. Nose: ripe fruit, floral. Palate: powertul, flavourful, spicy.

PORTENTO TEMPRANILLO 2011 T ROBLE
tempranillo

88 Colour: bright cherry. Nose: ripe fruit, sweet spices, creamy oak, balsamic herbs. Palate: flavourful, fruity, toasty, correct.

DO LA MANCHA / D.O.P.

BODEGAS SAN ISIDRO DE PEDRO MUÑOZ

Ctra. El Toboso, 1
13620 Pedro Muñoz (Ciudad Real)
☎: +34 926 586 057 - Fax: +34 926 568 380
www.viacotos.com
administracion@viacotos.com

GRAN AMIGO SANCHO 2008 T
100% tempranillo

86 Colour: bright cherry. Nose: ripe fruit, sweet spices, creamy oak. Palate: flavourful, fruity, toasty.

LA HIJUELA 2012 B
100% airén

84

LA HIJUELA TEMPRANILLO T
100% tempranillo

75

BODEGAS VERDÚGUEZ

Los Hinojosos, 1
45810 Villanueva de Alcardete (Toledo)
☎: +34 925 167 493 - Fax: +34 925 166 148
www.bodegasverduguez.com
export@bodegasverduguez.com

HIDALGO CASTILLA 2009 TR
tempranillo

89 Colour: cherry, garnet rim. Nose: ripe fruit, creamy oak, toasty, complex, sweet spices. Palate: powerful, flavourful, toasty, round tannins.

IMPERIAL TOLEDO OAKED SELECTION 2010 T

87 Colour: bright cherry. Nose: ripe fruit, sweet spices, expressive, roasted coffee. Palate: flavourful, fruity, toasty, round tannins.

IMPERIAL TOLEDO OLD VINE SELECTION 2009 T
tempranillo

88 Colour: bright cherry. Nose: ripe fruit, sweet spices, roasted coffee. Palate: flavourful, fruity, toasty, round tannins.

VEREDA MAYOR TEMPRANILLO 2011 T
tempranillo

84

BODEGAS VERUM

Ctra. Argamasilla de Alba, km. 0,800
13700 Tomelloso (Ciudad Real)
☎: +34 926 511 404 - Fax: +34 926 515 047
www.bodegasverum.com
administracion@bodegasverum.com

VERUM GRAN CUEVA 2007 ESP
100% chardonnay

86 Colour: bright golden. Nose: powerfull, candied fruit, citrus fruit, fragrant herbs, dry nuts. Palate: powerful, sweetness, spicy.

BODEGAS VID Y ESPIGA

San Antón, 30
16415 Villamayor de Santiago (Cuenca)
☎: +34 969 139 069 - Fax: +34 969 139 069
www.vidyespiga.es
export@vidyespiga.es

VEGABRISA 2012 T
tempranillo

84

VEGABRISA AIREN 2012 B
airén

83

VEGABRISA SAUVIGNON/VERDEJO 2012 B
sauvignon blanc, verdejo

85 Colour: bright straw. Nose: fresh, fresh fruit, white flowers. Palate: flavourful, fruity, good acidity, balanced.

BODEGAS VOLVER

Pza. de Grecia, 1 Local 1B
45005 Toledo (Toledo)
☎: +34 925 167 493 - Fax: +34 925 167 059
www.bodegasvolver.com
export@bodegasvolver.com

PASO A PASO TEMPRANILLO 2012 T
tempranillo

90 Colour: deep cherry, garnet rim. Nose: spicy, wild herbs, ripe fruit. Palate: flavourful, round tannins, fruity aftertaste.

PASO A PASO VERDEJO 2012 B
verdejo

84

VOLVER 2011 T
tempranillo

92 Colour: cherry, garnet rim. Nose: ripe fruit, spicy, creamy oak, toasty, complex. Palate: powerful, flavourful, toasty, round tannins.

BODEGAS Y VIÑEDOS BRO VALERO

Ctra. Las Mesas, Km. 11
2600 Villarrobledo (Albacete)
☎: +34 649 985 103 - Fax: +34 914 454 675
www.brovalero.es
bodegas@brovalero.es

BRO VALERO SYRAH 2009 T
syrah

85 Colour: cherry, garnet rim. Nose: ripe fruit, balsamic herbs, sweet spices, balanced. Palate: powerful, flavourful, correct.

BODEGAS Y VIÑEDOS DE CINCO CASAS

Virgen de las Nieves, 2
13720 Cinco Casas (Ciudad Real)
☎: +34 926 529 010
www.bodegascasadelavina.com
ventas@bodegascasadelavina.com

VIÑA SANTA AURORA 2007 TR
tempranillo

88 Colour: bright cherry. Nose: ripe fruit, sweet spices, creamy oak. Palate: flavourful, fruity, toasty, round tannins.

VIÑA SANTA ELENA 2012 B
macabeo

84

VIÑA SANTA ELENA 2012 RD

81

VIÑA SANTA ELENA TEMPRANILLO 2012 T
tempranillo

85 Colour: cherry, purple rim. Nose: lactic notes, ripe fruit, scrubland. Palate: grainy tannins, balsamic, green.

BODEGAS Y VIÑEDOS LADERO S.L.

Ctra. Alcázar, s/n
13700 Tomelloso (Ciudad Real)
☎: +34 926 505 653 - Fax: +34 926 505 652
ladero@allozo.com

LADERO 2006 TR
100% tempranillo

86 Colour: cherry, garnet rim. Nose: ripe fruit, spicy, creamy oak, toasty. Palate: powerful, flavourful, toasty.

LADERO 2008 TC
100% tempranillo

84

LADERO 2012 B
100% airén

84

LADERO SELECCIÓN 2012 T
100% tempranillo

84

BODEGAS YUNTERO

Pol. Ind., s/n
13200 Manzanares (Ciudad Real)
☎: +34 926 610 309 - Fax: +34 926 610 516
www.yuntero.com
yuntero@yuntero.com

EPÍLOGO 2011 T ROBLE
65% tempranillo, 35% merlot

86 Colour: bright cherry. Nose: ripe fruit, expressive, spicy, toasty. Palate: flavourful, fruity, toasty, correct.

EPÍLOGO 2012 B
90% sauvignon blanc, 10% moscatel

86 Colour: bright straw. Nose: fresh, fresh fruit, white flowers, honeyed notes. Palate: flavourful, fruity, good acidity, balanced.

MUNDO DE YUNTERO 2012 T
85% tempranillo, 15% syrah

88 Colour: cherry, purple rim. Nose: red berry notes, floral, ripe fruit, characterful. Palate: flavourful, fruity, good acidity, round tannins.

DO LA MANCHA / D.O.P.

MUNDO DE YUNTERO 2010 T ROBLE
100% tempranillo

85 Colour: garnet rim. Nose: ripe fruit, powerfull, balsamic herbs, spicy. Palate: flavourful, spicy, correct.

MUNDO DE YUNTERO 2012 B
50% airén, 25% macabeo, 25% verdejo

85 Colour: bright straw. Nose: fresh, fresh fruit, white flowers, lactic notes. Palate: flavourful, fruity, good acidity.

YUNTERO 2007 TR
100% tempranillo

86 Colour: cherry, garnet rim. Nose: ripe fruit, balsamic herbs, spicy, creamy oak. Palate: powerful, flavourful, toasty.

YUNTERO 2008 TC
85% tempranillo, 15% syrah

86 Colour: cherry, garnet rim. Nose: ripe fruit, spicy, creamy oak, toasty, complex. Palate: powerful, flavourful, toasty.

YUNTERO 2012 RD
100% tempranillo

83

YUNTERO 2011 T
85% tempranillo, 15% syrah

84

YUNTERO 2012 B
85% macabeo, 15% sauvignon blanc

84

BODEGAS ZAGARRON

Camino del Campo de Criptana, s/n
16630 Mota del Cuervo (Cuenca)
☎: +34 967 180 025 - Fax: +34 967 181 120
www.zagarron.com
enologia@zagarron.com

ZAGARRON 2011 T ROBLE
75% tempranillo, 25% petit verdot

80

ZAGARRON SAUVIGNON BLANC 2012 B
sauvignon blanc

86 Colour: bright straw. Nose: fresh, fresh fruit, faded flowers. Palate: flavourful, fruity, good acidity, balanced.

ZAGARRON VERDEJO 2012 B
verdejo

85 Colour: pale. Nose: fresh fruit, citrus fruit. Palate: flavourful, fruity.

BOGARVE 1915

Reyes Católicos, 10
45710 Madridejos (Toledo)
☎: +34 925 460 820 - Fax: +34 925 467 006
www.bogarve1915.com
bogarve@bogarve1915.com

LACRUZ VEGA 2011 B
100% sauvignon blanc

83

LACRUZ VEGA SYRAH 2011 T
100% syrah

86 Colour: cherry, garnet rim. Nose: red berry notes, ripe fruit, sweet spices, dark chocolate. Palate: powerful, flavourful, easy to drink.

LACRUZ VEGA VERDEJO 2011 B
100% verdejo

83

CAMPOS DE VIENTO

Avda. Diagonal, 590 - 5º 1ª
8021 (Barcelona)
☎: +34 660 445 464
www.vinergia.com
vinergia@vinergia.com

CAMPOS DE VIENTO 2012 T
100% tempranillo

84

CARREFOUR

Campezo, 16
28022 Madrid (Madrid)
☎: +34 902 202 000
www.carrefour.es

DOMINIO DE LA FUENTE 2007 TR
tempranillo

86 Colour: cherry, garnet rim. Nose: ripe fruit, spicy, creamy oak, toasty. Palate: powerful, flavourful, toasty, round tannins.

DOMINIO DE LA FUENTE 2010 TC
tempranillo

85 Colour: bright cherry. Nose: ripe fruit, sweet spices, roasted coffee. Palate: flavourful, fruity, round tannins.

DOMINIO DE LA FUENTE 2012 B
100% verdejo

85 Colour: bright straw, greenish rim. Nose: fresh fruit, wild herbs, varietal. Palate: correct, good acidity, easy to drink.

DOMINIO DE LA FUENTE 2012 T
tempranillo

88 Colour: cherry, purple rim. Nose: expressive, fresh fruit, red berry notes, floral. Palate: flavourful, fruity, good acidity, round tannins.

CASA GUALDA

Casa Gualda
16708 Pozoamargo (Cuenca)
☎: +34 969 387 173 - Fax: +34 969 387 202
www.casagualda.com
info@casagualda.com

CASA GUALDA 2010 TC
tempranillo, cabernet sauvignon

88 Colour: cherry, garnet rim. Nose: ripe fruit, spicy, creamy oak, toasty, complex. Palate: powerful, flavourful, toasty.

CASA GUALDA SELECCIÓN C&J 2008 T
tempranillo

87 Colour: bright cherry. Nose: ripe fruit, sweet spices, creamy oak, wet leather. Palate: flavourful, toasty, round tannins.

CASA GUALDA TEMPRANILLO 2012 T
tempranillo

84

COOP. SAN ANTONIO ABAD

Afueras, 17
45860 Villacañas (Toledo)
☎: +34 925 160 414 - Fax: +34 925 162 015
www.sanantonioabad.es
export@sanantonioabad.es

ALBARDIALES 2012 T
tempranillo

88 Colour: cherry, purple rim. Nose: expressive, fresh fruit, red berry notes, floral. Palate: flavourful, fruity, good acidity, round tannins.

ESPANILLO 2012 B
airén

85 Colour: bright straw. Nose: expressive, ripe fruit, dried herbs. Palate: flavourful, fruity.

ESPANILLO 2012 T
100% tempranillo

87 Colour: cherry, purple rim. Nose: red berry notes, floral, ripe fruit, varietal. Palate: flavourful, fruity, good acidity, round tannins.

VILLA ABAD 2010 T
100% tempranillo

85 Colour: cherry, garnet rim. Nose: overripe fruit, powerfull, roasted coffee. Palate: confected, fine bitter notes, toasty.

VILLA ABAD 2012 B
100% macabeo

84

VILLA ABAD 2012 T
50% tempranillo, 50% syrah

87 Colour: cherry, purple rim. Nose: expressive, red berry notes, floral, ripe fruit. Palate: flavourful, fruity, good acidity, round tannins.

VILLA ABAD TEMPRANILLO 2012 T ROBLE
100% tempranillo

87 Colour: bright cherry. Nose: ripe fruit, sweet spices, creamy oak. Palate: flavourful, fruity, toasty, round tannins.

FAMILIA MATEOS DE LA HIGUERA

Ctra. La Solana - Infantes, km. 7,1
13240 La Solana (Ciudad Real)
☎: +34 676 920 905
www.vegamara.es
info@vegamara.es

VEGA DEMARA 2011 T ROBLE
tempranillo

84

VEGA DEMARA TEMPRANILLO 2012 T
tempranillo

84

VEGA DEMARA VERDEJO 2012 B
verdejo

80

FÉLIX SOLÍS S.L.

Otumba, 2
45840 La Puebla de Almoradiel (Toledo)
☎: +34 925 178 626 - Fax: +34 925 178 626
www.felixsolis.com
lamancha@felixsolis.com

CALIZA 2012 B
chardonnay, verdejo, viura

85 Colour: bright straw. Nose: fresh, fresh fruit, white flowers. Palate: flavourful, fruity, good acidity, balanced.

CALIZA 2012 RD
tempranillo

86 Colour: rose, purple rim. Nose: powerfull, ripe fruit, red berry notes, floral, expressive. Palate: powerful, fruity, fresh.

VIÑA SAN JUAN 2012 B
chardonnay, verdejo, viura

86 Colour: bright straw. Nose: fresh, fresh fruit, white flowers, expressive. Palate: flavourful, fruity, good acidity, balanced.

VIÑA SAN JUAN 2012 RD
tempranillo

85 Colour: rose, purple rim. Nose: ripe fruit, red berry notes, floral, balsamic herbs. Palate: powerful, fruity, fresh, easy to drink.

FINCA ANTIGUA

Ctra. Quintanar - Los Hinojosos, Km. 11,5
16417 Los Hinojosos (Cuenca)
☎: +34 969 129 700 - Fax: +34 969 129 496
www.familiamartinezbujanda.com
info@fincaantigua.com

CICLOS DE FINCA ANTIGUA 2005 T
50% merlot, 25% cabernet sauvignon, 25% syrah

89 Colour: cherry, garnet rim. Nose: aromatic coffee, spicy, dark chocolate, ripe fruit. Palate: powerful, flavourful, fine bitter notes.

CLAVIS 2006 TR

90 Colour: cherry, garnet rim. Nose: ripe fruit, spicy, creamy oak, toasty, complex, fine reductive notes. Palate: powerful, flavourful, toasty, round tannins.

FINCA ANTIGUA 2009 TC
50% tempranillo, 20% cabernet sauvignon, 20% merlot, 10% syrah

90 Colour: cherry, garnet rim. Nose: ripe fruit, spicy, creamy oak, toasty, complex, earthy notes. Palate: powerful, flavourful, toasty, round tannins, balanced.

FINCA ANTIGUA CABERNET SAUVIGNON 2010 T
100% cabernet sauvignon

87 Colour: cherry, garnet rim. Nose: ripe fruit, balsamic herbs, fragrant herbs. Palate: powerful, flavourful, spicy.

FINCA ANTIGUA GARNACHA 2010 T
100% garnacha

87 Colour: bright cherry. Nose: ripe fruit, creamy oak, fragrant herbs. Palate: flavourful, fruity, toasty.

FINCA ANTIGUA MERLOT 2010 T ROBLE
100% merlot

86 Colour: cherry, garnet rim. Nose: ripe fruit, balsamic herbs, wild herbs, floral, creamy oak. Palate: powerful, flavourful, spicy.

FINCA ANTIGUA MOSCATEL 2011 B
moscatel

91 Colour: golden. Nose: powerfull, floral, honeyed notes, candied fruit, fragrant herbs, petrol notes. Palate: flavourful, sweet, fresh, fruity, good acidity, long.

FINCA ANTIGUA PETIT VERDOT 2010 T
100% petit verdot

88 Colour: cherry, garnet rim. Nose: ripe fruit, spicy, creamy oak, toasty, complex. Palate: powerful, flavourful, toasty, round tannins.

FINCA ANTIGUA SYRAH 2010 T
100% syrah

91 Colour: bright cherry. Nose: ripe fruit, sweet spices, creamy oak. Palate: flavourful, fruity, toasty, round tannins.

FINCA ANTIGUA TEMPRANILLO 2010 T
100% tempranillo

86 Colour: cherry, garnet rim. Nose: red berry notes, fruit liqueur notes, powerfull, creamy oak. Palate: powerful, flavourful, long.

FINCA ANTIGUA VIURA 2012 B
100% viura

85 Colour: bright yellow. Nose: ripe fruit, floral, fragrant herbs. Palate: correct, good acidity, rich.

FONTANA

Extramuros, s/n
16411 Fuente de Pedro Naharro (Cuenca)
☎: +34 969 125 433 - Fax: +34 969 125 387
www.bodegasfontana.com
gemag@bodegasfontana.com

FONTAL 2009 TC
85% tempranillo, 15% cabernet sauvignon

88 Colour: cherry, garnet rim. Nose: spicy, creamy oak, toasty, raspberry. Palate: powerful, flavourful, toasty, round tannins.

FONTAL 2012 B
60% verdejo, 40% sauvignon blanc

88 Colour: bright straw. Nose: fresh, fresh fruit, white flowers, expressive Palate: flavourful, fruity, good acidity, balanced.

FONTAL 2012 RD
70% merlot, 30% syrah

85 Colour: rose, purple rim. Nose: powerfull, ripe fruit, red berry notes, floral. Palate: powerful, fruity, fresh.

FONTAL TEMPRANILLO 2011 T ROBLE
100% tempranillo

88 Colour: cherry, garnet rim. Nose: ripe fruit, spicy, creamy oak, toasty, characterful. Palate: powerful, flavourful, toasty, round tannins.

GRAN CASTILLO ROYAL

Nicanor Piñole, 6
33420 Lugones (Asturias)
☎: +34 984 040 747
www.grancastilloroyal.bullanddragon.es
info@bullanddragon.es

GRAN CASTILLO ROYAL 2008 TC
100% tempranillo
84

GRAN CASTILLO ROYAL 2008 TR
100% tempranillo
84

GRAN CASTILLO ROYAL 2012 B
verdejo
83

J. GARCÍA CARRIÓN LA MANCHA

Guarnicionero, s/n
13250 Daimiel (Ciudad Real)
☎: +34 926 260 104 - Fax: +34 926 260 091
www.garciacarrion.es
mvillanueva@jgc.es

DON LUCIANO 2009 TR
tempranillo

85 Colour: garnet rim. Nose: fruit preserve, balsamic herbs, fine reductive notes. Palate: powerful, spicy, balsamic.

DON LUCIANO 2010 TC
tempranillo

85 Colour: cherry, garnet rim. Nose: spicy, wet leather, toasty. Palate: fine bitter notes, good acidity, fine tannins.

OPERA PRIMA CABERNET 2012 T
cabernet sauvignon
78

OPERA PRIMA CHARDONNAY 2012 B
chardonnay
82

OPERA PRIMA MERLOT 2012 T
merlot
82

OPERA PRIMA SHIRAZ 2012 T
syrah

85 Colour: cherry, purple rim. Nose: expressive, red berry notes, floral, ripe fruit, violet drops. Palate: flavourful, fruity, good acidity, round tannins.

OPERA PRIMA TEMPRANILLO 2012 T
tempranillo

80

PAGO DE LA JARABA

Ctra. Nacional 310, Km. 142,7
2600 Villarrobledo (Albacete)
☎: +34 967 138 250 - Fax: +34 967 138 252
www.lajaraba.com
info@lajaraba.com

AZAGADOR 2008 TR
70% tempranillo, 20% cabernet sauvignon, 10% merlot

82

AZAGADOR 2009 TC
80% tempranillo, 10% cabernet sauvignon, 10% merlot

84

PAGO DE LA JARABA 2009 TC
70% tempranillo, 20% cabernet sauvignon, 10% merlot

86 Colour: light cherry, garnet rim. Nose: earthy notes, ripe fruit, aged wood nuances, fine reductive notes. Palate: powerful, flavourful, spicy.

VIÑA JARABA 2008 TR
70% tempranillo, 20% cabernet sauvignon, 10% merlot

83

VIÑA JARABA 2009 TC
80% tempranillo, 10% cabernet sauvignon, 10% merlot

87 Colour: bright cherry. Nose: ripe fruit, spicy. Palate: flavourful, fruity, toasty, round tannins.

VIÑA JARABA SELECCIÓN 2009 TC
70% tempranillo, 20% cabernet sauvignon, 10% merlot

87 Colour: deep cherry. Nose: fruit liqueur notes, toasty, spicy. Palate: powerful, fine bitter notes, correct.

S.C.V. DE C-LM VIRGEN DE LAS VIÑAS

Ctra. Argamasilla de Alba, s/n
13700 Tomelloso (Ciudad Real)
☎: +34 926 510 865 - Fax: +34 926 512 130
www.vinostomillar.com
atencion.cliente@vinostomillar.com

LORENZETE 2012 B
100% airén

83

TOMILLAR 2008 TR
cabernet sauvignon

86 Colour: cherry, garnet rim. Nose: ripe fruit, fine reductive notes. Palate: flavourful, sweetness.

TOMILLAR CHARDONNAY 2012 B
100% chardonnay

85 Colour: bright straw. Nose: candied fruit, citrus fruit. Palate: flavourful, fruity.

TOMILLAR TEMPRANILLO 2012 T
100% tempranillo

84

SAN ISIDRO LABRADOR SOC. COOP. CLM

Ramón y Cajal, 42
16640 Belmonte (Cuenca)
☎: +34 967 170 289 - Fax: +34 967 170 289
www.castibell.es
isbelmonte@ucaman.es

CASTIBELL 2008 TC
tempranillo

72

VISIBEL 2012 B

84

SANTA CATALINA

Cooperativa, 2
13240 La Solana (Ciudad Real)
☎: +34 926 632 194 - Fax: +34 926 631 085
www.santacatalina.es
central@santacatalina.es

CAMPECHANO 2012 B
100% verdejo

82

CAMPECHANO 2012 T
tempranillo

85 Colour: cherry, purple rim. Nose: red berry notes, floral, ripe fruit. Palate: flavourful, fruity, good acidity.

LOS GALANES 2008 TR
100% tempranillo

86 Colour: cherry, garnet rim. Nose: ripe fruit, creamy oak, toasty. Palate: powerful, flavourful, toasty, round tannins.

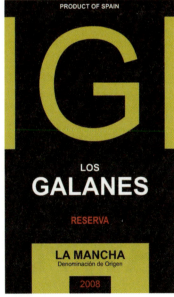

LOS GALANES 2009 TC
100% tempranillo

85 Colour: cherry, garnet rim. Nose: medium intensity, slightly evolved, candied fruit, toasty. Palate: fine bitter notes, good acidity, correct.

LOS GALANES 2012 T
100% tempranillo

86 Colour: cherry, purple rim. Nose: fresh fruit, red berry notes, floral. Palate: flavourful, fruity, good acidity, round tannins.

LOS GALANES AIRÉN 2012 B
airén

85 Colour: pale. Nose: ripe fruit, citrus fruit, faded flowers. Palate: flavourful, good acidity.

LOS GALANES MACABEO 2012 B
100% macabeo

84

VIHUCAS

Mayor, 3
45860 Villacañas (Toledo)
☎: +34 925 160 309 - Fax: +34 925 160 176
www.vihucas.com
info@vihucas.com

VIHUCAS BOREALIS 18 MESES 2008 TR
100% merlot

89 Colour: cherry, garnet rim. Nose: ripe fruit, spicy, creamy oak, toasty, complex. Palate: powerful, flavourful, toasty, round tannins.

VIHUCAS COLECCIÓN FAMILIAR 2010 TC
100% merlot

88 Colour: cherry, garnet rim. Nose: creamy oak, sweet spices, dark chocolate, ripe fruit. Palate: fine bitter notes, good acidity, long, spicy.

VIHUCAS DOBLE 10/11 TC
merlot, tempranillo

89 Colour: cherry, garnet rim. Nose: ripe fruit, spicy, creamy oak, toasty, complex. Palate: powerful, flavourful, toasty, round tannins.

VIHUCAS ENBLANCO 2012 B
100% chardonnay

85 Colour: bright golden. Nose: fresh, fresh fruit, white flowers. Palate: flavourful, fruity, good acidity, balanced.

VIHUCAS QUINCE 2007 TC

87 Colour: cherry, garnet rim. Nose: ripe fruit, spicy, creamy oak, toasty. Palate: powerful, flavourful, toasty, round tannins.

VINÍCOLA DE CASTILLA

Pol. Ind. Calle I, s/n
13200 Manzanares (Ciudad Real)
☎: +34 926 647 800 - Fax: +34 926 610 466
www.vinicoladecastilla.com
nacional@vinicoladecastilla.com

GUADIANEJA RESERVA ESPECIAL 2003 TR
tempranillo

88 Colour: cherry, garnet rim. Nose: spicy, creamy oak, toasty, overripe fruit, wet leather. Palate: powerful, flavourful, toasty, round tannins.

SEÑORÍO DE GUADIANEJA 2012 RD
100% tempranillo

84

SEÑORÍO DE GUADIANEJA 2001 TGR
100% tempranillo

87 Colour: cherry, garnet rim. Nose: ripe fruit, spicy, creamy oak, toasty, wet leather. Palate: powerful, flavourful, toasty, round tannins.

SEÑORÍO DE GUADIANEJA 2005 TR
100% tempranillo

84

SEÑORÍO DE GUADIANEJA 2007 TC
100% tempranillo

86 Colour: cherry, garnet rim. Nose: ripe fruit, spicy, creamy oak, toasty. Palate: powerful, flavourful, toasty, round tannins.

SEÑORÍO DE GUADIANEJA CABERNET SAUVIGNON 2012 T
100% cabernet sauvignon

85 Colour: deep cherry, purple rim. Nose: grassy, candied fruit. Palate: flavourful, fine bitter notes, good acidity.

SEÑORÍO DE GUADIANEJA CHARDONNAY 2012 B
100% chardonnay

85 Colour: bright straw. Nose: fresh, white flowers, ripe fruit, fragrant herbs. Palate: flavourful, fruity, good acidity.

SEÑORÍO DE GUADIANEJA MACABEO 2012 B
100% macabeo

81

SEÑORÍO DE GUADIANEJA MERLOT 2012 T
merlot

83

SEÑORÍO DE GUADIANEJA PETIT VERDOT 2012 T
petit verdot

84

SEÑORÍO DE GUADIANEJA SAUVIGNON BLANC 2012 B
sauvignon blanc

82

SEÑORÍO DE GUADIANEJA SYRAH 2012 T
100% syrah

83

SEÑORÍO DE GUADIANEJA TEMPRANILLO 2012 T
100% tempranillo

82

SEÑORÍO DE GUADIANEJA VERDEJO 2012 B
verdejo

82

VINÍCOLA DE TOMELLOSO

Ctra. Toledo - Albacete, Km. 130,8
13700 Tomelloso (Ciudad Real)
☎: +34 926 513 004 - Fax: +34 926 538 001
www.vinicolatomelloso.com
vinicola@vinicolatomelloso.com

AÑIL 2012 B
macabeo

87 Colour: bright straw. Nose: fresh, fresh fruit, white flowers, expressive. Palate: flavourful, fruity, good acidity, balanced.

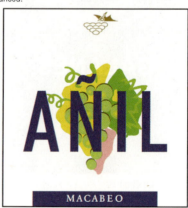

FINCA CERRADA 2005 TR
tempranillo, cabernet sauvignon

83

FINCA CERRADA 2007 TC
tempranillo, cabernet sauvignon, syrah

86 Colour: cherry, garnet rim. Nose: ripe fruit, spicy, creamy oak. Palate: flavourful, toasty, round tannins.

FINCA CERRADA 2012 B
macabeo

85 Colour: bright straw. Nose: fresh, white flowers, balanced, ripe fruit. Palate: flavourful, fruity, good acidity.

FINCA CERRADA 2012 RD
tempranillo

85 Colour: rose. Nose: red berry notes, candied fruit. Palate: light-bodied, fruity, fresh.

FINCA CERRADA TEMPRANILLO 2012 T
tempranillo

85 Colour: cherry, purple rim. Nose: expressive, red berry notes, floral, ripe fruit. Palate: flavourful, fruity, good acidity, round tannins.

GAZATE CHARDONNAY 2012 B
chardonnay

86 Colour: bright straw. Nose: powerfull, ripe fruit, white flowers. Palate: flavourful, light-bodied, fruity.

GAZATE MERLOT 2012 T
merlot

86 Colour: cherry, purple rim. Nose: expressive, fresh fruit, red berry notes, floral. Palate: flavourful, fruity, good acidity, round tannins.

GAZATE SAUVIGNON BLANC 2012 B
sauvignon blanc

86 Colour: bright straw. Nose: ripe fruit, white flowers. Palate: flavourful, fruity, fresh.

GAZATE SYRAH 2012 T
syrah

87 Colour: cherry, purple rim. Nose: expressive, red berry notes, ripe fruit. Palate: flavourful, fruity, good acidity, round tannins.

GAZATE VERDEJO 2012 B
verdejo

85 Colour: bright straw. Nose: fresh, fresh fruit, white flowers. Palate: flavourful, fruity, good acidity, balanced.

MANTOLÁN 2007 ESP
macabeo

85 Colour: bright straw. Nose: fresh fruit, dried herbs, floral. Palate: fresh, fruity, flavourful, good acidity.

TORRE DE GAZATE 2002 TGR
cabernet sauvignon

83

TORRE DE GAZATE 2005 TR
tempranillo, cabernet sauvignon

86 Colour: cherry, garnet rim. Nose: ripe fruit, spicy, creamy oak, toasty, characterful. Palate: powerful, flavourful, toasty, round tannins.

TORRE DE GAZATE 2008 TC
tempranillo, cabernet sauvignon

87 Colour: bright cherry. Nose: ripe fruit, sweet spices, creamy oak. Palate: flavourful, fruity, toasty, round tannins.

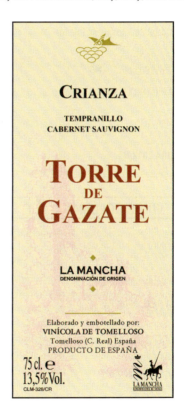

TORRE DE GAZATE 2010 T ROBLE
tempranillo

86 Colour: bright cherry. Nose: ripe fruit, sweet spices, creamy oak. Palate: flavourful, fruity, toasty, round tannins.

TORRE DE GAZATE 2012 RD
cabernet sauvignon

85 Colour: rose, purple rim. Nose: powerfull, ripe fruit, red berry notes, floral. Palate: powerful, fruity, fresh.

TORRE DE GAZATE 2012 T
tempranillo

87 Colour: bright cherry. Nose: ripe fruit, sweet spices, creamy oak. Palate: flavourful, fruity, toasty, round tannins.

TORRE DE GAZATE AIRÉN 2012 B
airén

82

VINOS 880

Sol, 11
45880 Corral de Almaguer (Toledo)
☎: +34 670 888 429
www.vinos880.com
info@vinos880.com

880 TEMPRANILLO 2011 T
100% tempranillo

88 Colour: deep cherry, purple rim. Nose: powerfull, ripe fruit, raspberry. Palate: flavourful, good acidity, ripe fruit.

880 VIURA 2012 B
100% viura

84

VINOS COLOMAN S.A.T.

Goya, 17
13620 Pedro Muñoz (Ciudad Real)
☎: +34 926 586 410 - Fax: +34 926 586 656
www.satcoloman.com
coloman@satcoloman.com

BESANA REAL 2009 TC
100% tempranillo

88 Colour: cherry, garnet rim. Nose: ripe fruit, spicy, creamy oak, toasty, complex. Palate: powerful, flavourful, toasty, round tannins.

BESANA REAL 2012 RD
tempranillo

84

BESANA REAL CABERNET SAUVIGNON 2011 T ROBLE
100% cabernet sauvignon

82

BESANA REAL MACABEO 2012 B
100% macabeo

84

BESANA REAL SYRAH 2008 T ROBLE
100% syrah

85 Colour: bright cherry. Nose: ripe fruit, sweet spices, spicy. Palate: flavourful, fruity, toasty.

BESANA REAL VERDEJO 2012 B
100% verdejo

84

VIÑA MAGUA

Finca La Navarra Ctra. Villarrobledo, Las Mesas, km. 11
2600 Villarrobledo (Albacete)
☎: +34 659 583 020
vinoecologicomagua.blogspot.com
vino.magua@gmail.com

VIÑA MAGUA 2011 T
tempranillo, syrah

86 Colour: cherry, garnet rim. Nose: ripe fruit, spicy, creamy oak, toasty. Palate: powerful, flavourful, toasty.

VIÑEDOS MEJORANTES S.L.

Ctra. de Villafranca, Km. 2
45860 Villacañas (Toledo)
☎: +34 925 200 023 - Fax: +34 925 200 023
www.portillejo.es
portillejo@portillejo.com

PORTILLEJO 2006 TC
cabernet sauvignon

84

PORTILLEJO CABERNET SAUVIGNON 2003 TR
100% cabernet sauvignon

80

PORTILLEJO CABERNET SAUVIGNON 2005 TC
100% cabernet sauvignon

80

PORTILLEJO CABERNET SAUVIGNON 2009 T ROBLE
100% cabernet sauvignon

81

PORTILLEJO MERLOT 2009 T ROBLE
100% merlot

84

DO LA PALMA / D.O.P.

LOCATION:

The production area covers the whole island of San Miguel de La Palma, and is divided into three distinct sub-regions: Hoyo de Mazo, Fuencaliente and Northern La Palma.

CLIMATE:

Variable according to the altitude and the direction that the vineyards face. The relief is a fundamental aspect in La Palma, seeing as it gives rise to different climates and microclimates; one must not forget that it has the highest altitudes in relation to surface area of all the Canary Islands. Nevertheless, as it is situated in the Atlantic, it benefits from the effects of the trade winds (humid and from the northwest), which temper the temperatures and tone down the climatic contrasts.

SOIL:

The vineyards are situated at altitudes of between 200 m and 1,400 m above sea level in a coastal belt ranging in width which surrounds the whole island. Due to the ragged topography, the vineyards occupy the steep hillsides in the form of small terraces. The soil is mainly of volcanic origin.

GRAPE VARIETIES:

WHITE: *Malvasía, Güal and Verdello* (main); *Albillo, Bastardo Blanco, Bermejuela, Bujariego, Burra Blanca, Forastera Blanca, Listán Blanco, Moscatel, Pedro Ximénez, Sabro* and *Torrontés.*
RED: *Negramol* (main), *Listán Negro* (Almuñeco), *Bastardo Negro, Malvasía Rosada, Moscatel Negro, Tintilla, Castellana, Listán Prieto* and *Vijariego Negro.*

SUB-REGIONS:

Hoyo de Mazo: It comprises the municipal districts of Villa de Mazo, Breña Baja, Breña Alta and Santa Cruz de La Palma, at altitudes of between 200 m and 700 m. The vines grow over the terrain on hillsides covered with volcanic stone ('Empedrados') or with volcanic gravel ('Picón Granado'). White and mainly red varieties are grown.
Fuencaliente: It comprises the municipal districts of Fuencaliente, El Paso, Los Llanos de Aridane and Tazacorte. The vines grow over terrains of volcanic ash at altitudes of between 200 m and 1900 m. The white varieties and the sweet Malvasia stand out.
Northern La Palma: Situated at an altitude of between 100 m and 200 m, It comprises the municipal areas of Puntallana, San Andrés and Sauces, Barlovento, Garafía, Puntagorda and Tijarafe. The region is richer in vegetation and the vines grow on trellises and using the goblet system. The traditional 'Tea' wines are produced here.

FIGURES:

Vineyard surface: 414,8 – **Wine-Growers:** 586 – **Wineries:** 18 – **2012 Harvest rating:** N/A – **Production:** 525.000 litres – **Market percentages:** 99% domestic. 1% export

CONSEJO REGULADOR
Esteban Acosta Gómez, 7 - 38740 Fuencaliente (La Palma) ☎: +34 922 444 404 - Fax: +34 922 444 432
vinoslapalma@ vinoslapalma.com   www.vinoslapalma.com

BODEGA CASTRO Y MOGAN

Cº Bellido Alto La Montaña, s/n
38780 Tijarafe (Santa Cruz de Tenerife)
☎: +34 626 485 811 - Fax: +34 922 490 066
www.vinostendal.com
contacto@vinostendal.com

TENDAL 2012 B
albillo, listán blanco

86 Colour: bright straw, greenish rim. Nose: ripe fruit, dried herbs. Palate: flavourful, full, good acidity, balanced.

TENDAL SELECCIÓN 2012 T
prieto picudo, listán blanco
81

TENDAL TRADICIÓN 2012 T
negramoll, listán blanco, prieto picudo
84

BODEGA JUAN MATÍAS TORRES

Fuencaliente de Ciudad Real, s/n Los Canarios
38740 Fuentecaliente de la Palma (Santa Cruz de Tenerife)
☎: +34 922 444 219
www.matiastorres.com
bodega@matiasitorres.com

LAS MACHUQUERAS 2012 B
100% listán blanco

88 Colour: bright golden. Nose: faded flowers, saline, spicy, dried herbs. Palate: powerful, flavourful, spicy, fine bitter notes.

MATIAS I TORRES MALVASÍA AROMÁTICA 2010 B
100% malvasía

94 Colour: old gold, amber rim. Nose: complex, expressive, candied fruit, cocoa bean, pattiserie. Palate: full, complex, balanced.

MATIAS I TORRES MALVASÍA AROMÁTICA 2011 B
100% malvasía

91 Nose: white flowers, ripe fruit, candied fruit, balanced, expressive. Palate: flavourful, long, good acidity, balanced, sweet.

MATÍAS I TORRES NEGRAMOLL 2011 T
negramoll
78

MATÍAS TORRES ALBILLO 2012 B
albillo

90 Colour: bright yellow. Nose: expressive, dried herbs, scrubland. Palate: full, flavourful, long, ripe fruit.

MATÍAS TORRES ALBILLO CRIOLLO 2012 B
albillo

91 Colour: bright golden. Nose: tropical fruit, ripe fruit, citrus fruit, faded flowers, scrubland. Palate: powerful, flavourful, spicy, long.

MATÍAS TORRES LISTÁN BLANCO 2012 B
listán blanco

90 Colour: bright yellow. Nose: expressive, ripe fruit, faded flowers. Palate: flavourful, fruity, good acidity, long, balanced.

VID SUR DULCE 2006 B
100% malvasía

94 Colour: golden. Nose: powerfull, floral, honeyed notes, candied fruit. Palate: flavourful, sweet, fresh, fruity, good acidity, long, balanced.

VID SUR DULCE 2008 B
100% malvasía

92 Colour: bright golden. Nose: candied fruit, sweet spices, honeyed notes. Palate: balanced, long, flavourful, fruity.

BODEGAS CARBALLO

Ctra. a Las Indias, 74
38740 Fuencaliente de La Palma (Santa Cruz de Tenerife)
☎: +34 922 444 140 - Fax: +34 922 211 744
www.bodegascarballo.com
info@bodegascarballo.com

CARBALLO 2011 T
negramoll
82

CARBALLO DULCE 2010 B
malvasía

92 Colour: golden. Nose: powerfull, floral, honeyed notes, candied fruit. Palate: flavourful, sweet, fresh, fruity, good acidity, long.

BODEGAS NOROESTE DE LA PALMA

Camino de Bellido, s/n
38780 Tijarafe (Santa Cruz de Tenerife)
☎: +34 922 491 075 - Fax: +34 922 491 075
www.vinosveganorte.com
administracion@vinosveganorte.com

VEGA NORTE 2012 T
negramoll, muñeco, castellana

86 Colour: light cherry, garnet rim. Nose: medium intensity, scrubland. Palate: flavourful, easy to drink, round tannins.

VEGA NORTE "VINO DE TEA" 2012 T
negramoll, muñeco, castellana

88 Colour: cherry, purple rim. Nose: expressive, red berry notes, ripe fruit, floral, scrubland. Palate: flavourful, ripe fruit, long. Personality.

VEGA NORTE 2012 B
78% listán blanco, 22% albillo

88 Colour: bright straw, greenish rim. Nose: medium intensity, fresh fruit, wild herbs. Palate: fruity, flavourful, balanced, fine bitter notes.

VEGA NORTE 2012 RD
100% negramoll

85 Colour: light cherry, bright. Nose: ripe fruit, fruit expression, lactic notes, powerfull, warm. Palate: rich, flavourful.

VEGA NORTE ALBILLO 2012 B
100% albillo

88 Colour: bright straw, greenish rim. Nose: balanced, ripe fruit, tropical fruit. Palate: fruity, flavourful, easy to drink.

VEGA NORTE LISTÁN PRIETO 2011 T
100% listán prieto

85 Colour: cherry, garnet rim. Nose: medium intensity, balanced, ripe fruit, wild herbs. Palate: fruity, correct, spicy.

VEGA NORTE VENDIMIA SELECCIONADA X ANIVERSARIO 2011 T
100% listán prieto

87 Colour: cherry, garnet rim. Nose: ripe fruit, toasty, spicy, dried herbs. Palate: fruity, round tannins, powerful, flavourful.

BODEGAS TAMANCA S.L.

Ctra. Gral. Tamanca, 75
38750 El Paso (Santa Cruz de Tenerife)
☎: +34 922 494 155 - Fax: +34 922 494 296
bioaad@telefonica.net

TAMANCA 2012 RD
negramoll, listán blanco

83

TAMANCA LISTÁN BLANCO 2012 B
listán blanco

87 Colour: bright straw, greenish rim. Nose: fresh fruit, balanced, dried herbs, citrus fruit. Palate: flavourful, good acidity.

TAMANCA MALVASÍA DULCE 2005 B BARRICA
malvasía

93 Colour: old gold. Nose: sweet spices, pattiserie, candied fruit, faded flowers, aromatic coffee. Palate: varietal, creamy.

TAMANCA MALVASÍA DULCE 2011 B
malvasía

89 Colour: bright golden. Nose: medium intensity, honeyed notes, floral, candied fruit. Palate: full, flavourful, rich.

TAMANCA NEGRAMOLL 2012 T
negramoll

82

TAMANCA PEDREGAL 2012 T ROBLE
negramoll, almuñeco, vijariego negro, castellana, baboso negro

86 Colour: light cherry, garnet rim. Nose: red berry notes, ripe fruit, spicy. Palate: correct, fruity, round tannins.

TAMANCA SABRO DULCE S/C B
sabro

87 Colour: bright golden. Nose: neat, sweet spices, honeyed notes, jasmine. Palate: fruity, flavourful, sweet.

TAMANCA SELECCIÓN 2012 B
albillo, vijariego blanco, malvasía, marmajuelo

87 Colour: bright straw, greenish rim. Nose: balanced, citrus fruit, dried flowers. Palate: flavourful, fruity, easy to drink, good acidity, fine bitter notes.

BODEGAS TENEGUÍA

Los Canarios, s/n
38740 Fuencaliente de La Palma (Santa Cruz de Tenerife)
☎: +34 922 444 078 - Fax: +34 922 444 394
www.vinosteneguia.com
enologia@vinosteneguia.com

TENEGUÍA MALVASÍA AROMÁTICA 2012 B
malvasía

89 Colour: bright golden. Nose: candied fruit, honeyed notes. Palate: flavourful, long, sweet.

TENEGUÍA MALVASÍA AROMÁTICA SECO 2012 B
malvasía

87 Colour: bright yellow, greenish rim. Nose: medium intensity, ripe fruit, sweet spices, dried flowers. Palate: correct, good acidity, toasty.

TENEGUÍA MALVASÍA DULCE 2006 B RESERVA
malvasía

95 Colour: golden. Nose: powerfull, floral, honeyed notes, candied fruit, fragrant herbs, complex, sweet spices. Palate: flavourful, sweet, fresh, fruity, good acidity, long.

TENEGUÍA MALVASÍA DULCE ESTELAR 1996 B RESERVA
malvasía

95 Colour: light mahogany. Nose: complex, sweet spices, rancio notes, roasted almonds, candied fruit. Palate: flavourful, fruity, creamy, long.

TENEGUÍA SABRO/GUAL DULCE 2011 B
sabro, gual

91 Colour: bright golden. Nose: white flowers, faded flowers, honeyed notes. Palate: rich, flavourful, full, good acidity.

TENEGUÍA VARIETALES 2012 T
negramoll, castellana, vijariego negro, baboso negro

84

EUFROSINA PÉREZ RODRÍGUEZ

Briesta, 3- El Castillo
38787 El Castillo (La Palma)
☎: +34 922 400 447
adali_12@msn.com

EL NÍSPERO 2011 BFB
100% albillo

89 Colour: bright yellow. Nose: faded flowers, spicy, balanced, ripe fruit. Palate: flavourful, good acidity, toasty.

EL NÍSPERO 2012 B
100% albillo

89 Colour: bright straw. Nose: fresh, fresh fruit, white flowers, citrus fruit. Palate: flavourful, fruity, good acidity, balanced.

LOCATION:

On the island of Lanzarote. The production area covers the municipal areas of Tinajo, Yaiza, San Bartolomé, Haría and Teguise.

CLIMATE:

Dry subtropical in nature, with low rainfall (about 200 mm per year) which is spread out irregularly throughout the year. On occasions, the Levante wind (easterly), characterised by its low humidity and which carries sand particles from the African continent, causes a considerable increase in the temperatures.

SOIL:

Volcanic in nature (locally known as 'Picón'). In fact, the cultivation of vines is made possible thanks to the ability of the volcanic sand to perfectly retain the water from dew and the scant rainfall. The island is relatively flat (the maximum altitude is 670 m) and the most characteristic form of cultivation is in 'hollows' surrounded by semicircular walls which protect the plants from the wind. This singular trainig system brings about an extremaly low density.

GRAPE VARIETIES:

WHITE: *Malvasía* (majority 75%), *Pedro Ximénez, Diego, Listán Blanco, Moscatel, Burrablanca, Breval.*
RED: *Listán Negra* (15%) and *Negramoll.*

FIGURES:

Vineyard surface: 1.975 – **Wine-Growers:** 1.723 – **Wineries:** 17 – **2012 Harvest rating:** Excellent – **Production:** 1.045.167 litres – **Market percentages:** 94% domestic. 6% export

2008	2009	2010	2011	2012
GOOD	GOOD	EXCELLENT	VERY GOOD	VERY GOOD

CONSEJO REGULADOR
Arrecife, 9 - 35550 San Bartolomé (Lanzarote) ☎: +34 928 521 313 - Fax: +34 928 521 049
info@dolanzarote.com   www.dolanzarote.com

BODEGA STRATVS

Ctra. La Geria, Km. 18
35570 Yaiza (Las Palmas)
☎: +34 928 809 977 - Fax: +34 928 524 651
www.stratvs.com
bodega@stratvs.com

STRATVS 2007 TC
listán negro, tinto conejera

86 Colour: cherry, garnet rim. Nose: powerfull, ripe fruit, old leather, spicy. Palate: flavourful, balsamic, round tannins.

STRATVS MALVASÍA SECO 2012 B
100% malvasía

88 Colour: yellow, greenish rim. Nose: slightly evolved, ripe fruit, floral. Palate: fruity, flavourful, long.

STRATVS MOSCATEL LICOR S/C B
100% moscatel de alejandría

91 Colour: old gold, amber rim. Nose: toasty, pattiserie, candied fruit, fruit liqueur notes. Palate: flavourful, fruity, sweet, unctuous.

STRATVS MOSCATEL SEMIDULCE 2010 B
moscatel de alejandría

91 Colour: bright yellow, greenish rim. Nose: expressive, ripe fruit, jasmine, varietal. Palate: flavourful, fruity, balanced, elegant.

BODEGA VULCANO DE LANZAROTE

Victor Fernández Gopar, 5
35572 Tías (Las Palmas)
☎: +34 928 524 469 - Fax: +34 928 524 384
www.bodegavulcano.es
info@bodegavulcano.es

VULCANO DE LANZAROTE 2012 B
100% malvasía

86 Colour: bright straw. Nose: citrus fruit, white flowers, medium intensity. Palate: correct, fruity, easy to drink.

VULCANO DE LANZAROTE 2012 B
100% malvasía

89 Colour: bright straw. Nose: balanced, mineral, medium intensity, dried flowers. Palate: ripe fruit, flavourful, fine bitter notes, good acidity.

VULCANO DE LANZAROTE 2012 RD
50% negramoll, 50% listán negro

82

VULCANO DE LANZAROTE 2012 T BARRICA
50% negramoll, 50% listán negro

87 Colour: cherry, garnet rim. Nose: balanced, spicy, ripe fruit, dried herbs. Palate: fruity, round tannins.

VULCANO DOLCE 2012 B
100% moscatel de alejandría

91 Colour: bright yellow. Nose: expressive, varietal, ripe fruit, jasmine, honeyed notes. Palate: flavourful, full, sweet, long.

BODEGAS LOS BERMEJOS

Camino a Los Bermejos, 7
35550 San Bartolomé de Lanzarote (Las Palmas)
☎: +34 928 522 463 - Fax: +34 928 522 641
www.losbermejos.com
bodegas@losbermejos.com

BERMEJO DIEGO 2012 B
diego

88 Colour: bright straw, greenish rim. Nose: medium intensity, balanced, fresh fruit, dried flowers, citrus fruit. Palate: easy to drink, fine bitter notes.

BERMEJO LISTÁN NEGRO 2012 T BARRICA
listán negro

87 Colour: cherry, purple rim. Nose: medium intensity, ripe fruit, toasty, spicy. Palate: flavourful, balsamic, round tannins.

BERMEJO LISTÁN NEGRO 2012
T MACERACIÓN CARBÓNICA
listán negro

88 Colour: deep cherry, purple rim. Nose: expressive, fruit expression, scrubland. Palate: flavourful, fruity, easy to drink, balanced.

BERMEJO LISTÁN ROSADO 2012 RD
listán negro

84

BERMEJO MALVASÍA 2012 BFB
malvasía

88 Colour: bright yellow. Nose: ripe fruit, sweet spices, medium intensity, faded flowers. Palate: flavourful, balanced.

BERMEJO MALVASIA 2011 BN
malvasía

86 Colour: bright yellow. Nose: ripe fruit, candied fruit, faded flowers. Palate: correct, light-bodied, easy to drink.

BERMEJO MALVASIA NATURALMENTE DULCE B
malvasía

92 Colour: old gold. Nose: sweet spices, cocoa bean, caramel, acetaldehyde, candied fruit. Palate: full, flavourful, complex, long.

BERMEJO MALVASÍA SECO 2012 B
malvasía

87 Colour: bright straw. Nose: medium intensity, citrus fruit, fresh, dried flowers. Palate: flavourful, good acidity, easy to drink.

BERMEJO MALVASÍA SEMIDULCE 2012 B
90% malvasía, 10% moscatel

88 Colour: straw, greenish rim. Nose: medium intensity, white flowers, balanced, varietal. Palate: fruity, elegant.

BERMEJO MOSCATEL NATURALMENTE DULCE 2012 B
moscatel

88 Colour: bright yellow. Nose: ripe fruit, candied fruit, pattiserie. Palate: easy to drink, correct, rich, fruity.

BODEGAS MALPAÍS DE MAGUEZ

Cueva de los Verdes, 5
35542 Punta Mujeres - Haria (Las Palmas)
☎: +34 616 908 484 - Fax: +34 928 848 110
bodegamalpais@gmail.com

LA GRIETA MALVASÍA SECO 2012 B
84

BODEGAS REYMAR

Pza. Virgen de Los Dolores, 19 Mancha Blanca
35560 Tinajo (Las Palmas)
☎: +34 649 993 096 - Fax: +34 928 840 737
reymar@losperdomos.com

LOS PERDOMOS 2012 T MACERACIÓN CARBÓNICA
100% listán negro

86 Colour: cherry, garnet rim. Nose: scrubland, ripe fruit. Palate: flavourful, fruity.

LOS PERDOMOS 2012 RD
100% listán negro
80

LOS PERDOMOS MALVASÍA MOSCATEL 2012 B
50% malvasía, moscatel de alejandría
84

LOS PERDOMOS MALVASÍA SECO 2012 B
90% malvasía, 10% moscatel de alejandría

87 Colour: yellow, greenish rim. Nose: white flowers, faded flowers, citrus fruit. Palate: fruity, flavourful, balanced.

LOS PERDOMOS MOSCATEL DULCE 2010 B
moscatel de alejandría

90 Colour: old gold. Nose: sweet spices, candied fruit, white flowers, medium intensity. Palate: fruity, balanced, good acidity, sweet.

LOS PERDOMOS MOSCATEL SECO 2012 B
85% moscatel de alejandría, 15% diego

85 Colour: yellow, greenish rim. Nose: white flowers, jasmine, expressive, ripe fruit. Palate: correct, flavourful, astringent.

BODEGAS RUBICÓN

Ctra. Teguise - Yaiza, 2
35570 La Geria - Yaiza (Las Palmas)
☎: +34 928 173 708
www.vinosrubicon.com
bodegasrubicon@gmail.com

AMALIA MALVASÍA SECO 2012 B
malvasía

88 Colour: bright yellow. Nose: balanced, ripe fruit, citrus fruit. Palate: flavourful, fruity, good acidity.

DON DIEGO 2012 B
90% diego, 10% moscatel de alejandría

89 Colour: bright yellow. Nose: balanced, medium intensity, white flowers, faded flowers. Palate: fruity, spicy.

DOÑA DULCE 2012 B
90% moscatel de alejandría, 10% diego

87 Colour: bright yellow. Nose: floral, ripe fruit, varietal. Palate: flavourful, fruity, sweet, easy to drink.

RUBICÓN MALVASÍA SEMIDULCE 2012 B
malvasía

86 Colour: bright yellow. Nose: ripe fruit, medium intensity, floral. Palate: fruity, sweet, easy to drink, good acidity.

RUBICÓN MOSCATEL 2012 B
moscatel

88 Colour: bright yellow. Nose: candied fruit, honeyed notes, jasmine, pattiserie. Palate: flavourful, rich, sweet.

RUBICÓN ROSADO 2012 RD
listán negro

81

SWEET GOLD 2009 B
moscatel

90 Colour: bright golden. Nose: candied fruit, sweet spices, pattiserie, honeyed notes. Palate: flavourful, full, long.

EL GRIFO MALVASÍA COLECCIÓN 2012 SEMIDULCE
malvasía

89 Colour: bright straw. Nose: expressive, elegant, white flowers, ripe fruit. Palate: flavourful, balanced, good acidity, fruity.

EL GRIFO MALVASÍA SECO COLECCIÓN 2012 B
100% malvasía

90 Colour: straw, greenish rim. Nose: expressive, balanced, jasmine, fresh fruit. Palate: balanced, flavourful, fruity, long.

EL GRIFO

Lugar de El Grifo, s/n
35550 San Bartolomé (Las Palmas de Gran Canaria)
☎: +34 928 524 036 - Fax: +34 928 832 634
www.elgrifo.com
malvasia@elgrifo.com

ARIANA 2011 T
60% listán negro, 40% syrah

91 Colour: very deep cherry, garnet rim. Nose: toasty, sweet spices, cocoa bean. Palate: flavourful, fruity, easy to drink, toasty.

EL GRIFO 2012 RD
listán negro

87 Colour: light cherry. Nose: medium intensity, red berry notes, ripe fruit, jasmine, balanced. Palate: flavourful, fruity, good acidity, good finish.

EL GRIFO 2012 T
listán negro

89 Colour: cherry, garnet rim. Nose: balanced, red berry notes, ripe fruit, violets. Palate: flavourful, fruity, long, good acidity.

EL GRIFO CANARI DULCE DE LICOR B
malvasía

95 Colour: old gold. Nose: sweet spices, aged wood nuances, fruit liqueur notes, acetaldehyde, varnish, complex. Palate: rich, flavourful, good acidity, fine bitter notes, spicy.

EL GRIFO MALVASÍA 2012 BFB
malvasía

89 Colour: bright straw, greenish rim. Nose: floral, sweet spices, ripe fruit. Palate: flavourful, balanced, fine bitter notes.

MÁLAGA

▽ Consejo Regulador
● DO Boundary

DO MÁLAGA Y SIERRAS DE MÁLAGA / D.O.P.

LOCATION:

In the province of Málaga. It covers 54 municipal areas along the coast (in the vicinity of Málaga and Estepona) and inland (along the banks of the river Genil), together with the new sub-region of Serranía de Ronda, a region to which the two new municipal districts of Cuevas del Becerro and Cortes de la Frontera have been added.

CLIMATE:

Varies depending on the production area. In the northern region, the summers are short with high temperatures, and the average rainfall is in the range of 500 mm; in the region of Axarquía, protected from the northerly winds by the mountain ranges and facing south, the climate is somewhat milder due to the influence of the Mediterranean; whilst in the west, the climate can be defined as dry subhumid.

SOIL:

It varies from red Mediterranean soil with limestone components in the northern region to decomposing slate on steep slopes of the Axarquía.

GRAPE VARIETIES:

WHITE: <u>DO Málaga</u>: *Pedro Ximénez* and *Moscatel*; <u>DO Sierras de Málaga</u>: *Chardonnay, Moscatel, Pedro Ximénez, Macabeo, Sauvignon Blanc* and *Colombard.*
RED (<u>only DO Sierras de Málaga</u>): *Romé, Cabernet Sauvignon, Merlot, Syrah, Tempranillo, Petit Verdot.*

TYPOLOGY OF CLASSIC WINES:

A) LIQUEUR WINES: from 15 to 22% vol.
B) NATURAL SWEET WINES: from 15 to 22 % vol. obtained from the *Moscatel* or *Pedro Ximénez* varieties, from musts with a minimum sugar content of 244 grams/litre.
C) NATURALLY SWEET WINES (with the same varieties, over 13% vol. and from musts with 300 grams of sugar/litre) and still wines (from 10 to 15% vol.).
Depending on their ageing:
- **Málaga Joven:** Unaged still wines.- **Málaga Pálido:** Unaged non-still wines.
- **Málaga:** Wines aged for between 6 and 24 months.- **Málaga Noble:** Wines aged for between 2 and 3 years.
- **Málaga Añejo:** Wines aged for between 3 and 5 years.- **Málaga Trasañejo:** Wines aged for over 5 years.

FIGURES:

Vineyard surface: 1.200– **Wine-Growers:** 456 – **Wineries:** 37 – **2012 Harvest rating:** N/A – **Production:** 2,.200.000 litres – **Market percentages:** 60% domestic. 40% export

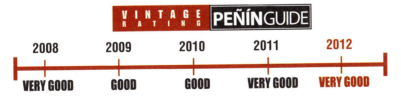

VINTAGE RATING PEÑÍNGUIDE				
2008	2009	2010	2011	2012
VERY GOOD	GOOD	GOOD	VERY GOOD	VERY GOOD

CONSEJO REGULADOR
Plaza de los Viñeros,1 - 29008 Málaga ☎: +34 952 227 990 - Fax: +34 952 227 990
info@vinomalaga.com www.vinomalaga.com

BODEGA ANTIGUA CASA DE GUARDIA

Ctra. Olias - Comares- El Romerillo
29197 (Málaga)
☎: +34 952 030 714 - Fax: +34 952 252 150
www.casadeguardia.com
info@casadeguardia.com

ISABEL II TRASAÑEJO
100% moscatel

93 Colour: light mahogany. Nose: neat, medium intensity, sweet spices, spicy. Palate: complex, good structure, rich, flavourful, balanced, fine bitter notes.

PAJARETE 1908 VINO DE LICOR
100% pedro ximénez

87 Colour: light mahogany. Nose: caramel, sweet spices, dried fruit, floral. Palate: long, balanced, fine bitter notes, sweet.

PEDRO XIMENEZ 1908 VINO DE LICOR
100% pedro ximénez

86 Colour: mahogany. Nose: dry nuts, candied fruit, cocoa bean, rancio notes, medium intensity. Palate: balanced, flavourful, long.

VERDIALES CONARTE AÑEJO VINO DE LICOR DULCE
70% pedro ximénez, 30% moscatel de alejandría

89 Colour: mahogany. Nose: medium intensity, candied fruit, pattiserie, dry nuts. Palate: flavourful, correct, fine bitter notes, long.

VERDIALES CR
100% pedro ximénez

87 Colour: light mahogany. Nose: caramel, pattiserie, medium intensity. Palate: flavourful, fruity, spicy.

VERDIALES SECO VINO DE LICOR
100% pedro ximénez

86 Colour: old gold, amber rim. Nose: spicy, varnish, rancio notes, candied fruit. Palate: balanced, fine bitter notes.

BODEGA ANTONIO MUÑOZ CABRERA

San Bartolomé, 5
29738 Moclinejo (Málaga)
☎: +34 952 400 594 - Fax: +34 952 400 743
www.dimobe.es
bodega@dimobe.es

EL LAGAR DE CABRERA SYRAH 2011 T
syrah

86 Colour: cherry, garnet rim. Nose: medium intensity, balanced, red berry notes, grassy. Palate: flavourful, fruity, long.

FINCA LA INDIANA 2010 T
petit verdot

86 Colour: deep cherry, garnet rim. Nose: powerfull, toasty, spicy. Palate: ripe fruit, round tannins.

LAGAR DE CABRERA 2009 TC
syrah

84

LAGAR DE CABRERA 2011 MOSCATEL
moscatel

83

PIAMATER 2010 B
moscatel

89 Colour: bright golden. Nose: expressive, balanced, varietal, white flowers, honeyed notes. Palate: fruity, rich, flavourful.

RUJAQ ANDALUSI TRASAÑEJO
moscatel

88 Colour: light mahogany. Nose: spicy, toasty, dried fruit, dry nuts, varnish. Palate: flavourful, balanced, fine bitter notes, long.

SEÑORÍO DE BROCHES MOSCATEL
moscatel

86 Colour: yellow. Nose: white flowers, ripe fruit, neat. Palate: fruity, flavourful, sweet.

ZUMBRAL MOSCATEL
moscatel

86 Colour: light mahogany. Nose: dried fruit, powerfull, varietal, pattiserie, honeyed notes. Palate: creamy, long, balanced.

BODEGA DOÑA FELISA

Cordel del Puerto al Quejigal s/n
29400 Ronda (Málaga)
☎: +34 951 166 033 - Fax: +34 951 166 033
www.chinchillawine.com
jlosantos@chinchillawine.com

CHINCHILLA CONARTE 2008 T
cabernet sauvignon, merlot, syrah

87 Colour: cherry, garnet rim. Nose: spicy, ripe fruit, warm. Palate: fruity, spicy, round tannins.

CHINCHILLA DOBLE DOCE 2007 T
cabernet sauvignon, merlot

87 Colour: deep cherry, garnet rim. Nose: balanced, toasty, ripe fruit, wild herbs. Palate: flavourful, fruity, correct.

CHINCHILLA SEIS + SEIS 2010 T ROBLE
tempranillo, syrah

86 Colour: cherry, garnet rim. Nose: red berry notes, ripe fruit, sweet spices. Palate: flavourful, fruity, correct, good acidity, fine bitter notes.

BODEGA ECOLÓGICA JOAQUÍN FERNÁNDEZ

Finca Los Frutales Paraje de los Frontones
29400 Ronda (Málaga)
☎: +34 665 899 200 - Fax: +34 951 166 043
www.bodegajf.com
info@bodegajf.es

FINCA LOS FRUTALES GARNACHA 2011 T
80% garnacha, 20% cabernet sauvignon

88 Colour: cherry, garnet rim. Nose: balanced, powerfull, sweet spices, ripe fruit. Palate: flavourful, good structure, spicy, good acidity.

FINCA LOS FRUTALES IGUALADOS 2008 T
50% cabernet sauvignon, 10% garnacha, 20% merlot, 20% syrah

87 Colour: cherry, garnet rim. Nose: ripe fruit, spicy, toasty, wild herbs. Palate: powerful, flavourful, toasty, round tannins.

FINCA LOS FRUTALES MERLOT SYRAH 2009 TC
50% merlot, 50% syrah

87 Colour: cherry, garnet rim. Nose: ripe fruit, sweet spices, medium intensity, balanced. Palate: flavourful, good acidity.

HACIENDA VIZCONDESA 2009 T ROBLE
40% merlot, 20% syrah, 40% cabernet sauvignon

86 Colour: bright cherry. Nose: ripe fruit, sweet spices, expressive. Palate: fruity, correct, good acidity, easy to drink.

ROSADO FINCA LOS FRUTALES 2012 RD ROBLE
33% merlot, 33% syrah, 33% cabernet sauvignon

87 Colour: rose, bright. Nose: red berry notes, citrus fruit, floral, lactic notes. Palate: flavourful, fruity, long, balanced, good acidity.

BODEGA F. SCHATZ

Finca Sanguijuela, s/n Apdo. Correos 131
29400 Ronda (Málaga)
☎: +34 952 871 313 - Fax: +34 952 871 313
www.f-schatz.com
bodega@f-schatz.com

FINCA SANGUIJUELA 2007 TC
25% tempranillo, 25% syrah, 25% merlot, 25% cabernet sauvignon

90 Colour: cherry, garnet rim. Nose: balanced, elegant, cocoa bean, ripe fruit. Palate: good structure, flavourful, fruity, fine tannins.

SCHATZ CHARDONNAY 2012 B
chardonnay

85 Colour: bright yellow. Nose: ripe fruit, white flowers, powerfull. Palate: flavourful, fruity, good acidity, easy to drink.

SCHATZ PETIT VERDOT 2007 TC
petit verdot

89 Colour: deep cherry, garnet rim. Nose: spicy, ripe fruit, balanced, scrubland. Palate: balanced, fine bitter notes, ripe fruit, good acidity.

SCHATZ PINOT NOIR 2007 TC
pinot noir

86 Colour: cherry, garnet rim. Nose: ripe fruit, cocoa bean, floral, medium intensity, slightly evolved. Palate: flavourful, good acidity, spicy.

BODEGA KIENINGER

Los Frontones, 67
29400 Ronda (Málaga)
☎: +34 952 879 554
www.bodegakieninger.com
martin@bodegakieninger.com

VINANA CABERNET FRANC 2011 T
100% cabernet franc

90 Colour: cherry, garnet rim. Nose: ripe fruit, balsamic herbs, dry stone, cocoa bean, creamy oak. Palate: good structure, complex, spicy, long.

VINANA PINOT NOIR 2011 T
85% pinot noir, 15% merlot

92 Colour: cherry, garnet rim. Nose: ripe fruit, dry stone, earthy notes, wild herbs, expressive, balanced. Palate: powerful, flavourful, spicy, long, elegant.

BODEGA PASOS LARGOS

Ctra. Ronda El Burgo, Km 1
29400 Ronda (Málaga)
☎: +34 673 235 072 - Fax: +34 952 161 309
www.hoteleljuncalronda.com
bodegapasoslargos@gmail.com

A PASOS 2009 T
60% cabernet sauvignon, 20% syrah, 15% merlot, 5% petit verdot

90 Colour: light cherry. Nose: ripe fruit, fruit liqueur notes, scrubland, spicy, damp earth. Palate: flavourful, spicy, toasty.

PASOS LARGOS 2008 T ROBLE
15% cabernet sauvignon, 15% cabernet franc, 20% petit verdot, 20% merlot, 15% syrah, 15% garnacha

90 Colour: deep cherry, garnet rim. Nose: powerfull, dried herbs, balanced, ripe fruit. Palate: flavourful, good acidity, balanced.

BODEGA VETAS

Con Nador Finca El Baco
29350 Arriate (Málaga)
☎: +34 647 177 620
www.bodegavetas.com
info@bodegavetas.com

VETAS PETIT VERDOT 2006 T
100% petit verdot

93 Colour: bright cherry, garnet rim. Nose: elegant, wild herbs, sweet spices. Palate: good structure, round tannins, good acidity.

BODEGA Y VIÑEDOS DE LA CAPUCHINA

Cortijo La Capuchina
29532 Mollina (Málaga)
☎: +34 952 111 565
www.bodegalacapuchina.es
info@bodegalacapuchina.es

CAPUCHINA VIEJA 2009 T
cabernet franc, syrah, cabernet sauvignon, merlot

91 Colour: cherry, garnet rim. Nose: expressive, balanced, ripe fruit, wild herbs, cocoa bean, creamy oak. Palate: flavourful, good structure, round tannins.

CAPUCHINA VIEJA MOSCATEL SECO 2011 B
moscatel de alejandría

89 Colour: bright yellow. Nose: dried flowers, ripe fruit. Palate: fruity, flavourful, long, fine bitter notes.

BODEGAS BENTOMIZ

Finca Almendro - Pago Cuesta Robano
29752 Sayalonga (Málaga)
☎: +34 952 115 939
www.bodegasbentomiz.com
info@bodegasbentomiz.com

ARIYANAS NATURALMENTE DULCE 2008 BLANCO DULCE
moscatel de alejandría

92 Colour: bright yellow. Nose: white flowers, honeyed notes, expressive, balanced. Palate: fruity, flavourful, sweet, rich, long.

ARIYANAS SECO SOBRE LÍAS 2011 B
100% moscatel de alejandría

89 Colour: bright straw. Nose: white flowers, varietal, balanced, ripe fruit. Palate: flavourful, long, fine bitter notes.

ARIYANAS TERRUÑO PIZARROSO 2008 B
100% moscatel de alejandría

94 Colour: bright golden. Nose: complex, candied fruit, jasmine, mineral, expressive, elegant. Palate: rich, ripe fruit, long.

ARIYANAS TINTO DE ENSAMBLAJE 2011 T
romé, petit verdot, tempranillo, cabernet franc

88 Colour: cherry, garnet rim. Nose: fruit expression, red berry notes, violets, medium intensity. Palate: light-bodied, fruity, easy to drink.

BODEGAS CONRAD

Ctra. El Burgo, Km. 4,0
29400 Ronda (Málaga)
☎: +34 351 166 035 - Fax: +34 951 166 035
www.vinosconrad.com
conrad@vinosconrad.com

CRISTINA 2009 T
malbec, cabernet franc

87 Colour: cherry, garnet rim. Nose: toasty, spicy, warm, ripe fruit. Palate: flavourful, ripe fruit, correct.

EL NIÑO LEÓN 2011 T
tempranillo, merlot, cabernet sauvignon

85 Colour: bright cherry. Nose: ripe fruit, sweet spices, expressive. Palate: flavourful, fruity.

EL PINSAPO 2011 T
cabernet franc

87 Colour: cherry, purple rim. Nose: powerfull, spicy, ripe fruit. Palate: fruity, flavourful, good acidity.

SAN LORENZO 2011 T
pinot noir

86 Colour: deep cherry, garnet rim. Nose: ripe fruit, fruit preserve, dark chocolate. Palate: flavourful, correct.

SOLEÓN 2009 T
cabernet sauvignon, merlot, cabernet franc

88 Colour: cherry, garnet rim. Nose: ripe fruit, medium intensity, warm, spicy. Palate: flavourful, fruity, spicy, good acidity.

BODEGAS EXCELENCIA

Almendra, 40-42
29400 Ronda (Málaga)
☎: +34 952 870 960 - Fax: +34 952 877 002
www.bodegasexcelencia.com
info@bodegasexcelencia.com

LOS FRONTONES 2009 T
cabernet sauvignon, cabernet franc, tempranillo, syrah

87 Colour: cherry, garnet rim. Nose: wild herbs, ripe fruit, toasty, spicy. Palate: flavourful, fruity, good structure.

BODEGAS GARCÍA HIDALGO

Partido Rural Los Morales- LLano de la Cruz s/n
29400 Ronda (Málaga)
☎: +34 600 487 284
www.bodegasgarciahidalgo.es
info@bodegasgarciahidalgo.es

ALCOBAZÍN 2009 T ROBLE
cabernet sauvignon, merlot, syrah

84

ALCOBAZÍN 2011 T ROBLE
cabernet sauvignon, merlot, syrah

85 Colour: deep cherry, garnet rim. Nose: ripe fruit, sweet spices, dark chocolate. Palate: fruity, flavourful, round tannins.

ALCOBAZÍN MERLOT SELECCIÓN 2009 TC
merlot

85 Colour: deep cherry, garnet rim. Nose: roasted coffee, dark chocolate. Palate: good structure, flavourful, correct.

BODEGAS GOMARA

Diseminado Maqueda Alto, 59
29590 Campanillas (Málaga)
☎: +34 952 434 195 - Fax: +34 952 626 312
www.gomara.com
bodegas@gomara.com

GOMARA PEDRO XIMÉNEZ PX
100% pedro ximénez

84

GRAN GOMARA TRASAÑEJO SOLERA
70% pedro ximénez, 30% moscatel de alejandría

91 Colour: mahogany. Nose: creamy oak, sweet spices, candied fruit, acetaldehyde. Palate: full, long, complex.

LACRIMAE CHRISTI NOBLE SOLERA
90% pedro ximénez, 10% moscatel de alejandría

87 Colour: mahogany. Nose: powerfull, dried fruit, caramel, pattiserie. Palate: long, flavourful, fine solera notes, sweet.

MÁLAGA DULCE MÁLAGA
90% pedro ximénez, 10% moscatel de alejandría

85 Colour: mahogany. Nose: candied fruit, sweet spices, cocoa bean, balanced, acetaldehyde. Palate: flavourful, sweet.

MÁLAGA TRASAÑEJO GOMARA TRASAÑEJO
100% pedro ximénez

90 Colour: dark mahogany. Nose: caramel, dark chocolate, pattiserie. Palate: good structure, spicy, balanced, long.

MOSCATEL MÁLAGA MOSCATEL
100% moscatel de alejandría

85 Colour: old gold, amber rim. Nose: floral, candied fruit, honeyed notes, toasty, cocoa bean. Palate: balanced, correct.

PAJARETE GOMARA
100% pedro ximénez

86 Colour: light mahogany. Nose: toasty, varnish, sweet spices, cocoa bean, candied fruit. Palate: sweet, flavourful, rich, toasty, fine bitter notes.

SECO AÑEJO GOMARA
100% pedro ximénez

85 Colour: light mahogany. Nose: cocoa bean, pattiserie, caramel, dry nuts. Palate: rich, correct, spirituous.

BODEGAS LUNARES DE RONDA

Almendra, 3
29400 Ronda (Málaga)
☎: +34 952 877 180
www.bodegaslunares.com
vinos@bodegaslunares.com

ALTOCIELO 2010 T
syrah, cabernet sauvignon, tintilla de rota

88 Colour: cherry, garnet rim. Nose: medium intensity, dried herbs, spicy. Palate: fruity, flavourful, good acidity.

LUNARES 2011 T
garnacha, syrah, tintilla de rota

89 Colour: cherry, purple rim. Nose: balanced, dark chocolate, dry stone, ripe fruit. Palate: flavourful, ripe fruit, good finish.

BODEGAS MÁLAGA VIRGEN

Autovía A-92, Km. 132
29520 Fuente de Piedra (Málaga)
☎: +34 952 319 454 - Fax: +34 952 359 819
www.bodegasmalagavirgen.com
bodegas@bodegasmalagavirgen.com

BARÓN DE RIVERO 2012 B
chardonnay, pedro ximénez

83

CARTOJAL PÁLIDO
moscatel de alejandría, moscatel morisco

86 Colour: bright straw. Nose: grapey, medium intensity, floral. Palate: sweet, light-bodied, easy to drink.

DON JUAN TRASAÑEJO
pedro ximénez

93 Colour: mahogany. Nose: acetaldehyde, varnish, candied fruit, sweet spices, complex. Palate: long, creamy, good structure, full.

DON SALVADOR MOSCATEL 30 AÑOS
moscatel de alejandría

93 Colour: mahogany. Nose: elegant, candied fruit, sweet spices, varnish, acetaldehyde. Palate: good structure, full, flavourful.

EL VIVILLO 2011 T
syrah

85 Colour: cherry, garnet rim. Nose: fruit preserve, balsamic herbs, floral, sweet spices, earthy notes. Palate: warm, powerful, flavourful.

MÁLAGA VIRGEN PX
pedro ximénez

86 Colour: mahogany. Nose: toasty, cocoa bean, medium intensity. Palate: flavourful, correct, easy to drink.

MOSCATEL IBERIA MALAGA
moscatel de alejandría

86 Colour: mahogany. Nose: toasty, fruit liqueur notes, pattiserie, sweet spices. Palate: flavourful, correct, sweet.

MOSCATEL RESERVA DE FAMILIA MOSCATEL
moscatel de alejandría

90 Colour: old gold, amber rim. Nose: balanced, expressive, elegant, varietal, honeyed notes, floral. Palate: flavourful, sweet, fruity.

PEDRO XIMÉNEZ RESERVA DE FAMILIA PX
pedro ximénez

92 Colour: mahogany. Nose: expressive, balanced, varietal, honeyed notes, dried fruit, dark chocolate. Palate: full, flavourful, long.

PERNALES SYRAH 2008 T
syrah

87 Colour: deep cherry, garnet rim. Nose: balanced, macerated fruit, ripe fruit, spicy. Palate: correct, good acidity, easy to drink.

SECO TRASAÑEJO B
pedro ximénez

93 Colour: light mahogany. Nose: acetaldehyde, candied fruit, caramel, toasty. Palate: good structure, rich, full, complex.

SOL DE MÁLAGA
pedro ximénez, moscatel de alejandría

88 Colour: dark mahogany. Nose: characterful, powerfull, dried fruit, caramel, pattiserie. Palate: balanced, sweet.

TRAJINERO AÑEJO
pedro ximénez

88 Colour: bright golden. Nose: candied fruit, pattiserie, sweet spices, cocoa bean. Palate: rich, correct, toasty, fine bitter notes.

TRES LEONES B
moscatel de alejandría

85 Colour: bright yellow. Nose: medium intensity, faded flowers. Palate: sweet, fruity, correct.

BODEGAS MOROSANTO

Ctra. Arriate - Setenil, Km. 1,6
29400 Ronda (Málaga)
☎: +34 619 124 208
www.bodegasmorosanto.com
bodega@bogasmorosanto.com

LUCIO 2011 T
55% syrah, 45% tempranillo

86 Colour: deep cherry, garnet rim. Nose: ripe fruit, sweet spices, balanced. Palate: flavourful, fruity, good finish.

LUNERA 2010 T
55% petit verdot, 30% cabernet sauvignon, 15% syrah

89 Colour: deep cherry, garnet rim. Nose: red berry notes, ripe fruit, cocoa bean, wild herbs. Palate: balanced, ripe fruit, long, round tannins.

BODEGAS PÉREZ HIDALGO

Avda. Virgen de las Flores, 15
29500 Álora (Málaga)
☎: +34 952 497 665 - Fax: +34 952 497 665
www.bodegasperezhidalgo.es
info@bodegasperezhidalgo.es

PÁRAMO DE CÁSSER 2008 TR

87 Colour: cherry, garnet rim. Nose: ripe fruit, spicy, creamy oak, toasty, complex. Palate: powerful, flavourful, toasty, round tannins.

VEGA DEL GEVA 2009 TC
syrah, cabernet sauvignon, merlot

84

VEGA DEL GEVA 2010 T ROBLE
syrah, merlot, cabernet sauvignon

85 Colour: light cherry, orangey edge. Nose: ripe fruit, spicy, creamy oak. Palate: powerful, flavourful, toasty.

BODEGAS QUITAPENAS

Ctra. de Guadalmar, 12
29004 Málaga (Málaga)
☎: +34 952 247 595 - Fax: +34 952 105 138
www.quitapenas.es
ventas@quitapenas.es

MÁLAGA PAJARETE NOBLE

87 Colour: bright golden. Nose: candied fruit, caramel, toasty, balanced, acetaldehyde. Palate: good structure, spirituous, full.

MÁLAGA PX NOBLE
pedro ximénez

87 Colour: mahogany. Nose: dried fruit, honeyed notes, caramel, powerfull. Palate: flavourful, unctuous, sweet, toasty.

QUITAPENAS MOSCATEL DORADO PÁLIDO
moscatel

84

SOL SALERO SOLERA
pedro ximénez

88 Colour: old gold, amber rim. Nose: pattiserie, dried fruit, honeyed notes. Palate: spirituous, full, fine bitter notes, sweetness.

BODEGAS VILORIA

Ronda La Vieja Km. 4,800 Puerto Quejigal Finca Bernardino
29400 Ronda (Málaga)
☎: +34 637 531 800
www.bodegasviloria.es
bodegasviloria@hotmail.es

LAGAREJO 2011 T
cabernet sauvignon

82

LAGAREJO 2012 RD
petit verdot, syrah

86 Colour: light cherry. Nose: powerfull, ripe fruit, faded flowers. Palate: flavourful, spicy, sweetness.

LAGAREJO SELECCIÓN 2007 T
tempranillo, cabernet sauvignon, syrah, merlot, petit verdot

86 Colour: cherry, garnet rim. Nose: ripe fruit, scrubland, spicy, fruit preserve. Palate: flavourful, fruity, good finish.

COMPAÑÍA DE VINOS TELMO RODRÍGUEZ

El Monte
1308 Lanciego (Álava)
☎: +34 945 628 315 - Fax: +34 945 628 314
www.telmorodriguez.com
contact@telmorodriguez.com

MOLINO REAL 2009 B
moscatel de alejandría

97 Colour: golden. Nose: powerfull, floral, honeyed notes, candied fruit, fragrant herbs, citrus fruit. Palate: flavourful, sweet, fresh, good acidity, long, ripe fruit.

MOUNTAIN 2011 B
moscatel de alejandría

93 Colour: bright straw. Nose: white flowers, ripe fruit, citrus fruit. Palate: fruity, fresh, good acidity.

CORTIJO LOS AGUILARES

Ctra. Ronda a Campillo. Puente de la Ventilla
29400 Ronda (Málaga)
☎: +34 952 874 457 - Fax: +34 951 166 000
www.cortijolosaguilares.com
bodega@cortijolosaguilares.com

CORTIJO LOS AGUILARES 2012 RD
tempranillo, petit verdot

88 Colour: rose, bright. Nose: fresh fruit, red berry notes, wild herbs, balanced. Palate: fruity, fresh, balanced.

CORTIJO LOS AGUILARES 2012 T
55% tempranillo, 30% merlot, 15% zalema

88 Colour: cherry, purple rim. Nose: balanced, expressive, red berry notes, ripe fruit. Palate: flavourful, fruity, good acidity.

CORTIJO LOS AGUILARES PAGO EL ESPINO 2010 T
39% petit verdot, 31% tempranillo, 30% merlot

91 Colour: deep cherry, garnet rim. Nose: cocoa bean, sweet spices, ripe fruit, elegant. Palate: flavourful, fruity, good structure, round tannins.

CORTIJO LOS AGUILARES PINOT NOIR 2012 T
100% pinot noir

92 Colour: cherry, purple rim. Nose: expressive, elegant, violets, red berry notes. Palate: flavourful, balanced, fine bitter notes, good acidity.

CORTIJO LOS AGUILARES TADEO 2010 T
100% petit verdot

95 Colour: very deep cherry. Nose: cocoa bean, creamy oak, ripe fruit, spicy, earthy notes. Palate: flavourful, good structure, fine tannins, elegant.

DESCALZOS VIEJOS

Finca Descalzos Viejos- Partido de los Molinos, s/n
29400 Ronda (Málaga)
☎: +34 952 874 696 - Fax: +34 952 874 696
www.descalzosviejos.com
info@descalzosviejos.com

DV CHARDONNAY 2011 B
chardonnay

86 Colour: bright yellow. Nose: ripe fruit, faded flowers, sweet spices. Palate: ripe fruit, correct.

DV CONARTE 2007 TC
petit verdot, syrah, cabernet sauvignon, merlot

92 Colour: dark-red cherry. Nose: wild herbs, ripe fruit, sweet spices, cocoa bean. Palate: concentrated, flavourful, round tannins, spicy, long.

DV DESCALZOS VIEJOS (+) 2007 TC
cabernet sauvignon, merlot, graciano

89 Colour: cherry, garnet rim. Nose: ripe fruit, spicy, creamy oak, toasty, warm. Palate: powerful, flavourful, toasty, round tannins.

DV DESCALZOS VIEJOS 2010 T
garnacha, syrah, merlot

83

FINCA LA MELONERA

Paraje Los Frontones, Camino Ronda-Setenil s/n
29400 Ronda (Malaga)
☎: +34 932 097 514 - Fax: +34 932 011 068
www.lamelonera.com
info@lamelonera.com

ENCINA DEL INGLÉS 2012 T
60% garnacha, 40% syrah

92 Colour: cherry, purple rim. Nose: expressive, red berry notes, floral. Palate: flavourful, fruity, good acidity, round tannins.

PAYOYA NEGRA 2010 T
garnacha, syrah, tintilla de rota

92 Colour: cherry, garnet rim. Nose: scrubland, ripe fruit, spicy, earthy notes. Palate: fruity, fine bitter notes, good acidity, long.

JORGE ORDÓÑEZ & CO

Bartolome Esteban Murillo, 11
29700 Velez-Málaga (Málaga)
☎: +34 952 504 706 - Fax: +34 951 284 796
www.jorgeordonez.es
info@jorgeordonez.es

JORGE ORDÓÑEZ & CO BOTANI 2012 B
100% moscatel de alejandría

92 Colour: bright straw. Nose: fresh, fresh fruit, white flowers, varietal. Palate: flavourful, fruity, good acidity, balanced, rich.

JORGE ORDÓÑEZ & CO BOTANI GARNACHA 2011 T
100% garnacha

88 Colour: very deep cherry. Nose: fruit preserve, red berry notes, spicy. Palate: fine bitter notes, sweetness.

JORGE ORDÓÑEZ & CO Nº 1 SELECCIÓN ESPECIAL 2011 B
100% moscatel de alejandría

92 Colour: bright straw. Nose: varietal, citrus fruit, fresh fruit. Palate: flavourful, good acidity, sweetness.

JORGE ORDÓÑEZ & CO Nº 2 VICTORIA 2012 BLANCO DULCE
100% moscatel de alejandría

95 Colour: bright straw. Nose: expressive, elegant, varietal, floral. Palate: fruity, flavourful, long, rich, balanced, complex.

JORGE ORDÓÑEZ & CO. Nº3 VIÑAS VIEJAS 2008 B
moscatel

96 Colour: golden. Nose: powerfull, floral, honeyed notes, candied fruit, fragrant herbs, petrol notes. Palate: flavourful, sweet, fresh, fruity, good acidity, long.

LA DONAIRA

Apartado de Correos 581
29400 Ronda (Málaga)
☎: +34 951 390 059
www.ladonaira.com
info@ladonaira.com

LA DONAIRA CABERNET FRANC 2010 T
100% cabernet franc

90 Colour: very deep cherry. Nose: closed, medium intensity, ripe fruit, creamy oak. Palate: fruity, good structure, round tannins, toasty.

LA DONAIRA PETIT VERDOT 2011 T
100% petit verdot

83

SEDELLA VINOS

Término Las Viñuelas, s/n
29715 Sedella (Málaga)
☎: +34 687 463 082 - Fax: +34 967 140 723
www.sedellavinos.com
info@sedellavinos.com

SEDELLA 2010 T
romé, garnacha

91 Colour: cherry, garnet rim. Nose: balanced, expressive, ripe fruit, tobacco, spicy. Palate: fruity, spicy, long, fine bitter notes.

TIERRAS DE MOLLINA

Avda. de las Américas, s/n (Cortijo Colarte)
29532 Mollina (Málaga)
☎: +34 952 841 451 - Fax: +34 952 842 555
www.montespejo.com
administracion@tierrasdemollina.net

CARPE DIEM MÁLAGA AÑEJO
90% pedro ximénez, 10% moscatel

87 Colour: mahogany. Nose: acetaldehyde, candied fruit, cocoa bean, sweet spices. Palate: balanced, fine bitter notes, sweet, flavourful.

CARPE DIEM DULCE NATURAL 2011 B
moscatel

88 Colour: bright yellow. Nose: floral, jasmine, expressive, varietal. Palate: fruity, rich, good acidity, sweetness.

CARPE DIEM MÁLAGA TRASAÑEJO MÁLAGA
90% pedro ximénez, 10% moscatel

88 Colour: mahogany. Nose: cocoa bean, dry nuts, sweet spices. Palate: flavourful, sweet, spicy, easy to drink.

MONTESPEJO 2010 T ROBLE
85% syrah, 15% merlot

87 Colour: deep cherry, purple rim. Nose: creamy oak, toasty, sweet spices, ripe fruit. Palate: flavourful, good structure, round tannins.

MONTESPEJO 2011 B
lairén, moscatel, doradilla

86 Colour: bright yellow. Nose: powerfull, ripe fruit, balanced, floral. Palate: flavourful, fruity, easy to drink.

MONTESPEJO 2011 T
100% syrah

85 Colour: cherry, purple rim. Nose: red berry notes, medium intensity. Palate: flavourful, fruity, good acidity, easy to drink.

MONTESPEJO CEPAS VIEJAS 2011 B ROBLE
doradilla

86 Colour: bright yellow. Nose: ripe fruit, sweet spices, creamy oak, floral. Palate: flavourful, spicy, toasty.

LOCATION:

The production area covers the territory situated in the southeast of the province of Cuenca and the northeast of Albacete, between the rivers Júcar and Cabriel. It comprises 70 municipal districts, 26 of which are in Albacete and the rest in Cuenca.

CLIMATE:

The climate is continental in nature, with cold winters and hot summers, although the cool and humid winds from the Mediterranean during the summer help to lower the temperatures at night, so creating favourable day-night temperature contrasts for a slow ripening of the grapes.

SOIL:

The vineyards are situated at an altitude ranging between 600 and 700 m above sea level. The terrain is mainly flat, except for the ravines outlined by the rivers. Regarding the composition of the terrain, below a clayey surface of gravel or sand, the soil is limy, which is an important quality factor for the region.

GRAPE VARIETIES:

WHITE: *Albillo, Chardonnay, Macabeo, Sauvignon Blanc, Verdejo, Pardillo, Viognier* and *Moscatel de Grano Menudo.*
RED: *Bobal, Cabernet Sauvignon, Cencibel (Tempranillo), Garnacha, Merlot, Monastrell, Moravia Dulce, Syrah, Garnacha Tintorera, Malbec, Moravia agria, Mazuelo, Graciano, Rojal, Frasco (Tinto Velasco), Petit Verdot, Cabernet Franc* and *Pinot Noir.*

FIGURES:

Vineyard surface: 5.500 – **Wine-Growers**: 800 – **Wineries**: 33 – **2012 Harvest rating:** Very Good– **Production**: 1.000.000 litres – **Market percentages**: 20% domestic. 80% export

CONSEJO REGULADOR
Avda. San Agustín, 9 - 02270 Villamalea (Albacete) ☎: +34 967 09 06 94 - Fax: +34 967 09 06 96
domanchuela@lamanchuela.es   www.do-manchuela.com

ALTOLANDÓN

Ctra. N-330, km. 242
16330 Landete (Cuenca)
☎: +34 962 300 662 - Fax: +34 962 300 662
www.altolandon.com
altolandon@altolandon.com

ALTOLANDÓN 2009 T
syrah, garnacha, cabernet franc

92 Colour: cherry, garnet rim. Nose: ripe fruit, balsamic herbs, cocoa bean, sweet spices, creamy oak, fine reductive notes. Palate: powerful, flavourful, spicy, long.

ALTOLANDÓN WHITE 2011 BFB
chardonnay, petit manseng

90 Colour: bright golden. Nose: tropical fruit, citrus fruit, ripe fruit, wild herbs, creamy oak. Palate: rich, powerful, flavourful, spicy.

CF DE ALTOLANDÓN 2010 T
100% cabernet franc

91 Colour: cherry, garnet rim. Nose: ripe fruit, spicy, creamy oak, toasty, dry stone, expressive. Palate: powerful, flavourful, toasty, round tannins.

RAYUELO 2009 T
bobal

93 Colour: cherry, garnet rim. Nose: red berry notes, fragrant herbs, floral, mineral, creamy oak, elegant. Palate: rich, flavourful, spicy, long.

BODEGA INIESTA

Ctra. Villamalea, km. 1,5
2260 Fuentealbilla (Albacete)
☎: +34 967 090 650 - Fax: +34 967 090 651
www.bodegainiesta.com
juanjo@bodegainiesta.com

CORAZÓN LOCO 2012 B
sauvignon blanc, verdejo

86 Colour: bright yellow. Nose: medium intensity, citrus fruit, ripe fruit. Palate: correct, easy to drink, balanced.

CORAZÓN LOCO 2012 RD
bobal

89 Colour: rose, purple rim. Nose: powerfull, ripe fruit, red berry notes, floral, expressive. Palate: powerful, fruity, fresh.

CORAZÓN LOCO 2012 T
tempranillo, syrah

88 Colour: bright cherry, purple rim. Nose: balanced, fruit expression, violets. Palate: flavourful, fruity, easy to drink, long.

CORAZÓN LOCO PREMIUM 2010 T
syrah, petit verdot, tempranillo, cabernet sauvignon

92 Colour: bright cherry. Nose: ripe fruit, sweet spices, creamy oak, earthy notes, spicy, balsamic herbs. Palate: flavourful, fruity, toasty, round tannins, balanced.

CORAZÓN LOCO SELECCIÓN 2010 T
syrah, petit verdot, tempranillo, cabernet sauvignon

89 Colour: cherry, garnet rim. Nose: ripe fruit, spicy, creamy oak, toasty, complex. Palate: powerful, flavourful, toasty, round tannins.

DULCE CORAZÓN 2012 B
moscatel

88 Colour: bright yellow. Nose: citrus fruit, candied fruit, floral, fragrant herbs. Palate: fresh, fruity, flavourful, balanced.

FINCA EL CARRIL 2011 T ROBLE
tempranillo, syrah, petit verdot

90 Colour: bright cherry. Nose: ripe fruit, sweet spices, creamy oak, expressive. Palate: flavourful, fruity, toasty, round tannins.

FINCA EL CARRIL 2012 B
macabeo, chardonnay

87 Colour: bright straw. Nose: fresh, fresh fruit, white flowers, expressive. Palate: flavourful, fruity, good acidity, balanced.

FINCA EL CARRIL HECHICERO 2010 T
tempranillo, syrah, petit verdot, cabernet sauvignon

91 Colour: cherry, garnet rim. Nose: ripe fruit, creamy oak, toasty. Palate: powerful, toasty, flavourful, balanced.

FINCA EL CARRIL VALERIA 2012 BFB
chardonnay, viognier

86 Colour: bright yellow. Nose: powerfull, ripe fruit, sweet spices, creamy oak, fragrant herbs. Palate: rich, smoky aftertaste, flavourful, fresh, good acidity.

BODEGA PARDO TOLOSA

Villatoya, 26
2215 Alborea (Albacete)
☎: +34 961 668 222
www.bodegapardotolosa.com
ventas@bodegapardotolosa.com

LA SIMA 2012 T
tempranillo, bobal

84

MIZARAN BOBAL 2012 RD
bobal

80

MIZARAN MACABEO 2012 B
macabeo

87 Colour: bright yellow. Nose: dried flowers, ripe fruit, sweet spices. Palate: rich, powerful, flavourful, spicy, balanced.

MIZARAN TEMPRANILLO 2009 T
tempranillo

83

SENDA DE LAS ROCHAS 2008 TC
tempranillo

90 Colour: cherry, garnet rim. Nose: ripe fruit, spicy, creamy oak, toasty, complex, fine reductive notes. Palate: powerful, flavourful, toasty, round tannins.

SENDA DE LAS ROCHAS BOBAL 2011 T
bobal

86 Colour: cherry, garnet rim. Nose: scrubland, ripe fruit, medium intensity. Palate: flavourful, ripe fruit.

BODEGA SAN ISIDRO

Ctra. de Albacete, s/n
16220 Quintanar del Rey (Cuenca)
☎: +34 967 495 052 - Fax: +34 967 495 067
www.bodegasanisidro.es
administracion@bodegasanisidro.es

MONTE DE LAS MOZAS 2012 B
macabeo

84

MONTE DE LAS MOZAS 2012 RD
bobal

83

QUINTA REGIA 2011 T
bobal

89 Colour: cherry, purple rim. Nose: balanced, spicy, ripe fruit. Palate: round tannins, balanced, long.

ZAÍNO ROBLE 2011 T ROBLE
syrah

87 Colour: cherry, garnet rim. Nose: red berry notes, ripe fruit, sweet spices, roasted coffee. Palate: powerful, flavourful, spicy, toasty.

ZAÍNO SYRAH 2012 T
syrah

84

BODEGAS RECIAL

Libertad, 1
2154 Pozo Lorente (Albacete)
☎: +34 630 418 264 - Fax: +34 967 572 063
gerencia@bodegasrecial.com

PÚRPURA 2012 RD
syrah

83

PÚRPURA POZO LORENTE 2008 TC
garnacha tintorera

86 Colour: cherry, garnet rim. Nose: ripe fruit, spicy, creamy oak, toasty, complex, mineral. Palate: powerful, flavourful, toasty, round tannins.

PÚRPURA POZO LORENTE 2010 TC
garnacha tintorera

84

PÚRPURA POZO LORENTE 2012 B
sauvignon blanc

84

BODEGAS VILLAVID

Niño Jesús, 25
16280 Villarta (Cuenca)
☎: +34 962 189 006 - Fax: +34 962 189 125
www.villavid.com
info@villavid.com

VILLAVID 2012 B
macabeo, verdejo

84

VILLAVID 2012 RD
bobal

84

VILLAVID 2012 T
tempranillo

83

BODEGAS VITIVINOS

Camino de Cabezuelas, s/n
2270 Villamalea (Albacete)
☎: +34 967 483 114 - Fax: +34 967 483 964
www.vitivinos.com
comercial@vitivinos.com

AZUA BOBAL 2012 RD
bobal

85 Colour: light cherry, bright. Nose: medium intensity, scrubland, ripe fruit. Palate: easy to drink, correct.

AZUA BOBAL 2012 T
bobal

88 Colour: bright cherry. Nose: ripe fruit, sweet spices, creamy oak. Palate: flavourful, fruity, toasty, harsh oak tannins.

AZUA CABERNET 2011 T ROBLE
cabernet sauvignon

86 Colour: cherry, garnet rim. Nose: ripe fruit, creamy oak, toasty, balsamic herbs. Palate: powerful, flavourful, toasty.

AZUA CRIANZA SELECCIÓN BOBAL VIEJO 2009 TC
bobal

87 Colour: cherry, garnet rim. Nose: balanced, red berry notes, ripe fruit, wild herbs, spicy. Palate: flavourful, fruity.

AZUA MACABEO 2012 B
macabeo

84

AZUA MACABEO SEMIDULCE 2012 B
macabeo

85 Colour: golden. Nose: powerfull, floral, honeyed notes, candied fruit, fragrant herbs. Palate: flavourful, sweet, fresh, fruity, good acidity, long.

AZUA RESERVA SELECCIÓN BOBAL VIEJO 2008 TR
bobal

88 Colour: cherry, garnet rim. Nose: balanced, spicy, scrubland, ripe fruit. Palate: flavourful, round tannins.

AZUA SYRAH 2011 T ROBLE
syrah

87 Colour: cherry, garnet rim. Nose: ripe fruit, red berry notes, dried herbs, spicy. Palate: fruity, easy to drink, good finish.

AZUA VERDEJO 2012 B
verdejo

85 Colour: bright straw. Nose: medium intensity, wild herbs, ripe fruit. Palate: correct, fine bitter notes, good acidity.

BODEGAS Y VIÑEDOS PONCE

La Virgen, 34
16235 Iniesta (Cuenca)
☎: +34 677 434 523 - Fax: +34 967 220 876
bodegasponce@gmail.com

CLOS LOJEN 2012 T
100% bobal

92 Colour: bright cherry, purple rim. Nose: medium intensity, balanced, ripe fruit, wild herbs. Palate: flavourful, fruity, long, easy to drink.

LA CASILLA (ESTRECHA) 2011 T
100% bobal

92 Colour: bright cherry. Nose: ripe fruit, sweet spices, creamy oak, violet drops, lactic notes. Palate: flavourful, fruity, toasty, round tannins, balanced.

P.F. 2011 T
100% bobal

93 Colour: cherry, purple rim. Nose: ripe fruit, fruit preserve, sweet spices. Palate: good structure, ripe fruit, long, round tannins.

PINO 2011 T
100% bobal

93 Colour: cherry, garnet rim. Nose: medium intensity, red berry notes, ripe fruit, balsamic herbs, spicy. Palate: flavourful, ripe fruit, round tannins.

RETO 2012 BFB
100% albilla

87 Colour: bright yellow. Nose: candied fruit, sweet spices, toasty. Palate: spicy, correct, rich.

CIEN Y PICO WINE S.L.

San Francisco, 19
2240 Mahora (Albacete)
☎: +34 610 239 186
www.cienypico.com
luisjimenaz@gmail.com

CIEN Y PICO DOBLE PASTA 2009 T
100% garnacha tintorera

87 Colour: black cherry, garnet rim. Nose: fruit preserve, cocoa bean, sweet spices. Palate: flavourful, balanced, round tannins.

CIEN Y PICO EN VASO 2011 T
100% bobal

88 Colour: deep cherry, garnet rim. Nose: powerfull, ripe fruit, dark chocolate, balsamic herbs. Palate: balanced, round tannins.

CIEN Y PICO WINEMAKER'S - GALLANT 2011 T
100% bobal

88 Colour: deep cherry. Nose: balsamic herbs, earthy notes, ripe fruit, medium intensity. Palate: flavourful, sweetness, long.

COOP DEL CAMPO VIRGEN DE LAS NIEVES, S.C. DE CLM

Paseo Virgen de las Nieves, 1
2247 Cenizate (Albacete)
☎: +34 967 482 006 - Fax: +34 967 482 805
www.virgendelasnieves.com
cooperativa@virgendelasnives.com

ARTESONES DE CENIZATE 2008 TR
tempranillo

84

ARTESONES DE CENIZATE 2012 B
macabeo

84

ARTESONES DE CENIZATE 2012 RD
bobal

87 Colour: rose, purple rim. Nose: red berry notes, lactic notes, raspberry, floral. Palate: powerful, flavourful, fresh, fruity.

ARTESONES DE CENIZATE 2012 T
syrah

84

ARTESONES DE CENIZATE TEMPRANILLO 2008 TC
tempranillo

83

COOP. DEL CAMPO SAN ISIDRO

Extramuros, s/n
2215 Alborea (Albacete)
☎: +34 967 477 096 - Fax: +34 967 477 096
www.vinosalborea.com
coopalborea@telefonica.net

ALTERÓN 2005 TGR
bobal

86 Colour: pale ruby, brick rim edge. Nose: spicy, fine reductive notes, wet leather, aged wood nuances, fruit liqueur notes. Palate: spicy, fine tannins, elegant, long.

ALTERÓN 2009 TC
bobal

83

ALTERÓN 2010 TC
cencibel

84

ALTERÓN 2012 B
macabeo

85 Colour: bright yellow. Nose: ripe fruit, wild herbs. Palate: fruity, correct, fine bitter notes.

COOP. NUESTRA SEÑORA DE LA ESTRELLA

Elías Fernández, 10
16290 El Herrumbar (Cuenca)
☎: +34 962 313 029 - Fax: +34 962 313 232
francisco@antaresvinos.es

ANTARES 2012 B
sauvignon blanc

83

ANTARES 2012 RD
bobal

85 Colour: rose, purple rim. Nose: red berry notes, ripe fruit, floral. Palate: fruity, flavourful.

ANTARES 2012 T ROBLE
syrah

87 Colour: cherry, purple rim. Nose: red berry notes, ripe fruit, sweet spices, creamy oak. Palate: toasty, long, powerful, flavourful.

ANTARES SAUVIGNON BLANC 2012 BFB
sauvignon blanc

87 Colour: yellow, greenish rim. Nose: wild herbs, balanced, spicy, toasty. Palate: fruity, ripe fruit, long.

COOPERATIVA SAN ANTONIO ABAD

Valencia, 41
2270 Villamalea (Albacete)
☎: +34 967 483 023 - Fax: +34 967 483 536
www.bodegas-saac.com
saac@bodegas-saac.com

ALTOS DEL CABRIEL 2012 B
macabeo

84

ALTOS DEL CABRIEL 2012 RD
bobal

88 Colour: rose. Nose: red berry notes, ripe fruit, lactic notes, balanced. Palate: powerful, flavourful, fruity, balanced.

ALTOS DEL CABRIEL 2012 T
tempranillo

87 Colour: cherry, purple rim. Nose: red berry notes, ripe fruit, balsamic herbs, floral. Palate: correct, fruity, flavourful, easy to drink.

GREDAS VIEJAS 2009 T ROBLE
syrah

87 Colour: cherry, garnet rim. Nose: ripe fruit, fruit preserve, spicy. Palate: flavourful, balanced, good structure, toasty.

FINCA SANDOVAL

Ctra. CM-3222, Km. 26,800
16237 Ledaña (Cuenca)
☎: +34 696 910 769
fincasandoval@gmail.com

FINCA SANDOVAL 2009 T
77% syrah, 13% monastrell, 10% bobal

94 Colour: cherry, garnet rim. Nose: ripe fruit, spicy, creamy oak, toasty, complex, earthy notes, mineral, balanced. Palate: powerful, flavourful, toasty, round tannins, complex, elegant.

FINCA SANDOVAL CUVÉE CECILIA 2011 T
80% syrah, 20% moscatel de alejandría

90 Colour: deep cherry, garnet rim. Nose: fruit preserve, dried fruit, cocoa bean, faded flowers. Palate: flavourful, rich, sweet, good acidity.

FINCA SANDOVAL CUVEE TNS MAGNUM 2009 T
67% touriga nacional, 33% syrah

95 Colour: bright cherry. Nose: ripe fruit, sweet spices, creamy oak, expressive, balanced. Palate: flavourful, fruity, toasty, round tannins, elegant, balanced.

SALIA 2010 T
51% syrah, 34% garnacha tintorera, 15% garnacha

92 Colour: cherry, garnet rim. Nose: old leather, ripe fruit, mineral, spicy. Palate: full, flavourful, good structure, round tannins.

SIGNO BOBAL 2010 T
91% bobal, 9% syrah

94 Colour: cherry, garnet rim. Nose: balanced, scrubland, spicy, ripe fruit. Palate: flavourful, full, fine tannins, good acidity, long.

SIGNO GARNACHA 2011 T
91% garnacha, 5% garnacha tintorera, moravia agria

94 Colour: bright cherry. Nose: ripe fruit, sweet spices, creamy oak, expressive. Palate: flavourful, fruity, toasty, round tannins, balanced, elegant.

MONTEAGUDO RUIZ

Plaza San pedro, 17
16234 Casas de Santa Cruz (Cuenca)
☎: +34 967 493 828 - Fax: +34 967 493 841
www.señoriodemonterruiz.es
reservas@monterruiz.com

SEÑORIO DE MONTERRUIZ 2012 T
bobal

87 Colour: deep cherry, purple rim. Nose: balanced, red berry notes, ripe fruit, violets. Palate: fruity, flavourful.

SEÑORIO DE MONTERRUIZ 2012 T MACERACIÓN CARBÓNICA
bobal

83

NUESTRA SEÑORA DE LA CABEZA DE CASAS IBÁÑEZ SOC. COOP. DE CLM

Avda. del Vino, 10
2200 Casas Ibáñez (Albacete)
☎: +34 967 460 266 - Fax: +34 967 460 105
www.coop-cabeza.com
info@hotmail.com

VIARIL 2012 B
100% macabeo

84

VIARIL 2012 BFB
100% macabeo

87 Colour: bright yellow. Nose: powerfull, ripe fruit, creamy oak, fragrant herbs. Palate: rich, flavourful, fresh, good acidity.

VIARIL 2007 TR
tempranillo, syrah, cabernet sauvignon

86 Colour: cherry, garnet rim. Nose: spicy, cocoa bean, tobacco, ripe fruit. Palate: flavourful, fruity, fine tannins.

VIARIL 2012 RD
100% bobal

88 Colour: rose, purple rim. Nose: powerfull, ripe fruit, red berry notes, floral, lactic notes. Palate: powerful, fruity, fresh.

VIARIL 2012 T
100% bobal

86 Colour: deep cherry, garnet rim. Nose: ripe fruit, wild herbs. Palate: flavourful, fruity, good structure.

VIARIL CABERNET SAUVIGNON 2012 T
100% cabernet sauvignon

84

VIARIL SELECCIÓN 2012 T
100% syrah

86 Colour: deep cherry, purple rim. Nose: ripe fruit, balsamic herbs, powerfull. Palate: flavourful, ripe fruit, correct.

PAGOS DE FAMILIA VEGA TOLOSA

Pol. Ind. Calle B, 11
2200 Casas Ibáñez (Albacete)
☎: +34 967 461 331
www.vegatolosa.com
info@vegatolosa.com

VEGA TOLOSA BLANCO SELECCIÓN 2012 B
50% macabeo, 35% sauvignon blanc, 15% chardonnay

84

VEGA TOLOSA BOBAL VIÑAS VIEJAS 2010 TC
100% bobal

89 Colour: cherry, garnet rim. Nose: ripe fruit, spicy, creamy oak, toasty. Palate: powerful, flavourful, toasty, round tannins.

VEGA TOLOSA BOBAL VIÑAS VIEJAS 2012 T BARRICA
bobal

85 Colour: cherry, purple rim. Nose: medium intensity, balsamic herbs, ripe fruit. Palate: flavourful, correct.

VEGA TOLOSA CABERNET SAUVIGNON MERLOT 2009 TC
50% cabernet sauvignon, 50% merlot

91 Colour: cherry, garnet rim. Nose: scrubland, ripe fruit, spicy, complex. Palate: balanced, long, round tannins.

VEGA TOLOSA CABERNET SAUVIGNON MERLOT 2012 T
50% cabernet sauvignon, 50% merlot

88 Colour: bright cherry. Nose: ripe fruit, sweet spices, creamy oak, expressive. Palate: flavourful, fruity, toasty, round tannins.

VEGA TOLOSA CHARDONNAY BARRICA 2011 B BARRICA
100% chardonnay

88 Colour: bright golden. Nose: ripe fruit, dry nuts, powerfull, toasty, aged wood nuances. Palate: flavourful, fruity, spicy, toasty, long.

VEGA TOLOSA NATURE 2012 T
50% tempranillo, 50% syrah

87 Colour: cherry, purple rim. Nose: medium intensity, red berry notes, violets. Palate: fruity, flavourful, balanced.

VEGA TOLOSA ROSADO LÁGRIMA DE SYRAH 2012 RD
100% syrah

84

VEGA TOLOSA SYRAH 2009 TR
100% syrah

91 Colour: cherry, garnet rim. Nose: red berry notes, ripe fruit, floral, balsamic herbs, expressive, sweet spices, creamy oak. Palate: correct, powerful, flavourful, long, toasty.

SAN ANTONIO ABAD
SOC. COOP. DE CLM

Barrio Arriba, 9
2260 Fuentealbilla (Albacete)
☎: +34 967 472 026 - Fax: +34 967 477 530
www.maricubas.com
lucio@sanantonioabad.com

MARICUBAS 2012 RD
bobal

84

MARICUBAS SENSACIÓN 2010
petit verdot, cabernet sauvignon

88 Colour: bright cherry. Nose: red berry notes, ripe fruit, sweet spices, balsamic herbs. Palate: powerful, flavourful, toasty.

SDAD. UNION CAMPESINA
INIESTENSE

San Idefonso, 1
16235 Iniesta (Cuenca)
☎: +34 967 490 120 - Fax: +34 967 490 777
www.cooperativauci.com
comercial@cooperativauci.com

REALCE BOBAL 2007 TR
100% bobal

83

REALCE BOBAL 2012 RD
bobal

85 Colour: rose, purple rim. Nose: red berry notes, floral, fragrant herbs. Palate: fresh, fruity, light-bodied, flavourful.

REALCE TEMPRANILLO 2006 TC
tempranillo

86 Colour: cherry, garnet rim. Nose: cocoa bean, sweet spices, ripe fruit. Palate: balanced, easy to drink, fine tannins.

REALCE TEMPRANILLO 2012 T
tempranillo

86 Colour: cherry, purple rim. Nose: red berry notes, ripe fruit, balsamic herbs. Palate: powerful, flavourful, spicy.

REALCE VIURA 2012 B
viura

80

VINICOLA EL MOLAR

Camino del Molar, s/n
2260 Fuentealbilla (Albacete)
☎: +34 913 312 155
gerencia@sonsagens.es

QUANTUM 2011 T ROBLE
cabernet sauvignon, merlot, syrah

83

QUANTUM 2012 T ROBLE
100% syrah

85 Colour: bright cherry. Nose: ripe fruit, sweet spices, creamy oak. Palate: flavourful, fruity, toasty.

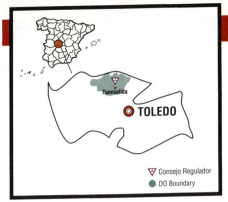

DO MÉNTRIDA / D.O.P.

LOCATION:

In the north of the province of Toledo. It borders with the provinces of Ávila and Madrid to the north, with the Tajo to the south, and with the Sierra de San Vicente to the west. It is made up of 51 municipal areas of the province of Toledo.

CLIMATE:

Continental, dry and extreme, with long, cold winters and hot summers. Late frosts in spring are quite common. The average rainfall is between 300 mm and 500 mm, and is irregularly distributed throughout the year.

SOIL:

The vineyards are at an altitude of between 400 m and 600 m, although some municipal districts of the Sierra de San Vicente reach an altitude of 800 m. The soil is mainly sandy-clayey, with a medium to loose texture.

GRAPE VARIETIES:

WHITE: *Albillo, Macabeo, Sauvignon Blanc, Chardonnay* and *Moscatel de Grano Menudo.*
RED: *Garnacha* (majority 85% of total), *Cencibel* (*Tempranillo*), *Cabernet Sauvignon, Merlot, Syrah, Petit Verdot, Cabernet Franc* and *Graciano.*

FIGURES:

Vineyard surface: 5.766,07 – **Wine-Growers:** 1.376 – **Wineries:** 27 – **2012 Harvest rating:** Good – **Production:** 15.880.494 litres – **Market percentages:** 80% domestic. 20% export

AGROVILLARTA

Ctra. Toledo-Ávila, Km. 48
45910 Escalona (Toledo)
☎: +34 913 441 990
comunicacion@haciendavillarta.com

BESANAS 2008 TR
tempranillo, cabernet sauvignon, syrah

88 Colour: cherry, garnet rim. Nose: ripe fruit, sweet spices, wild herbs, balanced. Palate: good structure, flavourful.

BESANAS 2009 TC
tempranillo, cabernet sauvignon, syrah

87 Colour: cherry, garnet rim. Nose: spicy, old leather, ripe fruit. Palate: flavourful, fruity, easy to drink.

BESANAS 2012 B
chardonnay, sauvignon blanc

83

YX 2010 B
chardonnay, sauvignon blanc

85 Colour: bright yellow. Nose: dried flowers, balsamic herbs, ripe fruit, expressive. Palate: fruity, easy to drink, correct, good finish.

ALONSO CUESTA

Pza. de la Constitución, 2
45920 La Torre de Esteban Hambrán (Toledo)
☎: +34 925 795 742 - Fax: +34 925 795 742
www.alonsocuesta.com
comercial@alonsocuesta.com

ALONSO CUESTA 2010 T
garnacha, tempranillo, cabernet sauvignon

93 Colour: deep cherry, garnet rim. Nose: powerfull, creamy oak, sweet spices, cocoa bean, ripe fruit. Palate: good structure, flavourful, round tannins.

ALONSO CUESTA 2012 B
verdejo, sauvignon blanc

87 Colour: bright straw. Nose: balanced, wild herbs, citrus fruit, tropical fruit. Palate: balanced, good acidity, fine bitter notes.

CAMARUS 2012 T
garnacha

85 Colour: cherry, purple rim. Nose: floral, fruit expression, medium intensity. Palate: flavourful, fruity, good acidity, round tannins.

HACIENDA VALPRIMERO 2010 T
garnacha, syrah

87 Colour: cherry, garnet rim. Nose: ripe fruit, fruit preserve, spicy, wild herbs. Palate: good structure, round tannins.

BODEGAS ABANICO

Pol. Ind Ca l'Avellanet - Susany, 6
8553 Seva (Barcelona)
☎: +34 938 125 676 - Fax: +34 938 123 213
www.bodegasabanico.com
info@exportiberia.com

TIERRA FUERTE 2011 T
graciano

89 Colour: deep cherry, purple rim. Nose: expressive, wild herbs, ripe fruit, spicy. Palate: flavourful, good structure, round tannins.

BODEGAS ARRAYÁN

Finca La Verdosa, s/n
45513 Santa Cruz del Retamar (Toledo)
☎: +34 916 633 131 - Fax: +34 916 632 796
www.arrayan.es
comercial@arrayan.es

ARRAYÁN 2012 RD
60% syrah, 40% merlot

89 Colour: light cherry. Nose: fruit expression, expressive, violets, wild herbs, floral. Palate: fine bitter notes, fruity.

ARRAYÁN PETIT VERDOT 2010 T
petit verdot

91 Colour: deep cherry, garnet rim. Nose: balanced, ripe fruit, spicy. Palate: flavourful, balanced, good acidity, round tannins.

ARRAYÁN PREMIUM 2009 T
syrah, merlot, cabernet sauvignon, petit verdot

91 Colour: cherry, garnet rim. Nose: creamy oak, toasty, spicy, ripe fruit. Palate: round tannins, good structure, balsamic.

ARRAYÁN SELECCIÓN 2010 T
syrah, merlot, cabernet sauvignon, petit verdot

88 Colour: cherry, garnet rim. Nose: red berry notes, ripe fruit, balanced, expressive, sweet spices. Palate: fruity, flavourful, fruity aftestaste.

ARRAYÁN SYRAH 2010 T
syrah

88 Colour: cherry, purple rim. Nose: ripe fruit, violet drops, lactic notes, balanced. Palate: round tannins, fruity aftestaste.

ESTELA DE ARRAYÁN 2009 T
syrah, merlot, cabernet sauvignon, petit verdot

93 Colour: cherry, garnet rim. Nose: ripe fruit, spicy, creamy oak, complex, wild herbs. Palate: powerful, flavourful, round tannins.

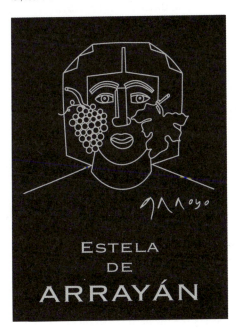

ESTELA DE ARRAYÁN

BODEGAS CANOPY

Avda. Barber, 71
45004 (Toledo)
☎: +34 619 244 878 - Fax: +34 925 283 681
achacon@bodegascanopy.com

CASTILLO DE BERLARFONSO 2012 T
garnacha

91 Colour: bright cherry. Nose: sweet spices, creamy oak, ripe fruit. Palate: flavourful, fruity, toasty, round tannins.

CONGO 2009 T
100% garnacha

94 Colour: deep cherry. Nose: balsamic herbs, ripe fruit, sweet spices, mineral. Palate: flavourful, powerful, good acidity, astringent.

LA VIÑA ESCONDIDA 2008 T
garnacha

94 Colour: cherry, garnet rim. Nose: powerfull, earthy notes, smoky, ripe fruit. Palate: powerful, spicy, ripe fruit, fine bitter notes.

LOCO 2012 B

93 Colour: bright straw. Nose: fine lees, ripe fruit, scrubland. Palate: flavourful, fruity, fresh, spicy.

TRES PATAS 2008 T
90% garnacha, 10% syrah

93 Colour: cherry, garnet rim. Nose: ripe fruit, spicy, creamy oak, toasty, complex, mineral, balsamic herbs. Palate: powerful, flavourful, toasty, round tannins.

BODEGAS GONZALO VALVERDE

Río Tajo, 19
45523 Alcabón (Toledo)
☎: +34 659 452 512
www.bodegasgonzalovalverde.es
info@bodegasgonzalovalverde.es

VALLELOBO 2012 T
tempranillo, cabernet sauvignon, syrah

83

DO MÉNTRIDA / D.O.P.

BODEGAS JIMÉNEZ LANDI

Avda. Solana, 39
45930 Méntrida (Toledo)
☎: +34 918 178 213 - Fax: +34 918 178 213
www.jimenezlandi.com
info@jimenezlandi.com

JIMÉNEZ-LANDI ATAULFOS 2011 T
garnacha

94 Colour: light cherry, garnet rim. Nose: expressive, complex, sweet spices, varietal. Palate: full, flavourful, fine tannins, elegant.

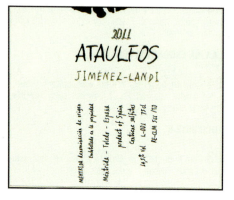

JIMÉNEZ-LANDI BAJONDILLO 2012 T
garnacha, syrah

87 Colour: cherry, purple rim. Nose: medium intensity, wild herbs, red berry notes. Palate: fruity, correct, easy to drink.

JIMÉNEZ-LANDI PIÉLAGO 2011 T
garnacha

94 Colour: cherry, garnet rim. Nose: medium intensity, red berry notes, ripe fruit, spicy, complex, varietal. Palate: good structure, full, flavourful, long.

JIMÉNEZ-LANDI SOTORRONDERO 2011 T
garnacha, syrah

91 Colour: cherry, garnet rim. Nose: ripe fruit, wild herbs, spicy. Palate: balanced, good acidity, round tannins.

BODEGAS LA CERCA

Lepanto, 15
45950 Casarrubios del Monte (Toledo)
☎: +34 918 172 456 - Fax: +34 918 172 456
bodegaslacerca@yahoo.es

MOLINO VIEJO TEMPRANILLO 2010 T ROBLE
tempranillo

84

MOLINO VIEJO TINTO CRIANZA 2011
tempranillo

81

BODEGAS TAVERA S.L.

Ctra. Valmojado - Toledo, Km. 22
45182 Arcicóllar (Toledo)
☎: +34 666 294 012
www.bodegastavera.com
info@bodegastavera.com

TAVERA 2012 T MACERACIÓN CARBÓNICA
40% syrah, 40% tempranillo, 20% garnacha

85 Colour: cherry, garnet rim. Nose: balanced, fruit expression, violets. Palate: fruity, flavourful, balanced, easy to drink.

TAVERA EDICIÓN SYRAH 2010 T FERMENTADO EN BARRICA
100% syrah

87 Colour: cherry, garnet rim. Nose: balanced, red berry notes, ripe fruit, spicy. Palate: good structure, flavourful, round tannins.

TAVERA ROSADO ANTIGUOS VIÑEDOS 2012 RD
100% garnacha

84

TAVERA TEMPRANILLO SYRAH 2011 T
50% tempranillo, 50% syrah

84

BODEGAS TORRESTEBAN

Ctra. Méntrida, s/n
45920 La Torre de Esteban Hambrán (Toledo)
☎: +34 925 795 114
coopcristo@gmail.com

REMURI 2012 T
syrah
82

SEÑORÍO DE ESTEBAN HAMBRÁN 2012 T
tempranillo, garnacha
82

TORRESTEBAN 2012 RD
83

COOPERATIVA CONDES DE FUENSALIDA

Avda. San Crispín, 129
45510 Fuensalida (Toledo)
☎: +34 925 784 823 - Fax: +34 925 784 823
www.condesdefuensalida.iespana.es
condesdefuensalida@hotmail.com

CONDES DE FUENSALIDA 2010 TC
tempranillo, cabernet sauvignon, garnacha
83

CONDES DE FUENSALIDA S/C T
garnacha, tempranillo
82

CONDES DE FUENSALIDA 2012 RD
100% garnacha
85 Colour: light cherry, bright. Nose: medium intensity, red berry notes, ripe fruit, citrus fruit. Palate: flavourful, easy to drink.

CONDES DE FUENSALIDA FRUIT ROSE 2012 RD
garnacha
83

COOPERATIVA NUESTRA SEÑORA DE LA NATIVIDAD

San Roque, 1
45930 Méntrida (Toledo)
☎: +34 918 177 004 - Fax: +34 918 177 004
www.cooperativamentrida.es
coopnatividad@gmail.com

VEGA BERCIANA 2012 RD
garnacha
83

VEGA BERCIANA 2012 T
garnacha
82

COOPERATIVA NUESTRA SEÑORA DE LINARES

Inmaculada, 95
45920 Torre de Esteban Hambrán (Toledo)
☎: +34 925 795 452 - Fax: +34 925 795 452
cooplina@futurnet.es

FORTITUDO 2012 T
garnacha
79

DANI LANDI

28640 Cadalso de los Vidrios (Madrid)
☎: +34 696 366 555
www.danilandi.com
daniel@danilandi.com

CANTOS DEL DIABLO 2011 T
100% garnacha
94 Colour: deep cherry. Nose: fruit expression, raspberry, spicy, scrubland. Palate: fruity, spicy, ripe fruit, balsamic.

FINCA LOS ALIJARES

Avda. de la Paz, 5
45180 Camarena (Toledo)
☎: +34 918 174 364 - Fax: +34 918 174 364
www.fincalosalijares.com
gerencia@fincalosalijares.com

**FINCA LOS ALIJARES PETIT
VERDOT GARNACHA 2011 T**
50% garnacha, 50% petit verdot

85 Colour: cherry, garnet rim. Nose: ripe fruit, grassy, spicy. Palate: powerful, harsh oak tannins.

HIBÉU BODEGAS

Camino Las Ventas, Pol 10 Parc. 90
45920 Torre de Esteban Hambrán (Toledo)
☎: +34 915 043 056
www.bodegashibeu.es
info@bodegashibeu.es

HIBEU 2011 T
syrah, cencibel

85 Colour: deep cherry, garnet rim. Nose: powerfull, ripe fruit, fruit preserve, sweet spices, warm. Palate: good structure, flavourful.

HIBEU 2012 RD
syrah, cencibel

84

SANTO DOMINGO DE GUZMÁN SOC. COOP.

Alameda del Fresno, 14
45940 Valmojado (Toledo)
☎: +34 918 170 904
www.santodomingodeguzman.es
info@santodomingodeguzman.es

VALDEJUANA GARNACHA 2012 T
garnacha

81

VALDEJUANA SYRAH 2012 T
syrah

86 Colour: deep cherry, purple rim. Nose: ripe fruit, violet drops, medium intensity. Palate: fruity, good finish.

UNVINOBENAYAS

Calle Vieja, 4
45542 El Casar de Escalona (Toledo)
☎: +34 655 907 640
www.unvinobenayas.es
unvinobenayas@gmail.com

CODICIOSO 2009 TC
syrah

83

VIÑEDOS DE CAMARENA, SDAD. COOPERATIVA DE CLM

Ctra. Toledo - Valmojado, km. 24,6
45180 Camarena (Toledo)
☎: +34 918 174 347 - Fax: +34 918 174 632
www.vdecamarena.com
vdecamarena@hotmail.com

BASTIÓN DE CAMARENA 2011 T ROBLE
cabernet sauvignon

83

BASTIÓN DE CAMARENA 2012 B

82

BASTIÓN DE CAMARENA 2012 RD

85 Colour: light cherry, bright. Nose: balanced, medium intensity, dried herbs, dried flowers. Palate: fruity, balanced.

BASTIÓN DE CAMARENA 2012 T

86 Colour: cherry, purple rim. Nose: medium intensity, red berry notes, ripe fruit, balanced. Palate: balanced, ripe fruit, good acidity.

VIÑEDOS Y BODEGAS GONZÁLEZ

45180 Camarena (Toledo)
☎: +34 918 174 063 - Fax: +34 918 174 063
www.vinobispo.com
bodegasgonzalez@yahoo.es

VIÑA BISPO 2008 TC
cabernet sauvignon, syrah

86 Colour: cherry, garnet rim. Nose: ripe fruit, spicy, toasty, cocoa bean. Palate: powerful, flavourful, toasty, round tannins.

VIÑA BISPO 2011 B
sauvignon blanc, verdejo, moscatel grano menudo

78

VIÑA BISPO 2011 RD
garnacha, cabernet sauvignon

80

VIÑA BISPO 2011 T
syrah

83

DO MONDÉJAR / D.O.P.

LOCATION:

In the southwest of the province of Guadalajara. It is made up of the municipal districts of Albalate de Zorita, Albares, Almoguera, Almonacid de Zorita, Driebes, Escariche, Escopete, Fuenteovilla, Illana, Loranca de Tajuña, Mazuecos, Mondéjar, Pastrana, Pioz, Pozo de Almoguera, Sacedón, Sayatón, Valdeconcha, Yebra and Zorita de los Canes.

CLIMATE:

Temperate Mediterranean. The average annual temperature is around 18°C and the average rainfall is 500 mm per year.

SOIL:

The south of the Denomination is characterized by red soil on lime-clayey sediments, and the north (the municipal districts of Anguix, Mondéjar, Sacedón, etc.) has brown limestone soil on lean sandstone and conglomerates.

GRAPE VARIETIES:

WHITE (40%): *Malvar* (majority 80% of white varieties), *Macabeo* and *Torrontés*.
RED (60%): *Cencibel* (*Tempranillo* – represents 95% of red varieties), *Cabernet Sauvignon* (5%) and *Syrah*.

FIGURES:

Vineyard surface: 3,000 – **Wine-Growers:** 300 – **Wineries:** 2 – **2012 Harvest rating:** N/A – **Production:** 421,130 litres – **Market percentages:** 100% domestic

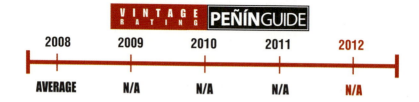

2008	2009	2010	2011	2012
AVERAGE	N/A	N/A	N/A	N/A

CONSEJO REGULADOR
Pza. Mayor, 15 - 19110 Mondéjar (Guadalajara) ☎: 949 385 284 - Fax: 949 385 284
crdom@crdomondejar.com   www.crdomondejar.com

DO MONTERREI / D.O.P.

LOCATION:

In the east of the province of Orense, on the border with Portugal. The vineyards occupy the valley of Monterrei, and it is made up of the municipal districts of Verín, Monterrei, Oimbra and Castrelo do Vall.

CLIMATE:

Midway between the Atlantic and Continental influences. Drier than in the rest of Galicia, with maximum temperatures of 35°C in summer and minimum of –5°C in winter.

SOIL:

The vineyards cover the slopes of the mountains and valleys irrigated by the Támega river and its tributaries. The soil is quite clayey, deep, rather heavy and, in some places, somewhat sandy.

GRAPE VARIETIES:

WHITE: *Dona Blanca, Verdello* (*Godello*) and *Treixadura* (*Verdello Louro*), *Albariño, Caiño Blanco, Loureira* and *Blanca de Monterrei*.
RED: *Aranxa (Tempranillo), Caiño Tinto, Mencía, Bastardo* (or *María Ardoña*) and *Sousón*.

SUB-REGIONS:

Val de Monterrei. Comprising the vineyards situated in the valley region (therefore, more level terrains) and covering the parishes and municipal districts belonging to the following city councils: Castrelo do Val (Castrelo do Val, Pepín and Nocedo); Monterrei (Albarellos, Infesta, Monterrei and Vilaza); Oimbra (Oimbra, Rabal, O Rosal and San Cibrao); Verín (Abedes, Cabreiroa, Feces da Baixo, Feces de Cima, Mandín, Mourazos, Pazos, Queizás, A Rasela, Tamagos, Tamaguelos, Tintores, Verín, Vilela and Vilamaior do Val).
Ladeira de Monterrei. These vineyards occupy the hills. The parishes and municipal districts that make up this sub-region are: Castrelo do Val (Gondulfes and Servoi), Oimbra (As Chas and A Granxa), Monterrey (Flariz, Medeiros, Mixós, Estevesiños and Vences) and Verín (Queirugas).

FIGURES:

Vineyard surface: 407 – **Wine-Growers:** 361 – **Wineries:** 24 – **2012 Harvest rating:** Very Good – **Production:** 1.857.600 – **Market percentages:** 88% domestic. 12% export

CONSEJO REGULADOR
Mercado Comarcal, 1 - 32600 Verín (Ourense) ☎: +34 988 410 634 - Fax: +34 988 410 634
info@domonterrei.com   www.domonterrei.com

ADEGA ABELEDOS

Avda. Portugal, 110 2ºA
32600 Verín (Ourense)
☎: +34 988 414 075 - Fax: +34 988 414 075
cristinabooparadela@hotmail.com

ABELEDO 2012 B
godello, treixadura

88 Colour: bright straw. Nose: fresh, fresh fruit, white flowers, varietal. Palate: flavourful, fruity, balanced.

ABELEDO 2012 T
mencía, tempranillo

87 Colour: cherry, purple rim. Nose: expressive, floral, overripe fruit, fresh. Palate: flavourful, fruity, good acidity, round tannins.

ADEGA VALDERELLO

Rua Máximo 1 Albarellos de Monterrey
32618 Monterrei (Ourense)
☎: +34 988 411 199
valderello@yahoo.es

VALDERELLO 2011 T
mencía

84

ADEGAS CHICHENO

Quintá de Arriba, s/n
32600 Queizas Verin (Ourense)
☎: +34 988 411 949
www.bodegaschicheno.com
bodegaschicheno@gmail.com

GALVÁN 2012 B
godello, treixadura

86 Colour: bright straw. Nose: fresh, white flowers, ripe fruit. Palate: flavourful, fruity, good acidity, balanced.

GALVÁN 2012 T
mencía

88 Colour: cherry, purple rim. Nose: expressive, fresh fruit, red berry notes, floral. Palate: flavourful, fruity, good acidity, round tannins.

ADEGAS TRIAY

Rua Ladairo, 36
32613 O'Rosal Oimbra (Ourense)
☎: +34 988 422 776 - Fax: +34 988 422 776
www.bodegastriay.com
triayadegas@gmail.com

TRIAY 2012 B
100% godello

87 Colour: pale. Nose: candied fruit, citrus fruit, medium intensity. Palate: easy to drink, spicy, ripe fruit.

BODEGA BOO-RIVERO

Touza, 22
32618 Villaza (Ourense)
☎: +34 988 425 950 - Fax: +34 988 425 950
bodegaboorivero@yahoo.es

FRAGAS DO LECER 2012 B

88 Colour: bright straw. Nose: fresh, fresh fruit, white flowers, varietal. Palate: flavourful, fruity, good acidity, balanced.

BODEGA GARGALO

Rua Do Castelo, 59
32619 Verín (Ourense)
☎: +34 988 590 203 - Fax: +34 988 590 295
www.gargalo.es
gargalo@verino.es

GARGALO ALBARIÑO & TREIXADURA 2012 B
treixadura, albariño

90 Colour: bright straw. Nose: fresh fruit, white flowers, balsamic herbs. Palate: flavourful, fruity, good acidity, balanced.

GARGALO GODELLO 2012 B
godello

91 Colour: bright straw. Nose: fresh, fresh fruit, white flowers, expressive, mineral, grassy. Palate: flavourful, fruity, good acidity, balanced.

TERRA DO GARGALO SOBRE LÍAS 2010 B
godello, treixadura

91 Colour: bright yellow. Nose: powerfull, ripe fruit, sweet spices. Palate: rich, flavourful, fresh, good acidity.

TERRA RUBIA GODELLO-TREIXADURA 2012 B
godello, treixadura

87 Colour: bright straw. Nose: medium intensity, ripe fruit, citrus fruit. Palate: flavourful, spicy, fine bitter notes.

BODEGA TABÚ

Plaza A Carreira, 6 O Rosal
32613 Oimbra (Ourense)
☎: +34 665 644 500
bodegatabu@gmail.com

STIBADÍA 2010 T BARRICA
mencía, tempranillo

90 Colour: bright cherry. Nose: ripe fruit, expressive. Palate: flavourful, fruity, toasty, round tannins.

STIBADÍA 2011 T BARRICA
mencía, tempranillo

88 Colour: cherry, garnet rim. Nose: ripe fruit, toasty, dark chocolate. Palate: toasty, ripe fruit, spicy.

STIBADÍA 2012 B
godello, treixadura

89 Colour: bright straw. Nose: fresh, fresh fruit, white flowers, expressive. Palate: flavourful, fruity, good acidity, balanced.

STIBADÍA 2012 T
mencía, tempranillo

89 Colour: cherry, purple rim. Nose: fresh fruit, red berry notes, floral, scrubland. Palate: flavourful, fruity, good acidity, round tannins.

BODEGAS ABANICO

Pol. Ind Ca l'Avellanet - Susany, 6
8553 Seva (Barcelona)
☎: +34 938 125 676 - Fax: +34 938 123 213
www.bodegasabanico.com
info@exportiberia.com

VIÑA TOEN 2012 B
50% godello, 50% treixadura

90 Colour: bright straw. Nose: fresh, fresh fruit, white flowers, grassy, balsamic herbs. Palate: flavourful, fruity, good acidity, balanced.

BODEGAS LADAIRO

Ctra. Ladairo, 42
32613 O'Rosal (Oimbra) (Ourense)
☎: +34 988 422 757 - Fax: +34 988 422 757
www.ladairo.com
info@bodegasladairo.com

LADAIRO 2011 BFB

90 Colour: bright yellow. Nose: powerfull, ripe fruit, sweet spices, creamy oak, fragrant herbs. Palate: rich, smoky aftertaste, flavourful, fresh, good acidity.

LADAIRO 2011 T

87 Colour: cherry, garnet rim. Nose: powerfull, overripe fruit, spicy. Palate: spicy, ripe fruit, toasty.

LADAIRO 2012 B
godello

89 Colour: bright straw. Nose: medium intensity, candied fruit, citrus fruit. Palate: good acidity, fine bitter notes.

BODEGAS MARTÍN CÓDAX MONTERREI

Ctra. Albarellos, 525
36618 Albarellos de Monterrei (Ourense)
☎: +34 986 526 040 - Fax: +34 986 526 901
www.almaatlantica.com
comercial@martincodax.com

MARA MARTIN GODELLO 2012 B
100% godello

88 Colour: bright straw. Nose: white flowers, fruit expression, ripe fruit. Palate: flavourful, fruity, good acidity, balanced.

BODEGAS Y VIÑEDOS QUINTA DA MURADELLA

Avda. Luis Espada, 99- Entresuelo, dcha.
32600 Verín (Ourense)
☎: +34 988 411 724 - Fax: +34 988 590 427
muradella@verin.net

ALANDA 2009 T BARRICA
mencía, bastardo negro, sousón

88 Colour: deep cherry. Nose: ripe fruit, scrubland, spicy. Palate: fruity, light-bodied, fine tannins, good acidity.

ALANDA 2011 B BARRICA
dona blanca, treixadura, godello

89 Colour: yellow. Nose: dry nuts, dried flowers, spicy, ripe fruit. Palate: balanced, good acidity, ripe fruit, fine bitter notes.

GORVIA 2009 T
100% mencía

92 Colour: deep cherry, garnet rim. Nose: ripe fruit, balsamic herbs, balanced, mineral. Palate: fruity, good acidity, balanced.

GORVIA FERMENTADO EN BARRICA 2010 BFB
100% dona blanca

92 Colour: bright yellow. Nose: powerfull, ripe fruit, sweet spices, creamy oak. Palate: rich, flavourful, fresh, good acidity.

MURADELLA 2010 B
treixadura, dona blanca

92 Colour: bright yellow. Nose: balanced, ripe fruit, faded flowers, spicy. Palate: full, fruity, long.

QUINTA DA MURADELLA BERRANDE 2009 T
100% mencía

94 Colour: deep cherry, garnet rim. Nose: red berry notes, ripe fruit, spicy, earthy notes, balsamic herbs. Palate: fruity, rich, full.

CREGO E MONAGUILLO S.L.

Rua Nova
32618 Salgueira (Ourense)
☎: +34 988 418 164 - Fax: +34 988 418 164
www.cregoemonaguillo.com
tito@cregoemonaguillo.com

CREGO E MONAGUILLO 2012 B
godello, treixadura

90 Colour: bright straw. Nose: fresh, fresh fruit, white flowers, grassy, characterful, varietal. Palate: flavourful, fruity, good acidity, balanced.

CREGO E MONAGUILLO 2012 T
mencía, arauxa

89 Colour: cherry, purple rim. Nose: expressive, red berry notes, floral, ripe fruit. Palate: flavourful, fruity, good acidity, round tannins.

FATHER 1943 2011 T
mencía, arauxa

90 Colour: black cherry. Nose: powerfull, overripe fruit, roasted coffee, dark chocolate. Palate: ripe fruit, pruney, toasty.

MANUEL GUERRA JUSTO

Ctra. Albarellos, 61
32618 Villaza (Monterrei) (Ourense)
☎: +34 687 409 618
viaarxentea@viaarxentea.com

VÍA ARXÉNTEA 2012 B
treixadura, godello

90 Colour: bright straw. Nose: fresh, fresh fruit, white flowers, mineral, complex. Palate: flavourful, fruity, good acidity, balanced.

PAZO DAS TAPIAS

Finca As Tapias - Pazos
32600 Verin (Ourense)
☎: +34 988 261 256 - Fax: +34 988 261 264
www.pazodastapias.com
info@pazodomar.com

ALMA DE BLANCO GODELLO 2012 B
100% godello

88 Colour: bright straw. Nose: fresh, fresh fruit, white flowers. Palate: flavourful, fruity, good acidity, balanced.

PAZO DE VALDECONDE

Mourazos
Verín (Ourense)
☎: +34 988 422 773 - Fax: +34 988 422 773
www.bodegapazodevaldeconde.com
info@bodegapazodevaldeconde.com

SOUTO DO REI 2012 B
godello, treixadura, albariño

87 Colour: straw. Nose: grassy, floral, candied fruit. Palate: flavourful, light-bodied, fruity.

PAZO DE VALDECONDE

Mourazos
Verín (Ourense)
☎: +34 988 422 773 - Fax: +34 988 422 773
www.bodegapazodevaldeconde.com
info@bodegapazodevaldeconde.com

SOUTO DO REI 2012 T

86 Colour: deep cherry. Nose: powerfull, warm, ripe fruit. Palate: powerful, concentrated.

PAZOS DEL REY

Carrero Blanco, 33- Albarellos
32618 Monterrei (Ourense)
☎: +34 988 425 959
www.pazosdelrey.com
info@pazosdelrey.com

PAZO DE MONTERREY 2012 B
100% godello

90 Colour: bright straw. Nose: fresh, fresh fruit, white flowers. Palate: flavourful, fruity, good acidity, balanced.

SILA GODELLO 2012 B
godello

87 Colour: bright straw. Nose: faded flowers, candied fruit, citrus fruit. Palate: fine bitter notes, correct, good acidity.

SILA MENCÍA 2011 T BARRICA
100% mencía

89 Colour: deep cherry. Nose: ripe fruit, balsamic herbs, overripe fruit. Palate: good acidity, correct, ripe fruit.

TERRAS DE CIGARRÓN

Ctra. de Albarellos, km. 525
32618 Albarellos de Monterrei (Ourense)
☎: +34 988 418 703
www.terrasdecigarron.com
bodega@terrasdecigarron.com

TERRAS DO CIGARRÓN 2012 B
100% godello

89 Colour: bright straw. Nose: fresh fruit, white flowers, ripe fruit, citrus fruit. Palate: flavourful, fruity, good acidity, balanced.

DO MONTILLA-MORILES / D.O.P.

CÓRDOBA

• Montilla

▽ Consejo Regulador
● DO Boundary

LOCATION:

To the south of Córdoba. It covers all the vineyards of the municipal districts of Montilla, Moriles, Montalbán, Puente Genil, Montruque, Nueva Carteya and Doña Mencía, and part of the municipal districts of Montemayor, Fernán-Núñez, La Rambla, Santaella, Aguilar de la Frontera, Lucena, Cabra, Baena, Castro del Río and Espejo.

CLIMATE:

Semi-continental Mediterranean, with long, hot, dry summers and short winters. The average annual temperature is 16.8°C and the average rainfall is between 500 mm and 1,000 mm per year.

SOIL:

The vineyards are situated at an altitude of between 125 m and 640 m. The soils are franc, franc-sandy and, in the higher regions, calcareous ('Albarizas'), which are precisely those of best quality, and which predominate in what is known as the Upper Sub-Region, which includes the municipal districts of Montilla, Moriles, Castro del Río, Cabra and Aguilar de la Frontera.

GRAPE VARIETIES:

WHITE: *Pedro Ximénez* (main variety), *Airén, Baladí, Moscatel, Torrontés* and *Verdejo*.
RED: *Tempranillo, Syrah* and *Cabernet Sauvignon*.

SUB-REGIONS:

We have to differentiate between the vineyards in the flatlands and those in higher areas —such as Sierra de Montilla and Moriles Alto–, prominently limestone soils of higher quality and hardly 2000 hectares planted.

FIGURES:

Vineyard surface: 5.333 – **Wine-Growers:** 2.277 – **Wineries:** 68 – **2012 Harvest rating:** N/A – **Production:** 27.682.783 litres – **Market percentages:** 92% domestic. 8% export

VINTAGE RATING PEÑÍNGUIDE

2008	2009	2010	2011	2012
VERY GOOD	VERY GOOD	GOOD	N/A	N/A

CONSEJO REGULADOR
Rita Pérez, s/n - 14550 Montilla (Córdoba) ☎: +34 957 652 110 - Fax: +34 957652 407
consejo@montillamoriles.es   www.montilla-moriles.org

ALVEAR

María Auxiliadora, 1
14550 Montilla (Córdoba)
☎: +34 957 650 100 - Fax: +34 957 650 135
www.alvear.es
alvearsa@alvear.es

ALVEAR DULCE VIEJO 2000 PX RESERVA
pedro ximénez

94 Colour: dark mahogany. Nose: expressive, dark chocolate, aromatic coffee, spicy, toasty. Palate: balanced, full. Personality.

ALVEAR FINO EN RAMA 2006 FI
100% pedro ximénez

90 Colour: bright yellow. Nose: elegant, balanced, dry nuts, fresh, saline, pungent. Palate: flavourful, balanced, fine bitter notes.

ALVEAR PX 1830 PX RESERVA
100% pedro ximénez

98 Colour: dark mahogany. Nose: elegant, dried fruit, cocoa bean, sweet spices, aromatic coffee. Palate: spirituous, creamy, long, elegant, round, fine solera notes.

ALVEAR PX 1927 PX
100% pedro ximénez

91 Colour: dark mahogany. Nose: complex, dried fruit, pattiserie, toasty, aromatic coffee. Palate: rich, unctuous, powerful, full, sweet.

ALVEAR PX DE AÑADA 2011 PX
100% pedro ximénez

92 Colour: light mahogany. Nose: balanced, varietal, creamy oak, toasty, spicy, dry nuts. Palate: good structure, flavourful, balanced.

ALVEAR SOLERA FUNDACIÓN AM
100% pedro ximénez

94 Colour: old gold. Nose: dry nuts, spicy, rancio notes, acetaldehyde, complex, sweet spices. Palate: balanced, round, fine bitter notes, long, fine solera notes.

ASUNCIÓN OL
100% pedro ximénez

91 Colour: old gold. Nose: sweet spices, candied fruit, varnish. Palate: flavourful, long, fine bitter notes, rich.

C.B. FI
100% pedro ximénez

90 Colour: bright yellow. Nose: balanced, expressive, pungent, dry nuts, complex, saline. Palate: full, fine bitter notes, long.

BODEGAS CRUZ CONDE

Ronda Canillo, 4
14550 Montilla (Córdoba)
☎: +34 957 651 250 - Fax: +34 957 653 619
www.bodegascruzconde.es
info@bodegascruzconde.es

CRUZ CONDE SOLERA FUNDACIÓN 1902 PX
100% pedro ximénez

92 Colour: dark mahogany. Nose: complex, dried fruit, aromatic coffee, fruit liqueur notes. Palate: sweet, unctuous, powerful, spirituous.

FINO CRUZ CONDE 1902 FI
100% pedro ximénez

85 Colour: bright yellow. Nose: dried flowers, medium intensity. Palate: flavourful, easy to drink, correct, fine bitter notes.

PEDRO XIMÉNEZ CRUZ CONDE 1902 PX
100% pedro ximénez

89 Colour: dark mahogany. Nose: dried fruit, honeyed notes, dark chocolate, sweet spices. Palate: concentrated, sweet, unctuous.

BODEGAS DELGADO

Cosano, 2
14500 Puente Genil (Córdoba)
☎: +34 957 600 085 - Fax: +34 957 604 571
www.bodegasdelgado.com
fino@bodegasdelgado.com

DELGADO 1874 AMONTILLADO NATURAL MUY VIEJO AM
pedro ximénez

93 Colour: old gold, amber rim. Nose: acetaldehyde, pungent, dried herbs, caramel, spicy, toasty. Palate: rich, powerful, flavourful, spicy, long, balanced, elegant.

DELGADO 1874 PX
pedro ximénez

92 Colour: dark mahogany. Nose: complex, fruit liqueur notes, dried fruit, pattiserie, toasty, damp earth. Palate: sweet, rich, unctuous, powerful.

DELGADO AM
pedro ximénez

91 Colour: iodine, amber rim. Nose: powerfull, complex, elegant, dry nuts, toasty, cocoa bean, dark chocolate, sweet spices. Palate: rich, fine bitter notes, fine solera notes, long, spicy.

["

BODEGAS NAVARRO S.A.

Avda. Antonio y Miguel Navarro, 1
14550 Montilla (Córdoba)
☎: +34 957 650 644 - Fax: +34 957 650 122
www.bodegasnavarro.com
export@bodegasnavarro.com

**FINO NATURAL NAVARRO
SOLERA FUNDACIÓN1830 FI**
100% pedro ximénez

86 Colour: bright straw. Nose: medium intensity, saline, balanced. Palate: flavourful, correct, fine bitter notes.

NAVARRO P.X. SOLERA FUNDACIÓN 1830 PX
100% pedro ximénez

90 Colour: dark mahogany. Nose: complex, fruit liqueur notes, dried fruit, pattiserie, toasty, aromatic coffee. Palate: sweet, rich, unctuous.

NAVARRO SOLERA FUNDACIÓN 1830 AM
100% pedro ximénez

87 Colour: old gold, amber rim. Nose: candied fruit, honeyed notes, acetaldehyde, sweet spices, dry nuts. Palate: correct, spicy, easy to drink.

BODEGAS SILLERO

Ctra. de La Redonda, s/n
14540 La Rambla (Córdoba)
☎: +34 957 684 464
www.bodegassillero.com
sillero@bodegassillero.com

ANACLETO FI
pedro ximénez

82

LAS CÁRMENES FI
pedro ximénez

85 Colour: bright yellow. Nose: saline, medium intensity, fresh. Palate: rich, powerful, fresh, fine bitter notes, long.

MORILES SILLERO FI
pedro ximénez

85 Colour: bright straw. Nose: faded flowers, dry nuts, rancio notes. Palate: flavourful, easy to drink, spicy.

SILLERO DULCE
pedro ximénez

84

SILLERO PX

86 Colour: mahogany. Nose: pattiserie, dried fruit, cocoa bean, caramel, powerfull. Palate: flavourful, varietal, unctuous, sweet.

VIEJO RONDALLA OL
pedro ximénez

86 Colour: light mahogany. Nose: medium intensity, balanced, ripe fruit, sweet spices. Palate: flavourful, fruity, balanced, fine bitter notes.

CARREFOUR

Campezo, 16
28022 Madrid (Madrid)
☎: +34 902 202 000
www.carrefour.es

DE NUESTRA TIERRA PX
pedro ximénez

92 Colour: dark mahogany. Nose: complex, fruit liqueur notes, dried fruit, pattiserie, toasty. Palate: sweet, rich, unctuous, powerful.

LA SULTANA CR

81

LA SULTANA FI

79

LA SULTANA MOSCATEL
moscatel

87 Colour: old gold. Nose: candied fruit, white flowers, citrus fruit. Palate: fruity, rich, full, correct.

LA SULTANA OL

83

LA SULTANA PX
pedro ximénez

88 Colour: light mahogany. Nose: dark chocolate, aromatic coffee, dried fruit. Palate: sweet, fine bitter notes.

CÍA. VINÍCOLA DEL SUR - TOMÁS GARCÍA

Avda. Luis de Góngora y Argote, s/n
14550 Montilla (Córdoba)
☎: +34 957 650 204 - Fax: +34 957 652 335
www.vinicoladelsur.com
info@vinicoladelsur.com

MONTE CRISTO AM
100% pedro ximénez

88 Colour: light mahogany. Nose: medium intensity, sweet spices, varnish, cocoa bean, acetaldehyde. Palate: spicy, long, fine bitter notes.

MONTE CRISTO FI
100% pedro ximénez

89 Colour: bright yellow. Nose: faded flowers, saline, dry nuts, fresh. Palate: flavourful, balanced, fine bitter notes, spicy.

MONTE CRISTO OL
100% pedro ximénez

92 Colour: light mahogany. Nose: acetaldehyde, candied fruit, sweet spices. Palate: flavourful, full, powerful, fine bitter notes, long.

MONTE CRISTO PX
100% pedro ximénez

87 Colour: dark mahogany. Nose: dried fruit, caramel, pattiserie, dark chocolate. Palate: sweet, flavourful, correct, concentrated.

PEDRO XIMÉNEZ VIEJO TOMÁS GARCÍA PX
100% pedro ximénez

89 Colour: dark mahogany. Nose: pattiserie, caramel, aromatic coffee, dried fruit. Palate: round, unctuous, sweet, elegant.

VERBENERA FI
pedro ximénez

88 Colour: bright yellow. Nose: medium intensity, faded flowers, saline. Palate: rich, correct, easy to drink, fine bitter notes.

CONDE DE LA CORTINA

María Auxiliadora, 1
14550 Montilla (Córdoba)
☎: +34 957 650 100 - Fax: +34 957 650 135
alvearsa@alvear.es

CONDE DE LA CORTINA FI
76

EQUIPO NAVAZOS

Cartuja, 1 - módulo 6
11401 Jerez de la Frontera (Cádiz)
www.equiponavazos.com
equipo@navazos.com

CASA DEL INCA 2011 PX
pedro ximénez

95 Colour: dark mahogany. Nose: fruit liqueur notes, dried fruit, pattiserie. Palate: sweet, rich, unctuous, powerful.

LA BOTA DE FINO (BOTA Nº 45) FI
pedro ximénez

93 Colour: bright yellow. Nose: candied fruit, citrus fruit, honeyed notes. Palate: ripe fruit, fine bitter notes, good acidity, long.

LA BOTA DE OLOROSO Nº46 OL
pedro ximénez

95 Colour: iodine, amber rim. Nose: powerfull, complex, elegant, dry nuts, toasty, characterful, candied fruit. Palate: rich, long, fine solera notes, spicy.

OVNI 2012 B
100% pedro ximénez

90 Colour: bright yellow. Nose: candied fruit, fruit preserve, complex, characterful. Palate: long, pruney, fine bitter notes, good acidity.

GRACIA HERMANOS

Avda. Marqués de la Vega de Armijo, 103
14550 Montilla (Córdoba)
☎: +34 957 650 162 - Fax: +34 957 652 335
www.bodegasgracia.com
info@bodegasgracia.com

FINO CORREDERA FI
100% pedro ximénez

86 Colour: bright yellow. Nose: medium intensity, dry nuts, saline. Palate: light-bodied, fresh, easy to drink, fine bitter notes.

GRACIA DULCE VIEJO PX
100% pedro ximénez

89 Colour: dark mahogany. Nose: balanced, expressive, varnish, sweet spices, cocoa bean. Palate: good structure, flavourful, sweet, spicy.

SOLERA FINA MARÍA DEL VALLE FI
100% pedro ximénez

88 Colour: bright yellow. Nose: balanced, fresh, pungent, dry nuts, saline. Palate: rich, flavourful, spicy, fine bitter notes.

SOLERA FINA TAUROMAQUIA FI
100% pedro ximénez

90 Colour: bright yellow. Nose: expressive, faded flowers, saline, dry nuts. Palate: full, flavourful, balanced, fine bitter notes, spicy.

TAUROMAQUIA AMONTILLADO VIEJO AM
100% pedro ximénez

90 Colour: light mahogany. Nose: toasty, sweet spices, acetaldehyde, dry nuts, expressive. Palate: flavourful, complex, long.

TAUROMAQUIA OL
100% pedro ximénez

88 Colour: old gold, amber rim. Nose: sweet spices, caramel, medium intensity, dry nuts. Palate: full, flavourful, good structure.

TAUROMAQUIA PX
100% pedro ximénez

91 Colour: dark mahogany. Nose: complex, fruit liqueur notes, dried fruit, pattiserie, varietal. Palate: sweet, rich, unctuous, powerful, full.

VIÑAVERDE 2012 B
pedro ximénez, torrontés, moscatel, verdejo, macabeo

85 Colour: bright straw. Nose: medium intensity, fresh, wild herbs, tropical fruit. Palate: fruity, correct, easy to drink.

NAVISA

Avda. José Padillo Delgado, s/n
14550 Montilla (Córdoba)
☎: +34 957 650 450 - Fax: +34 957 651 747
www.navisa.es
navisa@navisa.es

COBOS FI
pedro ximénez

85 Colour: bright straw. Nose: medium intensity, dried flowers, spicy, saline. Palate: correct, fine bitter notes.

DOS PASAS PX
pedro ximénez

87 Colour: mahogany. Nose: dried fruit, cocoa bean, caramel, pattiserie. Palate: good structure, flavourful, balanced.

MONTULIA OL
pedro ximénez

85 Colour: mahogany. Nose: fruit preserve, sweet spices, pattiserie. Palate: flavourful, long, spicy.

TRES PASAS PX
pedro ximénez

87 Colour: mahogany. Nose: dried fruit, toasty, dark chocolate, sweet spices. Palate: creamy, sweet, concentrated.

VEGA MARÍA 2012 B
chardonnay

81

PÉREZ BARQUERO S.A.

Avda. Andalucía, 27
14550 Montilla (Córdoba)
☎: +34 957 650 500 - Fax: +34 957 650 208
www.perezbarquero.com
info@perezbarquero.com

FINO LOS AMIGOS FI
100% pedro ximénez

87 Colour: bright yellow. Nose: complex, expressive, pungent, saline. Palate: rich, powerful, fresh, fine bitter notes.

GRAN BARQUERO AM
100% pedro ximénez

90 Colour: bright straw. Nose: candied fruit, sweet spices, pattiserie, acetaldehyde. Palate: spicy, long, balanced.

GRAN BARQUERO FI
100% pedro ximénez

90 Colour: bright yellow. Nose: balanced, pungent, saline, expressive, dry nuts, faded flowers. Palate: flavourful, spicy, long.

GRAN BARQUERO OL
100% pedro ximénez

90 Colour: old gold, amber rim. Nose: balanced, pattiserie, sweet spices, dry nuts. Palate: balanced, fine bitter notes.

GRAN BARQUERO PX
100% pedro ximénez

91 Colour: dark mahogany. Nose: fruit liqueur notes, dried fruit, pattiserie, toasty, dark chocolate. Palate: sweet, rich, unctuous, powerful.

LA CAÑADA PX
100% pedro ximénez

96 Colour: dark mahogany. Nose: complex, balanced, expressive, candied fruit, dried fruit, dark chocolate. Palate: good structure, complex, flavourful, spicy.

PÉREZ BARQUERO PEDRO XIMÉNEZ DE COSECHA PX
100% pedro ximénez

92 Colour: mahogany. Nose: dried fruit, pattiserie, caramel. Palate: flavourful, sweet, varietal, long.

VIÑA AMALIA 2012 B
pedro ximénez, moscatel, verdejo, torrontés

84

TORO ALBALÁ

Avda. Antonio Sánchez, 1
14920 Aguilar de la Frontera (Córdoba)
☎: +34 957 660 046 - Fax: +34 957 661 494
www.toroalbala.com
info@toroalbala.com

DON P.X. 1983 PX GRAN RESERVA
100% pedro ximénez

94 Colour: dark mahogany. Nose: expressive, complex, aromatic coffee, powerfull, fruit liqueur notes. Palate: full, varietal, unctuous, sweet, flavourful.

DON P.X. 2008 PX
100% pedro ximénez

90 Colour: mahogany. Nose: dried fruit, sweet spices, expressive, powerfull, pattiserie. Palate: flavourful, long, toasty, unctuous.

DO MONTSANT / D.O.P.

LOCATION:

In the region of Priorat (Tarragona). It is made up of Baix Priorat, part of Alt Priorat and various municipal districts of Ribera d'Ebre that were already integrated into the Falset sub-region. In total, 16 municipal districts: La Bisbal de Falset, Cabaces, Capçanes, Cornudella de Montsant, La Figuera, Els Guiamets, Marçá, Margalef, El Masroig, Pradell, La Torre de Fontaubella, Ulldemolins, Falset, El Molar, Darmós and La Serra d'Almos. The vineyards are located at widely variable altitudes, ranging between 200 m to 700 m above sea level.

CLIMATE:

Although the vineyards are located in a Mediterranean region, the mountains that surround the region isolate it from the sea to a certain extent, resulting in a somewhat more Continental climate. Due to this, it benefits from the contrasts in day/night temperatures, which is an important factor in the ripening of the grapes. However, it also receives the sea winds, laden with humidity, which help to compensate for the lack of rainfall in the summer. The average rainfall is between 500 and 600 mm per year.

SOIL:

There are mainly three types of soil: compact calcareous soils with pebbles on the borders of the DO; granite sands in Falset; and siliceous slate (the same stony slaty soil as Priorat) in certain areas of Falset and Cornudella.

GRAPE VARIETIES:

WHITE: *Chardonnay, Garnacha Blanca, Macabeo, Moscatel, Pansal, Parellada.*
RED: *Cabernet Sauvignon, Cariñena, Garnacha Tinta, Garnacha Peluda, Merlot, Monastrell, Picapoll, Syrah, Tempranillo* and *Mazuela.*

FIGURES:

Vineyard surface: 1.860 – **Wine-Growers:** 700 – **Wineries:** 61 – **2012 Harvest rating:** Good – **Production:** 4.800.000 litres – **Market percentages:** 51,2% domestic. 48,8% export

CONSEJO REGULADOR
Plaça de la Quartera, 6 - 43730 Falset (Tarragona) - ☎: +34 977 831 742 - Fax: +34 977 830 676
info@domontsant.com   ww.domontsant.com

ACUSTIC CELLER

Progrés s/n
43775 Marça (Tarragona)
☎: +34 672 432 691 - Fax: +34 977 660 867
www.acusticceller.com
acustic@acusticceller.com

ACÚSTIC 2010 T ROBLE
35% garnacha, 65% cariñena

92 Colour: bright cherry, garnet rim. Nose: balanced, ripe fruit, spicy, balsamic herbs, dry stone. Palate: full, good acidity.

ACÚSTIC 2011 BFB
60% garnacha, 10% garnacha roja, 25% macabeo, 5% pansal

89 Colour: bright yellow. Nose: powerfull, ripe fruit, sweet spices, fragrant herbs. Palate: rich, smoky aftertaste, flavourful, fresh, good acidity.

ACÚSTIC 2011 T ROBLE
65% cariñena, 35% garnacha

89 Nose: ripe fruit, sweet spices, creamy oak, expressive. Palate: flavourful, fruity, toasty, round tannins.

ACÚSTIC ROSAT 2012 RD
40% garnacha, 40% cariñena, 20% garnacha roja

87 Colour: rose, bright. Nose: medium intensity, ripe fruit, wild herbs. Palate: fruity, easy to drink, correct.

AUDITORI 2010 T
100% garnacha

93 Colour: very deep cherry. Nose: fruit preserve, sweet spices, balsamic herbs, complex, mineral, toasty. Palate: balanced, round tannins.

AUDITORI 2011 T
100% garnacha

92 Colour: cherry, garnet rim. Nose: expressive, ripe fruit, mineral, wild herbs. Palate: flavourful, round tannins, long, fruity aftestaste.

BRAÓ 2011 T
55% cariñena, 45% garnacha

93 Colour: cherry, garnet rim. Nose: ripe fruit, cocoa bean, balanced, sweet spices. Palate: good structure, full, round tannins, fruity.

AGRÍCOLA D'ULLDEMOLINS SANT JAUME

Avda. Verge de Montserrat, s/n
43363 Ulldemolins (Tarragona)
☎: +34 977 561 613 - Fax: +34 977 561 613
www.coopulldemolins.com
coopulldemolins@ono.com

LES PEDRENYERES 2009 T
garnacha

88 Colour: deep cherry, garnet rim. Nose: spicy, ripe fruit, old leather, balsamic herbs. Palate: good structure, spicy.

LES PEDRENYERES 2012 B
garnacha, macabeo

88 Colour: bright straw. Nose: medium intensity, balanced, ripe fruit, spicy, dried flowers. Palate: correct, good acidity.

ULLDEMOLINS 2012 T
garnacha

86 Colour: very deep cherry. Nose: powerfull, toasty, creamy oak. Palate: powerful, ripe fruit, spicy.

AGRÍCOLA I SC DE LA SERRA D'ALMOS

Avinguda de la Cooperativa, s/n
43746 La Serra D'Almos (Tarragona)
☎: +34 977 418 125 - Fax: +34 977 418 399
www.serradalmos.com
coopserra@telefonica.net

MUSSEFRES 2009 TC
cariñena, garnacha, cabernet sauvignon, ull de llebre

89 Colour: cherry, garnet rim. Nose: ripe fruit, spicy, creamy oak, balsamic herbs, dry stone. Palate: powerful, flavourful, toasty.

MUSSEFRES 2012 B
macabeo, garnacha blanca

79

MUSSEFRES NEGRE 2012 T
cariñena, garnacha, syrah

83

MUSSEFRES ROSAT 2012 RD
garnacha

84

ALFREDO ARRIBAS (D.O. MONTSANT)

Sort dels Capellans, 23
43730 Falset (Tarragona)
☎: +34 932 531 760 - Fax: +34 934 173 591
www.portaldelpriorat.com
info@portaldelpriorat.com

TROSSOS SANTS 2012 B
garnacha blanca, garnacha gris

92 Colour: bright straw. Nose: floral, fruit expression, fragrant herbs, mineral. Palate: rich, powerful, flavourful, spicy.

TROSSOS TROS BLANC 2011 B
garnacha blanca

92 Colour: bright yellow. Nose: elegant, ripe fruit, floral, balsamic herbs, sweet spices, creamy oak, dry stone. Palate: rich, flavourful, fruity, balanced, spicy, elegant.

TROSSOS TROS BLANC MAGNUM 2010 B
garnacha blanca

94 Colour: bright golden. Nose: powerfull, expressive, spicy, ripe fruit, mineral, wild herbs, creamy oak. Palate: long, rich, powerful, flavourful, balanced, good structure.

TROSSOS TROS NEGRE 2010 T
garnacha

94 Colour: cherry, garnet rim. Nose: spicy, creamy oak, toasty, complex, warm, candied fruit. Palate: powerful, flavourful, toasty, round tannins.

TROSSOS TROS NEGRE MAGNUM 2009 T
garnacha

93 Colour: cherry, garnet rim. Nose: mineral, balsamic herbs, complex, spicy. Palate: balanced, fruity, full, round tannins, good acidity.

TROSSOS VELLS 2011 T
cariñena

92 Colour: cherry, garnet rim. Nose: scrubland, spicy, expressive. Palate: balanced, spicy, ripe fruit, round tannins.

ANGUERA DOMENECH

Sant Pere, 2
43743 Darmós (Tarragona)
☎: +34 977 405 857
www.vianguera.com
angueradomenech@gmail.com

RECLOT 2012 T
tempranillo, garnacha, monastrell

86 Colour: deep cherry, garnet rim. Nose: powerfull, ripe fruit, fruit preserve, dried herbs. Palate: good structure, flavourful.

ROSAT ANGUERA DOMENECH 2012 RD
monastrell, garnacha

83

VINYA GASÓ 2011 TC
cariñena, garnacha, tempranillo

88 Colour: very deep cherry. Nose: powerfull, ripe fruit, sweet spices, dark chocolate. Palate: powerful, flavourful, fine bitter notes.

BODEGAS ORDÓÑEZ

Bartolomé Esteban Murillo, 11
29700 Vélez- Málaga (Málaga)
☎: +34 952 504 706 - Fax: +34 951 284 796
www.grupojorgeordonez.com
info@jorgeordoncz.es

ZERRÁN 2011 T
ferrol, mazuelo, syrah

92 Colour: bright cherry. Nose: ripe fruit, sweet spices, expressive. Palate: flavourful, fruity, toasty, round tannins, spicy.

CASTELL D'OR

Mare Rafols, 3- 1º 4º
8720 Vilafranca del Penedès (Barcelona)
☎: +34 938 905 446 - Fax: +34 938 905 446
www.castelldor.com
castelldor@castelldor.com

TEMPLER 2006 TR
40% cabernet sauvignon, 30% garnacha, 30% tempranillo

84

TEMPLER 2009 TC
50% garnacha, 50% tempranillo

85 Colour: deep cherry. Nose: fruit liqueur notes, spicy. Palate: powerful, fine bitter notes, warm.

CELLER CEDÓ ANGUERA

Ctra. La Serra d'Almos-Darmós, Km. 0,2
43746 La Serra d'Almos (Tarragona)
☎: +34 699 694 728 - Fax: +34 977 417 369
www.cedoanguera.com
celler@cedoanguera.com

ANEXE 2012 T
40% samsó, 40% garnacha, 20% syrah

85 Colour: cherry, garnet rim. Nose: mineral, balsamic herbs, ripe fruit. Palate: powerful, flavourful, good structure.

ANEXE VINYES VELLES DE SAMSO 2012 T
100% samsó

86 Colour: cherry, purple rim. Nose: overripe fruit, dry stone, balsamic herbs, powerfull. Palate: rich, full, powerful, flavourful.

CLÒNIC 2009 TC
60% samsó, 20% syrah, 20% cabernet sauvignon

89 Colour: cherry, garnet rim. Nose: spicy, creamy oak, fruit preserve. Palate: powerful, flavourful, toasty.

CLÒNIC VINYES VELLES DE SAMSO 2012 T
100% samsó

87 Colour: cherry, purple rim. Nose: ripe fruit, spicy, creamy oak, balanced. Palate: powerful, flavourful, spicy, long.

CELLER DE CAPÇANES

Llebaria, 4
43776 Capçanes (Tarragona)
☎: +34 977 178 319 - Fax: +34 977 178 319
www.cellercapcanes.com
cellercapcanes@cellercapcanes.com

2 PÁJAROS 2011 T
100% cariñena

93 Colour: very deep cherry. Nose: toasty, dark chocolate, overripe fruit, mineral, creamy oak. Palate: powerful, good structure, ripe fruit, round tannins.

CABRIDA 2011 T
100% garnacha

88 Colour: deep cherry. Nose: toasty, candied fruit, new oak. Palate: fine bitter notes, good acidity, spicy, fine tannins.

CABRIDA CALISSA 2010 T
100% garnacha

93 Colour: cherry, garnet rim. Nose: ripe fruit, creamy oak, toasty, complex, earthy notes. Palate: powerful, flavourful, toasty, round tannins.

COSTERS DEL GRAVET 2011 TC
50% cabernet sauvignon, 25% garnacha, 25% cariñena

91 Colour: bright cherry. Nose: ripe fruit, sweet spices, creamy oak, mineral. Palate: flavourful, fruity, toasty, round tannins.

LASENDAL GARNATXA 2012 T BARRICA
85% garnacha, 15% syrah

89 Colour: deep cherry, purple rim. Nose: balanced, medium intensity, ripe fruit, sweet spices. Palate: long, ripe fruit, round tannins.

MAS COLLET 2012 T BARRICA
35% garnacha, 25% cariñena, 25% tempranillo, 15% cabernet sauvignon

87 Colour: deep cherry, garnet rim. Nose: powerfull, dried herbs, ripe fruit, fruit preserve. Palate: full, fruity, rich.

MAS DONÍS 2012 T
80% garnacha, 20% syrah

86 Colour: cherry, purple rim. Nose: balanced, ripe fruit, wild herbs. Palate: flavourful, fruity, easy to drink.

MAS PICOSA 2012 T
40% garnacha, 40% cariñena, 10% merlot, 10% tempranillo

87 Colour: deep cherry, purple rim. Nose: medium intensity, ripe fruit, closed. Palate: good structure, round tannins.

MAS TORTÓ 2011 T
70% garnacha, 10% cabernet sauvignon, 10% merlot, 10% syrah

91 Colour: cherry, garnet rim. Nose: ripe fruit, spicy, creamy oak, toasty, complex. Palate: powerful, flavourful, toasty, round tannins.

PANSAL DEL CALÀS 2010 T
70% garnacha, 30% cariñena

88 Colour: garnet rim, purple rim. Nose: medium intensity, ripe fruit, fruit preserve. Palate: fruity, flavourful, balanced, good acidity.

PERAJ HA'ABIB FLOR DE PRIMAVERA 2011 T
40% cabernet sauvignon, 40% garnacha, 20% cariñena

93 Colour: bright cherry. Nose: ripe fruit, sweet spices, creamy oak, earthy notes, toasty. Palate: flavourful, fruity, toasty, round tannins.

VALL DEL CALÀS 2011 T
50% merlot, 35% garnacha, 15% macabeo

90 Colour: very deep cherry. Nose: spicy, ripe fruit, toasty, sweet spices. Palate: powerful, good acidity, fine bitter notes.

CELLER DE CORNUDELLA

Comte de Rius, 2
43360 Cornudella de Montsant (Tarragona)
☎: +34 977 821 329 - Fax: +34 977 821 329
www.cornudella.net
info@cornudella.net

CASTELL DE SIURANA GARNATXA DEL MONTSANT 2011
garnacha roja

89 Colour: ruby red. Nose: ripe fruit, candied fruit, balsamic herbs, spicy, balanced. Palate: rich, powerful, flavourful.

CASTELL DE SIURANA SELECCIÓ DE COSTERS 2010 T
70% garnacha, 30% cariñena

90 Colour: cherry, garnet rim. Nose: ripe fruit, wild herbs, earthy notes, spicy. Palate: powerful, flavourful, ripe fruit.

CASTELLA DE SIURANA MISTELA 2011 VINO DE LICOR
100% garnacha

88 Colour: cherry, garnet rim. Nose: ripe fruit, fruit preserve, balsamic herbs, sweet spices, creamy oak. Palate: powerful, flavourful, spicy.

EL CODOLAR 2010 T
50% garnacha, 50% cariñena

91 Colour: bright cherry. Nose: sweet spices, creamy oak, mineral, expressive, red berry notes, ripe fruit. Palate: flavourful, fruity, toasty, round tannins.

LES TROIES 2012 B
macabeo, garnacha roja

86 Colour: bright straw. Nose: ripe fruit, fragrant herbs, spicy, dry stone. Palate: powerful, flavourful, spicy.

LES TROIES 2012 RD
50% garnacha, 50% cariñena

87 Colour: light cherry. Nose: ripe fruit, balsamic herbs, fragrant herbs. Palate: powerful, flavourful, fruity.

LES TROIES 2012 T
50% garnacha, 50% cariñena

87 Colour: very deep cherry. Nose: earthy notes, over-ripe fruit. Palate: flavourful, powerful, fine bitter notes, good acidity.

CELLER DE L'ERA

Finca Mas de les Moreres
43360 Cornudella de Montsant (Tarragona)
☎: +34 977 262 031
www.cellerdelera.com
jordi.torella@cellerdelera.com

BRI CELLER DE L'ERA 2010 T
garnacha, samsó, cabernet sauvignon

91 Colour: cherry, garnet rim. Nose: ripe fruit, spicy, creamy oak, toasty, complex, earthy notes, mineral. Palate: powerful, flavourful, toasty, spicy, long.

CELLER DOSTERRAS

Ctra. Falset a Marça, Km. 2
43775 Marça (Tarragona)
☎: +34 678 730 596
www.dosterras.com
jgrau@dosterras.com

DOSTERRAS 2011 T
100% garnacha

92 Colour: cherry, garnet rim. Nose: ripe fruit, balsamic herbs, earthy notes, mineral, spicy, toasty. Palate: powerful, flavourful, spicy, long.

VESPRES 2011 T
80% garnacha, 20% samsó

91 Colour: cherry, garnet rim. Nose: ripe fruit, spicy, creamy oak, toasty. Palate: powerful, flavourful, toasty.

CELLER EL MASROIG

Passeig de L'Arbre, 3
43736 El Masroig (Tarragona)
☎: +34 977 825 026
www.cellermasroig.com
celler@cellermasroig.com

CASTELL DE LES PINYERES 2010 T
40% cariñena, 40% garnacha, 20% cabernet sauvignon, syrah

91 Colour: bright cherry. Nose: ripe fruit, creamy oak. Palate: flavourful, fruity, toasty, round tannins.

LES SORTS 2011 BFB
100% garnacha blanca

89 Colour: bright yellow. Nose: creamy oak, sweet spices, ripe fruit, white flowers. Palate: flavourful, ripe fruit, toasty.

LES SORTS 2012 T MACERACIÓN CARBÓNICA
cariñena, garnacha, syrah

87 Colour: cherry, purple rim. Nose: red berry notes, ripe fruit, powerfull, violet drops. Palate: fruity, flavourful, long.

LES SORTS ROSAT 2012 RD
90% garnacha, 10% cariñena

89 Colour: rose, purple rim. Nose: powerfull, ripe fruit, red berry notes, floral, expressive. Palate: powerful, fruity, fresh.

LES SORTS SYCAR 2010 T
70% cariñena, 30% syrah

93 Colour: cherry, garnet rim. Nose: powerfull, ripe fruit, fruit expression, sweet spices, creamy oak. Palate: powerful, concentrated, fruity.

LES SORTS VINYES VELLES 2008 TC
60% cariñena, 30% garnacha, 10% cabernet sauvignon

90 Colour: cherry, garnet rim. Nose: ripe fruit, spicy, creamy oak, toasty, earthy notes. Palate: powerful, flavourful, toasty, round tannins.

SOLA FRED 2012 B
75% macabeo, 25% garnacha blanca

85 Colour: bright straw. Nose: ripe fruit, citrus fruit, mineral. Palate: flavourful, fruity, fresh.

SOLÀ FRED 2012 T
90% cariñena, 10% garnacha

86 Colour: bright cherry, purple rim. Nose: violet drops, ripe fruit, warm. Palate: correct, round tannins.

SOLA FRED ROSAT 2012 RD
90% garnacha, 10% syrah

86 Colour: rose, purple rim. Nose: expressive, red berry notes. Palate: flavourful, fruity, fresh.

CELLER ELS GUIAMETS

Avinguda Ctra., 23
43777 Els Guiamets (Tarragona)
☎: +34 977 413 018
www.cellerelsguiamets.com
eguasch@cellerelsguiamets.com

FILS DE VELLUT 2010 TC

92 Colour: bright cherry. Nose: ripe fruit, sweet spices, creamy oak, violet drops. Palate: flavourful, fruity, toasty, round tannins.

FILS DE VELLUT 2012 T
garnacha, cariñena, syrah, tempranillo, merlot

88 Colour: cherry, purple rim. Nose: floral, fruit expression. Palate: flavourful, fruity, good acidity, round tannins.

GRAN METS 2007 TC
cabernet sauvignon, merlot, garnacha, cariñena

88 Colour: very deep cherry, garnet rim. Nose: expressive, wild herbs, spicy, dried fruit. Palate: rich, flavourful.

GRAN METS 2008 TC
cabernet sauvignon, merlot, garnacha, cariñena

88 Colour: dark-red cherry, orangey edge. Nose: ripe fruit, fruit liqueur notes, earthy notes, wild herbs, creamy oak. Palate: powerful, flavourful, spicy, long.

ISIS 2006 T
syrah, garnacha, cariñena, cabernet sauvignon

87 Colour: cherry, garnet rim. Nose: powerfull, fruit preserve. Palate: spicy, flavourful, round tannins.

MAS DELS METS 2012 T
garnacha, cariñena, syrah, tempranillo

87 Colour: deep cherry. Nose: powerfull, ripe fruit, red berry notes. Palate: flavourful, ripe fruit, long.

CELLER LAURONA S.A.

Ctra. Bellmunt, s/n
43730 Falset (Tarragona)
☎: +34 977 830 221 - Fax: +34 977 831 797
www.cellerlaurona.com
laurona@cellerlaurona.com

BLANC DE LAURONA 2012 B
90% garnacha, 10% macabeo

87 Colour: pale. Nose: white flowers, ripe fruit, mineral. Palate: powerful, fresh, flavourful.

LAURONA 2008 T
garnacha, cariñena, merlot, syrah

92 Colour: very deep cherry. Nose: expressive, ripe fruit, sweet spices. Palate: powerful, flavourful, fine bitter notes.

LAURONA PLINI 2009 T
garnacha, cariñena, syrah

93 Colour: cherry, garnet rim. Nose: ripe fruit, spicy, creamy oak, toasty, characterful. Palate: powerful, flavourful, toasty, round tannins.

CELLER LOS TROVADORES

Avda. de las Encinas, 25
28707 San Sebastián de los Reyes (Madrid)
☎: +34 679 459 074
www.lostrovadores.com
cgomez@lostrovadores.com

GALLICANT 2005 T
60% garnacha, 30% mazuelo, 10% syrah

88 Colour: cherry, garnet rim. Nose: elegant, spicy, fine reductive notes, wet leather, aged wood nuances. Palate: spicy, fine tannins, elegant, long.

KARMA DE DRAC 2010 T
50% garnacha, 50% mazuelo

89 Colour: cherry, garnet rim. Nose: ripe fruit, spicy, creamy oak, toasty, scrubland, dry stone. Palate: powerful, flavourful, toasty, round tannins.

CELLER MALONDRO

Miranda, 27
43360 Cornudella del Montsant (Tarragona)
☎: +34 636 595 736 - Fax: +34 977 821 451
www.malondro.es
jcestivill@malondro.es

LATRIA 2011 T
50% garnacha, 30% cariñena, 20% syrah

87 Colour: cherry, garnet rim. Nose: sweet spices, creamy oak, fruit preserve. Palate: flavourful, fruity, toasty.

MALONDRO 2011 T
50% garnacha, 50% cariñena

91 Colour: cherry, garnet rim. Nose: red berry notes, ripe fruit, balsamic herbs, mineral, sweet spices, creamy oak. Palate: powerful, flavourful, toasty, long.

CELLER RONADELLES

Finca La Plana, s/n
43360 Cornudella del Montsant (Tarragona)
☎: +34 977 821 104 - Fax: +34 977 274 913
www.ronadelles.com
eva.prim@ronadelles.com

CAP DE RUC BLANC 2012 B
garnacha blanca, macabeo

84

CAP DE RUC GARNACHA 2010 TC
garnacha, cariñena

87 Colour: cherry, garnet rim. Nose: ripe fruit, fruit liqueur notes, balsamic herbs, creamy oak, toasty. Palate: powerful, flavourful, spicy, rich.

CAP DE RUC GARNACHA 2012 T
garnacha

87 Colour: cherry, purple rim. Nose: ripe fruit, creamy oak, mineral. Palate: flavourful, fruity, toasty.

GIRAL VINYES VELLES 2006 TC
garnacha, cariñena

87 Colour: pale ruby, brick rim edge. Nose: spicy, fine reductive notes, wet leather, aged wood nuances, fruit liqueur notes. Palate: spicy, long, spirituous.

PETIT BLANC 2011 B
garnacha blanca, macabeo

87 Colour: bright straw. Nose: medium intensity, citrus fruit, fragrant herbs. Palate: flavourful, correct, good acidity.

PETIT CHARDONNAY 2012 B
chardonnay

86 Colour: yellow. Nose: powerfull, ripe fruit, faded flowers, citrus fruit. Palate: flavourful, fruity.

CELLER SERRA MAJOR

Alfons El Cast, s/n
43363 Ulldemolins (Tarragona)
☎: +34 647 986 960
santi@sarroges.com

TEIX 2009 T
garnacha, cabernet sauvignon, syrah
78

TEIX 2010 T
garnacha, cabernet sauvignon, syrah

89 Colour: cherry, garnet rim. Nose: ripe fruit, spicy, toasty. Palate: powerful, flavourful, toasty, round tannins.

CELLER VENDRELL RIVED

Bassa, 10
43775 Marçà (Tarragona)
☎: +34 637 537 383
www.vendrellrived.com
celler@vendrellrived.com

L'ALLEU 2009 T
garnacha

88 Colour: ruby red, brick rim edge. Nose: fruit liqueur notes, balsamic herbs, dry stone, spicy, creamy oak. Palate: flavourful, complex, spicy.

L'ALLEU 2011 T
garnacha, cariñena

89 Colour: cherry, garnet rim. Nose: ripe fruit, balsamic herbs, spicy, creamy oak, mineral. Palate: powerful, flavourful, complex, long.

SERÈ 2011 T
garnacha, cariñena

87 Colour: bright cherry. Nose: ripe fruit, sweet spices, creamy oak, dry stone. Palate: flavourful, fruity, toasty, round tannins.

CELLER VERMUNVER

Dalt, 29
43775 Marçà (Tarragona)
☎: +34 977 178 288 - Fax: +34 977 178 288
www.genesi.cat
info@genesi.cat

GÈNESI SELECCIÓ 2008 T
garnacha, cariñena

90 Colour: cherry, garnet rim. Nose: ripe fruit, spicy, creamy oak, toasty, complex. Palate: powerful, flavourful, toasty, round tannins.

GÈNESI VARIETAL 2010 T
100% samsó

92 Colour: cherry, garnet rim. Nose: ripe fruit, spicy, creamy oak, earthy notes. Palate: powerful, flavourful, toasty.

VINUM DOMI 2011 T
garnacha, carignan, merlot

88 Colour: bright cherry, purple rim. Nose: powerfull, fruit expression, violet drops. Palate: flavourful, fruity, round tannins.

CELLERS BARONÍA DEL MONTSANT S.L.

Comte de Rius, 1
43360 Cornudella de Montsant (Tarragona)
☎: +34 977 821 483 - Fax: +34 977 821 483
www.baronia-m.com
englora@baronia-m.com

B CLOS D'ENGLORA 2011 B
100% garnacha blanca

87 Colour: bright straw. Nose: powerfull, varietal, faded flowers. Palate: flavourful, ripe fruit, powerful.

CIMS DEL MONTSANT 2011 T
72% garnacha, 28% cariñena

90 Colour: deep cherry. Nose: powerfull, warm, ripe fruit, overripe fruit, earthy notes. Palate: powerful, sweetness, good structure.

CLOS D'ENGLORA AV 14 2009 T
64% garnacha, 10% garnacha peluda, 26% cariñena

91 Colour: bright cherry. Nose: ripe fruit, creamy oak, characterful. Palate: flavourful, fruity, toasty, round tannins.

CÒDOLS DEL MONTSANT 2012 T
100% garnacha

89 Colour: cherry, purple rim. Nose: ripe fruit, mineral, dry stone, balsamic herbs. Palate: flavourful, balanced, easy to drink.

ENGLORA 2010 TC
10% garnacha, 16% cariñena, 31% syrah, 20% merlot

92 Colour: bright cherry. Nose: ripe fruit, sweet spices, creamy oak, expressive, mineral, fragrant herbs. Palate: flavourful, fruity, toasty, round tannins.

FLOR D'ENGLORA GARNATXA 2012 T
100% garnacha

87 Colour: cherry, purple rim. Nose: expressive, fresh fruit, red berry notes, floral, mineral. Palate: flavourful, fruity, good acidity, round tannins.

FLOR D'ENGLORA ROURE 2011 T
72% garnacha, 28% cariñena

88 Colour: very deep cherry. Nose: powerfull, warm, ripe fruit, overripe fruit. Palate: powerful, flavourful, good acidity.

CELLERS CAN BLAU

Ctra. Bellmunt, s/n
43730 Falset (Tarragona)
☎: +34 629 261 379 - Fax: +34 968 716 051
www.orowines.com
info@orowines.com

BLAU 2011 T
50% cariñena, 25% syrah, 25% garnacha

90 Colour: cherry, purple rim. Nose: sweet spices, ripe fruit, balanced, dried herbs. Palate: rich, long, round tannins.

CAN BLAU 2011 T
40% mazuelo, 40% syrah, 20% garnacha

92 Colour: very deep cherry, garnet rim. Nose: powerfull, ripe fruit, cocoa bean. Palate: flavourful, full, powerful, ripe fruit.

MAS DE CAN BLAU 2009 T
40% mazuelo, 40% syrah, 20% garnacha

94 Colour: deep cherry, garnet rim. Nose: closed, creamy oak, cocoa bean, sweet spices. Palate: good structure, complex, full, good acidity, long, balsamic.

MAS DE CAN BLAU 2010 T
40% mazuelo, 40% syrah, 20% garnacha

93 Colour: cherry, garnet rim. Nose: spicy, creamy oak, toasty, roasted coffee, overripe fruit. Palate: powerful, flavourful, toasty, round tannins.

CELLERS SANT RAFEL

Ctra. La Torre, Km. 1,7
43774 Pradell de la Teixeta (Tarragona)
☎: +34 689 792 305 - Fax: +34 977 323 078
www.solpost.com
info@solpost.com

JOANA 2010 T
80% garnacha, 10% merlot, 10% cabernet sauvignon

90 Colour: cherry, garnet rim. Nose: powerfull, balanced, ripe fruit, spicy, scrubland. Palate: good structure, good acidity, fine bitter notes.

SOLPOST 2009 T
50% garnacha, 35% cariñena, 15% cabernet sauvignon

90 Colour: deep cherry, garnet rim. Nose: balanced, balsamic herbs, ripe fruit, cocoa bean. Palate: flavourful, fruity, round tannins.

SOLPOST BLANC 2011 B
100% garnacha blanca

91 Colour: bright yellow. Nose: expressive, balanced, faded flowers, fragrant herbs. Palate: flavourful, long, spicy, good acidity.

SOLPOST FRESC 2010 TC
80% garnacha, 10% merlot, 10% cabernet sauvignon

91 Colour: cherry, garnet rim. Nose: ripe fruit, wild herbs, spicy, mineral. Palate: balanced, full, round tannins.

CELLERS TERRA I VINS

43206 Reus (Tarragona)
☎: +34 633 289 267
jmra70@gmail.com

CLOS DEL GOS 2012 T
70% garnacha, 20% samsó, 10% syrah

86 Colour: deep cherry, purple rim. Nose: ripe fruit, wild herbs. Palate: spicy, round tannins, flavourful.

CELLERS UNIÓ

Joan Oliver, 16-24
43206 Reus (Tarragona)
☎: +34 977 330 055 - Fax: +34 977 330 070
www.cellersunio.com
info@cellersunio.com

DAIRO 2011 TC
40% garnacha, 40% mazuelo, 20% syrah

90 Colour: cherry, garnet rim. Nose: ripe fruit, spicy, toasty, complex. Palate: powerful, flavourful, toasty, round tannins.

PERLAT 2011 T
40% garnacha, 40% mazuelo, 20% syrah

87 Colour: very deep cherry. Nose: powerfull, ripe fruit, toasty, spicy. Palate: powerful, sweetness.

PERLAT GARNATXA 2009 T
100% garnacha

88 Colour: cherry, garnet rim. Nose: ripe fruit, fruit preserve, wild herbs, sweet spices. Palate: powerful, flavourful, balsamic, long.

PERLAT SELECCIÓ 2010 T
40% garnacha, 50% mazuelo, 10% syrah

89 Colour: cherry, garnet rim. Nose: ripe fruit, creamy oak, toasty, sweet spices, balsamic herbs, mineral. Palate: powerful, flavourful, toasty.

PERLAT SYRAH 2010 T
100% syrah

87 Colour: cherry, garnet rim. Nose: creamy oak, toasty, violet drops. Palate: powerful, flavourful, toasty.

CHARMIAN

Avda. Baix Penedès 77-81, 1º 1ª esc. A
43700 El Vendrell (Tarragona)
☎: +34 977 661 862 - Fax: +34 977 661 862
www.cataloniacava.net
j.murillo@cataloniacava.net

CHARMIAN 2012 T
garnacha, samsó, syrah, merlot, tempranillo

85 Colour: deep cherry, garnet rim. Nose: floral, violet drops, warm, fruit liqueur notes. Palate: flavourful, good structure.

CHARMIAN GARNATXA BLANCA 2012 B
100% garnacha blanca

88 Colour: bright straw. Nose: fresh, fresh fruit, dried herbs, dried flowers. Palate: flavourful, fruity, good acidity, balanced.

CHARMIAN GRENACHE OLD VINES 2007 T
85% garnacha, 15% cabernet sauvignon

90 Colour: cherry, garnet rim. Nose: ripe fruit, spicy, toasty, complex, dried herbs, earthy notes. Palate: flavourful, toasty, round tannins.

CHARMIAN NEGRE 2010 TC
garnacha, mazuelo, syrah

89 Colour: deep cherry. Nose: powerfull, warm, ripe fruit, aromatic coffee. Palate: powerful, spirituous, spicy, ripe fruit.

CINGLES BLAUS

Mas de les Moreres - Afueras de Cornudella
43360 Cornudella de Montsant (Tarragona)
☎: +34 977 326 080 - Fax: +34 977 323 928
www.cinglesblaus.com
info@cinglesblaus.com

CINGLES BLAUS MAS DE LES MORERES 2009 T
50% garnacha, 20% cariñena, 20% cabernet sauvignon, 10% merlot

90 Colour: bright cherry. Nose: ripe fruit, sweet spices, creamy oak, expressive. Palate: flavourful, fruity, toasty, round tannins.

CINGLES BLAUS OCTUBRE 2010 T
60% garnacha, 40% cariñena

90 Colour: cherry, garnet rim. Nose: ripe fruit, fruit preserve, wild herbs. Palate: fruity, toasty, spicy.

CINGLES BLAUS OCTUBRE 2011 B
60% macabeo, 40% garnacha blanca

88 Colour: bright straw. Nose: fresh, fresh fruit, white flowers. Palate: flavourful, fruity, good acidity, balanced.

SINGLES BLAUS OCTUBRE 2012 RD
60% garnacha, 40% cariñena

85 Colour: rose, bright. Nose: red berry notes, citrus fruit, medium intensity. Palate: easy to drink, correct.

CLOS MESORAH

Finca "Clos Mesorah" Ctra. T-300 Falset Marça, Km. 1
43775 Marça Priorat (Tarragona)
☎: +34 935 343 026 - Fax: +34 936 750 316
www.elviwines.com
moises@elviwines.com

CLOS MESORAH 2010 TR
40% cariñena, 30% garnacha, syrah

89 Colour: cherry, garnet rim. Nose: ripe fruit, spicy, wild herbs. Palate: powerful, flavourful, toasty, round tannins.

COCA I FITÓ

Avda. 11 de Setembre s/n
43736 El Masroig (Tarragona)
☎: +34 619 776 948 - Fax: +34 935 457 092
www.cocaifito.com
info@cocaifito.cat

COCA I FITÓ NEGRE 2009 T
50% syrah, 30% garnacha, 20% cariñena

93 Colour: cherry, garnet rim. Nose: ripe fruit, spicy, creamy oak, toasty, complex, earthy notes, warm. Palate: powerful, flavourful, toasty, round tannins.

COCA I FITÓ ROSA 2012 RD
100% syrah

87 Colour: rose. Nose: ripe fruit, wild herbs, spicy. Palate: flavourful, powerful, ripe fruit.

JASPI MARAGDA 2010 T
55% garnacha, 25% cariñena, 20% syrah

90 Colour: very deep cherry, garnet rim. Nose: wild herbs, spicy, ripe fruit. Palate: good structure, flavourful, good acidity.

JASPI NEGRE 2011 T
45% garnacha, 25% cariñena, 15% cabernet sauvignon, 15% syrah

86 Colour: bright cherry. Nose: ripe fruit, sweet spices. Palate: flavourful, fruity, toasty, round tannins.

COOPERATIVA FALSET - MARÇA

Miquel Barceló, 31
43730 Falset (Tarragona)
☎: +34 977 830 105
www.la-cooperativa.cat

AFINUS 2012 T
garnacha, samsó

86 Colour: cherry, purple rim. Nose: medium intensity, red berry notes, ripe fruit. Palate: flavourful, balanced, round tannins.

AFINUS BLANC SELECCIÓ 2012 B
garnacha

85 Colour: bright yellow. Nose: ripe fruit, spicy, dried herbs, floral. Palate: powerful, flavourful.

AFINUS SELECCIÓ 2009 T
garnacha

90 Colour: cherry, garnet rim. Nose: ripe fruit, balsamic herbs, spicy, creamy oak, earthy notes. Palate: powerful, flavourful, spicy, long.

AFINUS SELECCIÓ 2010 T
garnacha, samsó, syrah

89 Colour: cherry, garnet rim. Nose: ripe fruit, spicy, creamy oak, toasty, complex. Palate: powerful, flavourful, toasty, round tannins.

CASTELL DE FALSET 2006 TGR
garnacha, samsó, cabernet sauvignon

88 Colour: cherry, garnet rim. Nose: powerfull, characterful, ripe fruit, dark chocolate. Palate: sweetness, flavourful, powerful.

CASTELL DE FALSET 2009 BFB
garnacha blanca

92 Colour: bright yellow. Nose: powerfull, ripe fruit, sweet spices, fragrant herbs. Palate: rich, flavourful, fresh, good acidity.

ÈTIM 2012 B
garnacha blanca

88 Colour: bright straw. Nose: fresh, fresh fruit, expressive, wild herbs. Palate: flavourful, fruity, good acidity, balanced.

ÈTIM L'ESPARVER 2006 T
garnacha, syrah, cabernet sauvignon

89 Colour: bright cherry. Nose: ripe fruit, creamy oak, warm. Palate: flavourful, fruity, toasty, round tannins.

ÈTIM NEGRE 2010 T
garnacha, samsó, syrah

88 Colour: very deep cherry. Nose: dark chocolate, over-ripe fruit, characterful. Palate: powerful, good structure, good acidity.

ÈTIM NEGRE 2010 T
garnacha, samsó, syrah

88 Colour: cherry, garnet rim. Nose: ripe fruit, scrubland, spicy, creamy oak, earthy notes. Palate: powerful, flavourful, spicy, long.

ÈTIM OLD VINES GRENACHE 2008 TR
garnacha

89 Colour: pale ruby, brick rim edge. Nose: ripe fruit, spicy, balsamic herbs, dry stone, expressive. Palate: spicy, long, powerful, flavourful, complex.

ÈTIM RANCI AM
garnacha, samsó

92 Colour: iodine, amber rim. Nose: powerfull, complex, elegant, dry nuts, toasty. Palate: rich, fine bitter notes, fine solera notes, long, spicy.

ÈTIM SYRAH 2006 T
syrah

90 Colour: cherry, garnet rim. Nose: ripe fruit, spicy, creamy oak, toasty, complex. Palate: powerful, flavourful, toasty, round tannins.

ÈTIM VEREMA TARDANA BLANC 2011 B
garnacha

90 Colour: golden. Nose: powerfull, floral, honeyed notes, candied fruit, fragrant herbs. Palate: flavourful, sweet, fresh, fruity, good acidity, long.

ÈTIM VEREMA TARDANA NEGRE 2010 T
garnacha

91 Colour: very deep cherry. Nose: powerfull, character-ful, fruit liqueur notes, fruit liqueur notes. Palate: flavourful, powerful, sweet, good acidity.

IMUS SELECCIÓ DE VINYES 2012 T
garnacha, samsó

86 Colour: very deep cherry. Nose: characterful, candied fruit, warm. Palate: powerful, warm.

DIT CELLER

Avda. Setembre, s/n Baixos
43736 El Masroig (Tarragona)
☎: +34 619 777 419
www.ditceller.com
tonicoca@gmail.com

CABIROL 2011 T
garnacha, tempranillo

88 Colour: very deep cherry, purple rim. Nose: ripe fruit, violet drops, medium intensity, balsamic herbs. Palate: fla-vourful, balanced, round tannins.

SELENITA 2010 T
garnacha, syrah, cabernet sauvignon

87 Colour: very deep cherry, garnet rim. Nose: powerfull, ripe fruit, fruit preserve, sweet spices. Palate: rich, flavourful.

SELENITA 2012 RD
60% syrah, 40% garnacha

88 Colour: light cherry. Nose: medium intensity, red berry notes. Palate: flavourful, fruity, fresh.

SELENITA TERRER 2009 T
garnacha, cariñena

92 Colour: very deep cherry. Nose: earthy notes, ripe fruit, dark chocolate. Palate: powerful, flavourful, spicy.

EDICIONES I-LIMITADAS

Claravall, 2
8022 (Barcelona)
☎: +34 932 531 760 - Fax: +34 934 173 591
www.edicionesi-limitadas.com
info@edicionesi-limitadas.com

FAUNUS 2011 T
tempranillo, syrah, merlot, cariñena

90 Colour: bright cherry. Nose: sweet spices, creamy oak, expressive, overripe fruit. Palate: flavourful, fruity, toasty, round tannins.

LUNO 2011 T
garnacha, cariñena, syrah, cabernet sauvignon

93 Colour: very deep cherry. Nose: powerfull, fruit expres-sion, ripe fruit, spicy. Palate: powerful, fruity, ripe fruit, long.

NÚVOL 2012 B
garnacha blanca, macabeo

91 Colour: bright straw. Nose: white flowers, fragrant herbs, mineral, candied fruit. Palate: powerful, flavourful, balsamic.

ESTONES

Pl. Sort dels Capellans, Nau Bahaus
43730 Falset (Tarragona)
☎: +34 666 415 735
www.massersal.com
vins@massersal.com

ESTONES 2010 T
garnacha, samsó

88 Colour: cherry, garnet rim. Nose: ripe fruit, spicy, creamy oak, toasty, earthy notes. Palate: powerful, flavourful, toasty, spicy, long.

ESTONES DE MISHIMA "SET TOTA LA VIDA" 2011 T
garnacha, samsó

88 Colour: deep cherry, garnet rim. Nose: closed, ripe fruit, dried herbs. Palate: flavourful, round tannins, balanced.

FRANCK MASSARD

Rambla Arnau de Vilanova, 6 entlo. 4a
8880 Vilanova i La Geltrú (Barcelona)
☎. +34 938 956 541
www.epicure-wines.com
info@epicure-wines.com

EL BRINDIS 2010 T
cariñena, garnacha

90 Colour: very deep cherry. Nose: fruit preserve, overripe fruit. Palate: powerful, sweetness.

FINCA EL ROMERO 2011 TC
cariñena

87 Colour: very deep cherry. Nose: roasted coffee, aromatic coffee, overripe fruit. Palate: powerful, sweetness, spirituous.

I TANT VINS

Passeig del Ferrocarril, 337 Baixos
8860 Castelldefels (Barcelona)
☎: +34 936 628 253 - Fax: +34 934 517 628
www.aribau.es
albert@aribau.es

I TANT GARNATXA NEGRA 2012 T
100% garnacha

86 Colour: cherry, purple rim. Nose: ripe fruit, balsamic herbs, mineral, earthy notes, spicy. Palate: powerful, flavourful, slightly dry, soft tannins.

MAS D'EN CANONGE

Pol. Ind. 7, Parc. 27
43775 Marçà (Tarragona)
☎: +34 977 054 071 - Fax: +34 977 054 071
www.masdencanonge.com
info@masdencanonge.com

SOLEIES D'EN CANONGE 2012 B
garnacha blanca

88 Colour: bright straw. Nose: fresh, fresh fruit, white flowers, varietal. Palate: flavourful, fruity, good acidity, balanced.

SONS D'EN CANONGE 2012 T
garnacha, cariñena, syrah

86 Colour: cherry, purple rim. Nose: dried herbs, warm, ripe fruit. Palate: flavourful, fruity, long.

SORRES 2012 RD
garnacha, syrah, cariñena

82

MAS DE L'ABUNDÀNCIA VITICULTORS

Camí de Gratallops, s/n
43736 El Masroig (Tarragona)
☎: +34 627 471 444
www.masdelabundancia.com
info@masdelabundancia.com

DE CALPINO 2012 B
garnacha blanca

87 Colour: bright straw. Nose: candied fruit, citrus fruit, faded flowers. Palate: flavourful, spicy.

FLVMINIS 2011 T
50% cabernet sauvignon, 40% garnacha, 10% cariñena

84

MAS DE L'ABUNDÀNCIA 2007 T
50% cabernet sauvignon, 20% garnacha, 30% cariñena

91 Colour: cherry, garnet rim. Nose: balsamic herbs, balanced, spicy, earthy notes. Palate: fruity, good structure, good acidity, long, round tannins.

MAS PERINET

Finca Mas Perinet, s/n
43660 Cornudella de Montsant (Tarragona)
☎: +34 977 827 113 - Fax: +34 977 827 180
www.masperinet.com
info@masperinet.com

GOTIA 2006 T
36% garnacha, 33% merlot, 22% cabernet sauvignon, 9% syrah

93 Colour: pale ruby, brick rim edge. Nose: ripe fruit, balsamic herbs, spicy, earthy notes, creamy oak, expressive. Palate: powerful, flavourful, spicy, long.

NOGUERALS

Tou, 5
43360 Cornudella de Montsant (Tarragona)
☎: +34 650 033 546
www.noguerals.com
noguerals@hotmail.com

CORBATERA 2009 T
garnacha, cabernet sauvignon

88 Colour: deep cherry, garnet rim. Nose: toasty, balsamic herbs, ripe fruit, spicy, premature reduction notes. Palate: fruity, flavourful, fine bitter notes.

ORTO VINS

Afores s/n
43736 El Molar (Tarragona)
☎: +34 629 171 246
www.ortovins.com
info@ortovins.com

DOLÇ D'ORTO 2011 B
80% garnacha blanca, 20% macabeo

93 Colour: golden. Nose: powerfull, floral, honeyed notes, candied fruit, fragrant herbs. Palate: flavourful, sweet, fresh, fruity, good acidity, long.

DOLÇ D'ORTO NEGRE DULCE NATURAL 2011 T
garnacha

88 Colour: very deep cherry. Nose: fruit liqueur notes, dark chocolate, spicy. Palate: powerful, sweet, concentrated.

LA CARRERADA 2011 T
samsó

95 Colour: cherry, garnet rim. Nose: wild herbs, balsamic herbs, spicy, creamy oak, floral, earthy notes, dry stone. Palate: elegant, balanced, spicy, balsamic, long.

LES COMES D'ORTO 2011 T
50% garnacha, 45% samsó, 5% ull de llebre

88 Colour: cherry, garnet rim. Nose: ripe fruit, balsamic herbs, earthy notes, creamy oak, balanced. Palate: powerful, flavourful, complex, long.

LES PUJOLES 2011 TC
ull de llebre

93 Colour: cherry, garnet rim. Nose: ripe fruit, spicy, creamy oak, toasty, mineral. Palate: powerful, flavourful, toasty, round tannins, balanced.

LES TALLADES DE CAL NICOLAU 2011 TC
picapoll negro

92 Colour: cherry, garnet rim. Nose: spicy, wild herbs, ripe fruit, earthy notes, balsamic herbs. Palate: powerful, flavourful, balanced, elegant.

ORTO 2011 T
60% samsó, 30% garnacha, 6% ull de llebre, 4% cabernet sauvignon

87 Colour: cherry, garnet rim. Nose: ripe fruit, dry stone, spicy, creamy oak. Palate: powerful, flavourful, spicy, long.

PALELL 2011 TC
garnacha peluda

90 Colour: ruby red. Nose: ripe fruit, spicy, creamy oak, toasty, balsamic herbs, dry stone. Palate: powerful, flavourful, toasty.

PORTAL DEL MONTSANT

Carrer de Dalt, s/n
43775 Marçà (Tarragona)
☎: +34 933 950 811 - Fax: +34 933 955 500
www.portaldelmontsant.com
info@portaldelmontsant.es

BRUBERRY 2011 T
cariñena, garnacha, syrah

89 Colour: deep cherry, garnet rim. Nose: balanced, ripe fruit, wild herbs. Palate: good structure, flavourful, fruity.

BRUBERRY 2012 B
garnacha blanca, garnacha gris

88 Colour: bright straw. Nose: medium intensity, wild herbs, citrus fruit. Palate: flavourful, balanced, fine bitter notes.

BRUNUS 2010 T
cariñena, garnacha

91 Colour: cherry, garnet rim. Nose: ripe fruit, spicy, creamy oak, toasty, complex. Palate: powerful, flavourful, toasty, round tannins.

BRUNUS ROSÉ 2012 RD
garnacha

88 Colour: rose, bright. Nose: balanced, red berry notes, ripe fruit, floral, citrus fruit. Palate: correct, good acidity, ripe fruit.

SANTBRU 2009 T
cariñena, garnacha, syrah

93 Colour: cherry, garnet rim. Nose: spicy, complex, elegant, ripe fruit, creamy oak. Palate: powerful, flavourful, toasty, round tannins.

SANTBRU BLANC 2011 B
garnacha blanca, garnacha gris

89 Colour: bright straw. Nose: medium intensity, citrus fruit, balsamic herbs, dried flowers, spicy. Palate: balanced, good acidity, fine bitter notes.

SERRA & BARCELÓ S.L.

Sant Lluis, 12
43777 Els Guiamets (Tarragona)
☎: +34 649 670 430
josep@serra-barcelo.com

OCTONIA 2009 T
50% garnacha, 35% garnacha peluda, 15% mazuelo

91 Colour: cherry, garnet rim. Nose: ripe fruit, spicy, creamy oak, toasty, complex. Palate: powerful, flavourful, toasty, round tannins, balanced.

SOMSI

Apartado 96
43730 Falset (Tarragona)
☎: +34 662 214 291
www.somsis.es
info@somsis.es

SOMSIS 2010 TC
60% carignan, 30% garnacha, 5% cabernet sauvignon, 5% syrah

88 Colour: bright cherry. Nose: ripe fruit, sweet spices, creamy oak, cocoa bean, dark chocolate, mineral. Palate: flavourful, fruity, toasty.

SPECTACLE VINS

Camí Manyetes, s/n
43737 Gratallops (Tarragona)
☎: +34 977 839 171 - Fax: +34 977 839 426
www.espectaclevins.com
closmogador@closmogador.com

ESPECTACLE 2010 T
100% garnacha

96 Colour: bright cherry. Nose: ripe fruit, fruit expression, balsamic herbs, scrubland, spicy. Palate: flavourful, ripe fruit, spicy.

TERRA PERSONAS

Apartado 96
43730 Falset (Tarragona)
☎: +34 662 214 291
www.terrapersonas.festis.cat
ruud@terrapersonas.com

TERRA NEGRA 2010 T
60% carignan, 30% garnacha, 5% cabernet sauvignon, 5% syrah

88 Colour: cherry, garnet rim. Nose: ripe fruit, spicy, creamy oak, toasty, complex, mineral. Palate: powerful, flavourful, toasty, round tannins, balanced.

TERRA VERMELLA 2012 T
50% cariñena, 40% garnacha, 10% syrah

86 Colour: cherry, purple rim. Nose: ripe fruit, balsamic herbs, earthy notes, powerfull. Palate: warm, flavourful, powerful.

VENUS LA UNIVERSAL

Ctra. Porrera, s/n
43730 Falset (Tarragona)
☎: +34 699 435 154 - Fax: +34 977 262 348
www.venuslauniversal.com
info@venuslauniversal.com

DIDO 2011 T
garnacha, syrah, merlot, cabernet sauvignon

93 Colour: cherry, garnet rim. Nose: ripe fruit, spicy, creamy oak, toasty, characterful, mineral, balsamic herbs. Palate: powerful, flavourful, round tannins.

DIDO 2012 B
macabeo, garnacha blanca, cartujano

90 Colour: bright straw. Nose: powerfull, mineral, fruit preserve. Palate: flavourful, sweetness, powerful.

VENUS 2008 T
cariñena, syrah, garnacha

94 Colour: cherry, garnet rim. Nose: ripe fruit, balsamic herbs, sweet spices, creamy oak, dry stone. Palate: powerful, flavourful, spicy, long, round tannins, balanced, elegant.

VINATERRERS DEL COLL DE MORA

Pol. Ind. Sort dels Capellans Nau, 14
43730 Falset (Tarragona)
☎: +34 692 114 451
www.vinaterrers.com
info@vinaterrers.com

LLUNARA 2010 T
garnacha, cariñena, syrah, cabernet sauvignon

91 Colour: black cherry, garnet rim. Nose: closed, balsamic herbs, sweet spices, mineral. Palate: powerful, flavourful, good structure, round tannins.

VINYES DOMÈNECH

Camí del Collet, km. 3,8
43776 Capçanes (Tarragona)
☎: +34 670 297 395
www.vinyesdomenech.com
jidomenech@vinyesdomenech.com

BANCAL DEL BOSC 2011 T
60% garnacha, 15% samsó, 15% syrah, 10% cabernet sauvignon

88 Colour: very deep cherry. Nose: overripe fruit, warm, spicy. Palate: flavourful, spicy, ripe fruit.

FURVUS 2010 T
80% garnacha, 20% merlot

92 Colour: bright cherry. Nose: ripe fruit, sweet spices, creamy oak, expressive. Palate: flavourful, fruity, round tannins.

RITA 2012 B
garnacha blanca

90 Colour: bright straw. Nose: balanced, medium intensity, floral, fruit expression. Palate: flavourful, fruity, good acidity.

TEIXAR 2010 T
garnacha peluda

93 Colour: cherry, garnet rim. Nose: spicy, creamy oak, toasty, earthy notes, mineral, characterful. Palate: powerful, flavourful, toasty, round tannins.

TEIXAR MAGNUM 2009 T
garnacha peluda

94 Colour: dark-red cherry, garnet rim. Nose: wild herbs, creamy oak, sweet spices, mineral. Palate: flavourful, fruity, round tannins.

VIÑAS DEL MONTSANT

Partida Coll de Mora , s/n
43775 Marça (Tarragona)
☎: +34 977 831 309 - Fax: +34 977 831 356
www.morlanda.com
mariajose.bajon@morlanda.com

FRA GUERAU 2009 TC
merlot, garnacha, syrah

88 Colour: very deep cherry. Nose: sweet spices, ripe fruit, creamy oak. Palate: flavourful, powerful.

GARBÓ 2011 T
garnacha, syrah, cabernet sauvignon, merlot

86 Colour: cherry, garnet rim. Nose: powerfull, ripe fruit, warm. Palate: flavourful, powerful.

GARBÓ 2012 RD
70% garnacha, 30% syrah

86 Colour: light cherry. Nose: powerfull, ripe fruit, red berry notes, dried herbs. Palate: powerful, fruity, fresh.

Consejo Regulador
DO Boundary

PAMPLONA

Olite

LOCATION:

In the province of Navarra. It draws together areas of different climates and soils, which produce wines with diverse characteristics.

CLIMATE:

Typical of dry, sub-humid regions in the northern fringe, with average rainfall of between 593 mm and 683 mm per year. The climate in the central region is transitional and changes to drier conditions in southern regions, where the average annual rainfall is a mere 448 mm.

SOIL:

The diversity of the different regions is also reflected in the soil. Reddish or yellowish and stony in the Baja Montaña, brownish-grey limestone and limestone in Valdizarbe and Tierra Estella, limestone and alluvium marl in the Ribera Alta, and brown and grey semi-desert soil, brownish-grey limestone and alluvium in the Ribera Baja.

GRAPE VARIETIES:

WHITE: *Chardonnay* (2%), *Garnacha Blanca, Malvasía, Moscatel de Grano Menudo, Viura* (6% of total) and *Sauvignon Blanc.*
RED: *Cabernet Sauvignon* (9%), *Garnacha Tinta* (majority 42% of total), *Graciano, Mazuelo, Merlot, Tempranillo* (29%), *Syrah* and *Pinot Noir.*

SUB-REGIONS:

Baja Montaña. Situated northeast of Navarra, it comprises 22 municipal districts with around 2,500 Ha under cultivation.
Tierra Estella. In western central Navarra, it stretches along the Camino de Santiago. It has 1,800 Ha of vineyards in 38 municipal districts.
Valdizarbe. In central Navarra. It is the key centre of the Camino de Santiago. It comprises 25 municipal districts and has 1,100 Ha of vineyards.
Ribera Alta. In the area around Olite, it takes in part of central Navarra and the start of the southern region. There are 26 municipal districts and 3,300 Ha of vineyards.
Ribera Baja. In the south of the province, it is the most important in terms of size (4,600 Ha). It comprises 14 municipal districts.

FIGURES:

Vineyard surface: 11,700 – **Wine-Growers:** 2,716 – **Wineries:** 113 – **2012 Harvest rating:** Very Good – **Production:** --- litres – **Market percentages:** 68% domestic. 32% export

VINTAGE RATING PEÑÍNGUIDE

2008	2009	2010	2011	2012
VERY GOOD	GOOD	VERY GOOD	VERY GOOD	VERY GOOD

CONSEJO REGULADOR
Rúa Romana, s/n - 31390 Olite (Navarra) ☎: +34 948 741 812 - Fax: +34 948 741 776
consejoregulador@vinonavarra.com info@navarrawine.com www.navarrawine.com

AROA BODEGAS

Apalaz, 13
31292 Gorozin-Zurukoain (Navarra)
☎: +34 948 921 867
www.aroawines.com
info@aroawines.com

AROA GARNATXAS 2011 T
100% garnacha

88 Colour: bright cherry. Nose: ripe fruit, sweet spices, creamy oak. Palate: flavourful, fruity, toasty, round tannins.

AROA GORENA 2008 TR
70% cabernet sauvignon, 30% merlot

89 Colour: cherry, garnet rim. Nose: balsamic herbs, wild herbs, spicy. Palate: flavourful, ripe fruit, round tannins.

AROA JAUNA 2008 TC
41% cabernet sauvignon, 39% merlot

88 Colour: cherry, garnet rim. Nose: ripe fruit, spicy, creamy oak, damp earth. Palate: powerful, flavourful, toasty.

AROA LAIA 2012 B
100% garnacha blanca

86 Colour: bright straw. Nose: fresh, fresh fruit, white flowers, expressive. Palate: flavourful, fruity, good acidity, balanced.

AROA LARROSA 2012 RD
60% garnacha, 40% tempranillo

88 Colour: rose, purple rim. Nose: powerfull, ripe fruit, floral, expressive. Palate: powerful, fruity, fresh.

ASENSIO VIÑEDOS Y BODEGAS

Ctra. Los Arcos, s/n
31293 Sesma (Navarra)
☎: +34 948 698 078 - Fax: +34 948 698 097
www.bodegasasensio.com
info@bodegasasensio.com

JAVIER ASENSIO 2006 TR
90% merlot, 10% cabernet sauvignon

87 Colour: bright cherry, garnet rim. Nose: wild herbs, scrubland, fruit preserve. Palate: flavourful, fine tannins.

JAVIER ASENSIO 2009 TC
66% syrah, 44% merlot

88 Colour: cherry, garnet rim. Nose: ripe fruit, spicy, creamy oak, toasty. Palate: powerful, flavourful, toasty.

JAVIER ASENSIO 2012 B
55% chardonnay, 45% sauvignon blanc

86 Colour: bright straw. Nose: fresh, white flowers, lactic notes, ripe fruit, dried herbs. Palate: flavourful, fruity, good acidity.

AZUL Y GARANZA BODEGAS

San Juan, 19
31310 Carcastillo (Navarra)
☎: +34 636 406 939 - Fax: +34 948 725 677
www.azulygaranza.com
info@azulygaranza.com

ABRIL DE AZUL Y GARANZA 2012 T
95% tempranillo, 5% cabernet sauvignon

89 Colour: cherry, purple rim. Nose: expressive, fresh fruit, red berry notes, floral. Palate: flavourful, fruity, good acidity, round tannins, fruity aftestaste.

DESIERTO DE AZUL Y GARANZA 2009 T
100% cabernet sauvignon

91 Colour: cherry, garnet rim. Nose: elegant, complex, dried herbs, ripe fruit. Palate: fruity, flavourful, round tannins, balanced.

ROSA DE AZUL Y GARANZA 2012 RD
70% garnacha, 30% tempranillo

88 Colour: light cherry, bright. Nose: medium intensity, red berry notes. Palate: flavourful, fruity, long, good acidity, fine bitter notes.

SEIS DE AZUL Y GARANZA 2010 T
90% merlot, 10% cabernet sauvignon

88 Colour: cherry, garnet rim. Nose: balanced, fruit preserve, sweet spices. Palate: flavourful, fruity, round tannins.

VIURA DE AZUL Y GARANZA 2012 B
100% viura

88 Colour: bright straw. Nose: ripe fruit, candied fruit, floral, fragrant herbs. Palate: powerful, flavourful, fresh, fruity.

BLACKBOARD WINES

Conrado Albaladejo, 31 BW 61
3540 (Alicante)
☎: +34 686 097 742
www.blackboardwines.com
sales@blackboardwines.com

THE TAPAS WINE COLLECTION 2012 RD
garnacha

85 Colour: rose, purple rim. Nose: powerfull, ripe fruit, red berry notes, floral, expressive. Palate: powerful, fruity, fresh.

BODEGA DE SADA

Arrabal, 2
31491 Sada (Navarra)
☎: +34 948 877 013 - Fax: +34 948 877 433
www.bodegadesada.com
bodega@bodegadesada.com

PALACIO DE SADA 2010 TC

88 Colour: cherry, garnet rim. Nose: ripe fruit, spicy, creamy oak, toasty. Palate: powerful, flavourful, toasty.

PALACIO DE SADA 2012 RD
garnacha

87 Colour: raspberry rose. Nose: floral, candied fruit, balsamic herbs. Palate: easy to drink, fresh, fruity, light-bodied.

PALACIO DE SADA GARNACHA 2012 T
garnacha

87 Colour: light cherry. Nose: red berry notes, ripe fruit, floral, balsamic herbs. Palate: fresh, fruity, flavourful.

BODEGA DE SARRÍA

Finca Señorío de Sarría, s/n
31100 Puente La Reina (Navarra)
☎: +34 948 202 200 - Fax: +34 948 202 202
www.bodegadesarria.com
info@taninia.com

SEÑORÍO DE SARRÍA 2004 TGR
merlot, cabernet sauvignon

90 Colour: pale ruby, brick rim edge. Nose: fruit liqueur notes, balsamic herbs, aged wood nuances, cigar, waxy notes. Palate: powerful, flavourful, spicy, long, balanced.

SEÑORÍO DE SARRÍA 2005 TR
merlot, cabernet sauvignon

88 Colour: cherry, garnet rim. Nose: ripe fruit, spicy, creamy oak, toasty, fine reductive notes. Palate: powerful, flavourful, toasty.

SEÑORÍO DE SARRÍA 2010 TC
cabernet sauvignon, tempranillo

85 Colour: bright cherry, garnet rim. Nose: ripe fruit, spicy, wild herbs. Palate: fruity, flavourful, round tannins.

SEÑORÍO DE SARRÍA 2012 RD
garnacha

87 Colour: rose, bright. Nose: balanced, red berry notes, rose petals. Palate: flavourful, fruity, easy to drink.

SEÑORÍO DE SARRÍA CHARDONNAY 2012 B
chardonnay

86 Colour: bright straw. Nose: ripe fruit, dried flowers, fragrant herbs. Palate: fresh, fruity, powerful.

SEÑORÍO DE SARRÍA MOSCATEL 2011 BLANCO DULCE
moscatel grano menudo

87 Colour: bright straw. Nose: balanced, white flowers, jasmine, varietal. Palate: ripe fruit, sweet, good finish.

SEÑORÍO DE SARRÍA RESERVA ESPECIAL 2004 TR

91 Colour: pale ruby, brick rim edge. Nose: elegant, spicy, fine reductive notes, fruit liqueur notes, aged wood nuances, toasty. Palate: spicy, long, balsamic, fine tannins.

SEÑORÍO DE SARRÍA VIÑEDO Nº 3 2009 BFB
chardonnay

91 Colour: bright golden. Nose: ripe fruit, dry nuts, powerfull, toasty, aged wood nuances. Palate: flavourful, fruity, spicy, toasty, long.

SEÑORÍO DE SARRÍA VIÑEDO Nº 5 2012 RD
garnacha

88 Colour: rose, purple rim. Nose: powerfull, ripe fruit, red berry notes, floral, expressive. Palate: powerful, fruity, fresh, easy to drink.

SEÑORÍO DE SARRÍA VIÑEDO Nº 7 2008 TC
graciano

85 Colour: bright cherry, garnet rim. Nose: grassy, fruit preserve, waxy notes. Palate: flavourful, correct.

SEÑORÍO DE SARRÍA VIÑEDO Nº 8 2009 TC
mazuelo

88 Colour: bright cherry, garnet rim. Nose: medium intensity, ripe fruit, dark chocolate. Palate: good acidity, round tannins.

SEÑORÍO DE SARRÍA VIÑEDO SOTÉS 2009 TC
tempranillo, garnacha, cabernet sauvignon, mazuelo, merlot, graciano.

89 Colour: cherry, garnet rim. Nose: balsamic herbs, cocoa bean, creamy oak, toasty, ripe fruit. Palate: flavourful, powerful, balanced.

BODEGA INURRIETA

Ctra. Falces-Miranda de Arga, km. 30
31370 Falces (Navarra)
☎: +34 948 737 309 - Fax: +34 948 737 310
www.bodegainurrieta.com
info@bodegainurrieta.com

ALTOS DE INURRIETA 2009 TR
graciano, garnacha, syrah

92 Colour: cherry, garnet rim. Nose: ripe fruit, spicy, creamy oak, toasty, complex. Palate: powerful, flavourful, toasty, round tannins, balanced.

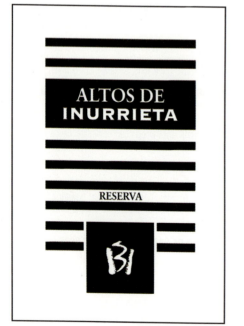

INURRIETA CUATROCIENTOS 2010 TC
cabernet sauvignon, merlot

89 Colour: bright cherry, purple rim. Nose: ripe fruit, cocoa bean, toasty. Palate: flavourful, good acidity, balanced, round tannins.

INURRIETA MEDIODÍA 2012 RD
garnacha

89 Colour: rose, purple rim. Nose: powerfull, ripe fruit, red berry notes, floral, expressive. Palate: powerful, fruity, fresh, balanced.

INURRIETA NORTE 2011 T ROBLE
cabernet sauvignon, merlot

90 Colour: bright cherry. Nose: ripe fruit, sweet spices, creamy oak. Palate: flavourful, fruity, toasty.

INURRIETA ORCHÍDEA 2012 B
sauvignon blanc

87 Colour: bright straw. Nose: fresh fruit, white flowers, fragrant herbs. Palate: flavourful, fruity, good acidity.

INURRIETA ORCHÍDEA CUVÉE 2011 B
100% sauvignon blanc

92 Colour: bright yellow. Nose: powerfull, ripe fruit, sweet spices, fragrant herbs. Palate: rich, flavourful, fresh, good acidity.

INURRIETA SUR 2011 T ROBLE
garnacha, syrah

88 Colour: cherry, garnet rim. Nose: roasted coffee, fruit preserve, dark chocolate. Palate: flavourful, round tannins.

LADERAS DE INURRIETA 2010 T
graciano

91 Colour: deep cherry, garnet rim. Nose: spicy, dark chocolate, balsamic herbs, ripe fruit. Palate: good structure, flavourful, round tannins.

BODEGA MARQUÉS DE MONTECIERZO

San José, 62
31590 Castejón (Navarra)
☎: +34 948 814 414 - Fax: +34 948 814 420
www.marquesdemontecierzo.com
info@marquesdemontecierzo.com

EMERGENTE 2009 TC
tempranillo, cabernet sauvignon, merlot, garnacha

86 Colour: cherry, garnet rim. Nose: sweet spices, cocoa bean. Palate: flavourful, good acidity, round tannins.

EMERGENTE 2011 T ROBLE
100% garnacha

85 Colour: bright cherry, garnet rim. Nose: medium intensity, ripe fruit, dried herbs. Palate: flavourful, spicy.

EMERGENTE 2012 B
chardonnay

84

EMERGENTE 2012 T
100% garnacha

88 Colour: light cherry. Nose: red berry notes, fruit liqueur notes, fragrant herbs. Palate: flavourful, long, balanced.

EMERGENTE GARNACHA SELECCIÓN 2010 T ROBLE
100% garnacha

88 Colour: cherry, garnet rim. Nose: ripe fruit, spicy, creamy oak, toasty, complex. Palate: powerful, flavourful, toasty, round tannins.

EMERGENTE MOSCATEL 2012 B
moscatel grano menudo

86 Colour: bright yellow. Nose: floral, candied fruit, dried herbs. Palate: sweet, flavourful, fruity.

EMERGENTE RESERVA NUMERADA 2006 TR
tempranillo, merlot, cabernet sauvignon

87 Colour: cherry, garnet rim. Nose: spicy, creamy oak, toasty, ripe fruit, fruit preserve. Palate: powerful, flavourful, toasty, round tannins.

EMERGENTE ROSADO DE LÁGRIMA 2012 RD
garnacha, cabernet sauvignon, merlot

84

MARQUES DE MONTECIERZO MERLOT SELECCIÓN 2006 TC
100% merlot

88 Colour: pale ruby, brick rim edge. Nose: ripe fruit, scrubland, cigar, waxy notes, creamy oak. Palate: powerful, flavourful, spicy.

BODEGA MÁXIMO ABETE

Ctra. Estella-Sangüesa, Km. 43,5
31495 San Martín de Unx (Navarra)
☎: +34 948 738 120 - Fax: +34 948 738 120
www.bodegasmaximoabete.com
info@bodegasmaximoabete.com

GUERINDA 2005 TR
garnacha, cabernet sauvignon, merlot

87 Colour: deep cherry, garnet rim. Nose: balanced, spicy, dried herbs. Palate: flavourful, good acidity, round tannins.

GUERINDA 2009 TC
garnacha, cabernet sauvignon, merlot, graciano

86 Colour: cherry, garnet rim. Nose: ripe fruit, spicy, creamy oak, toasty. Palate: powerful, flavourful, toasty.

GUERINDA CHARDONNAY 2012 B
100% chardonnay

85 Colour: bright yellow. Nose: ripe fruit, floral, fragrant herbs, honeyed notes. Palate: powerful, flavourful, correct.

GUERINDA GRACIANO SELECCIÓN 2008 T ROBLE
100% graciano

87 Colour: cherry, garnet rim. Nose: medium intensity, ripe fruit, spicy. Palate: ripe fruit, round tannins.

BODEGA NUESTRA SEÑORA DEL ROMERO

Ctra. de Tarazona, 33
31520 Cascante (Navarra)
☎: +34 948 851 411 - Fax: +34 948 844 504
www.bodegasdelromero.com
info@bodegasdelromero.com

MALÓN DE ECHAIDE 2009 TC
100% tempranillo

85 Colour: cherry, garnet rim. Nose: medium intensity, ripe fruit, spicy. Palate: fruity, correct, easy to drink.

MALÓN DE ECHAIDE 2012 RD
100% garnacha

86 Colour: rose, purple rim. Nose: fresh, red berry notes, balanced. Palate: fruity, correct, easy to drink.

MALÓN DE ECHAIDE CHARDONNAY 2012 B
100% chardonnay

85 Colour: yellow, greenish rim. Nose: medium intensity, varietal, faded flowers. Palate: correct, easy to drink, ripe fruit.

MALÓN DE ECHAIDE GARNACHA VIEJA 2009 T ROBLE
100% garnacha

86 Colour: bright cherry. Nose: ripe fruit, sweet spices, creamy oak. Palate: flavourful, fruity, toasty.

MALÓN DE ECHAIDE TEMPRANILLO 2012 T
100% tempranillo

85 Colour: cherry, purple rim. Nose: medium intensity, ripe fruit. Palate: correct, ripe fruit, flavourful.

VIÑA PAROT 2007 TR
85% cabernet sauvignon, 15% tempranillo

86 Colour: deep cherry, garnet rim. Nose: balanced, elegant, ripe fruit, spicy, cocoa bean. Palate: fruity, spicy, slightly dry, soft tannins.

BODEGA OTAZU

Señorío de Otazu, s/n
31174 Etxauri (Navarra)
☎: +34 948 329 200 - Fax: +34 948 329 353
www.otazu.com
otazu@otazu.com

OTAZU 2006 TC

88 Colour: ruby red, orangey edge. Nose: powerfull, ripe fruit, scrubland, spicy, fine reductive notes. Palate: powerful, spicy, aged character.

OTAZU 2011 RD

85 Colour: light cherry. Nose: fruit liqueur notes, scrubland, dried herbs. Palate: spicy, powerful, flavourful.

OTAZU CHARDONNAY 2011 B

88 Colour: bright straw. Nose: ripe fruit, floral, dried herbs. Palate: powerful, spicy, flavourful.

BODEGA SAN MARTÍN S. COOP.

Ctra. de Sanguesa, s/n
31495 San Martín de Unx (Navarra)
☎: +34 948 738 294 - Fax: +34 948 738 297
www.bodegasanmartin.com
enologia@bodegasanmartin.com

ALMA DE UNX 2008 T
100% garnacha

89 Colour: cherry, garnet rim. Nose: spicy, fine reductive notes, aged wood nuances, earthy notes. Palate: spicy, long, correct.

ALMA DE UNX 2011 B
100% garnacha blanca

88 Colour: bright yellow. Nose: ripe fruit, dried flowers, balsamic herbs, spicy, creamy oak. Palate: powerful, rich, flavourful.

ILAGARES 2012 B
100% viura

83

ILAGARES 2012 RD
100% garnacha

84

ILAGARES 2012 T
70% tempranillo, 30% garnacha

84

SEÑORÍO DE UNX 2006 TR
90% tempranillo, 10% garnacha

88 Colour: cherry, garnet rim. Nose: ripe fruit, dark chocolate, sweet spices, creamy oak. Palate: powerful, flavourful, spicy.

SEÑORÍO DE UNX 2009 TC
80% tempranillo, 20% garnacha

86 Colour: cherry, garnet rim. Nose: balanced, red berry notes, ripe fruit, spicy. Palate: fruity, easy to drink.

SEÑORÍO DE UNX GARNACHA 2012 T
100% garnacha

89 Colour: cherry, purple rim. Nose: balanced, red berry notes, ripe fruit. Palate: flavourful, fruity, long.

BODEGA SAN SALVADOR

Ctra. de Allo, 102
31243 Arróniz (Navarra)
☎: +34 948 537 128 - Fax: +34 948 537 662
galcibar.admon@consebro.com

CASTILUZAR 2008 TC
tempranillo

89 Colour: bright cherry. Nose: ripe fruit, sweet spices, creamy oak, expressive. Palate: flavourful, fruity, toasty, round tannins, easy to drink.

CASTILUZAR 2012 RD
garnacha

86 Colour: rose, bright. Nose: fresh, red berry notes, balanced. Palate: fruity, easy to drink, correct, good acidity.

CASTILUZAR 2012 T
tempranillo

85 Colour: cherry, purple rim. Nose: floral, ripe fruit, balsamic herbs. Palate: flavourful, fruity, good acidity.

GALCÍBAR 2006 TR
tempranillo

87 Colour: cherry, garnet rim. Nose: ripe fruit, spicy, creamy oak, toasty, fine reductive notes. Palate: powerful, flavourful, toasty.

GALCÍBAR 2009 TC
tempranillo

88 Colour: cherry, garnet rim. Nose: ripe fruit, spicy, creamy oak, toasty, complex. Palate: powerful, flavourful, toasty, round tannins.

GALCÍBAR 2011 T ROBLE
84

GALCÍBAR 2012 RD
garnacha

84

BODEGA TÁNDEM

Ctra. Pamplona - Logroño Km. 35,9
31292 Lácar (Navarra)
☎: +34 948 536 031 - Fax: +34 948 536 068
www.tandem.es
bodega@tandem.es

ARS IN VITRO 2010 T
tempranillo, merlot

88 Colour: cherry, garnet rim. Nose: spicy, scrubland, ripe fruit, fruit preserve. Palate: flavourful, fruity.

ARS MEMORIA 2007 T
cabernet sauvignon

90 Colour: cherry, garnet rim. Nose: ripe fruit, spicy, toasty, balsamic herbs, earthy notes, fine reductive notes. Palate: powerful, flavourful, toasty.

ARS NOVA 2007 T
tempranillo, cabernet sauvignon, merlot

89 Colour: bright cherry, orangey edge. Nose: expressive, scrubland, ripe fruit. Palate: good structure, round tannins.

MÁCULA 2006 T
cabernet sauvignon, merlot

89 Colour: pale ruby, brick rim edge. Nose: elegant, spicy, fine reductive notes, wet leather, aged wood nuances. Palate: spicy, elegant, long.

BODEGA Y VIÑAS VALDELARES

Ctra. Eje del Ebro, km. 60
31579 Carcar (Navarra)
☎: +34 656 849 602
www.valdelares.com
valdelares@valdelares.com

VALDELARES 2010 TC
cabernet sauvignon, tempranillo, merlot

89 Colour: cherry, garnet rim. Nose: ripe fruit, spicy, toasty, dark chocolate, sweet spices. Palate: powerful, flavourful, toasty.

VALDELARES 2012 RD
garnacha

90 Colour: rose, purple rim. Nose: powerfull, ripe fruit, red berry notes, floral, expressive. Palate: powerful, fruity, fresh, rich, balanced.

VALDELARES ALTA EXPRESIÓN 2010 TC

90 Colour: bright cherry. Nose: ripe fruit, sweet spices, creamy oak, expressive. Palate: flavourful, fruity, toasty, round tannins.

VALDELARES CHARDONNAY 2012 B
chardonnay

87 Colour: bright straw. Nose: balanced, expressive, white flowers, varietal. Palate: fine bitter notes, good acidity, fruity.

VALDELARES DULCE B

87 Colour: golden. Nose: powerfull, floral, honeyed notes, candied fruit, fragrant herbs, citrus fruit. Palate: flavourful, sweet, fresh, fruity, good acidity, long.

BODEGAS AGUIRRE

Placeta de Añorbe 1
31370 Falces (Navarra)
☎: - Fax: +34 948 714 773
info@bodegasaguirre.es

AGUIRRE 2009 TC
50% garnacha, 30% tempranillo, 20% cabernet sauvignon

85 Colour: cherry, garnet rim. Nose: ripe fruit, balsamic herbs, cocoa bean, sweet spices. Palate: powerful, flavourful, spicy.

CASTILLO DE FALCES 2012 RD
garnacha

86 Colour: rose, purple rim. Nose: red berry notes, ripe fruit, balanced, powerfull. Palate: correct, good acidity, fine bitter notes.

CASTILLO DE FALCES 2012 T JOVEN
garnacha

85 Colour: cherry, purple rim. Nose: fresh fruit, red berry notes, floral, balsamic herbs. Palate: flavourful, fruity, good acidity.

BODEGAS BERAMENDI

Ctra. Tafalla, s/n
31495 San Martín de Unx (Navarra)
☎: +34 948 738 262 - Fax: +34 948 738 080
www.bodegasberamendi.com
info@bodegasberamendi.com

BERAMENDI 2012 RD
100% garnacha

84

BERAMENDI 2012 T
80% tempranillo, 20% garnacha

84

BERAMENDI 3F 2012 B
60% chardonnay, 40% moscatel

85 Colour: bright straw. Nose: fresh, fresh fruit, white flowers, expressive. Palate: flavourful, fruity, good acidity, balanced.

BERAMENDI 3F 2012 RD
100% garnacha

86 Colour: rose, purple rim. Nose: powerfull, ripe fruit, floral, balsamic herbs. Palate: powerful, fruity, fresh.

BERAMENDI MERLOT 2008 TR
90% merlot, 10% graciano

87 Colour: cherry, garnet rim. Nose: ripe fruit, spicy, creamy oak, balsamic herbs. Palate: powerful, flavourful, toasty, spicy.

BERAMENDI TEMPRANILLO 2010 TC
100% tempranillo

85 Colour: cherry, garnet rim. Nose: ripe fruit, creamy oak, grassy. Palate: powerful, balsamic.

BODEGAS CAMILO CASTILLA

Santa Bárbara, 40
31591 Corella (Navarra)
☎: +34 948 780 006 - Fax: +34 948 780 515
www.bodegasab.com
info@camilocastilla.com

CAPRICHO DE GOYA AM
moscatel grano menudo

93 Colour: dark mahogany. Nose: powerfull, complex, dry nuts, toasty, acetaldehyde, aromatic coffee, varnish. Palate: rich, fine bitter notes, fine solera notes, long, spicy.

MONTECRISTO 2009 TC
tempranillo, cabernet sauvignon

85 Colour: cherry, garnet rim. Nose: toasty, spicy, grassy, ripe fruit. Palate: fruity, correct.

MONTECRISTO 2012 B
moscatel grano menudo

85 Colour: bright straw. Nose: floral, tropical fruit, candied fruit, citrus fruit, expressive. Palate: fresh, fruity, flavourful.

MONTECRISTO 2012 B
moscatel grano menudo

87 Colour: golden. Nose: powerfull, honeyed notes, candied fruit, fragrant herbs. Palate: flavourful, sweet, good acidity, long.

PINK 2012 RD
garnacha

85 Colour: rose, purple rim. Nose: ripe fruit, fruit preserve, faded flowers. Palate: powerful, flavourful, fruity.

BODEGAS CASTILLO DE MONJARDÍN

Viña Rellanada, s/n
31242 Villamayor de Monjardín (Navarra)
☎: +34 948 537 412 - Fax: +34 948 537 436
www.monjardin.es
sonia@monjardin.es

CASTILLO DE MONJARDÍN 2010 TC
cabernet sauvignon, tempranillo, merlot

87 Colour: bright cherry, garnet rim. Nose: medium intensity, ripe fruit, sweet spices. Palate: light-bodied, spicy, correct.

CASTILLO DE MONJARDÍN CHARDONNAY 2008 B RESERVA
chardonnay

90 Colour: bright yellow. Nose: faded flowers, sweet spices, ripe fruit, citrus fruit. Palate: balanced, spicy, rich.

CASTILLO DE MONJARDÍN CHARDONNAY 2010 BFB
chardonnay

93 Colour: bright yellow. Nose: powerfull, ripe fruit, sweet spices, creamy oak, fragrant herbs, elegant. Palate: rich, smoky aftertaste, flavourful, fresh, good acidity, varietal.

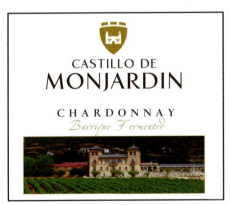

CASTILLO DE MONJARDÍN CHARDONNAY 2012 B
chardonnay

87 Colour: yellow. Nose: ripe fruit, faded flowers, balanced. Palate: flavourful, full, long, fine bitter notes.

CASTILLO DE MONJARDÍN DEYO 2009 TC
merlot

88 Colour: cherry, garnet rim. Nose: ripe fruit, balanced, expressive, sweet spices. Palate: flavourful, fruity, round tannins.

CASTILLO DE MONJARDÍN FINCA LOS CARASOLES 2005 TR
cabernet sauvignon, tempranillo

89 Colour: pale ruby, brick rim edge. Nose: spicy, fine reductive notes, wet leather, dark chocolate, earthy notes. Palate: spicy, long, flavourful.

CASTILLO DE MONJARDÍN GARNACHA OLD VINES 2011 T
garnacha

87 Colour: light cherry. Nose: red berry notes, ripe fruit, balsamic herbs, sweet spices. Palate: light-bodied, flavourful, balanced.

CASTILLO DE MONJARDÍN MERLOT 2012 RD
merlot

84

CASTILLO DE MONJARDÍN PINOT NOIR VIÑAS VIEJAS 2011 T
pinot noir

89 Colour: cherry, garnet rim. Nose: medium intensity, ripe fruit, violet drops, wild herbs. Palate: balanced, round tannins.

CASTILLO DE MONJARDÍN TEMPRANILLO 2012 T
tempranillo

85 Colour: cherry, purple rim. Nose: medium intensity, red berry notes, ripe fruit. Palate: flavourful, good acidity, good finish.

ESENCIA MONJARDÍN 2007 B
chardonnay

93 Colour: golden. Nose: powerfull, floral, candied fruit, fragrant herbs, varnish, sweet spices. Palate: flavourful, sweet, fresh, fruity, good acidity, long.

GURMÉ SAUVIGNON & CHARDONNAY 2012 B
sauvignon blanc, chardonnay

89 Colour: bright straw. Nose: balanced, citrus fruit, wild herbs, faded flowers. Palate: flavourful, fruity, good acidity.

GURMÉ TEMPRANILLO & CABERNET 2011 T
cabernet sauvignon, tempranillo

86 Colour: cherry, garnet rim. Nose: ripe fruit, fruit preserve, dried herbs, spicy, dark chocolate. Palate: correct, round tannins.

GURMÉ TEMPRANILLO & MERLOT 2011 T
merlot, tempranillo

84

BODEGAS CAUDALIA

San Francisco, 7
26300 Najera (La Rioja)
☎: +34 670 833 340
www.bodegascaudalia.com
info@bodegascaudalia.com

PAAL 01 2012 T
100% syrah

89 Colour: cherry, garnet rim. Nose: red berry notes, ripe fruit, grassy. Palate: rich, flavourful, easy to drink.

XI'IPAL 2012 T
100% syrah

88 Colour: cherry, garnet rim. Nose: red berry notes, ripe fruit, balsamic herbs, spicy. Palate: powerful, flavourful, fruity.

BODEGAS CORELLANAS

Santa Bárbara, 29
31591 Corella (Navarra)
☎: +34 948 780 029 - Fax: +34 948 781 542
www.bodegascorellanas.com
info@bodegascorellanas.com

MOSCATEL SARASATE EXPRESIÓN 2012 B
100% moscatel grano menudo

87 Colour: bright straw. Nose: fruit liqueur notes, ripe fruit, floral, dried herbs. Palate: correct, unctuous, powerful, flavourful.

VIÑA RUBICÁN 2009 TC
15% cabernet sauvignon, 85% tempranillo

84

VIÑA RUBICÁN 2012 B
60% viura, 40% moscatel grano menudo

85 Colour: bright yellow, greenish rim. Nose: white flowers, jasmine, medium intensity. Palate: fruity, flavourful, good acidity.

VIÑA RUBICÁN TEMPRANILLO 2011 T
100% tempranillo

80

VIÑA RUBICÁN ÚNICO 2007 TC
85% garnacha, 15% tempranillo

88 Colour: cherry, garnet rim. Nose: fruit preserve, spicy, tobacco. Palate: fruity, round tannins.

BODEGAS DE LA CASA DE LÚCULO

Ctra. Larraga, s/n
31150 Mendigorría (Navarra)
☎: +34 948 343 148 - Fax: +34 948 343 148
www.luculo.es
bodega@luculo.es

JARDÍN DE LÚCULO 2010 T
garnacha

92 Colour: light cherry. Nose: floral, red berry notes, balsamic herbs, spicy, creamy oak. Palate: balanced, elegant, flavourful, complex.

LOS BOHEMIOS 2012 T
garnacha

89 Colour: bright cherry, purple rim. Nose: medium intensity, dried herbs, red berry notes. Palate: ripe fruit, balanced.

BODEGAS FERNÁNDEZ DE ARCAYA

La Serna, 31
31210 Los Arcos (Navarra)
☎: +34 948 640 811
www.fernandezdearcaya.com
info@fernandezdearcaya.com

FERNÁNDEZ DE ARCAYA 2009 TR
100% cabernet sauvignon

90 Colour: bright cherry, orangey edge. Nose: balanced, cocoa bean, sweet spices. Palate: balsamic, ripe fruit, good acidity.

VIÑA PERGUITA 2010 TC
80% tempranillo, 15% cabernet sauvignon, 5% merlot

86 Colour: pale ruby, brick rim edge. Nose: ripe fruit, balsamic herbs, spicy, fine reductive notes. Palate: powerful, flavourful, spicy.

VIÑA PERGUITA 2012 T ROBLE
85% tempranillo, 10% cabernet sauvignon, 5% merlot

83

BODEGAS GRAN FEUDO

Ribera, 34
31592 Cintruénigo (Navarra)
☎: +34 948 811 000 - Fax: +34 948 811 407
www.granfeudo.com
info@granfeudo.com

GRAN FEUDO 2008 TR
tempranillo, cabernet sauvignon, merlot

90 Colour: cherry, garnet rim. Nose: ripe fruit, spicy, creamy oak, toasty. Palate: flavourful, toasty, round tannins.

GRAN FEUDO 2009 TC
tempranillo, garnacha, cabernet sauvignon

89 Colour: cherry, garnet rim. Nose: balanced, scrubland, spicy. Palate: flavourful, round tannins.

GRAN FEUDO 2012 RD
garnacha

89 Colour: rose, purple rim. Nose: ripe fruit, red berry notes, floral, expressive. Palate: powerful, fruity, fresh.

GRAN FEUDO CHARDONNAY 2012 B
chardonnay

88 Colour: bright yellow. Nose: ripe fruit, floral, balsamic herbs, spicy, warm. Palate: powerful, flavourful, rich, correct.

GRAN FEUDO EDICIÓN CHARDONNAY SOBRE LÍAS 2011 B

91 Colour: bright yellow. Nose: floral, dried herbs, spicy, creamy oak, citrus fruit, ripe fruit. Palate: powerful, flavourful, fruity, long, toasty.

GRAN FEUDO EDICIÓN DULCE DE MOSCATEL 2012 B
moscatel grano menudo

92 Colour: golden. Nose: powerfull, floral, honeyed notes, candied fruit, fragrant herbs. Palate: flavourful, sweet, fresh, fruity, good acidity, long, elegant.

GRAN FEUDO VIÑAS VIEJAS 2008 TR
tempranillo, garnacha

88 Colour: deep cherry, garnet rim. Nose: ripe fruit, balanced. Palate: fruity, spicy, easy to drink.

BODEGAS IRACHE

Monasterio de Irache, 1
31240 Ayegui (Navarra)
☎: +34 948 551 932 - Fax: +34 948 554 954
www.irache.com
irache@irache.com

CASTILLO IRACHE 2012 B
garnacha

82

CASTILLO IRACHE TEMPRANILLO 2012 T
tempranillo

83

GRAN IRACHE 2010 TC
tempranillo, cabernet sauvignon, merlot

85 Colour: cherry, garnet rim. Nose: medium intensity, ripe fruit, fruit preserve, spicy. Palate: correct, easy to drink.

IRACHE 2004 TR
tempranillo, cabernet sauvignon, merlot

84

BODEGAS ITURBIDE

Término la Torre, s/n
31350 Peralta (Navarra)
☎: +34 948 750 537 - Fax: +34 647 742 368
www.bodegasiturbide.com
bodegasiturbide@bodegasiturbide.com

NOVEM 2011 T
garnacha, tempranillo, cabernet sauvignon

86 Colour: cherry, garnet rim. Nose: medium intensity, ripe fruit, spicy, toasty. Palate: flavourful, round tannins.

NOVEM 2012 RD
garnacha

84

BODEGAS LEZAUN

Egiarte, 1
31292 Lakar (Navarra)
☎: +34 948 541 339
www.lezaun.com
info@lezaun.com

EGIARTE 2009 TC
tempranillo, merlot, cabernet sauvignon

87 Colour: bright cherry, garnet rim. Nose: medium intensity, sweet spices, cocoa bean, ripe fruit. Palate: flavourful, fruity aftertaste.

EGIARTE 2009 TR
tempranillo, merlot, cabernet sauvignon

88 Colour: cherry, garnet rim. Nose: ripe fruit, spicy, creamy oak, toasty, complex. Palate: powerful, flavourful, toasty.

EGIARTE 2012 T
tempranillo, merlot, garnacha

86 Colour: cherry, garnet rim. Nose: ripe fruit, wild herbs. Palate: powerful, flavourful, correct.

EGIARTE ROSADO 2012 RD
garnacha

86 Colour: raspberry rose. Nose: candied fruit, dried flowers, fragrant herbs. Palate: easy to drink, fresh, fruity.

LEZAUN 0,0 SULFITOS 2012 T
tempranillo

87 Colour: bright cherry, purple rim. Nose: ripe fruit, varietal. Palate: fruity, flavourful, good acidity.

LEZAUN 2007 TR
tempranillo, graciano, garnacha

87 Colour: cherry, garnet rim. Nose: ripe fruit, spicy. Palate: flavourful, good acidity, easy to drink.

LEZAUN 2009 TC
50% tempranillo, 10% merlot, 40% cabernet sauvignon

87 Colour: cherry, garnet rim. Nose: balanced, ripe fruit, fruit preserve, sweet spices. Palate: flavourful, round tannins.

LEZAUN GAZAGA 2010 T ROBLE
tempranillo, merlot, cabernet sauvignon

88 Colour: deep cherry, garnet rim. Nose: toasty, spicy, ripe fruit. Palate: fruity, flavourful, roasted-coffee aftertaste.

LEZAUN TEMPRANILLO 2012 T MACERACIÓN CARBÓNICA
tempranillo

89 Colour: cherry, purple rim. Nose: expressive, fresh fruit, red berry notes, floral, lactic notes. Palate: flavourful, fruity, good acidity.

LEZAUN TXURIA 2012 B
garnacha

83

LOGOS 2012 RD FERMENTADO EN BARRICA
100% garnacha

84

BODEGAS LOGOS

Avda. de los Fueros, 18
31522 Monteagudo (Navarra)
☎: +34 941 398 008 - Fax: +34 941 398 070
www.familiaescudero.com
info@familiaescudero.com

LOGOS I 2004 T
40% garnacha, 30% cabernet sauvignon, 30% tempranillo

89 Colour: pale ruby, brick rim edge. Nose: spicy, fine reductive notes, wet leather, aged wood nuances, fruit liqueur notes. Palate: spicy, fine tannins, long.

LOGOS II 2006 TC
40% cabernet sauvignon, 40% garnacha, 20% tempranillo

86 Colour: cherry, garnet rim. Nose: fruit liqueur notes, fruit preserve, old leather, cigar, waxy notes, toasty. Palate: powerful, flavourful, long.

PEDRO DE IVAR 2008 TC
70% tempranillo, 20% garnacha, 10% mazuelo

89 Colour: cherry, garnet rim. Nose: ripe fruit, spicy, creamy oak, toasty. Palate: powerful, flavourful, toasty.

PEDRO DE IVAR PRESTIGIO 2004 TR
60% garnacha, 40% tempranillo

90 Colour: pale ruby, brick rim edge. Nose: elegant, fine reductive notes, aged wood nuances, creamy oak, ripe fruit. Palate: spicy, elegant, long.

BODEGAS MACAYA

Ctra. Berbinzana, 74
31251 Larraga (Navarra)
☎: +34 948 711 549 - Fax: +34 948 711 788
www.bodegasmacaya.com
info@bodegasmacaya.com

ALMARA CABERNET SAUVIGNON 2009 TR
cabernet sauvignon

88 Colour: bright cherry, garnet rim. Nose: powerfull, varietal, spicy, balsamic herbs. Palate: flavourful, good structure, ripe fruit.

CONDADO DE ALMARA CRIANZA 2009 TC
tempranillo, cabernet sauvignon

86 Colour: cherry, garnet rim. Nose: ripe fruit, wild herbs, earthy notes. Palate: flavourful, spicy, balsamic.

CONDADO DE ALMARA RESERVA 2008 TR
tempranillo, cabernet sauvignon

88 Colour: cherry, garnet rim. Nose: spicy, ripe fruit, balsamic herbs, creamy oak. Palate: long, powerful, flavourful, spicy.

CONDADO DE ALMARA SELECCIÓN 2010 T
tempranillo

87 Colour: bright cherry. Nose: ripe fruit, sweet spices, creamy oak, expressive. Palate: flavourful, fruity, toasty.

FINCA LINTE 2011 T
tempranillo

85 Colour: cherry, garnet rim. Nose: ripe fruit, spicy, creamy oak. Palate: powerful, flavourful, toasty.

BODEGAS MARCO REAL

Ctra. Pamplona-Zaragoza, Km. 38
31390 Olite (Navarra)
☎: +34 948 712 193 - Fax: +34 948 712 343
www.familiabelasco.com
info@familiabelasco.com

HOMENAJE 2009 TC
tempranillo, merlot

88 Colour: cherry, garnet rim. Nose: ripe fruit, spicy, creamy oak, toasty. Palate: powerful, flavourful, toasty.

HOMENAJE 2012 B
viura, chardonnay

86 Colour: bright yellow. Nose: ripe fruit, floral, fragrant herbs. Palate: fresh, fruity, flavourful, easy to drink.

HOMENAJE 2012 RD
garnacha

85 Colour: rose, bright. Nose: slightly evolved, red berry notes. Palate: fruity, easy to drink, good acidity.

MARCO REAL COLECCIÓN PRIVADA 2010 TC
tempranillo, cabernet sauvignon, merlot, graciano

89 Colour: cherry, garnet rim. Nose: powerfull, ripe fruit, spicy, wild herbs. Palate: fruity, flavourful, easy to drink, spicy.

MARCO REAL PEQUEÑAS PRODUCCIONES GARNACHA 2011 T
100% garnacha

91 Colour: bright cherry. Nose: ripe fruit, sweet spices, creamy oak, expressive. Palate: flavourful, fruity, toasty, round tannins.

MARCO REAL PEQUEÑAS PRODUCCIONES SYRAH 2011 TC
100% syrah

89 Colour: bright cherry, garnet rim. Nose: ripe fruit, violet drops, balanced, toasty. Palate: fruity, round tannins.

MARCO REAL PEQUEÑAS PRODUCCIONES TEMPRANILLO 2011 TR
100% tempranillo

88 Colour: cherry, garnet rim. Nose: medium intensity, ripe fruit, varietal. Palate: balanced, easy to drink.

MARCO REAL RESERVA DE FAMILIA 2008 TR
tempranillo, cabernet sauvignon, merlot, graciano

91 Colour: bright cherry, garnet rim. Nose: complex, balanced, ripe fruit, spicy. Palate: balanced, good acidity, round tannins.

BODEGAS NAPARRALDE

Crtra. de Madrid s/n
31591 Corella (Navarra)
☎: +34 948 782 255 - Fax: +34 948 401 182
www.upain.es
administracion@naparralde.com

UPAIN 2012 RD
garnacha

85 Colour: rose, bright. Nose: medium intensity, red berry notes, ripe fruit. Palate: correct, fine bitter notes, good acidity.

UPAIN GARNACHA 2009 T
100% garnacha

85 Colour: cherry, garnet rim. Nose: ripe fruit, spicy, creamy oak, complex. Palate: powerful, flavourful, toasty.

UPAIN GARNACHA SELECCIÓN PRIVADA 2009 T
100% garnacha

86 Colour: cherry, garnet rim. Nose: ripe fruit, spicy, creamy oak, toasty. Palate: powerful, flavourful, toasty.

UPAIN SYRAH SELECCIÓN PRIVADA 2010 T
100% syrah

86 Colour: cherry, garnet rim. Nose: medium intensity, ripe fruit, sweet spices. Palate: correct, ripe fruit, round tannins.

UPAIN TEMPRANILLO 2007 T
tempranillo

85 Colour: pale ruby, brick rim edge. Nose: spicy, wet leather, aged wood nuances, fruit liqueur notes. Palate: spicy, long, flavourful.

UPAIN TEMPRANILLO MERLOT 2008 TC
80% tempranillo, 20% merlot

85 Colour: cherry, garnet rim. Nose: ripe fruit, spicy, creamy oak, toasty. Palate: powerful, flavourful, toasty.

UPAIN TRES VARIEDADES SELECCIÓN PRIVADA 2008 T
33% tempranillo, 33% garnacha, 33% cabernet sauvignon

87 Colour: cherry, garnet rim. Nose: scrubland, spicy, ripe fruit. Palate: flavourful, fruity, spicy.

UPAINBERRI 2009 T ROBLE
60% tempranillo, 15% merlot, 25% cabernet sauvignon

86 Colour: bright cherry, orangey edge. Nose: medium intensity, spicy, old leather. Palate: correct, fine bitter notes.

BODEGAS OCHOA

Alcalde Maillata, 2
31390 Olite (Navarra)
☎: +34 948 740 006 - Fax: +34 948 740 048
www.bodegasochoa.com
info@bodegasochoa.com

MOSCATO DE OCHOA 2012 B
moscatel grano menudo

86 Colour: bright straw. Nose: white flowers, candied fruit, fragrant herbs. Palate: sweetness, fresh, fruity.

OCHOA 2007 TR
tempranillo, cabernet sauvignon, merlot

86 Colour: cherry, garnet rim. Nose: ripe fruit, spicy, creamy oak, toasty. Palate: powerful, toasty, round tannins.

OCHOA CALENDAS 2010 T ROBLE
tempranillo, syrah

84

OCHOA CALENDAS 2012 B
viura, chardonnay

81

OCHOA FINCA MONTIJO 2007 T
merlot, cabernet sauvignon, tempranillo

89 Colour: cherry, garnet rim. Nose: ripe fruit, spicy, creamy oak, toasty, fine reductive notes. Palate: powerful, flavourful, toasty.

OCHOA MOSCATEL VENDIMIA TARDÍA 2012 BLANCO DULCE
moscatel grano menudo

89 Colour: bright straw. Nose: candied fruit, varietal, jasmine. Palate: rich, flavourful, balanced.

OCHOA ORIGEN 2007 TR
tempranillo, merlot, cabernet sauvignon

89 Colour: pale ruby, brick rim edge. Nose: fruit liqueur notes, aged wood nuances, waxy notes, fine reductive notes. Palate: powerful, flavourful, spicy, long.

OCHOA ROSADO DE LÁGRIMA 2012 RD
garnacha, cabernet sauvignon

86 Colour: light cherry, bright. Nose: balanced, fresh, red berry notes, wild herbs. Palate: light-bodied, fresh, easy to drink.

OCHOA SERIE 8A MIL GRACIAS 2008 TC
graciano

86 Colour: cherry, garnet rim. Nose: medium intensity, ripe fruit, sweet spices, animal reductive notes. Palate: fruity, good acidity.

OCHOA TEMPRANILLO 2009 TC
tempranillo

87 Colour: cherry, garnet rim. Nose: ripe fruit, spicy, creamy oak, toasty. Palate: powerful, flavourful, toasty.

BODEGAS OLIMPIA

Avda. Río Aragón, 1
31490 Cáseda (Navarra)
☎: +34 948 186 262 - Fax: +34 948 186 565
www.bodegasolimpia.com
export@bodegasolimpia.com

EDICIÓN LIMITADA (F. OLIMPIA BODEGAS Y VIÑEDOS) 2010 T
100% graciano

89 Colour: deep cherry, garnet rim. Nose: balanced, expressive, ripe fruit, dark chocolate. Palate: spicy, good acidity, varietal.

BODEGAS ORVALAIZ

Ctra. Pamplona-Logroño, s/n
31151 Óbanos (Navarra)
☎: +34 948 344 437 - Fax: +34 948 344 401
www.orvalaiz.es
bodega@orvalaiz.es

ORVALAIZ 2006 TR
tempranillo, cabernet sauvignon, merlot

85 Colour: pale ruby, brick rim edge. Nose: elegant, spicy, fine reductive notes, wet leather, aged wood nuances, fruit liqueur notes. Palate: spicy, fine tannins, long.

ORVALAIZ 2009 TC
tempranillo, cabernet sauvignon, merlot

86 Colour: cherry, garnet rim. Nose: ripe fruit, spicy, creamy oak, toasty, fine reductive notes. Palate: powerful, flavourful, toasty.

ORVALAIZ CABERNET SAUVIGNON 2011 T ROBLE
cabernet sauvignon

86 Colour: bright cherry. Nose: ripe fruit, sweet spices, balsamic herbs. Palate: flavourful, fruity, thin.

ORVALAIZ CHARDONNAY 2012 B
chardonnay

85 Colour: bright yellow. Nose: ripe fruit, floral, balsamic herbs, medium intensity. Palate: powerful, flavourful, ripe fruit.

ORVALAIZ GARNACHA 2010 T ROBLE
garnacha

82

ORVALAIZ MERLOT 2011 T ROBLE
merlot

85 Colour: cherry, garnet rim. Nose: balsamic herbs, wild herbs, ripe fruit, creamy oak. Palate: powerful, flavourful, thin.

ORVALAIZ ROSADO DE LÁGRIMA 2012 RD
cabernet sauvignon

87 Colour: light cherry. Nose: red berry notes, candied fruit, floral, fragrant herbs, powerfull, expressive. Palate: rich, powerful, long, flavourful.

ORVALAIZ TEMPRANILLO 2010 T ROBLE
tempranillo

83

SEPTENTRIÓN 2008 TC
tempranillo, cabernet sauvignon

85 Colour: cherry, garnet rim. Nose: ripe fruit, dried herbs, creamy oak, wet leather, tobacco. Palate: powerful, flavourful, spicy, long.

VIÑA ORVALAIZ 2011 T
tempranillo, cabernet sauvignon

83

VIÑA ORVALAIZ 2012 B
viura, chardonnay

84

VIÑA ORVALAIZ ROSADO 2012 RD
garnacha, tempranillo

86 Colour: rose, purple rim. Nose: powerfull, ripe fruit, red berry notes, floral, lactic notes. Palate: powerful, fruity, fresh.

BODEGAS PAGOS DE ARÁIZ

Camino de Araiz, s/n
31390 Olite (Navarra)
☎: +34 948 399 182
www.bodegaspagosdearaiz.com
info@bodegaspagosdearaiz.com

BLANEO BY PAGOS DE ARÁIZ 2011 T
100% syrah

89 Colour: bright cherry, garnet rim. Nose: creamy oak, sweet spices, cocoa bean. Palate: powerful, toasty, round tannins.

PAGOS DE ARÁIZ 2012 RD
100% garnacha

87 Colour: rose, purple rim. Nose: red berry notes, ripe fruit, balsamic herbs, fresh. Palate: powerful, flavourful, fruity.

BODEGAS PALACIO DE LA VEGA

Condesa de la Vega de Pozo, s/n
31263 Dicastillo (Navarra)
☎: +34 948 527 009 - Fax: +34 948 527 333
www.palaciodelavega.com

CONDE DE LA VEGA 2007 TR
tempranillo, cabernet sauvignon, merlot

89 Colour: dark-red cherry, orangey edge. Nose: ripe fruit, spicy, balsamic herbs, old leather, creamy oak. Palate: balanced, flavourful, spicy, long, round tannins.

PALACIO DE LA VEGA CABERNET SAUVIGNON 2006 TR
cabernet sauvignon

87 Colour: cherry, garnet rim. Nose: ripe fruit, wild herbs, spicy, old leather, tobacco. Palate: flavourful, spicy, correct.

PALACIO DE LA VEGA CABERNET SAUVIGNON TEMPRANILLO 2010 TC

88 Colour: cherry, garnet rim. Nose: ripe fruit, creamy oak, wild herbs, spicy. Palate: powerful, flavourful, toasty.

PALACIO DE LA VEGA CHARDONNAY 2012 B
chardonnay

90 Colour: bright golden. Nose: ripe fruit, dry nuts, powerfull, toasty, aged wood nuances. Palate: flavourful, fruity, spicy, toasty, long.

PALACIO DE LA VEGA GARNACHA 2012 RD
garnacha

89 Colour: rose, purple rim. Nose: powerfull, ripe fruit, red berry notes, floral, balsamic herbs. Palate: powerful, fruity, fresh.

BODEGAS PIEDEMONTE

Rua Romana, s/n
31390 Olite (Navarra)
☎: +34 948 712 406 - Fax: +34 948 740 090
www.piedemonte.com
bodega@piedemonte.com

PIEDEMONTE +DQUINCE 2009 T
merlot

88 Colour: bright cherry, orangey edge. Nose: fruit preserve, sweet spices, cocoa bean. Palate: good structure, flavourful, round tannins.

PIEDEMONTE 2006 TR
merlot, tempranillo, cabernet sauvignon

86 Colour: bright cherry, orangey edge. Nose: medium intensity, spicy, ripe fruit. Palate: easy to drink, round tannins, reductive nuances.

PIEDEMONTE 2009 TC
cabernet sauvignon, tempranillo, merlot

86 Colour: bright cherry. Nose: balanced, ripe fruit, scrubland. Palate: fruity, round tannins.

PIEDEMONTE 2012 RD
100% garnacha

87 Colour: rose, purple rim. Nose: powerfull, ripe fruit, red berry notes, floral, expressive. Palate: powerful, fruity, fresh.

PIEDEMONTE CABERNET SAUVIGNON 2009 TC
100% cabernet sauvignon

87 Colour: cherry, garnet rim. Nose: ripe fruit, spicy, toasty, balsamic herbs. Palate: powerful, flavourful, toasty.

PIEDEMONTE CHARDONNAY 2012 B
100% chardonnay

86 Colour: yellow. Nose: medium intensity, ripe fruit, white flowers. Palate: fruity, good finish, correct, easy to drink.

PIEDEMONTE GAMMA 2012 B
viura, chardonnay, moscatel

83

PIEDEMONTE MERLOT 2009 TC
100% merlot

89 Colour: bright cherry. Nose: ripe fruit, sweet spices, creamy oak, fragrant herbs. Palate: flavourful, fruity, toasty.

PIEDEMONTE MERLOT 2012 T
100% merlot

83

PIEDEMONTE MOSCATEL B
moscatel

89 Colour: bright yellow. Nose: floral, honeyed notes, candied fruit, fragrant herbs, elegant. Palate: flavourful, sweet, fresh, fruity, balanced.

BODEGAS PRÍNCIPE DE VIANA

Mayor, 191
31521 Murchante (Navarra)
☎: +34 948 838 640 - Fax: +34 948 818 574
www.principedeviana.com
info@principedeviana.com

PRÍNCIPE DE VIANA 1423 2007 TR
75% tempranillo, 10% cabernet sauvignon, 10% merlot, 5% garnacha

87 Colour: cherry, garnet rim. Nose: ripe fruit, smoky, scrubland, fine reductive notes, creamy oak. Palate: correct, powerful, flavourful.

PRÍNCIPE DE VIANA 2010 TC
40% tempranillo, 30% cabernet sauvignon, 30% merlot

88 Colour: cherry, garnet rim. Nose: ripe fruit, spicy, creamy oak. Palate: powerful, flavourful, toasty, balanced.

PRÍNCIPE DE VIANA CHARDONNAY 2012 B
100% chardonnay

88 Colour: bright straw. Nose: fresh, fresh fruit, white flowers, expressive. Palate: flavourful, fruity, good acidity.

PRÍNCIPE DE VIANA EDICIÓN LIMITADA 2009 TC
tempranillo, merlot, cabernet sauvignon

90 Colour: cherry, garnet rim. Nose: ripe fruit, spicy, toasty, earthy notes. Palate: powerful, flavourful, long, balanced.

PRÍNCIPE DE VIANA GARNACHA 2012 RD
garnacha

88 Colour: rose, purple rim. Nose: powerfull, ripe fruit, red berry notes, floral. Palate: powerful, fruity, fresh.

PRÍNCIPE DE VIANA GARNACHA 2012 T ROBLE
100% garnacha

88 Colour: cherry, garnet rim. Nose: medium intensity, wild herbs, dried herbs, ripe fruit. Palate: flavourful, fruity.

PRÍNCIPE DE VIANA SYRAH 2012 T ROBLE
100% syrah

89 Colour: bright cherry. Nose: expressive, violet drops, ripe fruit, sweet spices. Palate: balanced, good acidity.

PRÍNCIPE DE VIANA TEMPRANILLO 2012 T ROBLE
100% tempranillo

88 Colour: bright cherry, purple rim. Nose: balanced, red berry notes, ripe fruit, violet drops. Palate: flavourful, good acidity, spicy.

BODEGAS URABAIN

Ctra. Estella, 21
31262 Allo (Navarra)
☎: +34 948 523 011 - Fax: +34 948 523 409
www.bodegasurabain.com
vinos@bodegasurabain.com

PRADO DE CHICA 2010 TC
100% merlot

87 Colour: cherry, garnet rim. Nose: powerfull, fruit preserve, toasty, dark chocolate. Palate: good structure, flavourful, round tannins.

UN PASO MÁS 2009 TC
40% tempranillo, 40% cabernet sauvignon, 20% merlot

90 Colour: cherry, garnet rim. Nose: ripe fruit, spicy, creamy oak, toasty. Palate: powerful, flavourful, toasty.

URABAIN CABERNET SAUVIGNON TEMPRANILLO 2012 T
70% tempranillo, 30% cabernet sauvignon

84

URABAIN CHARDONNAY 2012 B
100% chardonnay

87 Colour: bright straw. Nose: floral, dried herbs, candied fruit. Palate: flavourful, correct, fruity, rich.

URABAIN CHARDONNAY BARRELL FERMENTED 2011 B
100% chardonnay

88 Colour: bright yellow. Nose: powerfull, ripe fruit, sweet spices, creamy oak, fragrant herbs. Palate: rich, flavourful, good acidity, toasty.

URABAIN ROSADO DE LÁGRIMA 2012 RD
100% merlot

87 Colour: rose, purple rim. Nose: powerfull, ripe fruit, red berry notes, floral, expressive. Palate: powerful, fruity, fresh.

BODEGAS VALCARLOS

Ctra. Circunvalación, s/n
31210 Los Arcos (Navarra)
☎: +34 948 640 806
www.bodegasvalcarlos.com
info@bodegasvalcarlos.com

ÉLITE DE FORTIUS 2009 TR
merlot, cabernet sauvignon

89 Colour: cherry, garnet rim. Nose: balanced, spicy, fine reductive notes, scrubland. Palate: correct, good acidity, balanced.

FORTIUS 2001 TGR
tempranillo, cabernet sauvignon

89 Colour: pale ruby, brick rim edge. Nose: spicy, fine reductive notes, wet leather, aged wood nuances, fruit liqueur notes. Palate: spicy, long, flavourful.

FORTIUS 2006 TR
tempranillo, cabernet sauvignon

87 Colour: bright cherry. Nose: old leather, spicy, ripe fruit. Palate: flavourful, round tannins, good acidity.

FORTIUS 2008 TC
tempranillo, cabernet sauvignon

85 Colour: cherry, garnet rim. Nose: ripe fruit, balsamic herbs, fine reductive notes, creamy oak. Palate: powerful, flavourful, spicy.

FORTIUS 2012 B
viura, chardonnay

85 Colour: bright straw. Nose: medium intensity, faded flowers, citrus fruit. Palate: flavourful, easy to drink, fine bitter notes.

FORTIUS 2012 RD
tempranillo, merlot

83

FORTIUS CHARDONNAY 2011 B
chardonnay

85 Colour: bright yellow. Nose: dried flowers, fragrant herbs, citrus fruit, ripe fruit. Palate: powerful, rich, fruity, flavourful.

FORTIUS CHARDONNAY 2012 B
100% chardonnay

84

FORTIUS MERLOT 2008 TC
100% merlot

86 Colour: cherry, garnet rim. Nose: medium intensity, fruit preserve, spicy. Palate: correct, easy to drink.

FORTIUS TEMPRANILLO 2010 T ROBLE
100% tempranillo

85 Colour: pale ruby, brick rim edge. Nose: fruit liqueur notes, fruit preserve, slightly evolved. Palate: powerful, flavourful, toasty.

MARQUÉS DE VALCARLOS 2001 TGR
tempranillo, cabernet sauvignon

87 Colour: bright cherry, orangey edge. Nose: ripe fruit, spicy, old leather. Palate: flavourful, spicy, fine tannins.

MARQUÉS DE VALCARLOS 2005 TR
tempranillo, cabernet sauvignon

83

MARQUÉS DE VALCARLOS 2008 TC
tempranillo, cabernet sauvignon

85 Colour: light cherry, orangey edge. Nose: balsamic herbs, aged wood nuances, creamy oak, fine reductive notes. Palate: spicy, powerful, flavourful.

MARQUÉS DE VALCARLOS 2012 B
viura, chardonnay

85 Colour: bright yellow. Nose: medium intensity, fresh fruit, citrus fruit. Palate: easy to drink, correct, fine bitter notes.

MARQUÉS DE VALCARLOS 2012 RD
tempranillo, merlot

85 Colour: rose, bright. Nose: red berry notes, ripe fruit, powerfull. Palate: fruity, correct, easy to drink, fruity aftestaste.

MARQUÉS DE VALCARLOS CHARDONNAY 2012 B
100% chardonnay

83

MARQUÉS DE VALCARLOS TEMPRANILLO 2010 T ROBLE
100% tempranillo

85 Colour: cherry, garnet rim. Nose: ripe fruit, spicy, creamy oak, toasty, fine reductive notes. Palate: powerful, flavourful, toasty.

BODEGAS VEGA DEL CASTILLO

Rua Romana, 7
31390 Olite (Navarra)
☎: +34 948 740 012 - Fax: +34 948 740 012
info@vegadelcastillo.com

CAPA ROJA 2011 T
tempranillo

88 Colour: bright cherry. Nose: ripe fruit, sweet spices, creamy oak. Palate: flavourful, fruity, toasty.

DUBHE 2008 T ROBLE
tempranillo, cabernet sauvignon, merlot

91 Colour: bright cherry. Nose: ripe fruit, sweet spices, creamy oak, expressive. Palate: flavourful, fruity, toasty, round tannins.

LLAVERO 2009 TC
cabernet sauvignon

86 Colour: cherry, garnet rim. Nose: ripe fruit, spicy, wild herbs. Palate: fruity, good acidity, correct.

MERAK 2008 T
tempranillo, cabernet sauvignon, merlot

89 Colour: cherry, garnet rim. Nose: medium intensity, ripe fruit, dried herbs. Palate: round, fruity, round tannins.

ROSADO VEGA DEL CASTILLO 2012 RD
garnacha

87 Colour: brilliant rose. Nose: candied fruit, lactic notes, floral. Palate: fresh, fruity, easy to drink, balanced.

VEGA DEL CASTILLO 2009 TC
tempranillo, cabernet sauvignon, merlot

88 Colour: cherry, garnet rim. Nose: ripe fruit, spicy, creamy oak, toasty. Palate: powerful, flavourful, toasty, round tannins.

BODEGAS VINÍCOLA NAVARRA

Avda. Pamplona, 25
31398 Tiebas (Navarra)
☎: +34 948 360 131 - Fax: +34 948 360 544
www.vinicolanavarra.com
vinicolanavarra@pernod-ricard.com

CASTILLO DE JAVIER 2012 RD
garnacha

88 Colour: rose, bright. Nose: medium intensity, fruit expression, rose petals. Palate: fruity, good acidity, correct.

LAS CAMPANAS 2012 RD
garnacha

85 Colour: raspberry rose. Nose: candied fruit, dried flowers, fragrant herbs. Palate: light-bodied, flavourful, good acidity.

LAS CAMPANAS CHARDONNAY 2012 B
chardonnay, viura

85 Colour: bright straw. Nose: floral, fragrant herbs, tropical fruit. Palate: light-bodied, fresh, fruity.

LAS CAMPANAS TEMPRANILLO 2012 T
tempranillo

88 Colour: cherry, purple rim. Nose: fresh fruit, red berry notes, floral, lactic notes. Palate: flavourful, fruity, good acidity.

BODEGAS VIÑA MAGAÑA

San Miguel, 9
31523 Barillas (Navarra)
☎: +34 948 850 034 - Fax: +34 948 851 536
www.vinamagana.com
bodegas@vinamagana.com

BARÓN DE MAGAÑA 2009 TC

90 Colour: cherry, garnet rim. Nose: toasty, cocoa bean, balsamic herbs, ripe fruit. Palate: powerful, flavourful, toasty, long.

MAGAÑA CALCHETAS 2010 T

91 Colour: cherry, garnet rim. Nose: ripe fruit, spicy, creamy oak, balsamic herbs. Palate: powerful, flavourful, toasty, round tannins.

MAGAÑA DIGNUS 2009 TC

89 Colour: cherry, garnet rim. Nose: red berry notes, ripe fruit, sweet spices. Palate: powerful, flavourful, toasty.

TORCAS 2009 T

92 Colour: cherry, garnet rim. Nose: red berry notes, ripe fruit, mineral, fragrant herbs, sweet spices, creamy oak. Palate: rich, flavourful, spicy, long, balanced.

BODEGAS Y VIÑEDOS ARTAZU

Mayor, 3
31109 Artazu (Navarra)
☎: +34 945 600 119 - Fax: +34 945 600 850
artazu@artadi.com

SANTA CRUZ DE ARTAZU 2011 T
100% garnacha

94 Colour: bright cherry. Nose: sweet spices, creamy oak, mineral, fruit expression, red berry notes. Palate: flavourful, fruity, toasty, round tannins.

CAMPOS DE ENANZO S.C.

Mayor, 189
31521 Murchante (Navarra)
☎: +34 948 838 031 - Fax: +34 948 838 677
www.enanzo.com
info@enanzo.com

ENANZO 2007 TR
70% tempranillo, 15% cabernet sauvignon, 15% merlot

86 Colour: cherry, garnet rim. Nose: ripe fruit, spicy, creamy oak, toasty. Palate: powerful, flavourful, toasty.

ENANZO 2008 TC
70% tempranillo, 15% cabernet sauvignon, 15% merlot

86 Colour: cherry, garnet rim. Nose: medium intensity, ripe fruit, cocoa bean. Palate: fruity, easy to drink, round tannins.

ENANZO 2012 RD
garnacha

87 Colour: rose, purple rim. Nose: fresh, fresh fruit, red berry notes, lactic notes. Palate: fruity, good acidity, correct.

ENANZO CHARDONNAY 2012 B BARRICA
100% chardonnay

88 Colour: bright yellow. Nose: faded flowers, ripe fruit, sweet spices. Palate: fruity, flavourful, ripe fruit.

REMONTE 2007 TR
70% tempranillo, 15% cabernet sauvignon, 15% merlot

86 Colour: deep cherry, garnet rim. Nose: toasty, spicy, ripe fruit, dark chocolate. Palate: correct, round tannins, good finish.

REMONTE 2009 TC
70% tempranillo, 15% cabernet sauvignon, 15% merlot

89 Colour: bright cherry. Nose: ripe fruit, sweet spices, creamy oak, toasty. Palate: flavourful, fruity, toasty, round tannins.

REMONTE 2012 RD
100% garnacha

87 Colour: rose, purple rim. Nose: powerfull, ripe fruit, red berry notes, floral, expressive. Palate: powerful, fruity, fresh.

REMONTE CHARDONNAY 2012 B
100% chardonnay

86 Colour: bright straw, greenish rim. Nose: medium intensity, dried flowers, ripe fruit. Palate: flavourful, good acidity, fine bitter notes.

CARREFOUR

Campezo, 16
28022 Madrid (Madrid)
☎: +34 902 202 000
www.carrefour.es

MONTE ESQUINZA 2007 TR

89 Colour: cherry, garnet rim. Nose: ripe fruit, spicy, creamy oak, toasty. Palate: powerful, flavourful, toasty, round tannins.

MONTE ESQUINZA 2010 TC
tempranillo, cabernet sauvignon, merlot

87 Colour: bright cherry. Nose: ripe fruit, sweet spices, creamy oak. Palate: flavourful, fruity, toasty, round tannins.

MONTE ESQUINZA 2012 B
viura

84

MONTE ESQUINZA 2012 MOSCATEL
moscatel

87 Colour: bright straw, greenish rim. Nose: ripe fruit, jasmine, white flowers, varietal. Palate: rich, sweet.

MONTE ESQUINZA 2012 RD
100% garnacha

83

MONTE ESQUINZA 2012 T
tempranillo

86 Colour: cherry, purple rim. Nose: fresh fruit, red berry notes, floral. Palate: flavourful, fruity, good acidity, round tannins.

MONTE ESQUINZA CABERNET SAUVIGNON 2012 T
cabernet sauvignon

81

DISTRIBUCIONES B. IÑAKI NÚÑEZ

Ctra. de Ablitas a Ribafora, Km. 5
31523 Ablitas (Navarra)
☎: +34 948 386 210 - Fax: +34 629 354 190
www.pagodecirsus.com
bodegasin@pagodecirsus.com

PAGO DE CIRSUS CHARDONNAY 2011 BFB
100% chardonnay

90 Colour: bright yellow. Nose: balanced, ripe fruit, sweet spices, faded flowers. Palate: fruity, flavourful, good acidity, spicy.

PAGO DE CIRSUS CHARDONNAY 2012 B
100% chardonnay

89 Colour: yellow. Nose: balanced, ripe fruit, citrus fruit, dried flowers. Palate: flavourful, fruity, good acidity.

PAGO DE CIRSUS DE IÑAKI NÚÑEZ CUVÉE ESPECIAL 2009 TR
tempranillo, merlot, syrah

91 Colour: bright cherry, garnet rim. Nose: ripe fruit, spicy, sweet spices. Palate: good structure, full, flavourful, round tannins.

PAGO DE CIRSUS DE IÑAKI NÚÑEZ SELECCIÓN DE FAMILIA 2009 T
tempranillo, syrah

91 Colour: cherry, garnet rim. Nose: ripe fruit, spicy, creamy oak, toasty, complex, earthy notes. Palate: powerful, flavourful, toasty, fine bitter notes.

PAGO DE CIRSUS DE IÑAKI NUÑEZ VENDIMIA SELECCIONADA 2010 TC
tempranillo, merlot, syrah

90 Colour: bright cherry. Nose: ripe fruit, sweet spices, creamy oak, expressive, balsamic herbs. Palate: flavourful, fruity, toasty, round tannins.

PAGO DE CIRSUS MOSCATEL VENDIMIA TARDÍA 2007 BFB
100% moscatel grano menudo

92 Colour: bright golden. Nose: balanced, candied fruit, honeyed notes, faded flowers. Palate: rich, full, flavourful, long.

PAGO DE CIRSUS OPUS 11 2009 T
syrah

93 Colour: cherry, garnet rim. Nose: red berry notes, ripe fruit, floral, sweet spices, creamy oak, mineral. Palate: spicy, long, powerful, flavourful, round tannins.

PAGO DE CIRSUS ROSÉ GRAN CUVÉE ESPECIAL 2012 RD
tempranillo, syrah

90 Colour: light cherry, bright. Nose: floral, ripe fruit, balanced, expressive. Palate: good acidity, fine bitter notes, spicy, long.

TE DEUM CHARDONNAY 2011 BFB
100% chardonnay

88 Colour: bright yellow. Nose: powerfull, ripe fruit, sweet spices, creamy oak, medium intensity. Palate: rich, smoky aftertaste, flavourful.

TE DEUM CHARDONNAY 2012 B
100% chardonnay

88 Colour: bright straw. Nose: citrus fruit, dried flowers, fragrant herbs, medium intensity. Palate: powerful, flavourful, fruity, balanced.

TE DEUM CUVÈE ESPECIAL 2009 T
tempranillo, merlot, syrah

88 Colour: bright cherry, garnet rim. Nose: balanced, ripe fruit, toasty, spicy. Palate: balanced, ripe fruit.

TE DEUM SELECCIÓN FAMILIA 2009 T
tempranillo, syrah

90 Colour: cherry, garnet rim. Nose: ripe fruit, spicy, creamy oak, toasty, complex. Palate: powerful, flavourful, toasty, round tannins.

TE DEUM VENDIMIA SELECCIONADA 2010 T
tempranillo, merlot, syrah

90 Colour: bright cherry. Nose: ripe fruit, balsamic herbs, sweet spices, cocoa bean, dark chocolate. Palate: flavourful, fruity, toasty, balanced.

DOMAINES LUPIER

Monseñor Justo Goizueta, 4
31495 San Martín de Unx (Navarra)
☎: +34 639 622 111
www.domaineslupier.com
info@domaineslupier.com

DOMAINES LUPIER EL TERROIR 2010 T
100% garnacha

93 Colour: cherry, garnet rim. Nose: ripe fruit, floral, earthy notes, spicy, creamy oak. Palate: rich, flavourful, spicy, long, balanced.

DOMAINES LUPIER LA DAMA VIÑAS VIEJAS 2010 T
100% garnacha

94 Colour: cherry, garnet rim. Nose: red berry notes, ripe fruit, balsamic herbs, dry stone, spicy, balanced. Palate: powerful, flavourful, balsamic, elegant.

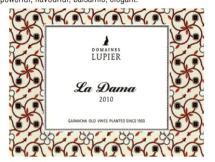

EMILIO VALERIO - LADERAS DE MONTEJURRA

Paraje de Argonga
31263 Dicastillo (Navarra)
www.laderasdemontejurra.com
info@laderasdemontejurra.com

AMBURZA 2010 T
80% cabernet sauvignon, 10% garnacha, 10% tempranillo

91 Colour: deep cherry, garnet rim. Nose: complex, ripe fruit, spicy. Palate: good acidity, fine bitter notes, ripe fruit.

ARANBELTZA 2011 T
100% garnacha

92 Colour: cherry, garnet rim. Nose: balanced, expressive, ripe fruit, dried herbs. Palate: good acidity, round tannins, spicy.

EMILIO VALERIO LADERAS DE MONTEJURRA 2011 T
25% garnacha, 10% tempranillo, 30% merlot, 35% cabernet sauvignon

93 Colour: cherry, garnet rim. Nose: ripe fruit, mineral, balanced, spicy. Palate: good structure, flavourful, full, round tannins.

LA MERCED 2011 B
100% malvasía

90 Colour: bright yellow. Nose: expressive, balanced, spicy, citrus fruit. Palate: fruity, good acidity, fine bitter notes, complex.

USUARAN 2011 T
50% garnacha, 25% tempranillo, 25% graciano

90 Colour: deep cherry, garnet rim. Nose: complex, fruit preserve, dark chocolate. Palate: full, round tannins, spicy.

VIÑA DE LEORÍN 2011 T
95% garnacha, 5% tempranillo

90 Colour: bright cherry. Nose: ripe fruit, sweet spices, creamy oak, expressive. Palate: flavourful, fruity, toasty.

VIÑA DE SAN MARTÍN 2011 T
95% garnacha, 5% tempranillo

93 Colour: cherry, garnet rim. Nose: powerfull, violet drops, ripe fruit, mineral. Palate: good structure, flavourful, spicy, good acidity.

FINCA ALBRET

Ctra. Cadreita-Villafranca, s/n
31515 Cadreita (Navarra)
☎: +34 948 406 806 - Fax: +34 948 406 699
www.fincaalbret.com
info@fincaalbret.com

ALBRET 2008 TR
85% tempranillo, 5% merlot, 10% cabernet sauvignon

91 Colour: cherry, garnet rim. Nose: red berry notes, ripe fruit, balsamic herbs, creamy oak. Palate: powerful, flavourful, spicy, long.

ALBRET 2012 RD
100% garnacha

88 Colour: rose, purple rim. Nose: powerfull, ripe fruit, red berry notes, floral, expressive. Palate: powerful, fruity, fresh.

ALBRET CHARDONNAY 2012 BFB
100% chardonnay

90 Colour: bright straw. Nose: citrus fruit, balsamic herbs, candied fruit, spicy, creamy oak. Palate: powerful, fresh, fruity, balanced.

ALBRET LA VIÑA DE MI MADRE 2008 TR
95% cabernet sauvignon, 5% merlot

92 Colour: cherry, garnet rim. Nose: ripe fruit, spicy, creamy oak, toasty, complex, earthy notes. Palate: powerful, flavourful, toasty, balanced.

JUAN DE ALBRET 2009 TC
60% tempranillo, 20% merlot, 20% cabernet sauvignon

90 Colour: cherry, garnet rim. Nose: red berry notes, ripe fruit, balsamic herbs, sweet spices, creamy oak. Palate: powerful, flavourful, spicy.

GARCÍA BURGOS

Finca La Cantera de Santa Ana, s/n
31521 Murchante (Navarra)
☎: +34 948 847 734 - Fax: +34 948 847 734
www.bodegasgarciaburgos.com
info@bodegasgarciaburgos.com

FINCA LA CANTERA DE SANTA ANA 2007 T
100% cabernet sauvignon

92 Colour: cherry, garnet rim. Nose: ripe fruit, spicy, creamy oak, toasty, complex, fine reductive notes. Palate: powerful, flavourful, toasty, round tannins.

GARCÍA BURGOS SH 2010 T
100% syrah

90 Colour: cherry, garnet rim. Nose: red berry notes, ripe fruit, sweet spices, creamy oak. Palate: powerful, flavourful, spicy, long.

GARCÍA BURGOS VENDIMIA SELECCIONADA 2009 T
40% cabernet sauvignon, 40% merlot, 20% syrah

89 Colour: bright cherry. Nose: ripe fruit, sweet spices, creamy oak, expressive. Palate: flavourful, fruity, toasty.

LOLA GARCÍA AS 2007 TR
100% merlot

89 Colour: cherry, garnet rim. Nose: fruit preserve, balsamic herbs, cocoa bean, sweet spices, fine reductive notes. Palate: powerful, flavourful, full, spicy.

J. CHIVITE FAMILY ESTATE

31264 Aberin (Navarra)
☎: +34 948 555 285 - Fax: +34 948 555 285
www.chivite.com
info@bodegaschivite.com

CHIVITE COLECCIÓN 125 2004 BFB
100% chardonnay

98 Colour: bright straw. Nose: fruit expression, candied fruit, citrus fruit, spicy, creamy oak. Palate: varietal, full, mineral, ripe fruit, good acidity.

CHIVITE COLECCIÓN 125 2009 TR
tempranillo

94 Colour: cherry, garnet rim. Nose: ripe fruit, spicy, creamy oak, toasty, mineral, earthy notes. Palate: powerful, flavourful, toasty, round tannins.

CHIVITE COLECCIÓN 125 2010 BFB
chardonnay

95 Colour: bright yellow. Nose: powerfull, sweet spices, creamy oak, fragrant herbs, mineral, ripe fruit. Palate: rich, smoky aftertaste, flavourful, fresh, good acidity.

CHIVITE COLECCIÓN 125 2011
RD FERMENTADO EN BARRICA
tempranillo, garnacha

93 Colour: onion pink. Nose: elegant, candied fruit, dried flowers, fragrant herbs, red berry notes. Palate: light-bodied, flavourful, good acidity, long, spicy.

CHIVITE COLECCIÓN 125
VENDIMIA TARDÍA 2009 B
moscatel grano menudo

95 Colour: golden. Nose: powerfull, floral, honeyed notes, candied fruit, fragrant herbs. Palate: flavourful, sweet, fresh, fruity, good acidity, long.

CHIVITE FINCA DE VILLATUERTA
CHARDONNAY SOBRE LÍAS 2011 B
chardonnay

92 Colour: bright straw. Nose: fruit expression, citrus fruit, ripe fruit. Palate: flavourful, fruity, ripe fruit, good acidity.

CHIVITE FINCA DE VILLATUERTA
SELECCIÓN ESPECIAL 2009 T
tempranillo, merlot

91 Colour: bright cherry. Nose: ripe fruit, expressive. Palate: flavourful, fruity, toasty, round tannins.

CHIVITE FINCA DE VILLATUERTA SYRAH 2010 T
syrah

93 Colour: deep cherry. Nose: ripe fruit, sweet spices, expressive, balanced. Palate: fruity, balanced, ripe fruit, round tannins.

LA CALANDRIA. PURA GARNACHA

Camino de Aspra, s/n
31521 Murchante (Navarra)
☎: +34 630 904 327
www.puragarnacha.com
luis@lacalandria.org

CIENTRUENOS 2011 T BARRICA
garnacha

91 Colour: light cherry. Nose: red berry notes, ripe fruit, floral, balsamic herbs, spicy. Palate: long, flavourful, fruity, balanced.

SONROJO 2012 RD
garnacha

88 Colour: rose, bright. Nose: medium intensity, red berry notes, fresh, scrubland. Palate: flavourful, fruity, easy to drink, good acidity.

VOLANDERA 2012 T MACERACIÓN CARBÓNICA
garnacha

90 Colour: bright cherry, purple rim. Nose: balanced, expressive, red berry notes, ripe fruit, wild herbs. Palate: flavourful, fruity.

NEKEAS

Las Huertas, s/n
31154 Añorbe (Navarra)
☎: +34 948 350 296 - Fax: +34 948 350 300
www.nekeas.com
nekeas@nekeas.com

EL CHAPARRAL DE VEGA SINDOA
OLD VINE GARNACHA 2011 T
100% garnacha

90 Colour: bright cherry, garnet rim. Nose: balanced, red berry notes, ripe fruit, cocoa bean. Palate: flavourful, varietal, fruity, round tannins.

NEKEAS CHARDONNAY "CUVÉE ALLIER" 2011 BFB
100% chardonnay

88 Colour: bright yellow. Nose: dried herbs, ripe fruit, toasty, sweet spices, pattiserie. Palate: powerful, flavourful, long, spicy.

NEKEAS 2010 TC
40% tempranillo, 60% cabernet sauvignon

89 Colour: cherry, garnet rim. Nose: ripe fruit, dark chocolate, creamy oak, toasty. Palate: powerful, flavourful, long, toasty.

NEKEAS CHARDONNAY 2012 B
100% chardonnay

89 Colour: bright straw. Nose: white flowers, fragrant herbs, ripe fruit, tropical fruit. Palate: rich, powerful, flavourful, correct.

NEKEAS TEMPRANILLO MERLOT 2012 T
70% tempranillo, 30% merlot

86 Colour: cherry, garnet rim. Nose: wild herbs, ripe fruit, medium intensity. Palate: correct, balsamic, flavourful.

NUEVOS VINOS

Alfafara, 12 Entlo.
3803 Alcoy (Alicante)
☎: +34 965 549 172 - Fax: +34 965 549 173
www.nuevosvinos.es
josecanto@nuevosvinos.es

TERRAPLEN BLANCO VIURA 2012 B
100% viura

83

TERRAPLEN ROSADO GARNACHA 2012 RD
100% garnacha

88 Colour: rose, purple rim. Nose: ripe fruit, red berry notes, floral, lactic notes. Palate: powerful, fruity, fresh.

TERRAPLEN TINTO GARNACHA 2012 T
100% garnacha

85 Colour: cherry, garnet rim. Nose: red berry notes, ripe fruit, balsamic herbs. Palate: warm, powerful, flavourful.

PACO & LOLA

Valdamor, 18 - XII
36968 Meaño (Pontevedra)
☎: +34 986 747 779 - Fax: +34 986 748 940
www.pacolola.com
internacional@pacolola.com

PACO 2011 T
50% garnacha, 50% tempranillo

88 Colour: cherry, garnet rim. Nose: red berry notes, ripe fruit, balsamic herbs, spicy, creamy oak. Palate: powerful, flavourful, rich, spicy.

PAGO DE LARRÁINZAR

Camino de la Corona, s/n
31240 Ayegui (Navarra)
☎: +34 948 550 421 - Fax: +34 948 556 120
www.pagodelarrainzar.com
info@pagodelarrainzar.com

PAGO DE LARRAINZAR 2007 T
40% merlot, 40% cabernet sauvignon, 15% tempranillo, 5% garnacha

92 Colour: bright cherry. Nose: ripe fruit, sweet spices, creamy oak, expressive. Palate: flavourful, fruity, toasty, round tannins, balanced, elegant.

RASO DE LARRAINZAR 2009 T
50% tempranillo, 30% merlot, 15% cabernet sauvignon, 5% garnacha

91 Colour: cherry, garnet rim. Nose: medium intensity, ripe fruit, spicy, scrubland. Palate: balanced, round tannins, full.

SEÑORÍO DE ANDIÓN

Ctra. Pamplona-Zaragoza, Km. 38
31390 Olite (Navarra)
☎: +34 948 712 193 - Fax: +34 948 712 343
www.familiabelasco.com
info@familiabelasco.com

SEÑORÍO DE ANDIÓN 2008 T
cabernet sauvignon, tempranillo, merlot, graciano

92 Colour: deep cherry, garnet rim. Nose: elegant, balanced, ripe fruit, sweet spices. Palate: balanced, good acidity, round tannins, spicy.

SEÑORÍO DE ANDIÓN MOSCATEL VENDIMIA TARDÍA 2007 B
moscatel grano menudo

93 Colour: old gold. Nose: sweet spices, cocoa bean, candied fruit, elegant, neat. Palate: rich, flavourful, full, complex, spicy.

VINÍCOLA CORELLANA

Ctra. del Villar, s/n
31591 Corella (Navarra)
☎: +34 948 780 617 - Fax: +34 948 401 794
www.vinicolacorellana.com
info@vinicolacorellana.com

VIÑA ZORZAL GARNACHA VIÑAS VIEJAS 2012 T
100% garnacha

86 Colour: deep cherry, purple rim. Nose: powerfull, fruit preserve. Palate: long, fruity, full.

VIÑA ZORZAL GRACIANO 2011 T
100% graciano

88 Colour: cherry, garnet rim. Nose: ripe fruit, balsamic herbs, spicy, fine reductive notes. Palate: powerful, flavourful.

VIÑA ZORZAL MERLOT 2012 T
100% merlot

86 Colour: cherry, garnet rim. Nose: red berry notes, ripe fruit, sweet spices. Palate: powerful, flavourful, spicy.

VINOS Y VIÑEDOS DOMINIO LASIERPE

Ribera, s/n
31592 Cintruénigo (Navarra)
☎: +34 948 811 033 - Fax: +34 948 815 160
www.dominiolasierpe.com
comercial@dominiolasierpe.com

FINCA LASIERPE BLANCO DE CHARDONNAY 2012 BR
100% chardonnay

87 Colour: bright yellow. Nose: ripe fruit, tropical fruit, powerfull. Palate: fruity, flavourful, balanced.

FINCA LASIERPE BLANCO DE VIURA 2012 B
100% viura

86 Colour: bright yellow. Nose: balanced, wild herbs, citrus fruit. Palate: fresh, fruity, flavourful, easy to drink.

FINCA LASIERPE GARNACHA 2012 RD
100% garnacha

86 Colour: light cherry, bright. Nose: fresh, red berry notes, rose petals. Palate: flavourful, good acidity, fine bitter notes.

FINCA LASIERPE TEMPRANILLO GARNACHA 2012 T
60% tempranillo, 40% garnacha

85 Colour: cherry, purple rim. Nose: balanced, ripe fruit, wild herbs. Palate: fruity, good finish, easy to drink.

FLOR DE LASIERPE GARNACHA VIÑAS VIEJAS 2009 T
100% garnacha

88 Colour: cherry, garnet rim. Nose: ripe fruit, spicy, creamy oak, complex, fine reductive notes. Palate: powerful, flavourful, toasty.

FLOR DE LASIERPE GRACIANO 2009 T
100% graciano

87 Colour: cherry, garnet rim. Nose: ripe fruit, spicy, creamy oak, toasty, complex. Palate: powerful, flavourful, toasty.

VIÑA ALIAGA

Camino del Villar. N-161, Km. 3
31591 Corella (Navarra)
☎: +34 948 401 321 - Fax: +34 948 781 414
www.vinaaliaga.com
sales@vinaaliaga.com

ALIAGA COLECCIÓN PRIVADA 2008 TC
80% tempranillo, 20% cabernet sauvignon

88 Colour: cherry, garnet rim. Nose: ripe fruit, spicy, creamy oak, toasty, fine reductive notes. Palate: powerful, flavourful, toasty, round tannins.

ALIAGA CUVÉE 2009 T
85% tempranillo, 15% cabernet sauvignon

86 Colour: bright cherry, garnet rim. Nose: medium intensity, balsamic herbs, dark chocolate. Palate: light-bodied, fine tannins, correct.

ALIAGA DOSCARLOS 2012 B
sauvignon blanc

86 Colour: bright yellow. Nose: dried flowers, dried herbs, ripe fruit, citrus fruit. Palate: fruity, easy to drink, correct.

ALIAGA GARNACHA VIEJA 2009 T
100% garnacha

86 Colour: cherry, garnet rim. Nose: ripe fruit, spicy, toasty, fine reductive notes. Palate: powerful, flavourful, toasty.

ALIAGA LÁGRIMA DE GARNACHA 2012 RD
100% garnacha

86 Colour: light cherry. Nose: red berry notes, violet drops, balsamic herbs. Palate: light-bodied, fresh, fruity, flavourful.

ALIAGA MOSCATEL VENDIMIA TARDÍA 2012 B
100% moscatel grano menudo

87 Colour: bright straw. Nose: floral, citrus fruit, candied fruit, fragrant herbs. Palate: powerful, flavourful, fruity, sweet.

ALIAGA RESERVA DE LA FAMILIA 2005 TR
75% tempranillo, 25% cabernet sauvignon

87 Colour: pale ruby, brick rim edge. Nose: ripe fruit, cigar, fine reductive notes, aged wood nuances, creamy oak. Palate: powerful, flavourful, balsamic, long.

ALIAGA TEMPRANILLO 2011 T
100% tempranillo

83

VIÑA ALIAGA ANTONIO CORPUS 2002 T
100% garnacha

86 Colour: light cherry, orangey edge. Nose: roasted coffee, spicy. Palate: correct, ripe fruit.

VIÑA VALDORBA

Ctra. de la Estación
31395 Garinoain (Navarra)
☎: +34 948 720 505 - Fax: +34 948 720 505
www.bodegasvaldorba.com
bodegasvaldorba@bodegasvaldorba.com

EOLO 2010 TC
cabernet sauvignon, merlot, garnacha, graciano

85 Colour: cherry, garnet rim. Nose: ripe fruit, medium intensity, sweet spices. Palate: fruity, good acidity, round tannins.

EOLO CAURO 2002 TR
cabernet sauvignon, graciano

88 Colour: bright cherry, orangey edge. Nose: cocoa bean, ripe fruit, tobacco. Palate: flavourful, ripe fruit, correct, good acidity.

EOLO CHARDONNAY 2011 B
100% chardonnay

85 Colour: yellow. Nose: powerfull, ripe fruit, faded flowers. Palate: flavourful, fine bitter notes.

EOLO MOSCATEL 2011 B
moscatel grano menudo

88 Colour: yellow. Nose: balanced, white flowers, honeyed notes, varietal. Palate: correct, sweet, fruity, rich.

EOLO SYRAH 2010 T
100% syrah

90 Colour: bright cherry. Nose: ripe fruit, sweet spices, creamy oak, violets, lactic notes. Palate: flavourful, fruity, toasty, round tannins.

GRAN EOLO 2008 TR
cabernet sauvignon, merlot, garnacha

87 Colour: light cherry. Nose: ripe fruit, balsamic herbs, fine reductive notes, spicy. Palate: powerful, flavourful, long.

DO NAVARRA / D.O.P.

VIÑEDOS DE CALIDAD

Ctra. Tudela, s/n
31591 Corella (Navarra)
☎: +34 948 782 014 - Fax: +34 948 782 164
www.vinosalex.com
inf@vinosalex.com

ALEX 2010 TC
tempranillo, merlot, graciano

88 Colour: bright cherry. Nose: sweet spices, creamy oak, red berry notes, ripe fruit. Palate: flavourful, fruity, toasty.

ALEX GARNACHA 2012 RD
garnacha

88 Colour: raspberry rose. Nose: floral, raspberry, red berry notes, fragrant herbs. Palate: fresh, fruity, flavourful, easy to drink.

ALEX MOSCATEL 2012 B
moscatel grano menudo

88 Colour: bright straw. Nose: fruit liqueur notes, faded flowers, powerfull. Palate: flavourful, rich, fruity, long, full.

ALEX TEMPRANILLO 2012 T
tempranillo

86 Colour: cherry, purple rim. Nose: medium intensity, ripe fruit, fruit preserve. Palate: fruity, flavourful.

ALEX VIURA 2012 B
viura

85 Colour: bright straw. Nose: fresh, fresh fruit, white flowers. Palate: flavourful, fruity, good acidity.

ONTINAR 2009 T
tempranillo, merlot

88 Colour: cherry, garnet rim. Nose: creamy oak, cocoa bean, sweet spices. Palate: fruity, flavourful, round tannins.

VIÑEDOS Y BODEGAS ALCONDE

Ctra. de Calahorra, s/n
31260 Lerín (Navarra)
☎: +34 948 530 058 - Fax: +34 948 530 589
www.bodegasalconde.com
info@bodegasalconde.com

ALCONDE 2005 TR
merlot, cabernet sauvignon, tempranillo, garnacha

90 Colour: cherry, garnet rim. Nose: ripe fruit, spicy, creamy oak, toasty, complex, fine reductive notes. Palate: powerful, flavourful, toasty, round tannins, balanced.

BODEGAS ALCONDE SELECCIÓN "TINTO ROBLE" 2010 T ROBLE
merlot, garnacha

86 Colour: cherry, garnet rim. Nose: spicy, ripe fruit, medium intensity, dried herbs. Palate: correct, ripe fruit.

BODEGAS ALCONDE SELECCIÓN 2007 TR
85% tempranillo, 10% merlot, 5% cabernet sauvignon

88 Colour: bright cherry, garnet rim. Nose: spicy, ripe fruit. Palate: flavourful, correct, good acidity, round tannins.

BODEGAS ALCONDE SELECCIÓN 2008 TC
tempranillo, garnacha, cabernet sauvignon

88 Colour: cherry, garnet rim. Nose: ripe fruit, spicy, toasty, fine reductive notes. Palate: powerful, flavourful, toasty, round.

BODEGAS ALCONDE SELECCIÓN GARNACHA 2007 TR
garnacha, cabernet sauvignon, merlot

88 Colour: bright cherry, garnet rim. Nose: medium intensity, balsamic herbs, ripe fruit. Palate: correct, good acidity, ripe fruit.

VIÑA SARDASOL 2006 TR
tempranillo, merlot, cabernet sauvignon

85 Colour: cherry, garnet rim. Nose: ripe fruit, balsamic herbs, creamy oak, toasty. Palate: powerful, flavourful, correct.

VIÑA SARDASOL 2009 TC
tempranillo

86 Colour: bright cherry, garnet rim. Nose: medium intensity, ripe fruit, toasty, spicy. Palate: fruity, flavourful, easy to drink.

VIÑA SARDASOL 2012 B
chardonnay

83

VIÑA SARDASOL 2012 RD
garnacha

86 Colour: rose, bright. Nose: fresh fruit, medium intensity, citrus fruit. Palate: flavourful, fruity, fresh.

VIÑA SARDASOL CABERNET SAUVIGNON 2007 TR
cabernet sauvignon

87 Colour: cherry, garnet rim. Nose: balanced, wild herbs, varietal, ripe fruit. Palate: balanced, fruity, round tannins.

VIÑA SARDASOL MERLOT 2007 TR
merlot

88 Colour: cherry, garnet rim. Nose: ripe fruit, spicy, creamy oak, toasty. Palate: powerful, flavourful, toasty.

VIÑA SARDASOL MERLOT 2011 T ROBLE
merlot

89 Colour: cherry, garnet rim. Nose: medium intensity, sweet spices, balanced, ripe fruit. Palate: flavourful, good acidity, easy to drink.

VIÑA SARDASOL TEMPRANILLO 2011 T
tempranillo

84

VIÑA SARDASOL TEMPRANILLO MERLOT 2011 T ROBLE
tempranillo, merlot

84

DO PENEDÈS / D.O.P.

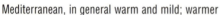

LOCATION:

In the province of Barcelona, between the pre-coastal Catalonian mountain range and the plains that lead to the Mediterranean coast. There are three different areas: Penedès Superior, Penedès Central or Medio and Bajo Penedès.

CLIMATE:

Mediterranean, in general warm and mild; warmer in the Bajo Penedès region due to the influence of the Mediterranean Sea, with slightly lower temperatures in Medio Penedès and Penedès Superior, where the climate is typically pre-coastal (greater contrasts between maximum and minimum temperatures, more frequent frosts and annual rainfall which at some places can reach 990 litres per square metre).

SOIL:

There is deep soil, not too sandy or too clayey, permeable, which retains the rainwater well. The soil is poor in organic matter and not very fertile.

GRAPE VARIETIES:

WHITE: *Macabeo, Xarel·lo, Parellada, Chardonnay, Riesling, Gewürztraminer, Chenin Blanc, Moscatel de Alejandría, Garnacha Blanca* and *Vioquier*.
RED: *Garnacha, Merlot, Cariñena, Ull de Llebre* (*Tempranillo*), *Pinot Noir, Monastrell, Cabernet Sauvignon, Petit Verdot, Syrah* and *Sumoll*.

SUB-REGIONS:

Penedès Superior. The vineyards reach an altitude of 800 m; the traditional, characteristic variety is the Parellada, which is better suited to the cooler regions.
Penedès Central or Medio. Cava makes up a large part of the production in this region; the most abundant traditional varieties are *Macabeo* and *Xarel-lo*.
Bajo Penedès. This is the closest region to the sea, with a lower altitude and wines with a markedly Mediterranean character.

FIGURES:

Vineyard surface: 19.679 – **Wine-Growers:** 4.379 – **Wineries:** 183 – **2012 Harvest rating:** white: Excellent. Red and Roses: Very Good – **Production:** 16.402.100 litres – **Market percentages:** 75% domestic. 25% export

VINTAGE RATING PENÍNGUIDE				
2008	2009	2010	2011	2012
VERY GOOD	EXCELLENT	VERY GOOD	VERY GOOD	GOOD

CONSEJO REGULADOR
Plaça Àgora. s/n. - Pol. Ind. Domenys, II - 08720 Vilafranca del Penedès (Barcelona) ☎: +34 938 904 811 - Fax: +34 938 904 754
dopenedes@dopenedes.cat www.dopenedes.es

1 + 1 = 3

Masía Navinés
8736 Guardiola de Font-Rubí (Barcelona)
☎: +34 938 974 069 - Fax: +34 938 974 724
www.umesufan3.com
umesu@umesufan3.com

1+1=3 XAREL.LO 2012 B
100% xarel.lo

88 Colour: bright straw. Nose: fresh, fresh fruit, white flowers, fragrant herbs. Palate: flavourful, fruity, good acidity, balanced.

DAHLIA 1 + 1 = 3 2011 B
75% viognier, 25% xarel.lo

90 Colour: bright straw. Nose: fresh, fresh fruit, white flowers, fragrant herbs. Palate: flavourful, fruity, good acidity, balanced.

DÉFORA 1 + 1 = 3 2010 T
75% garnacha, 25% cariñena

91 Colour: cherry, garnet rim. Nose: ripe fruit, spicy, creamy oak, toasty. Palate: powerful, flavourful, toasty, round tannins.

AGUSTÍ TORELLÓ MATA

La Serra, s/n (Camí de Ribalta)
8770 Sant Sadurní D'Anoia (Barcelona)
☎: +34 938 911 173 - Fax: +34 938 912 616
www.agustitorellomata.com
comunicacio@agustitorellomata.com

APTIÀ D'AGUSTÍ TORELLÓ MATA "COL.LECCIÓ TERRERS" 2012 BFB
100% macabeo

92 Colour: bright straw. Nose: balanced, ripe fruit, white flowers, tropical fruit. Palate: flavourful, fruity, long, good acidity.

XAREL.LO D'AGUSTÍ TORELLÓ MATA "COL.LECCIÓ TERRERS" 2012 B
100% xarel.lo

89 Colour: bright straw. Nose: medium intensity, varietal, dried flowers. Palate: flavourful, ripe fruit, good acidity.

XII SUBIRAT PARENT D'AGUSTÍ TORELLÓ MATA "COL.LECCIÓ TERRERS" 2012 B
100% subirat parent

89 Colour: bright straw. Nose: ripe fruit, faded flowers, mineral, expressive. Palate: flavourful, good acidity, good finish.

ALBET I NOYA

Camí Can Vendrell de la Codina, s/n
8739 Sant Pau D'Ordal (Barcelona)
☎: +34 938 994 812 - Fax: +34 938 994 930
www.albetinoya.cat
albetinoya@albetinoya.cat

ALBET I NOYA 3 MACABEUS 2012 B
macabeo

87 Colour: bright yellow. Nose: ripe fruit, dried flowers, fragrant herbs, spicy, mineral. Palate: powerful, flavourful, ripe fruit.

ALBET I NOYA COL.LECCIÓ CHARDONNAY 2011 B
chardonnay

92 Colour: bright yellow. Nose: powerfull, ripe fruit, sweet spices, creamy oak, fragrant herbs. Palate: rich, smoky aftertaste, flavourful, fresh, good acidity.

ALBET I NOYA COL.LECCIÓ SYRAH 2009 T
syrah

92 Colour: bright cherry, purple rim. Nose: balanced, expressive, ripe fruit, creamy oak. Palate: flavourful, fruity, good structure, round tannins.

ALBET I NOYA DOLÇ ADRIÀ 2007 TINTO DULCE
syrah, merlot

90 Colour: black cherry. Nose: powerfull, fruit preserve, toasty. Palate: powerful, sweet, concentrated, good acidity.

ALBET I NOYA EL BLANC XXV "ECOLÓGICO" 2011 B
viognier, vidal, marina rion

90 Colour: bright yellow. Nose: powerfull, ripe fruit, sweet spices, fragrant herbs, petrol notes, earthy notes. Palate: rich, flavourful, fresh, good acidity.

ALBET I NOYA EL FANIO 2011 B
xarel.lo

91 Colour: bright yellow. Nose: ripe fruit, mineral, spicy, expressive, faded flowers. Palate: balanced, good acidity, long.

ALBET I NOYA LIGNUM 2010 T
cabernet sauvignon, garnacha, merlot, syrah, tempranillo

90 Colour: bright cherry. Nose: ripe fruit, sweet spices, creamy oak, expressive. Palate: flavourful, fruity, toasty, round tannins.

ALBET I NOYA LIGNUM 2011 B
chardonnay, sauvignon blanc, xarel.lo

90 Colour: bright yellow. Nose: balanced, ripe fruit, faded flowers, dried herbs, spicy. Palate: fruity, rich.

ALBET I NOYA PETIT ALBET 2012 B
xarel.lo, macabeo, chardonnay

87 Colour: bright straw. Nose: dried herbs, fresh fruit, medium intensity, dried flowers. Palate: good acidity, balanced, good finish.

ALBET I NOYA PINOT NOIR MERLOT CLÀSSIC 2012 RD
pinot noir, merlot

87 Colour: rose, purple rim. Nose: powerfull, ripe fruit, red berry notes, floral. Palate: powerful, fruity, fresh.

ALBET I NOYA RESERVA MARTÍ 2007 TR
tempranillo, syrah, cabernet sauvignon, merlot

93 Colour: cherry, garnet rim. Nose: ripe fruit, spicy, creamy oak, toasty, fine reductive notes, earthy notes. Palate: powerful, flavourful, toasty, round tannins, long.

ALBET I NOYA RESERVA MARTÍ FENIX 1998 T
tempranillo, syrah, cabernet sauvignon, merlot

91 Colour: pale ruby, brick rim edge. Nose: elegant, spicy, fine reductive notes, wet leather, aged wood nuances, fruit liqueur notes. Palate: spicy, fine tannins, elegant, long.

ALBET I NOYA TEMPRANILLO CLÀSSIC 2012 T
tempranillo

91 Colour: cherry, purple rim. Nose: red berry notes, floral, ripe fruit. Palate: flavourful, fruity, good acidity, round tannins.

ALBET I NOYA XAREL-LO CLÀSSIC 2012 B
xarel.lo

88 Colour: bright yellow. Nose: balanced, white flowers, citrus fruit, ripe fruit. Palate: fruity, flavourful, correct, long.

ALBET I NOYA XAREL-LO NOSODOS + 2011 BN
xarel.lo

87 Colour: bright straw. Nose: medium intensity, fresh fruit, dried herbs, fine lees, floral. Palate: fresh, fruity, flavourful, good acidity.

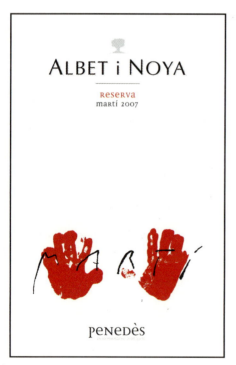

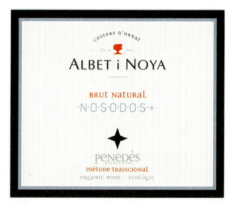

ALBET I NOYA XAREL-LO NOSODOS + 2012 B
xarel.lo

85 Colour: bright yellow. Nose: fruit expression, dried herbs, floral, jasmine, earthy notes. Palate: slightly evolved, powerful, flavourful, long.

BELAT 2008 T
belat

93 Colour: deep cherry, garnet rim. Nose: elegant, spicy, dried herbs, ripe fruit, mineral. Palate: fruity, fine tannins, spicy.

FINCA LA MILANA 2007 T
caladoc, tempranillo, cabernet sauvignon, merlot

90 Colour: cherry, garnet rim. Nose: balanced, expressive, ripe fruit, spicy. Palate: good structure, flavourful, round tannins.

MARINA RION "ECOLÓGICO" 2012 B
marina rion

87 Colour: bright straw. Nose: expressive, white flowers, citrus fruit, fresh fruit. Palate: fruity, balanced, fine bitter notes, easy to drink.

ALEMANY I CORRIO

Melió, 78
8720 Vilafranca del Penedès (Barcelona)
☎: +34 938 922 746 - Fax: +34 938 172 587
sotlefriec@sotlefriec.com

PAS CURTEI 2011 T
60% merlot, 20% cariñena, 20% cabernet sauvignon

90 Colour: black cherry. Nose: powerfull, fruit preserve, spicy. Palate: good structure, concentrated, round tannins, flavourful.

PRINCIPIA MATHEMATICA 2012 B
100% xarel.lo

89 Colour: straw. Nose: ripe fruit, citrus fruit, spicy. Palate: flavourful, powerful, fine bitter notes, good acidity.

SOT LEFRIEC 2007 T
cabernet sauvignon, cariñena, merlot

95 Colour: cherry, garnet rim. Nose: ripe fruit, spicy, toasty, complex, dark chocolate, earthy notes. Palate: powerful, flavourful, toasty, round tannins.

ALSINA SARDÁ

8770 Pla del Penedès (Barcelona)
☎: +34 938 988 132 - Fax: +34 938 988 671
www.alsinasarda.com
alsina@alsinasarda.com

ALSINA & SARDÁ BLANC DE BLANCS 2012 B
70% parellada, 30% macabeo

86 Colour: bright straw. Nose: fresh, fresh fruit, white flowers, expressive. Palate: flavourful, fruity, good acidity.

ALSINA & SARDÁ CHARDONNAY XAREL.LO 2012 B
50% chardonnay, 50% xarel.lo

84

ALSINA & SARDÁ FINCA CAL JANES 2010 T
100% merlot

86 Colour: bright cherry. Nose: ripe fruit, sweet spices, creamy oak. Palate: flavourful, fruity, toasty, round tannins.

ALSINA & SARDÁ FINCA LA BOLTANA 2012 B
100% xarel.lo

89 Colour: bright yellow. Nose: floral, citrus fruit, ripe fruit, fragrant herbs. Palate: rich, powerful, flavourful, balanced.

ALSINA & SARDÁ MERLOT LLÀGRIMA 2012 RD
100% merlot

85 Colour: rose. Nose: powerfull, ripe fruit, red berry notes, balanced. Palate: easy to drink, correct, balsamic.

ALSINA & SARDÁ MUSCAT LLÀGRIMA 2012 B
100% moscatel de alejandría

86 Colour: bright straw. Nose: fresh, fresh fruit, white flowers. Palate: flavourful, fruity, good acidity, balanced.

ALSINA & SARDÁ RESERVA DE FAMILIA 2008 T
100% merlot

88 Colour: deep cherry, garnet rim. Nose: balanced, ripe fruit, wild herbs. Palate: balanced, easy to drink, round tannins.

ARNAU 2012 T
100% merlot

84

AVINYÓ CAVAS

Masia Can Fontanals
8793 Avinyonet del Penedès (Barcelona)
☎: +34 938 970 055 - Fax: +34 938 970 691
www.avinyo.com
avinyo@avinyo.com

AVINYÓ CABERNET SAUVIGNON 2007 TC
100% cabernet sauvignon

89 Colour: deep cherry. Nose: powerfull, aromatic coffee, earthy notes. Palate: ripe fruit, powerful, fine bitter notes.

AVINYÓ MERLOT 2009 T
100% merlot

88 Colour: deep cherry. Nose: toasty, spicy, earthy notes. Palate: flavourful, powerful, spicy.

BERBAC VINS

Doctor Corberà, 4
8328 Alella (Barcelona)
☎: +34 695 173 522
www.berbacvins.com
bertran@berbacvins.com

IREU 2012 B

87 Colour: bright straw. Nose: white flowers, fresh fruit. Palate: flavourful, fruity, fresh.

BLANCHER-CAPDEVILA PUJOL

Plaça Pont Romà, Edificio Blancher
8770 Sant Sadurní D'Anoia (Barcelona)
☎: +34 938 183 286 - Fax: +34 938 911 961
www.blancher.es
blancher@blancher.es

BLANCHER GUIXERES 2012 B
xarel.lo

86 Colour: bright straw. Nose: fragrant herbs, citrus fruit. Palate: flavourful, fruity, fresh.

BLANCHER MERLOT 2012 RD
merlot

83

BODEGA J. MIQUEL JANÉ

Masia Cal Costas, s/n
8736 Font- Rubí (Barcelona)
☎: +34 934 140 948 - Fax: +34 932 015 901
www.jmiqueljane.com
info@jmiqueljane.com

BALTANA SELECCIO 2010 T
60% cabernet sauvignon, 40% merlot

87 Colour: cherry, garnet rim. Nose: ripe fruit, spicy, creamy oak, toasty. Palate: powerful, flavourful, toasty.

BARTHOMEUS NEGRE 2011 T
100% cabernet sauvignon

85 Colour: black cherry. Nose: powerfull, warm, characterful. Palate: powerful, sweetness, warm.

BARTHOMEUS ROSAT 2012 RD
100% cabernet sauvignon

82

J. MIQUEL JANÉ BLANC BALTANA 2012 B
50% macabeo, 35% parellada, 15% sauvignon blanc

88 Colour: bright straw. Nose: grassy, floral, ripe fruit. Palate: flavourful, fine bitter notes, spicy.

J. MIQUEL JANÉ CABERNET SAUVIGNON 2012 RD
85% cabernet sauvignon, 15% garnacha

85 Colour: rose, bright. Nose: ripe fruit, red berry notes, powerfull, dried herbs. Palate: correct, flavourful, fruity.

J. MIQUEL JANÉ SAUVIGNON BLANC 2012 B
100% sauvignon blanc

90 Colour: bright yellow. Nose: expressive, balanced, white flowers, citrus fruit, fresh fruit. Palate: fruity, good acidity, balanced.

MIQUEL JANÉ BALTANA NEGRE 2012 T
50% cabernet sauvignon, 30% grenache, 20% syrah

86 Colour: cherry, garnet rim. Nose: ripe fruit, spicy, creamy oak, toasty. Palate: powerful, flavourful, toasty.

BODEGAS CA N'ESTELLA

Masia Ca N'Estella, s/n
8635 Sant Esteve Sesrovires (Barcelona)
☎: +34 934 161 387 - Fax: +34 934 161 620
www.fincacanestella.com
a.vidal@fincacanestella.com

CLOT DELS OMS 2010 TC

87 Colour: cherry, garnet rim. Nose: ripe fruit, spicy, creamy oak, earthy notes. Palate: powerful, flavourful, toasty.

CLOT DELS OMS BLANC 2012 B
80% chardonnay, 20% malvasía

88 Colour: bright straw. Nose: fresh fruit, white flowers, fragrant herbs. Palate: flavourful, fruity, balanced.

CLOT DELS OMS CABERNET SAUVIGNON 2010 T

84

CLOT DELS OMS ROSAT 2012 RD
100% merlot

87 Colour: rose, purple rim. Nose: powerfull, ripe fruit, red berry notes, floral, expressive. Palate: powerful, fruity, fresh.

CLOT DELS OMS VI DOLÇ DE FRED ROSAT 2010 RD
merlot

85 Colour: ruby red. Nose: red berry notes, ripe fruit, fragrant herbs, spicy. Palate: rich, powerful, flavourful.

GRAN CLOT DELS OMS 2010 BFB
chardonnay

90 Colour: bright straw. Nose: spicy, ripe fruit, citrus fruit, toasty. Palate: flavourful, powerful, good structure.

GRAN CLOT DELS OMS NEGRE 2006 TR
40% merlot, 60% cabernet sauvignon

89 Colour: pale ruby, brick rim edge. Nose: spicy, fine reductive notes, wet leather, fruit liqueur notes. Palate: spicy, fine tannins, elegant, long.

GRAN CLOT DELS OMS XAREL.LO 2011 BFB
xarel.lo

90 Colour: bright yellow. Nose: powerfull, ripe fruit, sweet spices, creamy oak. Palate: rich, smoky aftertaste, flavourful, fresh, good acidity.

PETIT CLOT DELS OMS 2010 T
20% merlot, 80% cabernet sauvignon

88 Colour: bright cherry. Nose: ripe fruit, sweet spices, creamy oak, spicy, wild herbs. Palate: flavourful, fruity, toasty.

PETIT CLOT DELS OMS 2012 RD
cabernet sauvignon

86 Colour: rose, bright. Nose: powerfull, floral, red berry notes, ripe fruit. Palate: correct, fruity, flavourful.

PETIT CLOT DELS OMS BLANC 2012 B
20% macabeo, 40% xarel.lo, 30% chardonnay, 10% moscatel

85 Colour: bright straw. Nose: fresh, fruit expression. Palate: flavourful, fruity.

BODEGAS MUR BARCELONA

Rambla de la Generalitat, 1-9
8720 Sant Sadurni D'Anoia (Barcelona)
☎: +34 938 911 551 - Fax: +34 938 911 662
www.mur-barcelona.com
info@mur-barcelona.com

ROBERT J. MUR 2012 T
ull de llebre, merlot, cabernet sauvignon

85 Colour: cherry, garnet rim. Nose: ripe fruit, fruit preserve, balsamic herbs. Palate: powerful, flavourful, ripe fruit.

ROBERT J. MUR ROSADO SECO 2012 RD
garnacha, monastrell, ull de llebre

84

ROBERT MUR BLANCO SECO 2012 B
xarel.lo, parellada, macabeo

84

BODEGAS PINORD

Doctor Pasteur, 6
8720 Vilafranca del Penedès (Barcelona)
☎: +34 938 903 066 - Fax: +34 938 170 979
www.pinord.com
visites@pinord.com

PINORD CHATELDON 2006 TR
100% cabernet sauvignon

83

PINORD CLOS DE TORRIBAS 2006 TR
tempranillo, cabernet sauvignon

88 Colour: dark-red cherry, orangey edge. Nose: spicy, wild herbs, dried herbs, ripe fruit. Palate: flavourful, balanced, long.

PINORD CLOS DE TORRIBAS 2009 TC
85% tempranillo, 15% cabernet sauvignon

84

PINORD CLOS DE TORRIBAS 2012 B
52% xarel.lo, 30% macabeo, 11% parellada, 7% gewürztraminer

86 Colour: bright straw. Nose: varietal, white flowers, medium intensity, ripe fruit. Palate: correct, easy to drink, good finish.

PINORD DIORAMA CHARDONNAY 2012 B
chardonnay

88 Colour: bright straw. Nose: white flowers, faded flowers, ripe fruit. Palate: flavourful, fruity, good acidity, balanced.

PINORD DIORAMA MERLOT 2010 T
merlot

86 Colour: cherry, garnet rim. Nose: ripe fruit, wild herbs, spicy. Palate: correct, round tannins.

PINORD DIORAMA SYRAH 2009 T
syrah

89 Colour: cherry, garnet rim. Nose: ripe fruit, sweet spices, balsamic herbs. Palate: flavourful, correct, round tannins, balanced.

PINORD PI DEL NORD CABERNET SAUVIGNON 2003 T
cabernet sauvignon

83

BODEGAS TORRE DEL VEGUER

Urb. Torre de Veguer, s/n
8810 Sant Pere de Ribes (Barcelona)
☎: +34 938 963 190 - Fax: +34 938 962 967
www.torredelveguer.com
torredelveguer@torredelveguer.com

TORRE DEL VEGUER ECLECTIC 2009 T
70% cabernet sauvignon, 20% petite syrah, 10% merlot

91 Colour: cherry, garnet rim. Nose: ripe fruit, spicy, creamy oak, toasty, complex. Palate: powerful, flavourful, toasty, round tannins.

TORRE DEL VEGUER GALA 2012 B
80% moscatel de frontignan, 20% xarel.lo

86 Colour: bright straw. Nose: fresh, fresh fruit, white flowers. Palate: flavourful, fruity, balanced.

TORRE DEL VEGUER MARTA 2011 ESP
100% moscatel de frontignan

86 Colour: bright straw. Nose: dried herbs, fine lees, floral, candied fruit. Palate: fresh, fruity, flavourful, good acidity.

TORRE DEL VEGUER MUSCAT 2012 B
100% moscatel de frontignan

87 Colour: bright yellow. Nose: candied fruit, white flowers, fragrant herbs. Palate: light-bodied, fresh, fruity.

TORRE DEL VEGUER RAÏMS DE LA INMORTALITAT 2005 TR
85% cabernet sauvignon, 10% petite syrah, 5% merlot

87 Colour: pale ruby, brick rim edge. Nose: spicy, aromatic coffee, fruit liqueur notes. Palate: spicy, ripe fruit, fine tannins.

TORRE DEL VEGUER XAREL.LO 2012 B
100% xarel.lo

88 Colour: bright yellow. Nose: floral, balsamic herbs, citrus fruit, ripe fruit, balanced. Palate: flavourful, powerful, spicy.

BODEGUES SUMARROCA

El Rebato, s/n
8739 Subirats (Barcelona)
☎: +34 938 911 092 - Fax: +34 938 911 778
www.sumarroca.es
info@sumarroca.es

BÒRIA 2008 T
syrah, cabernet sauvignon, merlot

92 Colour: cherry, garnet rim. Nose: ripe fruit, spicy, creamy oak, toasty, complex, earthy notes. Palate: powerful, flavourful, toasty, round tannins.

SUMARROCA 2012 RD
45% tempranillo, 35% merlot, 20% syrah

85 Colour: raspberry rose. Nose: ripe fruit, wild herbs, faded flowers. Palate: powerful, flavourful, balsamic.

SUMARROCA BLANC DE BLANCS 2012 B
macabeo, xarel.lo, parellada, moscatel

88 Colour: bright straw. Nose: fresh, fresh fruit, white flowers. Palate: flavourful, good acidity, balanced.

SUMARROCA CHARDONNAY 2012 B
100% chardonnay

91 Colour: bright yellow. Nose: powerfull, ripe fruit, sweet spices, fragrant herbs. Palate: rich, flavourful, fresh, good acidity.

SUMARROCA GEWÜRZTRAMINER 2012 B
100% gewürztraminer

86 Colour: bright straw, greenish rim. Nose: balanced, ripe fruit, floral. Palate: correct, easy to drink, sweetness.

SUMARROCA MINUET 2010 BFB
xarel.lo, chardonnay

87 Colour: bright yellow. Nose: toasty, smoky, creamy oak, ripe fruit, candied fruit. Palate: rich, fruity, spicy.

SUMARROCA MUSCAT 2012 B
100% moscatel

88 Colour: bright straw. Nose: expressive, varietal, fresh fruit. Palate: flavourful, fruity.

SUMARROCA NEGRE 2011 T
merlot, tempranillo, cabernet sauvignon

90 Colour: bright cherry. Nose: ripe fruit, sweet spices, creamy oak. Palate: flavourful, fruity, toasty, round tannins.

SUMARROCA PINOT NOIR 2012 RD
100% pinot noir

90 Colour: onion pink. Nose: elegant, candied fruit, dried flowers, fragrant herbs. Palate: light-bodied, flavourful, good acidity, long, spicy, balanced, elegant.

SUMARROCA RIESLING 2012 B
100% riesling

86 Colour: bright straw. Nose: faded flowers, scrubland. Palate: fine bitter notes, good acidity, ripe fruit.

SUMARROCA SANTA CREU DE CREIXÀ 2010 T
garnacha, cabernet sauvignon, cabernet franc, syrah

90 Colour: bright cherry. Nose: ripe fruit, sweet spices. Palate: flavourful, fruity, toasty, round tannins.

SUMARROCA SAUVIGNON BLANC 2012 B
100% sauvignon blanc

91 Colour: bright straw. Nose: fresh, fresh fruit, white flowers, fine lees. Palate: flavourful, fruity, good acidity, balanced.

SUMARROCA TEMPRANILLO 2011 T
tempranillo

88 Colour: deep cherry. Nose: medium intensity, ripe fruit, red berry notes. Palate: flavourful, fruity.

SUMARROCA TEMPS DE FLORS 2012 B
50% moscatel, 25% gewürztraminer, 25% xarel.lo

87 Colour: bright straw. Nose: expressive, powerfull, white flowers, jasmine, ripe fruit. Palate: flavourful, fruity.

SUMARROCA XAREL.LO 2012 B
100% xarel.lo

88 Colour: bright straw. Nose: white flowers, ripe fruit. Palate: flavourful, good acidity, balanced.

TERRAL 2010 T
syrah, cabernet franc, merlot, cabernet sauvignon

92 Colour: cherry, garnet rim. Nose: earthy notes, mineral, ripe fruit. Palate: flavourful, fine bitter notes, good acidity.

BOLET VINS I CAVES

Finca Mas Lluet, s/n
8732 Castellvi de la Marca (Barcelona)
☎: +34 938 918 153
www.cavasbolet.com
cavasbolet@cavasbolet.com

BOLET MERLOT 2004 TC
merlot

85 Colour: pale ruby, brick rim edge. Nose: spicy, fine reductive notes, wet leather, aged wood nuances, fruit liqueur notes. Palate: spicy, long, light-bodied.

BOLET ULL DE LLEBRE 2011 T
ull de llebre

84

BOLET VINYA SOTA BOSC 2012 B

85 Colour: bright yellow. Nose: white flowers, varietal, powerfull. Palate: fruity, flavourful, good finish.

BOLET XAREL.LO 2012 B
xarel.lo

84

CAL RASPALLET VITICULTORS

Barri Sabanell, 11
8736 Font Rubí (Barcelona)
☎: +34 607 262 779
calraspallet@vinifera.cat

IMPROVISACIÓ 2011 B
xarel.lo

92 Colour: bright straw. Nose: fresh, fresh fruit, white flowers, expressive. Palate: flavourful, fruity, good acidity, balanced.

NUN VINYA DELS TAUS 2011 B

xarel.lo

94 Colour: bright golden. Nose: ripe fruit, dry nuts, powerfull, toasty. Palate: flavourful, fruity, spicy, toasty, long.

CAN CAMPS

Cam Camps, s/n
8810 Olivella (Barcelona)
☎: +34 938 970 013

PEDRADURA 2006 TR

90 Colour: cherry, garnet rim. Nose: scrubland, old leather, spicy, fruit liqueur notes. Palate: powerful, flavourful, spicy, long.

CAN FEIXES (HUGUET)

Finca Can Feixes, s/n
8718 Cabrera D'Anoia (Barcelona)
☎: +34 937 718 227 - Fax: +34 937 718 031
www.canfeixes.com
canfeixes@canfeixes.com

CAN FEIXES SELECCIÓ 2012 B

parellada, macabeo, chardonnay, malvasía

87 Colour: bright straw. Nose: floral, candied fruit, citrus fruit, faded flowers. Palate: fine bitter notes, easy to drink, ripe fruit.

CAN RÀFOLS DELS CAUS

Can Rafols del Caus s/n
8792 Avinyonet del Penedès (Barcelona)
☎: +34 938 970 013 - Fax: +34 938 970 370
www.canrafolsdelscaus.com
canrafolsdelscaus@canrafolsdelscaus.com

GRAN CAUS 2005 TR

cabernet franc, cabernet sauvignon, merlot

92 Colour: pale ruby, brick rim edge. Nose: elegant, spicy, fine reductive notes, fruit liqueur notes, toasty. Palate: spicy, fine tannins, elegant, long.

CANALS & MUNNÉ

Plaza Pau Casals, 6
8770 Sant Sadurní D'Anoia (Barcelona)
☎: +34 938 910 318 - Fax: +34 938 911 945
www.canalsimunne.com
info@canalsimunne.com

BLANC PRÍNCEPS MUSCAT 2012 B

moscatel de frontignan

87 Colour: bright straw. Nose: dried flowers, fragrant herbs. Palate: full, fresh, fruity.

GRAN BLANC PRÍNCEPS 2010 BFB

chardonnay, xarel.lo

89 Colour: bright yellow. Nose: medium intensity, ripe fruit, floral, spicy. Palate: good acidity, balanced, spicy, fine bitter notes.

GRAN PRÍNCEPS 2002 TR

cabernet sauvignon, tempranillo, merlot

81

NOIR PRÍNCEPS 2004 TC

cabernet sauvignon, tempranillo, merlot

88 Colour: deep cherry. Nose: wet leather, fruit liqueur notes, spicy. Palate: ripe fruit, fine bitter notes, good acidity.

PRÍNCEPS ECOLÓGICO 2012 B

xarel.lo, chardonnay, sauvignon blanc

85 Colour: bright straw. Nose: citrus fruit, dried flowers, fragrant herbs, medium intensity. Palate: full, fruity, fresh.

ROSE PRÍNCEPS MERLOT 2012 RD

merlot

84

CARREFOUR

Campezo, 16
28022 Madrid (Madrid)
☎: +34 902 202 000
www.carrefour.es

SANT LLACH 2012 B

xarel.lo, macabeo, parellada

84

SANT LLACH 2012 RD

tempranillo

83

SANT LLACH 2012 T
55% merlot, 45% tempranillo

82

SANT LLACH BARRICA 2009 T
merlot

85 Colour: very deep cherry, orangey edge. Nose: ripe fruit, fruit liqueur notes, old leather. Palate: spicy, ripe fruit.

SANT LLACH CABERNET 2012 T
cabernet sauvignon

83

SANT LLACH CHARDONNAY 2011 BFB
chardonnay

87 Colour: bright yellow. Nose: ripe fruit, sweet spices, creamy oak, fragrant herbs. Palate: rich, smoky aftertaste, flavourful, good acidity.

SANT LLACH MERLOT 2012 T
merlot

85 Colour: black cherry, purple rim. Nose: balanced, powerfull, ripe fruit, balsamic herbs. Palate: fruity, good finish, ripe fruit.

CASA RAVELLA

Casa Ravella, 1
8739 Ordal (Barcelona)
☎: +34 938 179 173 - Fax: +34 938 179 245
www.casaravella.com
bodega@condedeolzinellas.com

CASA RAVELLA 2008 TC
90% cabernet sauvignon, 10% merlot

90 Colour: deep cherry. Nose: powerfull, ripe fruit, warm, toasty. Palate: ripe fruit, spicy, fine bitter notes.

CASA RAVELLA 2010 BC
70% xarel.lo, 30% chardonnay

90 Colour: bright golden. Nose: ripe fruit, dry nuts, powerfull, toasty, aged wood nuances. Palate: flavourful, fruity, spicy, toasty, long.

CASA RAVELLA 2012 B
100% xarel.lo

84

CASA RAVELLA 2012 RD
100% merlot

85 Colour: onion pink. Nose: candied fruit, dried flowers, fragrant herbs, red berry notes. Palate: light-bodied, flavourful, good acidity, long, spicy.

CASA RAVELLA 2012 T ROBLE
100% merlot

88 Colour: bright cherry. Nose: ripe fruit, sweet spices, expressive, balsamic herbs. Palate: flavourful, fruity, toasty, round tannins.

CASTELL D'AGE

Ctra.de Martorell a Capellades, 6-8
8782 La Beguda Baixa (Barcelona)
☎: +34 937 725 181 - Fax: +34 937 727 061
www.castelldage.com
info@castelldage.com

CASTELL D'AGE BLANC DE BLANCS 2012 B
100% macabeo

84

CASTELL D'AGE CABERNET SAUVIGNON 2006 T
100% cabernet sauvignon

87 Colour: pale ruby, brick rim edge. Nose: fruit liqueur notes, wild herbs, tobacco, fine reductive notes, spicy. Palate: powerful, flavourful, long, balsamic.

CASTELL D'AGE MERLOT 2006 T
100% merlot

85 Colour: pale ruby, brick rim edge. Nose: fruit liqueur notes, scrubland, spicy, wet leather, cigar. Palate: powerful, flavourful, spirituous.

CASTELL D'AGE ROSAT MERLOT 2012 RD
100% merlot

85 Colour: light cherry. Nose: fruit expression, red berry notes. Palate: powerful, spicy.

CASTELL D'AGE TEMPRANILLO 2010 T
100% tempranillo

85 Colour: cherry, garnet rim. Nose: ripe fruit, spicy, creamy oak, toasty, balsamic herbs. Palate: powerful, flavourful, toasty.

FRUIT DE CASTELL D'AGE 2004 T
cabernet sauvignon, merlot, syrah

88 Colour: pale ruby, brick rim edge. Nose: elegant, spicy, fine reductive notes, aged wood nuances, fruit liqueur notes, fruit liqueur notes. Palate: spicy, elegant, long.

L'ESSÈNCIA DEL XAREL.LO 2012 B
100% xarel.lo

88 Colour: bright straw. Nose: fresh, fresh fruit, white flowers, expressive. Palate: flavourful, fruity, good acidity, balanced.

CASTELL D'OR

Mare Rafols, 3- 1º 4º
8720 Vilafranca del Penedès (Barcelona)
☎: +34 938 905 446 - Fax: +34 938 905 446
www.castelldor.com
castelldor@castelldor.com

COSSETÀNIA 2008 TR
100% cabernet sauvignon

90 Colour: cherry, garnet rim. Nose: ripe fruit, spicy, creamy oak, toasty, complex. Palate: powerful, flavourful, toasty, round tannins.

COSSETÀNIA 2009 TC
80% tempranillo, 20% merlot

88 Colour: deep cherry. Nose: spicy, powerfull, ripe fruit, toasty. Palate: spicy, ripe fruit.

COSSETÀNIA 2011 T
60% cabernet sauvignon, 40% merlot

89 Colour: bright cherry. Nose: ripe fruit, sweet spices, creamy oak, green pepper. Palate: flavourful, toasty, round tannins.

COSSETÀNIA 2012 RD
100% merlot

84

COSSETÀNIA CHARDONNAY 2012 B
100% chardonnay

90 Colour: bright straw, greenish rim. Nose: balanced, white flowers, dried flowers. Palate: fruity, correct, good acidity, fine bitter notes.

COSSETÀNIA XAREL.LO 2012 B
100% xarel.lo

86 Colour: bright straw, greenish rim. Nose: ripe fruit, floral, citrus fruit. Palate: flavourful, fruity, long.

CASTELLROIG - FINCA SABATÉ I COCA

Ctra. Sant Sadurní d'Anoia a Vilafranca del Penedès, Km. 1
8739 Subirats (Barcelona)
☎: +34 938 911 927 - Fax: +34 938 914 055
www.castellroig.com
info@castellroig.com

CASTELLROIG BLANC SELECCIÓ 2011 B
xarel.lo

89 Colour: bright yellow. Nose: sweet spices, faded flowers, ripe fruit, candied fruit, complex. Palate: flavourful, fruity.

CASTELLROIG NEGRE ULL DE LLEBRE 2010 T
tempranillo

88 Colour: cherry, garnet rim. Nose: ripe fruit, creamy oak, toasty. Palate: powerful, flavourful, round tannins.

CASTELLROIG SELECCIÓ NEGRE 2009 T
cabernet sauvignon, merlot

90 Colour: deep cherry. Nose: dark chocolate, ripe fruit, creamy oak, spicy. Palate: powerful, ripe fruit, good acidity.

CASTELLROIG XAREL.LO 2012 B
100% xarel.lo

89 Colour: bright straw. Nose: ripe fruit, floral, varietal, expressive. Palate: flavourful, fruity, balanced, good acidity.

TERROJA DE SABATÉ I COCA 2011 B
xarel.lo

89 Colour: bright yellow. Nose: ripe fruit, faded flowers. Palate: flavourful, fruity, ripe fruit, long.

CAVA & HOTEL MAS TINELL

Ctra. de Vilafranca a St. Martí Sarroca, Km. 0,5
8720 Vilafranca del Penedès (Barcelona)
☎: +34 938 170 586 - Fax: +34 938 170 500
www.mastinell.com
info@mastinell.com

MAS TINELL ARTE 2007 TR

88 Colour: cherry, garnet rim. Nose: ripe fruit, spicy, creamy oak, toasty, complex. Palate: powerful, flavourful, toasty, round tannins, balanced.

MAS TINELL CHARDONNAY 2012 B
100% chardonnay

86 Colour: bright straw. Nose: white flowers, citrus fruit, ripe fruit. Palate: flavourful, fruity, good acidity, balanced.

MAS TINELL CLOS SANT PAU 2008 B

89 Colour: bright yellow. Nose: white flowers, citrus fruit, candied fruit. Palate: flavourful, fruity, fresh.

MAS TINELL GISELE 2011 B
100% xarel.lo

88 Colour: bright yellow. Nose: sweet spices. Palate: rich, flavourful, ripe fruit, good acidity, spicy.

MAS TINELL L' ALBA BLANC DE LLUNA 2012 B
24% xarel.lo, 38% chardonnay, 38% moscatel

85 Colour: bright straw. Nose: floral, dried herbs, ripe fruit. Palate: fresh, fruity, easy to drink.

CAVA JOSEP M. FERRET GUASCH

Barri L'Alzinar, 68
8798 Font-Rubí (Barcelona)
☎: +34 938 979 037 - Fax: +34 938 979 414
www.ferretguasch.com
ferretguasch@ferretguasch.com

JOSEP M. FERRET GUASCH GEBRE 2012 RD
100% cabernet sauvignon

84

JOSEP M. FERRET GUASCH NADIA 2011 B
100% sauvignon blanc

87 Colour: bright straw. Nose: fresh, fresh fruit, white flowers, dried herbs. Palate: flavourful, fruity, good acidity.

CAVAS HILL

Bonavista, 2
8734 Moja (Barcelona)
☎: +34 938 900 588 - Fax: +34 938 170 246
www.cavashill.com
cavashill@cavashill.com

BLANC BRUC 2012 BFB
xarel.lo, chardonnay

85 Colour: bright yellow. Nose: ripe fruit, sweet spices, creamy oak, fragrant herbs. Palate: rich, flavourful, fresh, good acidity.

GRAN CIVET 2010 TC
cabernet sauvignon, tempranillo

88 Colour: deep cherry, garnet rim. Nose: varietal, scrubland, spicy. Palate: fruity, spicy, balsamic, round tannins.

GRAN TOC 2009 TR
merlot, tempranillo

90 Colour: deep cherry, garnet rim. Nose: balanced, ripe fruit, spicy, earthy notes. Palate: good structure, ripe fruit.

ORO PENEDÈS 2012 B
moscatel, xarel.lo

86 Colour: bright straw. Nose: fresh, fresh fruit, white flowers, expressive. Palate: flavourful, fruity, good acidity, balanced.

RESERVA HILL 2008 TR
merlot, tempranillo, syrah

91 Colour: deep cherry, garnet rim. Nose: balanced, varietal, expressive, wild herbs. Palate: flavourful, fruity, round tannins.

CAVAS LAVERNOYA

Masia La Porxada
8729 Sant Marçal (Barcelona)
☎: +34 938 912 202
www.lavernoya.com
lavernoya@lavernoya.com

LÁCRIMA BACCUS 2012 B
macabeo, xarel.lo, parellada

87 Colour: bright straw. Nose: fresh fruit, white flowers. Palate: flavourful, fruity, good acidity, balanced.

LÁCRIMA BACCUS 2012 RD
tempranillo, pinot noir

84

LÁCRIMA BACCUS 2012 T
cabernet sauvignon, tempranillo, merlot

90 Colour: bright cherry. Nose: ripe fruit, sweet spices, creamy oak, expressive. Palate: flavourful, fruity, toasty, round tannins.

LÁCRIMA BACCUS BLANC DE BLANCS 2012 B
xarel.lo, chardonnay, parellada, moscatel

87 Colour: bright straw. Nose: fresh, fresh fruit, white flowers, expressive. Palate: flavourful, fruity, good acidity, balanced.

CAVES NAVERÁN

Can Parellada Torrelavit
8735 Torrelavit (Barcelona)
☎: +34 938 988 274 - Fax: +34 938 989 027
www.naveran.com
naveran@naveran.com

CLOS ANTONIA 2012 B
viognier

93 Colour: bright straw. Nose: powerfull, ripe fruit, citrus fruit. Palate: flavourful, powerful, fruity, fine bitter notes, good acidity.

CLOS DEL PI 1996 T
cabernet sauvignon, merlot, syrah

91 Colour: pale ruby, brick rim edge. Nose: elegant, fine reductive notes, wet leather, aged wood nuances, spicy. Palate: spicy, fine tannins, elegant, long.

MANUELA DE NAVERÁN 2012 B
chardonnay

90 Colour: bright straw. Nose: fresh fruit, white flowers. Palate: flavourful, fruity, good acidity, balanced.

NAVERÁN CLOS DELS ANGELS 2011 T
syrah

93 Colour: dark-red cherry, garnet rim. Nose: complex, balanced, wild herbs, dried herbs. Palate: fruity, flavourful, round tannins.

NAVERÁN DON PABLO 1999 TGR
cabernet sauvignon

92 Colour: dark-red cherry, orangey edge. Nose: wild herbs, fine reductive notes, spicy, expressive, tobacco. Palate: spicy, balsamic, fine tannins.

CELLER CREDO

Tamarit, 10
8770 Sant Sadurní D'Anoia (Barcelona)
☎: +34 938 910 214 - Fax: +34 938 911 697
www.cellercredo.cat
vins@cellercredo.cat

ALOERS 2012 B
100% xarel.lo

90 Colour: bright straw. Nose: faded flowers, candied fruit, citrus fruit. Palate: flavourful, fine bitter notes, good acidity.

CAN CREDO 2010 B
100% xarel.lo

92 Colour: bright straw. Nose: powerfull, complex, characterful, ripe fruit. Palate: flavourful, powerful, fine bitter notes, good acidity. Personality.

CAPFICAT 2012 B
100% xarel.lo

88 Colour: bright straw. Nose: medium intensity, balanced, dried herbs. Palate: fruity, correct, fine bitter notes, good acidity.

ESTRANY 2011 B
100% xarel.lo

90 Colour: bright straw. Nose: expressive, ripe fruit, citrus fruit, balsamic herbs, dried herbs. Palate: flavourful, spicy, ripe fruit.

MIRANIUS 2012 B
50% xarel.lo, 47% macabeo, 3% chardonnay

88 Colour: bright straw. Nose: medium intensity, ripe fruit, citrus fruit. Palate: flavourful, fruity.

CELLER JORDI LLUCH

Barrio Les Casetes, s/n
8777 Sant Quintí de Mediona (Barcelona)
☎: +34 938 988 138 - Fax: +34 938 988 138
www.vinyaescude.com
vinyaescude@vinyaescude.com

VINYA ESCUDÉ MAIOLES 2008 BFB
chardonnay, xarel.lo

88 Colour: bright golden. Nose: ripe fruit, dry nuts, powerfull, toasty, aged wood nuances. Palate: flavourful, fruity, spicy, toasty, long.

VINYA ESCUDÉ MERLOT 2012 RD
merlot

83

VINYA ESCUDÉ NOGUERA 2005 TC
cabernet sauvignon, merlot

86 Colour: pale ruby, brick rim edge. Nose: spicy, fine reductive notes, wet leather, aged wood nuances, fruit liqueur notes. Palate: long, correct, slightly evolved.

CELLERS AVGVSTVS FORVM

Ctra. Sant Vicenç, s/n Apartado Correos 289
43700 El Vendrell (Tarragona)
☎: +34 977 666 910 - Fax: +34 977 666 590
www.avgvstvs.es
avgvstvs@avgvstvs.es

AVGVSTVS CABERNET FRANC 2011 T ROBLE
100% cabernet franc

91 Colour: bright cherry. Nose: ripe fruit, sweet spices, creamy oak, expressive, dry stone. Palate: flavourful, fruity, toasty.

AVGVSTVS CABERNET SAUVIGNON-MERLOT 2010 T ROBLE
57% cabernet sauvignon, 43% merlot

89 Colour: cherry, garnet rim. Nose: ripe fruit, spicy, creamy oak, premature reduction notes. Palate: powerful, flavourful, toasty.

AVGVSTVS CHARDONNAY 2012 BFB
100% chardonnay

91 Colour: bright yellow. Nose: candied fruit, toasty, smoky, citrus fruit. Palate: fruity, flavourful, ripe fruit, long, spicy.

AVGVSTVS CHARDONNAY MAGNUM 2011 B
100% chardonnay

94 Colour: bright straw. Nose: white flowers, expressive, ripe fruit, citrus fruit. Palate: flavourful, fruity, good acidity, balanced.

AVGVSTVS ROSÉ 2012 RD
62% cabernet sauvignon, 38% merlot

84

AVGVSTVS TRAJANVS 2009 TR
33,5% cabernet sauvignon, 33,5% merlot, 16,5% cabernet franc, 16,5% garnacha

91 Colour: light cherry, orangey edge. Nose: ripe fruit, balsamic herbs, spicy, earthy notes, tobacco, fine reductive notes. Palate: powerful, flavourful, spicy, long.

AVGVSTVS VI VARIETALES MAGNUM 2011 TC
58% syrah, 19% cabernet franc, 6,5% cabernet sauvignon, 6,5% merlot, 6,5% garnacha, 3,5% tempranillo

90 Colour: cherry, garnet rim. Nose: ripe fruit, spicy, creamy oak, toasty. Palate: powerful, flavourful, toasty, round tannins.

AVGVSTVS XAREL.LO 2011 BFB
100% xarel.lo

90 Colour: bright yellow, greenish rim. Nose: balanced, expressive, spicy, dried herbs. Palate: balanced, fruity, easy to drink.

CELLERS PLANAS ALBAREDA

Ctra. Guardiola, Km. 3
8735 Vilobí del Penedès (Barcelona)
☎: +34 938 922 143 - Fax: +34 938 922 143
www.planasalbareda.com
planasalbareda@yahoo.es

PLANAS ALBAREDA DESCLÒS 2011 T
merlot

88 Colour: bright cherry. Nose: ripe fruit, sweet spices, creamy oak, expressive. Palate: flavourful, fruity, toasty, round tannins.

PLANAS ALBAREDA L'AVENC 2012 B
xarel.lo

84

PLANAS ALBAREDA ROSAT 2012 RD
merlot

84

CLOS LENTISCUS 1939

Masía Can Ramón, s/n
8810 Sant Pere de Ribes (Barcelona)
☎: +34 667 517 659
www.closlentiscus.cat
closlentiscus@closlentiscus.cat

CLOS LENTISCUS 41 ROSÉ 2009 BN GRAN RESERVA
samsó

87 Colour: coppery red. Nose: fresh fruit, dried herbs, fine lees, floral. Palate: fresh, fruity, flavourful, good acidity.

CLOS LENTISCUS BLANC DE BLANCS ESP
malvasía

90 Colour: coppery red. Nose: fruit expression, citrus fruit. Palate: flavourful, fruity, fresh.

CLOS LENTISCUS CAN RAMÓN 2006 TGR
sumoll

84

CLOS LENTISCUS SUMOLL RESERVA DE FAMILIA 2008 T
sumoll

86 Colour: coppery red. Nose: characterful, ripe fruit, red berry notes. Palate: sweetness, fine bitter notes, good acidity.

CLOS LENTISCUS SUMOLL RESERVA DE FAMILIA MAGNUM 2007 BN GRAN RESERVA
sumoll

91 Colour: light cherry. Nose: fine lees, dry nuts, fragrant herbs, sweet spices, pattiserie. Palate: powerful, flavourful, good acidity, fine bead, fine bitter notes.

CLOS LENTISCUS SYRAH COLECTION ROSÉ 2009 BN GRAN RESERVA
syrah

87 Colour: deep cherry. Nose: candied fruit, red berry notes. Palate: flavourful, sweetness, spicy.

LENTISCUS BLANC 2010 ESP
xarel.lo, malvasía

87 Colour: bright golden. Nose: candied fruit, citrus fruit, honeyed notes. Palate: sweetness, powerful.

LENTISCUS ROSÉ 2010 BN
syrah, sumoll

84

X-PRESSIO BY CLOS LENTISCUS 2010
xarel.lo, vermell

84

COLET

Cami del Salinar, s/n
8796 Pacs del Penedès (Barcelona)
☎: +34 938 170 809 - Fax: +34 938 170 809
www.colet.cat sergi@colet.cat
info@colet.cat

A POSTERIORI ROSAT ESP
merlot

87 Colour: coppery red. Nose: fruit liqueur notes, red berry notes. Palate: sweetness, spicy, ripe fruit.

A PRIORI ESP
macabeo, chardonnay, riesling, gewürztraminer, moscatel

90 Colour: bright yellow. Nose: fine lees, dry nuts, fragrant herbs, smoky, saline. Palate: powerful, flavourful, good acidity, fine bead, fine bitter notes.

COLET ASSEMBLAGE BLANC DE NOIR ESP
chardonnay, pinot noir

91 Colour: bright straw. Nose: candied fruit, citrus fruit, spicy, cocoa bean. Palate: flavourful, ripe fruit, powerful.

COLET GRAND CUVEÉ ESP
chardonnay, macabeo, xarel.lo

90 Colour: bright yellow. Nose: spicy, medium intensity, dried herbs, dry nuts, elegant. Palate: fruity, good acidity.

COLET NAVAZOS 2008 EXTRA BRUT RESERVA
chardonnay

93 Colour: bright golden. Nose: fine lees, dry nuts, fragrant herbs, pattiserie, toasty, complex. Palate: powerful, flavourful, good acidity, fine bead, fine bitter notes, long.

COLET NAVAZOS 2009 ESP
xarel.lo

93 Colour: bright straw. Nose: fresh fruit, dried herbs, fine lees, saline, white flowers. Palate: fresh, fruity, flavourful, good acidity, balanced, elegant.

COLET NAVAZOS 2009 EXTRA BRUT
xarel.lo

94 Colour: bright golden. Nose: fine lees, dry nuts, fragrant herbs, complex, powerfull. Palate: powerful, flavourful, good acidity, fine bead, fine bitter notes.

COLET TRADICIONAL ESP
xarel.lo, macabeo, parellada

93 Colour: bright golden. Nose: fine lees, dry nuts, fragrant herbs, complex. Palate: powerful, flavourful, good acidity, fine bead, fine bitter notes.

VATUA ! ESP
moscatel, parellada, gewürztraminer

90 Colour: bright straw. Nose: ripe fruit, citrus fruit, fine lees, grassy. Palate: flavourful, fruity, fine bitter notes.

EMENDIS

Barrio de Sant Marçal, 67
8732 Castellet i La Gornal (Barcelona)
☎: +34 938 186 119 - Fax: +34 938 918 169
www.emendis.es
avalles@emendis.es

EMENDIS DUET VARIETAL 2010 T
ull de llebre

90 Colour: dark-red cherry, garnet rim. Nose: balanced, fruit expression, wild herbs. Palate: fruity, flavourful, round tannins.

EMENDIS MATER 2006 TC
merlot

90 Colour: dark-red cherry, garnet rim. Nose: ripe fruit, wild herbs, spicy. Palate: flavourful, fruity, round tannins.

EMENDIS NOX 2012 RD
syrah, pinot noir

83

EMENDIS TRÍO VARIETAL 2012 B
macabeo, chardonnay, moscatel

89 Colour: bright straw. Nose: white flowers, expressive, ripe fruit. Palate: flavourful, good acidity, balanced.

MAS SUAU BLANC 2012 B
macabeo, xarel.lo, moscatel

84

SOMIATRUITES 2012 B
chenin blanc, sauvignon blanc, xarel.lo, chardonnay

88 Colour: bright yellow. Nose: ripe fruit, earthy notes, dried herbs, floral, expressive. Palate: rich, powerful, flavourful.

SOY UN ROSADO 2012 RD
merlot

83

FERRE I CATASUS

Masía Gustems s/n Ctra. Sant Sadurní, Km. 8
8792 La Granada (Barcelona)
☎: +34 647 806 896 - Fax: +34 938 974 758
www.ferreicatasus.com
maracalvo@ferreicatasus.com

CAP DE TRONS 2012 T
syrah, cabernet sauvignon, merlot

88 Colour: very deep cherry. Nose: ripe fruit, wild herbs. Palate: correct, balanced, long.

FERRÉ I CATASÚS CAMERLOT 2008 T
merlot, cabernet sauvignon

87 Colour: pale ruby, brick rim edge. Nose: ripe fruit, scrubland, spicy, cigar, wet leather. Palate: flavourful, balsamic, long.

FERRÉ I CATASÚS GALL NEGRE 2008 T
merlot

89 Colour: cherry, garnet rim. Nose: ripe fruit, spicy, creamy oak, toasty, waxy notes, scrubland. Palate: powerful, flavourful, toasty, spicy.

FERRÉ I CATASÚS XAREL.LO 2011 B
xarel.lo

89 Colour: bright yellow. Nose: powerfull, ripe fruit, sweet spices, creamy oak, fragrant herbs. Palate: rich, flavourful, fresh, good acidity.

MAS SUAU 2012 T
cabernet sauvignon, tempranillo

86 Colour: cherry, purple rim. Nose: medium intensity, ripe fruit, violets. Palate: fruity, flavourful, easy to drink.

FINCA VALLDOSERA

Masia Les Garrigues, Urb. Can Trabal
8734 Olèrdola (Barcelona)
☎: +34 938 143 047 - Fax: +34 938 935 590
www.fincavalldosera.com
general@fincavalldosera.com

FINCA VALLDOSERA COLLITA 2011 T
65% merlot, 25% cabernet sauvignon, 10% tempranillo

88 Colour: cherry, garnet rim. Nose: fruit preserve, balsamic herbs, earthy notes, spicy, creamy oak. Palate: powerful, flavourful, spicy.

FINCA VALLDOSERA SUBIRAT PARENT 2012 B
subirat parent

89 Colour: bright straw. Nose: fresh, fresh fruit, white flowers, jasmine, balanced. Palate: flavourful, fruity, good acidity.

FINCA VALLDOSERA SUBIRAT PARENT VYNIA GERMADA 2012 B
subirat parent

90 Colour: bright straw. Nose: fresh, fresh fruit, white flowers, fragrant herbs, citrus fruit. Palate: flavourful, fruity, good acidity, balanced.

FINCA VALLDOSERA SYRAH MERLOT 2012 RD
60% syrah, 40% merlot

85 Colour: rose, purple rim. Nose: powerfull, ripe fruit, red berry notes, floral. Palate: powerful, fruity.

FINCA VALLDOSERA SYRAH MERLOT CABERNET 2012 T
50% syrah, 35% merlot, 15% cabernet sauvignon

86 Colour: cherry, purple rim. Nose: fresh fruit, red berry notes, floral, balsamic herbs. Palate: flavourful, fruity, good acidity.

FINCA VALLDOSERA XAREL.LO 2012 B
xarel.lo

87 Colour: bright straw. Nose: fresh, fresh fruit, white flowers, expressive. Palate: flavourful, fruity, good acidity, balanced.

FINCA VILADELLOPS

Celler Gran Viladellops
8734 Olérdola (Barcelona)
☎: +34 938 188 371 - Fax: +34 938 973 237
www.viladellops.com
info@viladellops.com

FINCA VILADELLOPS XAREL.LO 2011 BFB
xarel.lo

89 Colour: bright yellow. Nose: sweet spices, faded flowers, ripe fruit. Palate: flavourful, fruity, spicy, balanced.

FINCA VILADELLOPS 2010 T
60% garnacha, 40% syrah

87 Colour: deep cherry. Nose: overripe fruit, powerfull, warm. Palate: powerful, ripe fruit, fine bitter notes.

TURÓ DE LES ABELLES 2010 T
50% garnacha, 50% syrah

92 Colour: deep cherry. Nose: dark chocolate, sweet spices, ripe fruit, fruit expression. Palate: powerful, flavourful, good acidity.

VILADELLOPS GARNATXA 2012 T
garnacha

89 Colour: deep cherry, purple rim. Nose: fruit expression, wild herbs, violet drops. Palate: fruity, flavourful.

VILADELLOPS XAREL.LO 2012 B
xarel.lo

86 Colour: bright straw. Nose: medium intensity, fresh, citrus fruit, wild herbs. Palate: flavourful, good acidity, fine bitter notes.

GIRÓ RIBOT, S.L.

Finca El Pont, s/n
8792 Santa Fe del Penedès (Barcelona)
☎: +34 938 974 050 - Fax: +34 938 974 311
www.giroribot.es
giroribot@giroribot.es

GIRÓ RIBOT BLANC DE BLANCS 2012 B
30% macabeo, 50% xarel.lo, 15% parellada, 5% chardonnay

84

GIRÓ RIBOT GIRO 2 B
100% giró

91 Colour: bright yellow. Nose: powerfull, ripe fruit, sweet spices, creamy oak, fragrant herbs. Palate: rich, smoky aftertaste, flavourful, fresh, good acidity.

GIRÓ RIBOT MUSCAT DE FRONTIGNAC 2012 B
100% moscatel de frontignan

87 Colour: bright yellow. Nose: varietal, balanced, ripe fruit, white flowers. Palate: flavourful, balanced, ripe fruit, long.

GRAMONA

Industria, 36
8770 Sant Sadurní D'Anoia (Barcelona)
☎: +34 938 910 113 - Fax: +34 938 183 284
www.gramona.com
nerea@gramona.com

GRAMONA GESSAMÍ 2012 B
moscatel de alejandría, moscatel de frontignan, gewürztraminer, sauvignon blanc

90 Colour: bright straw. Nose: powerfull, floral, candied fruit, fragrant herbs. Palate: flavourful, sweet, fresh, fruity, good acidity, long, balanced.

GRAMONA GRA A GRA 2011 B

94 Colour: golden. Nose: powerfull, floral, honeyed notes, candied fruit, fragrant herbs. Palate: flavourful, sweet, fresh, fruity, good acidity, long.

GRAMONA SAUVIGNON BLANC 2012 BFB
100% sauvignon blanc

91 Colour: bright yellow. Nose: ripe fruit, citrus fruit, mineral, wild herbs, spicy, creamy oak. Palate: concentrated, powerful, flavourful, spicy, long.

GRAMONA XAREL.LO FONT JUI 2012 B
100% xarel.lo

90 Colour: bright straw. Nose: powerfull, candied fruit, citrus fruit, spicy. Palate: flavourful, sweetness.

VI DE GLASS GEWÜRZTRAMINER 0,375 2010 B
100% gewürztraminer

92 Colour: golden. Nose: powerfull, floral, honeyed notes, candied fruit, citrus fruit. Palate: flavourful, sweet, fresh, fruity, good acidity, long.

VI DE GLASS GEWÜRZTRAMINER 0,75 2007 BC
100% gewürztraminer

94 Colour: golden. Nose: honeyed notes, candied fruit, fragrant herbs. Palate: flavourful, sweet, fresh, fruity, good acidity, long.

HERETAT MONT-RUBÍ

L'Avellà, 1
8736 Font- Rubí (Barcelona)
☎: +34 938 979 066 - Fax: +34 938 979 066
www.montrubi.com
hmr@montrubi.com

ADVENT SAMSO DULCE NATURAL 2010 RD
samsó

95 Colour: iodine, amber rim. Nose: powerfull, complex, elegant, dry nuts, toasty, acetaldehyde, saline. Palate: rich, long, fine solera notes, spicy.

ADVENT SUMOLL DULCE 2009 T
sumoll

93 Colour: light mahogany. Nose: powerfull, complex, elegant, dry nuts, toasty, acetaldehyde. Palate: rich, long, fine solera notes, spicy.

ADVENT XAREL.LO 2009 B
xarel.lo

91 Colour: golden. Nose: powerfull, floral, honeyed notes, candied fruit, fragrant herbs. Palate: flavourful, sweet, fresh, fruity, good acidity, long.

BLACK HMR 2012 T
garnacha

91 Colour: cherry, purple rim. Nose: expressive, fresh fruit, red berry notes, floral. Palate: flavourful, fruity, good acidity, round tannins.

DURONA 2007 T
sumoll, garnacha, samsó

90 Colour: very deep cherry. Nose: mineral, scrubland, balsamic herbs, toasty, aromatic coffee. Palate: fine bitter notes, good acidity, fruity.

GAINTUS 2009 T
sumoll

92 Colour: cherry, garnet rim. Nose: ripe fruit, spicy, creamy oak, toasty, varietal. Palate: powerful, flavourful, toasty, round tannins.

GAINTUS VN 2012 T
sumoll

90 Colour: bright cherry. Nose: ripe fruit, sweet spices, creamy oak, mineral. Palate: flavourful, fruity, toasty.

WHITE HMR 2012 B
xarel.lo

88 Colour: bright straw. Nose: fresh, fresh fruit, white flowers, fragrant herbs. Palate: flavourful, fruity, good acidity, balanced, elegant.

JANÉ VENTURA

Ctra. Calafell, 2
43700 El Vendrell (Tarragona)
☎: +34 977 660 118 - Fax: +34 977 661 239
www.janeventura.com
janeventura@janeventura.com

JANÉ VENTURA "FINCA ELS CAMPS" MACABEU 2011 BFB
97% macabeo, 3% malvasía

92 Colour: bright yellow. Nose: powerfull, ripe fruit, sweet spices, creamy oak, fragrant herbs. Palate: rich, smoky aftertaste, flavourful, fresh, good acidity.

JANÉ VENTURA "MAS VILELLA" COSTERS DEL ROTLLAN 2010 T
95% cabernet sauvignon, 5% sumoll

91 Colour: cherry, garnet rim. Nose: ripe fruit, toasty, complex, spicy, mineral. Palate: flavourful, toasty, round tannins, balsamic.

JANÉ VENTURA BLANC SELECCIÓ 2012 B
72% xarel.lo, 14% macabeo, 8% garnacha blanca, 6% malvasía

88 Colour: bright straw. Nose: white flowers, characterful, ripe fruit. Palate: flavourful, fruity, good acidity, balanced.

JANÉ VENTURA FINCA ELS CAMPS ULL DE LLEBRE 2007 T
ull de llebre

90 Colour: deep cherry, garnet rim. Nose: balanced, expressive, cocoa bean, ripe fruit. Palate: good structure, flavourful, good acidity, round tannins.

JANÉ VENTURA MALVASÍA DE SITGES 2012 B BARRICA
100% malvasía

93 Colour: bright straw. Nose: fresh, fresh fruit, white flowers, expressive, varietal. Palate: flavourful, fruity, good acidity, balanced.

JANÉ VENTURA NEGRE SELECCIÓ 2010 T
40% ull de llebre, 20% merlot, 10% syrah, 20% cabernet sauvignon, 10% sumoll

91 Colour: deep cherry, garnet rim. Nose: medium intensity, balanced, dried herbs. Palate: fruity, ripe fruit, round tannins.

JANÉ VENTURA ROSAT SELECCIÓ 2012 RD
15% sumoll, 35% ull de llebre, 35% merlot, 15% syrah

87 Colour: rose, bright. Nose: balanced, red berry notes, ripe fruit, wild herbs. Palate: correct, good acidity, flavourful.

JANÉ VENTURA SUMOLL 2011 T
100% sumoll

93 Colour: deep cherry, purple rim. Nose: expressive, balsamic herbs, spicy, ripe fruit, earthy notes. Palate: flavourful, good acidity, balanced, round tannins.

JAUME LLOPART ALEMANY

Font Rubí, 9
8736 Font-Rubí (Barcelona)
☎: +34 938 979 133 - Fax: +34 938 979 133
www.jaumellopartalemany.com
info@jaumellopartalemany.com

JAUME LLOPART ALEMANY 2012 B
100% xarel.lo

88 Colour: bright straw. Nose: floral, expressive, ripe fruit, powerfull. Palate: fruity, flavourful, good acidity.

JAUME LLOPART ALEMANY 2012 RD
100% cabernet sauvignon

85 Colour: rose, purple rim. Nose: powerfull, ripe fruit, dried herbs, balanced. Palate: powerful, fruity, easy to drink.

JAUME LLOPART ALEMANY VINYA D'EN LLUC SAUVIGNON BLANC 2012 B
100% sauvignon blanc

89 Colour: bright straw. Nose: ripe fruit, white flowers, tropical fruit. Palate: long, flavourful, fruity.

JAUME SERRA

Ctra. de Vilanova a Vilafranca, Km. 2,5
8800 Vilanova i la Geltru (Barcelona)
☎: +34 938 936 404 - Fax: +34 938 147 482
www.garciacarrion.es
jaumeserra@jgc.es

JAUME SERRA 2009 TC
65% cabernet sauvignon, 20% merlot, 15% tempranillo

81

JAUME SERRA 2012 B
100% macabeo

82

JAUME SERRA CHARDONNAY 2012 BFB
100% chardonnay

86 Colour: bright yellow. Nose: ripe fruit, candied fruit, sweet spices, faded flowers. Palate: fruity, easy to drink.

JAUME SERRA MACABEO 2012 B
100% macabeo

81

JAUME SERRA MERLOT 2012 RD
100% merlot

84

JAUME SERRA TEMPRANILLO 2012 T
100% tempranillo

83

JEAN LEON

Pago Jean León, s/n
8775 Torrelavit (Barcelona)
☎: +34 938 995 512 - Fax: +34 938 995 517
www.jeanleon.com
jeanleon@jeanleon.com

JEAN LEÓN 3055 2012 RD
merlot, cabernet sauvignon

89 Colour: onion pink. Nose: elegant, candied fruit, dried flowers, fragrant herbs, red berry notes. Palate: light-bodied, flavourful, good acidity, long, spicy, elegant.

JEAN LEÓN 3055 CHARDONNAY 2012 B
100% chardonnay

92 Colour: bright yellow. Nose: ripe fruit, expressive, floral, varietal. Palate: full, flavourful, fruity, good acidity, long.

JEAN LEÓN 3055 MERLOT PETIT VERDOT 2012 T ROBLE
60% merlot, 40% petit verdot

91 Colour: bright cherry. Nose: ripe fruit, sweet spices, creamy oak, expressive. Palate: flavourful, fruity, toasty, round tannins.

JEAN LEÓN VINYA LA SCALA CABERNET SAUVIGNON 2003 TGR
100% cabernet sauvignon

93 Colour: cherry, garnet rim. Nose: ripe fruit, spicy, creamy oak, toasty, characterful, earthy notes. Palate: powerful, flavourful, toasty, round tannins.

JEAN LEÓN VINYA LE HAVRE 2006 TR
cabernet sauvignon, cabernet franc

90 Colour: deep cherry. Nose: ripe fruit, spicy, toasty. Palate: flavourful, ripe fruit, fine bitter notes, good acidity.

JEAN LEÓN VINYA PALAU MERLOT 2009 TC
100% merlot

91 Colour: dark-red cherry. Nose: powerfull, warm, scrubland. Palate: good acidity, fine bitter notes, ripe fruit, round tannins.

JEAN LEÓN VIÑA GIGI CHARDONNAY 2011 BC
100% chardonnay

92 Colour: bright yellow. Nose: powerfull, ripe fruit, sweet spices, creamy oak, fragrant herbs, faded flowers. Palate: rich, flavourful, good acidity.

JEAN LEÓN VIÑA GIGI CHARDONNAY 2012 B
100% chardonnay

91 Colour: bright yellow. Nose: ripe fruit, citrus fruit, floral, fragrant herbs, sweet spices, creamy oak. Palate: rich, powerful, spicy, long.

JOAN SARDÀ

Ctra. Vilafranca a St. Jaume dels Domenys, Km. 8,1
8732 Castellvi de la Marca (Barcelona)
☎: +34 937 720 900 - Fax: +34 937 721 495
www.joansarda.com
joansarda@joansarda.com

BLANC MARINER 2012 B
xarel.lo, chardonnay

87 Colour: bright yellow. Nose: citrus fruit, ripe fruit, wild herbs. Palate: powerful, flavourful, balsamic.

JOAN SARDÀ 2009 TC
merlot, cabernet sauvignon

87 Colour: deep cherry. Nose: aromatic coffee, toasty, ripe fruit. Palate: powerful, ripe fruit.

JOAN SARDÀ 2009 TR
cabernet sauvignon, tempranillo, merlot

89 Colour: cherry, garnet rim. Nose: ripe fruit, creamy oak, toasty. Palate: powerful, flavourful, toasty, round tannins.

JOAN SARDÀ CABERNET SAUVIGNON 2010 TC
cabernet sauvignon

88 Colour: deep cherry. Nose: ripe fruit, warm, characterful, spicy, toasty. Palate: powerful, fine bitter notes, good acidity.

JOAN SARDÀ CABERNET SAUVIGNON 2012 RD
cabernet sauvignon

86 Colour: rose, purple rim. Nose: ripe fruit, red berry notes, floral, varietal. Palate: powerful, fruity.

JOAN SARDÀ CHARDONNAY 2012 B
chardonnay

85 Colour: bright yellow. Nose: candied fruit, ripe fruit, fragrant herbs. Palate: powerful, flavourful, thin.

VINYA SARDÀ 2012 B
xarel.lo

85 Colour: bright yellow. Nose: medium intensity, dried flowers, dried herbs. Palate: correct, good acidity, good finish.

VINYA SARDÀ 2012 RD
merlot

82

VINYA SARDÀ 2012 T
merlot, tempranillo, syrah

88 Colour: cherry, purple rim. Nose: fresh fruit, red berry notes. Palate: flavourful, fruity, good acidity, round tannins.

JOSEP Mª RAVENTÓS I BLANC

Plaça del Roure, s/n
8770 Sant Sadurní D'Anoia (Barcelona)
☎: +34 938 183 262 - Fax: +34 938 912 500
www.raventos.com
raventos@raventos.com

11 DE ISABEL NEGRA 2007 T
monastrell, cabernet sauvignon

91 Colour: cherry, garnet rim. Nose: ripe fruit, expressive, balanced, wild herbs. Palate: balanced, flavourful, ripe fruit, long.

11 DE ISABEL NEGRA 2008 T
monastrell

92 Colour: cherry, garnet rim. Nose: medium intensity, ripe fruit, dark chocolate, dried herbs. Palate: flavourful, round tannins.

ISABEL NEGRA 2010 T
cabernet sauvignon, monastrell

90 Colour: cherry, garnet rim. Nose: ripe fruit, spicy, creamy oak, complex, wild herbs. Palate: flavourful, toasty, round tannins.

LA ROSA DE RAVENTÓS I BLANC 2012 RD
pinot noir

85 Colour: onion pink. Nose: dried flowers, fragrant herbs. Palate: light-bodied, flavourful, good acidity, long, spicy.

PERFUM DE VI BLANC 2012 B
macabeo, moscatel, chardonnay

87 Colour: bright straw. Nose: floral, fruit expression, fragrant herbs, medium intensity. Palate: fresh, fruity.

SILENCIS 2012 B
xarel.lo

91 Colour: bright straw. Nose: balanced, ripe fruit, white flowers, citrus fruit. Palate: flavourful, good acidity, fine bitter notes.

JUVÉ Y CAMPS

Sant Venat, 1
8770 Sant Sadurní D'Anoia (Barcelona)
☎: +34 938 911 000 - Fax: +34 938 912 100
www.juveycamps.com
juveycamps@juveycamps.com

CASA VELLA D'ESPIELLS 2008 T
80% cabernet sauvignon, 20% merlot

90 Colour: cherry, garnet rim. Nose: ripe fruit, spicy, creamy oak, fine reductive notes, balsamic herbs. Palate: powerful, flavourful, toasty, round tannins.

CASA VELLA D'ESPIELLS MAGNUM 2008 T
80% cabernet sauvignon, 20% merlot

91 Colour: pale ruby, brick rim edge. Nose: ripe fruit, scrubland, spicy, aged wood nuances, creamy oak, fine reductive notes. Palate: powerful, flavourful, spicy, long.

ERMITA D'ESPIELLS 2012 B
32% macabeo, 56% xarel.lo, 12% parellada

88 Colour: bright straw. Nose: fresh, fresh fruit, white flowers. Palate: flavourful, fruity, good acidity, balanced.

ERMITA D'ESPIELLS ROSÉ 2012 RD
85% pinot noir, 15% syrah

86 Colour: rose, purple rim. Nose: powerfull, ripe fruit, red berry notes, floral, expressive. Palate: powerful, fruity, fresh.

FLOR D'ESPIELLS 2011 BFB
100% chardonnay

89 Colour: bright straw. Nose: ripe fruit, citrus fruit, fruit expression, powerfull. Palate: fruity, ripe fruit.

GREGAL D'ESPIELLS 2012 B
79% moscatel, 14% garnacha, 7% malvasía

87 Colour: bright straw. Nose: powerfull, white flowers, ripe fruit, citrus fruit. Palate: flavourful, fruity, fresh.

IOHANNES 2008 T
45% cabernet sauvignon, 55% merlot

92 Colour: pale ruby, brick rim edge. Nose: ripe fruit, spicy, aged wood nuances, wild herbs, creamy oak, sweet spices. Palate: powerful, flavourful, long, round.

MIRANDA D'ESPIELLS 2012 B
100% chardonnay

89 Colour: bright straw. Nose: white flowers, expressive, ripe fruit, citrus fruit. Palate: flavourful, fruity, good acidity, balanced.

VIÑA ESCARLATA 2008 T
100% merlot

89 Colour: ruby red, orangey edge. Nose: ripe fruit, scrubland, spicy, damp earth, wet leather. Palate: flavourful, balsamic, long.

LLOPART

Ctra. de Sant Sadurni - Ordal, Km. 4
8739 Subirats (Els Casots) (Barcelona)
☎: +34 938 993 125 - Fax: +34 938 993 038
www.llopart.com
llopart@llopart.com

LLOPART CASTELL DE SUBIRATS 2009 TC
40% merlot, 30% tempranillo, 30% cabernet sauvignon

89 Colour: cherry, garnet rim. Nose: spicy, creamy oak, toasty. Palate: powerful, flavourful, toasty, round tannins.

LLOPART CLOS DELS FÒSSILS 2012 B
85% chardonnay, 15% xarel.lo

87 Colour: bright straw. Nose: balanced, ripe fruit, white flowers, faded flowers. Palate: fruity, flavourful, good acidity.

LLOPART VITIS 2012 B
60% xarel.lo, 30% subirat parent, 10% moscatel

85 Colour: bright straw. Nose: medium intensity, wild herbs, dried flowers. Palate: fruity, easy to drink, fine bitter notes.

LOXAREL

Can Mayol, s/n
8735 Vilobí del Penedès (Barcelona)
☎: +34 938 978 001 - Fax: +34 938 978 111
www.loxarel.com
loxarel@loxarel.com

790 LOXAREL 2008 T
cabernet sauvignon

88 Colour: cherry, garnet rim. Nose: fruit preserve, spicy, powerfull, creamy oak, dried herbs. Palate: round tannins, flavourful.

999 DE LOXAREL ROSADO BN
pinot noir, xarel.lo

89 Colour: onion pink. Nose: medium intensity, fresh fruit, dried herbs, fine lees, floral. Palate: fresh, fruity, flavourful, good acidity.

AMALTEA DE LOXAREL 2011 T
cabernet sauvignon, merlot

89 Colour: bright cherry, purple rim. Nose: ripe fruit, spicy, medium intensity, expressive. Palate: balsamic, round tannins.

AMALTEA DE LOXAREL 2012 B
garnacha blanca

88 Colour: bright straw. Nose: white flowers, wild herbs, dry stone, balanced. Palate: powerful, flavourful, balsamic, easy to drink.

CORA DE LOXAREL 2012 B
xarel.lo, sauvignon blanc, moscatel

88 Colour: bright straw. Nose: fresh, white flowers, candied fruit. Palate: flavourful, fruity, good acidity, balanced.

EOS DE LOXAREL SYRAH 2011 T
syrah

87 Colour: bright cherry. Nose: ripe fruit, sweet spices. Palate: flavourful, fruity, toasty, round tannins.

GAL GRAN ARNAU DE LOXAREL 2012 RD
merlot

85 Colour: deep cherry. Nose: overripe fruit, violet drops. Palate: powerful, sweetness.

LOXAREL RESERVA FAMILIA 2007 BN GRAN RESERVA
xarel.lo, macabeo, chardonnay

90 Colour: bright yellow. Nose: balanced, faded flowers, fine lees, ripe fruit. Palate: spicy, good acidity, balanced.

LOXAREL VINTAGE 2008 BN RESERVA

90 Colour: bright golden. Nose: fine lees, dry nuts, fragrant herbs, complex. Palate: powerful, flavourful, good acidity, fine bead, fine bitter notes.

LOXAREL VINTAGE 2009 BN RESERVA

89 Colour: bright straw. Nose: fresh fruit, dried herbs, fine lees, floral, expressive. Palate: fresh, fruity, flavourful, good acidity.

LXV DE LOXAREL XAREL.LO VERMELL 2012 B
100% xarel.lo vermell

82

MAS CARGOLS DE LOXAREL 2008 T
pinot noir

87 Colour: deep cherry, garnet rim. Nose: balanced, expressive, ripe fruit, dark chocolate. Palate: good structure, fruity, grainy tannins.

MM DE LOXAREL BN GRAN RESERVA
pinot noir, xarel.lo

88 Colour: yellow, pale. Nose: balanced, faded flowers, spicy, fine lees. Palate: flavourful, good acidity, balanced.

PETIT ARNAU DE LOXAREL 2012 RD
pinot noir, merlot

82

REFUGI DE LOXAREL 2009 BN RESERVA

85 Colour: bright yellow. Nose: ripe fruit, faded flowers, slightly evolved. Palate: correct, good acidity.

XAREL.LO FERMENTAT EN ÁMFORES 2012 B
xarel.lo

90 Colour: bright yellow. Nose: powerfull, ripe fruit, sweet spices, creamy oak, fragrant herbs. Palate: rich, flavourful, fresh, good acidity.

MARQUÉS DE GELIDA - L'ALZINAR

Can Llopart de Les Alzines
8770 Sant Sadurní D'Anoia (Barcelona)
☎: +34 938 912 353 - Fax: +34 938 183 956
www.vinselcep.com
crami@vinselcep.com

MARQUÉS DE GÉLIDA CLOT DEL ROURE 2011 B BARRICA
xarel.lo

92 Colour: bright yellow. Nose: ripe fruit, sweet spices, balanced, powerfull. Palate: flavourful, spicy, ripe fruit.

MARQUÉS DE GÉLIDA XAREL.LO 2012 B
xarel.lo

87 Colour: bright straw. Nose: white flowers, ripe fruit, tropical fruit. Palate: fruity, flavourful, balanced.

MAS BERTRAN

Ctra. BP - 2121, Vilafranca a Sant Martí km. 7,7
8731 St. Martí Sarroca (Barcelona)
☎: +34 938 990 859 - Fax: +34 938 990 859
www.masbertran.com
info@masbertran.com

ARGILA 2009 BN GRAN RESERVA
100% xarel.lo

93 Colour: bright straw. Nose: medium intensity, fresh fruit, dried herbs, fine lees, floral. Palate: fresh, fruity, flavourful, good acidity.

ARGILA ROSÉ 2010 BN RESERVA
100% sumoll

88 Colour: coppery red, bright. Nose: medium intensity, fresh fruit, balanced, dried flowers. Palate: fresh, fruity, easy to drink.

ARGILA ROSÉ 2011 BN RESERVA
100% sumoll

86 Colour: coppery red, bright. Nose: medium intensity, ripe fruit. Palate: fruity, flavourful, long, ripe fruit.

BALMA 2010 BN RESERVA
45% xarel.lo, 40% macabeo, 15% parellada

89 Colour: bright straw. Nose: medium intensity, fresh fruit, dried herbs, fine lees, floral. Palate: fresh, fruity, flavourful, good acidity.

BALMA 2010 BR RESERVA
45% xarel.lo, 40% macabeo, 15% parellada

86 Colour: bright yellow. Nose: citrus fruit, dried flowers, medium intensity. Palate: fruity, correct, easy to drink.

NUTT 2011 B
100% xarel.lo

88 Colour: bright yellow. Nose: powerfull, ripe fruit, sweet spices, creamy oak, fragrant herbs. Palate: rich, flavourful, fresh, good acidity.

NUTT 2012 B
100% xarel.lo

87 Colour: bright straw. Nose: white flowers, dried herbs, candied fruit. Palate: fresh, fruity, flavourful, easy to drink.

NUTT ROSÉ SUMOLL 2012 RD
100% sumoll

88 Colour: raspberry rose. Nose: dried flowers, fragrant herbs, red berry notes. Palate: light-bodied, flavourful, good acidity, long, spicy.

MAS CAN COLOMÉ

Masies Sant Marçal s/n
8720 Castellet i La Gornal (Barcelona)
☎: +34 938 918 203 - Fax: +34 938 918 203
www.mascancolome.com
info@mascancolome.com

BLANC MEDITERRANI 2012 B
xarel.lo, macabeo, parellada, moscatel

88 Colour: bright straw. Nose: fresh, fresh fruit, white flowers. Palate: flavourful, fruity, good acidity, balanced.

MAS CAN COLOMÉ VITICULTORS 2011 BN
xarel.lo, macabeo, parellada

89 Colour: bright straw. Nose: medium intensity, fresh fruit, dried herbs, fine lees, floral. Palate: fresh, fruity, flavourful, good acidity.

ROSADENC 2012 RD
garnacha, syrah, pinot noir

86 Colour: rose. Nose: powerfull, warm, ripe fruit. Palate: powerful, sweetness.

SERENOR 2010 BN
xarel.lo, parellada, macabeo, chardonnay, pinot noir

90 Colour: bright straw. Nose: medium intensity, fresh fruit, dried herbs, fine lees, floral. Palate: fresh, fruity, flavourful, good acidity.

TURÓ 2011 T
garnacha, syrah, samsó

85 Colour: cherry, garnet rim. Nose: ripe fruit, balsamic herbs, floral, spicy. Palate: flavourful, spicy, long, balsamic.

TURONET 2012 B
chardonnay, xarel.lo, sauvignon blanc

88 Colour: bright straw. Nose: ripe fruit, citrus fruit, spicy, toasty. Palate: flavourful, fine bitter notes, good acidity.

MAS CANDÍ

Ctra. de Les Gunyoles, s/n
8793 Les Gunyoles (Avinyonet del Penedès) (Barcelona)
☎: +34 680 765 275
www.mascandi.com
info@mascandi.com

MAS CANDI COVA DE L'OMETLIÓ DULCE 2011
cabernet sauvignon

87 Colour: dark mahogany. Nose: ripe fruit, cocoa bean, sweet spices, creamy oak, acetaldehyde. Palate: slightly evolved, spicy, long.

MAS CANDI DESIG 2012 B
xarel.lo

86 Colour: bright straw. Nose: varietal, medium intensity, dried herbs, dried flowers. Palate: fruity, good acidity.

MAS CANDÍ LES FORQUES 2009 T
cabernet sauvignon, sumoll, garnacha, mandó y mónica

89 Colour: dark-red cherry. Nose: balanced, ripe fruit, spicy. Palate: flavourful, good acidity, slightly dry, soft tannins.

MAS CANDÍ LES FORQUES 2010 T
cabernet sauvignon, sumoll, garnacha, mandó y mónica

91 Colour: deep cherry, garnet rim. Nose: medium intensity, ripe fruit, balsamic herbs. Palate: good structure, good acidity, balanced.

MAS CANDÍ OVELLA NEGRA 2011 B
garnacha blanca

86 Colour: yellow. Nose: dried herbs, medium intensity. Palate: correct, easy to drink, good acidity.

MAS CANDÍ QUATRE XAREL.LO QX 2011 BFB
xarel.lo

91 Colour: bright yellow. Nose: sweet spices, smoky, ripe fruit, faded flowers. Palate: rich, flavourful, spicy, long.

MAS CANDÍ QUATRE XAREL.LO QX MAGNUM 2009 BFB
xarel.lo

89 Colour: bright golden. Nose: expressive, ripe fruit, mineral, faded flowers. Palate: balanced, fine bitter notes, spicy, ripe fruit.

MAS CODINA

Barri El Gorner, s/n - Mas Codina
8797 Puigdalber (Barcelona)
☎: +34 938 988 166 - Fax: +34 938 988 166
www.mascodina.com
info@mascodina.com

MAS CODINA 2012 B
macabeo, xarel.lo, chardonnay, moscatel

88 Colour: bright straw. Nose: fresh, white flowers, citrus fruit. Palate: flavourful, fruity, good acidity, balanced.

MAS CODINA VINYA FERRER 2008 TR
cabernet sauvignon

88 Colour: cherry, garnet rim. Nose: ripe fruit, spicy, scrubland, creamy oak. Palate: flavourful, powerful, spicy.

MAS CODINA VINYA MIQUEL 2009 TC
syrah

88 Colour: cherry, garnet rim. Nose: ripe fruit, sweet spices, creamy oak. Palate: flavourful, fruity, toasty.

MAS COMTAL

Mas Comtal, 1
8793 Avinyonet del Penedès (Barcelona)
☎: +34 938 970 052 - Fax: +34 938 970 591
www.mascomtal.com
mascomtal@mascomtal.com

ANTISTIANA 2010 T
merlot, cabernet sauvignon

90 Colour: deep cherry. Nose: spicy, dark chocolate, ripe fruit. Palate: good structure, powerful, fine bitter notes.

**MAS COMTAL 20 ANIVERSARI
ROSADO 2010 ESP RESERVA**
merlot

88 Colour: light cherry. Nose: ripe fruit, fragrant herbs, dried flowers. Palate: fresh, fruity, powerful, flavourful.

MAS COMTAL NEGRE D'ANYADA 2011 T
cabernet sauvignon, merlot

88 Colour: deep cherry. Nose: powerfull, characterful, toasty, sweet spices. Palate: powerful, good acidity, ripe fruit, spicy.

MAS COMTAL POMELL DE BLANCS 2012 B
xarel.lo, chardonnay

85 Colour: bright yellow. Nose: ripe fruit, dried flowers, fragrant herbs. Palate: powerful, flavourful, correct.

MAS COMTAL PREMIUM 2011 BR
xarel.lo, chardonnay

86 Nose: medium intensity, fresh fruit, dried herbs. Palate: fresh, fruity, flavourful, good acidity.

MAS COMTAL ROSAT DE LLÀGRIMA 2012 RD
merlot

86 Colour: rose, bright. Nose: balanced, balsamic herbs, citrus fruit. Palate: flavourful, fruity, correct.

MAS RODÓ

Km. 2 Ctra. Sant Pere Sacarrera a Sant Joan de Mediona (Alto Penedès)
8773 Sant Joan de Mediona (Barcelona)
☎: +34 932 385 780 - Fax: +34 932 174 356
www.masrodo.com
info@masrodo.com

MAS RODÓ CABERNET SAUVIGNON 2009 T
100% cabernet sauvignon

89 Colour: cherry, garnet rim. Nose: spicy, balanced, ripe fruit, balsamic herbs. Palate: good structure, flavourful, round tannins.

MAS RODÓ MACABEO 2011 B
100% macabeo

88 Colour: bright straw. Nose: ripe fruit, citrus fruit, spicy. Palate: flavourful, powerful, toasty.

MAS RODÓ MERLOT 2009 TR
100% merlot

84

MAS RODÓ MONTONEGA 2011 B
100% montonega

88 Colour: bright straw. Nose: mineral, ripe fruit, white flowers. Palate: flavourful, fruity.

MAS RODÓ RIESLING 2011 BFB
85% riesling, 15% montonega

88 Colour: bright yellow. Nose: powerfull, sweet spices, creamy oak. Palate: rich, flavourful, fresh, good acidity.

MASET DEL LLEÓ

C-244, Km. 32,5
8792 La Granada del Penedès (Barcelona)
☎: +34 902 200 250 - Fax: +34 938 921 333
www.maset.com
info@maset.com

MASET DEL LLEÓ CABERNET SAUVIGNON 2010 TC
cabernet sauvignon

86 Colour: cherry, garnet rim. Nose: ripe fruit, spicy, creamy oak, grassy. Palate: powerful, flavourful, toasty.

**MASET DEL LLEÓ CHARDONNAY
FLOR DE MAR 2012 B**
chardonnay

86 Colour: bright straw. Nose: fresh, fresh fruit, white flowers, expressive. Palate: flavourful, fruity, good acidity, balanced.

MASET DEL LLEÓ MERLOT 2012 RD
merlot

84

MASET DEL LLEÓ MERLOT FOC 2010 TR
merlot

90 Colour: cherry, garnet rim. Nose: red berry notes, ripe fruit, fragrant herbs, earthy notes. Palate: powerful, correct, balanced.

MASET DEL LLEÓ SELECCIÓN 2011 T
ull de llebre

90 Colour: cherry, purple rim. Nose: expressive, fresh fruit, red berry notes, floral. Palate: flavourful, fruity, good acidity, round tannins.

MASET DEL LLEÓ XAREL.LO BLANC DE BLANCS 2012 B
xarel.lo

87 Colour: bright straw. Nose: fresh, fresh fruit, white flowers, dried herbs. Palate: flavourful, fruity, balanced.

MIGUEL TORRES S.A.

Miguel Torres i Carbó, 6
8720 Vilafranca del Penedès (Barcelona)
☎: +34 938 177 400 - Fax: +34 938 177 444
www.torres.es
mailadmin@torres.es

ATRIUM CABERNET SAUVIGNON 2010 T
cabernet sauvignon

88 Colour: cherry, garnet rim. Nose: balanced, ripe fruit, spicy, wild herbs. Palate: fruity, flavourful, good acidity.

ATRIUM CHARDONNAY 2011 B
chardonnay

90 Colour: bright yellow. Nose: powerfull, ripe fruit, sweet spices, creamy oak, fragrant herbs. Palate: rich, flavourful, fresh, good acidity.

ATRIUM MERLOT 2011 T
merlot

89 Colour: cherry, garnet rim. Nose: balanced, scrubland, varietal, ripe fruit. Palate: fruity, easy to drink, round tannins.

FRANSOLA 2011 B
sauvignon blanc, parellada

91 Colour: bright yellow. Nose: citrus fruit, fruit expression, fragrant herbs, herbaceous, spicy, creamy oak. Palate: long, balsamic, powerful, flavourful.

FRANSOLA 2012 B
sauvignon blanc

90 Colour: bright straw. Nose: fresh, white flowers, citrus fruit, balsamic herbs. Palate: flavourful, fruity, good acidity, balanced.

GRAN CORONAS 2010 TC
cabernet sauvignon, tempranillo

90 Colour: deep cherry, garnet rim. Nose: spicy, scrubland, ripe fruit. Palate: balsamic, long, round tannins.

MAS LA PLANA CABERNET SAUVIGNON 2009 TGR
cabernet sauvignon

92 Colour: cherry, garnet rim. Nose: ripe fruit, spicy, complex, scrubland, varietal. Palate: powerful, flavourful, toasty, round tannins.

RESERVA REAL 2009 TGR
cabernet sauvignon, merlot, cabernet franc

93 Colour: black cherry, garnet rim. Nose: balanced, expressive, complex, ripe fruit. Palate: good structure, full, flavourful, round tannins.

WALTRAUD 2012 B
riesling

90 Colour: bright yellow. Nose: expressive, elegant, white flowers, citrus fruit. Palate: balanced, fine bitter notes, long, good acidity.

MONT MARÇAL

Finca Manlleu
8732 Castellví de la Marca (Barcelona)
☎: +34 938 918 281 - Fax: +34 938 919 045
www.mont-marcal.com
mrivas@mont-marcal.com

MONT MARÇAL 2009 TC
50% cabernet sauvignon, 50% merlot

84

MONT MARÇAL 2012 B
50% xarel.lo, 30% sauvignon blanc, 20% chardonnay

85 Colour: bright straw. Nose: dried flowers, balsamic herbs, citrus fruit, wild herbs. Palate: fresh, fruity, easy to drink.

OLIVELLA I BONET

Casetes Puigmoltó, 15
43720 L'Arboç del Penedès (Tarragona)
☎: +34 977 670 433 - Fax: +34 977 670 433
www.olivellaibonet.com
info@olivellaibonet.com

MONT CARANAC BN
macabeo, xarel.lo, parellada

87 Colour: bright golden. Nose: fine lees, dry nuts, fragrant herbs, complex. Palate: powerful, flavourful, good acidity, fine bead, fine bitter notes.

MONT CARANAC CHARDONNAY BR
90% chardonnay, 10% macabeo, xarel.lo, parellada

86 Colour: bright yellow. Nose: candied fruit, ripe fruit, dried flowers, dried herbs. Palate: powerful, flavourful, easy to drink.

OLIVELLA I BONET BN
macabeo, xarel.lo, parellada

85 Colour: bright straw. Nose: floral, fine lees, dried herbs, citrus fruit, ripe fruit. Palate: fresh, flavourful, easy to drink.

OLIVELLA I BONET BR
macabeo, xarel.lo, parellada

84

OLIVELLA I BONET ESPECIAL ARTESÀ BN
macabeo, xarel.lo, parellada

86 Colour: bright straw. Nose: fresh fruit, dried herbs, fine lees, floral, expressive. Palate: fresh, fruity, flavourful, good acidity.

OLIVELLA I BONET ESPECIAL ARTESÀ EXTRA BRUT
macabeo, xarel.lo, parellada

84

OLIVELLA I BONET SS
macabeo, xarel.lo, parellada

84

ORIOL ROSSELL

Propietat Can Cassanyes, s/n
8732 St. Marçal (Barcelona)
☎: +34 977 670 207 - Fax: +34 977 670 207
www.oriolrossell.com
oriolrossell@oriolrossell.com

LES CERVERES XAREL.LO 2011 B
xarel.lo

89 Colour: bright yellow. Nose: ripe fruit, sweet spices, creamy oak, fragrant herbs. Palate: rich, smoky aftertaste, flavourful, fresh.

ROCAPLANA 2011 TC
syrah

89 Colour: bright cherry. Nose: ripe fruit, sweet spices, creamy oak, expressive. Palate: flavourful, fruity, toasty, round tannins.

VIROLET XAREL.LO 2012 B
xarel.lo

90 Colour: bright straw. Nose: fresh, fresh fruit, white flowers, expressive. Palate: flavourful, fruity, good acidity, balanced.

PARATÓ

Can Respall de Renardes
8733 El Pla del Penedès (Barcelona)
☎: +34 938 988 182 - Fax: +34 938 988 510
www.parato.es
info@parato.es

ÁTICA PINOT NOIR 2007 T
pinot noir

85 Colour: deep cherry. Nose: powerfull, overripe fruit, warm. Palate: powerful, sweetness.

FINCA RENARDES 2011 T
tempranillo, cabernet sauvignon, cariñena

89 Colour: cherry, garnet rim. Nose: red berry notes, ripe fruit, balsamic herbs, spicy, creamy oak. Palate: powerful, flavourful, spicy, long.

FINCA RENARDES MACABEU + COUPAGE 2012 B
macabeo, chardonnay, xarel.lo, parellada

86 Colour: bright straw. Nose: white flowers, ripe fruit. Palate: flavourful, fruity, good acidity, balanced.

PARATÓ ÁTICA TRES X TRES 2011 B
xarel.lo, macabeo, chardonnay

86 Colour: bright yellow. Nose: powerfull, ripe fruit, sweet spices, creamy oak, fragrant herbs. Palate: rich, smoky aftertaste, flavourful, fresh, good acidity.

PARATÓ PINOT NOIR 2012 RD
pinot noir

85 Colour: bright cherry. Nose: ripe fruit, balsamic herbs, powerfull. Palate: concentrated, powerful, flavourful, rich.

PARATÓ SAMSÓ 2008 TR
cariñena

90 Colour: deep cherry. Nose: mineral, ripe fruit, spicy. Palate: flavourful, complex, fine bitter notes.

PARATÓ XAREL.LO 2012 B
xarel.lo

86 Colour: bright straw. Nose: medium intensity, white flowers, dried herbs, varietal. Palate: correct, balanced, fine bitter notes.

XAREL.LO XXV 2010 B
xarel.lo

86 Colour: golden. Nose: floral, honeyed notes, candied fruit, fragrant herbs. Palate: flavourful, sweet, fresh, fruity, long.

PARDAS

Finca Can Comas, s/n
8775 Torrelavit (Barcelona)
☎: +34 938 995 005
www.pardas.net
pardas@cancomas.com

PARDAS ASPRIU 2010 B
xarel.lo

92 Colour: bright straw. Nose: smoky, spicy. Palate: fruity, balanced, fine bitter notes, long, spicy, good acidity.

PARDAS COLLITA ROJA 2009 T
90% sumoll, 10% marselan

90 Colour: cherry, garnet rim. Nose: medium intensity, balanced, balsamic herbs, spicy, varnish. Palate: good structure, flavourful, good acidity.

PARDAS NEGRE FRANC 2009 T
66% cabernet franc, 23% cabernet sauvignon, 11% sumoll

91 Colour: deep cherry. Nose: ripe fruit, sweet spices, mineral. Palate: flavourful, powerful, fine bitter notes, round tannins.

PARDAS RUPESTRIS 2012 B
81% xarel.lo, 6% xarel.lo vermell, 13% malvasía

89 Colour: bright straw. Nose: fresh, white flowers, expressive. Palate: flavourful, fruity, balanced.

PARDAS XAREL.LO 2010 B
100% xarel.lo

90 Colour: bright straw. Nose: ripe fruit, citrus fruit, dried herbs. Palate: flavourful, spicy, ripe fruit.

PARÉS BALTÀ

Masía Can Baltá, s/n
8796 Pacs del Penedès (Barcelona)
☎: +34 938 901 399 - Fax: +34 938 901 143
www.paresbalta.com
paresbalta@paresbalta.com

BLANC DE PACS 2012 B
45% parellada, 34% macabeo, 21% xarel.lo

87 Colour: bright straw. Nose: fragrant herbs, white flowers, ripe fruit. Palate: flavourful, fruity, fresh.

CALCARI XAREL.LO 2012 B
100% xarel.lo

91 Colour: bright straw. Nose: fresh, fresh fruit, white flowers, expressive, mineral. Palate: flavourful, fruity, good acidity, balanced.

ELECTIO XAREL.LO 2010 B
100% xarel.lo

92 Colour: bright yellow. Nose: powerfull, ripe fruit, sweet spices, fragrant herbs. Palate: rich, flavourful, fresh, good acidity.

HISENDA MIRET GARNATXA 2010 T
100% garnacha

88 Colour: dark-red cherry, garnet rim. Nose: powerfull, fruit preserve, balsamic herbs. Palate: fruity, flavourful, round tannins.

INDÍGENA 2011 T
100% garnacha

89 Colour: dark-red cherry, garnet rim. Nose: powerfull, toasty, ripe fruit. Palate: flavourful, round tannins.

INDÍGENA 2012 B
100% garnacha blanca

92 Colour: bright straw. Nose: fresh, fresh fruit, white flowers, expressive. Palate: flavourful, fruity, good acidity, balanced.

MARTA DE BALTÀ 2008 T
100% syrah

89 Colour: deep cherry, garnet rim. Nose: ripe fruit, expressive, sweet spices. Palate: flavourful, round tannins, spicy.

MAS ELENA 2010 T
merlot, cabernet sauvignon, cabernet franc

92 Colour: cherry, garnet rim. Nose: medium intensity, ripe fruit, expressive, balanced. Palate: elegant, spicy, complex, full.

MAS IRENE 2009 T
72% merlot, 28% cabernet franc

93 Colour: cherry, garnet rim. Nose: medium intensity, ripe fruit, spicy, dried herbs, varietal. Palate: good structure, good acidity, round tannins.

MAS PETIT 2010 T
76% garnacha, 24% cabernet sauvignon

87 Colour: dark-red cherry, garnet rim. Nose: ripe fruit, powerfull, sweet spices. Palate: flavourful, round tannins.

RADIX 2012 RD
100% syrah

86 Colour: dark-red cherry, garnet rim. Nose: powerfull, ripe fruit, floral, expressive. Palate: powerful, fruity, fresh, concentrated.

ROCAMAR

Major, 80
8755 Castellbisbal (Barcelona)
☎: +34 937 720 900 - Fax: +34 937 721 495
www.rocamar.net
info@rocamar.net

ROCAMAR TEMPRANILLO 2012 T
tempranillo

88 Colour: bright cherry. Nose: ripe fruit, sweet spices, creamy oak. Palate: flavourful, fruity, toasty, round tannins.

ROVELLATS

Finca Rovellats - Bº La Bleda
8731 Sant Marti Sarroca (Barcelona)
☎: +34 934 880 575 - Fax: +34 934 880 819
www.cavasrovellats.com
rovellats@cavasrovellats.com

ROVELLATS BLANC PRIMAVERA 2012 B
chardonnay, xarel.lo, macabeo

87 Colour: bright straw. Nose: dried herbs, fresh fruit, citrus fruit. Palate: flavourful, fruity, fresh.

ROVELLATS BRUT DE TARDOR 2008 T
garnacha, cabernet sauvignon, merlot, syrah

88 Colour: light cherry, orangey edge. Nose: violet drops, wild herbs, spicy, creamy oak. Palate: powerful, flavourful, balsamic, spicy, long.

ROVELLATS MERLOT 2012 RD
merlot

85 Colour: rose, purple rim. Nose: powerfull, ripe fruit, red berry notes, expressive. Palate: powerful, fruity, fresh.

SEGURA VIUDAS

Ctra. Sant Sadurní a St. Pere de Riudebitlles, Km. 5
8775 Torrelavit (Barcelona)
☎: +34 938 917 070 - Fax: +34 938 996 006
www.seguraviudas.com
seguraviudas@seguraviudas.es

CREU DE LAVIT 2011 BFB
xarel.lo

86 Colour: bright straw. Nose: citrus fruit, ripe fruit, dried herbs, floral, creamy oak. Palate: flavourful, fruity, spicy.

VIÑA HEREDAD 2012 B
macabeo, xarel.lo, parellada

84

VIÑA HEREDAD CABERNET SAUVIGNON 2011 T
cabernet sauvignon

86 Colour: cherry, garnet rim. Nose: ripe fruit, spicy, toasty, balsamic herbs. Palate: powerful, flavourful, round tannins.

TERRAPRIMA

Can Ràfols dels Caus, s/n
8792 Avinyonet del Penedès (Barcelona)
☎: +34 938 970 013 - Fax: +34 938 970 370
www.terraprima.es
info@terraprima.es

TERRAPRIMA 2011 T

90 Colour: bright cherry. Nose: red berry notes, wild herbs, floral, dry stone. Palate: fresh, fruity, balsamic, round tannins.

TERRAPRIMA 2012 B

90 Colour: bright straw. Nose: fresh, fresh fruit, white flowers. Palate: flavourful, fruity, good acidity.

TORELLÓ

Can Martí de Baix (Apartado Correos nº8)
8770 Sant Sadurní D'Anoia (Barcelona)
☎: +34 938 910 793 - Fax: +34 938 910 877
www.torello.com
torello@torello.es

PETJADES 2012 RD
merlot

86 Colour: light cherry, bright. Nose: red berry notes, ripe fruit, warm. Palate: flavourful, fruity, easy to drink.

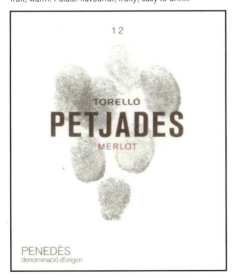

CRISALYS 2012 BFB
xarel.lo

89 Colour: yellow, pale. Nose: sweet spices, creamy oak, ripe fruit, faded flowers. Palate: balanced, rich, flavourful.

RAIMONDA 2007 TR
cabernet sauvignon, merlot

90 Colour: pale ruby, brick rim edge. Nose: spicy, scrubland, wet leather, tobacco, sweet spices, creamy oak. Palate: powerful, flavourful, spicy, long.

TORELLÓ MALVAREL.LO 2012 B
malvasía, xarel.lo

88 Colour: bright straw. Nose: white flowers, citrus fruit, expressive. Palate: flavourful, fruity, easy to drink, good acidity, correct.

VITTIOS VENDIMIA TARDÍA 2012 B
xarel.lo

88 Colour: golden. Nose: powerfull, floral, candied fruit, fragrant herbs. Palate: flavourful, sweet, fresh, fruity, good acidity, long.

TRIAS BATLLE

Pere El Gran, 21
8720 Vilafranca del Penedès (Barcelona)
☎: +34 677 497 892
www.triasbatlle.com
peptrias@triasbatlle.com

TRIAS BATLLE 2009 TC
cabernet sauvignon

87 Colour: cherry, garnet rim. Nose: ripe fruit, spicy, toasty, balsamic herbs. Palate: powerful, flavourful, toasty.

TRIAS BATLLE 2012 B
macabeo, xarel.lo, parellada, moscatel

85 Colour: bright straw. Nose: fresh, fresh fruit, white flowers. Palate: flavourful, fruity, good acidity.

TRIAS BATLLE 2012 RD
merlot, syrah

84

TRIAS BATLLE CHARDONNAY 2011 BC
chardonnay

84

VALLDOLINA

Plaça de la Creu, 1
8795 Olesa de Bonesvalls (Barcelona)
☎: +34 938 984 181 - Fax: +34 938 984 181
www.valldolina.com
info@valldolina.com

BONES VALLS CABERNET SAUVIGNON 2010 T
cabernet sauvignon

88 Colour: cherry, garnet rim. Nose: ripe fruit, spicy, creamy oak, damp earth. Palate: powerful, flavourful, toasty.

VALL DOLINA XAREL.LO "ECOLÓGICO" 2012 B
xarel.lo

90 Colour: bright straw. Nose: mineral, fresh fruit, fruit expression. Palate: flavourful, fruity, fresh.

VALL DOLINA ROSAT ECO 2012 RD
merlot

85 Colour: light cherry. Nose: powerfull, ripe fruit, red berry notes. Palate: powerful, flavourful, sweetness.

VALLDOLINA MERLOT ECO 2011 T
merlot

86 Colour: deep cherry. Nose: medium intensity, warm, scrubland. Palate: spicy, fine bitter notes.

VALLFORMOSA

La Sala, 45
8735 Vilobi del Penedès (Barcelona)
☎: +34 938 978 286 - Fax: +34 938 978 355
www.vallformosa.com
vallformosa@vallformosa.es

LA.SALA MERLOT SUMOLL TEMPRANILLO 2012 RD
50% merlot, 35% sumoll, 15% tempranillo

87 Colour: raspberry rose. Nose: floral, candied fruit, fragrant herbs. Palate: fresh, fruity, flavourful.

LA.SALA TEMPRANILLO CABERNET SAUVIGNON GARNACHA 2011 T
50% tempranillo, 45% cabernet sauvignon, 5% garnacha

89 Colour: cherry, purple rim. Nose: expressive, fresh fruit, red berry notes, floral, fragrant herbs. Palate: flavourful, fruity, good acidity.

MASIA FREYÈ MERLOT SUMOLL 2012 RD
90% merlot, 10% sumoll

85 Colour: brilliant rose. Nose: powerfull, ripe fruit, red berry notes, floral. Palate: powerful, fruity, fresh.

MASIA FREYÈ PARELLADA MUSCAT 2012 B
55% parellada, 45% moscatel

88 Colour: bright straw. Nose: ripe fruit, citrus fruit, white flowers. Palate: flavourful, fruity, fresh.

MASIA FREYÈ SYRAH TEMPRANILLO 2011 T
60% syrah, 40% tempranillo

88 Colour: bright cherry. Nose: ripe fruit, sweet spices, creamy oak. Palate: flavourful, fruity, toasty.

MASIA FREYÈ XAREL.LO CHARDONNAY 2012 B
85% xarel.lo, 15% chardonnay

88 Colour: bright straw. Nose: fresh, fresh fruit, white flowers, expressive. Palate: flavourful, fruity, good acidity, balanced.

MASIA LA.SALA XAREL.LO MACABEO CHARDONNAY 2012 B
55% xarel.lo, 30% macabeo, 15% chardonnay

88 Colour: bright straw. Nose: expressive, fresh, ripe fruit, citrus fruit. Palate: flavourful, powerful, fruity.

VILARNAU

Ctra. d'Espiells, Km. 1,4 Finca "Can Petit"
8770 Sant Sadurní D'Anoia (Barcelona)
☎: +34 938 912 361 - Fax: +34 938 912 913
www.vilarnau.es
vilarnau@vilarnau.es

VILARNAU CABERNET SAUVIGNON 2012 T
100% cabernet sauvignon

88 Colour: cherry, purple rim. Nose: fresh fruit, red berry notes. Palate: flavourful, fruity, good acidity, round tannins.

VILARNAU XAREL.LO 2012 B
100% xarel.lo

87 Colour: bright straw. Nose: fresh, fresh fruit, white flowers. Palate: flavourful, fruity, good acidity, balanced.

VINS I CAVES CUSCÓ BERGA

Esplugues, 7
8793 Avinyonet del Penedès (Barcelona)
☎: +34 938 970 164
www.cuscoberga.com
cuscoberga@cuscoberga.com

CUSCÓ BERGA CABERNET MERLOT 2009 TC
80% cabernet sauvignon, 20% merlot

84

CUSCÓ BERGA MERLOT SELECCIÓ 2012 RD
100% merlot

84

CUSCÓ BERGA MERLOT ULL DE LLEBRE 2011 T
60% merlot, 40% tempranillo

84

CUSCÓ BERGA MUSCAT D'ALEJANDRÍA 2012 B
100% moscatel de alejandría

83

CUSCÓ BERGA XAREL.LO SELECCIÓ 2012 B
100% xarel.lo

85 Colour: bright straw. Nose: fresh fruit, white flowers, dried herbs. Palate: flavourful, fruity, good acidity.

VINYA OCULTA

Cal Banyeres s/n
8731 Sant Martí Sarroca (Barcelona)
www.vinyaoculta.com
amos@vinyaoculta.com

V.O. VINYA OCULTA 2011 B
xarel.lo

92 Colour: bright yellow. Nose: powerfull, ripe fruit, sweet spices, creamy oak. Palate: rich, flavourful, fresh, good acidity.

V.O. VINYA OCULTA DIABLES 2012 B
macabeo

80

V.O. VINYA OCULTA SENSE 2012 B
xarel.lo

90 Colour: bright golden. Nose: powerfull, ripe fruit, citrus fruit, white flowers, sweet spices. Palate: powerful, sweetness, fruity.

DO PLA DE BAGES / D.O.P.

LOCATION:

Covering one of the eastern extremes of the Central Catalonian Depression; it covers the natural region of Bages, of which the city of Manresa is the urban centre. To the south the region is bordered by the Montserrat mountain range, the dividing line which separates it from Penedés. It comprises the municipal areas of Fonollosa, Monistrol de Caldres, Sant Joan de Vilatorrada, Artés, Avinyó, Balsareny, Calders, Callús, Cardona, Castellgalí, Castellfollit del Boix, Castellnou de Bages, Manresa, Mura, Navarcles, Navàs, El Pont de Vilomara, Rajadell, Sallent, Sant Fruitós de Bages, Sant Mateu de Bages, Sant Salvador de Guardiola, Santpedor, Santa María d'Oló, Súria and Talamanca.

CLIMATE:

Mid-mountain Mediterranean, with little rainfall (500 mm to 600 mm average annual rainfall) and greater temperature contrasts than in the Penedès.

SOIL:

The vineyards are situated at an altitude of about 400 m. The soil is franc-clayey, franc-sandy and franc-clayey-sandy.

GRAPE VARIETIES:

WHITE: *Chardonnay, Gewürztraminer, Macabeo, Picapoll, Parellada, Sauvignon Blanc.*
RED: *Sumoll, Ull de Llebre (Tempranillo), Merlot, Cabernet Franc, Cabernet Sauvignon, Syrah* and *Garnacha.*

FIGURES:

Vineyard surface: 450 – **Wine-Growers:** 94 – **Wineries:** 12 – **2012 Harvest rating:** Very Good– **Production:** - litres – **Market percentages:** 70% domestic. 30% export

CONSEJO REGULADOR
Casa de La Culla - La Culla, s/n - 08240 Manresa (Barcelona) ☎: +34 938 748 236 - Fax: +34 938 748 094
info@dopladebages.com   www.dopladebages.com

ABADAL

Santa María d'Horta d'Avinyó
8279 Santa María D'Horta D'Avinyó (Barcelona)
☎: +34 938 743 511 - Fax: +34 938 737 204
www.abadal.net
info@abadal.net

ABADAL 3.9 2009 TR
85% cabernet sauvignon, 15% syrah

91 Colour: cherry, garnet rim. Nose: ripe fruit, spicy, creamy oak, earthy notes. Palate: powerful, flavourful, toasty, spicy, long.

ABADAL 5 MERLOT 2009 TR
100% merlot

87 Colour: cherry, garnet rim. Nose: spicy, creamy oak, toasty, fruit preserve, fine reductive notes. Palate: powerful, flavourful, toasty, balsamic.

ABADAL CABERNET SAUVIGNON 2012 RD
90% cabernet sauvignon, 10% sumoll

88 Colour: rose, purple rim. Nose: powerfull, ripe fruit, red berry notes, floral, expressive. Palate: powerful, fruity, fresh.

ABADAL PICAPOLL 2012 B
100% picapoll

91 Colour: bright straw. Nose: white flowers, fragrant herbs, tropical fruit, wild herbs. Palate: rich, fresh, fruity, balanced.

ABADAL SELECCIÓ 2007 TR
40% cabernet sauvignon, 40% cabernet franc, 15% syrah, 5% sumoll, 5% mando

92 Colour: cherry, garnet rim. Nose: ripe fruit, spicy, creamy oak, toasty, complex. Palate: powerful, flavourful, toasty, round tannins.

BODEGA EL MOLI

8241 Manresa (Barcelona)
☎: +34 931 021 965
www.cellerelmoli.com
collbaix@cellerelmoli.com

COLLBAIX CUPATGE 2009 T
cabernet sauvignon, cabernet franc, tempranillo, merlot

88 Colour: cherry, garnet rim. Nose: ripe fruit, balsamic herbs, damp earth, creamy oak, toasty. Palate: balanced, flavourful, round tannins.

COLLBAIX LA LLOBETA 2009 T
cabernet sauvignon, merlot, cabernet franc

89 Colour: cherry, garnet rim. Nose: ripe fruit, spicy, creamy oak, toasty, balsamic herbs, dry stone. Palate: powerful, flavourful, toasty, round tannins.

COLLBAIX PICAPOLL MACABEO 2012 B
macabeo, picapoll

89 Colour: bright straw. Nose: ripe fruit, white flowers, fragrant herbs, expressive. Palate: powerful, flavourful, correct, long.

COLLBAIX SINGULAR 2009 T
100% cabernet sauvignon

93 Colour: deep cherry, garnet rim. Nose: red berry notes, ripe fruit, wild herbs, earthy notes, sweet spices, toasty. Palate: rich, powerful, flavourful, long, balanced, elegant.

COLLBAIX SINGULAR 2011 B BARRICA
macabeo, picapoll

91 Colour: bright golden. Nose: ripe fruit, floral, balsamic herbs, wild herbs, spicy, creamy oak. Palate: powerful, flavourful, spicy, long, balanced, elegant.

CELLER SOLERGIBERT

Barquera, 40
8271 Artés (Barcelona)
☎: +34 938 305 084 - Fax: +34 938 305 763
www.cellersolergibert.com
josep@cellersolergibert.com

ENRIC SOLERGIBERT 2002 T
cabernet sauvignon, cabernet franc

88 Colour: pale ruby, brick rim edge. Nose: elegant, spicy, wet leather, aged wood nuances, fruit liqueur notes. Palate: spicy, elegant, long.

PD'A DE SOLERGILABERT 2011 B
picapoll

89 Colour: bright yellow. Nose: powerfull, ripe fruit, sweet spices, creamy oak, fragrant herbs, citrus fruit. Palate: rich, flavourful, fresh, good acidity, balanced.

PIC SOLERGIBERT 2011 B
picapoll

91 Colour: bright yellow. Nose: ripe fruit, fragrant herbs, sweet spices, creamy oak. Palate: rich, fresh, powerful, flavourful.

SOLERGIBERT 20 ANIVERSARI 2007 TR
cabernet sauvignon, cabernet franc, merlot

89 Colour: pale ruby, brick rim edge. Nose: spicy, fine reductive notes, wet leather, aged wood nuances. Palate: spicy, fine tannins, long.

SOLERGIBERT DE MATACANS 2011 T
50% cabernet sauvignon, 50% cabernet franc

91 Colour: cherry, garnet rim. Nose: red berry notes, ripe fruit, balsamic herbs, creamy oak, mineral. Palate: powerful, flavourful, spicy, long, balanced.

TOC DE SOLERGIBERT 2011 T
85% merlot, 15% cabernet sauvignon

88 Colour: light cherry. Nose: red berry notes, ripe fruit, fragrant herbs, sweet spices, toasty. Palate: powerful, flavourful, correct, toasty.

HERETAT OLLER DEL MAS

Ctra. de Igualada (C-37), km. 91
8241 Manresa (Barcelona)
☎: +34 938 768 315
www.ollerdelmas.com
info@ollerdelmas.com

ARNAU OLLER SELECCIÓ DE LA FAMILIA 2007 T
90% merlot, 10% picapoll negro

89 Colour: cherry, garnet rim. Nose: ripe fruit, spicy, creamy oak, complex, waxy notes, tobacco. Palate: powerful, flavourful, round tannins.

BERNAT OLLER 2007 T
70% merlot, 30% picapoll negro

89 Colour: pale ruby, brick rim edge. Nose: fruit preserve, scrubland, spicy, creamy oak, fine reductive notes. Palate: powerful, flavourful, long, fine tannins.

BERNAT OLLER BLANC DE PICAPOLLS 2012 B
50% picapoll, 50% picapoll negro

89 Colour: bright straw. Nose: damp earth, floral, wild herbs, ripe fruit, citrus fruit. Palate: powerful, fruity, fresh, flavourful.

BERNAT OLLER ROSAT 2012 RD
70% merlot, 30% picapoll negro

82

PETIT BERNAT 2012 B
80% picapoll, 20% macabeo

87 Colour: bright straw. Nose: fresh, fresh fruit, white flowers, expressive. Palate: flavourful, fruity, good acidity, balanced.

PETIT BERNAT 2012 T
picapoll negro, merlot, syrah, cabernet franc, cabernet sauvignon

86 Colour: bright cherry. Nose: ripe fruit, sweet spices, creamy oak, dark chocolate, balsamic herbs. Palate: flavourful, fruity, toasty.

JAUME GRAU - VINS GRAU S.L.

Ctra. C-37, Km. 75,5
8255 Maians (Barcelona)
☎: +34 938 356 002 - Fax: +34 938 356 812
www.vinsgrau.com
info@vinsgrau.com

JAUME GRAU I GRAU "GRATVS" 2009 TC
merlot, tempranillo

87 Colour: cherry, garnet rim. Nose: ripe fruit, spicy, creamy oak, grassy. Palate: powerful, flavourful, toasty.

JAUME GRAU I GRAU AVRVM 2012 B
sauvignon blanc, chardonnay

84

JAUME GRAU I GRAU MERLOT 2012 RD
merlot

85 Colour: rose, purple rim. Nose: red berry notes, ripe fruit, floral, fragrant herbs. Palate: powerful, fresh, fruity.

JAUME GRAU I GRAU PICAPOLL 2012 B
picapoll

87 Colour: bright straw. Nose: fresh, fresh fruit, white flowers. Palate: flavourful, fruity, good acidity.

JAUME GRAU I GRAU SENSVS 2007 TC
cabernet franc, syrah

89 Colour: cherry, garnet rim. Nose: ripe fruit, acetaldehyde, spicy, creamy oak, mineral. Palate: powerful, flavourful, correct.

JAUME GRAU SELECCIÓN ESPECIAL 2011 T
tempranillo, merlot, cabernet franc, syrah

88 Colour: bright cherry. Nose: ripe fruit, sweet spices, creamy oak. Palate: flavourful, fruity, toasty.

VINS I CAVES ARTIUM

Cr. Rocafort, 44
8271 Artés (Barcelona)
☎: +34 938 305 325 - Fax: +34 938 306 289
www.cavesartium.com
artium@cavesartium.com

ARTIUM CABERNET SAUVIGNON 2009 T ROBLE
90% cabernet sauvignon, 10% merlot

87 Colour: cherry, garnet rim. Nose: ripe fruit, spicy, creamy oak, toasty, balsamic herbs. Palate: powerful, flavourful, toasty, round tannins.

ARTIUM MERLOT CAPRICI 2012 T
100% merlot

85 Colour: cherry, garnet rim. Nose: red berry notes, fruit liqueur notes, balsamic herbs, scrubland. Palate: powerful, flavourful, balsamic.

ARTIUM PICAPOLL 2012 B
100% picapoll

84

ARTIUM ROQUES ALBES 2008 TC
50% cabernet sauvignon, 50% merlot

85 Colour: pale ruby, brick rim edge. Nose: spicy, fine reductive notes, wet leather, aged wood nuances, fruit liqueur notes. Palate: spicy, long, powerful, flavourful.

DO PLA I LLEVANT / D.O.P.

Consejo Regulador
DO Boundary

LOCATION:

The production region covers the eastern part of Majorca and consists of 18 municipal districts: Algaida, Ariany, Artá, Campos, Capdepera, Felanitx, Lluchamajor, Manacor, Mª de la Salud, Montuiri, Muro, Petra, Porreres, Sant Joan, Sant Llorens des Cardasar, Santa Margarita, Sineu and Vilafranca de Bonany.

CLIMATE:

Mediterranean, with an average temperature of 16°C and with slightly cool winters and dry, hot summers. The constant sea breeze during the summer has a notable effect on these terrains close to the coast. The wet season is in autumn and the average annual rainfall is between 450 mm and 500 mm.

SOIL:

The soil is made up of limestone rocks, which give limy-clayey soils. The reddish Colour: of the terrain is due to the presence of iron oxide. The clays and calcium and magnesium carbonates, in turn, provide the whitish Colour: which can also be seen in the vineyards.

GRAPE VARIETIES:

WHITE: *Prensal Blanc, Macabeo, Parellada, Moscatel* and *Chardonnay.*
RED: *Callet* (majority), *Manto Negro, Fogoneu, Tempranillo, Monastrell, Cabernet Sauvignon, Merlot* and *Syrah.*

FIGURES:

Vineyard surface: 359 – **Wine-Growers:** 84 – **Wineries:** 14 – **2012 Harvest rating:** Very Good– **Production:** 1.108.800 litres – **Market percentages:** 90% domestic. 10% export

2008	2009	2010	2011	2012
VERY GOOD	EXCELLENT	VERY GOOD	VERY GOOD	VERY GOOD

CONSEJO REGULADOR
Molí de N'Amengual. Dusai, 3 - 07260 Porreres (Illes Balears) ☎: +34 971 168 569 - Fax: +34 971 184 49 34
info@plaillevantmallorca.es   www.plaillevantmallorca.es

ARMERO I ADROVER

Camada Real s/n
7200 Mallorca (Illes Ballears)
☎: +34 971 827 103 - Fax: +34 971 580 305
www.armeroiadrover.com
luisarmero@armeroiadrover.com

ARMERO ADROVER 2009 T
callet, cabernet sauvignon, merlot

87 Colour: cherry, garnet rim. Nose: medium intensity, short, neat. Palate: fruity, spirituous, flavourful, lacks expression.

ARMERO ADROVER CHARDONNAY PRENSAL 2012 B
chardonnay

87 Colour: bright straw. Nose: faded flowers, ripe fruit. Palate: flavourful, good acidity.

ARMERO ADROVER SYRAH-CALLET ROSAT 2012 RD
syrah, callet

87 Colour: salmon. Nose: medium intensity, neat, fresh, balanced, fresh fruit. Palate: correct, fresh, fruity.

ARMERO ADROVER SYRAH-MERLOT ROSAT 2012 RD
syrah, merlot

87 Colour: light cherry. Nose: elegant, candied fruit, dried flowers, fragrant herbs, red berry notes. Palate: light-bodied, flavourful, good acidity, long, spicy.

ARMERO I ADROVER COLLITA DE FRUITS 2009 T
callet, cabernet sauvignon, merlot

88 Colour: cherry, garnet rim. Nose: medium intensity, short, spicy. Palate: sweetness, powerful, flavourful.

ARMERO I ADROVER COLLITA DE FRUITS CALLET 2012 RD
callet

87 Colour: onion pink. Nose: elegant, candied fruit, dried flowers, fragrant herbs, red berry notes. Palate: light-bodied, flavourful, good acidity, long, spicy.

ARMERO I ADROVER SELECCION FAMILIAR 2009 T
100% callet

87 Colour: cherry, garnet rim. Nose: medium intensity, fruit liqueur notes, spicy. Palate: flavourful, spirituous, reductive nuances, ripe fruit.

BODEGA JAUME MESQUIDA

Vileta, 7
7260 Porreres (Illes Ballears)
☎: +34 971 168 646
www.jaumemesquida.com
vinsdemallorca@jaumemesquida.org

VIÑA DEL ALBARICOQUE 2010 T

91 Colour: bright cherry. Nose: sweet spices, creamy oak, expressive, earthy notes, smoky. Palate: flavourful, fruity, toasty, round tannins.

BODEGA MESQUIDA MORA

Pas des Frare - Cantonada Cami de Sa
7260 Porreres (Illes Balears)
☎: +34 971 647 106 - Fax: +34 971 168 205
www.mesquidamora.com
info@mesquidamora.com

TRISPOL 2010 T
cabernet sauvignon, syrah, merlot

92 Colour: bright cherry. Nose: ripe fruit, sweet spices, creamy oak, expressive, earthy notes, damp earth, balanced, characterful. Palate: flavourful, fruity, toasty, round tannins.

BODEGAS BORDOY

Camí de Muntanya s/n
7609 Lluchmajor (Illes Ballears)
☎: +34 646 619 776 - Fax: +34 971 771 246
www.bodegasbordoy.es
sarota@bodegasbordoy.com

SA ROTA 2008 TC
50% cabernet sauvignon, 25% merlot, 25% syrah

88 Colour: cherry, garnet rim. Nose: powerfull, spicy, ripe fruit. Palate: fruity, powerful, sweetness, flavourful.

SA ROTA 2008 TR
50% cabernet sauvignon, 30% merlot, 20% syrah

88 Colour: dark-red cherry. Nose: spicy, ripe fruit. Palate: sweetness, powerful, flavourful, spicy, creamy.

SA ROTA 2011 T
90% cabernet sauvignon, 10% callet

87 Colour: light cherry. Nose: ripe fruit, spicy. Palate: sweetness, powerful, flavourful, spirituous.

SA ROTA BLANC 2012 B
80% chardonnay, 20% prensal

90 Colour: bright straw. Nose: fresh, fresh fruit, white flowers, expressive. Palate: flavourful, fruity, good acidity, balanced.

SA ROTA BLANC CHARDONNAY 2011 BFB
100% chardonnay

88 Colour: bright yellow. Nose: closed, elegant, expressive, fresh, medium intensity. Palate: short, fruity, fresh, flavourful.

SA ROTA DULCE 2011 T
60% syrah, 40% merlot

85 Colour: cherry, garnet rim. Nose: balsamic herbs, fruit preserve, spicy, creamy oak. Palate: powerful, flavourful, long, spicy.

SA ROTA MERLOT 2008 T
100% merlot

87 Colour: dark-red cherry. Nose: spicy, fruit preserve, ripe fruit. Palate: sweet tannins, flavourful, spirituous, sweetness.

SA ROTA ROSAT 2012 RD
65% merlot, 35% cabernet sauvignon

86 Colour: light cherry. Nose: neat, fresh, short. Palate: flavourful, powerful, fruity.

SA ROTA SELECCIÓN 2010 T
75% cabernet sauvignon, 15% syrah, 10% merlot

92 Colour: dark-red cherry. Nose: complex, expressive, dry stone, spicy, cocoa bean. Palate: powerful, flavourful, spirituous, good structure, spicy.

SA ROTA SYRAH 2007 T
100% syrah

86 Colour: dark-red cherry. Nose: ripe fruit, spicy, medium intensity. Palate: powerful, spirituous, ripe fruit, spicy.

BODEGAS PERE SEDA

Cid Campeador, 22
7500 Manacor (Illes Ballears)
☎: +34 971 605 087
www.pereseda.com
pereseda@pereseda.com

CHARDONNAY PERE SEDA 2012 B
100% chardonnay

86 Colour: bright straw. Nose: floral, candied fruit. Palate: good acidity, fine bitter notes.

GVIVM MERLOT-CALLET 2009 T
70% merlot, 30% callet

90 Colour: cherry, garnet rim. Nose: spicy, creamy oak, toasty, characterful. Palate: powerful, flavourful, toasty, round tannins.

L'ARXIDUC PERE SEDA 2012 RD
70% merlot, 30% tempranillo

87 Colour: brilliant rose. Nose: elegant, candied fruit, dried flowers, red berry notes. Palate: light-bodied, flavourful, good acidity, long.

L'ARXIDUC PERE SEDA BLANC 2012 B
moscatel, chardonnay, parellada

88 Colour: bright straw. Nose: fresh, fresh fruit, white flowers, honeyed notes. Palate: flavourful, fruity, good acidity, balanced.

L'ARXIDUC PERE SEDA NEGRE 2010 T
merlot, tempranillo, cabernet sauvignon, callet

87 Colour: deep cherry. Nose: fruit preserve, overripe fruit, toasty. Palate: powerful, fine bitter notes.

MOSSÈN ALCOVER 2009 T
cabernet sauvignon, callet

89 Colour: very deep cherry. Nose: fruit liqueur notes, spicy, toasty. Palate: fine bitter notes, good acidity, powerful.

PERE SEDA 2008 TR
cabernet sauvignon, merlot, syrah, callet

87 Colour: deep cherry. Nose: spicy, sweet spices, ripe fruit. Palate: spicy, ripe fruit.

PERE SEDA 2011 BN
95% parellada, 5% chardonnay

86 Colour: bright straw. Nose: medium intensity, fresh fruit, dried herbs, fine lees, floral. Palate: fresh, fruity, flavourful, good acidity.

PERE SEDA 2009 TC
merlot, cabernet sauvignon, syrah, callet

90 Colour: cherry, garnet rim. Nose: candied fruit, spicy, toasty, earthy notes. Palate: balsamic, ripe fruit, long.

PERE SEDA BLANC 2012 B
prensal, macabeo, chardonnay, parellada

87 Colour: bright straw. Nose: fresh, fresh fruit, white flowers. Palate: flavourful, fruity, good acidity, balanced.

PERE SEDA NEGRE 2011 T
tempranillo, cabernet sauvignon, merlot, manto negro, syrah, callet.

85 Colour: light cherry, garnet rim. Nose: medium intensity, short, macerated fruit. Palate: fruity, correct, lacks expression.

PERE SEDA ROSAT 2012 RD
tempranillo, merlot, cabernet sauvignon, callet

87 Colour: rose, purple rim. Nose: powerfull, ripe fruit, red berry notes, floral. Palate: powerful, fruity, fresh.

MIQUEL OLIVER VINYES I BODEGUES

Font, 26
7520 Petra-Mallorca (Illes Ballears)
☎: +34 971 561 117 - Fax: +34 971 561 117
www.miqueloliver.com
bodega@miqueloliver.com

AIA 2010 T
merlot

91 Colour: cherry, garnet rim. Nose: ripe fruit, spicy, creamy oak, toasty, complex, balsamic herbs. Palate: powerful, flavourful, toasty, round tannins.

ORIGINAL MUSCAT MIQUEL OLIVER 2012 B
moscatel

90 Colour: bright straw. Nose: fruit expression, powerfull, varietal, neat, fresh, complex. Palate: correct, elegant, powerful, flavourful.

SES FERRITGES 2009 TC
callet, cabernet sauvignon, merlot, syrah

92 Colour: cherry, garnet rim. Nose: ripe fruit, spicy, creamy oak, toasty, complex, balsamic herbs. Palate: powerful, flavourful, toasty, round tannins.

SYRAH NEGRE MIQUEL OLIVER 2010 T
syrah

88 Colour: cherry, garnet rim. Nose: neat, medium intensity, ripe fruit. Palate: easy to drink, ripe fruit, flavourful.

XPERIMENT 2011 T
callet

92 Colour: bright cherry. Nose: ripe fruit, sweet spices, creamy oak, toasty. Palate: flavourful, toasty, round tannins.

VID'AUBA

5 Volta, 2
7200 Folanitx (Mallorca)
☎: +34 699 096 295
www.vidauba.com
vidauba@vidauba.com

PICOT BLANC 2012 B
chardonnay, prensal, moscatel

86 Colour: bright straw. Nose: fresh, fresh fruit, white flowers. Palate: flavourful, fruity, good acidity, balanced.

PICOT NEGRE 2009 T
callet, cabernet sauvignon, merlot, syrah

86 Colour: bright cherry. Nose: ripe fruit, sweet spices, creamy oak. Palate: flavourful, fruity, toasty, round tannins.

PICOT NEGRE 2010 T
callet, cabernet sauvignon, merlot, syrah

90 Colour: cherry, garnet rim. Nose: ripe fruit, spicy, creamy oak, toasty, complex. Palate: powerful, flavourful, toasty, round tannins.

SINGLO BLANC DE BOTA 2010 B
chardonnay, giró

92 Colour: bright yellow. Nose: powerfull, ripe fruit, sweet spices, creamy oak, fragrant herbs. Palate: rich, smoky aftertaste, flavourful, fresh, good acidity.

VINS MIQUEL GELABERT

Carrer d'en Sales, 50
7500 Manacor (Illes Balears)
☎: +34 971 821 444 - Fax: +34 971 596 441
www.vinsmiquelgelabert.com
vinsmg@vinsmiquelgelabert.com

CHARDONNAY ROURE 2011 BFB
chardonnay

90 Colour: bright yellow. Nose: powerfull, neat, creamy oak, fresh fruit. Palate: creamy, ripe fruit, flavourful, complex.

DOLÇ DE VALL B
moscatel

90 Colour: golden. Nose: powerfull, floral, honeyed notes, candied fruit. Palate: flavourful, sweet, fresh, fruity, good acidity, long.

DOLÇ DES MORRO B
moscatel, callet

87 Colour: light mahogany. Nose: powerfull, floral, honeyed notes, candied fruit, fragrant herbs. Palate: flavourful, fruity, good acidity, long.

GOLÓS 2010 T
callet, manto negro, fogoneu

91 Colour: bright cherry. Nose: sweet spices, creamy oak, fruit expression. Palate: flavourful, fruity, toasty, round tannins.

GOLÓS 2012 RD
pinot noir

87 Colour: light cherry. Nose: elegant, candied fruit, dried flowers, red berry notes. Palate: light-bodied, flavourful, good acidity, long, spicy.

GOLÓS BLANC 2011 B
riesling, moscatel

86 Colour: bright straw. Nose: medium intensity, wild herbs, ripe fruit. Palate: correct, round, powerful, fruity.

GRAN VINYA SON CAULES 2007 T
callet

89 Colour: deep cherry. Nose: fruit liqueur notes, toasty, spicy. Palate: flavourful, good acidity, long.

PETIT TORRENT 2007 T
cabernet sauvignon, merlot, callet

90 Colour: bright cherry. Nose: ripe fruit, sweet spices, creamy oak. Palate: flavourful, fruity, toasty, round tannins.

SA VALL SELECCIÓ PRIVADA 2011 BFB
chardonnay, prensal, moscatel

88 Colour: bright straw. Nose: closed, short, fresh, neat. Palate: fresh, fruity, flavourful.

TORRENT NEGRE 2007 T
cabernet sauvignon, merlot, syrah

88 Colour: cherry, garnet rim. Nose: toasty, aromatic coffee, warm. Palate: powerful, sweetness.

TORRENT NEGRE SELECCIÓ PRIVADA SYRAH 2007 T
syrah

90 Colour: pale ruby, brick rim edge. Nose: spicy, aromatic coffee, ripe fruit, fruit liqueur notes. Palate: good acidity, ripe fruit, spicy.

VINYA DES MORÉ 2007 T
pinot noir

88 Colour: pale ruby, brick rim edge. Nose: medium intensity, ripe fruit, aromatic coffee, spicy. Palate: sweetness, light-bodied.

VINS TONI GELABERT

Camí dels Horts de Llodrá Km. 1,3
7500 Manacor (Illes Balears)
☎: +34 610 789 531
www.vinstonigelabert.com
info@vinstonigelabert.com

EQUILIBRI 2009 T
callet, syrah, cabernet sauvignon

89 Colour: dark-red cherry. Nose: toasty, medium intensity, warm, ripe fruit. Palate: sweet tannins, powerful, flavourful, spirituous, sweetness.

FANGOS BLANC 2012 B
prensal, moscatel

87 Colour: straw. Nose: wild herbs, fresh fruit, short. Palate: elegant, good acidity, fruity, powerful, flavourful.

FANGOS NEGRE 2009 T
callet, cabernet sauvignon, merlot, syrah

90 Colour: dark-red cherry, garnet rim. Nose: roasted coffee, warm, earthy notes. Palate: sweet tannins, spirituous, fruity, powerful, full, flavourful.

NEGRE DE SA COLONIA 2010 T
callet

89 Colour: cherry, garnet rim. Nose: ripe fruit, medium intensity, complex, sweet spices. Palate: correct, rich, powerful, flavourful.

SES HEREVES 2006 T
cabernet sauvignon, merlot, syrah

90 Colour: dark-red cherry, orangey edge. Nose: earthy notes, ripe fruit, spicy.

TONI GELABERT CHARDONNAY 2012 BFB
chardonnay

89 Colour: bright straw. Nose: candied fruit, neat, fresh, closed. Palate: creamy, fruity, powerful, flavourful, rich, sweetness.

DO Ca. PRIORAT / D.O.P.

LOCATION:

In the province of Tarragona. It is made up of the municipal districts of La Morera de Montsant, Scala Dei, La Vilella, Gratallops, Bellmunt, Porrera, Poboleda, Torroja, Lloá, Falset and Mola.

CLIMATE:

Although with Mediterranean influences, it is temperate and dry. One of the most important characteristics is the practical absence of rain during the summer, which ensures very healthy grapes. The average rainfall is between 500 and 600 mm per year.

SOIL:

This is probably the most distinctive characteristic of the region and precisely what has catapulted it to the top positions in terms of quality, not only in Spain, but around the world. The soil, thin and volcanic, is composed of small pieces of slate (llicorella), which give the wines a markedly mineral character. The vineyards are located on terraces and very steep slopes.

GRAPE VARIETIES:

WHITE: *Chenin Blanc, Macabeo, Garnacha Blanca, Pedro Ximénez.*
RED: *Cariñena, Garnacha, Garnacha Peluda, Cabernet Sauvignon, Merlot, Syrah.*

FIGURES:

Vineyard surface: 1.893 – **Wine-Growers:** 617 – **Wineries:** 97 – **2012 Harvest rating:** N/A – **Production:** 3.039.668 litres – **Market percentages:** 51% domestic. 49% export

2008	2009	2010	2011	2012
VERY GOOD	EXCELLENT	GOOD	VERY GOOD	VERY GOOD

CONSEJO REGULADOR
Major, 2 - 43737 Torroja del Priorat (Tarragona) ☎: +34 977 83 94 95 - Fax. +34 977 83 94 72
info@doqpriorat.org   www.doqpriorat.org

AGNÈS DE CERVERA

Ctra. El Molar - El Lloar, Km. 10
43736 El Molar (Tarragona)
☎: +34 977 054 851 - Fax: +34 977 054 851
www.agnesdecervera.com
bodega@agnesdecervera.com

ARGELES 2011 T
50% garnacha, 40% mazuelo, 10% cabernet sauvignon

87 Colour: deep cherry. Nose: powerfull, warm, ripe fruit, toasty. Palate: powerful, concentrated, spicy, ripe fruit.

KALOS 2011 T
85% mazuelo, 15% syrah

89 Colour: black cherry. Nose: mineral, overripe fruit, toasty, dark chocolate. Palate: powerful, concentrated.

LA PETITE AGNÈS 2012 T
85% garnacha, 15% mazuelo

87 Colour: cherry, purple rim. Nose: ripe fruit, balsamic herbs, earthy notes. Palate: powerful, flavourful, ripe fruit.

LYTOS 2011 T
30% garnacha, 15% syrah, 5% cabernet sauvignon, 45% mazuelo

89 Colour: very deep cherry. Nose: spicy, toasty. Palate: powerful, flavourful, spicy, ripe fruit.

ALVARO PALACIOS

Afores, s/n
43737 Gratallops (Tarragona)
☎: +34 977 839 195 - Fax: +34 977 839 197
info@alvaropalacios.com

CAMINS DEL PRIORAT 2012 T
40% garnacha, 25% samsó, 10% cabernet sauvignon, 10% syrah, 7% merlot

92 Colour: bright cherry. Nose: ripe fruit, creamy oak, mineral, expressive. Palate: flavourful, fruity, toasty, round tannins.

FINCA DOFÍ 2011 TC
95% garnacha, 5% otras

94 Colour: cherry, garnet rim. Nose: creamy oak, toasty, complex, earthy notes. Palate: powerful, flavourful, toasty, round tannins.

GRATALLOPS VI DE LA VILA 2011 T
65% garnacha, 35% samsó

94 Colour: cherry, garnet rim. Nose: spicy, complex, overripe fruit, fruit expression. Palate: powerful, flavourful, toasty, round tannins.

L'ERMITA 2011 TC
90% garnacha, 8% samsó, 2% uva blanca

97 Colour: deep cherry. Nose: elegant, ripe fruit, red berry notes, spicy, mineral, earthy notes. Palate: flavourful, fruity, fresh, spicy.

LES TERRASSES 2011 T
50% garnacha, 50% samsó

92 Colour: bright cherry. Nose: ripe fruit, sweet spices, earthy notes, fruit preserve. Palate: flavourful, fruity, toasty, round tannins.

BLAI FERRÉ JUST

Piró, 28
43737 Gratallops (Tarragona)
☎: +34 647 217 751 - Fax: +34 977 839 507
blaiferrejust@yahoo.es

BILLO 2010 T
35% syrah, 35% garnacha, 20% cariñena, 10% cabernet sauvignon

88 Colour: cherry, garnet rim. Nose: powerfull, toasty, dried herbs. Palate: flavourful, fruity, round tannins.

BILLO 2011 T
35% syrah, 35% garnacha, 20% cariñena, 10% cabernet sauvignon

88 Colour: bright cherry. Nose: sweet spices, creamy oak, expressive, candied fruit, warm. Palate: flavourful, fruity, toasty, round tannins.

DESNIVELL 2010 TC
80% garnacha, 20% cariñena

88 Colour: cherry, garnet rim. Nose: ripe fruit, fruit preserve, balsamic herbs, mineral, spicy, creamy oak. Palate: powerful, flavourful, spicy, long.

BODEGA PUIG PRIORAT

Ctra. T-710, km. 8,3
43737 Gratallops (Tarragona)
☎: +34 977 054 032
www.puigpriorat.com
mail@puigpriorat.com

AKYLES 2009 TC
45% garnacha, 40% cariñena, 15% cabernet sauvignon

91 Colour: cherry, garnet rim. Nose: ripe fruit, spicy, creamy oak. Palate: flavourful, toasty, correct, good structure.

DOMINICUS 2009 TC
50% garnacha, 35% cariñena, 15% syrah

87 Colour: cherry, garnet rim. Nose: ripe fruit, spicy, creamy oak, toasty. Palate: powerful, flavourful, toasty.

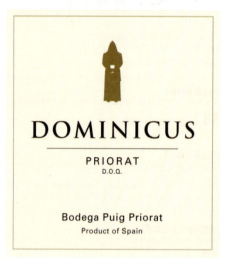

ODYSSEUS CLÀSSIC (ETIQUETA ROJA) 2009 TR
40% garnacha, garnacha peluda, 40% cariñena, 10% syrah, 10% cabernet sauvignon

91 Colour: very deep cherry. Nose: powerfull, spicy, aromatic coffee, dark chocolate. Palate: flavourful, powerful, fine bitter notes, good acidity.

ODYSSEUS GARNACHA BLANCA 2012 B
100% garnacha blanca

85 Colour: bright yellow. Nose: ripe fruit, tropical fruit, warm. Palate: rich, flavourful, lacks balance.

ODYSSEUS PEDRO XIMÉNEZ 2012 B
100% pedro ximénez

86 Colour: bright straw. Nose: fresh, fresh fruit, white flowers, dried herbs. Palate: flavourful, fruity, good acidity, balanced.

ODYSSEUS ÚNICO 2008 TR
22% cariñena, 36% garnacha, 9% garnacha peluda, 22% syrah, 11% cabernet sauvignon

90 Colour: ruby red, orangey edge. Nose: ripe fruit, balsamic herbs, spicy, fine reductive notes. Palate: powerful, flavourful, spicy, long.

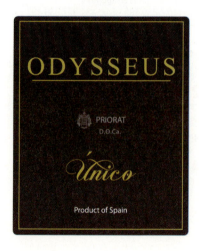

BODEGAS CASA ROJO

Sánchez Picazo, 53
30332 Balsapintada (Murcia)
☎: +34 968 151 520 - Fax: +34 968 151 690
www.casarojo.com
info@casarojo.com

FAUNO DE CASA ROJO 2009 T
100% garnacha

88 Colour: cherry, garnet rim. Nose: ripe fruit, spicy, acetaldehyde, toasty, mineral. Palate: powerful, flavourful, toasty, round tannins.

BODEGAS MAS ALTA

Ctra. T-702 Km. 16,8
43375 La Vilella Alta (Tarragona)
☎: +34 977 054 151 - Fax: +34 977 817 194
www.bodegasmasalta.com
info@bodegasmasalta.com

ARTIGAS 2008 T
garnacha, cariñena, cabernet sauvignon

92 Colour: deep cherry, garnet rim. Nose: powerfull, ripe fruit, spicy, mineral. Palate: flavourful, full, good structure, powerful.

ARTIGAS 2012 B
garnacha blanca, macabeo, pedro ximénez

92 Colour: bright straw. Nose: fruit preserve, citrus fruit, ripe fruit. Palate: flavourful, powerful, sweetness.

CIRERETS 2010 T
cariñena, garnacha

94 Colour: bright cherry. Nose: sweet spices, creamy oak, expressive, red berry notes. Palate: flavourful, fruity, toasty, round tannins.

ELS PICS 2011 T
garnacha, cariñena, syrah, cabernet sauvignon

92 Colour: bright cherry. Nose: ripe fruit, sweet spices, creamy oak, expressive, earthy notes, mineral. Palate: flavourful, fruity, toasty, round tannins.

LA BASSETA 2010 T
100% garnacha

95 Colour: cherry, garnet rim. Nose: spicy, creamy oak, toasty, complex, mineral, varietal. Palate: powerful, flavourful, toasty, round tannins.

LA CREU ALTA 2007 T
cariñena, garnacha, syrah

94 Colour: deep cherry, garnet rim. Nose: mineral, expressive, complex, balsamic herbs. Palate: ripe fruit, long, round tannins.

BUIL & GINÉ

Ctra. de Gratallops - Vilella Baixa, Km. 11,5
43737 Gratallops (Tarragona)
☎: +34 977 839 810 - Fax: +34 977 839 811
www.builgine.com
info@builgine.com

GINÉ GINÉ 2011 T
garnacha, cariñena

90 Colour: cherry, garnet rim. Nose: ripe fruit, spicy, creamy oak, toasty, complex. Palate: powerful, flavourful, toasty, round tannins.

JOAN GINÉ 2008 T
garnacha, cariñena, cabernet sauvignon

89 Colour: bright cherry. Nose: ripe fruit, sweet spices, creamy oak, expressive. Palate: flavourful, fruity, toasty, round tannins.

JOAN GINÉ 2012 B
garnacha blanca, pedro ximénez, macabeo, viognier

88 Colour: bright straw. Nose: spicy, ripe fruit, citrus fruit. Palate: flavourful, fruity.

PLERET 2006 T
garnacha, cariñena, cabernet sauvignon, merlot, syrah

91 Colour: cherry, garnet rim. Nose: ripe fruit, spicy, creamy oak, toasty, complex. Palate: powerful, flavourful, toasty, round tannins.

BURGOS PORTA

Finca Mas Sinén, s/n
43202 Poboleda (Tarragona)
☎: +34 696 094 509
www.massinen.com
burgosporta@massinen.com

MAS SINÉN 2008 TC
garnacha, cariñena, cabernet sauvignon, syrah

91 Colour: cherry, garnet rim. Nose: ripe fruit, spicy, creamy oak, toasty, complex. Palate: powerful, flavourful, toasty, round tannins.

MAS SINÉN COSTER 2009 TC
garnacha, cariñena

90 Colour: deep cherry, garnet rim. Nose: balanced, ripe fruit, wild herbs, cocoa bean, mineral. Palate: good structure, rich, fruity.

PETIT MAS SINÉN 2010 T
garnacha, cariñena, syrah, cabernet sauvignon, merlot

88 Colour: very deep cherry. Nose: overripe fruit, toasty, sweet spices. Palate: powerful, spicy, fine bitter notes.

CARREFOUR

Campezo, 16
28022 Madrid (Madrid)
☎: +34 902 202 000
www.carrefour.es

MAS D'ALBA 2012 T
garnacha, cariñena, syrah

88 Colour: bright cherry. Nose: ripe fruit, creamy oak, expressive. Palate: flavourful, fruity, round tannins.

CASA GRAN DEL SIURANA

Mayor, 3
43738 Bellmunt del Priorat (Tarragona)
☎: +34 932 233 022 - Fax: +34 932 231 370
www.castilloperelada.com
perelada@castilloperelada.com

CRUOR 2008 T
30% garnacha, 20% syrah, 10% merlot, 20% cabernet sauvignon, 20% cariñena

90 Colour: cherry, garnet rim. Nose: spicy, creamy oak, toasty, overripe fruit. Palate: powerful, flavourful, toasty, round tannins.

GR-174 2012 T
33% garnacha, 33% cariñena, 15% cabernet sauvignon, 10% syrah, 9% merlot, 3% cabernet franc

89 Colour: deep cherry, purple rim. Nose: balanced, scrubland, closed. Palate: ripe fruit, long, fruity aftestaste.

GRAN CRUOR 2008 T
20% cariñena, 70% syrah, 10% garnacha

92 Colour: cherry, garnet rim. Nose: ripe fruit, spicy, creamy oak, toasty, mineral. Palate: powerful, flavourful, toasty, round tannins, balanced, elegant.

CASTELL D'OR

Mare Rafols, 3- 1º 4º
8720 Vilafranca del Penedès (Barcelona)
☎: +34 938 905 446 - Fax: +34 938 905 446
www.castelldor.com
castelldor@castelldor.com

ABADÍA MEDITERRÀNIA 2010 TC
garnacha, cariñena, cabernet sauvignon

89 Colour: cherry, garnet rim. Nose: ripe fruit, fruit preserve, balsamic herbs, spicy, creamy oak. Palate: powerful, flavourful, ripe fruit.

ESPLUGEN 2010 T
garnacha, cariñena, cabernet sauvignon

89 Colour: cherry, garnet rim. Nose: ripe fruit, spicy, creamy oak, toasty, complex. Palate: powerful, flavourful, toasty, round tannins.

CELLER AIXALÀ I ALCAIT

Carrer Balandra, 8
43737 Torroja del Priorat (Tarragona)
☎: +34 629 507 807
www.pardelasses.com
pardelasses@gmail.com

DESTRANKIS 2011 T
80% garnacha, 20% cariñena

85 Colour: cherry, garnet rim. Nose: fruit liqueur notes, powerfull, sweet spices. Palate: powerful, flavourful.

EL COSTER DE L'ALZINA 2011 TC
100% cariñena

86 Colour: cherry, garnet rim. Nose: spicy, creamy oak, toasty, fruit preserve. Palate: powerful, flavourful, toasty.

PARDELASSES 2010 T
50% garnacha, 50% cariñena

87 Colour: cherry, garnet rim. Nose: ripe fruit, fruit preserve, waxy notes, tobacco, spicy. Palate: rich, powerful, flavourful.

PARDELASSES 2011 T
50% garnacha, 50% cariñena

90 Colour: cherry, purple rim. Nose: powerfull, ripe fruit, fruit preserve, sweet spices, cocoa bean. Palate: good structure, flavourful, full.

CELLER BARTOLOMÉ

Major, 23
43738 Bellmunt del Priorat (Tarragona)
☎: +34 977 830 098 - Fax: +34 977 320 448
www.cellerbartolome.com
cellerbartolome@hotmail.com

CLOS BARTOLOME 2008 T
50% garnacha, 40% cariñena, 10% cabernet sauvignon

89 Colour: cherry, garnet rim. Nose: ripe fruit, fruit liqueur notes, earthy notes, balsamic herbs, spicy, creamy oak. Palate: powerful, flavourful, spicy, long.

CLOS BARTOLOME 2009 T
50% garnacha, 40% cariñena, 10% cabernet sauvignon

90 Colour: very deep cherry, garnet rim. Nose: ripe fruit, dried herbs, balanced, waxy notes. Palate: long, round tannins, flavourful.

PRIMITIU DE BELLMUNT 2005 T
50% garnacha, 50% cariñena

90 Colour: cherry, garnet rim. Nose: dark chocolate, sweet spices, fruit liqueur notes, toasty.

PRIMITIU DE BELLMUNT 2008 T
50% garnacha, 50% cariñena

93 Colour: cherry, garnet rim. Nose: ripe fruit, spicy, creamy oak, toasty, complex, earthy notes, mineral. Palate: powerful, flavourful, toasty, round tannins, elegant.

CELLER CECILIO

Piró, 28
43737 Gratallops (Tarragona)
☎: +34 977 839 507 - Fax: +34 977 839 507
www.cellercecilio.com
celler@cellercecilio.com

CELLER CECILIO BLANC 2012 B
garnacha blanca

87 Colour: golden. Nose: powerfull, floral, honeyed notes, fragrant herbs, citrus fruit. Palate: flavourful, fresh, fruity, good acidity, long.

CELLER CECILIO NEGRE 2011 T
garnacha, cariñena, cabernet sauvignon, syrah

85 Colour: very deep cherry. Nose: medium intensity, premature reduction notes, fruit preserve. Palate: correct, flavourful.

L'ESPILL 2009 TC
garnacha, cariñena, cabernet sauvignon

88 Colour: deep cherry. Nose: spicy, ripe fruit. Palate: toasty, ripe fruit, round tannins.

CELLER CLO93

43737 El Lloar (Tarragona)
☎: +34 620 215 770
www.clos93.com
clos93@clos93.com

L'INTERROGANT 2011 T
40% garnacha, 40% cariñena, 20% cabernet sauvignon

90 Colour: bright cherry. Nose: ripe fruit, sweet spices, creamy oak, mineral. Palate: flavourful, fruity, toasty, round tannins, balanced.

CELLER DE L'ABADÍA

Font, 38
43737 Gratallops (Tarragona)
☎: +34 627 032 134 - Fax: +34 977 054 078
www.cellerabadia.com
jeroni@cellerabadia.com

ALICE 2008 T
40% garnacha, 40% cariñena, 10% cabernet sauvignon, 10% syrah

88 Colour: very deep cherry. Nose: fruit liqueur notes, caramel, aromatic coffee. Palate: powerful, toasty, spicy.

SANT JERONI BLANC DE L'AUBADA 2012 B
60% pedro ximénez, 40% garnacha blanca

80

SANT JERONI CARIÑENA DEL FORN 2010 T
80% cariñena, 20% cabernet sauvignon

92 Colour: cherry, garnet rim. Nose: ripe fruit, spicy, creamy oak, toasty, complex, mineral. Palate: powerful, flavourful, toasty, round tannins.

CELLER DE L'ENCASTELL

Castell, 7
43739 Porrera (Tarragona)
☎: +34 630 941 959
www.roquers.com
roquers@roquers.com

MARGE 2011 T
60% garnacha, 40% cabernet sauvignon, merlot, syrah

88 Colour: very deep cherry. Nose: toasty, fruit liqueur notes. Palate: powerful, spirituous, spicy.

ROQUERS DE PORRERA 2010 TR
40% garnacha, 40% cariñena, 20% merlot, syrah

90 Colour: cherry, garnet rim. Nose: ripe fruit, spicy, creamy oak, toasty, complex. Palate: powerful, flavourful, toasty, round tannins.

CELLER DEVINSSI

43737 Gratallops (Tarragona)
☎: +34 977 839 523
www.devinssi.com
devinssi@il-lia.com

CUPATGE DEVINSSI 2010 T
garnacha, cariñena, cabernet sauvignon

92 Colour: cherry, garnet rim. Nose: ripe fruit, spicy, creamy oak, toasty, complex. Palate: powerful, flavourful, toasty, round tannins.

IL.LIA 2008 T
garnacha, cariñena, cabernet sauvignon

88 Colour: very deep cherry. Nose: powerfull, overripe fruit, warm, spicy. Palate: powerful, spicy, ripe fruit.

MAS DE LES VALLS 2009 TC
garnacha, cariñena, cabernet sauvignon

88 Colour: cherry, garnet rim. Nose: ripe fruit, spicy, creamy oak, toasty. Palate: powerful, flavourful, toasty, round tannins.

CELLER ESCODA PALLEJÀ

La Font, 16
43737 Torroja del Priorat (Tarragona)
☎: +34 977 839 200
perescoda@yahoo.es

PALET 11 2011 T
garnacha, cabernet sauvignon, syrah, cariñena

86 Colour: bright cherry. Nose: sweet spices, creamy oak, ripe fruit. Palate: flavourful, fruity, toasty, round tannins.

CELLER HIDALGO ALBERT

Finca Les Salanques, Pol. Ind. 14, Parc. 102
43376 Poboleda (Tarragona)
☎: +34 977 842 064 - Fax: +34 977 842 064
www.cellerhidalgoalbert.es
hialmi@yahoo.es

1270 A VUIT 2008 T
garnacha, syrah, cabernet sauvignon, merlot, cariñena

92 Colour: cherry, garnet rim. Nose: ripe fruit, spicy, creamy oak, toasty, complex. Palate: powerful, flavourful, toasty, round tannins.

1270 A VUIT 2009 T
garnacha, syrah, cabernet sauvignon, merlot, cariñena

90 Colour: very deep cherry. Nose: powerfull, characterful, ripe fruit. Palate: powerful, good structure, spirituous.

1270 A VUIT 2011 B
garnacha blanca

90 Colour: bright yellow. Nose: powerfull, ripe fruit, sweet spices, creamy oak, fragrant herbs. Palate: rich, smoky aftertaste, flavourful, fresh, good acidity.

FINA 2010 T
garnacha, merlot, syrah, cabernet sauvignon

89 Colour: cherry, garnet rim. Nose: spicy, creamy oak, toasty, fruit preserve. Palate: powerful, flavourful, toasty.

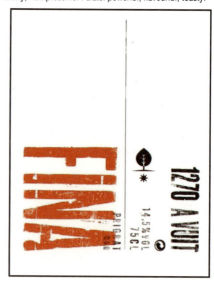

CELLER JOAN SIMÓ

11 de Setembre, 5-7
43739 Porrera (Tarragona)
☎: +34 627 563 713 - Fax: +34 977 830 993
www.cellerjoansimo.com
leseres@cellerjoansimo.com

LES ERES 2009 T
70% cariñena, 20% garnacha, 10% cabernet sauvignon

92 Colour: cherry, garnet rim. Nose: ripe fruit, spicy, creamy oak, toasty, violet drops. Palate: powerful, flavourful, toasty, round tannins.

LES ERES ESPECIAL DELS CARNERS 2009 T
75% garnacha, 25% cariñena

90 Colour: deep cherry, garnet rim. Nose: powerfull, fruit preserve, cocoa bean. Palate: good structure, flavourful, full, round tannins.

SENTIUS 2009 T
60% garnacha, 20% syrah, 20% cabernet sauvignon

88 Colour: bright cherry. Nose: ripe fruit, sweet spices, creamy oak, expressive. Palate: flavourful, fruity, toasty, round tannins.

CELLER JORDI DOMENECH

Finca Les Comes
43376 Poboleda (Tarragona)
☎: +34 646 169 210
www.cellerjordidomenech.com
jordidomenech@live.com

CLOS PENAT 2009 TC
garnacha, syrah

90 Colour: very deep cherry. Nose: powerfull, toasty, creamy oak. Palate: powerful, ripe fruit, spicy.

PETIT CLOS PENAT 2010 T
garnacha, syrah

88 Colour: deep cherry. Nose: powerfull, warm, overripe fruit. Palate: flavourful, toasty, ripe fruit.

CELLER MAS BASTE

Font, 38
43737 Gratallops (Tarragona)
☎: +34 629 300 291
www.cellermasbaste.com
info@cellermasbaste.com

CLOS PEITES 2010 T
80% cariñena, 10% cabernet sauvignon, 10% syrah

86 Colour: cherry, garnet rim. Nose: fruit preserve, spicy. Palate: powerful, flavourful, pruney, round tannins.

PEITES 2011 TC
80% cariñena, 10% cabernet sauvignon, 10% syrah

88 Colour: very deep cherry. Nose: overripe fruit, toasty, aromatic coffee. Palate: powerful, sweetness, spirituous.

PEITES 2012 T
70% garnacha, 30% syrah

88 Colour: very deep cherry, purple rim. Nose: ripe fruit, balanced, balsamic herbs, mineral. Palate: flavourful, sweetness, long.

CELLER MAS DE LES PERERES

Mas de Les Pereres, s/n
43376 Poboleda (Tarragona)
☎: +34 977 827 257 - Fax: +34 977 827 257
www.nunci.com
dirk@nunci.com

NUNCI ABOCAT 2010 B
macabeo, garnacha, moscatel de alejandría, moscatel grano menudo

89 Colour: bright yellow. Nose: dried herbs, ripe fruit, dried flowers, damp earth. Palate: powerful, flavourful, spicy, balsamic.

NUNCI ABOCAT 2011 B
macabeo, garnacha, moscatel de alejandría, moscatel grano menudo

88 Colour: bright straw. Nose: fresh, fresh fruit, white flowers, citrus fruit. Palate: flavourful, fruity, sweet, balanced.

NUNCI BLANC 2009 BFB
garnacha, macabeo

91 Colour: bright golden. Nose: ripe fruit, powerfull, toasty, aged wood nuances, petrol notes. Palate: flavourful, fruity, spicy, toasty, long.

NUNCI BLANC 2010 BFB
garnacha, macabeo

90 Colour: bright yellow. Nose: powerfull, ripe fruit, sweet spices, creamy oak, fragrant herbs. Palate: rich, flavourful, fresh, good acidity.

NUNCI COSTERO 2006 T
55% mazuelo, 40% garnacha, 5% merlot

90 Colour: bright cherry, garnet rim. Nose: ripe fruit, spicy, mineral. Palate: balanced, good acidity, round tannins.

NUNCI COSTERO 2007 T
55% mazuelo, 40% garnacha, 5% merlot

89 Colour: deep cherry, garnet rim. Nose: ripe fruit, balsamic herbs, spicy. Palate: rich, flavourful.

NUNCI NEGRE 2006 T
garnacha, syrah, mazuelo, cabernet franc, merenzao, cabernet sauvignon.

88 Colour: very deep cherry. Nose: fruit liqueur notes, spicy, toasty. Palate: flavourful, powerful, sweetness.

NUNCI NEGRE 2007 T
garnacha, syrah, mazuelo, cabernet franc, merlot, cabernet sauvignon.

87 Colour: very deep cherry. Nose: spicy, balsamic herbs, mineral, overripe fruit. Palate: flavourful, good acidity, balanced, round tannins.

NUNCITO 2009 T BARRICA
garnacha, syrah, mazuelo

90 Colour: bright cherry. Nose: ripe fruit, sweet spices, creamy oak, expressive, balsamic herbs, spicy. Palate: flavourful, fruity, toasty, round tannins.

NUNCITO 2010 T BARRICA
garnacha, syrah, mazuelo

91 Colour: deep cherry. Nose: fruit liqueur notes, balsamic herbs, scrubland, toasty. Palate: powerful, concentrated, spicy.

CELLER MAS DOIX

Carme, 115
43376 Poboleda (Tarragona)
☎: +34 639 356 172 - Fax: +34 933 216 790
www.masdoix.com
info@masdoix.com

LES CRESTES 2011 T

92 Colour: bright cherry. Nose: ripe fruit, sweet spices, creamy oak, red berry notes. Palate: flavourful, fruity, toasty, round tannins.

SALANQUES 2011 T

93 Colour: cherry, garnet rim. Nose: ripe fruit, spicy, creamy oak, toasty, complex, mineral. Palate: powerful, flavourful, round tannins.

CELLER PAHÍ

Carrer del Carme, 57
43376 Poboleda (Tarragona)
☎: +34 977 762 042
www.celler-pahi.com
ramon@cellerpahi.com

GAUBANÇA 2011 T
garnacha, cariñena, merlot, syrah

87 Colour: very deep cherry, purple rim. Nose: toasty, ripe fruit, fruit preserve. Palate: flavourful, spicy, round tannins.

CELLER PRIOR PONS

Del Rey, 4
43375 La Vilella Alta (Tarragona)
☎: +34 606 547 865
www.priorpons.com
info@priorpons.com

PLANETS DE PRIOR PONS 2010 T
40% garnacha, 40% mazuelo, 10% cabernet sauvignon, 5% syrah, 5% merlot

89 Colour: very deep cherry. Nose: ripe fruit, spicy, warm. Palate: fruity, flavourful, round tannins, pruney.

PRIOR PONS 2010 T
40% garnacha, 45% mazuelo, 15% cabernet sauvignon

91 Colour: very deep cherry, garnet rim. Nose: balanced, wild herbs, expressive. Palate: good structure, round tannins.

CELLER SABATÉ

Nou, 6
43374 La Vilella Baixa (Tarragona)
☎: +34 977 839 209
www.cellersabate.com
cellersabate@cellersabate.com

MAS D'EN BERNAT 2012 T
garnacha

88 Colour: cherry, purple rim. Nose: red berry notes, ripe fruit, balsamic herbs, earthy notes. Palate: powerful, flavourful, spicy.

MAS PLANTADETA 2007 TC
garnacha, cariñena, cabernet sauvignon

88 Colour: cherry, garnet rim. Nose: ripe fruit, toasty, old leather. Palate: powerful, flavourful, toasty, round tannins.

MAS PLANTADETA 2011 T ROBLE
garnacha

88 Colour: deep cherry. Nose: powerfull, warm, ripe fruit. Palate: powerful, flavourful, spicy.

MAS PLANTADETA 2012 BFB
garnacha

86 Colour: bright yellow. Nose: powerfull, warm, fruit liqueur notes. Palate: powerful, fine bitter notes, long.

CELLER VALL-LLACH

Pont, 9
43739 Porrera (Tarragona)
☎: +34 977 828 244 - Fax: +34 977 828 325
www.vallllach.com
celler@vallllach.com

AIGUA DE LLUM 2012 B
70% viognier, 30% garnacha

84

EMBRUIX DE VALL-LLACH 2010 T
27% cariñena, 23% garnacha, 15% syrah, 27% cabernet sauvignon, 15% merlot

90 Colour: very deep cherry. Nose: fruit liqueur notes, toasty, warm. Palate: powerful, sweetness, spicy.

IDUS DE VALL-LLACH 2010 T
45% cariñena, 13% garnacha, 20% cabernet sauvignon, 12% syrah, 10% merlot

89 Colour: bright cherry. Nose: creamy oak, expressive, earthy notes, ripe fruit. Palate: flavourful, fruity, toasty, round tannins.

PORRERA VI DE VILA 2009 TC
70% cariñena, 30% garnacha

92 Colour: cherry, garnet rim. Nose: ripe fruit, spicy, creamy oak, earthy notes, mineral. Palate: rich, powerful, flavourful, balanced, elegant.

PORRERA VI DE VILA 2010 TC
70% cariñena, 30% garnacha

91 Colour: cherry, garnet rim. Nose: spicy, creamy oak, toasty, complex, overripe fruit. Palate: powerful, toasty, round tannins, fine bitter notes.

VALL-LLACH VI DE FINCA DE LA ROSA 2010 TC
90% cariñena, 10% cabernet sauvignon

93 Colour: cherry, garnet rim. Nose: spicy, creamy oak, toasty, complex, earthy notes, fruit expression. Palate: powerful, flavourful, toasty, round tannins.

CELLERS COSTERS DEL ROS

Les Valls, 8
43737 Gratallops (Tarragona)
☎: +34 610 664 135
www.costersdelros.com
info@costersdelros.com

L'ALBADA 2009 T
garnacha, cariñena, cabernet sauvignon

89 Colour: cherry, garnet rim. Nose: ripe fruit, spicy, complex, balanced. Palate: powerful, flavourful, toasty, round tannins.

CELLERS DE SCALA DEI

Rambla de la Cartoixa, s/n
43379 Scala Dei (Tarragona)
☎: +34 977 827 027 - Fax: +34 977 827 044
www.grupocodorniu.com
codinfo@codorniu.es

LA CREU NEGRA 2010 T
garnacha, cariñena, cabernet sauvignon

92 Colour: cherry, garnet rim. Nose: red berry notes, ripe fruit, spicy, balsamic herbs, mineral, earthy notes. Palate: powerful, flavourful, complex, long.

LES TRES CREUS 2012 T
60% garnacha, 40% syrah

88 Colour: cherry, garnet rim. Nose: red berry notes, fruit liqueur notes, balsamic herbs, dry stone. Palate: powerful, flavourful, spicy.

SCALA DEI CARTOIXA 2007 TR
60% garnacha, 25% cariñena, 10% syrah, 5% cabernet sauvignon

90 Colour: cherry, garnet rim. Nose: spicy, toasty, characterful, fruit liqueur notes. Palate: powerful, flavourful, toasty, round tannins.

SCALA DEI PRIOR 2009 TC
45% garnacha, 20% samsó, 20% cabernet sauvignon, 15% syrah

89 Colour: cherry, garnet rim. Nose: ripe fruit, spicy, creamy oak, toasty. Palate: powerful, flavourful, toasty, round tannins.

CELLERS UNIÓ

Joan Oliver, 16-24
43206 Reus (Tarragona)
☎: +34 977 330 055 - Fax: +34 977 330 070
www.cellersunio.com
info@cellersunio.com

ROUREDA LLICORELLA BLANC
PEDRO XIMÉNEZ 2011 B
100% pedro ximénez

87 Colour: bright golden. Nose: balanced, faded flowers, spicy. Palate: long, balanced, good acidity, good finish.

ROUREDA LLICORELLA CLASSIC 2007 T
40% garnacha, 40% cariñena, 15% cabernet sauvignon, 5% merlot

87 Colour: cherry, garnet rim. Nose: fruit preserve, balsamic herbs, spicy, creamy oak, earthy notes. Palate: powerful, flavourful, spicy, long.

ROUREDA LLICORELLA VITIS 60 2006 T
40% garnacha, 40% cariñena, 10% cabernet sauvignon, 10% syrah

88 Colour: deep cherry. Nose: spicy, aromatic coffee, fruit liqueur notes. Palate: powerful, spirituous, sweetness.

SEÑORÍO DE CONVEY 2010 T
40% cariñena, 60% garnacha

88 Colour: deep cherry. Nose: fruit liqueur notes, spicy, ripe fruit. Palate: powerful, spicy, ripe fruit.

TENDRAL SELECCIÓN 2009 T
60% garnacha, 40% cariñena

87 Colour: very deep cherry. Nose: spicy, fruit liqueur notes. Palate: spicy, ripe fruit, fine bitter notes.

CLOS BERENGUER

Ctra. T-734 del Masroig, km. 8,3
43735 El Molar (Tarragona)
☎: +34 977 361 390
www.closberenguer.com
info@closberenguer.com

CLOS BERENGUER SELECCIÓ 2008 T
garnacha, samsó, syrah, cabernet sauvignon

88 Colour: cherry, garnet rim. Nose: ripe fruit, spicy, creamy oak, toasty, complex. Palate: powerful, flavourful, toasty, round tannins.

CLOS DE TAFALL 2010 T
garnacha, samsó, syrah, cabernet sauvignon

88 Colour: cherry, garnet rim. Nose: ripe fruit, spicy, creamy oak, roasted coffee. Palate: powerful, flavourful, toasty.

CLOS DE TAFALL SELECCIO DE VINYES 2011 T
garnacha, samsó, syrah, cabernet sauvignon

89 Colour: bright cherry, purple rim. Nose: balanced, ripe fruit, violet drops, toasty, fruit preserve. Palate: balanced, ripe fruit.

CLOS DE L'OBAC

Camí Manyetes, s/n
43737 Gratallops (Tarragona)
☎: +34 977 839 276 - Fax: +34 977 839 371
www.obac.es
info@obac.es

CLOS DE L'OBAC 2009 TC
garnacha, cabernet sauvignon, cariñena, merlot, syrah

93 Colour: cherry, garnet rim. Nose: spicy, creamy oak, toasty, complex, scrubland, expressive, earthy notes. Palate: powerful, flavourful, toasty, round tannins.

KYRIE 2009 BC
garnacha blanca, macabeo, xarel.lo, moscatel de alejandría

92 Colour: bright golden. Nose: ripe fruit, dry nuts, powerfull, toasty, aged wood nuances, dry stone. Palate: flavourful, fruity, spicy, toasty, long.

MISERERE 2009 TC
garnacha, cabernet sauvignon, tempranillo, cariñena, merlot

93 Colour: cherry, garnet rim. Nose: ripe fruit, spicy, creamy oak, toasty, powerfull, warm. Palate: powerful, flavourful, toasty, round tannins.

CLOS DEL PORTAL

Pista del Lloar a Bellmunt
43376 Vila del Lloar (Tarragona)
☎: +34 932 531 760 - Fax: +34 934 173 591
www.portaldelpriorat.com
info@portaldelpriorat.com

GOTES DEL PRIORAT 2012 T
garnacha, cariñena

89 Colour: cherry, garnet rim. Nose: ripe fruit, spicy, wild herbs. Palate: powerful, flavourful, balanced.

GOTES DEL PRIORAT MAGNUM 2011 T
garnacha, cariñena

92 Colour: deep cherry, garnet rim. Nose: powerfull, fruit expression, balanced, dry stone, scrubland. Palate: spicy, round tannins.

NEGRE DE NEGRES 2011 T
garnacha, cariñena, cabernet sauvignon, syrah

93 Colour: cherry, garnet rim. Nose: red berry notes, ripe fruit, fragrant herbs, floral, dry stone, sweet spices. Palate: powerful, flavourful, long, spicy, balanced, elegant.

NEGRE DE NEGRES MAGNUM 2010 T

93 Colour: deep cherry, garnet rim. Nose: earthy notes, balanced, spicy, neat. Palate: good structure, balanced, fruity, good acidity.

SOMNI 2011 T
cariñena, syrah

93 Colour: very deep cherry. Nose: spicy, mineral, dark chocolate, powerfull, dried herbs. Palate: full, good structure, complex, spicy, long.

SOMNI MAGNUM 2010 T
cariñena, syrah, garnacha

96 Colour: deep cherry, garnet rim. Nose: complex, mineral, balsamic herbs, expressive, balanced, ripe fruit. Palate: good structure, round tannins, long, balsamic.

TROS DE CLOS 2011 T
cariñena

92 Colour: deep cherry, purple rim. Nose: toasty, ripe fruit, balsamic herbs, mineral, cocoa bean. Palate: good structure, ripe fruit, long.

CLOS FIGUERAS

Carrer La Font, 38
43737 Gratallops (Tarragona)
☎: +34 977 830 217 - Fax: +34 627 471 732
www.desfigueras.com
info@closfigueras.com

CLOS FIGUERES 2010 T
garnacha, cariñena, syrah, cabernet sauvignon

92 Colour: deep cherry, garnet rim. Nose: balanced, ripe fruit, mineral, dried herbs. Palate: elegant, balanced, round tannins.

FONT DE LA FIGUERA 2010 T
garnacha, cariñena, syrah, cabernet sauvignon

90 Colour: bright cherry. Nose: ripe fruit, sweet spices, creamy oak. Palate: flavourful, fruity, toasty, round tannins.

FONT DE LA FIGUERA 2012 B
viognier, garnacha blanca, chenin blanc

89 Colour: bright yellow. Nose: medium intensity, faded flowers, wild herbs. Palate: fruity, flavourful, balanced.

SERRAS DEL PRIORAT 2012 T
garnacha, cariñena, syrah, cabernet sauvignon

89 Colour: cherry, purple rim. Nose: balanced, red berry notes, ripe fruit, mineral. Palate: fruity, flavourful, round tannins.

SWEET CLOS FIGUERES DULCE 2011 T
garnacha

88 Colour: bright cherry. Nose: ripe fruit, sweet spices, creamy oak, dark chocolate. Palate: flavourful, fruity, toasty, correct.

CLOS GALENA

Camino de la Solana, s/n
43736 El Molar (Tarragona)
☎: +34 619 790 956
www.closgalena.com
info@closgalena.com

CLOS GALENA 2009 TC
40% garnacha, 20% cariñena, 20% syrah, 20% cabernet sauvignon

92 Colour: cherry, garnet rim. Nose: spicy, creamy oak, toasty, characterful. Palate: powerful, flavourful, toasty, round tannins.

CROSSOS 2011 T
60% garnacha, 20% cabernet sauvignon, 20% cariñena

88 Colour: bright cherry. Nose: sweet spices, creamy oak, overripe fruit. Palate: flavourful, fruity, toasty, round tannins.

FORMIGA DE VELLUT 2011 T
60% garnacha, 20% cariñena, 20% syrah

91 Colour: cherry, garnet rim. Nose: ripe fruit, spicy, creamy oak, toasty, complex. Palate: powerful, flavourful, toasty, round tannins.

GALENA 2010 T
35% garnacha, 15% cariñena, 25% merlot, 25% cabernet sauvignon

90 Colour: cherry, garnet rim. Nose: ripe fruit, spicy, creamy oak, toasty, complex. Palate: powerful, flavourful, toasty, round tannins.

CLOS MOGADOR

Camí Manyetes, s/n
43737 Gratallops (Tarragona)
☎: +34 977 839 171 - Fax: +34 977 839 426
closmogador@closmogador.com

CLOS MOGADOR 2010 T
garnacha, cariñena, cabernet sauvignon, syrah

95 Colour: cherry, garnet rim. Nose: spicy, creamy oak, toasty, complex, earthy notes. Palate: powerful, flavourful, toasty, round tannins.

MANYETES 2010 T
cariñena, garnacha

94 Colour: deep cherry. Nose: powerfull, characterful, overripe fruit, fruit expression. Palate: flavourful, powerful, fine bitter notes, good acidity.

NELIN 2011 B
garnacha, macabeo, viognier, escanyavelles

88 Colour: bright yellow. Nose: citrus fruit, ripe fruit, aged wood nuances, balsamic herbs, spicy. Palate: flavourful, spicy, correct.

COSTERS DEL PRIORAT

Finca Sant Martí
43738 Bellmunt del Priorat (Tarragona)
☎: +34 610 203 473
www.costersdelpriorat.com
info@costersdelpriorat.com

CLOS CYPRES 2011 T
100% cariñena

91 Colour: very deep cherry, purple rim. Nose: medium intensity, ripe fruit, spicy. Palate: flavourful, good structure, round tannins.

ELIOS 2011 T
55% garnacha, 45% cariñena

91 Colour: cherry, garnet rim. Nose: spicy, creamy oak, toasty, fruit expression. Palate: powerful, flavourful, toasty, round tannins.

PISSARRES 2011 T
60% cariñena, 35% garnacha

92 Colour: cherry, garnet rim. Nose: red berry notes, ripe fruit, balsamic herbs, mineral, sweet spices, creamy oak. Palate: powerful, flavourful, spicy.

DE MULLER

Camí Pedra Estela, 34
43205 Reus (Tarragona)
☎: +34 977 757 473 - Fax: +34 977 771 129
www.demuller.es
lab@demuller.es

DOM JOAN FORT 1865 SOLERA
moscatel, garnacha, garnacha blanca

94 Colour: light mahogany. Nose: powerfull, complex, elegant, dry nuts, toasty. Palate: rich, fine bitter notes, fine solera notes, long, spicy.

LEGITIM 2011 TC
garnacha, merlot, syrah, mazuelo

86 Colour: pale ruby, brick rim edge. Nose: slightly evolved, warm, fruit liqueur notes. Palate: spicy, warm.

LES PUSSES DE MULLER 2009 TC
merlot, syrah

90 Colour: deep cherry, garnet rim. Nose: wild herbs, ripe fruit, fruit preserve, expressive. Palate: balanced, fine bitter notes.

LO CABALÓ 2008 TR
garnacha, merlot, syrah, mazuelo

89 Colour: cherry, garnet rim. Nose: ripe fruit, spicy, scrubland, old leather. Palate: powerful, flavourful, toasty, round tannins.

DURAN'S

Unió, 4
43739 Porrera (Tarragona)
☎: +34 686 963 385
www.calporrera.com
dicduran@hotmail.com

TROSSET DE PORRERA 2009 TC
60% cariñena, 20% garnacha, 20% merlot, cabernet sauvignon, syrah

91 Colour: cherry, garnet rim. Nose: ripe fruit, spicy, creamy oak, toasty, complex, earthy notes, dry stone. Palate: powerful, flavourful, toasty.

EDICIONES I-LIMITADAS

Claravall, 2
8022 (Barcelona)
☎: +34 932 531 760 - Fax: +34 934 173 591
www.edicionesi-limitadas.com
info@edicionesi-limitadas.com

FLORS 2011 T
cariñena, syrah, garnacha

91 Colour: bright cherry. Nose: ripe fruit, creamy oak, expressive. Palate: flavourful, fruity, toasty, round tannins.

ELVIWINES

Antoni Caballé, 8
8197 Valldoreix- St Cugat del Vallès (Tarragona)
☎: +34 935 343 026 - Fax: +34 936 750 316
www.elviwines.com
moises@elviwines.com

EL26 2008 TR
40% cabernet sauvignon, 25% syrah, 20% garnacha, 15% cariñena

92 Colour: cherry, garnet rim. Nose: spicy, creamy oak, toasty, characterful, overripe fruit. Palate: powerful, flavourful, toasty, round tannins.

FERRER BOBET

Ctra. Falset a Porrera, Km. 6,5
43730 Falset (Tarragona)
☎: +34 609 945 532 - Fax: +34 935 044 265
www.ferrerbobet.com
eguerre@ferrerbobet.com

FERRER BOBET SELECCIÓ ESPECIAL VINYES VELLES 2010 T
cariñena

94 Colour: cherry, garnet rim. Nose: ripe fruit, spicy, creamy oak, toasty, characterful. Palate: powerful, flavourful, toasty, round tannins.

FERRER BOBET VINYES VELLES 2011 T
cariñena, garnacha

94 Colour: cherry, garnet rim. Nose: red berry notes, ripe fruit, balsamic herbs, mineral, spicy, creamy oak. Palate: powerful, flavourful, spicy, long, balanced.

GENIUM CELLER

Nou, 92- Bajos
43376 Poboleda (Tarragona)
☎: +34 977 827 146 - Fax: +34 977 827 146
www.geniumceller.com
genium@geniumceller.com

GENIUM CELLER 2007 TC
60% garnacha, 20% cariñena, 15% merlot, 5% syrah

89 Colour: cherry, garnet rim. Nose: spicy, creamy oak, toasty, balsamic herbs, ripe fruit, fruit preserve. Palate: powerful, flavourful, toasty.

GENIUM COSTERS 2009 TR
50% cariñena, 30% garnacha, 10% merlot, 10% syrah

87 Colour: deep cherry. Nose: overripe fruit, fruit liqueur notes, warm. Palate: powerful, sweetness.

GENIUM ECOLÒGIC 2008 TC
50% garnacha, 30% merlot, 10% cariñena, 10% syrah

88 Colour: deep cherry, garnet rim. Nose: scrubland, spicy, ripe fruit. Palate: fruity, good acidity, round tannins.

GENIUM XIMENIS 2011 BFB
90% pedro ximénez, 10% garnacha blanca

88 Colour: bright yellow. Nose: expressive, candied fruit, fruit liqueur notes. Palate: powerful, sweetness, fine bitter notes.

POBOLEDA VI DE VILA 2009 TR
70% garnacha, 30% cariñena

88 Colour: deep cherry. Nose: fruit liqueur notes, warm, toasty, dark chocolate. Palate: sweetness, fine bitter notes.

GRAN CLOS

Montsant, 2
43738 Bellmunt (Tarragona)
☎: +34 977 830 675
www.granclos.com
cellersfuentes@granclos.com

CARTUS 2006 T
76% garnacha, 24% cariñena

91 Colour: cherry, garnet rim. Nose: ripe fruit, spicy, creamy oak, toasty, complex. Palate: powerful, flavourful, toasty, round tannins.

FINCA EL PUIG 2007 T
60% garnacha, 20% syrah, 20% cabernet sauvignon

91 Colour: deep cherry, garnet rim. Nose: powerfull, cocoa bean, balsamic herbs, spicy. Palate: good acidity, balanced, round tannins.

FINCA EL PUIG 2008 T
60% garnacha, 20% syrah, 20% cabernet sauvignon

90 Colour: bright cherry. Nose: sweet spices, creamy oak, expressive, overripe fruit. Palate: flavourful, fruity, toasty, round tannins.

GRAN CLOS 2006 T
54% garnacha, 34% cariñena, 12% cabernet sauvignon

91 Colour: cherry, garnet rim. Nose: ripe fruit, spicy, creamy oak, toasty, characterful, mineral. Palate: powerful, flavourful, round tannins.

GRAN CLOS 2009 B
78% garnacha blanca, 22% macabeo

91 Colour: bright straw. Nose: powerfull, candied fruit, citrus fruit, dried herbs. Palate: flavourful, powerful, full.

LES MINES 2010 T
70% garnacha, 20% cariñena, 10% merlot

87 Colour: cherry, garnet rim. Nose: fruit preserve, powerfull, cocoa bean. Palate: flavourful, fruity, round tannins.

SOLLUNA 2010 T
75% garnacha, 15% cabernet sauvignon, 10% merlot

86 Colour: cherry, garnet rim. Nose: ripe fruit, spicy, toasty, complex, warm. Palate: powerful, round tannins.

GRATAVINUM

Antic Camí Vilella Baixa a El Lloar. Mas d'en Serres s/n
43737 Gratallops (Tarragona)
☎: +34 938 901 399 - Fax: +34 938 901 143
www.gratavinum.com
gratavinum@gratavinum.com

GRATAVINUM 2 PI R 2010 T
garnacha, cariñena, cabernet sauvignon, syrah

91 Colour: cherry, garnet rim. Nose: ripe fruit, expressive, balsamic herbs, spicy, mineral. Palate: good structure, flavourful, round tannins.

GRATAVINUM GV5 2010 T
cariñena, garnacha, cabernet sauvignon

90 Colour: cherry, garnet rim. Nose: spicy, creamy oak, toasty, complex, earthy notes. Palate: powerful, flavourful, toasty, round tannins.

GRATAVINUM SILVESTRIS 2011 T
garnacha, cabernet sauvignon

87 Colour: cherry, garnet rim. Nose: fruit preserve, balsamic herbs, spicy, toasty. Palate: spicy, long, powerful, flavourful.

JOAN AMETLLER

Ctra. La Morera de Monsant - Cornudella, km. 3,2
43361 La Morera de Monsant (Tarragona)
☎: +34 933 208 439 - Fax: +34 933 208 437
www.ametller.com
ametller@ametller.com

CLOS CORRIOL 2010 T
70% garnacha, 15% merlot, 15% cabernet sauvignon

87 Colour: deep cherry. Nose: fruit preserve, spicy, toasty. Palate: powerful, spicy, ripe fruit.

CLOS CORRIOL 2012 B
100% garnacha blanca

87 Colour: yellow, greenish rim. Nose: ripe fruit, white flowers. Palate: flavourful, correct, ripe fruit.

CLOS CORRIOL 2012 RD
65% cabernet sauvignon, 35% garnacha

85 Colour: rose, purple rim. Nose: powerfull, ripe fruit, red berry notes, floral. Palate: powerful, fruity, fresh.

CLOS MUSTARDÓ 2011 BFB
100% garnacha blanca

90 Colour: bright straw. Nose: candied fruit, citrus fruit, mineral. Palate: flavourful, sweetness, good acidity.

L'INFERNAL (TRÍO INFERNAL)

Pol. 8 Parcela 148
43737 Torroja del Priorat (Tarragona)
☎: - Fax: +34 977 828 380
contact@linfernal.es

L'INFERNAL AGUILERA 2008 TC
100% cariñena

91 Colour: pale ruby, brick rim edge. Nose: ripe fruit, scrubland, mineral, earthy notes, fine reductive notes, spicy, creamy oak. Palate: powerful, flavourful, spicy, long.

L'INFERNAL CARA NORD 2011 T
100% syrah

92 Colour: cherry, purple rim. Nose: red berry notes, ripe fruit, violet drops, balsamic herbs, spicy, creamy oak. Palate: powerful, flavourful, balanced, long.

L'INFERNAL EL CASOT 2011 T
100% garnacha

89 Colour: cherry, garnet rim. Nose: spicy, creamy oak, toasty, complex, fruit preserve. Palate: powerful, flavourful, toasty, round tannins.

L'INFERNAL FONS CLAR 2011 T
100% cariñena

90 Colour: cherry, garnet rim. Nose: red berry notes, fruit liqueur notes, wild herbs, mineral, sweet spices, creamy oak. Palate: full, powerful, flavourful, spicy.

RIU BY TRÍO INFERNAL 2010 T
garnacha, cariñena, syrah

91 Colour: cherry, garnet rim. Nose: spicy, creamy oak, toasty. Palate: powerful, flavourful, toasty, round tannins.

TRÍO INFERNAL Nº 0/3 2011 B
macabeo, garnacha blanca

89 Colour: bright yellow. Nose: medium intensity, faded flowers, balanced. Palate: flavourful, fruity, complex, good acidity.

LA CONRERIA D'SCALA DEI

Carrer Mitja Galta, s/n - Finca Les Brugueres
43379 Scala Dei (Tarragona)
☎: +34 977 827 055 - Fax: +34 977 827 055
www.vinslaconreria.com
laconreria@vinslaconreria.com

IUGITER 2009 T
garnacha, merlot, cabernet sauvignon, cariñena

88 Colour: very deep cherry. Nose: overripe fruit, sweet spices, dark chocolate. Palate: powerful, ripe fruit, spicy.

IUGITER SELECCIÓ VINYES VELLES 2009 TC
garnacha, cariñena, cabernet sauvignon

89 Colour: bright cherry, garnet rim. Nose: expressive, mineral. Palate: good structure, full, round tannins.

LA CONRERIA 2010 T
garnacha, syrah, merlot, cabernet sauvignon, cariñena

90 Colour: cherry, garnet rim. Nose: ripe fruit, spicy, creamy oak, toasty, complex. Palate: powerful, flavourful, toasty, round tannins.

LES BRUGUERES 2012 B
100% garnacha blanca

89 Colour: bright straw. Nose: fresh, fresh fruit, white flowers, expressive. Palate: flavourful, fruity, good acidity, balanced.

LLICORELLA VINS

Carrer de l'Era, 11
43737 Torroja del Priorat (Tarragona)
☎: +34 977 839 049 - Fax: +34 977 839 049
www.llicorellavins.com
comercial@llicorellavins.com

AÒNIA 2010 T
garnacha, cariñena, cabernet sauvignon

90 Colour: deep cherry, purple rim. Nose: ripe fruit, dried herbs, sweet spices. Palate: flavourful, good acidity.

GRAN NASARD 2008 TC
garnacha, cariñena

90 Colour: cherry, garnet rim. Nose: spicy, creamy oak, toasty, complex, mineral, ripe fruit. Palate: powerful, flavourful, toasty, round tannins.

MAS SAURA 2008 TC
garnacha, cabernet sauvignon, syrah, cariñena

90 Colour: cherry, garnet rim. Nose: ripe fruit, spicy, creamy oak, toasty, complex. Palate: powerful, flavourful, toasty, round tannins.

MAIUS

Santa María, 17
8172 Sant Cugat del Vallès (Barcelona)
☎: +34 936 752 897 - Fax: +34 936 752 897
www.maiusviticultors.com
jgomez@maiusviticultors.com

MAIUS BARRANC DE LA BRUIXA 2009 T
cabernet sauvignon, garnacha, cariñena, syrah

91 Colour: deep cherry. Nose: ripe fruit, spicy, scrubland. Palate: flavourful, good acidity, fine bitter notes.

MAS BLANC PINORD PRIORAT

Dr. Pasteur, 6
8720 Vilafranca del Penedès (Barcelona)
☎: +34 938 903 066 - Fax: +34 938 170 979
www.pinord.com
visites@pinord.es

+ 7 2008 T
36% cabernet sauvignon, 33% garnacha, 22% merlot, 7% syrah, 2% cariñena

89 Colour: cherry, garnet rim. Nose: powerfull, ripe fruit, fruit liqueur notes, spicy, toasty, mineral. Palate: powerful, flavourful, spicy, long.

BALCONS 2006 T
36% cabernet sauvignon, 36% garnacha, 20% merlot, 8% cariñena

86 Colour: pale ruby, brick rim edge. Nose: fruit liqueur notes, overripe fruit, toasty. Palate: sweetness, powerful.

CLOS DEL MAS 2009 T
38,5% cabernet sauvignon, 29,5% garnacha, 19,5% merlot, 10% syrah, 2,5% cariñena

87 Colour: deep cherry, garnet rim. Nose: powerfull, over-ripe fruit, spicy. Palate: correct, good structure, flavourful.

CLOS DEL MUSIC 2008 T
45% cabernet sauvignon, 45% garnacha, 10% syrah

91 Colour: cherry, garnet rim. Nose: spicy, creamy oak, toasty, characterful. Palate: powerful, flavourful, round tannins.

MAS IGNEUS

Ctra. Falset a Vilella Baixa T-710, Km. 11,1
43737 Gratallops (Tarragona)
☎: +34 977 262 259 - Fax: +34 977 054 027
www.masigneus.com
celler@masigneus.com

BARRANC DELS CLOSOS BLANC 2012 B
90% garnacha blanca, 10% pedro ximénez

91 Colour: bright straw. Nose: fresh, fresh fruit, white flowers, expressive, mineral. Palate: flavourful, fruity, good acidity, balanced.

BARRANC DELS CLOSOS NEGRE 2011 T
garnacha, cariñena

88 Colour: cherry, garnet rim. Nose: ripe fruit, sweet spices, creamy oak. Palate: flavourful, fruity, toasty.

COSTERS DE L'ERMITA 2011 T
garnacha, cariñena

92 Colour: bright cherry. Nose: ripe fruit, sweet spices, creamy oak, expressive, balsamic herbs. Palate: flavourful, fruity, toasty, round tannins.

FA 104 BLANC 2012 B
100% garnacha blanca

92 Colour: bright yellow. Nose: ripe fruit, sweet spices, fragrant herbs. Palate: rich, smoky aftertaste, flavourful, fresh, good acidity.

FA 112 2011 T
garnacha, cariñena

93 Colour: cherry, purple rim. Nose: mineral, scrubland, cocoa bean. Palate: fruity, flavourful, good structure, round tannins.

FA 206 NEGRE 2011 T
garnacha, cariñena

88 Colour: deep cherry, purple rim. Nose: wild herbs, spicy, ripe fruit, fruit liqueur notes. Palate: fruity, round tannins.

MAS LA MOLA

Raval, 4
43376 Poboleda (Tarragona)
www.maslamola.com
info@maslamola.com

L'EXPRESSIÓ DEL PRIORAT 2011 T
40% garnacha, 40% cariñena, 20% cabernet sauvignon

84

MAS LA MOLA 2012 B
75% macabeo, 25% garnacha blanca

83

MAS LA MOLA NEGRE 2009 T
garnacha peluda, garnacha, syrah

88 Colour: cherry, garnet rim. Nose: spicy, creamy oak, toasty, powerfull. Palate: powerful, flavourful, toasty, round tannins.

MAS MARTINET

Ctra. Falset - Gratallops, Km. 6
43730 Falset (Tarragona)
☎: +34 629 238 236 - Fax: +34 977 262 348
www.masmartinet.com
masmartinet@masmartinet.com

CAMI PESSEROLES 2010 T
cariñena, garnacha

93 Colour: cherry, garnet rim. Nose: ripe fruit, spicy, creamy oak, toasty, damp earth. Palate: powerful, flavourful, toasty, round tannins.

CLOS MARTINET 2010 T
garnacha, cariñena, merlot, cabernet sauvignon, syrah

93 Colour: deep cherry, garnet rim. Nose: balanced, ripe fruit, balsamic herbs, waxy notes. Palate: fruity, balanced, long, round tannins.

ELS ESCURÇONS 2010 T
garnacha

92 Colour: cherry, garnet rim. Nose: spicy, creamy oak, toasty, overripe fruit, characterful. Palate: powerful, flavourful, toasty, round tannins.

MARTINET BRU 2010 T
garnacha, syrah

93 Colour: cherry, garnet rim. Nose: ripe fruit, spicy, creamy oak, toasty, complex, mineral, balsamic herbs, dried herbs. Palate: powerful, flavourful, toasty, round tannins.

MAS PERINET

Finca Mas Perinet, s/n - T-702, Km. 1,6
43361 La Morera de Montsant (Tarragona)
☎: +34 977 827 113 - Fax: +34 977 827 180
www.masperinet.com
info@masperinet.com

PERINET + PLUS 2006 T
51% mazuelo, 41% garnacha, 8% syrah

93 Colour: cherry, garnet rim. Nose: spicy, creamy oak, toasty, characterful, mineral. Palate: powerful, flavourful, toasty, round tannins.

PERINET 2005 T
40% mazuelo, 20% syrah, 20% cabernet sauvignon, 10% garnacha, 10% merlot

92 Colour: cherry, garnet rim. Nose: powerfull, characterful, mineral, earthy notes. Palate: powerful, flavourful, concentrated.

PERINET 2006 T
36% mazuelo, 19% syrah, 16% garnacha, 15% cabernet sauvignon, 14% merlot

92 Colour: deep cherry. Nose: powerfull, ripe fruit, sweet spices, creamy oak, aromatic coffee. Palate: powerful, good structure, round tannins.

MASET DEL LLEÓ

C-244, Km. 32,5
8792 La Granada del Penedès (Barcelona)
☎: +34 902 200 250 - Fax: +34 938 921 333
www.maset.com
info@maset.com

CLOS GRAN VILÓ 2009 T
cariñena

90 Colour: cherry, garnet rim. Nose: spicy, creamy oak, toasty, overripe fruit. Palate: powerful, flavourful, toasty, round tannins.

CLOS VILÓ 2010 T
garnacha, cariñena, syrah

89 Colour: deep cherry, purple rim. Nose: balanced, ripe fruit, sweet spices, cocoa bean. Palate: ripe fruit, flavourful.

MAS VILÓ 2011 T
garnacha, cariñena

87 Colour: cherry, garnet rim. Nose: toasty, dark chocolate, fruit liqueur notes, overripe fruit. Palate: powerful, concentrated, sweetness.

MERITXELL PALLEJÀ

Carrer Major, 32
43737 Gratallops (Tarragona)
☎: +34 670 960 735
www.nita.cat
info@nita.cat

NITA 2011 T
garnacha, samsó, cabernet sauvignon, syrah

88 Colour: cherry, garnet rim. Nose: spicy, creamy oak, toasty, characterful, overripe fruit. Palate: powerful, flavourful, toasty, round tannins.

NOGUERALS

Tou, 5
43360 Cornudella de Montsant (Tarragona)
☎: +34 650 033 546
www.noguerals.com
noguerals@hotmail.com

TITÍ 2009 TC
garnacha, cabernet sauvignon, syrah

88 Colour: cherry, garnet rim. Nose: ripe fruit, spicy, creamy oak, toasty. Palate: powerful, flavourful, toasty, round tannins.

RITME CELLER

Sindicat s/n
43375 Vilella Alta (Tarragona)
☎: +34 672 432 691 - Fax: +34 977 660 867
www.ritmeceller.com
ritme@ritmrceller.com

+ RITME BLANC 2010 B
70% garnacha blanca, 30% macabeo

91 Colour: bright straw. Nose: floral, citrus fruit, ripe fruit, petrol notes, dried herbs, dry stone. Palate: powerful, flavourful, spicy, balanced.

DO Ca. PRIORAT / D.O.P.

+ RITME BLANC 2011 B
70% garnacha blanca, 30% macabeo

90 Colour: bright yellow. Nose: powerfull, ripe fruit, sweet spices, creamy oak, fragrant herbs. Palate: rich, flavourful, fresh, good acidity, fine bitter notes.

ETERN 2011 T
cariñena, garnacha

91 Colour: cherry, garnet rim. Nose: balsamic herbs, dry stone, sweet spices, creamy oak, fruit preserve. Palate: powerful, flavourful, balsamic, mineral, elegant.

PLAER 2011 T
cariñena, garnacha

94 Colour: cherry, garnet rim. Nose: ripe fruit, spicy, earthy notes, mineral, wild herbs, scrubland. Palate: flavourful, powerful, spicy, long.

RITME NEGRE 2011 T
70% cariñena, 30% garnacha

91 Colour: bright cherry, garnet rim. Nose: ripe fruit, sweet spices, creamy oak, expressive, mineral. Palate: flavourful, fruity, toasty, balanced.

RODRÍGUEZ SANZO

Manuel Azaña, 9
47014 (Valladolid)
☎: +34 983 150 150 - Fax: +34 983 150 151
www.rodriguezsanzo.com
comunicacion@valsanzo.com

NASSOS 2009 T
garnacha

92 Colour: cherry, garnet rim. Nose: red berry notes, ripe fruit, wild herbs, dry stone, creamy oak. Palate: spicy, balsamic, round tannins.

NASSOS 2010 T
garnacha

93 Colour: cherry, garnet rim. Nose: ripe fruit, spicy, creamy oak, toasty, mineral, balsamic herbs. Palate: powerful, flavourful, toasty, round tannins.

ROTLLAN TORRA

Balandra, 6
43737 Torroja del Priorat (Tarragona)
☎: +34 977 839 285
www.rotllantorra.com
comercial@rotllantorra.com

AUTOR 2008 TR
garnacha, samsó, cabernet sauvignon

90 Colour: cherry, garnet rim. Nose: ripe fruit, fruit preserve, spicy, balsamic herbs, creamy oak, mineral. Palate: powerful, flavourful, spicy, long.

MISTIK 2008 T
garnacha, mazuelo, cabernet sauvignon

91 Colour: cherry, garnet rim. Nose: ripe fruit, fruit preserve, balsamic herbs, spicy, creamy oak, mineral. Palate: flavourful, spicy, balanced.

SANGENÍS I VAQUÉ

Pl. Catalunya, 3
43739 Porrera (Tarragona)
☎: +34 977 828 252
www.sangenisivaque.com
celler@sangenisivaque.com

CLOS MONLLEÓ 2006 T
50% garnacha, 50% cariñena

91 Colour: pale ruby, brick rim edge. Nose: elegant, spicy, fine reductive notes, aged wood nuances, ripe fruit. Palate: spicy, fine tannins, elegant, long.

LO COSTER BLANC 2011 B
50% garnacha, 50% macabeo

91 Colour: bright yellow. Nose: powerfull, characterful, candied fruit. Palate: flavourful, sweetness, ripe fruit.

SIMFONIA EN DOLÇ 2007 T
90% garnacha, 10% cariñena

92 Colour: cherry, garnet rim. Nose: ripe fruit, spicy, creamy oak, cocoa bean, aromatic coffee. Palate: powerful, flavourful, spicy.

VALL POR 2006 TR
35% garnacha, 35% cariñena, 15% cabernet sauvignon, 15% merlot

88 Colour: cherry, garnet rim. Nose: spicy, creamy oak, toasty, characterful, warm. Palate: powerful, flavourful, toasty, round tannins.

SAÓ DEL COSTER

De Les Valls, 28
43737 Gratallops (Priorat)
☎: +34 977 839 298
www.saodelcoster.com
info@saodelcoster.com

"S" 2011 T
garnacha, merlot, cabernet sauvignon, syrah

87 Colour: cherry, garnet rim. Nose: fruit preserve, scrubland, spicy, toasty. Palate: powerful, flavourful, spicy, long.

PLANASSOS 2008 T
cariñena

90 Colour: dark-red cherry, orangey edge. Nose: earthy notes, mineral, balsamic herbs, spicy, cigar, tobacco, creamy oak. Palate: powerful, flavourful, spicy, long.

TERRAM 2009 T
cariñena, garnacha, syrah, cabernet sauvignon

88 Colour: very deep cherry. Nose: powerfull, creamy oak, fruit liqueur notes. Palate: powerful, spirituous, sweetness.

TERROIR AL LIMIT

Baixa Tont, 10
43737 Torroja del Priorat (Tarragona)
☎: +34 699 732 707
www.terroir-al-limit.com
vi@terroir-al-limit.com

ARBOSSAR 2010 T

93 Colour: cherry, garnet rim. Nose: balanced, ripe fruit, wild herbs, mineral. Palate: elegant.

DITS DEL TERRA 2010 T

90 Colour: bright cherry, garnet rim. Nose: medium intensity, balsamic herbs, spicy. Palate: fruity, round tannins, balanced.

LES MANYES 2010 T

92 Colour: deep cherry. Nose: ripe fruit, spicy, scrubland, balsamic herbs, wet leather. Palate: flavourful, powerful, spicy, ripe fruit.

LES TOSSES 2010 T

93 Colour: cherry, garnet rim. Nose: spicy, creamy oak, toasty, complex, wet leather. Palate: powerful, flavourful, toasty, round tannins.

PEDRA DE GUIX 2010 B

89 Colour: bright yellow. Nose: medium intensity, mineral, dried flowers, citrus fruit. Palate: flavourful, good acidity, balanced.

TERRA DE CUQUES 2011 B

90 Colour: bright yellow. Nose: floral, dried herbs, citrus fruit, ripe fruit, spicy, dry stone. Palate: flavourful, rich, spicy, balsamic.

TORROJA VI DE LA VILA 2010 T

94 Colour: deep cherry. Nose: fruit expression, violet drops, toasty, spicy. Palate: flavourful, fruity, balsamic, long.

TORRES PRIORAT

Finca La Soleta, s/n
43737 El Lloar (Tarragona)
☎: +34 938 177 400 - Fax: +34 938 177 444
www.torres.es
admin@torres.es

SALMOS 2011 TC
cariñena, garnacha, syrah

89 Colour: cherry, garnet rim. Nose: ripe fruit, spicy, toasty, mineral, smoky. Palate: powerful, flavourful, toasty, round tannins.

ABRACADABRA 2011 B
70% garnacha blanca, 30% macabeo

92 Colour: bright golden. Nose: ripe fruit, dry nuts, toasty, spicy. Palate: flavourful, fruity, spicy, long, balanced.

LO MÓN 2010 T
60% garnacha, 25% cariñena, syrah, cabernet sauvignon

93 Colour: cherry, garnet rim. Nose: spicy, creamy oak, toasty, characterful. Palate: powerful, flavourful, toasty, round tannins.

LO PETIT DE LA CASA 2010 TC
80% garnacha, 20% cabernet sauvignon

90 Colour: cherry, garnet rim. Nose: ripe fruit, spicy, creamy oak, toasty, mineral. Palate: powerful, flavourful, toasty, round tannins.

PAM DE NAS 2009 T
60% garnacha, 40% cariñena

94 Colour: cherry, garnet rim. Nose: ripe fruit, spicy, creamy oak, toasty, complex, earthy notes, mineral. Palate: powerful, flavourful, toasty, balanced, elegant.

VINÍCOLA DEL PRIORAT

Piró, s/n
43737 Gratallops (Tarragona)
☎: +34 977 839 167 - Fax: +34 977 839 201
www.vinicoladelpriorat.com
info@vinicoladelpriorat.com

CLOS GEBRAT 2010 TC
garnacha, cabernet sauvignon, mazuelo

90 Colour: cherry, garnet rim. Nose: spicy, creamy oak, toasty, complex, earthy notes, fruit expression. Palate: powerful, flavourful, toasty, round tannins.

CLOS GEBRAT 2012 T
garnacha, mazuelo, cabernet sauvignon, merlot, syrah

89 Colour: dark-red cherry, cherry, purple rim. Nose: powerful, balanced, ripe fruit, mineral. Palate: fruity, flavourful, round tannins.

L'OBAGA 2011 T
garnacha, syrah

88 Colour: bright cherry. Nose: ripe fruit, sweet spices, creamy oak, expressive. Palate: flavourful, fruity, toasty, round tannins.

NADIU 2012 T
garnacha, mazuelo, cabernet sauvignon, merlot, syrah

87 Colour: cherry, garnet rim. Nose: ripe fruit, fruit liqueur notes, balsamic herbs, earthy notes. Palate: powerful, flavourful, spicy.

ÒNIX CLÀSSIC 2012 B
viura, garnacha blanca, pedro ximénez

87 Colour: yellow. Nose: ripe fruit, balsamic herbs, medium intensity. Palate: fruity, flavourful, correct.

ÒNIX CLÀSSIC 2012 T
garnacha, mazuelo

88 Colour: deep cherry, purple rim. Nose: medium intensity, ripe fruit, balsamic herbs. Palate: fruity, flavourful, round tannins.

ÒNIX EVOLUCIÓ 2010 T
mazuelo, garnacha, cabernet sauvignon

90 Colour: cherry, garnet rim. Nose: spicy, creamy oak, toasty, overripe fruit. Palate: powerful, flavourful, toasty, round tannins.

ÒNIX FUSIÓ 2011 T
garnacha, syrah, mazuelo

88 Colour: cherry, garnet rim. Nose: spicy, creamy oak, toasty, characterful, overripe fruit. Palate: powerful, toasty, round tannins.

VITICULTORS DEL PRIORAT

Partida Palells - Mas Subirat
43738 Bellmunt del Priorat (Tarragona)
☎: +34 977 262 268 - Fax: +34 977 262 268
www.morlanda.com
morlanda@morlanda.com

MORLANDA 2009 TR
garnacha, cariñena

89 Colour: bright cherry. Nose: sweet spices, creamy oak, overripe fruit. Palate: flavourful, fruity, toasty, round tannins.

MORLANDA 2012 B
garnacha blanca, macabeo

88 Colour: bright straw. Nose: powerfull, ripe fruit, creamy oak, dried herbs. Palate: rich, smoky aftertaste, flavourful.

VITICULTORS MAS D'EN GIL

Finca Mas d'en Gil
43738 Bellmunt del Priorat (Tarragona)
☎: +34 977 830 192 - Fax: +34 977 830 152
www.masdengil.com
mail@masdengil.com

CLOS FONTÀ 2010 TR
40% garnacha peluda, 30% garnacha país, 30% cariñena

93 Colour: cherry, garnet rim. Nose: creamy oak, toasty, complex, fruit expression, ripe fruit. Palate: powerful, flavourful, toasty, round tannins.

COMA BLANCA 2011 BC
50% macabeo, 50% garnacha blanca

91 Colour: bright yellow. Nose: powerfull, ripe fruit, sweet spices, fragrant herbs, smoky. Palate: rich, flavourful, good acidity, ripe fruit.

COMA VELLA 2010 T
50% garnacha peluda, 20% garnacha país, 20% cariñena, 10% syrah

90 Colour: very deep cherry. Nose: ripe fruit, expressive, medium intensity, spicy, mineral. Palate: flavourful, fruity, toasty, round tannins.

NUS 2010 DULCE NATURAL
80% garnacha, 15% syrah, 5% viognier

93 Colour: very deep cherry. Nose: sweet spices, toasty, dark chocolate, fruit liqueur notes. Palate: powerful, sweet, good acidity.

Consejo Regulador
DO Boundary

DO RÍAS BAIXAS / D.O.P.

LOCATION:

In the southwest of the province of Pontevedra, covering five distinct sub-regions: Val do Salnés, O Rosal, Condado do Tea, Soutomaior and Ribeira do Ulla.

CLIMATE:

Atlantic, with moderate, mild temperatures due to the influence of the sea, high relative humidity and abundant rainfall (the annual average is around 1600 mm). There is less rainfall further downstream of the Miño (Condado de Tea), and as a consequence the grapes ripen earlier.

SOIL:

Sandy, shallow and slightly acidic, which makes fine soil for producing quality wines. The predominant type of rock is granite, and only in the Concellos of Sanxenxo, Rosal and Tomillo is it possible to find a narrow band of metamorphous rock. Quaternary deposits are very common in all the sub-regions.

GRAPE VARIETIES:

WHITE: *Albariño* (majority), *Loureira Blanca* or *Marqués*, *Treixadura* and Caíño *Blanco* (preferred); *Torrontés* and *Godello* (authorized). **RED:** *Caíño Tinto, Espadeiro, Loureira Tinta* and *Sousón* (preferred); *Tempranillo, Mouratón, Garnacha Tintorera, Mencía* and *Brancellao* (authorized).

SUB-REGIONS:

Val do Salnés. This is the historic sub-region of the *Albariño* (in fact, here, almost all the white wines are produced as single-variety wines from this variety) and is centred around the municipal district of Cambados. It has the flattest relief of the four sub-regions.
Condado do Tea. The furthest inland, it is situated in the south of the province on the northern bank of the Miño. It is characterized by its mountainous terrain. The wines must contain a minimum of 70% of *Albariño* and *Treixadura*.
O Rosal. In the extreme southwest of the province, on the right bank of the Miño river mouth. The warmest sub-region, where river terraces abound. The wines must contain a minimum of 70% of *Albariño* and *Loureira*.
Soutomaior. Situated on the banks of the Verdugo River, about 10 km from Pontevedra, it consists only of the municipal district of Soutomaior. It produces only single-varietals of *Albariño*.
Ribeira do Ulla. A new sub-region along the Ulla River, which forms the landscape of elevated valleys further inland. It comprises the municipal districts of Vedra and part of Padrón, Dco, Boquixon, Touro, Estrada, Silleda and Vila de Cruce. Red wines predominate.

FIGURES:

Vineyard surface: 4.080 – **Wine-Growers:** 6.712 – **Wineries:** 175 – **2012 Harvest rating:** Very Good – **Production:** 11.995.640 litres – **Market percentages:** 75% domestic. 25% export

VINTAGE RATING **PEÑÍN**GUIDE				
2008	2009	2010	2011	2012
EXCELLENT	EXCELLENT	GOOD	VERY GOOD	VERY GOOD

CONSEJO REGULADOR
Plaza de la Pedreira, 10 - Edif. Pazo de Mugartegui - 36002 Pontevedra ☎: +34 986 854 850 - Fax: +34 986 864 546
consejo@doriasbaixas.com   www.doriasbaixas.com

A. PAZOS DE LUSCO

Grixó - Alxén s/n
36458 Salvaterra do Miño (Pontevedra)
☎: +34 987 514 550 - Fax: +34 987 514 570
www.lusco.es
info@lusco.es

LUSCO 2012 B
100% albariño

93 Colour: bright straw. Nose: fresh fruit, floral, mineral, grassy. Palate: flavourful, fruity, good acidity, balanced.

PAZO DE PIÑEIRO 2010 B
albariño

95 Colour: bright straw. Nose: candied fruit, fruit expression, citrus fruit, honeyed notes. Palate: flavourful, powerful, sweetness, ripe fruit, long.

ZIOS DE LUSCO 2012 B
albariño

92 Colour: bright straw. Nose: fresh, fresh fruit, white flowers, mineral, varietal. Palate: flavourful, fruity, good acidity, balanced.

ADEGA CONDES DE ALBAREI

Lugar a Bouza, 1 Castrelo
36639 Cambados (Pontevedra)
☎: +34 986 543 535 - Fax: +34 986 524 251
www.condesdealbarei.com
inf@condesdealbarei.com

CARBALLO GALEGO 2011 BFB
100% albariño

92 Colour: bright yellow. Nose: powerfull, ripe fruit, sweet spices. Palate: rich, flavourful, fresh, good acidity.

CONDES DE ALBAREI 2012 B
100% albariño

88 Colour: bright yellow. Nose: faded flowers, dried herbs. Palate: sweetness, good acidity.

CONDES DE ALBAREI EN RAMA 2006 B
100% albariño

93 Colour: bright yellow. Nose: spicy, cocoa bean, fruit expression, candied fruit, citrus fruit. Palate: flavourful, fruity, fresh, spicy, ripe fruit.

ENXEBRE 2011 B
100% albariño

89 Colour: bright straw. Nose: candied fruit, citrus fruit, dried herbs. Palate: flavourful, powerful, fine bitter notes, good acidity.

ADEGA EIDOS

Padriñán, 65
36960 Sanxenxo (Pontevedra)
☎: +34 986 690 009 - Fax: +34 986 720 307
www.adegaeidos.com
info@adegaeidos.com

CONTRAAPAREDE 2008 B
100% albariño

93 Colour: bright yellow. Nose: powerfull, candied fruit, citrus fruit, honeyed notes. Palate: flavourful, good structure.

EIDOS DE PADRIÑÁN 2012 B
100% albariño

91 Colour: bright straw. Nose: fresh, white flowers, grassy. Palate: flavourful, fruity, good acidity, balanced.

VEIGAS DE PADRIÑÁN 2011 B
100% albariño

92 Colour: bright straw. Nose: fresh, fresh fruit, white flowers, grassy, varietal. Palate: flavourful, fruity, good acidity, balanced.

ADEGA FAMILIAR ELADIO PIÑEIRO

Sobrán, 38 - Vilaxoan
36611 Vilagarcía de Arousa (Pontevedra)
☎: +34 986 511 771 - Fax: +34 986 501 218
www.eladiopineiro.es
adegafamiliar@eladiopineiro.es

ENVIDIACOCHINA 2011 B
albariño

90 Colour: bright straw. Nose: fresh, fresh fruit, white flowers, expressive. Palate: flavourful, fruity, good acidity, balanced.

FRORE DE CARME 2009 B
albariño

91 Colour: bright yellow. Nose: powerfull, varietal, ripe fruit, citrus fruit, dried herbs. Palate: flavourful, good acidity, sweetness, ripe fruit.

ADEGA VALDÉS

Finca As Regas Santa Cruz de Rivadulla
15885 Vedra (A Coruña)
☎: +34 981 512 439 - Fax: +34 981 509 226
www.adegavaldes.com
ventas@gundian.com

ALBARIÑO GUNDIAN 2012 B
100% albariño

91 Colour: bright straw. Nose: fresh, fresh fruit, white flowers, expressive, grassy. Palate: flavourful, fruity, good acidity, balanced.

PAZO VILADOMAR 2012 B
albariño, treixadura

91 Colour: bright straw. Nose: fresh, fresh fruit, dried flowers, mineral. Palate: flavourful, fruity, good acidity, balanced.

XIRADELLA 2012 B
100% albariño

89 Colour: bright straw. Nose: grassy, floral, fresh fruit. Palate: flavourful, fruity, fresh.

ADEGAS AROUSA

Tirabao, 15 - Baión
36614 Vilanova de Arousa (Pontevedra)
☎: +34 986 506 113 - Fax: +34 986 715 454
www.adegasarousa.com
grupoarousaboucina@gmail.com

PAZO DA BOUCIÑA 2012 B
100% albariño

92 Colour: bright straw. Nose: grassy, wild herbs, ripe fruit. Palate: flavourful, varietal, round

VALDEMONXES 2012 B
albariño

90 Colour: bright straw. Nose: fresh fruit, ripe fruit, grassy. Palate: flavourful, fruity, fresh.

ADEGAS CASTROBREY

Camanzo, s/n
36587 Vila de Cruces (Pontevedra)
☎: +34 986 583 643 - Fax: +34 986 411 612
www.castrobrey.com
bodegas@castrobrey.com

SEÑORÍO DE CRUCES 2012 B
100% albariño

88 Colour: bright straw. Nose: citrus fruit, dried herbs, ripe fruit. Palate: sweetness, spicy.

SIN PALABRAS CASTRO VALDÉS 2012 B
100% albariño

90 Colour: bright straw. Nose: fragrant herbs, grassy, ripe fruit, citrus fruit. Palate: flavourful, fruity, ripe fruit.

ADEGAS GALEGAS

Meder, s/n
36457 Salvaterra de Miño (Pontevedra)
☎: +34 986 657 143 - Fax: +34 986 526 901
www.adegasgalegas.es
comercial@adegasgalegas.es

BAGO AMARELO 2012 B
100% albariño

89 Colour: bright straw. Nose: fresh fruit, white flowers, varietal, grassy. Palate: flavourful, fruity, good acidity, balanced.

DIONISOS 2012 B
100% albariño

87 Colour: bright straw. Nose: medium intensity, floral, fresh fruit. Palate: good acidity, fine bitter notes, correct.

DON PEDRO SOUTOMAIOR 2012 B
100% albariño

91 Colour: bright straw. Nose: fresh, white flowers, mineral, dry stone, citrus fruit. Palate: flavourful, fruity, good acidity, balanced.

ADEGAS GRAN VINUM

Fermín Bouza Brei, 9 - 5ºB
36600 Vilagarcía de Arousa (Pontevedra)
☎: +34 986 555 742 - Fax: +34 986 555 742
www.granvinum.com
info@adegasgranvinum.com

ESENCIA DIVIÑA 2012 B
100% albariño

91 Colour: bright straw. Nose: dried herbs, ripe fruit, citrus fruit. Palate: fruity, flavourful.

GRAN VINUM 2011 B
100% albariño

90 Colour: bright yellow. Nose: expressive, characterful, candied fruit. Palate: long, ripe fruit, flavourful.

MAR DE VIÑAS 2012 B
100% albariño

87 Colour: bright straw. Nose: medium intensity, citrus fruit, grassy. Palate: flavourful, light-bodied.

NESSA 2012 B
100% albariño

88 Colour: bright straw. Nose: candied fruit, citrus fruit, floral. Palate: flavourful, sweetness, good acidity, fine bitter notes.

ADEGAS TERRA SANTA

Avda. de Villagarcía, 100
36630 Cambados (Pontevedra)
☎: +34 986 542 947
www.adegasterrasanta.com
terrasanta@adegasterrasanta.com

TERRA SANTA ALBARIÑO 2012 B
albariño

89 Colour: bright yellow. Nose: floral, citrus fruit, ripe fruit, balsamic herbs. Palate: flavourful, fresh, balanced.

ADEGAS TOLLODOURO

Ctra. de Puxeiros a Peinador, 59 Tameiga-Mos
36416 Mos (Pontevedra)
☎: +34 986 609 810 - Fax: +34 986 609 811
www.tollodouro.com
adegastollodouro@tollodouro.com

ALBANTA 2012 B
100% albariño

90 Colour: bright straw. Nose: white flowers, fresh fruit, citrus fruit, grassy. Palate: flavourful, fruity, fresh.

PONTELLÓN ALBARIÑO 2012 B
100% albariño

90 Colour: bright straw. Nose: fresh, fresh fruit, white flowers, grassy. Palate: flavourful, fruity, good acidity, balanced.

TOLLODOURO ROSAL 2012 B
albariño, loureiro, caiño, treixadura

87 Colour: bright straw. Nose: candied fruit, citrus fruit, floral. Palate: flavourful, light-bodied.

TORRES DE ERMELO 2012 B
100% albariño

90 Colour: bright straw. Nose: fresh, fresh fruit, white flowers, expressive, mineral. Palate: flavourful, fruity, good acidity, balanced.

ADEGAS VALMIÑOR

Adega Valmiñor
36370 O'Rosal (Pontevedra)
☎: +34 986 609 060 - Fax: +34 986 609 313
www.adegasvalminor.com
valminor@valminorebano.com

DÁVILA 2011 B
albariño, loureiro, treixadura

91 Colour: bright yellow. Nose: characterful, citrus fruit, candied fruit. Palate: long, ripe fruit, fine bitter notes.

SERRA DA ESTRELA 2012 B
albariño

86 Colour: bright straw. Nose: candied fruit, dried herbs. Palate: ripe fruit, spicy.

TORROXAL 2012 B
albariño

89 Colour: bright straw. Nose: expressive, varietal, ripe fruit, grassy. Palate: flavourful, good acidity.

VALMIÑOR 2012 B
albariño

90 Colour: bright straw. Nose: fresh fruit, white flowers, varietal. Palate: flavourful, fruity, good acidity, balanced.

ADEGAS VALTEA

Lg. Portela, 14
36429 Crecente (Pontevedra)
☎: +34 986 666 344 - Fax: +34 986 644 914
www.vilarvin.com
vilarvin@vilarvin.com

VALTEA 2012 B
100% albariño

89 Colour: bright straw. Nose: candied fruit, citrus fruit, faded flowers. Palate: flavourful, spicy, ripe fruit, good acidity.

ALDEA DE ABAIXO

Novas, s/n
36770 O'Rosal (Pontevedra)
☎: +34 986 626 121 - Fax: +34 986 626 121
www.bodegasorosal.com
senoriodatorre@grannovas.com

GRAN NOVAS ALBARIÑO 2011 B
100% albariño

88 Colour: bright straw. Nose: candied fruit, citrus fruit, honeyed notes. Palate: sweetness, fine bitter notes, good acidity.

SEÑORÍO DA TORRE ROSAL 2011 B
70% albariño, 25% loureiro, 5% caíño

87 Colour: bright straw. Nose: citrus fruit, ripe fruit, medium intensity. Palate: flavourful, fruity, fresh.

SEÑORÍO DA TORRE ROSAL SOBRE LÍAS 2010 B
albariño

92 Colour: bright straw. Nose: fresh, white flowers, expressive, candied fruit, ripe fruit. Palate: flavourful, fruity, balanced, fine bitter notes, round.

ATTIS BODEGAS Y VIÑEDOS

Morouzos, 16 - Dena
36967 Meaño (Pontevedra)
☎: +34 986 744 790 - Fax: +34 986 744 790
www.attisbyv.com
info@attisbyv.com

ATTIS 2012 B
100% albariño

89 Colour: bright straw. Nose: ripe fruit, citrus fruit, white flowers, grassy. Palate: flavourful, fruity, sweetness.

NANA 2011 B
100% albariño

89 Colour: bright yellow. Nose: expressive, powerfull, candied fruit, citrus fruit. Palate: flavourful, powerful, spicy, ripe fruit.

XIÓN 2012 B
100% albariño

89 Colour: bright straw. Nose: fresh, varietal, floral, ripe fruit. Palate: flavourful, fruity, good acidity, balanced.

BENJAMÍN MIGUEZ NOVAL

Porto de Abaixo, 10 - Porto
36458 Salvaterra de Miño (Pontevedra)
☎: +34 986 122 705
www.mariabargiela.com
enoturismo@mariabargiela.com

MARÍA BARGIELA 2010 B
90% albariño, 8% treixadura, 2% loureiro

86 Colour: bright straw. Nose: balsamic herbs, candied fruit, powerfull. Palate: powerful, flavourful, sweetness.

BLACKBOARD WINES

Conrado Albaladejo, 31 BW 61
3540 (Alicante)
☎: +34 686 097 742
www.blackboardwines.com
sales@blackboardwines.com

VISTAS AL MAR 2011 B
albariño

90 Colour: bright yellow. Nose: citrus fruit, ripe fruit, balsamic herbs, dried flowers, powerfull, creamy oak. Palate: flavourful, spicy, long, rich.

BODEGA CASTRO BAROÑA

Cabèiro - San Martín
36637 Meis (Pontevedra)
☎: +34 981 134 847 - Fax: +34 981 174 030
www.castrobarona.com
castrobarona@castrobarona.com

CASTRO BAROÑA 2012 B
100% albariño

91 Colour: bright straw. Nose: fresh, fresh fruit, white flowers, varietal. Palate: flavourful, fruity, good acidity, balanced.

LAGAR DO CASTELO 2012 B
100% albariño

89 Colour: bright straw. Nose: fresh fruit, citrus fruit, grassy. Palate: good acidity, flavourful, fine bitter notes.

MONTELOURO 2012 B
100% albariño

89 Colour: bright straw. Nose: expressive, ripe fruit, citrus fruit. Palate: flavourful, fruity, fresh, long.

BODEGA FORJAS DEL SALNÉS

As Covas, 5
36968 Meaño (Pontevedra)
☎: +34 699 446 113 - Fax: +34 986 744 428
goliardovino@gmail.com

GOLIARDO ATELLEIRA 2011 B BARRICA
100% albariño

93 Colour: bright straw. Nose: fresh, white flowers, ripe fruit, mineral. Palate: flavourful, fruity, good acidity, balanced.

LEIRANA 2012 B
100% albariño

92 Colour: bright straw. Nose: citrus fruit, floral, dried herbs, dry stone, expressive. Palate: rich, powerful, flavourful, balanced, elegant.

LEIRANA FINCA GENOVEVA 2011 B
albariño

93 Colour: bright yellow. Nose: white flowers, citrus fruit, ripe fruit, fragrant herbs, expressive, mineral. Palate: powerful, flavourful, spicy, long, balanced, elegant.

LEIRANA LUISA LÁZARO 2005 B
100% albariño

94 Colour: bright yellow. Nose: candied fruit, citrus fruit, expressive, lees reduction notes, scrubland. Palate: flavourful, fruity, fresh, sweetness.

BODEGA GRANBAZÁN

Lg. Tremoedo, 46
36628 Vilanova de Arousa (Pontevedra)
☎: +34 986 555 562 - Fax: +34 986 555 799
www.agrodebazan.com
jesus@agrodebazan.com

CONTRAPUNTO 2012 B
100% albariño

88 Colour: bright straw. Nose: white flowers, dried herbs, fruit expression. Palate: fresh, fruity, easy to drink.

GRANBAZÁN DON ALVARO DE BAZÁN 2010 B
100% albariño

93 Colour: bright yellow. Nose: dried flowers, citrus fruit, ripe fruit, balsamic herbs, powerfull, sweet spices. Palate: flavourful, spicy, long, round.

GRANBAZÁN ETIQUETA ÁMBAR 2012 B
100% albariño

91 Colour: bright yellow. Nose: white flowers, fragrant herbs, fruit expression, expressive. Palate: rich, powerful, flavourful, balsamic, long, balanced.

GRANBAZÁN ETIQUETA VERDE 2012 B
100% albariño

90 Colour: bright yellow. Nose: floral, fresh fruit, citrus fruit, wild herbs, expressive. Palate: rich, flavourful, balanced, long.

GRANBAZÁN LIMOUSIN 2011 B
100% albariño

93 Colour: bright yellow. Nose: powerfull, ripe fruit, sweet spices, creamy oak, fragrant herbs. Palate: rich, flavourful, fresh, good acidity.

BODEGA Y VIÑEDOS VEIGA DA PRINCESA

Pol. Ind. de Arbo, Parc. 2
Arbo (Pontevedra)
☎: +34 988 261 256
www.pazodomar.com
info@pazodomar.com

VEIGA DA PRINCESA 2012 B
100% albariño

90 Colour: bright straw. Nose: fresh, fresh fruit, white flowers, expressive. Palate: flavourful, fruity, good acidity, balanced.

BODEGAS ABANICO

Pol. Ind Ca l'Avellanet - Susany, 6
8553 Seva (Barcelona)
☎: +34 938 125 676 - Fax: +34 938 123 213
www.bodegasabanico.com
info@exportiberia.com

DILUVIO 2012 B
100% albariño

91 Colour: bright straw. Nose: expressive, varietal, characterful, ripe fruit, citrus fruit. Palate: flavourful, powerful, fine bitter notes, good acidity.

BODEGAS AGRUPADAS PONTE

Eduardo Pondal, 3 Entpa B
36001 (Pontevedra)
☎: +34 986 840 064 - Fax: +34 986 710 230
www.bodegasagrupadasponte.com
info@bodegasagrupadasponte.com

LA RECOMENDACIÓN DE EVA 2011 B
100% albariño

90 Colour: bright yellow. Nose: ripe fruit, citrus fruit, floral, dried herbs. Palate: rich, powerful, flavourful, spicy, long.

BODEGAS ALBAMAR

O Adro, 11 - Castrelo
36639 Cambados (Pontevedra)
☎: +34 660 292 750 - Fax: +34 986 520 048
info@bodegasalbamar.com

ALBAMAR 2012 B
albariño

88 Colour: bright straw. Nose: white flowers, candied fruit. Palate: flavourful, fruity, good acidity, balanced.

ALBAMAR FINCA O PEREIRO 2012 B
100% albariño

90 Colour: bright straw. Nose: floral, wild herbs, dry stone, citrus fruit, fruit expression. Palate: rich, flavourful, fruity, balanced.

ALMA DE MAR SOBRE LÍAS 2011 B
albariño

88 Colour: bright straw. Nose: candied fruit, citrus fruit, lees reduction notes. Palate: rich, powerful, fine bitter notes.

PEPE LUIS SOBRE LÍAS 2011 B
albariño

91 Colour: bright straw. Nose: spicy, candied fruit, citrus fruit, honeyed notes. Palate: flavourful, spicy, ripe fruit.

BODEGAS ALTOS DE TORONA

Vilachán s/n
36740 Tomiño (Pontevedra)
☎: +34 986 288 212 - Fax: +34 986 401 185
www.altosdetorona.com
info@reginaviarum.es

ALTOS DE TORONA 2012 B
albariño, caíño blanco, loureiro

89 Colour: bright straw. Nose: lactic notes, candied fruit, citrus fruit. Palate: flavourful, light-bodied, fruity.

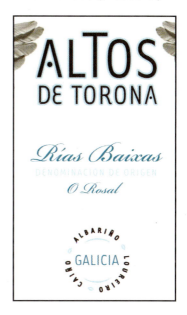

BODEGAS AQUITANIA

Bouza, 17 Castrelo
36639 Cambados (Pontevedra)
☎: +34 986 520 895 - Fax: +34 986 520 895
www.bodegasaquitania.com
info@bodegasaquitania.com

AQUITANIA 2012 B
100% albariño

90 Colour: bright straw. Nose: fresh, fresh fruit, white flowers, grassy. Palate: flavourful, fruity, good acidity.

AQUITANIA 2012 T
mencía

86 Colour: cherry, purple rim. Nose: red berry notes, ripe fruit. Palate: flavourful, good acidity, round tannins.

BERNON 2012 B
albariño

88 Colour: straw. Nose: citrus fruit, floral, ripe fruit. Palate: flavourful, fruity, fresh.

RAIOLAS D'OUTONO 2012 B
albariño

87 Colour: bright straw. Nose: candied fruit, citrus fruit, tropical fruit. Palate: fresh, fruity.

BODEGAS AS LAXAS

As Laxas, 16
36430 Arbo (Pontevedra)
☎: +34 986 665 444 - Fax: +34 986 665 554
www.bodegasaslaxas.com
info@bodegasaslaxas.com

BÁGOA DO MIÑO 2012 B
100% albariño

92 Colour: bright straw. Nose: white flowers, varietal, grassy, wild herbs. Palate: flavourful, good acidity, balanced.

LAXAS 2012 B
100% albariño

90 Colour: bright straw. Nose: white flowers, ripe fruit. Palate: flavourful, fruity, good acidity, balanced.

SENSUM LAXAS ESP
100% albariño

85 Colour: bright straw. Nose: powerfull, fine lees, pattiserie, fresh fruit. Palate: fresh, fine bitter notes, slightly acidic.

VAL DO SOSEGO 2012 B
100% albariño

88 Colour: bright yellow. Nose: powerfull, ripe fruit, cocoa bean, sweet spices. Palate: flavourful, sweetness, good acidity.

BODEGAS DEL PALACIO DE FEFIÑANES

Pza. de Fefiñanes, s/n
36630 Cambados (Pontevedra)
☎: +34 986 542 204 - Fax: +34 986 524 512
www.fefinanes.com
fefinanes@fefinanes.com

1583 ALBARIÑO DE FEFIÑANES 2011 BFB
100% albariño

92 Colour: bright straw. Nose: candied fruit, citrus fruit, grassy, wild herbs. Palate: flavourful, powerful, good acidity.

1583 ALBARIÑO DE FEFIÑANES 2012 B
100% albariño

93 Colour: bright yellow. Nose: citrus fruit, fruit expression, wild herbs, dried flowers. Palate: powerful, rich, flavourful, balanced, elegant.

ALBARIÑO DE FEFIÑANES 2012 B
100% albariño

92 Colour: bright straw. Nose: varietal, ripe fruit, fruit expression, mineral. Palate: flavourful, fruity, fresh, full.

ALBARIÑO DE FEFIÑANES III AÑO 2010 B
100% albariño

94 Colour: bright yellow. Nose: characterful, complex, candied fruit, spicy. Palate: flavourful, ripe fruit, long.

BODEGAS EIDOSELA

Eidos de Abaixo, s/n - Sela
36494 Arbo (Pontevedra)
☎: +34 986 665 550 - Fax: +34 986 665 299
www.bodegaseidosela.com
info@bodegaseidosela.com

ARBASTRUM 2012 B
albariño, loureiro, treixadura

89 Colour: bright straw. Nose: fresh, fresh fruit, white flowers. Palate: flavourful, fruity, good acidity, balanced.

EIDOSELA 2012 B
100% albariño

91 Colour: bright straw. Nose: fresh, fresh fruit, white flowers. Palate: flavourful, fruity, good acidity, balanced.

EIDOSELA BURBUJAS DEL ATLÁNTICO 2012 ESP
100% albariño

88 Colour: bright straw. Nose: medium intensity, fresh fruit, dried herbs, fine lees, floral. Palate: fresh, fruity, flavourful, fine bitter notes.

ETRA ALBARIÑO 2012 B
100% albariño

90 Colour: bright straw. Nose: fresh fruit, white flowers. Palate: flavourful, fruity, good acidity, balanced.

BODEGAS ETHEREO

Arbo
36495 Arbo (Pontevedra)
☎: +34 626 833 060
www.bodegasethereo.com

ETHEREO 2012 B
100% albariño

88 Colour: bright straw. Nose: medium intensity, candied fruit. Palate: spicy, ripe fruit.

BODEGAS FILLABOA

Lugar de Fillaboa, s/n
36450 Salvaterra do Miño (Pontevedra)
☎: +34 986 658 132
www.bodegasfillaboa.com
info@bodegasfillaboa.masaveu.com

FILLABOA 2012 B
albariño

92 Colour: bright straw. Nose: fresh, fresh fruit, white flowers, mineral, grassy. Palate: flavourful, fruity, good acidity, fine bitter notes.

BODEGAS GERARDO MÉNDEZ

Galiñanes, 10 - Lores
36968 Meaño (Pontevedra)
☎: +34 986 747 046 - Fax: +34 986 748 915
www.bodegasgerardomendez.com
info@bodegasgerardomendez.com

ALBARIÑO DO FERREIRO 2012 B
100% albariño

92 Colour: bright straw. Nose: white flowers, fragrant herbs, fruit expression, mineral, balanced. Palate: fresh, flavourful, spicy, long, balsamic.

BODEGAS GÓMEZ Y RIAL

Piro, 15 - Oza
15886 Teo (A Coruña)
☎: +34 981 806 260
www.gomezrial.com
aagorial@yahoo.es

ALARGO 2011 B
albariño

88 Colour: bright straw. Nose: ripe fruit, candied fruit, citrus fruit. Palate: flavourful, fresh.

COMPOSTELAE 2011 B
100% albariño

89 Colour: bright straw. Nose: medium intensity, elegant, ripe fruit. Palate: flavourful, fruity, fresh.

BODEGAS LA CANA

Bartolome Esteban Murillo, 11 - Pol Ind La Pañoleta
29700 Vélez (Málaga)
☎: +34 952 504 706 - Fax: +34 951 284 796
www.lacana.es
info@jorgeordonez.es

LA CAÑA 2012 B
100% albariño

91 Colour: bright straw. Nose: floral, varietal, citrus fruit. Palate: balanced, good acidity, fine bitter notes.

BODEGAS LA VAL

Lugar Muguiña, s/n - Arantei
36458 Salvaterra de Miño (Pontevedra)
☎: +34 986 610 728 - Fax: +34 986 611 635
www.bodegaslaval.com
laval@bodegaslaval.com

FINCA ARANTEI 2012 B
albariño

90 Colour: bright straw. Nose: ripe fruit, fruit expression, grassy. Palate: flavourful, fruity, fresh, good acidity.

LA VAL ALBARIÑO 2010 BFB
100% albariño

90 Colour: bright yellow. Nose: powerfull, ripe fruit, sweet spices, creamy oak. Palate: rich, flavourful, good acidity.

LA VAL ALBARIÑO 2012 B
100% albariño

91 Colour: bright straw. Nose: fresh fruit, white flowers, varietal. Palate: flavourful, fruity, good acidity, balanced.

LA VAL CRIANZA SOBRE LÍAS 2005 BC
100% albariño

93 Colour: bright yellow. Nose: powerfull, ripe fruit, sweet spices, fragrant herbs. Palate: rich, flavourful, fresh, good acidity.

ORBALLO 2012 B
100% albariño

90 Colour: bright straw. Nose: citrus fruit, ripe fruit, fruit expression. Palate: flavourful, light-bodied, fruity.

TABOEXA 2012 B
100% albariño

90 Colour: bright straw. Nose: fresh fruit, white flowers, ripe fruit. Palate: flavourful, fruity, good acidity, balanced.

VIÑA LUDY 2012 B
100% albariño

90 Colour: bright straw. Nose: fresh, fresh fruit, white flowers, expressive. Palate: flavourful, fruity, good acidity, balanced.

BODEGAS MAR DE FRADES

Lg. Arosa, 16 - Finca Valiñas
36637 Meis (Pontevedra)
☎: +34 986 680 911 - Fax: +34 986 680 926
www.mardefrades.es
info@mardefrades.es

FINCA VALIÑAS "CRIANZA SOBRE LÍAS" 2012 B
albariño

93 Colour: bright yellow. Nose: fragrant herbs, candied fruit, ripe fruit, spicy, balanced. Palate: powerful, flavourful, long, good acidity, elegant.

MAR DE FRADES 2012 B
albariño

90 Colour: bright yellow. Nose: citrus fruit, ripe fruit, balsamic herbs, floral, expressive. Palate: rich, flavourful, fresh, fruity, balanced.

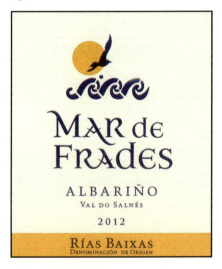

MAR DE FRADES S/C BN
100% albariño

88 Colour: bright straw. Nose: fresh fruit, dried herbs, fine lees, dried flowers, citrus fruit. Palate: fresh, fruity, flavourful, powerful.

BODEGAS MARQUÉS DE VIZHOJA

Finca La Moreira s/n
36438 Cequeliños Arbo (Pontevedra)
☎: +34 986 665 825 - Fax: +34 986 665 960
www.marquesdevizhoja.com
marquesdevizhoja@marquesdevizhoja.com

SEÑOR DA FOLLA VERDE 2012 B
70% albariño, 15% treixadura, 15% loureiro

88 Colour: bright straw. Nose: white flowers, ripe fruit, dried herbs, grassy. Palate: flavourful, fruity, fresh.

TORRE LA MOREIRA 2012 B
100% albariño

88 Colour: bright straw. Nose: ripe fruit, tropical fruit. Palate: good acidity, fine bitter notes, sweetness.

BODEGAS MARTÍN CÓDAX

Burgáns, 91
36633 Vilariño-Cambados (Pontevedra)
☎: +34 986 526 040 - Fax: +34 986 526 901
www.martincodax.com
comercial@martincodax.com

ALBA MARTÍN 2012 B
100% albariño

91 Colour: bright straw. Nose: ripe fruit, citrus fruit, grassy, balsamic herbs. Palate: flavourful, fresh, ripe fruit.

ANXO MARTÍN 2012 B
85% albariño, 10% caíño blanco, 5% loureiro

93 Colour: bright straw. Nose: fresh, fresh fruit, white flowers, expressive, mineral, grassy. Palate: flavourful, fruity, good acidity, balanced.

BURGÁNS 2012 B
100% albariño

89 Colour: bright straw. Nose: fresh, white flowers, ripe fruit. Palate: flavourful, fruity, good acidity, balanced.

MARIETA 2012 B
100% albariño

87 Colour: bright straw. Nose: medium intensity, white flowers, candied fruit, citrus fruit. Palate: flavourful, sweetness, good acidity.

MARTÍN CÓDAX 2012 B
100% albariño

90 Colour: bright straw. Nose: white flowers, characterful, varietal, ripe fruit. Palate: flavourful, fruity, good acidity, balanced.

MARTÍN CÓDAX GALLAECIA 2009 B
100% albariño

91 Colour: bright yellow. Nose: powerfull, ripe fruit, sweet spices, creamy oak. Palate: rich, flavourful, fresh, good acidity.

MARTIN CODAX LÍAS 2010 B
100% albariño

92 Colour: bright yellow. Nose: powerfull, ripe fruit, sweet spices, fragrant herbs. Palate: rich, flavourful, fresh, good acidity.

ORGANISTRUM 2010 B
100% albariño

90 Colour: bright straw. Nose: scrubland, candied fruit, powerfull. Palate: fine bitter notes, good acidity.

BODEGAS NANCLARES

Castriño - Castrelo, 13
36639 Cambados (Pontevedra)
☎: +34 986 520 763
www.bodegasnanclares.com
bodega@bodegasnanclares.es

ALBERTO NANCLARES SOBRE LÍAS 2011 B
100% albariño

90 Colour: bright yellow. Nose: candied fruit, citrus fruit, dried herbs. Palate: flavourful, sweetness, ripe fruit.

DANDELION 2011 B
100% albariño

87 Colour: bright straw. Nose: white flowers, fresh fruit, ripe fruit. Palate: flavourful, fruity, fresh, fine bitter notes.

SOVERRIBAS DE NANCLARES 2011 BFB
100% albariño

88 Colour: bright straw. Nose: ripe fruit, citrus fruit. Palate: flavourful, light-bodied, good acidity, fine bitter notes.

TEMPUS VIVENDI 2011 B
100% albariño

87 Colour: bright straw. Nose: candied fruit, citrus fruit, spicy, faded flowers. Palate: flavourful, easy to drink.

BODEGAS PABLO PADÍN

Ameiro, 24 - Dena
36967 Meaño (Pontevedra)
☎: +34 986 743 231 - Fax: +34 986 745 791
www.pablopadin.com

ALBARIÑO EIRAL 2012 B
100% albariño

88 Colour: bright straw. Nose: fresh, fresh fruit, white flowers. Palate: flavourful, fruity, balanced.

ALBARIÑO SEGREL 2012 B
100% albariño

88 Colour: bright straw. Nose: floral, ripe fruit, grassy. Palate: flavourful, fruity, fresh.

ALBARIÑO SEGREL ÁMBAR 2012 B
albariño

89 Colour: bright straw. Nose: fresh, white flowers, candied fruit, citrus fruit. Palate: flavourful, fruity, good acidity, balanced.

FEITIZO DA NOITE ESP
albariño

89 Colour: bright yellow. Nose: expressive, balanced, faded flowers. Palate: good acidity, correct.

BODEGAS SANTIAGO ROMA

Catariño, 5 - Besomaño
36636 Ribadumia (Pontevedra)
☎: +34 679 469 218
www.santiagoroma.com
bodega@santiagoroma.com

ALBARIÑO SANTIAGO ROMA 2012 B
albariño

91 Colour: bright yellow. Nose: dried flowers, wild herbs, citrus fruit, fruit expression. Palate: balanced, fresh, fruity, easy to drink.

ALBARIÑO SANTIAGO ROMA SELECCIÓN ALBARIÑO 2012 B
albariño

92 Colour: bright yellow. Nose: citrus fruit, tropical fruit, floral, balsamic herbs. Palate: powerful, flavourful, rich, long, balanced, elegant.

COLLEITA DE MARTIS ALBARIÑO 2012 B
albariño

90 Colour: bright straw. Nose: dried herbs, citrus fruit, fresh fruit, floral, fragrant herbs. Palate: fresh, fruity, flavourful, balanced.

BODEGAS SEÑORÍO DE VALEI

La Granja, s/n
36494 Arbo (Pontevedra)
☎: +34 698 146 950 - Fax: +34 986 665 390
www.bodegasenoriodevalei.com
info@bodegasenoriodevalei.com

JORGE PARIS 2012 B
100% albariño

90 Colour: bright straw. Nose: grassy, dried herbs, white flowers, fresh fruit. Palate: flavourful, fruity, varietal.

ORO VALEI 2012 B
100% albariño

88 Colour: bright straw. Nose: ripe fruit, dried flowers. Palate: flavourful, fruity, fine bitter notes.

PAZO DE VALEI 2012 B
albariño

91 Colour: bright straw. Nose: ripe fruit, dried herbs, floral. Palate: flavourful, fruity, fresh.

SEÑORÍO DE VALEI 2012 B
100% albariño

91 Colour: bright straw. Nose: fresh, fresh fruit, white flowers, citrus fruit. Palate: flavourful, fruity, good acidity, balanced.

BODEGAS TERRAS GAUDA

Ctra. Tui - A Guarda, Km. 55
36760 O´Rosal (Pontevedra)
☎: +34 986 621 001 - Fax: +34 986 621 084
www.terrasgauda.com
terrasgauda@terrasgauda.com

ABADÍA DE SAN CAMPIO 2012 B
100% albariño

90 Colour: bright straw. Nose: fresh, fresh fruit, white flowers, expressive. Palate: flavourful, fruity, good acidity, balanced.

LA MAR 2011 B
85% caíño blanco, 10% albariño, 5% loureiro

93 Colour: bright yellow. Nose: dried flowers, ripe fruit, wild herbs, dried herbs, earthy notes. Palate: powerful, flavourful, spicy, long, balanced.

TERRAS GAUDA 2012 B
70% albariño, 18% loureiro, 12% caíño blanco

92 Colour: bright yellow. Nose: floral, dried herbs, mineral, citrus fruit, ripe fruit, expressive. Palate: rich, flavourful, spicy, balsamic, round.

TERRAS GAUDA ETIQUETA NEGRA 2010 BFB
70% albariño, 20% loureiro, 10% caíño blanco

92 Colour: bright yellow. Nose: powerfull, ripe fruit, sweet spices, creamy oak, fragrant herbs. Palate: rich, smoky aftertaste, flavourful, fresh, good acidity.

BODEGAS VICENTE GANDÍA

Ctra. Cheste a Godelleta, s/n
46370 Chiva (Valencia)
☎: +34 962 524 242 - Fax: +34 962 524 243
www.vicentegandia.es
info@vicentegandia.com

CON UN PAR ALBARIÑO 2011 B
100% albariño

90 Colour: bright golden. Nose: citrus fruit, ripe fruit, dried flowers, fragrant herbs. Palate: powerful, flavourful, long, spicy, balanced, elegant.

BODEGAS VINUM TERRAE

Lugar de Axis - Simes, s/n
36968 Meaño (Pontevedra)
☎: +34 986 747 566 - Fax: +34 986 747 621
www.vinumterrae.com
pepa.formoso@vinumterrae.com

AGNUSDEI ALBARIÑO 2012 B
albariño

92 Colour: bright straw. Nose: fresh, fresh fruit, white flowers, citrus fruit. Palate: flavourful, fruity, good acidity, balanced.

YOU & ME WHITE EXPERIENCE 2012 B
albariño

91 Colour: bright straw. Nose: white flowers, candied fruit, fragrant herbs, expressive. Palate: fresh, fruity, flavourful, round.

BODEGAS Y VIÑEDOS DON OLEGARIO

Refoxos, s/n - Corbillón
36634 Cambados (Pontevedra)
☎: +34 986 520 886 - Fax: +34 986 520 886
www.donolegario.com
info@donolegario.com

DON OLEGARIO ALBARIÑO 2012 B
100% albariño

93 Colour: bright straw. Nose: citrus fruit, fresh fruit, white flowers, fragrant herbs, expressive. Palate: fresh, fruity, flavourful, balanced, elegant.

BOUZA DO REI

Lugar de Puxafeita, s/n
36636 Ribadumia (Pontevedra)
☎: +34 986 710 257 - Fax: +34 986 718 393
www.bouzadorei.com
bouzadorei@bouzadorei.com

ALBARIÑO BOUZA DO REI 2012 B
100% albariño

90 Colour: bright straw. Nose: fresh, white flowers, expressive, mineral. Palate: flavourful, fruity, good acidity, balanced.

BOUZA DO REI ALBARIÑO GRAN LAGAR 2012 B
100% albariño

88 Colour: bright straw. Nose: fresh, white flowers, candied fruit. Palate: flavourful, fruity, balanced.

BOUZA DO REI ALBARIÑO GRAN SELECCIÓN 2011 B
100% albariño

91 Colour: bright yellow. Nose: powerfull, citrus fruit, candied fruit, sweet spices, toasty. Palate: powerful, fine bitter notes, good acidity.

CASTEL DE BOUZA 2012 B
100% albariño

90 Colour: bright straw. Nose: fresh, fresh fruit, white flowers, grassy. Palate: flavourful, fruity, good acidity, balanced.

CAMPOS DE CELTAS

Avda. Diagonal, 590, 5º 1ª
8021 (Barcelona)
☎: +34 660 445 464
www.vinergia.com
vinergia@vinergia.com

CAMPOS DE CELTAS 2012 B
100% albariño

90 Colour: bright straw. Nose: fresh, fresh fruit, white flowers, grassy. Palate: flavourful, fruity, good acidity, balanced.

CARREFOUR

Campezo, 16
28022 Madrid (Madrid)
☎: +34 902 202 000
www.carrefour.es

SANTEIRO 2012 B
albariño

90 Colour: bright straw. Nose: fresh, fresh fruit, white flowers, varietal. Palate: flavourful, fruity, good acidity, balanced.

COMERCIAL GRUPO FREIXENET S.A.

Joan Sala, 2
8770 Sant Sadurní D'Anoia (Barcelona)
☎: +34 938 917 000 - Fax: +34 938 183 095
www.freixenet.es
freixenet@freixenet.es

VIONTA 2012 B
albariño

90 Colour: bright straw. Nose: fresh, fresh fruit, white flowers, grassy. Palate: flavourful, fruity, balanced.

COMPAÑIA DE VINOS TRICÓ

Rua A Caleira, 2 Bajo
36210 Vigo (Pontevedra)
☎: +34 637 507 311
j.lopez@espaciovital.es

NICOLAS 2010 B
100% albariño

93 Colour: bright straw. Nose: fresh fruit, white flowers, expressive, mineral, earthy notes. Palate: flavourful, fruity, good acidity, balanced.

TRICÓ 2010 B
100% albariño

92 Colour: bright straw. Nose: fresh fruit, white flowers, expressive, grassy, varietal. Palate: flavourful, fruity, good acidity, balanced.

COTO REDONDO

Bouza do Rato, s/n - Rubiós
36449 As Neves (Pontevedra)
☎: +34 986 667 212 - Fax: +34 986 648 279
www.bodegas-cotoredondo.com
info@bodegas-cotoredondo.com

MANUEL D'AMARO PEDRAL 2011 T
100% pedral

88 Colour: deep cherry. Nose: balsamic herbs, grassy, medium intensity. Palate: fruity, fresh.

SEÑORÍO DE RUBIÓS ALBARIÑO 2012 B
100% albariño

91 Colour: bright straw. Nose: fresh, fresh fruit, white flowers, characterful, varietal, grassy. Palate: flavourful, fruity, good acidity, balanced.

SEÑORÍO DE RUBIÓS CONDADO BLANCO 2011 ESP
treixadura, albariño, loureiro, godello, torrontés

90 Colour: bright straw. Nose: medium intensity, fresh fruit, dried herbs, fine lees, floral. Palate: fresh, fruity, flavourful, good acidity.

SEÑORÍO DE RUBIÓS CONDADO BLANCO DO TEA 2012 B
treixadura, albariño, loureiro, godello, torrontés

91 Colour: bright straw. Nose: fresh, fresh fruit, white flowers, complex. Palate: flavourful, fruity, good acidity, balanced.

SEÑORÍO DE RUBIÓS CONDADO DO TEA BARRICA 2010 B
treixadura, albariño, loureiro, godello, torrontés

90 Colour: bright straw. Nose: fresh, white flowers, expressive, sweet spices. Palate: flavourful, fruity, good acidity, balanced.

SEÑORÍO DE RUBIÓS CONDADO TINTO 2012 T
sousón, espadeiro, caíño, mencía, pedral, loureiro tinto

87 Colour: cherry, purple rim. Nose: reduction notes, red berry notes. Palate: flavourful, fruity, good acidity, round tannins.

SEÑORÍO DE RUBIÓS MENCÍA 2012 T
100% mencía

88 Colour: cherry, purple rim. Nose: red berry notes, floral, balsamic herbs, grassy. Palate: flavourful, fruity, good acidity, round tannins.

SEÑORÍO DE RUBIÓS SOUSÓN 2011 T
100% sousón

89 Colour: cherry, purple rim. Nose: floral, overripe fruit. Palate: flavourful, fruity, round tannins.

SEÑORÍO DE RUBIÓS VINO NOVO 2012 T MACERACIÓN CARBÓNICA
sousón, espadeiro, caíño, mencía, pedral, loureiro tinto.

90 Colour: deep cherry. Nose: fruit expression, balsamic herbs, scrubland. Palate: flavourful, fine bitter notes.

DOS DE UVAS

Campo das Fontes, Lg. de Teizosas
36880 A Cañiza (Pontevedra)

TABLA DE SUMAR 2011 B
albariño

90 Colour: bright straw. Nose: white flowers, ripe fruit, grassy. Palate: flavourful, fruity, fresh.

EL ESCOCÉS VOLANTE

Barrio La Rosa Bajo, 16
50300 Calatayud (Zaragoza)
☎: +34 637 511 133
www.escocesvolante.es
info@escocesvolante.es

THE CUP AND RINGS ALBARIÑO SOBRE LÍAS 2011 B
100% albariño

92 Colour: bright yellow. Nose: citrus fruit, ripe fruit, balsamic herbs, floral, mineral, balanced. Palate: powerful, flavourful, spicy, long.

JOSÉ CARLOS QUINTAS PÉREZ

Fonte, 20 Quintela
36492 Crecente (Pontevedra)
☎: +34 639 630 050 - Fax: +34 986 267 145
www.oreidecampoverde.es
quintas.aviso@gmail.com

DAINSUA 2012 B
albariño, loureiro, treixadura

84

O REI DE CAMPOVERDE 2012 B
100% albariño

89 Colour: bright straw. Nose: medium intensity, fresh fruit, dried herbs. Palate: flavourful, fruity, fresh.

KATAME

Berlin, 5 1ºC
28850 Torrejón de Ardo (Madrid)
☎: +34 916 749 427
katame@katamesl.com

PEKADO MORTAL 2011 B
albariño

91 Colour: bright straw. Nose: white flowers, characterful, complex. Palate: flavourful, fruity, good acidity, balanced.

LAGAR DE BESADA

Pazo, 11
36968 Xil-Meaño (Pontevedra)
☎: +34 986 747 473 - Fax: +34 986 747 826
www.lagardebesada.com
info@lagardebesada.com

AÑADA DE BALADIÑA 2006 B
100% albariño

90 Colour: bright yellow. Nose: closed, characterful, candied fruit, citrus fruit. Palate: fine bitter notes, ripe fruit, long.

BALADIÑA 2011 B
100% albariño

90 Colour: bright straw. Nose: candied fruit, fruit expression, citrus fruit, grassy. Palate: flavourful, fresh, good acidity.

LAGAR DE BESADA 2012 B
100% albariño

88 Colour: bright straw. Nose: fresh fruit, ripe fruit, citrus fruit. Palate: light-bodied, fresh.

LAGAR DE CERVERA

Estrada de Loureza, 86
36770 O Rosal (Pontevedra)
☎: +34 986 625 875 - Fax: +34 986 625 011
www.riojalta.com
lagar@riojalta.com

LAGAR DE CERVERA 2012 B
100% albariño

92 Colour: bright straw. Nose: fresh, white flowers, varietal, candied fruit, ripe fruit. Palate: flavourful, fruity, good acidity, balanced.

LUAR DE MINARELLOS

Plaza de Matute 12
28012 (Madrid)
☎: +34 609 119 248
www.miravinos.es
info@miravinos.es

MINARELLOS 2011 B
albariño

92 Colour: bright straw. Nose: fresh, fresh fruit, white flowers, varietal. Palate: flavourful, fruity, good acidity, balanced.

M. CONSTANTINA SOTELO ARES

Castelo Castriño,
36639 Cambados (Pontevedra)
☎: +34 639 835 073
adegasotelo@yahoo.es

ADEGA SOTELO 2012 B
albariño

88 Colour: bright straw. Nose: ripe fruit, fruit expression. Palate: flavourful, fruity, fresh.

ROSALÍA 2012 B
albariño

90 Colour: bright straw. Nose: ripe fruit, citrus fruit, grassy. Palate: flavourful, fruity, fresh.

ROSALÍA DE CASTRO 2012 B
albariño

91 Colour: bright straw. Nose: fresh, fresh fruit, white flowers, expressive, grassy, varietal. Palate: flavourful, fruity, good acidity, balanced.

MAIOR DE MENDOZA

Rúa de Xiabre, 58
36600 Villagarcía de Arosa (Pontevedra)
☎: +34 986 508 896 - Fax: +34 986 507 924
www.maiordemendoza.com
maiordemendoza@hotmail.es

FULGET 2012 B
100% albariño

89 Colour: bright straw. Nose: candied fruit, citrus fruit. Palate: flavourful, fruity, fresh.

MAIOR DE MENDOZA 2012 B
100% albariño

89 Colour: bright straw. Nose: fresh, white flowers, candied fruit. Palate: flavurful, fruity, good acidity, balanced.

MAIOR DE MENDOZA 3 CRIANZAS 2010 B
100% albariño

91 Colour: bright yellow. Nose: powerfull, ripe fruit, sweet spices, fragrant herbs. Palate: rich, flavourful, fresh, good acidity.

MAIOR DE MENDOZA MACERACIÓN CARBÓNICA 2012 B MACERACIÓN CARBÓNICA
100% albariño

87 Colour: bright straw. Nose: dried herbs, medium intensity. Palate: flavourful, fruity, fresh.

MAR DE ENVERO

Lugar Quintáns, 17
36638 Ribadumia (Pontevedra)
☎: +34 981 577 083 - Fax: +34 981 569 552
www.mardeenvero.es
bodega@mardeenvero.es

MAR DE ENVERO 2011 B
albariño

92 Colour: bright yellow. Nose: citrus fruit, ripe fruit, dried flowers, sweet spices, balsamic herbs. Palate: powerful, rich, flavourful, long, balanced.

TROUPE 2012 B
albariño

90 Colour: bright straw. Nose: citrus fruit, white flowers, fragrant herbs, mineral. Palate: fresh, fruity, easy to drink, elegant.

MIGUEL TORRES S.A.

Miguel Torres i Carbó, 6
8720 Vilafranca del Penedès (Barcelona)
☎: +34 938 177 400 - Fax: +34 938 177 444
www.torres.es
mailadmin@torres.es

PAZO DAS BRUXAS 2012 B
100% albariño

90 Colour: bright straw. Nose: expressive, ripe fruit, fruit expression, mineral. Palate: flavourful, fruity, fresh.

ORO WINES

Ctra. de Fuentealamo - Paraje de la Aragona
30520 Jumilla (Murcia)
☎: +34 968 435 022 - Fax: +34 968 716 051
www.orowines.com
info@orowines.com

KENTIA 2012 B
100% albariño

90 Colour: bright straw. Nose: ripe fruit, citrus fruit, white flowers. Palate: ripe fruit, long, good acidity, varietal.

PACO & LOLA

Valdamor, 18 - XII
36968 Meaño (Pontevedra)
☎: +34 986 747 779 - Fax: +34 986 748 940
www.pacolola.com
internacional@pacolola.com

FOLLAS NOVAS 2012 B
albariño

90 Colour: bright yellow. Nose: fresh, fresh fruit, white flowers, wild herbs. Palate: flavourful, fruity, good acidity, balanced.

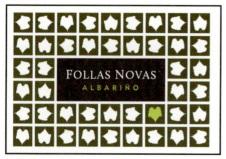

IWINE 2011 B
albariño

90 Colour: bright straw. Nose: floral, wild herbs, balsamic herbs, fruit expression, mineral. Palate: rich, powerful, flavourful, balanced, elegant.

LOLO 2012 B
albariño

89 Colour: bright yellow. Nose: ripe fruit, white flowers, wild herbs. Palate: fresh, fruity, easy to drink.

OPHALUM 2012 B
albariño

89 Colour: bright yellow. Nose: white flowers, balsamic herbs, citrus fruit, ripe fruit. Palate: balanced, fresh, fruity, easy to drink.

PACO & LOLA 2012 B
albariño

93 Colour: bright yellow. Nose: citrus fruit, fruit expression, fragrant herbs, mineral, expressive. Palate: balanced, elegant, flavourful, spicy, rich, long.

PAZO BAIÓN

Abelleira 4, 5, 6 - Baión
36614 Vilanova de Arousa (Pontevedra)
☎: +34 986 543 535 - Fax: +34 986 524 251
www.pazobaion.com
info@pazobaion.com

PAZO BAIÓN 2011 B
100% albariño

92 Colour: bright straw. Nose: mineral, fresh fruit, ripe fruit, floral, dried herbs. Palate: flavourful, light-bodied, fruity, good acidity.

PAZO DE BARRANTES

Finca Pazo de Barrantes
36636 Barrantes (Pontevedra)
☎: +34 986 718 211 - Fax: +34 986 710 424
www.pazodebarrantes.com
bodega@pazodebarrantes.com

LA COMTESSE 2009 B
100% albariño

94 Colour: bright yellow. Nose: powerfull, ripe fruit, sweet spices, creamy oak, fragrant herbs. Palate: rich, smoky aftertaste, flavourful, fresh, good acidity.

LA COMTESSE 2010 B
100% albariño

95 Colour: bright yellow. Nose: powerfull, ripe fruit, sweet spices, fragrant herbs. Palate: rich, flavourful, fresh, good acidity, roasted-coffee aftertaste.

PAZO DE BARRANTES ALBARIÑO 2012 B
100% albariño

92 Colour: bright straw. Nose: ripe fruit, mineral, grassy. Palate: flavourful, fruity, fresh, fine bitter notes.

PAZO DE SAN MAURO

Pombal, 3 - Lugar de Porto
36458 Salvaterra de Miño (Pontevedra)
☎: +34 986 658 285 - Fax: +34 986 664 208
www.marquesdevargas.com
info@pazosanmauro.com

PAZO SAN MAURO 2012 B
100% albariño

91 Colour: bright straw. Nose: fresh, fresh fruit, white flowers, expressive. Palate: flavourful, fruity, good acidity, balanced.

SANAMARO 2010 B
albariño, loureiro

89 Colour: bright straw. Nose: medium intensity, candied fruit, citrus fruit. Palate: good acidity, spicy, ripe fruit.

PAZO DE SEÑORANS

Vilanoviña, s/n
36616 Meis (Pontevedra)
☎: +34 986 715 373 - Fax: +34 986 715 569
www.pazodesenorans.com
info@pazodesenorans.com

PAZO SEÑORANS 2012 B
100% albariño

93 Colour: bright yellow. Nose: dried flowers, citrus fruit, ripe fruit, fragrant herbs, expressive, elegant. Palate: powerful, flavourful, spicy, long, balsamic.

PAZO SEÑORANS SELECCIÓN DE AÑADA 2006 B
100% albariño

95 Colour: bright yellow. Nose: powerfull, ripe fruit, sweet spices, fragrant herbs, mineral. Palate: rich, smoky aftertaste, flavourful, fresh, good acidity.

PAZO DE VILLAREI

Arousa San Martiño
36637 Meis (Pontevedra)
☎: +34 986 710 827 - Fax: +34 986 710 827
www.domecqbodegas.com
info@hgabodegas.com

ABADÍA DO SEIXO 2012 B
100% albariño

89 Colour: bright straw. Nose: fresh fruit, white flowers, grassy. Palate: flavourful, fruity, good acidity, balanced.

PAZO DE VILLAREI 2012 B
100% albariño

90 Colour: bright straw. Nose: powerfull, candied fruit, citrus fruit, dried herbs. Palate: powerful, flavourful, sweetness.

PAZO PONDAL

Coto, s/n - Cabeiras
36436 Arbo (Pontevedra)
☎: +34 986 665 551 - Fax: +34 986 665 949
www.pazopondal.com
info@pazopondal.com

LEIRA 2012 B
100% albariño

89 Colour: bright straw. Nose: white flowers, ripe fruit. Palate: flavourful, fruity, good acidity, balanced.

LENDA 2012 B
albariño

86 Colour: bright straw. Nose: candied fruit, citrus fruit, cocoa bean. Palate: flavourful, sweetness, fine bitter notes, good acidity.

PAZO PONDAL ALBARIÑO 2012 B
100% albariño

88 Colour: bright straw. Nose: fresh, white flowers, ripe fruit. Palate: flavourful, fruity, good acidity, balanced.

QUINTA COUSELO

Barrio de Couselo, 13
36770 O'Rosal (Pontevedra)
☎: +34 986 625 051 - Fax: +34 986 626 267
www.quintacouselo.com
quintacouselo@quintacouselo.com

QUINTA DE COUSELO 2012 B
albariño, loureiro, caíño

90 Colour: bright straw. Nose: fresh, fresh fruit, white flowers, fragrant herbs. Palate: flavourful, fruity, good acidity.

RECTORAL DO UMIA

Plg. de Rua do Pan, 9
36636 Ribadumia (Pontevedra)
☎: +34 986 716 360 - Fax: +34 986 718 252
www.rectoraldoumia.com
jmanuel@rectoraldoumia.com

MIUDIÑO 2012 B
albariño

89 Colour: bright straw. Nose: fresh fruit, white flowers, varietal. Palate: flavourful, fruity, good acidity, balanced.

RECTORAL DO UMIA 2012 B
albariño

89 Colour: bright straw. Nose: fresh, fresh fruit, white flowers, expressive. Palate: flavourful, fruity, good acidity, balanced.

RED BOTTLE INTERNATIONAL

Rosales, 6
9400 Aranda de Duero (Burgos)
☎: +34 947 515 884 - Fax: +34 947 515 886
www.redbottleint.com
rbi@redbottleint.com

ELAS 2012 B
100% albariño

90 Colour: bright straw. Nose: fresh fruit, white flowers, varietal, ripe fruit, citrus fruit. Palate: flavourful, fruity, balanced.

SANTIAGO RUIZ

Rua do Vinicultor Santiago Ruiz
36760 San Miguel de Tabagón - O Rosal (Pontevedra)
☎: +34 986 614 083 - Fax: +34 986 614 142
www.bodegasantiagoruiz.com
info@bodegasantiagoruiz.com

SANTIAGO RUIZ 2012 B
70% albariño, 10% loureiro, 10% godello, caíño blanco, 10% treixadura

91 Colour: bright straw. Nose: fresh, fresh fruit, white flowers, expressive. Palate: flavourful, fruity, good acidity, balanced.

TERRA DE ASOREI

San Francisco, 2 - 1º C-D
36630 Cambados (Pontevedra)
☎: +34 986 198 882 - Fax: +34 986 520 813
www.terradeasorei.com
info@terradeasorei.com

NAI E SEÑORA 2012 B
100% albariño

90 Colour: bright straw. Nose: expressive, ripe fruit, citrus fruit, grassy. Palate: flavourful, fruity, fresh.

PAZO TORRADO 2012 B
100% albariño

88 Colour: straw. Nose: medium intensity, ripe fruit, citrus fruit, dried herbs. Palate: flavourful, fruity, fresh.

TERRA DE ASOREI 2012 B
100% albariño

89 Colour: bright straw. Nose: fresh, fresh fruit, white flowers. Palate: flavourful, fruity, good acidity, balanced.

TOMADA DE CASTRO

Travesía do Freixo, 3
36636 Ribadumia (Pontevedra)
☎: +34 986 710 550 - Fax: +34 986 718 552
www.tomadadecastro.com
info@tomadadecastro.com

RÍA DE AROSA 2012 B
100% albariño

89 Colour: bright straw. Nose: medium intensity, white flowers, fresh fruit. Palate: flavourful, fruity, fresh.

TOMADA DE CASTRO 2012 B
100% albariño

87 Colour: bright straw. Nose: mineral, fresh fruit, ripe fruit. Palate: flavourful, fruity, fresh.

UVAS FELICES

Agullers, 7
8003 Barcelona (Barcelona)
☎: +34 902 327 777
www.vilaviniteca.es

EL JARDÍN DE LUCIA 2012 B
albariño

90 Colour: bright straw. Nose: fresh, fresh fruit, white flowers. Palate: flavourful, fruity, good acidity, balanced.

LA LOCOMOTORA 2009 TC

90 Colour: cherry, garnet rim. Nose: ripe fruit, spicy, toasty. Palate: powerful, flavourful, toasty, round tannins.

VEIGA NAÚM

Villarreis, 21 - Dena
36967 Meaño (Pontevedra)
☎: +34 941 454 050 - Fax: +34 941 454 529
www.bodegasriojanas.com
bodega@bodegasriojanas.com

VEIGA NAÚM 2012 B
100% albariño

87 Colour: bright straw. Nose: tropical fruit, floral, wild herbs. Palate: fresh, fruity, easy to drink.

VIÑA ALMIRANTE

Peroxa, 5
36658 Portas (Pontevedra)
☎: +34 620 294 293 - Fax: +34 986 541 471
www.vinaalmirante.com
info@vinaalmirante.com

PIONERO MACCERATO 2012 B
100% albariño

90 Colour: bright straw. Nose: fresh fruit, white flowers, grassy, characterful. Palate: flavourful, fruity, good acidity, balanced.

PIONERO MUNDI 2012 B
100% albariño

90 Colour: bright straw. Nose: fresh, white flowers. Palate: flavourful, fruity, good acidity, balanced.

VANIDADE 2012 B
100% albariño

89 Colour: bright straw. Nose: candied fruit, citrus fruit, powerfull. Palate: flavourful, fruity, fresh.

VIÑA CARTIN

Baceiro, 1 - Lantaño
36657 Portas (Pontevedra)
☎: +34 615 646 442
www.terrasdelantano.com
bodegas@montino.es

TERRAS DE LANTAÑO 2012 B
100% albariño

92 Colour: bright straw. Nose: white flowers, fragrant herbs, fruit expression, mineral. Palate: fresh, fruity, flavourful, rich, balanced, elegant.

VIÑA CARTIN 2012 B
100% albariño

90 Colour: bright straw. Nose: fresh, fresh fruit, white flowers, expressive. Palate: flavourful, fruity, good acidity, balanced.

VIÑA NORA

Bruñeiras, 7
36440 As Neves (Pontevedra)
☎: +34 986 667 210
www.vinanora.com
info@vinanora.com

NORA 2012 B
100% albariño

92 Colour: bright straw. Nose: fresh, fresh fruit, white flowers, characterful, varietal. Palate: flavourful, fruity, good acidity, balanced.

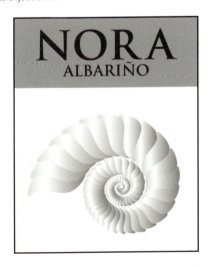

NORA DA NEVE 2010 BFB
100% albariño

95 Colour: bright yellow. Nose: powerfull, ripe fruit, sweet spices, creamy oak, fragrant herbs, mineral. Palate: rich, smoky aftertaste, flavourful, fresh, good acidity.

VAL DE NORA 2012 B
100% albariño

90 Colour: bright straw. Nose: fresh, fresh fruit, white flowers, varietal. Palate: flavourful, fruity, good acidity, balanced.

VIÑEDOS SINGULARES

Cuzco, 26 - 28, Nave 8
8030 (Barcelona)
☎: +34 609 168 191 - Fax: +34 934 807 076
www.vinedossingulares.com
info@vinedossingulares.com

LUNA CRECIENTE 2012 B
albariño

90 Colour: bright straw. Nose: fresh, fresh fruit, white flowers, expressive. Palate: flavourful, fruity, good acidity, balanced.

ZÁRATE

Bouza, 23 -
36638 Padrenda - Meaño (Pontevedra)
☎: +34 986 718 503 - Fax: +34 986 718 549
www.albarino-zarate.com
info@zarate.es

ZÁRATE 2012 B
albariño

90 Colour: bright straw, greenish rim. Nose: balanced, varietal, expressive, floral. Palate: flavourful, full, fruity, good acidity.

ZÁRATE CAIÑO TINTO 2011 T
caiño

88 Colour: deep cherry. Nose: scrubland, balsamic herbs, ripe fruit. Palate: lacks balance, slightly acidic, powerful.

ZÁRATE EL BALADO 2011 B
albariño

93 Colour: bright straw. Nose: white flowers, fresh fruit, citrus fruit, dried herbs. Palate: flavourful, fruity, fresh, good acidity.

ZÁRATE EL PALOMAR 2011 BFB
albariño

92 Colour: bright yellow. Nose: powerfull, ripe fruit, sweet spices, floral, earthy notes. Palate: rich, smoky aftertaste, flavourful, fresh, good acidity.

ZÁRATE ESPADEIRO TINTO 2011 T
espadeiro

92 Colour: deep cherry. Nose: powerfull, expressive, scrubland, balsamic herbs. Palate: ripe fruit, spicy, balsamic. Personality.

ZÁRATE LOUREIRO TINTO 2011 T
loureiro tinto

90 Colour: deep cherry, purple rim. Nose: balanced, medium intensity, ripe fruit, balsamic herbs. Palate: balanced, good acidity, round tannins.

ZÁRATE TRAS DA VIÑA 2009 B
albariño

93 Colour: bright straw. Nose: powerfull, ripe fruit, citrus fruit. Palate: flavourful, fruity, fine bitter notes, long.

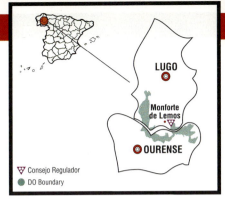

Consejo Regulador
DO Boundary

LOCATION:

The region extends along the banks of the rivers Miño and Sil in the south of the province of Lugo and the northern region of the province of Orense; it is made up of 17 municipal districts in this region.

CLIMATE:

Quite variable depending on the specific area. Less rain and slightly cooler climate and greater Continental influence in the Sil valley, and greater Atlantic character in the Miño valley. Altitude, on the other hand, also has an effect, with the vineyards closer to the rivers and with a more favourable orientation (south-southeast) being slightly warmer.

SOIL:

In general, the soil is highly acidic, although the composition varies greatly from one area to another. The vineyards are located on steep terraces and are no higher than 400 m to 500 m above sea level.

GRAPE VARIETIES:

WHITE: *Albariño, Loureira, Treixadura, Godello, Dona Blanca* and *Torrontés*.
RED: Main: *Mencía, Brancellao Merenzao, Garnacha Tintorera, Tempranillo, Sausón, Caiño Tinto* and *Mouratón*.

SUB-REGIONS:

Amandi, Chantada, Quiroga-Bibei, Ribeiras do Miño (in the province of Lugo) and **Ribeiras do Sil**.

FIGURES:

Vineyard surface: 1.263 – **Wine-Growers:** 2.964 – **Wineries:** 96 – **2012 Harvest rating:** Very Good **Production:** 5.452.206 litres – **Market percentages:** 90% domestic. 10% export

CONSEJO REGULADOR
Rúa do Comercio, 6-8 - 27400 Monforte de Lemos (Lugo) ☎: +34 982 410 968 - Fax: +34 982 411 265
info@ribeirasacra.org   www.ribeirasacra.org

ADEGA CRUCEIRO

Vilachá de Doade, 140
27424 Sober (Lugo)
☎: +34 982 152 285
www.adegacruceiro.es
info@adegacruceiro.es

CRUCEIRO 2012 T
mencía, merenzao

90 Colour: cherry, purple rim. Nose: red berry notes, floral, fragrant herbs, ripe fruit. Palate: flavourful, fruity, good acidity, round tannins.

CRUCEIRO REXIO 2010 T
mencía, albarello, caiño

88 Colour: cherry, garnet rim. Nose: ripe fruit, spicy, toasty, balsamic herbs, scrubland. Palate: powerful, flavourful, toasty, round tannins.

ADEGA DON RAMÓN

Rubín - Rozabales, 3
27413 Monforte de Lemos (Lugo)
☎: +34 982 404 237
donramonsl@gmail.com

DON RAMÓN 2012 B

87 Colour: bright straw. Nose: medium intensity, fresh fruit, grassy. Palate: light-bodied, flavourful.

DON RAMÓN MENCÍA 2012 T
mencía

87 Colour: deep cherry. Nose: varietal, ripe fruit, scrubland. Palate: flavourful, spicy, ripe fruit.

ADEGAS CONDADO DE SEQUEIRAS

Sequeiras, 1 - Camporramiro
27514 Chantada (Lugo)
☎: +34 982 446 238 - Fax: +34 944 120 227
www.condadodesequeiras.com
condadodesequeiras@grupopeago.com

CONDADO DE SEQUEIRAS 2010 T BARRICA
100% mencía

87 Colour: bright cherry. Nose: ripe fruit, sweet spices, roasted coffee. Palate: flavourful, fruity, toasty, round tannins.

CONDADO DE SEQUEIRAS 2011 T
100% mencía

86 Colour: bright cherry. Nose: scrubland, sulphur notes, characterful, candied fruit. Palate: fine bitter notes, good acidity.

CONDADO DE SEQUEIRAS 2012 B
godello, treixadura

88 Colour: bright straw. Nose: fresh, fresh fruit, white flowers. Palate: flavourful, fruity, good acidity, balanced.

ADEGAS MOURE

Avda. Buenos Aires, 12
27540 Escairón (Lugo)
☎: +34 982 452 031 - Fax: +34 982 452 700
www.adegasmoure.com
abadiadacova@adegasmoure.com

A FUGA 2012 T
mencía

86 Colour: bright cherry. Nose: medium intensity, ripe fruit, red berry notes. Palate: flavourful, fruity, fresh.

ABADÍA DA COVA 2011 T BARRICA
100% mencía

92 Colour: bright cherry. Nose: ripe fruit, sweet spices, creamy oak, expressive, mineral, balsamic herbs. Palate: flavourful, fruity, toasty, round tannins.

ABADÍA DA COVA 2012 B
85% albariño, 15% godello

91 Colour: bright straw. Nose: white flowers, expressive, characterful, ripe fruit. Palate: flavourful, fruity, good acidity, balanced.

ABADÍA DA COVA 2012 T BARRICA
mencía

92 Colour: bright cherry. Nose: ripe fruit, sweet spices, creamy oak, scrubland, characterful. Palate: flavourful, fruity, toasty, round tannins.

ABADÍA DA COVA DE AUTOR 2011 T
100% mencía

93 Colour: bright cherry. Nose: ripe fruit, fruit expression, balsamic herbs, scrubland. Palate: flavourful, fruity, toasty, round tannins.

ABADÍA DA COVA DE AUTOR MAGNUM 2012 T
100% mencía

95 Colour: cherry, garnet rim. Nose: ripe fruit, spicy, creamy oak, toasty, characterful, powerfull. Palate: powerful, flavourful, toasty, round tannins.

ABADÍA DA COVA MENCÍA 2012 T
mencía

90 Colour: cherry, purple rim. Nose: red berry notes, floral, characterful, varietal, ripe fruit. Palate: flavourful, fruity, good acidity, round tannins.

CEPA VELLA 2012 T
mencía

87 Colour: cherry, purple rim. Nose: red berry notes, floral, ripe fruit. Palate: flavourful, fruity, round tannins.

ADEGAS SAN JOSÉ

Santa Mariña - Eiré
27439 Pantón (Lugo)
☎: +34 982 456 545 - Fax: +34 982 456 697
www.adegassanjose.com
info@adegassanjose.com

FINCA CUARTA 2011 T
100% mencía

91 Colour: deep cherry. Nose: ripe fruit, toasty, spicy. Palate: powerful, spicy, ripe fruit.

FINCA CUARTA 2012 B
godello

88 Colour: bright straw. Nose: fresh, white flowers, ripe fruit, citrus fruit. Palate: flavourful, fruity, good acidity, balanced.

ALGUEIRA

Doade, s/n
27424 Sober (Lugo)
☎: +34 982 410 290 - Fax: +34 982 410 299
www.algueira.com
info@algueira.com

ALGUEIRA BRANCELLAO 2010 T ROBLE
100% brancellao

94 Colour: deep cherry. Nose: floral, balsamic herbs, scrubland, spicy. Palate: light-bodied, fresh, flavourful, balsamic.

ALGUEIRA CARRAVEL 2009 T
mencía

93 Colour: cherry, garnet rim. Nose: ripe fruit, spicy, toasty, complex, mineral, balsamic herbs, scrubland. Palate: powerful, flavourful, toasty, round tannins.

ALGUEIRA CORTEZADA 2011 B
godello, albariño, treixadura

91 Colour: bright straw. Nose: expressive, ripe fruit, citrus fruit, spicy. Palate: flavourful, fruity, sweetness.

ALGUEIRA ESCALADA 2011 B
godello

92 Colour: bright yellow. Nose: powerfull, sweet spices, fragrant herbs, candied fruit. Palate: rich, flavourful, fresh, good acidity.

ALGUEIRA FINCAS 2010 T ROBLE
caiño, sousón

93 Colour: bright cherry. Nose: balsamic herbs, scrubland, fruit expression, candied fruit. Palate: good acidity, fine bitter notes, elegant.

ALGUEIRA MADIALEVA MAGNUM 2011 T
garnacha

90 Colour: dark-red cherry. Nose: powerfull, ripe fruit, fruit preserve, spicy. Palate: powerful, flavourful, concentrated.

ALGUEIRA MENCÍA 2012 T
mencía

89 Colour: very deep cherry. Nose: powerfull, varietal, characterful, earthy notes, ripe fruit. Palate: good acidity, fine bitter notes, powerful.

ALGUEIRA MERENZAO 2011 T ROBLE
100% merenzao

93 Colour: bright cherry. Nose: ripe fruit, creamy oak, expressive, balsamic herbs, scrubland. Palate: flavourful, fruity, toasty, round tannins.

ALGUEIRA PIZARRA 2010 T ROBLE
mencía

93 Colour: bright cherry. Nose: ripe fruit, sweet spices, creamy oak, expressive, mineral, balsamic herbs. Palate: flavourful, fruity, toasty, round tannins.

BRANDÁN GODELLO 2012 B
godello

88 Colour: bright straw. Nose: floral, medium intensity, grassy. Palate: flavourful, fruity, fresh.

BODEGA CASTRO BAROÑA

Cabeiro - San Martín
36637 Meis (Pontevedra)
☎: +34 981 134 847 - Fax: +34 981 174 030
www.castrobarona.com
castrobarona@castrobarona.com

PAZO DE BEXÁN 2012 T
100% mencía

88 Colour: cherry, purple rim. Nose: floral, fruit expression. Palate: flavourful, fruity, good acidity, round tannins.

BODEGA RECTORAL DE AMANDI

Santa Cruz de Arrabaldo, 49
32990 Ourense
☎: +34 988 384 200 - Fax: +34 988 384 068
www.bodegasgallegas.com
sonia@bodegasgallegas.com

RECTORAL DE AMANDI 2012 T
100% mencía

90 Colour: cherry, purple rim. Nose: ripe fruit, fruit expression. Palate: flavourful, fruity, good acidity.

BODEGA VICTORINO ÁLVAREZ

Lugar Os Vazquez, s/n
32765 A Teixeira (Ourense)
☎: +34 988 207 418
adegasollio@yahoo.es

SOLLIO GODELLO 2012 B
100% godello

89 Colour: bright straw. Nose: fresh, white flowers, expressive, grassy. Palate: flavourful, fruity, good acidity, balanced.

SOLLÍO MENCÍA 2012 T
90% mencía, 10% brancellao

88 Colour: very deep cherry. Nose: warm, ripe fruit, medium intensity. Palate: flavourful, powerful, fruity.

BODEGAS ALBAMAR

O Adro, 11 - Castrelo
36639 Cambados (Pontevedra)
☎: +34 660 292 750 - Fax: +34 986 520 048
info@bodegasalbamar.com

FUSCO 2012 T
mencía

89 Colour: cherry, garnet rim. Nose: violet drops, sweet spices, ripe fruit, candied fruit, mineral. Palate: fruity, good acidity, balanced.

CARLOS DÍAZ DIAZ

Vilachá - Doabe
27424 Sober (Lugo)
☎: +34 982 152 425

ESTRELA 2012 T
mencía

88 Colour: cherry, purple rim. Nose: red berry notes, ripe fruit. Palate: flavourful, fruity, good acidity, round tannins, fine bitter notes.

CASA MOREIRAS

San Martín de Siós, s/n
27430 Pantón (Pontevedra)
☎: +34 982 456 129 - Fax: +34 982 456 129
www.casamoreiras.com
bodega@casamoreiras.com

CASA MOREIRAS 2012 B
godello, albariño

88 Colour: bright straw. Nose: fresh, fresh fruit, white flowers, expressive. Palate: flavourful, fruity, good acidity, balanced.

CASA MOREIRAS 2012 T
mencía, tempranillo, sousón

88 Colour: cherry, purple rim. Nose: red berry notes, powerfull, ripe fruit. Palate: flavourful, fruity, round tannins.

DOMINIO DO BIBEI

Langullo, s/n
32781 Manzaneda (Ourense)
☎: +34 670 704 028 - Fax: +34 988 269 053
www.dominiododobibei.com
info@dominiododobibei.com

DOMINIO DO BIBEI B 2010 T
100% brancellao

96 Colour: bright cherry. Nose: complex, expressive, raspberry, macerated fruit, ripe fruit, balsamic herbs, wild herbs. Palate: full, elegant, ripe fruit, long, fine tannins.

LACIMA 2010 T
100% mencía

94 Colour: bright cherry. Nose: scrubland, balsamic herbs, red berry notes, mineral. Palate: flavourful, fruity, fresh, good acidity.

LALAMA 2010 T
mencía, brancellao, mouratón, sousón, garnacha tintorera

92 Colour: deep cherry. Nose: red berry notes, faded flowers, fragrant herbs. Palate: flavourful, spicy, ripe fruit.

LAPENA 2010 B
100% godello

94 Colour: bright yellow. Nose: powerfull, ripe fruit, sweet spices, creamy oak, balsamic herbs. Palate: rich, smoky aftertaste, flavourful, fresh, good acidity.

LAPOLA 2011 B
godello, albariño, dona blanca

92 Colour: bright straw. Nose: powerfull, candied fruit, citrus fruit, faded flowers. Palate: flavourful, spicy, ripe fruit.

DON BERNARDINO

Santa Cruz de Brosmos, 9
27425 Sober (Lugo)
☎: +34 670 882 449 - Fax: +34 982 403 600
www.donbernardino.com
info@donbernardino.com

DON BERNARDINO 2010 T BARRICA
mencía

90 Colour: bright cherry. Nose: ripe fruit, sweet spices, expressive, red berry notes, fruit expression. Palate: flavourful, fruity, toasty, round tannins.

DON BERNARDINO 2012 T
mencía

90 Colour: cherry, purple rim. Nose: expressive, fresh fruit, red berry notes, floral. Palate: flavourful, fruity, good acidity, round tannins.

ENVINATE

Gran Vía, 2 1ºC
27600 Sarría (Lugo)
☎: +34 682 207 160
asesoria@envinate.es

LOUSAS PARCELA CAMIÑO NOVO 2012 T
mencía

92 Colour: cherry, garnet rim. Nose: red berry notes, ripe fruit, wild herbs, mineral, spicy. Palate: flavourful, spicy, balanced, elegant, mineral.

LOUSAS PARCELA SEOANE 2012 T
mencía

94 Colour: cherry, garnet rim. Nose: red berry notes, floral, violet drops, balsamic herbs, dry stone. Palate: rich, powerful, flavourful, spicy, balanced, elegant.

LOUSAS VINO DE ALDEAS 2012 T
mencía

93 Colour: cherry, purple rim. Nose: scrubland, earthy notes, spicy, red berry notes, ripe fruit. Palate: powerful, flavourful, spicy, long.

JAVIER FERNÁNDEZ GONZÁLEZ

Pacios - Espasantes
27450 Pantón (Lugo)
☎: +34 982 456 228 - Fax: +34 982 456 228
javier.fdez@hotmail.com

JAVIER FERNÁNDEZ VENDIMIA SELECCIONADA 2012 T
mencía

85 Colour: deep cherry. Nose: medium intensity, ripe fruit. Palate: fine bitter notes, spicy.

SAIÑAS 2010 T

90 Colour: cherry, garnet rim. Nose: ripe fruit, spicy, creamy oak, toasty, complex. Palate: powerful, flavourful, toasty, round tannins.

SAIÑAS 2011 T BARRICA
mencía

88 Colour: bright cherry. Nose: ripe fruit, sweet spices, creamy oak. Palate: flavourful, fruity, toasty.

SAIÑAS 2012 T
mencía

90 Colour: cherry, purple rim. Nose: mineral, ripe fruit, complex, characterful. Palate: flavourful, spicy, ripe fruit.

JORGE FEIJÓO GONZÁLEZ

Eirexa, 14
32614 Abeleda - A Teixeira (Ourense)
☎: +34 606 807 897
www.adegavella.com
adegavella@terra.es

12 ADEGA VELLA 2011 T
mencía

88 Colour: deep cherry. Nose: spicy, toasty, scrubland. Palate: flavourful, spicy, ripe fruit.

ADEGA VELLA GODELLO 2012 B
godello, loureiro, treixadura

88 Colour: bright straw. Nose: white flowers, expressive, ripe fruit, citrus fruit. Palate: flavourful, fruity, good acidity, balanced.

ADEGA VELLA MENCÍA 2012 T
mencía, brancellao, merenzao

90 Colour: cherry, purple rim. Nose: fresh fruit, red berry notes, floral. Palate: flavourful, fruity, good acidity.

BALUCE 2011 T
mencía

86 Colour: deep cherry. Nose: powerfull, candied fruit, toasty, spicy. Palate: fine bitter notes, spicy.

JOSÉ IGNACIO RODRÍGUEZ PÉREZ

Barantes de Arriba
27421 Sober (Lugo)
☎: +34 982 152 570
bodegasregueiral@gmail.com

VIÑA REGUEIRAL 2011 T
mencía

85 Colour: deep cherry. Nose: spicy, ripe fruit. Palate: powerful, sweetness, good acidity.

JOSÉ MANUEL RODRÍGUEZ GONZÁLEZ

Vilachá - Doade
27424 Sober (Lugo)
☎: +34 982 460 613

DÉCIMA 2012 T
mencía

85 Colour: very deep cherry. Nose: expressive, varietal, ripe fruit. Palate: spicy, ripe fruit.

LEIRABELLA

Leirabella - Sacardebois
32748 Parada do Sil (Ourense)
☎: +34 630 882 558
martin.lagaron@hotmal.es

MARTÍN LAGARÓN 2011 T
mencía, tempranillo, garnacha

90 Colour: bright cherry. Nose: ripe fruit, creamy oak, expressive. Palate: flavourful, fruity, toasty, round tannins.

M. DEL CARMEN PRADO FERREIRO

Lobios, 30
27423 Sober (Lugo)
☎: +34 982 152 575

GULLUFRE 2012 T
mencía

88 Colour: cherry, purple rim. Nose: red berry notes, floral, ripe fruit. Palate: flavourful, fruity, good acidity.

MANUEL CALVO MÉNDEZ

San Fiz
27513 Chantada (Lugo)
☎: +34 619 319 589 - Fax: +34 982 441 579
vinaribada@telefonica.net

RIBADA 2012 B
godello

90 Colour: bright yellow. Nose: powerfull, ripe fruit, characterful. Palate: flavourful, powerful, fruity.

RIBADA SELECCION 2010 T
mencía

90 Colour: cherry, garnet rim. Nose: spicy, toasty, complex, candied fruit, overripe fruit. Palate: powerful, flavourful, toasty, round tannins.

VIÑA RIBADA 2012 T

88 Colour: deep cherry. Nose: characterful, ripe fruit, cocoa bean. Palate: flavourful, fruity, good acidity, fine bitter notes.

MARÍA JESÚS LÓPEZ CRISTÓBAL

Outeiro 20 - Bolmente
27425 Sober (Lugo)
☎: +34 982 152 981

CIVIDADE 2012 T
mencía, brancellao

88 Colour: cherry, purple rim. Nose: fresh fruit, red berry notes, floral, mineral. Palate: flavourful, fruity, good acidity, round tannins.

MOURE VIÑOS ARTESANS

Saviñao (Lugo)
☎: +34 982 452 031

MOURE TRADICIÓN 2012 T
mencía, garnacha, garnacha tintorera, mouratón

93 Colour: cherry, garnet rim. Nose: floral, ripe fruit, fruit expression, scrubland, balsamic herbs. Palate: flavourful, fruity, fresh.

NAZ

Naz de Abaixo, 55
27466 Sober (Lugo)
☎: +34 982 460 110
www.naz.es
comercial@naz.es

NAZ 2012 T
90% mencía, 7% tempranillo, 3% garnacha

85 Colour: deep cherry. Nose: warm, characterful. Palate: fine bitter notes, spicy, ripe fruit.

NOVA TOURAL

Mardoñedo, 22
27004 Lugo (Lugo)
☎: +34 620 825 362
info@novatoural.es

SOMBRERO 2011 T ROBLE
mencía, tempranillo

88 Colour: very deep cherry. Nose: fruit liqueur notes, spicy, toasty, balsamic herbs. Palate: fine bitter notes, spicy.

SOMBRERO MENCÍA 2012 T
mencía, tempranillo

90 Colour: cherry, purple rim. Nose: fresh fruit, red berry notes, floral. Palate: flavourful, fruity, good acidity, round tannins.

OS CIPRESES

Tarrio-San Fiz
27500 Chantada (Lugo)
☎: +34 982 440 809 - Fax: +34 982 440 880
www.oscipreses.com
cristina@oscipreses.com

OS CIPRESES 2011 T BARRICA
90% mencía, 10% tempranillo

90 Colour: very deep cherry. Nose: powerfull, candied fruit, ripe fruit, toasty. Palate: flavourfull, powerful, spicy, ripe fruit.

PEDRO MANUEL RODRÍGUEZ PÉREZ

Sanmil, 43 - Santa Cruz de Brosmos
27425 Sober (Lugo)
☎: +34 982 152 508 - Fax: +34 982 402 000
adegasguimaro@gmail.com

FINCA CAPELIÑOS 2011 T
100% mencía

93 Colour: deep cherry, purple rim. Nose: expressive, balsamic herbs, ripe fruit. Palate: good structure, fruity, round tannins, good acidity.

FINCA POMBEIRAS 2011 T
100% mencía

92 Colour: deep cherry, garnet rim. Nose: powerfull, ripe fruit, aromatic coffee, spicy. Palate: good structure, complex, round tannins.

GUIMARO 2012 B
100% godello

91 Colour: yellow, greenish rim. Nose: balanced, expressive, dried herbs. Palate: fruity, full, balsamic, fine bitter notes.

GUIMARO MENCÍA 2012 T
mencía

92 Colour: cherry, purple rim. Nose: expressive, fresh fruit, red berry notes. Palate: flavourful, fruity, good acidity, round tannins.

PENA DAS DONAS

Pombeiro
27470 Pantón (Lugo)
☎: +34 988 200 045 - Fax: +34 988 200 045
www.penadasdonas.com
adega@penadasdonas.com

ALMALARGA 2012 B
godello

88 Colour: bright straw. Nose: ripe fruit, citrus fruit, fruit expression. Palate: flavourful, fruity, fine bitter notes.

ALMALARGA 2012 B BARRICA

91 Colour: bright straw. Nose: fresh, fresh fruit, white flowers, creamy oak, sweet spices. Palate: flavourful, fruity, good acidity, balanced.

VERDES MATAS MENCÍA 2012 T
mencía

88 Colour: cherry, purple rim. Nose: red berry notes, floral, sweet spices, ripe fruit. Palate: flavourful, fruity, good acidity, round tannins.

PONTE DA BOGA

Lugar do Couto - Sampaio
32760 Castro Caldelas (Ourense)
☎: +34 988 203 306 - Fax: +34 988 203 299
www.pontedaboga.es
ruben@pontedaboga.es

ALAIS 2010 T
mencía

89 Colour: bright cherry. Nose: sweet spices, expressive. Palate: flavourful, fruity, toasty, round tannins.

PONTE DA BOGA BANCALES OLVIDADOS MENCÍA 2011 T
mencía

92 Colour: cherry, garnet rim. Nose: ripe fruit, spicy, creamy oak, toasty, complex, scrubland. Palate: powerful, flavourful, toasty, round tannins.

PONTE DA BOGA BLANCO DE BLANCOS 2011 B
godello, albariño

94 Colour: bright yellow. Nose: powerfull, sweet spices, creamy oak, fragrant herbs, mineral. Palate: rich, flavourful, fresh, good acidity.

PONTE DA BOGA CAPRICHO DE MERENZAO 2010 T
merenzao

92 Colour: deep cherry. Nose: powerfull, spicy, toasty. Palate: flavourful, fine bitter notes, good acidity, round tannins.

PONTE DA BOGA EXPRESIÓN ROMÁNTICA 2011 T
mencía, sousón, merenzao, brancellao

90 Colour: bright cherry. Nose: creamy oak, fruit expression, spicy, balsamic herbs. Palate: flavourful, fruity, toasty, round tannins.

PONTE DA BOGA GODELLO 2012 B
godello

90 Colour: bright straw. Nose: floral, fragrant herbs, fruit expression, dry stone, spicy, citrus fruit. Palate: balanced, flavourful, fresh, fruity.

PONTE DA BOGA MENCÍA 2012 T
mencía

89 Colour: cherry, purple rim. Nose: red berry notes, floral, balsamic herbs, scrubland, ripe fruit. Palate: flavourful, fruity, good acidity, round tannins.

REGINA VIARUM

Doade, s/n
27424 Sober (Lugo)
☎: +34 986 288 212 - Fax: +34 986 401 185
www.reginaviarum.es
info@reginaviarum.es

REGINA EXPRESIÓN 2010 T BARRICA
mencía

87 Colour: deep cherry. Nose: spicy, aromatic coffee. Palate: fruity, light-bodied, flavourful.

REGINA VIARUM 2012 T
mencía

90 Colour: cherry, purple rim. Nose: red berry notes, floral, ripe fruit. Palate: flavourful, fruity, good acidity, round tannins.

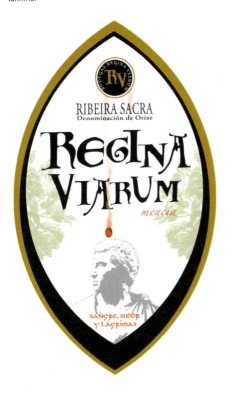

REGINA VIARUM EDICIÓN LIMITADA 2011 T
mencía

88 Colour: bright cherry. Nose: ripe fruit, sweet spices, creamy oak, toasty. Palate: flavourful, fruity, toasty, round tannins.

REGINA VIARUM GODELLO 2012 B
godello

90 Colour: bright straw. Nose: white flowers, powerfull, ripe fruit, citrus fruit. Palate: flavourful, powerful, complex, ripe fruit.

VÍA APPIA 2012 T
mencía

88 Colour: deep cherry. Nose: expressive, varietal, balsamic herbs. Palate: light-bodied, flavourful.

VÍA IMPERIAL 2012 T
mencía

87 Colour: deep cherry. Nose: ripe fruit, fruit expression, medium intensity. Palate: flavourful, good acidity.

RONSEL DO SIL

Sacardebois
34740 Parada de Sil (Ourense)
☎: +34 988 984 923
www.ronseldosil.com
info@ronseldosil.com

ALPENDRE 2011 T
merenzao

93 Colour: light cherry. Nose: red berry notes, fruit liqueur notes, balsamic herbs, wild herbs, spicy, creamy oak, dry stone. Palate: complex, powerful, flavourful, round tannins, balanced.

ARPEGIO 2011 T
mencía

91 Colour: cherry, garnet rim. Nose: red berry notes, ripe fruit, balsamic herbs, spicy, mineral. Palate: flavourful, spicy, long, round tannins.

OURIVE 2011 B
godello

90 Colour: bright straw. Nose: white flowers, fragrant herbs, mineral, fruit expression. Palate: fresh, fruity, flavourful, elegant, balanced.

VEL'UVEYRA GODELLO 2011 B
godello

88 Colour: bright straw. Nose: citrus fruit, ripe fruit, wild herbs, floral, expressive. Palate: fresh, fruity, flavourful, balanced.

VEL'UVEYRA MENCÍA 2011 T
mencía

92 Colour: cherry, garnet rim. Nose: floral, red berry notes, raspberry, fruit liqueur notes, wild herbs, dry stone, spicy. Palate: balanced, elegant, balsamic, fruity.

TOMÁS ARIAS FERNÁNDEZ

Sanxillao - Proendos
27460 Sober (Lugo)
☎: +34 982 460 055
proencia1@gmail.com

PROENCIA AMANDI 2009 T BARRICA
mencía

91 Colour: bright cherry. Nose: ripe fruit, sweet spices, aromatic coffee, toasty. Palate: flavourful, fruity, toasty, round tannins.

PROENCIA AMANDI 2012 T
mencía

86 Colour: deep cherry. Nose: grassy, balsamic herbs, ripe fruit. Palate: light-bodied, flavourful.

TOMÁS RODRÍGUEZ GONZÁLEZ

Proendos, 104
27460 Sober (Lugo)
☎: +34 982 460 489 - Fax: +34 982 460 489

ADEGA BARBADO 2012 T
mencía

85 Colour: deep cherry. Nose: medium intensity, warm, candied fruit. Palate: powerful, fine bitter notes, spicy.

AS MURAS 2012 T
mencía

88 Colour: cherry, purple rim. Nose: fresh fruit, floral, characterful, varietal. Palate: flavourful, fruity, good acidity.

VAL DA LENDA

Cantón - Amandi, 22
27423 Sober (Lugo)
☎: +34 619 665 783
www.valdalenda.com
info@valdalenda.com

VAL DA LENDA 2012 T
100% mencía

89 Colour: cherry, purple rim. Nose: fresh fruit, red berry notes. Palate: flavourful, fruity, good acidity, round tannins.

VÍA ROMANA

A Ermida - Belesar, s/n
27500 Chantada (Lugo)
☎: +34 982 454 005 - Fax: +34 982 454 094
www.viaromana.es
viaromana@viaromana.es

VÍA ROMANA MENCÍA 2011 T
mencía

87 Colour: cherry, garnet rim. Nose: balsamic herbs, scrubland, ripe fruit, spicy. Palate: powerful, balsamic, fine bitter notes.

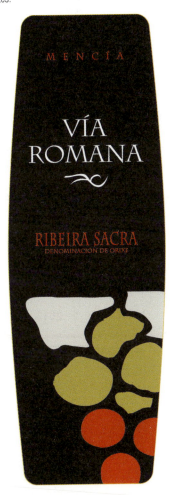

VÍA ROMANA GODELLO 2011 B
godello

88 Colour: bright straw. Nose: white flowers, varietal, ripe fruit. Palate: flavourful, fruity, good acidity, balanced.

VÍA ROMANA MENCÍA 2009 T BARRICA
100% mencía

90 Colour: cherry, garnet rim. Nose: ripe fruit, spicy, creamy oak, toasty, characterful. Palate: powerful, flavourful, toasty, round tannins.

VIRXEN DOS REMEDIOS

Diomondi, 56
27548 O Saviñao (Lugo)
☎: +34 982 171 720 - Fax: +34 982 171 720
www.virxendosremedios.es
info@virxendosremedios.es

VIÑA VELLA 2012 B
60% godello, 20% albariño, 20% treixadura

88 Colour: bright straw. Nose: fresh, fresh fruit, white flowers, expressive. Palate: flavourful, fruity, good acidity, balanced.

VIÑA VELLA MENCÍA 2012 T
100% mencía

87 Colour: deep cherry. Nose: medium intensity, warm, ripe fruit. Palate: spicy, ripe fruit, fine bitter notes.

DO RIBEIRO / D.O.P.

LOCATION:

In the west of the province of Ourense. The region comprises 13 municipal districts marked by the Miño and its tributaries.

CLIMATE:

Atlantic, with low temperatures in winter, a certain risk of spring frosts, and high temperatures in the summer months. The average annual rainfall varies between 800 mm and 1,000 mm.

▼ Consejo Regulador
● DO Boundary

SOIL:

Predominantly granite, deep and rich in organic matter, although in some areas clayey soils predominate. The vineyards are on the slopes of the mountains (where higher quality wines are produced) and on the plains.

GRAPE VARIETIES :

WHITE: Preferred: *Treixadura, Torrontés, Palomino, Godello, Macabeo, Loureira* and *Albariño*. Authorized: *Albilla, Macabeo, Jerez*. Experimental: *Lado*.
RED: Preferred: *Caíño, Alicante, Sousón, Ferrón, Mencía, Tempranillo, Brancellao*. Authorized: *Tempranillo, Garnacha*.

FIGURES:

Vineyard surface: 2.842.132 – **Wine-Growers:** 6,054 – **Wineries:** 101– **2012 Harvest rating:** Very Good– **Production:** 9.560.684 litres – **Market percentages:** 95% domestic. 5% export

2008	2009	2010	2011	2012
VERY GOOD	EXCELLENT	VERY GOOD	VERY GOOD	VERY GOOD

CONSEJO REGULADOR
Salgado Moscoso, 11 - 32400 Ribadavia (Ourense) ☎: +34 988 477 200 - Fax: +34 988 477 201
info@ribeiro.es   www.ribeiro.es

ADEGA DE ACINUS

Bº de Gomariz, 9
32429 Leiro (Ourense)
☎: +34 988 488 165
alfredo.acinus@gmail.com

ACINUS 2011 B
albariño, treixadura

87 Colour: bright straw. Nose: expressive, varietal, candied fruit.

ADEGA MANUEL FORMIGO

Adega Manuel Formigo
32431 Beade (Ourense)
☎: +34 988 480 173
www.fincateira.com
info@fincateira.com

FINCA TEIRA 2012 B
70% treixadura, 20% godello, 10% torrontés

90 Colour: bright straw. Nose: fresh, fresh fruit, white flowers, grassy. Palate: flavourful, fruity, good acidity, balanced.

FORMIGO 2012 B
treixadura, godello, otras

89 Colour: bright straw. Nose: fresh, white flowers, dried herbs, scrubland, ripe fruit. Palate: flavourful, fruity, good acidity, balanced.

TEIRA X 2011 B
65% treixadura, 15% loureiro, 10% albariño, 10% albilla

86 Colour: bright straw. Nose: faded flowers, spicy, honeyed notes. Palate: fine bitter notes, good acidity.

TOSTADO DE TEIRA B
treixadura

93 Colour: golden. Nose: powerfull, floral, honeyed notes, candied fruit, acetaldehyde. Palate: flavourful, sweet, fresh, good acidity, long.

ADEGA MANUEL ROJO

Chaos s/n Arnoia
32417 Vigo (Pontevedra)
☎: +34 670 309 688
www.adegamanuelrojo.es
info@adegamanuelrojo.es

MANUEL ROJO 2010 B
treixadura, godello, lado

91 Colour: bright straw. Nose: scrubland, dried herbs, ripe fruit. Palate: light-bodied, flavourful, fruity.

MANUEL ROJO 2011 B
treixadura, lado, godello

92 Colour: bright straw. Nose: fragrant herbs, dried herbs, ripe fruit, citrus fruit, white flowers. Palate: flavourful, powerful, fruity, spicy.

MANUEL ROJO 2011 T
mencía, brancellao, ferrón, sousón

86 Colour: deep cherry. Nose: closed, ripe fruit, red berry notes. Palate: flavourful, powerful, ripe fruit.

MANUEL ROJO 2012 B
treixadura, godello, lado

90 Colour: bright straw. Nose: fresh, fresh fruit, white flowers, expressive. Palate: flavourful, fruity, good acidity, balanced.

ADEGA MARÍA DO PILAR

Casardeita, 14 Macendo
32430 Castrelo de Miño (Ourense)
☎: +34 988 475 236 - Fax: +34 988 475 236
www.adegamariadopilar.com
adega@adegamariadopilar.com

RECHAMANTE 2012 T
mencía, brancellao

86 Colour: deep cherry. Nose: balsamic herbs, scrubland, red berry notes. Palate: light-bodied, fine bitter notes, spicy.

ADEGAS ÁUREA LUX

Rúa do Ribeiro, 29
32400 Ribadavia (Ourense)
☎: +34 988 470 368
www.aurealux.com
info@aurealux.com

LEIVE RELIQUIA 2011 BFB
50% treixadura, 35% albariño, 15% loureiro

90 Colour: bright yellow. Nose: powerfull, ripe fruit, sweet spices, cocoa bean, honeyed notes. Palate: rich, smoky aftertaste, flavourful, fresh, good acidity.

LEIVE TREIXADURA 2012 B
100% treixadura

85 Colour: pale. Nose: white flowers, fresh fruit. Palate: light-bodied, fruity, fresh.

PARADIGMA LEIVE 2012 B
50% treixadura, 35% albariño, 15% loureiro

89 Colour: bright straw. Nose: ripe fruit, citrus fruit, fruit expression, fragrant herbs. Palate: flavourful, fruity, fresh.

PRETO DE LEIVE 2012 T
25% caíño, 25% sousón, 25% brancellao, 25% mencía

86 Colour: very deep cherry. Nose: overripe fruit, scrubland, toasty. Palate: spicy, ripe fruit, powerful.

ADEGAS PAZO DO MAR

Ctra. Ourense-Castrelo, Km. 12,5
32940 Toén (Ourense)
☎: +34 988 261 256 - Fax: +34 988 261 264
www.pazodomar.com
info@pazodomar.com

EXPRESIÓN DE PAZO DO MAR 2012 B
100% treixadura

88 Colour: bright straw. Nose: characterful, expressive, fresh fruit, citrus fruit. Palate: flavourful, fruity, fresh.

PAZO DO MAR 2012 B
treixadura, torrontés, godello

88 Colour: bright straw. Nose: expressive, ripe fruit, grassy. Palate: flavourful, light-bodied, fruity.

ADEGAS VALDAVIA

Cuñas, s/n
32454 Cenlle (Ourense)
☎: +34 669 892 681 - Fax: +34 986 367 016
www.adegasvaldavia.com
comercial@adegasvaldavia.com

CUÑAS DAVIA 2011 BFB
80% treixadura, 20% albariño

90 Colour: bright yellow. Nose: powerfull, ripe fruit, creamy oak. Palate: rich, smoky aftertaste, flavourful, fresh, good acidity.

CUÑAS DAVIA 2011 T
35% mencía, 35% brancellao, 20% caíño, 10% sousón

84

CUÑAS DAVIA 2012 B JOVEN
70% treixadura, 20% albariño, 8% godello, 2% lado

91 Colour: bright straw. Nose: fresh, fresh fruit, white flowers, fine lees. Palate: flavourful, fruity, good acidity, balanced.

AILALA-AILALELO

Lugar o Cotiño, s/n
32415 Ribadavia (Ourense)
☎: +34 695 220 256 - Fax: +34 988 488 741
www.ailalawine.com
export@ailalawine.com

AILALÁ 2012 B
100% treixadura

89 Colour: bright straw. Nose: fresh, fresh fruit, white flowers, fragrant herbs. Palate: flavourful, fruity, good acidity, balanced.

ALFONSO ALBOR RODRÍGUEZ

Coedo Cenlle
32454 (Ourense)
☎: +34 626 903 725

PAZOS DE ALBOR 2012 B
treixadura, godello, loureiro

91 Colour: bright straw. Nose: fresh, white flowers, expressive, varietal, characterful. Palate: flavourful, fruity, good acidity, balanced.

ANTONIO MONTERO

Santa María, 7
32430 Castrelo do Miño (Ourense)
☎: +34 607 856 002
www.antoniomontero.com
antoniomontero@antoniomontero.com

ALEJANDRVS 2010 B
treixadura

90 Colour: bright yellow. Nose: powerfull, ripe fruit, creamy oak, dried herbs. Palate: rich, flavourful, fresh, good acidity.

ANTONIO MONTERO "AUTOR" 2012 B
80% treixadura, 10% torrontés, 5% albariño, 5% loureiro

90 Colour: bright straw. Nose: white flowers, varietal, ripe fruit. Palate: flavourful, fruity, good acidity, balanced.

BENITO ELADIO RODRÍGUEZ FERNÁNDEZ

Arco da Vella a Adega de Eladio
32431 Beade (Ourense)
☎: +34 607 487 060 - Fax: +34 986 376 800
www.bodegaeladio.com
bodega@bodegaeladio.com

TARABELO 2008 TC
60% sousón, 40% caiño, brancellao, ferrol

87 Colour: deep cherry. Nose: powerfull, characterful, ripe fruit. Palate: ripe fruit, spicy, fine bitter notes.

TARABELO 2011 TC
60% sousón, 40% caiño, brancellao, ferrol

85 Colour: deep cherry. Nose: scrubland, balsamic herbs, ripe fruit. Palate: ripe fruit, spicy.

TORQUES DO CASTRO 2012 B
60% treixadura, 20% torrontés, 15% godello, 5% albariño

89 Colour: bright straw. Nose: fresh, white flowers, grassy. Palate: flavourful, fruity, good acidity, balanced.

BODEGA ALANÍS

Santa Cruz de Arrabaldo, 49
32990 (Ourense)
☎: +34 988 384 200 - Fax: +34 988 384 068
www.bodegasgallegas.com
sonia@bodegasgallegas.com

GRAN ALANÍS 2012 B
85% treixadura, 15% godello

90 Colour: bright straw. Nose: fresh, white flowers, ripe fruit, citrus fruit, tropical fruit. Palate: flavourful, fruity, good acidity, balanced.

BODEGAS AGRUPADAS PONTE

Eduardo Pondal, 3 Entpa B
36001 (Pontevedra)
☎: +34 986 840 064 - Fax: +34 986 710 230
www.bodegasagrupadasponte.com
info@bodegasagrupadasponte.com

LA INVITACIÓN DE PEPA 2011 T
100% mencía

86 Colour: cherry, garnet rim. Nose: warm, wild herbs, ripe fruit, dried flowers, spicy. Palate: balsamic, sweetness, ripe fruit.

LA PROPUESTA DE MARÍA 2011 B
100% godello

85 Colour: bright yellow. Nose: ripe fruit, floral, balsamic herbs, spicy. Palate: powerful, rich, flavourful.

LA SUGERENCIA DE MANOLA 2011 B
60% treixadura, 40% torrontés

86 Colour: bright straw. Nose: fresh fruit, white flowers, fragrant herbs. Palate: flavourful, fruity, balanced.

BODEGAS CAMPANTE

Finca Reboreda, s/n
32941 Puga (Ourense)
☎: +34 988 261 212 - Fax: +34 988 261 213
www.campante.com
info@campante.com

GRAN REBOREDA 2012 B
treixadura, godello, loureiro

90 Colour: bright straw. Nose: fresh, fresh fruit, mineral, floral. Palate: flavourful, fruity, good acidity, balanced.

BODEGAS DOCAMPO

Lg. Sampaio
32414 Ribadavia (Ourense)
☎: +34 988 470 258 - Fax: +34 988 470 421
www.bodegasdocampo.com
admin@bodegasdocampo.com

SEÑORÍO DA VILA 2011 B
treixadura

91 Colour: bright straw. Nose: candied fruit, citrus fruit, fruit expression, honeyed notes, cocoa bean. Palate: flavourful, powerful, good acidity, round.

VIÑA DO CAMPO 2011 BFB
treixadura, torrontés

85 Colour: bright yellow. Nose: scrubland, candied fruit, honeyed notes. Palate: good acidity, spicy, ripe fruit, smoky aftertaste.

VIÑA DO CAMPO 2012 B
treixadura, torrontés

88 Colour: bright straw. Nose: white flowers, characterful, ripe fruit. Palate: flavourful, fruity, good acidity, balanced.

VIÑA DO CAMPO MENCÍA 2012 T
mencía

90 Colour: cherry, purple rim. Nose: expressive, fresh fruit, red berry notes, floral, powerfull. Palate: flavourful, fruity, good acidity, round tannins.

BODEGAS EL PARAGUAS

Lugar de Esmelle, 111
15594 Ferrol (A Coruña)
☎: +34 636 161 479
www.bodegaselparaguas.com
info@bodegaselparaguas.com

EL PARAGUAS ATLÁNTICO 2011 B
85% treixadura, 10% godello, 5% albariño

90 Colour: bright yellow. Nose: ripe fruit, citrus fruit, floral, fragrant herbs, mineral. Palate: fresh, rich, flavourful, long, balanced.

EL PARAGUAS ATLÁNTICO 2012 B
85% treixadura, 10% godello, 5% albariño

91 Colour: bright straw. Nose: white flowers, fragrant herbs, mineral, fruit expression, expressive. Palate: flavourful, balsamic, good acidity, round.

BODEGAS NAIROA

A Ponte, 2
32417 Arnoia (Ourense)
☎: +34 988 492 867
www.bodegasnairoa.com
info@bodegasnairoa.com

ALBERTE 2012 B
90% treixadura, 10% albariño

89 Colour: bright straw. Nose: grassy, dried herbs, fresh fruit, citrus fruit, floral. Palate: flavourful, light-bodied, fruity.

NAIROA 2012 B
treixadura, torrontés, palomino

86 Colour: bright straw. Nose: white flowers, tropical fruit. Palate: flavourful, fruity, good acidity, balanced.

VAL DO COUSO 2012 B
treixadura, torrontés, otras

89 Colour: bright straw. Nose: candied fruit, citrus fruit, grassy, dried herbs. Palate: flavourful, powerful.

BODEGAS O'VENTOSELA

Ctra. Ribadavia - Carballiño, km. 8,8 San Clodio
32420 Leiro (Ourense)
☎: +34 981 635 829 - Fax: +34 981 635 870
www.oventosela.com
bodegasydestilerias@oventosela.com

GRAN LEIRIÑA 2012 B

85 Colour: bright straw. Nose: dried herbs, medium intensity, candied fruit. Palate: fine bitter notes, ripe fruit.

CASAL DE ARMÁN

Lugar O Cotiño, s/n. San Andrés de Camporredondo
32400 Ribadavia (Ourense)
☎: +34 699 060 464 - Fax: +34 988 491 809
www.casaldearman.net
bodega@casaldearman.net

ARMÁN FINCA MISENHORA 2011 B
treixadura, godello, albariño

90 Colour: bright yellow. Nose: citrus fruit, ripe fruit, floral, fragrant herbs, expressive. Palate: powerful, rich, flavourful, balsamic, long, balanced.

ARMAN FINCA OS LOUREIROS 2011 B
100% treixadura

93 Colour: bright yellow. Nose: powerfull, ripe fruit, sweet spices, creamy oak, fragrant herbs. Palate: rich, flavourful, fresh, good acidity, balanced, elegant.

CASAL DE ARMÁN 2012 B
90% treixadura, 5% albariño, 5% godello

92 Colour: bright straw. Nose: fresh, fresh fruit, white flowers, mineral, citrus fruit. Palate: flavourful, fruity, good acidity, balanced, elegant.

COTO DE GOMARIZ

Barrio de Gomariz
32429 Leiro (Ourense)
☎: +34 610 602 672 - Fax: +34 988 488 174
www.cotodegomariz.com
gomariz@cotodegomariz.com

ABADÍA DE GOMARIZ 2010 T
sousón, brancellao, ferrol, mencía

93 Colour: cherry, garnet rim. Nose: powerfull, red berry notes, ripe fruit, wild herbs, dry stone, expressive. Palate: powerful, flavourful, spicy, long.

COTO DE GOMARIZ 2012 B
80% treixadura, 20% godello, loureiro, torrontés

92 Colour: bright yellow. Nose: floral, balsamic herbs, mineral, fruit expression, expressive.

COTO DE GOMARIZ COLLEITA SELECCIONADA 2010 B
treixadura, godello, albariño, loureiro, lado

93 Colour: bright golden. Nose: ripe fruit, floral, balsamic herbs, sweet spices, creamy oak. Palate: rich, powerful, flavourful, spicy, long, elegant.

GOMARIZ X 2012 B
95% albariño, 5% treixadura

91 Colour: bright straw. Nose: white flowers, fragrant herbs, fruit expression. Palate: fresh, fruity, flavourful, balanced.

SEICA 2008 T
sousón, carabuñeira, garnacha

91 Colour: cherry, garnet rim. Nose: ripe fruit, spicy, creamy oak, toasty, mineral. Palate: flavourful, toasty, round tannins, balanced, elegant.

THE FLOWER AND THE BEE (TREIXADURA) 2012 B
treixadura

90 Colour: bright straw. Nose: fresh, fresh fruit, white flowers, expressive. Palate: flavourful, fruity, good acidity, balanced.

CUNQUEIRO

Prado de Miño, 4
32430 Castrelo de Miño (Ourense)
☎: +34 988 489 023 - Fax: +34 988 489 082
www.bodegascunqueiro.es
info@bodegascunqueiro.es

CUNQUEIRO III MILENIUM 2012 B
treixadura, loureiro, godello, albariño

90 Colour: bright straw. Nose: fresh fruit, white flowers, expressive, varietal. Palate: flavourful, fruity, good acidity, balanced.

CUQUEIRA 2011 B
treixadura, torrontés

86 Colour: bright straw. Nose: ripe fruit, citrus fruit, dried herbs. Palate: flavourful, fruity, fresh, good acidity.

MAIS DE CUNQUEIRO 2012 B
torrontés

88 Colour: bright straw. Nose: characterful, ripe fruit, citrus fruit, white flowers. Palate: flavourful, spicy, aged character, fine bitter notes.

EDUARDO PEÑA

Barral - Castelo do Miño
32430 Barral (Ourense)
☎: +34 629 872 130 - Fax: +34 988 239 704
www.bodegaeduardopenha.es
bodega@bodegaeduardopenha.es

EDUARDO PEÑA 2012 B
treixadura, albariño, godello, loureiro

90 Colour: bright straw. Nose: mineral, ripe fruit, candied fruit, faded flowers, dried herbs. Palate: ripe fruit, fruity, spicy.

EMILIO DOCAMPO DIÉGUEZ

San Andrés, 57
32415 Ribadavia (Ourense)
☎: +34 639 332 790 - Fax: +34 988 275 318
edocampodieguez@hotmail.com

CASAL DE PAULA 2012 B
treixadura, torrontés, albariño, godello

90 Colour: bright straw. Nose: ripe fruit, citrus fruit, fragrant herbs. Palate: flavourful, fruity, fresh, fine bitter notes.

CASAL DE PAULA 2012 T
25% sausón, 25% ferrón, 25% mencía, 25% brancellao

87 Colour: deep cherry. Nose: candied fruit, red berry notes, characterful. Palate: flavourful, fruity, balsamic.

FINCA VIÑOA

A Viñoa, s/n, Banga
32821 O Carballiño (Ourense)
☎: +34 695 220 256 - Fax: +34 988 488 741
www.fincavinoa.com
info@fincavinoa.com

FINCA VIÑOA 2012 B
treixadura, godello, loureiro, albariño

92 Colour: bright yellow. Nose: white flowers, fragrant herbs, dry stone, fresh fruit. Palate: fresh, fruity, flavourful, elegant.

FRANCISCO FERNÁNDEZ SOUSA

Prado, 14
32430 Castrelo do Miño (Ourense)
☎: +34 678 530 898
www.terraminei.com
info@terraminei.com

LAGAR DE BRAIS 2011 B
palomino, torrontés

87 Colour: bright straw. Nose: faded flowers, medium intensity, candied fruit. Palate: sweetness, fine bitter notes.

TERRA MINEI 2011 B
100% treixadura

88 Colour: bright straw. Nose: candied fruit, citrus fruit, expressive. Palate: flavourful, fruity, fresh.

TERRA MINEI 2012 B
100% treixadura

88 Colour: bright straw. Nose: fresh, white flowers, complex, ripe fruit. Palate: flavourful, fruity, good acidity, balanced.

JOSÉ ESTÉVEZ FERNÁNDEZ

Ponte, 21
32417 Arnoia (Ourense)
☎: +34 696 402 970
joseestevezarnoia@gmail.com

MAURO ESTEVEZ 2012 B
treixadura, lado, albariño, loureiro

93 Colour: bright straw. Nose: fresh, white flowers, characterful, complex, citrus fruit. Palate: flavourful, fruity, good acidity, balanced.

JOSÉ GONZÁLEZ ALVAREZ

Pazo Lalón Barro de Gomariz
32427 Leiro (Ourense)
☎: +34 653 131 487
www.eduardobravo.es
eduardogonzalezbravo@gmail.com

EDUARDO BRAVO 2012 B
treixadura, albariño, torrontés

89 Colour: bright straw. Nose: fresh, white flowers, ripe fruit, citrus fruit. Palate: flavourful, fruity, good acidity, balanced.

JULIO VÁZQUEZ QUINTELA

Barón - Carvalliño
32500 (Ourense)
☎: +34 988 243 426
carmenandreajulio@hotmail.com

PAZO LODEIRO 2011 B
treixadura, godello, torrontés, loureiro

89 Colour: bright straw. Nose: fresh, white flowers, expressive, mineral. Palate: flavourful, fruity, good acidity.

PAZO LODEIRO 2012 B
treixadura, godello, torrontés, loureiro, albariño

89 Colour: bright straw. Nose: fresh, fresh fruit, white flowers, expressive. Palate: flavourful, fruity, good acidity, balanced.

LAGAR DO MERENS

Lagar do Merens
32430 Arnoia (Ourense)
☎: +34 607 533 314
www.lagardomerens.com
info@lagardomerens.com

30 COPELOS 2011 T
brancellao, sousón, caiño, ferrón

91 Colour: bright cherry. Nose: ripe fruit, sweet spices, creamy oak, expressive, balsamic herbs. Palate: flavourful, fruity, round tannins.

LAGAR DO MERENS 2011 B
treixadura, lado, torrontés

89 Colour: bright straw. Nose: ripe fruit, citrus fruit. Palate: fine bitter notes, good acidity, spicy.

LAGAR DO MERENS 2011 BFB
treixadura, godello, albariño

92 Colour: bright yellow. Nose: powerfull, ripe fruit, sweet spices, creamy oak, fragrant herbs. Palate: rich, flavourful, fresh, good acidity.

LUIS A. RODRÍGUEZ VÁZQUEZ

Laxa, 7
32417 Arnoia (Ourense)
☎: +34 988 492 977 - Fax: +34 988 492 977

A TORNA DOS PASAS 2010 T

88 Colour: deep cherry. Nose: fruit preserve, powerfull, characterful. Palate: powerful, sweetness.

VIÑA DE MARTÍN "OS PASÁS" 2011 B

90 Colour: bright yellow. Nose: candied fruit, citrus fruit, scrubland. Palate: ripe fruit, spicy, balsamic.

VIÑA DE MARTÍN ESCOLMA 2009 BFB

92 Colour: bright yellow. Nose: expressive, characterful, complex, powerfull, candied fruit. Palate: powerful, spicy, ripe fruit.

VIÑA DE MARTÍN ESCOLMA 2009 T

90 Colour: deep cherry. Nose: powerfull, balsamic herbs, scrubland, candied fruit. Palate: spicy, ripe fruit, balsamic.

PAZO CASANOVA

Camiño Souto do Río, 1 Santa Cruz de Arrabaldo
32990 (Ourense)
☎: +34 988 384 196 - Fax: +34 988 384 196
www.pazocasanova.com
casanova@pazocasanova.com

CASANOVA 2012 B
80% treixadura, 20% godello, albariño, loureiro

88 Colour: bright straw. Nose: white flowers, candied fruit, citrus fruit. Palate: flavourful, fruity, fresh.

PAZO DE VIEITE

Ctra. OU-504 (Ribadavia a Carballiño, Km. 6)
32419 Vieite Leiro (Ourense)
☎: +34 988 488 229 - Fax: +34 988 488 229
www.pazodevieite.es
info@pazodevieite.es

1932 2011 B
100% treixadura

87 Colour: bright straw. Nose: candied fruit, medium intensity, dried herbs. Palate: flavourful, spicy, ripe fruit.

VIÑA FARNADAS 2011 B
85% treixadura, 5% torrontés, 10% godello

87 Colour: bright straw. Nose: dried herbs, grassy, ripe fruit. Palate: flavourful, good acidity, fine bitter notes.

PAZO TIZÓN

Rua do San Casares, 20
32514 Boboras (Orense)
☎: +34 902 120 915 - Fax: +34 916 913 553
www.pazotizon.com
admon@pazotizon.com

EXTRAMUNDI 2012 B
treixadura, albariño

88 Colour: bright straw. Nose: powerfull, candied fruit, citrus fruit, dried herbs. Palate: fruity, spicy, ripe fruit.

PRODUCCIONES A MODIÑO

Cubilledo-Gomariz
32420 Leiro (Ourense)
☎: +34 686 961 681
www.vinosanclodio.com
sanclodiovino@gmail.com

SANCLODIO 2011 B
treixadura, godello, loureiro, torrontés, albariño

90 Colour: bright straw. Nose: white flowers, expressive, ripe fruit, candied fruit. Palate: flavourful, fruity, good acidity, balanced.

SAMEIRÁS

San Andrés, 98
32415 Ribadavia (Ourense)
☎: +34 988 491 812 - Fax: +34 988 470 591
sameiras@terra.es

1040 SAMEIRÁS 2012 B
treixadura, albariño, godello

91 Colour: bright yellow. Nose: powerfull, ripe fruit, sweet spices, creamy oak. Palate: rich, flavourful, fresh, good acidity.

SAMEIRÁS 2011 T
40% sousón, 30% caíño, 20% brancellao, 10% otras

89 Colour: cherry, purple rim. Nose: fresh fruit, red berry notes, cocoa bean, scrubland, balsamic herbs. Palate: flavourful, fruity, good acidity, round tannins.

SAMEIRÁS 2012 B
55% treixadura, 20% albariño, 12% godello, 8% lado, 2% loureiro, 3% otras

91 Colour: bright straw. Nose: fresh, fresh fruit, white flowers, varietal, mineral. Palate: flavourful, fruity, good acidity, balanced.

SEÑORÍO DE BEADE

Piñeiros, s/n
32431 Beade (Ourense)
☎: +34 988 480 050 - Fax: +34 988 480 050
www.beadeprimacia.com
beade@beadeprimacia.com

BEADE PRIMACÍA 2012 B
95% treixadura, 5% albariño, 5% loureiro

90 Colour: bright straw. Nose: fresh, fresh fruit, white flowers, citrus fruit. Palate: flavourful, fruity, good acidity, fine bitter notes.

SEÑORÍO DE BEADE 2012 B
treixadura, torrontés, godello, otras

86 Colour: bright straw. Nose: candied fruit, citrus fruit, grassy. Palate: flavourful, light-bodied.

SEÑORÍO DE BEADE 2012 T
mencía, caíño

90 Colour: cherry, garnet rim. Nose: ripe fruit, fruit expression, balsamic herbs, scrubland. Palate: flavourful, fruity, balsamic.

TERRA DO CASTELO

Ctra. Ribadavia - Carballiño, Km. 4
32431 Beade (Ourense)
☎: +34 988 471 522 - Fax: +34 988 471 502
www.terradocastelo.com
adegas@terradocastelo.com

TERRA DO CASTELO "SENSACIÓN" 2012 B
palomino, torrontés, godello, treixadura

87 Colour: bright straw. Nose: medium intensity, candied fruit, citrus fruit, tropical fruit. Palate: flavourful, sweetness.

TERRA DO CASTELO GODELLO 2012 B
100% godello

87 Colour: bright straw. Nose: ripe fruit, citrus fruit, dried herbs. Palate: flavourful, light-bodied, fruity.

TERRA DO CASTELO TREIXADURA 2012 B
100% treixadura

87 Colour: bright straw. Nose: fresh fruit, ripe fruit, citrus fruit, grassy. Palate: fruity, fresh, light-bodied.

TERRA DO CASTELO TREIXADURA SELECCIÓN 2011 B
100% treixadura

88 Colour: bright straw. Nose: ripe fruit, citrus fruit, fruit expression. Palate: flavourful, fruity, ripe fruit.

VAL DE SOUTO

Souto, 34
32430 (Ourense)
☎: +34 988 489 028 - Fax: +34 988 489 028
www.valdesouto.com
info@valdesouto.com

VAL DE SOUTO 2012 B
treixadura, godello, loureiro

88 Colour: bright straw. Nose: floral, ripe fruit, citrus fruit, grassy. Palate: flavourful, powerful, fruity.

BODEGA CONVENTO SAN FRANCISCO

Calvario, 22
47300 Peñafiel (Valladolid)
☎: +34 983 878 052 - Fax: +34 983 873 052
www.bodegaconvento.com
bodega@bodegaconvento.com

CONVENTO SAN FRANCISCO 2009 T
tinta del país

90 Colour: cherry, garnet rim. Nose: ripe fruit, spicy, creamy oak, toasty, complex. Palate: powerful, flavourful, toasty, round tannins.

BODEGA COOPERATIVA VIRGEN DE LA ASUNCIÓN

Las Afueras, s/n
9311 La Horra (Burgos)
☎: +34 947 542 057 - Fax: +34 947 542 057
www.virgendelaasuncion.com
info@virgendelaasuncion.com

VIÑA VALERA 6 MESES BARRICA 2011 T ROBLE
tempranillo

84

VIÑA VALERA JOVEN 2012 RD
tempranillo

80

VIÑA VALERA RESERVA 2007 TR
tempranillo

88 Colour: cherry, garnet rim. Nose: scrubland, ripe fruit. Palate: ripe fruit, spicy, correct.

VIÑA VALERA VENDIMIA SELECCIONADA 2009 T
tempranillo

89 Colour: cherry, garnet rim. Nose: ripe fruit, fruit preserve, balsamic herbs, fine reductive notes, spicy, creamy oak. Palate: powerful, flavourful, spicy, long.

ZARZUELA 2012 RD
tempranillo

85 Colour: rose, purple rim. Nose: ripe fruit, red berry notes, floral, citrus fruit. Palate: powerful, fruity, fresh.

VIÑA VALERA 2011 T JOVEN
tempranillo

84

VIÑA VALERA 2009 TC
tempranillo

89 Colour: cherry, garnet rim. Nose: ripe fruit, spicy, creamy oak. Palate: powerful, flavourful, toasty, round tannins.

ZARZUELA 2012 T
100% tinta del país

88 Colour: cherry, purple rim. Nose: expressive, fresh fruit, red berry notes, floral. Palate: flavourful, fruity, good acidity, round tannins.

ZARZUELA RESERVA 2006 TR
tempranillo

90 Colour: cherry, garnet rim. Nose: ripe fruit, spicy, complex, cocoa bean, tobacco. Palate: powerful, flavourful, round tannins.

ZARZUELA CRIANZA 2009 TC
tempranillo

87 Colour: cherry, garnet rim. Nose: ripe fruit, spicy, toasty, complex, medium intensity. Palate: powerful, flavourful, toasty, round tannins.

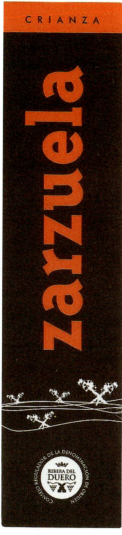

ZARZUELA SELECCIÓN 2009 T ROBLE
tempranillo

90 Colour: very deep cherry. Nose: powerfull, ripe fruit, toasty, dark chocolate. Palate: powerful, fine bitter notes, toasty.

ZARZUELA TINTO JOVEN 2012 T ROBLE
tempranillo

87 Colour: cherry, purple rim. Nose: ripe fruit, aromatic coffee, creamy oak. Palate: powerful, flavourful, toasty.

ZARZUELA VIÑAS VIEJAS 2011 T
tempranillo

90 Colour: cherry, garnet rim. Nose: ripe fruit, sweet spices, creamy oak, expressive. Palate: flavourful, fruity, toasty, harsh oak tannins.

BODEGA CUESTA ROA

Malpica, s/n
9311 La Horra (Burgos)
www.cuestaroa.es
cuestaroa@cuestaroa.es

CUESTA ROA 2009 TC
100% tempranillo

89 Colour: cherry, garnet rim. Nose: ripe fruit, spicy, creamy oak, toasty, mineral. Palate: powerful, flavourful, toasty, round tannins.

BODEGA EMINA

Ctra. San Bernardo, s/n
47359 Valbuena de Duero (Valladolid)
☎: +34 983 683 315 - Fax: +34 902 430 189
www.emina.es
emina@emina.es

EMINA 2010 TC
100% tempranillo

89 Colour: cherry, garnet rim. Nose: ripe fruit, creamy oak, roasted coffee, dark chocolate. Palate: powerful, flavourful, toasty, round tannins.

EMINA ATIO 2005 T
100% tempranillo

87 Colour: pale ruby, brick rim edge. Nose: scrubland, wet leather, fruit preserve, spicy, creamy oak. Palate: long, powerful, flavourful.

EMINA PASIÓN 2012 T ROBLE
100% tempranillo

88 Colour: deep cherry, purple rim. Nose: ripe fruit, creamy oak, dark chocolate, roasted coffee. Palate: full, flavourful, long, round tannins.

EMINA PRESTIGIO 2006 T
100% tempranillo

88 Colour: cherry, garnet rim. Nose: ripe fruit, spicy, creamy oak, toasty, fragrant herbs. Palate: powerful, flavourful, toasty, correct.

BODEGA HEMAR

La Iglesia, 48
9315 Fuentecén (Burgos)
☎: +34 947 532 718 - Fax: +34 947 532 768
www.bodegahemar.com
info@bodegahemar.com

HEMAR 12 MESES 2011 T
tempranillo

85 Colour: cherry, garnet rim. Nose: fruit preserve, toasty. Palate: powerful, good acidity, toasty.

HEMAR 7 MESES 2011 T
tempranillo

87 Colour: bright cherry. Nose: sweet spices, creamy oak, varietal. Palate: flavourful, fruity, toasty, round tannins.

LLANUM 2006 T
tempranillo

91 Colour: cherry, garnet rim. Nose: ripe fruit, spicy, creamy oak, toasty, mineral, complex. Palate: powerful, flavourful, toasty, round tannins.

BODEGA HNOS. PÁRAMO ARROYO

Ctra. de Roa Pedrosa, Km. 4
9314 Pedrosa de Duero (Burgos)
☎: +34 947 530 041 - Fax: +34 947 530 036
www.paramoarroyo.com
bodega@paramoarroyo.com

EREMUS 2008 TC
100% tempranillo

88 Colour: cherry, garnet rim. Nose: ripe fruit, spicy, creamy oak, toasty. Palate: powerful, flavourful, toasty, balanced.

EREMUS 2012 T
tempranillo

85 Colour: cherry, purple rim. Nose: ripe fruit, candied fruit. Palate: flavourful, ripe fruit, good finish.

BODEGA MATARROMERA

Ctra. Renedo-Pesquera, Km. 30
47359 Valbuena de Duero (Valladolid)
☎: +34 983 107 100 - Fax: +34 902 430 189
www.grupomatarromera.com
matarromera@matarromera.es

MATARROMERA 2001 TGR
100% tempranillo

92 Colour: dark-red cherry, orangey edge. Nose: elegant, spicy, fine reductive notes, wet leather, fruit liqueur notes. Palate: spicy, fine tannins, elegant, long.

MATARROMERA 2009 TR
100% tempranillo

90 Colour: cherry, garnet rim. Nose: ripe fruit, spicy, creamy oak, toasty, complex. Palate: powerful, flavourful, toasty, round tannins.

MATARROMERA 2010 TC
100% tempranillo

90 Colour: very deep cherry. Nose: overripe fruit, toasty, dark chocolate. Palate: powerful, fine bitter notes, round.

MATARROMERA EDICIÓN LIMITADA 25 ANIVERSARIO 2010 T
100% tempranillo

93 Colour: cherry, garnet rim. Nose: ripe fruit, spicy, creamy oak, toasty, complex. Palate: powerful, flavourful, toasty, round tannins.

MELIOR 2012 T ROBLE
100% tempranillo

85 Colour: cherry, purple rim. Nose: ripe fruit, fruit preserve, balsamic herbs, creamy oak. Palate: powerful, flavourful, toasty.

BODEGA NEXUS

Santiago, 17 - 4º
47001 (Valladolid)
☎: +34 983 360 284 - Fax: +34 983 345 546
www.bodegasfrontaura.com
info@bodegasfrontaura.es

NEXUS + 2006 T
100% tempranillo

92 Colour: cherry, garnet rim. Nose: ripe fruit, spicy, creamy oak, toasty. Palate: powerful, flavourful, toasty, round tannins.

NEXUS 2008 TC
100% tempranillo

92 Colour: very deep cherry. Nose: ripe fruit, toasty, aromatic coffee. Palate: fine bitter notes, good acidity, round.

NEXUS 2011 T
100% tempranillo

91 Colour: cherry, purple rim. Nose: balanced, ripe fruit, red berry notes, spicy, dried herbs. Palate: flavourful, round tannins, fruity.

TIERRAS GUINDAS 2011 T
100% tempranillo

88 Colour: cherry, purple rim. Nose: red berry notes, fruit liqueur notes, balsamic herbs, sweet spices, creamy oak. Palate: powerful, flavourful, spicy.

TIERRAS GUINDAS 2011 T
100% tempranillo

89 Colour: bright cherry. Nose: sweet spices, creamy oak, red berry notes. Palate: flavourful, fruity, toasty, round tannins.

VEGA MURILLO 2011 T
100% tempranillo

87 Colour: deep cherry, garnet rim. Nose: violet drops, ripe fruit, sweet spices. Palate: correct, balanced.

BODEGA RENTO

Santa María, 36
47359 Olivares de Duero (Valladolid)
☎: +34 983 683 315 - Fax: +34 902 430 189
www.bodegarento.es
emina@emina.es

OINOZ 2008 TC
100% tempranillo

86 Colour: cherry, garnet rim. Nose: fruit preserve, balsamic herbs, aged wood nuances, toasty. Palate: powerful, flavourful, spicy.

OINOZ 2011 T
100% tempranillo

86 Colour: cherry, purple rim. Nose: ripe fruit, fruit preserve, wild herbs, spicy. Palate: powerful, flavourful, correct.

RENTO 2005 T
100% tempranillo

89 Colour: pale ruby, brick rim edge. Nose: fruit preserve, scrubland, dark chocolate, fine reductive notes. Palate: powerful, flavourful, spicy, long.

BODEGA S. ARROYO

Avda. del Cid, 99
9441 Sotillo de la Ribera (Burgos)
☎: +34 947 532 444 - Fax: +34 947 532 444
www.tintoarroyo.com
info@tintoarroyo.com

TINTO ARROYO 2007 TGR
100% tempranillo

89 Colour: deep cherry, orangey edge. Nose: elegant, spicy, fine reductive notes, wet leather, aged wood nuances. Palate: spicy, elegant, long.

TINTO ARROYO 2008 TR
100% tempranillo

88 Colour: deep cherry, garnet rim. Nose: varietal, medium intensity, balsamic herbs, ripe fruit. Palate: fruity, flavourful.

TINTO ARROYO 2010 TC
100% tempranillo

91 Colour: cherry, garnet rim. Nose: ripe fruit, spicy, creamy oak, toasty, complex. Palate: powerful, flavourful, toasty, round tannins, balanced, elegant.

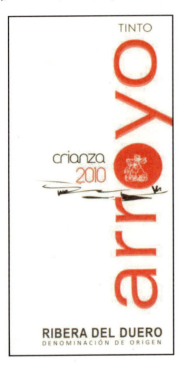

TINTO ARROYO 2011 T ROBLE
100% tempranillo

86 Colour: cherry, garnet rim. Nose: medium intensity, varietal, ripe fruit, dried herbs. Palate: fruity, correct, easy to drink.

TINTO ARROYO 2012 T
100% tempranillo

88 Colour: cherry, purple rim. Nose: expressive, fresh fruit, red berry notes, floral. Palate: flavourful, fruity, good acidity.

TINTO ARROYO VENDIMIA SELECCIONADA 2010 T
100% tempranillo

92 Colour: bright cherry. Nose: ripe fruit, sweet spices, creamy oak, expressive. Palate: flavourful, fruity, toasty, round tannins.

VIÑA ARROYO 2012 RD
100% tempranillo

88 Colour: rose, purple rim. Nose: powerfull, ripe fruit, red berry notes, floral, expressive. Palate: powerful, fruity, fresh.

BODEGA SAN MAMÉS

Ctra. Valladolid, s/n
9315 Fuentecén (Burgos)
☎: +34 947 532 693 - Fax: +34 947 532 653
www.bodegasanmames.com
info@bodegasanmames.com

DOBLE R (5 MESES) 2011 T
tempranillo

87 Colour: cherry, garnet rim. Nose: ripe fruit, aromatic coffee, creamy oak. Palate: powerful, flavourful, toasty.

DOBLE R 2009 TC
tempranillo

89 Colour: cherry, garnet rim. Nose: ripe fruit, spicy, creamy oak, toasty, complex. Palate: powerful, flavourful, toasty, round tannins.

DOBLE R 2011 T
tempranillo

87 Colour: cherry, garnet rim. Nose: fruit preserve, balsamic herbs, sweet spices. Palate: powerful, flavourful, spicy, toasty.

BODEGA SAN ROQUE DE LA ENCINA, SDAD. COOP.

San Roque, 73
9391 Castrillo de la Vega (Burgos)
☎: +34 947 536 001 - Fax: +34 947 536 183
www.bodegasanroquedelaencina.com
info@bodegasanroquedelaencina.com

CERRO PIÑEL 2010 TC
100% tempranillo

88 Colour: cherry, garnet rim. Nose: ripe fruit, spicy, creamy oak, toasty. Palate: powerful, flavourful, toasty, harsh oak tannins.

CERRO PIÑEL 2012 T
100% tempranillo

87 Colour: bright cherry. Nose: ripe fruit, sweet spices, creamy oak. Palate: flavourful, fruity, toasty, round tannins, smoky aftertaste.

MONTE DEL CONDE 2010 TC
100% tempranillo

88 Colour: cherry, garnet rim. Nose: scrubland, ripe fruit, varietal. Palate: balanced, ripe fruit, round tannins.

MONTE DEL CONDE 2012 T
100% tempranillo

87 Colour: cherry, purple rim. Nose: medium intensity, balanced, ripe fruit, red berry notes. Palate: flavourful, fruity.

MONTE PINADILLO 2010 TC
100% tempranillo

89 Colour: cherry, garnet rim. Nose: ripe fruit, spicy, creamy oak, toasty. Palate: powerful, flavourful, toasty, round tannins.

MONTE PINADILLO 2012 RD
100% tempranillo

87 Colour: rose, purple rim. Nose: powerfull, ripe fruit, red berry notes, lactic notes. Palate: powerful, fruity, fresh.

MONTE PINADILLO 2012 T
100% tempranillo

87 Colour: very deep cherry, purple rim. Nose: ripe fruit, creamy oak, sweet spices. Palate: fruity, flavourful, round tannins.

MONTE PINADILLO 2012 T ROBLE
100% tempranillo

88 Colour: cherry, purple rim. Nose: expressive, red berry notes, floral, toasty. Palate: flavourful, fruity, good acidity.

BODEGA SEVERINO SANZ

Del Rio, s/n
40542 Montejo De La Vega De La Serrezuela (Segovia)
☎: +34 944 659 659 - Fax: +34 944 531 442
www.bodegaseverinosanz.es
erika@picmatic.es

HERENCIA DE LLANOMINGOMEZ 2010 T
tempranillo

91 Colour: very deep cherry. Nose: medium intensity, toasty, aromatic coffee, dark chocolate. Palate: sweetness, concentrated, fine bitter notes.

MURON 2010 T
tempranillo

90 Colour: bright cherry. Nose: sweet spices, creamy oak, ripe fruit, expressive. Palate: flavourful, fruity, toasty, round tannins.

MURON 2011 T ROBLE
tempranillo

89 Colour: bright cherry. Nose: sweet spices, creamy oak, varietal. Palate: flavourful, toasty, round tannins.

MURON EDICIÓN LIMITADA 2010 T
tempranillo

88 Colour: bright cherry. Nose: sweet spices, creamy oak. Palate: flavourful, fruity, toasty, round tannins.

BODEGA VIÑA BUENA

Avda. Portugal, 96
9400 Aranda de Duero (Burgos)
☎: +34 947 546 414 - Fax: +34 947 506 694
www.vinabuena.com
vinabuena@vinabuena.com

FUERO REAL 2009 TC

87 Colour: cherry, garnet rim. Nose: fruit preserve, sweet spices, waxy notes, old leather. Palate: powerful, flavourful.

VIÑA BUENA 2012 T
tempranillo

83

VIÑA BUENA 2010 TC
tempranillo

87 Colour: cherry, garnet rim. Nose: ripe fruit, spicy, toasty, balsamic herbs. Palate: flavourful, round tannins, fruity.

BODEGA VIÑA VILANO S. COOP.

Ctra. de Anguix, 10
9314 Pedrosa de Duero (Burgos)
☎: +34 947 530 029 - Fax: +34 947 530 037
www.vinavilano.com
info@vinavilano.com

TERRA INCÓGNITA 2009 T
100% tempranillo

91 Colour: cherry, garnet rim. Nose: spicy, creamy oak, toasty, mineral, overripe fruit. Palate: powerful, flavourful, toasty, round tannins, balanced, elegant.

VIÑA VILANO 2009 TR
100% tempranillo

87 Colour: pale ruby, brick rim edge. Nose: ripe fruit, balsamic herbs, spicy, tobacco, waxy notes, fine reductive notes. Palate: flavourful, spicy, long.

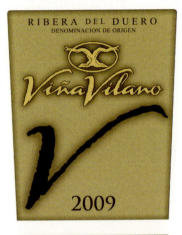

VIÑA VILANO 2010 TC
100% tempranillo

87 Colour: cherry, garnet rim. Nose: ripe fruit, creamy oak, toasty. Palate: powerful, flavourful, toasty.

VIÑA VILANO 2012 RD
100% tempranillo

88 Colour: rose, purple rim. Nose: powerfull, ripe fruit, red berry notes, floral, lactic notes. Palate: powerful, fruity, fresh.

VIÑA VILANO 2012 T
100% tempranillo

87 Colour: cherry, purple rim. Nose: expressive, fresh fruit, red berry notes, floral. Palate: flavourful, fruity, good acidity, easy to drink.

VIÑA VILANO 2012 T ROBLE
100% tempranillo

85 Colour: bright cherry. Nose: ripe fruit, sweet spices, creamy oak. Palate: flavourful, fruity, toasty, easy to drink.

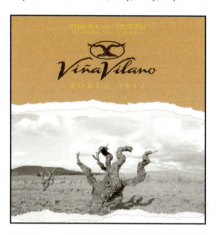

BODEGAS ABADÍA LA ARROYADA

La Tejera, s/n
9442 Terradillos de Esgueva (Burgos)
☎: +34 947 545 309 - Fax: +34 947 545 309
www.abadialaarroyada.es
bodegas@abadialaarroyada.es

ABADÍA LA ARROYADA 2009 TC
tempranillo

90 Colour: bright cherry. Nose: ripe fruit, sweet spices, creamy oak, expressive. Palate: flavourful, fruity, toasty, round tannins.

ABADÍA LA ARROYADA 2011 T ROBLE
tempranillo

87 Colour: bright cherry. Nose: ripe fruit, sweet spices, creamy oak. Palate: flavourful, fruity, toasty.

ABADÍA LA ARROYADA 2012 RD
tempranillo

85 Colour: rose, purple rim. Nose: powerfull, red berry notes, floral, fruit preserve. Palate: powerful, fruity.

BODEGAS ALTOGRANDE

Crta. Peñafiel Pesquera, Km 6
47316 Curiel de Duero (Valladolid)
☎: +34 983 880 489 - Fax: +34 983 880 489
www.haciendadelarte.com
bodega@altogrande.es

HACIENDA DEL ARTE 2010 TC

87 Colour: cherry, garnet rim. Nose: spicy, creamy oak, toasty. Palate: powerful, flavourful, toasty, round tannins.

HACIENDA DEL ARTE VENDIMIA SELECCIONADA 2012 T

85 Colour: bright cherry. Nose: sweet spices, creamy oak, fruit preserve. Palate: flavourful, fruity, toasty, round tannins.

VALDECURIEL 2010 TC

88 Colour: cherry, garnet rim. Nose: ripe fruit, spicy, creamy oak, toasty. Palate: powerful, toasty, round tannins.

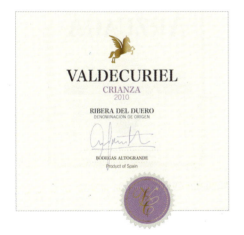

VALDECURIEL 2012 T ROBLE

87 Colour: cherry, purple rim. Nose: expressive, red berry notes, floral, citrus fruit, fragrant herbs. Palate: flavourful, fruity, good acidity, spicy.

VALDECURIEL VENDIMIA SELECCIONADA 2011 T

87 Colour: cherry, garnet rim. Nose: ripe fruit, spicy, creamy oak, toasty. Palate: powerful, flavourful, toasty.

VALDECURIEL VENDIMIA SELECCIONADA 2012 T

86 Colour: bright cherry. Nose: ripe fruit, sweet spices, creamy oak. Palate: flavourful, fruity, toasty.

BODEGAS ANTÍDOTO

Elias Alvarez nº31, 1ºB
42330 San Esteban de Gormaz (Soria)

ANTÍDOTO 2011 T
100% tinto fino

91 Colour: cherry, garnet rim. Nose: ripe fruit, fruit expression, sweet spices. Palate: fruity, fresh, long, ripe fruit, fine tannins.

BODEGAS ARROCAL

Eras de Santa María, s/n
9443 Gumiel de Mercado (Burgos)
☎: +34 947 561 290 - Fax: +34 947 561 290
www.arrocal.com
info@arrocal.com

ARROCAL 2011 T BARRICA
tempranillo

87 Colour: cherry, garnet rim. Nose: red berry notes, ripe fruit, cocoa bean, sweet spices. Palate: powerful, flavourful, long, toasty.

ARROCAL ANGEL 2009 T
tempranillo

91 Colour: cherry, garnet rim. Nose: red berry notes, ripe fruit, balsamic herbs, mineral, creamy oak, cocoa bean, sweet spices. Palate: powerful, rich, flavourful, balanced, elegant.

ARROCAL PASSIÓN 2010 T
tempranillo

90 Colour: cherry, garnet rim. Nose: red berry notes, ripe fruit, fragrant herbs, sweet spices, creamy oak. Palate: good acidity, flavourful, balanced, toasty.

ARROCAL SELECCIÓN 2008 T
tempranillo

90 Colour: cherry, garnet rim. Nose: ripe fruit, spicy, creamy oak, toasty, scrubland. Palate: powerful, flavourful, toasty, balanced, elegant.

ROSA DE ARROCAL 2012 RD
tempranillo

87 Colour: rose, purple rim. Nose: powerfull, ripe fruit, red berry notes, floral, fragrant herbs. Palate: powerful, fruity, fresh.

BODEGAS ARZUAGA NAVARRO

Ctra. N-122, Km. 325
47350 Quintanilla de Onésimo (Valladolid)
☎: +34 983 681 146 - Fax: +34 983 681 147
www.arzuaganavarro.com
bodeg@arzuaganavarro.com

AMAYA ARZUAGA AUTOR 2009 T
95% tinto fino, 5% albillo

93 Colour: cherry, garnet rim. Nose: ripe fruit, spicy, creamy oak, complex, mineral. Palate: powerful, flavourful, toasty, round tannins.

ARZUAGA 2010 TC
90% tinto fino, 7% cabernet sauvignon, 3% merlot

91 Colour: cherry, garnet rim. Nose: ripe fruit, powerfull, roasted coffee. Palate: powerful, flavourful, round tannins.

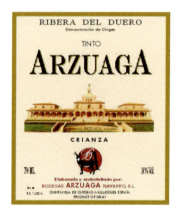

ARZUAGA 2011 TC

89 Colour: bright cherry, garnet rim. Nose: red berry notes, ripe fruit, sweet spices, roasted coffee. Palate: flavourful, fruity, toasty.

ARZUAGA 2004 TGR
90% tinto fino, 5% cabernet sauvignon, 5% merlot

91 Colour: deep cherry. Nose: ripe fruit, spicy, expressive, sweet spices. Palate: round tannins, spicy, long.

ARZUAGA 2009 TR
95% tinto fino, 5% cabernet sauvignon, 5% merlot

89 Colour: cherry, garnet rim. Nose: ripe fruit, spicy, creamy oak. Palate: powerful, flavourful, toasty, round tannins.

ARZUAGA 2010 TR

92 Colour: cherry, garnet rim. Nose: ripe fruit, spicy, creamy oak, toasty. Palate: powerful, flavourful, toasty, round tannins, balanced.

ARZUAGA ECOLÓGICO 2010 TC
90% tinto fino, 7% cabernet sauvignon, 3% merlot

90 Colour: cherry, garnet rim. Nose: ripe fruit, creamy oak, toasty. Palate: flavourful, toasty, round tannins, good acidity.

ARZUAGA
VINO ELABORADO CON
UVAS ECOLÓGICAS

RIBERA DEL DUERO
CRIANZA

ARZUAGA RESERVA ESPECIAL 2009 TR
95% tinto fino, 5% blanca del país

93 Colour: cherry, garnet rim. Nose: ripe fruit, spicy, creamy oak, toasty, mineral. Palate: powerful, flavourful, toasty, round tannins, long.

BODEGAS Y VIÑEDOS LA PLANTA 2011 T
100% tinto fino

89 Colour: bright cherry. Nose: sweet spices, creamy oak, fruit preserve. Palate: flavourful, fruity, toasty, round tannins.

RIBERA DEL DUERO
DENOMINACIÓN DE ORIGEN

LA PLANTA

COSECHA

GRAN ARZUAGA 2009 T
75% tinto fino, 20% cabernet sauvignon, 5% albillo

94 Colour: cherry, garnet rim. Nose: spicy, creamy oak, roasted coffee. Palate: powerful, flavourful, toasty, round tannins.

BODEGAS ASENJO & MANSO

Ctra. Palencia, km. 58,200
9311 La Horra (Burgos)
☎: +34 636 972 524 - Fax: +34 947 505 269
www.asenjo-manso.com
info@asenjo-manso.com

A&M AUTOR 2009 T
100% tempranillo

92 Colour: very deep cherry, garnet rim. Nose: complex, fruit preserve, sweet spices, dried herbs. Palate: powerful, good structure, round tannins.

CERES 2009 TC
100% tempranillo

88 Colour: cherry, garnet rim. Nose: medium intensity, fruit preserve, sweet spices. Palate: fruity, round tannins.

MANSO 2009 TC
100% tempranillo

89 Colour: cherry, garnet rim. Nose: ripe fruit, complex, sweet spices, dry stone. Palate: round tannins, fruity, easy to drink.

SILVANUS 2009 TC
100% tempranillo

90 Colour: cherry, garnet rim. Nose: red berry notes, ripe fruit, balsamic herbs, sweet spices. Palate: powerful, flavourful, balanced.

SILVANUS EDICIÓN LIMITADA 2009 T
100% tempranillo

89 Colour: cherry, garnet rim. Nose: creamy oak, dark chocolate, sweet spices, ripe fruit. Palate: good structure, flavourful, fruity, round tannins, smoky aftertaste.

BODEGAS BALBÁS

La Majada, s/n
9311 La Horra (Burgos)
☎: +34 947 542 111 - Fax: +34 947 542 112
www.balbas.es
bodegas@balbas.es

ALITUS 2005 TR
75% tempranillo, 20% cabernet sauvignon, 5% merlot

93 Colour: bright cherry, garnet rim. Nose: complex, powerfull, cocoa bean, sweet spices, creamy oak. Palate: good structure, flavourful, round tannins, toasty.

ARDAL 2008 TR
80% tempranillo, 20% cabernet sauvignon

91 Colour: cherry, garnet rim. Nose: ripe fruit, spicy, creamy oak, toasty, mineral. Palate: powerful, flavourful, toasty, round tannins.

ARDAL 2010 TC
80% tempranillo, 20% cabernet sauvignon

89 Colour: cherry, garnet rim. Nose: ripe fruit, spicy, creamy oak, toasty, fine reductive notes. Palate: powerful, flavourful, toasty.

BALBÁS 2010 TC
90% tempranillo, 10% cabernet sauvignon

93 Colour: cherry, garnet rim. Nose: spicy, creamy oak, toasty, complex, fruit expression. Palate: powerful, flavourful, toasty, round tannins, creamy.

RITUS 2010 T
75% tempranillo, 25% merlot

89 Colour: deep cherry, garnet rim. Nose: cocoa bean, sweet spices, ripe fruit. Palate: powerful, roasted-coffee aftertaste.

BODEGAS BALUARTE

Ribera, 34
31592 Cintruénigo (Navarra)
☎: +34 948 811 000 - Fax: +34 948 811 407
www.chivite.com
info@bodegaschivite.com

BALUARTE 2011 T ROBLE
tempranillo

86 Colour: very deep cherry. Nose: fruit preserve, sweet spices, powerfull. Palate: fruity, flavourful.

BODEGAS BOHÓRQUEZ

Ctra. Peñafiel, Km. 4
47315 Pesquera de Duero (Valladolid)
☎: +34 915 640 508 - Fax: +34 915 618 602
www.bodegasbohorquez.com
info@bodegasbohorquez.com

BOHÓRQUEZ 2009 TR
tempranillo, cabernet sauvignon, merlot

88 Colour: cherry, garnet rim. Nose: ripe fruit, spicy, creamy oak, toasty. Palate: powerful, flavourful, toasty.

CARDELA 2009 TC
tempranillo, cabernet sauvignon, merlot

89 Colour: cherry, garnet rim. Nose: candied fruit, sweet spices. Palate: powerful, flavourful, balsamic.

BODEGAS BRIEGO

Ctra. Cuellar, s/n
47311 Fompedraza (Valladolid)
☎: +34 983 892 156 - Fax: +34 983 892 156
www.bodegasbriego.com
info@bodegasbriego.com

ANKAL 2005 TR
100% tempranillo

90 Colour: cherry, garnet rim. Nose: ripe fruit, spicy, toasty, balsamic herbs. Palate: powerful, flavourful, toasty, round tannins.

ANKAL 2009 TC
100% tempranillo

91 Colour: cherry, garnet rim. Nose: ripe fruit, spicy, creamy oak, toasty, complex. Palate: powerful, flavourful, toasty, round tannins.

ANKAL 2011 T ROBLE
100% tempranillo

86 Colour: cherry, garnet rim. Nose: ripe fruit, fruit preserve, balsamic herbs. Palate: flavourful, fruity, round tannins.

BRIEGO ADALID 2009 TR
100% tempranillo

88 Colour: cherry, garnet rim. Nose: sweet spices, fruit preserve, ripe fruit. Palate: fruity, long.

BRIEGO VENDIMIA SELECCIONADA 2011 T ROBLE
100% tempranillo

92 Colour: cherry, garnet rim. Nose: spicy, creamy oak, toasty, complex, characterful. Palate: powerful, flavourful, toasty, round tannins.

SUPERNOVA 2009 TC
100% tempranillo

90 Colour: bright cherry. Nose: sweet spices, creamy oak, aromatic coffee, ripe fruit. Palate: flavourful, fruity, toasty, round tannins.

SUPERNOVA EDICIÓN LIMITADA 2009 T
100% tempranillo

91 Colour: cherry, garnet rim. Nose: ripe fruit, spicy, creamy oak, toasty, fine reductive notes. Palate: powerful, flavourful, toasty, round tannins.

SUPERNOVA ROBLE 2011 T ROBLE
100% tempranillo

92 Colour: cherry, garnet rim. Nose: ripe fruit, spicy, creamy oak, toasty, complex, mineral, varietal, red berry notes. Palate: powerful, flavourful, toasty, round tannins.

TIEMPO BRIEGO 2011 TC
100% tempranillo

91 Colour: cherry, garnet rim. Nose: ripe fruit, spicy, creamy oak. Palate: powerful, flavourful, toasty, round tannins.

BODEGAS BRIONES ABAD

Bodegas Briones Abad
9300 Roa (Burgos)
☎: +34 947 540 613 - Fax: +34 947 540 613
www.cantamuda.com
brionesabad@cantamuda.com

CANTA MUDA 2011 T ROBLE
100% tempranillo

88 Colour: bright cherry. Nose: ripe fruit, sweet spices, creamy oak, aromatic coffee. Palate: flavourful, fruity, toasty.

CANTA MUDA PARCELA 64 2010 T
100% tempranillo

90 Colour: cherry, garnet rim. Nose: red berry notes, ripe fruit, balsamic herbs, mineral, sweet spices, creamy oak. Palate: powerful, flavourful, spicy, long.

BODEGAS BRIONES BANIANDRÉS

Camino Valdeguzmán, s/n
9314 Quintanamanvirgo (Burgos)
☎: +34 947 561 385 - Fax: +34 947 561 386
www.apricus.es
bodegas@apricus.es

APRICUS 2009 TC
100% tempranillo

89 Colour: cherry, garnet rim. Nose: spicy, creamy oak, toasty, fruit preserve. Palate: flavourful, toasty, round tannins.

APRICUS 2011 T BARRICA
100% tempranillo

88 Colour: bright cherry. Nose: sweet spices, creamy oak. Palate: flavourful, fruity, toasty, round tannins.

APRICUS SENSUS 2009 T
100% tempranillo

90 Colour: cherry, garnet rim. Nose: spicy, creamy oak, toasty, fruit liqueur notes. Palate: powerful, flavourful, toasty, round tannins.

BODEGAS CASTILLO DE GUMIEL

Avda. de Extremadura, 55
9400 Aranda de Duero (Burgos)
☎: +34 947 510 839 - Fax: +34 947 510 839
www.silenciovaldiruela.com
castillodegumiel@hotmail.com

SILENCIO DE VALDIRUELA 2007 TR
tinta del país

89 Colour: cherry, garnet rim. Nose: balanced, medium intensity, ripe fruit, varietal. Palate: spicy, ripe fruit, long.

SILENCIO DE VALDIRUELA 2009 TC
tinta del país

88 Colour: cherry, garnet rim. Nose: ripe fruit, spicy, creamy oak, toasty. Palate: powerful, flavourful, toasty, round tannins.

SILENCIO DE VALDIRUELA 2011 T ROBLE
tinta del país

88 Colour: cherry, garnet rim. Nose: spicy, creamy oak, toasty. Palate: powerful, flavourful, toasty, round tannins.

SILENCIO DE VALDIRUELA 2012 T
tinta del país

88 Colour: deep cherry, purple rim. Nose: balanced, ripe fruit, violet drops. Palate: balanced, fruity, long.

SILENCIO VIÑAS CENTENARIAS 2009 T BARRICA
tinta del país

92 Colour: deep cherry, garnet rim. Nose: expressive, balanced, ripe fruit, sweet spices. Palate: flavourful, ripe fruit, long, fine tannins.

BODEGAS CEPA 21

Ctra. N-122, Km. 297
47318 Castrillo de Duero (Valladolid)
☎: +34 983 484 083 - Fax: +34 983 480 017
www.cepa21.com
bodega@cepa21.com

CEPA 21 2010 T
100% tinto fino

92 Colour: cherry, garnet rim. Nose: spicy, creamy oak, toasty, complex, fruit expression. Palate: powerful, flavourful, toasty, round tannins.

HITO 2011 T
100% tinto fino

84

MALABRIGO 2010 T
100% tinto fino

93 Colour: cherry, garnet rim. Nose: ripe fruit, spicy, creamy oak, toasty, complex, mineral, dry stone. Palate: powerful, flavourful, round tannins, good acidity.

BODEGAS COOPERATIVA NUESTRA SEÑORA DE LA ASUNCIÓN

Eras de Arriba, s/n
9454 Quemada (Burgos)
☎: +34 947 553 133 - Fax: +34 947 553 133
roquesanq@terra.es

ROQUESÁN 2011 T ROBLE

85 Colour: cherry, purple rim. Nose: medium intensity, ripe fruit. Palate: fruity, correct, easy to drink, good finish.

BODEGAS CRUZ DE ALBA

Síndico, 4 y 5
47350 Quintanilla de Onésimo (Valladolid)
☎: +34 941 310 295 - Fax: +34 941 310 832
www.cruzdealba.es
info@cruzdealba.es

CRUZ DE ALBA 2011 TC
100% tempranillo

90 Colour: black cherry, garnet rim. Nose: ripe fruit, fruit liqueur notes, sweet spices, toasty. Palate: powerful, flavourful, spicy, long.

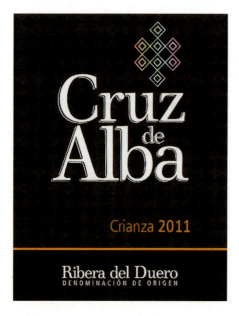

LUCERO DE ALBA 2012 T ROBLE
100% tempranillo

87 Colour: cherry, purple rim. Nose: ripe fruit, balsamic herbs, spicy, creamy oak. Palate: powerful, flavourful, toasty.

BODEGAS CUEVAS JIMÉNEZ - FERRATUS

Ctra. Madrid-Irún, A-I km. 165
9370 Gumiel de Izán (Burgos)
☎: +34 947 679 999 - Fax: +34 947 613 873
www.ferratus.es
bodega@ferratus.es

FERRATUS 2008 T
100% tempranillo

93 Colour: cherry, garnet rim. Nose: mineral, ripe fruit, spicy, toasty. Palate: flavourful, spicy, ripe fruit, round tannins.

FERRATUS A0 2011 T ROBLE
tempranillo

89 Colour: bright cherry. Nose: sweet spices, toasty, dark chocolate, powerfull. Palate: flavourful, fruity, toasty.

FERRATUS A0 2012 T ROBLE
100% tempranillo

90 Colour: deep cherry, purple rim. Nose: toasty, creamy oak, ripe fruit. Palate: spicy, good acidity, long.

FERRATUS SENSACIONES 2008 T
100% tempranillo

93 Colour: cherry, garnet rim. Nose: powerfull, ripe fruit, spicy, toasty, creamy oak. Palate: flavourful, powerful, good acidity, spicy.

FERRATUS SENSACIONES DÉCIMO 2003 T
100% tempranillo

96 Colour: very deep cherry. Nose: powerfull, ripe fruit, cocoa bean, spicy, dark chocolate. Palate: flavourful, fine bitter notes, good acidity, elegant, round, fine tannins.

BODEGAS DE LOS RÍOS PRIETO

Ctra. Pesquera - Renedo, 1
47315 Pesquera de Duero (Valladolid)
☎: +34 983 880 383 - Fax: +34 983 878 032
www.bodegasdelosriosprieto.com
info@bodegasdelosriosprieto.com

LARA PRIOS MAXIMUS VINO DE AUTOR 2009 T
tempranillo

90 Colour: cherry, garnet rim. Nose: balanced, dried herbs, spicy, ripe fruit. Palate: spicy, flavourful, round tannins.

PRIOS MAXIMUS 2009 TR
tempranillo

90 Colour: cherry, garnet rim. Nose: ripe fruit, spicy, creamy oak, cigar. Palate: powerful, flavourful, spicy, long.

PRIOS MAXIMUS 2011 TC
tempranillo

88 Colour: cherry, garnet rim. Nose: candied fruit, spicy. Palate: flavourful, fruity, spicy.

PRIOS MAXIMUS 2012 T ROBLE
tempranillo

87 Colour: very deep cherry, purple rim. Nose: powerfull, ripe fruit, candied fruit, sweet spices. Palate: flavourful, correct.

BODEGAS DEL CAMPO

Camino Fuentenavares, s/n
9370 Quintana del Pidío (Burgos)
☎: +34 947 561 034 - Fax: +34 947 561 038
www.pagosdequintana.com
bodegas@pagosdequintana.com

PAGOS DE QUINTANA 2009 TC
100% tinto fino

88 Colour: cherry, garnet rim. Nose: medium intensity, ripe fruit, fruit preserve, sweet spices. Palate: fruity, round tannins.

PAGOS DE QUINTANA ROBLE 2011 T ROBLE
100% tinto fino

88 Colour: deep cherry, garnet rim. Nose: powerfull, violets, ripe fruit, sweet spices. Palate: fruity, flavourful, round tannins.

PAGOS DE QUINTANA VENDIMIA SELECCIONADA 2009 T
100% tinto fino

90 Colour: bright cherry. Nose: ripe fruit, sweet spices, creamy oak. Palate: flavourful, fruity, toasty, round tannins.

BODEGAS DÍEZ LLORENTE

Ctra. Circunvalación, s/n
9300 Roa (Burgos)
☎: +34 615 293 031 - Fax: +34 947 540 341
www.diezllorente.com
bodegas@diezllorente.com

DÍEZ LLORENTE 2010 TC
tempranillo

86 Colour: deep cherry, garnet rim. Nose: ripe fruit, scrubland, sweet spices. Palate: flavourful, ripe fruit.

DÍEZ LLORENTE 2011 T ROBLE
tempranillo

86 Colour: bright cherry. Nose: sweet spices, expressive, overripe fruit, toasty. Palate: flavourful, toasty, round tannins.

GRAN SALINERO 2009 TC
tempranillo

84

GRAN SALINERO SELECCIÓN 2011 T ROBLE
tempranillo

88 Colour: cherry, garnet rim. Nose: expressive, toasty, dark chocolate, creamy oak. Palate: flavourful, smoky aftertaste.

SEÑORÍO DE BRENDA 2011 T ROBLE
tempranillo

87 Colour: cherry, garnet rim. Nose: ripe fruit, spicy, creamy oak. Palate: powerful, flavourful, toasty, round tannins.

BODEGAS DOMINIO DE CAIR

Ctra. Aranda a la Aguilera. km. 9
9370 La Aguilera (Burgos)
☎: +34 947 545 276 - Fax: +34 947 545 383
www.dominiodecair.com
bodegas@dominiodecair.com

CAIR 2009 T
100% tempranillo

90 Colour: cherry, garnet rim. Nose: ripe fruit, spicy, creamy oak, mineral. Palate: powerful, flavourful, spicy, long.

CAIR 2010 TC
100% tempranillo

92 Colour: cherry, garnet rim. Nose: red berry notes, ripe fruit, sweet spices, expressive, mineral, elegant. Palate: rich, fruity, flavourful, long, balanced.

CAIR CUVÉE 2010 T
85% tempranillo, 15% merlot

91 Colour: cherry, garnet rim. Nose: ripe fruit, spicy, toasty, characterful. Palate: powerful, flavourful, toasty, round tannins.

TIERRAS DE CAIR 2008 TR
100% tempranillo

93 Colour: cherry, garnet rim. Nose: ripe fruit, spicy, creamy oak, toasty, complex. Palate: powerful, flavourful, toasty, round tannins.

TIERRAS DE CAIR 2009 T
100% tempranillo

94 Colour: cherry, garnet rim. Nose: red berry notes, ripe fruit, balsamic herbs, mineral, sweet spices, expressive. Palate: rich, flavourful, spicy, long, balanced, elegant.

BODEGAS EMILIO MORO

Ctra. Peñafiel - Valoria, s/n
47315 Pesquera de Duero (Valladolid)
☎: +34 983 878 400 - Fax: +34 983 870 195
www.emiliomoro.com
bodega@emiliomoro.com

EMILIO MORO 2010 T
tinto fino

93 Colour: very deep cherry. Nose: ripe fruit, medium intensity, dark chocolate, creamy oak. Palate: good structure, flavourful, round tannins.

FINCA RESALSO 2012 T
100% tinto fino

90 Colour: bright cherry. Nose: sweet spices, creamy oak, red berry notes. Palate: flavourful, fruity, toasty, round tannins.

MALLEOLUS 2010 T
100% tinto fino

93 Colour: very deep cherry. Nose: creamy oak, complex, ripe fruit. Palate: round, good structure, round tannins, ripe fruit.

MALLEOLUS DE SANCHOMARTÍN 2009 T
100% tinto fino

94 Colour: very deep cherry, garnet rim. Nose: red berry notes, ripe fruit, balsamic herbs, mineral, sweet spices, creamy oak, balanced, elegant. Palate: flavourful, elegant, long, spicy.

MALLEOLUS DE VALDERRAMIRO 2009 T
100% tinto fino

93 Colour: bright cherry, garnet rim. Nose: ripe fruit, sweet spices, creamy oak, cocoa bean, toasty, expressive. Palate: flavourful, fruity, toasty, round tannins.

BODEGAS EPIFANIO RIVERA

Onésimo Redondo, 47
47315 Pesquera de Duero (Valladolid)
☎: +34 983 870 109 - Fax: +34 983 870 109
www.epifaniorivera.com
info@epifaniorivera.com

ERIAL 2010 T
100% tinto fino

91 Colour: cherry, garnet rim. Nose: red berry notes, ripe fruit, sweet spices, creamy oak. Palate: powerful, flavourful, spicy, long.

ERIAL TF 2010 T
100% tinto fino

90 Colour: cherry, garnet rim. Nose: toasty, spicy, ripe fruit. Palate: fruity, flavourful, good acidity.

BODEGAS FÉLIX CALLEJO

Avda. del Cid, km. 16
9441 Sotillo de la Ribera (Burgos)
☎: +34 947 532 312 - Fax: +34 947 532 304
www.bodegasfelixcallejo.com
callejo@bodegasfelixcallejo.com

CALLEJO 2010 TC
100% tempranillo

89 Colour: very deep cherry. Nose: varietal, ripe fruit, balsamic herbs, spicy. Palate: good structure, flavourful, round tannins.

FÉLIX CALLEJO SELECCIÓN 2010 T
tempranillo

92 Colour: cherry, garnet rim. Nose: ripe fruit, fruit preserve, balsamic herbs, mineral, sweet spices, creamy oak. Palate: powerful, flavourful, rich, balanced.

FLORES DE CALLEJO 2011 T
tempranillo

88 Colour: cherry, garnet rim. Nose: powerfull, fruit preserve, roasted coffee. Palate: flavourful, powerful, sweetness.

MAJUELOS DE CALLEJO 2010 T
tempranillo

91 Colour: cherry, garnet rim. Nose: ripe fruit, spicy, creamy oak, toasty, complex. Palate: powerful, flavourful, toasty, round tannins.

VIÑA PILAR 2012 RD
tempranillo

86 Colour: rose, purple rim. Nose: medium intensity, citrus fruit, ripe fruit. Palate: fruity, good acidity, balanced.

BODEGAS FÉLIX SANZ

Ronda Aradillas, s/n
47490 Rueda (Valladolid)
☎: +34 983 868 044 - Fax: +34 983 868 133
www.bodegasfelixsanz.es
pedidos@bodegasfelixsanz.es

MONTENEGRO 2005 TR
tempranillo

85 Colour: deep cherry. Nose: medium intensity, slightly evolved, spicy, toasty. Palate: sweetness, warm.

MONTENEGRO 2006 TC
tempranillo

87 Colour: cherry, garnet rim. Nose: ripe fruit, spicy, creamy oak. Palate: powerful, flavourful, round tannins.

MONTENEGRO 2011 T ROBLE
tempranillo

86 Colour: cherry, garnet rim. Nose: roasted coffee, powerfull, aromatic coffee. Palate: flavourful, ripe fruit, long.

BODEGAS FUENTENARRO

Ctra. Burgos, s/n Cruce
9311 La Horra (Burgos)
☎: +34 947 542 092 - Fax: +34 947 542 083
www.fuentenarro.com
bodegas@fuentenarro.com

VIÑA FUENTENARRO 2006 TR
tempranillo

91 Colour: cherry, garnet rim. Nose: ripe fruit, spicy, creamy oak, toasty. Palate: powerful, flavourful, toasty, round tannins.

VIÑA FUENTENARRO 2010 TC
tempranillo

92 Colour: cherry, garnet rim. Nose: ripe fruit, spicy, creamy oak, toasty, complex, powerfull, varietal, mineral. Palate: powerful, flavourful, toasty, round tannins.

VIÑA FUENTENARRO CUATRO MESES BARRICA 2011 T BARRICA
tempranillo

87 Colour: cherry, garnet rim. Nose: fruit preserve, roasted coffee. Palate: powerful, sweetness.

VIÑA FUENTENARRO VENDIMIA SELECCIONADA 2011 T
tempranillo

90 Colour: bright cherry. Nose: ripe fruit, sweet spices, toasty, balsamic herbs. Palate: flavourful, fruity, toasty, round tannins.

BODEGAS FUENTESPINA

Bodegas Fuentespina
40460 Fuentespina (Burgos)
☎: +34 921 596 002 - Fax: +34 921 596 035
www.avelinovegas.com
ana@avelinovegas.com

CORONA DE CASTILLA PRESTIGIO 2010 TC
tempranillo

92 Colour: cherry, garnet rim. Nose: ripe fruit, spicy, creamy oak, toasty, complex. Palate: powerful, flavourful, toasty, round tannins.

F DE FUENTESPINA 2009 TR
tempranillo

90 Colour: cherry, garnet rim. Nose: ripe fruit, spicy, toasty. Palate: powerful, flavourful, toasty, round tannins.

FUENTESPINA 2010 TC
tempranillo

90 Colour: cherry, garnet rim. Nose: ripe fruit, spicy, creamy oak, toasty. Palate: powerful, flavourful, toasty.

FUENTESPINA 2008 TR
tempranillo

89 Colour: cherry, garnet rim. Nose: ripe fruit, spicy, aromatic coffee. Palate: spicy, ripe fruit, fine bitter notes.

FUENTESPINA 2012 T ROBLE
tempranillo

86 Colour: deep cherry, purple rim. Nose: toasty, aromatic coffee. Palate: flavourful, fruity, correct.

FUENTESPINA GRANATE 2012 T
tempranillo

87 Colour: cherry, purple rim. Nose: medium intensity, balanced, ripe fruit, faded flowers. Palate: fruity, easy to drink, correct.

FUENTESPINA SELECCIÓN 2010 T
tempranillo

92 Colour: cherry, garnet rim. Nose: red berry notes, ripe fruit, balsamic herbs, dry stone, expressive. Palate: powerful, long, spicy, balanced.

BODEGAS GARCÍA DE ARANDA

Ctra. de Soria, s/n
9400 Aranda de Duero (Burgos)
☎: +34 947 501 817 - Fax: +34 947 506 355
www.bodegasgarcia.com
bodega@bodegasgarcia.com

EDADES DE BALDÍOS 2011 T ROBLE
tempranillo
84

PG PEDRO GARCÍA 2010 T
tempranillo

90 Colour: cherry, garnet rim. Nose: spicy, creamy oak, toasty, balsamic herbs, fruit preserve. Palate: powerful, flavourful, toasty.

SEÑORÍO DE LOS BALDÍOS 2008 TR
tempranillo

87 Colour: cherry, garnet rim. Nose: medium intensity, balsamic herbs, ripe fruit. Palate: fruity, spicy, good finish.

SEÑORÍO DE LOS BALDÍOS 2010 TC
tempranillo

88 Colour: cherry, garnet rim. Nose: ripe fruit, spicy, creamy oak, toasty, earthy notes. Palate: powerful, flavourful, toasty.

SEÑORÍO DE LOS BALDÍOS 2012 T
tempranillo

85 Colour: cherry, purple rim. Nose: fresh fruit, red berry notes, floral. Palate: flavourful, fruity, good acidity.

SEÑORÍO DE LOS BALDÍOS 2012 T ROBLE
tempranillo

84

SEÑORÍO DE LOS BALDÍOS DON ANASTASIO GARCÍA 2012 RD
tempranillo

85 Colour: light cherry. Nose: ripe fruit, dried herbs. Palate: flavourful, balanced, long.

BODEGAS HACIENDA MONASTERIO

Ctra. Pesquera - Valbuena, s/n
47315 Pesquera de Duero (Valladolid)
☎: +34 983 484 002 - Fax: +34 983 484 079
www.haciendamonasterio.com
bmonasterio@haciendamonasterio.com

HACIENDA MONASTERIO 2008 TR
80% tinto fino, 20% cabernet sauvignon

91 Colour: cherry, garnet rim. Nose: expressive, ripe fruit, sweet spices, toasty. Palate: flavourful, spicy, ripe fruit.

HACIENDA MONASTERIO 2009 T
80% tinto fino, 15% merlot, 5% cabernet sauvignon

91 Colour: very deep cherry. Nose: ripe fruit, fruit preserve, sweet spices. Palate: good structure, flavourful, good acidity, round tannins.

HACIENDA MONASTERIO 2010 T
80% tinto fino, 10% merlot, 10% cabernet sauvignon

92 Colour: cherry, garnet rim. Nose: powerfull, characterful, complex, cocoa bean. Palate: flavourful, long, good acidity, fine tannins.

HACIENDA MONASTERIO RESERVA ESPECIAL 2009 TR
78% tinto fino, 22% cabernet sauvignon

91 Colour: black cherry, garnet rim. Nose: dark chocolate, sweet spices, ripe fruit, fruit preserve. Palate: flavourful, rich, round tannins.

BODEGAS HERMANOS PÉREZ PASCUAS

Ctra. Roa, s/n
9314 Pedrosa de Duero (Burgos)
☎: +34 947 530 100 - Fax: +34 947 530 002
www.perezpascuas.com
vinapedrosa@perezpascuas.com

CEPA GAVILÁN 2011 T
100% tinta del país

90 Colour: bright cherry, garnet rim. Nose: ripe fruit, sweet spices, creamy oak, mineral. Palate: flavourful, fruity, toasty.

PÉREZ PASCUAS GRAN SELECCIÓN 2006 TGR
100% tinta del país

94 Colour: deep cherry, orangey edge. Nose: ripe fruit, spicy, balsamic herbs, earthy notes, creamy oak. Palate: flavourful, spicy, long, balanced, elegant.

VIÑA PEDROSA 2006 TGR
90% tinta del país, 10% cabernet sauvignon

90 Colour: pale ruby, brick rim edge. Nose: spicy, fine reductive notes, wet leather, aged wood nuances, fruit liqueur notes. Palate: spicy, fine tannins, elegant, long.

VIÑA PEDROSA 2010 TR
90% tinta del país, 10% cabernet sauvignon

94 Colour: cherry, garnet rim. Nose: ripe fruit, spicy, balsamic herbs, cocoa bean, dark chocolate, creamy oak, expressive. Palate: spicy, toasty, long, balanced.

VIÑA PEDROSA 2011 TC
100% tinta del país

92 Colour: cherry, garnet rim. Nose: red berry notes, ripe fruit, cocoa bean, dark chocolate, toasty, powerfull. Palate: flavourful, easy to drink, long, toasty.

VIÑA PEDROSA LA NAVILLA 2010 T
100% tinta del país

93 Colour: cherry, garnet rim. Nose: red berry notes, ripe fruit, mineral, sweet spices, creamy oak, earthy notes. Palate: powerful, flavourful, spicy, long, balanced.

BODEGAS HERMANOS SASTRE

San Pedro, s/n
9311 La Horra (Burgos)
☎: +34 947 542 108 - Fax: +34 947 542 108
www.vinasastre.com
sastre@vinasastre.com

VIÑA SASTRE 2011 T ROBLE
100% tempranillo

90 Colour: bright cherry. Nose: ripe fruit, sweet spices, cocoa bean, dark chocolate. Palate: flavourful, fruity, toasty, balanced.

VIÑA SASTRE PAGO DE SANTA CRUZ 2010 T
100% tempranillo

94 Colour: cherry, garnet rim. Nose: mineral, creamy oak, sweet spices. Palate: powerful, flavourful, concentrated, long, round tannins.

VIÑA SASTRE PESUS 2010 T
80% tempranillo, 20% merlot, cabernet sauvignon

97 Colour: very deep cherry. Nose: creamy oak, sweet spices, ripe fruit, toasty, earthy notes. Palate: flavourful, fruity, powerful, ripe fruit, round tannins.

VIÑA SASTRE 2010 TC
100% tempranillo

93 Colour: deep cherry, garnet rim. Nose: balanced, medium intensity, cocoa bean, sweet spices, ripe fruit. Palate: flavourful, round tannins.

REGINA VIDES 2010 T
100% tempranillo

96 Colour: cherry, garnet rim. Nose: ripe fruit, spicy, creamy oak, toasty, powerfull, varietal, mineral. Palate: powerful, flavourful, toasty, round tannins.

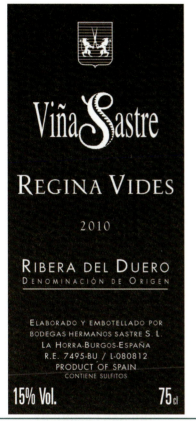

BODEGAS HESVERA

Ctra. Peñafiel - Pesquera, Km. 5,5
47315 Pesquera de Duero (Valladolid)
☎: +34 983 870 137 - Fax: +34 983 870 201
www.hesvera.es
hesvera@hesvera.es

HESVERA 2009 TC
tempranillo

88 Colour: cherry, garnet rim. Nose: ripe fruit, fruit preserve, scrubland, creamy oak. Palate: powerful, flavourful, spicy.

HESVERA COSECHA LIMITADA 2009 T
tempranillo, merlot

89 Colour: cherry, garnet rim. Nose: ripe fruit, spicy, creamy oak, balsamic herbs, fine reductive notes. Palate: powerful, flavourful, balanced, elegant.

HESVERA SEIS MESES 2011 T
tempranillo

84

BODEGAS IMPERIALES

Ctra. Madrid - Irun, Km. 171
9370 Gumiel de Izán (Burgos)
☎: +34 947 544 070 - Fax: +34 947 525 759
www.bodegasimperiales.com
direccion@bodegasimperiales.com

ABADÍA DE SAN QUIRCE 2005 TR
100% tempranillo

90 Colour: cherry, garnet rim. Nose: ripe fruit, spicy, toasty. Palate: powerful, flavourful, toasty, round tannins.

ABADÍA DE SAN QUIRCE 2009 TC
100% tempranillo

92 Colour: cherry, garnet rim. Nose: ripe fruit, spicy, creamy oak, toasty, characterful, varietal. Palate: powerful, flavourful, toasty, round tannins.

ABADÍA DE SAN QUIRCE 2012 T ROBLE
100% tempranillo

91 Colour: bright cherry. Nose: sweet spices, creamy oak, expressive, fruit expression. Palate: flavourful, fruity, toasty, round tannins.

ABADÍA DE SAN QUIRCE FINCA HELENA AUTOR 2008 T
100% tempranillo

92 Colour: cherry, garnet rim. Nose: spicy, dry stone, ripe fruit, complex. Palate: balanced, good acidity, fine bitter notes, round tannins.

BODEGAS ISMAEL ARROYO - VALSOTILLO

Los Lagares, 71
9441 Sotillo de la Ribera (Burgos)
☎: +34 947 532 309 - Fax: +34 947 532 487
www.valsotillo.com
bodega@valsotillo.com

MESONEROS DE CASTILLA 2011 T ROBLE
100% tinta del país

87 Colour: bright cherry. Nose: ripe fruit, sweet spices, creamy oak. Palate: flavourful, fruity, toasty.

VALSOTILLO 2004 TGR
100% tinta del país

91 Colour: pale ruby, brick rim edge. Nose: elegant, spicy, fine reductive notes, wet leather, aged wood nuances, fruit liqueur notes. Palate: spicy, fine tannins, elegant, long.

VALSOTILLO 2006 TR
100% tinta del país

88 Colour: cherry, garnet rim. Nose: toasty, fruit preserve, spicy. Palate: flavourful, reductive nuances, spicy.

VALSOTILLO 2010 TC
100% tinta del país

92 Colour: cherry, garnet rim. Nose: spicy, creamy oak, toasty. Palate: powerful, flavourful, toasty, round tannins.

VALSOTILLO VS 2004 TR
100% tinta del país

92 Colour: pale ruby, brick rim edge. Nose: elegant, spicy, fine reductive notes, aged wood nuances, fruit liqueur notes. Palate: spicy, fine tannins, elegant, long, balanced.

BODEGAS LA HORRA

Camino de Anguix, s/n
9311 La Horra (Burgos)
☎: +34 947 613 963 - Fax: +34 947 613 963
www.bodegaslahorra.es
rodarioja@roda.es

CORIMBO 2010 T
100% tinta del país

92 Colour: cherry, garnet rim. Nose: ripe fruit, creamy oak, toasty, sweet spices. Palate: powerful, flavourful, toasty, round tannins.

CORIMBO I 2010 T
100% tinta del país

94 Colour: cherry, garnet rim. Nose: ripe fruit, spicy, creamy oak, toasty, complex, characterful, varietal. Palate: powerful, flavourful, toasty, round tannins.

PRODUCT OF SPAIN   ESTATE BOTTLED

CORIMBO I

EMBOTELLADO EN LA PROPIEDAD

75 cl. e

BODEGAS LA HORRA, S.L.
LA HORRA - BURGOS - ESPAÑA

ALC.14,5%VOL.

RIBERA DEL DUERO
DENOMINACIÓN DE ORIGEN

R.E. 8457-BU

BODEGAS LAMBUENA

Ctra. Fuentecén, s/n
9300 Roa (Burgos)
☎: +34 947 540 016 - Fax: +34 947 540 614
www.bodegaslambuena.com
lambuena@bodegaslambuena.com

LAMBUENA 2010 TC
tempranillo

87 Colour: deep cherry. Nose: medium intensity, overripe fruit, spicy, toasty. Palate: powerful, fine bitter notes, good acidity.

LAMBUENA 2011 T ROBLE
tempranillo

86 Colour: cherry, garnet rim. Nose: ripe fruit, creamy oak, toasty, complex. Palate: powerful, flavourful, toasty.

LAMBUENA ROSADO SELECCIÓN 2012 RD
tempranillo

86 Colour: light cherry, bright. Nose: medium intensity, red berry notes, ripe fruit. Palate: fruity, flavourful, correct.

LAMBUENA VIÑAS VIEJAS 2009 T
tempranillo

90 Colour: cherry, garnet rim. Nose: toasty, spicy. Palate: good structure, ripe fruit, balanced, round tannins.

BODEGAS LIBA Y DELEITE

Paseo De Zorrilla, 77 – 3º Dcha.
47007 (Valladolid)
☎: +34 983 355 543 - Fax: +34 983 340 824
www.acontia.es
info@cepasybodegas.com

ACONTIA 2009 TC
100% tempranillo

90 Colour: cherry, garnet rim. Nose: ripe fruit, spicy, creamy oak, toasty, fine reductive notes. Palate: powerful, flavourful, toasty, round tannins.

ACONTIA 2012 T
100% tempranillo

88 Colour: deep cherry, purple rim. Nose: ripe fruit, fruit preserve, balsamic herbs, spicy, creamy oak. Palate: powerful, flavourful.

BODEGAS LÓPEZ CRISTÓBAL

Barrio Estación, s/n
9300 Roa de Duero (Burgos)
☎: +34 947 561 136 - Fax: +34 947 540 606
www.lopezcristobal.com
info@lopezcristobal.com

BAGÚS 2010 T
100% tempranillo

94 Colour: bright cherry. Nose: ripe fruit, sweet spices, creamy oak, expressive. Palate: flavourful, fruity, toasty, harsh oak tannins.

LÓPEZ CRISTOBAL 2009 TR
95% tempranillo, 5% merlot

91 Colour: cherry, garnet rim. Nose: ripe fruit, spicy, creamy oak, characterful. Palate: powerful, flavourful, toasty, round tannins.

LÓPEZ CRISTOBAL 2010 TC
95% tempranillo, 5% merlot

90 Colour: cherry, garnet rim. Nose: ripe fruit, spicy, creamy oak, toasty, complex. Palate: powerful, flavourful, toasty.

LÓPEZ CRISTOBAL 2012 T ROBLE
95% tempranillo, 5% merlot

89 Colour: bright cherry. Nose: ripe fruit, sweet spices, creamy oak. Palate: flavourful, fruity, toasty, round tannins, balanced.

LÓPEZ CRISTOBAL SELECCIÓN 2010 T
100% tempranillo

90 Colour: cherry, purple rim. Nose: red berry notes, ripe fruit, sweet spices, creamy oak. Palate: powerful, flavourful, toasty.

BODEGAS MUÑOZ Y MAZÓN

Avda. Valle Esgueva, 12
9310 Villatuelda (Burgos)
☎: +34 941 454 050 - Fax: +34 941 454 529
www.bodegasriojanas.com
bodega@bodegasriojanas.com

AZUEL 2009 TC
100% tempranillo

87 Colour: cherry, garnet rim. Nose: powerfull, fruit preserve, pattisserie. Palate: flavourful, round tannins.

AZUEL ROBLE 2012 T
100% tempranillo

86 Colour: deep cherry, purple rim. Nose: powerfull, ripe fruit, toasty, sweet spices. Palate: powerful, correct.

BODEGAS PAGOS DE MOGAR

Ctra. Pesquera, km. 0,2
47359 Valbuena de Duero (Valladolid)
☎: +34 983 683 011
www.bodegaspagosdemogar.com
comercial@bodegaspagosdemogar.com

MOGAR 2011 T ROBLE
100% tinta del país

86 Colour: cherry, garnet rim. Nose: fruit preserve, balsamic herbs, spicy, creamy oak. Palate: powerful, flavourful, toasty.

MOGAR VENDIMIA SELECCIONADA 2009 TC
100% tinta del país

89 Colour: very deep cherry. Nose: spicy, powerfull. Palate: flavourful, fine bitter notes, warm.

MOGAR VENDIMIA SELECCIONADA 2010 T
100% tinta del país

86 Colour: cherry, garnet rim. Nose: toasty, sweet spices. Palate: flavourful, round tannins, smoky aftertaste.

BODEGAS PASCUAL

Ctra. de Aranda, Km. 5
9471 Fuentelcesped (Burgos)
☎: +34 947 557 351 - Fax: +34 947 557 312
www.bodegaspascual.com
export@bodegaspascual.com

BURÓ DE PEÑALOSA 2008 TR
100% tempranillo

88 Colour: cherry, garnet rim. Nose: ripe fruit, fine reductive notes, spicy, creamy oak. Palate: powerful, flavourful, correct.

BURÓ DE PEÑALOSA 2010 TC
100% tempranillo

89 Colour: cherry, garnet rim. Nose: fruit preserve, balsamic herbs, sweet spices, creamy oak. Palate: powerful, flavourful, spicy, long.

BURÓ SELECCIÓN 2010 T
100% tempranillo

91 Colour: cherry, garnet rim. Nose: ripe fruit, spicy, creamy oak, toasty, complex. Palate: powerful, flavourful, toasty, round tannins.

DIODORO AUTOR 2005 T
100% tempranillo

90 Colour: deep cherry, orangey edge. Nose: ripe fruit, scrubland, powerfull, spicy, creamy oak. Palate: powerful, flavourful, balanced.

HEREDAD DE PEÑALOSA 2012 T ROBLE
100% tempranillo

88 Colour: deep cherry, purple rim. Nose: powerfull, ripe fruit, violet drops, sweet spices. Palate: flavourful, powerful, long.

BODEGAS PEÑAFIEL

Ctra. N-122, Km. 311
47300 Peñafiel (Valladolid)
☎: +34 983 881 622 - Fax: +34 983 881 944
www.bodegaspenafiel.com
bodegaspenafiel@bodegaspenafiel.com

MIROS 2011 T ROBLE
85% tempranillo, 10% merlot, 5% cabernet sauvignon

87 Colour: cherry, garnet rim. Nose: ripe fruit, balsamic herbs, spicy, creamy oak. Palate: powerful, flavourful, warm.

MIROS DE RIBERA 2007 TR
100% tempranillo

89 Colour: pale ruby, brick rim edge. Nose: ripe fruit, sweet spices, creamy oak, fine reductive notes. Palate: powerful, flavourful, long.

MIROS DE RIBERA 2008 TC
85% tempranillo, 11% merlot, 4% cabernet sauvignon

90 Colour: cherry, garnet rim. Nose: ripe fruit, creamy oak, toasty, elegant. Palate: powerful, flavourful, toasty, round tannins, balanced.

BODEGAS PEÑALBA HERRAIZ

Sol de las Moreras, 3
9400 Aranda de Duero (Burgos)
☎: +34 947 508 249 - Fax: +34 947 511 145
miguelpma@ono.com

APTUS 2011 T ROBLE
tempranillo

87 Colour: cherry, garnet rim. Nose: fruit preserve, balsamic herbs, spicy. Palate: powerful, flavourful, long, toasty.

CARRAVID 2009 T
90% tempranillo, 10% garnacha

90 Colour: deep cherry. Nose: balsamic herbs, ripe fruit, creamy oak. Palate: flavourful, powerful, round tannins.

BODEGAS PINGÓN

Ctra. N-122, Km. 311
47300 Peñafiel (Valladolid)
☎: +34 983 880 623 - Fax: +34 983 880 623
www.bodegaspingon.com
carramimbre@bodegaspingon.com

ALTAMIMBRE 2010 T
100% tempranillo

92 Colour: deep cherry, garnet rim. Nose: balsamic herbs, spicy, ripe fruit, dry stone. Palate: long, fruity, balanced.

CARRAMIMBRE 2009 TC
95% tempranillo, 5% cabernet sauvignon

90 Colour: cherry, garnet rim. Nose: balanced, ripe fruit, spicy, violets. Palate: fruity, flavourful, easy to drink.

CARRAMIMBRE 2009 TR
95% tempranillo, 5% cabernet sauvignon

92 Colour: deep cherry, garnet rim. Nose: ripe fruit, balanced, balsamic herbs. Palate: flavourful, balanced, round tannins.

CARRAMIMBRE 2011 T ROBLE
95% tempranillo, 5% cabernet sauvignon

88 Colour: cherry, purple rim. Nose: ripe fruit, sweet spices, medium intensity. Palate: flavourful, fruity, long.

BODEGAS PORTIA

Antigua Ctra. N-I, km. 170
9370 Gumiel de Izán (Burgos)
☎: +34 947 102 700
www.bodegasportia.com
info@bodegasportia.com

EBEIA DE PORTIA 2012 T ROBLE
tempranillo

88 Colour: bright cherry. Nose: ripe fruit, sweet spices, creamy oak. Palate: flavourful, fruity, toasty, round tannins.

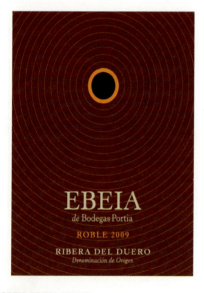

PORTIA PRIMA 2011 T
tempranillo

90 Colour: cherry, garnet rim. Nose: ripe fruit, creamy oak, toasty, balsamic herbs. Palate: powerful, flavourful, toasty.

PORTIA 2010 TC
tempranillo

90 Colour: cherry, garnet rim. Nose: ripe fruit, spicy, creamy oak, toasty. Palate: powerful, flavourful, toasty, round tannins.

TRIENNIA 2010 T
tempranillo

91 Colour: bright cherry, garnet rim. Nose: ripe fruit, sweet spices, creamy oak, toasty. Palate: flavourful, fruity, toasty, round tannins.

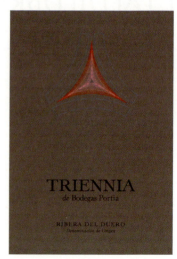

BODEGAS PRADO DE OLMEDO

Paraje El Salegar, s/n
9370 Quintana del Pidío (Burgos)
☎: +34 947 546 960 - Fax: +34 947 546 960
www.pradodeolmedo.com
pradodeolmedo@pradodeolmedo.com

MONASTERIO DE SAN MIGUEL 2010 T
tempranillo

93 Colour: cherry, garnet rim. Nose: spicy, creamy oak, toasty, complex. Palate: powerful, flavourful, toasty, round tannins.

VALDESANTOS 2010 T
tempranillo

88 Colour: bright cherry. Nose: ripe fruit, sweet spices, creamy oak. Palate: flavourful, fruity, toasty, harsh oak tannins.

VALDESANTOS 2012 T
tempranillo

86 Colour: cherry, purple rim. Nose: expressive, fresh fruit, red berry notes, balsamic herbs. Palate: flavourful, fruity, good acidity.

BODEGAS RAIZ

Ctra. Circunvalación R-30, s/n
9300 Roa (Burgos)
☎: +34 947 541 191 - Fax: +34 947 541 192
www.paramodeguzman.es
paramodeguzman@paramodeguzman.es

RAÍZ DE GUZMÁN 2009 TR
100% tempranillo

91 Colour: cherry, garnet rim. Nose: ripe fruit, spicy, creamy oak, toasty, mineral, expressive. Palate: powerful, flavourful, toasty, round tannins, balanced.

RAÍZ DE GUZMÁN 2010 TC
100% tempranillo

93 Colour: cherry, garnet rim. Nose: ripe fruit, spicy, creamy oak, toasty, complex. Palate: powerful, flavourful, toasty, round tannins, elegant.

RAÍZ DE GUZMÁN 2012 RD
100% tempranillo

90 Colour: rose, purple rim. Nose: powerfull, ripe fruit, red berry notes, floral, lactic notes. Palate: powerful, fruity, fresh.

RAÍZ DE GUZMÁN 2012 T ROBLE
100% tempranillo

91 Colour: cherry, garnet rim. Nose: red berry notes, ripe fruit, sweet spices, creamy oak. Palate: powerful, flavourful, toasty.

RAIZ PROFUNDA 2009 T
100% tempranillo

94 Colour: cherry, garnet rim. Nose: spicy, creamy oak, toasty, powerfull, characterful, ripe fruit. Palate: powerful, flavourful, toasty, round tannins.

BODEGAS RECOLETAS

Ctra. Quintanilla, s/n
47359 Olivares de Duero (Valladolid)
☎: +34 983 687 017 - Fax: +34 983 687 017
www.bodegasrecoletas.es
bodegas@bodegasrecoletas.es

RECOLETAS 2005 TR
tempranillo

88 Colour: cherry, garnet rim. Nose: ripe fruit, creamy oak, warm. Palate: powerful, flavourful, toasty, round tannins.

RECOLETAS 2009 TC
tempranillo

90 Colour: cherry, garnet rim. Nose: sweet spices, ripe fruit, creamy oak. Palate: toasty, correct, round.

RECOLETAS 2011 T ROBLE
tempranillo

85 Colour: bright cherry. Nose: ripe fruit, creamy oak, spicy. Palate: flavourful, fruity, toasty.

RECOLETAS VENDIMIA SELECCIONADA 2009 T
tempranillo

92 Colour: pale ruby, brick rim edge. Nose: fruit preserve, balsamic herbs, spicy, creamy oak, fine reductive notes. Palate: balanced, round, flavourful, fine tannins.

BODEGAS RESALTE DE PEÑAFIEL

Ctra. N-122, Km. 312
47300 Peñafiel (Valladolid)
☎: +34 983 878 160 - Fax: +34 983 880 601
www.resalte.com
s.garcia@resalte.com

GRAN RESALTE 2001 TGR
100% tempranillo

87 Colour: pale ruby, brick rim edge. Nose: spicy, fine reductive notes, wet leather, aged wood nuances, fruit liqueur notes, scrubland, earthy notes. Palate: spicy, fine tannins, long.

LECCO 2006 TR
100% tempranillo

91 Colour: cherry, garnet rim. Nose: spicy, creamy oak. Palate: powerful, flavourful, toasty, round tannins.

LECCO 2007 TC
100% tempranillo

90 Colour: cherry, garnet rim. Nose: balanced, cocoa bean, sweet spices, medium intensity. Palate: flavourful, full, long.

LECCO 2012 T
100% tempranillo

89 Colour: cherry, purple rim. Nose: red berry notes, ripe fruit, violet drops, medium intensity, sweet spices. Palate: fruity, balanced, good finish.

PEÑA ROBLE 2006 TR
100% tempranillo

88 Colour: dark-red cherry. Nose: ripe fruit, fruit preserve, old leather, spicy. Palate: fruity, spicy, flavourful.

PEÑA ROBLE 2007 TC
100% tempranillo

88 Colour: cherry, garnet rim. Nose: medium intensity, balanced, ripe fruit, sweet spices. Palate: flavourful, fruity.

PEÑA ROBLE 2012 T
100% tempranillo

87 Colour: cherry, purple rim. Nose: powerfull, ripe fruit, sweet spices. Palate: ripe fruit, round tannins, easy to drink.

RESALTE 2006 TR
100% tempranillo

90 Colour: cherry, garnet rim. Nose: ripe fruit, spicy, toasty. Palate: powerful, flavourful, toasty, round tannins.

RESALTE 2009 TC
100% tempranillo

89 Colour: cherry, garnet rim. Nose: balanced, varietal, sweet spices. Palate: fruity, spicy, round tannins.

RESALTE VENDIMIA SELECCIONADA 2011 T
100% tempranillo

91 Colour: cherry, purple rim. Nose: expressive, ripe fruit, sweet spices. Palate: fruity, flavourful, round tannins, long.

BODEGAS REYES

Ctra. Valladolid - Soria, Km. 54
47300 Peñafiel (Valladolid)
☎: +34 983 873 015 - Fax: +34 983 873 017
www.bodegasreyes.com
info@teofiloreyes.com

TAMIZ 2011 T ROBLE
tempranillo

86 Colour: cherry, garnet rim. Nose: spicy, powerfull, ripe fruit. Palate: good structure, flavourful, round tannins.

TEÓFILO REYES 2009 TC
tempranillo

89 Colour: cherry, garnet rim. Nose: fruit preserve, spicy. Palate: balanced, long, balsamic, round tannins.

TEÓFILO REYES 2009 TR
tempranillo

91 Colour: cherry, garnet rim. Nose: medium intensity, varietal, ripe fruit, cocoa bean. Palate: flavourful, round tannins, good acidity.

BODEGAS RODERO

Ctra. Boada, s/n
9314 Pedrosa de Duero (Burgos)
☎: +34 947 530 046 - Fax: +34 947 530 097
www.bodegasrodero.com
rodero@bodegasrodero.com

CARMELO RODERO 2009 TR
90% tempranillo, 10% cabernet sauvignon

93 Colour: cherry, garnet rim. Nose: complex, ripe fruit, dark chocolate, spicy. Palate: flavourful, ripe fruit, round tannins.

CARMELO RODERO 2010 TC
90% tempranillo, 10% cabernet sauvignon

93 Colour: cherry, garnet rim. Nose: ripe fruit, spicy, toasty, dark chocolate, cocoa bean. Palate: powerful, flavourful, toasty, round tannins, balanced.

CARMELO RODERO 2012 T
100% tempranillo

90 Colour: cherry, purple rim. Nose: expressive, fresh fruit, red berry notes, fragrant herbs. Palate: flavourful, fruity, good acidity.

CARMELO RODERO 9 MESES 2012 T
100% tempranillo

88 Colour: cherry, purple rim. Nose: cocoa bean, dark chocolate, sweet spices, creamy oak, ripe fruit. Palate: flavourful, spicy, toasty, long.

CARMELO RODERO TSM 2009 T
75% tempranillo, 10% cabernet sauvignon, 15% merlot

94 Colour: cherry, garnet rim. Nose: red berry notes, ripe fruit, balsamic herbs, spicy, toasty, creamy oak. Palate: long, elegant, spicy, toasty, balanced.

PAGO DE VALTARREÑA 2009 T
100% tempranillo

93 Colour: cherry, garnet rim. Nose: ripe fruit, spicy, creamy oak, toasty, powerfull, varietal, characterful. Palate: round tannins.

BODEGAS SANTA EULALIA

Malpica, s/n
9311 La Horra (Burgos)
☎: +34 983 586 868 - Fax: +34 947 580 180
www.bodegasfrutosvillar.com
bodegasfrutosvillar@bodegasfrutosvillar.com

CONDE DE SIRUELA 2006 TR
100% tinta del país

88 Colour: cherry, garnet rim. Nose: ripe fruit, spicy, creamy oak, toasty, cigar, tobacco. Palate: powerful, flavourful, toasty, balanced.

CONDE DE SIRUELA 2009 TC
100% tinta del país

92 Colour: cherry, garnet rim. Nose: spicy, creamy oak, toasty, fruit expression. Palate: powerful, flavourful, toasty, round tannins.

CONDE DE SIRUELA 2011 T ROBLE
100% tinta del país

86 Colour: cherry, purple rim. Nose: ripe fruit, candied fruit, powerfull, warm. Palate: ripe fruit, long, flavourful, sweet tannins.

CONDE DE SIRUELA 2012 T
100% tinta del país

88 Colour: deep cherry, purple rim. Nose: balanced, ripe fruit, violet drops. Palate: fruity, ripe fruit, long.

CONDE DE SIRUELA ELITE 2006 T
100% tinta del país

86 Colour: pale ruby, brick rim edge. Nose: spicy, fine reductive notes, wet leather, aged wood nuances, fruit liqueur notes. Palate: spicy, elegant, long.

BODEGAS SEÑORÍO DE NAVA

Ctra. Valladolid - Soria, s/n
9318 Nava de Roa (Burgos)
☎: +34 987 209 712 - Fax: +34 987 209 800
www.senoriodenava.es
snava@senoriodenava.es

SEÑORÍO DE NAVA 2006 TR
tinta del país

88 Colour: cherry, garnet rim. Nose: toasty, aromatic coffee, fruit liqueur notes. Palate: fine bitter notes, good acidity, round tannins.

SEÑORÍO DE NAVA 2009 TC
tinta del país

89 Colour: cherry, garnet rim. Nose: ripe fruit, balsamic herbs, spicy, creamy oak. Palate: powerful, flavourful, spicy.

SEÑORÍO DE NAVA 2011 T ROBLE
85% tinta del país, 15% cabernet sauvignon

86 Colour: cherry, garnet rim. Nose: ripe fruit, spicy, creamy oak, complex. Palate: powerful, flavourful, toasty.

SEÑORÍO DE NAVA 2012 RD
95% tinta del país, 5% albillo

87 Colour: rose, purple rim. Nose: red berry notes, ripe fruit, lactic notes. Palate: flavourful, fruity, good finish, ripe fruit.

SEÑORÍO DE NAVA 2012 T
100% tinta del país

88 Colour: cherry, purple rim. Nose: fresh fruit, red berry notes, floral. Palate: flavourful, fruity, good acidity.

SEÑORÍO DE NAVA FINCA SAN COBATE 2005 TR
tinta del país

91 Colour: dark-red cherry, orangey edge. Nose: fine reductive notes, medium intensity, ripe fruit, spicy. Palate: fruity, flavourful.

BODEGAS TAMARAL

Ctra. N-122, Km. 310,6
47300 Peñafiel (Valladolid)
☎: +34 983 878 017 - Fax: +34 983 878 089
www.tamaral.com
exterior@tamaral.com

TAMARAL 2008 TR
100% tempranillo

91 Colour: bright cherry, garnet rim. Nose: fruit preserve, sweet spices, scrubland. Palate: flavourful, fruity, round tannins.

TAMARAL 2010 TC
100% tempranillo

90 Colour: cherry, garnet rim. Nose: spicy, creamy oak, toasty, characterful, mineral. Palate: powerful, flavourful, toasty, round tannins.

TAMARAL 2011 T ROBLE
100% tempranillo

88 Colour: bright cherry. Nose: ripe fruit, sweet spices, creamy oak, expressive. Palate: flavourful, fruity, toasty, round tannins.

TAMARAL FINCA LA MIRA 2009 T
100% tempranillo

90 Colour: cherry, garnet rim. Nose: ripe fruit, balsamic herbs, spicy, creamy oak. Palate: powerful, flavourful, spicy.

BODEGAS TARSUS

Ctra. de Roa - Anguix, Km. 3
9313 Anguix (Burgos)
☎: +34 947 554 218 - Fax: +34 947 541 804
www.bodegastarsus.com
tarsus@pernod-ricard.com

QUINTA DE TARSUS 2010 TC
tinta del país

91 Colour: cherry, garnet rim. Nose: red berry notes, ripe fruit, balsamic herbs, mineral, sweet spices, toasty. Palate: powerful, flavourful, balanced.

TARSUS 2008 TR
tinta del país, cabernet sauvignon

90 Colour: deep cherry. Nose: toasty, dark chocolate, ripe fruit. Palate: ripe fruit, long, good acidity.

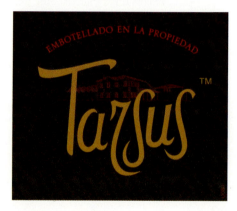

TARSUS 2011 T ROBLE
tinta del país

90 Colour: cherry, garnet rim. Nose: spicy, creamy oak, toasty. Palate: powerful, flavourful, toasty, round tannins.

TARSUS MANOLÁCTICA 2008 T
tinta del país, cabernet sauvignon

89 Colour: garnet rim. Nose: red berry notes, balsamic herbs, spicy, creamy oak, fine reductive notes. Palate: flavourful, balanced, spicy, long.

BODEGAS THESAURUS

Ctra. Cuellar - Villafuerte, s/n
47359 Olivares de Duero (Valladolid)
☎: +34 983 250 319 - Fax: +34 983 250 329
www.bodegasthesaurus.com.com
exportacion@ciadevinos.com

CASA CASTILLA 2010 TC

89 Colour: cherry, garnet rim. Nose: ripe fruit, spicy, creamy oak, toasty, complex. Palate: powerful, flavourful, toasty, round tannins.

CASTILLO DE PEÑAFIEL TR
tempranillo

90 Colour: pale ruby, brick rim edge. Nose: elegant, spicy, fine reductive notes, wet leather, aged wood nuances, fruit liqueur notes. Palate: spicy, fine tannins, elegant, long.

CASTILLO DE PEÑAFIEL 2010 TC

88 Colour: cherry, garnet rim. Nose: ripe fruit, spicy, creamy oak, toasty. Palate: powerful, flavourful, toasty, harsh oak tannins.

CASTILLO DE PEÑAFIEL 2011 T ROBLE

85 Colour: cherry, garnet rim. Nose: ripe fruit, fruit preserve, balsamic herbs, creamy oak. Palate: powerful, flavourful, correct.

DORIVM 2010 TC

89 Colour: cherry, garnet rim. Nose: sweet spices, creamy oak, ripe fruit. Palate: correct, flavourful, spicy, toasty.

DORIVM 2011 T ROBLE

87 Colour: cherry, garnet rim. Nose: ripe fruit, spicy, creamy oak, toasty. Palate: powerful, flavourful, toasty.

BODEGAS TIONIO

Carretera de Valoria, Km 7
47315 Pesquera de Duero (Valladolid)
☎: +34 933 950 811 - Fax: +34 933 955 500
www.tionio.com
info@parxet.es

AUSTUM 2012 T
tinto fino

89 Colour: cherry, purple rim. Nose: red berry notes, ripe fruit, balsamic herbs, balanced. Palate: powerful, flavourful, complex, elegant.

TIONIO 2010 TC
tinto fino

92 Colour: cherry, garnet rim. Nose: ripe fruit, spicy, creamy oak, toasty, complex, varietal, mineral. Palate: powerful, flavourful, toasty, round tannins.

BODEGAS TORREDEROS

Ctra. Valladolid, Km. 289,300
9318 Fuentelisendo (Burgos)
☎: +34 947 532 627 - Fax: +34 947 532 731
www.torrederos.com
administracion@torrederos.com

TORREDEROS 2009 TR
100% tempranillo

91 Colour: cherry, garnet rim. Nose: ripe fruit, creamy oak, toasty, sweet spices, cocoa bean. Palate: powerful, flavourful, toasty, round tannins.

TORREDEROS 2010 TC
100% tempranillo

90 Colour: deep cherry, garnet rim. Nose: medium intensity, ripe fruit, sweet spices, complex. Palate: balanced, ripe fruit, long.

BODEGAS TORREMORÓN

Ctra. Boada, s/n
9314 Quintanamanvirgo (Burgos)
☎: +34 947 554 075 - Fax: +34 947 554 036
www.bodegastorremoron.com
torremoron@wanadoo.es

TORREMORÓN 2010 TC
tempranillo

90 Colour: cherry, garnet rim. Nose: ripe fruit, sweet spices, creamy oak, expressive. Palate: flavourful, fruity, toasty, round tannins.

TORREMORÓN TEMPRANILLO 2012 T
tempranillo

84

BODEGAS TRUS

Ctra. Pesquera - Encinas, Km. 3
47316 Piñel de Abajo (Valladolid)
☎: +34 983 872 033 - Fax: +34 983 872 041
www.bodegastrus.com
trus@bodegastrus.com

KREL 2010 TC
100% tinto fino

92 Colour: cherry, garnet rim. Nose: red berry notes, ripe fruit, balsamic herbs, sweet spices, creamy oak. Palate: powerful, flavourful, spicy, toasty.

TRAMUZ 2012 T
100% tinto fino

89 Colour: bright cherry. Nose: sweet spices, creamy oak, powerfull, red berry notes, ripe fruit. Palate: flavourful, fruity, toasty.

TRUS 2006 TR
100% tinto fino

92 Colour: deep cherry. Nose: candied fruit, spicy, wet leather. Palate: good acidity, elegant, round.

TRUS 2010 TC
100% tinto fino

92 Colour: cherry, garnet rim. Nose: ripe fruit, creamy oak, toasty, characterful, varietal. Palate: powerful, flavourful, toasty, round tannins.

TRUS 2012 T ROBLE
tinto fino

90 Colour: bright cherry. Nose: ripe fruit, sweet spices, creamy oak, expressive, toasty. Palate: flavourful, fruity, toasty, round tannins.

BODEGAS VALDEMAR

Camino Viejo, s/n
1320 Oyón (Álava)
☎: +34 945 622 188 - Fax: +34 945 622 111
www.valdemar.es
info@valdemar.es

FINCAS VALDEMACUCO 2012 T ROBLE
100% tempranillo

88 Colour: bright cherry. Nose: ripe fruit, sweet spices, creamy oak. Palate: flavourful, fruity, toasty.

BODEGAS VALDUBÓN

Antigua N-I, Km. 151
9460 Milagros (Burgos)
☎: +34 947 546 251 - Fax: +34 947 546 250
www.valdubon.es
valdubon@valdubon.es

HONORIS DE VALDUBÓN 2007 T
84% tempranillo, 6% cabernet sauvignon, 9% merlot

91 Colour: deep cherry, garnet rim. Nose: expressive, wild herbs, ripe fruit, varietal. Palate: flavourful, round tannins.

VALDUBÓN 2007 TR
100% tempranillo

86 Colour: cherry, garnet rim. Nose: fruit preserve, cocoa bean, creamy oak. Palate: flavourful, toasty, smoky aftertaste.

VALDUBÓN 2010 TC
100% tempranillo

89 Colour: deep cherry, garnet rim. Nose: ripe fruit, dark chocolate, sweet spices. Palate: good structure, long, round tannins.

VALDUBÓN 2011 T ROBLE
100% tempranillo

86 Colour: cherry, garnet rim. Nose: powerfull, creamy oak, sweet spices, ripe fruit. Palate: good structure, flavourful, round tannins.

VALDUBÓN 2012 T
100% tempranillo

88 Colour: cherry, purple rim. Nose: red berry notes, ripe fruit, wild herbs, expressive. Palate: powerful, flavourful, balsamic, balanced.

VALDUBÓN DIEZ 2010 T
100% tempranillo

89 Colour: cherry, garnet rim. Nose: ripe fruit, spicy, creamy oak, toasty. Palate: powerful, flavourful, toasty.

BODEGAS VALLE DE MONZÓN

Paraje El Salegar, s/n
9370 Quintana del Pidío (Burgos)
☎: +34 947 545 694 - Fax: +34 947 545 694
www.vallemonzon.com
bodega@vallemonzon.com

EL SALEGAR 2010 TR
100% tinta del país

89 Colour: cherry, garnet rim. Nose: cocoa bean, fragrant herbs, ripe fruit. Palate: ripe fruit, toasty, smoky aftertaste, round tannins.

GROMEJÓN 2010 TC
100% tinta del país

89 Colour: deep cherry. Nose: red berry notes, ripe fruit, sweet spices, balanced. Palate: fruity, flavourful, good acidity, round tannins.

HOYO DE LA VEGA 2010 TC
100% tinta del país

89 Colour: cherry, garnet rim. Nose: ripe fruit, spicy, toasty. Palate: flavourful, toasty, round tannins.

HOYO DE LA VEGA 2010 TR
100% tinta del país

90 Colour: cherry, garnet rim. Nose: ripe fruit, spicy, creamy oak, toasty, complex. Palate: powerful, flavourful, toasty, round tannins.

HOYO DE LA VEGA 2011 T BARRICA
100% tinta del país

88 Colour: bright cherry. Nose: ripe fruit, sweet spices, creamy oak, expressive. Palate: flavourful, fruity, toasty, round tannins.

HOYO DE LA VEGA 2012 RD
100% tinta del país

87 Colour: light cherry. Nose: floral, red berry notes, candied fruit, lactic notes. Palate: fresh, fruity, flavourful.

BODEGAS VALPARAISO

Paraje los Llanillos, s/n
9370 Quintana del Pidío (Burgos)
☎: +34 947 545 286 - Fax: +34 947 545 163
www.bodegasvalparaiso.com
info@bodegasvalparaiso.com

FINCA EL ENCINAL 2010 TC
100% tempranillo

88 Colour: dark-red cherry. Nose: ripe fruit, toasty, spicy. Palate: flavourful, powerful, concentrated.

FINCA EL ENCINAL 2011 T ROBLE
100% tempranillo

85 Colour: bright cherry. Nose: ripe fruit, sweet spices, creamy oak. Palate: flavourful, fruity, toasty.

VALPARAÍSO 2010 TC
100% tempranillo

88 Colour: bright cherry. Nose: sweet spices, creamy oak, fruit preserve. Palate: flavourful, fruity, round tannins.

VALPARAÍSO 2011 T ROBLE
100% tempranillo

85 Colour: cherry, purple rim. Nose: herbaceous, ripe fruit. Palate: fruity, flavourful, correct.

BODEGAS VALPINCIA

Ctra. de Melida, 3,5
47300 Peñafiel (Valladolid)
☎: +34 983 878 007 - Fax: +34 983 880 620
www.bodegasvalpincia.com
comunicacion@bodegasvalpincia.com

GLORIA MAYOR 2009 T
100% tempranillo

89 Colour: cherry, garnet rim. Nose: ripe fruit, sweet spices, dark chocolate, balsamic herbs. Palate: powerful, flavourful, long, toasty, balanced.

PAGOS DE VALCERRACÍN 2009 TC
100% tempranillo

88 Colour: cherry, garnet rim. Nose: ripe fruit, spicy, creamy oak, toasty. Palate: powerful, flavourful, toasty.

PAGOS DE VALCERRACÍN 2011 T ROBLE
100% tempranillo

86 Colour: bright cherry. Nose: ripe fruit, sweet spices, creamy oak, expressive. Palate: flavourful, fruity, toasty, harsh oak tannins.

PAGOS DE VALCERRACÍN 2012 T
100% tempranillo

86 Colour: cherry, purple rim. Nose: red berry notes, ripe fruit, balsamic herbs. Palate: rich, flavourful, balanced.

VALPINCIA 2007 TR
100% tempranillo

86 Colour: cherry, garnet rim. Nose: ripe fruit, aged wood nuances, creamy oak, fine reductive notes. Palate: long, classic aged character, powerful, flavourful.

VALPINCIA 2010 TC
100% tempranillo

85 Colour: cherry, garnet rim. Nose: ripe fruit, spicy, creamy oak, toasty. Palate: powerful, flavourful, toasty.

VALPINCIA 2011 T ROBLE
100% tempranillo

84

VALPINCIA 2012 T
100% tempranillo

85 Colour: cherry, purple rim. Nose: red berry notes, floral, balsamic herbs. Palate: flavourful, fruity, good acidity, round tannins.

BODEGAS VEGA SICILIA

Ctra. N-122, Km. 323
47359 Valbuena de Duero (Valladolid)
☎: +34 983 680 147 - Fax: +34 983 680 263
www.vega-sicilia.com
vegasicilia@vega-sicilia.com

VALBUENA 5º 2009 T
95% tinto fino, 5% merlot

95 Colour: bright cherry. Nose: sweet spices, creamy oak, expressive, balsamic herbs, scrubland. Palate: flavourful, fruity, toasty, round tannins.

VEGA SICILIA RESERVA ESPECIAL 94/95/00 T

97 Colour: pale ruby, brick rim edge. Nose: elegant, spicy, fine reductive notes, wet leather, fruit liqueur notes, characterful. Palate: spicy, fine tannins, elegant, long.

VEGA SICILIA ÚNICO 2004 T
87% tinto fino, 13% cabernet sauvignon

97 Colour: very deep cherry. Nose: elegant, spicy, fine reductive notes, wet leather, aged wood nuances, fruit liqueur notes. Palate: spicy, fine tannins, elegant, long.

BODEGAS VEGANZONES

Rosario, 4
47311 Fompedraza (Valladolid)
☎: +34 983 036 010 - Fax: +34 983 036 010
www.bodegasveganzones.com
administracion@bodegasveganzones.com

912 DE ALTITUD 2009 TC
95% tempranillo, 5% merlot

91 Colour: cherry, garnet rim. Nose: ripe fruit, spicy, creamy oak, balsamic herbs. Palate: powerful, flavourful, toasty, round tannins.

912 DE ALTITUD 2011 TC
100% tempranillo

87 Colour: cherry, garnet rim. Nose: fruit preserve, powerfull. Palate: flavourful, correct, round tannins.

BODEGAS VEGARANDA

Avda. Arangón, s/n
9400 Aranda de Duero (Burgos)
☎: +34 626 996 974
www.bodegasvegaranda.com
comercial@bodegasvegaranda.com

VEGARANDA 2008 TR
tempranillo

90 Colour: cherry, garnet rim. Nose: spicy, creamy oak, toasty. Palate: powerful, flavourful, toasty, round tannins.

VEGARANDA 2010 TC
tempranillo

87 Colour: cherry, garnet rim. Nose: powerfull, ripe fruit, sweet spices. Palate: flavourful, powerful.

VEGARANDA 2012 T
tempranillo

86 Colour: cherry, purple rim. Nose: red berry notes, candied fruit, balsamic herbs. Palate: fruity, flavourful, easy to drink.

VEGARANDA 2012 T ROBLE
tempranillo

87 Colour: bright cherry. Nose: ripe fruit, sweet spices, creamy oak. Palate: flavourful, fruity, toasty.

BODEGAS VICENTE GANDÍA

Ctra. Cheste a Godelleta, s/n
46370 Chiva (Valencia)
☎: +34 962 524 242 - Fax: +34 962 524 243
www.vicentegandia.es
info@vicentegandia.com

**DOLMO TEMPRANILLO VENDIMIA
SELECCIONADA 2011 T**
100% tempranillo

87 Colour: bright cherry. Nose: ripe fruit, sweet spices, creamy oak. Palate: flavourful, fruity, toasty.

BODEGAS VITULIA

Sendín, 49
9400 Aranda de Duero (Burgos)
☎: +34 947 515 051 - Fax: +34 947 515 051
www.bodegasvitulia.com
bvitulia@bodegasvitulia.com

**HACIENDA VITULIA VENDIMIA
SELECCIONADAS 2009 T**
90% tinto fino, 10% merlot

91 Colour: cherry, garnet rim. Nose: ripe fruit, spicy, creamy oak, toasty, complex. Palate: powerful, flavourful, toasty, round tannins, balanced.

VITULIA 2009 TC
tinto fino

90 Colour: bright cherry. Nose: ripe fruit, sweet spices, creamy oak. Palate: flavourful, fruity, toasty, round tannins.

VITULIA 2011 T ROBLE
tinto fino

90 Colour: cherry, garnet rim. Nose: ripe fruit, balsamic herbs, sweet spices, creamy oak. Palate: rich, fruity, flavourful.

VITULIA 2012 RD
90% tinto fino, 10% otras

86 Colour: rose, purple rim. Nose: ripe fruit, red berry notes, floral. Palate: powerful, fruity, flavourful.

VITULIA 2012 T
tinto fino

87 Colour: cherry, purple rim. Nose: fresh fruit, red berry notes, floral. Palate: flavourful, fruity, good acidity, round tannins.

BODEGAS VIYUELA

Ctra. de Quintanamanvirgo, s/n
9314 Boada de Roa (Burgos)
☎: +34 947 530 072 - Fax: +34 947 530 075
www.bodegasviyuela.com
viyuela@bodegasviyuela.com

SOLEIL ROUGE 2010 TC
100% tempranillo

90 Colour: bright cherry. Nose: ripe fruit, sweet spices, creamy oak, mineral. Palate: flavourful, fruity, toasty, round tannins.

VALDECABAÑAS 2005 TR
100% tempranillo

89 Colour: deep cherry, garnet rim. Nose: medium intensity, balanced, fruit preserve, spicy. Palate: flavourful, spicy.

VALDECABAÑAS 2006 TC
100% tempranillo

87 Colour: cherry, garnet rim. Nose: ripe fruit, spicy, toasty, fine reductive notes. Palate: powerful, flavourful, toasty.

VALDECABAÑAS 2007 TGR
100% tempranillo

91 Colour: deep cherry, orangey edge. Nose: ripe fruit, fragrant herbs, mineral, fine reductive notes, sweet spices, creamy oak. Palate: powerful, flavourful, long, correct.

VALDECABAÑAS 2010 T ROBLE
100% tempranillo

87 Colour: cherry, garnet rim. Nose: ripe fruit, spicy, creamy oak, toasty, complex. Palate: powerful, flavourful, toasty, harsh oak tannins.

VALDECABAÑAS 2011 T
tempranillo

86 Colour: cherry, garnet rim. Nose: powerfull, ripe fruit, candied fruit, cocoa bean. Palate: flavourful, round tannins, toasty.

VIYUELA 10 2007 T
100% tempranillo

88 Colour: deep cherry. Nose: ripe fruit, spicy, toasty. Palate: flavourful, spicy.

VIYUELA 2004 TR
100% tempranillo

88 Colour: cherry, garnet rim. Nose: medium intensity, toasty, spicy. Palate: fruity, flavourful, correct, good acidity.

VIYUELA 2010 TC
100% tempranillo

89 Colour: cherry, garnet rim. Nose: ripe fruit, fragrant herbs, sweet spices. Palate: ripe fruit, round tannins.

VIYUELA 2011 T FERMENTADO EN BARRICA
100% tempranillo

88 Colour: cherry, garnet rim. Nose: medium intensity, balanced, ripe fruit. Palate: fruity, easy to drink, correct.

VIYUELA 3 + 3 2011 T
100% tempranillo

86 Colour: cherry, garnet rim. Nose: ripe fruit, spicy, creamy oak. Palate: powerful, flavourful, toasty.

VIYUELA SELECCIÓN 2005 T
100% tempranillo

89 Colour: cherry, garnet rim. Nose: sweet spices, fruit preserve, cocoa bean, dark chocolate. Palate: fruity, round tannins.

BODEGAS VIZCARRA

Finca Chirri, s/n
9317 Mambrilla de Castrejón (Burgos)
☎: +34 947 540 340 - Fax: +34 947 540 340
www.vizcarra.es
bodegas@vizcarra.es

VIZCARRA 2011 T
100% tinto fino

91 Colour: cherry, garnet rim. Nose: ripe fruit, spicy, creamy oak, toasty, dark chocolate. Palate: powerful, flavourful, toasty, balanced.

VIZCARRA SENDA DEL ORO 2012 T
100% tinto fino

91 Colour: cherry, purple rim. Nose: powerfull, red berry notes, balsamic herbs, mineral, expressive. Palate: powerful, flavourful, concentrated, fruity.

BODEGAS Y VIÑEDOS ALIÓN

Ctra. N-122, Km. 312,4 Padilla de Duero
47300 Peñafiel (Valladolid)
☎: +34 983 881 236 - Fax: +34 983 881 246
www.bodegasalion.com
imartin@bodegasalion.com

ALIÓN 2010 T
100% tinto fino

95 Colour: very deep cherry. Nose: spicy, ripe fruit, sweet spices, earthy notes. Palate: fruity, fine bitter notes, good acidity, round tannins.

BODEGAS Y VIÑEDOS ESCUDERO

Camino El Ramo, s/n
9311 Olmedillo de Roa (Burgos)
☎: +34 629 857 575 - Fax: +34 947 551 070
www.costaval.com
info@costaval.com

COSTAVAL 2005 TR
100% tempranillo

90 Colour: cherry, garnet rim. Nose: ripe fruit, dried herbs, sweet spices, cocoa bean. Palate: powerful, flavourful, toasty, round tannins.

COSTAVAL 2009 TC
100% tempranillo

87 Colour: cherry, garnet rim. Nose: ripe fruit, spicy, toasty, complex, sweet spices. Palate: powerful, flavourful, toasty.

COSTAVAL 2010 TC
100% tempranillo

88 Colour: cherry, garnet rim. Nose: ripe fruit, spicy, creamy oak, toasty, complex. Palate: powerful, flavourful, toasty, round tannins.

COSTAVAL 2011 T
100% tempranillo

85 Colour: bright cherry. Nose: sweet spices, creamy oak, expressive, fruit preserve. Palate: flavourful, fruity, toasty.

ELOY ESCUDERO 2006 T
100% tempranillo

88 Colour: cherry, garnet rim. Nose: ripe fruit, spicy, creamy oak. Palate: powerful, flavourful, toasty, round tannins.

BODEGAS Y VIÑEDOS GALLEGO ZAPATERO

Segunda Travesía de la Olma, 4
9313 Anguix (Burgos)
☎: +34 648 180 777
www.bodegasgallegozapatero.com
info@bodegasgallegozapatero.com

YOTUEL 2011 T ROBLE
100% tinta del país

88 Colour: very deep cherry. Nose: sweet spices, ripe fruit. Palate: flavourful, fine bitter notes.

YOTUEL FINCA LA NAVA 2010 T
100% tinta del país

93 Colour: cherry, garnet rim. Nose: spicy, creamy oak, toasty, mineral, fruit expression. Palate: powerful, flavourful, toasty, round tannins.

YOTUEL FINCA SAN MIGUEL 2009 T
100% tinta del país

90 Colour: cherry, garnet rim. Nose: spicy, creamy oak, toasty. Palate: powerful, flavourful, toasty, round tannins.

YOTUEL FINCA VALDEPALACIOS 2007 T
100% tinta del país

91 Colour: cherry, garnet rim. Nose: wild herbs, spicy, ripe fruit. Palate: fruity, round tannins, flavourful.

YOTUEL SELECCIÓN 2010 T
100% tinta del país

90 Colour: cherry, garnet rim. Nose: red berry notes, ripe fruit, creamy oak, sweet spices, mineral. Palate: powerful, flavourful, spicy, long.

BODEGAS Y VIÑEDOS JUAN MANUEL BURGOS

Aranda, 39
9471 Fuentelcesped (Burgos)
☎: +34 635 525 272 - Fax: +34 947 557 443
www.byvjuanmanuelburgos.com
juanmanuelburgos@byvjuanmanuelburgos.com

AVAN CEPAS CENTENARIAS 2010 T BARRICA
tempranillo

93 Colour: cherry, garnet rim. Nose: powerfull, characterful, ripe fruit, fruit preserve, earthy notes. Palate: powerful, round, round tannins.

AVAN CONCENTRACIÓN 2010 T BARRICA
tempranillo

92 Colour: cherry, garnet rim. Nose: powerfull, toasty, red berry notes, ripe fruit, sweet spices, expressive. Palate: flavourful, powerful, good acidity, balanced.

AVAN NACIMIENTO 2011 T
tempranillo

90 Colour: cherry, garnet rim. Nose: ripe fruit, spicy, creamy oak, toasty. Palate: powerful, flavourful, toasty, round tannins.

AVAN TERRUÑO DE VALDEHERNANDO 2010 T
tempranillo

91 Colour: deep cherry. Nose: powerfull, warm, fruit preserve, roasted coffee. Palate: powerful, sweetness, unctuous.

AVAN VIÑEDO DEL TORRUBIO 2010 T
tempranillo

93 Colour: cherry, garnet rim. Nose: ripe fruit, spicy, creamy oak, toasty, complex. Palate: powerful, flavourful, toasty, round tannins.

BODEGAS Y VIÑEDOS LLEIROSO

Ctra. Monasterio, s/n
47359 Valbuena del Duero (Valladolid)
☎: +34 983 683 300
www.bodegaslleiroso.com
bodega@bodegaslleiroso.com

BORQUE 2009 TC
tempranillo

90 Colour: cherry, garnet rim. Nose: balanced, dry stone, ripe fruit, varietal. Palate: ripe fruit, flavourful, fruity aftestaste.

LLEIROSO 2007 T
tempranillo

88 Colour: cherry, garnet rim. Nose: ripe fruit, scrubland, spicy, creamy oak. Palate: powerful, flavourful, spicy, long.

LVZMILLAR 2009 TC
tempranillo

90 Colour: cherry, garnet rim. Nose: ripe fruit, spicy, creamy oak, toasty, complex. Palate: powerful, flavourful, toasty, round tannins.

LVZMILLAR 2012 T
tempranillo

88 Colour: bright cherry, purple rim. Nose: medium intensity, violet drops, ripe fruit. Palate: good structure, flavourful, round tannins.

MARÍA 1926 2012 T
tempranillo

88 Colour: bright cherry. Nose: ripe fruit, sweet spices, creamy oak, expressive. Palate: flavourful, fruity, toasty, round tannins.

BODEGAS Y VIÑEDOS MARTÍN BERDUGO

Ctra. de la Colonia, s/n
9400 Aranda de Duero (Burgos)
☎: +34 947 506 331 - Fax: +34 947 506 612
www.martinberdugo.com
bodega@martinberdugo.com

MARTÍN BERDUGO 2010 TC
tempranillo

91 Colour: cherry, garnet rim. Nose: ripe fruit, spicy, creamy oak, toasty, complex. Palate: powerful, flavourful, toasty, round tannins, balanced.

MARTÍN BERDUGO 2011 T BARRICA
tempranillo

89 Colour: bright cherry. Nose: ripe fruit, sweet spices, creamy oak. Palate: flavourful, fruity, toasty, balanced.

MARTÍN BERDUGO 2012 RD
tempranillo

87 Colour: raspberry rose. Nose: red berry notes, candied fruit, floral. Palate: flavourful, fresh, fruity, easy to drink.

MARTÍN BERDUGO 2012 T
tempranillo

87 Colour: cherry, purple rim. Nose: expressive, fresh fruit, red berry notes, floral. Palate: flavourful, fruity, good acidity, round tannins.

MB MARTÍN BERDUGO 2008 T
tempranillo

92 Colour: cherry, garnet rim. Nose: ripe fruit, spicy, creamy oak, toasty. Palate: powerful, flavourful, toasty, round tannins.

BODEGAS Y VIÑEDOS MONTEABELLÓN

Calvario, s/n
9318 Nava de Roa (Burgos)
☎: +34 947 550 000 - Fax: +34 947 550 219
www.monteabellon.com
info@monteabellon.com

MONTEABELLÓN 14 MESES EN BARRICA 2010 T
tempranillo

89 Colour: cherry, garnet rim. Nose: ripe fruit, fruit preserve, spicy, creamy oak. Palate: powerful, flavourful, spicy, long.

MONTEABELLÓN 24 MESES EN BARRICA 2008 T
tempranillo

92 Colour: cherry, garnet rim. Nose: ripe fruit, aged wood nuances, spicy, creamy oak, fine reductive notes. Palate: powerful, flavourful, long, spicy.

MONTEABELLÓN 5 MESES EN BARRICA 2012 T
tempranillo

89 Colour: deep cherry, purple rim. Nose: red berry notes, ripe fruit, balanced, expressive, floral. Palate: balanced, ripe fruit, long.

MONTEABELLÓN FINCA LA BLANQUERA 2009 T
tempranillo

90 Colour: cherry, garnet rim. Nose: fruit preserve, sweet spices, dark chocolate. Palate: long, ripe fruit, good structure, flavourful.

BODEGAS Y VIÑEDOS NEO

Ctra. N-122, Km. 274,5
9391 Castrillo de la Vega (Burgos)
☎: +34 947 514 393 - Fax: +34 947 515 445
www.bodegasneo.com
info@bodegasconde.com

DISCO 2012 T
100% tempranillo

88 Colour: deep cherry, purple rim. Nose: powerfull, ripe fruit, dried herbs, warm. Palate: powerful, long.

EL ARTE DE VIVIR 2012 T
tempranillo

89 Colour: cherry, purple rim. Nose: ripe fruit, wild herbs, powerfull, balanced. Palate: powerful, flavourful, easy to drink, balanced.

NEO 2010 T
100% tempranillo

89 Colour: very deep cherry. Nose: powerfull, closed, sweet spices, creamy oak, ripe fruit. Palate: good structure, flavourful, round tannins.

NEO PUNTA ESENCIA 2010 T
100% tempranillo

93 Colour: cherry, garnet rim. Nose: ripe fruit, spicy, creamy oak, complex, dry stone. Palate: powerful, flavourful, round tannins.

SENTIDO 2011 T
100% tempranillo

89 Colour: cherry, garnet rim. Nose: sweet spices, ripe fruit, creamy oak. Palate: fine bitter notes, good acidity, flavourful, ripe fruit.

BODEGAS Y VIÑEDOS ORTEGA FOURNIER

Finca El Pinar, s/n
9316 Berlangas de Roa (Burgos)
☎: +34 947 533 006 - Fax: +34 947 533 010
www.ofournier.com
jmortega@ofournier.com

ALFA SPIGA 2007 T
100% tinta del país

93 Colour: cherry, garnet rim. Nose: ripe fruit, balsamic herbs, spicy, dry stone, expressive. Palate: flavourful, spicy, long, balanced, elegant.

O. FOURNIER 2005 T
100% tinta del país

92 Colour: ruby red, orangey edge. Nose: ripe fruit, spicy, creamy oak, wild herbs, fine reductive notes. Palate: fine tannins, elegant, balanced, flavourful.

SPIGA 2008 T
100% tinta del país

91 Colour: cherry, garnet rim. Nose: ripe fruit, spicy, creamy oak, toasty, complex. Palate: powerful, flavourful, toasty, round tannins.

URBAN RIBERA 2010 T ROBLE
100% tinta del país

89 Colour: bright cherry. Nose: ripe fruit, sweet spices, creamy oak, expressive. Palate: flavourful, fruity, toasty, round tannins.

BODEGAS Y VIÑEDOS QUMRÁN

Pago de las Bodegas, s/n
47300 Padilla de Duero (Valladolid)
☎: +34 983 882 103 - Fax: +34 983 881 514
www.bodegasqumran.es
info@bodegasqumran.es

PROVENTUS 2010 T

92 Colour: cherry, garnet rim. Nose: ripe fruit, balsamic herbs, spicy, creamy oak. Palate: flavourful, long, toasty, spicy.

QUMRÁN 2012 T ROBLE

89 Colour: cherry, purple rim. Nose: balanced, ripe fruit, red berry notes, sweet spices. Palate: flavourful, good structure, fruity.

BODEGAS Y VIÑEDOS RAUDA

Ctra. de Pedrosa, s/n
9300 Roa de Duero (Burgos)
☎: +34 947 540 224 - Fax: +34 947 541 811
www.vinosderauda.com
informacion@vinosderauda.com

TINTO ROA 2007 TR
tinta del país

89 Colour: cherry, garnet rim. Nose: spicy, creamy oak, toasty. Palate: powerful, flavourful, toasty, round tannins.

TINTO ROA 2010 TC
tinta del país

91 Colour: cherry, garnet rim. Nose: ripe fruit, spicy, characterful, new oak. Palate: powerful, flavourful, toasty, round tannins.

TINTO ROA 2012 T
tinta del país

86 Colour: bright cherry, purple rim. Nose: medium intensity, ripe fruit, citrus fruit, dried herbs. Palate: correct, easy to drink.

BODEGAS Y VIÑEDOS ROBEAL

Ctra. Anguix, s/n
9300 Roa (Burgos)
☎: +34 947 484 706 - Fax: +34 947 482 817
www.bodegasrobeal.com
info@bodegasrobeal.com

BUEN MIÑÓN 2012 T
tempranillo

87 Colour: cherry, purple rim. Nose: ripe fruit, medium intensity, dried herbs, faded flowers. Palate: fruity, light-bodied, easy to drink.

LA CAPILLA 2009 TR
tempranillo

90 Colour: cherry, garnet rim. Nose: spicy, aged wood nuances, ripe fruit, fine reductive notes. Palate: powerful, flavourful, long, spicy.

LA CAPILLA 2010 TC
tempranillo

89 Colour: bright cherry. Nose: ripe fruit, sweet spices, creamy oak. Palate: flavourful, fruity, toasty, round tannins.

VALNOGAL 6 MESES 2011 T ROBLE
tempranillo

86 Colour: bright cherry. Nose: ripe fruit, sweet spices, balsamic herbs. Palate: flavourful, fruity, toasty, correct.

BODEGAS Y VIÑEDOS TÁBULA

Ctra. de Valbuena, km. 2
47359 Olivares de Duero (Valladolid)
☎: +34 608 219 019 - Fax: +34 983 107 300
www.bodegastabula.es
armando@bodegastabula.es

CLAVE DE TÁBULA 2010 T
100% tempranillo

93 Colour: cherry, garnet rim. Nose: red berry notes, ripe fruit, spicy, scrubland, dry stone, creamy oak, complex. Palate: powerful, flavourful, long, toasty, balanced.

DAMANA 2010 TC
100% tempranillo

91 Colour: cherry, garnet rim. Nose: ripe fruit, fruit liqueur notes, balsamic herbs, earthy notes, spicy, creamy oak. Palate: powerful, flavourful, spicy.

DAMANA 5 2011 T
100% tempranillo

88 Colour: bright cherry. Nose: ripe fruit, sweet spices, creamy oak, expressive. Palate: flavourful, fruity, toasty.

GRAN TÁBULA 2009 T
100% tempranillo

92 Colour: very deep cherry, garnet rim. Nose: aged wood nuances, spicy, creamy oak, toasty, ripe fruit, tobacco, waxy notes. Palate: powerful, flavourful, oaky.

TÁBULA 2009 T
100% tempranillo

93 Colour: deep cherry, garnet rim. Nose: varietal, red berry notes, ripe fruit, mineral, spicy, creamy oak, toasty. Palate: rich, powerful, flavourful, spicy, long.

BODEGAS Y VIÑEDOS VALDERIZ

Ctra. Pedrosa, Km. 1
9300 Roa (Burgos)
☎: +34 947 540 460 - Fax: +34 947 541 032
www.valderiz.com
bodega@valderiz.com

VALDEHERMOSO 2011 TC
100% tinta del país

90 Colour: cherry, garnet rim. Nose: ripe fruit, spicy, creamy oak, toasty, wild herbs. Palate: powerful, flavourful, toasty.

VALDEHERMOSO 2012 T
100% tinta del país

88 Colour: cherry, purple rim. Nose: red berry notes, ripe fruit, balsamic herbs. Palate: fruity, flavourful, easy to drink.

VALDEHERMOSO ROBLE 2012 T
100% tinta del país

89 Colour: bright cherry. Nose: ripe fruit, sweet spices, creamy oak. Palate: flavourful, fruity, toasty.

VALDERIZ JUEGABOLOS 2011 T
100% tinta del país

91 Colour: cherry, garnet rim. Nose: ripe fruit, spicy, toasty, creamy oak, aged wood nuances, mineral. Palate: powerful, rich, flavourful, spicy, long.

VALDERIZ TOMÁS ESTEBAN 2009 T
100% tinta del país

94 Colour: cherry, garnet rim. Nose: red berry notes, ripe fruit, fragrant herbs, dry stone, sweet spices, creamy oak. Palate: balanced, elegant, rich, flavourful, spicy, long.

BODEGAS Y VIÑEDOS VEGA DE YUSO S.L.

Basilón, 9 - Cañada Real, s/n
47350 Quintanilla de Onésimo (Valladolid)
☎: +34 983 680 054 - Fax: +34 983 680 294
www.vegadeyuso.com
export@vegadeyuso.com

POZO DE NIEVE 2012 T BARRICA
100% tempranillo

86 Colour: cherry, purple rim. Nose: medium intensity, ripe fruit. Palate: correct, spicy, fruity.

TRES MATAS 2009 TR
100% tempranillo

90 Colour: cherry, garnet rim. Nose: ripe fruit, spicy, creamy oak, toasty, complex. Palate: powerful, flavourful, toasty, round tannins.

TRES MATAS 2010 TC
100% tempranillo

91 Colour: cherry, garnet rim. Nose: ripe fruit, sweet spices, toasty. Palate: powerful, flavourful, good acidity.

TRES MATAS VENDIMIA SELECCIONADA 2009 T
100% tempranillo

91 Colour: cherry, garnet rim. Nose: powerfull, fruit preserve, creamy oak, cocoa bean. Palate: fruity, flavourful, long.

VEGANTIGUA 10 MESES 2011 T BARRICA
100% tempranillo

86 Colour: cherry, garnet rim. Nose: ripe fruit, spicy, creamy oak, toasty. Palate: powerful, flavourful, toasty.

BODEGAS Y VIÑEDOS VIÑA MAYOR

Ctra. Valladolid - Soria, Km. 325,6
47350 Quintanilla de Onésimo (Valladolid)
☎: +34 983 680 461 - Fax: +34 983 027 217
www.vina-mayor.es
rrpp@vina-mayor.com

SECRETO 2006 TR
tinta del país

91 Colour: deep cherry. Nose: spicy, ripe fruit, toasty. Palate: ripe fruit, toasty.

SECRETO VENDIMIA SELECCIONADA 2011 T ROBLE
tinta del país

88 Colour: cherry, garnet rim. Nose: medium intensity, ripe fruit, spicy, cocoa bean. Palate: fruity, flavourful.

VIÑA MAYOR 2008 TR
tinta del país

89 Colour: cherry, garnet rim. Nose: spicy, dried herbs, ripe fruit, varietal. Palate: ripe fruit, long.

VIÑA MAYOR 2010 TC
tinta del país

88 Colour: cherry, garnet rim. Nose: powerfull, ripe fruit. Palate: flavourful, fine bitter notes.

VIÑA MAYOR 2012 T ROBLE
tinta del país

89 Colour: cherry, purple rim. Nose: creamy oak, sweet spices, ripe fruit. Palate: good acidity, flavourful, fine bitter notes.

BODEGAS ZIFAR

Afueras de D. Juan Manuel, 9-11
47300 Peñafiel (Valladolid)
☎: +34 983 873 147 - Fax: +34 983 880 287
www.zifar.com
bodegaszifar@zifar.com

ZIFAR 2008 TC
tempranillo

90 Colour: cherry, garnet rim. Nose: ripe fruit, spicy, creamy oak, toasty. Palate: powerful, flavourful, toasty, round tannins.

ZIFAR SELECCIÓN 2009 T
tempranillo

92 Colour: cherry, garnet rim. Nose: ripe fruit, spicy, creamy oak, complex, mineral. Palate: powerful, flavourful, toasty, round tannins.

BODEGUEROS QUINTA ESENCIA

47520 Castronuño (Valladolid)
☎: +34 605 887 100 - Fax: +34 983 866 391
www.bodeguerosquintaesencia.com
info@bodeguerosquintaesencia.com

AL-NABIZ 2011 T
tempranillo

88 Colour: cherry, garnet rim. Nose: powerfull, sweet spices, creamy oak, cocoa bean, ripe fruit. Palate: good structure, flavourful.

BOSQUE DE MATA ASNOS

Sendin, s/n Parc. 5
9400 Aranda de Duero (Burgos)
☎: +34 915 630 590 - Fax: +34 915 630 704
www.bosquedematasnos.es
jaimep@bosquedematasnos.es

BOSQUE DE MATASNOS 2010 T
95% tempranillo, 5% merlot

94 Colour: cherry, garnet rim. Nose: spicy, creamy oak, toasty, characterful, ripe fruit. Palate: powerful, flavourful, toasty, round tannins.

BOSQUE DE MATASNOS SELECCIÓN PRIVADA 2009 T
tempranillo, merlot

95 Colour: cherry, garnet rim. Nose: red berry notes, ripe fruit, balsamic herbs, sweet spices, creamy oak, mineral. Palate: rich, powerful, flavourful, spicy, balsamic, long, balanced, elegant.

CAMPOS GÓTICOS

Parcela 622
9312 Anguix (Burgos)
☎: +34 979 165 121
www.camposgoticos.es
clientedirecto@camposgoticos.es

7 LUNAS VENDIMIA SELECCIONADA 2005 TC
100% tempranillo

91 Colour: dark-red cherry, garnet rim. Nose: medium intensity, fragrant herbs, spicy, ripe fruit. Palate: flavourful, round tannins.

7 LUNAS VIÑEDOS DE LA JOYA 2004 T
100% tempranillo

90 Colour: pale ruby, brick rim edge. Nose: elegant, spicy, fine reductive notes, aged wood nuances, fruit liqueur notes. Palate: spicy, elegant, long.

CAMPOS GÓTICOS 2004 TR
100% tempranillo

90 Colour: cherry, garnet rim. Nose: fruit preserve, tobacco, spicy, wild herbs. Palate: varietal.

CAMPOS GÓTICOS 2005 TC
100% tempranillo

90 Colour: cherry, garnet rim. Nose: ripe fruit, spicy, creamy oak, toasty, cigar, waxy notes, fine reductive notes. Palate: powerful, flavourful, toasty, round tannins.

CAMPOS GÓTICOS 2009 TC
100% tempranillo

88 Colour: cherry, garnet rim. Nose: medium intensity, varietal, ripe fruit, sweet spices. Palate: fruity, easy to drink.

CAMPOS GÓTICOS 2010 T ROBLE
100% tempranillo

89 Colour: bright cherry. Nose: ripe fruit, sweet spices, balanced. Palate: flavourful, fruity, toasty, round tannins.

CARRASVILLA

Ctra. Pesquera Va-101, P.K. 3,700
47300 Peñafiel (Valladolid)
☎: +34 983 218 925 - Fax: +34 983 218 926
www.carrasvilla.es
comercial@carrasvilla.es

GONZALVILLA 2011 T
tempranillo

87 Colour: cherry, garnet rim. Nose: ripe fruit, spicy, creamy oak, balsamic herbs. Palate: powerful, flavourful, toasty.

TERRALUX 2010 T
tempranillo

91 Colour: deep cherry, garnet rim. Nose: balanced, ripe fruit, sweet spices. Palate: flavourful, fruity, good structure, good acidity.

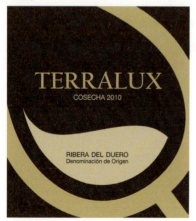

TERRALUX 2011 T
tempranillo

89 Colour: cherry, garnet rim. Nose: ripe fruit, spicy, new oak, aged wood nuances. Palate: powerful, flavourful, spicy.

CARREFOUR

Campezo, 16
28022 Madrid (Madrid)
☎: +34 902 202 000
www.carrefour.es

CAMINO DE LA DEHESA 2006 TR
tinta del país

87 Colour: deep cherry. Nose: ripe fruit, toasty, fruit liqueur notes, fine reductive notes. Palate: flavourful, fine bitter notes, good acidity.

CAMINO DE LA DEHESA 2010 TC
tinta del país

88 Colour: cherry, garnet rim. Nose: ripe fruit, spicy, creamy oak, toasty. Palate: powerful, flavourful, toasty, round tannins.

CAMINO DE LA DEHESA 2011 T ROBLE
tinta del país

86 Colour: bright cherry. Nose: ripe fruit, sweet spices, creamy oak. Palate: flavourful, fruity, toasty, round tannins.

CAMINO DE LA DEHESA 2012 RD
tinta del país

87 Colour: rose, purple rim. Nose: powerfull, ripe fruit, red berry notes, floral, expressive. Palate: powerful, fruity, fresh.

CAMINO DE LA DEHESA 2012 T
tinta del país

85 Colour: bright cherry. Nose: medium intensity, ripe fruit. Palate: fine bitter notes, good acidity, fruity.

GOMELLANO 2006 TR
100% tempranillo

84

GOMELLANO 2009 TC
100% tempranillo

89 Colour: cherry, garnet rim. Nose: ripe fruit, spicy, toasty. Palate: powerful, flavourful, toasty, round tannins, long.

GOMELLANO 2011 T ROBLE
100% tempranillo

88 Colour: deep cherry, purple rim. Nose: ripe fruit, balanced, spicy. Palate: good structure, round tannins.

GOMELLANO 2012 T
100% tempranillo

87 Colour: bright cherry, purple rim. Nose: medium intensity, red berry notes, ripe fruit. Palate: balanced, fruity, flavourful.

CILLAR DE SILOS

Paraje El Soto, s/n
9370 Quintana del Pidio (Burgos)
☎: +34 947 545 126 - Fax: +34 947 545 605
www.cillardesilos.es
bodega@cillardesilos.es

CILLAR DE SILOS 2009 TC
100% tempranillo

92 Colour: cherry, garnet rim. Nose: spicy, creamy oak, toasty, complex, mineral, earthy notes. Palate: powerful, flavourful, round tannins.

EL QUINTANAL 2012 T
100% tempranillo

87 Colour: cherry, purple rim. Nose: medium intensity, ripe fruit, floral, balanced, sweet spices. Palate: balanced, flavourful.

EL QUINTANAL
TEMPRANILLO
2012

RIBERA DEL DUERO
DENOMINACIÓN DE ORIGEN

LA VIÑA DE AMALIO 2009 T
100% tempranillo

94 Colour: bright cherry, garnet rim. Nose: ripe fruit, violets, expressive, balanced. Palate: flavourful, fruity, round tannins.

TORRESILO 2009 T
100% tempranillo

91 Colour: cherry, garnet rim. Nose: spicy, creamy oak, toasty, complex, earthy notes, mineral. Palate: powerful, flavourful, toasty, round tannins.

CINEMA WINES

Felipe Gómez, 1
47140 Laguna de Duero (Valladolid)
☎: +34 983 544 696 - Fax: +34 983 545 539
www.cinemawines.es
info@cinemawines.es

CINEMA 2010 TC
100% tempranillo

89 Colour: cherry, garnet rim. Nose: ripe fruit, cocoa bean, sweet spices, creamy oak, mineral. Palate: powerful, flavourful, correct.

CINEMA 2011 T ROBLE
100% tempranillo

87 Colour: bright cherry. Nose: sweet spices, creamy oak. Palate: flavourful, fruity, toasty, round tannins.

COMENGE BODEGAS Y VIÑEDOS

Camino del Castillo, s/n
47316 Curiel de Duero (Valladolid)
☎: +34 983 880 363 - Fax: +34 983 880 717
www.comenge.com
admin@comenge.com

BIBERIUS 2012 T

89 Colour: very deep cherry. Nose: ripe fruit, fruit expression, earthy notes. Palate: ripe fruit, spicy.

COMENGE 2009 T
100% tempranillo

90 Colour: cherry, garnet rim. Nose: ripe fruit, spicy, creamy oak, toasty. Palate: powerful, flavourful, round tannins.

DON MIGUEL COMENGE 2009 T
tempranillo, cabernet sauvignon

95 Colour: cherry, garnet rim. Nose: earthy notes, spicy, toasty, ripe fruit. Palate: powerful, flavourful, good acidity, elegant.

DON MIGUEL COMENGE 2010 T
90% tempranillo, 10% cabernet sauvignon

94 Colour: cherry, garnet rim. Nose: ripe fruit, spicy, creamy oak, toasty. Palate: powerful, flavourful, toasty, round tannins.

COMPAÑÍA VINÍCOLA SOLTERRA

9300 Roa (Burgos)
☎: +34 915 196 651 - Fax: +34 914 135 907
www.cvsolterra.com
m.antonia@cvsolterra.com

ALTO DE LOS ZORROS 2009 TC
100% tempranillo

89 Colour: deep cherry. Nose: ripe fruit, sweet spices, creamy oak. Palate: flavourful, powerful, ripe fruit.

ALTO DE LOS ZORROS 2010 T ROBLE
100% tempranillo

89 Colour: bright cherry. Nose: sweet spices, creamy oak. Palate: flavourful, fruity, toasty, round tannins.

CONVENTO DE LAS CLARAS S.L.

Calvario s/n
47316 Curiel de Duero (Valladolid)
☎: +34 983 880 481
www.bodegasconventodelasclaras.com
info@bodegasconventodelasclaras.com

CONVENTO LAS CLARAS TEMPRANILLO 2011 T
100% tempranillo

92 Colour: cherry, garnet rim. Nose: ripe fruit, spicy, creamy oak, toasty, complex. Palate: powerful, flavourful, toasty, round tannins.

CONVENTO DE OREJA

Avda. Palencia, 1
47010 (Valladolid)
☎: +34 685 990 596
www.conventooreja.net
convento@conventooreja.es

CONVENTO OREJA 2008 TC
100% tinta del país

89 Colour: pale ruby, brick rim edge. Nose: ripe fruit, creamy oak, sweet spices, toasty, fine reductive notes. Palate: flavourful, spicy, long.

CONVENTO OREJA 2009 TC
100% tinta del país

90 Colour: cherry, garnet rim. Nose: ripe fruit, spicy, creamy oak, smoky. Palate: powerful, flavourful, toasty, round tannins.

CONVENTO OREJA 2011 T ROBLE
100% tinta del país

87 Colour: cherry, garnet rim. Nose: red berry notes, ripe fruit, balsamic herbs, spicy, creamy oak. Palate: powerful, flavourful, spicy.

CVNE - COMPAÑÍA VINÍCOLA DEL NORTE DE ESPAÑA

Barrio de la Estación, s/n
26200 Haro (La Rioja)
☎: +34 941 304 800 - Fax: +34 941 304 815
www.cvne.com
marketing@cvne.com

BLACK 2010 TC
100% tempranillo

88 Colour: cherry, garnet rim. Nose: ripe fruit, spicy, creamy oak, toasty. Palate: powerful, flavourful, toasty.

BLACK 2011 T ROBLE
100% tempranillo

86 Colour: cherry, garnet rim. Nose: ripe fruit, balsamic herbs, spicy, medium intensity. Palate: flavourful, spicy, thin.

DEHESA DE LOS CANÓNIGOS S.A.

Ctra. Renedo - Pesquera, Km. 39
47315 Pesquera de Duero (Valladolid)
☎: +34 983 484 001 - Fax: +34 983 484 040
www.bodegadehesadeloscanonigos.com
bodega@dehesacanonigos.com

DEHESA DE LOS CANÓNIGOS 2006 TR
85% tempranillo, 12% cabernet sauvignon, 3% albillo

90 Colour: dark-red cherry, orangey edge. Nose: fine reductive notes, tobacco, ripe fruit, spicy. Palate: flavourful, balanced, fine bitter notes, spicy, long.

DEHESA DE LOS CANÓNIGOS 2009 T
88% tinto fino, 12% cabernet sauvignon

88 Colour: deep cherry. Nose: powerfull, fruit preserve, dried herbs, cocoa bean. Palate: flavourful, fruity, round tannins.

DEHESA VALDELAGUNA

Ctra. Valoria, Km. 16
47315 Pesquera de Duero (Valladolid)
☎: +34 619 460 308 - Fax: +34 921 142 325
www.montelaguna.es
montelaguna@montelaguna.es

MONTELAGUNA 2010 TC
tempranillo

90 Colour: cherry, garnet rim. Nose: aromatic coffee, sweet spices, creamy oak, ripe fruit. Palate: powerful, flavourful, spicy, long.

MONTELAGUNA 6 MESES 2011 T
tempranillo

87 Colour: bright cherry, garnet rim. Nose: ripe fruit, sweet spices, creamy oak. Palate: flavourful, fruity, toasty.

MONTELAGUNA SELECCIÓN 2009 T
tempranillo

92 Colour: cherry, garnet rim. Nose: ripe fruit, spicy, creamy oak, toasty, complex. Palate: powerful, flavourful, toasty, round tannins, balanced.

DO RIBERA DEL DUERO / D.O.P.

RA 08 2008 TR
tempranillo

90 Colour: dark-red cherry, orangey edge. Nose: ripe fruit, spicy, creamy oak, fine reductive notes. Palate: spicy, long, flavourful.

RA 09 2009 T
tempranillo

91 Colour: black cherry, garnet rim. Nose: ripe fruit, toasty, dark chocolate, sweet spices. Palate: rich, powerful, flavourful, toasty.

RA VENDIMIA SELECCIONADA 2009 T
tempranillo

92 Colour: cherry, garnet rim. Nose: red berry notes, ripe fruit, spicy, mineral, creamy oak, expressive. Palate: powerful, flavourful, fruity, spicy, balanced, elegant, round tannins.

DÍAZ BAYO HERMANOS

Camino de los Anarinos, s/n
9471 Fuentelcésped (Burgos)
☎: +34 947 561 020 - Fax: +34 947 561 204
www.bodegadiazbayo.com
info@bodegadiazbayo.com

DARDANELOS 2012 T BARRICA
tempranillo

87 Colour: bright cherry. Nose: ripe fruit, creamy oak, aromatic coffee. Palate: flavourful, fruity, toasty.

DIAZ BAYO MAJUELO DE LA HOMBRÍA 2009 T BARRICA
tempranillo

92 Colour: cherry, garnet rim. Nose: dry stone, ripe fruit, balsamic herbs, varietal, complex. Palate: balanced, round tannins, fruity.

FDB 2006 T BARRICA
tempranillo

91 Colour: cherry, garnet rim. Nose: ripe fruit, spicy, creamy oak, toasty, balsamic herbs. Palate: powerful, flavourful, toasty, fine tannins, balanced.

MAGUNUS MAXIMUS 2009 TC
100% tempranillo

90 Colour: cherry, garnet rim. Nose: ripe fruit, spicy, toasty, complex, balsamic herbs. Palate: powerful, flavourful, toasty, balanced.

MAGUNUS MAXIMUS 2010 TC
tempranillo

89 Colour: bright cherry. Nose: ripe fruit, spicy, dried herbs. Palate: flavourful, fruity, toasty, round tannins.

NUESTRO 12 MESES 2011 T BARRICA
tempranillo

89 Colour: bright cherry. Nose: ripe fruit, sweet spices, creamy oak. Palate: flavourful, fruity, toasty, round tannins.

NUESTRO 20 MESES 2007 T BARRICA
tempranillo

93 Colour: cherry, garnet rim. Nose: ripe fruit, spicy, creamy oak, mineral. Palate: powerful, flavourful, toasty, round tannins.

NUESTRO CRIANZA 2009 TC
tempranillo

90 Colour: very deep cherry. Nose: fruit preserve, overripe fruit. Palate: long, spicy, ripe fruit.

DISTRIBUCIONES B. IÑAKI NÚÑEZ

Ctra. de Ablitas a Ribafora, Km. 5
31523 Ablitas (Navarra)
☎: +34 948 386 210 - Fax: +34 629 354 190
www.pagodecirsus.com
bodegasin@pagodecirsus.com

SENDA DE LOS OLIVOS EDICIÓN ESPECIAL 2006 T
100% tinto fino

88 Colour: cherry, garnet rim. Nose: fruit preserve, balsamic herbs, spicy, old leather, tobacco, toasty. Palate: rich, powerful, warm.

SENDA DE LOS OLIVOS FINCA LA CARRASCA 2009 T
100% tinto fino

89 Colour: cherry, garnet rim. Nose: ripe fruit, spicy, creamy oak, fruit expression. Palate: powerful, flavourful, toasty, round tannins.

SENDA DE LOS OLIVOS VENDIMIA SELECCIONADA 2010 T
100% tinto fino

90 Colour: very deep cherry, garnet rim. Nose: complex, balanced, ripe fruit. Palate: flavourful, round tannins, long.

DOMINIO BASCONCILLOS

Condado de Treviño, 55
9001 (Burgos)
☎: +34 947 473 000 - Fax: +34 947 473 360
www.dominiobasconcillos.com
info@dominiobasconcillos.com

DOMINIO BASCONCILLOS 2011 T ROBLE
100% tempranillo

88 Colour: bright cherry. Nose: ripe fruit, sweet spices, creamy oak, expressive. Palate: flavourful, fruity, toasty, round tannins.

DOMINIO BASCONCILLOS ECOLÓGICO 6 MESES 2011 T
100% tempranillo

89 Colour: cherry, purple rim. Nose: red berry notes, ripe fruit, fragrant herbs, sweet spices, creamy oak. Palate: correct, powerful, flavourful.

VIÑA MAGNA 2009 TR
85% tempranillo, 10% cabernet sauvignon, 5% merlot

91 Colour: cherry, garnet rim. Nose: ripe fruit, spicy, creamy oak. Palate: powerful, flavourful, toasty, round tannins.

VIÑA MAGNA 2010 TC
95% tempranillo, 5% cabernet sauvignon

92 Colour: cherry, garnet rim. Nose: sweet spices, dry stone, ripe fruit, expressive. Palate: good structure, balanced, round tannins, spicy, long.

DOMINIO DE ATAUTA

Ctra. a Morcuera, s/n
42345 Atauta (Soria)
☎: +34 975 351 349
www.dominiodeatauta.com
info@dominiodeatauta.com

DOMINIO DE ATAUTA 2009 T
100% tinto fino

94 Colour: deep cherry. Nose: ripe fruit, spicy, toasty, earthy notes. Palate: powerful, good acidity, fine bitter notes, round tannins.

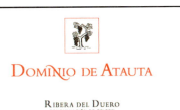

DOMINIO DE ATAUTA 2010 T
100% tinto fino

94 Colour: cherry, garnet rim. Nose: fresh fruit, fruit expression, scrubland, balsamic herbs, sweet spices. Palate: flavourful, spicy, ripe fruit, long, fine tannins.

DOMINIO DE ATAUTA LA MALA 2009 TC
100% tinto fino

95 Colour: cherry, garnet rim. Nose: ripe fruit, spicy, toasty, fruit expression. Palate: ripe fruit, warm, round, round tannins.

DOMINIO DE ATAUTA LLANOS DEL ALMENDRO 2009 T
100% tinto fino

97 Colour: cherry, garnet rim. Nose: ripe fruit, spicy, creamy oak, toasty, complex, mineral, earthy notes. Palate: powerful, flavourful, toasty, round tannins, round.

DOMINIO DE ATAUTA VALDEGATILES 2009 T
100% tinto fino

96 Colour: very deep cherry, garnet rim. Nose: elegant, complex, varietal, spicy, balsamic herbs. Palate: good structure, ripe fruit, full, round, round tannins.

PARADA DE ATAUTA 2010 T
100% tinto fino

95 Colour: cherry, garnet rim. Nose: red berry notes, ripe fruit, toasty, sweet spices, mineral. Palate: flavourful, spicy, balanced.

DOMINIO DE ES

Avenida Manuel de Falla, nº 37 2ºE
26007 Logroño (La Rioja)
☎: +34 676 536 390

DOMINIO DE ES 2011 T
100% tinto fino

95 Colour: very deep cherry. Nose: powerfull, complex, characterful, mineral, spicy, cocoa bean. Palate: flavourful, varietal, fruity, spicy, fine tannins.

DOMINIO DE PINGUS S.L.

Hospital, s/n - Apdo. 93, Peñafiel
47350 Quintanilla de Onésimo (Valladolid)
☎: +34 639 833 854
www.dominiopingus.com

FLOR DE PINGUS 2011 T
100% tinto fino

95 Colour: very deep cherry. Nose: ripe fruit, spicy, scrubland, sweet spices, creamy oak. Palate: flavourful, ripe fruit, spicy, round tannins.

PINGUS 2011 T
tinto fino

97 Colour: cherry, garnet rim. Nose: fruit expression, ripe fruit, sweet spices, cocoa bean, earthy notes. Palate: flavourful, fruity, ripe fruit, round, round tannins.

PSI 2011 T

94 Colour: bright cherry, garnet rim. Nose: balanced, expressive, ripe fruit, spicy, mineral. Palate: full, flavourful, long, fruity, round tannins.

DOMINIO ROMANO

Lagares, s/n
47319 Rábano (Valladolid)
☎: +34 983 871 661 - Fax: +34 938 901 143
www.dominioromano.es
dominioromano@dominioromano.es

CAMINO ROMANO 2011 T
tinto fino

90 Colour: cherry, garnet rim. Nose: spicy, creamy oak, toasty, characterful. Palate: powerful, flavourful, toasty, round tannins.

DOMINIO ROMANO 2010 T
tinto fino

89 Colour: bright cherry. Nose: sweet spices, creamy oak, fruit expression. Palate: flavourful, fruity, toasty, round tannins.

DOMINIO ROMANO RDR 2011 T
tinto fino

91 Colour: cherry, garnet rim. Nose: spicy, creamy oak, toasty, complex, fruit preserve, mineral. Palate: powerful, flavourful, toasty, round tannins.

ÉBANO VIÑEDOS Y BODEGAS

Ctra. N-122 Km., 299,6 Pol. Ind. 1 Parcela 32
47318 Castrillo de Duero (Valladolid)
☎: +34 983 106 440 - Fax: +34 986 609 313
www.ebanovinedosybodegas.com
ebano@valminorebano.com

ÉBANO 2009 T
100% tempranillo

91 Colour: cherry, garnet rim. Nose: ripe fruit, spicy, creamy oak, toasty. Palate: powerful, flavourful, toasty.

ÉBANO 6 2012 T
100% tempranillo

87 Colour: dark-red cherry, purple rim. Nose: medium intensity, ripe fruit, sweet spices. Palate: flavourful, easy to drink.

EL LAGAR DE ISILLA

Camino Real, 1
9471 La Vid (Burgos)
☎: +34 947 530 434 - Fax: +34 947 504 316
www.lagarisilla.es
bodegas@lagarisilla.es

EL LAGAR DE ISILLA 2009 TR
100% tempranillo

90 Colour: cherry, garnet rim. Nose: ripe fruit, spicy, creamy oak, toasty, mineral. Palate: powerful, flavourful, toasty, harsh oak tannins.

EL LAGAR DE ISILLA 2010 TC
100% tempranillo

89 Colour: deep cherry, garnet rim. Nose: balanced, ripe fruit, dark chocolate. Palate: good structure, round tannins, long.

EL LAGAR DE ISILLA 9 MESES GESTACIÓN 2011 T ROBLE
100% tempranillo

87 Colour: cherry, garnet rim. Nose: ripe fruit, fragrant herbs, mineral, creamy oak. Palate: flavourful, long, spicy.

EL LAGAR DE ISILLA VENDIMIA SELECCIONADA 2009 T
100% tempranillo

91 Colour: cherry, garnet rim. Nose: ripe fruit, spicy, toasty. Palate: powerful, flavourful, toasty, round tannins, good structure, sweet tannins.

FINCA TORREMILANOS

Finca Torremilanos, s/n
9400 Aranda de Duero (Burgos)
☎: +34 947 510 377 - Fax: +34 947 508 044
www.torremilanos.com
torremilanos@torremilanos.com

CYCLO 2009 T

92 Colour: deep cherry, garnet rim. Nose: cocoa bean, sweet spices, creamy oak. Palate: fruity, good structure, round tannins.

CYCLO 2010 T

93 Colour: cherry, garnet rim. Nose: balanced, neat, ripe fruit, spicy. Palate: round tannins, good acidity.

LOS CANTOS DE TORREMILANOS 2010 T
tempranillo, merlot

91 Colour: deep cherry, garnet rim. Nose: wild herbs, ripe fruit, spicy. Palate: balanced, round tannins.

LOS CANTOS DE TORREMILANOS 2011 T
tempranillo, merlot

90 Colour: deep cherry, garnet rim. Nose: ripe fruit, fruit preserve, sweet spices. Palate: good structure, full, round tannins.

MONTECASTRILLO 2011 RD
tempranillo

85 Colour: rose. Nose: powerfull, ripe fruit, red berry notes, floral. Palate: powerful, fruity, fresh.

MONTECASTRILLO 2011 T ROBLE
tempranillo

87 Colour: cherry, garnet rim. Nose: spicy, dried herbs, ripe fruit. Palate: ripe fruit, round tannins.

TORRE ALBÉNIZ 2009 TR
tempranillo, tempranillo blanco

88 Colour: deep cherry. Nose: roasted coffee, dark chocolate. Palate: good structure, powerful, flavourful, toasty.

TORREMILANOS 2010 TC
tempranillo, cabernet sauvignon

90 Colour: deep cherry, garnet rim. Nose: varietal, spicy, ripe fruit. Palate: good acidity, balanced, round tannins.

FINCA VILLACRECES

Ctra. N-122 Km. 322
47350 Quintanilla de Onésimo (Valladolid)
☎: +34 983 680 437 - Fax: +34 983 683 314
www.grupoartevino.com
villacreces@villacreces.com

FINCA VILLACRECES 2009 T
86% tinto fino, 10% cabernet sauvignon, 4% merlot

92 Colour: cherry, garnet rim. Nose: ripe fruit, spicy, creamy oak, toasty, characterful. Palate: powerful, flavourful, toasty, round tannins.

FINCA VILLACRECES NEBRO 2011 TC
100% tinto fino   1

95 Colour: very deep cherry. Nose: powerfull, characterful, ripe fruit, fruit expression, creamy oak, cocoa bean. Palate: powerful, flavourful, fine bitter notes, good acidity, round tannins.

PRUNO 2011 T
90% tinto fino, 10% cabernet sauvignon

92 Colour: bright cherry. Nose: ripe fruit, sweet spices, creamy oak, balanced. Palate: flavourful, fruity, toasty, round tannins.

GRANDES BODEGAS

Ctra. de Sotillo de la Ribera, s/n
9311 La Horra (Burgos)
☎: +34 947 542 166 - Fax: +34 947 542 165
www.marquesdevelilla.com
bodega@marquesdevelilla.com

DONCEL DE MATAPERRAS 2009 TC
100% tinta del país

93 Colour: cherry, garnet rim. Nose: creamy oak, toasty, spicy, ripe fruit. Palate: ripe fruit, round tannins, long.

MARQUÉS DE VELILLA 2009 TC
100% tinta del país

87 Colour: cherry, garnet rim. Nose: fruit preserve, scrubland, aged wood nuances. Palate: rich, powerful, flavourful.

MARQUÉS DE VELILLA FINCA LA MARÍA 2010 T
100% tempranillo

90 Colour: cherry, garnet rim. Nose: powerfull, ripe fruit, balsamic herbs. Palate: good structure, round tannins, ripe fruit.

GRUPO VINÍCOLA MARQUÉS DE VARGAS - CONDE SAN CRISTÓBAL

Ctra. Valladolid a Soria, Km. 303
47300 Peñafiel (Valladolid)
☎: +34 983 878 055 - Fax: +34 983 878 196
www.marquesdevargas.com
bodega@condesancristobal.com

CONDE DE SAN CRISTÓBAL 2010 T
tempranillo

91 Colour: cherry, garnet rim. Nose: ripe fruit, spicy, creamy oak, characterful. Palate: powerful, flavourful, toasty, round tannins.

GRUPO YLLERA

A-6 Madrid - Coruña, Km. 173, 5
47490 Rueda (Valladolid)
☎: +34 983 868 097 - Fax: +34 983 868 177
www.grupoyllera.com
grupoyllera@grupoyllera.com

BOADA 2009 TC
tempranillo

89 Colour: cherry, garnet rim. Nose: red berry notes, ripe fruit, balsamic herbs, creamy oak. Palate: flavourful, spicy, long.

BOADA 2009 TR
tempranillo

88 Colour: cherry, garnet rim. Nose: ripe fruit, spicy, balsamic herbs, creamy oak. Palate: flavourful, spicy, long.

BOADA 2011 T ROBLE
tempranillo

86 Colour: bright cherry. Nose: ripe fruit, sweet spices, balsamic herbs. Palate: flavourful, fruity, toasty, balanced.

BRACAMONTE 2009 TC
tempranillo

92 Colour: cherry, garnet rim. Nose: spicy, creamy oak, toasty, varietal, expressive. Palate: powerful, flavourful, toasty, round tannins.

BRACAMONTE 2009 TR
tempranillo

89 Colour: cherry, garnet rim. Nose: ripe fruit, spicy, creamy oak, toasty. Palate: powerful, flavourful, toasty, harsh oak tannins.

BRACAMONTE 2011 T ROBLE
tempranillo

87 Colour: bright cherry. Nose: ripe fruit, sweet spices, creamy oak, balsamic herbs. Palate: flavourful, fruity, toasty.

VIÑA DEL VAL 2012 RD
tempranillo

87 Colour: rose, purple rim. Nose: powerfull, ripe fruit, red berry notes, floral, expressive. Palate: powerful, fruity, flavourful.

VIÑA DEL VAL 2012 T
tempranillo

88 Colour: cherry, purple rim. Nose: ripe fruit, red berry notes, violet drops, balanced. Palate: powerful, fruity.

HACIENDA URBIÓN

Ctra. Nalda, km. 9
26120 Albelda de Iregua (Rioja)
☎: +34 941 444 233 - Fax: +34 941 444 427
www.vinicolareal.com
info@vinicolareal.com

VEGA VIEJA 2011 TC
90% tempranillo, 10% garnacha

84

VEGA VIEJA 2012 T ROBLE
100% tempranillo

86 Colour: deep cherry, garnet rim. Nose: spicy, toasty, ripe fruit, fruit preserve. Palate: flavourful, round tannins, ripe fruit.

VEGA VIEJA COSECHA 2012 T
100% tempranillo

85 Colour: bright cherry, purple rim. Nose: powerfull, fruit preserve, dried herbs. Palate: flavourful, ripe fruit, correct.

HACIENDAS DE ESPAÑA

Hacienda Abascal, N-122, Km. 321,5
47360 Quintanilla de Onésimo (Valladolid)
☎: +34 914 365 924
www.haciendas-espana.com
comunicacion@arcoinvest-group.com

HACIENDA ABASCAL (MARQUÉS DE LA CONCORDIA FAMILY OF WINES) 2010 TC
tempranillo

89 Colour: cherry, garnet rim. Nose: red berry notes, ripe fruit, sweet spices, creamy oak. Palate: powerful, flavourful, spicy.

HACIENDA ABASCAL PREMIUM (MARQUÉS DE LA CONCORDIA FAMILY OF WINES) 2010 T
tempranillo

90 Colour: cherry, garnet rim. Nose: spicy, creamy oak, toasty, complex, fruit preserve. Palate: powerful, flavourful, toasty, round tannins.

HIJOS DE ANTONIO POLO

La Olma, 5
47300 Peñafiel (Valladolid)
☎: +34 983 873 183 - Fax: +34 983 881 808
www.pagopenafiel.com
info@pagopenafiel.com

PAGOS DE PEÑAFIEL 2009 TC
tempranillo

91 Colour: cherry, garnet rim. Nose: ripe fruit, spicy, creamy oak, toasty, complex. Palate: powerful, flavourful, toasty, round tannins.

PAGOS DE PEÑAFIEL 2010 T ROBLE
tempranillo

88 Colour: cherry, garnet rim. Nose: powerfull, ripe fruit, aromatic coffee, cocoa bean. Palate: flavourful, good acidity.

PAGOS DE PEÑAFIEL VENDIMIA SELECCIÓN 2009 T
tempranillo

88 Colour: cherry, garnet rim. Nose: ripe fruit, fragrant herbs, creamy oak, mineral. Palate: long, ripe fruit, balanced.

HORNILLOS BALLESTEROS

Camino Tenerías, 9
9300 Roa de Duero (Burgos)
☎: +34 947 541 071 - Fax: +34 947 541 071
www.hornillosballesteros.es
hornillosballesteros@telefonica.net

MIBAL 2009 TC
100% tempranillo

88 Colour: cherry, garnet rim. Nose: ripe fruit, toasty, sweet spices. Palate: flavourful, toasty, round tannins, easy to drink.

MIBAL 2011 T
100% tempranillo

88 Colour: bright cherry. Nose: sweet spices, creamy oak, red berry notes, ripe fruit. Palate: flavourful, fruity, toasty.

MIBAL SELECCIÓN 2008 T
100% tempranillo

88 Colour: cherry, garnet rim. Nose: balanced, ripe fruit, fruit preserve, spicy. Palate: flavourful, round tannins.

PERFIL 2009 T
100% tempranillo

91 Colour: cherry, garnet rim. Nose: ripe fruit, balsamic herbs, mineral, sweet spices, creamy oak. Palate: complex, flavourful, balanced.

J.A. CALVO CASAJÚS S.L.

Cercados s/n
9443 Quintana del Pidío (Burgos)
☎: +34 947 545 699 - Fax: +34 947 545 626
www.bodegascasajus.com
info@bodegascasajus.com

CASAJÚS 2010 T BARRICA

87 Colour: cherry, garnet rim. Nose: ripe fruit, fruit preserve, balsamic herbs, spicy, aged wood nuances. Palate: powerful, flavourful, toasty.

CASAJÚS 2010 TC

93 Colour: bright cherry. Nose: sweet spices, creamy oak, characterful, varietal. Palate: flavourful, fruity, toasty, round tannins.

LA VIÑA DEL LOCO

Plaza de Matute 12
28012 (Madrid)
☎: +34 609 119 248
www.miravinos.es
info@miravinos.es

TOGA 2010 T
tinto fino

94 Colour: cherry, garnet rim. Nose: ripe fruit, spicy, creamy oak, toasty, complex, powerfull, mineral. Palate: powerful, flavourful, toasty, round tannins.

TOGA XL 2011 T
tinto fino

96 Colour: cherry, garnet rim. Nose: spicy, creamy oak, toasty, complex, earthy notes, varietal. Palate: powerful, flavourful, toasty, round tannins.

VENTA EL LOCO 2010 TC
tinto fino

91 Colour: cherry, garnet rim. Nose: ripe fruit, powerfull, sweet spices, toasty. Palate: flavourful, powerful, fine bitter notes, good acidity.

LEGARIS

Ctra. Peñafiel - Encinas de Esgueva, km. 2,5
47316 Curiel de Duero (Valladolid)
☎: +34 983 878 088 - Fax: +34 983 881 034
www.grupocodorniu.com
info@legaris.com

LEGARIS 2009 TR
100% tinto fino

90 Colour: cherry, garnet rim. Nose: ripe fruit, spicy, creamy oak, toasty. Palate: powerful, flavourful, toasty, round tannins.

LEGARIS 2010 TC
96% tinto fino, 4% cabernet sauvignon

90 Colour: bright cherry. Nose: ripe fruit, sweet spices, creamy oak, expressive, dried herbs, varietal. Palate: flavourful, fruity, toasty, round tannins.

LEGARIS 2011 T ROBLE
100% tinto fino

88 Colour: cherry, garnet rim. Nose: red berry notes, ripe fruit, dark chocolate, creamy oak. Palate: powerful, flavourful, balanced, toasty.

LOESS

El Monte, 7- Bajo
47195 Arroyo de la Encomienda (Valladolid)
☎: +34 983 664 898 - Fax: +34 983 406 579
www.loess.es
loess@loess.es

LOESS 2010 T
tinta del país

91 Colour: cherry, garnet rim. Nose: ripe fruit, spicy, creamy oak, toasty, mineral, dry stone. Palate: powerful, flavourful, toasty, round tannins.

LOESS COLLECTION 2010 T
tinta del país

90 Colour: cherry, garnet rim. Nose: red berry notes, ripe fruit, spicy, creamy oak. Palate: rich, flavourful, balanced.

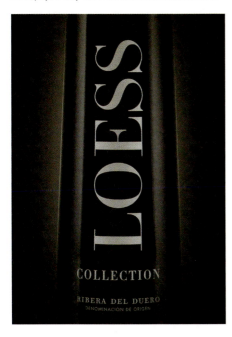

LONG WINES

Avda. del Puente Cultural, 8 Bloque B Bajo 7
28702 San Sebastián de los Reyes (Madrid)
☎: +34 916 221 305 - Fax: +34 916 220 029
www.longwines.com
adm@longwines.com

LAMATUM 2009 TC
100% tempranillo

88 Colour: cherry, garnet rim. Nose: balanced, fruit preserve, sweet spices. Palate: good structure, ripe fruit, good acidity.

LAMATUM 2010 T
100% tempranillo

86 Colour: bright cherry. Nose: sweet spices, creamy oak, fruit preserve. Palate: flavourful, fruity, toasty, round tannins.

MAGICAL WINES

Pio Baroja, 21
28939 Arroyomolinos (Madrid)
☎: +34 916 096 025
www.magicalwines.com
info@magicalwines.com

ALAKAZAM 2010 T
100% tempranillo

88 Colour: cherry, garnet rim. Nose: ripe fruit, spicy, creamy oak, toasty. Palate: powerful, flavourful, toasty.

ALAKAZAM 2012 T
100% tempranillo

86 Colour: bright cherry. Nose: ripe fruit, creamy oak, balsamic herbs. Palate: flavourful, fruity, toasty.

MARÍA ASCENSIÓN REPISO BOCOS

Ctra. de Valbuena, s/n
47315 Pesquera de Duero (Valladolid)
☎: +34 983 870 178 - Fax: +34 983 870 178
www.ascensionpagodetasio.net
info@ascensionpagodetasio.net

VERÓNICA SALGADO 2009 T

90 Colour: cherry, garnet rim. Nose: red berry notes, fragrant herbs, floral, sweet spices, creamy oak. Palate: powerful, flavourful, spicy, long.

MONTEBACO

Finca Montealto
47359 Valbuena de Duero (Valladolid)
☎: +34 983 485 128 - Fax: +34 983 485 033
www.bodegasmontebaco.com
montebaco@bodegasmontebaco.com

MONTEBACO 2011 TC
tempranillo

89 Colour: cherry, garnet rim. Nose: ripe fruit, spicy, creamy oak, toasty. Palate: powerful, flavourful, toasty.

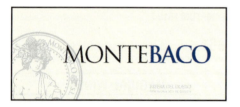

MONTEBACO VENDIMIA SELECCIONADA 2008 T
tempranillo

91 Colour: cherry, garnet rim. Nose: ripe fruit, spicy, creamy oak, dark chocolate. Palate: powerful, flavourful, toasty, round tannins.

SEMELE 2011 TC
90% tempranillo, 10% merlot

90 Colour: cherry, garnet rim. Nose: powerfull, fruit preserve, toasty, creamy oak. Palate: good acidity, sweetness.

MONTEGAREDO

Ctra. Boada a Pedrosa, s/n
9314 Boada de Roa (Burgos)
☎: +34 947 530 003 - Fax: +34 947 530 140
www.montegaredo.com
info@montegaredo.com

MONTEGAREDO 2011 TC
100% tinto fino

87 Colour: very deep cherry. Nose: powerfull, fruit preserve, toasty, spicy. Palate: powerful, spirituous, spicy.

MONTEGAREDO 2012 T ROBLE
100% tinto fino

88 Colour: bright cherry. Nose: ripe fruit, sweet spices, creamy oak. Palate: flavourful, fruity, toasty, round tannins.

PIRÁMIDE 2011 T
100% tinto fino

91 Colour: cherry, garnet rim. Nose: ripe fruit, spicy, creamy oak, toasty, complex. Palate: powerful, flavourful, toasty, round tannins.

MONTEVANNOS

Paraje Tiemblos, Pol 509 - Parcela 5146
9441 Sotillo de la Ribera (Burgos)
☎: +34 947 534 277 - Fax: +34 947 534 016
bodega@montevannos.es

MONTEVANNOS 2006 TR
92% tempranillo, 8% merlot

87 Colour: cherry, garnet rim. Nose: ripe fruit, spicy, creamy oak, toasty, old leather. Palate: powerful, flavourful, toasty, round tannins.

MONTEVANNOS 2009 TC
85% tempranillo, 15% merlot

83

MONTEVANNOS 2010 T ROBLE
80% tempranillo, 20% merlot

82

MONTEVANNOS 2012 T
85% tempranillo, 15% merlot

84

OPIMIUS 2007 T
100% tempranillo

90 Colour: cherry, garnet rim. Nose: ripe fruit, spicy, creamy oak, toasty, characterful. Palate: powerful, flavourful, toasty, round tannins.

OLID INTERNACIONAL

Juan García Hortelano, 21
47014 (Valladolid)
☎: +34 983 132 690
www.olidinternacional.com
olid@olidinternacional.com

983 2006 TC
tinta del país

91 Colour: bright cherry. Nose: ripe fruit, sweet spices, creamy oak. Palate: flavourful, fruity, toasty, round tannins.

983 2011 T ROBLE
tinta del país

89 Colour: cherry, purple rim. Nose: powerfull, ripe fruit, fruit preserve, roasted coffee. Palate: fine bitter notes, sweetness.

OSBORNE RIBERA DEL DUERO

Crta. Fuenmayor - Navarrete, km. 2
26360 Fuenmayor (La Rioja)
☎: +34 925 860 990 - Fax: +34 925 860 905
www.osborne.es
carolina.cerrato@osborne.es

SEÑORÍO DEL CID 2011 T ROBLE
tinto fino

88 Colour: cherry, garnet rim. Nose: toasty, powerfull, ripe fruit, sweet spices. Palate: flavourful, ripe fruit, long.

PAGO DE CARRAOVEJAS

Camino de Carraovejas, s/n
47300 Peñafiel (Valladolid)
☎: +34 983 878 020 - Fax: +34 983 878 022
www.pagodecarraovejas.com
administracion@pagodecarraovejas.com

PAGO DE CARRAOVEJAS "CUESTA DE LAS LIEBRES" VENDIMIA SELECCIONADA 2009 TR
96% tinto fino, 3% cabernet sauvignon, 1% merlot

96 Colour: cherry, garnet rim. Nose: ripe fruit, spicy, creamy oak, toasty, complex, earthy notes. Palate: powerful, flavourful, toasty, round tannins, spicy.

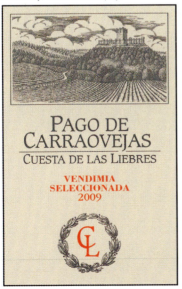

PAGO DE CARRAOVEJAS 2010 TR
97% tinto fino, 2% cabernet sauvignon, 1% merlot

95 Colour: cherry, garnet rim. Nose: sweet spices, ripe fruit, earthy notes, mineral. Palate: flavourful, round, unctuous, spicy, long.

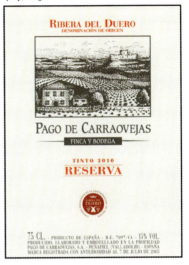

PAGO DE CARRAOVEJAS 2011 TC
93% tinto fino, 5% cabernet sauvignon, 2% merlot

94 Colour: cherry, garnet rim. Nose: ripe fruit, spicy, creamy oak, complex. Palate: powerful, flavourful, toasty, round tannins.

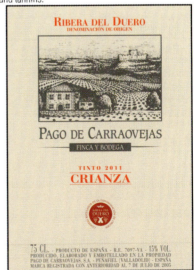

PAGO DE CARRAOVEJAS EL ANEJÓN DE LA CUESTA DE LAS LIEBRES 2009 T
93% tinto fino, 6% cabernet sauvignon, 1% merlot

95 Colour: deep cherry. Nose: mineral, earthy notes, ripe fruit, red berry notes, dark chocolate, sweet spices, creamy oak. Palate: flavourful, fine bitter notes, good acidity.

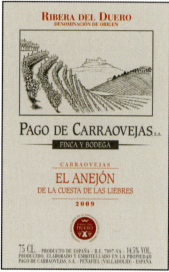

PAGO DE CARRAOVEJAS 2010 TC
95% tinto fino, 5% cabernet sauvignon

93 Colour: cherry, garnet rim. Nose: ripe fruit, spicy, creamy oak, toasty, complex, earthy notes. Palate: powerful, flavourful, toasty, round tannins.

PAGO DE LOS CAPELLANES

Camino de la Ampudia, s/n
9314 Pedrosa de Duero (Burgos)
☎: +34 947 530 068 - Fax: +34 947 530 111
www.pagodeloscapellanes.com
comunicacion@pagodeloscapellanes.com

PAGO DE LOS CAPELLANES 2009 TR
tempranillo

92 Colour: very deep cherry, garnet rim. Nose: spicy, cocoa bean, medium intensity, balsamic herbs. Palate: flavourful, good structure, spicy, good acidity, round tannins.

PAGO DE LOS CAPELLANES 2010 TC
tempranillo

94 Colour: cherry, garnet rim. Nose: spicy, creamy oak, toasty, complex, earthy notes. Palate: powerful, flavourful, toasty, round tannins.

PAGO DE LOS CAPELLANES 2012 T ROBLE
tempranillo

90 Colour: deep cherry, purple rim. Nose: balanced, red berry notes, ripe fruit, spicy. Palate: flavourful, ripe fruit, long.

PAGO DE LOS CAPELLANES PARCELA EL NOGAL 2009 T
tempranillo

94 Colour: cherry, garnet rim. Nose: ripe fruit, spicy, creamy oak, toasty, complex, characterful, expressive, powerfull. Palate: powerful, flavourful, toasty, round tannins.

PAGO DE LOS CAPELLANES PARCELA EL PICÓN 2009 T
tempranillo

94 Colour: cherry, garnet rim. Nose: ripe fruit, spicy, creamy oak, toasty, balsamic herbs, fine reductive notes, balanced. Palate: powerful, flavourful, toasty, round tannins.

PAGOS DE MATANEGRA

Ctra. Santa María, 27
9311 Olmedillo de Roa (Burgos)
☎: +34 947 551 310 - Fax: +34 947 551 309
www.pagosdematanegra.es
info@pagosdematanegra.es

MATANEGRA VENDIMIA SELECCIONADA 2009 T
tempranillo

91 Colour: bright cherry, garnet rim. Nose: spicy, tobacco, ripe fruit. Palate: flavourful, slightly dry, soft tannins.

MATANEGRA 2009 TC
tempranillo

91 Colour: cherry, garnet rim. Nose: spicy, ripe fruit, dried herbs. Palate: correct, fine bitter notes, round tannins.

MATANEGRA 2012 T
tempranillo

88 Colour: bright cherry. Nose: sweet spices, creamy oak, overripe fruit. Palate: flavourful, fruity, toasty, round tannins.

PAGOS DEL REY

Ctra. Palencia-Aranda, Km. 53
9311 Olmedillo de Roa (Burgos)
☎: +34 926 322 400 - Fax: +34 926 322 417
www.felixsolisavantis.com
fsa@pagosdelrey.com

ALTOS DE TAMARÓN 2012 T
tempranillo

87 Colour: cherry, garnet rim. Nose: powerfull, characterful, red berry notes. Palate: flavourful, powerful, good acidity.

ALTOS DE TAMARÓN 2012 T ROBLE
tempranillo

85 Colour: bright cherry. Nose: ripe fruit, sweet spices, creamy oak, toasty. Palate: flavourful, fruity, toasty.

ALTOS DE TAMARÓN 2009 TR
tempranillo

88 Colour: cherry, garnet rim. Nose: ripe fruit, warm, spicy, balsamic herbs. Palate: fruity, round tannins.

ALTOS DE TAMARÓN 2011 TC
tempranillo

87 Colour: cherry, garnet rim. Nose: sweet spices, ripe fruit, dried herbs. Palate: balanced, spicy, ripe fruit.

CONDADO DE ORIZA 2009 TR
tempranillo

90 Colour: deep cherry, garnet rim. Nose: cocoa bean, balsamic herbs, ripe fruit, violets, red berry notes. Palate: balanced, long, round tannins.

CONDADO DE ORIZA 2011 TC
tempranillo

89 Colour: cherry, garnet rim. Nose: spicy, creamy oak, ripe fruit. Palate: flavourful, good acidity.

CONDADO DE ORIZA 2012 T
tempranillo

88 Colour: cherry, purple rim. Nose: fresh fruit, floral. Palate: flavourful, fruity, good acidity, round tannins.

CONDADO DE ORIZA 2012 T ROBLE
tempranillo

91 Colour: bright cherry. Nose: ripe fruit, sweet spices, creamy oak, expressive. Palate: flavourful, fruity, toasty, round tannins.

MORALINOS 20012 T
tempranillo

87 Colour: cherry, purple rim. Nose: floral, red berry notes, fresh. Palate: flavourful, fruity, good acidity.

PEPE LÓPEZ VINOS Y VIÑEDOS

Avda. Soria 53 - Bajos Buzón 136
47300 Peñafiel (Valladolid)
☎: +34 983 106 207 - Fax: +34 916 048 322
www.arrotos.es
info@arrotos.es

ARROTOS 2009 TR
100% tempranillo

89 Colour: cherry, garnet rim. Nose: ripe fruit, spicy, creamy oak, toasty, complex. Palate: powerful, flavourful, toasty.

ARROTOS 2011 TC
95% tempranillo, 5% cabernet sauvignon

87 Colour: very deep cherry. Nose: cocoa bean, candied fruit, ripe fruit. Palate: ripe fruit, long.

ARROTOS 2012 T ROBLE
100% tempranillo

86 Colour: cherry, purple rim. Nose: red berry notes, ripe fruit, sweet spices, creamy oak. Palate: powerful, harsh oak tannins.

PICO CUADRO

Del Río, 22
47350 Quintanilla de Onésimo (Valladolid)
☎: +34 620 547 057
www.picocuadro.com
picocuadro@picocuadro.com

PICO CUADRO 2010 T
100% tempranillo

91 Colour: cherry, garnet rim. Nose: spicy, balanced, ripe fruit, balsamic herbs. Palate: good structure, round tannins.

PICO CUADRO VENDIMIA SELECCIONADA 2010 T
100% tempranillo

92 Colour: cherry, garnet rim. Nose: ripe fruit, complex, sweet spices. Palate: powerful, flavourful, toasty, round tannins.

PINNA FIDELIS

Camino Llanillos, s/n
47300 Peñafiel (Valladolid)
☎: +34 983 878 034 - Fax: +34 983 878 035
www.pinnafidelis.com
info@pinnafidelis.com

PINNA FIDELIS 2009 TC
tinta del país

90 Colour: cherry, garnet rim. Nose: ripe fruit, spicy, creamy oak, toasty, characterful. Palate: powerful, flavourful, toasty, round tannins.

PINNA FIDELIS 2004 TGR
tinta del país

90 Colour: cherry, garnet rim. Nose: ripe fruit, spicy, toasty, tobacco. Palate: flavourful, round tannins, spicy, fruity.

PINNA FIDELIS 2006 TR
tinta del país

87 Colour: cherry, garnet rim. Nose: powerfull, cigar, balsamic herbs, dark chocolate. Palate: flavourful, spicy, long.

PINNA FIDELIS 2012 T ROBLE
tinta del país

88 Colour: cherry, purple rim. Nose: ripe fruit, violet drops, balanced. Palate: fruity, correct, good acidity.

PINNA FIDELIS ROBLE ESPAÑOL 2006 T
tinta del país

90 Colour: cherry, garnet rim. Nose: ripe fruit, spicy, creamy oak, toasty, characterful. Palate: powerful, flavourful, toasty, round tannins.

PINNA FIDELIS VENDIMIA SELECCIONADA 2006 T
100% tinta del país

89 Colour: bright cherry, garnet rim. Nose: cocoa bean, sweet spices, balsamic herbs. Palate: flavourful, reductive nuances.

PROTOS BODEGAS RIBERA DUERO DE PEÑAFIEL

Bodegas Protos, 24-28
47300 Peñafiel (Valladolid)
☎: +34 983 878 011 - Fax: +34 983 878 012
www.bodegasprotos.com
bodega@bodegasprotos.com

PROTOS 2006 TGR
100% tinto fino

91 Colour: cherry, garnet rim. Nose: ripe fruit, spicy, toasty, complex, aromatic coffee. Palate: powerful, flavourful, toasty, round tannins.

PROTOS 2009 TC
100% tinto fino

92 Colour: cherry, garnet rim. Nose: ripe fruit, spicy, creamy oak, toasty, characterful, varietal. Palate: powerful, flavourful, toasty, round tannins.

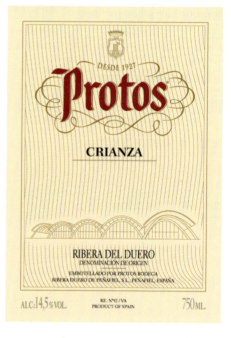

PROTOS 2009 TR
100% tinto fino

92 Colour: cherry, garnet rim. Nose: balanced, varietal, cocoa bean. Palate: ripe fruit, long, round tannins, balanced.

PROTOS 2011 T ROBLE
tinto fino

91 Colour: cherry, garnet rim. Nose: ripe fruit, spicy, creamy oak, toasty, characterful. Palate: powerful, flavourful, toasty, round tannins.

PROTOS SELECCIÓN FINCA EL GRAJO VIEJO 2009 T
tinto fino

94 Colour: cherry, garnet rim. Nose: ripe fruit, spicy, creamy oak, toasty, characterful, earthy notes, mineral. Palate: powerful, flavourful, toasty, round tannins.

QUINTA MILÚ

Camino El Val, s/n
9370 La Aguilera (Burgos)
☎: +34 661 328 504
www.quintamilu.com
info@quintamilu.com

MILÚ 2012 T
tempranillo

89 Colour: cherry, purple rim. Nose: fresh fruit, red berry notes, sweet spices. Palate: flavourful, fruity, good acidity, round tannins.

QUINTA MILÚ EL MALO 2009 TC
tempranillo

90 Colour: cherry, garnet rim. Nose: expressive, balsamic herbs, ripe fruit, fruit preserve. Palate: good structure, flavourful, spicy, long.

QUINTA MILÚ LA COMETA 2011 TC
tempranillo

90 Colour: cherry, garnet rim. Nose: ripe fruit, spicy, creamy oak, toasty, characterful, varietal. Palate: powerful, flavourful, toasty, round tannins.

REAL SITIO DE VENTOSILLA

Ctra. CL-619 (Magaz - Aranda) Km. 66,1
9443 Gumiel del Mercado (Burgos)
☎: +34 947 546 900 - Fax: +34 947 546 999
www.pradorey.com
bodega@pradorey.com

ADARO DE PRADOREY 2010 TC
tempranillo

93 Colour: cherry, garnet rim. Nose: red berry notes, ripe fruit, powerfull, mineral, sweet spices, creamy oak. Palate: rich, powerful, flavourful.

LÍA DE PRADOREY 2012 RD
100% tempranillo

88 Colour: raspberry rose. Nose: elegant, candied fruit, dried flowers, fragrant herbs, red berry notes. Palate: light-bodied, flavourful, good acidity, long, spicy.

PRADOREY 2004 TGR
tempranillo, cabernet sauvignon, merlot

91 Colour: cherry, garnet rim. Nose: medium intensity, spicy, ripe fruit, toasty. Palate: fruity, good acidity, balanced.

PRADOREY 2011 T ROBLE
tempranillo, cabernet sauvignon, merlot

87 Colour: cherry, garnet rim. Nose: ripe fruit, candied fruit, spicy, dried herbs. Palate: flavourful, correct, toasty.

PRADOREY 2012 RD
tempranillo, merlot

88 Colour: raspberry rose. Nose: red berry notes, ripe fruit, cocoa bean, dark chocolate, creamy oak. Palate: rich, powerful, spicy, toasty.

PRADOREY ÉLITE 2009 T
tempranillo

93 Colour: deep cherry, garnet rim. Nose: expressive, balanced, ripe fruit, varietal, sweet spices. Palate: round tannins, good structure, ripe fruit.

PRADOREY ÉLITE 2010 T
tempranillo

94 Colour: deep cherry. Nose: closed, ripe fruit, sweet spices, complex. Palate: good structure, round tannins, long, balanced.

PRADOREY FINCA LA MINA 2009 TR
tempranillo, cabernet sauvignon, merlot

92 Colour: cherry, garnet rim. Nose: powerfull, varietal, ripe fruit, toasty. Palate: flavourful, fruity, mineral.

PRADOREY FINCA VALDELAYEGUA 2010 TC
tempranillo, cabernet sauvignon, merlot

91 Colour: cherry, garnet rim. Nose: ripe fruit, spicy, creamy oak, toasty, complex. Palate: powerful, flavourful, toasty, round tannins.

RED BOTTLE INTERNATIONAL

Rosales, 6
9400 Aranda de Duero (Burgos)
☎: +34 947 515 884 - Fax: +34 947 515 886
www.redbottleint.com
rbi@redbottleint.com

ADMIRACIÓN SELECCIÓN ESPECIAL 2009 T
100% tempranillo

90 Colour: cherry, garnet rim. Nose: ripe fruit, spicy, creamy oak, toasty, balsamic herbs, earthy notes. Palate: powerful, flavourful, toasty.

RIVENDEL 2009 TC
100% tempranillo

88 Colour: cherry, garnet rim. Nose: ripe fruit, spicy, creamy oak, toasty. Palate: powerful, flavourful, toasty.

RIVENDEL 2011 T ROBLE
100% tempranillo

87 Colour: cherry, garnet rim. Nose: ripe fruit, spicy, creamy oak, fine reductive notes. Palate: powerful, flavourful, spicy.

RODRÍGUEZ SANZO

Manuel Azaña, 9
47014 (Valladolid)
☎: +34 983 150 150 - Fax: +34 983 150 151
www.rodriguezsanzo.com
comunicacion@valsanzo.com

VALL SANZO 2009 TC
100% tempranillo

91 Colour: cherry, garnet rim. Nose: ripe fruit, fruit preserve, toasty, sweet spices. Palate: powerful, flavourful, spicy, long.

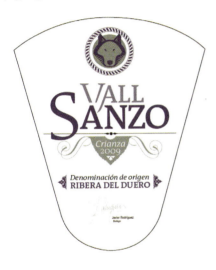

RUDELES - TIERRAS EL GUIJARRAL

Trasterrera, 10
42345 Peñalba de San Esteban (Soria)
☎: +34 618 644 633 - Fax: +34 975 350 082
www.rudeles.com
jmartin@rudeles.com

FINCA LA NACIÓN 2008 T
100% tempranillo

89 Colour: cherry, garnet rim. Nose: red berry notes, ripe fruit, balsamic herbs, earthy notes, dry stone. Palate: powerful, flavourful, long.

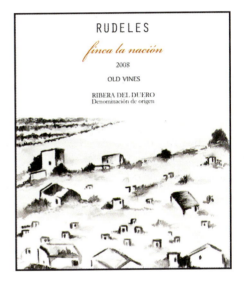

RUDELES "23" 2009 T
95% tempranillo, 5% garnacha

92 Colour: cherry, garnet rim. Nose: ripe fruit, spicy, creamy oak, toasty, complex. Palate: powerful, flavourful, toasty, round tannins.

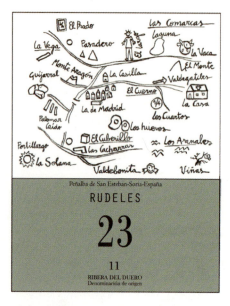

RUDELES CERRO EL CUBERILLO 2007 T
100% tempranillo

92 Colour: cherry, garnet rim. Nose: spicy, creamy oak, toasty, earthy notes. Palate: powerful, flavourful, toasty, round tannins.

RUDELES LOS ARENALES 2006 T
97% tempranillo, 3% garnacha

88 Colour: pale ruby, brick rim edge. Nose: elegant, spicy, fine reductive notes, wet leather, aged wood nuances, fruit liqueur notes. Palate: spicy, fine tannins, long.

RUDELES SELECCIÓN 2006 T
97% tempranillo, 3% garnacha

90 Colour: cherry, garnet rim. Nose: ripe fruit, spicy, creamy oak, toasty. Palate: powerful, flavourful, toasty, round tannins.

SÁNCHEZ ROMATE

Lealas, 26
11404 Jerez de la Frontera (Cádiz)
☎: +34 956 182 212 - Fax: +34 956 185 276
www.romate.com
romate@romate.com

MOMO 2009 T
85% tempranillo, 12% cabernet sauvignon, 3% merlot

89 Colour: cherry, garnet rim. Nose: ripe fruit, spicy, creamy oak, toasty. Palate: powerful, flavourful, toasty, correct.

SELECCIÓN CÉSAR MUÑOZ

Acera de Recoletos, 14 6A
47004 (Valladolid)
☎: +34 666 548 751
www.cesarmunoz.es
info@cesarmunoz.es

MAGALLANES 2010 TC
100% tempranillo

92 Colour: cherry, garnet rim. Nose: ripe fruit, spicy, creamy oak, earthy notes, mineral. Palate: powerful, flavourful, toasty, round tannins.

SELECCIÓN TORRES

Del Rosario, 56
47311 Fompedraza (Valladolid)
☎: +34 938 177 400 - Fax: +34 938 177 444
www.torres.es
mailadmin@torres.es

CELESTE 2010 TC
100% tinto fino

90 Colour: cherry, garnet rim. Nose: ripe fruit, spicy, creamy oak, toasty. Palate: powerful, flavourful, toasty, round tannins.

CELESTE 2012 T ROBLE
100% tinto fino

87 Colour: bright cherry. Nose: sweet spices, creamy oak, medium intensity, red berry notes. Palate: flavourful, fruity, toasty, round tannins.

SEÑORIO DE BOCOS

Camino La Canaleja, s/n
47317 Bocos de Duero (Valladolid)
☎: +34 983 880 988 - Fax: +34 983 880 988
www.senoriodebocos.com
bodegas@senoriodebocos.com

SEÑORIO DE BOCOS 2009 TC
tempranillo

88 Colour: ruby red. Nose: ripe fruit, sweet spices, aged wood nuances, fine reductive notes. Palate: powerful, flavourful, spicy.

SEÑORIO DE BOCOS 2012 T ROBLE
tempranillo

87 Colour: bright cherry. Nose: ripe fruit, sweet spices, creamy oak, expressive. Palate: flavourful, fruity, toasty, round tannins.

THE GRAND WINES

Razón social : Ramón y Cajal 7, 1ºA
1007 Vitoria (Alava)
☎: +34 945 158 282 - Fax: +34 945 158 283
www.thegrandwines.com

ROLLAND GALARRETA 2010 T
tempranillo, merlot

92 Colour: cherry, garnet rim. Nose: ripe fruit, spicy, creamy oak, dry stone. Palate: powerful, flavourful, toasty, fine tannins, elegant.

TOMÁS POSTIGO

Estación, 12
47300 Peñafiel (Valladolid)
☎: +34 983 873 019 - Fax: +34 983 880 258
www.tomaspostigo.es
administracion@tomaspostigo.es

TOMÁS POSTIGO 2010 TC
tempranillo, cabernet sauvignon, merlot

94 Colour: cherry, garnet rim. Nose: ripe fruit, spicy, creamy oak, toasty, cocoa bean, dark chocolate. Palate: powerful, flavourful, toasty, round tannins, balanced.

TOMÁS POSTIGO 2011 TC
tempranillo, cabernet sauvignon, merlot

92 Colour: cherry, purple rim. Nose: red berry notes, ripe fruit, expressive, balsamic herbs, sweet spices, creamy oak. Palate: rich, flavourful, toasty, balanced, elegant.

TORRES DE ANGUIX

Camino La Tejera, s/n
9400 Anguix (Burgos)
☎: +34 947 554 008 - Fax: +34 947 554 129
www.torresdeanguix.com
bodega@torresdeanguix.com

A D'ANGUIX 2004 T
tinta del país

93 Colour: black cherry, garnet rim. Nose: dark chocolate, sweet spices, ripe fruit. Palate: flavourful, long, spicy, round tannins, good acidity.

D'ANGUIX 2007 T
tinta del país

90 Colour: pale ruby, brick rim edge. Nose: spicy, fine reductive notes, wet leather, aged wood nuances, balsamic herbs. Palate: spicy, elegant, long.

R D'ANGUIX 2012 RD
tinta del país

87 Colour: light cherry, bright. Nose: medium intensity, balanced, red berry notes, ripe fruit, lactic notes. Palate: fruity, flavourful.

T D'ANGUIX 2003 TGR
tinta del país

90 Colour: pale ruby, brick rim edge. Nose: elegant, spicy, fine reductive notes, wet leather, aged wood nuances. Palate: spicy, fine tannins, elegant, long, balanced.

T D'ANGUIX 2005 TR
tinta del país

89 Colour: pale ruby, brick rim edge. Nose: ripe fruit, creamy oak, toasty, fine reductive notes. Palate: powerful, flavourful, toasty, round tannins.

T D'ANGUIX 2009 TC
tinta del país

88 Colour: deep cherry. Nose: roasted coffee, dark chocolate, ripe fruit. Palate: spicy, ripe fruit, toasty.

T D'ANGUIX 2011 T ROBLE
tinta del país

87 Colour: deep cherry. Nose: ripe fruit, creamy oak. Palate: flavourful, fine bitter notes, good acidity.

UNESDI DISTRIBUCIONES S.A

Aurora, 11
11500 El Puerto de Santa María (Cádiz)
☎: +34 956 541 329
www.unesdi.com
info@unesdi.com

MATAVERAS 2010 T
88% tempranillo, 8% cabernet sauvignon, 4% merlot

88 Colour: cherry, garnet rim. Nose: ripe fruit, scrubland, medium intensity. Palate: fruity, good acidity, spicy.

UVAS FELICES

Agullers, 7
8003 Barcelona (Barcelona)
☎: +34 902 327 777
www.vilaviniteca.es

VENTA LAS VACAS 2011 T

90 Colour: very deep cherry. Nose: sweet spices, ripe fruit, creamy oak. Palate: good structure, powerful, sweetness.

VALLEBUENO

Ctra. Valbuena, 20
47315 Pesquera de Duero (Valladolid)
☎: +34 983 868 116 - Fax: +34 983 868 432
www.vallebueno.com
info@taninia.com

VALLEBUENO 2009 TC
tinta del país

88 Colour: cherry, garnet rim. Nose: ripe fruit, spicy, creamy oak, toasty, complex. Palate: powerful, flavourful, toasty.

VALLEBUENO 2010 T ROBLE
tinta del país

89 Colour: bright cherry. Nose: ripe fruit, sweet spices, creamy oak, balanced. Palate: flavourful, fruity, toasty.

VALTOÑAR

Ctra. de Roa, Km. 5
9313 Anguix (Burgos)
☎: +34 617 196 323
www.valtonar.com
riojalopez@valtonar.com

VALTOÑAR 2010 TC
95% tempranillo, 5% cabernet sauvignon

85 Colour: cherry, garnet rim. Nose: ripe fruit, spicy, creamy oak, toasty. Palate: powerful, flavourful, toasty.

VALTRAVIESO

Finca La Revilla, s/n
47316 Piñel de Arriba (Valladolid)
☎: +34 983 484 030 - Fax: +34 983 484 037
www.valtravieso.com
valtravieso@valtravieso.com

VALTRAVIESO 2009 TR

90 Colour: dark-red cherry. Nose: candied fruit, fruit liqueur notes, toasty, spicy. Palate: concentrated, powerful.

VALTRAVIESO 2010 TC
tinto fino, cabernet sauvignon, merlot

89 Colour: cherry, garnet rim. Nose: ripe fruit, fruit preserve, balsamic herbs, sweet spices, creamy oak. Palate: powerful, flavourful, spicy.

VALTRAVIESO 2011 T ROBLE

89 Colour: cherry, garnet rim. Nose: spicy, creamy oak, toasty, characterful. Palate: powerful, flavourful, toasty, round tannins.

VALTRAVIESO VT TINTA FINA 2009 T
tinto fino

89 Colour: bright cherry, garnet rim. Nose: medium intensity, ripe fruit, spicy, varietal. Palate: flavourful, round tannins.

VALTRAVIESO VT VENDIMIA SELECCIONADA 2009 T
tinto fino, cabernet sauvignon, merlot

91 Colour: cherry, garnet rim. Nose: ripe fruit, balsamic herbs, spicy, creamy oak, mineral. Palate: correct, flavourful, spicy, long.

VEGA CLARA

Ctra. N-122, Km 328
47350 Quintanilla De Onesimo (Valladolid)
☎: +34 677 570 779 - Fax: +34 983 361 005
www.vegaclara.com
vegaclara@vegaclara.com

MARIO VC 2010 T
75% tempranillo, 25% cabernet sauvignon

92 Colour: cherry, garnet rim. Nose: ripe fruit, spicy, creamy oak, toasty, complex, earthy notes, mineral. Palate: powerful, flavourful, toasty, round tannins.

VEGA REAL

Ctra. N-122, Km. 298,6
47318 Castrillo de Duero (Valladolid)
☎: +34 983 881 580 - Fax: +34 983 873 188
www.vegareal.com
visitas@vegareal.net

VEGA REAL 2007 TR
tempranillo, cabernet sauvignon

88 Colour: cherry, garnet rim. Nose: ripe fruit, spicy, toasty, old leather, tobacco. Palate: flavourful, toasty, round tannins.

VEGA REAL 2009 TC
tempranillo

86 Colour: cherry, garnet rim. Nose: medium intensity, premature reduction notes, old leather, fruit preserve. Palate: fruity, flavourful.

VEGA REAL 2011 T ROBLE
tempranillo

84

VELVETY WINES

Ctra. Peñafiel (Valoria), s/n
47315 Pesquera de Duero (Valladolid)
☎: +34 983 870 199
www.velvetywines.com
info@velvetywines.com

VELVETY 2011 T
100% tempranillo

90 Colour: cherry, garnet rim. Nose: spicy, creamy oak, toasty, fruit expression. Palate: powerful, flavourful, toasty, round tannins.

VELVETY 2012 T
100% tempranillo

89 Colour: deep cherry, purple rim. Nose: ripe fruit, sweet spices, scrubland. Palate: balanced, long, round tannins.

VINNICO

Muela, 16
3730 Jávea (Alicante)
☎: +34 965 791 967 - Fax: +34 966 461 471
www.vinnico.com
info@vinnico.com

AVENTINO 2010 TC
100% tempranillo

88 Colour: cherry, garnet rim. Nose: ripe fruit, spicy, creamy oak. Palate: powerful, flavourful, toasty, correct.

AVENTINO 2011 T ROBLE
100% tempranillo

88 Colour: bright cherry. Nose: ripe fruit, sweet spices, cocoa bean, aromatic coffee. Palate: flavourful, fruity, toasty.

AVENTINO TEMPRANILLO 2011 T
100% tempranillo

87 Colour: bright cherry. Nose: ripe fruit, sweet spices, creamy oak. Palate: flavourful, fruity, toasty, round tannins.

IMAGINAERUM 2010 T

91 Colour: cherry, garnet rim. Nose: ripe fruit, spicy, creamy oak, toasty, complex. Palate: powerful, flavourful, toasty, round tannins.

ORACULO BARREL SELECT 2010 T
100% tempranillo

90 Colour: cherry, garnet rim. Nose: ripe fruit, spicy, creamy oak, toasty, mineral. Palate: powerful, flavourful, toasty, round tannins, elegant.

VINOS HERCAL

Santo Domingo, 2
9300 Roa (Burgos)
☎: +34 947 541 281
www.somanilla.es
ventas@somanilla.es

BOCCA 2011 T ROBLE
tempranillo

90 Colour: deep cherry. Nose: ripe fruit, toasty, spicy. Palate: powerful, flavourful, ripe fruit.

BOCCA 2012 RD
albilla, tempranillo

82

SOMANILLA 2006 T

87 Colour: cherry, garnet rim. Nose: ripe fruit, creamy oak, complex. Palate: powerful, toasty, round tannins, balanced.

SOMANILLA 2009 TC
tinto fino

91 Colour: cherry, garnet rim. Nose: red berry notes, ripe fruit, expressive, sweet spices, creamy oak. Palate: powerful, flavourful, spicy, long.

VINOS SANTOS ARRANZ

Ctra. de Valbuena, s/n
47315 Pesquera de Duero (Valladolid)
☎: +34 983 870 008 - Fax: +34 983 870 008
www.lagrima-negra.com
lagrimanegra82@hotmail.com

LÁGRIMA NEGRA 2010 TC
100% tempranillo

86 Colour: cherry, garnet rim. Nose: fruit preserve, balsamic herbs, creamy oak, toasty. Palate: powerful, flavourful, spicy, long.

LÁGRIMA NEGRA 2011 T ROBLE
100% tempranillo

87 Colour: bright cherry. Nose: ripe fruit, sweet spices, creamy oak, expressive. Palate: flavourful, fruity, toasty, round tannins.

VIÑA ARNAIZ

Ctra. N-122, km. 281
9463 Haza (Burgos)
☎: +34 947 536 227 - Fax: +34 947 536 216
www.garciacarrion.es
info@jgc.es

CASTILLO DE AZA 2007 TR
100% tempranillo

87 Colour: cherry, garnet rim. Nose: ripe fruit, spicy, toasty, complex, balsamic herbs. Palate: powerful, flavourful, toasty.

CASTILLO DE AZA 2009 TC
100% tempranillo

86 Colour: cherry, garnet rim. Nose: sweet spices, red berry notes, ripe fruit, spicy. Palate: flavourful, spicy, long.

CASTILLO DE AZA 2011 T ROBLE
100% tempranillo

86 Colour: cherry, garnet rim. Nose: ripe fruit, fruit preserve, sweet spices. Palate: flavourful, round tannins.

MAYOR DE CASTILLA 2006 TGR
100% tempranillo

90 Colour: deep cherry. Nose: spicy, toasty, fruit liqueur notes. Palate: spicy, ripe fruit, fine tannins.

MAYOR DE CASTILLA 2008 TR
100% tempranillo

87 Colour: cherry, garnet rim. Nose: ripe fruit, creamy oak, toasty, cocoa bean, fine reductive notes. Palate: powerful, flavourful, toasty, harsh oak tannins.

MAYOR DE CASTILLA 2010 TC
100% tempranillo

88 Colour: bright cherry. Nose: ripe fruit, sweet spices. Palate: flavourful, fruity, toasty, round tannins.

MAYOR DE CASTILLA 2011 T ROBLE
100% tempranillo

88 Colour: cherry, garnet rim. Nose: powerfull, ripe fruit. Palate: powerful, flavourful, ripe fruit.

VIÑA ARNÁIZ 2008 TR
85% tempranillo, 10% cabernet sauvignon, 5% merlot

88 Colour: pale ruby, brick rim edge. Nose: ripe fruit, spicy, creamy oak, balsamic herbs, fine reductive notes. Palate: powerful, spicy, long.

VIÑA ARNÁIZ 2009 TC
100% tempranillo

87 Colour: deep cherry, garnet rim. Nose: ripe fruit, varietal, sweet spices. Palate: balanced, fruity, good finish.

VIÑA ARNÁIZ 2011 T ROBLE
95% tempranillo, 3% cabernet sauvignon, 2% merlot

87 Colour: cherry, garnet rim. Nose: red berry notes, ripe fruit, sweet spices, creamy oak. Palate: powerful, flavourful, spicy, toasty.

VIÑA MAMBRILLA

Ctra. Pedrosa s/n
9317 Mambrilla de Castrejón (Burgos)
☎: +34 947 540 234 - Fax: +34 947 540 234
www.mambrilla.com
bodega@mambrilla.com

ALIDIS 6 MESES BARRICA 2012 T
tempranillo

87 Colour: deep cherry, purple rim. Nose: powerfull, fruit preserve, ripe fruit, spicy. Palate: flavourful, long.

ALIDIS CRIANZA 2010 TC
tempranillo

89 Colour: cherry, garnet rim. Nose: ripe fruit, spicy, toasty, dried herbs. Palate: powerful, flavourful, toasty, round tannins.

ALIDIS EXPRESIÓN 2010 TC
tempranillo

90 Colour: very deep cherry. Nose: sweet spices, dark chocolate, ripe fruit. Palate: powerful, flavourful, unctuous.

ALIDIS GRAN RESERVA 2007 TGR
tempranillo

92 Colour: pale ruby, brick rim edge. Nose: elegant, spicy, fine reductive notes, wet leather, aged wood nuances, fruit preserve. Palate: spicy, fine tannins, long.

ALIDIS RESERVA 2009 TR
tempranillo

90 Colour: cherry, garnet rim. Nose: ripe fruit, spicy, creamy oak, toasty. Palate: powerful, flavourful, toasty, harsh oak tannins.

ALIDIS VS 2009 T

91 Colour: dark-red cherry, garnet rim. Nose: expressive, balsamic herbs, ripe fruit, sweet spices. Palate: flavourful, long, round tannins.

VIÑA SOLORCA

Ctra. Circunvalación, s/n
9300 Roa (Burgos)
☎: +34 947 541 823 - Fax: +34 947 540 035
www.bodegassolorca.com
info@bodegassolorca.com

GRAN SOLORCA 2008 TR
100% tempranillo

91 Colour: bright cherry, garnet rim. Nose: balanced, medium intensity, varietal, ripe fruit. Palate: good structure, flavourful, long.

VIÑA SOLORCA 2009 TC
100% tempranillo

88 Colour: deep cherry. Nose: dark chocolate, aromatic coffee. Palate: flavourful, powerful, fine bitter notes, good acidity.

VIÑA SOLORCA 2011 T
100% tempranillo

82

VIÑA TUELDA

Camino de las Bodegas, 26
9310 Villatuelda (Burgos)
☎: +34 947 551 145 - Fax: +34 947 551 145
www.vintuelda.com
alvarog@vintuelda.com

VIÑA TVELDA 2010 TC
100% tinto fino

88 Colour: cherry, garnet rim. Nose: fruit preserve, over-ripe fruit, sweet spices, dark chocolate. Palate: powerful, fine bitter notes, good acidity.

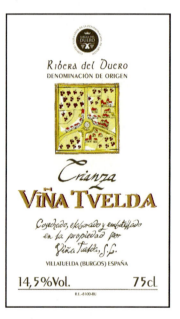

VIÑA TVELDA 2011 T ROBLE
100% tinto fino

88 Colour: bright cherry. Nose: sweet spices, creamy oak, ripe fruit. Palate: flavourful, fruity, toasty, round tannins.

VIÑA TVELDA 2012 RD
100% tinto fino

88 Colour: rose, purple rim. Nose: powerfull, ripe fruit, red berry notes, floral, expressive. Palate: powerful, fruity, fresh, balanced.

VIÑA VALDEMAZÓN

Pza. Sur, 3
47359 Olivares de Duero (Valladolid)
☎: +34 983 680 220
www.valdemazon.com
info@valdemazon.com

VIÑA VALDEMAZÓN VENDIMIA SELECCIONADA 2010 T
tempranillo

90 Colour: cherry, garnet rim. Nose: ripe fruit, spicy, creamy oak, toasty. Palate: powerful, flavourful, toasty, round tannins.

VIÑEDOS ALONSO DEL YERRO

Finca Santa Marta - Ctra. Roa-Anguix, Km. 1,8
9300 Roa (Burgos)
☎: +34 913 160 121 - Fax: +34 913 160 121
www.alonsodelyerro.es
mariadelyerro@vay.es

"MARÍA" ALONSO DEL YERRO 2010 T
100% tempranillo

93 Colour: cherry, garnet rim. Nose: ripe fruit, spicy, creamy oak, toasty, complex, powerfull, varietal, mineral. Palate: powerful, flavourful, toasty, round tannins.

ALONSO DEL YERRO 2010 T
100% tempranillo

93 Colour: cherry, garnet rim. Nose: ripe fruit, spicy, creamy oak, toasty, characterful. Palate: powerful, flavourful, toasty, round tannins.

VIÑEDOS HIJOS DE MARCOS REDONDO ,S.L.

Avd.Santander, 141
47011 (Valladolid)
☎: +34 983 320 315 - Fax: +34 983 320 315
www.viñedosmr.com
jcredondo@vinedosmr.com

MONTEREDONDO 2010 TC
100% tempranillo

92 Colour: cherry, garnet rim. Nose: ripe fruit, spicy, creamy oak, toasty, complex. Palate: powerful, flavourful, toasty, round tannins.

MONTEREDONDO 2012 T
100% tempranillo

86 Colour: cherry, purple rim. Nose: fresh fruit, red berry notes. Palate: flavourful, fruity, good acidity, round tannins.

VIÑEDOS SINGULARES

Cuzco, 26 - 28, Nave 8
8030 (Barcelona)
☎: +34 609 168 191 - Fax: +34 934 807 076
www.vinedossingulares.com
info@vinedossingulares.com

ENTRELOBOS 2011 T
tinto fino

88 Colour: deep cherry. Nose: ripe fruit, fruit preserve, sweet spices, powerfull. Palate: good structure, round tannins, long.

VIÑEDOS Y BODEGAS GARCÍA FIGUERO

Ctra. La Horra - Roa, Km. 2,2
9311 La Horra (Burgos)
☎: +34 947 542 127 - Fax: +34 947 542 033
www.tintofiguero.com
bodega@tintofiguero.com

FIGUERO NOBLE 2009 T
100% tempranillo

90 Colour: cherry, garnet rim. Nose: red berry notes, ripe fruit, balsamic herbs, spicy, toasty. Palate: powerful, rich, flavourful, round, elegant.

FIGUERO TINUS 2010 T
tempranillo

93 Colour: cherry, garnet rim. Nose: elegant, red berry notes, ripe fruit, sweet spices, creamy oak, mineral. Palate: powerful, flavourful, spicy, long, balsamic, balanced.

TINTO FIGUERO 12 MESES BARRICA 2010 TC
100% tempranillo

90 Colour: cherry, garnet rim. Nose: ripe fruit, spicy, creamy oak, toasty, complex. Palate: powerful, flavourful, toasty.

VIÑEDOS Y BODEGAS GORMAZ

Ctra. de Soria, s/n
42330 San Esteban de Gormaz (Soria)
☎: +34 975 350 404 - Fax: +34 975 351 513
www.hispanobodegas.com
carlos.garcia@hispanobodegas.com

12 LINAJES 2008 TR
tempranillo

93 Colour: cherry, garnet rim. Nose: ripe fruit, spicy, creamy oak, toasty, characterful, varietal. Palate: powerful, flavourful, toasty, round tannins.

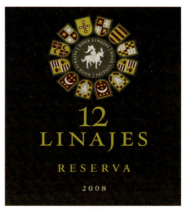

12 LINAJES 2010 TC
tempranillo

90 Colour: deep cherry, garnet rim. Nose: sweet spices, cocoa bean, ripe fruit. Palate: ripe fruit, long, round tannins, good acidity.

12 LINAJES 2011 T ROBLE
tempranillo

88 Colour: cherry, garnet rim. Nose: spicy, ripe fruit, toasty. Palate: ripe fruit, fine bitter notes, good acidity.

ANIER VENDIMIA SELECCIONADA 2010 T
tempranillo

94 Colour: very deep cherry. Nose: complex, balsamic herbs, cocoa bean, creamy oak, ripe fruit. Palate: balanced, spicy, round tannins.

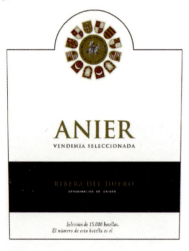

CATANIA 2010 TC
tempranillo

91 Colour: bright cherry. Nose: ripe fruit, sweet spices, creamy oak, expressive, mineral. Palate: flavourful, fruity, toasty, round tannins, balanced.

CATANIA 2012 T
tempranillo

87 Colour: cherry, garnet rim. Nose: red berry notes, ripe fruit, balsamic herbs, medium intensity. Palate: flavourful, fresh, fruity, easy to drink.

VIÑA GORMAZ 2010 TC
tempranillo

90 Colour: deep cherry, garnet rim. Nose: ripe fruit, balanced, sweet spices. Palate: flavourful, spicy, round tannins.

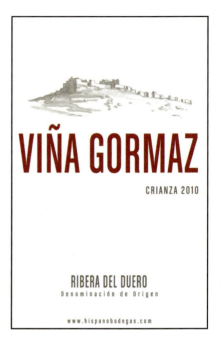

VIÑA GORMAZ 2012 T
tempranillo

88 Colour: cherry, purple rim. Nose: medium intensity, ripe fruit, dried flowers. Palate: ripe fruit, balanced, good acidity.

VIÑEDOS Y BODEGAS RIBÓN

Basilón, 15
47350 Quintanilla de Onésimo (Valladolid)
☎: +34 983 680 015 - Fax: +34 983 680 015
www.bodegasribon.com
info@bodegasribon.com

TINTO RIBÓN 2010 TC
100% tempranillo

92 Colour: cherry, garnet rim. Nose: balanced, ripe fruit, spicy, scrubland. Palate: flavourful, fruity, round tannins.

TINTO RIBÓN 2011 T ROBLE
100% tempranillo

89 Colour: bright cherry. Nose: ripe fruit, sweet spices, creamy oak, expressive. Palate: flavourful, fruity, toasty, round tannins.

VITIVINÍCOLA DE VALBUENA

Real de Abajo, 4
47359 Valbuena de Duero (Valladolid)
☎: +34 646 242 262 - Fax: +34 983 683 014
www.tintocarme.es
info@tintocarme.es

CARME 2010 TC
tinto fino

86 Colour: cherry, garnet rim. Nose: old leather, ripe fruit, spicy, cocoa bean. Palate: fruity, spicy, correct.

CARME 2011 T
tinto fino

84

WINNER WINES

Avda. del Mediterráneo, 38
28007 Madrid (Madrid)
☎: +34 915 019 042 - Fax: +34 915 019 042
www.entornoalvino.com
winnerwines@ibernoble.com

IBERNOBLE 2007 TR
90% tempranillo, 10% cabernet sauvignon

87 Colour: pale ruby, brick rim edge. Nose: spicy, fine reductive notes, wet leather, aged wood nuances, ripe fruit. Palate: spicy, long, correct.

IBERNOBLE 2009 T ROBLE
100% tempranillo

86 Colour: deep cherry, garnet rim. Nose: cocoa bean, toasty. Palate: flavourful, slightly dry, soft tannins.

IBERNOBLE 2009 TC
90% tempranillo, 10% cabernet sauvignon

88 Colour: cherry, garnet rim. Nose: ripe fruit, waxy notes, cigar, spicy, creamy oak. Palate: powerful, flavourful.

IBERNOBLE 2011 T ROBLE
90% tempranillo, 10% cabernet sauvignon

85 Colour: cherry, purple rim. Nose: toasty, spicy, fragrant herbs. Palate: fruity, correct.

LOCATION:

Covering the 6 wine-growing regions of Extremadura, with a total surface of more than 87,000 Ha as described below.

GRAPE VARIETIES:

WHITE: *Alarije, Borba, Cayetana Blanca, Pardina, Macabeo, Chardonnay, Chelva or Montua, Malvar, Parellada, Pedro Ximénez, Verdejo, Eva, Cigüente, Perruno, Moscatel de Alejandría, Moscatel de Grano Menudo, Sauvignon Blanc* and *Bobal Blanca*.

RED: *Garnacha Tinta, Tempranillo, Bobal, Cabernet Sauvignon, Garnacha Tintorera, Graciano, Mazuela, Merlot, Monastrell, Syrah, Pinot Noir* and *Jaén Tinto*.

(Map:)
CÁCERES
Almendralejo
BADAJOZ
▼ Consejo Regulador
● DO Boundary

SUB-REGIONS:

Cañamero. To the south east of the province of Cáceres, in the heart of the Sierra de Guadalupe. It comprises the municipal districts of Alia, Berzocana, Cañamero, Guadalupe and Valdecaballeros. The vineyards are located on the mountainside, at altitudes of between 600 m to 800 m. The terrain is rugged and the soil is slaty and loose. The climate is mild without great temperature contrasts, and the average annual rainfall is 750 mm to 800 mm. The main grape variety is the white *Alarije*. **Montánchez.** Comprising 27 municipal districts. It is characterised by its complex terrain, with numerous hills and small valleys. The vineyards are located on brown acidic soil. The climate is Continental in nature and the average annual rainfall is between 500 mm and 600 mm. The white grape variety *Borba* occupies two thirds of the vineyards in the region. **Ribera Alta.** This covers the Vegas del Guadiana and the plains of La Serena and Campo de Castuera and comprises 38 municipal districts. The soil is very sandy. The most common varieties are *Alarije, Borba* (white), *Tempranillo* and *Garnacha* (red). **Ribera Baja.** Comprising 11 municipal districts. The vineyards are located on clayey-limy soil. The climate is Continental, with a moderate Atlantic influence and slight contrasts in temperature. The most common varieties are: *Cayetana Blanca* and *Pardina* among the whites, and *Tempranillo* among the reds. **Matanegra.** Rather similar to Tierra de Barros, but with a milder climate. It comprises 8 municipal districts, and the most common grape varieties are *Beba, Montua* (whites), *Tempranillo, Garnacha* and *Cabernet Sauvignon* (reds). **Tierra de Barros.** Situated in the centre of the province of Badajoz and the largest (4475 Ha and 37 municipal districts). It has flat plains with fertile soils which are rich in nutrients and have great water retention capacity (Rainfall is low: 350 mm to 450 mm per year). The most common varieties are the white *Cayetana Blanca* and *Pardina*, and the red *Tempranillo, Garnacha* and *Cabernet Sauvignon*.

FIGURES:

Vineyard surface: 32.135– **Wine-Growers:** 2.770 – **Wineries:** 23 – **2012 Harvest rating:** S/C– **Production:** 8.017.059 litres – **Market percentages:** 64% domestic. 36% export

VINTAGE RATING PEÑÍNGUIDE				
2008	2009	2010	2011	2012
VERY GOOD	GOOD	VERY GOOD	GOOD	GOOD

CONSEJO REGULADOR
Ctra. Sevilla-Gijón, km. 114. Apdo. 299. - 06200 Almendralejo (Badajoz). ☎: +34 924 671 302 - Fax: +34 924 664 703
info@riberadelguadiana.eu   www.riberadelguadiana.eu

BODEGA CARABAL

Ctra. Alía - Castilblanco, Km. 10
10137 Alía (Cáceres)
☎: +34 917 346 152 - Fax: +34 913 720 440
www.carabal.es
info@carabal.es

CARABAL CAVEA 2009 TC
35% syrah, 39% cabernet sauvignon, 15% graciano, 10% tempranillo

91 Colour: cherry, garnet rim. Nose: powerfull, ripe fruit, fruit preserve, dark chocolate, sweet spices. Palate: balanced, long, round tannins.

CARABAL RASGO 2010 T
70% syrah, 30% tempranillo

88 Colour: deep cherry. Nose: powerfull, ripe fruit, sweet spices, characterful. Palate: good structure, round tannins, flavourful, fruity.

BODEGA SAN MARCOS

Ctra. Aceuchal, s/n
6200 Almendralejo (Badajoz)
☎: +34 924 670 410 - Fax: +34 924 665 505
www.campobarro.com
ventas@bodegasanmarcos.com

CAMPOBARRO 2005 TR
tempranillo

85 Colour: deep cherry, garnet rim. Nose: spicy, dark chocolate, tobacco, ripe fruit. Palate: balanced, correct.

CAMPOBARRO 2009 TC
tempranillo

85 Colour: cherry, garnet rim. Nose: ripe fruit, spicy, toasty. Palate: powerful, flavourful, toasty, round tannins.

CAMPOBARRO MACABEO 2012 B
macabeo

84

CAMPOBARRO PARDINA 2012 B
pardina

86 Colour: bright straw. Nose: balanced, fresh fruit, jasmine. Palate: balanced, flavourful, fruity.

CAMPOBARRO SELECCIÓN 2010 T
tempranillo, mazuelo

85 Colour: deep cherry, garnet rim. Nose: medium intensity, balanced, ripe fruit, spicy. Palate: fruity, correct.

CAMPOBARRO SELECCIÓN 2011 T
tempranillo, mazuelo

84

CAMPOBARRO TEMPRANILLO 2012 T
tempranillo

84

HEREDAD DE BARROS 2005 TR
100% tempranillo

85 Colour: cherry, garnet rim. Nose: spicy, ripe fruit, old leather. Palate: flavourful, long.

HEREDAD DE BARROS 2009 TC
tempranillo

85 Colour: cherry, garnet rim. Nose: medium intensity, ripe fruit, spicy. Palate: correct, easy to drink.

BODEGAS MARTÍNEZ PAIVA SAT

Ctra. Gijón - Sevilla N-630, Km. 646 Apdo. Correos 87
6200 Almendralejo (Badajoz)
☎: +34 924 671 130 - Fax: +34 924 663 056
www.payva.es
info@payva.es

56 BARRICAS 2008 TC
tempranillo

86 Colour: very deep cherry. Nose: dark chocolate, toasty, ripe fruit. Palate: balanced, fine bitter notes, round tannins.

DOÑA FRANCISQUITA 2011 T
tempranillo

85 Colour: cherry, purple rim. Nose: faded flowers, ripe fruit. Palate: flavourful, fruity, easy to drink, good acidity.

PAYVA 2007 TR
80% tempranillo, 20% graciano

87 Colour: cherry, garnet rim. Nose: medium intensity, ripe fruit, spicy. Palate: flavourful, round tannins.

PAYVA 2009 TC
80% tempranillo, 10% cabernet sauvignon, 10% graciano

84

PAYVA 2012 T
tempranillo

84

PAYVA CAYETANA BLANCA 2012 B
cayetana blanca

86 Colour: bright yellow. Nose: medium intensity, floral, citrus fruit. Palate: fresh, fruity, good acidity.

PAYVA MACABEO 2012 B
macabeo

86 Colour: bright yellow. Nose: fresh fruit, white flowers, citrus fruit. Palate: flavourful, good acidity, fresh.

PAYVA MOSCATEL 2012 B
moscatel grano menudo

86 Colour: bright yellow. Nose: medium intensity, white flowers, faded flowers. Palate: flavourful, sweetness, balanced.

BODEGAS ORAN

Hiedra, 21
6200 Almendralejo (Badajoz)
☎: +34 662 952 800
www.bodegasoran.com
info@bodegasoran.com

FLOR DEL SEÑORÍO DE ORÁN 2011 T
tempranillo

87 Colour: cherry, garnet rim. Nose: red berry notes, ripe fruit, balsamic herbs, floral, spicy, creamy oak. Palate: rich, powerful, flavourful, fruity.

SEÑORÍO DE ORÁN 2009 TC
tempranillo

85 Colour: cherry, garnet rim. Nose: powerfull, ripe fruit, fruit preserve, cocoa bean. Palate: correct, good finish.

SEÑORÍO DE ORÁN 2012 B
pardina

85 Colour: bright yellow. Nose: balanced, white flowers, medium intensity, fresh fruit. Palate: fresh, easy to drink.

VIÑA ROJA TEMPRANILLO 2012 T
tempranillo

85 Colour: cherry, purple rim. Nose: medium intensity, red berry notes, ripe fruit. Palate: fruity, easy to drink.

BODEGAS ROMALE

Pol. Ind. Parc. 6, Manz. D
6200 Almendralejo (Badajoz)
☎: +34 924 667 255 - Fax: +34 924 665 877
www.romale.com
romale@romale.com

PRIVILEGIO DE ROMALE 2008 TR
tempranillo

87 Colour: cherry, garnet rim. Nose: ripe fruit, spicy, dark chocolate. Palate: powerful, flavourful, toasty, round tannins.

PRIVILEGIO DE ROMALE 2010 TC
tempranillo

85 Colour: cherry, garnet rim. Nose: powerfull, smoky, sweet spices, ripe fruit. Palate: flavourful, round tannins.

VIÑA ROMALE MACABEO 2012 B
macabeo

83

BODEGAS RUIZ TORRES

Ctra. EX 116, km.33,8
10136 Cañamero (Cáceres)
☎: +34 927 369 027 - Fax: +34 927 369 383
www.ruiztorres.com
info@ruiztorres.com

ATTELEA 2008 TC
tempranillo, cabernet sauvignon

83

ATTELEA 2011 T ROBLE
tempranillo

85 Colour: deep cherry, garnet rim. Nose: toasty, spicy, ripe fruit. Palate: flavourful, smoky aftertaste, ripe fruit.

BODEGAS TORIBIO

Real Provisión - Avda. Constitución 12A
6230 Los Santos de Maimona (Badajoz)
☎: +34 924 551 449
www.doloresmorenas.com
realprovision@hotmail.com

REAL PROVISIÓN 2009 TC
tempranillo, cabernet sauvignon, syrah

88 Colour: cherry, garnet rim. Nose: ripe fruit, spicy, creamy oak, toasty, complex. Palate: powerful, flavourful, toasty, round tannins.

REAL PROVISIÓN 2012 B
100% macabeo

84

REAL PROVISIÓN 2012 T
100% tempranillo

86 Colour: cherry, purple rim. Nose: medium intensity, ripe fruit, red berry notes. Palate: ripe fruit, easy to drink, correct.

BODEGAS TORIBIO VIÑA PUEBLA

Luis Chamizo, 12-21
6310 Puebla de Sancho Pérez (Badajoz)
☎: +34 924 551 449
www.bodegastoribio.com
info@bodegastoribio.com

MADRE DEL AGUA 2010 TC
garnacha tintorera

91 Colour: cherry, garnet rim. Nose: expressive, fruit preserve, cocoa bean, sweet spices, toasty. Palate: full, good structure, round tannins, balsamic.

VIÑA PUEBLA 2012 BFB
macabeo

90 Colour: bright yellow. Nose: ripe fruit, sweet spices, creamy oak. Palate: flavourful, toasty, smoky aftertaste.

VIÑA PUEBLA SELECCIÓN 2011 T ROBLE
cabernet sauvignon, tempranillo, garnacha, syrah

89 Colour: cherry, garnet rim. Nose: balanced, ripe fruit, wild herbs, spicy. Palate: flavourful, good structure, round tannins.

VIÑA PUEBLA VERDEJO 2012 B
verdejo

84

LUIS GURPEGUI MUGA

Avda. Celso Muerza, 8
31560 San Adrián (Navarra)
☎: +34 948 670 050 - Fax: +34 948 670 259
www.gurpegui.es
bodegas@gurpegui.es

CINCO VIÑAS 2012 T
tempranillo, garnacha

85 Colour: cherry, purple rim. Nose: expressive, fresh fruit, red berry notes, floral. Palate: flavourful, fruity, good acidity, easy to drink.

GURPEGUI 2012 T
tempranillo, cabernet sauvignon

86 Colour: cherry, purple rim. Nose: red berry notes, ripe fruit, fragrant herbs, spicy. Palate: powerful, flavourful, balsamic.

PAGO LOS BALANCINES

Paraje la Agraria, s/n
6475 Oliva de Mérida (Badajoz)
☎: +34 916 295 841
www.pagolosbalancines.com
info@pagolosbalancines.com

LOS BALANCINES MATANEGRA 2009 TC
cabernet sauvignon, tempranillo, garnacha tintorera

94 Colour: cherry, garnet rim. Nose: balsamic herbs, spicy, creamy oak, dry stone, earthy notes, scrubland. Palate: balanced, elegant, spicy, flavourful, long.

LOS BALANCINES HUNO 2010 T
50% garnacha tintorera, 20% cabernet sauvignon, 20% tempranillo, 10% syrah

91 Colour: cherry, garnet rim. Nose: ripe fruit, fruit preserve, balsamic herbs, spicy, mineral. Palate: powerful, flavourful, spicy, long, round tannins.

VASO DE LUZ 2009 TR
cabernet sauvignon

94 Colour: cherry, garnet rim. Nose: elegant, expressive, ripe fruit, fruit expression, spicy. Palate: good acidity, fine bitter notes, elegant, balanced, round tannins.

PALACIO QUEMADO

Ctra. Almendralejo - Alange, km 6,9
6200 Almendralejo (Badajoz)
☎: +34 924 120 082 - Fax: +34 924 120 028
www.palacioquemado.com
palacioquemado@alvear.es

"PQ" PRIMICIA 2011 T
60% tempranillo, 20% syrah, 20% garnacha

88 Colour: bright cherry, purple rim. Nose: ripe fruit, violet drops, powerfull. Palate: flavourful, fruity, round tannins.

PALACIO QUEMADO 2007 TR
100% tempranillo

88 Colour: deep cherry, garnet rim. Nose: spicy, ripe fruit, cocoa bean, tobacco. Palate: flavourful, good structure, round tannins.

PALACIO QUEMADO 2010 TC
95% tempranillo, 5% cabernet sauvignon

88 Colour: bright cherry, garnet rim. Nose: ripe fruit, spicy, medium intensity. Palate: easy to drink, good finish.

PALACIO QUEMADO LA ZARCITA 2010 T
40% tempranillo, 40% syrah, 20% cabernet sauvignon

90 Colour: cherry, garnet rim. Nose: medium intensity, dried herbs, wild herbs, spicy. Palate: flavourful, fine bitter notes, round tannins.

PALACIO QUEMADO LOS ACILATES 2010 T
50% tempranillo, 50% syrah

90 Colour: cherry, garnet rim. Nose: ripe fruit, spicy, toasty, complex, scrubland. Palate: powerful, flavourful, toasty, round tannins.

SANTA MARTA VIRGEN

Cooperativa, s/n
6150 Santa Marta de los Barros (Badajoz)
☎: +34 924 690 218 - Fax: +34 924 690 043
www.bodegasantamarta.com
info@bodegasantamarta.com

BLASÓN DEL TURRA 2012 RD
tempranillo
83

BLASÓN DEL TURRA 2012 T
tempranillo
83

BLASÓN DEL TURRA MACABEO 2012 B
macabeo
83

BLASÓN DEL TURRA PARDINA 2012 B
pardina
84

COMPASS 2011 T
tempranillo

85 Colour: cherry, garnet rim. Nose: powerfull, ripe fruit, fruit preserve. Palate: flavourful, correct, sweet tannins.

COMPASS 2012 RD
syrah

85 Colour: light cherry, bright. Nose: red berry notes, ripe fruit. Palate: fruity, flavourful, good finish.

VALDEAURUM 2010 T
tempranillo

86 Colour: bright cherry. Nose: ripe fruit, sweet spices, creamy oak. Palate: fruity, round tannins, light-bodied.

VIÑAOLIVA SOCIEDAD COOPERATIVA

Pol. Ind., Parcela 4-17
6200 Almendralejo (Badajoz)
☎: +34 924 677 321 - Fax: +34 924 660 989
www.zaleo.es
acoex@bme.es

ZALEO 2012 RD
tempranillo
84

ZALEO MOSCATEL 2012 B
moscatel
84

ZALEO PARDINA 2012 B
pardina
84

ZALEO PREMIUM 2010 T
tempranillo

87 Colour: cherry, garnet rim. Nose: medium intensity, sweet spices, ripe fruit. Palate: flavourful, fruity, easy to drink.

ZALEO SELECCIÓN 2010 T
tempranillo

85 Colour: cherry, garnet rim. Nose: spicy, ripe fruit, fruit preserve. Palate: flavourful, correct.

ZALEO SEMIDULCE 2012 B
pardina
83

ZALEO TEMPRANILLO 2012 T
tempranillo

85 Colour: cherry, purple rim. Nose: medium intensity, ripe fruit, red berry notes. Palate: correct, easy to drink.

ZALEO TEMPRANILLO SEMIDULCE 2012 T
tempranillo
83

VITICULTORES DE BARROS

Ctra. de Badajoz, s/n
6200 Almendralejo (Badajoz)
☎: +34 924 664 852 - Fax: +34 924 664 852
www.viticultoresdebarros.com
bodegas@viticultoresdebarros.com

EMPERADOR DE BARROS CAYETANA 2012 B
cayetana blanca

87 Colour: bright straw. Nose: expressive, white flowers, jasmine. Palate: fruity, balanced, fine bitter notes, good acidity.

EMPERADOR DE BARROS TEMPRANILLO 2012 T
tempranillo

86 Colour: very deep cherry, purple rim. Nose: ripe fruit. Palate: flavourful, fruity, good structure, correct.

VIZANA 2009 TC
tempranillo

87 Colour: cherry, garnet rim. Nose: ripe fruit, warm, sweet spices. Palate: long, ripe fruit, round tannins.

DO RIBERA DEL JÚCAR / D.O.P.

LOCATION:

The 7 wine producing municipal districts that make up the DO are located on the banks of the Júcar, in the south of the province of Cuenca. They are: Casas de Benítez, Casas de Guijarro, Casas de Haro, Casas de Fernando Alonso, Pozoamargo, Sisante and El Picazo. The region is at an altitude of between 650 and 750 m above sea level.

CLIMATE:

Continental in nature, dry, and with very cold winters and very hot summers. The main factor contributing to the quality of the wine is the day-night temperature contrasts during the ripening season of the grapes, which causes the process to be carried out slowly.

SOIL:

The most common type of soil consists of pebbles on the surface and a clayey subsoil, which provides good water retention capacity in the deeper levels.

GRAPE VARIETIES:

RED: *Cencibel* or *Tempranillo, Cabernet Sauvignon, Merlot, Syrah, Bobal, Cabernet Franc* and *Petit Verdot.*
WHITE: *Moscatel de Grano Menudo* and *Sauvignon Blanc.*

FIGURES:

Vineyard surface: 9,141 – **Wine-Growers:** 970 – **Wineries:** 11 – **2012 Harvest rating:** Very Good – **Production:** 631,507 litres – **Market percentages:** 35% domestic. 65% export

VINTAGE RATING PEÑINGUIDE				
2008	2009	2010	2011	2012
VERY GOOD	GOOD	VERY GOOD	VERY GOOD	VERY GOOD

CONSEJO REGULADOR
Deportes, 4. - 16700 Sisante (Cuenca) ☎: +34 969 387 182 - Fax: +34 969 387 208
do@vinosriberadeljucar.com   www.vinosriberadeljucar.com

BODEGA SAN GINÉS

Virgen del Carmen, 6
16707 Casas de Benítez (Cuenca)
☎: +34 969 382 037 - Fax: +34 969 382 998
www.cincoalmudes.es
juancarlos@bodegasangines.es

5 ALMUDES 2010 TC
tempranillo
84

5 ALMUDES TEMPRANILLO 2012 T
tempranillo
84

ALMUDES 5 DÉCADAS 2008 TR
tempranillo
90 Colour: cherry, garnet rim. Nose: spicy, creamy oak, toasty, expressive, elegant. Palate: powerful, flavourful, toasty, round tannins.

LAS ERAS TRADICIÓN 2010 T
bobal
88 Colour: deep cherry. Nose: sweet spices, toasty. Palate: powerful, flavourful, good structure, toasty.

BODEGAS Y VIÑEDOS ILLANA

Finca Buenavista, s/n
16708 Pozoamargo (Cuenca)
☎: +34 969 147 039 - Fax: +34 969 147 057
www.bodegasillana.com
info@bodegasillana.com

CASA DE ILLANA EXPRESSION 2012 T
85% tempranillo, 15% bobal
87 Colour: cherry, purple rim. Nose: red berry notes, floral, ripe fruit. Palate: flavourful, fruity, good acidity, round tannins.

CASA DE ILLANA SELECCIÓN 2009 T
syrah, petit verdot
90 Colour: cherry, garnet rim. Nose: ripe fruit, spicy, creamy oak, toasty, mineral. Palate: powerful, flavourful, toasty, round tannins.

CASA DE ILLANA TRESDECINCO 2009 TC
58% merlot, 16% syrah, 16% cabernet sauvignon, 10% petit verdot
88 Colour: very deep cherry. Nose: toasty, ripe fruit, over-ripe fruit. Palate: ripe fruit, toasty.

PETIT YLLANA BOBAL 2012 T
bobal
90 Colour: deep cherry. Nose: expressive, ripe fruit, dried herbs, mineral. Palate: flavourful, good acidity, spicy.

PETIT YLLANA PETIT VERDOT 2011 T
87 Colour: bright cherry. Nose: powerfull, ripe fruit, over-ripe fruit, spicy. Palate: fine bitter notes, powerful tannins.

CASA GUALDA

Casa Gualda
16708 Pozoamargo (Cuenca)
☎: +34 969 387 173 - Fax: +34 969 387 202
www.casagualda.com
info@casagualda.com

CASA GUALDA SAUVIGNON BLANC 2012 B
sauvignon blanc
84

CASA GUALDA SYRAH 2012 T
syrah
84

ELVIWINES

Antoni Caballé, 8
8197 Valldoreix- St Cugat del Vallès (Tarragona)
☎: +34 935 343 026 - Fax: +34 936 750 316
www.elviwines.com
moises@elviwines.com

ADAR 2008 T
cabernet sauvignon, petit verdot, syrah
90 Colour: cherry, garnet rim. Nose: spicy, creamy oak, toasty, characterful. Palate: powerful, flavourful, toasty, round tannins.

NESS 2011 B
56% sauvignon blanc, 44% moscatel
85 Colour: bright straw. Nose: white flowers, ripe fruit. Palate: flavourful, fruity, balanced.

NUESTRO PADRE JESÚS DE NAZARENO SDAD. COOP.

Deportes, 4
16700 Sisante (Cuenca)
☎: +34 969 387 094 - Fax: +34 969 387 094
www.cooperativasisante.com
sisante_nazareno@yahoo.es

CASA DON JUAN 2011 T
84

TEATINOS

Ctra. Minaya - San Clemente, Km. 10
16610 Casas de Fernando Alonso (Cuenca)
☎: +34 969 383 043 - Fax: +34 969 383 153
www.vinoteatino.com
info@vinoteatinos.com

TEATINOS BOBAL S/C RD
82

TEATINOS CLAROS DE CUBA 2006 TR
90 Colour: cherry, garnet rim. Nose: ripe fruit, spicy, creamy oak, toasty, complex. Palate: powerful, flavourful, toasty, round tannins.

TEATINOS DULCE MOSCATEL BLANCO DULCE
88 Colour: bright yellow. Nose: candied fruit, citrus fruit, floral. Palate: sweetness, concentrated, good acidity.

TEATINOS S/C B
70

TEATINOS SELECCIÓN 40 BARRICAS TEMPRANILLO 2007 TR
87 Colour: cherry, garnet rim. Nose: spicy, toasty, char-acterful, roasted coffee. Palate: powerful, flavourful, toasty, round tannins.

TEATINOS SIGNVM 2009 TC
85 Colour: very deep cherry. Nose: powerfull, overripe fruit, toasty, dark chocolate. Palate: powerful, concentrated, toasty.

TEATINOS SYRAH 2012 T
87 Colour: deep cherry. Nose: red berry notes, ripe fruit, powerfull. Palate: powerful, flavourful, ripe fruit.

TEATINOS TEMPRANILLO 2012 T
89 Colour: cherry, purple rim. Nose: fresh fruit, red berry notes. Palate: flavourful, fruity, good acidity, round tannins.

VIÑEDOS Y BODEGAS LA MAGDALENA

Ctra. La Roda, s/n
16611 Casas de Haro (Cuenca)
☎: +34 969 380 722 - Fax: +34 969 380 722
www.vegamoragona.com
vinos@vegamoragona.com

VEGA MORAGONA 2012 B
100% moscatel grano menudo

86 Colour: bright straw. Nose: faded flowers, ripe fruit, honeyed notes. Palate: powerful, ripe fruit.

VEGA MORAGONA DULCE B
100% moscatel grano menudo

89 Colour: golden. Nose: powerfull, floral, honeyed notes, candied fruit. Palate: flavourful, sweet, fine bitter notes.

VEGA MORAGONA TEMPRANILLO 2012 T JOVEN
100% tempranillo

87 Colour: deep cherry. Nose: powerfull, expressive, ripe fruit, red berry notes. Palate: flavourful, fruity, ripe fruit.

Consejo Regulador
DO Boundary

DO Ca. RIOJA / D.O.P.

LOCATION:

Occupying the Ebro valley. To the north it borders with the Sierra de Cantabria and to the south with the Sierra de la Demanda, and is made up of different municipal districts of La Rioja, the Basque Country and Navarra. The most western region is Haro and the easternmost, Alfaro, with a distance of 100 km between the two. The region is 40 km wide.es de 40 kilómetros.

CLIMATE:

Quite variable depending on the different sub-regions. In general, there is a combination of Atlantic and Mediterranean influences, the latter becoming more dominant as the terrain descends from west to east, becoming drier and hotter. The average annual rainfall is slightly over 400 mm.

SOIL:

Various types: the clayey calcareous soil arranged in terraces and small plots which are located especially in Rioja Alavesa, la Sonsierra and some regions of Rioja Alta; the clayey ferrous soil, scattered throughout the region, with vineyards located on reddish, strong soil with hard, deep rock; and the alluvial soil in the area close to the rivers; these are the most level vineyards with larger plots; here the soil is deeper and has pebbles.

GRAPE VARIETIES:

WHITE: *Viura* (7,045 Ha), *Malvasía, Garnacha Blanca, Chardonnay, Sauvignon Blanc, Verdejo, Maturana Blanca, Tempranillo Blanco* and *Torrontés*.
RED: *Tempranillo* (majority with 38,476 Ha), *Garnacha, Graciano, Mazuelo* and *Maturana Tinta*.

SUB-REGIONS:

Rioja Alta. This has Atlantic influences; it is the most extensive with some 20,500 Ha and produces wines well suited for ageing. **Rioja Alavesa.** A mixture of Atlantic and Mediterranean influences, with an area under cultivation of some 11,500 Ha; both young wines and wines suited for ageing are produced. **Rioja Baja.** With approximately 18,000 Ha, the climate is purely Mediterranean; white wines and rosés with a higher alcohol content and extract are produced.

FIGURES:

Vineyard surface: 63.297 – **Wine-Growers:** 16.983 – **Wineries:** 788 – **2012 Harvest rating:** Very Good – **Production:** 244.590.000 litres – **Market percentages:** 64% domestic. 36% export

VINTAGE RATING — PEÑÍN GUIDE

2008	2009	2010	2011	2012
VERY GOOD	VERY GOOD	EXCELLENT	EXCELLENT	VERY GOOD

CONSEJO REGULADOR
Estambrera, 52 - 26006 Logroño (La Rioja) ☎: +34 941 500 400 - Fax: +34 941 500 672
info@riojawine.com   www.riojawine.com

ALTOS DE ONTAÑÓN

Altos de Ontañón
9315 Fuentecen (Burgos)
☎: +34 941 234 200 - Fax: +34 941 270 482
www.ontanon.es
comercial@ontanon.es

ARTESO 2008 TC
75% tempranillo, 15% graciano, 10% garnacha

94 Colour: deep cherry. Nose: cocoa bean, fruit expression, complex. Palate: fine tannins, powerful, flavourful, fruity, complex, fruity aftestaste.

COLECCIÓN MITOLÓGICA ONTAÑÓN 2004 TGR
95% tempranillo, 5% graciano

89 Colour: deep cherry. Nose: fine reductive notes, spicy, cedar wood, creamy oak. Palate: round, spicy, good finish, reductive nuances, flavourful, powerful.

ONTAÑÓN 2004 TGR
95% tempranillo, 5% graciano

90 Colour: deep cherry. Nose: powerfull, complex, spicy, creamy oak, toasty, fruit preserve. Palate: ripe fruit, flavourful, powerful, spicy.

ONTAÑÓN 2005 TR
95% tempranillo, 5% graciano

88 Colour: deep cherry. Nose: spicy, aged wood nuances, ripe fruit. Palate: round tannins, powerful, flavourful, spicy.

ONTAÑÓN 2010 TC
90% tempranillo, 10% garnacha

91 Colour: dark-red cherry. Nose: cocoa bean, aromatic coffee, spicy, fruit expression. Palate: balsamic, creamy, powerful, flavourful, fruity, good structure, complex.

VETIVER 2012 B
100% viura

88 Colour: bright straw. Nose: ripe fruit, cocoa bean, sweet spices. Palate: flavourful, fine bitter notes, good acidity.

ALTOS DE RIOJA VITICULTORES Y BODEGUEROS

Ctra. Logroño, s/n
1300 Laguardia (Alava)
☎: +34 945 600 693 - Fax: +34 945 600 692
www.altosderioja.com
altosderioja@altosderioja.com

ALTOS R 2007 TR
100% tempranillo

90 Colour: bright cherry. Nose: ripe fruit, sweet spices, creamy oak. Palate: flavourful, fruity, toasty, round tannins.

ALTOS R 2009 TC
100% tempranillo

88 Colour: cherry, garnet rim. Nose: ripe fruit, creamy oak, toasty, complex. Palate: powerful, flavourful, toasty, round tannins.

ALTOS R 2010 TC
tempranillo

90 Colour: deep cherry, garnet rim. Nose: ripe fruit, balanced, spicy, wild herbs. Palate: good structure, round tannins.

ALTOS R 2012 B
60% viura, 40% malvasía

91 Colour: straw. Nose: ripe fruit, floral, expressive. Palate: balanced, flavourful, fruity, ripe fruit, long, good acidity.

ALTOS R PIGEAGE 2009 T
90% tempranillo, 10% graciano

91 Colour: very deep cherry. Nose: powerfull, ripe fruit, toasty, wet leather. Palate: ripe fruit, spicy, fine bitter notes.

ALTOS R PIGEAGE GRACIANO 2009 T
100% graciano

91 Colour: cherry, garnet rim. Nose: spicy, creamy oak, toasty, fruit preserve, balsamic herbs. Palate: powerful, flavourful, toasty, round tannins.

ALTOS R PIGEAGE GRACIANO 2010 T
100% graciano

92 Colour: cherry, garnet rim. Nose: ripe fruit, spicy, creamy oak, toasty, characterful, scrubland. Palate: powerful, flavourful, toasty, round tannins.

ALTOS R TEMPRANILLO 2010 T
100% tempranillo

90 Colour: bright cherry. Nose: ripe fruit, sweet spices, creamy oak, expressive. Palate: flavourful, fruity, toasty, round tannins.

ALTÚN

Las Piscinas, 30
1307 Baños de Ebro (Álava)
☎: +34 945 609 317 - Fax: +34 945 609 309
www.bodegasaltun.com
altun@bodegasaltun.com

ALBIKER 2012 T MACERACIÓN CARBÓNICA
97% tempranillo, 3% viura

89 Colour: cherry, purple rim. Nose: tropical fruit, red berry notes, expressive. Palate: easy to drink, fresh, fruity, light-bodied.

ALTÚN 2007 TR

89 Colour: cherry, garnet rim. Nose: ripe fruit, balsamic herbs, spicy, creamy oak, fine reductive notes. Palate: flavourful, spicy, long.

ALTÚN 2010 TC
100% tempranillo

90 Colour: cherry, garnet rim. Nose: ripe fruit, creamy oak, toasty, sweet spices. Palate: powerful, flavourful, toasty.

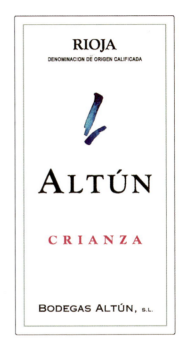

ANA DE ALTÚN 2012 B
80% viura, 20% malvasía

86 Colour: pale. Nose: floral, ripe fruit. Palate: light-bodied, fruity, ripe fruit, long.

EVEREST 2011 T
100% tempranillo

93 Colour: cherry, purple rim. Nose: red berry notes, violet drops, balsamic herbs, sweet spices, toasty. Palate: powerful, rich, flavourful, toasty, elegant.

SECRETO DE ALTÚN 2010 T
100% tempranillo

93 Colour: cherry, garnet rim. Nose: spicy, creamy oak, complex, red berry notes, ripe fruit. Palate: powerful, flavourful, toasty, long, rich.

ALVAREZ ALFARO

Ctra. Comarcal 384, Km. 0,8
26559 Aldeanueva de Ebro (La Rioja)
☎: +34 941 144 210 - Fax: +34 941 144 210
www.bodegasalvarezalfaro.com
info@bodegasalvarezalfaro.com

ALVAREZ ALFARO 2007 TR
tempranillo

88 Colour: deep cherry, garnet rim. Nose: ripe fruit, spicy, balanced. Palate: balanced, good acidity.

ALVAREZ ALFARO 2010 TC
80% tempranillo, 10% mazuelo, 8% garnacha, 2% graciano

87 Colour: bright cherry. Nose: sweet spices, aromatic coffee, ripe fruit. Palate: flavourful, fruity, toasty, round tannins.

ALVAREZ ALFARO SELECCIÓN FAMILIAR 2010 T
100% tempranillo

90 Colour: cherry, garnet rim. Nose: ripe fruit, spicy, creamy oak, toasty, complex. Palate: powerful, flavourful, toasty, round tannins.

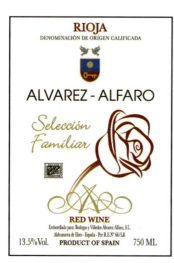

AMADOR GARCÍA CHAVARRI

Avda. Río Ebro, 68 - 70
1307 Baños de Ebro (Álava)
☎: +34 945 623 322 - Fax: +34 975 290 373
www.bodegasamadorgarcia.com

AMADOR GARCÍA 2012 BFB
100% viura

87 Colour: bright straw. Nose: creamy oak, fragrant herbs, fresh fruit. Palate: balsamic, flavourful, dry, fresh.

AMADOR GARCÍA VENDIMIA SELECCIONADA 2010 TC
tempranillo, mazuelo, garnacha

89 Colour: dark-red cherry. Nose: short, ripe fruit, spicy. Palate: spicy, toasty, ripe fruit, powerful, flavourful.

PEÑAGUDO 2010 TC
tempranillo, graciano, garnacha

87 Colour: cherry, garnet rim. Nose: medium intensity, balanced, spicy. Palate: flavourful, fruity, spicy.

PEÑAGUDO 2012 B
100% viura

83

PEÑAGUDO 2012 T
tempranillo, viura

87 Colour: dark-red cherry. Nose: maceration notes, candied fruit, powerfull, varietal. Palate: sweetness, fresh, fruity, powerful, flavourful.

ARRIAGA Y MIMÉNDEZ COMPAÑÍA DE VINOS

Capitán Cortés, 6. Piso 4º Puerta 3
26003 Logroño (La Rioja)
☎: +34 941 210 448 - Fax: +34 941 287 072
www.arriagaymimendez.com

LA INVIERNA CORTE UNO 2007 T
100% tempranillo

91 Colour: cherry, garnet rim. Nose: ripe fruit, spicy, creamy oak, toasty, sweet spices. Palate: powerful, flavourful, toasty, round tannins.

ARTUKE BODEGAS Y VIÑEDOS

Artuke Bodegas y Viñedos
1307 Baños de Ebro (Álava)
☎: +34 945 623 323 - Fax: +34 945 623 323
www.artuke.com
artuke@artuke.com

ARTUKE 2012 T MACERACIÓN CARBÓNICA
95% tempranillo, 5% viura

90 Colour: cherry, purple rim. Nose: red berry notes, raspberry, lactic notes, floral, powerfull, expressive. Palate: fresh, fruity, flavourful, easy to drink.

ARTUKE FINCA DE LOS LOCOS 2011 T
80% tempranillo, 20% graciano

95 Colour: bright cherry. Nose: ripe fruit, sweet spices, creamy oak, expressive, red berry notes. Palate: flavourful, fruity, toasty, round tannins.

ARTUKE K4 2011 T
75% tempranillo, 25% graciano

96 Colour: bright cherry. Nose: ripe fruit, sweet spices, creamy oak, neat, red berry notes, varietal, balsamic herbs. Palate: flavourful, fruity, toasty, round tannins.

ARTUKE PIES NEGROS 2011 TC
90% tempranillo, 10% graciano

92 Colour: cherry, purple rim. Nose: mineral, ripe fruit, fruit expression, sweet spices. Palate: flavourful, powerful, ripe fruit.

ARTUKE VENDIMIA SELECCIONADA 2012 T
95% tempranillo, 5% graciano

91 Colour: bright cherry. Nose: sweet spices, creamy oak, raspberry, red berry notes, ripe fruit. Palate: flavourful, fruity, toasty.

BAIGORRI

Ctra. Vitoria-Logroño, Km. 53
1307 Samaniego (Álava)
☎: +34 945 609 420
www.bodegasbaigorri.com
mail@bodegasbaigorri.com

BAIGORRI 2007 TR
100% tempranillo

92 Colour: cherry, garnet rim. Nose: ripe fruit, spicy, wild herbs, earthy notes, old leather. Palate: powerful, flavourful, long, round, balanced.

BAIGORRI 2011 BFB
95% viura, 5% malvasía

91 Colour: bright yellow. Nose: ripe fruit, sweet spices, fragrant herbs, toasty. Palate: rich, smoky aftertaste, flavourful, fresh, good acidity.

BAIGORRI 2012 BFB
95% viura, 5% malvasía

90 Colour: bright yellow. Nose: powerfull, ripe fruit, sweet spices, creamy oak, fragrant herbs. Palate: rich, smoky aftertaste, flavourful, fresh, good acidity.

BAIGORRI 2012 T MACERACIÓN CARBÓNICA
100% tempranillo

88 Colour: cherry, purple rim. Nose: red berry notes, lactic notes, floral, expressive. Palate: fresh, fruity, balsamic, flavourful.

BAIGORRI 2006 TR
100% tempranillo

90 Colour: cherry, garnet rim. Nose: ripe fruit, fruit liqueur notes, scrubland, aromatic coffee, cigar, wet leather. Palate: powerful, flavourful, spicy, long.

BAIGORRI 2008 TR
100% tempranillo

91 Colour: cherry, garnet rim. Nose: ripe fruit, balsamic herbs, spicy, creamy oak, fine reductive notes. Palate: powerful, flavourful, spicy, long.

BAIGORRI 2009 TC
90% tempranillo, 5% garnacha, 5% otras

91 Colour: cherry, garnet rim. Nose: ripe fruit, spicy, creamy oak, toasty, complex. Palate: powerful, flavourful, toasty, round tannins.

BAIGORRI 2010 B
95% viura, 5% malvasía

91 Colour: bright yellow. Nose: ripe fruit, cocoa bean, dark chocolate, sweet spices, balsamic herbs. Palate: rich, fruity, flavourful, balanced.

BAIGORRI 2010 TC
90% tempranillo, 10% otras

90 Colour: cherry, garnet rim. Nose: red berry notes, ripe fruit, sweet spices, creamy oak, earthy notes. Palate: powerful, flavourful, long, elegant.

BAIGORRI BELUS 2008 T
80% tempranillo, 15% mazuelo, 5% otras

90 Colour: cherry, garnet rim. Nose: ripe fruit, scrubland, earthy notes, sweet spices, creamy oak. Palate: powerful, flavourful, toasty, correct.

BAIGORRI DE GARAGE 2008 T
tempranillo

91 Colour: cherry, garnet rim. Nose: balsamic herbs, earthy notes, sweet spices, creamy oak, aromatic coffee, fruit preserve. Palate: powerful, flavourful, spicy, long.

BAIGORRI GARNACHA 2010 T
100% garnacha

93 Colour: cherry, garnet rim. Nose: red berry notes, ripe fruit, balsamic herbs, mineral, spicy, creamy oak. Palate: powerful, flavourful, spicy, long, balanced, elegant.

BARÓN DE LEY

Ctra. Mendavia - Lodosa, Km. 5,5
31587 Mendavia (Navarra)
☎: +34 948 694 303 - Fax: +34 948 694 304
www.barondeley.com
info@barondeley.com

BARÓN DE LEY 2007 TGR
100% tempranillo

88 Colour: cherry, garnet rim. Nose: earthy notes, spicy, toasty. Palate: spicy, ripe fruit, classic aged character.

BARÓN DE LEY 2009 TR
100% tempranillo

88 Colour: bright cherry. Nose: sweet spices, creamy oak. Palate: flavourful, fruity, toasty, round tannins.

BARÓN DE LEY 2012 B
85% viura, 15% malvasía

89 Colour: straw. Nose: powerfull, fresh, expressive, elegant, fruit expression. Palate: fresh, fruity, powerful, flavourful, dry.

BARÓN DE LEY 2012 RD
60% tempranillo, 40% garnacha

88 Colour: light cherry, bright. Nose: balanced, dried herbs, faded flowers, citrus fruit. Palate: fruity, flavourful, good acidity.

BARON DE LEY 3 VIÑAS 2008 B RESERVA
75% viura, 15% malvasía, 15% garnacha blanca

93 Colour: bright golden. Nose: powerfull, complex, petrol notes, candied fruit, roasted almonds, creamy oak. Palate: powerful, flavourful, dry, classic aged character, ripe fruit.

BARON DE LEY 7 VIÑAS 2005 TR
55% tempranillo, 15% graciano, 15% garnacha, 7% mazuelo, 5% viura, 3% otras.

92 Colour: cherry, garnet rim. Nose: powerfull, scrubland, ripe fruit. Palate: fine bitter notes, powerful, flavourful, round tannins.

BARÓN DE LEY FINCA MONASTERIO 2010 T
90% tempranillo, 10% otras

90 Colour: cherry, garnet rim. Nose: powerfull, ripe fruit, roasted coffee. Palate: powerful, ripe fruit, spicy.

BARÓN DE LEY VARIETALES GARNACHA 2011 T
100% garnacha

91 Colour: deep cherry. Nose: expressive, varietal, fruit expression, grassy. Palate: flavourful, fruity, fresh, sweet tannins.

BARÓN DE LEY VARIETALES GRACIANO 2010 T
100% graciano

90 Colour: bright cherry. Nose: ripe fruit, sweet spices, creamy oak. Palate: flavourful, fruity, toasty, round tannins.

BARÓN DE LEY VARIETALES MATURANA 2010 T
100% maturana

89 Colour: cherry, purple rim. Nose: creamy oak, ripe fruit, cocoa bean. Palate: flavourful, good acidity, fine bitter notes.

BARÓN DE LEY VARIETALES TEMPRANILLO 2010 T
100% tempranillo

92 Colour: cherry, garnet rim. Nose: ripe fruit, spicy, creamy oak, toasty. Palate: powerful, flavourful, toasty, round tannins.

BERARTE VIÑEDOS Y BODEGAS

Mayor, 37
1307 Villabuena De Alava (Alava)
☎: +34 945 609 034
www.berarte.es
info@berarte.es

BERARTE 2008 TR
100% tempranillo

86 Colour: dark-red cherry, orangey edge. Nose: scrubland, fruit preserve, spicy, creamy oak, fine reductive notes. Palate: flavourful, spicy, correct.

BERARTE 2009 TC
100% tempranillo

84

BERARTE 2012 T
95% tempranillo, 5% viura

83

BOD. PEDRO Y JAIME MARTÍNEZ PRADO

Del Prado, 7
26310 Badarán (La Rioja)
☎: +34 941 367 117 - Fax: +34 941 367 117
www.rivalia.com
chaval@rivalia.com

CHAVAL 2012 B
90% viura, 10% malvasía

83

CHAVAL 2012 T
75% tempranillo, 25% garnacha

86 Colour: cherry, purple rim. Nose: floral, ripe fruit, fruit preserve. Palate: flavourful, fruity, good acidity.

RIVALIA VENDIMIA SELECCIONADA 2009 TC
100% tempranillo

89 Colour: cherry, garnet rim. Nose: powerfull, ripe fruit, dark chocolate, dried herbs. Palate: flavourful, fruity, round tannins.

BODEGA ABEL MENDOZA MONGE

Ctra. Peñacerrada, 7
26338 San Vicente de la Sonsierra (La Rioja)
☎: +34 941 308 010 - Fax: +34 941 308 010
jarrarte.abelmendoza@gmail.com

ABEL MENDOZA GRACIANO GRANO A GRANO 2010 T
100% graciano

94 Colour: cherry, garnet rim. Nose: red berry notes, violet drops, fragrant herbs, sweet spices, creamy oak, mineral. Palate: rich, flavourful, spicy, long, balanced, elegant.

ABEL MENDOZA SELECCIÓN PERSONAL 2010 T
100% tempranillo

93 Colour: cherry, garnet rim. Nose: red berry notes, ripe fruit, balsamic herbs, mineral, sweet spices. Palate: powerful, rich, flavourful, spicy, long, balanced.

ABEL MENDOZA TEMPRANILLO BLANCO 2012 B
tempranillo blanco

90 Colour: bright yellow. Nose: powerfull, ripe fruit, sweet spices, creamy oak, fragrant herbs. Palate: rich, flavourful, fresh, good acidity.

ABEL MENDOZA TEMPRANILLO GRANO A GRANO 2010 T
100% tempranillo

95 Colour: cherry, garnet rim. Nose: ripe fruit, fragrant herbs, elegant, spicy, creamy oak. Palate: rich, fruity, spicy, balanced.

JARRARTE 2008 T
100% tempranillo

88 Colour: cherry, garnet rim. Nose: ripe fruit, spicy, creamy oak, toasty. Palate: flavourful, toasty, round tannins.

JARRARTE 2012 T MACERACIÓN CARBÓNICA
100% tempranillo

86 Colour: cherry, purple rim. Nose: ripe fruit, fruit preserve, wild herbs. Palate: fresh, fruity, easy to drink.

BODEGA CONTADOR

Ctra. Baños de Ebro, Km. 1
26338 San Vicente de la Sonsierra (La Rioja)
☎: +34 941 334 228 - Fax: +34 941 334 537
www.bodegacontador.com
info@bodegacontador.com

CARMEN 2008 T
82% tempranillo, 10% garnacha, 4% graciano, 4% mazuelo

94 Colour: cherry, garnet rim. Nose: spicy, toasty, fruit liqueur notes, fine reductive notes. Palate: powerful, flavourful, toasty, round tannins.

CONTADOR 2011 T
94% tempranillo, 3% graciano, 3% mazuelo

97 Colour: cherry, garnet rim. Nose: spicy, creamy oak, fruit expression, ripe fruit, sweet spices. Palate: powerful, flavourful, toasty, round tannins.

LA CUEVA DEL CONTADOR 2011 T
100% tempranillo

96 Colour: bright cherry. Nose: sweet spices, creamy oak, expressive, red berry notes, fruit expression, earthy notes. Palate: flavourful, fruity, toasty, round tannins.

LA VIÑA DE ANDRÉS ROMEO 2011 T
100% tempranillo

96 Colour: cherry, garnet rim. Nose: spicy, toasty, dry stone, mineral, creamy oak. Palate: powerful, flavourful, toasty, round tannins.

PREDICADOR 2011 T
91% tempranillo, 9% mazuelo

94 Colour: cherry, garnet rim. Nose: spicy, creamy oak, toasty, fruit expression, red berry notes. Palate: powerful, flavourful, toasty, round tannins.

PREDICADOR 2012 B
33% viura, 25% malvasía, garnacha blanca

92 Colour: bright straw. Nose: fresh, white flowers, ripe fruit, spicy. Palate: flavourful, fruity, good acidity, balanced.

QUÉ BONITO CACAREABA 2012 B
15% viura, 35% malvasía, 50% garnacha blanca

95 Colour: bright yellow. Nose: powerfull, sweet spices, creamy oak, fragrant herbs. Palate: rich, smoky aftertaste, flavourful, fresh, good acidity.

BODEGA I. PETRALANDA

Avda. La Estación, 44
26360 Fuenmayor (La Rioja)
☎: +34 608 893 732 - Fax: +34 941 450 620
www.vinoart.es
nonno@vinoart.es

NONNO 2008 TC
tempranillo, mazuelo

89 Colour: bright cherry. Nose: sweet spices, creamy oak. Palate: flavourful, fruity, toasty, round tannins.

BODEGA MONTEALTO

Las Piscinas, s/n
1307 Baños del Ebro (Alava)
☎: +34 918 427 013 - Fax: +34 918 427 013
www.meddissl.com
contacta@meddissl.com

ROBATIE 2009 TC
100% tempranillo

89 Colour: cherry, garnet rim. Nose: ripe fruit, spicy, creamy oak, toasty, expressive. Palate: powerful, flavourful, toasty.

ROBATIE 2012 T
95% tempranillo, 5% viura

89 Colour: cherry, purple rim. Nose: fresh fruit, red berry notes, macerated fruit. Palate: flavourful, fruity, good acidity, round tannins.

BODEGA SAN PRUDENCIO

Ctra. de Viana, Km. 1
1322 Moreda (Álava)
☎: +34 945 601 034 - Fax: +34 945 622 451
www.bodegasanprudencio.com
info@bodegasanprudencio.es

CONCLAVE 2005 TR
60% tempranillo, 35% garnacha, 5% mazuelo

88 Colour: pale ruby, brick rim edge. Nose: cocoa bean, dark chocolate, creamy oak, fruit liqueur notes, cigar, waxy notes. Palate: rich, powerful, flavourful.

CONCLAVE ESENCIA 2008 T
65% garnacha, 20% tempranillo, 15% graciano

87 Colour: pale ruby, brick rim edge. Nose: spicy, wet leather, aged wood nuances, fruit liqueur notes. Palate: spicy, long, correct.

CONCLAVE ESENCIA 2010 B
90% viura, 10% malvasía

87 Colour: bright golden. Nose: fruit preserve, faded flowers, slightly evolved. Palate: concentrated, sweetness, powerful.

DEPADRE 2009 T
50% tempranillo, 50% garnacha

86 Colour: cherry, garnet rim. Nose: fruit preserve, spicy, wet leather, tobacco, reduction notes. Palate: long, spicy, classic aged character.

ENVITE 2010 TC
60% tempranillo, 25% garnacha, 15% mazuelo

84

ENVITE 2012 B
90% viura, 10% malvasía

87 Colour: bright straw. Nose: fresh, fresh fruit, white flowers, expressive. Palate: flavourful, fruity, good acidity, balanced.

ENVITE 2012 T
70% tempranillo, 25% garnacha, 5% graciano

86 Colour: dark-red cherry. Nose: ripe fruit, powerfull, fresh, spicy. Palate: correct, fine bitter notes, balsamic.

MALIZIA (VINO DE HIELO) 2009 T
60% tempranillo, 40% garnacha

90 Colour: coppery red. Nose: candied fruit, sweet spices, toasty, pattiserie. Palate: spirituous, fine bitter notes.

SEDUCCIÓN 2012 B
90% viura, 10% malvasía

90 Colour: bright straw. Nose: powerfull, floral, honeyed notes, candied fruit, fragrant herbs. Palate: flavourful, sweet, fresh, fruity, good acidity, long.

BODEGA VIÑA EGUILUZ

Camino de San Bartolomé, 10
26339 Abalos (La Rioja)
☎: +34 941 334 064 - Fax: +34 941 583 022
www.bodegaseguiluz.es
info@bodegaseguiluz.es

EGUILUZ 2008 TC
100% tempranillo

88 Colour: dark-red cherry, garnet rim. Nose: ripe fruit, spicy, balanced. Palate: flavourful, correct, round tannins.

EGUILUZ 2012 T
100% tempranillo

87 Colour: dark-red cherry. Nose: ripe fruit, fruit expression, toasty. Palate: sweetness, good structure, spirituous, full, powerful, flavourful.

BODEGA Y VIÑEDOS SOLABAL

Camino San Bartolomé, 6
26339 Abalos (La Rioja)
☎: +34 941 334 492 - Fax: +34 941 308 164
www.solabal.com
solabal@solabal.com

ESCULLE DE SOLABAL 2010 T
tempranillo

87 Colour: deep cherry. Nose: sweet spices, cocoa bean. Palate: spicy, ripe fruit, fine bitter notes.

MUÑARRATE DE SOLABAL 2012 B
viura

88 Colour: bright straw. Nose: white flowers. Palate: flavourful, fruity, good acidity, balanced.

MUÑARRATE DE SOLABAL 2012 RD
40% garnacha, 30% tempranillo, 30% viura

84

**MUÑARRATE DE SOLABAL 2012
T MACERACIÓN CARBÓNICA**
tempranillo

88 Colour: cherry, purple rim. Nose: expressive, red berry notes, floral. Palate: flavourful, fruity, good acidity, round tannins.

SOLABAL 2008 TR
tempranillo

88 Colour: bright cherry. Nose: ripe fruit, sweet spices, creamy oak, expressive. Palate: flavourful, fruity, toasty, round tannins.

SOLABAL 2010 TC
tempranillo

89 Colour: cherry, garnet rim. Nose: spicy, creamy oak, toasty. Palate: powerful, flavourful, toasty, round tannins.

VALA DE SOLABAL 2010 T
tempranillo

91 Colour: black cherry. Nose: powerfull, fruit preserve, roasted coffee. Palate: ripe fruit, long, toasty, round tannins.

BODEGAS 1808

Ctra. El Villar Polígono 7 Biribil, 33 Apdo. 26
1300 Laguardia (Alava)
☎: +34 685 752 384 - Fax: +34 945 293 450
www.rioja1808.com

1808 TEMPERAMENTO NATURAL 2010 TC
100% tempranillo

90 Colour: cherry, garnet rim. Nose: ripe fruit, spicy, creamy oak, toasty, complex. Palate: powerful, flavourful, toasty, round tannins.

BODEGAS ABANICO

Pol. Ind Ca l'Avellanet - Susany, 6
8553 Seva (Barcelona)
☎: +34 938 125 676 - Fax: +34 938 123 213
www.bodegasabanico.com
info@exportiberia.com

HAZAÑA 2006 TR
100% tempranillo

87 Colour: cherry, garnet rim. Nose: powerfull, ripe fruit. Palate: flavourful, fine bitter notes, good acidity.

HAZAÑA 2009 TC
100% tempranillo

84

HAZAÑA CUVE 2011 T
100% tempranillo

83

HAZAÑA VENDIMIA SELECCIONADA 2005 T
100% tempranillo

90 Colour: cherry, garnet rim. Nose: ripe fruit, creamy oak, toasty, characterful, balsamic herbs. Palate: powerful, flavourful, toasty, round tannins.

BODEGAS AGE

Barrio de la Estación, s/n
26360 Fuenmayor (La Rioja)
☎: +34 941 293 500 - Fax +34 941 293 501
www.bodegasage.com
bodegasage@pernod-ricard.com

SIGLO 2005 TGR
tempranillo, graciano, mazuelo

88 Colour: dark-red cherry, orangey edge. Nose: fruit liqueur notes, powerfull, sweet spices, short. Palate: round, full, powerful, flavourful.

SIGLO 2008 TR
tempranillo, graciano, mazuelo

87 Colour: deep cherry. Nose: spicy, sweet spices, cocoa bean, ripe fruit. Palate: flavourful, light-bodied, lacks expression.

SIGLO SACO 2009 TC
tempranillo, garnacha, mazuelo

89 Colour: dark-red cherry. Nose: cocoa bean, ripe fruit, short. Palate: light-bodied, flavourful, soft tannins.

BODEGAS AGRUPADAS PONTE

Eduardo Pondal, 3 Entpa B
36001 (Pontevedra)
☎: +34 986 840 064 - Fax: +34 986 710 230
www.bodegasagrupadasponte.com
info@bodegasagrupadasponte.com

EL CONSEJO DE PACA 2009 T
80% tempranillo, 20% garnacha

88 Colour: cherry, garnet rim. Nose: ripe fruit, spicy, creamy oak, toasty, complex. Palate: powerful, flavourful, toasty, round tannins.

BODEGAS ALABANZA

Avda. de Cameros, 27 Pol. Sequero
26150 Agoncillo (La Rioja)
☎: +34 941 437 051
www.bodegasalabanza.com
bodegasalabanza@bodegasalabanza.com

ALABANZA 2008 TR
70% tempranillo, 30% graciano

88 Colour: cherry, garnet rim. Nose: ripe fruit, creamy oak, balsamic herbs. Palate: powerful, flavourful, spicy.

ALABANZA 2012 T
80% tempranillo, 20% garnacha

84

ALABANZA 2010 TC
70% tempranillo, 20% garnacha, 10% graciano

88 Colour: cherry, garnet rim. Nose: red berry notes, ripe fruit, balsamic herbs, sweet spices, creamy oak. Palate: powerful, flavourful, spicy.

ALABANZA EDICIÓN LIMITADA 2005 TC
70% tempranillo, 30% graciano

88 Colour: dark-red cherry, orangey edge. Nose: ripe fruit, fruit liqueur notes, spicy, creamy oak. Palate: powerful, flavourful, spicy, long.

BODEGAS ALADRO

Barco, 23
1340 Elciego (Álava)
☎: +34 679 822 754
www.aladro.es
aladro@aladro.es

ALADRO 2012 B
viura

87 Colour: bright straw. Nose: fruit expression, fragrant herbs, fresh, neat, powerfull. Palate: balanced, powerful, flavourful, balsamic, ripe fruit.

ALADRO 2012 T
tempranillo

87 Colour: cherry, garnet rim. Nose: varietal, fruit expression, earthy notes, damp earth. Palate: sweet tannins, spirituous, sweetness, powerful, flavourful.

BODEGAS ALONSO GONZÁLEZ

Hospital, 9
26339 Abalos (La Rioja)
☎: +34 669 897 630 - Fax: +34 941 334 554
www.bodegasalonsogonzalez.es
bodegasalonsogonzalez@hotmail.com

CANTAURI 2007 TR
90% tempranillo, 10% mazuelo, graciano

91 Colour: cherry, garnet rim. Nose: ripe fruit, spicy. Palate: flavourful, good acidity, spicy.

CANTAURI 2012 T MACERACIÓN CARBÓNICA
100% tempranillo

85 Colour: dark-red cherry. Nose: ripe fruit, reduction notes, fresh. Palate: carbonic notes, fruity, powerful, pruney.

CARLOS ALONSO 2012 B
100% viura

84

CARTURI VENDIMIA SELECCIONADA 2009 T
100% tempranillo

90 Colour: bright cherry. Nose: ripe fruit, sweet spices, creamy oak. Palate: flavourful, fruity, toasty, round tannins.

BODEGAS ALTANZA

Ctra. Nacional 232, Km. 419,5
26360 Fuenmayor (Rioja)
☎: +34 941 450 860 - Fax: +34 941 450 804
www.bodegasaltanza.com
altanza@bodegasaltanza.com

CLUB LEALTANZA 2008 TR
tempranillo

88 Colour: light cherry, orangey edge. Nose: animal reductive notes, tobacco, ripe fruit. Palate: correct, balanced, spicy, reductive nuances.

COLECCIÓN ARTISTAS ESPAÑOLES GOYA 2008 TR
tempranillo

89 Colour: light cherry, orangey edge. Nose: cedar wood, toasty, fine reductive notes, candied fruit. Palate: spicy, smoky aftertaste, flavourful.

LEALTANZA 2008 TR
tempranillo

89 Colour: cherry, garnet rim. Nose: toasty, spicy, ripe fruit. Palate: spicy, ripe fruit, toasty.

LEALTANZA 2012 B
viura, sauvignon blanc

88 Colour: bright straw. Nose: ripe fruit, tropical fruit, fragrant herbs, dried flowers. Palate: powerful, flavourful, warm.

LEALTANZA RESERVA DE FAMILIA 2008 TR
tempranillo

87 Colour: dark-red cherry, orangey edge. Nose: spicy, toasty, fruit preserve. Palate: flavourful, good structure, reductive nuances, ripe fruit.

BODEGAS ALTOS DEL MARQUÉS

Ctra. Navarrete, 1
26372 Hornos de Moncalvillo (La Rioja)
☎: +34 941 286 728 - Fax: +34 941 286 729
www.altosdelmarques.com
info@altosdelmarques.com

ALTOS DEL MARQUÉS 2009 TC
100% tempranillo

86 Colour: cherry, garnet rim. Nose: ripe fruit, balsamic herbs, sweet spices, creamy oak. Palate: powerful, flavourful, spicy.

ALTOS DEL MARQUÉS 2011 T
85% tempranillo, 10% garnacha, 5% mazuelo

85 Colour: cherry, garnet rim. Nose: ripe fruit, balsamic herbs, spicy, creamy oak. Palate: powerful, flavourful, spicy.

BODEGAS AMAREN

Ctra. Baños de Ebro, s/n
1307 Villabuena (Álava)
☎: +34 945 175 240 - Fax: +34 945 174 566
bodegas@bodegasamaren.com

AMAREN 2011 BFB
85% viura, 15% malvasía

91 Colour: bright yellow. Nose: powerfull, ripe fruit, sweet spices, creamy oak, fragrant herbs. Palate: rich, smoky aftertaste, flavourful, fresh, good acidity.

AMAREN GARNACHA 2007 T
100% garnacha

91 Colour: black cherry, garnet rim. Nose: ripe fruit, violet drops, scrubland. Palate: balanced, spicy, long.

AMAREN GRACIANO 2009 T
100% graciano

94 Colour: deep cherry. Nose: complex, expressive, balsamic herbs, balanced, ripe fruit. Palate: balanced, long, round tannins, good acidity.

AMAREN TEMPRANILLO 2006 TR
100% tempranillo

92 Colour: very deep cherry, garnet rim. Nose: balanced, expressive, varietal, toasty, spicy. Palate: flavourful, full, long, powerful.

ÁNGELES DE AMAREN 2008 T
85% tempranillo, 15% graciano

93 Colour: bright cherry, garnet rim. Nose: balanced, spicy, cocoa bean, dried herbs. Palate: good structure, flavourful, round tannins.

BODEGAS AMÉZOLA DE LA MORA S.A.

Paraje Viña Vieja, s/n
26359 Torremontalbo (La Rioja)
☎: +34 941 454 532 - Fax: +34 941 454 537
www.bodegasamezola.es
info@bodegasamezola.es

IÑIGO AMÉZOLA 2010 BFB
100% viura

90 Colour: yellow, greenish rim. Nose: dried herbs, faded flowers, ripe fruit, sweet spices. Palate: flavourful, fruity, spicy, long.

IÑIGO AMÉZOLA 2010 T
100% tempranillo

86 Colour: dark-red cherry. Nose: aged wood nuances, spicy, woody, fruit preserve. Palate: powerful, good structure, creamy, spicy, toasty.

SEÑORÍO AMÉZOLA 2007 TR
85% tempranillo, 10% mazuelo, 5% graciano

88 Colour: cherry, garnet rim. Nose: fine reductive notes, waxy notes, ripe fruit, cedar wood, creamy oak. Palate: correct, powerful, flavourful, sweetness, fruity, creamy, toasty, smoky aftertaste.

SOLAR AMÉZOLA 2004 TGR
85% tempranillo, 10% mazuelo, 5% graciano

86 Colour: dark-red cherry, brick rim edge. Nose: wet leather, cigar, cocoa bean, cedar wood. Palate: creamy, roasted-coffee aftertaste, spicy.

VIÑA AMÉZOLA 2009 TC
85% tempranillo, 10% mazuelo, 5% graciano

88 Colour: dark-red cherry. Nose: ripe fruit, sweet spices, aged wood nuances, woody. Palate: toasty, lacks expression, powerful, oaky.

BODEGAS ANTONIO ALCARAZ

Ctra. Vitoria-Logroño, Km. 57
1300 Laguardia (Álava)
☎: +34 658 959 745 - Fax: +34 965 888 359
www.antonio-alcaraz.es
rioja@antonio-alcaraz.es

ALTEA DE ANTONIO ALCARAZ 2009 TC

88 Colour: cherry, garnet rim. Nose: ripe fruit, spicy, characterful. Palate: powerful, flavourful, toasty, round tannins.

ANTONIO ALCARAZ 2008 TR
tempranillo, graciano, mazuelo

90 Colour: cherry, garnet rim. Nose: spicy, toasty, aromatic coffee, cocoa bean. Palate: powerful, flavourful, toasty, round tannins.

ANTONIO ALCARAZ 2009 TC
tempranillo, mazuelo

88 Colour: cherry, garnet rim. Nose: spicy, creamy oak, toasty, wet leather. Palate: powerful, flavourful, toasty, round tannins.

GLORIA ANTONIO ALCARAZ 2009 TC
tempranillo

90 Colour: cherry, garnet rim. Nose: ripe fruit, spicy, creamy oak, toasty, complex. Palate: powerful, flavourful, toasty, round tannins.

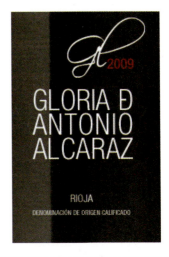

LES FONTS D'ALGAR ANTONIO ALCARAZ 2010 TC

91 Colour: bright cherry. Nose: ripe fruit, sweet spices, creamy oak, expressive, powerfull. Palate: flavourful, fruity, toasty, round tannins.

LES FONTS D'ALGAR SELECCIÓN 2010 T

90 Colour: cherry, garnet rim. Nose: spicy, creamy oak, toasty, powerfull, overripe fruit. Palate: powerful, flavourful, toasty, round tannins.

LES FONTS D'ALGAR

RIOJA
Denominación de Origen Calificada

El esmero con el que se seleccionan y recolectan los mejores racimos de uva tempranillo y una reposada maduración de 18 meses en bodega con trasiegos realizados en menguante de luna, sustentan y casi garantizan la excelente calidad de este vino. Los paladares más exigentes, también notan las dosis de cariño que se añaden en su elaboración.

SELECCIÓN PERSONAL
ANTONIO ALCARAZ

Botella nº 001/1000

BODEGAS ARACO

Ctra. Lapuebla, s/n
1300 Laguardia (Álava)
☎: +34 945 600 209 - Fax: +34 945 600 067
www.bodegasaraco.com
araco@bodegasaraco.com

ARACO 2005 TR
100% tempranillo

85 Colour: pale ruby, brick rim edge. Nose: spicy, fine reductive notes, wet leather, aged wood nuances, fruit liqueur notes. Palate: spicy, long, toasty.

ARACO 2010 TC
100% tempranillo

85 Colour: cherry, garnet rim. Nose: ripe fruit, spicy, creamy oak, toasty. Palate: powerful, flavourful, toasty.

ARACO 2012 B
100% viura

87 Colour: bright straw. Nose: ripe fruit, grassy, dried herbs. Palate: flavourful, good acidity.

ARACO 2012 T
100% tempranillo

88 Colour: deep cherry. Nose: violets, fruit expression, varietal, powerfull, fresh. Palate: powerful, flavourful, fresh, fruity.

ARACO 25 ANIVERSARIO 2005 T
100% tempranillo

90 Colour: cherry, garnet rim. Nose: ripe fruit, spicy, creamy oak, toasty, complex, earthy notes. Palate: powerful, flavourful, toasty, round tannins.

ARACO COLECCIÓN 2008 T
100% tempranillo

86 Colour: cherry, garnet rim. Nose: fruit preserve, spicy, woody, balsamic herbs. Palate: flavourful, powerful, oaky.

BODEGAS BASAGOITI

Torrent, 38
8391 Tiana (Barcelona)
☎: +34 933 950 811 - Fax: +34 933 955 500
www.basagoiti.es
info@parxet.es

BASAGOITI 2010 TC
tempranillo, garnacha

91 Colour: cherry, garnet rim. Nose: ripe fruit, spicy, creamy oak, toasty, complex. Palate: powerful, flavourful, toasty, round tannins.

BUHO CHICO 2012 T
tempranillo

87 Colour: cherry, garnet rim. Nose: red berry notes, ripe fruit, balsamic herbs, spicy. Palate: powerful, flavourful, correct.

FUERA DEL REBAÑO 2011 T
tempranillo

90 Colour: bright cherry, garnet rim. Nose: ripe fruit, sweet spices, creamy oak, expressive. Palate: flavourful, fruity, toasty, round tannins.

NABARI 2012 T
tempranillo, garnacha

89 Colour: cherry, purple rim. Nose: red berry notes, ripe fruit, scrubland. Palate: powerful, flavourful, easy to drink.

BODEGAS BENJAMÍN DE ROTHS- CHILD & VEGA SICILIA S.A.

Ctra. Logroño - Vitoria, km. 61
1309 Leza (Alava)
☎: +34 983 680 147 - Fax: +983 680 263
www.vegasicilia.com
irodriguez@vega-sicilia.com

MACÁN 2010 T
100% tempranillo

96 Colour: cherry, garnet rim. Nose: ripe fruit, spicy, creamy oak, toasty, complex, mineral, earthy notes. Palate: powerful, flavourful, toasty, round tannins.

MACÁN CLÁSICO 2010 T
100% tempranillo

95 Colour: cherry, garnet rim. Nose: ripe fruit, spicy, creamy oak, toasty, complex. Palate: powerful, flavourful, toasty, round tannins.

BODEGAS BERBERANA

Ctra. El Ciego s/n
26350 Cenicero (La Rioja)
☎: +34 913 878 612
www.berberana.com
abasilio@unitedwineries.com

BERBERANA CARTA DE ORO 2008 TR
80% tempranillo, 20% garnacha

86 Colour: pale ruby, brick rim edge. Nose: spicy, fine reductive notes, wet leather, aged wood nuances, fruit liqueur notes. Palate: spicy, long, easy to drink.

BERBERANA VIÑA ALARDE 2008 TR
80% tempranillo, 20% garnacha

86 Colour: pale ruby, brick rim edge. Nose: spicy, fine reductive notes, wet leather, aged wood nuances, fruit liqueur notes. Palate: long, spicy, balsamic.

BODEGAS BERCEO

Cuevas, 32-34-36
26200 Haro (La Rioja)
☎: +34 941 310 744 - Fax: +34 948 670 259
www.gurpegui.es
bodegas@gurpegui.es

BERCEO "NUEVA GENERACIÓN" 2010 TC
tempranillo, graciano, mazuelo

90 Colour: bright cherry. Nose: ripe fruit, sweet spices. Palate: flavourful, fruity, toasty, round tannins.

BERCEO SELECCIÓN 2010 T
tempranillo, mazuelo, graciano

91 Colour: cherry, garnet rim. Nose: powerfull, ripe fruit, toasty, sweet spices. Palate: powerful, flavourful, spicy, ripe fruit.

GONZALO DE BERCEO 2005 TGR
tempranillo, graciano, mazuelo

88 Colour: cherry, garnet rim. Nose: fruit liqueur notes, spicy. Palate: correct, long, round tannins.

GONZALO DE BERCEO 2008 TR
tempranillo, graciano, mazuelo, garnacha

88 Colour: cherry, garnet rim. Nose: spicy, creamy oak, toasty, wet leather. Palate: powerful, flavourful, toasty, round tannins.

LOS DOMINIOS DE BERCEO "RESERVA 36" 2008 TR
tempranillo

89 Colour: cherry, garnet rim. Nose: fruit expression, ripe fruit, toasty. Palate: fine bitter notes, spicy, long, harsh oak tannins.

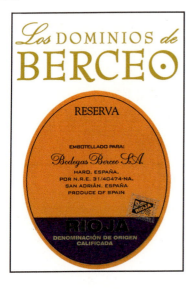

LOS DOMINIOS DE BERCEO 2012 T
tempranillo

89 Colour: deep cherry. Nose: fruit preserve, toasty, sweet spices. Palate: powerful, concentrated, round tannins.

VIÑA BERCEO 2010 TC
tempranillo, garnacha, graciano

91 Colour: cherry, garnet rim. Nose: ripe fruit, spicy, creamy oak, toasty, complex. Palate: powerful, flavourful, toasty, round tannins.

BODEGAS BERONIA

Ctra. Ollauri - Nájera, Km. 1,8
26220 Ollauri (La Rioja)
☎: +34 941 338 000 - Fax: +34 941 338 266
www.beronia.es
beronia@beronia.es

BERONIA 2006 TGR
92% tempranillo, 4% mazuelo, 4% graciano

90 Colour: pale ruby, brick rim edge. Nose: fine reductive notes, wet leather, ripe fruit, expressive. Palate: spicy, elegant, long, balanced.

BERONIA 2008 TR
93% tempranillo, 5% graciano, 2% mazuelo

89 Colour: cherry, garnet rim. Nose: ripe fruit, spicy, fine reductive notes, wet leather. Palate: powerful, flavourful, spicy, long.

BERONIA 2010 TC
88% tempranillo, 10% garnacha, 2% mazuelo

88 Colour: cherry, garnet rim. Nose: ripe fruit, creamy oak, toasty. Palate: powerful, flavourful, toasty.

BERONIA GRACIANO 2010 T
100% graciano

89 Colour: cherry, purple rim. Nose: red berry notes, ripe fruit, balsamic herbs, spicy, creamy oak. Palate: powerful, flavourful, spicy, toasty.

BERONIA MAZUELO 2008 TR
100% mazuelo

88 Colour: cherry, garnet rim. Nose: ripe fruit, spicy, creamy oak, fine reductive notes. Palate: powerful, flavourful, toasty.

BERONIA SELECCIÓN 198 BARRICAS 2006 TR
90% tempranillo, 9% mazuelo, 1% graciano

91 Colour: pale ruby, brick rim edge. Nose: elegant, spicy, fine reductive notes, wet leather, aged wood nuances, fruit liqueur notes. Palate: spicy, fine tannins, elegant, long.

BERONIA TEMPRANILLO ELABORACIÓN ESPECIAL 2011 T
100% tempranillo

90 Colour: bright cherry. Nose: ripe fruit, sweet spices, creamy oak, toasty. Palate: flavourful, fruity, toasty.

BERONIA VIÑAS VIEJAS 2010 T
100% tempranillo

90 Colour: cherry, garnet rim. Nose: ripe fruit, spicy, balsamic herbs. Palate: fruity, flavourful, good acidity, balanced.

III A.C., BERONIA 2010 T
94% tempranillo, 3% graciano, 3% mazuelo

92 Colour: cherry, garnet rim. Nose: ripe fruit, balsamic herbs, aromatic coffee, creamy oak. Palate: rich, powerful, flavourful, balanced.

BODEGAS BILBAÍNAS

Estación, 3
26200 Haro (La Rioja)
☎: +34 941 310 147
www.bodegasbilbainas.com
m.oyono@bodegasbilbainas.com

BODEGAS BILBAINAS GARNACHA 2010 T
100% garnacha

92 Colour: cherry, garnet rim. Nose: sweet spices, balsamic herbs, balanced. Palate: good structure, full, round tannins, good acidity.

BODEGAS BILBAINAS GRACIANO 2007 T
100% graciano

91 Colour: dark-red cherry, garnet rim. Nose: tobacco, fine reductive notes, candied fruit, powerfull, varietal, creamy oak, toasty, spicy. Palate: powerful, flavourful, spirituous, good structure, spicy.

LA VICALANDA 2005 TGR
100% tempranillo

93 Colour: deep cherry. Nose: fruit preserve, powerfull, expressive, spicy, sweet spices, cocoa bean, tobacco, premature reduction notes. Palate: powerful, spicy, creamy.

LA VICALANDA 2008 TR
100% tempranillo

91 Colour: dark-red cherry. Nose: candied fruit, red berry notes, cocoa bean, spicy, creamy oak. Palate: powerful, flavourful, creamy, spicy.

VIÑA POMAL "ALTO DE LA CASETA" 2008 T
100% tempranillo

90 Colour: deep cherry. Nose: roasted coffee, spicy, caramel, ripe fruit. Palate: good structure, powerful, flavourful, creamy, toasty, roasted-coffee aftertaste.

VIÑA POMAL 2004 TGR
90% tempranillo, 10% graciano

92 Colour: deep cherry. Nose: fruit preserve, creamy oak, spicy, cedar wood, fine reductive notes, tobacco. Palate: powerful, full, flavourful, round, spicy, creamy.

VIÑA POMAL 2008 TR
100% tempranillo

89 Colour: deep cherry. Nose: powerfull, expressive, caramel, spicy, creamy oak, macerated fruit. Palate: powerful, flavourful, dry, spicy.

VIÑA POMAL 2010 TC
100% tempranillo

88 Colour: dark-red cherry, orangey edge. Nose: spicy, creamy oak, fruit preserve. Palate: fruity, powerful, flavourful, creamy, spicy.

VIÑA ZACO 2010 T
100% tempranillo

90 Colour: deep cherry. Nose: elegant, powerfull, toasty, creamy oak, spicy. Palate: powerful, flavourful, spicy, balsamic.

BODEGAS CAMPILLO

Ctra. de Logroño, s/n
1300 Laguardia (Álava)
☎: +34 945 600 826 - Fax: +34 945 600 837
www.bodegascampillo.es
info@bodegascampillo.es

CAMPILLO 2001 TGR
95% tempranillo, 5% graciano

90 Colour: deep cherry, garnet rim. Nose: expressive, balanced, ripe fruit, dark chocolate, creamy oak. Palate: good structure, flavourful.

CAMPILLO 2009 TC
100% tempranillo

90 Colour: cherry, garnet rim. Nose: ripe fruit, spicy, creamy oak, toasty. Palate: powerful, flavourful, toasty.

CAMPILLO 2012 BFB
85% viura, 10% malvasía, 5% chardonnay

90 Colour: bright straw. Nose: expressive, reduction notes, varietal, wild herbs, smoky, toasty. Palate: creamy, spicy, powerful, flavourful, fruity.

CAMPILLO 2012 RD
100% tempranillo

85 Colour: rose, purple rim. Nose: slightly evolved, fresh, medium intensity. Palate: fruity, fresh, flavourful.

CAMPILLO FINCA CUESTA CLARA 2005 TR
tempranillo

92 Colour: cherry, garnet rim. Nose: dark chocolate, fruit preserve, creamy oak. Palate: ripe fruit, long, flavourful, toasty, round tannins.

CAMPILLO RESERVA ESPECIAL 2005 TR
85% tempranillo, 10% graciano, 5% cabernet sauvignon

91 Colour: cherry, garnet rim. Nose: ripe fruit, spicy, cocoa bean. Palate: powerful, flavourful, toasty, round tannins.

CAMPILLO RESERVA SELECTA 2005 TR
100% tempranillo

93 Colour: bright cherry, garnet rim. Nose: spicy, ripe fruit, balanced. Palate: flavourful, good acidity, round tannins.

BODEGAS CAMPO VIEJO

Camino de la Puebla, 50
26006 Logroño (La Rioja)
☎: +34 941 273 500 - Fax: +34 941 293 501
www.campoviejo.com
campoviejo@pernod-ricard.com

ALCORTA & FRIENDS 2012 RD

85 Colour: rose, purple rim. Nose: macerated fruit, fragrant herbs. Palate: spirituous, powerful, flavourful, fine bitter notes, slightly tart, fruity.

ALCORTA & FRIENDS 2012 T
tempranillo

86 Colour: deep cherry. Nose: varietal, powerfull, neat, fresh, fresh fruit. Palate: fruity, dry, flavourful, lacks expression.

ALCORTA 2008 TR
tempranillo

88 Colour: deep cherry. Nose: dark chocolate, ripe fruit, toasty. Palate: spicy, ripe fruit, good acidity, fine bitter notes.

ALCORTA 2009 TC
tempranillo

89 Colour: cherry, garnet rim. Nose: spicy, creamy oak, toasty. Palate: powerful, flavourful, toasty, round tannins.

ALCORTA GARNACHA 2012 T
garnacha

86 Colour: cherry, purple rim. Nose: red berry notes, floral, ripe fruit, wild herbs. Palate: flavourful, fruity, good acidity, round tannins.

AZPILICUETA 2008 TR
tempranillo, graciano, mazuelo

91 Colour: cherry, garnet rim. Nose: ripe fruit, spicy, creamy oak, toasty. Palate: powerful, flavourful, toasty, round tannins.

AZPILICUETA 2010 TC
tempranillo, graciano, mazuelo

92 Colour: cherry, garnet rim. Nose: toasty, complex, red berry notes, ripe fruit, sweet spices, creamy oak. Palate: powerful, flavourful, toasty, balanced.

AZPILICUETA 2012 B
viura

90 Colour: bright straw. Nose: fresh, fresh fruit, white flowers, expressive. Palate: flavourful, fruity, good acidity, balanced.

CAMPO VIEJO 2005 TGR
tempranillo, graciano, mazuelo

89 Colour: cherry, garnet rim. Nose: spicy, creamy oak, toasty, ripe fruit. Palate: powerful, flavourful, toasty, round tannins.

CAMPO VIEJO 2008 TR
tempranillo, graciano, mazuelo

87 Colour: cherry, garnet rim. Nose: ripe fruit, balsamic herbs, aged wood nuances, toasty, fine reductive notes. Palate: powerful, flavourful, spicy.

CAMPO VIEJO 2009 TC
tempranillo, garnacha, mazuelo

88 Colour: bright cherry. Nose: sweet spices, creamy oak. Palate: flavourful, fruity, toasty, round tannins.

CAMPO VIEJO 2012 B
viura

85 Colour: straw. Nose: fresh fruit, grassy, fresh, neat. Palate: fresh, fruity, flavourful.

CAMPO VIEJO ROSÉ 2012 RD
tempranillo, viura

87 Colour: coppery red. Nose: candied fruit, red berry notes, sweet spices, creamy oak. Palate: flavourful, spicy, ripe fruit, easy to drink.

CAMPO VIEJO S/C RD
tempranillo

79

CAMPO VIEJO SEMIDULCE
viura

82

CV DE CAMPO VIEJO 2009 TC
tempranillo, garnacha, graciano

88 Colour: cherry, garnet rim. Nose: ripe fruit, spicy, varietal. Palate: flavourful, round tannins, easy to drink.

CV DE CAMPO VIEJO 2012 B
viura

88 Colour: bright straw. Nose: ripe fruit, tropical fruit. Palate: flavourful, fruity, good acidity, spicy.

CV DE CAMPO VIEJO 2012 RD
tempranillo

85 Colour: rose, purple rim. Nose: powerfull, ripe fruit, red berry notes, floral. Palate: powerful, fruity, fresh.

DOMINIO CAMPO VIEJO 2007 T
tempranillo, graciano, mazuelo

90 Colour: cherry, garnet rim. Nose: ripe fruit, spicy, complex. Palate: powerful, flavourful, round tannins, balanced.

FÉLIX AZPILICUETA COLECCIÓN PRIVADA 2008 T
tempranillo, graciano, mazuelo

93 Colour: deep cherry, garnet rim. Nose: balanced, expressive, balsamic herbs, ripe fruit. Palate: balanced, round tannins.

FÉLIX AZPILICUETA COLECCIÓN PRIVADA 2012 B
viura

90 Colour: bright straw. Nose: powerfull, expressive, creamy oak, ripe fruit. Palate: powerful, flavourful, fruity, fresh, creamy.

BODEGAS CASA PRIMICIA

Camino de la Hoya, 1
1300 Laguardia (Álava)
☎: +34 945 600 296 - Fax: +34 945 621 252
www.bodegasprimicia.com
info@bodegascasaprimicia.com

JULIÁN MADRID 2008 TR
80% tempranillo, 20% otras

87 Colour: cherry, garnet rim. Nose: creamy oak, toasty, fruit preserve. Palate: powerful, flavourful, toasty, balanced.

VIÑA DIEZMO 2007 TR
100% tempranillo

87 Colour: cherry, garnet rim. Nose: ripe fruit, fruit preserve, scrubland, spicy, fine reductive notes. Palate: powerful, flavourful, spicy, correct.

VIÑA DIEZMO 2010 TC
100% tempranillo

88 Colour: cherry, garnet rim. Nose: ripe fruit, balsamic herbs, spicy, creamy oak, toasty, damp earth. Palate: powerful, flavourful, spicy, long.

BODEGAS CASTILLO DE MENDOZA, S.L.

Paraje San Juan, s/n
26338 San Vicente de la Sonsierra (La Rioja)
☎: +34 941 334 496 - Fax: +34 941 334 566
www.castillomendoza.com
bodegas@castillodemendoza.com

CASTILLO DE MENDOZA 2006 TR
100% tempranillo

88 Colour: black cherry. Nose: ripe fruit, spicy, creamy oak, toasty. Palate: powerful, flavourful, toasty, round tannins.

EVENTO CASTILLO DE MENDOZA 2006 T
100% tempranillo

90 Colour: cherry, garnet rim. Nose: balanced, ripe fruit, wild herbs, spicy. Palate: good structure, round tannins.

MOMILDE VENDIMIA SELECCIÓN 2008 TC
100% tempranillo

88 Colour: deep cherry, garnet rim. Nose: ripe fruit, cocoa bean, dried herbs. Palate: ripe fruit, correct, balanced.

NORALBA AGRICULTURA ECOLÓGICA 2010 TC
95% tempranillo, 5% graciano

87 Colour: deep cherry, garnet rim. Nose: powerfull, cocoa bean, ripe fruit. Palate: flavourful, round tannins.

VIÑA VITARÁN 2008 TC
tempranillo

86 Colour: cherry, garnet rim. Nose: medium intensity, ripe fruit, dried herbs. Palate: fruity, easy to drink, good finish.

VITARÁN 2011 B
100% viura

80

BODEGAS CASTILLO DE SAJAZARRA

Del Río, s/n
26212 Sajazarra (La Rioja)
☎: +34 941 320 066 - Fax: +34 941 320 251
www.castillodesajazarra.com
bodega@castillodesajazarra.com

CASTILLO DE SAJAZARRA 2006 TR
100% tempranillo

90 Colour: deep cherry. Nose: fruit liqueur notes, creamy oak, toasty, characterful. Palate: spicy, ripe fruit, fine bitter notes.

DIGMA 2006 TR
100% tempranillo

93 Colour: cherry, garnet rim. Nose: ripe fruit, spicy, creamy oak, mineral, fine reductive notes. Palate: powerful, flavourful, toasty, round tannins.

SOLAR DE LÍBANO 2008 TR
97% tempranillo, 3% graciano, garnacha

90 Colour: cherry, garnet rim. Nose: balanced, spicy, ripe fruit. Palate: good structure, round tannins, spicy.

SOLAR DE LÍBANO 2009 TC
97% tempranillo, 3% graciano, garnacha

89 Colour: cherry, garnet rim. Nose: dry stone, ripe fruit, dried herbs. Palate: flavourful, ripe fruit, round tannins.

SOLAR DE LÍBANO 2010 TC
94% tempranillo, 6% graciano

87 Colour: bright cherry. Nose: sweet spices, creamy oak, fruit expression. Palate: flavourful, fruity, toasty, round tannins.

BODEGAS CERROLAZA

Ctra. Navarrete, 1
26372 Hornos de Moncalvillo (La Rioja)
☎: +34 941 286 728 - Fax: +34 941 286 729
www.altosdelmarques.com
info@altosdelmarques.com

ATICUS 2006 TR
100% tempranillo

86 Colour: pale ruby, brick rim edge. Nose: ripe fruit, balsamic herbs, wet leather, tobacco. Palate: powerful, flavourful, toasty.

ATICUS 2008 T
100% tempranillo

87 Colour: cherry, garnet rim. Nose: ripe fruit, spicy, creamy oak, toasty. Palate: powerful, flavourful, toasty.

ATICUS 2009 TC
100% tempranillo

86 Colour: cherry, garnet rim. Nose: ripe fruit, spicy, creamy oak, toasty, complex. Palate: powerful, flavourful, spicy.

BODEGAS CORRAL

Ctra. de Logroño, Km. 10
26370 Navarrete (La Rioja)
☎: +34 941 440 193 - Fax: +34 941 440 195
www.donjacobo.es
info@donjacobo.es

ALTOS DE CORRAL SINGLE ESTATE 2004 TR
100% tempranillo

89 Colour: deep cherry. Nose: roasted coffee, dark chocolate, candied fruit. Palate: powerful, concentrated, flavourful, creamy, spicy.

DON JACOBO 1996 TGR
85% tempranillo, 15% garnacha

87 Colour: dark-red cherry, brick rim edge. Nose: waxy notes, tobacco, old leather. Palate: spicy, toasty, good structure, lacks expression.

DON JACOBO 2005 TR
90% tempranillo, 10% garnacha, mazuelo

87 Colour: deep cherry. Nose: slightly evolved, overripe fruit, sweet spices, aromatic coffee. Palate: powerful, spirituous, oaky, spicy, toasty.

DON JACOBO 2008 TC
85% tempranillo, 10% garnacha, 5% mazuelo, graciano

84

DON JACOBO 2012 B
100% viura

84

DON JACOBO 2012 RD
60% tempranillo, 40% garnacha

85 Colour: light cherry, bright. Nose: ripe fruit, faded flowers, lactic notes, dried herbs. Palate: correct, easy to drink.

BODEGAS COVILA

Camino del Soto, 26
1306 La Puebla de Labarca (Álava)
☎: +34 945 627 232 - Fax: +34 945 627 295
www.covila.es
comercial@covila.es

COVILA 2006 TR
100% tempranillo

89 Colour: cherry, garnet rim. Nose: ripe fruit, waxy notes, wet leather, spicy, toasty. Palate: powerful, flavourful, toasty, long.

COVILA 2009 TC
100% tempranillo

88 Colour: cherry, garnet rim. Nose: ripe fruit, spicy, creamy oak. Palate: powerful, flavourful, toasty, harsh oak tannins.

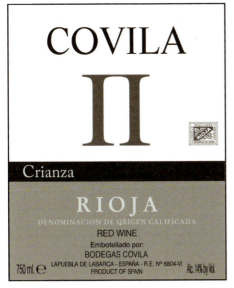

BODEGAS CRUZ VALLE

Santa Engracia, 52
1300 Laguardia (Álava)
☎: +34 605 039 811
www.cruzvalle.com
bodega@cruzvalle.com

CRUZ VALLE 2009 TC
100% tempranillo

87 Colour: cherry, garnet rim. Nose: spicy, toasty, aromatic coffee. Palate: flavourful, powerful, concentrated.

CRUZ VALLE 2012 T MACERACIÓN CARBÓNICA
100% tempranillo

88 Colour: cherry, purple rim. Nose: red berry notes, raspberry, fruit liqueur notes, balsamic herbs. Palate: fresh, fruity, flavourful.

BODEGAS DAVID MORENO

Ctra. de Villar de Torre, s/n
26310 Badarán (La Rioja)
☎: +34 941 367 338 - Fax: +34 941 418 685
www.davidmoreno.es
davidmoreno@davidmoreno.es

DAVID MORENO 2005 TGR
90% tempranillo, 10% garnacha

90 Colour: pale ruby, brick rim edge. Nose: elegant, spicy, fine reductive notes, wet leather, aged wood nuances, fruit liqueur notes. Palate: spicy, fine tannins, long.

DAVID MORENO 2007 TR
90% tempranillo, 10% garnacha

88 Colour: pale ruby, brick rim edge. Nose: ripe fruit, balsamic herbs, spicy, creamy oak, wet leather, tobacco. Palate: flavourful, spicy, long.

DAVID MORENO 2010 TC
85% tempranillo, 15% garnacha

89 Colour: cherry, garnet rim. Nose: ripe fruit, spicy, creamy oak, toasty, complex. Palate: powerful, flavourful, toasty, round tannins.

DAVID MORENO 2012 B
100% viura

85 Colour: bright straw. Nose: ripe fruit, dried flowers. Palate: flavourful, fruity, good acidity.

DAVID MORENO 2012 RD
50% viura, 50% garnacha

86 Colour: coppery red. Nose: medium intensity, fruit expression, ripe fruit. Palate: fruity, fresh.

DAVID MORENO 2012 T
85% tempranillo, 15% garnacha

88 Colour: dark-red cherry. Nose: powerfull, reduction notes, fresh, macerated fruit. Palate: powerful, flavourful, sweetness, spirituous, fruity.

DMORENO SELECCIÓN DE LA FAMILIA 2008 TC
90% tempranillo, 10% garnacha

89 Colour: bright cherry. Nose: ripe fruit, sweet spices, creamy oak, balsamic herbs. Palate: flavourful, fruity, toasty, round tannins, balanced.

BODEGAS DE CRIANZA MARQUÉS DE GRIÑÓN

Ctra. de El Ciego, s/n
26350 Cenicero (La Rioja)
☎: +34 913 878 612
abasilio@unitedwineries.com

MARQUÉS DE GRIÑÓN ALEA 2009 TC
100% tempranillo

87 Colour: cherry, garnet rim. Nose: ripe fruit, scrubland, spicy, fine reductive notes. Palate: powerful, flavourful, spicy.

BODEGAS DE LOS HEREDEROS DEL MARQUÉS DE RISCAL S.L.

Torrea, 1
1340 Elciego (Álava)
☎: +34 945 606 000
www.marquesderiscal.com
marketing@marquesderiscal.com

ARIENZO 2010 TC
tempranillo, graciano, mazuelo

90 Colour: cherry, garnet rim. Nose: spicy, creamy oak, toasty, complex, fruit expression. Palate: powerful, flavourful, toasty, round tannins.

BARÓN DE CHIREL 2010 TR
70% tempranillo, 30% otras

93 Colour: cherry, garnet rim. Nose: ripe fruit, spicy, creamy oak, characterful, roasted coffee. Palate: powerful, flavourful, toasty, round tannins.

FINCA TORREA 2010 T
tempranillo, graciano

94 Colour: cherry, garnet rim. Nose: spicy, creamy oak, toasty, complex, mineral, fruit expression. Palate: powerful, flavourful, toasty, round tannins.

MARQUÉS DE RISCAL 150 ANIVERSARIO 2004 TGR
tempranillo, graciano, otras

93 Colour: pale ruby, brick rim edge. Nose: elegant, spicy, fine reductive notes, wet leather, aged wood nuances, fruit liqueur notes. Palate: spicy, fine tannins, elegant, long.

MARQUÉS DE RISCAL 2008 TR
90% tempranillo, 10% graciano, mazuelo

90 Colour: cherry, garnet rim. Nose: spicy, creamy oak, toasty, ripe fruit. Palate: powerful, flavourful, toasty, round tannins.

BODEGAS DE SANTIAGO

Avda. del Ebro, 50
1307 Baños de Ebro (Álava)
☎: +34 945 609 201 - Fax: +34 945 609 201
www.bodegasdesantiago.es
info@bodegasdesantiago.es

LAGAR DE SANTIAGO 2010 TC
tempranillo

88 Colour: cherry, purple rim. Nose: toasty, spicy, dried herbs. Palate: flavourful, ripe fruit, round tannins.

LAGAR DE SANTIAGO 2012 BFB
viura, verdejo

86 Colour: bright straw. Nose: fresh, fresh fruit, white flowers. Palate: flavourful, good acidity, balanced.

LAGAR DE SANTIAGO 2012 T MACERACIÓN CARBÓNICA
tempranillo, viura

87 Colour: very deep cherry, purple rim. Nose: red berry notes, ripe fruit, floral. Palate: flavourful, fruity.

BODEGAS DEL MEDIEVO

Circunvalación San Roque, s/n
26559 Aldeanueva de Ebro (La Rioja)
☎: +34 941 163 141 - Fax: +34 941 144 204
www.bodegasdelmedievo.com
info@bodegasdelmedievo.com

COFRADE 2012 T
tempranillo

87 Colour: cherry, purple rim. Nose: medium intensity, ripe fruit, violet drops. Palate: ripe fruit, easy to drink, round tannins.

MEDIEVO 2007 TGR
90% tempranillo, 10% graciano

88 Colour: cherry, garnet rim. Nose: ripe fruit, spicy, creamy oak, toasty, complex. Palate: powerful, flavourful, toasty, round tannins.

MEDIEVO 2007 TR
80% tempranillo, 10% garnacha, 5% mazuelo, 5% graciano

88 Colour: deep cherry. Nose: creamy oak, roasted coffee, ripe fruit. Palate: powerful tannins, flavourful, fruity, creamy, spicy.

MEDIEVO 2009 TC
80% tempranillo, 10% garnacha, 5% mazuelo, 5% graciano

88 Colour: dark-red cherry. Nose: fresh, sweet spices, spicy, toasty, roasted coffee. Palate: fruity, powerful, flavourful.

TUERCE BOTAS 2010 TC
100% graciano

88 Colour: deep cherry. Nose: sweet spices, toasty, damp undergrowth. Palate: spirituous, good structure, powerful, flavourful, varietal, balsamic, toasty.

TUERCEBOTAS 2012 B
tempranillo blanco

89 Colour: bright yellow. Nose: dried flowers, balsamic herbs, ripe fruit, tropical fruit. Palate: rich, flavourful, long, balsamic, spicy.

BODEGAS DINASTÍA VIVANCO

Ctra. Nacional 232, s/n
26330 Briones (La Rioja)
☎: +34 941 322 013 - Fax: +34 941 322 316
www.dinastiavivanco.com

COLECCIÓN VIVANCO 4 VARIETALES 2010 T
70% tempranillo, 15% graciano, 10% garnacha, 5% mazuelo

90 Colour: deep cherry. Nose: reduction notes, fruit preserve, sweet spices, toasty. Palate: powerful, flavourful, fruity, creamy, spicy, pruney.

COLECCIÓN VIVANCO 4 VARIETALES DULCE DE INVIERNO 2010 T
50% tempranillo, 20% graciano, 20% garnacha, 10% mazuelo

95 Colour: pale ruby, brick rim edge. Nose: candied fruit, red berry notes, fruit preserve. Palate: sweetness, full, flavourful, round.

COLECCIÓN VIVANCO 4 VARIETALES DULCE DE INVIERNO 2011 T
tempranillo, graciano, garnacha, mazuelo

92 Colour: pale ruby, brick rim edge. Nose: fruit liqueur notes, candied fruit, fruit liqueur notes, sweet spices. Palate: good acidity, long, ripe fruit.

COLECCIÓN VIVANCO PARCELAS DE GARNACHA 2010 T
100% garnacha

92 Colour: dark-red cherry, garnet rim. Nose: spicy, cocoa bean, fruit expression, varietal, complex. Palate: creamy, ripe fruit, balsamic, flavourful, powerful.

COLECCIÓN VIVANCO PARCELAS DE GRACIANO 2008 T
100% graciano

91 Colour: deep cherry. Nose: spicy, aged wood nuances, fruit preserve. Palate: complex, good structure, fruity, fresh, varietal.

COLECCIÓN VIVANCO PARCELAS DE MATURANA 2010 T
100% maturana

93 Colour: deep cherry. Nose: violet drops, fruit expression, sweet spices, cocoa bean. Palate: flavourful, powerful, varietal, fruity, complex.

COLECCIÓN VIVANCO PARCELAS DE MAZUELO 2011 T
100% mazuelo

88 Nose: spicy, creamy oak, toasty, fruit preserve. Palate: powerful, flavourful, fruity, spicy, roasted-coffee aftertaste.

DINASTÍA VIVANCO 2007 TR
90% tempranillo, 10% graciano

88 Colour: dark-red cherry. Nose: medium intensity, reduction notes, creamy oak, spicy. Palate: creamy, spicy, flavourful.

DINASTÍA VIVANCO 2009 TC
100% tempranillo

89 Colour: dark-red cherry, orangey edge. Nose: cocoa bean, spicy, ripe fruit. Palate: balanced, round, flavourful, rich, fruity.

VIVANCO TEMPRANILLO GARNACHA 2012 RD
80% tempranillo, 20% garnacha

90 Colour: rose, purple rim. Nose: powerfull, red berry notes, floral, expressive. Palate: powerful, fruity, fresh.

VIVANCO VIURA MALVASÍA TEMPRANILLO BLANCO 2012 B
60% viura, 20% malvasía, 20% tempranillo blanco

88 Colour: bright straw. Nose: fruit expression, fragrant herbs, balanced, expressive, neat, fresh. Palate: elegant, balanced, powerful, flavourful, light-bodied.

BODEGAS DOMECO DE JARAUTA

Camino Sendero Royal, 5
26559 Aldeanueva de Ebro (La Rioja)
☎: +34 941 163 078 - Fax: +34 941 163 078
www.bodegasdomecodejarauta.com
info@bodegasdomecodejarauta.com

VIÑA MARRO 2008 TR
85% tempranillo, 10% graciano, 5% mazuelo

86 Colour: cherry, garnet rim. Nose: ripe fruit, spicy, fine reductive notes. Palate: powerful, flavourful, toasty.

VIÑA MARRO 2010 TC
100% tempranillo

85 Colour: cherry, garnet rim. Nose: ripe fruit, spicy, creamy oak, toasty, woody. Palate: powerful, flavourful, toasty.

VIÑA MARRO ECOLÓGICO 2011 T
100% tempranillo

90 Colour: cherry, purple rim. Nose: red berry notes, fruit liqueur notes, balsamic herbs, expressive. Palate: rich, flavourful, fresh, fruity, easy to drink.

VIÑA MARRO VENDIMIA SELECCIONADA 2011 T
90% tempranillo, 10% graciano

90 Colour: bright cherry. Nose: ripe fruit, sweet spices, cocoa bean, balsamic herbs. Palate: flavourful, fruity, toasty.

BODEGAS DUNVIRO

Ctra. Logroño, Km. 362
26500 Calahorra (La Rioja)
☎: +34 941 130 626 - Fax: +34 941 130 626
www.bodegasdunviro.com
info@bodegasdunviro.com

DUNVIRO 2007 TR
90% tempranillo, 10% graciano

87 Colour: cherry, garnet rim. Nose: ripe fruit, spicy, cocoa bean, toasty, fine reductive notes, wild herbs. Palate: flavourful, long, balsamic.

DUNVIRO 2011 BFB
viura

87 Colour: bright yellow. Nose: ripe fruit, sweet spices, creamy oak. Palate: rich, flavourful, fresh, good acidity.

DUNVIRO 2012 RD
garnacha

87 Colour: rose, purple rim. Nose: ripe fruit, red berry notes, floral, expressive. Palate: powerful, fruity, fresh.

DUNVIRO TEMPRANILLO 2012 T
tempranillo

84

DUNVIRO VENDIMIA SELECCIONADA 2012 T
tempranillo

88 Colour: bright cherry. Nose: ripe fruit, sweet spices, creamy oak. Palate: flavourful, toasty, easy to drink.

DUNVIRO VIÑAS VIEJAS 2010 TC
80% tempranillo, 20% graciano

89 Colour: cherry, garnet rim. Nose: ripe fruit, spicy, creamy oak, toasty. Palate: powerful, flavourful, toasty.

DUNVIRO VIURA 2012 B
viura

87 Colour: pale. Nose: ripe fruit, white flowers. Palate: flavourful, good acidity.

BODEGAS EL CIDACOS

Ctra. de Carbonera, s/n
26512 Tudelilla (La Rioja)
☎: +34 941 152 058 - Fax: +34 941 152 303
www.bodegaselcidacos.com
info@bodegaselcidacos.com

CONDE OTIÑANO 2008 TR
tempranillo, garnacha, graciano

85 Colour: deep cherry. Nose: dark chocolate, sweet spices. Palate: flavourful, fine bitter notes, good acidity.

CONDE OTIÑANO 2010 TC
tempranillo, garnacha

87 Colour: deep cherry. Nose: fruit liqueur notes, spicy, aromatic coffee. Palate: fine bitter notes, spicy, ripe fruit.

MARQUÉS DE ABADÍA 2007 TR
tempranillo, garnacha, graciano

86 Colour: cherry, garnet rim. Nose: spicy, creamy oak, toasty. Palate: powerful, flavourful, toasty, round tannins.

MARQUÉS DE ABADÍA 2009 TC
tempranillo, garnacha

87 Colour: deep cherry. Nose: fruit liqueur notes, spicy, toasty. Palate: flavourful, powerful, fine bitter notes, good acidity.

BODEGAS ESCUDERO

Ctra. de Arnedo, s/n
26587 Grávalos (La Rioja)
☎: +34 941 398 008 - Fax: +34 941 398 070
www.familiaescudero.com
info@familiaescudero.com

ARVUM 2005 T
100% vidau

91 Colour: cherry, garnet rim. Nose: ripe fruit, spicy, creamy oak, toasty, complex. Palate: powerful, flavourful, toasty, round tannins.

BECQUER 2010 T
70% tempranillo, 30% garnacha

88 Colour: deep cherry. Nose: powerfull, wet leather, toasty. Palate: powerful, flavourful, fine bitter notes.

BECQUER 2012 BFB
60% chardonnay, 40% viura

87 Colour: bright yellow. Nose: powerfull, ripe fruit, sweet spices, fragrant herbs. Palate: rich, flavourful, fresh, good acidity.

SOLAR DE BECQUER 2005 TR
70% tempranillo, 20% mazuelo, 10% garnacha

87 Colour: cherry, garnet rim. Nose: ripe fruit, creamy oak, roasted coffee, dark chocolate. Palate: powerful, flavourful, toasty, round tannins.

SOLAR DE BECQUER 2010 TC
70% tempranillo, 20% mazuelo, 10% garnacha

87 Colour: cherry, garnet rim. Nose: ripe fruit, spicy, toasty. Palate: powerful, flavourful, toasty, round tannins.

SOLAR DE BECQUER 2012 T
40% tempranillo, 60% garnacha

89 Colour: cherry, purple rim. Nose: floral, red berry notes. Palate: flavourful, fruity, good acidity, round tannins.

VIDAU 2005 T
75% tempranillo, 25% garnacha

90 Colour: cherry, garnet rim. Nose: ripe fruit, toasty, spicy. Palate: fine bitter notes, good acidity, spicy.

BODEGAS ESCUDERO & VALSACRO

Finca La Legua Ctra. N-232, Km. 364
26510 Pradejón (La Rioja)
☎: +34 947 398 008 - Fax: +34 941 398 070
www.familiaescudero.com
info@familiaescudero.com

VALSACRO 2010 T
40% vidau, 50% tempranillo, 10% mazuelo

88 Colour: cherry, garnet rim. Nose: ripe fruit, spicy, creamy oak. Palate: powerful, flavourful, toasty, round tannins.

VALSACRO DIORO 2005 T
100% vidau

90 Colour: cherry, garnet rim. Nose: spicy, toasty, characterful. Palate: powerful, flavourful, toasty, round tannins.

VALSACRO DIORO 2008 T
100% vidau

89 Colour: cherry, garnet rim. Nose: spicy, creamy oak, toasty, characterful. Palate: powerful, flavourful, toasty, round tannins.

BODEGAS EXOPTO

Ctra. de Elvillar, 26
1300 Laguardia (Álava)
☎: +34 650 213 993
www.exopto.net
info@exopto.net

BOZETO DE EXOPTO 2012 T
50% garnacha, 40% tempranillo, 10% graciano

87 Colour: very deep cherry, purple rim. Nose: ripe fruit, powerfull, balsamic herbs, damp earth. Palate: fruity, fine bitter notes, ripe fruit.

DOMINIO DEL VIENTO 2010 TC
80% tempranillo, 20% graciano

88 Colour: cherry, garnet rim. Nose: red berry notes, ripe fruit, balsamic herbs, sweet spices, creamy oak. Palate: powerful, flavourful, fruity.

EXOPTO 2010 T
60% graciano, 30% tempranillo, 10% garnacha

92 Colour: cherry, garnet rim. Nose: ripe fruit, spicy, creamy oak, toasty, complex. Palate: powerful, flavourful, toasty, round tannins.

HORIZONTE DE EXOPTO 2011 B
85% viura, 10% garnacha blanca, 5% malvasía

91 Colour: bright straw. Nose: fresh, fresh fruit, white flowers, expressive. Palate: flavourful, fruity, good acidity, balanced, spicy.

HORIZONTE DE EXOPTO 2011 T
80% tempranillo, 10% graciano, 10% garnacha

91 Colour: bright cherry. Nose: ripe fruit, sweet spices, creamy oak, expressive. Palate: flavourful, fruity, toasty, balanced.

BODEGAS FAUSTINO

Ctra. de Logroño, s/n
1320 Oyón (Álava)
☎: +34 945 622 500 - Fax: +34 945 622 511
www.bodegasfaustino.es
info@bodegasfaustino.es

FAUSTINO 2010 TC
100% tempranillo

87 Colour: cherry, garnet rim. Nose: ripe fruit, waxy notes, cigar, spicy, creamy oak. Palate: powerful, flavourful, spicy, long.

FAUSTINO DE AUTOR EDICIÓN ESPECIAL 2004 T
100% tempranillo

89 Colour: pale ruby, brick rim edge. Nose: spicy, aged wood nuances, fruit liqueur notes, waxy notes, tobacco. Palate: spicy, long, correct.

FAUSTINO DE AUTOR RESERVA ESPECIAL 2006 TR
86% tempranillo, 14% graciano

89 Colour: pale ruby, brick rim edge. Nose: spicy, fine reductive notes, wet leather, aged wood nuances, fruit liqueur notes. Palate: spicy, long, spirituous.

FAUSTINO I 2001 TGR
85% tempranillo, 10% graciano, 5% mazuelo

94 Colour: pale ruby, brick rim edge. Nose: elegant, spicy, fine reductive notes, wet leather, aged wood nuances, fruit liqueur notes. Palate: spicy, fine tannins, elegant, long.

FAUSTINO I 75 ANIVERSARIO 2004 TGR
92% tempranillo, 8% graciano

93 Colour: pale ruby, brick rim edge. Nose: ripe fruit, aged wood nuances, spicy, wet leather, tobacco. Palate: flavourful, spicy, correct, balanced, elegant.

FAUSTINO V 2008 TR
91% tempranillo, 9% mazuelo

86 Colour: cherry, garnet rim. Nose: ripe fruit, spicy, fine reductive notes, wet leather, tobacco. Palate: powerful, flavourful, spicy.

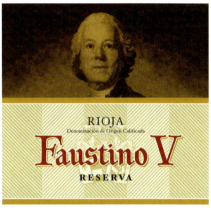

FAUSTINO V 2012 B
75% viura, 25% chardonnay

88 Colour: pale. Nose: fresh, expressive, ripe fruit. Palate: flavourful, good acidity, correct.

FAUSTINO V 2012 RD
100% tempranillo

88 Colour: rose, purple rim. Nose: red berry notes, ripe fruit, balanced, rose petals. Palate: fruity, flavourful, long.

BODEGAS FERNÁNDEZ EGUILUZ

Los Morales, 7 bajo
26339 Abalos (La Rioja)
☎: +34 941 334 166 - Fax: +34 941 308 055
www.penalarosa.com
p.larosa@hotmail.es

PEÑA LA ROSA 2012 T MACERACIÓN CARBÓNICA
tempranillo

87 Colour: deep cherry, purple rim. Nose: balanced, fruit expression, violets. Palate: flavourful, fruity, easy to drink.

PEÑA LA ROSA VENDIMIA SELECCIONADA 2008
tempranillo

90 Colour: cherry, garnet rim. Nose: ripe fruit, spicy, creamy oak, toasty. Palate: powerful, flavourful, toasty, round tannins, balanced.

BODEGAS FIN DE SIGLO

Camino Arenzana de Arriba
26311 Arenzana de Abajo (La Rioja)
☎: +34 941 410 042 - Fax: +34 941 410 043
www.bodegasfindesiglo.com
bfs@bodegasfindesiglo.com

RIBAGUDA 2008 TC
100% tempranillo

88 Colour: bright cherry. Nose: sweet spices, creamy oak, scrubland. Palate: flavourful, fruity, toasty, round tannins.

RIBAGUDA CEPAS VIEJAS 2006 TR
70% tempranillo, 25% garnacha, 5% mazuelo

89 Colour: deep cherry. Nose: expressive, balsamic herbs, aromatic coffee, toasty. Palate: spicy, ripe fruit, round tannins.

RIBAGUDA CEPAS VIEJAS 2007 TC
70% tempranillo, 25% garnacha, 5% mazuelo

88 Colour: deep cherry. Nose: spicy, toasty, ripe fruit, fruit expression. Palate: fruity, good acidity, spicy.

RIBAGUDA CEPAS VIEJAS GARNACHA 2012 T
100% garnacha

90 Colour: cherry, purple rim. Nose: expressive, red berry notes, floral, wild herbs. Palate: flavourful, fruity, good acidity, round tannins, spicy.

RIBAGUDA GARNACHA 2011 T
100% garnacha

90 Colour: bright cherry. Nose: ripe fruit, sweet spices. Palate: flavourful, fruity, toasty, round tannins.

BODEGAS FOS

Término de Vialba, s/n
1340 Elciego (Álava)
☎: +34 945 606 681 - Fax: +34 945 606 608
www.bodegasfos.com
fos@bodegasfos.com

FOS 2008 TR
85% tempranillo, 15% graciano

89 Colour: cherry, garnet rim. Nose: ripe fruit, spicy, creamy oak, toasty, fine reductive notes. Palate: powerful, flavourful, toasty, balanced.

FOS 2009 TC

90 Colour: cherry, garnet rim. Nose: red berry notes, ripe fruit, spicy, creamy oak, expressive. Palate: powerful, flavourful, long, balanced.

FOS 2010 TC
95% tempranillo, 5% graciano

90 Colour: cherry, garnet rim. Nose: ripe fruit, spicy, creamy oak, toasty, complex, balsamic herbs, elegant. Palate: powerful, flavourful, toasty.

FOS 2012 B
100% viura

87 Colour: bright straw. Nose: white flowers, dried herbs, spicy. Palate: flavourful, fruity, good acidity, balanced.

FOS 2012 T MACERACIÓN CARBÓNICA
100% tempranillo

88 Colour: deep cherry, purple rim. Nose: balanced, red berry notes, ripe fruit, violets, fragrant herbs. Palate: fruity, flavourful.

FOS BARANDA 2010 T
90% tempranillo, 10% graciano

92 Colour: cherry, garnet rim. Nose: red berry notes, ripe fruit, mineral, sweet spices, creamy oak. Palate: powerful, flavourful, spicy, long, balanced, elegant.

BODEGAS FRANCO ESPAÑOLAS

Cabo Noval, 2
26009 Logroño (La Rioja)
☎: +34 941 251 300 - Fax: +34 941 262 948
www.francoespanolas.com
info@francoespanolas.com

BARBARO 2007 TR
tempranillo, garnacha

90 Colour: cherry, garnet rim. Nose: ripe fruit, spicy, toasty, waxy notes. Palate: powerful, flavourful, toasty, round tannins.

BARBARO 2011 T
100% tempranillo

87 Colour: cherry, purple rim. Nose: fruit preserve, spicy, varietal. Palate: flavourful, correct, round tannins.

BARON D'ANGLADE 2007 TR
80% tempranillo, 10% mazuelo, 10% graciano

91 Colour: deep cherry, garnet rim. Nose: cocoa bean, spicy, ripe fruit, fruit preserve. Palate: flavourful, correct, round tannins.

RIOJA BORDÓN 2005 TGR
85% tempranillo, 10% garnacha, 5% mazuelo

89 Colour: cherry, garnet rim. Nose: balanced, spicy, scrubland, fine reductive notes. Palate: fruity, easy to drink, fine tannins.

RIOJA BORDÓN 2007 TR
85% tempranillo, 10% garnacha, 5% mazuelo

89 Colour: cherry, garnet rim. Nose: ripe fruit, spicy, creamy oak, toasty, fine reductive notes. Palate: powerful, flavourful, toasty.

RIOJA BORDÓN 2009 TC
75% tempranillo, 25% garnacha

86 Colour: cherry, garnet rim. Nose: old leather, medium intensity, spicy, premature reduction notes. Palate: fruity, round tannins.

VIÑA SOLEDAD 2012 B
100% viura

86 Colour: bright straw. Nose: expressive, ripe fruit, tropical fruit, dried herbs. Palate: easy to drink, good finish.

BODEGAS FUENMAYOR S.A.

Buicio, 5 - 6
26360 Fuenmayor (La Rioja)
☎: +34 941 450 935 - Fax: +34 941 450 936
www.bodegasfuenmayor.es
bodegasfuenmayor@bodegasfuenmayor.com

NOCEDAL 2001 TGR
tempranillo

88 Colour: cherry, garnet rim. Nose: spicy, ripe fruit, toasty. Palate: fine bitter notes, spicy.

NOCEDAL 2005 TR
tempranillo

84

BODEGAS FUIDIO

San Bartolome, 32
1322 Yécora (Álava)
☎: +34 945 601 883
bodegasfuidio@hotmail.com

FUIDIO 2012 B
viura

82

FUIDIO 2012 T
tempranillo

87 Colour: very deep cherry. Nose: characterful, ripe fruit, sweet spices, creamy oak. Palate: powerful, flavourful, fine bitter notes.

FUIDIO IRALEY 2012 T
tempranillo

85 Colour: cherry, garnet rim. Nose: red berry notes, ripe fruit, balsamic herbs, spicy. Palate: powerful, flavourful, balsamic, ripe fruit.

BODEGAS GARCÍA DE OLANO

Ctra. Vitoria, s/n
1309 Paganos (Álava)
☎: +34 945 621 146 - Fax: +34 945 621 146
www.bodegasgarciadeolano.com
garciadeolano@telefonica.net

3 DE OLANO 2009 T
100% tempranillo

90 Colour: cherry, garnet rim. Nose: powerfull, ripe fruit, fruit preserve, sweet spices. Palate: flavourful, round tannins, toasty.

3 DE OLANO SELECCIÓN 2010 T
100% tempranillo

93 Colour: very deep cherry, garnet rim. Nose: fruit expression, balanced, cocoa bean. Palate: ripe fruit, good structure, balanced, complex.

HEREDAD GARCÍA DE OLANO 2009 TC
100% tempranillo

88 Colour: deep cherry, purple rim. Nose: sweet spices, ripe fruit, red berry notes. Palate: correct, easy to drink, spicy.

HEREDAD GARCÍA DE OLANO 2011 T BARRICA
100% tempranillo

88 Colour: dark-red cherry, garnet rim. Nose: ripe fruit, fruit preserve, sweet spices. Palate: flavourful, ripe fruit, long.

HEREDAD GARCÍA DE OLANO 2012 B
100% viura

86 Colour: yellow. Nose: medium intensity, ripe fruit, dried herbs. Palate: fruity, flavourful, easy to drink, good acidity.

HEREDAD GARCÍA DE OLANO 2012 T
95% tempranillo, 5% viura

84

MAULEÓN 2006 TR
100% tempranillo

84

OLANUM VENDIMIA SELECCIONADA 2009 T BARRICA
100% tempranillo

88 Colour: cherry, garnet rim. Nose: medium intensity, sweet spices. Palate: flavourful, fruity, balanced, round tannins.

BODEGAS GARCÍA RAMÍREZ

Ctra. de Ventas Blancas, s/n
26143 Murillo del Río Leza (La Rioja)
☎: +34 941 432 372 - Fax: +34 941 432 156
www.bodegasgarciaramirez.com
info@bodegasgarciaramirez.com

HEREDAD GARBLO 2008 TC
85% tempranillo, 5% graciano, 5% mazuelo, 5% garnacha

88 Colour: cherry, garnet rim. Nose: ripe fruit, spicy, toasty, medium intensity, varietal, balsamic herbs. Palate: flavourful, round tannins.

BODEGAS GÓMEZ CRUZADO

Avda. Vizcaya, 6
26200 Haro (La Rioja)
☎: +34 941 312 502 - Fax: +34 941 303 567
www.gomezcruzado.com
bodega@gomezcruzado.com

GÓMEZ CRUZADO 2008 TR
tempranillo

89 Colour: cherry, garnet rim. Nose: ripe fruit, spicy, creamy oak. Palate: powerful, flavourful, toasty, round tannins.

GÓMEZ CRUZADO 2010 TC
tempranillo

90 Colour: cherry, garnet rim. Nose: ripe fruit, creamy oak, sweet spices. Palate: powerful, flavourful, toasty, round tannins.

GÓMEZ CRUZADO VENDIMIA SELECCIONADA 2012 T
50% tempranillo, 50% garnacha

84

HONORABLE GÓMEZ CRUZADO 2010 T
tempranillo

92 Colour: cherry, garnet rim. Nose: creamy oak, toasty, sweet spices. Palate: powerful, flavourful, toasty, round tannins.

PANCRUDO DE GÓMEZ CRUZADO 2011 T
100% garnacha

93 Colour: cherry, garnet rim. Nose: ripe fruit, spicy, creamy oak, toasty, complex, expressive. Palate: powerful, flavourful, toasty, round tannins.

BODEGAS GÓMEZ DE SEGURA IBÁÑEZ

Barrio El Campillar
1300 Laguardia (Álava)
☎: +34 945 600 227 - Fax: +34 945 600 227
www.gomezdesegura.com
info@gomezdesegura.com

GÓMEZ DE SEGURA 2009 TR
tempranillo

87 Colour: very deep cherry. Nose: fruit liqueur notes, spicy, toasty. Palate: sweetness, fine bitter notes, spicy.

GÓMEZ DE SEGURA 2011 TC
tempranillo

88 Colour: cherry, garnet rim. Nose: spicy, creamy oak, toasty. Palate: powerful, flavourful, toasty, round tannins.

GÓMEZ DE SEGURA 2012 RD
tempranillo

83

GÓMEZ DE SEGURA 2012 B
50% malvasía, 50% viura

83

GÓMEZ DE SEGURA 2012 T MACERACIÓN CARBÓNICA
tempranillo

87 Colour: cherry, purple rim. Nose: expressive, red berry notes, macerated fruit. Palate: flavourful, fruity, good acidity, round tannins.

GÓMEZ DE SEGURA VENDIMIA SELECCIONADA 2012 T
tempranillo

90 Colour: cherry, garnet rim. Nose: spicy, creamy oak, toasty. Palate: powerful, flavourful, toasty, round tannins.

BODEGAS GREGORIO MARTÍNEZ

Polígono 1 Parcela, 12
26190 Nalda (La Rioja)
☎: +34 941 220 266 - Fax: +34 941 203 849
www.gregoriomartinez.com
bodegas@gregoriomartinez.com

GREGORIO MARTÍNEZ (FINCA) 2011 B
viura, malvasía, garnacha

87 Colour: bright straw. Nose: fresh fruit, smoky, wild herbs. Palate: sweetness, fresh, fruity, smoky aftertaste.

GREGORIO MARTÍNEZ (FINCA) 2012 T
mazuelo

88 Colour: very deep cherry, purple rim. Nose: ripe fruit, fragrant herbs. Palate: fruity, balsamic, spicy, flavourful.

GREGORIO MARTÍNEZ 2005 TR
tempranillo

87 Colour: bright cherry, garnet rim. Nose: ripe fruit, fruit preserve, dark chocolate, sweet spices. Palate: flavourful, fine tannins, reductive nuances.

GREGORIO MARTÍNEZ 2009 TC
tempranillo

83

GREGORIO MARTÍNEZ 2012 B
viura

85 Colour: bright straw. Nose: medium intensity, faded flowers. Palate: easy to drink, correct.

GREGORIO MARTÍNEZ VENDIMIA SELECCIONADA 2005 TC
tempranillo

86 Colour: dark-red cherry, garnet rim. Nose: tobacco, old leather, spicy. Palate: balanced, good acidity, flavourful.

BODEGAS HERMANOS PECIÑA

Ctra. de Vitoria, Km. 47
26338 San Vicente de la Sonsierra (La Rioja)
☎: +34 941 334 366 - Fax: +34 941 334 180
www.bodegashermanospecina.com
info@bodegashermanospecina.com

CHOBEO DE PECIÑA 2007 T
100% tempranillo

90 Colour: deep cherry, garnet rim. Nose: ripe fruit, balanced, spicy, balsamic herbs. Palate: balanced, round tannins.

CHOBEO DE PECIÑA 2011 BFB
100% viura

89 Colour: bright yellow. Nose: powerfull, ripe fruit, sweet spices, fragrant herbs. Palate: rich, smoky aftertaste, flavourful, fresh, good acidity.

GRAN CHOBEO DE PECIÑA 2008 T
100% tempranillo

89 Colour: cherry, garnet rim. Nose: ripe fruit, spicy, creamy oak, tobacco. Palate: powerful, flavourful, round tannins.

PECIÑA VENDIMIA SELECCIONADA 2001 TR
95% tempranillo, 3% garnacha, 2% graciano

87 Colour: dark-red cherry, orangey edge. Nose: fine reductive notes, spicy, fruit liqueur notes. Palate: correct, balanced, round tannins.

SEÑORÍO DE P. PECIÑA 2001 TGR
95% tempranillo, 3% garnacha, 2% graciano

88 Colour: dark-red cherry, orangey edge. Nose: spicy, dried herbs, fruit liqueur notes. Palate: spicy, balanced, fine tannins.

SEÑORÍO DE P. PECIÑA 2001 TR
95% tempranillo, 3% garnacha, 2% graciano

86 Colour: dark-red cherry, orangey edge. Nose: spicy, ripe fruit, old leather. Palate: ripe fruit, good acidity.

SEÑORÍO DE P. PECIÑA 2008 TC
95% tempranillo, 3% garnacha, 2% graciano

88 Colour: cherry, garnet rim. Nose: ripe fruit, spicy, creamy oak. Palate: powerful, flavourful, toasty, round tannins.

BODEGAS IZADI

Herrería Travesía II, 5
1307 Villabuena de Álava (Álava)
☎: +34 945 609 086 - Fax: +34 945 609 261
www.grupoartevino.com
izadi@izadi.com

IZADI 2009 TC
100% tempranillo

89 Colour: cherry, garnet rim. Nose: ripe fruit, spicy, creamy oak. Palate: flavourful, round tannins.

IZADI 2012 BFB
80% viura, 20% malvasía

89 Colour: bright yellow. Nose: powerfull, ripe fruit, sweet spices, fragrant herbs. Palate: rich, flavourful, fresh, good acidity.

IZADI EL REGALO 2007 TR
90% tempranillo, 10% graciano, mazuelo, garnacha

91 Colour: cherry, garnet rim. Nose: ripe fruit, toasty, sweet spices. Palate: powerful, flavourful, round tannins.

BODEGAS J.E.R.

Camino Nájera - Huércanos, Pol. 10
26314 Huércanos (La Rioja)
☎: +34 941 745 020 - Fax: +34 941 745 021
www.bodegasjer.es
info@bodegasjer.es

J. CANTERA 2012 B JOVEN
viura

83

J. CANTERA 2012 CLARETE
garnacha, viura

89 Colour: raspberry rose. Nose: raspberry, fresh fruit, expressive, fresh, neat, varietal. Palate: fruity, fresh, light-bodied, powerful, flavourful.

J. CANTERA 2012 T JOVEN
tempranillo

85 Colour: cherry, purple rim. Nose: red berry notes, ripe fruit, balsamic herbs. Palate: fresh, fruity, easy to drink.

LARGO PLAZO 2007 TR
tempranillo

87 Colour: deep cherry. Nose: fruit preserve, overripe fruit, roasted coffee. Palate: powerful, spirituous, concentrated.

LARGO PLAZO 2010 TC
tempranillo

88 Colour: cherry, garnet rim. Nose: ripe fruit, spicy, creamy oak. Palate: powerful, flavourful, toasty, round tannins.

THALER 2006 T
garnacha

89 Colour: pale ruby, brick rim edge. Nose: ripe fruit, fruit preserve, balsamic herbs, spicy, creamy oak. Palate: flavourful, spicy, correct, balanced.

BODEGAS LA CATEDRAL - BODEGAS OLARRA

Avda. de Mendavia, 30
26009 Logroño (La Rioja)
☎: +34 941 235 299 - Fax: +34 941 253 703

RIVALLANA 2008 T
90% tempranillo, 5% garnacha, 5% mazuelo, graciano

88 Colour: cherry, garnet rim. Nose: ripe fruit, balsamic herbs, sweet spices, creamy oak. Palate: powerful, flavourful, spicy, long.

RIVALLANA 2011 TC
80% tempranillo, 10% garnacha, 10% mazuelo, graciano

87 Colour: cherry, garnet rim. Nose: ripe fruit, spicy, balsamic herbs, toasty. Palate: flavourful, spicy, long.

RIVALLANA SEGUNDO AÑO 2011 T
80% tempranillo, 10% garnacha, 10% mazuelo

89 Colour: cherry, purple rim. Nose: red berry notes, ripe fruit, balsamic herbs, mineral, expressive. Palate: fresh, fruity, easy to drink.

BODEGAS LA EMPERATRIZ

Finca La Emperatriz, s/n
26241 Baños de Rioja (La Rioja)
☎: +34 941 300 105 - Fax: +34 941 300 231
www.bodegaslaemperatriz.com
correo@bodegaslaemperatriz.com

FINCA LA EMPERATRIZ 2008 TR
90% tempranillo, 10% mazuelo, graciano, viura

90 Colour: cherry, garnet rim. Nose: spicy, creamy oak, toasty. Palate: powerful, flavourful, toasty, round tannins.

FINCA LA EMPERATRIZ 2010 TC
tempranillo, viura, garnacha

92 Colour: cherry, garnet rim. Nose: toasty, spicy, cocoa bean, mineral. Palate: flavourful, spicy, ripe fruit, long.

FINCA LA EMPERATRIZ GARNACHA CEPAS VIEJAS 2011 T
garnacha

93 Colour: cherry, garnet rim. Nose: ripe fruit, fruit expression, fragrant herbs. Palate: flavourful, long, ripe fruit, fine tannins.

FINCA LA EMPERATRIZ PARCELA Nº 1 2011 T
tempranillo

95 Colour: cherry, garnet rim. Nose: ripe fruit, spicy, creamy oak, toasty, complex, expressive. Palate: powerful, flavourful, toasty, round tannins.

FINCA LA EMPERATRIZ TEMPRANILLO 2012 T
tempranillo

88 Colour: cherry, purple rim. Nose: fresh fruit, red berry notes, floral, wild herbs. Palate: flavourful, fruity.

FINCA LA EMPERATRIZ TERRUÑO 2009 T
100% tempranillo

93 Colour: bright cherry. Nose: ripe fruit, sweet spices, creamy oak, expressive. Palate: flavourful, fruity, toasty, round tannins.

FINCA LA EMPERATRIZ TERRUÑO 2010 T
tempranillo

95 Colour: cherry, garnet rim. Nose: creamy oak, toasty, ripe fruit, fruit expression. Palate: flavourful, good acidity, round, round tannins.

FINCA LA EMPERATRIZ VIURA 2012 B
viura

89 Colour: bright straw. Nose: varietal, powerfull, fresh, macerated fruit. Palate: good acidity, balanced, fruity, powerful, flavourful.

BODEGAS LACUS

Cervantes, 18
26559 Aldeanueva de Ebro (La Rioja)
☎: +34 649 331 799 - Fax: +34 941 144 128
www.bodegaslacus.com
inedito@bodegaslacus.com

INÉDITO 2010 BFB
garnacha

87 Colour: bright straw. Nose: powerfull, toasty, spicy. Palate: flavourful, good acidity, smoky aftertaste.

INÉDITO 3/3 2011 T
54% graciano, 25% tempranillo, 21% garnacha

90 Colour: bright cherry, garnet rim. Nose: fragrant herbs, ripe fruit. Palate: concentrated, fruity, flavourful, round tannins.

INÉDITO H12 2009 T
93% graciano, 7% garnacha

88 Colour: deep cherry, garnet rim. Nose: expressive, varietal, fragrant herbs, spicy. Palate: flavourful, long, ripe fruit.

INÉDITO S 2009 T
60% graciano, 40% garnacha

88 Colour: deep cherry, garnet rim. Nose: powerfull, scrubland, ripe fruit. Palate: correct, spicy, balsamic.

BODEGAS LAGUNILLA

Ctra. de Elciego, s/n
26350 Cenicero (La Rioja)
☎: +34 913 878 612
www.unitedwineries.com
abasilio@unitedwineries.com

LAGUNILLA (MARQUÉS DE LA CONCORDIA FAMILY OF WINES) 2006 TR
tempranillo, garnacha

85 Colour: pale ruby, brick rim edge. Nose: spicy, fine reductive notes, wet leather, aged wood nuances, fruit liqueur notes, cigar, waxy notes. Palate: spicy, fine tannins, long.

LAGUNILLA 2008 TR
80% tempranillo, 20% garnacha

87 Colour: cherry, garnet rim. Nose: ripe fruit, balsamic herbs, spicy, creamy oak, fine reductive notes. Palate: powerful, flavourful, balanced.

LAGUNILLA 2010 TC
80% tempranillo, 20% garnacha

87 Colour: cherry, garnet rim. Nose: spicy, ripe fruit, balsamic herbs, fine reductive notes. Palate: flavourful, spicy, long.

LAGUNILLA CASA DEL COMENDADOR 2006 TGR
80% tempranillo, 20% garnacha

88 Colour: deep cherry, orangey edge. Nose: ripe fruit, balsamic herbs, spicy, toasty, wet leather, fine reductive notes. Palate: powerful, flavourful, spicy, long.

LAGUNILLA CASA DEL COMENDADOR 2007 TR
80% tempranillo, 20% garnacha

89 Colour: light cherry, garnet rim. Nose: red berry notes, ripe fruit, balsamic herbs, sweet spices, creamy oak. Palate: powerful, balanced, spicy, long.

LAGUNILLA CASA DEL COMENDADOR 2009 TC
80% tempranillo, 20% garnacha

88 Colour: cherry, garnet rim. Nose: ripe fruit, fine reductive notes, spicy, creamy oak. Palate: powerful, flavourful, long.

LAGUNILLA OPTIMUS 2008 T
100% tempranillo

90 Colour: cherry, garnet rim. Nose: ripe fruit, balsamic herbs, spicy, creamy oak. Palate: powerful, flavourful, balanced, elegant.

BODEGAS LANDALUCE

Ctra. Los Molinos, s/n
1300 Laguardia (Álava)
☎: +34 620 824 314
www.bodegaslandaluce.es
asier@bodegaslandaluce.es

CAPRICHO DE LANDALUCE 2007 T
100% tempranillo

90 Colour: deep cherry, garnet rim. Nose: balsamic herbs, ripe fruit, sweet spices. Palate: balanced, good acidity, round tannins.

ELLE DE LANDALUCE 2009 TC
80% tempranillo, 20% graciano

90 Colour: cherry, garnet rim. Nose: ripe fruit, spicy, dried herbs. Palate: flavourful, toasty, round tannins, good acidity.

ELLE DE LANDALUCE 2012 B
60% viura, 40% malvasía

88 Colour: bright straw. Nose: white flowers, candied fruit. Palate: flavourful, fruity, good acidity, balanced.

FINCAS DE LANDALUCE 2008 TR
100% tempranillo

90 Colour: dark-red cherry, garnet rim. Nose: dark chocolate, spicy, ripe fruit. Palate: balanced, ripe fruit, long, round tannins.

FINCAS DE LANDALUCE 2010 TC
100% tempranillo

91 Colour: bright cherry, garnet rim. Nose: ripe fruit, balanced, sweet spices. Palate: good structure, flavourful, good acidity, round tannins.

LANDALUCE 2012 T MACERACIÓN CARBÓNICA
95% tempranillo, 5% viura

89 Colour: bright cherry, purple rim. Nose: violets, fruit expression, expressive. Palate: flavourful, fruity, ripe fruit.

BODEGAS LAR DE PAULA

Coscojal, s/n
1309 Elvillar (Álava)
☎: +34 945 604 068 - Fax: +34 945 604 105
www.lardepaula.com
info@lardepaula.com

LAR DE PAULA 2008 TR
100% tempranillo

90 Colour: cherry, garnet rim. Nose: ripe fruit, spicy, varietal, medium intensity. Palate: flavourful, round tannins, reductive nuances.

LAR DE PAULA 2009 TC
100% tempranillo

88 Colour: deep cherry, garnet rim. Nose: ripe fruit, balanced. Palate: fruity, flavourful, balanced.

LAR DE PAULA 2012 BFB
60% malvasía, 40% viura

84

LAR DE PAULA CEPAS VIEJAS 2010 T
100% tempranillo

88 Colour: dark-red cherry, garnet rim. Nose: powerfull, spicy, toasty, ripe fruit. Palate: flavourful, fruity, correct, round tannins.

LAR DE PAULA MADURADO 2011 T
100% tempranillo

90 Colour: cherry, garnet rim. Nose: powerfull, sweet spices, creamy oak. Palate: flavourful, balanced, round tannins, good structure.

MERUS.4 2010 T
100% tempranillo

91 Colour: bright cherry. Nose: ripe fruit, sweet spices, creamy oak, expressive. Palate: flavourful, fruity, toasty, round tannins.

BODEGAS LARRAZ

Paraje Ribarrey. Pol. 12- Parcela 50
26350 Cenicero (La Rioja)
☎: +34 639 728 581
www.bodegaslarraz.com
info@bodegaslarraz.com

CAUDUM BODEGAS LARRAZ 2008 T
tempranillo

90 Colour: cherry, garnet rim. Nose: toasty, dark chocolate, ripe fruit. Palate: fine bitter notes, good acidity, spicy.

CAUDUM BODEGAS LARRAZ SELECCIÓN ESPECIAL 2007 T
tempranillo

88 Colour: cherry, garnet rim. Nose: spicy, toasty, characterful, fruit liqueur notes, roasted coffee. Palate: powerful, flavourful, toasty, round tannins.

CAUDUM BODEGAS LARRAZ SELECCIÓN ESPECIAL 2009 T
tempranillo

91 Colour: cherry, garnet rim. Nose: ripe fruit, spicy, toasty, characterful. Palate: powerful, flavourful, toasty, round tannins.

BODEGAS LEZA GARCÍA

San Ignacio, 26
26313 Uruñuela (La Rioja)
☎: +34 941 371 142 - Fax: +34 941 371 035
www.bodegasleza.com
bodegasleza@bodegasleza.com

LEZA GARCÍA 2004 TGR
90% tempranillo, 10% garnacha

88 Colour: dark-red cherry, garnet rim. Nose: spicy, fragrant herbs, old leather, ripe fruit. Palate: fruity, flavourful.

LEZA GARCÍA 2006 TR
90% tempranillo, 10% garnacha

88 Colour: deep cherry. Nose: ripe fruit, spicy, creamy oak, toasty. Palate: powerful, flavourful, toasty, round tannins.

LEZA GARCÍA TINTO FAMILIA 2008 T
100% tempranillo

88 Colour: deep cherry. Nose: spicy, ripe fruit, toasty. Palate: fine bitter notes, spicy.

LG DE LEZA GARCÍA 2009 T
90% tempranillo, 10% graciano

89 Colour: cherry, garnet rim. Nose: ripe fruit, spicy, varietal, toasty, tobacco. Palate: flavourful, round tannins, good acidity.

NUBE DE LEZA GARCÍA 2012 B
100% viura

85 Colour: bright straw. Nose: white flowers, ripe fruit, dried herbs. Palate: flavourful, fruity, good acidity.

NUBE DE LEZA GARCÍA 2012 RD
100% garnacha

83

VALDEPALACIOS 2009 TC
90% tempranillo, 10% garnacha

87 Colour: cherry, garnet rim. Nose: ripe fruit, spicy, toasty, dried herbs. Palate: flavourful, toasty, round tannins.

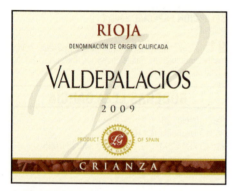

VALDEPALACIOS 2012 T
85% tempranillo, 10% garnacha, 5% mazuelo

85 Colour: cherry, garnet rim. Nose: ripe fruit, balsamic herbs, medium intensity. Palate: powerful, flavourful, correct.

VALDEPALACIOS VENDIMIA SELECCIONADA 2011 T
95% tempranillo, 5% garnacha

87 Colour: deep cherry. Nose: ripe fruit, toasty, sweet spices. Palate: flavourful, fine bitter notes, good acidity.

BODEGAS LOLI CASADO

Avda. La Poveda, 46
1306 Lapuebla de Labarca (Álava)
☎: +34 945 607 096 - Fax: +34 945 607 412
www.bodegaslolicasado.com
loli@bodegaslolicasado.com

JAUN DE ALZATE 2005 TGR
90% tempranillo, 5% graciano, 5% mazuelo

88 Colour: pale ruby, brick rim edge. Nose: spicy, fine reductive notes, wet leather, aged wood nuances. Palate: spicy, long, balsamic.

JAUN DE ALZATE 2009 TR
90% tempranillo, 5% graciano, 5% mazuelo

88 Colour: cherry, garnet rim. Nose: ripe fruit, balsamic herbs, spicy, creamy oak. Palate: rich, powerful, flavourful.

JAUN DE ALZATE 2010 TC
90% tempranillo, 5% graciano, 5% mazuelo

89 Colour: cherry, garnet rim. Nose: ripe fruit, spicy, sweet spices. Palate: powerful, flavourful, toasty.

JAUN DE ALZATE 2011 T
90% tempranillo, 5% graciano, 5% mazuelo

86 Colour: cherry, purple rim. Nose: fresh fruit, red berry notes, floral, balsamic herbs. Palate: flavourful, fruity, good acidity.

JAUN DE ALZATE 2012 T JOVEN
90% tempranillo, 5% graciano, 5% mazuelo

87 Colour: very deep cherry, purple rim. Nose: red berry notes, ripe fruit, dried herbs. Palate: flavourful, ripe fruit, long.

POLUS 2009 TR
100% tempranillo

88 Colour: cherry, garnet rim. Nose: spicy, fine reductive notes, wet leather, aged wood nuances, fruit liqueur notes. Palate: spicy, toasty, balanced.

POLUS 2010 TC
100% tempranillo

87 Colour: cherry, garnet rim. Nose: ripe fruit, spicy, creamy oak. Palate: powerful, flavourful, toasty.

POLUS GRACIANO 2010 T
85% graciano, 15% tempranillo

86 Colour: cherry, purple rim. Nose: scrubland, damp earth, fruit preserve. Palate: powerful, flavourful, spicy.

POLUS TEMPRANILLO 2011 T
100% tempranillo

88 Colour: bright cherry. Nose: ripe fruit, sweet spices, creamy oak, cocoa bean. Palate: flavourful, fruity, toasty.

POLUS VIURA 2009 BC
100% viura

88 Colour: bright golden. Nose: ripe fruit, dry nuts, powerfull, toasty. Palate: flavourful, fruity, spicy, toasty.

POLUS VIURA 2011 BFB
100% viura

86 Colour: bright yellow, greenish rim. Nose: ripe fruit, faded flowers, sweet spices. Palate: rich, fruity, toasty.

POLUS VIURA 2012 B
100% viura

84

BODEGAS LUIS ALEGRE

Ctra. Navaridas, s/n
1300 Laguardia (Álava)
☎: +34 945 600 089 - Fax: +34 945 600 729
www.luisalegre.com
luisalegre@bodegasluisalegre.com

FINCA LA REÑANA 2011 BFB
90% viura, 10% malvasía

90 Colour: bright yellow. Nose: powerfull, ripe fruit, sweet spices, creamy oak, fragrant herbs. Palate: rich, smoky aftertaste, flavourful, fresh.

GRAN VINO PONTAC 2009 T
95% tempranillo, 5% graciano

92 Colour: cherry, garnet rim. Nose: ripe fruit, spicy, creamy oak, balsamic herbs. Palate: powerful, flavourful, toasty, round tannins.

KODEN DE LUIS ALEGRE 2011 T
100% tempranillo

90 Colour: deep cherry, garnet rim. Nose: ripe fruit, fruit preserve, cocoa bean, varietal, balsamic herbs. Palate: ripe fruit, round tannins.

LUIS ALEGRE PARCELA Nº 5 2008 TR
100% tempranillo

90 Colour: deep cherry, garnet rim. Nose: ripe fruit, fruit preserve, spicy. Palate: flavourful, balanced, round tannins.

LUIS ALEGRE SELECCIÓN ESPECIAL 2009 TR
95% tempranillo, graciano, mazuelo

90 Colour: cherry, garnet rim. Nose: ripe fruit, spicy, toasty. Palate: powerful, flavourful, toasty, round tannins, balanced.

PONTAC DE PORTILES 2010 T
90% tempranillo, 10% garnacha

93 Colour: very deep cherry, garnet rim. Nose: balanced, sweet spices, cocoa bean, fragrant herbs, ripe fruit. Palate: good structure, flavourful, round tannins.

VITICULTUA DE PRECISIÓN 2010 TC
85% tempranillo, graciano, mazuelo, garnacha

89 Colour: cherry, garnet rim. Nose: red berry notes, ripe fruit, spicy, balanced. Palate: fruity, flavourful, round tannins.

BODEGAS LUIS CAÑAS

Ctra. Samaniego, 10
1307 Villabuena (Álava)
☎: +34 945 623 373 - Fax: +34 945 609 289
www.luiscanas.com
bodegas@luiscanas.com

LUIS CAÑAS 2005 TGR
95% tempranillo, 5% graciano

93 Colour: cherry, garnet rim. Nose: spicy, creamy oak, toasty, complex, powerfull, ripe fruit. Palate: powerful, flavourful, toasty, round tannins.

LUIS CAÑAS 2007 TR
85% tempranillo, 5% graciano

91 Colour: cherry, garnet rim. Nose: spicy, creamy oak, roasted coffee. Palate: powerful, flavourful, toasty, round tannins.

LUIS CAÑAS 2010 TC
95% tempranillo, 5% garnacha

91 Colour: cherry, garnet rim. Nose: ripe fruit, spicy, creamy oak, toasty. Palate: powerful, flavourful, toasty, round tannins.

LUIS CAÑAS 2012 BFB
85% viura, 15% malvasía

89 Colour: bright yellow. Nose: ripe fruit, sweet spices, fragrant herbs, faded flowers. Palate: rich, flavourful, fresh, good acidity.

LUIS CAÑAS HIRU 3 RACIMOS 2007 T
90% tempranillo, 10% graciano

92 Colour: deep cherry. Nose: ripe fruit, spicy, dark chocolate, toasty. Palate: powerful tannins, fruity, powerful, flavourful, concentrated, complex.

LUIS CAÑAS SELECCIÓN DE FAMILIA 2006 TR
85% tempranillo, 15% otras

92 Nose: elegant, spicy, fine reductive notes, wet leather, aged wood nuances, fruit liqueur notes. Palate: spicy, fine tannins, elegant, long.

BODEGAS MARQUÉS DE ARVIZA

Bodegas San Cristóbal, 34 A
26360 Fuenmayor (La Rioja)
☎: +34 941 451 245
www.marquesdearviza.com
info@marquesdearviza.es

EL TRACTOR 2008 T
tempranillo, graciano

90 Colour: cherry, garnet rim. Nose: red berry notes, ripe fruit, spicy, creamy oak, earthy notes. Palate: rich, powerful, flavourful, toasty.

MARQUÉS DE ARVIZA 2006 TR
90% tempranillo, 10% garnacha

88 Colour: pale ruby, brick rim edge. Nose: ripe fruit, earthy notes, spicy, toasty, fine reductive notes. Palate: powerful, flavourful, spicy, long.

MARQUÉS DE ARVIZA 2008 TC
90% tempranillo, 5% garnacha, 5% graciano

87 Colour: cherry, garnet rim. Nose: ripe fruit, spicy, creamy oak, toasty. Palate: powerful, flavourful, toasty, round tannins.

BODEGAS MARQUÉS DE CÁCERES

Ctra. Logroño, s/n
26350 Cenicero (La Rioja)
☎: +34 941 454 026 - Fax: +34 941 454 400
www.marquesdecaceres.com
export@marquesdecaceres.com

GAUDIUM GRAN VINO 2008 TR
95% tempranillo, 5% graciano

95 Colour: cherry, garnet rim. Nose: red berry notes, ripe fruit, fragrant herbs, sweet spices, expressive. Palate: flavourful, spicy, long, balanced, elegant, fine tannins.

MARQUÉS DE CÁCERES 2005 TGR
85% tempranillo, 15% garnacha, graciano

92 Colour: dark-red cherry, brick rim edge. Nose: spicy, creamy oak, cocoa bean, ripe fruit. Palate: creamy, spicy, powerful, flavourful, fruity, complex, smoky aftertaste, reductive nuances.

MARQUÉS DE CÁCERES 2008 TR
85% tempranillo, 15% garnacha, graciano

92 Colour: cherry, garnet rim. Nose: ripe fruit, balsamic herbs, spicy, creamy oak, fine reductive notes. Palate: powerful, flavourful, long, balanced.

MARQUÉS DE CÁCERES 2009 TR
85% tempranillo, 15% garnacha, graciano

91 Colour: dark-red cherry. Nose: complex, elegant, cocoa bean, creamy oak. Palate: complex, flavourful, powerful, spicy, creamy.

MARQUÉS DE CÁCERES 2010 TC
85% tempranillo, 15% garnacha, graciano

90 Colour: dark-red cherry. Nose: fruit expression, cocoa bean. Palate: elegant, flavourful, fruity, fruity aftestaste, spicy.

MARQUÉS DE CÁCERES 2012 B
100% viura

87 Colour: bright straw. Nose: powerfull, fresh fruit, ripe fruit. Palate: flavourful, fruity, fresh.

MARQUÉS DE CÁCERES 2012 RD
85% tempranillo, 15% garnacha

88 Colour: coppery red. Nose: powerfull, ripe fruit, red berry notes, floral, expressive. Palate: powerful, fruity, fresh.

MARQUÉS DE CÁCERES ANTEA 2012 BFB
viura, malvasía

89 Colour: bright yellow. Nose: ripe fruit, sweet spices, creamy oak, fragrant herbs. Palate: rich, flavourful, fresh, good acidity.

MARQUÉS DE CÁCERES ECOLÓGICO BIO 2012 T
90% tempranillo, 10% graciano

90 Colour: cherry, purple rim. Nose: fresh fruit, red berry notes, floral. Palate: flavourful, fruity, good acidity, round tannins.

MC MARQUÉS DE CÁCERES 2011 T
100% tempranillo

92 Colour: deep cherry. Nose: sweet spices, toasty, fresh fruit. Palate: creamy, complex, fruity, flavourful, powerful.

SATINELA SEMI-DULCE 2012 B
95% viura, 5% malvasía

86 Colour: bright straw. Nose: fresh, white flowers, expressive. Palate: flavourful, fruity, good acidity, balanced.

BODEGAS MARQUÉS DE TERÁN - REGALÍA DE OLLAURI

Ctra. de Nájera, Km. 1
26220 Ollauri (La Rioja)
☎: +34 941 338 373 - Fax: +34 941 338 374
www.marquesdeteran.com
info@marquesdeteran.com

AZENTO 2008 TR
tempranillo

86 Colour: cherry, garnet rim. Nose: ripe fruit, creamy oak, roasted coffee. Palate: powerful, flavourful, toasty.

MARQUÉS DE TERÁN 2007 TR
90% tempranillo, 5% mazuelo, 5% garnacha

88 Colour: pale ruby, brick rim edge. Nose: ripe fruit, balsamic herbs, waxy notes, spicy, creamy oak, fine reductive notes. Palate: spicy, long, flavourful.

MARQUÉS DE TERÁN 2008 TC
95% tempranillo, 5% mazuelo

87 Colour: cherry, garnet rim. Nose: ripe fruit, spicy, creamy oak, toasty. Palate: powerful, flavourful, toasty.

MARQUÉS DE TERÁN SELECCIÓN ESPECIAL 2009 T
tempranillo

91 Colour: cherry, garnet rim. Nose: ripe fruit, spicy, creamy oak, toasty, mineral. Palate: powerful, flavourful, toasty, round tannins.

OLLAMENDI 2007 T
tempranillo

90 Colour: cherry, garnet rim. Nose: ripe fruit, spicy, creamy oak, toasty, fine reductive notes. Palate: powerful, flavourful, toasty.

VERSUM 2010 T
tempranillo

90 Colour: cherry, garnet rim. Nose: balanced, red berry notes, ripe fruit, balsamic herbs, creamy oak. Palate: flavourful, spicy, elegant.

BODEGAS MARQUÉS DE VITORIA

Camino de Santa Lucía, s/n
1320 Oyón (Álava)
☎: +34 945 622 134 - Fax: +34 945 601 496
www.marquesdevitoria.com
info@bodegasmarquesdevitoria.es

MARQUÉS DE VITORIA 2004 TGR
100% tempranillo

90 Colour: pale ruby, brick rim edge. Nose: elegant, spicy, fine reductive notes, wet leather, aged wood nuances, fruit liqueur notes. Palate: spicy, fine tannins, elegant, long.

MARQUÉS DE VITORIA 2007 TR
100% tempranillo

90 Colour: cherry, garnet rim. Nose: spicy, creamy oak, toasty. Palate: powerful, flavourful, toasty, round tannins.

MARQUÉS DE VITORIA 2009 TC
100% tempranillo

90 Colour: cherry, garnet rim. Nose: ripe fruit, spicy, creamy oak, toasty. Palate: powerful, flavourful, toasty, round tannins.

MARQUÉS DE VITORIA 2012 B
100% viura

87 Colour: bright straw. Nose: ripe fruit, dried flowers, fragrant herbs. Palate: flavourful, fruity, good acidity.

MARQUÉS DE VITORIA 2012 RD
100% tempranillo

88 Colour: onion pink. Nose: elegant, candied fruit, dried flowers, fragrant herbs. Palate: light-bodied, flavourful, good acidity, long, spicy.

MARQUÉS DE VITORIA ECCO 2012 T
100% tempranillo

89 Colour: cherry, purple rim. Nose: fresh fruit, red berry notes, floral. Palate: flavourful, fruity, good acidity, round tannins.

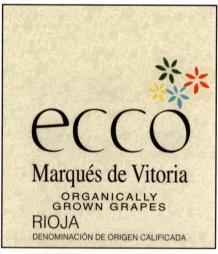

PEDRO MARTÍNEZ ALESANCO 2005 TGR
50% tempranillo, 50% garnacha

88 Colour: cherry, garnet rim. Nose: characterful, expressive, ripe fruit, toasty. Palate: flavourful, spicy, ripe fruit.

PEDRO MARTÍNEZ ALESANCO 2008 TR
90% tempranillo, 10% garnacha

90 Colour: bright cherry. Nose: sweet spices, creamy oak. Palate: flavourful, fruity, toasty, round tannins.

PEDRO MARTÍNEZ ALESANCO 2010 TC
80% tempranillo, 20% garnacha

88 Colour: deep cherry. Nose: powerfull, sweet spices, cocoa bean. Palate: fine bitter notes, good acidity, long, ripe fruit.

PEDRO MARTÍNEZ ALESANCO 2012 BFB
100% viura

84

PEDRO MARTÍNEZ ALESANCO 2012 RD FERMENTADO EN BARRICA
100% garnacha

87 Colour: onion pink. Nose: fruit expression, slightly evolved, fresh, candied fruit. Palate: fresh, fruity, smoky aftertaste.

PEDRO MARTÍNEZ ALESANCO 2012 T
100% tempranillo

77

PEDRO MARTÍNEZ ALESANCO CLARETE 2012 CLARETE
95% garnacha, 5% viura

82

PEDRO MARTÍNEZ ALESANCO SELECCIÓN 2007 TR
40% maturana, 30% tempranillo, 30% garnacha

88 Colour: cherry, garnet rim. Nose: ripe fruit, spicy, creamy oak, toasty. Palate: powerful, flavourful, toasty, round tannins.

BODEGAS MARTÍNEZ ALESANCO

José García, 20
26310 Badarán (La Rioja)
☎: +34 941 367 075 - Fax: +34 941 367 075
www.bodegasmartinezalesanco.com
info@bodegasmartinezalesanco.com

NADA QUE VER 2009 TC
100% maturana

91 Colour: cherry, garnet rim. Nose: spicy, creamy oak, toasty, warm. Palate: powerful, flavourful, toasty, round tannins.

BODEGAS MARTÍNEZ CORTA

Ctra. Cenicero, s/n
20313 Uruñuela (La Rioja)
☎: +34 670 937 520
www.bodegasmartinezcorta.com
administracion@bodegasmartinezcorta.com

CEPAS ANTIGUAS SELECCIÓN PRIVADA 2011 T
100% tempranillo

89 Colour: cherry, garnet rim. Nose: ripe fruit, spicy, creamy oak, toasty, complex. Palate: powerful, flavourful, toasty, round tannins.

MARTÍNEZ CORTA CEPAS ANTIGUAS 2010 TC
100% tempranillo

88 Colour: deep cherry. Nose: powerfull, woody, ripe fruit. Palate: powerful, spicy, ripe fruit.

MARTÍNEZ CORTA CEPAS ANTIGUAS 2012 T
100% tempranillo

87 Colour: cherry, garnet rim. Nose: ripe fruit, red berry notes, balanced. Palate: fruity, correct, round tannins.

MARTÍNEZ CORTA SELECCIÓN ESPECIAL 2007 T
100% tempranillo

89 Colour: cherry, garnet rim. Nose: sweet spices, toasty, ripe fruit. Palate: flavourful, spicy, ripe fruit, round tannins.

SOROS 2009 T
80% tempranillo, 10% garnacha, 10% graciano

88 Colour: very deep cherry. Nose: roasted coffee, fruit preserve, overripe fruit. Palate: powerful, concentrated, spicy, fine bitter notes, good acidity.

SOROS 2010 TC
100% tempranillo

88 Colour: bright cherry. Nose: sweet spices, creamy oak, balanced. Palate: flavourful, fruity, toasty, round tannins.

TENTACIÓN GARNACHA 2011 T
100% garnacha

87 Colour: cherry, garnet rim. Nose: powerfull, fruit preserve, fine reductive notes. Palate: powerful, fine bitter notes, good acidity.

BODEGAS MARTÍNEZ PALACIOS

Real, 22
26220 Ollauri (Rioja)
☎: +34 941 338 023 - Fax: +34 941 338 023
www.bodegasmartinezpalacios.com
bodega@bodegasmartinezpalacios.com

MARTÍNEZ PALACIOS 2006 TR
95% tempranillo, 5% graciano

87 Colour: cherry, garnet rim. Nose: ripe fruit, spicy, toasty. Palate: powerful, flavourful, toasty, round tannins.

MARTÍNEZ PALACIOS 2009 TC
100% tempranillo

88 Colour: cherry, garnet rim. Nose: ripe fruit, spicy, creamy oak, toasty. Palate: powerful, flavourful, toasty, round tannins.

MARTÍNEZ PALACIOS 2012 T
100% tempranillo

89 Colour: deep cherry. Nose: medium intensity, fruit expression, red berry notes. Palate: fine bitter notes, good acidity.

MARTÍNEZ PALACIOS PAGO CANDELA 2008 T
90% tempranillo, 10% graciano

91 Colour: cherry, garnet rim. Nose: ripe fruit, spicy, creamy oak, toasty, complex. Palate: powerful, flavourful, toasty, round tannins.

BODEGAS MEDRANO IRAZU S.L.

San Pedro, 14
1309 Elvillar (Álava)
☎: +34 945 604 066 - Fax: +34 945 604 126
www.bodegasmedranoirazu.com
info@bodegasmedranoirazu.com

LUIS MEDRANO GRACIANO 2010 T
100% graciano

87 Colour: pale ruby, brick rim edge. Nose: spicy, fine reductive notes, wet leather, aged wood nuances, fruit liqueur notes. Palate: spicy, fine tannins, elegant, long.

LUIS MEDRANO TEMPRANILLO 2010 T
100% tempranillo

90 Colour: cherry, garnet rim. Nose: ripe fruit, scrubland, spicy, creamy oak. Palate: long, spicy, powerful, flavourful.

MAS DE MEDRANO 2010 T
100% tempranillo

90 Colour: cherry, garnet rim. Nose: ripe fruit, scrubland, spicy, fine reductive notes, earthy notes. Palate: powerful, spicy, toasty.

MEDRANO IRAZU 2007 TR
100% tempranillo

88 Colour: pale ruby, brick rim edge. Nose: spicy, fine reductive notes, wet leather, aged wood nuances, earthy notes. Palate: spicy, long, round tannins.

MEDRANO IRAZU 2010 TC
100% tempranillo

90 Colour: cherry, garnet rim. Nose: red berry notes, ripe fruit, sweet spices, cocoa bean, creamy oak. Palate: rich, fruity, flavourful, long, toasty.

MEDRANO IRAZU RESERVA DE FAMILIA 2007 TR
100% tempranillo

91 Colour: cherry, garnet rim. Nose: toasty, creamy oak, ripe fruit, balsamic herbs, earthy notes. Palate: spicy, long, powerful, flavourful, round tannins.

BODEGAS MENTOR

San Antón, 4-Entpta. dcha.
26002 Logroño (La Rioja)
☎: +34 941 270 795 - Fax: +34 941 244 577
www.puertagotica.es
info@puertagotica.es

MENTOR 2005 TR
100% tempranillo

91 Colour: cherry, garnet rim. Nose: ripe fruit, spicy, toasty, complex. Palate: powerful, flavourful, toasty, round tannins.

MENTOR 2010 TC
100% tempranillo

91 Colour: bright cherry, garnet rim. Nose: ripe fruit, dried herbs, closed. Palate: good acidity, balanced, round tannins.

MENTOR ROBERTO TORRETTA 2010 T
100% tempranillo

95 Colour: deep cherry, garnet rim. Nose: ripe fruit, spicy, mineral, complex, expressive. Palate: round tannins, good structure, fruity, good acidity.

BODEGAS MITARTE

Avda. La Rioja, 5
1330 Labastida (Álava)
☎: +34 945 331 069
www.mitarte.com
bodegas@mitarte.com

DE FAULA 2007 TR
tempranillo

88 Colour: cherry, garnet rim. Nose: ripe fruit, spicy, creamy oak, complex. Palate: powerful, flavourful, toasty, round tannins.

MITARTE 2007 TR
100% tempranillo

92 Colour: cherry, garnet rim. Nose: balanced, expressive, balsamic herbs, ripe fruit. Palate: long, flavourful, round tannins.

MITARTE 2010 TC
100% tempranillo

86 Colour: very deep cherry, garnet rim. Nose: medium intensity, ripe fruit, spicy. Palate: flavourful, spicy, correct.

MITARTE 2012 B
100% viura

87 Colour: bright straw. Nose: ripe fruit, citrus fruit, balanced. Palate: fruity, flavourful, easy to drink, balanced.

MITARTE 2012 BFB
100% viura

85 Colour: bright straw. Nose: sweet spices, ripe fruit, faded flowers, warm. Palate: flavourful, toasty, long, rich.

MITARTE 2012 RD
50% tempranillo, 50% garnacha

86 Colour: rose, purple rim. Nose: powerfull, ripe fruit, red berry notes, floral. Palate: powerful, fruity, fresh.

MITARTE 3ª HOJA 2012 T
tempranillo

85 Colour: very deep cherry, purple rim. Nose: red berry notes, ripe fruit, balanced. Palate: flavourful, slightly dry, soft tannins.

MITARTE MAZUELO 2008 T
100% mazuelo

88 Colour: deep cherry, garnet rim. Nose: medium intensity, ripe fruit, dried herbs, spicy. Palate: fruity, flavourful.

MITARTE TEMPRANILLO 2012 T MACERACIÓN CARBÓNICA
80% tempranillo, 15% garnacha, 5% viura

84

MITARTE VENDIMIA SELECCIONADA 2010 TC
100% tempranillo

87 Colour: cherry, garnet rim. Nose: ripe fruit, spicy, toasty. Palate: powerful, flavourful, toasty, round tannins.

S Y C DE MITARTE 2008 B
100% viura

88 Colour: bright golden. Nose: candied fruit, characterful, powerfull. Palate: powerful, sweetness, good acidity.

S Y C DE MITARTE 2010 T
100% tempranillo

89 Colour: black cherry, garnet rim. Nose: ripe fruit, fruit preserve, aromatic coffee, cocoa bean. Palate: flavourful, good structure, round tannins.

BODEGAS MONTECILLO

Ctra. Navarrete-Fuenmayor, Km. 2
26360 Fuenmayor (La Rioja)
☎: +34 925 860 990 - Fax: +34 925 860 905
www.osborne.es
carolina.cerrato@osborne.es

CUMBRE MONTECILLO 2006 T
90% tempranillo, 10% mazuelo

91 Colour: dark-red cherry. Nose: complex, fresh, varietal, fresh fruit, cocoa bean, creamy oak. Palate: correct, elegant, round, varietal, fruity, spicy.

MONTECILLO 2005 TGR
tempranillo

90 Colour: dark-red cherry, orangey edge. Nose: fine reductive notes, tobacco, candied fruit, powerfull, complex, spicy, cocoa bean, creamy oak. Palate: creamy, toasty, ripe fruit, round tannins.

MONTECILLO 2009 TC
100% tempranillo

87 Colour: dark-red cherry, orangey edge. Nose: spicy, cedar wood, sweet spices, powerfull, reduction notes. Palate: dry, flavourful, lacks expression.

VIÑA CUMBRERO 2008 TR
100% tempranillo

89 Colour: dark-red cherry, orangey edge. Nose: fine reductive notes, spicy, cedar wood, ripe fruit. Palate: spicy, creamy, toasty.

VIÑA CUMBRERO 2009 TC
100% tempranillo

88 Colour: dark-red cherry. Nose: spicy, creamy oak, ripe fruit. Palate: spicy, ripe fruit, round tannins.

VIÑA MONTY 2007 TR
100% tempranillo

90 Colour: cherry, garnet rim. Nose: cedar wood, spicy, aromatic coffee, fruit expression. Palate: creamy, spicy, fruity, flavourful.

VIÑA MONTY 2009 TC
90% tempranillo, 10% mazuelo

89 Colour: dark-red cherry. Nose: spicy, aromatic coffee, smoky, candied fruit. Palate: flavourful, round, toasty, smoky aftertaste.

BODEGAS MORAZA

Ctra. Peñacerrada, s/n
26338 San Vicente de la Sonsierra (La Rioja)
☎: +34 941 334 473 - Fax: +34 941 334 473
www.bodegasmoraza.com
info@bodegasmoraza.com

ALESAGO 2012 T
100% tempranillo

88 Colour: cherry, purple rim. Nose: red berry notes, floral, ripe fruit. Palate: flavourful, fruity, good acidity, round tannins.

MORAZA 2010 TC
100% tempranillo

85 Colour: cherry, garnet rim. Nose: spicy, creamy oak, toasty. Palate: powerful, flavourful, toasty, round tannins.

MORAZA VENDIMIA SELECCIONADA 2008 T BARRICA
100% tempranillo

87 Colour: cherry, garnet rim. Nose: toasty, spicy, aromatic coffee. Palate: powerful, flavourful, balsamic.

SEÑORÍO DE MORAZA 2007 TR
100% tempranillo

85 Colour: cherry, garnet rim. Nose: ripe fruit, spicy, creamy oak. Palate: powerful, flavourful, toasty, round tannins.

BODEGAS MUGA

Barrio de la Estación, s/n
26200 Haro (La Rioja)
☎: +34 941 311 825
www.bodegasmuga.com
juan@bodegasmuga.com

ARO 2009 T
70% tempranillo, 30% graciano

95 Colour: cherry, garnet rim. Nose: spicy, creamy oak, toasty, characterful. Palate: powerful, flavourful, toasty, powerful tannins, ripe fruit.

MUGA 2009 TC
70% tempranillo, 20% garnacha, 10% mazuelo, graciano

90 Colour: cherry, garnet rim. Nose: ripe fruit, spicy, creamy oak, toasty, wet leather. Palate: powerful, flavourful, toasty, round tannins.

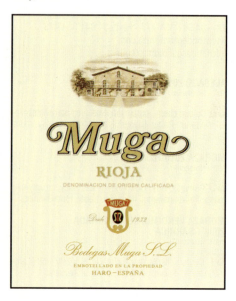

MUGA 2012 BFB
90% viura, 10% malvasía

90 Colour: bright straw. Nose: fresh, fresh fruit, white flowers, spicy, toasty. Palate: flavourful, fruity, good acidity, balanced.

MUGA 2012 RD
60% garnacha, 30% viura, 10% tempranillo

90 Nose: elegant, candied fruit, dried flowers, fragrant herbs, red berry notes. Palate: light-bodied, flavourful, good acidity, long, spicy.

MUGA SELECCIÓN ESPECIAL 2009 TR
70% tempranillo, 20% garnacha, 10% mazuelo, graciano

91 Colour: cherry, garnet rim. Nose: ripe fruit, spicy, creamy oak, toasty, complex. Palate: powerful, flavourful, toasty, round tannins.

PRADO ENEA 2005 TGR
80% tempranillo, 20% garnacha, mazuelo, graciano

94 Colour: cherry, garnet rim. Nose: spicy, ripe fruit, creamy oak. Palate: powerful, long, spicy, round tannins.

TORRE MUGA 2009 T
75% tempranillo, 15% mazuelo, 10% graciano

94 Colour: cherry, garnet rim. Nose: ripe fruit, spicy, creamy oak, toasty, characterful. Palate: powerful, flavourful, toasty, round tannins.

BODEGAS MURÚA

Ctra. Laguardia
1340 Elciego (Álava)
☎: +34 945 606 260
www.bodegasmurua.com
info@bodegasmurua.masaveu.com

MURÚA 2005 TR
90% tempranillo, 8% graciano, 2% mazuelo

90 Colour: cherry, garnet rim. Nose: wet leather, ripe fruit, sweet spices. Palate: flavourful, powerful, round tannins.

MURÚA 2009 BFB
50% viura, 30% malvasía, 20% garnacha blanca

88 Colour: bright yellow. Nose: powerfull, ripe fruit, sweet spices, creamy oak. Palate: rich, smoky aftertaste, flavourful, fresh, good acidity.

VS MURÚA 2010 T
92% tempranillo, 5% graciano, 3% mazuelo

92 Colour: cherry, garnet rim. Nose: ripe fruit, spicy, toasty, characterful. Palate: powerful, flavourful, toasty, round tannins.

BODEGAS NAVA-RIOJA S.A.T.

Ctra. Eje del Ebro, s/n
31261 Andosilla (Navarra)
☎: +34 948 690 454 - Fax: +34 948 674 491
www.bodegasnavarioja.com
info@bodegasnavarioja.com

OTIS TARDA 2010 TC

89 Colour: cherry, garnet rim. Nose: ripe fruit, spicy, toasty, complex, dried herbs. Palate: powerful, flavourful, round tannins.

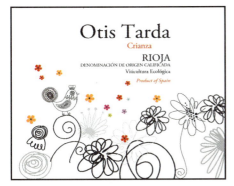

OTIS TARDA 2012 T

87 Colour: cherry, garnet rim. Nose: powerfull, scrubland, ripe fruit. Palate: fruity, easy to drink, good acidity.

PARDOÑO 2012 T

85 Colour: cherry, garnet rim. Nose: medium intensity, ripe fruit, varietal. Palate: correct, balanced.

BODEGAS NAVAJAS

Camino Balgarauz, 2
26370 Navarrete (La Rioja)
☎: +34 941 440 140 - Fax: +34 941 440 657
www.bodegasnavajas.com
info@bodegasnavajas.com

NAVAJAS 2007 TR
95% tempranillo, 5% mazuelo

89 Colour: deep cherry, garnet rim. Nose: sweet spices, dried herbs, ripe fruit. Palate: fruity, flavourful, good acidity.

NAVAJAS 2010 BC
100% viura

87 Colour: bright yellow. Nose: fresh, spicy, aged wood nuances, wild herbs. Palate: fine bitter notes, powerful, flavourful, classic aged character.

NAVAJAS GRACIANO 2009 TC
graciano

89 Colour: deep cherry, garnet rim. Nose: ripe fruit, balsamic herbs, cocoa bean. Palate: flavourful, fruity, round tannins.

BODEGAS NAVARRSOTILLO

Ctra. N-232, km. 354
26500 Calahorra (La Rioja)
☎: +34 948 690 523 - Fax: +34 948 690 523
www.navarrsotillo.com
info@navarrsotillo.com

COMISATIO 2008 T
tempranillo

82

MAGISTER BIBENDI 2005 TGR
tempranillo, garnacha, graciano

86 Colour: cherry, garnet rim. Nose: spicy, balsamic herbs, fruit preserve. Palate: flavourful, reductive nuances.

MAGISTER BIBENDI 2006 TR
tempranillo, garnacha

82

MAGISTER BIBENDI 2009 TC
tempranillo, garnacha

83

MAGISTER BIBENDI GARNACHA 2008 T
garnacha

85 Colour: deep cherry. Nose: expressive, ripe fruit, spicy. Palate: spicy, ripe fruit, good acidity.

MAGISTER BIBENDI GRACIANO 2008 T
graciano

84

MAGISTER BIBENDI MAZUELO 2008 T
mazuelo

88 Colour: deep cherry. Nose: ripe fruit, spicy, toasty. Palate: flavourful, good acidity, ripe fruit.

NAVARRSOTILLO 2012 RD

82

NOEMUS 2012 B
viura

84

NOEMUS 2012 RD
garnacha

83

NOEMUS 2012 T
tempranillo, mazuelo, garnacha

85 Colour: cherry, purple rim. Nose: ripe fruit, medium intensity. Palate: flavourful, easy to drink, good finish.

SEÑORÍO DE ARRIEZU 2005 TR
tempranillo, garnacha

84

SEÑORÍO DE ARRIEZU 2009 TC
tempranillo, garnacha

84

SEÑORÍO DE ARRIEZU 2012 B
viura

84

SEÑORÍO DE ARRIEZU 2012 RD
garnacha

80

SEÑORÍO DE ARRIEZU 2012 T
tempranillo, garnacha

86 Colour: dark-red cherry. Nose: ripe fruit, earthy notes, toasty. Palate: balsamic, fruity, powerful, flavourful.

BODEGAS NESTARES EGUIZÁBAL

Alberto Villanueva 82-84
26144 Galilea (La Rioja)
☎: +34 941 480 351 - Fax: +34 941 480 351
www.nestareseguizabal.com
info@nestareseguizabal.com

SEGARES 2009 TC
100% tempranillo

86 Colour: cherry, garnet rim. Nose: fruit preserve, balsamic herbs, spicy, creamy oak. Palate: flavourful, spicy, long.

SEGARES 2012 T
100% tempranillo

85 Colour: cherry, purple rim. Nose: floral, red berry notes, ripe fruit. Palate: flavourful, fruity, good acidity.

SEGARES LAS LLECAS 2011 T
100% tempranillo

85 Colour: cherry, garnet rim. Nose: ripe fruit, scrubland, smoky, creamy oak. Palate: powerful, flavourful, spicy, long.

BODEGAS NIVARIUS

Camino Vecinal de Nalda a Viguera, 50
26190 Nalda (La Rioja)
☎: +34 941 444 418 - Fax: +34 941 490 086
www.nivarius.com
info@nivarius.com

NIVARIUS 2012 B
55% tempranillo blanco, 45% viura

89 Colour: pale. Nose: powerfull, warm, candied fruit. Palate: flavourful, powerful, fine bitter notes.

BODEGAS OBALO

Ctra. 232 A, Km. 26
26339 Abalos (Rioja)
☎: +34 941 744 056
www.bodegaobalo.com
info@bodegasobalo.com

ALTINO 2010 TC
100% tempranillo

93 Colour: cherry, garnet rim. Nose: ripe fruit, spicy, creamy oak, toasty, complex. Palate: powerful, flavourful, toasty, round tannins, elegant.

OBALO 2010 TC
100% tempranillo

93 Colour: cherry, garnet rim. Nose: ripe fruit, sweet spices, creamy oak, toasty, dark chocolate, expressive. Palate: flavourful, fruity, toasty, round tannins, balanced.

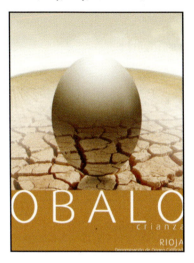

OBALO 2012 T
100% tempranillo

90 Colour: cherry, garnet rim. Nose: red berry notes, ripe fruit, spicy, wild herbs. Palate: powerful, rich, fruity, flavourful.

PINTURAS 2010 TC
100% tempranillo

89 Colour: cherry, garnet rim. Nose: ripe fruit, spicy, creamy oak, toasty. Palate: powerful, flavourful, toasty.

BODEGAS OLARRA

Avda. de Mendavia, 30
26009 Logroño (La Rioja)
☎: +34 941 235 299 - Fax: +34 941 253 703
www.bodegasolarra.es
bodegasolarra@bodegasolarra.es

AÑARES 2008 TR
90% tempranillo, 5% garnacha, 5% mazuelo, 5% graciano

87 Colour: cherry, garnet rim. Nose: creamy oak, toasty, ripe fruit, fine reductive notes. Palate: powerful, flavourful, toasty.

AÑARES 2011 TC
90% tempranillo, 5% garnacha, 5% mazuelo, 5% graciano

86 Colour: cherry, garnet rim. Nose: ripe fruit, sweet spices, creamy oak. Palate: powerful, flavourful, easy to drink.

CERRO AÑÓN 2008 TR
80% tempranillo, 5% garnacha, 15% mazuelo, graciano

90 Colour: cherry, garnet rim. Nose: ripe fruit, spicy, creamy oak, toasty, complex. Palate: powerful, flavourful, toasty.

CERRO AÑÓN 2011 TC
80% tempranillo, 10% garnacha, 10% mazuelo, 10% graciano

89 Colour: cherry, garnet rim. Nose: ripe fruit, spicy, creamy oak, toasty, balsamic herbs, sweet spices. Palate: powerful, flavourful, toasty.

OTOÑAL 2008 TR
75% tempranillo, 10% garnacha, 15% mazuelo, graciano

87 Colour: cherry, garnet rim. Nose: spicy, balsamic herbs, creamy oak, ripe fruit. Palate: powerful, flavourful, spicy, long.

OTOÑAL 2011 TC
90% tempranillo, 5% garnacha, 5% mazuelo, graciano

87 Colour: cherry, garnet rim. Nose: ripe fruit, spicy, toasty. Palate: powerful, flavourful, toasty, round tannins.

OTOÑAL 2012 T
100% tempranillo

84

SUMMA 2008 TR
85% tempranillo, 10% graciano, 5% mazuelo

91 Colour: cherry, garnet rim. Nose: ripe fruit, spicy, creamy oak, toasty, complex. Palate: powerful, flavourful, toasty, round tannins.

BODEGAS ONDALÁN

Ctra. de Logroño, 22
1320 Oyón - Oion (Álava)
☎: +34 945 622 537 - Fax: +34 945 622 538
www.ondalan.es
ondalan@ondalan.es

100 ABADES GRACIANO SELECCIÓN 2010 T
100% graciano

90 Colour: cherry, garnet rim. Nose: ripe fruit, spicy, creamy oak, toasty, complex. Palate: powerful, flavourful, toasty, balanced.

ONDALÁN 2008 TR
70% tempranillo, 30% graciano

89 Colour: cherry, garnet rim. Nose: ripe fruit, spicy, creamy oak, toasty. Palate: powerful, flavourful, toasty.

ONDALÁN 2010 TC
80% tempranillo, 20% graciano

85 Colour: cherry, garnet rim. Nose: ripe fruit, scrubland, woody. Palate: spicy, toasty.

ONDALÁN 2012 B
100% viura

87 Colour: bright straw. Nose: fruit expression, fragrant herbs, balanced, neat, fresh. Palate: sweetness, fresh, fruity, powerful, flavourful.

ONDALÁN 2012 T
90% tempranillo, 10% garnacha

86 Colour: cherry, purple rim. Nose: floral, red berry notes, ripe fruit. Palate: flavourful, fruity, good acidity.

ONDALÁN TEMPRANILLO SELECCIÓN 2010 T
100% tempranillo

87 Colour: cherry, garnet rim. Nose: ripe fruit, aged wood nuances, woody. Palate: spicy, toasty.

BODEGAS ONDARRE

Ctra. de Aras, s/n
31230 Viana (Navarra)
☎: +34 948 645 300 - Fax: +34 948 646 002
www.bodegasondarre.es
bodegasondarre@bodegasondarre.es

MAYOR DE ONDARRE 2008 TR
88% tempranillo, 12% mazuelo

91 Colour: cherry, garnet rim. Nose: ripe fruit, spicy, creamy oak, toasty, complex. Palate: powerful, flavourful, toasty, round tannins, balanced, elegant.

ONDARRE 2008 TR
85% tempranillo, 5% garnacha, 10% mazuelo

90 Colour: cherry, garnet rim. Nose: ripe fruit, fruit liqueur notes, balsamic herbs, creamy oak, earthy notes. Palate: powerful, flavourful, spicy, long.

BODEGAS ORBEN

Ctra. Laguardia, Km. 60
1300 Laguardia (Álava)
☎: +34 945 609 086 - Fax: +34 945 609 261
www.grupoartevino.com
izadi@izadi.com

MALPUESTO 2011 T
100% tempranillo

95 Colour: cherry, garnet rim. Nose: creamy oak, toasty, complex, mineral, earthy notes, fruit expression. Palate: powerful, flavourful, toasty, round tannins.

ORBEN 2009 T
100% tempranillo

93 Colour: deep cherry. Nose: ripe fruit, spicy, creamy oak, complex. Palate: powerful, flavourful, toasty, round tannins.

BODEGAS OSTATU

Ctra. Vitoria, 1
1307 Samaniego (Álava)
☎: +34 945 609 133 - Fax: +34 945 623 338
www.ostatu.com
ostatu@ostatu.com

GLORIA DE OSTATU 2007 T
100% tempranillo

93 Colour: deep cherry, garnet rim. Nose: complex, ripe fruit, varietal, spicy, toasty. Palate: balanced, long, ripe fruit, round tannins.

LADERAS OSTATU 2009 T
tempranillo, viura

90 Colour: bright cherry, garnet rim. Nose: complex, spicy, varietal, ripe fruit, roasted coffee. Palate: good structure, round tannins.

LORE DE OSTATU 2010 B
viura, malvasía

92 Colour: bright yellow. Nose: powerfull, ripe fruit, sweet spices, creamy oak, fragrant herbs. Palate: rich, smoky aftertaste, flavourful, fresh, good acidity.

OSTATU 2008 TR
tempranillo

91 Colour: bright cherry, garnet rim. Nose: expressive, varietal, spicy, dried herbs. Palate: flavourful, good structure, round tannins.

OSTATU 2010 TC
tempranillo, graciano, mazuelo, garnacha

90 Colour: cherry, garnet rim. Nose: spicy, dried herbs, red berry notes, ripe fruit. Palate: powerful, flavourful, round tannins.

OSTATU 2012 B
viura, malvasía

90 Colour: bright straw. Nose: ripe fruit, citrus fruit, floral, dried herbs. Palate: powerful, flavourful, creamy, long, balanced.

OSTATU 2012 T
tempranillo, graciano, mazuelo, viura

89 Colour: cherry, purple rim. Nose: red berry notes, ripe fruit, fragrant herbs, expressive. Palate: powerful, flavourful, fresh, fruity.

OSTATU SELECCIÓN 2009 T
tempranillo, graciano

89 Colour: bright cherry, garnet rim. Nose: ripe fruit, spicy, dried herbs. Palate: flavourful, fruity, round tannins.

BODEGAS PACO GARCÍA

Crta. de Ventas Blancas s/n
26143 Murillo de Rio Leza (La Rioja)
☎: +34 941 432 372 - Fax: +34 941 432 156
www.bodegaspacogarcia.com
info@bodegaspacogarcia.com

BEAUTIFUL THINGS DE PACO GARCÍA 2009 T
90% tempranillo, 10% graciano

90 Colour: cherry, garnet rim. Nose: ripe fruit, spicy, balsamic herbs. Palate: powerful, flavourful, toasty, round tannins.

PACO GARCÍA 2010 TC
90% tempranillo, 10% garnacha

90 Colour: cherry, garnet rim. Nose: ripe fruit, spicy, creamy oak, complex. Palate: flavourful, round tannins, complex.

PACO GARCÍA SEIS 2011 T
100% tempranillo

90 Colour: bright cherry, purple rim. Nose: toasty, sweet spices, ripe fruit, fruit preserve. Palate: fruity, flavourful, easy to drink.

BODEGAS PALACIO

San Lázaro, 1
1300 Laguardia (Álava)
☎: +34 945 600 057 - Fax: +34 945 600 297
www.bodegaspalacio.es
rrpp@bodegaspalacio.es

COSME PALACIO 2008 TR
100% tempranillo

90 Colour: cherry, garnet rim. Nose: sweet spices, ripe fruit, earthy notes. Palate: ripe fruit, fine bitter notes, good acidity.

COSME PALACIO VENDIMIA SELECCIONADA 2010 TC
100% tempranillo

91 Colour: cherry, garnet rim. Nose: ripe fruit, spicy, creamy oak, toasty, complex, mineral. Palate: powerful, flavourful, toasty, round tannins.

COSME PALACIO VENDIMIA SELECCIONADA 2011 B

88 Colour: bright yellow. Nose: powerfull, expressive, waxy notes, wet leather, macerated fruit. Palate: powerful, flavourful, fruity, fresh, good finish, fruity aftestaste.

GLORIOSO 2006 TGR
tempranillo

90 Colour: pale ruby, brick rim edge. Nose: medium intensity, ripe fruit, sweet spices, wet leather. Palate: light-bodied, fine bitter notes, elegant.

GLORIOSO 2008 TR
100% tempranillo

91 Colour: cherry, garnet rim. Nose: spicy, creamy oak, toasty, ripe fruit. Palate: powerful, flavourful, toasty, round tannins.

GLORIOSO 2009 TR
100% tempranillo

92 Colour: cherry, garnet rim. Nose: spicy, creamy oak, toasty, fruit expression. Palate: powerful, flavourful, toasty, round tannins.

GLORIOSO 2010 TC
100% tempranillo

90 Colour: cherry, garnet rim. Nose: spicy, creamy oak, toasty, fruit expression. Palate: powerful, flavourful, toasty, round tannins.

MILFLORES 2012 T
100% tempranillo

91 Colour: dark-red cherry. Nose: fruit expression, violet drops, powerfull, varietal, characterful. Palate: powerful, flavourful, light-bodied, fresh, fruity.

BODEGAS PALACIOS REMONDO

Avda. Zaragoza, 8
26540 Alfaro (La Rioja)
☎: +34 941 180 207 - Fax: +34 941 181 628
info@palaciosremondo.com

LA MONTESA 2010 TC
75% garnacha, 20% tempranillo, 5% mazuelo

90 Colour: deep cherry. Nose: ripe fruit, spicy, toasty, scrubland. Palate: fine bitter notes, good acidity, spicy.

LA MONTESA 2011 TC
75% garnacha, 20% tempranillo, 5% mazuelo

91 Colour: bright cherry. Nose: ripe fruit, sweet spices, creamy oak, spicy. Palate: flavourful, fruity, toasty, round tannins.

LA VENDIMIA 2012 T
50% garnacha, 50% tempranillo

91 Colour: dark-red cherry, garnet rim. Nose: fruit expression, wild herbs, maceration notes, varietal, powerfull. Palate: correct, elegant, good acidity, fruity, full, powerful.

PLÁCET VALTOMELLOSO 2010 B
100% viura

93 Colour: bright yellow. Nose: powerfull, ripe fruit, sweet spices, creamy oak, fragrant herbs. Palate: rich, flavourful, fresh, good acidity.

PROPIEDAD VIÑAS TRADICIONALES 2010 T
100% garnacha

92 Colour: deep cherry. Nose: ripe fruit, scrubland, spicy, mineral. Palate: spicy, flavourful, good acidity, fine bitter notes.

BODEGAS PATERNINA

Avda. Santo Domingo, 11
26200 Haro (La Rioja)
☎: +34 941 310 550 - Fax: +34 941 312 778
www.paternina.com
info@paternina.com

BANDA AZUL 2009 TC
75% tempranillo, 25% garnacha

86 Colour: cherry, garnet rim. Nose: ripe fruit, fruit pre-serve, aged wood nuances, creamy oak. Palate: flavourful, spicy, toasty.

BANDA DORADA 2012 B
100% viura

86 Colour: bright straw. Nose: neat, fresh, medium intensity. Palate: fresh, fruity, light-bodied, flavourful.

BANDA ROSA 2012 RD
95% garnacha, 5% viura

84

CLISOS 2012 T
100% tempranillo

82

CONDES DE LOS ANDES 2005 TGR
80% tempranillo, 10% mazuelo, 10% graciano

88 Colour: pale ruby, brick rim edge. Nose: elegant, spicy, fine reductive notes, wet leather, aged wood nuances, fruit liqueur notes. Palate: spicy, fine tannins, elegant, long.

CONDES DE LOS ANDES 2008 TR
85% tempranillo, 10% mazuelo, 5% garnacha

88 Colour: pale ruby, brick rim edge. Nose: ripe fruit, balsamic herbs, fruit liqueur notes, spicy, toasty. Palate: powerful, long, correct, classic aged character.

**FEDERICO PATERNINA SELECCIÓN
ESPECIAL 2010 T**
100% tempranillo

90 Colour: cherry, garnet rim. Nose: ripe fruit, spicy, creamy oak, toasty. Palate: powerful, flavourful, toasty.

LACORT 2009 T
100% tempranillo

87 Colour: bright cherry. Nose: ripe fruit, sweet spices, creamy oak, toasty. Palate: flavourful, fruity, toasty.

LACORT 2012 B
viura, malvasía

84

VIÑA VIAL 2008 TR
85% tempranillo, 10% mazuelo, 5% garnacha

85 Colour: pale ruby, brick rim edge. Nose: spicy, wet leather, aged wood nuances, fruit liqueur notes. Palate: spicy, long, correct.

BODEGAS PATROCINIO

Ctra. Cenicero
26313 Uruñuela (La Rioja)
☎: +34 941 371 319 - Fax: +34 941 371 435
info@bodegaspatrocinio.com

LÁGRIMAS DE MARÍA 2008 TR
100% tempranillo

88 Colour: cherry, garnet rim. Nose: ripe fruit, spicy, creamy oak, toasty. Palate: powerful, flavourful, toasty, round tannins.

LÁGRIMAS DE MARÍA 2010 TC
100% tempranillo

91 Colour: cherry, garnet rim. Nose: spicy, creamy oak, toasty. Palate: powerful, flavourful, toasty, round tannins.

LÁGRIMAS DE MARÍA 2012 B
100% viura

85 Colour: bright straw. Nose: fresh fruit, grassy, balanced, neat. Palate: fruity, fresh, flavourful.

LÁGRIMAS DE MARÍA 2012 RD
100% tempranillo

86 Colour: light cherry, bright. Nose: red berry notes, ripe fruit, medium intensity. Palate: flavourful, fruity, easy to drink.

LÁGRIMAS DE MARÍA 2012 T
100% tempranillo

85 Colour: cherry, purple rim. Nose: ripe fruit, powerfull. Palate: flavourful, fruity, ripe fruit, long, round tannins.

LÁGRIMAS DE MARÍA MADURADO 2010 TC
100% tempranillo

86 Colour: very deep cherry. Nose: powerfull, ripe fruit, sweet spices. Palate: powerful, flavourful, spicy.

SANCHO GARCÉS 2008 TR
100% tempranillo

88 Colour: cherry, garnet rim. Nose: ripe fruit, creamy oak, toasty. Palate: powerful, flavourful, toasty, round tannins.

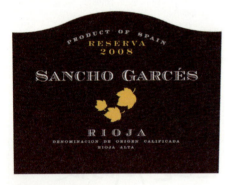

SANCHO GARCÉS 2010 TC
100% tempranillo

88 Colour: cherry, garnet rim. Nose: ripe fruit, spicy, creamy oak, toasty. Palate: powerful, flavourful, round tannins.

SANCHO GARCÉS 2012 T
100% tempranillo

88 Colour: cherry, garnet rim. Nose: spicy, creamy oak, toasty. Palate: powerful, flavourful, toasty, round tannins.

SEÑORÍO DE UÑUELA 2008 TR
100% tempranillo

87 Colour: very deep cherry. Nose: dark chocolate, spicy. Palate: flavourful, fine bitter notes, good acidity.

SEÑORÍO DE UÑUELA 2010 TC
100% tempranillo

89 Colour: cherry, garnet rim. Nose: spicy, creamy oak, toasty, scrubland, balsamic herbs. Palate: powerful, flavourful, toasty, round tannins.

SEÑORÍO DE UÑUELA 2012 B
100% viura

89 Colour: bright straw. Nose: fragrant herbs, fresh fruit, fruit expression, varietal, neat, complex. Palate: sweetness, fresh, fruity, powerful, flavourful.

SEÑORÍO DE UÑUELA 2012 RD
100% tempranillo

85 Colour: light cherry. Nose: ripe fruit, faded flowers, balsamic herbs. Palate: powerful, flavourful, warm.

SEÑORÍO DE UÑUELA 2012 T
100% tempranillo

85 Colour: cherry, garnet rim. Nose: reduction notes, varietal, macerated fruit. Palate: sweetness, carbonic notes, flavourful.

SEÑORÍO DE UÑUELA GARNACHA 2011 T
100% garnacha

88 Colour: deep cherry. Nose: fruit expression, violet drops. Palate: flavourful, fruity, fresh.

ZINIO 2012 B
2,25% viura

89 Colour: bright straw. Nose: fresh fruit, white flowers. Palate: flavourful, fruity, good acidity, balanced.

ZINIO 2012 RD
100% tempranillo

86 Colour: light cherry, bright. Nose: ripe fruit, medium intensity, faded flowers. Palate: flavourful, fruity.

ZINIO GARNACHA 2011 T
100% garnacha

88 Colour: cherry, purple rim. Nose: floral, ripe fruit, fruit liqueur notes, fragrant herbs. Palate: flavourful, fruity, good acidity.

ZINIO ORGÁNICO 2009 T
70% tempranillo, 30% garnacha

88 Colour: cherry, garnet rim. Nose: ripe fruit, balsamic herbs, spicy, creamy oak. Palate: flavourful, spicy, correct.

ZINIO VENDIMIA SELECCIONADA 2006 TR
100% tempranillo

88 Colour: deep cherry. Nose: wet leather, ripe fruit, sweet spices. Palate: ripe fruit, spicy.

ZINIO VENDIMIA SELECCIONADA 2010 T
85% tempranillo, 15% graciano

89 Colour: cherry, garnet rim. Nose: ripe fruit, spicy, creamy oak, toasty, complex. Palate: powerful, flavourful, toasty.

ZINIO VENDIMIA SELECCIONADA 2010 TC
100% tempranillo

89 Colour: cherry, garnet rim. Nose: ripe fruit, sweet spices, creamy oak, expressive. Palate: flavourful, fruity, toasty.

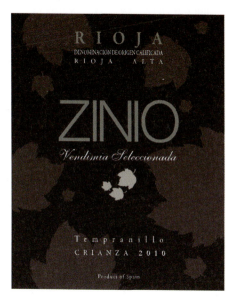

BODEGAS PERICA

Avda. de la Rioja, 59
26340 San Asensio (La Rioja)
☎: +34 941 457 152 - Fax: +34 941 457 240
www.bodegasperica.com
info@bodegasperica.com

6 CEPAS 6 2011 T
100% tempranillo

90 Colour: black cherry, purple rim. Nose: powerfull, dark chocolate, ripe fruit, creamy oak. Palate: good structure, flavourful, round tannins.

6 CEPAS 6 2012 B
60% viura, 40% verdejo

88 Colour: bright yellow. Nose: powerfull, ripe fruit, sweet spices, creamy oak, fragrant herbs. Palate: rich, flavourful, fresh, good acidity.

MI VILLA 2012 T
85% tempranillo, 15% garnacha

89 Colour: cherry, purple rim. Nose: red berry notes, floral, ripe fruit, fruit expression. Palate: flavourful, fruity, good acidity, round tannins.

OLAGOSA 2008 TR
90% tempranillo, 5% garnacha, 5% mazuelo

87 Colour: cherry, garnet rim. Nose: ripe fruit, spicy, toasty. Palate: powerful, flavourful, toasty, round tannins.

OLAGOSA 2010 TC
90% tempranillo, 5% garnacha, 5% mazuelo

89 Colour: very deep cherry. Nose: sweet spices, medium intensity, ripe fruit. Palate: flavourful, fruity, smoky aftertaste.

OLAGOSA 2012 BFB
95% viura, 5% malvasía

87 Colour: bright yellow. Nose: ripe fruit, sweet spices, creamy oak, fragrant herbs. Palate: rich, flavourful, fresh, good acidity.

PERICA ORO RESERVA ESPECIAL 2008 TR
95% tempranillo, 5% garnacha

92 Colour: very deep cherry, garnet rim. Nose: expressive, ripe fruit, creamy oak, sweet spices, complex. Palate: full, flavourful, long, round tannins.

BODEGAS PUELLES

Bodegas Puelles
26339 Ábalos (La Rioja)
☎: +34 941 334 415 - Fax: +34 941 334 132
www.bodegaspuelles.com
informacion@bodegaspuelles.com

PUELLES 2007 TR
tempranillo

88 Colour: cherry, garnet rim. Nose: expressive, ripe fruit, spicy, toasty. Palate: flavourful, spicy, fine bitter notes.

PUELLES 2010 TC
tempranillo

87 Colour: bright cherry. Nose: ripe fruit, sweet spices, creamy oak. Palate: flavourful, fruity, toasty, round tannins.

PUELLES 2011 T
tempranillo

84

PUELLES 2012 B
viura

85 Colour: bright straw. Nose: ripe fruit, floral, dried herbs. Palate: powerful, easy to drink, correct.

BODEGAS RAMÍREZ DE LA PISCINA

Ctra. Vitoria-Logroño, s/n
26338 San Vicente de la Sonsierra (La Rioja)
☎: +34 941 334 505 - Fax: +34 941 334 506
www.ramirezdelapiscina.es
rampiscina@knet.es

RAMÍREZ DE LA PISCINA 2007 TR
100% tempranillo

88 Colour: pale ruby, brick rim edge. Nose: toasty, spicy. Palate: spicy, good acidity, fine bitter notes.

RAMÍREZ DE LA PISCINA 2009 T
100% tempranillo

90 Colour: cherry, garnet rim. Nose: toasty, aromatic coffee, dark chocolate, ripe fruit. Palate: flavourful, powerful, spicy, ripe fruit.

RAMÍREZ DE LA PISCINA 2012 RD
50% viura, 50% garnacha

85 Colour: coppery red. Nose: red berry notes, medium intensity. Palate: flavourful, fruity, fresh.

RAMÍREZ DE LA PISCINA 2012 B
100% viura

84

RAMÍREZ DE LA PISCINA 2012
T MACERACIÓN CARBÓNICA
100% tempranillo

86 Colour: cherry, purple rim. Nose: red berry notes, ripe fruit, wild herbs. Palate: powerful, flavourful, fruity.

RAMÍREZ DE LA PISCINA SELECCIÓN 2005 TR
100% tempranillo

90 Colour: cherry, garnet rim. Nose: ripe fruit, spicy, creamy oak, toasty. Palate: powerful, flavourful, toasty, round tannins.

RAMÍREZ DE LA PISCINA SELECCIÓN 2009 TC
100% tempranillo

88 Colour: cherry, garnet rim. Nose: ripe fruit, spicy, creamy oak. Palate: powerful, flavourful, toasty, round tannins.

SANTA MARÍA DE LA PISCINA 2005 TGR
100% tempranillo

88 Colour: deep cherry. Nose: spicy, toasty, waxy notes, tobacco, fruit liqueur notes. Palate: light-bodied, spicy, ripe fruit.

BODEGAS RAMÓN BILBAO

Avda. Santo Domingo, 34
26200 Haro (La Rioja)
☎: +34 941 310 295 - Fax: +34 941 310 832
www.bodegasramonbilbao.es
info@bodegasramonbilbao.es

MIRTO DE RAMÓN BILBAO 2009 T
100% tempranillo

93 Colour: cherry, garnet rim. Nose: red berry notes, ripe fruit, sweet spices, creamy oak, mineral, balanced, expressive. Palate: rich, powerful, flavourful, spicy, long, round, elegant.

RAMÓN BILBAO 2005 TGR
90% tempranillo, 5% mazuelo, 5% graciano

92 Colour: pale ruby, brick rim edge. Nose: elegant, spicy, fine reductive notes, creamy oak. Palate: spicy, fine tannins, elegant, long.

RAMÓN BILBAO 2009 TR
90% tempranillo, 5% mazuelo, 5% graciano

91 Colour: cherry, garnet rim. Nose: red berry notes, ripe fruit, balsamic herbs, spicy, tobacco, wet leather, expressive. Palate: elegant, flavourful, long, spicy.

RAMÓN BILBAO ROSÉ 2012 RD
100% garnacha

89 Colour: raspberry rose. Nose: elegant, candied fruit, fragrant herbs, red berry notes, floral, lactic notes. Palate: light-bodied, flavourful, good acidity, long.

RAMÓN BILBAO 2011 TC
100% tempranillo

89 Colour: cherry, garnet rim. Nose: ripe fruit, balsamic herbs, creamy oak, spicy. Palate: powerful, flavourful, toasty.

RAMÓN BILBAO EDICIÓN LIMITADA 2011 T
100% tempranillo

91 Colour: cherry, garnet rim. Nose: complex, ripe fruit, aromatic coffee, creamy oak, balsamic herbs. Palate: rich, round, long, spicy, flavourful.

RAMÓN BILBAO VIÑEDOS DE ALTURA 2011 TC
50% tempranillo, 50% garnacha

90 Colour: cherry, garnet rim. Nose: ripe fruit, spicy, creamy oak, toasty, complex. Palate: powerful, flavourful, toasty, balanced.

BODEGAS REAL DIVISA

Barrio del Montalvo, s/n
26339 Abalos (La Rioja)
☎: +34 941 334 118 - Fax: +34 941 334 118
www.realdivisa.com
realdivisa@fer.es

MARQUÉS DE LEGARDA 2010 TC
tempranillo

83

BODEGAS REMÍREZ DE GANUZA

Constitución, 1
1307 Samaniego (Álava)
☎: +34 945 609 022 - Fax: +34 945 623 335
www.remirezdeganuza.com
cristina@remirezdeganuza.com

REMÍREZ DE GANUZA 2005 TGR
90% tempranillo, 10% graciano

93 Colour: deep cherry. Nose: ripe fruit, fruit preserve, fine reductive notes, spicy. Palate: good structure, flavourful, good acidity, balanced, round tannins.

REMÍREZ DE GANUZA 2007 TR
90% tempranillo, 5% graciano, 5% viura, malvasía

94 Colour: bright cherry, garnet rim. Nose: expressive, complex, elegant. Palate: flavourful, good structure, round tannins, complex, full.

TRASNOCHO 2008 T
90% tempranillo, 5% graciano, 5% viura, malvasía

93 Colour: cherry, garnet rim. Nose: medium intensity, balanced, ripe fruit, spicy. Palate: complex, flavourful, round tannins, good acidity.

VIÑA COQUETA 2007 TR
90% tempranillo, 5% graciano, 5% viura, malvasía

92 Colour: deep cherry, garnet rim. Nose: balanced, ripe fruit, spicy, elegant, scrubland.

ERRE PUNTO 2011 BFB
70% viura, 30% malvasía

89 Colour: bright yellow. Nose: ripe fruit, spicy, dried flowers, medium intensity. Palate: balanced, ripe fruit.

ERRE PUNTO 2012 T MACERACIÓN CARBÓNICA
90% tempranillo, 5% garnacha, 5% viura, malvasía

91 Colour: cherry, purple rim. Nose: red berry notes, violet drops. Palate: fruity, flavourful, balanced, round tannins.

FINCAS DE GANUZA 2006 TR
90% tempranillo, 10% graciano

92 Colour: dark-red cherry, garnet rim. Nose: spicy, balanced, ripe fruit. Palate: flavourful, full, round tannins, elegant, balanced.

BODEGAS RIOJANAS

Avda. Ruiz de Azcárraga, 1
26350 Cenicero (La Rioja)
☎: +34 941 454 050 - Fax: +34 941 452 929
www.bodegasriojanas.com
rrpp@bodegasriojanas.com

CANCHALES 2011 T
100% tempranillo

88 Colour: dark-red cherry. Nose: candied fruit, balsamic herbs. Palate: fresh, fruity, green, powerful, flavourful, good acidity.

GRAN ALBINA 2006 TR
34% tempranillo, 33% mazuelo, 33% graciano

89 Colour: dark-red cherry, brick rim edge. Nose: candied fruit, powerfull, toasty. Palate: powerful, dry, oaky, ripe fruit, grainy tannins.

GRAN ALBINA 2007 TR
tempranillo, mazuelo, graciano

90 Colour: dark-red cherry. Nose: fruit expression, powerfull, varietal, cedar wood, creamy oak. Palate: powerful, flavourful, spicy.

MONTE REAL 2005 TGR
100% tempranillo

88 Colour: cherry, garnet rim. Nose: expressive, fine reductive notes, powerfull, complex, spicy. Palate: toasty, spicy, reductive nuances.

MONTE REAL 2007 TR
100% tempranillo

89 Colour: cherry, garnet rim. Nose: ripe fruit, aged wood nuances, balsamic herbs, spicy, creamy oak, wet leather, cigar. Palate: powerful, flavourful, spicy, long.

MONTE REAL 2010 TC
100% tempranillo

88 Colour: deep cherry. Nose: spicy, toasty, cocoa bean, powerfull. Palate: fine bitter notes, powerful, flavourful, creamy, spicy.

MONTE REAL RESERVA DE FAMILIA 2007 TR
100% tempranillo

91 Colour: light cherry. Nose: complex, expressive, powerfull, spicy, cocoa bean, fruit preserve. Palate: round, good acidity, powerful, flavourful, complex.

PUERTA VIEJA 2008 TR
80% tempranillo, 15% mazuelo, 5% graciano

88 Colour: cherry, garnet rim. Nose: ripe fruit, spicy, creamy oak, tobacco, waxy notes. Palate: powerful, flavourful, toasty.

PUERTA VIEJA 2010 TC
80% tempranillo, 15% mazuelo, 5% graciano

87 Colour: dark-red cherry. Nose: wet leather, spicy, cedar wood, creamy oak, ripe fruit. Palate: grainy tannins, powerful, flavourful, dry, spicy.

PUERTA VIEJA 2012 B
100% viura

86 Colour: straw. Nose: medium intensity, fresh, neat, macerated fruit. Palate: fresh, fruity, light-bodied, flavourful.

PUERTA VIEJA SELECCIÓN 2010 TC
80% tempranillo, 15% mazuelo, 5% graciano

87 Colour: deep cherry. Nose: powerfull, expressive, candied fruit, toasty. Palate: good structure, powerful, flavourful, spicy, oaky.

VIÑA ALBINA 2012 BFB
90% viura, 10% malvasía

87 Colour: bright yellow. Nose: candied fruit, creamy oak. Palate: fruity, fresh, smoky aftertaste.

VIÑA ALBINA 2001 B RESERVA
90% viura, 10% malvasía

93 Colour: golden. Nose: powerfull, floral, honeyed notes, candied fruit, fragrant herbs. Palate: flavourful, sweet, fresh, fruity, good acidity, long.

VIÑA ALBINA 2005 TGR
80% tempranillo, 15% mazuelo, 5% graciano

88 Colour: dark-red cherry, orangey edge. Nose: complex, old leather, fine reductive notes, tobacco, spicy, pattiserie. Palate: round, good acidity, powerful, flavourful, spicy, creamy.

VIÑA ALBINA 2007 TR
80% tempranillo, 15% mazuelo, 5% graciano

87 Colour: light cherry, orangey edge. Nose: fine reductive notes, fruit preserve, cedar wood, sweet spices. Palate: powerful, flavourful, spicy, lacks expression, roasted-coffee aftertaste.

VIÑA ALBINA SELECCIÓN 2007 TR
80% tempranillo, 15% mazuelo, 5% graciano

89 Colour: dark-red cherry, orangey edge. Nose: cedar wood, sweet spices, ripe fruit. Palate: powerful, dry, spicy, toasty.

VIÑA ALBINA SEMIDULCE 2012 B
viura, malvasía

85 Colour: bright straw. Nose: dried herbs, fine lees, floral, candied fruit. Palate: fresh, fruity, flavourful, good acidity.

BODEGAS RIOLANC

Curillos, 36
1308 Lanciego (Álava)
☎: +34 945 608 140 - Fax: +34 945 608 140
www.riolanc.com
riolanc@riolanc.com

RIOLANC 2009 TC
100% tempranillo

84

RIOLANC VENDIMIA SELECCIONADA 2012 T
85% tempranillo, 15% mazuelo

87 Colour: cherry, purple rim. Nose: red berry notes, ripe fruit, wild herbs. Palate: powerful, flavourful, fruity.

BODEGAS RODA

Avda. de Vizcaya, 5
26200 Haro (La Rioja)
☎: +34 941 303 001 - Fax: +34 941 312 703
www.roda.es
rodarioja@roda.es

CIRSION 2010 T
100% tempranillo

96 Colour: dark-red cherry. Nose: powerfull, expressive, complex, fruit expression, creamy oak, spicy, toasty. Palate: creamy, ripe fruit, powerful, flavourful, full, complex.

RODA 2008 TR
89% tempranillo, 11% graciano

91 Colour: dark-red cherry. Nose: powerfull, complex, spicy, creamy oak, toasty. Palate: creamy, spicy, toasty, round tannins.

RODA 2009 TR

91 Colour: dark-red cherry. Nose: fruit expression, cocoa bean, spicy, creamy oak. Palate: round, elegant, full, powerful, flavourful.

RODA I 2007 TR
100% tempranillo

94 Colour: dark-red cherry. Nose: aromatic coffee, sweet spices, candied fruit. Palate: complex, fruity, powerful, flavourful, spicy, creamy, roasted-coffee aftertaste.

PRODUCT OF SPAIN — ESTATE BOTTLED

RODA I
RESERVA
2007

EMBOTELLADO EN LA PROPIEDAD

BODEGAS RODA, S.A.
HARO - ESPAÑA

ALC.14,5%VOL.

75 cl.e

RIOJA
DENOMINACIÓN DE ORIGEN CALIFICADA

R.E. 7276-LO

SELA 2010 T
95% tempranillo, 5% graciano

89 Colour: dark-red cherry. Nose: complex, expressive, varietal, fresh fruit, spicy, creamy oak. Palate: balanced, powerful, flavourful, roasted-coffee aftertaste.

SELA 2011 T
95% tempranillo, 3% graciano, 2% garnacha

90 Colour: cherry, garnet rim. Nose: fruit expression, sweet spices, creamy oak, toasty. Palate: powerful, flavourful, fruity, complex, spicy.

BODEGAS RUCONIA

Ctra. de San Asensio, s/n
26300 Nájera (La Rioja)
☎: +34 941 362 059 - Fax: +34 941 362 467
www.bodegasruconia.com
info@bodegasruconia.com

ALUÉN + 2008 T
100% tempranillo

89 Colour: cherry, garnet rim. Nose: spicy, creamy oak, toasty, complex, ripe fruit, fruit preserve. Palate: powerful, flavourful, toasty, rich.

RUCONIA 2007 TR
100% tempranillo

87 Colour: pale ruby, brick rim edge. Nose: waxy notes, cigar, balsamic herbs, spicy, ripe fruit. Palate: powerful, flavourful, spicy, long.

RUCONIA 2008 TC
100% tempranillo

84

RUCONIA 2010 TC
100% tempranillo

86 Colour: cherry, garnet rim. Nose: woody, ripe fruit, balsamic herbs, fine reductive notes. Palate: flavourful, toasty, correct.

RUCONIA 2012 T
100% tempranillo

84

TUBAL 2008 TC
100% tempranillo

85 Colour: cherry, garnet rim. Nose: ripe fruit, balsamic herbs, spicy, woody. Palate: flavourful, long, slightly evolved.

TUBAL 2010 TC
100% tempranillo

87 Colour: cherry, garnet rim. Nose: ripe fruit, spicy, creamy oak, toasty, balsamic herbs. Palate: powerful, flavourful, toasty.

BODEGAS SAN MARTÍN DE ABALOS

Camino del Prado s/n
26211 Fonzaleche (La Rioja)
☎: +34 941 300 423 - Fax: +34 941 300 423
www.sanmartindeabalos.com
comercial@bodegasanmartindeabalos.com

DOÑA CASILDA 2012 T

82

PORTALON DE SAN MARTÍN 2010 T
80% tempranillo, 15% viura, 5% garnacha

90 Colour: cherry, garnet rim. Nose: ripe fruit, spicy, creamy oak, toasty. Palate: powerful, flavourful, toasty.

PRADO DE FONZALECHE 2007 TR
85% tempranillo, 10% garnacha, 5% viura

87 Colour: cherry, garnet rim. Nose: ripe fruit, spicy, creamy oak, toasty, fine reductive notes. Palate: powerful, flavourful, toasty.

VIÑA VEREDA DEL RÍO 2008 TC
80% tempranillo, 15% garnacha, 5% viura

82

BODEGAS SANTALBA

Avda. de la Rioja, s/n
26221 Gimileo (La Rioja)
☎: +34 941 304 231 - Fax: +34 941 304 326
www.santalba.com
santalba@santalba.com

ERMITA DE SAN FELICES 2008 TR
tempranillo

88 Colour: cherry, garnet rim. Nose: sweet spices, red berry notes, ripe fruit, balsamic herbs, creamy oak. Palate: powerful, flavourful, spicy.

NABOT 2005 T
tempranillo

89 Colour: dark-red cherry. Nose: ripe fruit, balsamic herbs, sweet spices, creamy oak, fine reductive notes. Palate: powerful, flavourful, spicy, long.

OGGA 2008 TR
tempranillo

90 Colour: cherry, garnet rim. Nose: ripe fruit, creamy oak, toasty, balanced, elegant. Palate: powerful, flavourful, toasty, round tannins.

SANTALBA ECOLÓGICO RESVERATROL 2011 T
tempranillo

90 Colour: bright cherry. Nose: ripe fruit, sweet spices, creamy oak, aromatic coffee. Palate: flavourful, fruity, toasty.

SANTALBA EDICIÓN LIMITADA 2008 T
tempranillo

89 Colour: cherry, garnet rim. Nose: ripe fruit, spicy, toasty. Palate: powerful, flavourful, toasty, balanced.

VIÑA HERMOSA 2008 TR
tempranillo

88 Colour: cherry, garnet rim. Nose: ripe fruit, balsamic herbs, sweet spices, creamy oak. Palate: powerful, flavourful, spicy.

BODEGAS SEÑORÍA DE YERGA

Barrio Bodegas, s/n
26142 Villamediana (La Rioja)
☎: +34 941 435 003
info@senoriodeyerga.com

CASTILLO DE YERGA 2009 TC
90% tempranillo, 10% garnacha

88 Colour: deep cherry. Nose: spicy, fruit liqueur notes, toasty. Palate: flavourful, toasty, fine bitter notes.

CASTILLO YERGA 2007 TR
90% tempranillo, 10% mazuelo

86 Colour: deep cherry. Nose: medium intensity, ripe fruit, spicy. Palate: flavourful, fine bitter notes, good acidity.

SEÑORÍO DE YERGA 2004 TGR
85% tempranillo, 10% graciano, 5% mazuelo

88 Colour: pale ruby, brick rim edge. Nose: old leather, fruit liqueur notes, toasty, spicy. Palate: flavourful, light-bodied, aged character.

BODEGAS SIDERALES

Senda Soto, 9
1306 Lapuebla de Labarca (Alava)
☎: +34 945 627 250 - Fax: +34 945 607 257
bodega@siderales.com

SIDERAL 2007 T
tempranillo

88 Colour: cherry, garnet rim. Nose: powerfull, ripe fruit, sweet spices. Palate: flavourful, powerful, fine bitter notes, round tannins.

SIDERAL I 2008 T
tempranillo

90 Colour: cherry, garnet rim. Nose: ripe fruit, spicy, creamy oak, toasty. Palate: powerful, flavourful, toasty, round tannins.

BODEGAS SOLAR VIEJO

Camino de la Hoya, s/n
1300 Laguardia (Álava)
☎: +34 945 600 113 - Fax: +34 945 600 600
www.solarviejo.com
solarviejo@solarviejo.com

AMOR DE MADRE 2010 T
tempranillo

87 Colour: cherry, garnet rim. Nose: ripe fruit, spicy, creamy oak, toasty. Palate: powerful, flavourful, spicy.

ORUBE 2010 T
tempranillo

90 Colour: cherry, garnet rim. Nose: red berry notes, ripe fruit, balsamic herbs, mineral, sweet spices, creamy oak. Palate: rich, flavourful, spicy, long.

SOLAR VIEJO 2007 TR
tempranillo, graciano

89 Colour: dark-red cherry, orangey edge. Nose: ripe fruit, balsamic herbs, spicy, creamy oak. Palate: balanced, flavourful, spicy, round tannins.

SOLAR VIEJO 2010 TC
tempranillo

87 Colour: cherry, garnet rim. Nose: ripe fruit, spicy, creamy oak, aged wood nuances. Palate: powerful, flavourful, toasty, spicy.

SOLAR VIEJO 2012 T
tempranillo

88 Colour: cherry, purple rim. Nose: fresh fruit, red berry notes, floral, balsamic herbs. Palate: flavourful, fruity, good acidity.

BODEGAS SONSIERRA, S. COOP.

El Remedio, s/n
26338 San Vicente de la Sonsierra (La Rioja)
☎: +34 941 334 031 - Fax: +34 941 334 245
www.sonsierra.com
administracion@sonsierra.com

PAGOS DE LA SONSIERRA 2008 TR
tempranillo

90 Colour: very deep cherry. Nose: powerfull, ripe fruit, fruit preserve, spicy. Palate: balanced, toasty, long, round tannins.

PERFUME DE SONSIERRA DAVID DELFÍN 2010 T
tempranillo

91 Colour: bright cherry. Nose: ripe fruit, sweet spices, creamy oak, expressive. Palate: flavourful, fruity, toasty, round tannins.

SONSIERRA 2008 TR
100% tempranillo

88 Colour: cherry, garnet rim. Nose: spicy, old leather, ripe fruit. Palate: fruity, correct, balanced.

SONSIERRA 2010 TC
tempranillo

89 Colour: bright cherry, garnet rim. Nose: balanced, ripe fruit, varietal. Palate: flavourful, good acidity, easy to drink.

SONSIERRA 2012 B
100% viura

87 Colour: bright straw. Nose: dried herbs, faded flowers. Palate: fruity, easy to drink, fine bitter notes.

SONSIERRA 2012 RD
tempranillo

85 Colour: rose. Nose: lactic notes, ripe fruit, fragrant herbs. Palate: powerful, flavourful, warm.

SONSIERRA TEMPRANILLO 2012 T
tempranillo

87 Colour: cherry, purple rim. Nose: red berry notes, ripe fruit, floral. Palate: powerful, flavourful, balanced.

SONSIERRA VENDIMIA SELECCIONADA 2009 TC

90 Colour: cherry, garnet rim. Nose: ripe fruit, creamy oak, toasty. Palate: powerful, flavourful, toasty, round tannins.

BODEGAS TARÓN

Ctra. de Miranda, s/n
26211 Tirgo (La Rioja)
☎: +34 941 301 650 - Fax: +34 941 301 817
www.bodegastaron.com
info@bodegastaron.com

TARÓN 2005 TR
90% tempranillo, 10% mazuelo

88 Colour: cherry, garnet rim. Nose: spicy, creamy oak, toasty. Palate: powerful, flavourful, round tannins.

TARÓN 2009 TC
95% tempranillo, 5% mazuelo

86 Colour: deep cherry. Nose: dark chocolate, toasty, aromatic coffee. Palate: spicy, ripe fruit.

TARÓN 2012 B
100% viura

88 Colour: bright straw. Nose: white flowers, ripe fruit. Palate: flavourful, fruity, good acidity, balanced.

TARÓN 2012 RD
50% viura, 50% garnacha

85 Colour: coppery red. Nose: medium intensity, elegant, fruit expression. Palate: flavourful, light-bodied, fruity.

TARÓN 4MB 2010 T
100% tempranillo

90 Colour: deep cherry. Nose: expressive, ripe fruit, creamy oak, cocoa bean. Palate: flavourful, spicy.

TARÓN CEPAS CENTENARIAS 2010 TR
100% tempranillo

92 Colour: cherry, garnet rim. Nose: spicy, creamy oak, toasty, complex, earthy notes. Palate: powerful, flavourful, toasty, round tannins.

TARÓN TEMPRANILLO 2012 T
100% tempranillo

87 Colour: cherry, purple rim. Nose: red berry notes, ripe fruit, balanced. Palate: flavourful, fruity, good acidity, round tannins.

BODEGAS TOBÍA

Paraje Senda Rutia, s/n
26214 Cuzcurrita de Río Tirón (La Rioja)
☎: +34 941 301 789 - Fax: +34 941 328 045
www.bodegastobia.com
tobia@bodegastobia.com

ALMA DE TOBÍA 2009 T
50% tempranillo, 35% graciano, 15% otras

91 Colour: deep cherry. Nose: damp undergrowth, varietal, powerfull, complex. Palate: powerful, flavourful, varietal, complex.

ALMA DE TOBÍA 2012 RD
FERMENTADO EN BARRICA
55% tempranillo, 35% graciano, 10% otras

90 Colour: rose, purple rim. Nose: powerfull, ripe fruit, red berry notes, sweet spices, creamy oak. Palate: powerful, fruity, fresh, spicy.

DAIMON 2011 T
50% tempranillo, 50% garnacha

89 Colour: cherry, garnet rim. Nose: spicy, toasty, ripe fruit. Palate: harsh oak tannins, powerful, flavourful.

DAIMON 2012 B
30% viura, 25% malvasía, 15% tempranillo blanco, 30% sauvignon blanc

86 Colour: bright yellow. Nose: spicy, slightly evolved, medium intensity. Palate: correct, flavourful, powerful, lacks expression, smoky aftertaste.

OSCAR TOBÍA 2007 T
95% tempranillo, 5% graciano

89 Colour: deep cherry. Nose: powerfull, roasted coffee, ripe fruit. Palate: powerful, flavourful, good structure.

TOBÍA GRACIANO 2010 T
100% graciano

87 Colour: very deep cherry. Nose: closed, spicy, aged wood nuances, ripe fruit. Palate: powerful, spicy, toasty.

TOBÍA SELECCIÓN 2009 TC
80% tempranillo, 10% graciano, 10% garnacha

90 Colour: dark-red cherry. Nose: spicy, creamy oak, toasty, ripe fruit, balsamic herbs. Palate: correct, balanced, flavourful, powerful.

VIÑA TOBÍA 2012 RD
100% garnacha

88 Colour: rose, purple rim. Nose: raspberry, fruit liqueur notes, powerfull, varietal, earthy notes. Palate: sweetness, fruity, fresh, powerful, flavourful.

VIÑA TOBÍA 2012 B
50% viura, 20% verdejo, 10% tempranillo blanco, 10% malvasía

88 Colour: pale. Nose: jasmine, fruit expression, fragrant herbs. Palate: fresh, fruity, light-bodied, flavourful.

VIÑA TOBÍA 2012 T
100% tempranillo

88 Colour: cherry, purple rim. Nose: fresh fruit, red berry notes, floral, balsamic herbs. Palate: flavourful, fruity, good acidity.

BODEGAS URBINA

Campillo, 33
26214 Cuzcurrita de Río Tirón (La Rioja)
☎: +34 941 224 272 - Fax: +34 941 224 272
www.urbinavinos.com
urbina@fer.es

URBINA 2008 TC
95% tempranillo, 2,5% mazuelo, 2,5% graciano

79

URBINA GARNACHA 2012 T
100% garnacha

86 Colour: cherry, purple rim. Nose: floral, ripe fruit, fresh. Palate: flavourful, fruity, good acidity, round tannins.

URBINA TEMPRANILLO 2012 T
100% tempranillo

82

URBINA VIURA 2012 B
100% viura

83

BODEGAS VALDELACIERVA

Ctra. Burgos, Km. 13
26370 Navarrete (La Rioja)
☎: +34 941 440 620 - Fax: +34 941 440 787
www.hispanobodegas.com
carlos.garcia@hispanobodegas.com

ALFAR 2012 BFB
viura

91 Colour: bright straw. Nose: white flowers, ripe fruit, fragrant herbs, sweet spices, toasty. Palate: powerful, flavourful, spicy, long.

IMPAR VENDIMIA SELECCIONADA 2011 T

90 Colour: cherry, garnet rim. Nose: ripe fruit, spicy, creamy oak, toasty, complex. Palate: powerful, flavourful, toasty, round tannins.

VALDELACIERVA 2010 TC
tempranillo

90 Colour: cherry, garnet rim. Nose: red berry notes, ripe fruit, sweet spices, creamy oak. Palate: spicy, powerful, flavourful.

ALFAR VENDIMIA SELECCIONADA 2011 T
tempranillo

90 Colour: cherry, garnet rim. Nose: ripe fruit, spicy, creamy oak, toasty. Palate: powerful, flavourful, toasty, balanced.

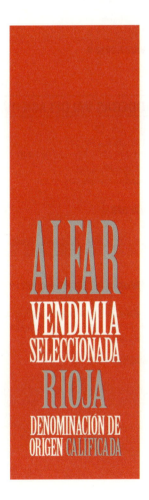

BODEGAS VALDELANA

Puente Barricuelo, 67-69
1340 Elciego (Álava)
☎: +34 945 606 055 - Fax: +34 945 606 587
www.bodegasvaldelana.com
info@bodegasvaldelana.com

AGNUS 2010 TC
95% tempranillo, 5% graciano

91 Colour: cherry, garnet rim. Nose: creamy oak, toasty, red berry notes, raspberry, ripe fruit. Palate: powerful, flavourful, toasty, balanced.

AGNUS DE VALDELANA DE AUTOR 2012 T
95% tempranillo, 5% graciano

87 Colour: bright cherry. Nose: ripe fruit, sweet spices, creamy oak. Palate: flavourful, fruity, toasty, round tannins.

DUQUESA DE LA VICTORIA 2010 TC
95% tempranillo, 5% mazuelo

90 Colour: cherry, garnet rim. Nose: ripe fruit, spicy, creamy oak, toasty, complex. Palate: powerful, flavourful, toasty, rich.

DUQUESA DE LA VICTORIA 2012 T
95% tempranillo, 5% viura

89 Colour: cherry, purple rim. Nose: fresh fruit, red berry notes, floral. Palate: flavourful, fruity, round tannins.

LADRÓN DE GUEVARA 2008 TR
95% tempranillo, 5% graciano

89 Colour: cherry, garnet rim. Nose: ripe fruit, balsamic herbs, sweet spices, creamy oak, expressive. Palate: powerful, flavourful, long, balsamic.

LADRÓN DE GUEVARA 2010 TC
95% tempranillo, 5% mazuelo

89 Colour: cherry, garnet rim. Nose: ripe fruit, spicy, creamy oak, toasty. Palate: powerful, flavourful, toasty.

LADRÓN DE GUEVARA 2012 B
viura

87 Colour: bright straw. Nose: fresh, fresh fruit, white flowers, expressive. Palate: flavourful, fruity, good acidity, balanced.

LADRÓN DE GUEVARA 2012 T
95% tempranillo, 5% viura

88 Colour: very deep cherry, purple rim. Nose: powerfull, fruit expression, ripe fruit, violet drops. Palate: flavourful, rich, round tannins.

LADRÓN DE GUEVARA DE AUTOR 2010 TC
95% tempranillo, 5% graciano

92 Colour: cherry, garnet rim. Nose: ripe fruit, spicy, creamy oak, toasty, complex, expressive. Palate: powerful, flavourful, toasty, round tannins, balanced.

LADRÓN DE GUEVARA DE AUTOR 2012 T
95% tempranillo, 5% graciano

89 Colour: bright cherry. Nose: ripe fruit, sweet spices, creamy oak. Palate: flavourful, fruity, toasty.

VALDELANA 2008 TR
95% tempranillo, 5% graciano

90 Colour: cherry, garnet rim. Nose: ripe fruit, creamy oak, toasty, complex, fine reductive notes. Palate: powerful, flavourful, toasty.

VALDELANA 2010 TC
95% tempranillo, 5% mazuelo

91 Colour: cherry, garnet rim. Nose: red berry notes, fruit preserve, balsamic herbs, sweet spices, creamy oak. Palate: powerful, flavourful, spicy.

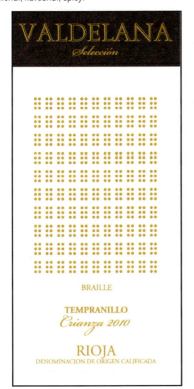

VALDELANA 2012 B
100% malvasía

88 Colour: bright straw. Nose: fresh fruit, white flowers, fragrant herbs. Palate: flavourful, fruity, good acidity, easy to drink.

VALDELANA 2012 T
95% tempranillo, 5% viura

90 Colour: deep cherry, purple rim. Nose: fruit expression, violet drops, expressive, floral. Palate: flavourful, fruity, long, fruity aftestaste.

BODEGAS VALDEMAR

Camino Viejo, s/n
1320 Oyón (Álava)
☎: +34 945 622 188 - Fax: +34 945 622 111
www.valdemar.es
info@valdemar.es

CONDE DE VALDEMAR 2006 TGR
85% tempranillo, 10% graciano, 5% maturana

90 Colour: deep cherry. Nose: ripe fruit, macerated fruit, cocoa bean, cedar wood, toasty, complex. Palate: powerful, flavourful, good structure, classic aged character, ripe fruit.

CONDE DE VALDEMAR 2008 TR
85% tempranillo, 10% graciano, 5% garnacha

87 Colour: deep cherry. Nose: spicy, dark chocolate, ripe fruit. Palate: powerful, creamy, spicy.

CONDE DE VALDEMAR 2009 TC
90% tempranillo, 10% mazuelo

87 Colour: dark-red cherry. Nose: ripe fruit, spicy, toasty. Palate: oaky, toasty, powerful, good structure, ripe fruit.

CONDE DE VALDEMAR 2012 RD

88 Colour: rose, purple rim. Nose: rose petals, fruit expression, fresh fruit. Palate: balanced, spirituous, fruity, fresh, powerful, flavourful, sweetness.

CONDE DE VALDEMAR FINCA ALTO CANTABRIA 2012 BFB
100% viura

87 Colour: bright straw. Nose: fresh, white flowers, ripe fruit. Palate: flavourful, fruity, good acidity, balanced.

CONDE DE VALDEMAR GARNACHA 2010 T
100% garnacha

87 Colour: dark-red cherry. Nose: short, spicy, toasty. Palate: toasty, smoky aftertaste, ripe fruit.

CONDE DE VALDEMAR VIURA 2012 B
90% viura, 10% malvasía

84

INSPIRACIÓN DE VALDEMAR LAS CANTERAS 2010 T
70% tempranillo, 30% graciano

92 Colour: deep cherry, garnet rim. Nose: red berry notes, ripe fruit, expressive, balsamic herbs, mineral. Palate: powerful, flavourful, round, spicy, long.

INSPIRACIÓN VALDEMAR EDICIÓN LIMITADA 2008 T
70% tempranillo, 20% experimental, 10% graciano

92 Colour: dark-red cherry, orangey edge. Nose: ripe fruit, powerfull, reduction notes, spicy, dark chocolate, sweet spices. Palate: powerful, varietal, fruity, balsamic.

INSPIRACIÓN VALDEMAR GRACIANO 2005 T
100% graciano

91 Colour: deep cherry. Nose: damp earth, earthy notes, powerfull, varietal, ripe fruit, creamy oak, toasty, spicy. Palate: spicy, balsamic, powerful, flavourful, varietal.

INSPIRACIÓN VALDEMAR MATURANA 2008 T
92% maturana, 8% tempranillo

92 Colour: dark-red cherry. Nose: powerfull, varietal, expressive, complex. Palate: fresh, flavourful, roasted-coffee aftertaste.

INSPIRACIÓN VALDEMAR SELECCIÓN 2010 T
80% tempranillo, 10% graciano, 5% maturana, 5% garnacha

88 Colour: dark-red cherry. Nose: ripe fruit, spicy, premature reduction notes. Palate: fine tannins, good structure, powerful, reductive nuances.

INSPIRACIÓN VALDEMAR TEMPRANILLO BLANCO 2012 BFB
100% tempranillo blanco

88 Colour: bright yellow. Nose: ripe fruit, sweet spices, creamy oak, fragrant herbs. Palate: rich, flavourful, fresh, good acidity.

VALDEMAR 2012 RD
70% garnacha, 30% viura

86 Colour: salmon. Nose: slightly evolved, fresh, varietal. Palate: fruity, fresh, light-bodied, flavourful.

VALDEMAR TEMPRANILLO 2012 T
100% tempranillo

89 Colour: cherry, purple rim. Nose: red berry notes, ripe fruit, balsamic herbs. Palate: flavourful, fruity, good acidity.

BODEGAS VALLEMAYOR

Ctra. Logroño-Vitoria, 38
26360 Fuenmayor (La Rioja)
☎: +34 941 450 142 - Fax: +34 941 450 376
www.vallemayor.com
vallemayor@fer.es

COLECCIÓN VALLE MAYOR VIÑA CERRADILLA 2006 TC
90% tempranillo, 10% mazuelo

86 Colour: cherry, garnet rim. Nose: old leather, animal reductive notes, ripe fruit, fruit liqueur notes. Palate: spicy, correct, toasty.

COLECCIÓN VALLE MAYOR VIÑA ENCINEDA 2011 T
100% tempranillo

90 Colour: very deep cherry. Nose: toasty, spicy, expressive, powerfull. Palate: powerful, good acidity, elegant, correct.

SEÑORÍO DE LA LUZ 2012 T
100% tempranillo

84

VALLE MAYOR 2012 B
100% viura

84

VALLEMAYOR 2005 TGR
80% tempranillo, 10% mazuelo, 10% graciano

86 Colour: pale ruby, brick rim edge. Nose: elegant, spicy, wet leather, aged wood nuances, fruit liqueur notes. Palate: spicy, fine tannins, long.

VALLEMAYOR 2007 TR
85% tempranillo, 10% mazuelo, 5% graciano

88 Colour: pale ruby, brick rim edge. Nose: elegant, spicy, fine reductive notes, wet leather, aged wood nuances, fruit liqueur notes. Palate: spicy, fine tannins, long.

VALLEMAYOR 2010 TC
90% tempranillo, 5% mazuelo, 5% graciano

86 Colour: cherry, garnet rim. Nose: fruit liqueur notes, spicy, warm, toasty. Palate: aged character, light-bodied.

BODEGAS VALLOBERA S.L.

Camino de la Hoya, s/n
1300 Laguardia (Álava)
☎: +34 945 621 204 - Fax: +34 945 600 040
www.vallobera.com
bsanpedro@vallobera.com

CAUDALIA 2012 B
100% viura

89 Colour: bright straw. Nose: medium intensity, dried flowers, dried herbs. Palate: fresh, fruity, thin.

FINCA VALLOBERA 2011 T
100% tempranillo

91 Colour: cherry, garnet rim. Nose: ripe fruit, spicy, creamy oak, toasty, complex. Palate: powerful, flavourful, toasty, round tannins.

PAGO MALARINA 2011 T
100% tempranillo

88 Colour: bright cherry. Nose: ripe fruit, sweet spices, creamy oak. Palate: flavourful, fruity, toasty, correct.

TERRAN 2009 T
100% tempranillo

92 Colour: cherry, garnet rim. Nose: red berry notes, ripe fruit, cocoa bean, sweet spices, creamy oak. Palate: correct, flavourful, spicy, long, elegant.

TERRAN 2010 T
100% tempranillo

91 Colour: cherry, garnet rim. Nose: ripe fruit, spicy, creamy oak, toasty. Palate: powerful, flavourful, toasty, spicy, long.

VALLOBERA 2010 TC
100% tempranillo

91 Colour: cherry, garnet rim. Nose: ripe fruit, spicy, creamy oak, toasty, complex. Palate: powerful, flavourful, toasty, round tannins.

VALLOBERA 2012 B
100% viura

88 Colour: bright straw. Nose: dried flowers, ripe fruit, dried herbs, earthy notes, medium intensity. Palate: fresh, fruity, light-bodied.

BODEGAS VICENTE GANDÍA

Ctra. Cheste a Godelleta, s/n
46370 Chiva (Valencia)
☎: +34 962 524 242 - Fax: +34 962 524 243
www.vicentegandia.es
info@vicentegandia.com

ALTOS DE RAIZA TEMPRANILLO 2011 T
100% tempranillo

86 Colour: cherry, garnet rim. Nose: ripe fruit, wild herbs, spicy. Palate: balsamic, correct, flavourful, easy to drink.

RAIZA TEMPRANILLO 2005 TGR
100% tempranillo

88 Colour: pale ruby, brick rim edge. Nose: spicy, wet leather, aged wood nuances, fruit liqueur notes, balanced. Palate: spicy, fine tannins, elegant, long.

RAIZA TEMPRANILLO 2008 TR
100% tempranillo

88 Colour: cherry, garnet rim. Nose: ripe fruit, scrubland, spicy, creamy oak, fine reductive notes. Palate: powerful, flavourful.

RAIZA TEMPRANILLO 2009 TC
100% tempranillo

88 Colour: cherry, garnet rim. Nose: ripe fruit, creamy oak, sweet spices. Palate: powerful, flavourful, toasty.

BODEGAS VINÍCOLA REAL

Ctra. Nalda, km. 9
26120 Albelda de Iregua (La Rioja)
☎: +34 941 444 233 - Fax: +34 941 444 427
www.vinicolareal.com
info@vinicolareal.com

200 MONGES 2007 TR
85% tempranillo, 10% graciano, 5% mazuelo

90 Colour: deep cherry. Nose: ripe fruit, spicy, complex, dried herbs. Palate: powerful, flavourful, round tannins, balanced.

CUEVA DEL MONGE 2010 T
100% tempranillo

89 Colour: deep cherry, garnet rim. Nose: varietal, ripe fruit, spicy. Palate: correct, flavourful, round tannins.

CUEVA DEL MONGE 2011 B
70% viura, 20% malvasía, 5% garnacha blanca, 5% moscatel

87 Colour: bright yellow. Nose: powerfull, ripe fruit, sweet spices, creamy oak, fragrant herbs. Palate: rich, smoky aftertaste, flavourful, fresh.

VIÑA LOS VALLES 2012 T
100% tempranillo

88 Colour: bright cherry, garnet rim. Nose: balanced, ripe fruit, dried herbs. Palate: fruity, round tannins, good finish.

VIÑA LOS VALLES 50 & 50 2010 TC
50% garnacha, 50% graciano

89 Colour: cherry, garnet rim. Nose: ripe fruit, spicy, toasty, fruit preserve. Palate: powerful, flavourful, toasty, round tannins, balsamic.

VIÑA LOS VALLES 70 & 30 2010 TC
70% tempranillo, 30% graciano

89 Colour: bright cherry, garnet rim. Nose: balanced, scrubland, spicy. Palate: balanced, long, round tannins, balsamic.

VIÑA LOS VALLES 80 & 20 2010 TC
80% tempranillo, 20% mazuelo

88 Colour: deep cherry, garnet rim. Nose: ripe fruit, dried herbs, spicy. Palate: good structure, flavourful.

BODEGAS VIÑA HERMINIA

Camino de los Agudos, 1
26559 Aldeanueva de Ebro (La Rioja)
☎: +34 941 142 305 - Fax: +34 941 142 303
www.viñaherminia.es

VIÑA HERMINIA 2007 TR
85% tempranillo, 10% garnacha, 5% graciano

88 Colour: cherry, garnet rim. Nose: ripe fruit, spicy, creamy oak, toasty. Palate: powerful, flavourful, toasty, round tannins.

VIÑA HERMINIA 2010 TC
85% tempranillo, 15% garnacha

88 Colour: deep cherry. Nose: ripe fruit, spicy. Palate: spicy, ripe fruit.

VIÑA HERMINIA EXCELSUS 2011 T
50% tempranillo, 50% garnacha

90 Colour: cherry, garnet rim. Nose: spicy, creamy oak, toasty. Palate: powerful, flavourful, toasty, round tannins.

VIÑA HERMINIA GARNACHA 2010 T
100% garnacha

88 Colour: cherry, garnet rim. Nose: spicy, creamy oak, toasty. Palate: powerful, flavourful, toasty, round tannins.

VIÑA HERMINIA GRACIANO 2010 T
100% graciano

89 Colour: cherry, garnet rim. Nose: spicy, creamy oak, toasty. Palate: powerful, flavourful, toasty, round tannins.

BODEGAS VIÑA LAGUARDIA

Ctra. Laguardia s/n
1309 Elvillar (Álava)
☎: +34 945 604 143 - Fax: +34 945 604 150
www.vinalaguardia.es
bodegas@vinalaguardia.es

BILUN 2006 T
100% tempranillo

90 Colour: black cherry. Nose: powerfull, characterful, warm, fruit liqueur notes. Palate: flavourful, spicy, ripe fruit, long.

ECANIA 2010 TC
100% tempranillo

85 Colour: very deep cherry. Nose: spicy, toasty, fruit liqueur notes. Palate: spicy, classic aged character.

ECANIA VENDIMIA SELECCIÓN 2008 T
100% tempranillo

88 Colour: dark-red cherry, garnet rim. Nose: spicy, ripe fruit, medium intensity. Palate: balanced, round tannins.

BODEGAS Y VIÑAS DEL CONDE

Calle Bodegas, 98
1306 La Puebla de Labarca (Álava)
☎: +34 673 736 155
www.casadomorales.es
condedealtava@gmail.com

CONDE DE ALTAVA 2007 TR
100% tempranillo

87 Colour: deep cherry. Nose: ripe fruit, spicy. Palate: spicy, aged character, fine tannins.

CONDE DE ALTAVA 2009 TC
100% tempranillo

88 Colour: cherry, garnet rim. Nose: ripe fruit, spicy, creamy oak, toasty, complex. Palate: powerful, flavourful, toasty, round tannins.

CONDE DE ALTAVA 2012 T
100% tempranillo

89 Colour: dark-red cherry. Nose: wild herbs, maceration notes, ripe fruit. Palate: sweetness, fresh, powerful, flavourful.

BODEGAS Y VIÑAS SENDA GALIANA

Barrio Bodegas, s/n
26142 Villamediana (La Rioja)
☎: +34 941 435 375 - Fax: +34 941 436 072
info@sendagaliana.com

SENDA GALIANA 2004 TGR
85% tempranillo, 10% graciano, 5% mazuelo

91 Colour: cherry, garnet rim. Nose: fruit liqueur notes, old leather, tobacco. Palate: spicy, ripe fruit, fine bitter notes, fine tannins.

SENDA GALIANA 2007 TR
90% tempranillo, 10% mazuelo

85 Colour: cherry, garnet rim. Nose: ripe fruit, spicy. Palate: flavourful, varietal, fruity, correct.

SENDA GALIANA 2009 TC
90% tempranillo, 10% garnacha

82

BODEGAS Y VIÑEDOS ALVAR

Camino de Ventosa, s/n
26371 Ventosa (La Rioja)
☎: +34 941 441 905 - Fax: +34 941 441 917
www.bodegasalvar.com
alvar@bodegasalvar.com

LIVIUS 2008 BFB
70% viura, 30% malvasía

90 Colour: bright yellow. Nose: powerfull, sweet spices, creamy oak, fragrant herbs. Palate: rich, smoky aftertaste, flavourful, fresh, good acidity.

LIVIUS GARNACHA 2007 T
100% garnacha

90 Colour: bright cherry, garnet rim. Nose: balanced, ripe fruit, medium intensity. Palate: fruity, balsamic, round tannins.

LIVIUS TEMPRANILLO 2008 T
100% tempranillo

89 Colour: cherry, garnet rim. Nose: ripe fruit, spicy, toasty, complex, dried herbs. Palate: powerful, flavourful, toasty, round tannins.

PRIMUM VITAE TEMPRANILLO 2007 TR
100% tempranillo

86 Colour: cherry, garnet rim. Nose: ripe fruit, spicy, old leather, tobacco. Palate: flavourful, toasty, round tannins.

BODEGAS Y VIÑEDOS ARRANZ-ARGOTE

Mayor Alta, 43
26370 Navarrete (La Rioja)
☎: +34 699 046 043
www.vinoarar.com
bodega@vinoarar.com

ARAR 2010 TC
tempranillo, graciano, garnacha

89 Colour: cherry, garnet rim. Nose: spicy, creamy oak, toasty, ripe fruit. Palate: powerful, flavourful, toasty, correct.

ARAR 2012 B
viura, malvasía, tempranillo blanco

86 Colour: bright straw. Nose: fresh, fresh fruit, white flowers, expressive. Palate: flavourful, fruity, good acidity.

ARAR 2012 T
tempranillo, graciano

85 Colour: cherry, purple rim. Nose: medium intensity, ripe fruit, dried herbs. Palate: fruity, good acidity, round tannins.

ARAR AUTOR 2005 T
tempranillo, graciano, garnacha, maturana

87 Colour: pale ruby, brick rim edge. Nose: spicy, fine reductive notes, wet leather, aged wood nuances, fruit liqueur notes. Palate: spicy, long, reductive nuances.

BODEGAS Y VIÑEDOS ARTADI

Ctra. de Logroño, s/n
1300 Laguardia (Álava)
☎: +34 945 600 119 - Fax: +34 945 600 850
www.artadi.com
info@artadi.com

ARTADI EL CARRETIL 2011 T
100% tempranillo

98 Colour: very deep cherry. Nose: sweet spices, fruit expression, red berry notes, spicy. Palate: flavourful, powerful, good acidity, round, round tannins.

ARTADI LA POZA DE BALLESTEROS 2011 T
100% tempranillo

97 Colour: cherry, garnet rim. Nose: fruit expression, red berry notes, sweet spices, cocoa bean. Palate: flavourful, powerful, fruity, good acidity, round.

ARTADI PAGOS VIEJOS 2011 T
100% tempranillo

95 Colour: cherry, garnet rim. Nose: spicy, creamy oak, toasty, characterful. Palate: powerful, flavourful, toasty, round tannins, good acidity.

ARTADI VALDEGINÉS 2011 T
100% tempranillo

96 Colour: bright cherry. Nose: sweet spices, creamy oak, red berry notes, fruit expression, violet drops, scrubland. Palate: flavourful, fruity, toasty, round tannins.

ARTADI VIÑA EL PISÓN 2011 T
100% tempranillo

97 Colour: very deep cherry. Nose: powerfull, characterful, ripe fruit, red berry notes, sweet spices. Palate: powerful, flavourful, fine bitter notes, good acidity, round tannins.

ARTADI VIÑAS DE GAIN 2010 B
100% viura

93 Colour: bright yellow. Nose: ripe fruit, sweet spices, fragrant herbs. Palate: rich, smoky aftertaste, flavourful, fresh, good acidity.

ARTADI VIÑAS DE GAIN 2011 T
100% tempranillo

94 Colour: bright cherry. Nose: ripe fruit, sweet spices, creamy oak, red berry notes, mineral. Palate: flavourful, fruity, toasty, round tannins.

BODEGAS Y VIÑEDOS CASADO MORALES, S.L.

Avda. La Póveda 12-14
1306 Lapuebla de Labarca (Alava)
☎: +34 945 607 017 - Fax: +34 945 063 173
www.casadomorales.es
info@casadomorales.es

CASADO MORALES 2009 T
90% tempranillo, 10% graciano

90 Colour: bright cherry, garnet rim. Nose: ripe fruit, sweet spices, cocoa bean. Palate: flavourful, round tannins, spicy.

CASADO MORALES SELECCIÓN PRIVADA 2007 TR
95% tempranillo, 5% garnacha

93 Colour: cherry, garnet rim. Nose: ripe fruit, spicy, creamy oak, toasty, complex, elegant. Palate: powerful, flavourful, toasty, round tannins.

NOBLEZA CASADO MORALES 2012 T
90% tempranillo, 10% viura

88 Colour: cherry, purple rim. Nose: red berry notes, balsamic herbs, expressive, lactic notes. Palate: flavourful, fruity, rich.

NOBLEZA DIMIDIUM 2010 T
100% tempranillo

90 Colour: bright cherry. Nose: sweet spices, creamy oak, fruit expression, varietal. Palate: flavourful, fruity, round tannins.

BODEGAS Y VIÑEDOS HERAS CORDÓN

Ctra. Lapuebla, Km. 2
26360 Fuenmayor (La Rioja)
☎: +34 608 176 743 - Fax: +34 941 450 265
www.herascordon.com
bodegas@herascordon.com

HERAS CORDÓN 2005 TR
90% tempranillo, 5% mazuelo, 5% graciano

87 Colour: pale ruby, brick rim edge. Nose: spicy, fine reductive notes, wet leather, fruit liqueur notes. Palate: spicy, long, balsamic, balanced.

HERAS CORDÓN VENDIMIA SELECCIONADA 2010 TC
90% tempranillo, 5% mazuelo, 5% graciano

87 Colour: cherry, garnet rim. Nose: ripe fruit, balsamic herbs, spicy, creamy oak. Palate: powerful, flavourful, spicy.

BODEGAS Y VIÑEDOS ILURCE

Ctra. Alfaro - Grávalos (LR-289), km. 23
26540 Alfaro (La Rioja)
☎: +34 941 180 829 - Fax: +34 941 183 897
www.ilurce.com
info@ilurce.com

ILURCE 2012 RD
100% garnacha

90 Colour: rose. Nose: fresh fruit, fruit expression, varietal, powerfull. Palate: powerful, flavourful, fruity, fresh, fruity aftestaste.

ILURCE 2012 T
100% tempranillo

83

ILURCE GRACIANO 2006 TC
100% graciano

86 Colour: cherry, garnet rim. Nose: ripe fruit, spicy, creamy oak, balsamic herbs. Palate: powerful, flavourful, toasty.

ILURCE VENDIMIA SELECCIONADA 2001 TR
60% tempranillo, 40% garnacha

87 Colour: pale ruby, brick rim edge. Nose: spicy, fine reductive notes, wet leather, aged wood nuances, fruit liqueur notes. Palate: spicy, fine tannins, long.

ILURCE VENDIMIA SELECCIONADA 2005 TC
60% garnacha, 40% tempranillo

85 Colour: pale ruby, brick rim edge. Nose: fruit preserve, spicy, balsamic herbs, wet leather, cigar. Palate: powerful, spicy, spirituous.

BODEGAS Y VIÑEDOS
LABASTIDA - SOLAGÜEN

Avda. Diputación, 22
1330 Labastida (Álava)
☎: +34 945 331 161 - Fax: +34 945 331 118
www.bodegaslabastida.com
info@bodegaslabastida.com

R&G 2010 T
tempranillo

91 Colour: cherry, garnet rim. Nose: ripe fruit, spicy, creamy oak, toasty, characterful, mineral. Palate: powerful, flavourful, toasty, round tannins.

SOLAGÜEN 2008 TR
100% tempranillo

89 Colour: dark-red cherry. Nose: creamy oak, ripe fruit. Palate: powerful, flavourful, round, elegant.

SOLAGÜEN 2010 TC
100% tempranillo

89 Colour: dark-red cherry. Nose: fresh, neat, ripe fruit, aromatic coffee. Palate: balsamic, creamy, flavourful, rich, fruity.

SOLAGÜEN VIURA 2012 B
100% viura

84

BODEGAS Y VIÑEDOS
MARQUÉS DE CARRIÓN

Ctra. Logroño, s/n
1330 Labastida (Álava)
☎: +34 945 331 643 - Fax: +34 945 331 694
www.vinosdefamilia.com
eromero@jgc.es

ANTAÑO 2009 TR
tempranillo, graciano, mazuelo, garnacha

83

ANTAÑO 2010 TC
tempranillo, graciano, mazuelo, garnacha

83

ANTAÑO GRACIANO 2008 T
graciano

85 Colour: deep cherry. Nose: overripe fruit, aged wood nuances, spicy. Palate: round, good structure, powerful, spicy, grainy tannins.

ANTAÑO TEMPRANILLO 2012 T
tempranillo

84

MARQUÉS DE CARRIÓN 2009 TR
tempranillo, graciano, mazuelo

79

MARQUÉS DE CARRIÓN 2010 TC
tempranillo, graciano, mazuelo

82

BODEGAS Y VIÑEDOS
MONTEABELLÓN

Calvario, s/n
9318 Nava de Roa (Burgos)
☎: +34 947 550 000 - Fax: +34 947 550 219
www.monteabellon.com
info@monteabellon.com

FINCA ATHUS 2010 TC
90% tempranillo, 10% mazuelo

90 Colour: cherry, garnet rim. Nose: ripe fruit, creamy oak, toasty, complex. Palate: powerful, flavourful, toasty.

BODEGAS Y VIÑEDOS PUERTA DE LABASTIDA

Ctra. de Autol - Calahorra, km. 6,5
26500 Calahorra (La Rioja)
☎ +34 941 163 021 - Fax: +34 941 163 493
www.puertadelabastida.com
c.ribeiro@puertadelabastida.com

MARQUÉS DE CARABÁS 2012 T
tempranillo, graciano

84

MARQUÉS DE CARABÁS 2009 TC
tempranillo, graciano

87 Colour: cherry, garnet rim. Nose: ripe fruit, spicy, creamy oak. Palate: powerful, flavourful, toasty.

BODEGAS Y VIÑEDOS PUJANZA

Ctra. del Villar, s/n
1300 Laguardia (Álava)
☎ +34 945 600 548 - Fax: +34 945 600 522
www.bodegaspujanza.com
info@bodegaspujanza.com

PUJANZA 2009 T
100% tempranillo

93 Colour: cherry, garnet rim. Nose: ripe fruit, spicy, creamy oak, toasty, characterful. Palate: powerful, flavourful, toasty, round tannins.

PUJANZA HADO 2011 T
100% tempranillo

90 Colour: bright cherry. Nose: ripe fruit, sweet spices, creamy oak, fragrant herbs. Palate: flavourful, fruity, toasty.

PUJANZA NORTE 2010 T
90% tempranillo, 10% otras

94 Colour: cherry, garnet rim. Nose: spicy, creamy oak, aromatic coffee, dark chocolate. Palate: powerful, flavourful, toasty, round tannins.

BODEGAS Y VIÑEDOS VARAL

San Vicente
1307 Baños de Ebro (Álava)
☎: +34 945 623 321 - Fax: +34 945 623 321
www.bodegasvaral.com
bodegasvaral@bodegasvaral.com

BLANCO DE VARAL 2012 B
100% viura

85 Colour: bright straw. Nose: fresh, fresh fruit, white flowers, citrus fruit. Palate: fruity, good acidity, correct.

CRIANZA DE VARAL 2010 T
100% tempranillo

90 Colour: cherry, garnet rim. Nose: ripe fruit, spicy, creamy oak, toasty, characterful. Palate: powerful, flavourful, toasty, round tannins.

ECOS DE VARAL 2012 T
90% tempranillo, 10% viura

88 Colour: cherry, purple rim. Nose: fresh fruit, red berry notes, floral. Palate: flavourful, fruity, good acidity, round tannins.

ESENCIAS DE VARAL 2009 T
100% tempranillo

90 Colour: bright cherry. Nose: ripe fruit, sweet spices, creamy oak. Palate: flavourful, fruity, toasty, round tannins.

JOVEN DE VARAL 2012 T
95% tempranillo, 5% viura

86 Colour: cherry, purple rim. Nose: red berry notes, floral, ripe fruit. Palate: fruity, good acidity, round tannins, easy to drink.

RESERVA DE VARAL 2006 TR
100% tempranillo

88 Colour: cherry, garnet rim. Nose: spicy, creamy oak, toasty. Palate: powerful, flavourful, toasty, round tannins.

VARAL VENDIMIA SELECCIONADA 2008 T
100% tempranillo

90 Colour: cherry, garnet rim. Nose: spicy, creamy oak, toasty, fruit liqueur notes. Palate: powerful, flavourful, toasty, round tannins.

BODEGAS Y VIÑEDOS ZUAZO GASTÓN

Las Norias, 2
1320 Oyón (Álava)
☎: +34 945 601 526 - Fax: +34 945 622 917
www.zuazogaston.com
zuazogaston@zuazogaston.com

FINCA COSTANILLAS 2011 T
90% tempranillo, 10% graciano

90 Colour: dark-red cherry. Nose: powerfull, expressive, sweet spices, toasty, creamy oak, fruit expression. Palate: ripe fruit, creamy, spicy, toasty.

ZUAZO GASTÓN 2008 TR
tempranillo

89 Colour: dark-red cherry. Nose: fruit preserve, powerfull, expressive, spicy, aromatic coffee, creamy oak. Palate: powerful, full, creamy, spicy.

ZUAZO GASTÓN 2010 TC
tempranillo

88 Colour: cherry, garnet rim. Nose: ripe fruit, spicy, toasty, balanced. Palate: powerful, flavourful, toasty.

ZUAZO GASTÓN 2012 B
viura

85 Colour: bright straw, greenish rim. Nose: ripe fruit, tropical fruit, medium intensity. Palate: correct, fruity.

BODEGAS YSIOS

Camino de la Hoya, s/n
1300 Laguardia (Álava)
☎: +34 945 600 640 - Fax: +34 945 600 520
www.ysios.com
ysios@pernod-ricard.com

ESENCIA DE YSIOS 2007 T
tempranillo

92 Colour: cherry, garnet rim. Nose: ripe fruit, spicy, creamy oak, toasty, balanced. Palate: powerful, flavourful, toasty, elegant.

YSIOS 2007 TR
tempranillo

90 Colour: cherry, garnet rim. Nose: ripe fruit, aromatic coffee, sweet spices, toasty. Palate: rich, flavourful, toasty, balanced, elegant.

YSIOS EDICIÓN LIMITADA 2007 TR
tempranillo

94 Colour: cherry, garnet rim. Nose: ripe fruit, spicy, creamy oak, toasty, complex, mineral, dry stone. Palate: powerful, flavourful, toasty, round tannins.

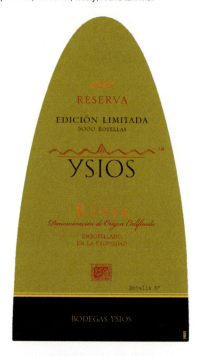

BODEGAS ZUGOBER

Tejerías, 13-15
1306 Lapuebla de Labarca (Álava)
☎: +34 945 627 228 - Fax: +34 945 627 281
www.zugober.com
contacto@belezos.com

BELEZOS 2007 TR
95% tempranillo, 5% graciano

88 Colour: dark-red cherry, garnet rim. Nose: ripe fruit, balsamic herbs, spicy, creamy oak, fine reductive notes. Palate: powerful, flavourful, spicy, long.

BELEZOS 2009 TC
95% tempranillo, 5% graciano

89 Colour: cherry, garnet rim. Nose: ripe fruit, balsamic herbs, sweet spices, creamy oak. Palate: powerful, flavourful, spicy, long.

BELEZOS ECOLÓGICO 2010 T
85% tempranillo, 15% graciano

90 Colour: cherry, purple rim. Nose: red berry notes, ripe fruit, balsamic herbs, sweet spices, creamy oak. Palate: flavourful, spicy, balanced.

BELEZOS VENDIMIA SELECCIONADA 2010 T
100% tempranillo

91 Colour: bright cherry. Nose: ripe fruit, sweet spices, creamy oak, toasty. Palate: flavourful, fruity, toasty, round tannins.

CUNA DE MARAS 2012 T
MACERACIÓN CARBÓNICA
100% tempranillo

89 Colour: very deep cherry, purple rim. Nose: fruit expression, violet drops, balanced, expressive. Palate: flavourful, fruity.

CUNA DE MARAS VENDIMIA SELECCIÓN 2011 T
100% tempranillo

90 Colour: bright cherry. Nose: ripe fruit, sweet spices, creamy oak, cocoa bean. Palate: flavourful, fruity, toasty, round tannins.

CAMPOS DE HOJAS

Avda. Diagonal, 590, 5º 1ª
8021 (Barcelona)
☎: +34 660 445 464
www.vinergia.com
vinergia@vinergia.com

CAMPOS DE HOJAS 2010 TC
80% tempranillo, 20% garnacha

89 Colour: garnet rim. Nose: ripe fruit, balsamic herbs, spicy, creamy oak. Palate: powerful, flavourful, spicy, long.

CAMPOS DE HOJAS TEMPRANILLO 2012 T
80% tempranillo, 20% garnacha

84

CARLOS SAN PEDRO
PÉREZ DE VIÑASPRE

Páganos, 44- Bajo
1300 Laguardia (Álava)
☎: +34 945 600 146 - Fax: +34 945 600 146
www.bodegascarlossampedro.com
info@bodegascarlossampedro.com

CARLOS SAN PEDRO 2010 T
tempranillo

91 Colour: cherry, garnet rim. Nose: ripe fruit, spicy, creamy oak, toasty, sweet spices. Palate: powerful, flavourful, toasty, round tannins.

VIÑASPERI 2009 TC
tempranillo

87 Colour: cherry, garnet rim. Nose: ripe fruit, spicy, creamy oak, earthy notes, balsamic herbs. Palate: powerful, flavourful, spicy.

VIÑASPERI SELECCIÓN 2010 T
tempranillo

90 Colour: cherry, purple rim. Nose: red berry notes, ripe fruit, sweet spices, creamy oak. Palate: powerful, flavourful, harsh oak tannins.

CARLOS SERRES

Avda. Santo Domingo, 40
26200 Haro (La Rioja)
☎: +34 941 310 279 - Fax: +34 941 310 418
www.carlosserres.com
info@carlosserres.com

CARLOS SERRES 2005 TGR
100% garnacha

88 Colour: pale ruby, brick rim edge. Nose: spicy, fine reductive notes, wet leather, aged wood nuances, ripe fruit. Palate: spicy, long, correct.

CARLOS SERRES 2007 TR
90% tempranillo, 10% graciano

89 Colour: dark-red cherry. Nose: fine reductive notes, ripe fruit, spicy, toasty. Palate: fine tannins, full, flavourful, complex.

CARLOS SERRES 2009 TC
85% tempranillo, 15% garnacha

89 Colour: dark-red cherry. Nose: sweet spices, toasty, candied fruit. Palate: creamy, spicy, toasty, powerful, flavourful.

ONOMÁSTICA 2007 TR
80% tempranillo, 10% graciano, 10% mazuelo

90 Colour: dark-red cherry, orangey edge. Nose: fine reductive notes, tobacco, powerfull, complex, spicy, sweet spices. Palate: complex, powerful, flavourful, creamy, toasty, smoky aftertaste.

ONOMÁSTICA 2009 B RESERVA
100% viura

89 Colour: bright yellow. Nose: balanced, medium intensity, faded flowers, sweet spices. Palate: fruity, long, rich.

SERRES TEMPRANILLO 2012 T
100% tempranillo

86 Colour: cherry, purple rim. Nose: medium intensity, varietal, ripe fruit. Palate: correct, easy to drink, fruity.

SERRES TEMPRANILLO GARNACHA 2012 RD
80% tempranillo, 20% garnacha

86 Colour: rose, bright. Nose: red berry notes, ripe fruit, dried flowers. Palate: flavourful, fruity, good finish, good acidity.

SERRES VIURA 2012 B
100% viura

86 Colour: bright straw. Nose: medium intensity, dried herbs, faded flowers. Palate: correct, good finish.

CARREFOUR

Campezo, 16
28022 Madrid (Madrid)
☎: +34 902 202 000
www.carrefour.es

TRES REINOS 2008 TR
tempranillo, garnacha, graciano, mazuelo

84

TRES REINOS 2010 TC
tempranillo, garnacha, graciano, mazuelo

82

TRES REINOS 2012 B
viura

78

TRES REINOS 2012 RD
garnacha

83

TRES REINOS 2012 T
tempranillo, garnacha, graciano, mazuelo

82

VIÑA ESPOLON 2007 TR
tempranillo, garnacha

86 Colour: dark-red cherry. Nose: balanced, spicy, medium intensity, ripe fruit. Palate: easy to drink, ripe fruit.

VIÑA ESPOLON 2009 TC
tempranillo, garnacha

84

VIÑA ESPOLON 2012 B
viura

83

VIÑA ESPOLON 2012 T
90% tempranillo, 7% garnacha, 3% mazuelo

84

VIÑA ESPOLON 37,5 CL 2009 TC
tempranillo, garnacha

84

VIÑA ESPOLON PREMIUM 2012 RD
garnacha

86 Colour: rose, purple rim. Nose: ripe fruit, red berry notes, floral, expressive. Palate: powerful, fruity, fresh.

VITES VIRIDES 2010 TC
tempranillo, garnacha

84

VITES VIRIDES 2012 RD
garnacha

84

VITES VIRIDES COSECHA 2012 T
tempranillo, mazuelo, garnacha

87 Colour: deep cherry. Nose: expressive, ripe fruit, balsamic herbs. Palate: flavourful, good acidity.

CASTILLO CLAVIJO

Ctra. de Clavijo, s/n
26141 Alberite (La Rioja)
☎: +34 941 436 702 - Fax: +34 941 436 440
www.criadoresderioja.com
info@castilloclavijo.com

CASTILLO CLAVIJO 2005 TGR
80% tempranillo, 10% garnacha, 10% mazuelo

85 Colour: pale ruby, brick rim edge. Nose: spicy, fine reductive notes, wet leather, aged wood nuances, fruit liqueur
notes. Palate: spicy, long, flavourful.

CASTILLO CLAVIJO 2007 TR
90% tempranillo, 10% mazuelo

88 Colour: pale ruby, brick rim edge. Nose: ripe fruit,
spicy, creamy oak, fine reductive notes. Palate: flavourful,
spicy, long.

CASTILLO CLAVIJO 2009 TC
80% tempranillo, 20% garnacha

87 Colour: dark-red cherry, orangey edge. Nose: ripe fruit,
spicy, creamy oak, toasty. Palate: flavourful, spicy, long.

CASTILLO CLAVIJO 2011 BFB
viura, malvasía, garnacha blanca

87 Colour: bright yellow. Nose: powerfull, ripe fruit, sweet
spices, fragrant herbs. Palate: rich, smoky aftertaste, flavourful, good acidity, ripe fruit.

CASTILLO DE CUZCURRITA

San Sebastián, 1
26214 Cuzcurrita del Río Tirón (La Rioja)
☎: +34 941 328 022 - Fax: +34 941 301 620
www.castillodecuzcurrita.com
info@castillodecuzcurrita.com

CERRADO DEL CASTILLO 2008 T
100% tempranillo

91 Colour: cherry, garnet rim. Nose: spicy, creamy oak,
toasty, ripe fruit. Palate: powerful, flavourful, toasty, round
tannins.

COMPAÑÍA DE VINOS TELMO RODRÍGUEZ

El Monte
1308 Lanciego (Álava)
☎: +34 945 628 315 - Fax: +34 945 628 314
www.telmorodriguez.com
contact@telmorodriguez.com

ALTOS DE LANZAGA 2009 T
tempranillo, graciano, garnacha

95 Colour: cherry, garnet rim. Nose: ripe fruit, spicy,
creamy oak, toasty, complex, mineral, scrubland. Palate:
powerful, flavourful, toasty, round tannins, spicy.

LANZAGA 2009 T
tempranillo, graciano, garnacha

92 Colour: cherry, garnet rim. Nose: ripe fruit, fruit expression, balsamic herbs, scrubland. Palate: fruity, fresh, spicy,
fine bitter notes, round tannins.

LZ 2012 T
tempranillo, graciano, garnacha

93 Colour: bright cherry. Nose: ripe fruit, sweet spices,
fruit expression. Palate: flavourful, fruity, toasty, round tannins.

CREACIONES EXEO

Costanilla del Hospital s/n
1330 Labastida (Álava)
☎: +34 649 940 040
www.bodegasexeo.com
carlos@bodegasexeo.com

CIFRAS 2010 T
100% garnacha

92 Colour: bright cherry, garnet rim. Nose: balanced, fruit
expression, sweet spices, fragrant herbs. Palate: flavourful,
good structure, round tannins.

CIFRAS 2011 B
100% garnacha blanca

88 Colour: bright straw. Nose: ripe fruit, spicy, fragrant
herbs, medium intensity. Palate: powerful, flavourful, spicy.

CIFRAS 2011 T
100% garnacha

93 Colour: very deep cherry, garnet rim. Nose: balanced,
violet drops, ripe fruit, balsamic herbs. Palate: fruity, flavourful, long.

LETRAS 2010 T
100% tempranillo

93 Colour: cherry, garnet rim. Nose: balanced, creamy oak, sweet spices, ripe fruit. Palate: good structure, flavourful, round tannins.

LETRAS MINÚSCULAS 2011 T
70% tempranillo, 30% garnacha

90 Colour: deep cherry, garnet rim. Nose: ripe fruit, cocoa bean. Palate: powerful, round tannins, smoky aftertaste.

CVNE - COMPAÑÍA VINÍCOLA DEL NORTE DE ESPAÑA

Barrio de la Estación, s/n
26200 Haro (La Rioja)
☎: +34 941 304 800 - Fax: +34 941 304 815
www.cvne.com
marketing@cvne.com

CORONA SEMIDULCE 2012 B
85% viura, 15% malvasía, garnacha blanca

92 Colour: bright straw. Nose: fresh, fresh fruit, white flowers, candied fruit. Palate: flavourful, fruity, good acidity, balanced.

CUNE 2007 TGR
85% tempranillo, 10% graciano, 5% mazuelo

89 Colour: cherry, garnet rim. Nose: spicy, creamy oak, toasty. Palate: powerful, flavourful, toasty, round tannins.

CUNE 2009 TR
85% tempranillo, 15% mazuelo, garnacha, graciano

91 Colour: cherry, garnet rim. Nose: ripe fruit, spicy, creamy oak, toasty, complex. Palate: powerful, flavourful, toasty, round tannins.

CUNE 2011 TC
80% tempranillo, 20% garnacha, mazuelo

90 Colour: bright cherry. Nose: ripe fruit, sweet spices, creamy oak, fruit expression. Palate: flavourful, fruity, toasty, round tannins.

CUNE 2012 RD
100% tempranillo

87 Colour: rose. Nose: fresh, neat, fresh fruit. Palate: sweetness, fresh, fruity, powerful.

CUNE SEMIDULCE B
85% viura, 15% garnacha blanca, malvasía

88 Colour: bright straw. Nose: characterful, fruit expression, candied fruit. Palate: sweetness, fine bitter notes, good acidity.

CUNE WHITE 2012 B
100% viura

90 Colour: bright yellow. Nose: powerfull, ripe fruit, sweet spices, creamy oak. Palate: rich, smoky aftertaste, flavourful, fresh, good acidity.

IMPERIAL 2005 TGR
85% tempranillo, 10% graciano, 5% mazuelo

93 Colour: pale ruby, brick rim edge. Nose: elegant, spicy, fine reductive notes, wet leather, aged wood nuances, fruit liqueur notes. Palate: spicy, fine tannins, elegant, long.

IMPERIAL 2008 TR
85% tempranillo, 10% graciano, 5% mazuelo

92 Colour: cherry, garnet rim. Nose: ripe fruit, spicy, characterful, aromatic coffee. Palate: powerful, flavourful, toasty, round tannins.

MONOPOLE 2012 B
100% viura

89 Colour: bright straw. Nose: fragrant herbs, fresh fruit, fresh, neat. Palate: flavourful, powerful, fruity, fresh.

DELICIAS GÓMEZ

1306 La Puebla de Labarca (Alava)
☎: +34 945 607 028 - Fax: +34 945 607 028
www.heredadluzuriaga.com
m.luzuriaga@heredadluzuriaga.com

HEREDAD DE LUZURIAGA 2007 T
90% tempranillo, 5% graciano, 5% mazuelo

83

DIEZ-CABALLERO

Barrihuelo, 53
1340 Elciego (Álava)
☎: +34 944 807 295
www.diez-caballero.es
diez-caballero@diez-caballero.es

DÍEZ-CABALLERO 2011 TC
tempranillo

87 Colour: deep cherry, garnet rim. Nose: smoky, spicy. Palate: flavourful, fruity, spicy, round tannins.

DÍEZ-CABALLERO 2009 TR
tempranillo

87 Colour: cherry, garnet rim. Nose: aromatic coffee, toasty, spicy. Palate: flavourful, fruity, round tannins.

DÍEZ-CABALLERO VENDIMIA SELECCIONADA 2007 TR
100% tempranillo

88 Colour: very deep cherry, garnet rim. Nose: powerfull, fruit preserve, creamy oak, dried herbs. Palate: good structure, flavourful.

VICTORIA DÍEZ-CABALLERO 2010 T
100% tempranillo

91 Colour: very deep cherry, garnet rim. Nose: ripe fruit, sweet spices, cocoa bean. Palate: flavourful, ripe fruit, good acidity.

DIOS ARES

Ctra. de Navaridas s/n
1300 Laguardia (Alava)
☎: +34 945 600 678 - Fax: +34 945 600 619
export@bodegasdiosares.com

ARES 2010 TC

90 Colour: cherry, garnet rim. Nose: ripe fruit, spicy, creamy oak, toasty. Palate: powerful, flavourful, toasty.

DOMINIO DE BERZAL

Término Río Salado, s/n
1307 Baños de Ebro (Álava)
☎: +34 945 623 368 - Fax: +34 945 623 368
www.dominioberzal.com
info@dominioberzal.com

DOMINIO DE BERZAL 2010 TC
95% tempranillo, 5% graciano

90 Colour: cherry, garnet rim. Nose: red berry notes, fruit preserve, sweet spices, creamy oak, balsamic herbs. Palate: full, flavourful, spicy, long.

DOMINIO DE BERZAL 2012 B
90% viura, 10% malvasía

86 Colour: bright straw. Nose: white flowers, dried herbs, ripe fruit. Palate: powerful, flavourful, warm.

DOMINIO DE BERZAL 2012 T MACERACIÓN CARBÓNICA
90% tempranillo, 10% viura

85 Colour: dark-red cherry. Nose: overripe fruit, slightly evolved. Palate: powerful, flavourful, sweetness, toasty.

DOMINIO DE BERZAL 7 VARIETALES 2010 T
40% maturana, 10% graciano, 10% merlot, 10% cabernet sauvignon, 10% syrah, 10% prieto picudo

89 Colour: cherry, garnet rim. Nose: red berry notes, ripe fruit, balsamic herbs, spicy, creamy oak. Palate: powerful, flavourful, correct.

DOMINIO DE BERZAL SELECCIÓN PRIVADA 2010 T
100% tempranillo

91 Colour: cherry, garnet rim. Nose: ripe fruit, spicy, creamy oak, toasty, complex. Palate: powerful, flavourful, toasty, balanced.

DSG VINEYARDS

Ctra. Assa
1309 Elvillar (Alava)
☎: +34 619 600 425
www.dsgvineyards.es

VUELTA DE TERCAS 2010 T

92 Colour: bright cherry. Nose: ripe fruit, sweet spices, creamy oak, expressive. Palate: flavourful, fruity, toasty, round tannins.

EGUREN UGARTE

Ctra. A-124, Km. 61
1309 Laguardia (Álava)
☎: +34 945 282 844 - Fax: +34 945 271 319
www.egurenugarte.com
info@egurenugarte.com

ANASTASIO 2007 T
100% tempranillo

91 Colour: cherry, garnet rim. Nose: powerfull, ripe fruit, toasty, dark chocolate. Palate: flavourful, fine bitter notes, good acidity.

CEDULA REAL 2004 TGR
90% tempranillo, 10% mazuelo

91 Colour: pale ruby, brick rim edge. Nose: elegant, spicy, fine reductive notes, wet leather, aged wood nuances, fruit liqueur notes. Palate: spicy, fine tannins, elegant, long.

CINCUENTA UGARTE 2009 T
100% tempranillo

88 Colour: cherry, garnet rim. Nose: ripe fruit, spicy, creamy oak. Palate: powerful, flavourful, toasty, round tannins.

DOMINIO DE UGARTE 2008 TR
92% tempranillo, 8% graciano

89 Colour: cherry, garnet rim. Nose: ripe fruit, spicy, creamy oak, toasty. Palate: powerful, flavourful, toasty, round tannins.

HEREDAD UGARTE 2010 TC
92% tempranillo, 8% garnacha

87 Colour: cherry, garnet rim. Nose: ripe fruit, spicy, creamy oak, toasty, complex. Palate: powerful, flavourful, toasty, round tannins.

MARTÍN CENDOYA 2008 TR
80% tempranillo, 15% graciano, 5% mazuelo

91 Colour: cherry, garnet rim. Nose: ripe fruit, spicy, toasty. Palate: powerful, flavourful, toasty, round tannins.

MARTÍN CENDOYA MALVASÍA 2012 B
100% malvasía

87 Colour: bright straw. Nose: fresh, fresh fruit, white flowers, expressive. Palate: flavourful, fruity, good acidity, balanced.

UGARTE 2010 TC
80% tempranillo, 20% garnacha

89 Colour: bright cherry. Nose: ripe fruit, sweet spices. Palate: flavourful, fruity, toasty, round tannins.

UGARTE TEMPRANILLO 2012 T
90% tempranillo, 10% garnacha

85 Colour: deep cherry. Nose: spicy, fruit liqueur notes, ripe fruit. Palate: fine bitter notes, spicy.

UGARTE VIURA 2012 B
100% viura

80

EL CONJURO DEL CIEGO

Barrihuelo, 77
1340 Elciego (Alava)
☎: +34 945 264 866 - Fax: +34 945 264 866
www.elconjurodelciego.com
lur@elconjurodelciego.com

LUR TEMPRANILLO 2009 T
100% tempranillo

88 Colour: bright cherry. Nose: sweet spices, creamy oak. Palate: flavourful, fruity, toasty, round tannins.

EL COTO DE RIOJA

Camino Viejo de Logroño, 26
1320 Oyón (Álava)
☎: +34 945 622 216 - Fax: +34 945 622 315
www.elcoto.com
cotorioja@elcoto.com

COTO DE IMAZ 2004 TGR
100% tempranillo

90 Colour: pale ruby, brick rim edge. Nose: spicy, fine reductive notes, wet leather, aged wood nuances. Palate: spicy, fine tannins, elegant, long.

COTO DE IMAZ 2008 TR
100% tempranillo

89 Colour: cherry, garnet rim. Nose: ripe fruit, spicy, creamy oak, waxy notes, old leather. Palate: powerful, flavourful, toasty.

COTO DE IMAZ SELECCIÓN ANIVERSARIO 2008 TR
100% tempranillo

90 Colour: cherry, garnet rim. Nose: ripe fruit, spicy, creamy oak, wet leather, tobacco. Palate: spirituous, powerful, flavourful.

COTO MAYOR 2009 TC
90% tempranillo, 10% graciano

89 Colour: cherry, garnet rim. Nose: ripe fruit, spicy, creamy oak, toasty, fine reductive notes. Palate: powerful, flavourful, toasty.

COTO REAL 2008 TR
80% tempranillo, 10% garnacha, 10% graciano

89 Colour: pale ruby, brick rim edge. Nose: ripe fruit, balsamic herbs, spicy, creamy oak, fine reductive notes. Palate: powerful, flavourful, long.

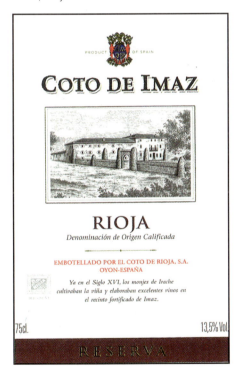

EL COTO 2010 TC
100% tempranillo

90 Colour: cherry, garnet rim. Nose: ripe fruit, spicy, creamy oak, toasty, complex. Palate: powerful, flavourful, toasty.

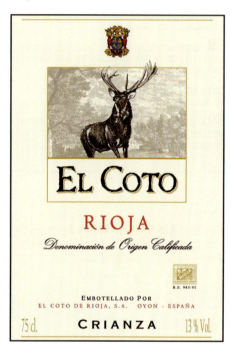

EL COTO 2012 B
100% viura

87 Colour: bright straw. Nose: fresh, fresh fruit, white flowers. Palate: flavourful, fruity, good acidity, balanced.

EL COTO 2012 RD
80% garnacha, 20% tempranillo

88 Colour: rose, purple rim. Nose: powerfull, ripe fruit, red berry notes, floral, expressive. Palate: powerful, fruity, fresh.

ELVIWINES

Antoni Caballé, 8
8197 Valldoreix- St Cugat del Vallès (Tarragona)
☎: +34 935 343 026 - Fax: +34 936 750 316
www.elviwines.com
moises@elviwines.com

HERENZA 2009 TC
100% tempranillo

92 Colour: dark-red cherry, garnet rim. Nose: spicy, dried herbs, ripe fruit. Palate: balanced, ripe fruit, round tannins.

HERENZA KOSHER ELVIWINES 2010 TC
100% tempranillo

91 Colour: bright cherry. Nose: sweet spices, creamy oak, fruit expression. Palate: flavourful, fruity, toasty, round tannins.

MATI KOSHER ELVIWINES 2011 T
100% tempranillo

90 Colour: cherry, purple rim. Nose: expressive, fresh fruit, red berry notes, floral. Palate: flavourful, fruity, good acidity, round tannins.

EMPATÍA

Pza. Fermín Gurbindo, 2
26339 Abalos (La Rioja)
☎: +34 649 841 746 - Fax: +34 941 308 023
www.hotelvilladeabalos.com
direccion@hotelvilladeabalos.com

EMPATÍA 2010 BFB
80% viura, 20% malvasía, garnacha blanca

87 Colour: bright straw. Nose: sweet spices, faded flowers, candied fruit. Palate: flavourful, spicy, ripe fruit, good finish.

EMPATÍA VENDIMIA SELECCIONADA 2008 T
90% tempranillo, 10% garnacha

88 Colour: bright cherry. Nose: ripe fruit, sweet spices, creamy oak, toasty, aromatic coffee. Palate: flavourful, fruity, toasty.

ESPADA OJEDA S.C.

Avda. La Poveda, 8
1306 Lapuebla de Labarca (Álava)
☎: +34 945 627 349
www.espadaojeda.com
bodegas@espadaojeda.com

DA LAUSAN 2012 T
tempranillo

85 Colour: deep cherry, purple rim. Nose: medium intensity, red berry notes, ripe fruit. Palate: ripe fruit, flavourful.

FINCA ALLENDE

Pza. Ibarra, 1
26330 Briones (La Rioja)
☎: +34 941 322 301 - Fax: +34 941 322 302
www.finca-allende.com
info@finca-allende.com

ALLENDE 2010 B
90% viura, 10% malvasía

93 Colour: bright yellow. Nose: ripe fruit, citrus fruit, dried herbs, floral, sweet spices, creamy oak. Palate: sweetness, spicy, long, balanced.

ALLENDE 2010 T
100% tempranillo

93 Colour: cherry, garnet rim. Nose: red berry notes, ripe fruit, balsamic herbs, spicy, mineral. Palate: balanced, elegant, flavourful, long, round tannins.

ALLENDE DULCE 2009 B
100% viura

96 Colour: golden. Nose: powerfull, floral, honeyed notes, candied fruit, fragrant herbs, petrol notes. Palate: flavourful, sweet, fresh, fruity, good acidity, long, concentrated, balanced, elegant.

AVRVS 2010 T
85% tempranillo, 15% graciano

97 Colour: cherry, garnet rim. Nose: ripe fruit, fruit liqueur notes, powerfull, dry stone, earthy notes, characterful, toasty, dark chocolate. Palate: powerful, flavourful, concentrated, long, balanced, round tannins.

CALVARIO 2010 T
90% tempranillo, 8% garnacha, 2% graciano

96 Colour: cherry, garnet rim. Nose: ripe fruit, fruit preserve, fruit expression, earthy notes, mineral, spicy. Palate: round, flavourful, powerful, long, round tannins.

MÁRTIRES 2012 B
100% viura

96 Colour: bright yellow. Nose: ripe fruit, sweet spices, earthy notes, balanced, elegant. Palate: rich, smoky aftertaste, flavourful, fresh, good acidity.

FINCA DE LA RICA

Las Cocinillas, s/n
1330 Labastida (Rioja)
☎: +34 941 509 406
www.fincadelarica.com
info@fincadelarica.com

EL BUSCADOR DE FINCA DE LA RICA 2010 TC
tempranillo, garnacha

90 Colour: cherry, garnet rim. Nose: ripe fruit, spicy, creamy oak, toasty, complex. Palate: powerful, flavourful, toasty, round tannins.

EL BUSCADOR DE FINCA DE LA RICA 2011 TC
tempranillo, garnacha

89 Colour: bright cherry. Nose: sweet spices, fruit expression, fruit preserve. Palate: flavourful, fruity, toasty, round tannins.

EL GUÍA DE FINCA DE LA RICA 2012 T
tempranillo, viura

88 Colour: cherry, purple rim. Nose: expressive, red berry notes, ripe fruit, wild herbs. Palate: flavourful, fruity, good acidity, round tannins.

EL NÓMADA 2010 T
tempranillo, graciano

92 Colour: cherry, garnet rim. Nose: spicy, creamy oak, toasty, fruit expression. Palate: powerful, flavourful, toasty, round tannins.

FINCA DE LOS ARANDINOS

Ctra. LP 137, km. 4,6
26375 Entrena (La Rioja)
☎: +34 941 446 065 - Fax: +34 941 446 423
www.fincadelosarandinos.com
bodega@fincadelosarandinos.com

EL CONJURO 2011 T
85% tempranillo, 15% garnacha

91 Colour: cherry, garnet rim. Nose: ripe fruit, spicy, creamy oak, toasty, balsamic herbs. Palate: powerful, flavourful, toasty.

FINCA DE LOS ARANDINOS 2011 TC
75% tempranillo, 20% garnacha, 5% mazuelo

90 Colour: cherry, garnet rim. Nose: ripe fruit, spicy, creamy oak, toasty. Palate: powerful, flavourful, toasty.

MALACAPA 2012 T
95% tempranillo, 5% mazuelo

85 Colour: cherry, purple rim. Nose: ripe fruit, floral, fragrant herbs. Palate: correct, powerful, flavourful.

VIERO SOBRE LÍAS 2012 BFB
100% viura

89 Colour: bright straw. Nose: powerfull, ripe fruit, sweet spices, creamy oak, fragrant herbs. Palate: rich, flavourful, fresh, good acidity.

VIERO VENDIMIA TARDÍA 2011 B
100% viura

90 Colour: golden. Nose: powerfull, floral, honeyed notes, candied fruit, fragrant herbs. Palate: flavourful, sweet, fresh, fruity, good acidity, long.

FINCA EGOMEI

Ctra. Corella, s/n
26540 Alfaro (La Rioja)
☎: +34 948 780 006 - Fax: +34 948 780 515
www.bodegasab.com
info@egomei.es

EGOMEI 2009 T
tempranillo, graciano

90 Colour: cherry, garnet rim. Nose: ripe fruit, spicy, creamy oak, toasty. Palate: powerful, flavourful, toasty, round tannins.

EGOMEI ALMA 2009 T
tempranillo, graciano

93 Colour: cherry, garnet rim. Nose: ripe fruit, spicy, cocoa bean, mineral, expressive. Palate: flavourful, toasty, round, balanced, elegant.

FINCA MANZANOS

Ctra. NA-134, km. 49
31560 Azagra (Navarra)
☎: +34 948 692 500
www.manzanoswines.com
info@manzanosenterprises.com

FINCA MANZANOS 2007 TR
90% tempranillo, 5% garnacha, 5% mazuelo

88 Colour: cherry, garnet rim. Nose: spicy, toasty, tobacco, fruit liqueur notes. Palate: powerful, flavourful, toasty, round tannins.

FINCA MANZANOS 2009 TC
90% tempranillo, 5% garnacha, 5% mazuelo

87 Colour: bright cherry, garnet rim. Nose: dried herbs, ripe fruit, fruit preserve, spicy. Palate: fruity, ripe fruit.

FINCA MANZANOS 2012 B
100% chardonnay

89 Colour: bright straw. Nose: fresh, fresh fruit, white flowers, expressive. Palate: flavourful, fruity, good acidity, balanced.

LOS HERMANOS MANZANOS 2007 TR
70% tempranillo, 30% garnacha

86 Colour: dark-red cherry, garnet rim. Nose: ripe fruit, fruit preserve, spicy, old leather. Palate: balanced, spicy, long.

MAS DE VÍCTOR GRACIANO 2011 T
100% graciano

90 Colour: cherry, garnet rim. Nose: ripe fruit, spicy, balsamic herbs, varietal. Palate: powerful, flavourful, toasty, round tannins.

FINCA NUEVA

Las Eras, 16
26330 Briones (La Rioja)
☎: +34 941 322 301 - Fax: +34 941 322 302
www.fincanueva.com
info@fincanueva.com

FINCA NUEVA 2004 TGR
100% tempranillo

92 Colour: deep cherry, orangey edge. Nose: fruit liqueur notes, balsamic herbs, fine reductive notes. Palate: elegant, balanced, flavourful, spicy, long, fine tannins.

FINCA NUEVA 2007 TR
100% tempranillo

91 Colour: bright cherry, garnet rim. Nose: ripe fruit, aromatic coffee, spicy, wet leather, tobacco. Palate: flavourful, good acidity, fine bitter notes, classic aged character.

FINCA NUEVA 2008 TC
100% tempranillo

88 Colour: cherry, garnet rim. Nose: ripe fruit, spicy, creamy oak, toasty, complex. Palate: powerful, flavourful, toasty, round tannins.

FINCA NUEVA 2009 TC
100% tempranillo

89 Colour: cherry, garnet rim. Nose: ripe fruit, balsamic herbs, spicy, creamy oak. Palate: powerful, flavourful, toasty.

FINCA NUEVA 2012 BFB
100% viura

90 Colour: bright yellow. Nose: powerfull, ripe fruit, sweet spices, creamy oak, fragrant herbs. Palate: rich, flavourful, fresh, good acidity.

FINCA NUEVA 2012 RD
60% tempranillo, 40% garnacha

88 Colour: raspberry rose. Nose: floral, fragrant herbs, candied fruit. Palate: fresh, fruity, flavourful, fine bitter notes.

FINCA NUEVA TEMPRANILLO 2012 T
100% tempranillo

91 Colour: cherry, purple rim. Nose: red berry notes, raspberry, balsamic herbs, wild herbs, expressive. Palate: fresh, fruity, flavourful, easy to drink.

FINCA NUEVA VIURA 2012 B
100% viura

87 Colour: bright straw. Nose: dried herbs, floral, fruit expression, medium intensity. Palate: powerful, flavourful, good finish.

FINCA VALPIEDRA

El Montecillo, s/n
26360 Fuenmayor (La Rioja)
☎: +34 941 450 876 - Fax: +34 941 450 875
www.familiamartinezbujanda.com
info@bujanda.com

CANTOS DE VALPIEDRA 2010 T
tempranillo

91 Colour: cherry, garnet rim. Nose: ripe fruit, spicy, toasty. Palate: powerful, flavourful, toasty, round tannins.

FINCA VALPIEDRA 2008 TR
94% tempranillo, 3% graciano, 3% maturana

92 Colour: cherry, garnet rim. Nose: spicy, creamy oak, toasty, mineral, characterful. Palate: powerful, flavourful, toasty, round tannins.

GONZÁLEZ TESO

El Olmo, 34-36
1330 Labastida (Álava)
☎: +34 945 331 321 - Fax: +34 945 331 321
www.bodegasgonzalezteso.com
info@gontes.com

GONTÉS 2009 TC
95% tempranillo, 5% garnacha

89 Colour: cherry, garnet rim. Nose: ripe fruit, spicy, creamy oak, toasty, balsamic herbs. Palate: powerful, flavourful, toasty, round tannins.

GONTÉS 2012 T
85% tempranillo, 15% garnacha

85 Colour: cherry, purple rim. Nose: floral, red berry notes, ripe fruit. Palate: flavourful, fruity, good acidity.

GONTÉS EXPRESIÓN 2007 T
100% tempranillo

89 Colour: cherry, garnet rim. Nose: ripe fruit, scrubland, creamy oak, fine reductive notes, tobacco. Palate: powerful, flavourful, spicy.

GONTÉS EXPRESIÓN 2008 T
100% tempranillo

90 Colour: cherry, garnet rim. Nose: red berry notes, ripe fruit, cocoa bean, sweet spices, expressive. Palate: spicy, long, harsh oak tannins.

GONTÉS MEDIA CRIANZA 2011 T
100% tempranillo

87 Colour: cherry, garnet rim. Nose: ripe fruit, aromatic coffee, creamy oak. Palate: powerful, flavourful, toasty.

GONTÉS MEDIA CRIANZA 2012 T
100% tempranillo

88 Colour: bright cherry. Nose: sweet spices, creamy oak, expressive, red berry notes, ripe fruit. Palate: flavourful, fruity, toasty.

OLMO 34 2008 T
50% tempranillo, 30% garnacha, 20% graciano

89 Colour: cherry, garnet rim. Nose: ripe fruit, balsamic herbs, sweet spices, creamy oak. Palate: rich, flavourful, long, correct, spicy.

OLMO 34 2009 T
25% tempranillo, 25% garnacha, 25% graciano, 25% mazuelo

90 Colour: cherry, garnet rim. Nose: ripe fruit, spicy, creamy oak, toasty, complex. Palate: powerful, flavourful, toasty, round tannins, balanced.

GRANJA NUESTRA SEÑORA DE REMELLURI

Ctra. Rivas de Tereso, s/n
1330 Labastida (Álava)
☎: +34 945 331 801 - Fax: +34 945 331 802
www.remelluri.com
remelluri@remelluri.com

LINDES DE REMELLURI LABASTIDA 2010 T
tempranillo, graciano, garnacha, viura

93 Colour: cherry, garnet rim. Nose: spicy, ripe fruit, scrubland, earthy notes, mineral. Palate: fruity, fresh, good acidity.

LINDES DE REMELLURI SAN VICENTE 2010 T
tempranillo, graciano, garnacha, viura

91 Colour: bright cherry. Nose: ripe fruit, sweet spices, creamy oak. Palate: flavourful, fruity, toasty, round tannins.

REMELLURI 2008 TR
tempranillo, graciano, garnacha, viura, malvasía

93 Colour: very deep cherry. Nose: powerfull, ripe fruit, fruit liqueur notes, toasty, spicy. Palate: flavourful, spicy, ripe fruit, fine bitter notes, good acidity.

REMELLURI 2010 B
viura, sauvignon blanc, chardonnay, garnacha blanca, otras

96 Colour: bright yellow. Nose: powerfull, sweet spices, creamy oak, fragrant herbs, candied fruit. Palate: rich, flavourful, fresh, good acidity.

GRUPO VINÍCOLA MARQUÉS DE VARGAS

Ctra. Zaragoza, Km. 6
26006 Logroño (La Rioja)
☎: +34 941 261 401 - Fax: +34 941 238 696
www.marquesdevargas.com
bodega@marquesdevargas.com

MARQUÉS DE VARGAS 2008 TR
75% tempranillo, 10% mazuelo, 5% garnacha, 10% otras

91 Colour: pale ruby, brick rim edge. Nose: elegant, spicy, fine reductive notes, wet leather, ripe fruit. Palate: spicy, long, balanced, round tannins.

MARQUÉS DE VARGAS HACIENDA PRADOLAGAR 2005 TR
40% tempranillo, 10% mazuelo, 10% garnacha, 40% otras

93 Colour: pale ruby, brick rim edge. Nose: ripe fruit, fruit liqueur notes, balsamic herbs, spicy, toasty, fine reductive notes, old leather. Palate: rich, flavourful, spicy, long, balanced, elegant.

MARQUÉS DE VARGAS RESERVA PRIVADA 2005 TR
60% tempranillo, 10% mazuelo, 10% garnacha, 20% otras

92 Colour: pale ruby, brick rim edge. Nose: elegant, spicy, fine reductive notes, wet leather, aged wood nuances, fruit liqueur notes. Palate: spicy, fine tannins, elegant, long.

GRUPO YLLERA

A-6 Madrid - Coruña, Km. 173, 5
47490 Rueda (Valladolid)
☎: +34 983 868 097 - Fax: +34 983 868 177
www.grupoyllera.com
grupoyllera@grupoyllera.com

COELUS 2004 TR
tempranillo

83

COELUS 2009 TC
tempranillo

85 Colour: dark-red cherry. Nose: toasty, spicy, fruit expression, earthy notes. Palate: powerful, flavourful, fruity, creamy, toasty.

COELUS JOVEN 2012 T
tempranillo

88 Colour: deep cherry. Nose: ripe fruit, grassy. Palate: flavourful, spicy, long.

HACIENDA GRIMÓN

Gallera, 6
26131 Ventas Blancas (La Rioja)
☎: +34 941 482 184 - Fax: +34 941 482 184
www.haciendagrimon.com
info@haciendagrimon.com

FINCA LA ORACIÓN 2010 T
100% tempranillo

92 Colour: deep cherry. Nose: spicy, toasty, ripe fruit, sweet spices. Palate: fine bitter notes, good acidity, ripe fruit.

HACIENDA GRIMÓN 2010 TC
85% tempranillo, 10% garnacha, 5% graciano

91 Colour: cherry, garnet rim. Nose: sweet spices, ripe fruit, toasty. Palate: spicy, fine bitter notes, good acidity.

HACIENDA URBIÓN

Ctra. Nalda, km. 9
26120 Albelda de Iregua (Rioja)
☎: +34 941 444 233 - Fax: +34 941 444 427
www.vinicolareal.com
info@vinicolareal.com

PALACIO DE ALCÁNTARA 2010 TC
100% tempranillo

85 Colour: bright cherry, garnet rim. Nose: ripe fruit, fruit preserve, spicy, balanced. Palate: flavourful, round tannins.

PALACIO DE ALCÁNTARA 2012 T
100% tempranillo

83

URBIÓN 2006 TR
100% tempranillo

91 Colour: bright cherry, garnet rim. Nose: balanced, elegant, balsamic herbs. Palate: complex, spicy, round, round tannins.

URBIÓN CUVÉE 2011 T
90% tempranillo, 10% garnacha

88 Colour: bright cherry, garnet rim. Nose: toasty, sweet spices, ripe fruit. Palate: balanced, balsamic, round tannins.

URBIÓN VENDIMIA 2009 TC
90% tempranillo, 10% garnacha

87 Colour: cherry, garnet rim. Nose: dried herbs, ripe fruit, closed. Palate: good structure, spicy, balanced.

HACIENDA Y VIÑEDOS MARQUÉS DEL ATRIO

Ctra. de Logroño NA-134, Km. 86,2
31587 Mendavia (Navarra)
☎: +34 948 379 994 - Fax: +34 948 389 049
www.marquesdelatrio.com
info@marquesdelatrio.com

BARDESANO 2010 TC
85% tempranillo, 15% garnacha

86 Colour: bright cherry. Nose: ripe fruit, toasty. Palate: flavourful, fruity, toasty, round tannins.

BODEGAS RASILLO 2008 TR
85% tempranillo, 15% garnacha

89 Colour: ruby red, garnet rim. Nose: ripe fruit, fruit liqueur notes, sweet spices, creamy oak, fine reductive notes. Palate: powerful, flavourful, spicy, long.

BODEGAS RASILLO 2010 TC
85% tempranillo, 15% garnacha

87 Colour: cherry, garnet rim. Nose: spicy, creamy oak, ripe fruit, fruit preserve. Palate: powerful, flavourful, spicy, balsamic.

DON FABIAN 2010 TC
85% tempranillo, 15% garnacha

85 Colour: bright cherry. Nose: sweet spices, creamy oak, toasty. Palate: flavourful, fruity, toasty, round tannins.

FAUSTINO RIVERO UCLECIA 2008 TR
85% tempranillo, 15% garnacha

88 Colour: cherry, garnet rim. Nose: spicy, fine reductive notes, wet leather, aged wood nuances, fruit liqueur notes. Palate: spicy, long, powerful.

FAUSTINO RIVERO UCLECIA 2010 TC
85% tempranillo, 15% garnacha

87 Colour: cherry, garnet rim. Nose: ripe fruit, spicy, creamy oak, balsamic herbs, fine reductive notes. Palate: powerful, flavourful, toasty.

HERMANOS FRÍAS DEL VAL

Herrerías, 13
1307 Villabuena (Álava)
☎: +34 656 782 714
www.friasdelval.com
info@friasdelval.com

DON PEDUZ 2011 T
100% tempranillo

89 Colour: cherry, purple rim. Nose: complex, expressive, fruit expression, aromatic coffee, creamy oak. Palate: sweetness, fruity, powerful, flavourful.

HERMANOS FRÍAS DEL VAL 2008 TR
100% tempranillo

86 Colour: dark-red cherry. Nose: candied fruit, spicy, creamy oak, toasty. Palate: dry, fine bitter notes, flavourful, spicy.

HERMANOS FRÍAS DEL VAL 2012 T
90% tempranillo, 10% viura

89 Colour: cherry, purple rim. Nose: fresh fruit, red berry notes, floral, varietal. Palate: flavourful, fruity, good acidity, round tannins.

HERMANOS FRÍAS DEL VAL 2010 TC
100% tempranillo

87 Colour: dark-red cherry. Nose: spicy, creamy oak, toasty, candied fruit. Palate: powerful, creamy, spicy, grainy tannins.

HERMANOS FRÍAS DEL VAL 2011 B
60% viura, 40% malvasía

86 Colour: bright straw. Nose: white flowers, ripe fruit. Palate: flavourful, fruity, good acidity, balanced.

HERMANOS FRÍAS DEL VAL 2012 B
60% viura, 40% malvasía

86 Colour: bright straw. Nose: fresh, white flowers. Palate: flavourful, fruity, good acidity, balanced.

HERMANOS FRÍAS DEL VAL EXPRESIÓN 2010 T
100% tempranillo

86 Colour: deep cherry. Nose: woody, spicy. Palate: good structure, powerful, oaky, ripe fruit, lacks expression, toasty.

HNOS. CASTILLO PÉREZ

Camino la Estación, 15
26330 Briones (La Rioja)
☎: +34 667 730 651
www.bodegaszurbal.com
info@bodegaszurbal.com

ZURBAL 2008 TR
tempranillo

84

ZURBAL 2009 TC
tempranillo

88 Colour: cherry, garnet rim. Nose: varietal, ripe fruit, creamy oak, sweet spices. Palate: balanced, round tannins.

ZURBAL 2012 B
viura

87 Colour: bright straw. Nose: fresh, fresh fruit, white flowers. Palate: flavourful, fruity, good acidity.

ZURBAL VENDIMIA SELECCIONADA 2010 T
tempranillo

88 Colour: deep cherry, garnet rim. Nose: ripe fruit, fruit preserve, spicy. Palate: fruity, good finish, balanced.

IRADIER

Avda. La Rioja, 17
26339 Abalos (La Rioja)
☎: +34 945 290 081 - Fax: +34 945 290 081
vinosiradier@telefonica.net

IRADIER 2012 B
viura, garnacha

89 Colour: bright straw. Nose: dried herbs, ripe fruit. Palate: powerful, flavourful, full, sweetness, fresh.

IRADIER 2012 RD
viura, tempranillo, garnacha

85 Colour: onion pink. Nose: candied fruit, dried flowers, fragrant herbs. Palate: light-bodied, flavourful, good acidity, long, spicy.

IRADIER 2012 T
tempranillo

86 Colour: cherry, purple rim. Nose: red berry notes, ripe fruit, dried flowers. Palate: fruity, good acidity, round tannins.

JOSÉ BASOCO BASOCO

1330 Villabuena (Álava)
☎: +34 657 794 964
www.fincabarronte.com
info@fincabarronte.com

FINCA BARRONTE 2010 TC
tempranillo

90 Colour: very deep cherry. Nose: creamy oak, toasty, ripe fruit. Palate: flavourful, good acidity.

FINCA BARRONTE GRACIANO 2010 T
graciano

91 Colour: cherry, garnet rim. Nose: ripe fruit, spicy, creamy oak. Palate: powerful, flavourful, toasty, round tannins.

FINCA BARRONTE TEMPRANILLO 2012 T
tempranillo

88 Colour: dark-red cherry. Nose: ripe fruit, macerated fruit, toasty. Palate: sweetness, fruity, powerful, flavourful.

JUAN CARLOS SANCHA

Cº de Las Barreras, s/n
26320 Baños de Río Tobía (La Rioja)
☎: +34 639 216 011
www.juancarlossancha.com
juancarlossancha@yahoo.es

AD LIBITUM MATURANA TINTA 2011 T
100% maturana

90 Colour: dark-red cherry. Nose: fruit preserve, spicy, creamy oak. Palate: sweet tannins, flavourful, powerful, fruity, spirituous.

AD LIBITUM MONASTEL 2010 T
100% monastel

91 Colour: deep cherry. Nose: undergrowth, damp earth, complex, expressive, varietal, powerfull. Palate: complex, full, powerful, flavourful, varietal. Personality.

AD LIBITUM TEMPRANILLO BLANCO 2012 B
100% tempranillo blanco

88 Colour: bright yellow. Nose: ripe fruit, fragrant herbs, earthy notes, expressive. Palate: flavourful, balsamic, spicy.

PEÑA EL GATO GARNACHA DE VIÑAS VIEJAS 2011 T
100% garnacha

92 Colour: deep cherry. Nose: fruit expression, mineral, cocoa bean, spicy, complex, expressive. Palate: flavourful, full.

LA RIOJA ALTA S.A.

Avda. de Vizcaya, 8
26200 Haro (La Rioja)
☎: +34 941 310 346 - Fax: +34 941 312 854
www.riojalta.com
riojalta@riojalta.com

GRAN RESERVA 904 RIOJA ALTA 2001 TGR
90% tempranillo, 10% graciano

94 Colour: dark-red cherry, orangey edge. Nose: elegant, balanced, fragrant herbs, spicy, fine reductive notes. Palate: balanced, classic aged character, fine tannins.

LA RIOJA ALTA GRAN RESERVA 890 1998 TGR
95% tempranillo, 3% graciano, 2% mazuelo

92 Colour: pale ruby, brick rim edge. Nose: spicy, fine reductive notes, wet leather, aged wood nuances, fruit liqueur notes, expressive, elegant. Palate: spicy, fine tannins, elegant, long.

VIÑA ALBERDI 2007 TC
tempranillo

90 Colour: cherry, garnet rim. Nose: ripe fruit, spicy, old leather, fine reductive notes. Palate: flavourful, fine tannins, good acidity, balanced.

VIÑA ARANA 2005 TR
tempranillo, mazuelo

91 Colour: dark-red cherry, orangey edge. Nose: balanced, tobacco, old leather. Palate: flavourful, good acidity, fine tannins.

VIÑA ARDANZA 2004 TR
tempranillo, garnacha

93 Colour: deep cherry. Nose: expressive, spicy, fine reductive notes, dried herbs, ripe fruit. Palate: balanced, good acidity, fine tannins, classic aged character.

LAN

Paraje del Buicio, s/n
26360 Fuenmayor (La Rioja)
☎: +34 941 450 550 - Fax: +34 941 450 567
www.bodegaslan.com
info@bodegaslan.com

CULMEN 2007 TR
85% tempranillo, 15% graciano

94 Colour: cherry, garnet rim. Nose: spicy, creamy oak, ripe fruit, balsamic herbs, fine reductive notes, balanced, elegant. Palate: spicy, long, powerful, flavourful, balanced.

LAN 2005 TGR
85% tempranillo, 10% mazuelo, 5% graciano

90 Colour: cherry, garnet rim. Nose: spicy, toasty, ripe fruit, cocoa bean. Palate: flavourful, spicy, ripe fruit, fine bitter notes.

LAN 2007 TR
90% tempranillo, 5% mazuelo, 5% graciano

90 Colour: cherry, garnet rim. Nose: ripe fruit, spicy, toasty. Palate: powerful, flavourful, toasty, round tannins.

LAN 2010 TC
100% tempranillo

88 Colour: cherry, garnet rim. Nose: spicy, ripe fruit. Palate: ripe fruit, flavourful, powerful.

LAN A MANO 2009 T
80% tempranillo, 15% graciano, 5% mazuelo

94 Colour: cherry, garnet rim. Nose: red berry notes, ripe fruit, balsamic herbs, earthy notes, spicy, creamy oak. Palate: powerful, rich, flavourful, long, spicy, balanced, elegant.

LAN D-12 2010 T
100% tempranillo

91 Colour: cherry, garnet rim. Nose: spicy, creamy oak, toasty. Palate: powerful, flavourful, toasty, round tannins.

VIÑA LANCIANO 2007 TR
90% tempranillo, 10% mazuelo

90 Colour: dark-red cherry. Nose: powerfull, expressive, sweet spices, dark chocolate. Palate: powerful, flavourful, fruity, creamy.

LAUNA

Ctra. Vitoria-Logroño, Km. 57
1300 Laguardia (Alava)
☎: +34 946 824 108 - Fax: +34 956 824 108
www.bodegaslauna.com
info@bodegaslauna.com

LAUNA 2010 TC
90% tempranillo, 10% mazuelo

89 Colour: cherry, garnet rim. Nose: ripe fruit, creamy oak, sweet spices. Palate: powerful, flavourful, long.

LAUNA SELECCIÓN FAMILIAR 2009 TR
90% tempranillo, 10% mazuelo, graciano

91 Colour: cherry, garnet rim. Nose: ripe fruit, balsamic herbs, sweet spices, creamy oak, expressive. Palate: powerful, flavourful, toasty.

LAUNA SELECCIÓN FAMILIAR 2010 TC
100% tempranillo

90 Colour: cherry, garnet rim. Nose: ripe fruit, spicy, creamy oak, toasty, complex. Palate: powerful, flavourful, toasty, balanced.

TEO'S 2009 T
100% tempranillo

90 Colour: cherry, garnet rim. Nose: ripe fruit, balsamic herbs, spicy, mineral, creamy oak. Palate: powerful, flavourful, balanced, long.

LECEA

Cerrillo Verballe s/n
26340 San Asensio (La Rioja)
☎: +34 941 457 444 - Fax: +34 941 457 444
www.bodegaslecea.com
info@bodegaslecea.com

CORAZÓN DE LAGO 2012 T
tempranillo

86 Colour: cherry, garnet rim. Nose: powerfull, fruit preserve, red berry notes. Palate: powerful, fine bitter notes.

LECEA 2000 TGR
90% tempranillo, 10% mazuelo

88 Colour: light cherry. Nose: medium intensity, fine reductive notes, spicy. Palate: light-bodied, fruity, fine tannins.

LECEA 2007 TR
tempranillo

87 Colour: cherry, garnet rim. Nose: powerfull, ripe fruit, fruit preserve, sweet spices. Palate: correct, long.

LECEA 2009 TC
100% tempranillo

87 Colour: very deep cherry. Nose: fruit liqueur notes, spicy, toasty. Palate: fine bitter notes, warm, spicy, round tannins.

LECEA 2012 B
viura

87 Colour: straw. Nose: powerfull, fresh, neat, ripe fruit. Palate: dry, flavourful, fresh, fruity.

LECEA 2012 RD
75% garnacha, 25% viura

85 Colour: coppery red. Nose: candied fruit, medium intensity, fruit expression. Palate: flavourful, fruity.

LECEA 2012 T
tempranillo

84

LECEA VIURA-CHARDONNAY 2010 BC
chardonnay, viura

88 Colour: bright yellow. Nose: powerfull, expressive, ripe fruit, grapey, spicy, smoky. Palate: dry, powerful, fruity, spicy, smoky aftertaste.

LECEA VIURA-CHARDONNAY 2012 B
chardonnay, viura

85 Colour: bright yellow. Nose: macerated fruit, wild herbs. Palate: fresh, fruity, lacks expression.

LONG WINES

Avda. del Puente Cultural, 8 Bloque B Bajo 7
28702 San Sebastián de los Reyes (Madrid)
☎: +34 916 221 305 - Fax: +34 916 220 029
www.longwines.com
adm@longwines.com

FINCA MÓNICA 2010 TC
100% tempranillo

89 Colour: cherry, garnet rim. Nose: ripe fruit, spicy, creamy oak, toasty, complex. Palate: powerful, flavourful, toasty, round tannins.

FINCA MÓNICA TEMPRANILLO 2011 T
100% tempranillo

87 Colour: cherry, garnet rim. Nose: ripe fruit, balsamic herbs, medium intensity. Palate: powerful, flavourful, spicy.

LUBERRI MONJE AMESTOY

Camino de Rehoyos, s/n
1340 Elciego (Álava)
☎: +34 945 606 010 - Fax: +34 945 606 482
www.luberri.com
luberri@luberri.com

BIGA DE LUBERRI 2010 TC
tempranillo

91 Colour: cherry, garnet rim. Nose: spicy, creamy oak, toasty, complex, red berry notes, raspberry. Palate: powerful, flavourful, toasty.

LUBERRI 2012 T MACERACIÓN CARBÓNICA
95% tempranillo, 5% viura

90 Colour: cherry, purple rim. Nose: red berry notes, ripe fruit, balsamic herbs, expressive. Palate: powerful, flavourful, spicy, easy to drink.

LUBERRI CEPAS VIEJAS 2008 TC
tempranillo

89 Colour: cherry, garnet rim. Nose: ripe fruit, aged wood nuances, waxy notes, cigar, spicy, toasty. Palate: powerful, flavourful, spicy, long.

LUBERRI ZURI 2012 B
80% viura, 20% malvasía

84

MONJE AMESTOY DE LUBERRI 2007 TR
95% tempranillo, 5% cabernet sauvignon

90 Colour: cherry, garnet rim. Nose: ripe fruit, balsamic herbs, spicy, creamy oak, fine reductive notes. Palate: powerful, flavourful, spicy, long, balsamic.

SEIS DE LUBERRI 2010 T
tempranillo

92 Colour: bright cherry. Nose: ripe fruit, sweet spices, creamy oak, expressive. Palate: flavourful, fruity, toasty, round tannins.

LUIS GURPEGUI MUGA

Avda. Celso Muerza, 8
31570 San Adrián (Navarra)
☎: +34 948 670 050 - Fax: +34 948 670 259
www.gurpegui.es
bodegas@gurpegui.es

PRIMI 2012 T
tempranillo, graciano, garnacha

87 Colour: cherry, purple rim. Nose: expressive, fresh fruit. Palate: flavourful, fruity, good acidity, round tannins.

MAGICAL WINES

Pio Baroja, 21
28939 Arroyomolinos (Madrid)
☎: +34 916 096 025
www.magicalwines.com
info@magicalwines.com

HOCUS POCUS 2009 TC
85% tempranillo, 10% mazuelo, 5% graciano

85 Colour: cherry, garnet rim. Nose: ripe fruit, spicy, creamy oak, toasty. Palate: powerful, flavourful, toasty.

MARQUÉS DE LA CONCORDIA

Ctra. El Ciego, s/n
26350 Cenicero (La Rioja)
☎: +34 914 365 924
www.the-haciendas.com
abasilio@unitedwineries.com

HACIENDA SUSAR 2007 T
100% tempranillo

89 Colour: cherry, garnet rim. Nose: fruit preserve, scrubland, spicy, fine reductive notes. Palate: powerful, flavourful, spicy, long.

MARQUÉS DE LA CONCORDIA (MARQUÉS DE LA CONCORDIA FAMILY OF WINES) 2009 TC
100% tempranillo

89 Colour: cherry, garnet rim. Nose: ripe fruit, spicy, creamy oak, balsamic herbs. Palate: powerful, flavourful, toasty.

MARQUÉS DE LA CONCORDIA 2007 TR
100% tempranillo

88 Colour: cherry, garnet rim. Nose: ripe fruit, spicy, complex. Palate: powerful, flavourful, toasty, fine tannins.

MARQUÉS DE MURRIETA

Finca Ygay- Ctra. Logroño-Zaragoza, km. 5
26006 Logroño (La Rioja)
☎: +34 941 271 370 - Fax: +34 941 251 606
www.marquesdemurrieta.com
rrpp@marquesdemurrieta.com

CAPELLANIA 2008 B
100% viura

91 Colour: old gold, amber rim. Nose: candied fruit, acetaldehyde, sweet spices. Palate: good acidity, fine bitter notes, ripe fruit.

CASTILLO YGAY 2004 TGR
93% tempranillo, 7% mazuelo

96 Colour: cherry, garnet rim. Nose: ripe fruit, spicy, toasty. Palate: flavourful, spicy, fine bitter notes, good acidity.

CASTILLO YGAY 2005 TGR
89% tempranillo, 11% mazuelo

95 Colour: cherry, garnet rim. Nose: ripe fruit, toasty, sweet spices. Palate: flavourful, fine bitter notes, balanced, spicy.

DALMAU 2007 TR
85% tempranillo, 8% cabernet sauvignon, 7% graciano

96 Colour: cherry, garnet rim. Nose: spicy, creamy oak, toasty, complex, expressive. Palate: powerful, flavourful, toasty, round tannins.

DALMAU 2009 TR
74% tempranillo, 15% cabernet sauvignon, 11% graciano

95 Colour: cherry, garnet rim. Nose: ripe fruit, toasty, creamy oak, spicy. Palate: powerful, fine bitter notes, good acidity, elegant.

MARQUÉS DE MURRIETA 2008 TR
86% tempranillo, 8% garnacha, 4% mazuelo, 2% graciano

92 Colour: bright cherry. Nose: ripe fruit, sweet spices, creamy oak, expressive, fine reductive notes. Palate: flavourful, fruity, toasty, round tannins.

MARQUÉS DE REINOSA, S. COOP.

Ctra. Rincón de Soto, s/n
26560 Autol (La Rioja)
☎: +34 941 401 327 - Fax: +34 941 390 065
www.marquesdereinosa.com
bodegas@marquesdereinosa.com

MARQUÉS DE REINOSA 2007 TR
100% tempranillo

88 Colour: cherry, garnet rim. Nose: ripe fruit, spicy, creamy oak, toasty, fine reductive notes. Palate: powerful, flavourful, toasty.

MARQUÉS DE REINOSA 2010 TC
100% tempranillo

89 Colour: cherry, garnet rim. Nose: ripe fruit, balsamic herbs, spicy, toasty. Palate: powerful, flavourful, spicy, long.

MARQUÉS DE REINOSA 2012 B
90% viura, 10% verdejo

87 Colour: bright straw. Nose: ripe fruit, dried herbs. Palate: fruity, long, correct, good acidity, balanced.

MARQUÉS DE REINOSA 2012 RD
50% garnacha, 50% tempranillo

82

MARQUÉS DE REINOSA TEMPRANILLO 2012 T
100% tempranillo

87 Colour: cherry, purple rim. Nose: red berry notes, floral. Palate: flavourful, fruity, good acidity, round tannins.

MARQUÉS DE TOMARES

Ctra. de Cenicero, s/n
26360 Fuenmayor (La Rioja)
☎: +34 941 451 129 - Fax: +34 941 450 267
www.marquesdetomares.es
info@marquesdetomares.com

LORIÑÓN 2010 TC
100% tempranillo

89 Colour: bright cherry. Nose: ripe fruit, sweet spices, creamy oak. Palate: flavourful, fruity, toasty, round tannins.

MARQUÉS DE TOMARES 2010 TC
90% tempranillo, 7% mazuelo, 3% graciano

87 Colour: cherry, garnet rim. Nose: spicy, toasty. Palate: ripe fruit, aged character, fine bitter notes.

MARQUÉS DE TOMARES RESERVA DE FAMILIA 2008 TR
80% tempranillo, 15% graciano, 5% mazuelo

88 Colour: deep cherry. Nose: toasty, spicy, ripe fruit. Palate: spicy, fine bitter notes, good acidity.

MARQUÉS DE ULÍA

Paraje del Buicio, s/n
26360 Fuenmayor (La Rioja)
☎: +34 941 450 950 - Fax: +34 941 450 567
www.marquesdeulia.com
info@marquesdeulia.com

LA VENDIMIA MARQUÉS DE ULÍA 2007 TR
85% tempranillo, 15% graciano

88 Colour: dark-red cherry. Nose: powerfull, ripe fruit, roasted coffee, sweet spices. Palate: powerful, fruity, sweetness, spicy, creamy, toasty.

MARQUÉS DE ULÍA 2007 TR
85% tempranillo, 15% mazuelo

90 Colour: dark-red cherry. Nose: ripe fruit, spicy, creamy oak, toasty. Palate: sweetness, fruity, fresh, powerful, flavourful, ripe fruit, creamy, spicy.

MARQUÉS DE ULÍA 2009 TC
100% tempranillo

90 Colour: dark-red cherry. Nose: complex, expressive, spicy, cedar wood, creamy oak, toasty, ripe fruit. Palate: elegant, balanced, full, powerful.

MARQUÉS DEL PUERTO

26360 Fuenmayor (La Rioja)
☎: +34 941 450 001 - Fax: +34 941 450 051
www.bodegamarquesdelpuerto.com
bmp@mbrizard.com

MARQUÉS DEL PUERTO 2001 TGR
92% tempranillo, 6% mazuelo, 2% graciano

86 Colour: dark-red cherry. Nose: fruit preserve, spicy, old leather, balanced. Palate: flavourful, fine tannins, correct.

MARQUÉS DEL PUERTO 2005 TR
90% tempranillo, 10% mazuelo

86 Colour: cherry, garnet rim. Nose: balanced, waxy notes, ripe fruit, spicy. Palate: correct, balanced, good acidity.

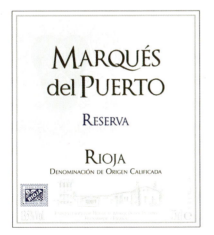

MARQUÉS DEL PUERTO 2009 TC
90% tempranillo, 10% mazuelo

87 Colour: cherry, garnet rim. Nose: ripe fruit, spicy, toasty. Palate: powerful, flavourful, toasty, round tannins.

MARTÍNEZ LACUESTA

Paraje de Ubieta, s/n
26200 Haro (La Rioja)
☎: +34 941 310 050 - Fax: +34 941 303 748
www.martinezlacuesta.com
bodega@martinezlacuesta.com

HINIA 2011 T
tempranillo

91 Colour: deep cherry. Nose: damp earth, macerated fruit, varietal, powerfull, sweet spices, cocoa bean. Palate: powerful, flavourful, fruity, full, fine tannins.

MARTÍNEZ LACUESTA 2007 TR
tempranillo, graciano, mazuelo

90 Colour: light cherry. Nose: fine reductive notes, tobacco, toasty, spicy. Palate: round, balanced, flavourful, powerful.

MARTÍNEZ LACUESTA 2010 TC
tempranillo, graciano, mazuelo

89 Colour: dark-red cherry. Nose: powerfull, elegant, ripe fruit. Palate: round, balanced, good acidity, flavourful.

MIGUEL ÁNGEL MURO

Avda. Diputación, 4
1306 Lapuebla de Labarca (Álava)
☎: +34 627 434 726
www.bodegasmuro.com
info@bodegasmiguelangelmuro.com

AMENITAL 2007 TC
85% tempranillo, 15% graciano

88 Colour: cherry, garnet rim. Nose: ripe fruit, creamy oak, toasty, aromatic coffee. Palate: powerful, flavourful, toasty, balanced.

AMENITAL 2011 T
85% tempranillo, 15% graciano

89 Colour: cherry, purple rim. Nose: expressive, fresh fruit, red berry notes. Palate: flavourful, fruity, good acidity, balanced.

MIGUEL ÁNGEL MURO 2012 T
MACERACIÓN CARBÓNICA
tempranillo

85 Colour: cherry, purple rim. Nose: varietal, characterful, red berry notes. Palate: sweetness, powerful.

MURO 2006 TR
90% tempranillo, 10% graciano

89 Colour: deep cherry. Nose: spicy, fine reductive notes, aged wood nuances, fruit liqueur notes, earthy notes. Palate: spicy, fine tannins, elegant, long.

MURO 2012 B
viura

87 Colour: bright straw. Nose: fresh, white flowers. Palate: flavourful, fruity, good acidity, balanced.

MURO BUJANDA 2009 TC
95% tempranillo, 5% graciano

89 Colour: cherry, garnet rim. Nose: ripe fruit, spicy, creamy oak, toasty. Palate: powerful, flavourful, toasty.

MURO MATURANA 2011 T
maturana

87 Colour: cherry, purple rim. Nose: red berry notes, ripe fruit, wild herbs, spicy. Palate: powerful, flavourful, harsh oak tannins.

MIGUEL MERINO

Ctra. de Logroño, 16
26330 Briones (La Rioja)
☎: +34 941 322 263
www.miguelmerino.com
info@miguelmerino.com

MAZUELO DE LA QUINTA CRUZ 2010 T
100% mazuelo

86 Colour: cherry, garnet rim. Nose: ripe fruit, spicy, toasty, aromatic coffee. Palate: flavourful, toasty, round tannins.

MIGUEL MERINO 2005 TGR
96% tempranillo, 4% graciano, mazuelo

86 Colour: cherry, garnet rim. Nose: spicy, waxy notes, fruit preserve. Palate: flavourful, round tannins, spicy, reductive nuances.

MIGUEL MERINO VIÑAS JÓVENES 2009 T
100% tempranillo

87 Colour: bright cherry. Nose: sweet spices, ripe fruit, fruit preserve. Palate: flavourful, fruity, round tannins.

UNNUM 2009 TC
98% tempranillo, 2% graciano

90 Colour: cherry, garnet rim. Nose: ripe fruit, spicy, balanced. Palate: powerful, flavourful, toasty, round tannins, long.

VITOLA 2006 TR
93% tempranillo, 4% graciano, 3% mazuelo

89 Colour: cherry, garnet rim. Nose: ripe fruit, spicy. Palate: powerful, flavourful, toasty, round tannins, classic aged character.

MIRAVINOS RIOJA

Plaza de Matute 12
28012 (Madrid)
☎: +34 609 119 248
www.miravinos.es
info@miravinos.es

ATUENDO 2009 TR

87 Colour: cherry, garnet rim. Nose: ripe fruit, spicy, creamy oak, toasty, complex. Palate: powerful, flavourful, toasty, round tannins.

ATUENDO 2010 TC

86 Colour: deep cherry. Nose: ripe fruit, premature reduction notes, spicy. Palate: flavourful, fruity.

ATUENDO 2012 T
tempranillo

84

CATAURO 2009 T
tempranillo

91 Colour: deep cherry. Nose: powerfull, ripe fruit, spicy, cocoa bean. Palate: flavourful, ripe fruit, good acidity, round tannins.

OLIVIER RIVIÈRE VINOS

Pepe Blanco, 6 1C
26140 Lardero (La Rioja)
☎: +34 690 733 541 - Fax: +34 941 452 476
olive_riviere@yahoo.fr

GANKO 2011 T
garnacha, mazuelo

93 Colour: very deep cherry. Nose: mineral, ripe fruit, fruit expression, balsamic herbs, scrubland. Palate: flavourful, powerful, fruity.

IDEM 2012 T
graciano, tempranillo, garnacha

89 Colour: very deep cherry. Nose: powerfull, ripe fruit, fruit expression. Palate: fruity, flavourful.

JEQUITIBÁ 2012 B
viura, malvasía, garnacha blanca

89 Colour: bright yellow. Nose: ripe fruit, dried flowers, balsamic herbs, earthy notes. Palate: rich, spicy, balanced.

PAGO DE LARREA

Ctra. de Cenicero, Km. 0,2
1340 Elciego (Álava)
☎: +34 945 606 063 - Fax: +34 945 606 697
www.pagodelarrea.com
bodega@pagodelarrea.com

8 DE CAECUS 2008 T
100% tempranillo

88 Colour: deep cherry, garnet rim. Nose: old leather, spicy, ripe fruit. Palate: fruity, spicy, round tannins.

CAECUS 2007 TR
100% tempranillo

87 Colour: cherry, garnet rim. Nose: ripe fruit, spicy, varietal. Palate: powerful, flavourful, toasty, round tannins, spicy.

CAECUS 2010 TC
100% tempranillo

86 Colour: cherry, garnet rim. Nose: spicy, toasty, ripe fruit, fruit preserve, dried herbs. Palate: powerful, flavourful, round tannins.

CAECUS 2012 T
90% tempranillo, 10% garnacha

87 Colour: cherry, purple rim. Nose: ripe fruit, violet drops, balanced. Palate: fruity, flavourful, balanced

CAECUS VERDERÓN 2012 BFB
90% viura, 10% malvasía

85 Colour: pale. Nose: scrubland, candied fruit, smoky. Palate: ripe fruit, lacks expression, dry.

PAGOS DE LEZA

Ctra. Vitoria - Logroño A-124 s/n
1309 Leza (Álava)
☎: +34 945 621 212 - Fax: +34 945 621 222
www.pagosdeleza.com
pagosdeleza@pagosdeleza.com

ANGEL SANTAMARÍA 2008 TR
tempranillo

89 Colour: cherry, garnet rim. Nose: medium intensity, ripe fruit, fruit preserve. Palate: fruity, spicy, fine tannins.

ANGEL SANTAMARÍA 2010 BC
viura, malvasía

86 Colour: bright yellow, greenish rim. Nose: faded flowers, ripe fruit, sweet spices. Palate: fruity, spicy, easy to drink.

ANGEL SANTAMARÍA VENDIMIA SELECCIONADA 2009 TC
tempranillo

88 Colour: bright cherry, garnet rim. Nose: medium intensity, ripe fruit, spicy. Palate: good acidity, balanced, good finish.

ANGEL SANTAMARÍA VENDIMIA SELECCIONADA 2010 TC
tempranillo

89 Colour: deep cherry, garnet rim. Nose: sweet spices, ripe fruit, cocoa bean. Palate: fruity, flavourful, ripe fruit, good acidity.

EDITOR 2010 TC
tempranillo

88 Colour: bright cherry, garnet rim. Nose: medium intensity, varietal, ripe fruit, spicy. Palate: fruity, easy to drink.

EDITOR 2012 B
viura, malvasía

85 Colour: bright straw. Nose: faded flowers, fragrant herbs. Palate: balanced, easy to drink.

EDITOR 2012 T
tempranillo

85 Colour: very deep cherry, purple rim. Nose: red berry notes, ripe fruit, medium intensity. Palate: flavourful, fruity, good finish.

PAGOS DEL REY S.L.

Ctra. N-232, PK 422,7
26360 Fuenmayor (La Rioja)
☎: +34 941 450 818 - Fax: +34 941 450 818
www.felixsolisavantis.com
pdr@pagosdelrey.com

ARNEGUI 2008 TR
tempranillo

87 Colour: cherry, garnet rim. Nose: ripe fruit, spicy, powerfull. Palate: flavourful, round tannins, fruity.

ARNEGUI 2010 TC
tempranillo

89 Nose: balanced, fruit expression, spicy. Palate: fruity, round tannins, easy to drink.

ARNEGUI 2012 B
viura

86 Colour: bright straw. Nose: fresh fruit, white flowers. Palate: flavourful, fruity, good acidity, balanced.

ARNEGUI 2012 RD
garnacha

86 Colour: rose, purple rim. Nose: powerfull, ripe fruit, red berry notes, floral. Palate: powerful, fruity, fresh.

ARNEGUI 2012 T
tempranillo

86 Colour: cherry, purple rim. Nose: fruit liqueur notes, ripe fruit, balsamic herbs, powerfull. Palate: flavourful, correct, easy to drink.

CASTILLO DE ALBAI 2008 TR
tempranillo

86 Colour: cherry, garnet rim. Nose: ripe fruit, spicy, creamy oak, dried herbs. Palate: flavourful, round tannins, easy to drink.

CASTILLO DE ALBAI 2010 TC
tempranillo

86 Colour: cherry, garnet rim. Nose: ripe fruit, fruit preserve, spicy. Palate: fruity, easy to drink, correct.

CASTILLO DE ALBAI 2012 B
viura

89 Colour: bright straw. Nose: fresh, fresh fruit, white flowers, varietal. Palate: flavourful, fruity, good acidity, balanced.

CASTILLO DE ALBAI 2012 T
tempranillo

87 Colour: cherry, purple rim. Nose: ripe fruit, red berry notes, violet drops. Palate: flavourful, fruity, easy to drink.

PAISAJES Y VIÑEDOS

Pza. Ibarra, 1
26330 Briones (La Rioja)
☎: +34 941 322 301 - Fax: +34 941 322 302
comunicacio@vilaviniteca.es

PAISAJES CECIAS 2010 T
garnacha

90 Colour: cherry, garnet rim. Nose: balanced, spicy, wild herbs. Palate: flavourful, fruity, round tannins, good acidity.

PAISAJES LA PASADA 2010 T
100% tempranillo

93 Colour: cherry, garnet rim. Nose: ripe fruit, spicy, creamy oak, toasty, earthy notes. Palate: powerful, flavourful, toasty, round tannins.

PAISAJES VALSALADO 2010 T
40% tempranillo, 40% garnacha, 10% mazuelo, 10% graciano

92 Colour: bright cherry. Nose: ripe fruit, sweet spices. Palate: flavourful, fruity, toasty, round tannins.

QUIROGA DE PABLO

Antonio Pérez, 24
26323 Azofra (La Rioja)
☎: +34 941 379 334 - Fax: +34 941 379 334
www.bodegasquirogadepablo.es
info@bodegasquirogadepablo.es

QUIRUS 2010 TC
tempranillo

87 Colour: very deep cherry. Nose: spicy, toasty, fruit preserve. Palate: powerful, flavourful, toasty, round tannins.

HEREDAD DE JUDIMA 2008 TR
100% tempranillo

89 Colour: deep cherry, garnet rim. Nose: balanced, balsamic herbs, spicy, ripe fruit, medium intensity. Palate: flavourful, round tannins.

HEREDAD DE JUDIMA 2010 TC
tempranillo

88 Colour: cherry, garnet rim. Nose: balanced, ripe fruit, fruit preserve, dried herbs. Palate: flavourful, fruity.

QUIRUS 2012 RD
tempranillo, garnacha

88 Colour: onion pink. Nose: elegant, candied fruit, dried flowers, fragrant herbs. Palate: light-bodied, flavourful, good acidity, long, spicy.

QUIRUS 4MB 2011 T
tempranillo

89 Colour: bright cherry. Nose: ripe fruit, sweet spices, dried herbs, toasty. Palate: flavourful, fruity, round tannins.

QUIRUS SELECCIÓN DE FAMILIA 2008 T
tempranillo

89 Colour: bright cherry, garnet rim. Nose: ripe fruit, fruit preserve, varietal, spicy, aromatic coffee. Palate: ripe fruit, round tannins, balanced.

R. LÓPEZ DE HEREDIA VIÑA TONDONIA

Avda. Vizcaya 3
26200 Haro (La Rioja)
☎: +34 941 310 244 - Fax: +34 941 310 788
www.tondonia.com
bodega@lopezdeheredia.com

VIÑA TONDONIA 1998 B RESERVA

93 Colour: bright golden. Nose: ripe fruit, dry nuts, powerfull, toasty, aged wood nuances. Palate: flavourful, fruity, spicy, toasty, long.

VIÑA TONDONIA 2001 TR

92 Colour: pale ruby, brick rim edge. Nose: fine reductive notes, wet leather, aged wood nuances, fruit liqueur notes, complex. Palate: spicy, fine tannins, elegant, long.

RIOJA VEGA

Ctra. Logroño-Mendavia, Km. 92
31230 Viana (Navarra)
☎: +34 948 646 263 - Fax: +34 948 645 612
www.riojavega.com
info@riojavega.com

RIOJA VEGA 130 ANIVERSARIO 2006 TR
75% tempranillo, 20% graciano, 5% mazuelo

89 Colour: dark-red cherry, orangey edge. Nose: elegant, spicy, fine reductive notes, ripe fruit, creamy oak. Palate: spicy, powerful, long, balanced.

RIOJA VEGA 2008 TR
85% tempranillo, 10% graciano, 5% mazuelo

87 Colour: dark-red cherry. Nose: fruit preserve, macerated fruit, aged wood nuances, spicy. Palate: grainy tannins, powerful, dry, fine bitter notes, spicy, ripe fruit.

RIOJA VEGA EDICIÓN LIMITADA 2010 TC
90% tempranillo, 10% graciano

88 Colour: deep cherry. Nose: fresh fruit, red berry notes, powerfull, varietal, aromatic coffee, spicy. Palate: good acidity, fine bitter notes, powerful, flavourful, spicy, slightly dry, soft tannins.

RIOJA VEGA G Y G 2012 T
50% garnacha, 50% graciano

85 Colour: cherry, purple rim. Nose: red berry notes, ripe fruit, wild herbs. Palate: powerful, flavourful.

RODRÍGUEZ SANZO

Manuel Azaña, 9
47014 (Valladolid)
☎: +34 983 150 150 - Fax: +34 983 150 151
www.rodriguezsanzo.com
comunicacion@valsanzo.com

LA SENOBA 2009 T
50% tempranillo, 50% graciano

91 Colour: cherry, garnet rim. Nose: ripe fruit, spicy, creamy oak, mineral. Palate: powerful, rich, flavourful, toasty.

LACRIMUS 2009 TC
85% tempranillo, 15% graciano

90 Colour: cherry, garnet rim. Nose: ripe fruit, spicy, creamy oak, toasty, earthy notes. Palate: powerful, flavourful, toasty, round tannins.

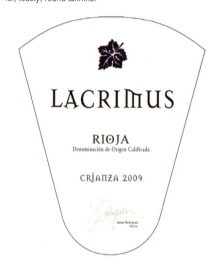

LACRIMUS
RIOJA
Denominación de Origen Calificada
CRIANZA 2009

LACRIMUS 5 2012 T
100% tempranillo

88 Colour: cherry, purple rim. Nose: red berry notes, ripe fruit, balsamic herbs, sweet spices. Palate: powerful, flavourful, balsamic, toasty.

LACRIMUS GARNACHA 2012 T
100% garnacha

88 Colour: cherry, purple rim. Nose: balsamic herbs, red berry notes, ripe fruit. Palate: flavourful, fruity, good acidity.

LACRIMUS REX 2010 T
75% graciano, 25% garnacha

90 Colour: deep cherry, garnet rim. Nose: grassy, wild herbs, ripe fruit. Palate: fruity, round tannins.

LACRIMUS ROSAE 2012 RD
100% graciano

85 Colour: rose. Nose: floral, red berry notes, ripe fruit, fragrant herbs. Palate: fresh, fruity, easy to drink.

SENDERO ROYAL

Ctra. LR 384 N- 232, Km. 0,08
26559 Aldeanueva de Ebro (La Rioja)
☎: +34 941 743 999 - Fax: +34 941 743 031
www.senderoroyal.com
info@senderoroyal.com

SENDERO ROYAL 2008 TC
80% tempranillo, 10% garnacha, 10% graciano

88 Colour: cherry, garnet rim. Nose: ripe fruit, spicy, creamy oak, toasty. Palate: powerful, flavourful, toasty.

SEÑORÍO DE ARANA

La Cadena, 20
1330 Labastida (Álava)
☎: +34 945 331 150 - Fax: +34 945 331 150
www.senoriodearana.com
info@senoriodearana.com

VIÑA DEL OJA 2004 TR
90% tempranillo, 5% mazuelo, 5% graciano

89 Colour: deep cherry. Nose: ripe fruit, spicy, toasty, dark chocolate, tobacco. Palate: powerful, flavourful, toasty, round tannins.

VIÑA DEL OJA 2009 TC
90% tempranillo, 10% mazuelo

87 Colour: cherry, garnet rim. Nose: varietal, balanced, spicy, ripe fruit. Palate: balanced, long, round tannins.

VIÑA DEL OJA 2012 T
100% tempranillo

85 Colour: cherry, purple rim. Nose: red berry notes, ripe fruit. Palate: flavourful, fruity, good acidity, round tannins.

SEÑORÍO DE SAN VICENTE

Los Remedios, 27
26338 San Vicente de la Sonsierra (La Rioja)
☎: +34 941 334 080 - Fax: +34 941 334 371
www.eguren.com
info@eguren.com

SAN VICENTE 2009 T
100% tempranillo

95 Colour: cherry, garnet rim. Nose: spicy, creamy oak, toasty, characterful, powerfull. Palate: powerful, flavourful, toasty, round tannins.

HEREDAD DE JUDIMA 2008 TR
100% tempranillo

89 Colour: deep cherry, garnet rim. Nose: balanced, balsamic herbs, spicy, ripe fruit, medium intensity. Palate: flavourful, round tannins.

HEREDAD DE JUDIMA 2010 TC
tempranillo

88 Colour: cherry, garnet rim. Nose: balanced, ripe fruit, fruit preserve, dried herbs. Palate: flavourful, fruity.

SAN VICENTE 2010 T
100% tempranillo

97 Colour: cherry, garnet rim. Nose: complex, new oak, sweet spices, dark chocolate, fruit expression, mineral. Palate: powerful, flavourful, toasty, round tannins.

SEÑORÍO DE SOMALO

Ctra. de Baños, 62
26321 Bobadilla (La Rioja)
☎: +34 941 202 351 - Fax: +34 941 202 351
www.bodegasomalo.com
info@bodegasomalo.com

SEÑORÍO DE SOMALO 2001 TGR
85% tempranillo, 15% garnacha

90 Colour: pale ruby, brick rim edge. Nose: elegant, spicy, fine reductive notes, wet leather, aged wood nuances, fruit liqueur notes. Palate: spicy, fine tannins, elegant, long.

HEREDAD DE JUDIMA 2008 TR
100% tempranillo

89 Colour: deep cherry, garnet rim. Nose: balanced, balsamic herbs, spicy, ripe fruit, medium intensity. Palate: flavourful, round tannins.

HEREDAD DE JUDIMA 2008 TR
100% tempranillo

89 Colour: deep cherry, garnet rim. Nose: balanced, balsamic herbs, spicy, ripe fruit, medium intensity. Palate: flavourful, round tannins.

HEREDAD DE JUDIMA 2010 TC
tempranillo

88 Colour: cherry, garnet rim. Nose: balanced, ripe fruit, fruit preserve, dried herbs. Palate: flavourful, fruity.

HEREDAD DE JUDIMA 2010 TC
tempranillo

88 Colour: cherry, garnet rim. Nose: balanced, ripe fruit, fruit preserve, dried herbs. Palate: flavourful, fruity.

SEÑORÍO DE SOMALO 2003 TR
90% tempranillo, 10% garnacha

88 Colour: cherry, garnet rim. Nose: ripe fruit, spicy, toasty. Palate: powerful, flavourful, toasty, round tannins.

SEÑORÍO DE SOMALO 2009 B RESERVA
95% viura, 5% garnacha blanca, malvasía

87 Colour: bright yellow. Nose: faded flowers, ripe fruit, medium intensity. Palate: spicy, ripe fruit, toasty.

SEÑORÍO DE SOMALO 2010 TC
85% tempranillo, 15% garnacha

87 Colour: cherry, garnet rim. Nose: spicy, creamy oak, toasty. Palate: powerful, flavourful, toasty, round tannins.

SEÑORÍO DE SOMALO 2012 B
95% viura, 5% garnacha blanca, malvasía

82

SEÑORÍO DE SOMALO 2012 RD
100% garnacha

85 Colour: raspberry rose. Nose: candied fruit, dried flowers, fragrant herbs, red berry notes. Palate: light-bodied, flavourful, good acidity, spicy.

SEÑORÍO DE SOMALO 2012 T
85% tempranillo, 15% garnacha

89 Colour: dark-red cherry. Nose: powerfull, ripe fruit, fruit expression. Palate: balsamic, fruity aftestaste, ripe fruit.

SEÑORÍO DE URARTE, S.L.

Calvo Sotelo, 16
1308 Lanciego (Álava)
☎: +34 670 885 050
www.urarte.es
senoriodeurarte@gmail.com

SEÑORÍO DE URARTE 2009 TC
garnacha

86 Colour: cherry, garnet rim. Nose: ripe fruit, spicy, creamy oak, toasty. Palate: powerful, flavourful, toasty.

SEÑORÍO DE URARTE 2012 T
garnacha

86 Colour: cherry, purple rim. Nose: expressive, fresh fruit, red berry notes, floral. Palate: flavourful, fruity, good acidity, round tannins.

SIERRA CANTABRIA

Amorebieta, 3
26338 San Vicente de la Sonsierra (La Rioja)
☎: +34 941 334 080 - Fax: +34 941 334 371
www.eguren.com
info@eguren.com

MURMURÓN 2012 T
100% tempranillo

90 Colour: cherry, purple rim. Nose: expressive, fresh fruit, red berry notes, floral, lactic notes. Palate: flavourful, fruity, good acidity.

SIERRA CANTABRIA 2004 TGR
97% tempranillo, 3% graciano

95 Colour: pale ruby, brick rim edge. Nose: fine reductive notes, wet leather, aged wood nuances, fruit liqueur notes, expressive. Palate: spicy, fine tannins, elegant, long.

SIERRA CANTABRIA 2005 TGR
97% tempranillo, 3% graciano

93 Colour: pale ruby, brick rim edge. Nose: elegant, spicy, fine reductive notes, wet leather, aged wood nuances, ripe fruit. Palate: spicy, fine tannins, elegant, long.

SIERRA CANTABRIA 2007 TR
tempranillo

92 Colour: cherry, garnet rim. Nose: red berry notes, ripe fruit, balsamic herbs, cocoa bean, creamy oak, fine reductive notes. Palate: flavourful, long, spicy.

SIERRA CANTABRIA 2009 TC
100% tempranillo

91 Colour: cherry, garnet rim. Nose: ripe fruit, spicy, creamy oak, toasty, balanced. Palate: powerful, flavourful, toasty.

SIERRA CANTABRIA 2012 RD
20% tempranillo, 30% garnacha, 50% viura

89 Colour: onion pink. Nose: elegant, candied fruit, dried flowers, fragrant herbs, red berry notes. Palate: light-bodied, flavourful, good acidity, long.

SIERRA CANTABRIA GARNACHA 2010 T
100% garnacha

95 Colour: bright cherry. Nose: ripe fruit, sweet spices, creamy oak, expressive, balsamic herbs, scrubland. Palate: flavourful, fruity, toasty, good acidity, fine tannins.

SIERRA CANTABRIA GARNACHA 2011 T
100% garnacha

94 Colour: bright cherry. Nose: candied fruit, red berry notes, balsamic herbs, spicy. Palate: flavourful, mineral, long, ripe fruit.

SIERRA CANTABRIA SELECCIÓN 2011 T
100% tempranillo

89 Colour: cherry, purple rim. Nose: red berry notes, floral, balsamic herbs, spicy. Palate: flavourful, fruity, good acidity.

SOC. COOP. SAN ESTEBAN P.

Ctra. Agoncillo s/n
26143 Murillo de Río Leza (La Rioja)
☎: +34 941 432 031 - Fax: +34 941 432 422
www.bodegassanesteban.com
administracion@bodegassanesteban.com

COLECCIÓN ANTIQUE 1 2011 T
tempranillo

89 Colour: cherry, garnet rim. Nose: ripe fruit, spicy, creamy oak, toasty, complex. Palate: powerful, flavourful, toasty, round tannins.

TIERRAS DE MURILLO 2010 TC
tempranillo

88 Colour: cherry, garnet rim. Nose: ripe fruit, spicy, creamy oak, toasty, balsamic herbs. Palate: powerful, flavourful, toasty.

TIERRAS DE MURILLO 2012 RD
tempranillo

85 Colour: raspberry rose. Nose: dried flowers, candied fruit, dried herbs. Palate: fresh, fruity, easy to drink.

TIERRAS DE MURILLO TEMPRANILLO 2012 T
tempranillo

85 Colour: cherry, garnet rim. Nose: ripe fruit, wild herbs, floral. Palate: light-bodied, fruity, flavourful.

TIERRAS DE MURILLO VIURA 2012 B
viura

85 Colour: bright straw. Nose: fresh, fresh fruit, expressive, floral, dried herbs. Palate: flavourful, fruity, balanced.

SOLANA DE RAMÍREZ RUIZ

Arana, 24
26339 Abalos (La Rioja)
☎: +34 941 334 354 - Fax: +34 941 308 049
www.valsarte.com
consultas@solanaderamirez.com

SOLANA DE RAMÍREZ 2008 TC
80% tempranillo, 20% graciano

87 Colour: dark-red cherry. Nose: fresh fruit, sweet spices, cocoa bean, creamy oak. Palate: creamy, spicy, balsamic, fruity aftestaste.

SOLANA DE RAMÍREZ 2012 B
90% viura, 10% otras

85 Colour: bright yellow. Nose: ripe fruit, dried flowers, dried herbs, powerfull. Palate: flavourful, balsamic, correct.

SOLANA DE RAMÍREZ 2012 RD
75% tempranillo, 20% garnacha, 5% viura

86 Colour: rose, purple rim. Nose: powerfull, ripe fruit, red berry notes, floral, expressive, lactic notes. Palate: powerful, fruity, fresh.

SOLANA DE RAMÍREZ 2012 T
90% tempranillo, 5% garnacha, 5% viura

85 Colour: deep cherry. Nose: roasted almonds, dried fruit, stalky. Palate: powerful, spirituous, grainy tannins.

SOLANA DE RAMÍREZ MADURADO EN BODEGA 2012 T
85% tempranillo, 15% graciano

86 Colour: cherry, purple rim. Nose: ripe fruit, spicy, wild herbs. Palate: powerful, flavourful, fruity.

VALSARTE 2001 TGR
80% tempranillo, 20% graciano

88 Colour: dark-red cherry. Nose: spicy, creamy oak, toasty, ripe fruit. Palate: powerful, flavourful, spicy.

VALSARTE 2004 TR
85% tempranillo, 15% graciano

89 Colour: deep cherry. Nose: fine reductive notes, complex, elegant, cocoa bean. Palate: balanced, flavourful, powerful, grainy tannins.

VALSARTE 2009 TC
100% tempranillo

86 Colour: deep cherry. Nose: short, toasty, fruit preserve. Palate: ripe fruit, flavourful, fruity, powerful, creamy, spicy.

VALSARTE VENDIMIA SELECCIONADA 2008 T
70% tempranillo, 30% otras

88 Colour: dark-red cherry. Nose: ripe fruit, expressive, varietal, complex. Palate: good structure, slightly tart, spicy, harsh oak tannins.

SOTO DE TORRES

Camino Los Arenales, s/n
1330 Labastida (Álava)
☎: +34 938 177 400 - Fax: +34 938 177 444
www.torres.es
mailadmin@torres.es

IBÉRICOS 2011 TC
100% tempranillo

89 Colour: cherry, purple rim. Nose: red berry notes, ripe fruit, balsamic herbs, sweet spices, creamy oak. Palate: powerful, flavourful, spicy, toasty.

THE GRAND WINES

Razón social : Ramón y Cajal 7, 1ºA
1007 Vitoria (Alava)
☎: +34 945 158 282 - Fax: +34 945 158 283
www.thegrandwines.com

R & G 2010 T
tempranillo

93 Colour: cherry, garnet rim. Nose: ripe fruit, spicy, balsamic herbs, creamy oak, toasty, mineral. Palate: powerful, rich, flavourful, balanced.

TIERRA AGRÍCOLA LABASTIDA

El Olmo, 16
1330 Labastida (Álava)
☎: +34 945 331 230 - Fax: +34 945 331 257
www.tierrayvino.com
info@tierrayvino.com

EL BELISARIO 2010 T
100% tempranillo

91 Colour: bright cherry. Nose: ripe fruit, sweet spices, creamy oak, expressive. Palate: flavourful, fruity, toasty, round tannins, smoky aftertaste.

EL PRIMAVERA 2012 T
100% tempranillo

88 Colour: dark-red cherry. Nose: fruit expression, dark chocolate, aged wood nuances, aromatic coffee. Palate: sweet tannins, powerful, flavourful, spicy.

FERNÁNDEZ GÓMEZ MC 2012 T
80% tempranillo, 10% viura, 10% garnacha

90 Colour: cherry, purple rim. Nose: fresh fruit, red berry notes, floral. Palate: flavourful, fruity, good acidity, round tannins.

LA HOJA 2010 TC
90% tempranillo, 5% garnacha, 5% viura

89 Colour: deep cherry, garnet rim. Nose: cocoa bean, ripe fruit, sweet spices. Palate: ripe fruit, balanced.

LA HOJA TEMPRANILLO 2012 T
100% tempranillo

88 Colour: dark-red cherry. Nose: macerated fruit, ripe fruit. Palate: good acidity, correct, powerful, flavourful, sweetness.

TIERRA 2010 TC
100% tempranillo

90 Colour: cherry, garnet rim. Nose: creamy oak, complex, ripe fruit. Palate: powerful, flavourful, toasty, round tannins.

TIERRA DE FERNÁNDEZ GÓMEZ 2012 B
70% viura, 20% garnacha blanca, 10% malvasía

89 Colour: bright yellow. Nose: ripe fruit, sweet spices, creamy oak. Palate: rich, flavourful, fresh, balanced.

TIERRA DE FIDEL 2010 BFB
20% garnacha blanca, 20% viura, 20% malvasía, 40% otras

90 Colour: bright yellow. Nose: complex, fresh, neat, powerfull. Palate: sweetness, fruity, fresh, powerful, flavourful, smoky aftertaste.

TIERRA FIDEL 2010 T
50% garnacha, 50% graciano

89 Colour: deep cherry, garnet rim. Nose: ripe fruit, wild herbs, spicy. Palate: flavourful, fruity, balanced.

TIERRA ANTIGUA

Urb. Monje Vigilia, 7
26120 Albelda de Iregua (La Rioja)
☎: +34 941 444 233 - Fax: +34 941 444 427
www.tierrantigua.com
info@tierrantigua.com

SARMIENTO 2009 T
90% tempranillo, 5% garnacha, 5% graciano

88 Colour: cherry, garnet rim. Nose: toasty, ripe fruit, scrubland, cocoa bean. Palate: good structure, flavourful, correct, round tannins.

TOBELOS BODEGAS Y VIÑEDOS

Ctra. N 124, Km. 45
26290 Briñas (La Rioja)
☎: +34 941 305 630 - Fax: +34 941 313 028
www.tobelos.com
tobelos@tobelos.com

TAHÓN DE TOBELOS 2009 TR

92 Colour: cherry, garnet rim. Nose: ripe fruit, spicy, creamy oak, characterful, dark chocolate. Palate: powerful, flavourful, toasty, round tannins.

TOBELOS 2011 BFB
80% viura, 20% garnacha blanca

88 Colour: straw, greenish rim. Nose: spicy, smoky, ripe fruit. Palate: balanced, flavourful, long.

TOBELOS GARNACHA 2010 T
100% tempranillo

89 Colour: deep cherry. Nose: ripe fruit, sweet spices, toasty. Palate: good acidity, flavourful, powerful.

TOBELOS TEMPRANILLO 2009 T
100% tempranillo

89 Colour: very deep cherry. Nose: sweet spices, ripe fruit, fruit expression. Palate: flavourful, fine bitter notes, good acidity.

TORRE DE OÑA

Finca San Martín
1309 Páganos (Álava)
☎: +34 945 621 154 - Fax: +34 945 621 171
www.torredeona.com
info@torredeona.com

FINCA SAN MARTÍN 2010 T
100% tempranillo

89 Colour: cherry, garnet rim. Nose: spicy, cocoa bean, ripe fruit. Palate: fruity, balanced, easy to drink, good acidity.

TORRE DE OÑA 2008 TR
95% tempranillo, 5% mazuelo

91 Colour: bright cherry, garnet rim. Nose: spicy, balanced, varietal, cocoa bean, ripe fruit. Palate: flavourful, good structure.

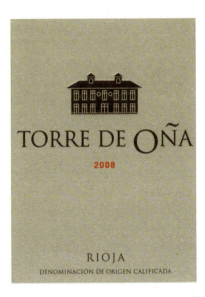

UNZU PROPIEDAD

Barón de la Torre, 4
31592 Cientruénigo (Navarra)
☎: +34 948 811 000 - Fax: +34 948 811 407
www.unzupropiedad.com
info@unzupropiedad.com

UNZU 2010 TC
100% tempranillo

90 Colour: deep cherry. Nose: ripe fruit, fruit expression, sweet spices. Palate: powerful, spicy, ripe fruit.

VALORIA

Ctra. de Burgos, Km. 5
26006 Logroño (La Rioja)
☎: +34 941 204 059 - Fax: +34 941 204 155
www.bvaloria.com
bodega@bvaloria.com

VIÑA VALORIA 2001 TGR
tempranillo

89 Colour: pale ruby, brick rim edge. Nose: medium intensity, fruit liqueur notes, spicy. Palate: flavourful, light-bodied, spicy.

VIÑA VALORIA 2008 TR
tempranillo

88 Colour: cherry, garnet rim. Nose: ripe fruit, spicy, creamy oak, toasty. Palate: powerful, flavourful, toasty, round tannins.

VIÑA VALORIA 2010 TC
tempranillo

88 Colour: deep cherry. Nose: ripe fruit, spicy, toasty. Palate: spicy, ripe fruit, fine bitter notes, good acidity.

ARADON 2010 TC
90% tempranillo, 5% garnacha, 5% mazuelo

86 Colour: cherry, garnet rim. Nose: ripe fruit, spicy, creamy oak. Palate: powerful, flavourful, toasty, round tannins.

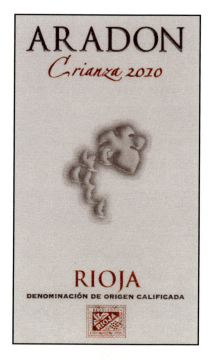

VINÍCOLA RIOJANA
DE ALCANADRE S.C.

San Isidro, 46
26509 Alcanadre (La Rioja)
☎: +34 941 165 036 - Fax: +34 941 165 289
www.riojanadealcanadre.com
vinicola@riojanadealcanadre.com

ARADON 2008 TR
90% tempranillo, 5% garnacha, 5% mazuelo

85 Colour: cherry, garnet rim. Nose: fruit preserve, powerfull, sweet spices. Palate: flavourful, correct, round tannins.

ARADON 2012 B
100% viura

85 Colour: bright straw. Nose: medium intensity, fresh fruit, floral. Palate: light-bodied, easy to drink, correct.

ARADON 2012 RD
100% garnacha

84

ARADON 2012 T
90% tempranillo, 10% garnacha

84

ARADON GARNACHA SELECCIÓN 2010 T
100% garnacha

83

VIÑA BUJANDA

Ctra. Logroño, s/n
1320 Oyón (Alava)
☎: +34 941 450 876 - Fax: +34 941 450 875
www.familiamartinezbujanda.com
info@bujanda.com

VIÑA BUJANDA 2008 TR
100% tempranillo

88 Colour: dark-red cherry, orangey edge. Nose: ripe fruit, balsamic herbs, spicy, creamy oak, fine reductive notes. Palate: powerful, flavourful, toasty.

HEREDAD DE JUDIMA 2008 TR
100% tempranillo

89 Colour: deep cherry, garnet rim. Nose: balanced, balsamic herbs, spicy, ripe fruit, medium intensity. Palate: flavourful, round tannins.

HEREDAD DE JUDIMA 2010 TC
tempranillo

88 Colour: cherry, garnet rim. Nose: balanced, ripe fruit, fruit preserve, dried herbs. Palate: flavourful, fruity.

VIÑA BUJANDA 2010 TC
100% tempranillo

86 Colour: cherry, garnet rim. Nose: ripe fruit, spicy, creamy oak, toasty, fine reductive notes. Palate: powerful, flavourful, toasty.

VIÑA BUJANDA 2012 B
100% viura

85 Colour: bright yellow. Nose: faded flowers, ripe fruit. Palate: easy to drink, ripe fruit.

VIÑA BUJANDA 2012 RD
100% tempranillo

85 Colour: rose, purple rim. Nose: powerfull, ripe fruit, red berry notes, floral. Palate: fruity, fresh.

VIÑA BUJANDA 2012 T
100% tempranillo

88 Colour: cherry, purple rim. Nose: expressive, fresh fruit, red berry notes, floral. Palate: flavourful, fruity, good acidity.

VIÑA EIZAGA

Camino de la Hoya s/n
1300 Laguardia (Alava)
☎: +34 677 450 759
www.vinoseizaga.com
contacto@vinoseizaga.com

LAGAR DE EIZAGA 2010 TC
100% tempranillo

89 Colour: cherry, garnet rim. Nose: ripe fruit, spicy, creamy oak, toasty. Palate: powerful, flavourful, toasty, round tannins.

VIÑA EIZAGA 2008 TR
100% tempranillo

86 Colour: cherry, garnet rim. Nose: ripe fruit, balsamic herbs, spicy, creamy oak, wet leather, tobacco.

VIÑA EIZAGA 2010 TC
100% tempranillo

88 Colour: cherry, garnet rim. Nose: ripe fruit, toasty, spicy. Palate: powerful, flavourful, spicy, long.

VIÑA IJALBA

Ctra. Pamplona, Km. 1
26006 Logroño (La Rioja)
☎: +34 941 261 100 - Fax: +34 941 261 128
www.ijalba.com
vinaijalba@ijalba.com

DIONISIO RUIZ IJALBA 2011 T
100% maturana

92 Colour: deep cherry. Nose: fruit liqueur notes, aromatic coffee, dark chocolate, varietal, balsamic herbs. Palate: spicy, fine bitter notes, spirituous.

GENOLI 2012 B
100% viura

87 Colour: yellow, greenish rim. Nose: fragrant herbs, ripe fruit, balanced. Palate: balanced, correct, good acidity.

IJALBA 2008 TR
80% tempranillo, 20% graciano

89 Colour: deep cherry. Nose: ripe fruit, spicy, toasty. Palate: ripe fruit, fruity, fine bitter notes, good acidity.

IJALBA 2009 TC
90% tempranillo, 10% graciano

89 Colour: cherry, garnet rim. Nose: spicy, creamy oak, toasty. Palate: powerful, flavourful, toasty, round tannins.

IJALBA GRACIANO 2011 TC
100% graciano

88 Colour: very deep cherry. Nose: powerfull, toasty, dark chocolate, dried fruit. Palate: powerful, flavourful, good acidity.

IJALBA MATURANA BLANCA 2012 B
100% maturana blanca

88 Colour: bright yellow. Nose: balanced, ripe fruit, faded flowers. Palate: flavourful, fruity, long.

IJALBA SELECCIÓN ESPECIAL 2005 TR
50% tempranillo, 50% graciano

91 Colour: cherry, garnet rim. Nose: spicy, creamy oak, toasty, complex, powerfull. Palate: powerful, flavourful, toasty, round tannins.

LIVOR 2012 T JOVEN
100% tempranillo

87 Colour: cherry, purple rim. Nose: floral, ripe fruit. Palate: flavourful, fruity, good acidity, round tannins.

MÚRICE 2009 TC
90% tempranillo, 10% graciano

90 Colour: cherry, garnet rim. Nose: spicy, creamy oak, toasty, fruit expression. Palate: powerful, flavourful, toasty, round tannins.

SOLFERINO 2011 T
100% tempranillo

88 Colour: bright cherry. Nose: sweet spices, creamy oak. Palate: flavourful, fruity, toasty, round tannins.

VIÑA OLABARRI

Ctra. Haro - Anguciana, s/n
26200 Haro (La Rioja)
☎: +34 941 310 937 - Fax: +34 941 311 602
www.bodegasolabarri.com
info@bodegasolabarri.com

VIÑA OLABARRI 2005 TGR
100% tempranillo

88 Colour: black cherry. Nose: spicy, fine reductive notes, tobacco. Palate: spicy, fine tannins, long, balanced.

VIÑA OLABARRI 2008 TR
80% tempranillo, 20% mazuelo, graciano

87 Colour: cherry, garnet rim. Nose: balanced, ripe fruit, fruit preserve, sweet spices, old leather. Palate: flavourful, fruity.

VIÑA REAL

Ctra. Logroño - Laguardia, Km. 4,8
1300 Laguardia (Álava)
☎: +34 945 625 255 - Fax: +34 945 625 211
www.cvne.com
marketing@cvne.com

VIÑA REAL 2006 TGR
95% tempranillo, 5% graciano

90 Colour: cherry, garnet rim. Nose: spicy, creamy oak, toasty, wet leather. Palate: powerful, toasty, round tannins.

VIÑA REAL 2009 TR
90% tempranillo, 10% graciano, garnacha, mazuelo

92 Colour: deep cherry. Nose: powerfull, ripe fruit, spicy, creamy oak. Palate: flavourful, good acidity, correct, round.

VIÑA REAL 2011 TC
90% tempranillo, 10% garnacha, mazuelo, graciano

92 Colour: cherry, garnet rim. Nose: ripe fruit, spicy, creamy oak, toasty, fruit expression. Palate: powerful, flavourful, toasty, round tannins.

VIÑA SALCEDA

Ctra. Cenicero, Km. 3
1340 Elciego (Álava)
☎: +34 945 606 125 - Fax: +34 945 606 069
www.vinasalceda.com
info@vinasalceda.com

PUENTE DE SALCEDA 2009 T
100% tempranillo

91 Colour: bright cherry, garnet rim. Nose: ripe fruit, balanced, expressive, cocoa bean. Palate: rich, balanced, good acidity.

VIÑA SALCEDA 2008 TR
95% tempranillo, 5% graciano

91 Colour: deep cherry, garnet rim. Nose: creamy oak, cocoa bean, ripe fruit. Palate: good structure, round tannins, spicy.

VIÑA SALCEDA 2010 TC
95% tempranillo, 5% mazuelo, graciano

88 Colour: cherry, garnet rim. Nose: medium intensity, ripe fruit, sweet spices. Palate: correct, round tannins.

VIÑASPRAL

Camino Del Soto s/n
1309 Elvillar (Álava)
☎: - Fax: +34 628 132 151
www.maisulan.com
info@maisulan.com

HONORATUS AURUM 2009 BC
100% viura

90 Colour: bright yellow. Nose: cedar wood, spicy, ripe fruit, wild herbs. Palate: fruity, powerful, classic aged character.

HONORATUS FRUCTUS VENDIMIA SELECCIONADA 2010 T
85% tempranillo, 10% graciano, 5% garnacha

89 Colour: cherry, garnet rim. Nose: ripe fruit, sweet spices, cocoa bean, fruit preserve. Palate: balanced, flavourful, round tannins.

MAISULAN 2009 TC
90% tempranillo, 5% garnacha, 5% graciano

90 Colour: cherry, garnet rim. Nose: ripe fruit, spicy, varietal. Palate: powerful, flavourful, toasty, round tannins, good acidity.

VIÑEDOS DE ALDEANUEVA

Avda. Juan Carlos I, 100
26559 Aldeanueva de Ebro (La Rioja)
☎: +34 941 163 039 - Fax: +34 941 163 585
www.aldeanueva.com
va@aldeanueva.com

AZABACHE 2012 RD
100% garnacha

86 Colour: light cherry. Nose: ripe fruit, fragrant herbs, faded flowers. Palate: powerful, warm, ripe fruit.

AZABACHE GARNACHA 2010 T
100% garnacha

86 Colour: cherry, garnet rim. Nose: ripe fruit, spicy, toasty, complex, wild herbs. Palate: powerful, flavourful, toasty.

AZABACHE GRACIANO 2008 TR
100% graciano

84

AZABACHE VENDIMIA SELECCIONADA 2009 TC
70% tempranillo, 20% garnacha, 10% mazuelo

84

CULTO 2010 T
60% graciano, 40% tempranillo

90 Colour: cherry, garnet rim. Nose: ripe fruit, spicy, creamy oak, toasty, complex. Palate: powerful, flavourful, toasty, round tannins.

VIÑEDOS DE ALFARO

Camino de los Agudos s/n
26559 Aldeanueva de Ebro (La Rioja)
☎: +34 941 142 389 - Fax: +34 941 142 386
www.vinedosdealfaro.com
info@vinedosdealfaro.com

CONDE DEL REAL AGRADO 2005 TR
garnacha, tempranillo, graciano, mazuelo

86 Colour: cherry, garnet rim. Nose: spicy, toasty, characterful, overripe fruit. Palate: powerful, flavourful, toasty, round tannins.

CONDE DEL REAL AGRADO 2008 TC
garnacha, tempranillo, graciano, mazuelo

89 Colour: bright cherry. Nose: ripe fruit, sweet spices, toasty, aromatic coffee. Palate: flavourful, fruity, toasty, round tannins.

REAL AGRADO 2012 B
viura

86 Colour: bright straw. Nose: fresh fruit, white flowers. Palate: flavourful, good acidity.

REAL AGRADO 2012 RD
garnacha

86 Colour: brilliant rose. Nose: candied fruit, floral, dried herbs. Palate: fresh, fruity, flavourful.

REAL AGRADO 2012 T
garnacha

85 Colour: cherry, purple rim. Nose: fresh fruit, red berry notes. Palate: flavourful, fruity, good acidity, round tannins.

RODILES 2005 T
garnacha, tempranillo, graciano, mazuelo

88 Colour: cherry, garnet rim. Nose: ripe fruit, spicy, creamy oak, toasty, wet leather. Palate: powerful, flavourful, toasty, round tannins.

RODILES VENDIMIA SELECCIONADA 2005 T
graciano

90 Colour: cherry, garnet rim. Nose: ripe fruit, spicy, creamy oak, toasty, roasted coffee. Palate: powerful, flavourful, toasty, round tannins.

VIÑEDOS DE PÁGANOS

Ctra. Navaridas, s/n
1309 Páganos (Álava)
☎: +34 945 600 590 - Fax: +34 945 600 885
www.eguren.com
info@eguren.com

EL PUNTIDO 2005 TGR
100% tempranillo

92 Colour: deep cherry. Nose: spicy, fine reductive notes, wet leather, aged wood nuances, fruit liqueur notes, characterful. Palate: spicy, fine tannins, long.

EL PUNTIDO 2009 T
100% tempranillo

96 Colour: cherry, garnet rim. Nose: ripe fruit, creamy oak, toasty, complex, cocoa bean, aromatic coffee. Palate: powerful, flavourful, toasty, round tannins.

EL PUNTIDO 2010 T
100% tempranillo

96 Colour: cherry, garnet rim. Nose: ripe fruit, spicy, creamy oak, toasty, complex, powerfull, fresh, expressive. Palate: powerful, flavourful, toasty, round tannins.

LA NIETA 2010 T
100% tempranillo

96 Colour: bright cherry. Nose: sweet spices, creamy oak, expressive, aromatic coffee, dark chocolate, mineral, fruit expression. Palate: flavourful, fruity, toasty, round tannins.

LA NIETA 2011 T
100% tempranillo

95 Colour: bright cherry. Nose: sweet spices, creamy oak, expressive, mineral, cocoa bean, aromatic coffee. Palate: flavourful, fruity, toasty, round tannins.

VIÑEDOS DEL CONTINO

Finca San Rafael, s/n
1321 Laserna (Álava)
☎: +34 945 600 201 - Fax: +34 945 621 114
www.contino.es

CONTINO 2007 TGR
70% tempranillo, 15% graciano, 15% garnacha

90 Colour: cherry, garnet rim. Nose: earthy notes, mineral, ripe fruit, creamy oak. Palate: powerful, concentrated, fine bitter notes.

CONTINO 2008 TR
85% tempranillo, 10% graciano, 5% garnacha, mazuelo

91 Colour: deep cherry. Nose: sweet spices, ripe fruit, toasty. Palate: fine bitter notes, good acidity, ripe fruit.

CONTINO 2009 TR
85% tempranillo, 10% graciano, 5% garnacha, mazuelo

92 Colour: cherry, garnet rim. Nose: ripe fruit, spicy, creamy oak, toasty. Palate: powerful, flavourful, toasty, round tannins.

CONTINO 2011 B
80% viura, 15% garnacha blanca, 5% malvasía

91 Colour: bright yellow. Nose: powerfull, ripe fruit, sweet spices, creamy oak, fragrant herbs. Palate: rich, smoky aftertaste, flavourful, fresh, good acidity.

CONTINO GARNACHA 2010 T
100% garnacha

92 Colour: bright cherry. Nose: sweet spices, creamy oak, red berry notes. Palate: flavourful, fruity, toasty, round tannins.

CONTINO GRACIANO 2009 T
100% graciano

92 Colour: cherry, garnet rim. Nose: sweet spices, ripe fruit, balsamic herbs. Palate: spicy, fine bitter notes, good acidity.

CONTINO VIÑA DEL OLIVO 2009 T
90% tempranillo, 10% graciano

93 Colour: cherry, garnet rim. Nose: ripe fruit, spicy, creamy oak, toasty. Palate: powerful, flavourful, toasty, round tannins.

VIÑEDOS DEL TERNERO

Finca El Ternero
9200 Miranda de Ebro (Burgos)
☎: +34 941 320 021 - Fax: +34 941 302 719
www.vinedosdelternero.com

HACIENDA TERNERO 2012 BFB
viura

87 Colour: bright straw. Nose: fresh fruit, white flowers, fragrant herbs. Palate: flavourful, fruity, balanced.

MIRANDA 2008 TC
tempranillo, mazuelo

90 Colour: dark-red cherry, orangey edge. Nose: cocoa bean, complex, elegant, fruit expression. Palate: good acidity, round, powerful, flavourful, complex.

MIRANDA 2009 TR
tempranillo, mazuelo

92 Colour: cherry, garnet rim. Nose: ripe fruit, spicy, creamy oak, balsamic herbs. Palate: powerful, flavourful, toasty, round tannins.

PICEA 650 2009 TR
tempranillo, mazuelo

93 Colour: dark-red cherry, orangey edge. Nose: varietal, aromatic coffee, complex. Palate: elegant, round, powerful, flavourful, complex, spicy.

VIÑEDOS SIERRA CANTABRIA

Calle Fuente de la Salud, s/n
26338 San Vicente de la Sonsierra (La Rioja)
☎: +34 945 600 590 - Fax: +34 945 600 885
www.eguren.com
info@eguren.com

AMANCIO 2009 T
100% tempranillo

95 Colour: bright cherry. Nose: sweet spices, creamy oak, neat, characterful, complex. Palate: flavourful, fruity, toasty, good acidity, powerful tannins.

AMANCIO 2010 T
100% tempranillo

96 Colour: cherry, garnet rim. Nose: spicy, creamy oak, complex, dark chocolate, aromatic coffee, fruit expression. Palate: powerful, flavourful, toasty, round tannins.

FINCA EL BOSQUE 2010 T
100% tempranillo

97 Colour: cherry, garnet rim. Nose: spicy, creamy oak, toasty, complex, powerfull, ripe fruit. Palate: powerful, flavourful, toasty, round tannins.

FINCA EL BOSQUE 2011 T
100% tempranillo

96 Colour: cherry, garnet rim. Nose: ripe fruit, spicy, toasty, complex, mineral, earthy notes, new oak. Palate: powerful, flavourful, toasty, round tannins.

SIERRA CANTABRIA COLECCIÓN PRIVADA 2010 T
100% tempranillo

95 Colour: cherry, garnet rim. Nose: spicy, creamy oak, toasty, complex, mineral, earthy notes, fruit expression. Palate: powerful, flavourful, toasty, round tannins.

SIERRA CANTABRIA COLECCIÓN PRIVADA 2011 T
100% tempranillo

96 Colour: cherry, garnet rim. Nose: creamy oak, toasty, complex, fruit expression, red berry notes. Palate: powerful, flavourful, toasty, round tannins.

SIERRA CANTABRIA CUVÈE ESPECIAL 2009 T
100% tempranillo

93 Colour: bright cherry. Nose: ripe fruit, sweet spices, creamy oak, expressive. Palate: flavourful, fruity, toasty, round tannins.

SIERRA CANTABRIA ORGANZA 2011 B
50% viura, 30% malvasía, 20% garnacha blanca

93 Colour: bright yellow. Nose: powerfull, ripe fruit, sweet spices, creamy oak, fragrant herbs. Palate: rich, smoky aftertaste, flavourful, fresh, good acidity.

SIERRA CANTABRIA ORGANZA 2012 B
55% viura, 25% malvasía, 20% garnacha blanca

92 Colour: bright straw. Nose: fresh, fresh fruit, white flowers, expressive, lactic notes, fine lees. Palate: flavourful, fruity, good acidity, balanced.

VIÑEDOS SINGULARES

Cuzco, 26 - 28, Nave 8
8030 (Barcelona)
☎: +34 609 168 191 - Fax: +34 934 807 076
www.vinedossingulares.com
info@vinedossingulares.com

JARDÍN ROJO 2012 T
tempranillo

88 Colour: cherry, garnet rim. Nose: ripe fruit, spicy, varietal. Palate: powerful, flavourful, toasty, round tannins.

VIÑEDOS Y BODEGAS DE LA MARQUESA - VALSERRANO

Herrería, 76
1307 Villabuena (Álava)
☎: +34 945 609 085 - Fax: +34 945 623 304
www.valserrano.com
info@valserrano.com

NICO BY VALSERRANO 2010 T
90% tempranillo, 10% graciano, garnacha, mazuelo

92 Colour: cherry, garnet rim. Nose: red berry notes, ripe fruit, sweet spices, creamy oak, balsamic herbs. Palate: powerful, flavourful, spicy, long, elegant.

VALSERRANO 2005 TGR
90% tempranillo, 10% graciano

88 Colour: pale ruby, brick rim edge. Nose: spicy, fine reductive notes, wet leather, aged wood nuances, fruit liqueur notes. Palate: spicy, elegant, long.

VALSERRANO 2008 TR
90% tempranillo, 10% graciano

91 Colour: cherry, garnet rim. Nose: ripe fruit, balsamic herbs, spicy, fine reductive notes. Palate: powerful, flavourful, balanced, elegant.

VALSERRANO 2010 TC
90% tempranillo, 10% mazuelo

90 Colour: cherry, garnet rim. Nose: ripe fruit, spicy, creamy oak, toasty, complex. Palate: powerful, flavourful, toasty, round tannins.

VALSERRANO 2012 BFB
95% viura, 5% malvasía

89 Colour: bright straw. Nose: ripe fruit, white flowers, dried herbs. Palate: fruity, flavourful, long.

VALSERRANO FINCA MONTEVIEJO 2008 T
95% tempranillo, 5% graciano, garnacha

91 Colour: cherry, garnet rim. Nose: ripe fruit, spicy, creamy oak, toasty, complex. Palate: powerful, flavourful, toasty.

VALSERRANO GARNACHA 2009 T
100% garnacha

90 Colour: bright cherry. Nose: ripe fruit, creamy oak, fragrant herbs. Palate: flavourful, fruity, toasty, round tannins.

VALSERRANO GRACIANO 2009 T
100% graciano

90 Colour: cherry, garnet rim. Nose: red berry notes, raspberry, ripe fruit, balsamic herbs, sweet spices, creamy oak. Palate: rich, powerful, flavourful, balsamic.

VALSERRANO MAZUELO 2008 T
100% mazuelo

89 Colour: cherry, garnet rim. Nose: ripe fruit, aged wood nuances, spicy, creamy oak. Palate: powerful, flavourful, toasty, long.

WINNER WINES

Avda. del Mediterráneo, 38
28007 Madrid (Madrid)
☎: +34 915 019 042 - Fax: +34 915 019 042
www.entornoalvino.com
winnerwines@ibernoble.com

VIÑA SASETA 2004 TGR
tempranillo

86 Colour: deep cherry. Nose: powerfull, ripe fruit, toasty, spicy, aromatic coffee. Palate: powerful, concentrated, ripe fruit.

VIÑA SASETA 2006 TR
tempranillo, graciano, mazuelo

88 Colour: deep cherry. Nose: medium intensity, fruit liqueur notes, fruit liqueur notes, toasty, spicy. Palate: powerful, fine bitter notes, spicy.

VIÑA SASETA 2009 TC
95% tempranillo, 5% graciano, mazuelo

87 Colour: deep cherry. Nose: fruit liqueur notes, spicy, ripe fruit. Palate: powerful, spicy, ripe fruit.

VIÑA SASETA 2012 T
100% tempranillo

88 Colour: deep cherry. Nose: medium intensity, ripe fruit, fruit expression. Palate: easy to drink, ripe fruit.

Consejo Regulador
DO Boundary

DO RUEDA / D.O.P.

LOCATION:

In the provinces of Valladolid (53 municipal districts), Segovia (17 municipal districts) and Ávila (2 municipal districts). The vineyards are situated on the undulating terrain of a plateau and are conditioned by the influence of the river Duero that runs through the northern part of the region.

CLIMATE:

Continental in nature, with cold winters and short hot summers. Rainfall is concentrated in spring and autumn. The average altitude of the region is between 600 m and 700 m, and only in the province of Segovia does it exceed 800 m.

SOIL:

Many pebbles on the surface. The terrain is stony, poor in organic matter, with good aeration and drainage. The texture of the soil is variable although, in general, sandy limestone and limestone predominate.

GRAPE VARIETIES:

WHITE: *Verdejo* (52%), *Viura* (22%), *Sauvignon Blanc* (7%) and *Palomino Fino* (19%).
RED: *Tempranillo, Cabernet Sauvignon, Merlot* and *Garnacha.*

FIGURES:

Vineyard surface: 12.826– **Wine-Growers:** 1.517 – **Wineries:** 62 – **2012 Harvest rating:** Good– **Production:** 55.203.495 litres – **Market percentages:** 81,39% domestic. 18,61% export

2008	2009	2010	2011	2012
VERY GOOD	VERY GOOD	EXCELLENT	VERY GOOD	VERY GOOD

CONSEJO REGULADOR
Real, 8 - 47490 Rueda (Valladolid) ☎: +34 983 868 248 - Fax: +34 983 868 135
crdo.rueda@dorueda.com   www.dorueda.com

AGRÍCOLA CASTELLANA.
BODEGA CUATRO RAYAS

Ctra. Rodilana, s/n
47491 La Seca (Valladolid)
☎: +34 983 816 320 - Fax: +34 983 816 562
www.cuatrorayas.org
info@cuatrorayas.org

APOTEOSIS 2012 B
100% verdejo

87 Colour: bright straw. Nose: candied fruit, tropical fruit, medium intensity. Palate: fruity, sweetness.

AZUMBRE VERDEJO VIÑEDOS CENTENARIOS 2012 B
100% verdejo

88 Colour: bright straw. Nose: ripe fruit, floral, dried herbs, medium intensity. Palate: flavourful, correct, fine bitter notes.

BITÁCORA VERDEJO 2012 B
100% verdejo

88 Colour: bright straw. Nose: fresh, white flowers, ripe fruit. Palate: flavourful, fruity, good acidity, balanced.

CUATRO RAYAS 2010 BFB
100% verdejo

90 Colour: bright yellow. Nose: powerfull, ripe fruit, sweet spices, creamy oak, fragrant herbs. Palate: rich, smoky aftertaste, flavourful, fresh, good acidity.

CUATRO RAYAS ECOLÓGICO 2012 B
100% verdejo

90 Colour: bright straw. Nose: fresh, fresh fruit, white flowers, fragrant herbs. Palate: flavourful, fruity, good acidity, good structure.

CUATRO RAYAS ORGANIC WINE 2012 B
100% verdejo

90 Colour: bright straw. Nose: fresh fruit, white flowers, expressive. Palate: flavourful, fruity, good acidity, balanced, easy to drink.

CUATRO RAYAS SAUVIGNON 2012 B
100% sauvignon blanc

90 Colour: bright straw. Nose: fresh, fresh fruit, white flowers, neat. Palate: flavourful, fruity, good acidity, balanced.

CUATRO RAYAS VERDEJO 2012 B
100% verdejo

89 Colour: bright straw. Nose: fresh, fresh fruit, dried flowers, balsamic herbs. Palate: flavourful, fruity, good acidity.

CUATRO RAYAS VIÑEDOS CENTENARIOS 2012 B
100% verdejo

90 Colour: bright straw. Nose: ripe fruit, dried flowers, dried herbs, earthy notes. Palate: flavourful, fruity, good acidity, fine bitter notes.

PALACIO DE VIVERO 2012 B
100% verdejo

86 Colour: bright straw. Nose: ripe fruit, medium intensity, balsamic herbs. Palate: flavourful, correct.

PÁMPANO 2012 SEMIDULCE
100% verdejo

86 Colour: bright straw. Nose: medium intensity, fresh fruit, dried herbs, floral. Palate: fresh, fruity, flavourful, good acidity, sweetness.

VACCEOS 2010 TC
100% tempranillo

87 Colour: cherry, garnet rim. Nose: overripe fruit, toasty. Palate: fine bitter notes, sweetness.

VACCEOS 2012 RD
100% tempranillo

86 Colour: onion pink. Nose: elegant, candied fruit, dried flowers, red berry notes. Palate: light-bodied, flavourful, good acidity, long, spicy.

VACCEOS TEMPRANILLO 2011 T ROBLE
100% tempranillo

88 Colour: cherry, purple rim. Nose: fresh fruit, red berry notes, floral. Palate: flavourful, fruity, good acidity, round tannins.

VELITERRA 2012 B
100% verdejo

86 Colour: bright straw. Nose: fresh, white flowers, medium intensity, candied fruit. Palate: flavourful, fruity, good acidity.

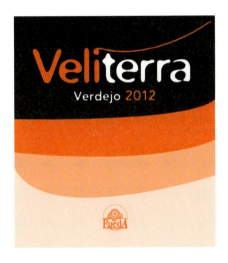

VISIGODO VERDEJO 2012 B
100% verdejo

87 Colour: bright straw. Nose: fresh fruit, white flowers, medium intensity. Palate: flavourful, fruity, correct.

ALIUS TAEDA S.L.

Calle Real, 19
47238 Hornillos de Eresma (Valladolid)
☎: +34 651 377 680
www.taeda.eu
buzon@taeda.eu

LIMIÉ VIÑEDOS CENTENARIOS 2012 B
verdejo

88 Colour: bright straw. Nose: fresh, fresh fruit, white flowers, expressive, balsamic herbs. Palate: flavourful, fruity, good acidity, balanced.

ÁLVAREZ Y DÍEZ

Juan Antonio Carmona, 12
47500 Nava del Rey (Valladolid)
☎: +34 983 850 136 - Fax: +34 983 850 761
www.alvarezydiez.com
bodegas@alvarezydiez.com

MANTEL BLANCO 2009 BFB
verdejo

90 Colour: bright yellow. Nose: powerfull, sweet spices, creamy oak, candied fruit. Palate: rich, smoky aftertaste, flavourful, fresh, good acidity.

MANTEL BLANCO SAUVIGNON BLANC 2012 B
sauvignon blanc

88 Colour: bright straw. Nose: fresh fruit, white flowers, earthy notes. Palate: flavourful, fruity, good acidity.

MANTEL BLANCO VERDEJO 2012 B
verdejo

90 Colour: bright straw. Nose: fresh, fresh fruit, white flowers. Palate: flavourful, fruity, good acidity, balanced.

MONTE ALINA 2012 B
verdejo, viura

86 Colour: bright straw. Nose: fresh, white flowers, ripe fruit. Palate: flavourful, fruity, good acidity, balanced.

ÁNGEL RODRÍGUEZ VIDAL

Torcido, 1
47491 La Seca (Valladolid)
☎: +34 983 816 302 - Fax: +34 983 816 302
martinsancho@martinsancho.com

MARTÍNSANCHO 2012 B
100% verdejo

91 Colour: bright straw. Nose: fresh, fresh fruit, white flowers, expressive, floral. Palate: flavourful, fruity, good acidity, balanced.

AVELINO VEGAS

Real del Pino, 36
40460 Santiuste (Segovia)
☎: +34 921 596 002 - Fax: +34 921 596 035
www.avelinovegas.com
ana@avelinovegas.com

CASA DE LA VEGA VERDEJO 2012 B JOVEN
verdejo

87 Colour: bright straw. Nose: fresh, white flowers, candied fruit. Palate: flavourful, fruity, fine bitter notes.

CIRCE 2012 B
verdejo

89 Colour: bright straw. Nose: fresh, fresh fruit, white flowers, balsamic herbs. Palate: flavourful, fruity, good acidity.

MONTESPINA SAUVIGNON 2012 B JOVEN
sauvignon blanc

89 Colour: bright straw. Nose: fresh, fresh fruit, dried flowers. Palate: flavourful, fruity, good acidity, correct.

MONTESPINA VERDEJO 2012 B JOVEN
verdejo

89 Colour: bright straw. Nose: fresh, ripe fruit, dried flowers. Palate: flavourful, fruity, good acidity, balanced.

NICTE 2012 RD
prieto picudo

87 Colour: rose, purple rim. Nose: powerfull, ripe fruit, red berry notes, floral, expressive. Palate: powerful, fruity, fresh, sweetness.

AXIAL

Pla-za Calle Castillo de Capua, 10 Nave 7
50197 (Zaragoza)
☎: +34 976 780 136 - Fax: +34 976 303 035
www.axialvinos.com
info@axialvinos.com

ESPERANZA RUEDA VERDEJO 2012 B
100% verdejo

88 Colour: bright straw. Nose: fragrant herbs, dried flowers, candied fruit, balanced. Palate: flavourful, balsamic, correct.

ESPERANZA VERDEJO VIURA 2012 B
70% verdejo, 30% viura

87 Colour: bright straw. Nose: citrus fruit, wild herbs, dried flowers, expressive. Palate: powerful, fresh, fruity, flavourful.

BELONDRADE

Quinta San Diego - Camino del Puerto, s/n
47491 La Seca (Valladolid)
☎: +34 983 481 001
www.belondrade.com
info@belondrade.com

BELONDRADE Y LURTON 2011 BFB
verdejo

95 Colour: bright yellow. Nose: powerfull, sweet spices, fragrant herbs, fruit expression. Palate: rich, smoky aftertaste, flavourful, fresh, good acidity.

BODEGA ALTAENCINA

Cañada Real, 30 1ºA
47008 (Valladolid)
☎: +34 639 780 716 - Fax: +34 983 868 905
www.altaencina.com
pablo@altaencina.com

QUIVIRA VERDEJO 2012 B
verdejo

87 Colour: bright straw. Nose: citrus fruit, candied fruit, dried herbs. Palate: correct, fresh, fruity, balsamic.

BODEGA AYUNTAMIENTO MADRIGAL DE LAS ALTAS TORRES

Plaza Santa María n1
5220 Madrigal de las Altas Torres (Ávila)
☎: +34 920 320 001
ayuntamientodemadrigal@aytomadrigal.es

CUNA DE YSABEL 2012 B
verdejo

90 Colour: bright straw. Nose: fresh, white flowers, expressive, varietal. Palate: flavourful, fruity, good acidity, balanced.

DON VASCO 2012 B
verdejo

91 Colour: bright straw. Nose: fresh, white flowers, expressive, mineral. Palate: flavourful, fruity, good acidity, balanced.

BODEGA EL ALBAR LURTON

Camino Magarin, s/n
47529 Villafranca del Duero (Valladolid)
☎: +34 983 034 030 - Fax: +34 983 034 040
www.francoislurton.es
bodega@francoislurton.es

HERMANOS LURTON SAUVIGNON BLANC 2012 B
sauvignon blanc

90 Colour: bright straw. Nose: fresh, fresh fruit, white flowers, tropical fruit. Palate: flavourful, fruity, good acidity, balanced.

HERMANOS LURTON VERDEJO 2012 B
verdejo

90 Colour: bright straw. Nose: white flowers, expressive, candied fruit, complex. Palate: flavourful, fruity, good acidity, balanced.

BODEGA EMINA RUEDA

Ctra. Medina del Campo - Olmedo, Km. 1,5
47400 Medina del Campo (Valladolid)
☎: +34 983 803 346 - Fax: +34 902 430 189
www.eminarueda.es
eminarueda@emina.es

EMINA SS
100% verdejo

83

EMINA BRUT NATURE ESP
verdejo

83

EMINA RUEDA 2012 B
90% verdejo, 10% viura

88 Colour: bright straw. Nose: grassy, ripe fruit, citrus fruit, tropical fruit. Palate: flavourful, ripe fruit, good acidity.

MELIOR VERDEJO 2012 B
100% verdejo

88 Colour: bright straw. Nose: white flowers, ripe fruit, dried herbs. Palate: flavourful, fruity, good acidity.

SELECCIÓN PERSONAL CARLOS MORO EMINA VERDEJO 2009 B
100% verdejo

91 Colour: bright yellow. Nose: powerfull, ripe fruit, sweet spices, creamy oak, fragrant herbs. Palate: rich, smoky after-taste, flavourful, fresh, good acidity.

BODEGA GÓTICA

Ctra. Rueda - La Seca, Km. 1,2
47490 Rueda (Valladolid)
☎: +34 620 752 642 - Fax: +34 983 868 387
www.bodegagotica.com
mjhmonsalve@ya.com

CAMINO LA FARA VERDEJO 2012 B
100% verdejo

86 Colour: bright straw. Nose: medium intensity, ripe fruit, dried herbs. Palate: fine bitter notes, flavourful.

MONSALVE VERDEJO 2012 B
100% verdejo

89 Colour: bright straw. Nose: white flowers, ripe fruit, balsamic herbs. Palate: flavourful, fruity, good acidity.

MOYORIDO 2012 B
100% verdejo

85 Colour: bright yellow. Nose: ripe fruit, faded flowers, balsamic herbs. Palate: powerful, easy to drink.

POLÍGONO 10 VERDEJO 2012 B
100% verdejo

88 Colour: bright straw. Nose: fruit expression, floral, balsamic herbs, medium intensity. Palate: easy to drink, fresh, fruity.

TRASCAMPANAS SAUVIGNON 2012 B
100% sauvignon blanc

89 Colour: bright straw. Nose: fresh, fresh fruit, white flowers, tropical fruit. Palate: flavourful, fruity, good acidity, balanced.

TRASCAMPANAS SELECCIÓN 2012 B
100% verdejo

90 Colour: bright golden. Nose: powerfull, ripe fruit, sweet spices, creamy oak, fragrant herbs. Palate: rich, smoky aftertaste, flavourful, fresh.

TRASCAMPANAS VERDEJO 2012 B
100% verdejo

89 Colour: bright straw. Nose: dried herbs, ripe fruit, floral. Palate: correct, fine bitter notes, flavourful, balsamic.

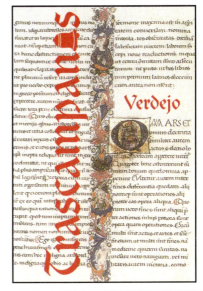

BODEGA HERMANOS DEL VILLAR

Zarcillo, s/n
47490 Rueda (Valladolid)
☎: +34 983 868 904 - Fax: +34 983 868 905
www.orodecastilla.com
pablo@orodecastilla.com

ORO DE CASTILLA SAUVIGNON BLANC 2012 B
sauvignon blanc

86 Colour: bright straw. Nose: fresh, fresh fruit, tropical fruit. Palate: flavourful, fruity, good acidity.

ORO DE CASTILLA VERDEJO 2012 B
verdejo

89 Colour: bright straw. Nose: expressive, fresh, ripe fruit, floral, fragrant herbs. Palate: flavourful, fruity, good acidity.

BODEGA LA SOTERRAÑA

Ctra. N-601, Km. 151
47410 Olmedo (Valladolid)
☎: +34 983 601 026 - Fax: +34 983 601 026
www.bodegaslasoterrana.com
info@bodegaslasoterrana.com

ERESMA 2011 BFB
verdejo

90 Colour: bright yellow. Nose: powerfull, ripe fruit, fragrant herbs, toasty. Palate: rich, smoky aftertaste, flavourful, fresh, good acidity.

ERESMA SAUVIGNON 2012 B
sauvignon blanc

91 Colour: bright straw. Nose: fresh, fresh fruit, white flowers, expressive. Palate: flavourful, fruity, balanced, easy to drink.

ERESMA VERDEJO 2012 B
verdejo

89 Colour: bright straw. Nose: ripe fruit, tropical fruit, floral. Palate: easy to drink, flavourful, fruity.

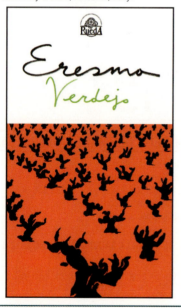

BODEGA MATARROMERA

Ctra. Renedo-Pesquera, Km. 30
47359 Valbuena de Duero (Valladolid)
☎: +34 983 107 100 - Fax: +34 902 430 189
www.grupomatarromera.com
matarromera@matarromera.es

MATARROMERA VERDEJO EDICIÓN LIMITADA 25 ANIVERSARIO 2012 B
100% verdejo

89 Colour: bright yellow. Nose: powerfull, ripe fruit, sweet spices, creamy oak, fragrant herbs. Palate: rich, smoky aftertaste, flavourful, fresh, good acidity.

BODEGA MONTE BLANCO

Ctra. Valladolid, Km. 24,5
47239 Serrada (Valladolid)
☎: +34 941 310 295 - Fax: +34 941 310 832
www.bodegas-monteblanco.es
info@bodegas-monteblanco.es

MONTE BLANCO DE RAMÓN BILBAO VERDEJO 2012 B
100% verdejo

90 Colour: bright straw. Nose: fresh, white flowers, ripe fruit, citrus fruit, balanced. Palate: flavourful, good acidity, balanced.

BODEGA NOS RIQUEZA

Sánchez Calvo, 6
33402 Avilés (Asturias)
☎: +34 984 836 826 - Fax: +34 985 931 074
www.nosriqueza.com
exportmanager@nosriqueza.com

NOS RIQUEZA 2012 B

89 Colour: bright straw. Nose: fresh, fresh fruit, white flowers, scrubland, grassy. Palate: flavourful, fruity, good acidity, balanced.

BODEGA REINA DE CASTILLA

Ctra. La Seca - Serrada
47491 La Seca (Valladolid)
☎: +34 983 816 667 - Fax: +34 983 816 663
www.reinadecastilla.es
bodega@reinadecastilla.es

EL BUFÓN VERDEJO 2012 B
100% verdejo

91 Colour: bright straw. Nose: fresh, fresh fruit, white flowers, balsamic herbs. Palate: flavourful, fruity, good acidity, easy to drink.

ISABELINO RUEDA 2012 B
70% verdejo, 30% viura

86 Colour: bright yellow. Nose: ripe fruit, honeyed notes, balsamic herbs. Palate: powerful, warm, correct.

REINA DE CASTILLA VERDEJO 2011 BFB
100% verdejo

90 Colour: bright yellow. Nose: powerfull, ripe fruit, sweet spices, creamy oak, fragrant herbs. Palate: rich, smoky aftertaste, flavourful, fresh, good acidity.

REINA DE CASTILLA VERDEJO 2012 B
100% verdejo

90 Colour: bright straw. Nose: ripe fruit, floral, fragrant herbs, balanced. Palate: powerful, flavourful, fruity, varietal.

BODEGA VALDEHERMOSO

Pasión, 13 4ºD
47001 (Valladolid)
☎: +34 651 993 680
www.valdehermoso.com
valdehermoso@valdehermoso.com

LAGAR DEL REY VERDEJO 2012 B
100% verdejo

88 Colour: bright straw. Nose: fresh fruit, white flowers, expressive, tropical fruit. Palate: flavourful, fruity, good acidity.

VIÑA PEREZ 2012 B
100% verdejo

90 Colour: bright straw. Nose: fresh, fresh fruit, white flowers, varietal, grassy. Palate: flavourful, fruity, good acidity, balanced.

BODEGA VIÑA VILANO S. COOP.

Ctra. de Anguix, 10
9314 Pedrosa de Duero (Burgos)
☎: +34 947 530 029 - Fax: +34 947 530 037
www.vinavilano.com
info@vinavilano.com

VIÑA VILANO VERDEJO 2012 B
100% verdejo

88 Colour: bright straw. Nose: fresh fruit, white flowers, elegant. Palate: flavourful, fruity, good acidity, balanced.

BODEGAS ABANICO

Pol. Ind Ca l'Avellanet - Susany, 6
8553 Seva (Barcelona)
☎: +34 938 125 676 - Fax: +34 938 123 213
www.bodegasabanico.com
info@exportiberia.com

FINCA REMENDIO RUEDA 2012 B
50% viura, 50% verdejo

87 Colour: bright straw. Nose: fresh, fresh fruit, white flowers, expressive. Palate: flavourful, fruity, good acidity, balanced.

FINCA REMENDIO VERDEJO 2012 B
100% verdejo

89 Colour: bright straw. Nose: fresh fruit, white flowers, fragrant herbs. Palate: flavourful, fruity, balanced.

BODEGAS AURA

Autovía del Noroeste, Km. 175
47490 Rueda (Valladolid)
☎: +34 983 868 286 - Fax: +34 983 868 148
www.domecqbodegas.com
aura@pernod-ricard.com

AURA VERDEJO 2012 B
85% verdejo, 15% sauvignon blanc

88 Colour: bright straw. Nose: ripe fruit, floral, balsamic herbs. Palate: fresh, fruity, flavourful.

BODEGAS BALUARTE

Ribera, 34
31592 Cintruénigo (Navarra)
☎: +34 948 811 000 - Fax: +34 948 811 407
www.chivite.com
info@bodegaschivite.com

BALUARTE VERDEJO 2012 B
verdejo

90 Colour: bright yellow. Nose: floral, fragrant herbs, ripe fruit. Palate: powerful, flavourful, easy to drink.

BODEGAS CASTELO DE MEDINA

Ctra. CL-602, Km. 48
47465 Villaverde de Medina (Valladolid)
☎: +34 983 831 884 - Fax: +34 983 831 857
www.castelodemedina.com
comunicacion@castelodemedina.com

CASTELO ÁMBAR SEMIDULCE 2012 B
100% sauvignon blanc

85 Colour: golden. Nose: powerfull, floral, honeyed notes, candied fruit, fragrant herbs. Palate: flavourful, sweet, fresh, fruity, good acidity, long.

CASTELO DE LA DEHESA 2012 B
50% verdejo, 30% viura, 20% sauvignon blanc

88 Colour: bright straw. Nose: fresh, fresh fruit, dried flowers, balsamic herbs. Palate: flavourful, fruity, balanced.

CASTELO DE MEDINA SAUVIGNON BLANC 2012 B
100% sauvignon blanc

91 Colour: bright straw. Nose: white flowers, ripe fruit, tropical fruit. Palate: flavourful, fruity, good acidity, balanced.

CASTELO DE MEDINA VERDEJO 2012 B
100% verdejo

91 Colour: bright straw. Nose: fresh, fresh fruit, white flowers. Palate: flavourful, fruity, good acidity, balanced.

CASTELO DE MEDINA VERDEJO VENDIMIA SELECCIONADA 2012 B
100% verdejo

91 Colour: bright yellow. Nose: tropical fruit, ripe fruit, citrus fruit, floral, fragrant herbs. Palate: powerful, flavourful, spicy, long.

CASTELO NOBLE 2011 BFB
85% verdejo, 15% sauvignon blanc

90 Colour: bright yellow. Nose: powerfull, ripe fruit, sweet spices, creamy oak, fragrant herbs. Palate: rich, smoky aftertaste, flavourful, fresh, good acidity.

REAL CASTELO 2012 B
85% verdejo, 15% sauvignon blanc

91 Colour: bright straw. Nose: fresh, fresh fruit, white flowers. Palate: flavourful, fruity, good acidity, balanced.

BODEGAS CERROSOL

Camino Villagonzalo, s/n
40460 Santituste de San Juan Bautista (Segovia)
☎: +34 921 596 326 - Fax: +34 921 596 351
www.bodegascerrosol.com
calidad@bodegascerrosol.com

DOÑA BEATRIZ RUEDA VERDEJO 2012 B
100% verdejo

86 Colour: bright straw. Nose: fresh, fresh fruit, white flowers. Palate: flavourful, fruity, good acidity, fine bitter notes.

DOÑA BEATRIZ SAUVIGNON 2012 B
100% sauvignon blanc

86 Colour: bright straw. Nose: fresh, fresh fruit, white flowers, expressive. Palate: flavourful, fruity, good acidity, balanced.

DOÑA BEATRIZ VERDEJO VIURA 2012 B
85% verdejo, 15% viura

87 Colour: bright straw. Nose: fresh, ripe fruit, dried flowers. Palate: flavourful, fruity, good acidity, balanced.

BODEGAS COPABOCA

N-122, Km. 407
47114 Torrecilla de la Abadesa (Valladolid)
☎: +34 983 486 010 - Fax: +34 983 307 729
www.copaboca.com
copaboca@copaboca.com

COPABOCA VERTICAL 2012 B
100% verdejo

88 Colour: bright straw. Nose: fresh, fresh fruit, white flowers. Palate: flavourful, fruity, good acidity, balanced.

FEROES 2012 B
100% verdejo

87 Colour: bright straw. Nose: medium intensity, ripe fruit, citrus fruit. Palate: flavourful, fruity, light-bodied.

GORGORITO VERDEJO 2012 B
100% verdejo

89 Colour: bright straw. Nose: fresh fruit, white flowers, grassy. Palate: flavourful, fruity, good acidity, balanced.

BODEGAS DE LOS HEREDEROS DEL MARQUÉS DE RISCAL

Ctra. N-VI, km. 172,600
47490 Rueda (Valladolid)
☎: +34 983 868 083 - Fax: +34 983 868 563
www.marquesderiscal.com
comunicacion@marquesderiscal.com

MARQUÉS DE RISCAL FINCA MONTICO 2012 B
100% verdejo

93 Colour: bright golden. Nose: mineral, powerfull, varietal, characterful, ripe fruit. Palate: flavourful, powerful, good acidity, long.

MARQUÉS DE RISCAL LIMOUSIN 2012 BFB
100% verdejo

91 Colour: bright golden. Nose: powerfull, ripe fruit, fruit expression, dried herbs, toasty, aromatic coffee. Palate: powerful, flavourful, ripe fruit.

MARQUÉS DE RISCAL RUEDA SAUVIGNON 2012 B
100% sauvignon blanc

91 Colour: bright straw. Nose: fresh fruit, white flowers, varietal. Palate: flavourful, fruity, good acidity, balanced.

MARQUÉS DE RISCAL RUEDA VERDEJO 2012 B
95% verdejo, 5% viura

90 Colour: bright straw. Nose: white flowers, ripe fruit, dried herbs. Palate: flavourful, fruity, good acidity, balanced.

VIÑA CALERA RUEDA VERDEJO 2012 B
85% verdejo, 10% viura, 5% sauvignon blanc

88 Colour: bright straw. Nose: white flowers, ripe fruit, dried herbs. Palate: flavourful, fine bitter notes.

BODEGAS DE LOS RÍOS PRIETO

Ctra. Pesquera - Renedo, 1
47315 Pesquera de Duero (Valladolid)
☎: +34 983 880 383 - Fax: +34 983 878 032
www.bodegasdelosriosprieto.com
info@bodegasdelosriosprieto.com

PRIOS MAXIMUS VERDEJO 2012 B
100% verdejo

88 Colour: bright straw. Nose: fresh, fresh fruit, white flowers, varietal. Palate: flavourful, fruity, good acidity, balanced.

BODEGAS FÉLIX LORENZO CACHAZO S.L.

Ctra. Medina del Campo, Km. 9
47220 Pozáldez (Valladolid)
☎: +34 983 822 008 - Fax: +34 983 822 008
www.cachazo.com
bodega@cachazo.com

CARRASVIÑAS ESPUMOSO BR
100% verdejo

87 Colour: bright straw. Nose: medium intensity, fresh fruit, dried herbs, floral, lactic notes. Palate: fresh, fruity, flavourful, good acidity.

CARRASVIÑAS VERDEJO 2012 B
100% verdejo

89 Colour: bright straw. Nose: dried flowers, ripe fruit, fragrant herbs. Palate: flavourful, fruity, balanced.

GRAN CARDIEL RUEDA VERDEJO B
100% verdejo

88 Colour: bright straw. Nose: fresh, fresh fruit, white flowers. Palate: flavourful, fruity, good acidity.

MANIA RUEDA VERDEJO 2012 B
100% verdejo

91 Colour: bright straw. Nose: fresh, white flowers, ripe fruit. Palate: flavourful, fruity, good acidity, balanced.

MANIA SAUVIGNON 2012 B
100% sauvignon blanc

90 Colour: bright straw. Nose: fresh fruit, white flowers, fragrant herbs. Palate: flavourful, fruity, good acidity, fine bitter notes.

QUIETUS VERDEJO 2012 B
100% verdejo

88 Colour: bright straw. Nose: white flowers, ripe fruit, fragrant herbs. Palate: flavourful, fruity, good acidity.

BODEGAS FÉLIX SANZ

Ronda Aradillas, s/n
47490 Rueda (Valladolid)
☎: +34 983 868 044 - Fax: +34 983 868 133
www.bodegasfelixsanz.es
pedidos@bodegasfelixsanz.es

VIÑA CIMBRÓN 2011 BFB
100% verdejo

89 Colour: bright golden. Nose: ripe fruit, dry nuts, powerfull, toasty, aged wood nuances. Palate: flavourful, fruity, spicy, toasty, long.

VIÑA CIMBRÓN 2012 RD
69% tempranillo, 31% cabernet sauvignon

90 Colour: rose, purple rim. Nose: powerfull, ripe fruit, red berry notes, floral, expressive. Palate: powerfull, fruity, fresh.

VIÑA CIMBRÓN RUEDA 2012 B
65% verdejo, 35% viura

87 Colour: bright straw. Nose: ripe fruit, tropical fruit, citrus fruit. Palate: flavourful, fruity, balanced.

VIÑA CIMBRÓN SAUVIGNON 2012 B
sauvignon blanc

87 Colour: bright straw. Nose: fresh fruit, white flowers, grassy. Palate: flavourful, fruity.

VIÑA CIMBRÓN VERDEJO 2012 B
100% verdejo

88 Colour: bright straw. Nose: fresh, white flowers, ripe fruit. Palate: flavourful, fruity, good acidity, balanced.

BODEGAS FRONTAURA

Santiago, 17 - 4º
47001 (Valladolid)
☎: +34 983 360 284 - Fax: +34 983 345 546
www.bodegasfrontaura.com
info@bodegasfrontaura.es

VEGA MURILLO VERDEJO 2011 B
100% verdejo

87 Colour: bright yellow. Nose: powerfull, ripe fruit, sweet spices, fragrant herbs. Palate: rich, flavourful, good acidity.

BODEGAS FRUTOS VILLAR

Ctra. Burgos-Portugal Km. 113,7
47270 Cigales (Valladolid)
☎: +34 983 586 868 - Fax: +34 983 580 180
www.bodegasfrutosvillar.com
bodegasfrutosvillar@bodegasfrutosvillar.com

MARÍA MOLINA RUEDA 2012 B
verdejo, viura

87 Colour: bright straw. Nose: white flowers, ripe fruit, tropical fruit. Palate: flavourful, fruity, correct.

MARÍA MOLINA VERDEJO 2012 B
100% verdejo

89 Colour: bright straw. Nose: fresh, fresh fruit, white flowers, varietal. Palate: flavourful, fruity, good acidity, balanced.

VIÑA CANSINA VERDEJO 2012 B
100% verdejo

87 Colour: bright straw. Nose: fresh fruit, white flowers, expressive. Palate: flavourful, fruity, good acidity.

VIÑA MOREJONA RUEDA 2012 B
verdejo, viura

87 Colour: bright straw. Nose: fragrant herbs, tropical fruit, floral. Palate: fine bitter notes, fruity, easy to drink.

VIÑA MOREJONA VERDEJO 2012 B
100% verdejo

88 Colour: bright straw. Nose: ripe fruit, dried flowers, dried herbs. Palate: flavourful, fruity, good acidity, balanced.

BODEGAS GARCÍA DE ARANDA

Ctra. de Soria, s/n
9400 Aranda de Duero (Burgos)
☎: +34 947 501 817 - Fax: +34 947 506 355
www.bodegasgarcia.com
bodega@bodegasgarcia.com

ORO BLANCO VERDEJO 2012 B
verdejo

88 Colour: bright straw. Nose: fresh, fresh fruit, white flowers, medium intensity. Palate: flavourful, fruity, balanced.

BODEGAS GARCÍAREVALO

Pza. San Juan, 4
47230 Matapozuelos (Valladolid)
☎: +34 983 832 914 - Fax: +34 983 832 986
www.garciarevalo.com
enologo@garciarevalo.com

TRES OLMOS CLASSIC 2012 B
100% verdejo

89 Colour: bright straw. Nose: fresh, fresh fruit, white flowers, expressive. Palate: flavourful, fruity, good acidity, balanced.

TRES OLMOS LÍAS 2012 B
100% verdejo

90 Colour: bright straw. Nose: floral, ripe fruit, fine lees, wild herbs. Palate: correct, fine bitter notes, powerful, flavourful, balanced.

VIÑA ADAJA VERDEJO 2012 B
100% verdejo

88 Colour: bright straw. Nose: fragrant herbs, ripe fruit. Palate: flavourful, fruity, good acidity, fine bitter notes.

BODEGAS GARCIGRANDE

Aradillas s/n
57490 Rueda (Valladolid)
☎: +34 983 868 561 - Fax: +34 983 868 449
www.hispanobodegas.com
info@hispanobodegas.com

12 LINAJES VERDEJO 2012 B
100% verdejo

90 Colour: bright straw. Nose: fresh, fresh fruit, floral, citrus fruit, ripe fruit. Palate: flavourful, fruity, good acidity, balanced.

ANIER VENDIMIA SELECCIONADA 2012 B
100% verdejo

92 Colour: bright straw. Nose: fresh, white flowers, expressive, mineral, ripe fruit. Palate: flavourful, fruity, good acidity, balanced, rich.

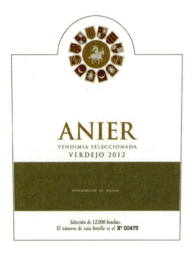

SEÑORÍO DE GARCI GRANDE VERDEJO 2012 B
100% verdejo

90 Colour: bright straw. Nose: fresh fruit, white flowers, expressive. Palate: flavourful, fruity, good acidity, balanced.

BODEGAS IMPERIALES

Ctra. Madrid - Irun, Km. 171
9370 Gumiel de Izán (Burgos)
☎: +34 947 544 070 - Fax: +34 947 525 759
www.bodegasimperiales.com
direccion@bodegasimperiales.com

ABADÍA DE SAN QUIRCE VERDEJO 2012 B

90 Colour: bright straw. Nose: ripe fruit, tropical fruit, floral, fragrant herbs. Palate: powerful, balsamic, flavourful.

BODEGAS JOSÉ PARIENTE

Ctra. de Rueda, km. 2.5
47491 La Seca (Valladolid)
☎: +34 983 816 600 - Fax: +34 983 816 620
www.josepariente.com
info@josepariente.com

JOSÉ PARIENTE 2010 BFB
100% verdejo

92 Colour: bright yellow. Nose: powerfull, ripe fruit, sweet spices, creamy oak. Palate: rich, smoky aftertaste, flavourful, fresh, good acidity.

JOSÉ PARIENTE SAUVIGNON BLANC 2012 B
100% sauvignon blanc

91 Colour: bright straw. Nose: fresh, fresh fruit, white flowers, expressive. Palate: flavourful, fruity, good acidity, balanced, elegant.

JOSÉ PARIENTE VERDEJO 2012 B
100% verdejo

91 Colour: bright straw. Nose: expressive, floral, citrus fruit, fruit expression, fragrant herbs. Palate: powerful, flavourful, fresh, elegant.

BODEGAS MARQUÉS DE ARVIZA

Bodegas San Cristóbal, 34 A
26360 Fuenmayor (La Rioja)
☎: +34 941 451 245
www.marquesdearviza.com
info@marquesdearviza.es

CAUTO 2012 B
100% verdejo

89 Colour: bright straw. Nose: fresh, fresh fruit, white flowers, citrus fruit. Palate: flavourful, fruity, good acidity.

BODEGAS MOCEN

Arribas, 7-9
47490 Rueda (Valladolid)
☎: +34 983 868 533 - Fax: +34 983 868 514
www.bodegasantano.com
info@bodegasmocen.com

MOCÉN SAUVIGNON 2012 B
100% sauvignon blanc

90 Colour: bright straw. Nose: fresh, fresh fruit, white flowers, fragrant herbs. Palate: flavourful, fruity, good acidity, balanced.

MOCÉN VERDEJO 2011 BFB
100% verdejo

87 Colour: bright yellow. Nose: sweet spices, creamy oak, ripe fruit. Palate: toasty, correct, fine bitter notes.

ALTA PLATA VERDEJO 2012 B
100% verdejo

90 Colour: bright straw. Nose: fresh fruit, citrus fruit, fragrant herbs. Palate: fruity, flavourful, fine bitter notes, varietal.

AÑ 2011 BN ESPUMOSO
100% verdejo

83

MOCÉN VERDEJO 2012 B
100% verdejo

89 Colour: bright straw. Nose: fresh, fresh fruit, white flowers, fragrant herbs. Palate: flavourful, fruity, good acidity.

MOCÉN VERDEJO VIURA 2012 B
50% verdejo, 50% viura

85 Colour: bright straw. Nose: fresh, fresh fruit, dried flowers. Palate: flavourful, fruity.

BODEGAS NAIA

Camino San Martín, s/n
47491 La Seca (Valladolid)
☎: +34 628 434 933
www.bodegasnaia.com
info@bodegasnaia.com

DUCADO DE ALTÁN 2012 B
verdejo

91 Colour: bright straw. Nose: fresh, fresh fruit, white flowers, balsamic herbs. Palate: flavourful, fruity, good acidity, balanced.

K-NAIA 2012 B
sauvignon blanc, verdejo

90 Colour: bright straw. Nose: ripe fruit, balsamic herbs, dried flowers. Palate: powerful, flavourful, fresh, easy to drink.

NAIA 2012 B
100% verdejo

93 Colour: bright straw. Nose: fragrant herbs, ripe fruit, floral, expressive. Palate: powerful, flavourful, correct, fine bitter notes, balanced.

NAIADES 2010 BFB
100% verdejo

95 Colour: bright yellow. Nose: powerfull, ripe fruit, sweet spices, creamy oak, fragrant herbs. Palate: rich, smoky aftertaste, flavourful, fresh, good acidity.

BODEGAS NILO

Federico García Lorca, 7
47490 Rueda (Valladolid)
☎: +34 690 068 682 - Fax: +34 983 868 366
www.bodegasnilo.com
info@bodegasnilo.com

BIANCA 2012 B
100% verdejo

90 Colour: bright straw. Nose: citrus fruit, ripe fruit, floral, balsamic herbs, wild herbs. Palate: fresh, fruity, flavourful, easy to drink.

BODEGAS ORDÓÑEZ

Bartolomé Esteban Murillo, 11
29700 Vélez- Málaga (Málaga)
☎: +34 952 504 706 - Fax: +34 951 284 796
www.grupojorgeordonez.com
info@jorgeordonez.es

NISIA 2012 B
100% verdejo

94 Colour: bright straw. Nose: ripe fruit, fruit expression, varietal. Palate: flavourful, good acidity, ripe fruit, long.

BODEGAS PEÑAFIEL

Ctra. N-122, Km. 311
47300 Peñafiel (Valladolid)
☎: +34 983 881 622 - Fax: +34 983 881 944
www.bodegaspenafiel.com
bodegaspenafiel@bodegaspenafiel.com

ALBA MIROS 2012 B
verdejo

89 Colour: bright yellow. Nose: ripe fruit, dried herbs, faded flowers, medium intensity. Palate: rich, powerful, flavourful, easy to drink.

BODEGAS PRADOREY

Ctra. Nacional VI, Km. 172,5
47490 Rueda (Valladolid)
☎: +34 983 444 048 - Fax: +34 983 868 564
www.pradorey.com
bodega@pradorey.com

BIRLOCHO 2012 B
95% verdejo, 5% sauvignon blanc

88 Colour: bright straw. Nose: fresh, fresh fruit, white flowers. Palate: flavourful, fruity, good acidity.

PR 3 BARRICAS 2009 BFB
100% verdejo

93 Colour: bright yellow. Nose: powerfull, ripe fruit, sweet spices, creamy oak, fragrant herbs. Palate: rich, smoky aftertaste, flavourful, fresh, good acidity.

PRADOREY SAUVIGNON BLANC 2012 B
100% sauvignon blanc

90 Colour: bright straw. Nose: white flowers, expressive. Palate: flavourful, fruity, good acidity, balanced, sweetness.

PRADOREY VERDEJO 2012 B
100% verdejo

91 Colour: bright straw. Nose: fresh, fresh fruit, white flowers, expressive. Palate: flavourful, fruity, good acidity, balanced.

PROTOS VERDEJO 2012 B
verdejo

91 Colour: bright straw. Nose: fresh, white flowers, ripe fruit, grassy. Palate: flavourful, fruity, good acidity, balanced.

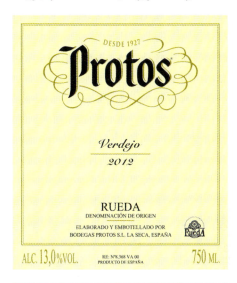

BODEGAS PROTOS S.L.

Ctra. CL 610, Km. 32,5
47491 La Seca (Valladolid)
☎: +34 983 878 011 - Fax: +34 983 878 012
www.bodegasprotos.com
bodega@bodegasprotos.com

PROTOS 2010 BFB
verdejo

94 Colour: bright yellow. Nose: powerfull, ripe fruit, sweet spices, creamy oak, fragrant herbs. Palate: rich, smoky aftertaste, flavourful, fresh, good acidity.

BODEGAS RUEDA PÉREZ

Boyón
47220 Pozáldez (Valladolid)
☎: +34 983 822 049 - Fax: +34 983 822 049
www.bodegasruedaperez.es
satruedaperez@terra.es

JOSÉ GALO VERDEJO SELECCIÓN 2012 B
100% verdejo

92 Colour: bright straw. Nose: fresh, fresh fruit, white flowers, fragrant herbs. Palate: flavourful, fruity, good acidity, balanced, elegant.

VIÑA BURÓN VERDEJO 2012 B
100% verdejo

91 Colour: bright straw. Nose: fresh, fresh fruit, white flowers, lactic notes. Palate: flavourful, fruity, good acidity, balanced.

ZAPADORADO VERDEJO 2012 B
100% verdejo

87 Colour: bright straw. Nose: fresh, fresh fruit, expressive, dried flowers. Palate: flavourful, fruity, good acidity, balanced.

BODEGAS SEÑORÍO DE NAVA

Ctra. Valladolid - Soria, s/n
9318 Nava de Roa (Burgos)
☎: +34 987 209 712 - Fax: +34 987 209 800
www.senoriodenava.es
snava@senoriodenava.es

SEÑORÍO DE NAVA VERDEJO 100% 2012 B
100% verdejo

86 Colour: bright straw. Nose: fresh, fresh fruit, white flowers, expressive. Palate: flavourful, fruity, good acidity, balanced.

VAL DE LAMAS VERDEJO 100% 2012 B
100% verdejo

85 Colour: bright straw. Nose: white flowers, ripe fruit, balsamic herbs. Palate: flavourful, fruity, good acidity.

VIÑA MARIAN VERDEJO 100% 2012 B
100% verdejo

85 Colour: bright straw. Nose: fragrant herbs, ripe fruit, dried flowers. Palate: flavourful, fruity, correct.

BODEGAS TAMARAL

Ctra. N-122, Km. 310,6
47300 Peñafiel (Valladolid)
☎: +34 983 878 017 - Fax: +34 983 878 089
www.tamaral.com
exterior@tamaral.com

TAMARAL VERDEJO 2012 B
100% verdejo

87 Colour: bright straw. Nose: ripe fruit, tropical fruit, dried herbs. Palate: rich, flavourful, correct.

BODEGAS TIONIO

Carretera de Valoria, Km 7
47315 Pesquera de Duero (Valladolid)
☎: +34 933 950 811 - Fax: +34 933 955 500
www.tionio.com
info@parxet.es

AUSTUM VERDEJO 2012 B
100% verdejo

86 Colour: bright yellow. Nose: warm, ripe fruit, dried flowers, balsamic herbs. Palate: powerful, rich, fruity, warm.

BODEGAS VAL DE VID

Ctra. Valladolid - Medina, Km. 23,6
47231 Serrada (Valladolid)
☎: +34 983 559 914 - Fax: +34 983 559 914
www.valdevid.es
info@valdevid.es

CONDESA EYLO 2012 B
100% verdejo

89 Colour: bright straw. Nose: white flowers, ripe fruit, balsamic herbs. Palate: flavourful, fruity, good acidity, balanced.

EYLO RUEDA 2012 B
70% verdejo, 30% viura

88 Colour: bright straw. Nose: fresh, fresh fruit, white flowers, balsamic herbs. Palate: flavourful, fruity, balanced.

MUSGO 2012 B
100% verdejo

85 Colour: bright straw. Nose: floral, ripe fruit, balsamic herbs. Palate: powerful, flavourful, easy to drink.

VAL DE VID RUEDA 2012 B
70% verdejo, 30% viura

90 Colour: bright straw. Nose: fresh, white flowers, ripe fruit. Palate: flavourful, fruity, good acidity, balanced.

VAL DE VID VERDEJO 2012 B
100% verdejo

90 Colour: bright straw. Nose: dried flowers, fragrant herbs, tropical fruit, citrus fruit. Palate: flavourful, fresh, fruity.

BODEGAS VALPINCIA

Ctra. de Melida, 3,5
47300 Peñafiel (Valladolid)
☎: +34 983 878 007 - Fax: +34 983 880 620
www.bodegasvalpincia.com
comunicacion@bodegasvalpincia.com

VALPINCIA VERDEJO VIURA 2012 B
50% verdejo, 50% viura

86 Colour: bright straw. Nose: fresh, fresh fruit, tropical fruit. Palate: flavourful, fruity, good acidity.

BODEGAS VERACRUZ S.L.

Juan A. Carmona, 1
47500 Nava del Rey (Valladolid)
☎: +34 983 850 136 - Fax: +34 983 850 761
www.bodegasveracruz.com
j.benito@bodegasveracruz.com

ERMITA VERACRUZ VERDEJO 2012 B
100% verdejo

92 Colour: bright straw. Nose: fresh, fresh fruit, white flowers, characterful, varietal, grassy. Palate: flavourful, fruity, good acidity, balanced.

BODEGAS VERDEAL

Nueva, 8
40200 Cuéllar (Segovia)
☎: +34 921 140 125 - Fax: +34 921 142 421
www.bodegasverdeal.com
info@bodegasverdeal.com

AYRE 2012 B
100% verdejo

88 Colour: bright straw. Nose: floral, tropical fruit, fragrant herbs. Palate: fresh, fruity, easy to drink.

VERDEAL 2012 B
100% verdejo

92 Colour: bright straw. Nose: fresh, fresh fruit, white flowers, wild herbs. Palate: flavourful, fruity, good acidity, balanced.

BODEGAS VETUS

Ctra. Toro a Salamanca, Km. 9,5
49800 Toro (Zamora)
☎: +34 945 609 086 - Fax: +34 980 056 012
grupoartevino.combodegasvetus.com
vetus@bodegasvetus.com

FLOR DE VETUS VERDEJO 2012 B
100% verdejo

89 Colour: bright straw. Nose: fresh, fresh fruit, white flowers, grassy. Palate: flavourful, fruity, good acidity, balanced.

BODEGAS VICENTE GANDÍA

Ctra. Cheste a Godelleta, s/n
46370 Chiva (Valencia)
☎: +34 962 524 242 - Fax: +34 962 524 243
www.vicentegandia.es
info@vicentegandia.com

NEBLA VERDEJO 2012 B
100% verdejo

88 Colour: bright straw. Nose: fragrant herbs, ripe fruit, dried flowers, medium intensity. Palate: powerful, flavourful, balanced.

BODEGAS VIÑA MAGNA

Jerónimo Roure, 45 Pol. Ind. Ingruinsa
46520 Puerto de Sagunto (Valencia)
☎: +34 962 691 090 - Fax: +34 962 690 963
www.vinamagna.es
direccioncomercial@vinamagna.es

DINASTÍA DE HELENIO 2012 B
100% verdejo

89 Colour: bright straw. Nose: fresh, white flowers, balsamic herbs, tropical fruit. Palate: flavourful, fruity, good acidity.

NAXUS 2012 B
100% verdejo

88 Colour: bright straw. Nose: expressive, candied fruit, tropical fruit. Palate: flavourful, fruity, good acidity.

OPTIMUS 2012 B
100% verdejo

87 Colour: bright straw. Nose: ripe fruit, citrus fruit, balsamic herbs, faded flowers. Palate: light-bodied, fresh, easy to drink.

THESEUS 2011 B

86 Colour: bright yellow. Nose: dried flowers, ripe fruit, fragrant herbs. Palate: rich, powerful, flavourful.

BODEGAS VIORE

Camino de la Moy, s/n
47491 La Seca (Valladolid)
☎: +34 941 454 050 - Fax: +34 941 454 529
www.bodegasriojanas.com
rrpp@bodegasriojanas.com

VIORE RUEDA 2012 B
70% verdejo, 30% viura

87 Colour: bright yellow. Nose: ripe fruit, floral, dried herbs. Palate: powerful, fruity, easy to drink.

VIORE VERDEJO 2012 B
100% verdejo

89 Colour: bright yellow. Nose: floral, ripe fruit, fragrant herbs, medium intensity. Palate: powerful, balsamic, flavourful, good acidity.

BODEGAS Y VIÑEDOS ÁNGEL LORENZO CACHAZO

Estación, 53
47220 Pozaldez (Valladolid)
☎: +34 983 822 481 - Fax: +34 983 822 012
www.martivilli.com
comercial@martivilli.com

LORENZO CACHAZO 2012 B
50% verdejo, 50% viura

87 Colour: bright straw. Nose: fresh, ripe fruit, tropical fruit. Palate: flavourful, fruity, good acidity.

MARTIVILLÍ 2011 BFB

88 Colour: bright straw. Nose: closed, candied fruit, smoky. Palate: fine bitter notes, spicy.

MARTIVILLÍ SAUVIGNON BLANC 2012 B
100% sauvignon blanc

87 Colour: bright straw. Nose: fresh fruit, white flowers, fragrant herbs. Palate: flavourful, fruity.

MARTIVILLÍ VERDEJO 2012 B
100% verdejo

91 Colour: bright straw. Nose: fresh, fresh fruit, white flowers, expressive. Palate: flavourful, fruity, good acidity, balanced.

BODEGAS Y VIÑEDOS MARTÍN BERDUGO

Ctra. de la Colonia, s/n
9400 Aranda de Duero (Burgos)
☎: +34 947 506 331 - Fax: +34 947 506 612
www.martinberdugo.com
bodega@martinberdugo.com

MARTÍN BERDUGO VERDEJO 2012 B
verdejo

88 Colour: bright straw. Nose: white flowers, dried herbs, ripe fruit. Palate: flavourful, fruity, good acidity, balanced.

BODEGAS Y VIÑEDOS MONTEABELLÓN

Calvario, s/n
9318 Nava de Roa (Burgos)
☎: +34 947 550 000 - Fax: +34 947 550 219
www.monteabellon.com
info@monteabellon.com

MONTEABELLÓN VERDEJO 2012 B
100% verdejo

90 Colour: bright straw. Nose: fresh, fresh fruit, white flowers, expressive. Palate: flavourful, fruity, good acidity, balanced.

BODEGAS Y VIÑEDOS NEO

Ctra. N-122, Km. 274,5
9391 Castrillo de la Vega (Burgos)
☎: +34 947 514 393 - Fax: +34 947 515 445
www.bodegasneo.com
info@bodegasconde.com

PRIMER MOTIVO VERDEJO 2012 B
100% verdejo

90 Colour: bright straw. Nose: medium intensity, fresh fruit, grassy. Palate: flavourful, fruity, fresh.

BODEGAS Y VIÑEDOS SHAYA

Ctra. Aldeanueva del Codonal s/n
40642 Aldeanueva del Codonal (Segovia)
☎: +34 968 435 022 - Fax: +34 968 716 051
www.orowines.com
info@orowines.com

ARINDO 2012 B
100% verdejo

88 Colour: bright straw. Nose: powerfull, tropical fruit, expressive. Palate: fruity, fresh, good acidity.

SHAYA 2012 B
100% verdejo

93 Colour: bright straw. Nose: fresh, fresh fruit, white flowers, expressive, mineral, grassy. Palate: flavourful, fruity, good acidity, balanced.

SHAYA HABIS 2010 BFB
100% verdejo

94 Colour: bright yellow. Nose: powerfull, ripe fruit, fragrant herbs, sweet spices, creamy oak. Palate: rich, smoky aftertaste, flavourful, good acidity, elegant.

BODEGAS Y VIÑEDOS TÁBULA

Ctra. de Valbuena, km. 2
47359 Olivares de Duero (Valladolid)
☎: +34 608 219 019 - Fax: +34 983 107 300
www.bodegastabula.es
armando@bodegastabula.es

DAMANA VERDEJO 2012 B
100% verdejo

88 Colour: bright straw. Nose: fresh, fresh fruit, floral. Palate: flavourful, fruity, good acidity, balanced.

CAMPOS DE SUEÑOS

Avda. Diagonal, 590, 5º 1ª
8021 (Barcelona)
☎: +34 660 445 464
www.vinergia.com
vinergia@vinergia.com

CAMPOS DE SUEÑOS 2012 B
100% verdejo

87 Colour: bright yellow. Nose: ripe fruit, dried flowers, fragrant herbs. Palate: rich, powerful, ripe fruit.

CAMPOS GÓTICOS

Parcela 622
9312 Anguix (Burgos)
☎: +34 979 165 121
www.camposgoticos.es
clientedirecto@camposgoticos.es

CAMPOS GÓTICOS VERDEJO VENDIMIA TARDÍA 2011 B
100% verdejo

90 Colour: bright yellow. Nose: ripe fruit, dried flowers, fragrant herbs, petrol notes. Palate: powerful, rich, flavourful.

CARREFOUR

Campezo, 16
28022 Madrid (Madrid)
☎: +34 902 202 000
www.carrefour.es

CAMINO DE LA DEHESA VERDEJO 2012 B
verdejo

87 Colour: yellow, greenish rim. Nose: balsamic herbs, ripe fruit. Palate: fruity, flavourful, varietal.

CAMINO DE LA DEHESA VIURA VERDEJO 2012 B
viura, verdejo

86 Colour: bright yellow. Nose: ripe fruit, dry nuts, dried flowers. Palate: fruity, flavourful, easy to drink, fine bitter notes.

COMENGE BODEGAS Y VIÑEDOS

Camino del Castillo, s/n
47316 Curiel de Duero (Valladolid)
☎: +34 983 880 363 - Fax: +34 983 880 717
www.comenge.com
admin@comenge.com

COMENGE VERDEJO 2012 B
100% verdejo

90 Colour: bright straw. Nose: white flowers, citrus fruit, dried herbs. Palate: flavourful, fruity, good acidity, balanced.

COMERCIAL GRUPO FREIXENET S.A.

Joan Sala, 2
8770 Sant Sadurní D'Anoia (Barcelona)
☎: +34 938 917 000 - Fax: +34 938 183 095
www.freixenet.es
freixenet@freixenet.es

ETCÉTERA 2011 B
verdejo, viura

85 Colour: bright straw. Nose: floral, ripe fruit, balsamic herbs. Palate: fresh, fruity, flavourful.

FRAY GERMÁN SAUVIGNON BLANC 2011 B
sauvignon blanc

84

FRAY GERMÁN VERDEJO 2011 B
verdejo, viura

88 Colour: bright straw. Nose: fresh, fresh fruit, grassy. Palate: flavourful, fruity, good acidity, balanced.

COMPAÑÍA DE VINOS MIGUEL MARTÍN

Ctra. Burgos - Portugal, Km. 101
47290 Cubillas de Santa María (Valladolid)
☎: +34 983 250 319 - Fax: +34 983 250 329
www.ciadevinos.com
exportacion@ciadevinos.com

CASA CASTILLA 2012 B
100% verdejo

87 Colour: bright straw. Nose: ripe fruit, floral, dried herbs. Palate: powerful, rich, flavourful, balanced.

DÒMINE 2012 B
10% sauvignon blanc, 90% verdejo

85 Colour: bright yellow. Nose: ripe fruit, dried flowers, dried herbs. Palate: powerful, rich, balsamic.

COMPAÑÍA DE VINOS TELMO RODRÍGUEZ

El Monte
1308 Lanciego (Álava)
☎: +34 945 628 315 - Fax: +34 945 628 314
www.telmorodriguez.com
contact@telmorodriguez.com

EL TRANSISTOR 2011 B
100% verdejo

94 Colour: bright yellow. Nose: powerfull, sweet spices, fragrant herbs. Palate: rich, smoky aftertaste, flavourful, fresh, good acidity.

CVNE - COMPAÑÍA VINÍCOLA DEL NORTE DE ESPAÑA

Barrio de la Estación, s/n
26200 Haro (La Rioja)
☎: +34 941 304 800 - Fax: +34 941 304 815
www.cvne.com
marketing@cvne.com

CUNE RUEDA 2012 B
verdejo

87 Colour: bright straw. Nose: fresh fruit, white flowers, balsamic herbs, medium intensity. Palate: flavourful, fruity, balanced.

MONOPOLE S. XXI 2012 B
verdejo

89 Colour: bright straw. Nose: fresh, white flowers, expressive, varietal. Palate: flavourful, fruity, good acidity, balanced.

DE ALBERTO

Ctra. de Valdestillas, 2
47231 Serrada (Valladolid)
☎: +34 983 559 107 - Fax: +34 983 559 084
www.dealberto.com
info@dealberto.com

DE ALBERTO VERDEJO 2012 B
100% verdejo

91 Colour: bright straw. Nose: fresh, fresh fruit, white flowers, fragrant herbs. Palate: flavourful, fruity, good acidity, balanced, elegant.

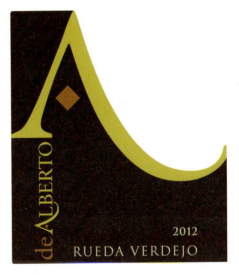

GUTI 2012 B
100% verdejo

88 Colour: bright straw. Nose: fresh, candied fruit, floral. Palate: flavourful, fruity, good acidity.

MONASTERIO DE PALAZUELOS SAUVIGNON BLANC 2012 B
100% sauvignon blanc

85 Colour: bright straw. Nose: fresh, fresh fruit, tropical fruit. Palate: flavourful, fruity, correct.

MONASTERIO DE PALAZUELOS VERDEJO 2012 B
100% verdejo

87 Colour: bright straw. Nose: fresh, ripe fruit, dried herbs, floral. Palate: flavourful, fruity, good acidity.

DIEZ SIGLOS DE VERDEJO

Ctra. Valladolid Km. 24,5
47231 Serrada (Valladolid)
☎: +34 983 559 910 - Fax: +34 983 559 020
www.diezsiglos.es
comercial1@diezsiglos.es

CANTO REAL 2012 B
verdejo

90 Colour: bright straw. Nose: fresh, white flowers, grassy. Palate: flavourful, fruity, good acidity, balanced.

CASTILLO DE LA MOTA 2012 B
verdejo

88 Colour: bright straw. Nose: floral, fragrant herbs, fruit expression. Palate: fine bitter notes, flavourful, easy to drink.

DIEZ SIGLOS 2011 BFB
verdejo

90 Colour: bright yellow. Nose: powerfull, ripe fruit, sweet spices, creamy oak, fragrant herbs. Palate: rich, smoky after-taste, flavourful, fresh, good acidity.

DIEZ SIGLOS 2012 B
verdejo

90 Colour: bright straw. Nose: fresh, fresh fruit, white flowers, characterful. Palate: flavourful, fruity, good acidity, balanced.

NEKORA 2012 B
verdejo

88 Colour: bright yellow. Nose: ripe fruit, dried flowers, fragrant herbs, expressive. Palate: flavourful, correct, fine bitter notes.

DISTRIBUCIONES B. IÑAKI NÚÑEZ

Ctra. de Ablitas a Ribafora, Km. 5
31523 Ablitas (Navarra)
☎: +34 948 386 210 - Fax: +34 629 354 190
www.pagodecirsus.com
bodegasin@pagodecirsus.com

SENDA DE LOS OLIVOS VENDIMIA SELECCIONADA VERDEJO 2012 B
100% verdejo

90 Colour: bright straw. Nose: citrus fruit, ripe fruit, floral, wild herbs. Palate: rich, fresh, fruity, balanced.

EMILIO GIMENO

Rueda (Valladolid)
☎: +34 686 487 007
emiliogimeno2011@yahoo.es

EMILIO GIMENO 2012 B
verdejo

86 Colour: bright straw. Nose: ripe fruit, floral, medium intensity. Palate: flavourful, fruity, correct.

ESTANCIA PIEDRA

Ctra. Toro a Salamanca (ZA-605) km. 8
49800 Toro (Zamora)
☎: +34 980 693 900 - Fax: +34 980 693 901
www.estanciapiedra.com
info@estanciapiedra.com

PIEDRA VERDEJO 2012 B
100% verdejo

89 Colour: bright straw. Nose: fresh, fresh fruit, white flowers, citrus fruit. Palate: flavourful, fruity, good acidity, balanced.

FINCA CASERÍO DE DUEÑAS

Ctra. Cl. 602, (Medina del Campo - Nava del Rey) km. 50,2
47465 Villaverde de Medina (Valladolid)
☎: +34 915 006 000 - Fax: +34 915 006 006
www.caserioduenas.es
rrpp@vina-mayor.es

VIÑA MAYOR 2011 BFB
100% verdejo

91 Colour: bright yellow. Nose: ripe fruit, sweet spices, creamy oak, fragrant herbs. Palate: rich, smoky aftertaste, flavourful, fresh.

VIÑA MAYOR VERDEJO 2012 B
100% verdejo

88 Colour: bright straw. Nose: fresh, fresh fruit, white flowers, expressive. Palate: flavourful, fruity, good acidity, balanced.

FINCA LAS CARABALLAS

Camino Velascálvaro, 2
47400 Medina del Campo (Valladolid)
☎: +34 650 986 185
www.lascaraballas.com
info@lascaraballas.com

FINCA LAS CARABALLAS 2012 B
verdejo

89 Colour: bright yellow. Nose: citrus fruit, ripe fruit, floral, fragrant herbs. Palate: powerful, rich, flavourful, balanced.

FINCA MONTEPEDROSO

Término La Morejona, s/n
47490 Rueda (Valladolid)
☎: +34 983 868 977 - Fax: +34 983 868 055
www.familiamartinezbujanda.com
acabezas@bujanda.com

FINCA MONTEPEDROSO VERDEJO 2012 B
100% verdejo

90 Colour: bright straw. Nose: fresh, fresh fruit, white flowers, expressive. Palate: flavourful, fruity, good acidity, balanced.

GRANDES BODEGAS

Ctra. de Sotillo de la Ribera, s/n
9311 La Horra (Burgos)
☎: +34 947 542 166 - Fax: +34 947 542 165
www.marquesdevelilla.com
bodega@marquesdevelilla.com

VIÑA DE MERCADO RUEDA VERDEJO 2012 B
verdejo

88 Colour: bright straw. Nose: fresh, fresh fruit, white flowers, expressive. Palate: flavourful, fruity, good acidity, balanced.

GRUPO YLLERA

A-6 Madrid - Coruña, Km. 173, 5
47490 Rueda (Valladolid)
☎: +34 983 868 097 - Fax: +34 983 868 177
www.grupoyllera.com
grupoyllera@grupoyllera.com

BOADA VERDEJO 2012 B
100% verdejo

87 Colour: bright straw. Nose: fresh, fresh fruit, white flowers, expressive. Palate: flavourful, fruity, good acidity.

BRACAMONTE VERDEJO 2012 B
100% verdejo

88 Colour: bright straw. Nose: fresh, fresh fruit, white flowers. Palate: flavourful, fruity, good acidity, balanced.

BRACAMONTE VERDEJO SUPERIOR 2012 B
100% verdejo

88 Colour: bright straw. Nose: fresh, fresh fruit, medium intensity. Palate: flavourful, fruity, good acidity, balanced.

CANTOSÁN BN
100% verdejo

82

CANTOSÁN BR
100% verdejo

85 Colour: bright straw. Nose: lees reduction notes, ripe fruit, dry nuts, medium intensity. Palate: correct, good acidity, fine bitter notes.

CANTOSÁN RESERVA ESPECIAL ESP
100% verdejo

86 Colour: bright straw. Nose: medium intensity, fresh fruit, dried herbs, floral. Palate: fresh, fruity, flavourful, balanced.

CANTOSÁN SS
100% verdejo

82

CANTOSÁN VERDEJO 2012 B
100% verdejo

89 Colour: bright straw. Nose: fresh, fresh fruit, white flowers, medium intensity. Palate: flavourful, fruity, good acidity, balanced.

TIERRA BUENA 2012 B
verdejo, viura, sauvignon blanc

89 Colour: bright straw. Nose: fresh, white flowers, ripe fruit. Palate: flavourful, fruity, good acidity, balanced.

VIÑA 65 2012 B
verdejo, viura, sauvignon blanc

89 Colour: bright straw. Nose: candied fruit, fruit expression, citrus fruit. Palate: light-bodied, fruity.

VIÑA GAREDO 2012 B
85% verdejo, 15% sauvignon blanc

90 Colour: bright straw. Nose: fresh, fresh fruit, white flowers, expressive. Palate: flavourful, fruity, good acidity, balanced.

YLLERA VERDEJO VENDIMIA NOCTURNA 2012 B
100% verdejo

90 Colour: bright straw. Nose: fresh, fresh fruit, white flowers, expressive, varietal. Palate: flavourful, fruity, good acidity, balanced.

J. GARCÍA CARRIÓN

Jorge Juan, 73
28009 (Madrid)
☎: +34 914 355 556 - Fax: +34 915 779 571
www.garciacarrion.com
jbrunet@jgc.es

ARRIBEÑO 2012 B
verdejo

88 Colour: bright straw. Nose: fresh fruit, white flowers, dried herbs. Palate: flavourful, fruity, good acidity.

CASTILLO DE AZA 2012 B
verdejo

87 Colour: bright straw. Nose: floral, candied fruit, tropical fruit. Palate: fresh, fruity, easy to drink.

MAYOR DE CASTILLA RUEDA 2012 B
verdejo, viura

87 Colour: bright straw. Nose: fresh fruit, dried flowers, balsamic herbs. Palate: flavourful, fruity, good acidity.

MAYOR DE CASTILLA VERDEJO 2012 B
verdejo

89 Colour: bright straw. Nose: fresh, fresh fruit, white flowers, expressive. Palate: flavourful, fruity, good acidity, balanced.

SOLAR DE LA VEGA 2012 B
verdejo, viura

85 Colour: bright straw. Nose: ripe fruit, floral, dried herbs. Palate: powerful, flavourful.

SOLAR DE LA VEGA VERDEJO 2012 B
verdejo

85 Colour: bright straw. Nose: faded flowers, dried herbs, ripe fruit. Palate: flavourful, fruity, good acidity.

JAVIER SANZ VITICULTOR

San Judas, 2
47491 La Seca (Valladolid)
☎: +34 983 816 669 - Fax: +34 983 816 639
www.bodegajaviersanz.com
info@bodegajaviersanz.com

JAVIER SANZ VITICULTOR 2011 BFB
100% verdejo

88 Colour: bright yellow. Nose: powerfull, ripe fruit, sweet spices, creamy oak, fragrant herbs. Palate: rich, smoky aftertaste, flavourful, fresh.

JAVIER SANZ VITICULTOR 2012 B
100% verdejo

92 Colour: bright straw. Nose: fresh, white flowers, ripe fruit, varietal. Palate: flavourful, fruity, good acidity, balanced.

JAVIER SANZ VITICULTOR SAUVIGNON 2012 B
100% sauvignon blanc

90 Colour: bright straw. Nose: fresh fruit, expressive, dried flowers. Palate: flavourful, fruity, good acidity, round.

JAVIER SANZ VITICULTOR V1863 2011 B
100% verdejo

91 Colour: bright straw. Nose: fresh, white flowers, fine lees, characterful. Palate: flavourful, fruity, good acidity, balanced.

ORDEN TERCERA VERDEJO B JOVEN
100% verdejo

89 Colour: bright straw. Nose: ripe fruit, floral, fragrant herbs. Palate: balanced, fine bitter notes, flavourful.

REY SANTO VERDEJO 2012 B
100% verdejo

90 Colour: bright straw. Nose: fresh, fresh fruit, white flowers, expressive. Palate: flavourful, fruity, good acidity, sweet.

VMARCORTA VERDEJO ATÍPICO 2012 B
verdejo malcorta

92 Colour: bright straw. Nose: fresh, fresh fruit, white flowers, fragrant herbs, mineral. Palate: flavourful, fruity, good acidity, balanced.

JUAN DAVID ALONSO RODRÍGUEZ

Juan de Juni, 4
47006 (Valladolid)
☎: +34 601 063 001
www.vinedosaequitas.es
vinedosaequitas@gmail.com

AÉQUITAS 2012 B
100% verdejo

87 Colour: bright yellow. Nose: candied fruit, fragrant herbs, floral. Palate: correct, balanced, easy to drink.

LEGARIS

Ctra. Peñafiel - Encinas de Esgueva, km. 2,5
47316 Curiel de Duero (Valladolid)
☎: +34 983 878 088 - Fax: +34 983 881 034
www.grupocodorniu.com
info@legaris.com

LEGARIS VERDEJO 2012 B
100% verdejo

89 Colour: bright straw. Nose: fresh, fresh fruit, white flowers, expressive. Palate: flavourful, fruity, good acidity, balanced.

LIBERALIA ENOLÓGICA

Camino del Palo, s/n
49800 Toro (Zamora)
☎: +34 980 692 571 - Fax: +34 980 692 571
www.liberalia.es
liberalia@liberalia.es

ENEBRAL 2012 B
100% verdejo

91 Colour: bright straw. Nose: fresh, fresh fruit, white flowers, characterful, powerfull, mineral. Palate: flavourful, fruity, good acidity, balanced.

LLANOS Y AYLLÓN S.L.

Rafael Alberti, 3
47490 Rueda (Valladolid)
☎: +34 627 400 316
www.verdejomaroto.es
ventas@verdejomaroto.es

MAROTO SELECCIÓN ESPECIAL 2012 B
100% verdejo

89 Colour: bright straw. Nose: fresh, fresh fruit, white flowers, expressive. Palate: flavourful, fruity, good acidity, balanced.

LOESS

El Monte, 7- Bajo
47195 Arroyo de la Encomienda (Valladolid)
☎: +34 983 664 898 - Fax: +34 983 406 579
www.loess.es
loess@loess.es

LOESS 2012 B
100% verdejo

88 Colour: bright straw. Nose: white flowers, fresh fruit, ripe fruit, citrus fruit. Palate: flavourful, light-bodied.

LOESS COLLECTION 2011 BFB
100% verdejo

92 Colour: bright yellow. Nose: powerfull, ripe fruit, sweet spices, fragrant herbs, expressive. Palate: rich, flavourful, fresh, good acidity, balanced.

LONG WINES

Avda. del Puente Cultural, 8 Bloque B Bajo 7
28702 San Sebastián de los Reyes (Madrid)
☎: +34 916 221 305 - Fax: +34 916 220 029
www.longwines.com
adm@longwines.com

CALAMAR VERDEJO 2012 B
100% verdejo

86 Colour: bright straw. Nose: white flowers, ripe fruit, fragrant herbs. Palate: flavourful, fruity, good acidity.

MAGICAL WINES

Pio Baroja, 21
28939 Arroyomolinos (Madrid)
☎: +34 916 096 025
www.magicalwines.com
info@magicalwines.com

ALAKAZAM VERDEJO 2012 B
100% verdejo

86 Colour: bright yellow. Nose: balanced, ripe fruit, tropical fruit. Palate: correct, easy to drink, ripe fruit.

MARQUÉS DE IRÚN

Nueva, 7-9
47491 La Seca (Valladolid)
☎: +34 913 080 420 - Fax: +34 913 080 458
www.marquesdeirun.com
marketing@caballero.es

MARQUÉS DE IRÚN VERDEJO 2012 B
100% verdejo

89 Colour: bright straw. Nose: citrus fruit, ripe fruit, medium intensity. Palate: good acidity, easy to drink, ripe fruit.

MARQUÉS DE LA CONCORDIA FAMILY OF WINES

Avenida Nava del Rey, 8
47490 Rueda (Valladolid)
☎: +34 913 878 612
www.the-haciendas.com
abasilio@unitedwineries.com

HACIENDA ZORITA VEGA DE LA REINA VERDEJO 2012 B
100% verdejo

90 Colour: bright yellow. Nose: citrus fruit, balsamic herbs, dried herbs, floral, jasmine. Palate: powerful, flavourful, rich, fruity, balsamic.

MENADE

Ctra. Rueda Nava del Rey, km. 1
47490 Rueda (Valladolid)
☎: +34 983 103 223 - Fax: +34 983 816 561
www.menade.es
info@menade.es

ANTONIO SANZ SAUVIGNON 2012 B
100% sauvignon blanc

92 Colour: bright straw. Nose: fresh, fresh fruit, white flowers, expressive, mineral, varietal. Palate: flavourful, fruity, good acidity, balanced.

ANTONIO SANZ VERDEJO 2012 B
100% verdejo

90 Colour: bright straw. Nose: ripe fruit, citrus fruit, white flowers, mineral. Palate: flavourful, fruity, ripe fruit.

MENADE SAUVIGNON BLANC 2012 B
100% sauvignon blanc

87 Colour: bright straw. Nose: candied fruit, tropical fruit, medium intensity. Palate: fine bitter notes, good acidity, fruity.

MENADE SAUVIGNON BLANC DULCE 2011 B
100% sauvignon blanc

88 Colour: bright straw. Nose: fresh, fresh fruit, white flowers, expressive. Palate: flavourful, fruity.

MENADE VERDEJO 2012 B
100% verdejo

90 Colour: bright straw. Nose: medium intensity, ripe fruit, white flowers. Palate: flavourful, fresh, fine bitter notes.

V3 2011 BFB
100% verdejo

93 Colour: bright yellow. Nose: powerfull, ripe fruit, sweet spices, creamy oak, fragrant herbs. Palate: rich, smoky aftertaste, flavourful, fresh, good acidity.

MIGUEL ARROYO IZQUIERDO

Calle Real, 34
47419 Puras (Valladolid)
☎: +34 983 626 095 - Fax: +34 983 626 095
info@arroyoizquierdo.com

DEMIMO 2012 B
verdejo

88 Colour: bright straw. Nose: ripe fruit, medium intensity, expressive. Palate: flavourful, fruity.

MIGUEL ARROYO IZQUIERDO 2010 T
tempranillo

90 Colour: cherry, garnet rim. Nose: ripe fruit, spicy, creamy oak, toasty, complex. Palate: powerful, flavourful, toasty, round tannins.

MIGUEL ARROYO IZQUIERDO 2012 B
verdejo

92 Colour: bright straw. Nose: fresh fruit, white flowers, varietal, ripe fruit. Palate: flavourful, fruity, good acidity, balanced.

MIGUEL TORRES S.A.

Miguel Torres i Carbó, 6
8720 Vilafranca del Penedès (Barcelona)
☎: +34 938 177 400 - Fax: +34 938 177 444
www.torres.es
mailadmin@torres.es

VERDEO 2012 B
100% verdejo

90 Colour: bright straw. Nose: fresh, fresh fruit, white flowers, expressive. Palate: flavourful, fruity, good acidity, balanced.

MIRAVINOS RUEDA

Plaza de Matute nº 12
28012 (Madrid)
☎: +34 609 119 248
www.miravinos.es
info@miravinos.es

INFRAGANTI 2012 B
verdejo

90 Colour: bright straw. Nose: ripe fruit, fresh fruit, grassy. Palate: flavourful, fruity, sweetness, light-bodied.

NAIPES 2012 B
verdejo

92 Colour: bright straw. Nose: mineral, ripe fruit, citrus fruit, grassy. Palate: flavourful, fruity, fresh, long, creamy.

NUEVOS VINOS

Alfafara, 12 Entlo.
3803 Alcoy (Alicante)
☎: +34 965 549 172 - Fax: +34 965 549 173
www.nuevosvinos.es
josecanto@nuevosvinos.es

PERLA MARIS VERDEJO 2012 B
100% verdejo

87 Colour: bright straw. Nose: fresh fruit, white flowers, expressive, citrus fruit. Palate: flavourful, fruity, good acidity.

OLID INTERNACIONAL

Juan García Hortelano, 21
47014 (Valladolid)
☎: +34 983 132 690
www.olidinternacional.com
olid@olidinternacional.com

983 2012 B
100% verdejo

88 Colour: bright straw. Nose: white flowers, ripe fruit. Palate: flavourful, good acidity, balanced.

PAGO TRASLAGARES

Autovía Noroeste (A-VI) km 166,4 Apdo. 507
47490 Rueda (Valladolid)
☎: +34 983 667 023
www.traslagares.com
export@traslagares.com

TRASLAGARES VERDEJO 2012 B
100% verdejo

88 Colour: bright straw. Nose: ripe fruit, tropical fruit. Palate: flavourful, powerful, sweetness.

PAGOS DEL REY S.L

Avda. Morejona, 6
47490 Rueda (Valladolid)
☎: +34 983 868 182 - Fax: +34 983 868 182
www.pagosdelrey.com
rueda@pagosdelrey.com

ANALIVIA RUEDA 2012 B
verdejo, viura

88 Colour: bright straw. Nose: fresh, expressive, ripe fruit, floral. Palate: flavourful, fruity, good acidity, balanced.

ANALIVIA SAUVIGNON BLANC 2012 B
sauvignon blanc

89 Colour: bright straw. Nose: fresh, white flowers, ripe fruit. Palate: flavourful, fruity aftestaste, good structure.

ANALIVIA VERDEJO 2012 B
verdejo

87 Colour: bright straw. Nose: faded flowers, dried herbs, ripe fruit. Palate: correct, fine bitter notes, flavourful.

BLUME RUEDA 2012 B
verdejo, viura

90 Colour: bright straw. Nose: fresh, fresh fruit, white flowers, grassy. Palate: flavourful, fruity, good acidity, balanced.

BLUME SAUVIGNON BLANC 2012 B
sauvignon blanc

90 Colour: bright straw. Nose: fresh, fresh fruit, white flowers, expressive. Palate: flavourful, fruity, good acidity, balanced.

BLUME VERDEJO 2012 B
verdejo

89 Colour: bright straw. Nose: fresh, fresh fruit, white flowers, varietal. Palate: flavourful, fruity, good acidity, balanced.

PALACIO DE BORNOS

Ctra. Madrid - Coruña, km. 170,6
47490 Rueda (Valladolid)
☎: +34 983 868 116 - Fax: +34 983 868 432
www.palaciodeborno.com
info@taninia.com

PALACIO DE BORNOS SAUVIGNON BLANC 2012 B
sauvignon blanc

88 Colour: bright straw. Nose: fresh, ripe fruit, fragrant herbs. Palate: flavourful, fruity, good acidity, balanced.

PALACIO DE BORNOS SEMIDULCE 2012 B
sauvignon blanc

84

PALACIO DE BORNOS VERDEJO VENDIMIA SELECCIONADA 2010 BFB
verdejo

92 Colour: bright golden. Nose: powerfull, characterful, ripe fruit, toasty. Palate: flavourful, fine bitter notes, good acidity.

PALACIOS DE BORNOS 2012 SS
verdejo

88 Colour: bright straw. Nose: candied fruit, citrus fruit. Palate: sweetness, flavourful.

PALACIOS DE BORNOS BN
verdejo

84

PALACIOS DE BORNOS LA CAPRICHOSA 2011 B
verdejo

91 Colour: bright straw. Nose: mineral, dried herbs, ripe fruit, citrus fruit. Palate: flavourful, fruity, fresh.

PALACIOS DE BORNOS ROSADO ESP
tempranillo

84

PALACIOS DE BORNOS SC BR
verdejo

84

PALACIOS DE BORNOS VERDEJO 2011 BFB
verdejo

89 Colour: bright yellow. Nose: powerfull, ripe fruit, sweet spices, fragrant herbs. Palate: rich, smoky aftertaste, flavourful, fresh, good acidity.

PALACIOS DE BORNOS VERDEJO 2012 B
verdejo

88 Colour: bright straw. Nose: white flowers, medium intensity, ripe fruit. Palate: flavourful, fruity, good acidity, balanced.

PALACIO DE VILLACHICA

Ctra. Nacional 122, Km. 433,2
49800 Toro (Zamora)
☎: +34 609 144 711 - Fax: +34 983 381 356
www.palaciodevillachica.com
bodegavillachica@yahoo.es

ABSIDE VERDEJO 2012 B
100% verdejo

88 Colour: bright straw. Nose: white flowers, fragrant herbs, tropical fruit. Palate: flavourful, fruity, easy to drink.

PREDIO DE VASCARLÓN

Ctra. Rueda, s/n
47491 La Seca (Valladolid)
☎: +34 983 816 325 - Fax: +34 983 816 326
www.prediodevascarlon.com
vascarlon@prediodevascarlon.com

ATELIER VERDEJO 2012 B
100% verdejo

90 Colour: bright straw. Nose: fresh, fresh fruit, white flowers, fragrant herbs. Palate: flavourful, fruity, good acidity, fine bitter notes.

TARDEVIENES 2012 B
50% verdejo, 50% viura

86 Colour: bright yellow. Nose: ripe fruit, dried herbs, balsamic herbs. Palate: powerful, flavourful.

RED BOTTLE INTERNATIONAL

Rosales, 6
9400 Aranda de Duero (Burgos)
☎: +34 947 515 884 - Fax: +34 947 515 886
www.redbottleint.com
rbi@redbottleint.com

PLUMA BLANCA 2012 B
100% verdejo

88 Colour: bright straw. Nose: ripe fruit, white flowers. Palate: flavourful, light-bodied, fresh, fruity.

RODRÍGUEZ SANZO

Manuel Azaña, 9
47014 (Valladolid)
☎: +34 983 150 150 - Fax: +34 983 150 151
www.rodriguezsanzo.com
comunicacion@valsanzo.com

DADOS VERDEJO 2012 B
100% verdejo

91 Colour: bright yellow. Nose: powerfull, ripe fruit, sweet spices, creamy oak, wild herbs. Palate: rich, smoky aftertaste, flavourful, fresh, good acidity.

VIÑA SANZO SOBRE LÍAS 2010 B
100% verdejo

92 Colour: bright yellow. Nose: citrus fruit, ripe fruit, balsamic herbs, spicy, floral, expressive. Palate: rich, flavourful, balanced, spicy, long.

VIÑA SANZO VERDEJO 2012 B
100% verdejo

90 Colour: bright straw. Nose: white flowers, fruit expression, fragrant herbs. Palate: fresh, fruity, easy to drink.

SÁNCHEZ ROMATE

Lealas, 26
11404 Jerez de la Frontera (Cádiz)
☎: +34 956 182 212 - Fax: +34 956 185 276
www.romate.com
romate@romate.com

MOMO 2012 B
80% verdejo, 20% viura

88 Colour: bright straw. Nose: fresh, fresh fruit, white flowers. Palate: flavourful, fruity, good acidity, balanced.

SOTO Y MANRIQUE

Arandano, 14
47008 (Valladolid)
☎: +34 626 290 408
info@sotoymanriquevo.com

TINITA VERDEJO 2012 B
verdejo

88 Colour: bright yellow. Nose: ripe fruit, citrus fruit, balsamic herbs, grassy. Palate: powerful, rich, fruity, flavourful.

THE GRAND WINES

Razón social : Ramón y Cajal 7, 1ºA
1007 Vitoria (Alava)
☎: +34 945 158 282 - Fax: +34 945 158 283
www.thegrandwines.com

ROLLAND GALARRETA 2012 B
verdejo

93 Colour: bright yellow. Nose: citrus fruit, balsamic herbs, dried herbs, white flowers, expressive. Palate: rich, powerful, flavourful, spicy, long.

TOMÁS POSTIGO

Estación, 12
47300 Peñafiel (Valladolid)
☎: +34 983 873 019 - Fax: +34 983 880 258
www.tomaspostigo.es
administracion@tomaspostigo.es

TOMÁS POSTIGO 2011 BFB
100% verdejo

90 Colour: bright yellow. Nose: powerfull, ripe fruit, citrus fruit, roasted coffee. Palate: rich, smoky aftertaste, flavourful, fresh, good acidity.

TRESCATORCE

Sayago, 6 1ºA
47008 (Valladolid)
☎: +34 667 467 321
www.bodegastrescatorce.com
info@bodegastrescatorce.com

TRESCATORCE 2012 B
verdejo

89 Colour: bright straw. Nose: fresh, fresh fruit, white flowers. Palate: flavourful, fruity, good acidity, easy to drink.

UNESDI DISTRIBUCIONES S.A

Aurora, 11
11500 El Puerto de Santa María (Cádiz)
☎: +34 956 541 329
www.unesdi.com
info@unesdi.com

PALOMO COJO 2012 B
100% verdejo

86 Colour: bright straw. Nose: dried flowers, ripe fruit, dried herbs. Palate: correct, flavourful, easy to drink.

UNZU PROPIEDAD

Barón de la Torre, 4
31592 Cientruénigo (Navarra)
☎: +34 948 811 000 - Fax: +34 948 811 407
www.unzupropiedad.com
info@unzupropiedad.com

LABORES DE UNZU VERDEJO 2012 B
verdejo

93 Colour: bright straw. Nose: fresh, fresh fruit, expressive, white flowers, grassy. Palate: flavourful, fruity, good acidity, balanced.

UVAS FELICES

Agullers, 7
8003 Barcelona (Barcelona)
☎: +34 902 327 777
www.vilaviniteca.es

EL PERRO VERDE 2012 B

90 Colour: bright yellow, greenish rim. Nose: balanced, ripe fruit, floral, wild herbs. Palate: flavourful, fruity, long.

FENOMENAL 2012 B

88 Colour: bright straw. Nose: fresh fruit, floral, white flowers, citrus fruit. Palate: flavourful, good acidity, fine bitter notes.

VEGA DEL PAS

Ctra. CL-602, Kilómetro 48
47465 Villaverde de Medina (Valladolid)
☎: +34 983 831 884 - Fax: +34 983 831 857
www.vegadelpas.com
comunicacion@vegadelpas.com

VEGA DEL PAS RUEDA 2012 B
50% verdejo, 30% viura, 20% sauvignon blanc

88 Colour: bright straw. Nose: fresh, fresh fruit, dried flowers. Palate: flavourful, fruity, good acidity, balanced, fine bitter notes.

VEGA DEL PAS RUEDA VERDEJO 2012 B
85% verdejo, 15% sauvignon blanc

86 Colour: bright straw. Nose: fresh, expressive, dried flowers, ripe fruit. Palate: flavourful, fruity, good acidity, balanced.

VEGA DEL PAS SAUVIGNON BLANC 2012 B
sauvignon blanc

87 Colour: bright straw. Nose: fresh, fresh fruit, white flowers. Palate: flavourful, fruity, balanced.

VEGA DEL PAS VERDEJO 2012 B
100% verdejo

88 Colour: bright straw. Nose: medium intensity, fresh fruit, ripe fruit, grassy. Palate: flavourful, fruity, fresh.

VEGA DEO

Ctra. CL-602, Kilómetro 48
47465 Villaverde de Medina (Valladolid)
☎: +34 983 831 884 - Fax: +34 983 831 857
www.vinosvegadeo.com
comunicacion@vinosvegadeo.com

VEGA DEO RUEDA 2012 B
50% verdejo, 30% viura, 20% sauvignon blanc

87 Colour: bright straw. Nose: candied fruit, complex, citrus fruit, tropical fruit. Palate: flavourful, light-bodied.

VEGA DEO RUEDA VERDEJO 2012 B
85% verdejo, 15% sauvignon blanc

88 Colour: bright straw. Nose: fresh, fresh fruit, white flowers, expressive. Palate: flavourful, fruity, good acidity, balanced.

VEGA DEO SAUVIGNON BLANC 2012 B
100% sauvignon blanc

86 Colour: bright straw. Nose: fresh fruit, white flowers, grassy. Palate: flavourful, fruity, good acidity.

VEGA DEO VERDEJO 2012 B
100% verdejo

87 Colour: bright straw. Nose: fresh, fresh fruit, dried herbs. Palate: flavourful, fruity, good acidity.

VEGA LACUESTA, S.L. (BELLORI VINOS)

Cobalto, 67
47012 (Valladolid)
☎: +34 983 314 522 - Fax: +34 983 314 522
www.bellorivinos.com
administracin@bellorivinos.com

BELLORI 2012 B
100% verdejo

90 Colour: bright straw. Nose: fresh, fresh fruit, white flowers, varietal. Palate: flavourful, fruity, good acidity, balanced.

VICENTE SANZ

Las Flores, 5
47240 Valdestillas (Valladolid)
☎: +34 610 525 188 - Fax: +34 983 551 197
www.bodegasvicentesanz.com
bodega@bodegasvicentesanz.com

CAÑADAREAL 2012 B JOVEN
100% verdejo

90 Colour: bright straw. Nose: fresh, fresh fruit, dried flowers, dried herbs. Palate: flavourful, fruity, good acidity, balanced.

VICARAL RUEDA VERDEJO 2012 B
100% verdejo

84

VINNICO

Muela, 16
3730 Jávea (Alicante)
☎: +34 965 791 967 - Fax: +34 966 461 471
www.vinnico.com
info@vinnico.com

AVENTINO VERDEJO 2012 B
verdejo

86 Colour: bright straw. Nose: fresh, fresh fruit, white flowers, expressive. Palate: flavourful, fruity, good acidity, balanced.

VIÑA ALTAMAR VERDEJO 2012 B
verdejo

83

VINOS JOC - JORDI OLIVER CONTI

Mas Marti
17467 Sant Mori (Girona)
☎: +34 607 222 002
www.vinojoc.com
info@vinojoc.com

JOC DE JORDI OLIVER 2012 B
verdejo

91 Colour: bright straw. Nose: fresh fruit, white flowers, varietal, characterful, powerfull. Palate: flavourful, fruity, good acidity, balanced.

VINOS SANZ

Ctra. Madrid - La Coruña, Km. 170,5
47490 Rueda (Valladolid)
☎: +34 983 868 100 - Fax: +34 983 868 117
www.vinossanz.com
vinossanz@vinossanz.com

FINCA LA COLINA SAUVIGNON BLANC 2012 B
100% sauvignon blanc

92 Colour: bright straw. Nose: fresh, fresh fruit, expressive, white flowers, powerfull, varietal. Palate: flavourful, fruity, good acidity, balanced.

FINCA LA COLINA VERDEJO CIEN X CIEN 2012 B
100% verdejo

92 Colour: bright straw. Nose: fresh, fresh fruit, white flowers, expressive, grassy, varietal. Palate: flavourful, fruity, good acidity, balanced.

SANZ CLÁSICO 2012 B
70% verdejo, 30% viura

89 Colour: bright straw. Nose: fresh fruit, white flowers, dried herbs, ripe fruit. Palate: flavourful, fruity, good acidity, balanced.

SANZ SAUVIGNON BLANC 2012 B
100% sauvignon blanc

90 Colour: bright straw. Nose: fresh, fresh fruit, white flowers. Palate: flavourful, fruity, good acidity, balanced.

SANZ VERDEJO 2012 B
100% verdejo

91 Colour: bright straw. Nose: fresh, fresh fruit, dried herbs. Palate: flavourful, fruity, good acidity, easy to drink.

VINOS TERRIBLES

Avda. Menendez Pelayo 13 B
28009 (Madrid)
☎: +34 914 092 131
esther@vinosterribles.com

TERRIBLE 2012 B
100% verdejo

90 Colour: bright straw. Nose: dried flowers, fragrant herbs, ripe fruit, tropical fruit. Palate: rich, fruity, complex, balanced.

TERRIBLE 2012 T BARRICA
100% tempranillo

88 Colour: cherry, garnet rim. Nose: red berry notes, ripe fruit, balsamic herbs, creamy oak. Palate: powerful, flavourful, spicy.

VIÑA DEL SOPIÉ

La Seca
47491 La Seca (Valladolid)
☎: +34 948 645 008 - Fax: +34 948 645 166
www.familiabelasco.com
info@familiabelasco.com

VIÑA DEL SOPIÉ 2012 B
verdejo, viura

85 Colour: bright straw. Nose: white flowers, ripe fruit. Palate: flavourful, good acidity.

VIÑA DEL SOPIÉ VERDEJO 2012 B
100% verdejo

89 Colour: bright straw. Nose: ripe fruit, floral, fragrant herbs. Palate: flavourful, fruity, fruity aftestaste.

VIÑEDO VALLELADO SÁNCHEZ

Fausto Herrero, 4 3ºB
47420 Iscar (Valladolid)
☎: +34 679 797 002
www.campogrande.com.es
info@campogrande.com.es

CAMPO GRANDE 2012 B
verdejo

88 Colour: bright yellow, greenish rim. Nose: balsamic herbs, citrus fruit, ripe fruit, dried flowers. Palate: rich, flavourful, balanced.

VIÑEDOS DE NIEVA

Camino Real, s/n
40447 Nieva (Segovia)
☎: +34 921 504 628 - Fax: +34 921 595 409
www.vinedosdenieva.com
info@vinedosdenieva.com

BLANCO NIEVA 2012 B
100% verdejo

91 Colour: bright straw. Nose: white flowers, expressive, mineral, ripe fruit. Palate: flavourful, fruity, good acidity, balanced.

BLANCO NIEVA PIE FRANCO 2009 BFB
100% verdejo

91 Colour: bright yellow. Nose: powerfull, ripe fruit, sweet spices, creamy oak. Palate: rich, smoky aftertaste, flavourful, fresh, good acidity.

BLANCO NIEVA PIE FRANCO 2012 B
100% verdejo

93 Colour: bright straw. Nose: fresh, fresh fruit, white flowers, characterful, earthy notes. Palate: flavourful, fruity, good acidity, balanced.

BLANCO NIEVA SAUVIGNON 2012 B
sauvignon blanc

90 Colour: bright straw. Nose: fresh, white flowers, varietal, tropical fruit. Palate: flavourful, fruity, good acidity, balanced.

LOS NAVALES VERDEJO 2012 B
100% verdejo

88 Colour: bright straw. Nose: fresh, white flowers, ripe fruit. Palate: flavourful, fruity, good acidity, balanced.

VIÑEDOS SINGULARES

Cuzco, 26 - 28, Nave 8
8030 (Barcelona)
☎: +34 609 168 191 - Fax: +34 934 807 076
www.vinedossingulares.com
info@vinedossingulares.com

AFORTUNADO 2012 B
verdejo

88 Colour: bright yellow. Nose: ripe fruit, tropical fruit, balsamic herbs, floral. Palate: fresh, fruity, easy to drink.

DO SOMONTANO / D.O.P.

Consejo Regulador

DO Boundary

LOCATION:

In the province of Huesca, around the town of Barbastro. The region comprises 43 municipal districts, mainly centred round the region of Somontano and the rest of the neighbouring regions of Ribagorza and Monegros.

CLIMATE:

Characterised by cold winters and hot summers, with sharp contrasts in temperature at the end of spring and autumn. The average annual rainfall is 500 mm, although the rains are scarcer in the south and east

SOIL:

The soil is mainly brownish limestone, not very fertile, with a good level of limestone and good permeability.

GRAPE VARIETIES:

WHITE: *Macabeo, Garnacha Blanca, Alcañón, Chardonnay, Riesling, Sauvignon Blanc* and *Gewürztraminer.*
RED: *Tempranillo, Garnacha Tinta, Cabernet Sauvignon, Merlot, Moristel, Parraleta, Pinot Noir* and *Syrah.*

FIGURES:

Vineyard surface: 4.310– **Wine-Growers:** 460 – **Wineries:** 30 – **2012 Harvest rating:** Very Good – **Production:** 10.342.400 litres – **Market percentages:** 67% domestic. 33% export

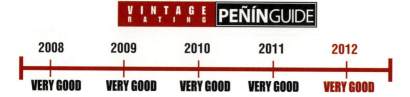

2008	2009	2010	2011	2012
VERY GOOD	VERY GOOD	VERY GOOD	VERY GOOD	VERY GOOD

CONSEJO REGULADOR
Avda. de la Merced, 64 - 22300 Barbastro (Huesca) ☎: +34 974 313 031 - Fax: +34 974 315 132
erio@dosomontano.com   www.dosomontano.com

ALIANZA DE GARAPITEROS

Plaza España, 6 Planta 1ª
50001 (Zaragoza)
☎: +34 976 094 033 - Fax: +34 976 094 033
www.alianzadegarapiteros.es
info@alianzadegarapiteros.es

GLÁRIMA 2011 T
45% tempranillo, 35% merlot, 20% syrah

89 Colour: cherry, purple rim. Nose: candied fruit, sweet spices, creamy oak, cocoa bean. Palate: flavourful, good acidity, toasty.

GLÁRIMA 2012 B
45% chardonnay, 35% sauvignon blanc, 20% gewürztraminer

90 Colour: bright yellow. Nose: powerfull, ripe fruit, dried herbs, spicy, faded flowers. Palate: rich, flavourful, fresh.

GLÁRIMA 2012 B
45% chardonnay, 35% sauvignon blanc, 20% gewürztraminer

90 Colour: bright yellow. Nose: candied fruit, sweet spices, balanced. Palate: ripe fruit, long, rich, flavourful.

BAL D'ISABENA BODEGAS

Ctra. A-1605, Km. 11,2
22587 Laguarres (Huesca)
☎: +34 605 785 178 - Fax: +34 974 310 151
www.baldisabena.com
info@baldisabena.com

COJÓN DE GATO 2011 T ROBLE
syrah, merlot, otras

89 Colour: bright cherry, garnet rim. Nose: ripe fruit, wild herbs, spicy, toasty. Palate: correct, round tannins.

COJÓN DE GATO 2012 B
gewürztraminer, chardonnay

88 Colour: bright straw. Nose: white flowers, ripe fruit, dried flowers. Palate: flavourful, fruity, good acidity.

GARNACHA DE BAL D'ISABENA 2011 T
garnacha

88 Colour: bright cherry. Nose: ripe fruit, spicy, creamy oak. Palate: flavourful, fruity, toasty.

IXEIA 2012 B
chardonnay

85 Colour: bright straw. Nose: floral, fragrant herbs, ripe fruit. Palate: powerful, flavourful, fruity.

IXEIA 2012 RD
merlot, garnacha

86 Colour: rose, purple rim. Nose: red berry notes, ripe fruit, dried flowers, fragrant herbs. Palate: powerful, flavourful, correct.

IXEIA 2012 T
cabernet sauvignon, merlot, tempranillo

86 Colour: cherry, purple rim. Nose: medium intensity, wild herbs, ripe fruit. Palate: fruity, easy to drink, good finish.

MORISTEL DE BAL D'ISABENA 2011 T
moristel

85 Colour: bright cherry, garnet rim. Nose: powerfull, slightly evolved, wild herbs. Palate: flavourful, correct.

REIS D'ISABENA 2009 T
merlot, cabernet sauvignon

89 Colour: very deep cherry, garnet rim. Nose: balanced, ripe fruit, wild herbs, spicy. Palate: balanced, good acidity, long.

BATAN DE SALAS DE BEROZ

Paraje El Ariño N-123, km. 5
22300 Barbastro (Huesca)
☎: +34 974 316 217 - Fax: +34 974 310 973
www.deberoz.es
bodega@deberoz.es

DE BEROZ CRIANZA ESPECIAL 2008 T
cabernet sauvignon, merlot, syrah

89 Colour: deep cherry, garnet rim. Nose: balanced, ripe fruit, cocoa bean, sweet spices. Palate: spicy, ripe fruit, long.

DE BEROZ ESENCIA DE BLANCOS 2012 B
chardonnay, gewürztraminer

88 Colour: bright straw. Nose: ripe fruit, floral, dried herbs, medium intensity. Palate: fresh, fruity, flavourful.

DE BEROZ ESENCIA DE GEWÜRZTRAMINER 2012 B
gewürztraminer

87 Colour: bright straw. Nose: white flowers, ripe fruit, fragrant herbs. Palate: powerful, rich, fruity, flavourful.

DE BEROZ ESENCIA DE TINTOS 2012 RD
cabernet sauvignon, merlot, syrah, garnacha

89 Colour: rose, purple rim. Nose: powerfull, ripe fruit, red berry notes, floral, expressive. Palate: powerful, fruity, flavourful.

DE BEROZ NUESTRO ROBLE 2010 T
40% merlot, 40% cabernet sauvignon, 10% tempranillo, 10% moristel

88 Colour: deep cherry, garnet rim. Nose: balanced, spicy, ripe fruit. Palate: fruity, spicy, good acidity, round tannins.

DE BEROZ RESERVA FAMILIA 2007 T
cabernet sauvignon, merlot, syrah, tempranillo

90 Colour: cherry, garnet rim. Nose: ripe fruit, scrubland, spicy, cigar, fine reductive notes. Palate: powerful, flavourful, toasty.

LAR DE BEROZ 2007 T
cabernet sauvignon, syrah, garnacha, moristel

90 Colour: cherry, garnet rim. Nose: ripe fruit, spicy, creamy oak, fine reductive notes. Palate: powerful, flavourful, balanced.

BLECUA

Ctra. Naval, Km. 3,7
22300 Barbastro (Huesca)
☎: +34 974 302 216 - Fax: +34 974 302 098
www.bodegablecua.com
marketing@vinasdelvero.es

BLECUA 2007 TR
garnacha, tempranillo, merlot, cabernet sauvignon

94 Colour: very deep cherry, garnet rim. Nose: elegant, balanced, ripe fruit, sweet spices. Palate: good structure, complex, round tannins.

BLECUA 2008 TR
garnacha, tempranillo, merlot, cabernet sauvignon

94 Colour: cherry, garnet rim. Nose: ripe fruit, spicy, creamy oak, toasty, complex. Palate: powerful, flavourful, toasty, round tannins, balanced, elegant.

BODEGA ALDAHARA

Ctra. Barbastro, 10
22423 Estadilla (Huesca)
☎: +34 974 305 236 - Fax: +34 974 305 236
www.aldahara.es
bodega@aldahara.es

ALDAHARA 2012 RD
merlot

84

ALDAHARA 2012 T
tempranillo, merlot, syrah

86 Colour: cherry, garnet rim. Nose: medium intensity, ripe fruit. Palate: flavourful, fruity, long.

ALDAHARA RASÉ 2010 T ROBLE
syrah

85 Colour: cherry, garnet rim. Nose: sweet spices, ripe fruit, creamy oak, floral. Palate: powerful, flavourful, toasty.

ALDAHARA SELECCIÓN 2010 B
100% chardonnay

85 Colour: bright straw. Nose: fresh, white flowers, dried herbs. Palate: flavourful, fruity, good acidity, balanced.

ALDAHARA TEMPRANILLO 2010 T
tempranillo

86 Colour: cherry, garnet rim. Nose: medium intensity, grassy, ripe fruit, sweet spices. Palate: flavourful, long.

VAL D'ALFERCHE 2010 TC
50% merlot, 40% cabernet sauvignon, 10% syrah

84

VAL D'ALFERCHE CHARDONNAY 2012 B
100% chardonnay

84

VAL D'ALFERCHE SYRAH 2010 T
100% syrah

88 Colour: cherry, garnet rim. Nose: ripe fruit, creamy oak, toasty, violet drops. Palate: powerful, flavourful, toasty.

BODEGA MIPANAS

Ctra. 138, Km. 14,600
22390 El Grado (Huesca)
☎: +34 682 688 521
www.bodegamipanas.com
info@bodegamipanas.com

MIPANAS 2009 TC
cabernet sauvignon, merlot, syrah, parraleta, garnacha

86 Colour: pale ruby, brick rim edge. Nose: spicy, fine reductive notes, wet leather, aged wood nuances, fruit liqueur notes. Palate: spicy, long, flavourful.

BODEGA OTTO BESTUÉ

Ctra. A-138, Km. 0,5
22312 Enate (Huesca)
☎: +34 974 305 157 - Fax: +34 974 305 157
www.bodega-ottobestue.com
info@bodega-ottobestue.com

OTTO BESTUÉ CABERNET SAUVIGNON TEMPRANILLO 2012 RD
50% cabernet sauvignon, 50% tempranillo

86 Colour: rose, purple rim. Nose: powerfull, ripe fruit, red berry notes, floral. Palate: powerful, fruity, sweetness.

OTTO BESTUÉ CHARDONNAY 2012 B
chardonnay

84

OTTO BESTUÉ FINCA RABLEROS 2009 T
50% cabernet sauvignon, 50% tempranillo

87 Colour: cherry, garnet rim. Nose: ripe fruit, spicy, creamy oak, balsamic herbs. Palate: powerful, flavourful, spicy, long.

OTTO BESTUÉ FINCA SANTA SABINA 2009 TC
80% cabernet sauvignon, 20% tempranillo

88 Colour: cherry, garnet rim. Nose: ripe fruit, spicy, creamy oak, toasty, complex. Palate: powerful, flavourful, toasty, round tannins.

BODEGA PIRINEOS

Ctra. Barbastro - Naval, Km. 3,5
22300 Barbastro (Huesca)
☎: +34 974 311 289 - Fax: +34 974 306 688
www.bodegapirineos.com
info@bodegapirineos.com

ALQUÉZAR 2012 RD
tempranillo, garnacha

87 Colour: light cherry, bright. Nose: red berry notes, ripe fruit, medium intensity. Palate: balanced, fine bitter notes, correct, easy to drink.

PIRINEOS MARBORÉ 2006 T
tempranillo, cabernet sauvignon, merlot, moristel, parraleta

90 Colour: cherry, garnet rim. Nose: ripe fruit, balsamic herbs, spicy, creamy oak, fine reductive notes. Palate: correct, complex, flavourful, spicy.

PIRINEOS MESACHE 2012 B
chardonnay, macabeo, gewürztraminer

88 Colour: bright yellow. Nose: ripe fruit, citrus fruit, floral, fragrant herbs. Palate: fresh, fruity, flavourful, balanced.

PIRINEOS MESACHE 2012 T
cabernet sauvignon, syrah, moristel, garnacha

88 Colour: cherry, purple rim. Nose: red berry notes, ripe fruit, floral, fragrant herbs. Palate: fresh, fruity, flavourful, easy to drink.

PIRINEOS SELECCIÓN 2012 RD
merlot, cabernet sauvignon

89 Colour: rose, purple rim. Nose: powerfull, ripe fruit, red berry notes, floral, expressive. Palate: powerful, fruity, fresh.

PIRINEOS SELECCIÓN GEWÜRZTRAMINER 2012 B
gewürztraminer

90 Colour: bright straw. Nose: fresh, fresh fruit, white flowers. Palate: flavourful, fruity, good acidity.

PIRINEOS SELECCIÓN MERLOT CABERNET 2008 TC
merlot, cabernet sauvignon

87 Colour: very deep cherry, garnet rim. Nose: powerfull, scrubland, spicy. Palate: ripe fruit, round tannins.

SEÑORÍO DE LAZÁN 2007 TR
tempranillo, cabernet sauvignon, moristel

89 Colour: cherry, garnet rim. Nose: ripe fruit, fragrant herbs, spicy, fine reductive notes. Palate: flavourful, spicy, long, harsh oak tannins.

BODEGAS ABINASA

Ctra. N 240, Km. 180
22124 Lascellas (Huesca)
☎: +34 974 319 156 - Fax: +34 974 319 156
www.bodegasabinasa.com
info@bodegasabinasa.com

ANA 2004 TR

87 Colour: pale ruby, brick rim edge. Nose: spicy, fine reductive notes, wet leather, aged wood nuances, fruit liqueur notes. Palate: spicy, fine tannins, long.

ANA 2010 T ROBLE
merlot, cabernet sauvignon

86 Colour: bright cherry, garnet rim. Nose: sweet spices, ripe fruit. Palate: flavourful, easy to drink.

ANA 2010 TC
merlot, cabernet sauvignon

84

BODEGAS ALODIA

Ctra. de Colungo, s/n
22147 Adahuesca (Huesca)
☎: +34 974 318 265
www.alodia.es
info@alodia.es

ALODIA ALCAÑÓN 2012 B
100% alcañon

87 Colour: bright straw. Nose: fresh, fresh fruit, white flowers, expressive. Palate: flavourful, fruity, good acidity.

ALODIA LUXURIA BN
macabeo, chardonnay

83

ALODIA LUXURIA S/C BN
garnacha, cabernet sauvignon

84

ALODIA PARRALETA 2009 T
parraleta

88 Colour: cherry, garnet rim. Nose: ripe fruit, wet leather, damp earth, expressive. Palate: powerful, flavourful, complex, balanced.

ALODIA SYRAH 2010 T
100% syrah

86 Colour: deep cherry, garnet rim. Nose: dark chocolate, ripe fruit, medium intensity. Palate: spicy, correct, easy to drink, round tannins.

ORACHE 2010 T
cabernet sauvignon, garnacha

85 Colour: cherry, garnet rim. Nose: ripe fruit, spicy, creamy oak, fine reductive notes. Palate: powerful, flavourful, toasty.

BODEGAS BALLABRIGA

Ctra. de Cregenzán, Km. 3
22300 Barbastro (Huesca)
☎: +34 974 310 216 - Fax: +34 974 306 163
www.bodegasballabriga.com
info@bodegasballabriga.com

AUCTOR SELECCIÓN FINCA ROSELLAS 2008 T
merlot, cabernet sauvignon, garnacha

87 Colour: cherry, garnet rim. Nose: ripe fruit, spicy, creamy oak, toasty. Palate: powerful, flavourful, toasty, round tannins.

NUNC 2008 TC
merlot, syrah, garnacha, parraleta, moristel

91 Colour: cherry, garnet rim. Nose: medium intensity, ripe fruit, dark chocolate, dried herbs. Palate: good structure, flavourful, round tannins.

PARRALETA EMOCIÓN 2008 TC
100% parraleta

91 Colour: cherry, garnet rim. Nose: ripe fruit, dark chocolate, tobacco, expressive, complex. Palate: flavourful, round tannins, good structure.

PETRET 2009 TC
cabernet sauvignon, merlot

89 Colour: cherry, garnet rim. Nose: medium intensity, spicy, balanced, ripe fruit. Palate: flavourful, good acidity, correct.

PETRET 2012 B
chardonnay, gewürztraminer, alcañón

86 Colour: bright straw. Nose: fresh, fresh fruit, white flowers, expressive. Palate: flavourful, fruity, good acidity, balanced.

PETRET 2012 RD
cabernet sauvignon, garnacha

88 Colour: rose, purple rim. Nose: lactic notes, raspberry, red berry notes, floral. Palate: powerful, flavourful, fresh, fruity.

SEÑOR JOSÉ 2012 T MACERACIÓN CARBÓNICA
100% syrah

86 Colour: cherry, purple rim. Nose: ripe fruit, medium intensity, violet drops. Palate: correct, good acidity, easy to drink.

BODEGAS EL GRILLO Y LA LUNA

Ctra. Berbegal, Km. 2,5
22300 Barbastro (Huesca)
☎: +34 974 269 188
www.elgrillo.net
info@elgrillo.net

12 LUNAS 2010 T
45% tempranillo, 25% cabernet sauvignon, 20% syrah, 10% garnacha

91 Colour: cherry, garnet rim. Nose: red berry notes, ripe fruit, fragrant herbs, creamy oak, toasty. Palate: powerful, flavourful, spicy, long, toasty.

12 LUNAS 2012 B
94% chardonnay, 6% gewürztraminer

90 Colour: bright yellow. Nose: ripe fruit, floral, fragrant herbs, expressive. Palate: powerful, flavourful, rich, balanced.

12 LUNAS 2012 RD
100% syrah

90 Colour: rose, purple rim. Nose: floral, rose petals, raspberry, candied fruit, fragrant herbs. Palate: powerful, flavourful, fresh, fruity, balanced.

BODEGAS ESTADA

Ctra. A-1232, Km. 6,4
22313 Castillazuelo (Huesca)
☎: +34 687 891 701
www.bodegasestada.com
info@bodegasestada.com

ESTADA 2008 TR
25% tempranillo, 15% syrah, 50% cabernet sauvignon, 10% garnacha

87 Colour: cherry, garnet rim. Nose: scrubland, ripe fruit, spicy, creamy oak. Palate: powerful, flavourful, spicy.

ESTADA 2011 T ROBLE
tempranillo, garnacha, cabernet sauvignon, syrah

85 Colour: bright cherry. Nose: ripe fruit, sweet spices, creamy oak, balsamic herbs. Palate: flavourful, fruity, toasty.

ESTADA 2020 VICIOUS 2009 T
20% tempranillo, 40% syrah, 20% cabernet sauvignon, 20% garnacha

90 Colour: cherry, garnet rim. Nose: sweet spices, ripe fruit, complex, balsamic herbs. Palate: ripe fruit, round tannins, good acidity.

ESTADA SAN CARBÁS 2012 B
chardonnay

86 Colour: bright yellow. Nose: citrus fruit, ripe fruit, dried herbs. Palate: powerful, flavourful, warm.

ESTATA 2020 VICIOUS 2012 BFB
chardonnay

90 Colour: bright yellow. Nose: ripe fruit, sweet spices, creamy oak, fragrant herbs. Palate: rich, flavourful, fresh.

VILLA ESTATA 2007 T
35% tempranillo, 35% garnacha, 30% cabernet sauvignon

91 Colour: cherry, garnet rim. Nose: ripe fruit, spicy, creamy oak, toasty, complex. Palate: powerful, flavourful, toasty, round tannins, elegant.

BODEGAS FÁBREGAS

Cerler, s/n
22300 Barbastro (Huesca)
☎: +34 974 310 498
www.bodegasfabregas.com
info@bodegasfabregas.com

FÁBREGAS PURO SYRAH 2007 TC
syrah

87 Colour: deep cherry, garnet rim. Nose: medium intensity, ripe fruit, sweet spices, tobacco. Palate: flavourful, good structure.

MINGUA 2012 B
garnacha blanca, chardonnay

86 Colour: bright straw. Nose: ripe fruit, white flowers, candied fruit, dried herbs. Palate: correct, fresh, fruity, sweetness.

MINGUA 2012 RD
cabernet sauvignon, garnacha

84

MINGUA 2012 T
merlot, cabernet sauvignon, garnacha

85 Colour: cherry, purple rim. Nose: grassy, floral, red berry notes. Palate: fresh, flavourful, easy to drink.

MINGUA GEWÜRZTRAMINER 2012 B
gewürztraminer

88 Colour: bright yellow. Nose: floral, fragrant herbs, ripe fruit. Palate: correct, powerful, flavourful, sweetness.

VEGA FERRERA 2007 TC
cabernet sauvignon, merlot, syrah

84

BODEGAS IRIUS

Ctra. N-240, Km. 154,5
22300 Barbastro (Huesca)
☎: +34 974 269 900
www.bodegairius.com
visitairius@bodegairius.com

ABSUM COLECCIÓN MERLOT 2010 T
merlot

92 Colour: bright cherry. Nose: ripe fruit, sweet spices, creamy oak, cocoa bean, expressive. Palate: flavourful, fruity, toasty, round tannins, balanced, elegant.

ABSUM COLECCIÓN SYRAH 2010 T

92 Colour: cherry, garnet rim. Nose: sweet spices, creamy oak, violet drops, red berry notes, expressive. Palate: spicy, long, round tannins, elegant, balanced.

ABSUM VARIETALES 2011 B
60% chardonnay, 25% gewürztraminer, 15% pinot noir

88 Colour: yellow, greenish rim. Nose: ripe fruit, faded flowers. Palate: rich, ripe fruit, flavourful.

ABSUM VARIETALES 2011 T
50% tempranillo, 35% merlot, 10% cabernet sauvignon, 5% syrah

91 Colour: bright cherry, garnet rim. Nose: ripe fruit, sweet spices, balanced. Palate: fine bitter notes, spicy, long, round tannins.

ALBAT ELIT 2011 T ROBLE

87 Colour: cherry, garnet rim. Nose: red berry notes, ripe fruit, lactic notes, cocoa bean, dark chocolate. Palate: powerful, flavourful, toasty.

IRIUS PREMIUM 2009 T
tempranillo, cabernet sauvignon, merlot

95 Colour: deep cherry, garnet rim. Nose: expressive, complex, ripe fruit, scrubland, spicy, elegant. Palate: good structure, round tannins, spicy.

IRIUS SELECCIÓN 2009 T
tempranillo, cabernet sauvignon, merlot

93 Colour: deep cherry, garnet rim. Nose: complex, balanced, creamy oak, dark chocolate, ripe fruit. Palate: good structure, round tannins.

BODEGAS LASIERRA - BESPEN

Baja, 12
22133 Bespén (Huesca)
☎: +34 652 791 187 - Fax: +34 974 260 365
www.bodegaslasierra.es
info@bodegaslasierra.es

BESPÉN 2010 TC
cabernet sauvignon

84

BESPÉN 2012 RD
cabernet sauvignon

85 Colour: rose. Nose: red berry notes, ripe fruit, floral, dried herbs. Palate: fine bitter notes, powerful, correct.

BESPÉN 2012 T
merlot, tempranillo

84

BESPÉN CHARDONNAY MACABEO 2012 B
chardonnay, macabeo

83

BESPÉN VENDIMIA SELECCIONADA MERLOT 2011 T
merlot

88 Colour: cherry, garnet rim. Nose: balanced, ripe fruit, fruit preserve, spicy. Palate: good structure, flavourful, round tannins.

BESPÉN VENDIMIA SELECCIONADA SYRAH 2010 T
syrah

87 Colour: cherry, garnet rim. Nose: red berry notes, ripe fruit, spicy, creamy oak. Palate: flavourful, correct, fruity.

BODEGAS LAUS

Ctra. N-240, km 154,8
22300 Barbastro (Huesca)
☎: +34 974 269 708 - Fax: +34 974 269 715
www.bodegaslaus.com
info@bodegaslaus.com

LAUS 2005 TR
100% cabernet sauvignon

89 Colour: cherry, garnet rim. Nose: ripe fruit, spicy, complex, wild herbs. Palate: powerful, flavourful, toasty, round tannins.

LAUS 2008 TC
30% merlot, 70% cabernet sauvignon

87 Colour: cherry, garnet rim. Nose: ripe fruit, spicy, creamy oak, toasty. Palate: powerful, flavourful, toasty, long.

LAUS 2010 T ROBLE
43% merlot, 41% cabernet sauvignon, 16% syrah

88 Colour: bright cherry, garnet rim. Nose: balanced, ripe fruit, sweet spices, creamy oak. Palate: flavourful, round tannins, spicy.

LAUS 700 ALT 2005 TC
40% syrah, 35% cabernet sauvignon, 25% merlot

88 Colour: bright cherry, garnet rim. Nose: medium intensity, ripe fruit, spicy, wild herbs. Palate: powerful, flavourful.

LAUS FLOR DE CHARDONNAY 2012 B
100% chardonnay

88 Colour: bright yellow. Nose: ripe fruit, tropical fruit, balanced. Palate: fruity, flavourful, rich, long.

LAUS FLOR DE GEWÜRZTRAMINER 2012 B
100% gewürztraminer

91 Colour: bright straw. Nose: fresh, fresh fruit, white flowers, expressive. Palate: flavourful, fruity, good acidity, balanced.

LAUS FLOR DE MERLOT 2012 RD
85% merlot, 15% cabernet sauvignon

87 Colour: light cherry, bright. Nose: balanced, ripe fruit, faded flowers. Palate: ripe fruit, flavourful.

BODEGAS MELER

Ctra. N-240, km. 154,4 Partida Las Almunietas
22300 (Huesca)
☎: +34 679 954 988 - Fax: +34 974 269 907
www.bodegasmeler.com
info@bodegasmeler.com

ANDRES MELER 2006 T
cabernet sauvignon

92 Colour: pale ruby, brick rim edge. Nose: elegant, spicy, fine reductive notes, aged wood nuances, fruit liqueur notes. Palate: spicy, fine tannins, elegant, long.

MELER 2006 TC
merlot, cabernet sauvignon

90 Colour: deep cherry, orangey edge. Nose: balanced, fragrant herbs, ripe fruit. Palate: flavourful, round tannins, long.

MELER CABERNET 2012 RD
cabernet sauvignon

86 Colour: rose, purple rim. Nose: powerfull, ripe fruit, red berry notes, floral. Palate: powerful, fruity, fresh.

MELER CHARDONNAY EDICIÓN LIMITADA 2012 B
chardonnay

87 Colour: bright yellow. Nose: balanced, ripe fruit, faded flowers. Palate: balanced, ripe fruit, easy to drink.

MELER LUMBRETA 2008 T ROBLE
cabernet sauvignon, garnacha, tempranillo

89 Colour: cherry, garnet rim. Nose: ripe fruit, spicy, dried herbs, tobacco. Palate: flavourful, good structure, round tannins.

BODEGAS MONTE ODINA

Monte Odina, s/n
22415 Ilche (Huesca)
☎: +34 974 343 480
www.monteodina.com
bodega@monteodina.com

MONTE ODINA 2009 TR

88 Colour: cherry, garnet rim. Nose: ripe fruit, spicy, complex, scrubland. Palate: powerful, flavourful, toasty, round tannins.

MONTE ODINA CABERNET SAUVIGNON 2010 T
100% cabernet sauvignon

87 Colour: cherry, garnet rim. Nose: medium intensity, balsamic herbs, spicy. Palate: fruity, correct, easy to drink.

VICTORIA DE MONTE ODINA 2012 B
gewürztraminer

86 Colour: bright straw. Nose: candied fruit, dried flowers, fragrant herbs. Palate: fresh, fruity, flavourful.

OBERGO VARIETALES 2011 T
100% cabernet sauvignon

91 Colour: cherry, garnet rim. Nose: ripe fruit, scrubland, balanced, spicy. Palate: long, flavourful, round tannins.

OBERGO VIÑA ANTIQUA 2011 T
garnacha

89 Colour: bright cherry. Nose: ripe fruit, sweet spices, creamy oak, balsamic herbs. Palate: flavourful, fruity, toasty.

BODEGAS OBERGO

Ctra. La Puebla, Km. 0,6
22439 Ubiergo (Huesca)
☎: +34 669 357 866
www.obergo.es
bodegasobergo@obergo.es

LÁGRIMAS DE OBERGO 2012 RD
garnacha, syrah

89 Colour: rose, purple rim. Nose: lactic notes, red berry notes, candied fruit, floral. Palate: correct, powerful, flavourful, fresh, fruity.

OBERGO "FINCA LA MATA" 2010 T
cabernet sauvignon, merlot, garnacha

91 Colour: cherry, garnet rim. Nose: ripe fruit, spicy, creamy oak. Palate: powerful, flavourful, toasty, round tannins, balanced.

OBERGO CARAMELOS 2012 T
garnacha

89 Colour: cherry, purple rim. Nose: ripe fruit, sweet spices. Palate: flavourful, round tannins, correct, fruity.

OBERGO EXPRESSION 2012 BFB
chardonnay, otras

89 Colour: bright straw. Nose: white flowers, jasmine, ripe fruit, spicy. Palate: rich, flavourful, fruity, balanced.

OBERGO MERLOT 2011 T
100% merlot

90 Colour: cherry, garnet rim. Nose: red berry notes, ripe fruit, balsamic herbs, floral, creamy oak. Palate: powerful, flavourful, toasty, balsamic.

OBERGO SYRAH 2010 T
100% syrah

91 Colour: cherry, garnet rim. Nose: ripe fruit, floral, violet drops, balsamic herbs. Palate: powerful, flavourful, toasty.

BODEGAS OSCA

La Iglesia, 1
22124 Ponzano (Huesca)
☎: +34 974 319 017 - Fax: +34 974 319 175
www.bodegasosca.com
bodega@bodegasosca.com

MASCÚN GARNACHA 2009 T
garnacha

85 Colour: cherry, garnet rim. Nose: ripe fruit, balsamic herbs, creamy oak, aged wood nuances. Palate: powerful, flavourful, correct.

MASCÚN GARNACHA 2012 RD
garnacha

85 Colour: light cherry, bright. Nose: medium intensity, balanced, red berry notes, ripe fruit. Palate: fruity, correct, easy to drink.

MASCÚN GARNACHA BLANCA 2012 B
100% garnacha blanca

85 Colour: yellow. Nose: ripe fruit, dried herbs. Palate: long, correct, good finish, good acidity, ripe fruit.

MASCÚN GRAN RESERVA DE LA FAMILIA 2006 T

88 Colour: cherry, garnet rim. Nose: ripe fruit, spicy, creamy oak, roasted coffee. Palate: powerful, flavourful, toasty.

MASCÚN SYRAH 2009 T
syrah

85 Colour: cherry, garnet rim. Nose: ripe fruit, spicy, creamy oak, toasty, fine reductive notes. Palate: powerful, flavourful, toasty.

OSCA 2009 TC
tempranillo, merlot

88 Colour: light cherry. Nose: ripe fruit, balsamic herbs, sweet spices, creamy oak. Palate: flavourful, spicy, correct.

OSCA 2012 RD

86 Colour: rose, purple rim. Nose: ripe fruit, red berry notes, floral, expressive. Palate: powerful, fruity, fresh.

OSCA COLECCIÓN 2009 TR

89 Colour: cherry, garnet rim. Nose: ripe fruit, spicy, creamy oak, toasty, complex. Palate: powerful, flavourful, toasty, round tannins.

OSCA SYRAH 2009 TR
100% syrah

88 Colour: cherry, garnet rim. Nose: ripe fruit, spicy, creamy oak, toasty. Palate: powerful, flavourful, toasty, round tannins.

OSCA 2012 B
macabeo, garnacha blanca

84

OSCA 2012 T
tempranillo, cabernet sauvignon

84

OSCA GRAN EROLES 2008 TR
cabernet sauvignon, tempranillo

88 Colour: cherry, garnet rim. Nose: ripe fruit, balsamic herbs, sweet spices, fine reductive notes. Palate: flavourful, complex, long, spicy.

OSCA MORISTEL 2009 TR
moristel

86 Colour: cherry, garnet rim. Nose: ripe fruit, spicy, creamy oak. Palate: powerful, flavourful, toasty.

OSCA MORISTEL 2010 TC
moristel

87 Colour: cherry, garnet rim. Nose: candied fruit, sweet spices, cocoa bean. Palate: fruity, round tannins, easy to drink.

BODEGAS SERS

Pza. Mayor, 7
22417 Cofita (Huesca)
☎: +34 652 979 718
www.bodegassers.es
info@bodegassers.es

SÈRS 2006 TGR
cabernet sauvignon, merlot, syrah

93 Colour: pale ruby, brick rim edge. Nose: elegant, spicy, fine reductive notes, wet leather, aged wood nuances, fruit liqueur notes. Palate: spicy, fine tannins, elegant, long.

SÈRS 2009 TR
cabernet sauvignon, syrah, merlot

89 Colour: cherry, garnet rim. Nose: ripe fruit, balsamic herbs, aged wood nuances, fine reductive notes. Palate: powerful, flavourful, complex, spicy, toasty.

SÈRS BLANQUÉ 2012 B
chardonnay

89 Colour: bright yellow. Nose: dried flowers, fragrant herbs, fruit expression, ripe fruit. Palate: powerful, flavourful, ripe fruit.

SÈRS PRIMER 2012 T
syrah

86 Colour: bright cherry, purple rim. Nose: ripe fruit, medium intensity, violet drops. Palate: good structure, flavourful.

SÈRS SINGULAR 2011 T
parraleta

90 Colour: cherry, garnet rim. Nose: expressive, ripe fruit, spicy. Palate: flavourful, ripe fruit, balanced, good acidity, long.

SÈRS TEMPLE 2010 TC
cabernet sauvignon, merlot

90 Colour: cherry, garnet rim. Nose: ripe fruit, wild herbs, cocoa bean, creamy oak. Palate: powerful, flavourful, balsamic, long.

BODEGAS SIERRA DE GUARA

Ctra. Abiego, Km. 0,1
22124 Lascellas (Huesca)
☎: +34 974 340 671
www.bodegassierradeguara.es
idrias@bodegassierradeguara.es

IDRIAS 2009 TC
cabernet sauvignon, tempranillo

89 Colour: cherry, garnet rim. Nose: ripe fruit, spicy, creamy oak, toasty, complex. Palate: powerful, flavourful, toasty, round tannins.

IDRIAS ABIEGO 2011 T
tempranillo, cabernet sauvignon

90 Colour: bright cherry. Nose: ripe fruit, sweet spices, creamy oak, expressive. Palate: flavourful, fruity, toasty, round tannins.

IDRIAS CHARDONNAY 2012 B
chardonnay

86 Colour: bright yellow. Nose: powerfull, faded flowers, candied fruit. Palate: flavourful, rich, long.

IDRIAS SEVIL 2008 T
cabernet sauvignon, merlot

88 Colour: deep cherry, garnet rim. Nose: toasty, spicy, scrubland. Palate: powerful, powerful tannins, ripe fruit.

BODEGAS VILLA D'ORTA

Ctra. Alquezar s/n
22313 Huerta de Vero (Huesca)
☎: +34 695 991 967 - Fax: +34 974 302 072
www.villadorta.com
villadorta@hotmail.com

VILLA D'ORTA 2009 TC

85 Colour: bright cherry. Nose: ripe fruit, sweet spices, creamy oak, wild herbs. Palate: flavourful, fruity, toasty.

CHESA

Autovía A-22, km. 57
22300 Barbastro (Huesca)
☎: +34 649 870 637 - Fax: +34 974 313 552
www.bodegaschesa.com
bodegaschesa@hotmail.com

CHESA 2010 T ROBLE
merlot, cabernet sauvignon

89 Colour: bright cherry. Nose: ripe fruit, creamy oak, fragrant herbs. Palate: flavourful, fruity, toasty.

CHESA 2010 TC
merlot, cabernet sauvignon

88 Colour: cherry, garnet rim. Nose: ripe fruit, balsamic herbs, aged wood nuances, spicy. Palate: flavourful, long, balanced.

CHESA 2012 RD
cabernet sauvignon

89 Colour: onion pink. Nose: candied fruit, dried flowers, fragrant herbs, red berry notes. Palate: light-bodied, flavourful, good acidity, long, spicy.

CHESA GEWÜRZTRAMINER 2012 B
gewürztraminer

85 Colour: bright straw. Nose: white flowers, medium intensity, ripe fruit. Palate: correct, easy to drink.

CHESA MERLOT CABERNET 2012 T
merlot, cabernet sauvignon

87 Colour: cherry, purple rim. Nose: scrubland, floral, earthy notes, red berry notes. Palate: fruity, flavourful, balanced.

DALCAMP

Pedanía Monte Odina s/n
22415 Monesma de San Juan (Huesca)
☎: +34 973 760 018 - Fax: +34 973 760 523
www.castillodemonesma.com
ramondalfo44@mixmail.com

CASTILLO DE MONESMA 2009 T ROBLE
20% merlot, 80% cabernet sauvignon

85 Colour: cherry, garnet rim. Nose: medium intensity, old leather, spicy. Palate: correct, fine bitter notes, good acidity.

CASTILLO DE MONESMA 2010 TC
cabernet sauvignon

87 Colour: dark-red cherry, orangey edge. Nose: fruit preserve, scrubland, spicy. Palate: flavourful, spicy, long.

CASTILLO DE MONESMA
CRIANZA
CABERNET SAUVIGNON - MERLOT
2010
EMBOTELLADO EN LA PROPIEDAD POR DALCAMP S.L.
22415 MONESMA DE SAN JUAN - ILCHE - ESPAÑA
PRODUCT OF SPAIN
14%vol   R.E. 40817 - HU   75cl.
CONTIENE SULFITOS
SOMONTANO
DENOMINACIÓN DE ORIGEN

CASTILLO DE MONESMA 2011 T ROBLE
70% merlot, 30% cabernet sauvignon

86 Colour: light cherry. Nose: ripe fruit, dried herbs, creamy oak. Palate: flavourful, spicy, balsamic.

CASTILLO DE MONESMA CABERNET SAUVIGNON 2007 TR
90% cabernet sauvignon, 10% merlot

88 Colour: cherry, garnet rim. Nose: ripe fruit, spicy. Palate: good structure, flavourful, ripe fruit, round tannins, toasty.

ENATE

Avda. de las Artes, 1
22300 Barbastro (Huesca)
☎: +34 974 302 580 - Fax: +34 974 300 046
www.enate.es
bodega@enate.es

ENATE 2012 RD
100% cabernet sauvignon

88 Colour: rose, purple rim. Nose: powerfull, ripe fruit, red berry notes, floral, expressive. Palate: powerful, fruity, fresh.

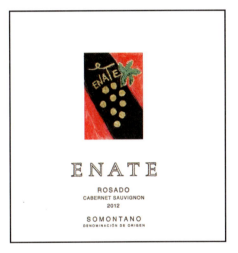

ENATE 2006 TR
100% cabernet sauvignon

92 Colour: cherry, garnet rim. Nose: ripe fruit, spicy, toasty, earthy notes. Palate: powerful, flavourful, toasty, fine tannins.

ENATE 2007 TC
70% tempranillo, 30% cabernet sauvignon

88 Colour: bright cherry, garnet rim. Nose: powerfull, ripe fruit, spicy, tobacco. Palate: flavourful, round tannins, spicy.

ENATE CABERNET SAUVIGNON MERLOT 2010 T
50% cabernet sauvignon, 50% merlot

89 Colour: cherry, garnet rim. Nose: balanced, expressive, ripe fruit, balsamic herbs, spicy. Palate: flavourful, easy to drink, good acidity.

ENATE CHARDONNAY 2010 BFB
100% chardonnay

92 Colour: bright yellow. Nose: creamy oak, candied fruit, balanced, sweet spices. Palate: flavourful, toasty, long.

ENATE MERLOT-MERLOT 2009 T
100% merlot

92 Colour: cherry, garnet rim. Nose: ripe fruit, spicy, creamy oak, toasty, complex. Palate: powerful, flavourful, toasty, round tannins, balanced.

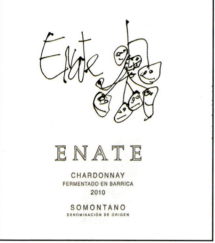

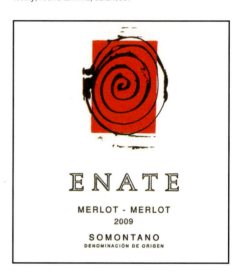

ENATE CHARDONNAY-234 2012 B
100% chardonnay

90 Colour: bright yellow. Nose: ripe fruit, white flowers, balanced, varietal. Palate: fine bitter notes, good acidity, long.

ENATE GEWÜRZTRAMINER 2012 B
100% gewürztraminer

91 Colour: bright straw. Nose: white flowers, candied fruit, fragrant herbs, mineral, expressive. Palate: powerful, flavourful, rich, balanced.

ENATE SYRAH-SHIRAZ 2009 T
100% syrah

91 Colour: cherry, garnet rim. Nose: ripe fruit, floral, violet drops, mineral, sweet spices. Palate: powerful, flavourful, complex, spicy.

ENATE TAPAS 2012 T
tempranillo, cabernet sauvignon, merlot

87 Colour: cherry, garnet rim. Nose: medium intensity, ripe fruit. Palate: flavourful, fruity, good acidity.

ENATE RESERVA ESPECIAL 2006 TR
65% cabernet sauvignon, 35% merlot

93 Colour: cherry, garnet rim. Nose: complex, ripe fruit, cocoa bean, old leather. Palate: balanced, good structure, flavourful, round tannins.

ENATE UNO 2009 T
40% cabernet sauvignon, 60% syrah

94 Colour: bright cherry, garnet rim. Nose: complex, expressive, ripe fruit, scrubland. Palate: full, flavourful, balanced, ripe fruit.

ENATE UNO CHARDONNAY 2011 BFB
100% chardonnay

94 Colour: bright golden. Nose: creamy oak, sweet spices, candied fruit, roasted coffee. Palate: long, ripe fruit, spicy, complex.

VIÑAS DEL VERO

Ctra. Naval, Km. 3,7
22300 Barbastro (Huesca)
☎: +34 974 302 216 - Fax: +34 974 302 098
www.vinasdelvero.es
marketing@vinasdelvero.es

VIÑAS DEL VERO CABERNET SAUVIGNON COLECCIÓN 2010 T
100% cabernet sauvignon

89 Colour: bright cherry, garnet rim. Nose: balanced, varietal, scrubland, ripe fruit. Palate: flavourful, good structure, round tannins.

VIÑAS DEL VERO CHARDONNAY COLECCIÓN 2012 B
100% chardonnay

91 Colour: bright straw. Nose: fresh, fresh fruit, white flowers, fragrant herbs. Palate: flavourful, fruity, good acidity, balanced, elegant.

VIÑAS DEL VERO CLARIÓN 2011 B

91 Colour: bright yellow. Nose: ripe fruit, sweet spices, creamy oak, fragrant herbs. Palate: rich, flavourful, fresh, good acidity.

VIÑAS DEL VERO GEWÜRZTRAMINER COLECCIÓN 2012 B
100% gewürztraminer

90 Colour: bright yellow. Nose: varietal, ripe fruit, expressive, jasmine. Palate: balanced, ripe fruit, fine bitter notes, fruity, full.

VIÑAS DEL VERO GRAN VOS 2006 TR

91 Colour: deep cherry, garnet rim. Nose: expressive, medium intensity, ripe fruit, spicy. Palate: complex, flavourful, good structure, round tannins.

VIÑAS DEL VERO GRAN VOS 2007 TR

90 Colour: deep cherry, garnet rim. Nose: balanced, ripe fruit, spicy, scrubland. Palate: flavourful, round tannins, fine bitter notes.

VIÑAS DEL VERO LA MIRANDA DE SECASTILLA 2011 T
garnacha, parraleta, syrah

90 Colour: deep cherry, purple rim. Nose: sweet spices, ripe fruit. Palate: balanced, fine bitter notes, round tannins.

VIÑAS DEL VERO MERLOT COLECCIÓN 2010 T
100% merlot

90 Colour: cherry, garnet rim. Nose: ripe fruit, balsamic herbs, balanced, spicy. Palate: flavourful, good acidity, round tannins.

VIÑAS DEL VERO RIESLING COLECCIÓN 2011 B
100% riesling

87 Colour: bright straw. Nose: floral, ripe fruit, balsamic herbs, medium intensity. Palate: powerful, flavourful, rich.

VIÑAS DEL VERO SECASTILLA 2009 T
garnacha

93 Colour: cherry, garnet rim. Nose: ripe fruit, spicy, creamy oak, toasty, complex. Palate: powerful, flavourful, toasty, round tannins, balanced, elegant.

VIÑAS DEL VERO SYRAH COLECCIÓN 2010 T
100% syrah

89 Colour: cherry, garnet rim. Nose: ripe fruit, violet drops, fragrant herbs, toasty. Palate: powerful, spicy, long.

VIÑEDOS DE HOZ

Mayor, 17
22312 Hoz de Barbastro (Huesca)
☎: +34 619 686 765
www.vinosdehoz.com
info@vinosdehoz.com

HOZ 2010 T ROBLE
cabernet sauvignon, syrah, garnacha

88 Colour: bright cherry, garnet rim. Nose: medium intensity, ripe fruit, spicy, dark chocolate. Palate: flavourful, balsamic.

HOZ 2010 TC
cabernet sauvignon, syrah, garnacha

88 Colour: bright cherry, garnet rim. Nose: balanced, ripe fruit, spicy, scrubland. Palate: correct, good acidity.

DO TACORONTE-ACENTEJO / D.O.P.

LOCATION:

Situated in the north of Tenerife, stretching for 23 km and is composed of 9 municipal districts: Tegueste, Tacoronte, El Sauzal, La Matanza de Acentejo, La Victoria de Acentejo, Santa Úrsula, La Laguna, Santa Cruz de Tenerife and El Rosario.

CLIMATE:

Typically Atlantic, affected by the orientation of the island and the relief which give rise to a great variety of microclimates. The temperatures are in general mild, thanks to the influence of the trade winds, which provide high levels of humidity, around 60%, although the rains are scarce.

SOIL:

The soil is volcanic, reddish, and is made up of organic matter and trace elements. The vines are cultivated both in the valleys next to the sea and higher up at altitudes of up to 1,000 m.

GRAPE VARIETIES:

WHITE: PREFERRED: *Güal, Malvasía, Listán Blanco* and *Marmajuelo.*
AUTHORIZED: *Pedro Ximénez, Moscatel, Verdello, Vijariego, Forastera Blanca, Albillo, Sabro, Bastardo Blanco, Breval, Burra Blanca* and *Torrontés.*
RED: PREFERRED: *Listán Negra* and *Negramoll.*
AUTHORIZED: *Tintilla, Moscatel Negro, Castellana Negra, Cabernet Sauvignon, Merlot, Pinot Noir, Ruby Cabernet, Syrah, Tempranillo, Bastardo Negro, Listán Prieto, Vijariego Negro* and *Malvasía Rosada.*

SUB-REGIONS:

Anaga (covering the municipal areas of La Laguna, Santa Cruz de Tenerife and Tegueste) which falls within the limits of the Anaga Rural Park.

FIGURES:

Vineyard surface: 1.156.075 – **Wine-Growers:** 1.882 – **Wineries:** 43 – **2012 Harvest rating:** Very Good – **Production:** 1.200.000 litres – **Market percentages:** 99% domestic.1% export

VINTAGE RATING · PEÑÍNGUIDE

2008	2009	2010	2011	2012
GOOD	AVERAGE	GOOD	AVERAGE	VERY GOOD

CONSEJO REGULADOR
Ctra. General del Norte, 97 - 38350 Tacoronte (Santa Cruz de Tenerife) ☎: +34 922 560 107 - Fax: +34 922 561 155
consejo@tacovin.com   www.tacovin.com

AGRYENCA

Fray Diego, 4
38350 Tacoronte (Tenerife)
☎: +34 922 564 013 - Fax: +34 922 564 013
www.agryenca.com
bodega@agryenca.com

TABAIBAL 2012 B
listán blanco, gual, verdello

84

TABAIBAL 2012 RD
listán negro, negramoll

82

TABAIBAL 2012 T
listán negro, negramoll

86 Colour: light cherry, garnet rim. Nose: medium intensity, wild herbs. Palate: fruity, easy to drink.

BODEGA DOMÍNGUEZ CUARTA GENERACIÓN

Calvario, 79
38350 Tacoronte (Santa Cruz de Tenerife)
☎: +34 922 572 435 - Fax: +34 922 572 435
www.bodegadominguez.com
administracion@bodegadominguez.es

DOMÍNGUEZ BLANCO DE UVA TINTA 2012 B
90% negramoll, 10% malvasía

85 Colour: coppery red. Nose: medium intensity, fresh, fresh fruit, fragrant herbs. Palate: easy to drink, correct, good acidity.

DOMÍNGUEZ CLÁSICO 2011 T
listán negro, negramoll, tintilla, listán blanco

84

DOMÍNGUEZ CON FIRMA 2010 T
castellana, tintilla

82

DOMÍNGUEZ MALVASÍA CLÁSICO 2010 B
malvasía

90 Colour: light mahogany. Nose: medium intensity, wild herbs, ripe fruit, faded flowers. Palate: fruity, good acidity, toasty.

DOMÍNGUEZ SELECCIÓN NEGRAMOLL 2008 T
negramoll

86 Colour: dark-red cherry, garnet rim. Nose: macerated fruit, fruit liqueur notes, tobacco, scrubland. Palate: easy to drink, correct.

BODEGA EL LOMO

Ctra. El Lomo, 18
38280 Tegueste (Santa Cruz de Tenerife)
☎: +34 922 545 254 - Fax: +34 922 546 453
www.bodegaellomo.com
oficina@bodegaellomo.com

EL LOMO 2012 B
95% listán blanco, malvasía, moscatel, gual, vijariego blanco

85 Colour: bright straw. Nose: medium intensity, fresh fruit, citrus fruit. Palate: fruity, easy to drink, fine bitter notes.

EL LOMO 2012 RD
90% listán negro, 10% negramoll, tintilla, ruby, tempranillo

80

EL LOMO 2012 T
90% listán negro, 10% negral, listán blanco

86 Colour: cherry, purple rim. Nose: ripe fruit, wild herbs, scrubland, powerfull. Palate: fruity, correct, good finish.

EL LOMO 2012 T BARRICA
90% listán negro, 10% negramoll, tintilla, ruby, tempranillo, listán blanco

84

EL LOMO 2012 T MACERACIÓN CARBÓNICA
96% listán negro, 4% negramoll, tintilla, ruby, tempranillo

88 Colour: cherry, purple rim. Nose: medium intensity, red berry notes, ripe fruit, balsamic herbs. Palate: fruity, flavourful, balanced.

BODEGA EL MOCANERO

38350 Tacoronte (Santa Cruz de Tenerife)
☎: +34 922 560 762 - Fax: +34 922 564 452
www.bodegaelmocanero.com
elmocanero@bodegaelmocanero.com

EL MOCANERO 2012 T
95% listán negro, 5% negramoll

84

EL MOCANERO 2012 T MACERACIÓN CARBÓNICA
95% listán negro, 5% negramoll

85 Colour: bright cherry, purple rim. Nose: ripe fruit, candied fruit, violet drops. Palate: flavourful, powerful.

EL MOCANERO AFRUTADO 2012 B
100% listán blanco

86 Colour: bright straw. Nose: scrubland, dried herbs, balanced, earthy notes. Palate: fruity, flavourful.

EL MOCANERO NEGRAMOLL 2012 T
100% negramoll

86 Colour: cherry, purple rim. Nose: spicy, ripe fruit, toasty. Palate: fruity, flavourful, round tannins.

BODEGA INSERCASA

Finca El Fresal - Juan Fernandez, 254 Valle Guerra
38270 La Laguna (Santa Cruz de Tenerife)
☎: +34 680 446 868 - Fax: +34 922 285 316
www.vinobronce.com
info@vinobronce.com

BRONCE ECOLÓGICO 2012 T
70% listán negro, 30% syrah

85 Colour: cherry, garnet rim. Nose: fruit preserve, sweet spices, dried herbs. Palate: correct, easy to drink, round tannins.

BRONCE SYRAH 2012 T
100% syrah

88 Colour: very deep cherry, garnet rim. Nose: balsamic herbs, ripe fruit, powerfull, warm. Palate: flavourful, good structure, round tannins.

BRONCE VENDIMIA SELECCIONADA 2012 T BARRICA
30% listán negro, 70% syrah

87 Colour: cherry, garnet rim. Nose: ripe fruit, dried herbs, spicy. Palate: fruity, balanced, round tannins, easy to drink.

BODEGAS CRATER

San Nicolás, 122
38360 El Sauzal (Santa Cruz de Tenerife)
☎: +34 922 573 273 - Fax: +34 922 573 272
www.craterbodegas.com
crater@bodegasbuten.com

CRÁTER 2010 TC
listán negro, negramoll

91 Colour: deep cherry, garnet rim. Nose: complex, ripe fruit, dark chocolate, creamy oak. Palate: full, flavourful, good structure, good acidity.

MAGMA DE CRÁTER 2008 TC
negramoll, syrah

93 Colour: cherry, garnet rim. Nose: ripe fruit, fruit preserve, dry stone, balsamic herbs, expressive. Palate: full, flavourful, round tannins.

BODEGAS INSULARES TENERIFE

Vereda del Medio, 48
38350 Tacoronte (Santa Cruz de Tenerife)
☎: +34 922 570 617 - Fax: +34 922 570 043
www.bodegasinsularestenerife.es
bitsa@bodegasinsularestenerife.es

HUMBOLDT 16 AÑOS BARRICA 1997 B
100% listán blanco

95 Colour: old gold. Nose: complex, expressive, aromatic coffee, cocoa bean, sweet spices, candied fruit. Palate: complex, concentrated, long, good acidity, round.

HUMBOLDT 1997 BLANCO DULCE
100% listán blanco

95 Colour: old gold. Nose: complex, expressive, cocoa bean, candied fruit, honeyed notes, pattiserie. Palate: long, flavourful, good acidity.

HUMBOLDT 2001 TINTO DULCE
100% listán negro

94 Colour: deep cherry, garnet rim. Nose: aromatic coffee, dark chocolate, complex, expressive. Palate: flavourful, good acidity, spirituous, round.

HUMBOLDT MALVASÍA 2008 B
100% malvasía

92 Colour: bright golden. Nose: elegant, candied fruit, sweet spices, caramel, faded flowers. Palate: flavourful, good acidity, unctuous.

HUMBOLDT VENDIMIA TARDÍA 2005 B
100% listán blanco

93 Colour: light mahogany. Nose: powerfull, candied fruit, sweet spices, cocoa bean, spicy. Palate: flavourful, long, good acidity.

HUMBOLDT VERDELLO 2005 BLANCO DULCE
100% verdello

94 Colour: old gold, amber rim. Nose: complex, acetaldehyde, sweet spices, creamy oak, dark chocolate, neat. Palate: good structure, balanced, good acidity, flavourful.

VIÑA NORTE 2012 T MACERACIÓN CARBÓNICA
95% listán negro, 5% negramoll

87 Colour: cherry, purple rim. Nose: medium intensity, red berry notes, balanced, wild herbs. Palate: fruity, easy to drink.

VIÑA NORTE 2012 T BARRICA
90% listán negro, 10% negramoll

88 Colour: deep cherry, purple rim. Nose: dried herbs, ripe fruit, varietal. Palate: balanced, flavourful, spicy, round tannins.

VIÑA NORTE PRIMER 2012 T MACERACIÓN CARBÓNICA

86 Colour: cherry, purple rim. Nose: fruit expression, scrubland, expressive. Palate: fruity, carbonic notes, easy to drink.

C.B. CUEVA EL INFIERNO

Subida Antonio Viera, 10. El Infierno
38280 Tegueste
☎: +34 670 842 462
www.cuevaelinfierno.com
bodega@cuevaelinfierno.com

TIBIZENA 2009 T

87 Colour: cherry, garnet rim. Nose: fruit preserve, sweet spices, honeyed notes. Palate: fruity, rich, sweet tannins.

VIDUEÑO DULCE 1998 B BARRICA

93 Colour: light mahogany. Nose: complex, candied fruit, cocoa bean, creamy oak, dry nuts. Palate: full, flavourful, long, good acidity, unctuous, spicy.

CÁNDIDO HERNÁNDEZ PÍO

Los Tomillos s/n
38530 Candelaria (Santa Cruz de Tenerife)
☎: +34 922 513 288 - Fax: +34 922 511 631
www.bodegaschp.es
almacenlahidalga@telefonica.net

BALCÓN CANARIO 2012 T
listán negro, negramoll, tintilla

85 Colour: cherry, purple rim. Nose: powerfull, ripe fruit, scrubland, expressive. Palate: flavourful, good finish.

PUNTA DEL SOL 2001 B
gual, albillo

85 Colour: bright yellow. Nose: scrubland, ripe fruit. Palate: fruity, easy to drink, good finish.

VIÑA RIQUELAS AFRUTADO 2012 B
moscatel, malvasía, listán blanco

86 Colour: bright straw. Nose: balanced, white flowers, expressive. Palate: fruity, rich, easy to drink, good finish.

VIÑA RIQUELAS BLANCO GUAL 2012 B
85% gual, 15% verdejo, malvasía

88 Colour: bright yellow. Nose: ripe fruit, sweet spices, powerfull. Palate: flavourful, fruity, good acidity, fine bitter notes.

VIÑA RIQUELAS NEGRAMOLL 2012 T
85% negramoll, 15% listán negro

86 Colour: light cherry. Nose: red berry notes, ripe fruit, medium intensity. Palate: balanced, correct, good acidity.

CARBAJALES

Barranco de San Juan, s/n
38350 Tacoronte (Santa Cruz de Tenerife)
☎: +34 639 791 608
www.carbajales.es
loscarbajales@gmail.com

CARBAJALES 2012 T BARRICA
listán negro, cabernet sauvignon, syrah

84

FINCA LA HORNACA

Camino Hacienda el Pino, 42
38350 Tacoronte (Santa Cruz de Tenerife)
☎: +34 922 560 676
www.hoyadelnavio.com
info@hoyadelnavio.com

HOYA DEL NAVÍO 2011 T
50% listán negro, 50% negramoll
84

HACIENDA DE ACENTEJO

Pérez Díaz, 44
38380 La Victoria de Acentejo (Santa Cruz de Tenerife)
☎: +34 922 581 003 - Fax: +34 922 581 831
almac.gutierrez@gmail.com

HACIENDA DE ACENTEJO 2012 B
listán blanco
83

HACIENDA DE ACENTEJO 2012 T
listán negro, negramoll
85 Colour: cherry, garnet rim. Nose: spicy, balsamic herbs, ripe fruit, balanced. Palate: good acidity, easy to drink, good finish.

JUAN J. FUENTES TABARES

Camino El Boquerón, s/n
38270 La Laguna (Santa Cruz de Tenerife)
☎: +34 922 541 500 - Fax: +34 922 541 000
info@orquidariolycaste.com

VIÑA EL DRAGO 2011 T
88 Colour: bright cherry. Nose: ripe fruit, balsamic herbs. Palate: flavourful, fruity, toasty, round tannins.

MARBA

Ctra. del Socorro, 253 - Portezuelo
38280 Tegueste (Santa Cruz de Tenerife)
☎: +34 639 065 015 - Fax: +34 922 638 400
www.bodegasmarba.es
marba@bodegasmarba.es

MARBA 2012 B
86 Colour: bright straw. Nose: fresh, fresh fruit, white flowers, expressive. Palate: flavourful, fruity, good acidity, balanced.

MARBA 2012 B BARRICA
88 Colour: bright yellow. Nose: powerfull, ripe fruit, sweet spices, fragrant herbs, white flowers. Palate: rich, smoky aftertaste, flavourful, fresh, good acidity.

MARBA 2012 RD
86 Colour: rose, purple rim. Nose: ripe fruit, red berry notes, floral, expressive. Palate: fruity, flavourful, fine bitter notes.

MARBA 2012 T BARRICA
86 Colour: bright cherry. Nose: ripe fruit, sweet spices, balsamic herbs. Palate: fruity, toasty, round tannins.

MARBA AFRUTADO 2012 B
87 Colour: bright straw. Nose: white flowers, ripe fruit, medium intensity. Palate: fruity, good acidity, balanced, sweetness.

MARBA TRADICIONAL 2012 T
85 Colour: very deep cherry, purple rim. Nose: ripe fruit, violet drops, powerfull, spicy, toasty. Palate: flavourful, round tannins.

MARCELO GONZÁLEZ SANTANA

Cuesta de San Bernabé, 103
38280 Tegueste (Santa Cruz de Tenerife)
☎: +34 676 681 480

MARCELO 2012 T
83

MODAS EL ARCA S.L.

El Torreón, s/n
38350 Tacoronte (Santa Cruz de Tenerife)
☎: +34 922 211 414 - Fax: +34 922 209 945
balmeid@bualamoda.es

EL GRANILETE 2011 T
70% listán negro, 20% tempranillo, 10% tintilla
83

MONJE

Camino Cruz de Leandro, 36
38359 El Sauzal (Santa Cruz de Tenerife)
☎: +34 922 585 027 - Fax: +34 922 585 027
www.bodegasmonje.com
monje@bodegasmonje.com

HOLLERA MONJE 2012 T
MACERACIÓN CARBÓNICA
listán negro
87 Colour: cherry, garnet rim. Nose: dried herbs, ripe fruit, powerfull. Palate: fruity, flavourful, long.

PRESAS OCAMPO

Los Alamos de San Juan, 5
38350 Tacoronte (Santa Cruz de Tenerife)
☎: +34 922 571 689 - Fax: +34 922 561 700
www.presasocampo.com
administracion@presasocampo.com

ALYSIUS 2011 T BARRICA
60% listán negro, 20% syrah, 10% tempranillo, 10% merlot
86 Colour: cherry, garnet rim. Nose: medium intensity, wild herbs, ripe fruit. Palate: fruity, spicy, easy to drink, round tannins.

ALYSIUS 2012 T
60% listán negro, 20% syrah, 10% tempranillo, 10% merlot
84

ALYSIUS 2012 T BARRICA
60% listán negro, 30% merlot, 5% syrah, 5% tempranillo
86 Colour: cherry, garnet rim. Nose: medium intensity, red berry notes, ripe fruit, spicy. Palate: easy to drink, round tannins, good acidity.

PRESAS OCAMPO 2012 T
90% listán negro, 5% tempranillo, 5% merlot
87 Colour: cherry, garnet rim. Nose: dried herbs, wild herbs, ripe fruit. Palate: good structure, flavourful, fruity.

PRESAS OCAMPO 2012 T
MACERACIÓN CARBÓNICA
100% listán negro
90 Colour: bright cherry, purple rim. Nose: balanced, fruit expression, violets. Palate: fruity, flavourful, long, easy to drink, fruity aftestaste.

TROPICAL MAR

Ctra. Los Angeles, 69
38360 Sauzal (Santa Cruz de Tenerife)
info@dongustavo.eu

DON GUSTAVO 2012 B
85 Colour: bright yellow. Nose: faded flowers, medium intensity. Palate: fruity, spicy, good finish.

DON GUSTAVO 2012 RD
79

DON GUSTAVO 2012 T
83

VIÑA EL MATO

Calvario, 270
38350 Tacoronte (Santa Cruz de Tenerife)
☎: +34 922 561 752 - Fax: +34 922 561 752
josesarabia@hotmail.com

VIÑA EL MATÓ 2012 B
82

VIÑA EL MATÓ 2012 T
83

VIÑA EL MATÓ 2012 T MACERACIÓN CARBÓNICA
79

VIÑA ESTEVEZ

Pérez Díaz, 80
38380 La Victoria (Santa Cruz de Tenerife)
☎: +34 922 580 779
elena.vinaestevez@gmail.com

VIÑA ESTÉVEZ 2012 T

86 Colour: cherry, purple rim. Nose: red berry notes, medium intensity, dried herbs. Palate: fruity, good acidity, round tannins.

TARRAGONA

▼ Consejo Regulador
● DO Boundary

LOCATION:

The region is situated in the province of Tarragona. It comprises two different wine-growing regions: El Camp and Ribera d'Ebre, with a total of 72 municipal areas.

CLIMATE:

Mediterranean in the region of El Camp, with an average annual rainfall of 500 mm. The region of the Ribera has a rather harsh climate with cold winters and hot summers; it also has the lowest rainfall in the region (385 mm per year).

SOIL:

El Camp is characterized by its calcareous, light terrain, and the Ribera has calcareous terrain and also some alluvial terrain.

GRAPE VARIETIES:

WHITE: *Chardonnay, Macabeo, Xarel·lo, Garnacha Blanca, Parellada, Moscatel de Alejandría, Moscatel de Frontignan, Sauvignon Blanc, Malvasía.*
RED: *Samsó* (*Cariñena*), *Garnacha, Ull de Llebre* (*Tempranillo*), *Cabernet Sauvignon, Merlot, Monastrell, Pinot Noir, Syrah.*

SUB-REGIONS:

El Camp and Ribera d'Ebre
(See specific characteristics in previous sections).

FIGURES:

Vineyard surface: 6.250 – **Wine-Growers:** 2.117 – **Wineries:** 33 – **2012 Harvest rating:** Very Good – **Production:** 4,000,000 litres – **Market percentages:** 50% domestic. 50% export

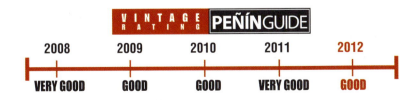

VINTAGE RATING PEÑÍNGUIDE				
2008	**2009**	**2010**	**2011**	**2012**
VERY GOOD	**GOOD**	**GOOD**	**VERY GOOD**	**GOOD**

CONSEJO REGULADOR
Avda. Catalunya, 50 - 43002 Tarragona ☎: +34 977 217 931 - Fax: +34 977 229 102
info@dotarragona.cat   www.dotarragona.cat

AGRÍCOLA I CAIXA AGRÀRIA I SEC-CIÓ DE CREDIT DE BRAFIM S.C.C.L.

Major, 50
43812 Brafim (Tarragona)
☎: +34 977 620 061 - Fax: +34 977 620 061
www.agricolabrafim.cat
oficina@agricolabrafim.cat

PUIG RODÓ 2012 RD
tempranillo

85 Colour: rose, purple rim. Nose: ripe fruit, red berry notes, floral, expressive. Palate: powerful, fruity, fine bitter notes.

PUIG RODÓ MACABEU 2012 B
100% macabeo

86 Colour: bright straw. Nose: medium intensity, fragrant herbs, citrus fruit. Palate: fresh, fine bitter notes, fruity, easy to drink.

PUIG RODÓ NEGRA 2008 T ROBLE
tempranillo, merlot

84

PUIG RODÓ NEGRA 2012 T
ull de llebre, merlot

84

PUIG RODÓ XAREL.LO 2012 B
xarel.lo

87 Colour: bright straw. Nose: medium intensity, white flowers, varietal. Palate: fresh, fruity, correct, easy to drink.

AGRÍCOLA I S.C. MONTBRIÓ DEL CAMP

Avda. Sant Jordi, 19-21
43340 Montbrió del Camp (Tarragona)
☎: +34 977 826 039 - Fax: +34 977 826 576
www.montebrione.cat
cooperative@montebrione.cat

MOSCATELL MONTEBRIONE 2012 BLANCO DULCE
moscatel romano

87 Colour: bright yellow. Nose: overripe fruit, fragrant herbs, sweet spices. Palate: rich, flavourful, long.

BODEGA COOPERATIVA VILA-RODONA

Ctra. Santes Creus, s/n
43814 Vila-Rodona (Tarragona)
☎: +34 977 638 004 - Fax: +34 977 639 075
www.coopvila-rodona.com
copvilar@copvilar.e.telefonica.net

VI RANCI VILA-RODONA RANCIO

83

VILA-RODONA MISTELA VINO DE LICOR

86 Colour: light mahogany. Nose: fruit liqueur notes, varnish, spicy, sweet spices, creamy oak. Palate: powerful, flavourful, rich, spicy.

CASTELL D'OR

Mare Rafols, 3- 1º 4º
8720 Vilafranca del Penedès (Barcelona)
☎: +34 938 905 446 - Fax: +34 938 905 446
www.castelldor.com
castelldor@castelldor.com

FLAMA ROJA 2009 TR
50% tempranillo, 50% merlot

73

FLAMA ROJA 2012 B
50% macabeo, 50% xarel.lo

84

FLAMA ROJA 2012 RD
100% tempranillo

84

FLAMA ROJA 2012 T
85% tempranillo, 15% garnacha

82

CELLER DPEGNA

Mas DPegna. Pol. 2 parcela 5
43747 Miravet
☎: +34 607 981 525
www.dpegna.com
info@dpegna.com

DAURAT 2011 B

85 Colour: pale. Nose: citrus fruit, fresh fruit, medium intensity, fresh. Palate: easy to drink, sweetness, fruity, fresh.

CELLER LA BOELLA

Autovía Reus - Tarragona (T-11), km. 12
43110 La Canonja (Tarragona)
☎: +34 977 771 515
www.cellerlaboella.com
celler@laboella.com

MAS LA BOELLA ROURE 2010 T
40% monastrell, 37% cabernet sauvignon, 23% merlot

87 Colour: bright cherry. Nose: ripe fruit, creamy oak, balanced. Palate: flavourful, fruity, toasty, round tannins.

MAS LA BOELLA VI DE GUARDA 2009 T
60% cabernet sauvignon, 40% merlot

89 Colour: cherry, garnet rim. Nose: ripe fruit, balsamic herbs, spicy. Palate: rich, powerful, flavourful, round tannins.

CELLER MANYÉ FORTUNY

Dr. Gaspà, 17 La Secuita
43765 El Masroig
☎: +34 977 611 206
cellermanye@gmail.com

MANYÉ ROBERT BN RESERVA
50% macabeo, 25% pinot noir, 25% chardonnay

86 Colour: bright straw. Nose: fresh, wild herbs. Palate: balanced, fruity, easy to drink, good acidity.

CELLER MAS BELLA

Sant Roc, 8 - Masmolets
43813 Valls (Tarragona)
☎: +34 600 269 786 - Fax: +34 977 613 092
www.cellermasbella.com
cellermasbella@gmail.com

BELLA BLANC 2012 B
75% macabeo, 25% parellada

85 Colour: bright yellow. Nose: candied fruit, citrus fruit. Palate: sweetness, good acidity.

BELLA NEGRE 2011 T
ull de llebre

83

BELLA ROSAT 2012 RD
ull de llebre

83

CELLER PEDROLA

Creu, 5
43747 Miravet (Tarragona)
☎: +34 650 093 906
pedrola97@yahoo.es

CAMÍ DE SIRGA 2012 B
50% moscatel, 50% macabeo

83

CAMÍ DE SIRGA 2012 T
25% syrah, 50% merlot, 25% cariñena

85 Colour: cherry, purple rim. Nose: balanced, warm, ripe fruit. Palate: powerful, round tannins.

CELLERS UNIÓ

Joan Oliver, 16-24
43206 Reus (Tarragona)
☎: +34 977 330 055 - Fax: +34 977 330 070
www.cellersunio.com
info@cellersunio.com

ROUREDA 2012 RD
merlot

87 Colour: salmon, bright. Nose: red berry notes, fresh, citrus fruit. Palate: balanced, fine bitter notes, good acidity, fruity.

ROUREDA BLANC DE BLANCS 2012 B
50% macabeo, 40% xarel.lo, 10% moscatel

84

ROUREDA CABERNET SAUVIGNON 2012 T
100% cabernet sauvignon

82

DE MULLER

Camí Pedra Estela, 34
43205 Reus (Tarragona)
☎: +34 977 757 473 - Fax: +34 977 771 129
www.demuller.es
lab@demuller.es

DE MULLER AVREO SECO AÑEJO
garnacha, garnacha blanca

91 Colour: iodine, amber rim. Nose: powerfull, complex, elegant, dry nuts, toasty. Palate: rich, long, fine solera notes, spicy.

DE MULLER AVREO SEMIDULCE AÑEJO
garnacha, garnacha blanca

93 Colour: light mahogany. Nose: candied fruit, caramel, aromatic coffee, sweet spices, creamy oak, varnish, acetaldehyde. Palate: balanced, elegant, powerful, flavourful, long, toasty.

DE MULLER CABERNET SAUVIGNON 2010 TC
100% cabernet sauvignon

83

DE MULLER CHARDONNAY 2012 BFB
chardonnay

90 Colour: bright yellow. Nose: powerfull, ripe fruit, sweet spices, creamy oak, fragrant herbs. Palate: rich, smoky aftertaste, flavourful, fresh, good acidity.

DE MULLER GARNACHA SOLERA 1926 SOLERA
garnacha

95 Colour: dark mahogany. Nose: complex, fruit liqueur notes, dried fruit, pattiserie, toasty. Palate: sweet, rich, unctuous, powerful.

DE MULLER MERLOT 2010 TC
merlot

86 Colour: cherry, garnet rim. Nose: fruit liqueur notes, balsamic herbs, fragrant herbs, creamy oak, toasty. Palate: powerful, flavourful, spicy, warm.

DE MULLER MOSCATEL AÑEJO VINO DE LICOR
moscatel de alejandría

91 Colour: iodine, amber rim. Nose: fruit liqueur notes, honeyed notes, acetaldehyde. Palate: flavourful, sweet, concentrated.

DE MULLER MUSCAT 2012 B
moscatel de alejandría

86 Colour: bright straw. Nose: fresh, white flowers, candied fruit. Palate: flavourful, fruity, good acidity, balanced.

DE MULLER RANCIO SECO VINO DE LICOR
garnacha, mazuelo

91 Colour: light mahogany. Nose: fruit liqueur notes, spicy, varnish. Palate: flavourful, sweetness, powerful.

DE MULLER SYRAH 2012 T
syrah

87 Colour: cherry, garnet rim. Nose: powerfull, ripe fruit, characterful. Palate: correct, round tannins, spicy, toasty.

MAS DE VALLS 2011 BN
macabeo, chardonnay, parellada

88 Colour: bright straw. Nose: fresh fruit, dried herbs, fine lees. Palate: fresh, fruity, flavourful, good acidity.

PAJARETE SOLERA 1851 RANCIO
moscatel, garnacha, garnacha blanca

95 Colour: dark mahogany. Nose: cocoa bean, creamy oak, dark chocolate, sweet spices, candied fruit. Palate: flavourful, full, long, elegant, creamy.

PORPORES DE MULLER 2008 TR
cabernet sauvignon, merlot, tempranillo

87 Colour: bright cherry. Nose: sweet spices, creamy oak, expressive. Palate: flavourful, fruity, toasty, round tannins.

RESERVA REINA VIOLANT 2009 ESP
chardonnay, pinot noir

88 Colour: bright straw. Nose: fine lees, ripe fruit, citrus fruit. Palate: fruity, good acidity, ripe fruit.

SOLIMAR 2010 TC
cabernet sauvignon, merlot

84

SOLIMAR 2012 B
moscatel de alejandría, sauvignon blanc, macabeo

87 Colour: bright straw. Nose: fresh, fresh fruit, white flowers, expressive. Palate: flavourful, fruity, good acidity, balanced.

SOLIMAR 2012 RD
pinot noir, syrah, merlot

84

TRILOGÍA CHARDONNAY RESERVA 2011 BN
chardonnay

88 Colour: bright straw. Nose: medium intensity, fresh fruit, dried herbs, fine lees, floral. Palate: fresh, fruity, flavourful, good acidity.

TRILOGÍA MUSCAT RESERVA 2011 BR
moscatel de alejandría

87 Colour: bright straw. Nose: white flowers, candied fruit, fragrant herbs, expressive. Palate: powerful, fresh, fruity, spicy, balsamic.

TRILOGÍA PINOT NOIR RESERVA 2010 BN
pinot noir

88 Colour: bright straw. Nose: fresh fruit, dried herbs, fine lees, floral. Palate: fresh, fruity, flavourful, good acidity, balanced.

VINO DE MISA DULCE SUPERIOR
garnacha blanca, macabeo

91 Colour: bright yellow. Nose: roasted almonds, pattiserie, cocoa bean, fruit liqueur notes, honeyed notes. Palate: spirituous, good acidity.

ESTUDI BL

Cases de Virgili s/n
43762 La Riera de Gaia (Tarragona)
☎: +34 977 130 939

TINTO TIERRA 2009 T
merlot, tempranillo

86 Colour: cherry, garnet rim. Nose: spicy, creamy oak, ripe fruit, fruit preserve. Palate: powerful, flavourful, toasty.

TINTO TIERRA 2011 T
merlot, tempranillo

82

MAS DEL BOTÓ

Bon Recer, 13
43007 (Tarragona)
☎: +34 630 982 747 - Fax: +34 977 236 396
www.masdelboto.cat
pep@masdelboto.cat

GANAGOT 2005 T
85% garnacha, 10% samsó, 5% cabernet sauvignon

90 Colour: cherry, garnet rim. Nose: ripe fruit, spicy, creamy oak, toasty. Palate: powerful, flavourful, toasty, round tannins.

GANAGOT 2006 T
85% garnacha, 10% samsó, 5% cabernet sauvignon

88 Colour: very deep cherry. Nose: aromatic coffee, creamy oak, overripe fruit, fruit liqueur notes. Palate: powerful, ripe fruit, long.

GANAGOT 2007 T
60% garnacha, 25% cabernet sauvignon, 15% samsó

86 Colour: cherry, garnet rim. Nose: powerfull, slightly evolved, fruit preserve, fruit liqueur notes, cocoa bean. Palate: flavourful.

GANAGOT 2008 T
60% garnacha, 40% samsó

89 Colour: cherry, garnet rim. Nose: medium intensity, balanced, spicy, ripe fruit. Palate: good structure, round tannins.

MAS DEL BOTÓ 2010 T
47% garnacha, 33% cabernot cauvignon, 20% samsó

87 Colour: bright cherry. Nose: ripe fruit, sweet spices, creamy oak. Palate: flavourful, toasty, round tannins.

MAS DELS FRARES (FACULTAT D'ENOLOGIA DE TARRAGONA)

Ctra. TV-7211, Km. 7,2
43120 Constantí (Tarragona)
☎: +34 977 520 197 - Fax: +34 977 522 156
fincafe@urv.cat

URV 2009 TC

87 Colour: cherry, garnet rim. Nose: ripe fruit, spicy, creamy oak, toasty. Palate: powerful, flavourful, toasty.

URV 2012 T

88 Colour: cherry, purple rim. Nose: red berry notes, fruit liqueur notes, balsamic herbs. Palate: flavourful, fruity, good acidity.

URV AROMATIC 2012 B

87 Colour: bright straw. Nose: fresh, fresh fruit, white flowers, expressive. Palate: flavourful, fruity, good acidity.

MAS VICENÇ

Mas Vicenç, s/n
43811 Cabra de Camp (Tarragona)
☎: +34 977 630 024
www.masvicens.com
masvicens@masvicens.com

NIT DE LLUNA 2011 TC
ull de llebre, syrah

85 Colour: cherry, garnet rim. Nose: ripe fruit, fruit liqueur notes, grassy, green pepper, creamy oak. Palate: powerful, flavourful.

ROMBES D'ARLEQUI 2009 TC
ull de llebre, cabernet sauvignon, cariñena

87 Colour: cherry, garnet rim. Nose: ripe fruit, spicy, toasty, complex. Palate: powerful, flavourful, slightly dry, soft tannins.

MOISES VIRGILI ROVIRA

Cases Noves, 19
43763 La Nou de Gaià
☎: +34 977 655 940

MEDOL 2012 T
84

SERRA ALTA 2012 B

86 Colour: bright straw. Nose: dried flowers, fragrant herbs, candied fruit. Palate: powerful, flavourful, spicy.

VINÍCOLA DE NULLES S.C.C.L.

Estació, s/n
43887 Nulles (Tarragona)
☎: +34 977 602 622 - Fax: +34 977 602 622
www.vinicoladenulles.com
botiga@vinicoladenulles.com

ADERNATS 2012 BFB
xarel.lo

87 Colour: bright yellow. Nose: powerfull, sweet spices, creamy oak, citrus fruit. Palate: rich, flavourful, fresh, good acidity.

ADERNATS ANGELUS 2011 T
ull de llebre, cabernet sauvignon, merlot
82

ADERNATS BLANC 2012 B
macabeo, xarel.lo, parellada, chardonnay

86 Colour: bright yellow. Nose: ripe fruit, citrus fruit. Palate: powerful, flavourful, good acidity.

ADERNATS IMPULS 2012 T
ull de llebre, merlot

88 Colour: ruby red. Nose: expressive, fresh fruit, red berry notes, floral. Palate: flavourful, fruity, good acidity, round tannins.

ADERNATS NEGRE JOVE 2011 T

85 Colour: very deep cherry. Nose: powerfull, ripe fruit, warm. Palate: powerful, sweetness.

ADERNATS ROSAT 2012 RD
ull de llebre, merlot

86 Colour: rose, purple rim. Nose: powerfull, red berry notes, floral. Palate: powerful, fruity.

ADERNATS SEDUCCIÓ 2012 B
moscatel, xarel.lo, chardonnay, macabeo

86 Colour: bright straw. Nose: expressive, honeyed notes, citrus fruit. Palate: flavourful, fruity.

VINOS PADRÓ

Avda. Catalunya, 64-70
43812 Brafim (Tarragona)
☎: +34 977 620 012 - Fax: +34 977 620 486
www.vinspadro.com
info@vinspadro.com

CAPITOL 2010 TC
tempranillo, merlot

88 Colour: bright cherry. Nose: ripe fruit, sweet spices, creamy oak. Palate: flavourful, fruity, toasty, round tannins.

CAPITOL TEMPRANILLO 2012 T

87 Colour: cherry, purple rim. Nose: red berry notes, floral, fresh, ripe fruit. Palate: flavourful, fruity, good acidity, round tannins.

IPSIS 2010 TC
tempranillo, merlot

85 Colour: cherry, garnet rim. Nose: ripe fruit, creamy oak, toasty, smoky. Palate: powerful, flavourful, toasty.

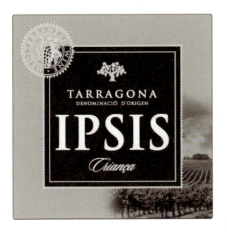

IPSIS BLANC FLOR 2012 B
xarel.lo, macabeo, moscatel

87 Colour: bright straw. Nose: fresh, fresh fruit, white flowers, dried herbs. Palate: flavourful, fruity, good acidity.

IPSIS CHARDONNAY 2012 B
chardonnay

88 Colour: bright straw. Nose: white flowers, ripe fruit. Palate: flavourful, fruity, good acidity, balanced.

IPSIS MUSCAT 2012 B
moscatel

86 Colour: bright straw. Nose: medium intensity, varietal, floral. Palate: correct, good acidity, fresh, easy to drink.

IPSIS TEMPRANILLO MERLOT 2012 T
tempranillo, merlot

84

VINS ECOLÒGICS HELGA HARBIG

Plaça St. Joan, 3
43513 Rasquera (Tarragona)
☎: +34 618 154 254
biopaumera@gmail.com

ADRIÀ DE PAUMERA 2010 T ROBLE
70% garnacha, 30% cabernet sauvignon

87 Colour: very deep cherry. Nose: powerfull, fruit preserve, overripe fruit, sweet spices. Palate: sweetness, powerful, toasty.

ERIKA DE PAUMERA 2012 RD
50% garnacha, 50% cabernet sauvignon

78

ESTHER DE PAUMERA 2010 TC
50% cabernet sauvignon, 50% garnacha

84

VINYA JANINE

Anselm Clavé, 1
43812 Rodonyá (Tarragona)
☎: +34 977 628 305 - Fax: +34 977 628 305
www.vinyajanine.com
vjanine@tinet.org

MOMENTS 2007 T

85 Colour: cherry, garnet rim. Nose: spicy, creamy oak, toasty, overripe fruit. Palate: powerful, flavourful, toasty, round tannins.

SYH 2011 T

85 Colour: deep cherry. Nose: powerfull, warm, characterful. Palate: powerful, fine bitter notes, good acidity.

VINYA JANINE XAREL.LO 2012 B
xarel.lo

87 Colour: bright straw. Nose: fresh, fresh fruit, white flowers. Palate: flavourful, fruity, good acidity, balanced.

VINYES DEL TERRER

Camí del Terrer, s/n
43480 Vila-Seca (Tarragona)
☎: +34 977 269 229 - Fax: +34 977 269 229
www.terrer.net
info@terrer.net

BLANC DEL TERRER 2012 B
100% sauvignon blanc

87 Colour: bright yellow. Nose: dried flowers, wild herbs, earthy notes, ripe fruit, spicy. Palate: powerful, flavourful, balsamic.

NUS DEL TERRER 2010 T
65% cabernet sauvignon, 35% garnacha

92 Colour: cherry, garnet rim. Nose: ripe fruit, spicy, creamy oak, toasty, mineral. Palate: powerful, flavourful, toasty, round tannins.

NUS DEL TERRER 2011 T
70% garnacha, 30% cabernet sauvignon

92 Colour: cherry, garnet rim. Nose: red berry notes, ripe fruit, wild herbs, sweet spices, mineral. Palate: spicy, balsamic, flavourful, long.

TERRER D'AUBERT 2010 T
95% cabernet sauvignon, 5% garnacha

93 Colour: cherry, garnet rim. Nose: ripe fruit, spicy, creamy oak, toasty, complex, mineral. Palate: powerful, flavourful, toasty, round tannins.

TERRER D'AUBERT 2011 T
95% cabernet sauvignon, 5% garnacha

90 Colour: cherry, garnet rim. Nose: ripe fruit, balsamic herbs, earthy notes, spicy, creamy oak. Palate: powerful, flavourful, spicy, long.

LOCATION:

In the southeast of Catalonia, in the province of Tarragona. It covers the municipal districts of Arnes, Batea, Bot, Caseres, Corbera d´Ebre, La Fatarella, Gandesa, Horta de Sant Joan, Pinell de Brai, La Pobla de Massaluca, Prat de Comte and Vilalba dels Arcs.

CLIMATE:

Mediterranean, with continental influences. It is characterized by its hot, dry summers and very cold winters, especially in the higher regions in the east. The average annual rainfall is 400 mm. Another vital aspect is the wind: the 'Cierzo' and the 'Garbi' (Ábrego) winds.

SOIL:

The vineyards are located on an extensive plateau at an altitude of slightly over 400 m. The soil is calcareous and the texture mainly clayey, poor in organic matter and with many pebbles.

GRAPE VARIETIES:

WHITE: *Chardonnay, Garnacha Blanca, Parellada, Macabeo, Moscatel, Sauvignon Blanc, Chenin, Pedro Ximénez.* Experimental: *Viognier.*
RED: *Cabernet Sauvigon, Cariñena, Garnacha Tinta, Garnacha Peluda, Syrah, Tempranillo, Merlot, Samsó, Cabernet Franc.* Experimental: *Petit Verdot, Marselane, Caladoc.*

FIGURES:

Vineyard surface: 6.000 – **Wine-Growers:** 1.500 – **Wineries:** 47– **2012 Harvest rating:** White: Very Good , Rest: Good– **Production:** 13.179.648 litres – **Market percentages:** 30% domestic. 70% export

2008	2009	2010	2011	2012
GOOD	VERY GOOD	VERY GOOD	GOOD	GOOD

CONSEJO REGULADOR
Ctra. Vilalba, 31 - 43780 Gandesa (Tarragona) ☎ +34 977 421 278- Fax: +34 977 421 623
info@terraaltawine.com   www.doterraalta.com

AGRÍCOLA CORBERA D'EBRE

Ponent, 21
43784 Corbera d'Ebre (Tarragona)
☎: +34 977 420 432
www.agricolacorberadebre.com
coop@corbera.tinet.org

MIRMIL-LÓ GARNACHA BLANCA 2012 B
garnacha blanca

84

MIRMIL-LÓ NEGRE 2012 T
garnacha, cariñena, tempranillo, syrah

84

MIRMIL-LÓ PARELLADA 2012 B
parellada

84

MIRMIL-LÓ ROSAT 2012 RD
garnacha

84

NAKENS 2012 B
parellada, moscatel de alejandría

85 Colour: bright straw. Nose: dried flowers, fragrant herbs, tropical fruit. Palate: fresh, fruity, easy to drink.

POBLE VELL BLANCO 2012 VINO DE LICOR BLANCO
100% garnacha blanca

85 Colour: old gold, amber rim. Nose: pattiserie, spicy, honeyed notes, candied fruit, caramel, fruit liqueur notes. Palate: flavourful, sweet.

POBLE VELL TINTO S/C VINO DE LICOR TINTO
garnacha

86 Colour: dark-red cherry, garnet rim. Nose: candied fruit, citrus fruit, powerfull, pattiserie. Palate: sweet, fruity, rich, correct.

VALL EXCELS 2010 TC
garnacha, ull de llebre

86 Colour: cherry, garnet rim. Nose: ripe fruit, spicy, creamy oak, toasty. Palate: powerful, flavourful, toasty.

VALL EXCELS 2011 BFB
100% garnacha blanca

70

AGRÍCOLA SANT JOSEP

Estació, 2
43785 Bot (Tarragona)
☎: +34 977 428 352 - Fax: +34 977 428 192
www.santjosepwines.com
info@santjosepwines.com

CLOT D'ENCÍS 2012 B
80% garnacha blanca, 5% chardonnay, 5% chenin blanc, 5% moscatel de alejandría, 5% sauvignon blanc

85 Colour: bright straw. Nose: medium intensity, balanced, white flowers. Palate: fruity, easy to drink, correct.

CLOT D'ENCIS 2012 RD
65% syrah, 35% garnacha

84

CLOT D'ENCÍS 2012 T
garnacha, samsó

85 Colour: cherry, garnet rim. Nose: red berry notes, fruit liqueur notes, scrubland. Palate: powerful, flavourful, warm.

CLOT D'ENCIS BLANC DE NEGRES 2012 B
100% garnacha

88 Colour: coppery red. Nose: white flowers, fragrant herbs, ripe fruit, mineral. Palate: flavourful, fresh, fruity, long.

LLÀGRIMES DE TARDOR 2007 TR
45% garnacha, 25% samsó, 20% syrah, 10% cabernet sauvignon

85 Colour: cherry, garnet rim. Nose: ripe fruit, spicy, dried herbs. Palate: correct, good finish, easy to drink.

LLÀGRIMES DE TARDOR 2008 TC
58% garnacha, 26% samsó, 15% syrah, 1% cabernet sauvignon

88 Colour: cherry, garnet rim. Nose: ripe fruit, spicy, toasty, complex. Palate: powerful, flavourful, toasty, round tannins.

LLÀGRIMES DE TARDOR 2010 BFB
100% garnacha blanca

91 Colour: bright yellow. Nose: ripe fruit, dry nuts, powerfull, toasty, aged wood nuances. Palate: flavourful, fruity, spicy, toasty, long.

LLÀGRIMES DE TARDOR MISTELA BLANCA 2010 B
100% garnacha blanca

89 Colour: golden. Nose: floral, honeyed notes, candied fruit, fragrant herbs. Palate: flavourful, sweet, fresh, fruity, good acidity, long.

LLÀGRIMES DE TARDOR MISTELA NEGRA 2011 VINO DE LICOR
100% garnacha

89 Colour: cherry, garnet rim. Nose: candied fruit, pattiserie, sweet spices. Palate: long, rich, balanced, spirituous.

LLÀGRIMES DE TARDOR SELECCIÓ 2006 T
30% samsó, 23% syrah, 23% cabernet sauvignon, 14% merlot, 10% garnacha

90 Colour: pale ruby, brick rim edge. Nose: elegant, spicy, fine reductive notes, wet leather, aged wood nuances, fruit liqueur notes. Palate: spicy, fine tannins, elegant, long.

NOVELL DE BOT 2012 T
100% garnacha

88 Colour: cherry, purple rim. Nose: expressive, fresh fruit, red berry notes, floral. Palate: flavourful, fruity, fresh.

ALTAVINS VITICULTORS

Ctra. Vilalba dels Arcs s/n
43786 Batea (Tarragona)
☎: +34 977 430 596 - Fax: +34 977 430 371
www.altavins.com
altavins@altavins.com

ALMODÍ 2012 T
garnacha, syrah

89 Colour: cherry, purple rim. Nose: balanced, red berry notes, ripe fruit, violets. Palate: good acidity, balanced, fruity, round tannins.

DOMUS PENSI 2009 TC
garnacha, syrah, cariñena

88 Colour: black cherry, garnet rim. Nose: ripe fruit, fruit preserve, balsamic herbs, dark chocolate. Palate: good structure, round tannins.

ILERCAVONIA 2012 B
garnacha blanca

88 Colour: coppery red. Nose: citrus fruit, ripe fruit, floral. Palate: flavourful, fruity, balanced, long.

TEMPUS 2010 T ROBLE
garnacha, syrah, cariñena

87 Colour: deep cherry, garnet rim. Nose: spicy, ripe fruit, medium intensity, fruit preserve. Palate: flavourful, balanced, round tannins.

BERNAVÍ

Finca Mas Vernet
43782 Vilalba dels Arcs (Tarragona)
☎: +34 651 031 835
www.bernavi.com
info@bernavi.com

3D3 2011 T
garnacha, syrah, merlot

85 Colour: cherry, garnet rim. Nose: ripe fruit, grassy, spicy. Palate: powerful, flavourful, balsamic.

CA'VERNET 2011 T
cabernet franc, cabernet sauvignon

86 Colour: very deep cherry. Nose: ripe fruit, scrubland, spicy. Palate: good structure, flavourful, round tannins.

NOTTE BIANCA 2012 B
garnacha blanca, viognier

86 Colour: bright yellow. Nose: dried flowers, fragrant herbs, citrus fruit, ripe fruit. Palate: powerful, flavourful, correct.

BODEGAS PINORD

Doctor Pasteur, 6
8720 Vilafranca del Penedès (Barcelona)
☎: +34 938 903 066 - Fax: +34 938 170 979
www.pinord.com
visites@pinord.com

PINORD DIORAMA GARNACHA BLANCA 2012 B
garnacha blanca

87 Colour: bright yellow. Nose: balanced, expressive, ripe fruit, citrus fruit. Palate: rich, fruity, correct, good acidity, good finish.

PINORD DIORAMA GARNACHA NEGRA 2012 T
garnacha

88 Colour: light cherry, garnet rim. Nose: ripe fruit, balanced, sweet spices. Palate: correct, ripe fruit, easy to drink.

CELLER BÁRBARA FORÉS

Santa Anna, 28
43780 Gandesa (Tarragona)
☎: +34 977 420 160 - Fax: +34 977 421 399
www.cellerbarbarafores.com
info@cellerbarbarafores.com

BÁRBARA FORÉS 2012 B
garnacha blanca, viognier

89 Colour: bright straw. Nose: medium intensity, balanced, white flowers, dried flowers, ripe fruit. Palate: fruity, flavourful.

BÁRBARA FORÉS 2012 RD
garnacha, syrah, cariñena

87 Colour: rose, purple rim. Nose: powerfull, ripe fruit, citrus fruit, floral. Palate: fruity, flavourful, long.

BÁRBARA FORÉS NEGRE 2011 T
60% garnacha, 33% syrah, 7% cariñena

88 Nose: ripe fruit, sweet spices, creamy oak, balsamic herbs. Palate: flavourful, fruity, toasty, balanced.

COMA D'EN POU BÀRBARA FORÉS 2010 T
55% garnacha, 24% syrah, 21% cabernet sauvignon

90 Colour: cherry, garnet rim. Nose: sweet spices, creamy oak, ripe fruit, dried herbs. Palate: full, flavourful, round tannins.

EL QUINTÀ BÁRBARA FORÉS 2011 BFB
garnacha blanca

90 Colour: bright yellow. Nose: ripe fruit, sweet spices, creamy oak, fragrant herbs. Palate: rich, flavourful, fresh.

EL QUINTÀ BÁRBARA FORÉS 2012 BFB
garnacha blanca

91 Colour: bright yellow. Nose: powerfull, ripe fruit, sweet spices, creamy oak, fragrant herbs. Palate: rich, flavourful, good acidity.

EL TEMPLARI BÁRBARA FORÉS 2011 T
65% morenillo, 35% garnacha

91 Colour: bright cherry. Nose: ripe fruit, sweet spices, creamy oak, expressive, earthy notes. Palate: flavourful, fruity, round tannins, long.

VI DOLÇ NATURAL BÁRBARA FORÉS 2010 B
garnacha blanca

90 Colour: bright golden. Nose: expressive, balanced, candied fruit, floral. Palate: rich, flavourful, good acidity, balanced.

CELLER BATEA

Moli, 30
43786 Batea (Tarragona)
☎: +34 977 430 056 - Fax: +34 977 430 589
www.cellerbatea.com
cellerbatea@cellerbatea.com

EQUINOX 2011 T
garnacha

90 Colour: cherry, garnet rim. Nose: fruit preserve, fruit liqueur notes, balsamic herbs, spicy, creamy oak, toasty, aromatic coffee, cocoa bean. Palate: powerful, flavourful, spirituous.

EQUINOX 2012 B
garnacha blanca

90 Colour: iodine, amber rim. Nose: complex, fruit liqueur notes, dried fruit, pattiserie, toasty. Palate: sweet, rich, unctuous, powerful.

L'AUBE "SELECCIO DE VINYES VELLES" 2008 TC
merlot, garnacha, cabernet sauvignon

90 Colour: cherry, garnet rim. Nose: ripe fruit, sweet spices, fine reductive notes, wild herbs. Palate: good structure, round tannins, spicy.

PRIMICIA CHARDONNAY 2012 B
chardonnay

85 Colour: bright yellow. Nose: powerfull, faded flowers, ripe fruit. Palate: fruity, good acidity, fine bitter notes.

PRIMICIA GARNACHA SYRAH 2010 TC
garnacha, syrah

86 Colour: cherry, garnet rim. Nose: ripe fruit, spicy, creamy oak, toasty, balsamic herbs. Palate: powerful, flavourful, toasty.

PRIMICIA GARNATXA BLANCA 2012 BFB
garnacha blanca

84

TIPICITAT 2009 T
garnacha, cariñena

89 Colour: cherry, garnet rim. Nose: ripe fruit, spicy, creamy oak, toasty, aromatic coffee. Palate: powerful, flavourful, toasty, round tannins, rich, elegant.

VALLMAJOR 2012 B
garnacha blanca

87 Colour: bright straw. Nose: fresh, fresh fruit, white flowers, expressive. Palate: flavourful, fruity, good acidity, balanced.

VALLMAJOR 2012 RD
garnacha, syrah

84

VALLMAJOR NEGRE 2012 T
garnacha, syrah

88 Colour: cherry, purple rim. Nose: red berry notes, balsamic herbs, earthy notes, floral. Palate: fresh, fruity, flavourful.

VIVERTELL 2008 TC
garnacha, tempranillo, syrah, cabernet sauvignon

88 Colour: cherry, garnet rim. Nose: ripe fruit, balsamic herbs, wet leather, spicy, creamy oak. Palate: powerful, flavourful, long.

CELLER COMA D'EN BONET

Camí de Les Comes d'En Bonet s/n
43780 Gandesa (Tarragona)
☎: +34 977 055 014 - Fax: +34 977 234 665
www.dardell.es
dardell@dardell.es

DARDELL 2009 T BARRICA
50% garnacha, 25% syrah, 25% cabernet sauvignon

84

DARDELL 2012 T
50% garnacha, 50% syrah

82

DARDELL GARNACHA BLANCA & VIOGNIER 2012 B
90% garnacha blanca, 10% viognier

85 Colour: pale, coppery red. Nose: ripe fruit, faded flowers, medium intensity. Palate: fruity, good finish.

PROHOM 2011 T
60% syrah, 20% garnacha, 10% cabernet sauvignon, 10% merlot

82

PROHOM 2012 B
70% garnacha blanca, 30% viognier

89 Colour: bright straw. Nose: fresh fruit, white flowers, fragrant herbs, expressive, mineral. Palate: flavourful, fruity, good acidity, balanced.

CELLER COOPERATIU GANDESA

Avda. Catalunya, 28
43780 Gandesa (Tarragona)
☎: +34 977 420 017 - Fax: +34 977 420 403
www.coopgandesa.com
info@coopgandesa.com

GANDESA MISTELA BLANCA 2011 VINO DE LICOR
garnacha blanca

83

GANDESOLA 2012 B
85% garnacha blanca, 15% macabeo

85 Colour: bright straw. Nose: floral, fragrant herbs, fruit preserve. Palate: flavourful, powerful, correct.

GANDESOLA 2012 RD
100% garnacha

85 Colour: onion pink. Nose: candied fruit, dried flowers, fragrant herbs, red berry notes. Palate: light-bodied, flavourful, long, spicy.

GANDESOLA 2012 T
75% garnacha, 25% tempranillo

86 Colour: cherry, purple rim. Nose: expressive, red berry notes. Palate: flavourful, fruity, good acidity, round tannins, balsamic.

PURESA 2007 T
cariñena

91 Colour: pale ruby, brick rim edge. Nose: ripe fruit, spicy, creamy oak, waxy notes, tobacco, aged wood nuances, earthy notes. Palate: powerful, flavourful, spicy, long.

SOMDINOU 2007 T
40% garnacha, 25% garnacha gris, 35% cariñena

85 Colour: dark-red cherry, garnet rim. Nose: ripe fruit, dried herbs, spicy, old leather. Palate: ripe fruit, round tannins.

SOMDINOU 2009 BFB
100% garnacha blanca

88 Colour: bright yellow. Nose: ripe fruit, sweet spices, creamy oak, fragrant herbs. Palate: rich, smoky aftertaste, flavourful, fresh, good acidity.

SOMDINOU BLANC JOVE 2012 B
90% garnacha blanca, 10% macabeo

89 Colour: bright straw. Nose: citrus fruit, ripe fruit, floral, balsamic herbs, mineral. Palate: powerful, flavourful, rich, long.

SOMDINOU NEGRE JOVE 2012 T
100% cariñena

85 Colour: cherry, garnet rim. Nose: red berry notes, fruit liqueur notes, fragrant herbs. Palate: powerful, flavourful, spicy, easy to drink.

VI DE LICOR 1919 RANCIO
garnacha blanca

90 Colour: iodine, amber rim. Nose: powerfull, complex, elegant, toasty. Palate: rich, fine bitter notes, fine solera notes, long, spicy, balanced.

CELLER JORDI MIRÓ

Sant Marc, 96
43784 Corbera d'Ebre (Tarragona)
☎: +34 650 010 639
www.cellerjordimiro.com
jordi@ennak.com

ENNAK 2011 TC
garnacha, cabernet sauvignon, merlot, tempranillo

89 Colour: very deep cherry, garnet rim. Nose: powerfull, characterful, spicy, ripe fruit. Palate: flavourful, round tannins.

JORDI MIRÓ 2012 T
garnacha, syrah

88 Colour: light cherry. Nose: expressive, fresh fruit, red berry notes, floral. Palate: flavourful, fruity, good acidity.

JORDI MIRÓ GARNATXA BLANCA 2012 B
garnacha blanca

84

CELLER LA BOLLIDORA

Carrer dels Tacons, 8
43782 Vilalba dels Arcs (Tarragona)
☎: +34 600 484 900
www.cellerlabollidora.com
laboratory@cellerlabollidora.com

NAEVOS 2011 T
garnacha, syrah

85 Colour: cherry, garnet rim. Nose: ripe fruit, spicy, creamy oak, toasty, fruit preserve. Palate: powerful, flavourful, toasty.

PLAN B 2009 T
garnacha, syrah, samsó, morenillo

81

CELLER MARIOL

Rosselló, 442
8025 (Barcelona)
☎: +34 934 367 628 - Fax: +34 934 500 281
www.casamariol.com
celler@cellermariol.es

CASA MARIOL CABERNET SAUVIGNON 2008 TR
cabernet sauvignon

81

CASA MARIOL CABERNET SAUVIGNON 2009 TC
cabernet sauvignon

83

CASA MARIOL CUPATGE DINÀMIC CHARDONNAY 2012 B

83

CASA MARIOL GARNATXA BLANCA 2012 B
garnacha blanca

84

CASA MARIOL SYRAH 2008 TR
syrah

86 Colour: pale ruby, brick rim edge. Nose: spicy, fine reductive notes, wet leather, aged wood nuances. Palate: spicy, elegant, long.

CELLER MENESCAL

Joan Amades, 2
43785 Bot (Tarragona)
☎: +34 977 428 095 - Fax: +34 977 428 261
www.cellermenescal.com
info@cellermenescal.com

AVUS BLANC 2011 BFB
garnacha blanca

83

AVUS DOLÇ 2010 T
garnacha

88 Colour: deep cherry, garnet rim. Nose: powerfull, dark chocolate, cocoa bean, sweet spices, candied fruit. Palate: balanced, spirituous, flavourful.

AVUS NEGRE 2011 T ROBLE
garnacha, syrah, merlot, ull de llebre

84

MAS DEL MENESCAL 2012 T
garnacha, syrah

85 Colour: cherry, garnet rim. Nose: fruit preserve, balsamic herbs, powerfull. Palate: rich, flavourful, powerful, balsamic.

CELLER PIÑOL

Avda. Aragón, 9
43786 Batea (Tarragona)
☎: +34 977 430 505 - Fax: +34 977 430 498
www.cellerpinol.com
info@cellerpinol.com

FINCA MORENILLO 2010 T
100% morenillo

89 Colour: ruby red, orangey edge. Nose: ripe fruit, spicy, balsamic herbs, creamy oak. Palate: powerful, flavourful, spicy, long.

JOSEFINA PIÑOL VENDIMIA TARDÍA 2011 TINTO DULCE
100% garnacha

90 Colour: cherry, garnet rim. Nose: ripe fruit, fruit preserve, balsamic herbs, cocoa bean, sweet spices, creamy oak. Palate: powerful, flavourful, spicy, long.

L'AVI ARRUFÍ 2009 T
60% cariñena, 30% garnacha, 10% syrah

92 Colour: deep cherry, garnet rim. Nose: spicy, ripe fruit, sweet spices, dried herbs, balanced. Palate: flavourful, spicy, ripe fruit, long, round tannins.

L'AVI ARRUFÍ 2011 BFB
100% garnacha blanca

91 Colour: bright yellow. Nose: ripe fruit, citrus fruit, sweet spices, balsamic herbs, creamy oak. Palate: powerful, flavourful, spicy, long.

l'Avi Arrufi 2011
Blanc fermentat en barrica
D.O Terra Alta
Celler Piñol

MATHER TERESINA SELECCIÓN DE VIÑAS VIEJAS 2009 T
50% garnacha, 30% cariñena, 20% morenillo

91 Colour: deep cherry, garnet rim. Nose: medium intensity, wild herbs, spicy. Palate: good structure, ripe fruit, round tannins.

PORTAL N. SRA. PORTAL 2011 T
60% garnacha, 15% cariñena, 15% syrah, 10% merlot

89 Colour: cherry, garnet rim. Nose: ripe fruit, creamy oak, wild herbs, spicy. Palate: flavourful, fruity, toasty.

PORTAL N. SRA. PORTAL 2012 B
90% garnacha, 5% macabeo, 5% sauvignon blanc, viognier

91 Colour: bright straw. Nose: balanced, elegant, citrus fruit, floral, mineral. Palate: full, flavourful, good acidity, balanced, long.

RAIG DE RAIM 2012 T
garnacha, cariñena, merlot, syrah

87 Colour: deep cherry, garnet rim. Nose: fruit preserve, wild herbs, spicy. Palate: flavourful, fruity, round tannins.

SA NATURA 2011 T
50% cariñena, 20% syrah, 10% tempranillo, 20% merlot

89 Colour: cherry, garnet rim. Nose: ripe fruit, spicy, creamy oak, toasty, fragrant herbs. Palate: powerful, flavourful, toasty, balsamic, spicy.

CELLER TERN

Ctra. Vilalba, s/n
43786 Batea (Tarragona)
☎: +34 646 047 861
www.ternobradordevi.com
ternobradordevi@gmail.com

TERN 2012 B
garnacha blanca

88 Colour: bright straw. Nose: ripe fruit, floral, fragrant herbs, balanced, expressive. Palate: long, flavourful, good acidity.

TERN GARNATXA NEGRA SYRAH 2011 T
50% garnacha, 20% syrah

87 Colour: deep cherry, garnet rim. Nose: sweet spices, creamy oak, powerfull, warm. Palate: fruity, flavourful, correct.

TERN SIRÀ 2012 T
syrah

87 Colour: very deep cherry, purple rim. Nose: powerfull, macerated fruit, ripe fruit, violet drops. Palate: rich, flavourful.

CELLER VINS FRISACH

Avda. Catalunya 26
43784 Corbera D'Ebre (Tarragona)
☎: +34 977 421 215 - Fax: +34 977 421 215
www.celler-frisach.com
celler-frisach@celler-frisach.com

FRISACH CUPATGE ECOLÒGIC 2012 T
garnacha, cariñena

85 Colour: cherry, garnet rim. Nose: powerfull, warm, ripe fruit, wild herbs. Palate: fruity, round tannins, easy to drink.

FRISACH SELECCIÓ ECOLÒGIC 2012 B
100% garnacha blanca

86 Colour: bright yellow. Nose: white flowers, powerfull, dried herbs. Palate: flavourful, fruity, long.

CELLERS TARRONÉ

Calvari, 22
43786 Batea (Tarragona)
☎: +34 977 430 109 - Fax: +34 977 430 183
www.cellerstarrone.com
info@cellerstarrone.com

MERIAN 2012 B
100% garnacha blanca

87 Colour: bright straw. Nose: white flowers, expressive. Palate: flavourful, fruity, good acidity, balanced.

MERIAN 2012 T
garnacha, syrah, merlot, cabernet sauvignon

87 Colour: deep cherry, purple rim. Nose: ripe fruit, powerfull, violets. Palate: fruity, balanced, long.

MERIAN DULCE NATURAL 2011 T
garnacha

89 Colour: cherry, garnet rim. Nose: fruit preserve, fruit liqueur notes, cocoa bean, sweet spices, balsamic herbs. Palate: powerful, flavourful, correct, spicy, toasty.

TORREMADRINA 2010 TC
garnacha, merlot, syrah, cabernet sauvignon

88 Colour: cherry, garnet rim. Nose: ripe fruit, spicy, creamy oak, toasty, complex. Palate: powerful, flavourful, toasty, round tannins.

TORREMADRINA ROBLE 2012 T
tempranillo, garnacha, merlot, cabernet sauvignon

87 Colour: bright cherry. Nose: ripe fruit, sweet spices, creamy oak. Palate: flavourful, fruity, toasty.

TORREMADRINA SELECCIÓN 2009 TC
garnacha, merlot, syrah, cabernet sauvignon

90 Colour: deep cherry, garnet rim. Nose: spicy, balsamic herbs, creamy oak, cocoa bean, dark chocolate. Palate: flavourful, good structure, powerful.

CELLERS UNIÓ

Joan Oliver, 16-24
43206 Reus (Tarragona)
☎: +34 977 330 055 - Fax: +34 977 330 070
www.cellersunio.com
info@cellersunio.com

CLOS DEL PINELL GARNATXA 2012 T
100% garnacha

85 Colour: cherry, purple rim. Nose: expressive, fresh fruit, red berry notes, floral. Palate: flavourful, fruity, easy to drink.

CLOS DEL PINELL GARNATXA BLANCA 2012 B
100% garnacha blanca

85 Colour: bright straw. Nose: fresh, fresh fruit, white flowers. Palate: flavourful, fruity, good acidity.

REINA ELIONOR 2009 TR
40% garnacha, 40% tempranillo, 20% cabernet sauvignon

84

COCA I FITÓ

Avda. 11 de Setembre s/n
43736 El Masroig (Tarragona)
☎: +34 619 776 948 - Fax: +34 935 457 092
www.cocaifito.com
info@cocaifito.cat

JASPI BLANC 2012 B
70% garnacha blanca, 30% macabeo

88 Colour: bright straw. Nose: fresh fruit, white flowers, citrus fruit. Palate: flavourful, fruity, good acidity, balanced.

EDETÀRIA

Finca El Mas - Ctra. Gandesa a Vilalba s/n
43780 Gandesa (Tarragona)
☎: +34 977 421 534 - Fax: +34 977 421 534
www.edetaria.com
info@edetaria.com

EDETANA MAGNUM 2010 B
70% garnacha blanca, 30% viognier

91 Colour: bright yellow. Nose: medium intensity, balanced, expressive, white flowers, faded flowers, spicy. Palate: balanced, long.

EDETÀRIA 2007 B
85% garnacha blanca, 15% macabeo

94 Colour: bright golden. Nose: ripe fruit, dry nuts, powerfull, toasty, aged wood nuances, petrol notes, sweet spices. Palate: flavourful, fruity, spicy, toasty, long.

EDETÀRIA 2007 T
60% garnacha peluda, 30% syrah, 5% cabernet sauvignon, 5% samsó

93 Colour: ruby red, brick rim edge. Nose: elegant, spicy, fine reductive notes, wet leather, damp earth, scrubland. Palate: spicy, fine tannins, elegant, long.

EDETÀRIA 2008 B
85% garnacha blanca, 15% macabeo

94 Colour: bright golden. Nose: ripe fruit, cocoa bean, sweet spices, expressive. Palate: full, complex, spicy, long.

EDETÀRIA 2008 T
60% garnacha peluda, 30% syrah, 5% cabernet sauvignon, 5% samsó

90 Colour: very deep cherry, garnet rim. Nose: creamy oak, sweet spices, wild herbs. Palate: flavourful, good structure, round tannins.

EDETÀRIA 2009 T
60% garnacha peluda, 30% syrah, 5% cabernet sauvignon, 5% samsó

91 Colour: cherry, garnet rim. Nose: ripe fruit, spicy, wild herbs, mineral. Palate: flavourful, round tannins, long, good acidity.

EDETÀRIA 2010 B
85% garnacha blanca, 15% macabeo

92 Colour: bright yellow. Nose: powerfull, ripe fruit, sweet spices, creamy oak, fragrant herbs, citrus fruit. Palate: rich, smoky aftertaste, flavourful.

EDETÀRIA 2011 B
85% garnacha blanca, 15% macabeo

92 Colour: bright yellow. Nose: sweet spices, toasty, powerfull, ripe fruit, faded flowers, mineral. Palate: flavourful, long, good acidity.

EDETÀRIA DOLÇ 2009 T
70% garnacha, 30% syrah

91 Colour: cherry, garnet rim. Nose: ripe fruit, fruit liqueur notes, spicy, varnish, creamy oak. Palate: powerful, flavourful, spicy, long, balanced, elegant.

VÍA EDETANA 2010 T
60% garnacha, 30% garnacha peluda, 10% samsó

89 Colour: cherry, garnet rim. Nose: ripe fruit, wild herbs, earthy notes, balanced. Palate: spicy, flavourful, round tannins.

VÍA EDETANA 2012 B
70% garnacha blanca, 30% viognier

90 Colour: bright yellow. Nose: floral, fragrant herbs, ripe fruit, citrus fruit, expressive. Palate: rich, flavourful, spicy, long.

VÍA TERRA 2012 B
100% garnacha blanca

90 Colour: bright straw. Nose: fresh, white flowers, medium intensity, citrus fruit. Palate: flavourful, fruity, good acidity, balanced.

VÍA TERRA 2012 RD
100% garnacha peluda

87 Colour: rose, purple rim. Nose: powerfull, ripe fruit, red berry notes, floral, expressive. Palate: powerful, fruity, flavourful.

VÍA TERRA 2012 T
100% garnacha

88 Colour: cherry, garnet rim. Nose: balsamic herbs, red berry notes, earthy notes, spicy. Palate: flavourful, correct, easy to drink.

ESCOLA AGRÀRIA DE GANDESA

Assis Garrote, s/n
43780 Gandesa (Tarragona)
☎: +34 977 420 164 - Fax: +34 977 420 607
www.gencat.cat/agricultura/eca/gandesa
aecagan.daam@gencat.cat

GARNATXES DEL PRAT 2012 T
garnacha, syrah, cabernet sauvignon, tempranillo

84

GLAUKA 2011 BFB
garnacha blanca

84

LES FEIXES EIXUTES 2011 T
garnacha, cariñena

86 Colour: bright cherry. Nose: sweet spices, ripe fruit, fruit preserve. Palate: flavourful, fruity, toasty, sweet tannins.

MACABEUS DEL PRAT 2011 B
macabeo, garnacha blanca, moscatel de alejandría

86 Colour: bright yellow. Nose: white flowers, medium intensity, balanced. Palate: flavourful, fruity, long, easy to drink.

FRANCK MASSARD

Rambla Arnau de Vilanova, 6 entlo. 4a
8880 Vilanova i La Geltrú (Barcelona)
☎: +34 938 956 541
www.epicure-wines.com
info@epicure-wines.com

EL MAGO 2011 T
garnacha

90 Colour: cherry, garnet rim. Nose: varietal, ripe fruit, balanced, scrubland. Palate: flavourful, fruity, round tannins.

HERÈNCIA ALTÉS

Joan Miró, 2
43786 Batea (Tarragona)
☎: +34 938 125 676 - Fax: +34 938 123 213
www.herenciaaltes.com
rdehaan@exportiberia.com

HERENCIA ALTÉS BENUFET 2012 B
garnacha blanca

89 Colour: bright straw. Nose: fresh, fresh fruit, white flowers. Palate: flavourful, fruity, good acidity, balanced.

HERENCIA ALTÉS GARNATXA NEGRA 2012 T
100% garnacha

85 Colour: cherry, garnet rim. Nose: expressive, fresh fruit, red berry notes, floral. Palate: flavourful, fruity, good acidity.

HERENCIA ALTÉS L'ESTEL 2011 T
80% garnacha, 20% syrah

86 Nose: ripe fruit, sweet spices, creamy oak, expressive. Palate: flavourful, fruity, toasty.

HERENCIA ALTÉS ROSAT 2012 RD
100% garnacha

86 Colour: onion pink. Nose: candied fruit, dried flowers, fragrant herbs, red berry notes. Palate: light-bodied, flavourful, good acidity, long, spicy.

I TANT VINS

Passeig del Ferrocarril, 337 Baixos
8860 Castelldefels (Barcelona)
☎: +34 936 628 253 - Fax: +34 934 517 628
www.aribau.es
albert@aribau.es

I TANT GARNATXA BLANCA 2012 B
100% garnacha blanca

89 Colour: bright straw. Nose: fresh, fresh fruit, white flowers, citrus fruit, expressive. Palate: flavourful, fruity, good acidity, balanced.

JOSEP VICENS VALLESPÍ

Aragó, 20
43780 Gandesa (Tarragona)
☎: +34 686 135 921 - Fax: +34 977 421 080
www.vinsjosepvicens.com
celler@vinsjosepvicens.com

VINYES DEL GRAU 2012 B
garnacha blanca

88 Colour: bright yellow. Nose: white flowers, candied fruit, fragrant herbs. Palate: fresh, fruity, light-bodied, easy to drink.

VINYES DEL GRAU 2012 RD
garnacha

84

VINYES DEL GRAU GRAN COUPATGE 2012 B
sauvignon blanc

85 Colour: bright straw. Nose: fresh fruit, white flowers, dried herbs. Palate: flavourful, fruity, good acidity.

VINYES DEL GRAU NEGRO 2012 T
garnacha, cariñena, syrah

84

VINYES DEL GRAU SYRAH 2009 TC
syrah

87 Colour: cherry, garnet rim. Nose: violet drops, fruit preserve, balsamic herbs. Palate: powerful, flavourful, spicy.

VINYES DEL GRAU SYRAH 2012 T
syrah

87 Colour: deep cherry, garnet rim. Nose: powerfull, ripe fruit, fruit preserve, spicy. Palate: good structure, flavourful, round tannins.

LAFOU CELLER

Plaça Catalunya, 34
43786 Batea (Tarragona)
☎: +34 938 743 511 - Fax: +34 938 737 204
www.lafou.net
info@lafou.net

LAFOU 2010 T
garnacha, syrah, cabernet sauvignon

90 Colour: cherry, garnet rim. Nose: spicy, creamy oak, toasty, overripe fruit. Palate: powerful, flavourful, toasty, round tannins.

LAFOU DE BATEA 2008 TR
75% garnacha, 15% syrah, 10% cabernet sauvignon

92 Colour: cherry, garnet rim. Nose: ripe fruit, creamy oak, complex, wild herbs, powerfull, earthy notes. Palate: powerful, flavourful, toasty, round tannins.

LAFOU EL SENDER 2011 TC
60% garnacha, 30% syrah, 10% morenillo

90 Colour: cherry, garnet rim. Nose: ripe fruit, spicy, creamy oak, toasty, complex, expressive. Palate: powerful, flavourful, toasty, round tannins.

LAFOU ELS AMELERS 2012 B
100% garnacha blanca

87 Colour: bright yellow. Nose: medium intensity, ripe fruit, floral. Palate: fruity, flavourful, fine bitter notes, good finish.

LES VINYES D'ANDREU

Sant Vicent, 31
43870 Amposta (Tarragona)
☎: +34 610 254 964 - Fax: +34 977 705 773
roca.andreu@gmail.com

VALL DE VINYES 2005 TC
garnacha, syrah

87 Colour: cherry, garnet rim. Nose: fruit expression, spicy. Palate: powerful, round tannins, flavourful.

VALL DE VINYES SEL-LECIO BLANC 2012 B
garnacha blanca, macabeo, chardonnay

86 Colour: bright straw. Nose: fresh fruit, white flowers, fragrant herbs. Palate: flavourful, fruity, good acidity, balanced.

SERRA DE CAVALLS

Bonaire, 1
43594 El Pinell de Brai (Tarragona)
☎: +34 977 426 049
www.serradecavalls.com
sat@serradecavalls.com

SERRA DE CAVALLS 2010 TC
merlot, cabernet sauvignon

81

SERRA DE CAVALLS 2012 B
chardonnay

87 Colour: bright straw. Nose: fresh, fresh fruit, white flowers, jasmine, citrus fruit. Palate: flavourful, fruity, good acidity, balanced.

SERRA DE CAVALLS 2012 T
garnacha, syrah

79

VINS ALGARS

Algars, 68
43786 Batea (Tarragona)
☎: +34 617 478 152
www.vinsalgars.com
vinsalgars@vinsalgars.com

DE NICANOR 2012 T
garnacha, merlot, syrah

82

VINS DE MESIES

La Verge, 6
43782 Vilalba dels Arcs (Tarragona)
☎: +34 977 438 196
www.ecovitres.com
info@ecovitres.com

BLANC DE MESIES 2012 B
garnacha blanca, macabeo

85 Colour: bright straw. Nose: fresh, fresh fruit, white flowers, expressive. Palate: flavourful, fruity, good acidity, balanced.

MESIES 2009 TC
garnacha, samsó, cabernet sauvignon

86 Colour: cherry, garnet rim. Nose: ripe fruit, spicy. Palate: powerful, flavourful, toasty, round tannins, balsamic.

MESIES GARNATXA 2011 T
100% garnacha

86 Colour: cherry, garnet rim. Nose: ripe fruit, powerfull, dried herbs, balanced. Palate: flavourful, round tannins, balsamic.

MESIES SELECCIÓ 2008 T
garnacha, samsó, syrah

87 Colour: cherry, garnet rim. Nose: ripe fruit, spicy, toasty, wild herbs. Palate: powerful, flavourful, toasty, round tannins.

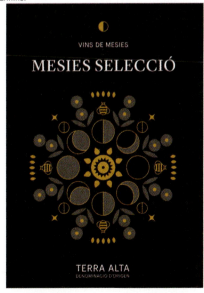

VINS DEL TROS

Major, 13
43782 Vilalba dels Arcs (Tarragona)
☎: +34 605 096 447 - Fax: +34 977 438 042
www.vinsdeltros.com
info@vinsdeltros.com

AY DE MÍ 2011 T
70% garnacha, 30% syrah

85 Colour: cherry, garnet rim. Nose: spicy, fruit preserve, scrubland. Palate: flavourful, balanced, warm.

CENT X CENT 2012 B
100% garnacha blanca

86 Colour: bright straw. Nose: medium intensity, citrus fruit, dried herbs. Palate: fruity, correct.

VINS LA BOTERA

Sant Roc, 26
43786 Batea (Tarragona)
☎: +34 977 430 009 - Fax: +34 977 430 801
www.labotera.com
labotera@labotera.com

BRUNA DOLÇ 2010 T
garnacha, syrah

91 Colour: dark-red cherry, garnet rim. Nose: balanced, overripe fruit, fruit liqueur notes, pattiserie. Palate: rich, flavourful.

MUDÈFER 2010 TC
garnacha, samsó, merlot, syrah

85 Colour: cherry, garnet rim. Nose: spicy, ripe fruit, balsamic herbs. Palate: flavourful, fruity, fine bitter notes.

VILA-CLOSA 2012 T
garnacha, cariñena, syrah

85 Colour: cherry, purple rim. Nose: ripe fruit, wild herbs. Palate: fruity, round tannins, easy to drink.

VILA-CLOSA CHARDONNAY 2012 BFB
chardonnay

87 Colour: bright yellow. Nose: powerfull, ripe fruit, sweet spices, creamy oak, fragrant herbs. Palate: rich, flavourful, fresh, good acidity.

VILA-CLOSA GARNATZA BLANCA 2012 B
garnacha blanca

85 Colour: bright yellow. Nose: ripe fruit, faded flowers. Palate: fruity, easy to drink, good finish.

VINYA D'IRTO

Plaça Comerç , 5
43780 Gandesa (Tarragona)
☎: +34 977 421 534 - Fax: +34 977 421 534
info@edetaria.com

VINYA D'IRTO 2012 B
70% garnacha blanca, 20% macabeo, 10% viognier

88 Colour: bright straw. Nose: white flowers, balanced, ripe fruit. Palate: fruity, flavourful, fine bitter notes, good acidity.

VINYA D'IRTO 2012 RD
100% garnacha peluda

84

VINYA D'IRTO 2012 T
70% garnacha, 30% syrah

87 Colour: cherry, garnet rim. Nose: powerfull, balsamic herbs, red berry notes, ripe fruit. Palate: rich, powerful, flavourful.

XAVIER CLUA COMA

Ctra. Vilalba, km. 9
43782 Vilalba dels Arcs (Tarragona)
☎: +34 977 263 069 - Fax: +34 977 439 003
www.cellerclua.com
rosa@cellerclua.com

CLUA MIL.LENNIUM 2008 TC
garnacha, cabernet sauvignon, merlot, syrah

88 Colour: ruby red, garnet rim. Nose: spicy, fine reductive notes, wet leather, aged wood nuances. Palate: spicy, long, round tannins.

IL.LUSIÓ DE CLUA 2012 B
100% garnacha blanca

90 Colour: bright straw. Nose: expressive, fresh fruit, floral. Palate: fruity, balanced, good acidity, long, balsamic.

MAS D'EN POL 2009 T BARRICA
garnacha, merlot, syrah, cabernet sauvignon

85 Colour: cherry, garnet rim. Nose: ripe fruit, spicy, creamy oak, balsamic herbs. Palate: flavourful, long, spicy.

MAS D'EN POL 2012 B
garnacha, chardonnay, sauvignon blanc

85 Colour: bright straw. Nose: fresh, fresh fruit, white flowers. Palate: flavourful, fruity, good acidity, balanced.

DO TERRA ALTA / D.O.P.

MAS D'EN POL 2012 T
garnacha, merlot, syrah, cabernet sauvignon

86 Colour: deep cherry, purple rim. Nose: balanced, red berry notes, ripe fruit. Palate: fruity, flavourful, correct, round tannins.

LEÓN
Valencia de
Don Juan
ZAMORA VALLADOLID

▽ Consejo Regulador
● DO Boundary

LOCATION:

In the southeast of Catalonia, in the province of Tarragona. It covers the municipal districts of Arnes, Batea, Bot, Caseres, Corbera d´Ebre, La Fatarella, Gandesa, Horta de Sant Joan, Pinell de Brai, La Pobla de Massaluca, Prat de Comte and Vilalba dels Arcs.

CLIMATE:

Mediterranean, with continental influences. It is characterized by its hot, dry summers and very cold winters, especially in the higher regions in the east. The average annual rainfall is 400 mm. Another vital aspect is the wind: the 'Cierzo' and the 'Garbi' (Ábrego) winds.

SOIL:

The vineyards are located on an extensive plateau at an altitude of slightly over 400 m. The soil is calcareous and the texture mainly clayey, poor in organic matter and with many pebbles.

GRAPE VARIETIES:

WHITE: *Chardonnay, Garnacha Blanca, Parellada, Macabeo, Moscatel, Sauvignon Blanc, Chenin, Pedro Ximénez.* Experimental: *Viognier.*
RED: *Cabernet Sauvigon, Cariñena, Garnacha Tinta, Garnacha Peluda, Syrah, Tempranillo, Merlot, Samsó, Cabernet Franc.* Experimental: *Petit Verdot, Marselane, Caladoc.*

FIGURES:

Vineyard surface: 1.318 – **Wine-Growers:** 370 – **Wineries:** 33 – **2012 Harvest rating:** Very Good – **Production:** 2.610.180 litres – **Market percentages:** --% domestic. --% export

VINTAGE RATING PEÑINGUIDE

2008	2009	2010	2011	2012
GOOD	VERY GOOD	VERY GOOD	VERY GOOD	VERY GOOD

CONSEJO REGULADOR
Alonso Castrillo, 29. - 24200 Valencia de Don Juan (León) ☎: +34 987 751 089 - Fax: +34 987 750 012
directortecnico@dotierradeleon.es   www.dotierradeleon.es

BODEGA 100 CEPAS

Pago de las Bodegas, s/n
24225 Corbillo de los Oteros (León)
☎: +34 987 570 059 - Fax: +34 987 570 059
cesar@100cepas.es

100 CEPAS 2011 T
100% prieto picudo

89 Colour: deep cherry. Nose: caramel, aromatic coffee, ripe fruit, fruit expression. Palate: warm, spirituous, good structure, concentrated, powerful.

BODEGAS JULIO CRESPO

Finca Villazán - Ctra. Sahagún, km. 6
24326 Joara, Sahagún (León)
☎: +34 987 130 010 - Fax: +34 987 130 010
www.bodegasjuliocrespo.com
info@bodegasjuliocrespo.com

ALEVOSÍA 2007 T
100% mencía

82

PREMEDITACIÓN 2008 T
prieto picudo

89 Colour: cherry, garnet rim. Nose: toasty, spicy, ripe fruit, powerfull. Palate: fruity, powerful, flavourful, fruity aftertaste, mineral.

BODEGAS MARCOS MIÑAMBRES

Camino de Pobladura, s/n
24234 Villamañán (León)
☎: +34 987 767 038
satvined@picos.com

LOS SILVARES 2005 TR
prieto picudo

89 Colour: dark-red cherry. Nose: undergrowth, medium intensity, short, ripe fruit, spicy. Palate: correct, balanced, powerful, flavourful.

BODEGAS MARGÓN

Avda de Valencia de Don Juan, s/n
24209 Pajares de los Oteros (León)
☎: +34 987 750 800 - Fax: +34 987 750 481
www.bodegasmargon.com
comercial@bodegasmargon.com

PRICUM 2012 RD
100% prieto picudo

90 Colour: onion pink, coppery red. Nose: powerfull, wild herbs, earthy notes, red clay notes. Palate: powerful, flavourful, fruity, concentrated, complex, sweetness.

PRICUM ALBARÍN VALDEMUZ 2011 B BARRICA
100% albarín

88 Colour: bright yellow. Nose: slightly evolved, characterful, new oak, creamy oak. Palate: oaky, balsamic, smoky aftertaste, fruity, powerful.

PRICUM EL VOLUNTARIO 2010 T
prieto picudo

92 Colour: dark-red cherry. Nose: fresh, varietal, complex, mineral. Palate: good acidity, elegant, fruity, fresh, powerful, balsamic.

PRICUM PARAJE DEL SANTO 2009 T
100% prieto picudo

90 Colour: dark-red cherry. Nose: creamy oak, expressive, complex. Palate: creamy, good structure, powerful, flavourful.

PRICUM PRIETO PICUDO 2008 T
100% prieto picudo

92 Colour: cherry, garnet rim. Nose: fruit expression, fresh fruit, complex, expressive, powerfull, varietal. Palate: mineral, fruity, powerful, flavourful, varietal, smoky aftertaste.

PRICUM PRIETO PICUDO 2009 T
100% prieto picudo

90 Colour: dark-red cherry. Nose: ripe fruit, spicy, earthy notes, wild herbs. Palate: powerful, flavourful, fruity, complex, ripe fruit, slightly dry, soft tannins.

PRICUM VALDEMUZ 2009 T
prieto picudo

91 Colour: deep cherry. Nose: undergrowth, damp earth, macerated fruit, varietal, expressive, complex. Palate: good structure, powerful, flavourful, creamy.

BODEGAS RIBERA DEL ORNIA

Madrid, 11
24765 Castrotierra de la Valduerna (León)
☎: +34 692 385 980 - Fax: +34 983 247 472
www.riberadelornia.es
comercial@riberadelornia.es

BAÑEIZA 2012 RD
prieto picudo

84

VAL D'ORNIA 2011 T ROBLE
prieto picudo

85 Colour: cherry, garnet rim. Nose: red berry notes, ripe fruit, balsamic herbs, cocoa bean, spicy. Palate: powerful, flavourful, toasty.

VENDIMIARIO SEDUCCIÓN 2009 TR
prieto picudo

85 Colour: cherry, garnet rim. Nose: spicy, creamy oak, toasty, fruit liqueur notes. Palate: powerful, flavourful, toasty.

BODEGAS VINOS DE LEÓN - VILE, S.A.

La Vega, s/n
24009 Armunia (León)
☎: +34 987 209 712 - Fax: +34 987 209 800
www.bodegasvinosdeleon.es
info@bodegasvinosdeleon.es

DON SUERO 2009 TR
100% prieto picudo

90 Colour: deep cherry. Nose: ripe fruit, damp earth, creamy oak, cedar wood, sweet spices. Palate: balanced, powerful, flavourful, good structure, toasty.

DON SUERO 2010 TC
tinta del país

89 Colour: deep cherry. Nose: toasty, spicy, woody, ripe fruit. Palate: spicy, ripe fruit, flavourful, powerful, fruity.

VALJUNCO 2012 RD
prieto picudo

86 Colour: rose, purple rim. Nose: balsamic herbs, powerfull, wild herbs, ripe fruit. Palate: ripe fruit, flavourful, fruity.

BODEGAS VITALIS

La Fragua, s/n
24324 Villeza (León)
☎: +34 987 263 710 - Fax: +34 987 263 710
aurora@bodegasvitalis.com

VITALIS 2009 TC
100% prieto picudo

88 Colour: cherry, garnet rim. Nose: medium intensity, ripe fruit, spicy. Palate: powerful, flavourful, fruity, fresh.

VITALIS 2010 T ROBLE
100% prieto picudo

88 Colour: dark-red cherry. Nose: ripe fruit, toasty, spicy. Palate: fresh, fruity, powerful, flavourful, spirituous, spicy, balsamic, varietal.

LÁGRIMA DE VITALIS 2012 RD
100% prieto picudo

90 Colour: rose. Nose: fresh fruit, fruit expression, complex, powerfull, varietal. Palate: sweetness, powerful, flavourful, complex, varietal.

BODEGAS Y VIÑEDOS CASIS

Las Bodegas, s/n
24325 Gordaliza del Pino (León)
☎: +34 987 699 618
www.bodegascasis.com
anacasis@gmail.com

CASIS 2006 TGR
100% prieto picudo

88 Colour: dark-red cherry. Nose: ripe fruit, short, spicy, smoky. Palate: powerful, flavourful, fruity, fresh, spicy, ripe fruit.

CASIS 2012 T
46% prieto picudo, 31% mencía, 23% tempranillo

89 Colour: cherry, garnet rim. Nose: fresh fruit, fruit expression. Palate: balsamic, light-bodied, powerful.

CASIS MENCÍA 2009 TC
mencía

88 Colour: dark-red cherry. Nose: spicy, toasty, fresh fruit, wild herbs, red clay notes. Palate: powerful, flavourful, fruity, soft tannins.

CASIS PRIETO PICUDO 2010 TC
prieto picudo

88 Colour: deep cherry. Nose: toasty, sweet spices, powerfull, macerated fruit. Palate: powerful, flavourful, good structure, ripe fruit, classic aged character.

CASIS PRIETO PICUDO 2011 T
prieto picudo

88 Colour: cherry, garnet rim. Nose: fruit expression, fresh fruit, characterful, fresh. Palate: fresh, fruity, flavourful.

CASIS PRIETO PICUDO 2012 RD
100% prieto picudo

87 Colour: rose. Nose: candied fruit, medium intensity, varietal. Palate: good structure, sweetness, powerful, flavourful, fruity.

BODEGAS Y VIÑEDOS LA SILVERA

La Barrera, 7
24209 Pajares de los Oteros (León)
☎: +34 618 174 176
oterobenito@gmail.com

PRETO 2012 RD
100% prieto picudo

83

COOP. VINÍCOLA COMARCAL VALDEVIMBRE

Ctra. de León, s/n
24230 Valdevimbre (León)
☎: +34 987 304 195 - Fax: +34 987 304 195
www.vinicoval.com
valdevim@hotmail.com

ABADÍA DE BALDEREDO 2012 RD
100% prieto picudo

87 Colour: rose. Nose: fresh fruit, fruit expression, varietal, powerfull, expressive. Palate: fruity, powerful, flavourful, balsamic.

SEÑORÍO DE VALDÉS 2012 RD
100% prieto picudo

86 Colour: rose, purple rim. Nose: fruit expression, fresh fruit, varietal, fresh. Palate: powerful, flavourful, fruity, lacks expression.

GORDONZELLO

Alto de Santa Marina, s/n
24294 Gordoncillo (León)
☎: +34 987 758 030 - Fax: +34 987 757 201
www.gordonzello.com
info@gordonzello.com

GURDOS 2012 RD
100% prieto picudo

89 Colour: rose, purple rim. Nose: fruit expression, macerated fruit. Palate: sweetness, full, powerful, flavourful.

KIRA PEREGRINO 2011 BFB
100% albarín

88 Colour: straw. Nose: macerated fruit, powerfull, medium intensity. Palate: powerful, flavourful, good structure, smoky aftertaste.

PEREGRINO 14 2008 TC
100% prieto picudo

89 Colour: cherry, garnet rim. Nose: earthy notes, fruit expression, spicy. Palate: balsamic, spicy, flavourful, powerful, fruity.

PEREGRINO 2008 TR
100% prieto picudo

90 Colour: cherry, garnet rim. Nose: fruit expression, mineral, dry stone, red berry notes, cocoa bean. Palate: fresh, fruity, full, powerful, flavourful, mineral.

PEREGRINO 2010 TC
100% prieto picudo

88 Colour: dark-red cherry. Nose: creamy oak, toasty, complex, fresh fruit. Palate: good structure, fruity, powerful, flavourful, spicy, roasted-coffee aftertaste.

PEREGRINO 2012 RD
100% prieto picudo

90 Colour: rose. Nose: fruit expression, raspberry, varietal. Palate: fruity, powerful, flavourful, complex, mineral, balsamic.

PEREGRINO 2012 T
100% prieto picudo

87 Colour: light cherry. Nose: medium intensity, balanced, expressive. Palate: good structure, powerful, flavourful, fresh.

DO TIERRA DE LEÓN / D.O.P.

PEREGRINO ALBARÍN 2012 B
100% albarín

87 Colour: bright straw. Nose: fragrant herbs, fruit expression, varietal, fresh, neat, medium intensity, complex. Palate: fruity, light-bodied, flavourful, thin.

PEREGRINO BLANCO 2012 B
100% verdejo

89 Colour: pale. Nose: fragrant herbs, fruit expression, citrus fruit, powerfull, varietal, fresh. Palate: powerful, flavourful, varietal, fruity.

PEREGRINO MIL 100 2008 T ROBLE
100% prieto picudo

90 Colour: dark-red cherry. Nose: ripe fruit, fruit expression, spicy, creamy oak, cocoa bean. Palate: spirituous, good structure, powerful, flavourful, creamy, toasty, powerful tannins.

PEREGRINO MIL 100 2011 T BARRICA
100% prieto picudo

89 Colour: dark-red cherry. Nose: fruit expression, fresh fruit, red berry notes. Palate: powerful, flavourful, good structure, fresh, fruity, creamy.

LEYENDA DEL PÁRAMO

Ctra. de León s/n, Paraje El Cueto
24230 Valdevimbre (León)
☎: +34 662 401 435 - Fax: +34 987 424 844
www.leyendadelparamo.com
info@leyendadelparamo.com

EL APRENDIZ 2011 T ROBLE
100% prieto picudo

89 Colour: dark-red cherry. Nose: wild herbs, fresh fruit, characterful, balanced, fresh. Palate: powerful, flavourful, concentrated, balanced.

EL APRENDIZ 2012 B
100% albarín

90 Colour: bright straw. Nose: expressive, powerfull, elegant, complex, varietal. Palate: powerful, flavourful, light-bodied, fruity, fresh.

EL APRENDIZ 2012 RD
100% prieto picudo

87 Colour: rose, purple rim. Nose: fresh fruit, fruit expression, medium intensity. Palate: powerful, flavourful, sweetness, carbonic notes, varietal.

EL MÉDICO 2011 T ROBLE
100% prieto picudo

93 Colour: bright cherry. Nose: ripe fruit, sweet spices, creamy oak, expressive, balsamic herbs, scrubland. Palate: flavourful, fruity, toasty, round tannins.

MITTEL 2012 B
100% albarín

91 Colour: bright straw. Nose: elegant, complex, characterful, powerfull, varietal. Palate: good acidity, elegant, fine bitter notes, powerful, flavourful.

MITTEL 2012 RD
100% prieto picudo

88 Colour: rose. Nose: fruit preserve, red berry notes, powerfull, varietal, earthy notes, red clay notes, fruit expression. Palate: concentrated, fruity, powerful, light-bodied, flavourful.

MEORIGA BODEGAS & VIÑEDOS

Ctra. de Alberite s/n
47680 Mayorga (Valladolid)
☎: +34 983 751 182 - Fax: +34 983 751 182
www.meoriga.com
bodegas@meoriga.com

ESENCIA 33 2012 B
100% verdejo

82

ESENCIA 33 2012 RD
100% prieto picudo

88 Colour: onion pink. Nose: fruit expression, macerated fruit, powerfull, varietal. Palate: good structure, spirituous, powerful, flavourful, sweetness.

MEORIGA ALTA EXPRESIÓN 2008 T ROBLE
100% prieto picudo

86 Colour: dark-red cherry. Nose: tar, spicy, aged wood nuances, ripe fruit. Palate: powerful, spicy, oaky, roasted-coffee aftertaste, lacks expression.

SEÑORÍO DE MOGROVEJO 2010 T JOVEN
100% prieto picudo

87 Colour: dark-red cherry. Nose: ripe fruit, fruit liqueur notes, fresh, neat, short. Palate: flavourful, fruity, ripe fruit.

SEÑORÍO DE MOGROVEJO 2010 T ROBLE
100% prieto picudo

86 Colour: dark-red cherry. Nose: toasty, balanced, ripe fruit, undergrowth. Palate: powerful tannins, fruity, spicy, oaky.

SDAD. COOP. VINOS DE LA RIBERA DEL CEA

Avda. Panduro y Villafañe, 15
24220 Valderas (León)
☎: +34 987 762 191 - Fax: +34 987 762 191
info@riberacea.e.telefonica.net

VIÑA TRASDERREY 2011 T
100% prieto picudo

89 Colour: cherry, garnet rim. Nose: fresh, powerfull, spicy, cedar wood, creamy oak, fresh fruit, macerated fruit. Palate: fruity, powerful, flavourful, slightly acidic, balsamic.

VIÑA TRASDERREY 2012 B
100% verdejo

87 Colour: straw. Nose: powerfull, varietal, expressive, fresh. Palate: fruity, light-bodied, flavourful, powerful, short.

VIÑA TRASDERREY 2012 RD
100% prieto picudo

85 Colour: rose. Nose: rose petals, macerated fruit, neat, expressive, fresh. Palate: fruity, lacks expression, fine bitter notes.

SEÑORÍO DE LOS ARCOS

Ctra. de Caboalles 332
24191 Villabalter (León)
☎: +34 987 226 594 - Fax: +34 987 226 594
admin@senoriodelosarcos.es

VEGA CARRIEGOS 2006 TC
100% prieto picudo

90 Colour: dark-red cherry. Nose: fruit expression, varietal, expressive, characterful. Palate: powerful, flavourful, fruity, easy to drink, soft tannins, fruity aftestaste.

VEGA CARRIEGOS 2011 T ROBLE
100% prieto picudo

88 Colour: dark-red cherry. Nose: spicy, ripe fruit, aged wood nuances. Palate: fruity, powerful, flavourful, sweetness, spicy, ripe fruit.

VEGA CARRIEGOS 2012 RD
100% prieto picudo

88 Colour: rose. Nose: varietal, powerfull, expressive, balanced, fresh fruit. Palate: sweetness, good structure, fruity, powerful, flavourful.

TAMPESTA

La Socollada, s/n
24240 Valdevimbre (León)
☎: +34 987 351 025 - Fax: +34 987 351 025
www.tampesta.com
bodegas@tampesta.com

GOLÁN TAMPESTA 2010 T ROBLE
100% prieto picudo

89 Colour: dark-red cherry. Nose: powerfull, balanced, ripe fruit, fruit liqueur notes, creamy oak, spicy. Palate: correct, balanced, powerful, flavourful, spicy, ripe fruit.

GOLÁN TAMPESTA 2011 T
100% prieto picudo

89 Colour: dark-red cherry. Nose: ripe fruit, warm, varietal. Palate: flavourful, powerful, fruity, fresh, varietal.

MANEKI 2012 B
100% albarín

90 Colour: straw. Nose: fresh fruit, varietal, scrubland. Palate: full, powerful, flavourful, fruity, good structure, spicy, smoky aftertaste.

ROCK 2011 T ROBLE

87 Colour: dark-red cherry. Nose: spicy, creamy oak, ripe fruit. Palate: fruity, powerful, spicy, oaky.

TAMPESTA 2011 T ROBLE
90% prieto picudo, 10% tempranillo

90 Colour: deep cherry. Nose: complex, neat, varietal, powerfull, earthy notes. Palate: powerful, flavourful, fruity, varietal, roasted-coffee aftertaste.

TAMPESTA 2012 RD
prieto picudo

88 Colour: rose. Nose: earthy notes, red clay notes, varietal, macerated fruit. Palate: good structure, powerful, flavourful.

TAMPESTA FINCA DE LOS VIENTOS 2010 T
prieto picudo

88 Colour: deep cherry. Nose: ripe fruit, red clay notes, earthy notes, fresh. Palate: good acidity, fine bitter notes, powerful, flavourful.

TAMPESTA GOLÁN 2011 RD
100% prieto picudo

86 Colour: onion pink. Nose: short, closed, fruit preserve. Palate: flavourful, powerful, fruity, good structure.

TAMPESTA GOLÁN 2012 RD
100% prieto picudo

84

TAMPESTA IMELDA 2010 T
100% prieto picudo

89 Colour: deep cherry. Nose: powerfull, ripe fruit, warm. Palate: ripe fruit, good finish, flavourful, fruity, varietal.

VIÑEDOS Y BODEGA PARDEVALLES

Ctra. de León, s/n
24230 Valdevimbre (León)
☎: +34 987 304 222 - Fax: +34 987 304 222
www.pardevalles.com
info@pardevalles.es

PARDEVALLES 2012 RD
100% prieto picudo

89 Colour: rose. Nose: varietal, neat, fresh, elegant, complex, balanced, fresh fruit. Palate: fruity, powerful, flavourful, balanced.

PARDEVALLES ALBARÍN 2012 B
100% albarín

93 Colour: bright straw. Nose: varietal, powerfull, expressive, characterful, fragrant herbs. Palate: flavourful, powerful, varietal, complex.

PARDEVALLES CARROLEÓN 2009 T
100% prieto picudo

90 Colour: dark-red cherry. Nose: ripe fruit, spicy, creamy oak, earthy notes. Palate: powerful, flavourful, ripe fruit, spicy, toasty.

PARDEVALLES CARROLEÓN 2010 T
100% prieto picudo

91 Colour: cherry, garnet rim. Nose: ripe fruit, spicy, creamy oak, fragrant herbs. Palate: powerful, flavourful, toasty, round tannins.

PARDEVALLES GAMONAL 2011 T
100% prieto picudo

90 Colour: deep cherry. Nose: earthy notes, damp earth, wild herbs, powerfull, complex, expressive. Palate: powerful, flavourful, good structure, spicy, toasty, smoky aftertaste.

WEINWERK EL LAGARTO

Renteilichtung 1
45134 Essen
☎: +34 980 700 043 - Fax: +34 980 700 043
www.gourmet-lagarto.de
info@gourmet-lagarto.de

EMILIA DE WEINWERK 2012 RD
100% prieto picudo

89 Colour: rose. Nose: elegant, candied fruit, dried flowers, red berry notes. Palate: light-bodied, flavourful, good acidity, long, spicy.

LUBY ALBARÍN 2012 B
100% albarín

92 Colour: bright straw. Nose: fresh fruit, white flowers, fruit expression. Palate: flavourful, fruity, good acidity, balanced.

![Map of Zamora and Salamanca regions showing DO boundary]

ZAMORA

Villanueva de Campeán

SALAMANCA

▽ Consejo Regulador
● DO Boundary

LOCATION:

In the southeast part of Zamora, on the Duero river banks. This region comprises 46 municipal districts in the province Zamora and 10 in neighbouring Salamanca. Average altitude is 750 meters.

CLIMATE:

Extreme temperatures as correspond to a dry continental pattern, with very hot summers and cold winters. It does not rain much and average annual rainfall hardly reaches 400 mm.

SOIL:

The character of the territory derives from the river Duero tributaries, so it is predominantly alluvial and clay in the lower strata that might not allow great drainage, though they vary a lot depending on the altitude. There are also some sandy patches on the plain land and stony ones on the hill side.

GRAPE VARIETIES:

WHITE: *Malvasía, Moscatel de grano menudo* and *Verdejo* (preferential); *Albillo, Palomino* and *Godello* (authorized).
RED: *Tempranillo* (main), *Cabernet Sauvignon* and *Garnacha*.

FIGURES:

Vineyard surface: 697 – **Wine-Growers:** 203– **Wineries:** 11 – **2012 Harvest rating:** N/A – **Production:** 597.389 litres – **Market percentages:** 60% domestic. 40% export

VINTAGE RATING PEÑÍNGUIDE				
2008	**2009**	**2010**	**2011**	**2012**
VERY GOOD	**GOOD**	**N/A**	**N/A**	**VERY GOOD**

CONSEJO REGULADOR
Plaza Mayor, 1 - 49708 Villanueva de Campeán (Zamora) ☎ +34 980 560 055 - Fax: +34 980 560 055
info@tierradelvino.net   www.tierradelvino.net

ALTER EGO BODEGA DE CRIANZA

Larga, 4
49709 Cabañas de Sayago (Zamora)
☎: +34 670 095 149

DOMINIO DE SEXMIL 2008 T
100% tempranillo

90 Colour: cherry, garnet rim. Nose: spicy, creamy oak, toasty, complex, overripe fruit, characterful. Palate: powerful, flavourful, toasty, round tannins.

DOMINIO DE SEXMIL EDICIÓN LIMITADA 2006 T
100% tempranillo

93 Colour: cherry, garnet rim. Nose: spicy, creamy oak, toasty, characterful, fruit expression. Palate: powerful, flavourful, toasty, round tannins.

BODEGAS EL SOTO

Ctra. de Circunvalación, s/n
49708 Villanueva de Campeán (Zamora)
☎: +34 980 560 330 - Fax: +34 980 560 330
www.bodegaselsoto.com
info@bodegaselsoto.com

PROCLAMA 2011 T
100% tempranillo

89 Colour: deep cherry. Nose: elegant, varietal, expressive. Palate: flavourful, fruity, spirituous, ripe fruit.

PROCLAMA 2012 B
malvasía

88 Colour: bright straw. Nose: fresh fruit, citrus fruit, white flowers. Palate: flavourful, good acidity.

PROCLAMA SELECCIÓN 2011 T
tempranillo

91 Colour: cherry, garnet rim. Nose: ripe fruit, spicy, creamy oak, toasty, complex, mineral. Palate: powerful, flavourful, toasty, round tannins, varietal.

BODEGAS TESO BLANCO

Larga, 12
49709 Cabañas de Sayago (Zamora)
☎: +34 980 577 820 - Fax: +34 980 560 055
tesoblanco@terra.es

BROCHERO FINCA MONTE CONCEJO 2006 T
tempranillo

87 Colour: light cherry. Nose: medium intensity, ripe fruit, spicy, toasty. Palate: flavourful, good acidity.

MALANDRÍN

Miguel S. Herrador, 3
47014 (Valladolid)
☎: +34 644 172 122
www.malandrinwines.com
info@malandrinwines.com

MALANDRÍN 2009 T
tempranillo

89 Colour: bright cherry. Nose: sweet spices, creamy oak, overripe fruit. Palate: flavourful, fruity, toasty, round tannins.

MALANDRÍN 2012 B
verdejo, godello, moscatel, malvasía

87 Colour: bright straw. Nose: medium intensity, candied fruit, ripe fruit. Palate: flavourful, light-bodied.

MICROBODEGA RODRÍGUEZ MORÁN

Del Prado, 16
49719 Villamor de los Escuderos (Zamora)
☎: +34 980 609 047
microbodegabio.blogspot.com.es
info@microbodega.es

ALUMBRO 2012 B
verdejo, godello, albillo, palomino

89 Colour: bright straw. Nose: fresh, fresh fruit, white flowers. Palate: flavourful, fruity, good acidity, balanced.

ALUMBRO 2012 T
tempranillo

88 Colour: bright cherry. Nose: ripe fruit, sweet spices, creamy oak, balsamic herbs, scrubland. Palate: flavourful, fruity, toasty, round tannins.

VIÑA ESCUDEROS S. COOP.

Ctra. Cubo del Vino, s/n
49719 Villamor de los Escuderos (Zamora)
☎: +34 980 609 204 - Fax: +34 980 609 154
www.vinaescuderos.com
bodega@vinaescuderos.com

GAVIÓN 2012 T ROBLE
tempranillo

89 Colour: bright cherry. Nose: sweet spices, creamy oak, fruit expression. Palate: flavourful, fruity, toasty, round tannins.

GAVIÓN 2007 TR
tempranillo

91 Colour: cherry, garnet rim. Nose: ripe fruit, spicy, creamy oak, toasty, mineral. Palate: powerful, flavourful, toasty, round tannins.

GAVIÓN 2009 TC
tempranillo

90 Colour: cherry, garnet rim. Nose: ripe fruit, spicy, creamy oak, toasty, complex, mineral. Palate: powerful, flavourful, toasty, round tannins.

GAVIÓN 2012 RD
tempranillo

88 Colour: rose, purple rim. Nose: powerfull, ripe fruit, red berry notes, floral, expressive. Palate: powerful, fruity, fresh.

GAVIÓN 2012 T
tempranillo

88 Colour: cherry, purple rim. Nose: fresh fruit, red berry notes, floral. Palate: flavourful, fruity, good acidity, round tannins.

GAVIÓN VERDEJO 2012 B

87 Colour: bright straw. Nose: fresh fruit, citrus fruit, short, neat. Palate: correct, good acidity, flavourful, light-bodied.

VIÑAS DEL CÉNIT

Ctra. de Circunvalación, s/n
49708 Villanueva de Campeán (Zamora)
☎: +34 980 569 346
www.bodegascenit.com
info@bodegascenit.com

CENIT 2009 T
100% tempranillo

94 Colour: deep cherry. Nose: ripe fruit, toasty, creamy oak, aromatic coffee, mineral. Palate: powerful, flavourful, rich, good structure, spirituous, complex.

VIA CENIT 2011 T
100% tempranillo

93 Colour: dark-red cherry. Nose: ripe fruit, complex, fruit expression. Palate: powerful, flavourful, full, spirituous, ripe fruit.

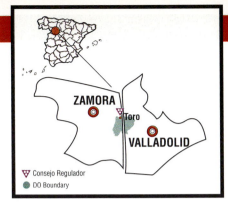

Consejo Regulador
DO Boundary

LOCATION:

Comprising 12 municipal districts of the province of Zamora (Argujillo, Boveda de Toro, Morales de Toro, El Pego, Peleagonzalo, El Piñero, San Miguel de la Ribera, Sanzoles, Toro, Valdefinjas, Venialbo and Villanueva del Puente) and three in the province of Valladolid (San Román de la Hornija, Villafranca de Duero and the vineyards of Villaester de Arriba and Villaester de Abajo in the municipal district of Pedrosa del Rey), which practically corresponds to the agricultural region of Bajo Duero. The production area is to the south of the course of the Duero, which crosses the region from east to west.

CLIMATE:

Extreme continental, with Atlantic influences and quite arid, with an average annual rainfall of between 350 mm and 400 mm. The winters are harsh (which means extremely low temperatures and long periods of frosts) and the summers short, although not excessively hot, with significant contrasts in day-night temperatures.

SOIL:

The geography of the DO is characterised by a gently-undulating terrain. The vineyards are situated at an altitude of 620 m to 750 m and the soil is mainly brownish-grey limestone. However, the stony alluvial soil is better.

GRAPE VARIETIES:

WHITE: *Malvasía* and *Verdejo*.
RED: *Tinta de Toro* (majority) and *Garnacha*.

FIGURES:

Vineyard surface: 5.607 – **Wine-Growers:** 1.329 – **Wineries:** 54 – **2012 Harvest rating:** Very Good– **Production:** 12.147.920 litres – **Market percentages:** 60% domestic. 40% export

VINTAGE RATING PEÑÍNGUIDE				
2008	2009	2010	2011	2012
EXCELLENT	GOOD	VERY GOOD	GOOD	VERY GOOD

CONSEJO REGULADOR
De la Concepción, 3 - Palacio de los Condes de Requena - 49800 Toro (Zamora) - ☎:+34 980 690 335 - Fax: +34 980 693 201
@ consejo@dotoro.es - www.dotoro.es

ÁLVAREZ Y DÍEZ

Juan Antonio Carmona, 12
47500 Nava del Rey (Valladolid)
☎: +34 983 850 136 - Fax: +34 983 850 761
www.alvarezydiez.com
bodegas@alvarezydiez.com

VALMORO 2008 T
tinta de Toro

87 Colour: cherry, garnet rim. Nose: red berry notes, ripe fruit, balsamic herbs, spicy, creamy oak. Palate: powerful, flavourful, balanced.

BODEGA BURDIGALA
(F. LURTON & M. ROLLAND)

Camino Magarín, s/n
47529 Villafranca del Duero (Valladolid)
☎: +34 983 034 030 - Fax: +34 983 034 040
www.burdigala.es
bodega@burdigala.es

CAMPESINO 2011 T
100% tinta de Toro

89 Colour: cherry, garnet rim. Nose: fruit preserve, over-ripe fruit, cocoa bean, balsamic herbs. Palate: flavourful, fruity, round tannins.

CAMPO ALEGRE 2010 T
100% tinta de Toro

89 Colour: cherry, garnet rim. Nose: ripe fruit, creamy oak, toasty, balsamic herbs. Palate: powerful, flavourful, toasty, round tannins.

CAMPO ELISEO 2008 T
100% tinta de Toro

93 Colour: bright cherry, garnet rim. Nose: ripe fruit, wild herbs, spicy, balanced. Palate: good structure, flavourful, long.

CAMPO ELISEO 2009 T
100% tinta de Toro

94 Colour: bright cherry. Nose: ripe fruit, sweet spices, expressive, complex. Palate: flavourful, fruity, round tannins, balsamic.

BODEGA CYAN

Ctra. Valdefinjas - Venialbo, Km. 9,2 Finca La Calera
49800 Toro (Zamora)
☎: +34 980 568 029 - Fax: +34 980 568 036
www.bodegacyan.es
cyan@matarromera.es

CYAN 12 MESES 2005 T
100% tinta de Toro

87 Colour: dark-red cherry. Nose: fruit preserve, wild herbs, spicy. Palate: flavourful, spicy, round tannins.

CYAN 8 MESES 2010 T
100% tinta de Toro

86 Colour: cherry, garnet rim. Nose: spicy, fruit preserve, varietal. Palate: fruity, correct, balanced.

CYAN PAGO DE LA CALERA 2004 T
100% tinta de Toro

90 Colour: pale ruby, brick rim edge. Nose: elegant, spicy, fine reductive notes, wet leather, aged wood nuances, fruit liqueur notes. Palate: spicy, long, toasty, balanced.

CYAN PRESTIGIO 2005 T

89 Colour: pale ruby, brick rim edge. Nose: spicy, fine reductive notes, wet leather, aged wood nuances. Palate: spicy, fine tannins, long.

SELECCIÓN PERSONAL CARLOS
MORO CYAN 2004 T
100% tinta de Toro

88 Colour: very deep cherry. Nose: powerfull, dark chocolate, aromatic coffee, fruit preserve, tobacco. Palate: good structure, full, round tannins.

BODEGA FLORENCIO SALGADO NARROS

Ctra. Toro - Salamanca, Km. 3,20
49800 Toro (Zamora)
cantogordo1926@yahoo.es

PICO ROYO 2008 T
80

PICO ROYO 2012 B
85 Colour: bright straw. Nose: ripe fruit, dried flowers, dried herbs. Palate: spicy, long, balsamic.

BODEGA NUMANTHIA

Real, s/n
49882 Valdefinjas (Zamora)
☎: +34 980 699 147 - Fax: +34 980 699 164
www.numanthia.com

TERMANTHIA 2010 T
tinta de Toro

96 Colour: black cherry. Nose: mineral, earthy notes, ripe fruit, fruit expression, spicy, toasty. Palate: concentrated, fruity, powerful, good acidity, round tannins.

TERMES 2011 T
tinta de Toro

95 Colour: cherry, garnet rim. Nose: spicy, creamy oak, toasty, complex, expressive, fruit expression. Palate: powerful, flavourful, toasty, round tannins.

NUMANTHIA 2010 T
tinta de Toro

96 Colour: cherry, garnet rim. Nose: sweet spices, toasty, ripe fruit, fruit expression, earthy notes. Palate: powerful, good acidity, full, good structure, long.

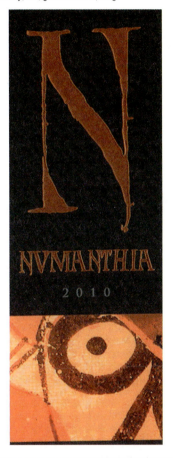

BODEGA PAGO DE CUBAS

Ctra. Toro Valdefinjas, Km. 6,9
49882 Valdefinjas (Zamora)
☎: +34 980 568 125 - Fax: +34 980 059 965
www.bodegapagodecubas.com

ASTERISCO 2011 T
100% tinta de Toro

84

INCRÉDULO 2009 T
100% tinta de Toro

91 Colour: cherry, garnet rim. Nose: ripe fruit, spicy, creamy oak, toasty, complex. Palate: powerful, flavourful, toasty, round tannins.

BODEGA VALDIGAL

Capuchinos, 6
49800 Toro (Zamora)
☎: +34 617 356 325 - Fax: +34 923 269 209
www.valdigal.com
valdigal@valdigal.com

VALDIGAL 2010 B
100% malvasía

90 Colour: bright golden. Nose: ripe fruit, dry nuts, powerfull, toasty, aged wood nuances. Palate: flavourful, fruity, spicy, toasty, long.

VALDIGAL 2010 T
100% tinta de Toro

91 Colour: cherry, garnet rim. Nose: ripe fruit, spicy, creamy oak, toasty, complex. Palate: powerful, flavourful, toasty, round tannins.

BODEGAS ABANICO

Pol. Ind Ca l'Avellanet - Susany, 6
8553 Seva (Barcelona)
☎: +34 938 125 676 - Fax: +34 938 123 213
www.bodegasabanico.com
info@exportiberia.com

ETERNUM VITI 2011 T
100% tinta de Toro

90 Colour: cherry, garnet rim. Nose: ripe fruit, spicy, creamy oak, toasty, complex. Palate: powerful, flavourful, toasty, round tannins.

LOS COLMILLOS 2011 T
100% tinta de Toro

91 Colour: bright cherry. Nose: ripe fruit, sweet spices, creamy oak, expressive, balsamic herbs. Palate: flavourful, fruity, toasty, round tannins.

BODEGAS CAMPIÑA

Ctra. Toro-Veniablo, Km. 6,9
49882 Valdefinjas (Zamora)
☎: +34 980 568 125 - Fax: +34 980 059 965
www.bodegascampina.com
info@bodegascampina.com

CAMPIÑA 2011 T ROBLE
100% tinta de Toro

86 Colour: cherry, garnet rim. Nose: fruit preserve, balsamic herbs. Palate: flavourful, fruity, round tannins, spicy.

CAMPIÑA 2012 T
100% tinta de Toro

85 Colour: cherry, purple rim. Nose: medium intensity, ripe fruit, macerated fruit. Palate: fruity, flavourful.

BODEGAS COVITORO

Ctra. de Tordesillas, 13
49800 Toro (Zamora)
☎: +34 980 690 347 - Fax: +34 980 690 143
www.covitoro.com
covitoro@covitoro.com

ARCO DEL RELOJ 2009 T
100% tinta de Toro

92 Colour: deep cherry, garnet rim. Nose: varietal, expressive, ripe fruit, sweet spices. Palate: balanced, round tannins, long.

CAÑUS VERUS VIÑAS VIEJAS 2009 T
100% tinta de Toro

89 Colour: bright cherry. Nose: ripe fruit, sweet spices, creamy oak, expressive. Palate: flavourful, fruity, toasty, round tannins.

CERMEÑO 2012 B
malvasía

86 Colour: bright straw. Nose: fresh fruit, white flowers, varietal. Palate: flavourful, fruity, good acidity, balanced.

CERMEÑO 2012 RD
tinta de Toro

87 Colour: rose, purple rim. Nose: powerfull, ripe fruit, red berry notes, floral, lactic notes. Palate: powerful, fruity, fresh.

CERMEÑO VENDIMIA SELECCIONADA 2012 T
100% tinta de Toro

88 Colour: bright cherry, purple rim. Nose: medium intensity, balanced, ripe fruit, scrubland. Palate: fruity, flavourful, easy to drink.

GRAN CERMEÑO 2009 TC
100% tinta de Toro

89 Colour: cherry, garnet rim. Nose: red berry notes, ripe fruit, balsamic herbs, cocoa bean, sweet spices.

MARQUÉS DE LA VILLA 2009 TC
100% tinta de Toro

86 Colour: cherry, garnet rim. Nose: medium intensity, ripe fruit, toasty. Palate: easy to drink, fruity, spicy.

MARQUÉS DE LA VILLA 2011 T ROBLE
100% tinta de Toro

87 Colour: bright cherry. Nose: ripe fruit, sweet spices. Palate: flavourful, fruity, toasty, round tannins.

BODEGAS FARIÑA

Camino del Palo, s/n
49800 Toro (Zamora)
☎: +34 980 577 673 - Fax: +34 980 577 720
www.bodegasfarina.com
comercial@bodegasfarina.com

COLEGIATA 2012 RD
100% tinta de Toro

88 Colour: light cherry, bright. Nose: red berry notes, ripe fruit, balanced. Palate: fruity, flavourful, easy to drink, long.

COLEGIATA 2012 T
100% tinta de Toro

89 Colour: cherry, purple rim. Nose: fresh fruit, red berry notes, floral, fragrant herbs. Palate: flavourful, fruity, good acidity.

GRAN COLEGIATA CAMPUS 2008 TC
100% tinto fino

93 Colour: cherry, garnet rim. Nose: ripe fruit, spicy, creamy oak, toasty, complex. Palate: powerful, flavourful, toasty, balanced.

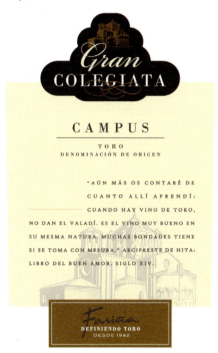

GRAN COLEGIATA ROBLE FRANCÉS 2008 TC
100% tinta de Toro

88 Colour: deep cherry, garnet rim. Nose: ripe fruit, spicy, fragrant herbs. Palate: correct, spicy, round tannins.

GRAN COLEGIATA VINO DE LÁGRIMA 2010 T ROBLE
100% tinta de Toro

89 Colour: bright cherry. Nose: ripe fruit, sweet spices, creamy oak, expressive. Palate: flavourful, fruity, toasty, roasted-coffee aftertaste.

PRIMERO 2012 T MACERACIÓN CARBÓNICA
100% tinta de Toro

88 Colour: cherry, purple rim. Nose: red berry notes, ripe fruit, balanced, violets. Palate: flavourful, long, good acidity, fruity.

BODEGAS FRANCISCO CASAS

Paseo de San Cosme, 6
28600 Navalcarnero (Madrid)
☎: +34 918 110 207 - Fax: +34 918 110 798
www.bodegascasas.com
f.casas@bodegascasas.com

ABBA 2008 T
tinta de Toro

86 Colour: cherry, garnet rim. Nose: spicy, ripe fruit, toasty. Palate: flavourful, toasty, smoky aftertaste.

CAMPARRÓN 2007 TR
tinta de Toro

88 Colour: cherry, garnet rim. Nose: cocoa bean, sweet spices, ripe fruit. Palate: flavourful, ripe fruit, spicy, long, balsamic.

CAMPARRÓN 2009 TC
tinta de Toro

88 Colour: cherry, garnet rim. Nose: ripe fruit, dark chocolate, aromatic coffee, creamy oak. Palate: powerful, flavourful, roasted-coffee aftertaste.

CAMPARRÓN 2012 B
84

CAMPARRÓN NOVUM 2012 T
tinta de Toro

88 Colour: cherry, purple rim. Nose: red berry notes, ripe fruit, violet drops, medium intensity. Palate: good structure, fruity, flavourful.

CAMPARRÓN SELECCION 2012 T
tinta de Toro

88 Colour: cherry, purple rim. Nose: red berry notes, ripe fruit, fragrant herbs. Palate: powerful, flavourful, fruity.

BODEGAS FRONTAURA

Santiago, 17 - 4º
47001 (Valladolid)
☎: +34 983 360 284 - Fax: +34 983 345 546
www.bodegasfrontaura.com
info@bodegasfrontaura.es

APONTE 2006 T
100% tempranillo

93 Colour: cherry, garnet rim. Nose: powerfull, scrubland, spicy, ripe fruit. Palate: full, good structure, complex, round tannins.

DOMINIO DE VALDELACASA 2009 T
100% tempranillo

90 Colour: cherry, garnet rim. Nose: fruit preserve, wild herbs, balsamic herbs, spicy, creamy oak. Palate: powerful, flavourful, correct.

FRONTAURA 2005 TR
100% tempranillo

92 Colour: cherry, garnet rim. Nose: ripe fruit, balsamic herbs, creamy oak, spicy. Palate: powerful, flavourful, long, balanced, elegant, fine tannins.

FRONTAURA 2006 TC
100% tempranillo

90 Colour: cherry, garnet rim. Nose: ripe fruit, spicy, creamy oak, toasty. Palate: powerful, flavourful, toasty, balanced.

FRONTAURA 2011 BFB
100% verdejo

90 Colour: bright golden. Nose: ripe fruit, dry nuts, powerfull, toasty, aged wood nuances. Palate: flavourful, fruity, spicy, toasty, long.

VEGA MURILLO 2011 T
100% tempranillo

87 Colour: bright cherry. Nose: ripe fruit, toasty. Palate: flavourful, fruity, toasty, round tannins.

BODEGAS GIL LUNA

Ctra. Toro - Salamanca, Km. 2
49800 Toro (Zamora)
☎: +34 980 698 509 - Fax: +34 980 698 294
www.giluna.com
pbgiluna@giluna.com

GIL LUNA 2005 T
100% tinta de Toro

88 Colour: cherry, garnet rim. Nose: spicy, old leather, ripe fruit, fruit liqueur notes. Palate: flavourful, good structure, long.

TRES LUNAS 2009 T
100% tinta de Toro

87 Colour: cherry, garnet rim. Nose: spicy, balsamic herbs, ripe fruit. Palate: easy to drink, correct, balanced.

TRES LUNAS 2010 T
100% tinta de Toro

86 Colour: bright cherry. Nose: ripe fruit, sweet spices, creamy oak. Palate: flavourful, fruity, toasty, round tannins.

TRES LUNAS ECOLÓGICO 2012 T
100% tinta de Toro

86 Colour: bright cherry. Nose: ripe fruit, creamy oak, balsamic herbs. Palate: flavourful, fruity, toasty, long.

TRES LUNAS VERDEJO 2012 B
100% verdejo

88 Colour: bright straw. Nose: ripe fruit, tropical fruit, citrus fruit. Palate: ripe fruit, balanced, flavourful.

BODEGAS ITURRIA

Avda. Torrecilla De La Abadesa 2,2E
47100 Tordesillas (Valladolid)
☎: +34 600 523 070
contact@bodegas-iturria.com

TINTO ITURRIA 2010 T
95% tinta de Toro, 5% garnacha

91 Colour: cherry, garnet rim. Nose: red berry notes, ripe fruit, wild herbs, mineral. Palate: powerful, flavourful, spicy, long.

VALDOSAN 2009 T
tinta de Toro

90 Colour: cherry, garnet rim. Nose: ripe fruit, wild herbs, spicy, varietal. Palate: fruity, flavourful, long.

BODEGAS LIBA Y DELEITE

Paseo De Zorrilla, 77 – 3º Dcha.
47007 (Valladolid)
☎: +34 983 355 543 - Fax: +34 983 340 824
www.acontia.es
info@cepasybodegas.com

ACONTIA 2010 TC
90% tinta de Toro, 10% garnacha

85 Colour: cherry, garnet rim. Nose: spicy, dried herbs, boiled fruit notes, ripe fruit. Palate: powerful, flavourful, round tannins.

ACONTIA 2012 T
90% tinta de Toro, 10% garnacha

86 Colour: cherry, garnet rim. Nose: ripe fruit, fruit liqueur notes, balsamic herbs, spicy, creamy oak. Palate: powerful, rich, flavourful.

BODEGAS MATARREDONDA

Ctra. Toro - Valdefinjas, km. 2,5
47195 Toro (Zamora)
☎: +34 980 059 981 - Fax: +34 980 059 981
www.vinolibranza.com
libranza@vinolibranza.com

JUAN ROJO 2008 T
100% tinta de Toro

90 Colour: cherry, garnet rim. Nose: spicy, creamy oak, toasty, balanced, fruit preserve. Palate: powerful, flavourful, toasty.

LIBRANZA 2008 T
100% tinta de Toro

88 Colour: bright cherry, garnet rim. Nose: ripe fruit, violet drops. Palate: balanced, round tannins, spicy.

VALDEFAMA 2011 T
100% tinta de Toro

87 Colour: cherry, garnet rim. Nose: ripe fruit, fruit liqueur notes, spicy, creamy oak. Palate: powerful, flavourful, spicy, long.

BODEGAS MONTE LA REINA

Ctra. Toro - Zamora, Km. 436,7
49881 Toro (Zamora)
☎: +34 980 082 011 - Fax: +34 980 082 012
www.montelareina.es
adm@montelareina.es

CASTILLO DE MONTE LA REINA 2008 TC
tempranillo

87 Colour: cherry, garnet rim. Nose: ripe fruit, spicy, creamy oak, toasty, complex. Palate: powerful, flavourful, toasty, round tannins.

CASTILLO DE MONTE LA REINA 2009 T FERMENTADO EN BARRICA
tempranillo

88 Colour: cherry, garnet rim. Nose: ripe fruit, spicy, creamy oak, toasty. Palate: powerful, flavourful, toasty.

CASTILLO DE MONTE LA REINA 2012 B
100% verdejo

85 Colour: bright straw. Nose: ripe fruit, dried herbs, floral. Palate: fresh, fruity, flavourful.

TERTIUS 2011 T ROBLE
tempranillo

85 Colour: cherry, garnet rim. Nose: ripe fruit, balsamic herbs, spicy, creamy oak. Palate: easy to drink, balsamic.

CASTILLO DE MONTE LA REINA 2011 T ROBLE
tempranillo

84

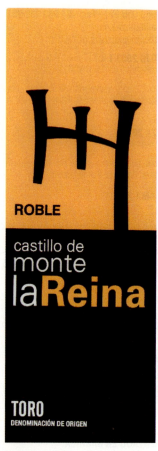

TERTIUS 2012 T
100% tempranillo

85 Colour: cherry, purple rim, cherry, garnet rim. Nose: medium intensity, red berry notes, dried herbs. Palate: fruity, easy to drink, good finish.

BODEGAS OLIVARA

Eras de Santa Catalina, s/n
49800 Toro (Zamora)
☎: +34 980 693 425 - Fax: +34 980 693 409
www.marquesdeolivara.com
marquesdeolivara@marquesdeolivara.com

OLIVARA 2010 TC
100% tinta de Toro

86 Colour: cherry, garnet rim. Nose: ripe fruit, spicy, toasty. Palate: flavourful, toasty, round tannins, ripe fruit.

OLIVARA 2012 T
100% tinta de Toro

85 Colour: cherry, purple rim. Nose: powerfull, ripe fruit, balsamic herbs, medium intensity. Palate: flavourful, rich, easy to drink.

OLIVARA VENDIMIA SELECCIONADA 2010 T
100% tinta de Toro

89 Colour: deep cherry, garnet rim. Nose: medium intensity, wild herbs, ripe fruit, dark chocolate. Palate: fruity, flavourful.

BODEGAS REJADORADA S.L.

Rejadorada, 11
49800 Toro (Zamora)
☎: +34 980 693 089 - Fax: +34 980 693 089
www.rejadorada.com
rejadorada@rejadorada.com

BRAVO DE REJADORADA 2010 T
100% tinta de Toro

92 Colour: cherry, garnet rim. Nose: ripe fruit, balsamic herbs, spicy, creamy oak, complex. Palate: powerful, flavourful, long, balanced, spicy.

NOVELLUM DE REJADORADA 2009 TC
100% tinta de Toro

88 Colour: cherry, garnet rim. Nose: red berry notes, ripe fruit, balsamic herbs, spicy, creamy oak. Palate: powerful, flavourful, long.

REJADORADA ROBLE 2011 T ROBLE
100% tinta de Toro

87 Colour: bright cherry. Nose: sweet spices, creamy oak, red berry notes, ripe fruit. Palate: flavourful, fruity, toasty, harsh oak tannins.

SANGO DE REJADORADA 2009 TR
100% tinta de Toro

91 Colour: deep cherry. Nose: ripe fruit, toasty, sweet spices, cocoa bean. Palate: powerful, flavourful, toasty, round tannins.

BODEGAS SIETECERROS

Finca Villaester N-122, km. 410
47540 Villaester de Arriba - Pedrosa del Rey (Valladolid)
☎: +34 983 784 083 - Fax: +34 983 784 142
www.bodegasietecerros.com
sietecerros@bodegasietecerros.com

QUEBRANTARREJAS 2012 T
100% tinta de Toro

86 Colour: cherry, purple rim. Nose: grassy, ripe fruit, medium intensity, wild herbs. Palate: easy to drink, fruity.

VALDELAZARZA 2009 TC
100% tinta de Toro

83

BODEGAS SOBREÑO

Ctra. N-122, Km. 423
49800 Toro (Zamora)
☎: +34 980 693 417 - Fax: +34 980 693 416
www.sobreno.com
sobreno@sobreno.com

FINCA SOBREÑO 2011 T ROBLE
tinta de Toro

86 Colour: cherry, garnet rim. Nose: red berry notes, fruit liqueur notes, spicy, creamy oak. Palate: powerful, flavourful, balsamic.

FINCA SOBREÑO CRIANZA 2010 TC
100% tinta de Toro

85 Colour: cherry, garnet rim. Nose: spicy, complex, fruit preserve. Palate: flavourful, toasty, round tannins, easy to drink.

FINCA SOBREÑO ECOLÓGICO 2011 T
100% tinta de Toro

85 Colour: cherry, garnet rim. Nose: ripe fruit, spicy, creamy oak, toasty, wild herbs. Palate: powerful, flavourful, toasty.

FINCA SOBREÑO ILDEFONSO 2009 T
100% tinta de Toro

89 Colour: cherry, garnet rim. Nose: ripe fruit, balsamic herbs, sweet spices, creamy oak. Palate: powerful, flavourful, long, elegant.

FINCA SOBREÑO SELECCIÓN ESPECIAL 2009 TR
100% tinta de Toro

89 Colour: cherry, garnet rim. Nose: ripe fruit, spicy, creamy oak, toasty, complex. Palate: powerful, flavourful, toasty, round tannins.

BODEGAS TORREDUERO

Pol. Ind. Norte - Parcela 5
49800 Toro (Zamora)
☎: +34 941 454 050 - Fax: +34 941 454 529
www.bodegasriojanas.com
bodega@bodegasriojanas.com

MARQUÉS DE PEÑAMONTE 2008 TR
100% tinta de Toro

87 Colour: cherry, garnet rim. Nose: ripe fruit, creamy oak, toasty, fine reductive notes. Palate: powerful, flavourful, toasty.

MARQUÉS DE PEÑAMONTE COLECCIÓN PRIVADA 2010 T
100% tinta de Toro

90 Colour: cherry, garnet rim. Nose: ripe fruit, spicy, toasty, mineral. Palate: powerful, flavourful, spicy, balanced.

PEÑAMONTE 2009 TC
100% tinta de Toro

87 Colour: cherry, garnet rim. Nose: ripe fruit, varietal, spicy. Palate: correct, balanced, round tannins.

PEÑAMONTE 2011 T BARRICA
100% tinta de Toro

88 Colour: bright cherry. Nose: ripe fruit, sweet spices, creamy oak, dark chocolate. Palate: flavourful, fruity, toasty, round tannins, balsamic.

PEÑAMONTE 2012 B
100% verdejo

83

PEÑAMONTE 2012 RD
85% tinta de Toro, 15% garnacha

86 Colour: rose, purple rim. Nose: powerfull, ripe fruit, red berry notes, floral, expressive. Palate: powerful, fruity, fresh.

PEÑAMONTE 2012 T
100% tinta de Toro

85 Colour: cherry, purple rim. Nose: red berry notes, ripe fruit, balsamic herbs. Palate: flavourful, fresh, fruity.

BODEGAS VEGA SAUCO

Avda. Comuneros, 108
49810 Morales de Toro (Zamora)
☎: +34 980 698 294 - Fax: +34 980 698 294
www.vegasauco.com
vegasauco@vegasauco.com

ADOREMUS 2006 TR
100% tinta de Toro

89 Colour: pale ruby, brick rim edge. Nose: spicy, fine reductive notes, wet leather, aged wood nuances, fruit liqueur notes. Palate: spicy, long.

ADOREMUS 1998 TGR
100% tinta de Toro

89 Colour: dark-red cherry, orangey edge. Nose: medium intensity, fine reductive notes, tobacco, spicy. Palate: flavourful, fine tannins, good acidity.

ADOREMUS 1999 TGR
100% tinta de Toro

87 Colour: dark-red cherry, orangey edge. Nose: old leather, cigar, fruit liqueur notes, spicy. Palate: fruity, correct, fine tannins.

ADOREMUS 2000 TGR
100% tinta de Toro

85 Colour: cherry, garnet rim. Nose: ripe fruit, spicy, creamy oak, toasty, cigar, waxy notes, old leather. Palate: powerful, flavourful, toasty, round tannins.

ADOREMUS 2001 TGR
100% tinta de Toro

84

ADOREMUS 2008 TR
100% tinta de Toro

88 Colour: cherry, garnet rim. Nose: ripe fruit, spicy, creamy oak, toasty, complex. Palate: powerful, flavourful, toasty.

ADOREMUS 2009 TR
100% tinta de Toro

86 Colour: black cherry. Nose: fruit preserve, overripe fruit, sweet spices. Palate: good structure, round tannins.

FLOR DEL SAUCO VENDIMIA TARDÍA TINTO DULCE NATURAL 2011 T
tempranillo

88 Colour: cherry, garnet rim. Nose: medium intensity, ripe fruit. Palate: flavourful, ripe fruit, long, round tannins.

VEGA SAÚCO EL BEYBI 2011 T ROBLE
100% tinta de Toro

87 Colour: bright cherry. Nose: ripe fruit, creamy oak, earthy notes, spicy. Palate: flavourful, fruity, toasty.

VEGA SAÚCO SELECCIÓN 2010 T
100% tinta de Toro

88 Colour: cherry, garnet rim. Nose: ripe fruit, spicy, creamy oak, toasty, complex. Palate: powerful, flavourful, toasty, round tannins.

BODEGAS VETUS

Ctra. Toro a Salamanca, Km. 9,5
49800 Toro (Zamora)
☎: +34 945 609 086 - Fax: +34 980 056 012
grupoartevino.combodegasvetus.com
vetus@bodegasvetus.com

CELSUS 2011 T
100% tinta de Toro

95 Colour: cherry, garnet rim. Nose: spicy, creamy oak, toasty, characterful. Palate: powerful, flavourful, toasty, round tannins.

FLOR DE VETUS 2011 T
100% tinta de Toro

91 Colour: bright cherry. Nose: sweet spices, creamy oak, fruit expression. Palate: flavourful, fruity, round tannins.

VETUS 2010 T
100% tinta de Toro

92 Colour: very deep cherry. Nose: powerfull, varietal, overripe fruit, toasty. Palate: powerful, toasty, fine bitter notes.

BODEGAS Y VIÑEDOS ANZIL

Ctra. Camino El Pego s/n, Ctra. Toro a Villabuena del Puente, km. 9,400
49800 Toro (Zamora)
☎: +34 915 006 000 - Fax: +34 915 006 006
www.bodegasanzil.es
rrpp@vina-mayor.es

FINCA ANZIL VENDIMIA SELECCIONADA 2011 T
100% tinta de Toro

92 Colour: bright cherry. Nose: ripe fruit, sweet spices, creamy oak, expressive. Palate: flavourful, fruity, toasty, round tannins.

VIÑA MAYOR TORO 2012 T
100% tinta de Toro

89 Colour: cherry, purple rim. Nose: expressive, red berry notes, ripe fruit, sweet spices. Palate: flavourful, fruity, good acidity, round tannins.

BODEGAS Y VIÑEDOS MAURODOS

Ctra. N-122, Km. 412 - Villaester
47112 Pedrosa del Rey (Valladolid)
☎: +34 983 784 118 - Fax: +34 983 784 018
www.bodegasanroman.com
comunicacion@bodegasmauro.com

PRIMA 2011 TC
90% tinta de Toro, 10% garnacha

89 Colour: bright cherry. Nose: ripe fruit, sweet spices, balsamic herbs. Palate: flavourful, fruity, toasty, round tannins.

SAN ROMÁN 2010 T
100% tinta de Toro

95 Colour: cherry, garnet rim. Nose: ripe fruit, spicy, creamy oak, toasty, earthy notes. Palate: powerful, flavourful, toasty, round tannins.

BODEGAS Y VIÑEDOS PINTIA

Ctra. de Morales, s/n
47530 San Román de Hornija (Valladolid)
☎: +34 983 680 147 - Fax: +34 983 680 263
www.bodegaspintia.com
rhernan-perez@vega-sicilia.com

PINTIA 2010 T
100% tinta de Toro

94 Colour: very deep cherry. Nose: powerfull, ripe fruit, toasty, spicy, new oak. Palate: powerful, spicy, ripe fruit, fine tannins.

BODEGUEROS QUINTA ESENCIA

47520 Castronuño (Valladolid)
☎: +34 605 887 100 - Fax: +34 983 866 391
www.bodeguerosquintaesencia.com
info@bodeguerosquintaesencia.com

SOFROS 2011 T
tinta de Toro

90 Colour: bright cherry. Nose: ripe fruit, sweet spices, creamy oak, expressive. Palate: flavourful, fruity, toasty, harsh oak tannins.

BOUTIQUE WINES

Jacinto Benavente, 2
47195 Arroyo de la Encomienda (Valladolid)
☎: +34 639 250 225
www.contaderowine.com
info@spanishboutiquewines.com

CAMPIÑA VIÑAS CENTENARIAS 2009 TC
100% tinta de Toro

87 Colour: cherry, garnet rim. Nose: ripe fruit, spicy, creamy oak, toasty, balsamic herbs. Palate: powerful, flavourful, long, spicy.

CONTADERO 2011 T
100% tinta de Toro

88 Colour: deep cherry, purple rim. Nose: ripe fruit, medium intensity. Palate: balanced, ripe fruit, long, round tannins.

CONTADERO VIÑAS CENTENARIAS 2009 T
100% tinta de Toro

88 Colour: cherry, garnet rim. Nose: ripe fruit, spicy, creamy oak, toasty. Palate: powerful, flavourful, toasty, balanced.

CARMEN RODRÍGUEZ MÉNDEZ

Ctra. Salamanca, ZA 605, Km. 1,650
49800 Toro (Zamora)
☎: +34 980 568 005
www.carodorum.com
info@carodorum.com

CARODORUM 2010 TC
100% tinta de Toro

89 Colour: very deep cherry. Nose: sweet spices, red berry notes, ripe fruit. Palate: good structure, flavourful, balsamic.

CARODORUM ISSOS 2010 TC
100% tinta de Toro

89 Colour: cherry, garnet rim. Nose: red berry notes, ripe fruit, balsamic herbs, sweet spices, toasty. Palate: rich, powerful, flavourful, spicy.

CARODORUM SELECCIÓN ESPECIAL 2010 TC
100% tinta de Toro

91 Colour: cherry, garnet rim. Nose: sweet spices, ripe fruit, fruit preserve. Palate: good structure, balsamic, long.

CARODORUM VENDIMIA SELECCIONADA 2012 T ROBLE
100% tinta de Toro

88 Colour: bright cherry. Nose: sweet spices, creamy oak, ripe fruit, fruit preserve. Palate: flavourful, fruity, toasty, round tannins.

COMPAÑÍA DE VINOS TELMO RODRÍGUEZ

El Monte
1308 Lanciego (Álava)
☎: +34 945 628 315 - Fax: +34 945 628 314
www.telmorodriguez.com
contact@telmorodriguez.com

GAGO 2010 T
100% tinta de Toro

91 Colour: cherry, garnet rim. Nose: spicy, creamy oak, toasty, fruit liqueur notes. Palate: powerful, flavourful, toasty, round tannins.

PAGO LA JARA 2009 T
100% tinta de Toro

94 Colour: cherry, garnet rim. Nose: creamy oak, toasty, complex, mineral, fruit expression. Palate: powerful, flavourful, toasty, round tannins.

CORAL DUERO

Ascensión, s/n
49154 El Pego (Zamora)
☎: +34 980 606 333 - Fax: +34 980 606 391
www.rompesedas.com
rompesedas@rompesedas.com

ROMPESEDAS 2007 T
100% tinta de Toro

90 Colour: cherry, garnet rim. Nose: balanced, ripe fruit, old leather. Palate: good structure, spicy, round tannins.

DIVINA PROPORCIÓN

Camino del Cristo s/n
49800 Toro
www.divinaproporcion.es
info@divinaproporcion.es

MADREMIA 2011 T
100% tinta de Toro

89 Colour: bright cherry. Nose: ripe fruit, sweet spices, balsamic herbs, creamy oak. Palate: flavourful, fruity, toasty, round tannins.

DOMAINES MAGREZ ESPAGNE

Pza. de la Trinidad, 5
49800 Toro (Zamora)
☎: +34 980 698 172 - Fax: +34 980 698 172
www.bernardmagrez.fr
info@vocarraje.es

PACIENCIA 2010 T
100% tinta de Toro

93 Colour: cherry, garnet rim. Nose: complex, balsamic herbs, spicy, ripe fruit. Palate: flavourful, good structure, good acidity.

DOMINIO DEL BENDITO

Pza. Santo Domingo, 8
49800 Toro (Zamora)
☎: +34 980 693 306 - Fax: +34 980 694 991
www.bodegadominiodelbendito.com
info@bodegadominiodelbendito.es

DOMINIO DEL BENDITO EL PRIMER PASO 2011 T ROBLE
100% tinta de Toro

91 Colour: deep cherry, garnet rim. Nose: medium intensity, balanced, ripe fruit, dried herbs. Palate: full, good structure, round tannins.

DOMINIO DEL BENDITO LAS SABIAS 16 MESES 2009 T
100% tinta de Toro

94 Colour: cherry, garnet rim. Nose: medium intensity, complex, ripe fruit, dried herbs. Palate: flavourful, fine tannins, balanced, long.

EL TITÁN DEL BENDITO 2009 T
100% tinta de Toro

95 Colour: cherry, garnet rim. Nose: ripe fruit, sweet spices, creamy oak, mineral, balsamic herbs. Palate: powerful, flavourful, rich, long, spicy, balanced.

ELÍAS MORA

Juan Mora, s/n
47530 San Román de Hornija (Valladolid)
☎: +34 983 784 029 - Fax: +34 983 784 190
www.bodegaseliasmora.com
info@bodegaseliasmora.com

2V PREMIUM 2009 T
100% tinta de Toro

93 Colour: cherry, garnet rim. Nose: ripe fruit, balsamic herbs, spicy, creamy oak, mineral. Palate: powerful, flavourful, spicy, long, balanced.

ELÍAS MORA 2008 TR
100% tinta de Toro

91 Colour: black cherry. Nose: ripe fruit, varietal, spicy, balanced, medium intensity. Palate: good structure, rich, round tannins.

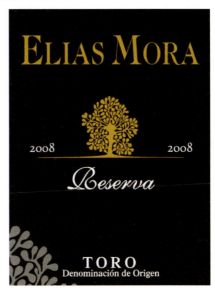

ELÍAS MORA 2010 TC
100% tinta de Toro

91 Colour: cherry, garnet rim. Nose: ripe fruit, spicy, creamy oak, toasty, complex. Palate: powerful, flavourful, toasty, harsh oak tannins.

GRAN ELÍAS MORA 2009 T
100% tinta de Toro

93 Colour: deep cherry, garnet rim. Nose: complex, expressive, cocoa bean, ripe fruit. Palate: good structure, flavourful, round tannins.

VIÑAS ELÍAS MORA 2011 T ROBLE
100% tinta de Toro

90 Colour: cherry, garnet rim. Nose: balanced, red berry notes, ripe fruit, spicy, scrubland, dried herbs. Palate: fruity, flavourful.

ESTANCIA PIEDRA

Ctra. Toro a Salamanca (ZA-605) km. 8
49800 Toro (Zamora)
☎: +34 980 693 900 - Fax: +34 980 693 901
www.estanciapiedra.com
info@estanciapiedra.com

LA GARONA 2008 T
75% tinta de Toro, 25% garnacha

89 Colour: cherry, garnet rim. Nose: ripe fruit, earthy notes, spicy, toasty. Palate: powerful, flavourful, spicy, long.

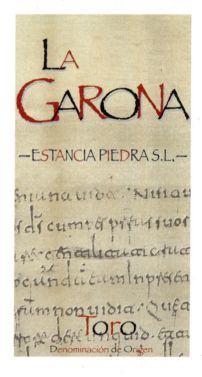

PAREDINAS 2007 TGR
100% tinta de Toro

92 Colour: ruby red, brick rim edge. Nose: elegant, spicy, fine reductive notes, wet leather. Palate: spicy, elegant, long.

PIEDRA AZUL 2012 T
100% tinta de Toro

90 Colour: cherry, garnet rim. Nose: red berry notes, balsamic herbs, powerfull, earthy notes, expressive. Palate: powerful, flavourful, spicy, fruity.

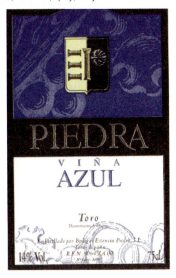

PIEDRA PLATINO 2007 TR
100% tinta de Toro

92 Colour: cherry, garnet rim. Nose: ripe fruit, balsamic herbs, damp earth, spicy, fine reductive notes. Palate: powerful, flavourful, long, toasty.

PIEDRA ROJA 2010 TC
100% tinta de Toro

93 Colour: cherry, garnet rim. Nose: ripe fruit, spicy, creamy oak, toasty, complex, mineral. Palate: powerful, flavourful, toasty, round tannins.

FRUTOS VILLAR

Eras de Santa Catalina, s/n
49800 Toro (Zamora)
☎: +34 983 586 868 - Fax: +34 983 580 180
www.bodegasfrutosvillar.com
bodegasfrutosvillar@bodegasfrutosvillar.com

MURUVE 2009 TC
100% tinta de Toro

87 Colour: cherry, garnet rim. Nose: ripe fruit, spicy, creamy oak, toasty, complex. Palate: powerful, flavourful, toasty.

MURUVE 2009 TR
100% tinta de Toro

91 Colour: cherry, garnet rim. Nose: balanced, varietal, sweet spices, balsamic herbs. Palate: flavourful, fruity, good acidity.

MURUVE 2012 T
100% tinta de Toro

86 Colour: cherry, purple rim. Nose: expressive, fresh fruit, red berry notes, floral. Palate: flavourful, fruity, good acidity.

MURUVE 2011 T ROBLE
100% tinta de Toro

86 Colour: deep cherry, garnet rim. Nose: ripe fruit, spicy, dark chocolate. Palate: fruity, round tannins, toasty.

MURUVE ÉLITE 2010 T
100% tinta de Toro

89 Colour: deep cherry, garnet rim. Nose: ripe fruit, fruit preserve, spicy, balsamic herbs. Palate: flavourful, round tannins.

HACIENDA TERRA D'URO

Campanas, 4, 1º A
47001 (Valladolid)
☎: +34 983 362 591 - Fax: +34 983 357 663
www.terraduro.com
manueldenicolas@gmail.com

TERRA D'URO FINCA LA RANA 2011 T
100% tinta de Toro

89 Colour: dark-red cherry, garnet rim. Nose: ripe fruit, creamy oak, expressive, earthy notes. Palate: flavourful, toasty, spicy.

TERRA D'URO SELECCIÓN 2009 T
100% tinta de Toro

90 Colour: cherry, garnet rim. Nose: fruit preserve, balsamic herbs, cocoa bean, sweet spices, toasty. Palate: rich, powerful, flavourful, spicy, long.

TERRA D'URO SELECCIÓN 2010 T
tinta de Toro

91 Colour: cherry, garnet rim. Nose: ripe fruit, balsamic herbs, spicy, creamy oak. Palate: powerful, rich, flavourful, spicy, long, correct.

URO 2010 T
tinta de Toro

93 Colour: cherry, garnet rim. Nose: ripe fruit, spicy, creamy oak, toasty, complex, mineral. Palate: powerful, flavourful, toasty, balanced.

LEGADO DE ORNIZ

Real de Pedrosa, 20
47530 San Román de Hornija (Valladolid)
☎: +34 669 545 976 - Fax: +34 983 784 116
legadodeorniz@gmail.com

EPITAFIO 2010 T
100% tinta de Toro

92 Colour: cherry, garnet rim. Nose: ripe fruit, spicy, creamy oak, toasty, earthy notes. Palate: powerful, flavourful, toasty, round tannins.

TRIENS 2010 T
100% tinta de Toro

89 Colour: very deep cherry. Nose: expressive, medium intensity, ripe fruit, dark chocolate. Palate: flavourful, round tannins, toasty.

LIBERALIA ENOLÓGICA

Camino del Palo, s/n
49800 Toro (Zamora)
☎: +34 980 692 571 - Fax: +34 980 692 571
www.liberalia.es
liberalia@liberalia.es

LIBER 2005 TGR
100% tinta de Toro

93 Colour: bright cherry, garnet rim. Nose: complex, expressive, ripe fruit, sweet spices, cocoa bean, elegant. Palate: full, long, spicy.

LIBERALIA CERO 2012 T
FERMENTADO EN BARRICA
100% tinta de Toro

90 Colour: bright cherry. Nose: ripe fruit, sweet spices, creamy oak, dark chocolate, aromatic coffee. Palate: flavourful, fruity, toasty.

LIBERALIA CINCO 2006 TR
100% tinta de Toro

92 Colour: cherry, garnet rim. Nose: ripe fruit, spicy, creamy oak, toasty, complex, fine reductive notes. Palate: powerful, flavourful, toasty, round tannins, balanced.

LIBERALIA CUATRO 2008 TC
100% tinta de Toro

91 Colour: cherry, garnet rim. Nose: ripe fruit, balsamic herbs, earthy notes, creamy oak. Palate: powerful, flavourful, spicy, long, varietal.

LIBERALIA TRES 2012 T ROBLE
100% tinta de Toro

89 Colour: cherry, garnet rim. Nose: ripe fruit, medium intensity, sweet spices. Palate: flavourful, fruity, round tannins.

LONG WINES

Avda. del Puente Cultural, 8 Bloque B Bajo 7
28702 San Sebastián de los Reyes (Madrid)
☎: +34 916 221 305 - Fax: +34 916 220 029
www.longwines.com
adm@longwines.com

EL BOS 2012 T ROBLE
100% tinta de Toro

85 Colour: cherry, purple rim. Nose: red berry notes, ripe fruit, balsamic herbs. Palate: correct, powerful, flavourful.

PAGOS DEL REY D.O. TORO

Avda. de los Comuneros, 90
49810 Morales de Toro (Zamora)
☎: +34 980 698 023 - Fax: +34 980 698 020
www.felixsolisavantis.com
toro@pagosdelrey.com

BAJOZ 2011 TC
tinta de Toro

88 Colour: cherry, garnet rim. Nose: ripe fruit, spicy, creamy oak, toasty, complex. Palate: powerful, flavourful, toasty, round tannins.

BAJOZ 2012 RD
tinta de Toro

85 Colour: rose, purple rim. Nose: balanced, ripe fruit, red berry notes, faded flowers. Palate: fruity, easy to drink, good finish.

BAJOZ 2012 T
tinta de Toro

88 Colour: deep cherry, purple rim. Nose: medium intensity, expressive, red berry notes, ripe fruit, violets. Palate: flavourful, fruity.

BAJOZ 2012 T ROBLE
tinta de Toro

88 Colour: bright cherry. Nose: ripe fruit, sweet spices, creamy oak, fragrant herbs. Palate: flavourful, fruity, toasty, round tannins.

BAJOZ MALVASÍA 2012 B
malvasía

85 Colour: bright straw. Nose: faded flowers, citrus fruit, ripe fruit. Palate: correct, good acidity, ripe fruit.

CAÑO 2012 T
50% tempranillo, 50% garnacha

85 Colour: cherry, purple rim. Nose: red berry notes, ripe fruit, balsamic herbs. Palate: powerful, flavourful, correct.

FINCA LA MEDA 2012 B
malvasía

84

FINCA LA MEDA 2012 RD
tinta de Toro

84

FINCA LA MEDA 2012 T
tinta de Toro

85 Colour: cherry, purple rim. Nose: fresh fruit, red berry notes, floral, fragrant herbs. Palate: flavourful, fruity, good acidity.

FINCA LA MEDA 2012 T ROBLE
tinta de Toro

87 Colour: cherry, purple rim. Nose: red berry notes, ripe fruit, wild herbs, sweet spices, creamy oak. Palate: powerful, flavourful, spicy, long.

FINCA LA MEDA ALTA EXPRESIÓN 2012 T
tinta de Toro

90 Colour: cherry, purple rim. Nose: red berry notes, ripe fruit, spicy, creamy oak. Palate: powerful, flavourful, long, balanced.

GRAN BAJOZ DE AUTOR 2012 T
tinta de Toro

90 Colour: bright cherry. Nose: ripe fruit, sweet spices, creamy oak, expressive. Palate: flavourful, fruity, toasty, round tannins.

OUNO 2012 T
100% tinta de Toro

85 Colour: cherry, purple rim. Nose: medium intensity, ripe fruit, violet drops. Palate: correct, balanced.

PALACIO DE VILLACHICA

Ctra. Nacional 122, Km. 433,2
49800 Toro (Zamora)
☎: +34 609 144 711 - Fax: +34 983 381 356
www.palaciodevillachica.com
bodegavillachica@yahoo.es

PALACIO DE VILLACHICA 2009 TC
tinta de Toro

87 Colour: cherry, garnet rim. Nose: medium intensity, scrubland, spicy. Palate: flavourful, fruity.

PALACIO DE VILLACHICA 2012 T
tinta de Toro

86 Colour: cherry, purple rim. Nose: floral, red berry notes, fruit liqueur notes. Palate: flavourful, fruity, good acidity, round tannins.

PALACIO DE VILLACHICA SELECCIÓN 2009 T
tinta de Toro

88 Colour: cherry, garnet rim. Nose: ripe fruit, spicy, creamy oak, toasty. Palate: powerful, flavourful, spicy.

QUINOLA SUÁREZ

Paseo de Zorrilla, 11- 4 izq.
47007 Valladolid (Valladolid)
☎: +34 625 227 321
www.quinola.es
garagewine@quinola.es

QUINOLA GARAGE WINE 2010 T ROBLE
100% tinta de Toro

93 Colour: cherry, garnet rim. Nose: expressive, ripe fruit, spicy, complex. Palate: good structure, flavourful, spicy, long.

QUINTA DE LA QUIETUD

Camino de Bardales, s/n
49800 Toro (Zamora)
☎: +34 980 568 019
www.quintaquietud.com
info@quintaquietud.com

CORRAL DE CAMPANAS 2011 T
100% tinta de Toro

90 Colour: bright cherry. Nose: ripe fruit, sweet spices, expressive. Palate: flavourful, fruity, toasty, round tannins.

QUINTA QUIETUD 2008 T
100% tinta de Toro

92 Colour: bright cherry, garnet rim. Nose: complex, varietal, balsamic herbs, fruit preserve. Palate: flavourful, good structure, round tannins, spicy.

TERRAS DE JAVIER RODRÍGUEZ TORO 2010 T
100% tinta de Toro

93 Colour: bright cherry. Nose: sweet spices, creamy oak, ripe fruit, earthy notes. Palate: flavourful, fruity, toasty, round tannins.

RODRÍGUEZ SANZO

Manuel Azaña, 9
47014 (Valladolid)
☎: +34 983 150 150 - Fax: +34 983 150 151
www.rodriguezsanzo.com
comunicacion@valsanzo.com

DAMALISCO 2009 TC
tinta de Toro

91 Colour: cherry, garnet rim. Nose: ripe fruit, spicy, creamy oak, toasty, dark chocolate. Palate: powerful, flavourful, toasty.

DAMALISCO 2010 TC
100% tinta de Toro

91 Colour: cherry, garnet rim. Nose: red berry notes, ripe fruit, cocoa bean, dark chocolate, toasty, balsamic herbs. Palate: rich, powerful, flavourful.

TESO LA MONJA

Paraje Valdebuey- Ctra. ZA-611, Km. 6,3
49882 Valdefinjas (Zamora)
☎: +34 980 568 143 - Fax: +34 980 508 144
www.eguren.com
info@eguren.com

ALABASTER 2010 T
100% tinta de Toro

95 Colour: cherry, garnet rim. Nose: spicy, creamy oak, dark chocolate, sweet spices, fruit expression, red berry notes. Palate: powerful, flavourful, toasty, round tannins.

ALABASTER 2011 T
100% tinta de Toro

96 Colour: cherry, garnet rim. Nose: spicy, creamy oak, toasty, complex, earthy notes, mineral, fruit expression, red berry notes. Palate: powerful, flavourful, toasty, fine bitter notes, good acidity, powerful tannins.

ALMIREZ 2010 T
100% tinta de Toro

94 Colour: bright cherry. Nose: ripe fruit, sweet spices, creamy oak, powerfull, varietal. Palate: flavourful, fruity, round tannins, ripe fruit.

ALMIREZ 2011 T
100% tinta de Toro

94 Colour: bright cherry. Nose: sweet spices, creamy oak, expressive, fruit expression. Palate: flavourful, toasty, round tannins, ripe fruit, spicy.

ROMANICO 2011 T
100% tinta de Toro

91 Colour: bright cherry. Nose: ripe fruit, sweet spices, creamy oak. Palate: flavourful, fruity, toasty, round tannins.

VICTORINO 2010 T
100% tinta de Toro

96 Colour: cherry, garnet rim. Nose: ripe fruit, spicy, creamy oak, toasty, characterful, expressive, varietal. Palate: powerful, flavourful, toasty, round tannins.

VICTORINO 2011 T
100% tinta de Toro

97 Colour: cherry, garnet rim. Nose: spicy, creamy oak, toasty, complex, earthy notes, mineral, fruit expression, red berry notes. Palate: powerful, flavourful, toasty, round tannins.

TORESANAS

Ctra. Tordesillas, s/n
49800 Toro (Zamora)
☎: +34 983 868 116 - Fax: +34 983 868 432
www.toresanas.com
info@taninia.com

AMANT 2011 T ROBLE
tinta de Toro

84

AMANT NOVILLO 2011 T
tinta del país

87 Colour: bright cherry. Nose: ripe fruit, sweet spices, creamy oak. Palate: flavourful, fruity, toasty.

OROT 2005 TC
tinta de Toro

88 Colour: cherry, garnet rim. Nose: ripe fruit, cocoa bean. Palate: flavourful, toasty, round tannins, balsamic.

VALBUSENDA

Ctra. Toro - Peleagonzalo s/n
49800 Toro (Zamora)
☎: +34 980 699 560 - Fax: +34 980 699 566
www.valbusenda.com
bodega@valbusenda.com

ABIOS VERDEJO 2012 B
100% verdejo

84

VALBUSENDA 2009 T ROBLE
100% tinta de Toro

88 Colour: bright cherry. Nose: ripe fruit, sweet spices, scrubland. Palate: flavourful, fruity, toasty, round tannins.

VALBUSENDA CEPAS VIEJAS 2008 T
100% tinta de Toro

90 Colour: bright cherry, garnet rim. Nose: balanced, varietal, spicy. Palate: flavourful, complex, ripe fruit, mineral.

VINNICO

Muela, 16
3730 Jávea (Alicante)
☎: +34 965 791 967 - Fax: +34 966 461 471
www.vinnico.com
info@vinnico.com

VIÑA ALTAMAR TEMPRANILLO 2011 T
tempranillo

86 Colour: bright cherry. Nose: ripe fruit, sweet spices, creamy oak. Palate: flavourful, fruity, toasty, round tannins.

VIÑA ALTAMAR TEMPRANILLO BARREL SELECT 2010 T
tempranillo

88 Colour: cherry, garnet rim. Nose: ripe fruit, balsamic herbs, sweet spices, creamy oak. Palate: powerful, flavourful, long, spicy.

VINOS Y VIÑEDOS DE LA CASA MAGUILA

Ctra. El Piñero P. 1 P. 715
49153 Venialbo (Zamora)
☎: +34 616 262 549 - Fax: +34 980 081 271
www.casamaguila.com
info@casamaguila.com

ANGELITOS NEGROS 2012 T
100% tinta de Toro

91 Colour: bright cherry. Nose: ripe fruit, sweet spices, creamy oak, expressive. Palate: flavourful, fruity, toasty, round tannins.

CACHITO MÍO 2012 T
100% tinta de Toro

90 Colour: cherry, garnet rim. Nose: ripe fruit, spicy, creamy oak, toasty, complex. Palate: powerful, flavourful, toasty, round tannins.

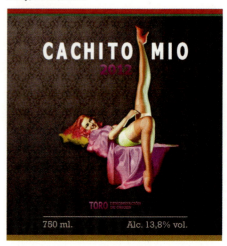

VIÑA ZANGARRÓN

San Esteban, s/n
49152 Sanzoles (Zamora)
☎: +34 619 149 062
www.vinovolvoreta.com
info@vinovolvoreta.com

EL VINO DEL BUEN AMOR 2012 T
100% tinta de Toro

88 Colour: bright cherry. Nose: ripe fruit, sweet spices, creamy oak. Palate: flavourful, fruity, toasty, balanced.

VOLVORETA SIN SULFITOS AÑADIDOS 2011 T
100% tinta de Toro

91 Colour: cherry, purple rim. Nose: balanced, expressive, balsamic herbs, spicy. Palate: fruity, flavourful, ripe fruit.

VIÑAGUAREÑA

Ctra. Toro a Salamanca, Km. 12,5
49800 Toro (Zamora)
☎: +34 980 568 013 - Fax: +34 980 568 134
www.vinotoro.com
info@vinotoro.com

IDUNA 2010 B
100% verdejo

89 Colour: bright yellow. Nose: powerfull, ripe fruit, sweet spices, creamy oak, fragrant herbs. Palate: rich, flavourful, fresh, good acidity.

LA MALANDA CINCO 2012 T
tinta de Toro

85 Colour: cherry, garnet rim. Nose: ripe fruit, spicy, creamy oak, toasty. Palate: powerful, flavourful, toasty.

LA MALANDA DOCE + UNO 2011 T
100% tinta de Toro

86 Colour: cherry, garnet rim. Nose: ripe fruit, spicy, creamy oak, toasty. Palate: powerful, flavourful, toasty.

MUNIA (14 MESES EN BARRICA) 2011 T ROBLE
100% tinta de Toro

90 Colour: very deep cherry, garnet rim. Nose: ripe fruit, balanced, dark chocolate. Palate: good structure, flavourful, round tannins.

MUNIA (6 MESES EN BARRICA) 2011 T ROBLE
100% tinta de Toro

89 Colour: cherry, purple rim. Nose: balanced, ripe fruit, dark chocolate, sweet spices. Palate: good structure, flavourful, round tannins.

MUNIA ESPECIAL 2010 T ROBLE
100% tinta de Toro

90 Colour: very deep cherry. Nose: creamy oak, cocoa bean, sweet spices. Palate: balanced, round tannins, ripe fruit.

VIÑEDOS ALONSO DEL YERRO

Finca Santa Marta - Ctra. Roa-Anguix, Km. 1,8
9300 Roa (Burgos)
☎: +34 913 160 121 - Fax: +34 913 160 121
www.alonsodelyerro.es
mariadelyerro@vay.es

PAYDOS 2009 T
100% tinta de Toro

89 Colour: cherry, garnet rim. Nose: spicy, creamy oak, toasty, complex, fruit preserve. Palate: powerful, flavourful, toasty, balanced.

PAYDOS 2010 T
100% tinta de Toro

93 Colour: cherry, garnet rim. Nose: balanced, complex, spicy, balsamic herbs. Palate: good structure, flavourful, long, round tannins.

VIÑEDOS DE VILLAESTER

49800 Toro (Zamora)
☎: +34 948 645 008 - Fax: +34 948 645 166
www.familiabelasco.com
info@familiabelasco.com

TAURUS 2007 T ROBLE
100% tinta de Toro

84

TAURUS 2007 TC
100% tinta de Toro

85 Colour: cherry, garnet rim. Nose: spicy, creamy oak, toasty, fruit preserve. Palate: powerful, flavourful, toasty.

VILLAESTER 2004 T
100% tinta de Toro

91 Colour: cherry, garnet rim. Nose: ripe fruit, toasty, dark chocolate, mineral. Palate: powerful, flavourful, toasty, round tannins, full.

VOCARRAJE

Ctra. San Román, s/n Calle Izq.
49810 Moral de Toro (Zamora)
☎: +34 980 698 172 - Fax: +34 980 698 172
www.vocarraje.es
info@vocarraje.es

ABDÓN SEGOVIA 2009 TC
100% tinta de Toro

89 Colour: cherry, garnet rim. Nose: fruit preserve, wild herbs, cigar, spicy. Palate: powerful, flavourful, spicy, long.

ABDÓN SEGOVIA 2011 T ROBLE
100% tinta de Toro

87 Colour: cherry, garnet rim. Nose: sweet spices, cocoa bean, ripe fruit, fruit preserve. Palate: ripe fruit, balanced.

WEINWERK EL LAGARTO

Renteilichtung 1
45134 Essen
☎: +34 980 700 043 - Fax: +34 980 700 043
www.gourmet-lagarto.de
info@gourmet-lagarto.de

TEGE WEINWERK 2010 T
garnacha, tinta de Toro

94 Colour: cherry, garnet rim. Nose: spicy, creamy oak, toasty, complex, earthy notes, mineral. Palate: powerful, flavourful, toasty, round tannins.

WEINWERK I. ROBLE 2010 T
tinta de Toro, garnacha

90 Colour: bright cherry. Nose: ripe fruit, sweet spices, creamy oak, expressive. Palate: flavourful, fruity, toasty, round tannins.

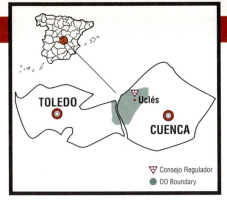

LOCATION:

Midway between Cuenca (to the west) and Toledo (to the northwest), this DO is made up of 25 towns from the first province and three from the second. However, the majority of vineyards are situated in Tarancón and the neighbouring towns of Cuenca, as far as Huete - where La Alcarria starts - the largest stretch of border in the DO.

CLIMATE:

The Altamira sierra forms gentle undulations that rise from an average of 600 metres in La Mancha, reaching 1,200 metres. These ups and downs produce variations in the continental climate, which is less extreme, milder and has a Mediterranean touch. As such, rain is scarce, more akin to a semi-dry climate.

SOIL:

Despite spreading over two provinces with different soil components, the communal soils are deep and not very productive, of a sandy and consistent texture, becoming more clayey as you move towards the banks of the rivers Riansares and Bendija.

GRAPE VARIETIES:

RED: *Tempranillo, Merlot, Cabernet Sauvignon, Garnacha* and *Syrah*.
WHITE: *Verdejo, Moscatel de Grano Menudo, Chardonnay, Sauvignon Blanc* and *Viura (macabeo)*.

FIGURES:

Vineyard surface: 1,700 – **Wine-Growers:** 122 – **Wineries:** 5 – **2012 Harvest rating:** Very Good – **Production:** 1,677,563 litres – **Market percentages:** 25% domestic. 75% export

VINTAGE RATING PEÑÍNGUIDE				
2008	**2009**	**2010**	**2011**	**2012**
AVERAGE	GOOD	VERY GOOD	VERY GOOD	GOOD

CONSEJO REGULADOR
Avda. Miguel Cervantes, 93 - 16400 Tarancón (Cuenca) ☎: +34 969 135 056 - Fax: +34 969 135 421
gerente@vinosdeucles.com   www.vinosdeucles.com

BODEGA SOLEDAD

Ctra. Tarancón, s/n
16411 Fuente de Pedro Naharro (Cuenca)
☎: +34 969 125 039 - Fax: +34 969 125 907
www.bodegasoledad.com
enologo@bodegasoledad.com

BISIESTO 2012 BFB
chardonnay
83

SOLMAYOR 2009 TC
tempranillo
87 Colour: cherry, garnet rim. Nose: balanced, ripe fruit, sweet spices, medium intensity. Palate: balanced, fine bitter notes, ripe fruit.

SOLMAYOR 2010 T ROBLE
tempranillo
85 Colour: bright cherry. Nose: ripe fruit, sweet spices, creamy oak. Palate: flavourful, fruity, toasty, easy to drink.

SOLMAYOR 2012 RD
tempranillo
85 Colour: light cherry, bright. Nose: red berry notes, ripe fruit, lactic notes. Palate: easy to drink, correct.

SOLMAYOR 2012 T
tempranillo
84

SOLMAYOR CHARDONNAY 2012 B
chardonnay
82

SOLMAYOR SAUVIGNON BLANC 2012 B
sauvignon blanc
83

BODEGAS FINCA LA ESTACADA

Ctra. N-400, Km. 103
16400 Tarancón (Cuenca)
☎: +34 969 327 099 - Fax: +34 969 327 199
www.laestacada.com
laestacada@laestacada.es

FINCA LA ESTACADA 2012 B
50% chardonnay, 50% sauvignon blanc
84

FINCA LA ESTACADA 6 MESES BARRICA 2011 T ROBLE
tempranillo
87 Colour: cherry, garnet rim. Nose: sweet spices, cocoa bean, ripe fruit. Palate: flavourful, fruity, spicy, fine bitter notes.

LA ESTACADA 2011 T ROBLE
80% syrah, 20% merlot
90 Colour: cherry, garnet rim. Nose: ripe fruit, sweet spices, cocoa bean. Palate: good structure, flavourful, round tannins.

BODEGAS LA ESTACIÓN

Avda Castilla la Mancha, 38
45370 Santa Cruz de la Zarza (Toledo)
☎: +34 925 143 234 - Fax: +34 925 125 154
www.bodegaslaestacion.es
enologia@bodegaslaestacion.es

VICUS 2009 TC
tempranillo
83

VICUS 2012 B
macabeo
85 Colour: bright straw. Nose: candied fruit, floral, fragrant herbs. Palate: fresh, fruity, easy to drink.

VICUS 2012 T
tempranillo
87 Colour: cherry, purple rim. Nose: ripe fruit, red berry notes, grassy. Palate: powerful, flavourful.

VICUS 6 MESES 2011 T
tempranillo
84

BODEGAS VID Y ESPIGA

San Antón, 30
16415 Villamayor de Santiago (Cuenca)
☎: +34 969 139 069 - Fax: +34 969 139 069
www.vidyespiga.es
export@vidyespiga.es

CAÑADA REAL 2009 TC
tempranillo
86 Colour: cherry, garnet rim. Nose: ripe fruit, candied fruit, sweet spices. Palate: fruity, spicy, correct.

CAÑADA REAL 2010 T
tempranillo

84

CAÑADA REAL 2012 B
sauvignon blanc, verdejo

84

CAÑADA REAL 2012 T
tempranillo

84

QUERCUS 2008 TC
100% tempranillo

91 Colour: cherry, garnet rim. Nose: dark chocolate, ripe fruit, spicy, creamy oak. Palate: good structure, round tannins, balanced.

FONTANA

Extramuros, s/n
16411 Fuente de Pedro Naharro (Cuenca)
☎: +34 969 125 433 - Fax: +34 969 125 387
www.bodegasfontana.com
gemag@bodegasfontana.com

ESENCIA DE FONTANA 2011 TC
90% tempranillo, 10% merlot

89 Colour: bright cherry. Nose: ripe fruit, sweet spices, creamy oak, powerfull. Palate: flavourful, fruity, toasty.

ESENCIA DE FONTANA SELECCIÓN 2009 T
100% tempranillo

90 Colour: cherry, garnet rim. Nose: ripe fruit, spicy, creamy oak, toasty, complex. Palate: powerful, flavourful, toasty, round tannins, balanced, elegant.

MESTA 2012 B
70% chardonnay, 30% moscatel grano menudo

84

MESTA 2012 RD
100% tempranillo

84

MESTA SELECCIÓN 2011 T ROBLE
85% tempranillo, 15% syrah

87 Colour: cherry, garnet rim. Nose: ripe fruit, spicy, creamy oak, complex. Palate: powerful, toasty.

MESTA TEMPRANILLO 2012 T
100% tempranillo

86 Colour: cherry, purple rim. Nose: ripe fruit, medium intensity. Palate: fruity, easy to drink, good finish.

DO UTIEL-REQUENA / D.O.P.

Consejo Regulador
DO Boundary

LOCATION:

In the west of the province of Valencia. It comprises the municipal districts of Camporrobles, Caudete de las Fuentes, Fuenterrobles, Requena, Siete Aguas, Sinarcas, Utiel, Venta del Moro and Villagordo de Cabriel.

CLIMATE:

Continental, with Mediterranean influences, cold winters and slightly milder summers than in other regions of the province. Rainfall is quite scarce with an annual average of 400 mm.

SOIL:

Mainly brownish-grey, almost red limestone, poor in organic matter and with good permeability. The horizon of the vineyards are broken by the silhouette of the odd tree planted in the middle of the vineyards, which, bordered by woods, offer a very attractive landscape.

GRAPE VARIETIES:

RED: *Bobal, Tempranillo, Garnacha, Cabernet Sauvignon, Merlot, Syrah, Pinot Noir, Garnacha Tintorera, Petit Verdot* and *Cabernet Franc.*
WHITE: *Tardana, Macabeo, Merseguera, Chardonnay, Sauvignon Blanc, Parellada, Xarel.lo, Verdejo, Moscatel de Grano Menudo, Viognier* and *Albariño.*

FIGURES:

Vineyard surface: 34.619– **Wine-Growers:** 7.000 – **Wineries:** 97 – **2012 Harvest rating:** Very Good– **Production:** 25.580.190 litres – **Market percentages**: 29,51% domestic.70,49% export

2008	2009	2010	2011	2012
GOOD	GOOD	VERY GOOD	VERY GOOD	VERY GOOD

CONSEJO REGULADOR
Sevilla, 12. Apdo. 61 - 46300 Utiel (Valencia) ☎: +34 962 171 062 - Fax:+34 962 172 185
info@utielrequena.org   www.utielrequena.org

BODEGA MAS DE BAZÁN

Ctra. Villar de Olmos, Km. 2
46340 Requena (Valencia)
☎: +34 986 555 562
www.agrodebazansa.es
export@agrodebazan.es

MAS DE BAZAN 2012 RD
100% bobal

85 Colour: rose, purple rim. Nose: powerfull, ripe fruit, red berry notes. Palate: powerful, fruity, fresh.

MAS DE BAZÁN BOBAL 2011 TC
100% bobal

85 Colour: cherry, purple rim. Nose: ripe fruit, balsamic herbs, sweet spices, creamy oak. Palate: powerful, flavourful, spicy.

BODEGA SEBIRAN

Pérez Galdos, 1
46352 Campo Arcis - Requena (Valencia)
☎: +34 962 303 321 - Fax: +34 962 301 560
www.sebiran.es
info@sebiran.es

SEBIRÁN "J" 2008 TC
bobal

84

SEBIRÁN "T" 2012 T FERMENTADO EN BARRICA
tempranillo

85 Colour: bright cherry. Nose: ripe fruit, sweet spices, creamy oak, balsamic herbs. Palate: flavourful, fruity, toasty.

SEBIRÁN "T" TERRÁNEO 2012 T
tempranillo

84

SEBIRÁN "Z" 2008 TC
bobal, tempranillo

87 Colour: cherry, garnet rim. Nose: ripe fruit, toasty, earthy notes. Palate: powerful, flavourful, toasty, slightly dry, soft tannins.

BODEGA Y VIÑEDOS CARRES

Francho, 1
46352 Casas de Eufema (Valencia)
☎: +34 675 515 729
www.bodegacarres.com
torrescarpiojl@gmail.com

EL OLIVASTRO 2009 T
100% bobal

89 Colour: cherry, garnet rim. Nose: powerfull, ripe fruit, spicy. Palate: good structure, balsamic, round tannins.

MEMBRILLERA 2011 T
100% bobal

84

BODEGAS ARANLEÓN

Ctra. Caudete, 3
46310 Los Marcos (Valencia)
☎: +34 963 631 640 - Fax: +34 962 185 150
www.aranleon.com
maria@aranleon.com

ARANLEÓN HELIX 2008 T ROBLE
tempranillo

88 Colour: cherry, garnet rim. Nose: ripe fruit, spicy, toasty, complex. Palate: powerful, flavourful, toasty, round tannins.

ARANLEÓN SÓLO 2010 T
80% bobal, 10% tempranillo, 10% syrah

87 Colour: deep cherry, garnet rim. Nose: ripe fruit, fruit preserve, balsamic herbs, spicy. Palate: flavourful, round tannins.

ARANLEÓN SÓLO 2012 B
50% chardonnay, 30% macabeo, 20% sauvignon blanc

88 Colour: yellow. Nose: medium intensity, dried herbs, faded flowers, citrus fruit. Palate: easy to drink, fruity, good acidity.

BODEGAS COVILOR

Antonio Bartual, 21
46313 Cuevas de Utiel (Valencia)
☎: +34 962 182 053 - Fax: +34 962 182 055
www.bodegascovilor.com
oficina@bodegascovilor.com

ALTO CUEVAS 2012 RD
100% bobal

86 Colour: rose, purple rim. Nose: powerfull, ripe fruit, red berry notes, floral, dried herbs. Palate: powerful, fruity, fresh.

ALTO CUEVAS BOBAL TEMPRANILLO 2011 T
50% bobal, 50% tempranillo

87 Colour: cherry, garnet rim. Nose: ripe fruit, wild herbs, medium intensity. Palate: fruity, correct, balanced.

ALTO CUEVAS MACABEO 2012 B
100% macabeo

83

ALTO CUEVAS TEMPRANILLO 2011 T
100% tempranillo

84

SUCESIÓN BOBAL 2011 T
100% bobal

89 Colour: cherry, purple rim. Nose: spicy, balanced, ripe fruit, balsamic herbs. Palate: fruity, flavourful, round tannins.

BODEGAS COVIÑAS

Avda. Rafael Duyos, s/n
46340 Requena (Valencia)
☎: +34 962 300 680 - Fax: +34 962 302 651
www.covinas.com
covinas@covinas.com

AL VENT BOBAL 2011 T

88 Colour: light cherry. Nose: floral, red berry notes, wild herbs, spicy. Palate: powerful, flavourful, fruity, balanced.

AL VENT BOBAL 2012 RD
bobal

87 Colour: light cherry. Nose: powerfull, ripe fruit, candied fruit, faded flowers, lactic notes. Palate: rich, flavourful, ripe fruit.

AL VENT SAUVIGNON BLANC 2012 B
sauvignon blanc

90 Colour: bright straw. Nose: wild herbs, fresh fruit, balanced, expressive. Palate: fruity, good acidity, fine bitter notes.

AULA CABERNET SAUVIGNON 2009 T
cabernet sauvignon

84

AULA MERLOT 2008 TC
merlot

89 Colour: cherry, garnet rim. Nose: spicy, creamy oak, fragrant herbs, ripe fruit. Palate: powerful, flavourful, toasty, round tannins.

AULA SYRAH 2008 TC
syrah

88 Colour: cherry, garnet rim. Nose: ripe fruit, spicy, toasty. Palate: powerful, flavourful, toasty, round tannins.

ENTERIZO 2006 TGR
garnacha

87 Colour: light cherry, orangey edge. Nose: medium intensity, ripe fruit, wild herbs, tobacco. Palate: fruity, easy to drink.

ENTERIZO 2009 TR
garnacha

86 Colour: light cherry, garnet rim. Nose: wild herbs, balanced, ripe fruit. Palate: fruity, spicy, good acidity.

VIÑA ENTERIZO 2010 TC
tempranillo, garnacha, bobal

86 Colour: cherry, garnet rim. Nose: spicy, old leather, medium intensity. Palate: balanced, good acidity, fine tannins.

VIÑA ENTERIZO BOBAL 2012 RD
bobal

87 Colour: rose, bright. Nose: red berry notes, ripe fruit, dried herbs. Palate: fruity, easy to drink.

VIÑA ENTERIZO MACABEO 2012 B
macabeo

83

VIÑA ENTERIZO TEMPRANILLO 2012 T
tempranillo

85 Colour: cherry, purple rim. Nose: medium intensity, ripe fruit, dried herbs. Palate: light-bodied, easy to drink, good finish.

BODEGAS FINCA ARDAL

Ctra. N-322, Km. 452 El Pontón
46340 Requena (Valencia)
☎: +34 962 302 835 - Fax: +34 962 302 835
www.fincaardal.com
bodega@fincaardal.com

COMO DESEES 2009 T
syrah

84

LAGAR DE LAR 2005 T
tempranillo, cabernet sauvignon, merlot

91 Colour: pale ruby, brick rim edge. Nose: ripe fruit, balsamic herbs, earthy notes, spicy, creamy oak. Palate: powerful, flavourful, spicy, long.

MATANZA SLAUGHTERHOUSE 2009 T

89 Colour: bright cherry. Nose: ripe fruit, sweet spices, creamy oak, toasty. Palate: flavourful, fruity, toasty, round tannins, balanced.

OCHO CUERDAS 2010 T
cabernet sauvignon, merlot, syrah

87 Colour: cherry, garnet rim. Nose: spicy, ripe fruit, scrubland, waxy notes. Palate: balsamic, powerful.

OCHO CUERDAS BOBAL 2011 TC
bobal

85 Colour: cherry, garnet rim. Nose: ripe fruit, spicy, creamy oak, toasty. Palate: powerful, flavourful, toasty.

BODEGAS HISPANO SUIZAS

Ctra. N-322, Km. 451,7 El Pontón
46357 Requena (Valencia)
☎: +34 661 894 200
www.bodegashispanosuizas.com
info@bodegashispanosuizas.com

BASSUS DULCE BOBAL-PINOT NOIR 2011 RD
bobal, pinot noir

90 Colour: coppery red, bright. Nose: faded flowers, citrus fruit, varnish, candied fruit. Palate: balanced, good acidity, flavourful.

BASSUS PINOT NOIR 2011 T
100% pinot noir

90 Colour: cherry, garnet rim. Nose: red berry notes, balsamic herbs, mineral, dry stone, spicy, creamy oak, roasted coffee. Palate: powerful, flavourful, long, spicy, balanced.

BASSUS PREMIUM 2010 T
bobal, petit verdot, cabernet franc, merlot, syrah

93 Colour: cherry, garnet rim. Nose: ripe fruit, complex, spicy, balsamic herbs. Palate: good structure, complex, ripe fruit, good acidity, fine tannins.

BOBOS FINCA CASA LA BORRACHA 2011 T
100% bobal

91 Colour: cherry, garnet rim. Nose: ripe fruit, spicy, toasty, earthy notes, creamy oak, wild herbs. Palate: powerful, flavourful, toasty, round tannins, balanced.

IMPROMPTU 2012 B
100% sauvignon blanc

92 Colour: bright yellow. Nose: citrus fruit, tropical fruit, floral, fragrant herbs, spicy, mineral. Palate: powerful, flavourful, rich, long, balsamic, balanced, elegant.

QUOD SUPERIUS 2009 T
bobal, syrah, cabernet franc, merlot

91 Colour: deep cherry, garnet rim. Nose: spicy, creamy oak, complex, ripe fruit, balsamic herbs. Palate: full, complex, round tannins, good acidity.

BODEGAS MURVIEDRO

Ampliación Pol. El Romeral, s/n
46340 Requena (Valencia)
☎: +34 962 329 003 - Fax: +34 962 329 002
www.bodegasmurviedro.es
murviedro@murviedro.es

COROLILLA 2008 TR
bobal

90 Colour: cherry, garnet rim. Nose: spicy, ripe fruit, balanced, balsamic herbs. Palate: good acidity, balanced, round tannins.

COROLILLA 2010 TC
bobal

89 Colour: cherry, garnet rim. Nose: ripe fruit, spicy, toasty. Palate: powerful, flavourful, toasty, round tannins.

CUEVA DE LA CULPA 2010 T
bobal, merlot

91 Colour: cherry, garnet rim. Nose: ripe fruit, spicy, scrubland. Palate: flavourful, fruity, spicy, balanced.

M DE MURVIEDRO TEMPRANILLO 2012 T
tempranillo, bobal

85 Colour: cherry, purple rim. Nose: floral, balsamic herbs, red berry notes, fruit liqueur notes. Palate: flavourful, fruity, good acidity.

MURVIEDRO COLECCIÓN SAUVIGNON BLANC 2012 B
sauvignon blanc

88 Colour: bright yellow. Nose: wild herbs, balanced. Palate: fresh, fruity, good acidity.

BODEGAS PALMERA

Partida Palomera, 345
46300 Utiel (Valencia)
☎: +34 626 706 394
www.bodegas-palmera.com
klauslauerbach@hotmail.com

BOBAL Y MERLOT 2011 T
bobal, merlot

85 Colour: cherry, garnet rim. Nose: red berry notes, fruit liqueur notes, balsamic herbs, spicy, creamy oak. Palate: powerful, flavourful, toasty.

BOBAL Y TEMPRANILLO 2010 T
bobal, tempranillo

88 Colour: cherry, garnet rim. Nose: red berry notes, ripe fruit, fragrant herbs, creamy oak, toasty. Palate: powerful, flavourful, spicy, long.

L'ANGELET 2010 TC
tempranillo, cabernet sauvignon, merlot

90 Colour: cherry, garnet rim. Nose: powerfull, balanced, sweet spices, balsamic herbs. Palate: flavourful, ripe fruit, long.

VIÑA CAPRICHO 2010 T
cabernet sauvignon, merlot, tempranillo

88 Colour: bright cherry, garnet rim. Nose: balanced, spicy, toasty, balsamic herbs. Palate: flavourful, round tannins.

BODEGAS PASIEGO

Avda. Virgen de Tejeda, 28
46320 Sinarcas (Valencia)
☎: +34 609 076 575 - Fax: +34 962 306 175
www.bodegaspasiego.com
bodega@bodegaspasiego.com

PASIEGO BOBAL 2010 T
85% bobal, 15% merlot

85 Colour: deep cherry, garnet rim. Nose: powerfull, scrubland, ripe fruit, fruit preserve, sweet spices. Palate: full, flavourful, round tannins.

PASIEGO DE AUTOR 2009 TC
55% cabernet sauvignon, 25% bobal, 20% merlot

90 Colour: bright cherry, garnet rim. Nose: complex, balsamic herbs, ripe fruit, spicy, tobacco. Palate: good structure, flavourful, round tannins.

PASIEGO LA BLASCA 2008 TC
39% cabernet sauvignon, 31% tempranillo, 27% merlot, 3% bobal

88 Colour: cherry, garnet rim. Nose: balanced, fine reductive notes, spicy. Palate: correct, balanced, ripe fruit.

PASIEGO LA SUERTES 2012 B
60% chardonnay, 40% sauvignon blanc

88 Colour: bright straw, greenish rim. Nose: balanced, wild herbs, floral. Palate: flavourful, good acidity, correct, spicy.

BODEGAS SIERRA NORTE

Pol. Ind. El Romeral. Transporte- Parc. C2
46340 Requena (Valencia)
☎: +34 962 323 099 - Fax: +34 962 323 048
www.bodegasierranorte.com
info@bodegasierranorte.com

CERRO BERCIAL 2007 TC
tempranillo, bobal

84

CERRO BERCIAL 2007 TR
bobal, cabernet sauvignon

91 Colour: cherry, garnet rim. Nose: spicy, balsamic herbs, complex, ripe fruit. Palate: balanced, round tannins, spicy.

CERRO BERCIAL 2009 T BARRICA
tempranillo, bobal

90 Colour: cherry, garnet rim. Nose: roasted coffee, balsamic herbs, red berry notes, ripe fruit. Palate: powerful, flavourful, toasty, balanced.

CERRO BERCIAL 2012 RD
bobal

87 Colour: rose, purple rim. Nose: fragrant herbs, floral, lactic notes, candied fruit. Palate: fresh, fruity, flavourful.

CERRO BERCIAL PARCELA "LADERA LOS CANTOS" 2006 T
bobal, cabernet sauvignon

91 Colour: pale ruby, brick rim edge. Nose: elegant, spicy, fine reductive notes, aged wood nuances, fruit liqueur notes. Palate: spicy, fine tannins, elegant, long.

CERRO BERCIAL SELECCIÓN 2012 B
macabeo, sauvignon blanc, chardonnay

90 Colour: bright yellow. Nose: powerfull, ripe fruit, sweet spices, creamy oak, fragrant herbs. Palate: rich, flavourful, fresh, good acidity.

FUENTESECA 2010 TC
tempranillo

87 Colour: cherry, garnet rim. Nose: balanced, ripe fruit, red berry notes, spicy. Palate: light-bodied, fruity, easy to drink.

FUENTESECA 2012 B
macabeo, sauvignon blanc

86 Colour: bright straw. Nose: fresh fruit, dried herbs, faded flowers. Palate: flavourful, fruity, good acidity.

FUENTESECA 2012 RD
bobal, cabernet sauvignon

86 Colour: light cherry, bright. Nose: medium intensity, floral, red berry notes, ripe fruit. Palate: fruity, flavourful, easy to drink.

FUENTESECA 2012 T
bobal, cabernet sauvignon

87 Colour: cherry, purple rim. Nose: expressive, fresh fruit, red berry notes, floral. Palate: flavourful, fruity, good acidity, round tannins.

PASION DE BOBAL 2011 T
bobal

91 Colour: deep cherry, garnet rim. Nose: spicy, toasty, dried herbs. Palate: fruity, flavourful, good acidity, round tannins.

PASION DE BOBAL 2012 RD
bobal

90 Colour: onion pink. Nose: elegant, candied fruit, dried flowers, fragrant herbs, red berry notes. Palate: light-bodied, flavourful, good acidity, long, spicy.

BODEGAS UTIELANAS

Avda. Marín Lázaro, 8
46300 Utiel (Valencia)
☎: +34 962 171 157 - Fax: +34 962 170 801
www.bodegasutielanas.com
administracion@bodegasutielanas.com

VEGA INFANTE 2012 B
100% macabeo

88 Colour: bright straw. Nose: fresh, fresh fruit, white flowers, expressive. Palate: flavourful, fruity, good acidity, balanced.

VEGA INFANTE 2012 RD
100% bobal

87 Colour: rose, purple rim. Nose: ripe fruit, red berry notes, expressive. Palate: powerful, fruity, fresh.

VEGA INFANTE 2012 T
100% bobal

83

BODEGAS VICENTE GANDÍA

Ctra. Cheste a Godelleta, s/n
46370 Chiva (Valencia)
☎: +34 962 524 242 - Fax: +34 962 524 243
www.vicentegandia.es
info@vicentegandia.com

BO - BOBAL ÚNICO 2011 T
100% bobal

89 Colour: bright cherry. Nose: ripe fruit, sweet spices, creamy oak, expressive. Palate: flavourful, fruity, toasty, round tannins, balanced.

CEREMONIA 2008 TR
60% tempranillo, 30% cabernet sauvignon, 10% bobal

89 Colour: cherry, garnet rim. Nose: ripe fruit, spicy, creamy oak, toasty, complex. Palate: toasty, flavourful, balanced.

FINCA DEL MAR CABERNET SAUVIGNON 2011 T
100% cabernet sauvignon

84

FINCA DEL MAR CHARDONNAY 2012 B
100% chardonnay

86 Colour: bright straw. Nose: dried herbs, faded flowers, ripe fruit. Palate: powerful, flavourful, balsamic.

FINCA DEL MAR MERLOT 2011 T
100% merlot

83

FINCA DEL MAR TEMPRANILLO 2011 T
100% tempranillo

85 Colour: deep cherry, garnet rim. Nose: ripe fruit, balsamic herbs, powerfull, spicy. Palate: rich, fruity, flavourful, correct.

GENERACIÓN 1 2007 T
100% tempranillo

88 Colour: pale ruby, brick rim edge. Nose: ripe fruit, balsamic herbs, damp earth, spicy, creamy oak. Palate: powerful, flavourful, spicy, balanced.

HOYA DE CADENAS 2012 B
50% chardonnay, 30% sauvignon blanc, 20% macabeo

83

HOYA DE CADENAS 2012 RD
100% bobal

86 Colour: brilliant rose. Nose: red berry notes, ripe fruit, floral, fragrant herbs. Palate: fruity, fresh, flavourful, balanced.

HOYA DE CADENAS CABERNET SAUVIGNON 2011 T
100% cabernet sauvignon

84

HOYA DE CADENAS CHARDONNAY 2012 B
100% chardonnay

84

HOYA DE CADENAS MERLOT 2011 T
100% merlot

87 Colour: cherry, garnet rim. Nose: fragrant herbs, spicy, ripe fruit. Palate: fresh, fruity, balsamic, balanced.

HOYA DE CADENAS RESERVA PRIVADA 2008 TR
85% tempranillo, 15% cabernet sauvignon

85 Colour: cherry, garnet rim. Nose: fruit preserve, spicy, creamy oak, fine reductive notes. Palate: correct, flavourful, toasty.

HOYA DE CADENAS SHIRAZ 2011 T
100% syrah

85 Colour: cherry, garnet rim. Nose: red berry notes, ripe fruit, medium intensity. Palate: easy to drink, fresh, fruity.

HOYA DE CADENAS TEMPRANILLO 2009 TR
100% tempranillo

84

MARQUÉS DE CHIVÉ 2009 TR
100% tempranillo

83

BODEGAS Y VIÑEDOS DE UTIEL

Finca El Renegado, s/n
46315 Caudete de las Fuentes (Valencia)
☎: +34 962 174 029 - Fax: +34 962 171 432
www.bodegasdeutiel.com
gestion@bodegasdeutiel.com

CAPELLANA 2012 B
macabeo

87 Colour: bright straw. Nose: medium intensity, citrus fruit, fresh fruit. Palate: correct, good acidity, fruity, fine bitter notes.

CAPELLANA 2012 RD
bobal

86 Colour: rose, purple rim. Nose: powerfull, ripe fruit, red berry notes, floral. Palate: powerful, fruity, fresh.

CAPELLANA 2012 T
tempranillo

85 Colour: cherry, purple rim. Nose: medium intensity, red berry notes, ripe fruit. Palate: fruity, easy to drink, good acidity.

CAPELLANA TINTO DE AUTOR 2010 TC
cabernet sauvignon, tempranillo

88 Colour: cherry, garnet rim. Nose: ripe fruit, spicy, creamy oak, toasty. Palate: powerful, flavourful, toasty.

NODUS BOBAL 2010 T
bobal

86 Colour: cherry, garnet rim. Nose: ripe fruit, spicy, toasty, balsamic herbs. Palate: powerful, flavourful, toasty, round tannins.

NODUS CHARDONNAY 2012 B
chardonnay

88 Colour: bright straw. Nose: floral, candied fruit, fragrant herbs, expressive. Palate: correct, powerful, flavourful, complex.

NODUS MERLOT DELIRIUM 2010 T
merlot

85 Colour: cherry, garnet rim. Nose: ripe fruit, spicy, creamy oak, toasty, old leather, cigar. Palate: powerful, flavourful, toasty.

NODUS TINTO DE AUTOR 2009 TC
merlot, syrah, cabernet sauvignon, bobal

90 Colour: cherry, garnet rim. Nose: red berry notes, ripe fruit, spicy, creamy oak, toasty. Palate: powerful, flavourful, spicy, long.

CERROGALLINA

Travesía Industria, 5
46352 Campo Arcis (Valencia)
☎: +34 962 338 135 - Fax +34 962 338 135
www.cerrogallina.com
info@cerrogallina.com

CERROGALLINA 2010 T
bobal

91 Colour: cherry, garnet rim. Nose: ripe fruit, spicy, creamy oak, toasty, complex, mineral. Palate: powerful, flavourful, toasty, round tannins, elegant.

CHOZAS CARRASCAL

Vereda Real de San Antonio s/n
46390 San Antonio de Requena (Valencia)
☎: +34 963 410 395
www.chozascarrascal.es
chozas@chozascarrascal.es

LAS DOSCES 2011 T
bobal

90 Colour: cherry, garnet rim. Nose: ripe fruit, fruit preserve, creamy oak, balsamic herbs. Palate: powerful, balsamic, flavourful, balanced.

LAS DOSCES 2012 B
80% macabeo, 20% sauvignon blanc

90 Colour: bright straw. Nose: fresh, fresh fruit, white flowers, expressive. Palate: flavourful, fruity, good acidity, balanced.

DOMINIO DE LA VEGA

Ctra. Madrid - Valencia, N-III Km. 270,6
46390 Requena (Valencia)
☎: +34 962 320 570 - Fax: +34 962 320 330
www.dominiodelavega.com
dv@dominiodelavega.com

AÑACAL DOMINIO DE LA VEGA 2012 B
macabeo, sauvignon blanc

85 Colour: bright straw. Nose: medium intensity, dried herbs, citrus fruit. Palate: fruity, easy to drink, good finish.

AÑACAL DOMINIO DE LA VEGA 2012 RD
bobal

87 Colour: rose, purple rim. Nose: powerfull, ripe fruit, red berry notes, floral, expressive. Palate: powerful, fruity, fresh.

ARTE MAYOR III 2005/2006/2007 2005/06/07 T
bobal

93 Colour: bright cherry, garnet rim. Nose: ripe fruit, creamy oak, spicy, dark chocolate, complex. Palate: full, flavourful, round tannins, balsamic.

DOMINIO DE LA VEGA 2008 TR
bobal, cabernet sauvignon, syrah

85 Colour: cherry, garnet rim. Nose: ripe fruit, spicy, creamy oak, toasty, fine reductive notes. Palate: powerful, flavourful, toasty.

DOMINIO DE LA VEGA 2010 TC
bobal, cabernet sauvignon, syrah

86 Colour: cherry, garnet rim. Nose: ripe fruit, spicy, creamy oak, toasty. Palate: powerful, flavourful, toasty.

DOMINIO DE LA VEGA 2011 T ROBLE
bobal, cabernet sauvignon, syrah

88 Colour: bright cherry. Nose: ripe fruit, sweet spices, creamy oak, expressive. Palate: flavourful, fruity, toasty, round tannins.

DOMINIO DE LA VEGA BOBAL 2011 T ROBLE
bobal

89 Colour: bright cherry, purple rim. Nose: red berry notes, ripe fruit, wild herbs. Palate: balanced, easy to drink, good acidity.

DOMINIO DE LA VEGA DULCE 2011 B
sauvignon blanc, chardonnay, macabeo

88 Colour: golden. Nose: powerfull, floral, honeyed notes, candied fruit, fragrant herbs. Palate: flavourful, sweet, fresh, fruity, good acidity, long.

DOMINIO DE LA VEGA DULCE 2012 T
bobal

86 Colour: bright cherry, purple rim. Nose: violets, balanced, ripe fruit, faded flowers. Palate: fruity, ripe fruit, good finish.

EMILIO CLEMENTE

Camino de San Blas, s/n
46340 Requena (Valencia)
☎: +34 962 323 391 - Fax: +34 963 173 726
www.eclemente.es
info@eclemente.es

EMILIO CLEMENTE 2005 TC
50% tempranillo, 15% cabernet sauvignon, 25% merlot, 10% bobal

86 Colour: light cherry, orangey edge. Nose: spicy, wet leather. Palate: spicy, long, fine bitter notes.

EXCELENCIA 2009 T
cabernet sauvignon, merlot

89 Colour: cherry, garnet rim. Nose: powerfull, balanced, complex, scrubland. Palate: flavourful, spicy, balsamic, long.

FLORANTE 2011 BFB
45% chardonnay, 32% macabeo, 20% tardana, 3% sauvignon blanc

86 Colour: bright yellow. Nose: faded flowers, ripe fruit, sweet spices. Palate: flavourful, spicy, fine bitter notes.

FLORANTE 2012 B
tardana, macabeo

83

PEÑAS NEGRAS MADURADO 2010 T
50% cabernet sauvignon, 50% merlot

79

FINCA SAN BLAS

Partida de San Blas, s/n
46340 Requena (Valencia)
☎: +34 963 375 617 - Fax: +34 963 370 707
www.fincasanblas.com
info@fincasanblas.com

FINCA SAN BLAS 2011 T
bobal

87 Colour: cherry, purple rim. Nose: ripe fruit, fruit liqueur notes, balsamic herbs, floral, creamy oak. Palate: long, spicy, powerful, flavourful.

FINCA SAN BLAS 2012 B
merseguera, chardonnay

88 Colour: bright yellow. Nose: medium intensity, faded flowers, ripe fruit. Palate: flavourful, rich, spicy, long.

LOMALTA M&S 2012 T
merlot, syrah

87 Colour: cherry, purple rim. Nose: red berry notes, ripe fruit, floral. Palate: fruity, flavourful, good acidity, correct.

LATORRE AGROVINÍCOLA

Ctra. Requena, 2
46310 Venta del Moro (Valencia)
☎: +34 962 185 028 - Fax: +34 962 185 422
www.latorreagrovinicola.com
luismiguel@latorreagrovinicola.com

DUQUE DE ARCAS 1999 TGR
bobal, tempranillo

85 Colour: dark-red cherry, orangey edge. Nose: fruit liqueur notes, fine reductive notes, old leather, spicy. Palate: fruity, good acidity.

DUQUE DE ARCAS 2001 TGR
bobal

85 Colour: pale ruby, brick rim edge. Nose: elegant, spicy, fine reductive notes, wet leather, aged wood nuances, fruit liqueur notes. Palate: spicy, fine tannins, elegant, long.

DUQUE DE ARCAS 2001 TR
bobal

83

DUQUE DE ARCAS 2003 TR
tempranillo

86 Colour: dark-red cherry, orangey edge. Nose: medium intensity, fruit liqueur notes, old leather, tobacco, aged wood nuances. Palate: fruity, spicy.

DUQUE DE ARCAS 2011 TC
bobal, tempranillo, cabernet sauvignon

81

DUQUE DE ARCAS 2012 T
tempranillo, cabernet sauvignon

84

PARREÑO 2012 T
tempranillo, cabernet sauvignon

85 Colour: cherry, purple rim. Nose: medium intensity, ripe fruit, scrubland. Palate: fruity, flavourful.

PARREÑO 2012 B
viura, verdejo

78

PARREÑO 2012 RD
bobal

84

PAGO DE THARSYS

Ctra. Nacional III, km. 274
46340 Requena (Valencia)
☎: +34 962 303 354 - Fax: +34 962 329 000
www.pagodetharsys.com
pagodetharsys@pagodetharsys.com

CARLOTA SURIA 2006 TR
70% tempranillo, 30% cabernet sauvignon

86 Colour: pale ruby, brick rim edge. Nose: fruit preserve, old leather, tobacco, waxy notes, spicy. Palate: long, balsamic, correct, flavourful.

THARSYS ÚNICO 2008 ESP RESERVA
bobal

86 Colour: bright straw, greenish rim. Nose: faded flowers, balanced, fresh. Palate: correct, good acidity, easy to drink, good finish.

PRIMUM BOBAL

Constitución, 50 pta. 6
46340 Requena (Valencia)
☎: +34 625 464 377
www.primumbobal.com
vinos@primumbobal.com

PRIMUM BOBAL 2012 T

90 Colour: cherry, purple rim. Nose: red berry notes, lactic notes, floral, fragrant herbs. Palate: powerful, flavourful, fruity, easy to drink.

UNIÓN VINÍCOLA DEL ESTE

Pl. Ind. El Romeral- Construcción, 74
46340 Requena (Valencia)
☎: +34 962 323 343 - Fax: +34 962 349 413
www.uveste.es
cava@uveste.es

BESO DE RECHENNA 2009 T
100% bobal

89 Colour: cherry, garnet rim. Nose: balsamic herbs, ripe fruit, roasted coffee. Palate: flavourful, long, complex.

VALSAN 1831

Ctra. Cheste - Godelleta, Km. 1
46370 Chiva (Valencia)
☎: +34 962 510 861 - Fax: +34 962 511 361
www.cherubino.es
cherubino@cherubino.es

BOBAL DESANJUAN 2011 T
bobal

88 Colour: light cherry, garnet rim. Nose: medium intensity, balsamic herbs, ripe fruit. Palate: easy to drink, good finish, spicy.

BOBAL DESANJUAN 2012 RD
bobal

88 Colour: rose, purple rim. Nose: floral, candied fruit, fragrant herbs, expressive. Palate: fresh, fruity, flavourful, easy to drink.

MARQUÉS DE CARO 2012 RD
bobal

85 Colour: light cherry, bright. Nose: medium intensity, wild herbs, balanced, fresh. Palate: fruity, good acidity.

VERA DE ESTENAS

Junto N-III, km. 266 - Paraje La Cabeuzela
46300 Utiel (Valencia)
☎: +34 962 171 141 - Fax: +34 962 174 352
www.estenas.es
estenas@estenas.es

CASA DON ÁNGEL BOBAL 2009 T
bobal

93 Colour: cherry, garnet rim. Nose: ripe fruit, spicy, creamy oak, toasty, complex, expressive. Palate: powerful, flavourful, toasty, round tannins, balanced, elegant.

VERA DE ESTENAS 2008 TR
bobal, cabernet sauvignon, tempranillo, merlot

89 Colour: cherry, garnet rim. Nose: spicy, balsamic herbs, fine reductive notes. Palate: balanced, flavourful, round tannins.

VERA DE ESTENAS 2009 TC
bobal, cabernet sauvignon, tempranillo, merlot

90 Colour: cherry, garnet rim. Nose: ripe fruit, balanced, sweet spices, floral. Palate: good acidity, fruity, flavourful.

VERA DE ESTENAS 2012 T BARRICA
cabernet sauvignon, tempranillo

85 Colour: cherry, purple rim. Nose: spicy, ripe fruit, dried herbs. Palate: fruity, easy to drink, good finish.

VERA DE ESTENAS BOBAL 2012 RD
bobal

87 Colour: rose, purple rim. Nose: balanced, ripe fruit, wild herbs. Palate: fruity, easy to drink.

VIÑA LIDÓN 2012 BFB

88 Colour: bright straw. Nose: floral, ripe fruit, sweet spices. Palate: fruity, correct, fine bitter notes, rich.

VIÑEDOS LA MADROÑERA

Traginers, 9
46014 (Valencia)
☎: +34 963 992 400 - Fax: +34 963 992 451
www.constantia.es
pguzman@grupoguzman.com

CONSTANTIA 2009 TC
bobal, merlot, cabernet sauvignon

83

DULCE DE CONSTANTIA 2011 T
tempranillo, cabernet sauvignon, merlot

90 Colour: light mahogany. Nose: fruit preserve, fruit liqueur notes, dry nuts, acetaldehyde, spicy, toasty. Palate: powerful, flavourful, spirituous, long.

VIÑEDOS Y BODEGAS VEGALFARO

Ctra. Pontón - Utiel, Km. 3
46430 Requena (Valencia)
☎: +34 962 320 680 - Fax: +34 962 321 126
www.vegalfaro.com
rodolfo@vegalfaro.com

REBEL.LIA 2012 T
garnacha tintorera, tempranillo, bobal

90 Colour: cherry, purple rim. Nose: ripe fruit, wild herbs. Palate: flavourful, ripe fruit, good finish.

VEGALFARO 2010 TC
merlot, syrah, tempranillo

88 Colour: bright cherry, garnet rim. Nose: dried herbs, ripe fruit, balanced. Palate: fruity, flavourful, spicy.

VEGALFARO 2012 RD
merlot, bobal

86 Colour: light cherry, bright. Nose: wild herbs, red berry notes, ripe fruit, medium intensity, citrus fruit. Palate: fruity, flavourful.

VEGALFARO 2012 T
merlot, bobal

88 Colour: bright cherry, purple rim. Nose: fruit expression, balanced, floral. Palate: fruity, flavourful, easy to drink.

VEGALFARO BARRICA 2011 T
merlot, bobal

86 Colour: bright cherry. Nose: ripe fruit, sweet spices, creamy oak, wild herbs. Palate: flavourful, fruity, toasty.

VEGALFARO CHARDONNAY 2012 B ROBLE
chardonnay

87 Colour: bright yellow. Nose: ripe fruit, white flowers, faded flowers, sweet spices. Palate: correct, fresh, fruity.

DO VALDEORRAS / D.O.P.

LOCATION:

The DO Valdeorras is situated in the northeast of the province of Orense. It comprises the municipal areas of Larouco, Petín, O Bolo, A Rua, Vilamartín, O Barco, Rubiá and Carballeda de Valdeorras.

CLIMATE:

Continental, with Atlantic influences. The average annual temperature is 11°C and the average annual rainfall ranges between 850 mm and 1,000 mm.

SOIL:

Quite varied. There are three types: the first type which is settled on shallow slate with many stones and a medium texture; the second type on deeper granite with a lot of sand and finally the type that lies on sediments and terraces, where there are usually a lot of pebbles.

GRAPE VARIETIES:

WHITE: *Godello, Dona Blanca, Palomino, Loureira, Treixadura, Dona Branca, Albariño, Torrontes, Lado* and *Palomino.*
RED: *Mencía, Merenzao, Grao Negro, Garnacha, Tempranillo (Araúxa), Brancellao, Sousón, Caíño Tinto, Espadeiro, Ferrón, Gran Negro, Garnacha Tintureira* and *Mouratón.*

FIGURES:

Vineyard surface: 1.157 – **Wine-Growers:** 1.489 – **Wineries:** 43 – **2012 Harvest rating:** Very Good – **Production:** 3.766.336 litres – **Market percentages:** 93% domestic. 7% export

2008	2009	2010	2011	2012
VERY GOOD	**VERY GOOD**	**VERY GOOD**	**EXCELLENT**	**EXCELLENT**

CONSEJO REGULADOR
Ctra. Nacional 120, km. 463 - 32340 Vilamartín de Valdeorras (Ourense) ☎: +34 988 300 295 - Fax: +34 988 300 455
consello@dovaldeorras.com   www.dovaldeorras.tv

ADEGA A COROA

A Coroa, s/n
32350 A Rúa (Ourense)
☎: +34 988 310 648 - Fax: +34 988 311 439
www.acoroa.com
acoroa@acoroa.com

A COROA "LÍAS" 2011 B
100% godello

91 Colour: bright yellow. Nose: spicy, ripe fruit, citrus fruit, dried herbs. Palate: flavourful, fruity, light-bodied.

A COROA 2012 B
100% godello

91 Colour: bright straw. Nose: fresh, fresh fruit, white flowers, dried herbs, varietal. Palate: flavourful, fruity, good acidity, balanced.

ADEGA DA PINGUELA

O Caraball - Petín de Valdeorras
32356 Petín de Valdeorras (Ourense)
☎: +34 654 704 753
www.adegadapinguela.com
adega@adegadapinguela.com

MEMORIA DE VENTURA GARNACHA 2011 T
garnacha tintorera

90 Colour: black cherry. Nose: powerfull, varietal, ripe fruit, fruit preserve, toasty, creamy oak. Palate: powerful, concentrated, fine bitter notes.

MEMORIA DE VENTURA GODELLO 2012 B
godello

90 Colour: bright straw. Nose: fresh, fresh fruit, white flowers, characterful, mineral. Palate: flavourful, fruity, good acidity, balanced.

MEMORIA DE VENTURA MENCÍA 2012 T
mencía

94 Colour: cherry, purple rim. Nose: expressive, fresh fruit, red berry notes, floral. Palate: flavourful, fruity, good acidity, round tannins.

VENTO 2011 BFB
godello

92 Colour: bright yellow. Nose: powerfull, ripe fruit, sweet spices, fragrant herbs. Palate: rich, flavourful, fresh, good acidity.

ADEGA JOSÉ ARISTEGUI

Avda. de Somoza, 9
32350 La Rua (Ourense)
☎: +34 626 647 356
aristanido@terra.com

JOSÉ ARISTEGUI GODELLO 2011 B
godello

90 Colour: bright straw. Nose: expressive, candied fruit, citrus fruit. Palate: flavourful, fruity, ripe fruit.

JOSÉ ARISTEGUI MENCÍA 2011 T
mencía

90 Colour: bright cherry. Nose: ripe fruit, sweet spices, creamy oak, expressive. Palate: flavourful, toasty, round tannins.

TRASTE 2011 T
garnacha tintorera, mencía

84

ADEGA O CASAL

Malladín, s/n
32310 Rubiá (Ourense)
☎: +34 689 675 800
www.casalnovo.es
casalnovo@casalnovo.es

CASAL NOVO GODELLO 2012 B
100% godello

92 Colour: bright straw. Nose: fresh, fresh fruit, white flowers, expressive, mineral. Palate: flavourful, fruity, good acidity, balanced.

CASAL NOVO MENCÍA 2012 T
90% mencía, 5% merenzao, 5% garnacha tintorera

90 Colour: cherry, purple rim. Nose: expressive, ripe fruit, red berry notes, fragrant herbs. Palate: fruity, fresh, full.

ADEGA O CEPADO

O Patal, 11
32310 Rubia de Valdeorras (Ourense)
☎: +34 686 611 589
www.cepado.com
info@cepado.com

CEPADO GODELLO 2012 B
100% godello

91 Colour: bright straw. Nose: fresh, white flowers, grassy. Palate: flavourful, fruity, good acidity, balanced.

CEPADO MENCÍA 2012 T
100% mencía

90 Colour: cherry, purple rim. Nose: fresh fruit, red berry notes, floral. Palate: flavourful, fruity, good acidity, round tannins.

ADEGA QUINTA DA PEZA

Ctra. Nacional 120, km.467
32350 A Rua de Valdeorras (Ourense)
☎: +34 988 311 537 - Fax: +34 981 232 642
www.quintadapeza.es
quintadapeza@gmail.com

QUINTA DA PEZA GODELLO 2012 B
100% godello

91 Colour: bright straw. Nose: fresh, fresh fruit, white flowers, sweet spices. Palate: flavourful, fruity, good acidity, balanced.

QUINTA DA PEZA MENCÍA 2012 T
100% mencía

87 Colour: cherry, garnet rim. Nose: medium intensity, ripe fruit, red berry notes. Palate: flavourful, fruity, good acidity, fine tannins.

QUINTA DA PEZA ORO MENCÍA BARRICA 2010 TC
100% mencía

90 Colour: cherry, garnet rim. Nose: ripe fruit, spicy, creamy oak, toasty, complex. Palate: powerful, flavourful, toasty, round tannins.

ALAN DE VAL

San Roque, 36
32350 A Rúa (Ourense)
☎: +34 988 310 431 - Fax +34 988 311 457
www.alandeval.com
alandeval@alandeval.com

A COSTIÑA 2008 T
100% brancellao

85 Colour: black cherry. Nose: powerfull, warm, overripe fruit, dried fruit. Palate: powerful, spirituous, sweetness.

ALAN DE VAL GODELLO 2012 B
100% godello

89 Colour: bright straw. Nose: fragrant herbs, dried herbs, ripe fruit. Palate: flavourful, fruity, fresh.

ALAN DE VAL MENCÍA 2012 T
100% mencía

89 Colour: cherry, purple rim. Nose: scrubland, ripe fruit, red berry notes. Palate: good acidity, fine bitter notes, long.

ESCADA GARNACHA 2010 T
100% garnacha tintorera

89 Colour: bright cherry. Nose: ripe fruit, sweet spices, creamy oak. Palate: flavourful, round tannins, sweetness.

ESCADA LEMBRANZAS 2011 T
100% garnacha tintorera

87 Colour: very deep cherry. Nose: fruit liqueur notes, fruit liqueur notes, cocoa bean. Palate: flavourful, powerful, sweetness.

PEDRAZAIS GODELLO 2011 BFB
100% godello

88 Colour: bright yellow. Nose: powerfull, ripe fruit, sweet spices, creamy oak. Palate: rich, flavourful, fresh, good acidity.

PEDRAZAIS GODELLO SOBRE LÍAS 2012 B
100% godello

94 Colour: bright straw. Nose: fresh, fresh fruit, white flowers, expressive, fine lees, dried herbs. Palate: flavourful, fruity, good acidity, balanced.

PEDRAZAIS MENCÍA 2011 T BARRICA
mencía

89 Colour: bright cherry. Nose: ripe fruit, creamy oak, expressive. Palate: fruity, toasty, round tannins.

AVELINA S.A.T.

Das Guerras, 4 Córgomo
32316 Vilamartín de Valdeorras (Ourense)
☎: +34 687 819 099
adegavelinasat@yahoo.com

CASAL DE FURCOS ROCIO GODELLO 2012 B
100% godello

86 Colour: bright straw. Nose: grassy, ripe fruit, citrus fruit. Palate: flavourful, light-bodied, fresh.

CASAL DE FURCOS ROCIO MENCÍA 2012 T
100% mencía

80

BODEGA COOPERATIVA JESÚS NAZARENO

Florencio Delgado Gurriarán, 62
32300 O Barco de Valdeorras (Ourense)
☎: +34 988 320 620 - Fax: +34 988 320 242
www.vinosbarco.com
coopbarco@infonegocio.com

MOZAFRESCA 2012 B
30% godello, 70% palomino

88 Colour: bright straw. Nose: fresh fruit, white flowers, mineral. Palate: flavourful, fruity, good acidity, balanced.

VIÑA ABAD GODELLO 2012 B
100% godello

88 Colour: bright straw. Nose: white flowers, ripe fruit, dried herbs. Palate: flavourful, fruity, fresh.

BODEGA COOPERATIVA VIRGEN DE LAS VIÑAS

Campo Grande, 97
32350 A Rua de Valdeorras (Ourense)
☎: +34 988 310 607 - Fax: +34 988 312 016
www.cooperativarua.com
info@cooperativarua.com

AMAVIA 2011 B
godello

88 Colour: bright yellow. Nose: powerfull, sweet spices, dried herbs. Palate: rich, flavourful, fresh, good acidity.

PINGADELO 2012 B
100% godello

87 Colour: bright straw. Nose: medium intensity, candied fruit, dried herbs. Palate: sweetness, fruity.

PINGADELO 2012 T
mencía

93 Colour: cherry, purple rim. Nose: red berry notes, raspberry, fruit expression, scrubland. Palate: flavourful, light-bodied, good acidity.

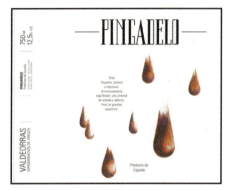

BODEGAS ABANICO

Pol. Ind Ca l'Avellanet - Susany, 6
8553 Seva (Barcelona)
☎: +34 938 125 676 - Fax: +34 938 123 213
www.bodegasabanico.com
info@exportiberia.com

BOCA DO MONTE 2012 B
30% godello, 70% palomino

88 Colour: bright straw. Nose: scrubland, fresh fruit, citrus fruit. Palate: light-bodied, fresh, good acidity.

TEMPESTAD 2012 B
100% godello

91 Colour: bright straw. Nose: white flowers, ripe fruit, dried herbs. Palate: flavourful, fruity, good acidity, balanced.

BODEGAS AVANTHIA

Bartolomé Esteban Murillo, 11
29700 Vélez- Málaga (Málaga)
☎: +34 952 504 706 - Fax: +34 951 284 796
www.grupojorgeordonez.com
info@jorgeordonez.es

AVANCIA CUVEE DE O 2012 B
100% godello

89 Colour: bright straw. Nose: fresh, fresh fruit, white flowers. Palate: flavourful, fruity, good acidity, balanced.

AVANCIA CUVEE MOSTEIRO 2011 T
100% mencía

92 Colour: cherry, garnet rim. Nose: ripe fruit, spicy, creamy oak, toasty, complex, roasted coffee. Palate: powerful, flavourful, toasty, round tannins.

AVANCIA GODELLO 2012 B

93 Colour: bright yellow. Nose: powerfull, ripe fruit, sweet spices, creamy oak, fragrant herbs. Palate: rich, smoky aftertaste, flavourful, fresh, good acidity.

AVANCIA ROSE 2012 RD
100% mencía

90 Colour: onion pink. Nose: elegant, candied fruit, dried flowers, fragrant herbs, red berry notes. Palate: light-bodied, flavourful, good acidity, spicy, sweetness.

BODEGAS CARBALLAL

Ctra. de Carballal, km 2,2
32356 Petín de Valdeorras (Ourense)
☎: +34 988 311 281 - Fax: +34 988 311 281
bodegascarballal@hotmail.com

EREBO GODELLO 2012 B
100% godello

92 Colour: bright straw. Nose: fresh, white flowers, ripe fruit, expressive, powerfull, varietal. Palate: flavourful, fruity, good acidity, balanced.

EREBO MENCÍA 2011 T
100% mencía

87 Colour: very deep cherry. Nose: complex, warm, overripe fruit. Palate: concentrated, sweetness, flavourful.

BODEGAS GODEVAL

Avda. de Galicia, 20
32300 El Barco de Valdeorras (Ourense)
☎: +34 988 108 282 - Fax: +34 988 325 309
www.godeval.com
godeval@godeval.com

GODEVAL 2011 B
100% godello

89 Colour: bright straw. Nose: white flowers, candied fruit, varietal. Palate: flavourful, fruity, good acidity, balanced.

GODEVAL 2012 B
100% godello

90 Colour: bright straw. Nose: ripe fruit, citrus fruit, varietal. Palate: flavourful, fine bitter notes, good acidity.

GODEVAL CEPAS VELLAS 2011 B
100% godello

92 Colour: bright yellow. Nose: powerfull, ripe fruit, sweet spices. Palate: rich, flavourful, fresh, good acidity.

GODEVAL CEPAS VELLAS 2012 B
100% godello

93 Colour: bright straw. Nose: fresh, fresh fruit, white flowers, earthy notes, mineral. Palate: flavourful, good acidity, balanced.

BODEGAS RUCHEL

Ctra. de Cernego, s/n
32340 Vilamartín de Valdeorras (Ourense)
☎: +34 986 253 345 - Fax +34 986 253 345
www.vinosruchel.com
info@vinosruchel.com

RUCHEL GODELLO 2011 B
100% godello

89 Colour: bright straw. Nose: fresh, white flowers, ripe fruit. Palate: flavourful, fruity, good acidity, balanced.

RUCHEL MENCÍA 2012 T
85% mencía, 15% tempranillo

90 Colour: cherry, purple rim. Nose: fresh fruit, red berry notes, floral. Palate: flavourful, fruity, good acidity, round tannins.

BODEGAS SAMPAYOLO

Ctra. de Barxela, s/n
32358 Petín de Valdeorras (Ourense)
☎: +34 679 157 977
www.sampayolo.com
info@sampayolo.com

GARNACHA VELLA DA CHAIRA DO RAMIRIÑO 2011 T
garnacha

89 Colour: bright cherry. Nose: ripe fruit, sweet spices, expressive, earthy notes. Palate: flavourful, fruity, toasty, round tannins.

SAMPAYOLO GODELLO 2011 B BARRICA
godello

88 Colour: bright straw. Nose: ripe fruit, powerfull, sweet spices, dried herbs. Palate: spicy, ripe fruit.

SAMPAYOLO GODELLO SOBRE LÍAS 2012 B
100% godello

90 Colour: bright straw. Nose: fresh fruit, white flowers, varietal, grassy. Palate: fruity, good acidity, balanced.

SAMPAYOLO MENCÍA 2012 T
100% mencía

89 Colour: deep cherry. Nose: sweet spices, creamy oak, ripe fruit, raspberry. Palate: flavourful, fruity, fresh.

COMPAÑÍA DE VINOS TELMO RODRÍGUEZ

El Monte
1308 Lanciego (Álava)
☎: +34 945 628 315 - Fax: +34 945 628 314
www.telmorodriguez.com
contact@telmorodriguez.com

AS CABORCAS 2010 T
mencía, merenzao, garnacha, godello

95 Colour: bright cherry. Nose: sweet spices, creamy oak, fresh fruit, red berry notes, scrubland, balsamic herbs. Palate: flavourful, fruity, round tannins.

GABA DO XIL GODELLO 2012 B
godello

92 Colour: bright straw. Nose: fresh, fresh fruit, white flowers, expressive, varietal. Palate: flavourful, fruity, good acidity, balanced.

ELADIO SANTALLA

Conde Fenosa, 36
32300 O Barco de Valdeorras (Ourense)
☎: +34 686 240 374
www.bodegaseladiosantalla.com
eladio@bodegaseladiosantalla.com

HACIENDA UCEDIÑOS 2012 B
godello

91 Colour: bright straw. Nose: fresh, white flowers, sweet spices, lactic notes. Palate: flavourful, fruity, good acidity, balanced.

HACIENDA UCEDIÑOS 2012 T
mencía

89 Colour: bright cherry. Nose: ripe fruit, sweet spices, creamy oak, expressive, scrubland, balsamic herbs. Palate: flavourful, fruity, toasty, round tannins.

GERMÁN RODRÍGUEZ SALGADO

Av. Barreais, 24
32350 A Rua (Ourense)
☎: +34 629 683 353 - Fax: +34 981 151 968
vinafornos@hotmail.com

VIÑA DE FORNOS 2012 B
godello

89 Colour: bright straw. Nose: fresh, fresh fruit, white flowers. Palate: flavourful, fruity, good acidity, balanced.

VIÑA DE FORNOS 2012 T
mencía

90 Colour: cherry, purple rim. Nose: expressive, varietal, red berry notes. Palate: flavourful, powerful, ripe fruit.

GUITIAN Y BLANCO

Córgomo
32340 Villamartín de Valdeorras (Ourense)
☎: +34 988 324 557 - Fax: +34 988 324 557
www.bodegasdberna.com
info@bodegasdberna.com

D'BERNA GODELLO 2012 B
godello

90 Colour: bright straw. Nose: dried herbs, white flowers, candied fruit. Palate: fine bitter notes, good acidity, ripe fruit.

D'BERNA GODELLO SOBRE LÍAS 2011 B
100% godello

89 Colour: bright straw. Nose: white flowers, warm, candied fruit. Palate: flavourful, fruity, balanced, fine bitter notes.

D'BERNA MENCÍA 2012 T
mencía

89 Colour: deep cherry. Nose: medium intensity, warm, candied fruit, dried herbs. Palate: fruity, sweetness.

D'BERNA MENCÍA BARRICA 2011 T
mencía

89 Colour: very deep cherry. Nose: powerfull, varietal, creamy oak, sweet spices, ripe fruit. Palate: flavourful, powerful, fine bitter notes.

JOAQUÍN REBOLLEDO

San Roque, 11
32350 A Rúa (Ourense)
☎: +34 988 372 307 - Fax: +34 988 371 427
www.joaquinrebolledo.com
info@joaquinrebolledo.com

JOAQUÍN REBOLLEDO 2011 T BARRICA
tempranillo, mencía

91 Colour: cherry, garnet rim. Nose: spicy, creamy oak, toasty, fruit liqueur notes. Palate: flavourful, toasty, round tannins.

JOAQUÍN REBOLLEDO GODELLO 2012 B
godello

92 Colour: bright straw. Nose: fresh, fresh fruit, white flowers, mineral. Palate: flavourful, fruity, good acidity, balanced.

JOAQUÍN REBOLLEDO MENCÍA 2012 T
mencía

93 Colour: cherry, purple rim. Nose: fresh fruit, red berry notes, floral, mineral. Palate: flavourful, fruity, good acidity, round tannins.

LA TAPADA

Finca A Tapada
32310 Rubiáde VAldeorras (Ourense)
☎: +34 988 324 197 - Fax: +34 988 324 197

GUITIÁN GODELLO 2011 BFB
100% godello

92 Colour: bright yellow. Nose: powerfull, ripe fruit, sweet spices, creamy oak, fragrant herbs. Palate: rich, smoky aftertaste, flavourful, fresh, good acidity.

GUITIÁN GODELLO 2012 B
100% godello

90 Colour: bright straw. Nose: fresh, white flowers, ripe fruit. Palate: flavourful, fruity, good acidity, balanced.

GUITIÁN GODELLO SOBRE LÍAS 2011 B
100% godello

93 Colour: bright straw. Nose: white flowers, expressive, mineral, candied fruit, characterful. Palate: flavourful, fruity, good acidity, balanced.

MENCÍA DE - DOS S.L.

La Reguera, 4
24540 Cacabelos (León)
☎: +34 616 920 648
alvaro.ollodegalo@gmail.com

OLLO DE GALO 2012 B
godello

90 Colour: bright straw. Nose: fresh fruit, white flowers, scrubland. Palate: flavourful, fruity, good acidity, balanced.

RAFAEL PALACIOS

Avda. de Somoza, 81
32350 A Rúa de Valdeorras (Ourense)
☎: +34 988 310 162 - Fax: +34 988 310 643
www.rafaelpalacios.com
bodega@rafaelpalacios.com

AS SORTES 2011 B
100% godello

95 Colour: bright yellow. Nose: powerfull, ripe fruit, sweet spices, creamy oak, fragrant herbs, mineral. Palate: rich, smoky aftertaste, flavourful, fresh, good acidity.

LOURO DO BOLO 2011 B
92% godello, 8% treixadura

93 Colour: bright straw. Nose: fresh, white flowers, expressive, ripe fruit, citrus fruit, dried herbs. Palate: flavourful, good acidity, balanced, full.

LOURO DO BOLO GODELLO 2012 B
94% godello, 6% treixadura

91 Colour: bright straw. Nose: fresh, white flowers, ripe fruit, warm, toasty. Palate: flavourful, fruity, balanced.

SORTE O SORO 2011 B
godello

97 Colour: bright yellow. Nose: powerfull, sweet spices, creamy oak, dried herbs, balsamic herbs, fruit expression. Palate: rich, flavourful, fresh, good acidity, mineral.

SANTA MARTA BODEGAS

32348 Villamartín de Ourense (Ourense)
☎: +34 988 324 559 - Fax: +34 988 324 559
www.vinaredo.com
info@vinaredo.com

VIÑAREDO GARNACHA CENTENARIA 2010 T
100% garnacha

88 Colour: cherry, garnet rim. Nose: ripe fruit, spicy, toasty, characterful. Palate: flavourful, toasty, round tannins.

VIÑAREDO GODELLO 2012 B
100% godello

92 Colour: bright straw. Nose: fresh, fresh fruit, white flowers, mineral, varietal. Palate: flavourful, fruity, good acidity, balanced.

VIÑAREDO GODELLO BARRICA 2011 B
100% godello

88 Colour: bright yellow. Nose: powerfull, ripe fruit, sweet spices, creamy oak. Palate: rich, smoky aftertaste, flavourful, fresh, good acidity.

VIÑAREDO MENCÍA 2012 T
100% mencía

84

VIÑAREDO SOUSÓN 2010 T BARRICA
100% sousón

89 Colour: bright cherry. Nose: ripe fruit, creamy oak, expressive, balsamic herbs, scrubland. Palate: flavourful, fruity, toasty, round tannins.

VIÑAREDO TOSTADO 2011 B
100% godello

95 Colour: golden. Nose: powerfull, floral, honeyed notes, candied fruit, fragrant herbs. Palate: flavourful, sweet, fresh, fruity, good acidity, long.

VALDESIL

Ctra. a San Vicente OU 807, km. 3
32348 Vilamartín de Valdeorras (Ourense)
☎: +34 988 337 900 - Fax: +34 988 337 901
www.valdesil.com
valdesil@valdesil.com

MONTENOVO GODELLO 2012 B
100% godello

91 Colour: bright straw. Nose: fresh, fresh fruit, white flowers, grassy, mineral. Palate: flavourful, fruity, good acidity, balanced.

PEZAS DA PORTELA 2011 BFB
100% godello

92 Colour: bright straw. Nose: fresh, white flowers, ripe fruit, mineral. Palate: flavourful, fruity, good acidity, balanced.

VALDERROA 2012 T
100% mencía

92 Colour: cherry, purple rim. Nose: scrubland, red berry notes, fruit expression. Palate: flavourful, fruity, fresh.

VALDESIL GODELLO SOBRE LÍAS 2012 B
100% godello

93 Colour: bright straw. Nose: fresh fruit, white flowers, powerfull, earthy notes, grassy. Palate: flavourful, fruity, good acidity, balanced.

VINIGALICIA

Ctra. Antigua Santiago, km. 3
27500 Chantada (Lugo)
☎: +34 982 454 005 - Fax: +34 982 454 094
www.vinigalicia.es
vinigalicia@vinigalicia.es

VERDES CASTROS 2011 B
100% godello

86 Colour: bright yellow. Nose: candied fruit, citrus fruit, warm. Palate: sweetness, spicy.

VERDES CASTROS 2011 T
100% mencía

90 Colour: cherry, garnet rim. Nose: complex, candied fruit, ripe fruit, cocoa bean, sweet spices, creamy oak. Palate: powerful, sweetness, fruity.

VIÑA SOMOZA BODEGAS Y VIÑEDOS

Pombar, s/n
32350 A Rúa (Ourense)
☎: +34 988 310 918 - Fax: +34 988 310 918
www.vinosomoza.com
bodega@vinosomoza.com

NENO VIÑA SOMOZA GODELLO SOBRE LIAS 2012 B
godello

90 Colour: bright straw. Nose: fresh, white flowers, candied fruit. Palate: flavourful, fruity, good acidity, balanced.

VIÑA SOMOZA GODELLO SELECCIÓN 2011 B ROBLE
godello

90 Colour: bright straw. Nose: ripe fruit, citrus fruit, fine lees, candied fruit, toasty. Palate: flavourful, good acidity, fine bitter notes.

VIRXE DE GALIR

Las Escuelas, s/n Estoma
32336 O Barco de Valdeorras (Ourense)
☎: +34 988 335 600 - Fax: +34 988 335 592
www.virxendegalir.es
bodega@virxendegalir.es

PAGOS DEL GALIR GODELLO 2012 B
100% godello

93 Colour: bright straw. Nose: fresh, fresh fruit, white flowers, expressive, mineral, fragrant herbs. Palate: flavourful, fruity, good acidity, balanced.

PAGOS DEL GALIR MENCÍA 2011 T ROBLE
100% mencía

88 Colour: cherry, garnet rim. Nose: ripe fruit, spicy, creamy oak, toasty. Palate: powerful, flavourful, round tannins.

VÍA NOVA MENCÍA 2012 T
100% mencía

90 Colour: cherry, purple rim. Nose: scrubland, ripe fruit, medium intensity. Palate: flavourful, good acidity, fine bitter notes.

LOCATION:

On the southern border of the southern plateau, in the province of Ciudad Real. It comprises the municipal districts of Alcubillas, Moral de Calatrava, San Carlos del Valle, Santa Cruz de Mudela, Torrenueva and Valdepeñas and part of Alhambra, Granátula de Calatrava, Montiel and Torre de Juan Abad.

CLIMATE:

Continental in nature, with cold winters, very hot summers and little rainfall, which is usually around 250 and 400 mm per year.

SOIL:

Mainly brownish-red and brownish-grey limestone soil with a high lime content and quite poor in organic matter.

GRAPE VARIETIES:

WHITE: *Airén, Macabeo, Chardonnay, Sauvignon Blanc, Moscatel de Grano Menudo* and *Verdejo.*
RED: *Cencibel (Tempranillo), Garnacha, Cabernet Sauvignon, Merlot, Syrah* and *Petit Verdot.*

FIGURES:

Vineyard surface: 22.003 – **Wine-Growers:** 2.691 – **Wineries:** 40 – **2012 Harvest rating:**Very Good – **Production:** 66.276.639 litres – **Market percentages:** 53% domestic. 47% export

VINTAGE RATING PEÑINGUIDE				
2008	2009	2010	2011	2012
EXCELLENT	GOOD	GOOD	GOOD	GOOD

CONSEJO REGULADOR
Constitución, 23 - 13300 Valdepeñas (Ciudad Real) - ☎: +34 926 322 788 - Fax: +34 926 321 054
dovaldepeñas@dovaldepenas.es   www.dovaldepenas.es

BODEGA HACIENDA LA PRINCESA

Ctra. San Carlos del Valle, km. 8 - Apdo. Correos 281
13300 Valdepeñas (Ciudad Real)
☎: +34 638 335 185
www.haciendalaprincesa.com
haciendalaprincesa@telefonica.net

**HACIENDA LA PRINCESA
DEBIR PRINCESA 2012 BFB**
100% chardonnay

84

BODEGAS CASA ROJO

Sánchez Picazo, 53
30332 Balsapintada (Murcia)
☎: +34 968 151 520 - Fax: +34 968 151 690
www.casarojo.com
info@casarojo.com

BALTHASAR 2002 TGR
100% tempranillo

83

BALTHASAR 2004 TR
100% tempranillo

84

BALTHASAR 2011 T
100% tempranillo

84

BODEGAS FERNANDO CASTRO

Paseo Castelar, 70
13730 Santa Cruz de Mudela (Ciudad Real)
☎: +34 926 342 168 - Fax: +34 926 349 029
www.bodegasfernandocastro.com
fernando@bodegasfernandocastro.com

CASTILLO SANTA BÁRBARA 2012 T
syrah, merlot

85 Colour: cherry, garnet rim. Nose: fruit preserve, ripe fruit, red berry notes. Palate: powerful, flavourful.

RAÍCES 2006 TGR
tempranillo

88 Colour: cherry, garnet rim. Nose: ripe fruit, spicy, creamy oak, toasty, complex. Palate: powerful, flavourful, toasty, round tannins.

RAÍCES 2007 TR
tempranillo

86 Colour: cherry, garnet rim. Nose: creamy oak, toasty, fruit preserve, sweet spices. Palate: powerful, flavourful, toasty.

RAÍCES 2008 TR
tempranillo

86 Colour: cherry, garnet rim. Nose: ripe fruit, spicy, toasty, tobacco. Palate: powerful, flavourful, toasty.

RAÍCES 2012 T
100% tempranillo

83

RAÍCES AIRÉN 2012 B
airén

84

RAÍCES SYRAH SELECCIÓN 2007 T
syrah

84

TABANICO T
cabernet sauvignon, syrah, merlot, tempranillo

86 Colour: cherry, garnet rim. Nose: ripe fruit, sweet spices, creamy oak, toasty, fragrant herbs. Palate: powerful, flavourful, spicy, toasty.

VALDEMONTE 2012 T
tempranillo

82

BODEGAS J. RAMÍREZ S.L.

Torrecilla, 138
13300 Valdepeñas (Ciudad Real)
☎: +34 926 322 021 - Fax: +34 926 320 495
www.bodegasjuanramirez.com
info@bodegasjuanramirez.com

TANIS 2005 T
tempranillo
84

BODEGAS LOS MARCOS

Cristo, 2
13730 Santa Cruz de Mudela (Ciudad Real)
☎: +34 926 349 028 - Fax: +34 926 349 029
www.bodeslosmarcos.com
fernando@bodegasfernandocastro.com

MONTECRUZ 2005 TGR
tempranillo

86 Colour: dark-red cherry, garnet rim. Nose: ripe fruit, sweet spices, creamy oak. Palate: flavourful, fruity, toasty, round tannins.

MONTECRUZ 2008 TR
tempranillo

85 Colour: ruby red, garnet rim. Nose: fine reductive notes, tobacco, ripe fruit. Palate: long, spicy, toasty.

BODEGAS MARÍN PERONA

Castellanos, 99
13300 Valdepeñas (Ciudad Real)
☎: +34 926 313 192 - Fax: +34 926 313 347
www.tejeruelas.com
bodega@tejeruela.com

CALAR VIEJO 2007 TC
tempranillo
83

MARÍN PERONA 2002 TGR
tempranillo

85 Colour: pale ruby, brick rim edge. Nose: spicy, wet leather, aged wood nuances, fruit liqueur notes. Palate: spicy, fine tannins, elegant, long.

MARÍN PERONA 2005 TR
tempranillo

85 Colour: ruby red, orangey edge. Nose: sweet spices, fruit liqueur notes, creamy oak, fine reductive notes. Palate: powerful, flavourful, long.

MARÍN PERONA VERDEJO 2012 B
verdejo

85 Colour: bright straw. Nose: fresh, fresh fruit, white flowers, expressive. Palate: flavourful, fruity, good acidity, balanced.

TEJERUELAS VIÑA ALDANTE 2012 B
airén
84

TEJERUELAS VIÑA ALDANTE 2012 T
tempranillo
82

BODEGAS MEGÍA E HIJOS -CORCOVO

Magdalena, 33
13300 Valdepeñas (Ciudad Real)
☎: +34 926 347 828 - Fax: +34 926 347 829
www.corcovo.com
jamegia@corcovo.com

CORCOVO 2007 TR
100% tempranillo

88 Colour: cherry, garnet rim. Nose: ripe fruit, spicy, creamy oak, toasty, complex. Palate: powerful, flavourful, toasty, round tannins.

CORCOVO 2009 TC
100% tempranillo

87 Colour: cherry, garnet rim. Nose: ripe fruit, spicy, creamy oak, toasty, complex. Palate: powerful, flavourful, toasty, round tannins.

CORCOVO 2012 RD
100% tempranillo

88 Colour: rose, purple rim. Nose: red berry notes, lactic notes, candied fruit, expressive. Palate: good acidity, powerful, flavourful.

CORCOVO AIREN 2012 B
100% airén

86 Colour: bright straw. Nose: fresh, fresh fruit, white flowers, expressive. Palate: flavourful, fruity, good acidity, balanced.

CORCOVO SYRAH 2012 T
100% syrah

89 Colour: cherry, purple rim. Nose: expressive, fresh fruit, red berry notes, floral. Palate: flavourful, fruity, good acidity, round tannins.

CORCOVO SYRAH 24 BARRICAS 2011 T ROBLE
100% syrah

88 Colour: cherry, garnet rim. Nose: spicy, creamy oak, ripe fruit, dried flowers. Palate: long, flavourful, powerful.

CORCOVO TEMPRANILLO 2011 T ROBLE
100% tempranillo

86 Colour: bright cherry. Nose: ripe fruit, sweet spices, creamy oak, expressive. Palate: flavourful, fruity, toasty, round tannins.

CORCOVO TEMPRANILLO 2012 T
100% tempranillo

88 Colour: cherry, purple rim. Nose: expressive, fresh fruit, red berry notes, floral, lactic notes. Palate: flavourful, fruity, good acidity, round tannins.

CORCOVO VERDEJO 2012 B
100% verdejo

87 Colour: bright straw. Nose: white flowers, expressive, ripe fruit, dried herbs. Palate: flavourful, fruity, good acidity.

CORCOVO VERDEJO 24 BARRICAS 2011 B ROBLE
100% verdejo

88 Colour: bright golden. Nose: ripe fruit, dry nuts, powerfull, toasty, sweet spices. Palate: flavourful, fruity, spicy, toasty, long.

BODEGAS MIGUEL CALATAYUD

Postas, 20
13300 Valdepeñas (Ciudad Real)
☎: +34 926 348 070 - Fax: +34 926 322 150
www.vegaval.com
vegaval@vegaval.com

VEGAVAL PLATA 2006 TGR
100% tempranillo

80

VEGAVAL PLATA 2008 TR
100% tempranillo

84

VEGAVAL PLATA 2009 TC
100% tempranillo

83

VEGAVAL PLATA AIRÉN 2012 B
100% airén

83

VEGAVAL PLATA VERDEJO 2012 B
100% verdejo

85 Colour: bright straw. Nose: fresh fruit, dried flowers, tropical fruit. Palate: flavourful, fruity, good acidity.

BODEGAS MUREDA

Ctra. N-IV, Km. 184,1
13300 Valdepeñas (Ciudad Real)
☎: +34 926 318 058 - Fax: +34 926 318 058
www.mureda.es
bmoreno@mureda.es

MUREDA CUVÉE BRUT 2008 ESP
airén, macabeo, sauvignon blanc

84

MUREDA CUVÉE BRUT ROSÉ 2008 ESP
garnacha

82

MUREDA GRAN CUVÉE BRUT NATURE 2007 ESP RESERVA
airén, macabeo, chardonnay

85 Colour: bright golden. Nose: fine lees, dry nuts, fragrant herbs, complex, sweet spices, toasty. Palate: powerful, flavourful, good acidity, fine bead.

BODEGAS NAVARRO LÓPEZ

Autovía Madrid - Cádiz, Km. 193
13210 Valdepeñas (Ciudad Real)
☎: +34 902 193 431 - Fax: +34 902 193 432
www.bodegasnavarrolopez.com
laboratorio2@navarrolopez.com

DON AURELIO 2007 TGR
100% tempranillo

86 Colour: deep cherry, orangey edge. Nose: waxy notes, tobacco, ripe fruit, spicy, aged wood nuances. Palate: fine bitter notes, powerful, flavourful.

DON AURELIO 2008 TR
100% tempranillo

86 Colour: cherry, garnet rim. Nose: ripe fruit, spicy, creamy oak, toasty, fine reductive notes. Palate: powerful, flavourful, toasty.

DON AURELIO 2010 TC
tempranillo

88 Colour: cherry, garnet rim. Nose: spicy, creamy oak, toasty, red berry notes. Palate: powerful, flavourful, toasty, round tannins.

DON AURELIO 2011 T BARRICA
tempranillo

86 Colour: bright cherry. Nose: ripe fruit, sweet spices, creamy oak. Palate: flavourful, fruity, toasty, round tannins.

DON AURELIO 2012 RD
tempranillo

87 Colour: raspberry rose. Nose: powerfull, ripe fruit, red berry notes, floral. Palate: powerful, fruity, fresh.

DON AURELIO GARNACHA 2012 T
garnacha

87 Colour: cherry, purple rim. Nose: red berry notes, floral, fragrant herbs. Palate: powerful, flavourful, easy to drink.

DON AURELIO TEMPRANILLO 2012 T
tempranillo

85 Colour: cherry, purple rim. Nose: red berry notes, floral, ripe fruit, lactic notes. Palate: flavourful, fruity, good acidity.

DON AURELIO VERDEJO MACABEO 2012 B
verdejo, macabeo

85 Colour: bright straw. Nose: dried flowers, balsamic herbs, ripe fruit. Palate: flavourful, fruity, good acidity.

BODEGAS REAL

Finca Marisánchez - Ctra. de Valdepeñas a Cózar, Km. 12,8
13300 Valdepeñas (Ciudad Real)
☎: +34 914 577 588 - Fax: +34 914 577 210
www.bodegas-real.com
comercial@bodegas-real.com

PALACIO DE IBOR 2007 TR

85 Colour: light cherry. Nose: fruit preserve, fruit liqueur notes, waxy notes, tobacco, old leather. Palate: light-bodied, spicy, correct.

CARREFOUR

Campezo, 16
28022 Madrid (Madrid)
☎: +34 902 202 000
www.carrefour.es

SEÑORÍO DE OJAILÉN 2009 TR
cencibel

85 Colour: deep cherry, brick rim edge. Nose: spicy, aromatic coffee, wet leather. Palate: flavourful, fine bitter notes.

SEÑORÍO DE OJAILÉN 2010 TC
cencibel

83

SEÑORÍO DE OJAILÉN 2012 B
airén

82

SEÑORÍO DE OJAILÉN 2012 RD
cencibel, mosto blanco

84

SEÑORÍO DE OJAILÉN 2012 T JOVEN
cencibel

87 Colour: cherry, purple rim. Nose: fresh fruit, red berry notes, floral. Palate: flavourful, fruity, good acidity.

FÉLIX SOLÍS

Autovía del Sur, Km. 199
13300 Valdepeñas (Ciudad Real)
☎: +34 926 322 400 - Fax: +34 926 322 417
www.felixsolisavantis.com
fsa@felixsolisavantis.com

AYRUM 2007 TGR
tempranillo

88 Colour: cherry, garnet rim. Nose: ripe fruit, spicy, creamy oak, wet leather. Palate: powerful, flavourful, toasty.

AYRUM 2008 TR
tempranillo

88 Colour: cherry, garnet rim. Nose: ripe fruit, spicy, toasty, complex, aged wood nuances. Palate: powerful, flavourful, toasty.

AYRUM 2009 TC
tempranillo

87 Colour: cherry, garnet rim. Nose: ripe fruit, spicy, creamy oak, toasty. Palate: powerful, flavourful, toasty, spicy.

AYRUM 2010 TC
tempranillo

88 Colour: cherry, garnet rim. Nose: ripe fruit, spicy, creamy oak, toasty, fine reductive notes. Palate: powerful, flavourful, toasty.

AYRUM 2012 RD
tempranillo

87 Colour: rose, purple rim. Nose: lactic notes, red berry notes, ripe fruit, expressive. Palate: correct, powerful, flavourful.

AYRUM VERDEJO 2012 B
verdejo

86 Colour: bright straw. Nose: fresh, fresh fruit, white flowers, tropical fruit. Palate: flavourful, fruity, good acidity.

LOS MOLINOS 2007 TGR
tempranillo

87 Colour: cherry, garnet rim. Nose: ripe fruit, spicy, creamy oak, toasty, fine reductive notes. Palate: powerful, flavourful, toasty.

VIÑA ALBALI 2007 TGR
tempranillo

86 Colour: pale ruby, brick rim edge. Nose: spicy, fine reductive notes, aged wood nuances, fruit liqueur notes, waxy notes, dark chocolate. Palate: spicy, long, correct.

VIÑA ALBALI 2008 TR
tempranillo

86 Colour: cherry, garnet rim. Nose: ripe fruit, spicy, creamy oak, toasty, complex. Palate: powerful, flavourful, toasty, round tannins.

VIÑA ALBALI 2009 TC
tempranillo

84

VIÑA ALBALI 2012 RD
tempranillo

86 Colour: rose, purple rim. Nose: powerfull, ripe fruit, red berry notes, floral, lactic notes. Palate: powerful, fruity, fresh.

VIÑA ALBALI GRAN RESERVA DE LA FAMILIA 2005 TGR
85% tempranillo, 15% cabernet sauvignon

87 Colour: pale ruby, brick rim edge. Nose: spicy, fine reductive notes, wet leather, aged wood nuances, fruit liqueur notes. Palate: spicy, long.

VIÑA ALBALI SELECCIÓN PRIVADA 2007 TGR
tempranillo

88 Colour: dark-red cherry, orangey edge. Nose: fruit liqueur notes, fruit liqueur notes, spicy, aged wood nuances, cigar. Palate: powerful, flavourful, spicy.

VIÑA ALBALI VERDEJO 2012 B
100% verdejo

84

GRUPO DE BODEGAS VINARTIS

Autovía Madrid - Cádiz, Km. 200,5
13300 Valdepeñas (Ciudad Real)
☎: +34 926 320 300 - Fax: +34 926 348 483
www.grupobodegasvinartis.com
jvnavarro@jgc.es

ARMONIOSO 2012 B
airén

82

ARMONIOSO 2012 RD
tempranillo

83

PATA NEGRA 2005 TGR
tempranillo

86 Colour: pale ruby, brick rim edge. Nose: spicy, fine reductive notes, aged wood nuances, fruit liqueur notes, waxy notes, tobacco. Palate: spicy, fine tannins, long.

PATA NEGRA 2006 TR
tempranillo
83

PATA NEGRA 2007 TC
tempranillo
82

PATA NEGRA 2010 T
tempranillo, cabernet sauvignon
84

PATA NEGRA 2011 T ROBLE
tempranillo
83

LA INVENCIBLE VINOS Y ACEITES, S.L.

Torrecilla, 130
13300 Valdepeñas (Ciudad Real)
☎: +34 926 321 700
www.lainvencible.eu
lainvencible@lainvencible.eu

VIÑA LASTRA AIRÉN 2012 B
airén
82

VIÑA LASTRA TEMPRANILLO 2012 T
tempranillo
82

DO VALENCIA / D.O.P.

LOCATION:

In the province of Valencia. It comprises 66 municipal districts in 4 different sub-regions: Alto Turia, Moscatel de Valencia, Valentino and Clariano.

CLIMATE:

Mediterranean, marked by strong storms and down-pours in summer and autumn. The average annual temperature is 15°C and the average annual rainfall is 500 mm.

SOIL:

Mostly brownish-grey with limestone content; there are no drainage problems.

GRAPE VARIETIES:

WHITE: *Macabeo, Malvasía, Merseguera, Moscatel de Alejandría, Moscatel de Grano Menudo, Pedro Ximénez, Plantafina, Plantanova, Tortosí, Verdil, Chardonnay, Semillon Blanc, Sauvignon Blanc, Verdejo, Riesling, Viognier* and *Gewüztraminer.*
RED: *Garnacha, Monastrell, Tempranillo, Tintorera, Forcallat Tinta, Bobal, Cabernet Cauvignon, Merlot, Pinot Noir, Syrah, Graciano, Malbec, Mandó, Marselan, Mencía, Merlot, Mazuelo* and *Petit Verdot.*

SUB-REGIONS:

There are four in total: **Alto Turia,** the highest sub-region (700 to 800 m above sea level) comprising 6 municipal districts; **Valentino** (23 municipal districts), in the centre of the province; the altitude varies between 250 m and 650 m; **Moscatel de Valencia** (9 municipal districts), also in the central region where the historical wine from the region is produced; and **Clariano** (33 municipal districts), to the south, at an altitude of between 400 m and 650 m.

FIGURES:

Vineyard surface: 13.050– **Wine-Growers:** 10.805 – **Wineries:** 88 – **2012 Harvest rating:** Very Good– **Production:** 72.000.000 litres – **Market percentages:** 24% domestic. 76% export

CONSEJO REGULADOR
Quart, 22 - 46001 Valencia ☎: +34 963 910 096 - Fax: +34 963 910 029
info@vinovalencia.org www.vinovalencia.org

ALVAREZ NÖLTING

Ctra. N-322, km. 431,25
46340 Requena (Valencia)
☎: +34 963 290 696 - Fax: +34 963 445 463
www.alvareznolting.com
info@alvareznolting.com

ALVAREZ NÖLTING 2010 T
50% bobal, 50% merlot

90 Colour: cherry, garnet rim. Nose: ripe fruit, spicy, creamy oak, toasty, balsamic herbs. Palate: powerful, flavourful, toasty, balanced.

ALVAREZ NÖLTING CHARDONNAY 2012 B
chardonnay

89 Colour: bright yellow. Nose: candied fruit, ripe fruit, sweet spices. Palate: powerful, spicy, ripe fruit.

ALVAREZ NÖLTING SYRAH 2011 T
syrah

88 Colour: bright cherry. Nose: sweet spices, creamy oak, fruit preserve. Palate: flavourful, fruity, toasty, balanced.

FINCA ALVAREZ 2012 T
bobal

88 Colour: cherry, purple rim. Nose: ripe fruit, fruit preserve, balsamic herbs. Palate: powerful, rich, flavourful.

BLACKBOARD WINES

Conrado Albaladejo, 31 BW 61
3540 (Alicante)
☎: +34 686 097 742
www.blackboardwines.com
sales@blackboardwines.com

THE TAPAS WINE COLLECTION 2011 T
tempranillo

87 Colour: cherry, purple rim. Nose: red berry notes, ripe fruit, violet drops, balsamic herbs. Palate: powerful, flavourful, fruity.

THE TAPAS WINE COLLECTION BLANCO 2012 ESP
moscatel

84

BODEGA J. BELDA

Avda. Conde Salvatierra, 54
46635 Fontanars dels Alforins (Valencia)
☎: +34 962 222 278 - Fax: +34 962 222 245
www.danielbelda.com
info@danielbelda.com

CA'BELDA 2007 T BARRICA
monastrell, garnacha tintorera

90 Colour: ruby red, brick rim edge. Nose: ripe fruit, balsamic herbs, spicy, creamy oak. Palate: powerful, flavourful, spirituous.

DANIEL BELDA CABERNET SAUVIGNON 2009 T
cabernet sauvignon

82

DANIEL BELDA CHARDONNAY 2011 B
chardonnay

85 Colour: bright yellow. Nose: wild herbs, citrus fruit, ripe fruit, floral. Palate: correct, easy to drink, flavourful.

DANIEL BELDA MERLOT 2007 TR
merlot

87 Colour: cherry, garnet rim. Nose: medium intensity, toasty, spicy. Palate: flavourful, correct, good acidity.

DANIEL BELDA PINOT NOIR 2011 T
pinot noir

87 Colour: bright cherry. Nose: ripe fruit, sweet spices, creamy oak, balsamic herbs. Palate: flavourful, fruity, toasty.

DANIEL BELDA SHIRAZ 2007 TR
syrah

84

DANIEL BELDA VERDIL 2012 B
verdil

86 Colour: bright yellow. Nose: medium intensity, faded flowers, ripe fruit, tropical fruit. Palate: correct, good acidity.

MIGJORN 2007 T
cabernet sauvignon, merlot, garnacha tintorera

84

TENDENCIA 2012 B
verdil, moscatel

86 Colour: bright yellow. Nose: medium intensity, dried flowers, grassy. Palate: fresh, balsamic.

BODEGAS 40 GRADOS NORTE

46635 Fontanars dels Alforins (Valencia)
☎: +34 615 167 040 - Fax: +34 960 963 724
www.40gradosnorte.com
amartin@40gradosnorte.com

COTA 830 2008 T
bobal, cabernet sauvignon, tempranillo

89 Colour: cherry, garnet rim. Nose: sweet spices, balsamic herbs, ripe fruit. Palate: flavourful, good acidity, round tannins.

MAR DE SO 2009 T
syrah, bobal, tempranillo

87 Colour: cherry, garnet rim. Nose: ripe fruit, spicy, creamy oak, toasty, scrubland. Palate: powerful, flavourful, toasty.

MAR DE SO BLANC 2012 B
merseguera, sauvignon blanc

88 Colour: bright straw. Nose: fresh, fresh fruit, white flowers, fragrant herbs. Palate: flavourful, fruity, good acidity, balanced.

SO DE SYRAH 2012 T JOVEN
syrah

85 Colour: cherry, purple rim. Nose: dried herbs, ripe fruit, medium intensity, warm. Palate: ripe fruit, flavourful.

BODEGAS ARANLEÓN

Ctra. Caudete, 3
46310 Los Marcos (Valencia)
☎: +34 963 631 640 - Fax: +34 962 185 150
www.aranleon.com
maria@aranleon.com

BLÉS CRIANZA DE ARANLEÓN 2011 TC
40% monastrell, 40% tempranillo, 20% cabernet sauvignon

89 Colour: cherry, garnet rim. Nose: ripe fruit, spicy, creamy oak, toasty. Palate: powerful, flavourful, toasty, round tannins.

BLÉS MADURADO 2012 T
70% tempranillo, 30% bobal

88 Colour: cherry, purple rim. Nose: red berry notes, fruit liqueur notes, balsamic herbs, spicy. Palate: powerful, flavourful, fruity.

BLÉS RESERVA DE ARANLEÓN 2010 TR
40% monastrell, 30% cabernet sauvignon, 10% petit verdot, 10% syrah, 10% marselan

90 Colour: cherry, garnet rim. Nose: ripe fruit, spicy, creamy oak, toasty, complex. Palate: powerful, flavourful, toasty, round tannins.

EL ÁRBOL DE ARANLEÓN 2008 TR
20% monastrell, 10% tempranillo, 20% syrah, 20% merlot, 20% cabernet sauvignon, 10% cabernet franc

92 Colour: cherry, garnet rim. Nose: ripe fruit, sweet spices, creamy oak, expressive. Palate: flavourful, fruity, toasty, round tannins.

BODEGAS ARRAEZ

Arcediano Ros, 35
46630 La Font de la Figuera (Valencia)
☎: +34 962 290 031 - Fax: +34 962 290 339
www.bodegasarraez.com
julian@bodegasarraez.com

A2 VERDIL 2012 B
verdil

88 Colour: bright straw. Nose: fresh, fresh fruit, white flowers, tropical fruit. Palate: flavourful, fruity, good acidity, elegant.

CASAS DE HERENCIA 2011 T BARRICA
tempranillo, monastrell

83

CASAS DE HERENCIA 2012 B
macabeo, merseguera

79

EDUARDO BERMEJO 2011 T
tempranillo

87 Colour: cherry, garnet rim. Nose: balsamic herbs, ripe fruit, medium intensity. Palate: fruity, spicy, good acidity.

EDUARDO BERMEJO 2012 B
moscatel, macabeo, merseguera

88 Colour: bright straw. Nose: floral, fragrant herbs, expressive, balanced. Palate: powerful, flavourful, balanced, elegant.

LAGARES 2006 TR
cabernet sauvignon, syrah, monastrell

85 Colour: cherry, garnet rim. Nose: ripe fruit, spicy, creamy oak, toasty, complex. Palate: powerful, flavourful, toasty, round tannins.

LAGARES 2009 TC
cabernet sauvignon

89 Colour: cherry, garnet rim. Nose: scrubland, powerfull, ripe fruit. Palate: flavourful, balsamic, spicy, ripe fruit.

MALA VIDA 2011 T ROBLE
tempranillo, monastrell, cabernet sauvignon, syrah

90 Colour: bright cherry. Nose: ripe fruit, sweet spices, creamy oak, expressive. Palate: flavourful, fruity, toasty, round tannins.

BODEGAS BATALLER

Camí Real, 94-96
46841 Castelló de Rugat (Valencia)
☎: +34 962 813 017 - Fax: +34 962 813 017
vinosbenicadell@telepolis.com

BENICADELL 2012 B
merseguera

80

BENICADELL TEMPRANILLO 2012 T
tempranillo

84

D'ALBA VARIETAL MOSCATEL 2012 B
100% moscatel

84

BODEGAS EL ANGOSTO

Finca Santa Rosa
46870 Ontinyent (Valencia)
☎: +34 962 380 638 - Fax: +34 962 911 349
www.bodegaelangosto.com
info@bodegaelangosto.com

ALMENDROS 2011 T
marselan, garnacha tintorera, syrah

93 Colour: bright cherry. Nose: ripe fruit, sweet spices, creamy oak, expressive. Palate: flavourful, fruity, toasty, round tannins.

ALMENDROS 2012 B
sauvignon blanc, verdejo

92 Colour: bright yellow, greenish rim. Nose: ripe fruit, floral, dried herbs, citrus fruit. Palate: flavourful, spicy, long.

ANGOSTO BLANCO 2012 B
chardonnay, verdejo, sauvignon blanc, moscatel grano menudo

91 Colour: bright straw. Nose: candied fruit, floral, fragrant herbs, spicy, elegant. Palate: powerful, flavourful, balanced, good acidity.

ANGOSTO TINTO 2011 T
syrah, garnacha, cabernet franc

91 Colour: deep cherry, purple rim. Nose: balanced, ripe fruit, cocoa bean. Palate: flavourful, fruity, long.

EL JEFE DE LA TRIBU 2011 T
touriga, marselan

92 Colour: deep cherry, garnet rim. Nose: complex, balanced, ripe fruit, sweet spices, creamy oak. Palate: flavourful, good structure.

LA TRIBU 2012 T
33% monastrell, 33% syrah, 34% garnacha tintorera

89 Colour: cherry, purple rim. Nose: violets, ripe fruit. Palate: flavourful, good structure, ripe fruit, good acidity.

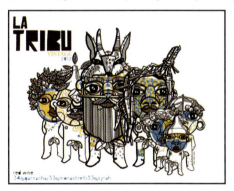

BODEGAS ELFESU

Jacquars, 14
46870 Onteniente
☎: +34 620 125 194 - Fax: +34 620 125 194
bodegas.elfesu.sl@gmail.com

CAMBRER 2009 TC
tempranillo, merlot, monastrell

86 Colour: cherry, garnet rim. Nose: ripe fruit, spicy, creamy oak, toasty. Palate: powerful, flavourful, toasty.

VIÑA BELMAR 2008 TR

86 Colour: ruby red, orangey edge. Nose: ripe fruit, spicy, creamy oak, toasty, fine reductive notes. Palate: powerful, flavourful, toasty.

BODEGAS ENGUERA

Ctra. CV - 590, Km. 51,5
46810 Enguera (Valencia)
☎: +34 962 224 318 - Fax: +34 963 415 999
www.bodegasenguera.com
oficina@bodegasenguera.com

BLANC D'ENGUERA 2012 B
verdil, chardonnay, viognier, sauvignon blanc

88 Colour: bright yellow. Nose: medium intensity, ripe fruit, tropical fruit, floral. Palate: flavourful, fruity, good acidity, correct.

MEGALA 2010 T
monastrell, syrah

91 Colour: cherry, garnet rim. Nose: ripe fruit, scrubland, spicy. Palate: good structure, flavourful, long, good acidity.

PARADIGMA 2008 T
100% monastrell

92 Colour: cherry, garnet rim. Nose: wild herbs, ripe fruit, fruit preserve, spicy. Palate: flavourful, balsamic, long.

SUEÑO DE MEGALA 2008 T
monastrell, merlot, tempranillo

93 Colour: cherry, garnet rim. Nose: complex, ripe fruit, balsamic herbs, spicy. Palate: flavourful, ripe fruit, long, good acidity.

BODEGAS LADRÓN DE LUNAS

Pintor Peiró, 10 - Bajo
46010 (Valencia)
☎: +349 610 505 553
www.ladrondelunas.es
administracion@ladrondelunas.es

BISILA BARRICA 2011 T
tempranillo

86 Colour: bright cherry. Nose: ripe fruit, sweet spices, creamy oak. Palate: flavourful, fruity, toasty.

BISILA SAUVIGNON 2012 B
sauvignon blanc

83

BODEGAS LOS PINOS

Casa Los Pinos, s/n
46635 Fontanars dels Alforins (Valencia)
☎: +34 600 584 397
www.bodegaslospinos.com
bodegaslospinos@bodegaslospinos.com

CA'LS PINS DE DOMINIO LOS PINOS 2012 T BARRICA
monastrell, cabernet sauvignon, merlot

89 Colour: cherry, purple rim. Nose: medium intensity, spicy, dried herbs. Palate: fruity, good acidity.

DOMINIO LOS PINOS 0 % 2012 T
garnacha, monastrell, syrah

87 Colour: cherry, purple rim. Nose: ripe fruit, dried herbs. Palate: fruity, flavourful, good finish.

DOMINIO LOS PINOS 2011 T BARRICA
tempranillo, syrah, cabernet sauvignon

89 Colour: cherry, garnet rim. Nose: sweet spices, red berry notes, ripe fruit. Palate: fruity, flavourful, round tannins.

DOMINIO LOS PINOS BROTE BLANCO 2012 BFB
verdil, viognier

87 Colour: bright straw. Nose: medium intensity, faded flowers. Palate: fruity, easy to drink, good finish, spicy.

DOMINIO LOS PINOS BROTE TINTO 2010 TC
monastrell, garnacha, merlot

88 Colour: cherry, garnet rim. Nose: powerfull, fruit preserve, lactic notes, sweet spices. Palate: flavourful, round tannins.

DX ROBLE DE DOMINIO LOS PINOS 2011 T
monastrell, cabernet sauvignon

87 Colour: bright cherry. Nose: ripe fruit, sweet spices, creamy oak. Palate: flavourful, fruity, toasty.

BODEGAS MURVIEDRO

Ampliación Pol. El Romeral, s/n
46340 Requena (Valencia)
☎: +34 962 329 003 - Fax: +34 962 329 002
www.bodegasmurviedro.es
murviedro@murviedro.es

ALBA DE MURVIEDRO 2012 B
sauvignon blanc, moscatel

90 Colour: bright straw, greenish rim. Nose: fresh, citrus fruit, floral. Palate: flavourful, balanced, fine bitter notes.

ALMA MÍSTICA MUSCAT 2012 B
85% moscatel, 15% viura

85 Colour: bright straw. Nose: white flowers, candied fruit, tropical fruit. Palate: light-bodied, fresh, fruity, easy to drink.

CUEVA DEL PECADO 2009 T
tempranillo, cabernet sauvignon

92 Colour: cherry, garnet rim. Nose: balanced, ripe fruit, toasty, cocoa bean, wild herbs. Palate: good structure, flavourful, good acidity, round tannins.

ESTRELLA DE MURVIEDRO FRIZZANTE 2012 B
moscatel de alejandría

84

LOS MONTEROS 2010 TC
monastrell, merlot

87 Colour: cherry, garnet rim. Nose: toasty, spicy, medium intensity. Palate: fruity, easy to drink.

LOS MONTEROS 2012 B
viura, moscatel

87 Colour: bright straw. Nose: floral, ripe fruit, honeyed notes. Palate: light-bodied, fresh, fruity, easy to drink.

MURVIEDRO 2009 TR
tempranillo, monastrell, cabernet sauvignon

89 Colour: light cherry, orangey edge. Nose: ripe fruit, balsamic herbs, sweet spices, creamy oak, fine reductive notes. Palate: powerful, flavourful, spicy, toasty.

MURVIEDRO 2010 TC
tempranillo, monastrell, syrah

89 Colour: cherry, garnet rim. Nose: red berry notes, ripe fruit, sweet spices, creamy oak. Palate: powerful, flavourful, spicy, long.

MURVIEDRO COLECCIÓN PETIT VERDOT 2012 T
petit verdot

91 Colour: deep cherry, purple rim. Nose: wild herbs, elegant, ripe fruit. Palate: balanced, ripe fruit, good acidity.

MURVIEDRO COLECCIÓN SYRAH 2012 T
syrah

88 Colour: cherry, purple rim. Nose: red berry notes, ripe fruit, floral. Palate: powerful, flavourful, fruity, balanced.

MURVIEDRO EXPRESIÓN 2010 TC
monastrell, garnacha

89 Colour: cherry, garnet rim. Nose: ripe fruit, spicy, creamy oak, toasty. Palate: powerful, flavourful, toasty, round tannins.

ROSA DE MURVIEDRO 2012 RD
cabernet sauvignon

88 Colour: rose, purple rim. Nose: balanced, red berry notes, ripe fruit, floral. Palate: fruity, fresh, long.

BODEGAS POLO MONLEÓN

Ctra. Valencia - Ademuz, Km. 86
46178 Titaguas (Valencia)
☎: +34 961 634 148
www.hoyadelcastillo.com
info@hoyadelcastillo.com

HOYA DEL CASTILLO 2012 B
75% merseguera, 25% macabeo

88 Colour: bright straw. Nose: fresh, fresh fruit, white flowers, tropical fruit. Palate: flavourful, fruity, good acidity, balanced.

BODEGAS SÁNCHEZ ZAHONERO

Ricardo Serrano, 13
46392 Siete Aguas (Valencia)
☎: +34 962 340 052
www.sanchezzahonero.com
bodega@sanchezzahonero.com

BRESSOL 2012 B
merseguera

88 Colour: bright straw. Nose: fragrant herbs, balanced, medium intensity, spicy. Palate: toasty, correct, good acidity.

LÉSSÈNCIA 2009 T
tempranillo, syrah

88 Colour: cherry, garnet rim. Nose: ripe fruit, spicy, warm, cocoa bean. Palate: flavourful, good structure, long.

BODEGAS SIERRA NORTE

Pol. Ind. El Romeral. Transporte- Parc. C2
46340 Requena (Valencia)
☎: +34 962 323 099 - Fax: +34 962 323 048
www.bodegasierranorte.com
info@bodegasierranorte.com

MARILUNA 2010 T
bobal, tempranillo, monastrell

89 Colour: deep cherry, garnet rim. Nose: spicy, ripe fruit, balanced. Palate: fruity, easy to drink, good finish.

MARILUNA 2012 B
macabeo, chardonnay, sauvignon blanc

85 Colour: bright straw. Nose: fresh, fresh fruit, dried flowers. Palate: flavourful, fruity, good acidity, balanced.

BODEGAS UTIELANAS

Avda. Marín Lázaro, 8
46300 Utiel (Valencia)
☎: +34 962 171 157 - Fax: +34 962 170 801
www.bodegasutielanas.com
administracion@bodegasutielanas.com

SUEÑOS DEL MEDITERRÁNEO 2012 B
100% macabeo

85 Colour: bright straw. Nose: ripe fruit, floral, fragrant herbs. Palate: fresh, fruity, light-bodied, easy to drink.

SUEÑOS DEL MEDITERRÁNEO 2012 RD
100% bobal

85 Colour: light cherry, bright. Nose: red berry notes, floral, balanced. Palate: correct, good acidity, fine bitter notes.

SUEÑOS DEL MEDITERRÁNEO 2012 T
100% bobal

85 Colour: cherry, purple rim. Nose: ripe fruit, balsamic herbs, floral. Palate: powerful, flavourful, correct, fruity.

BODEGAS VEGAMAR

Garcesa, s/n
46175 Calles (Valencia)
☎: +34 962 109 813
www.bodegasvegamar.com
info@bodegasvegamar.com

VEGAMAR 2007 TC
tempranillo, cabernet sauvignon, merlot

86 Colour: light cherry, orangey edge. Nose: spicy, scrubland, old leather. Palate: fruity, easy to drink, good finish.

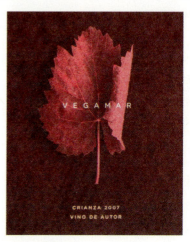

VEGAMAR 2007 TR
tempranillo, cabernet sauvignon

86 Colour: cherry, garnet rim. Nose: medium intensity, tobacco, spicy. Palate: flavourful, fruity, spicy, balsamic.

VEGAMAR COLECCIÓN PRIVADA 2009 TR
cabernet sauvignon

87 Colour: dark-red cherry, orangey edge. Nose: toasty, ripe fruit, old leather. Palate: correct, good acidity, balsamic.

VEGAMAR SYRAH 2011 TC
syrah

83

BODEGAS VICENTE GANDÍA

Ctra. Cheste a Godelleta, s/n
46370 Chiva (Valencia)
☎: +34 962 524 242 - Fax: +34 962 524 243
www.vicentegandia.es
info@vicentegandia.com

CASTILLO DE LIRIA 2008 TR
100% tempranillo

84

CASTILLO DE LIRIA 2009 TC
85% tempranillo, 15% syrah

84

CASTILLO DE LIRIA 2011 T
80% bobal, 20% syrah

85 Colour: bright cherry. Nose: ripe fruit, sweet spices, creamy oak. Palate: flavourful, fruity, toasty.

CASTILLO DE LIRIA 2012 B
80% viura, 20% sauvignon blanc

81

CASTILLO DE LIRIA 2012 RD
100% bobal

87 Colour: brilliant rose. Nose: lactic notes, fresh fruit, red berry notes, fragrant herbs. Palate: powerful, flavourful, easy to drink.

CASTILLO DE LIRIA MOSCATEL B
100% moscatel de alejandría

85 Colour: golden. Nose: powerfull, floral, honeyed notes, candied fruit, fragrant herbs. Palate: flavourful, sweet, fresh, fruity, long.

EL MIRACLE 120 2011 T
65% tempranillo, 35% syrah

87 Colour: cherry, garnet rim. Nose: ripe fruit, spicy, creamy oak, toasty. Palate: powerful, flavourful, toasty, round tannins.

EL MIRACLE 120 2012 B
60% chardonnay, 40% sauvignon blanc

86 Colour: bright straw. Nose: ripe fruit, floral, dried herbs. Palate: powerful, flavourful, correct, fine bitter notes.

EL MIRACLE BY MARISCAL 2010 T
100% garnacha tintorera

88 Colour: dark-red cherry, garnet rim. Nose: red berry notes, ripe fruit, balsamic herbs, creamy oak. Palate: powerful, flavourful, long, toasty.

FUSTA NOVA BLANC 2012 B
45% chardonnay, 35% sauvignon blanc, 20% moscatel de alejandría

84

FUSTA NOVA MOSCATEL B
moscatel de alejandría

86 Colour: golden. Nose: powerfull, floral, honeyed notes, fragrant herbs, balsamic herbs. Palate: flavourful, sweet, fresh, fruity, good acidity, long.

BODEGAS VIDAL

Valencia, 16
12550 Almazora (Castellón)
☎: +34 964 503 300 - Fax: +34 964 560 604
www.bodegasvidal.com
info@bodegasvidal.com

UVA D'OR MOSCATEL B
moscatel

90 Colour: bright golden. Nose: ripe fruit, honeyed notes, citrus fruit, sweet spices, toasty. Palate: creamy, long, powerful, flavourful, balanced, elegant.

BODEGAS XALÓ

Ctra. Xaló Alcalali, s/n
3727 Xaló (Alicante)
☎: +34 966 480 034 - Fax: +34 966 480 808
www.bodegasxalo.com
comercial@bodegasxalo.com

MALVARROSA 2012 RD
garnacha

83

BODEGAS Y VIÑEDOS DE UTIEL

Finca El Renegado, s/n
46315 Caudete de las Fuentes (Valencia)
☎: +34 962 174 029 - Fax: +34 962 171 432
www.bodegasdeutiel.com
gestion@bodegasdeutiel.com

ACTUM COLECCIÓN MACABEO CHARDONNAY 2011 B
macabeo, chardonnay

85 Colour: bright yellow. Nose: ripe fruit, fruit preserve, citrus fruit, dried herbs. Palate: powerful, flavourful, spicy.

ACTUM COLECCIÓN SYRAH TEMPRANILLO 2012 T
syrah, tempranillo

84

ACTUM FINCA EL RENEGADO 2010 T
bobal

90 Colour: cherry, garnet rim. Nose: dark chocolate, sweet spices, ripe fruit. Palate: flavourful, good acidity, ripe fruit.

BODEGUES I VINYES LA CASA DE LAS VIDES

Corral el Galtero, s/n
46890 Agullent (Valencia)
☎: +34 962 135 003 - Fax: +34 962 135 494
www.lacasadelasvides.com
bodega@lacasadelasvides.com

ABC 2012 T
tempranillo, petit verdot, garnacha, merlot

86 Colour: cherry, garnet rim. Nose: ripe fruit, grassy, spicy. Palate: powerful, flavourful.

ACVLIVS 2010 T
tempranillo, monastrell, syrah

89 Colour: cherry, garnet rim. Nose: ripe fruit, aromatic coffee, sweet spices, powerfull. Palate: complex, spicy, long, toasty.

CUP DE CUP 2010 T
40% tempranillo, 40% syrah, 20% garnacha

84

ROSA ROSAE 2012 RD
garnacha, cabernet sauvignon

82

VALLBLANCA 2012 B
verdil, gewürztraminer

85 Colour: bright yellow. Nose: wild herbs, citrus fruit, faded flowers. Palate: correct, good acidity.

BRUNO MURCIANO & DAVID SAMPEDRO GIL

8 Avenida Banda De Musica El Angel
46315 Caudete de las Fuentes (Valencia)
☎: +34 962 319 096
bru.murciano@yahoo.es

EL NOVIO PERFECTO 2012 B
50% moscatel, 50% macabeo

87 Colour: bright straw. Nose: fresh, fresh fruit, white flowers, varietal. Palate: flavourful, fruity, good acidity, sweetness.

CASA LOS FRAILES

Casa Los Frailes, s/n
46635 Fontanares dels Alforins (Valencia)
☎: +34 963 339 845 - Fax: +34 963 363 153
www.bodegaslosfrailes.com
info@bodegaslosfrailes.com

AFTER 3 2009 T
monastrell

88 Colour: bright cherry, garnet rim. Nose: overripe fruit, faded flowers. Palate: flavourful, fruity, fine bitter notes.

BILOGÍA 2009 T
monastrell, syrah

89 Colour: cherry, garnet rim. Nose: medium intensity, toasty, spicy, balsamic herbs. Palate: correct, good acidity, ripe fruit.

BLANC DE TRILOGÍA 2012 B
sauvignon blanc, moscatel, verdil

90 Colour: bright straw. Nose: fresh, fragrant herbs, citrus fruit, expressive, dried flowers. Palate: fruity, balanced, fine bitter notes, spicy.

CASA LOS FRAILES 1771 2011 T
monastrell

90 Colour: cherry, garnet rim. Nose: red berry notes, ripe fruit, balsamic herbs, sweet spices, creamy oak. Palate: powerful, flavourful, spicy.

LA DANZA DE LA MOMA 2009 T BARRICA
monastrell, marselan

92 Colour: cherry, purple rim. Nose: powerfull, warm, sweet spices, varnish, ripe fruit. Palate: good structure, ripe fruit.

LOS FRAILES BARRICA 2010 T BARRICA
monastrell, garnacha tintorera

87 Colour: cherry, garnet rim. Nose: ripe fruit, spicy, creamy oak, toasty, balsamic herbs. Palate: powerful, flavourful, toasty.

LOS FRAILES MONASTRELL 2012 T
monastrell

87 Colour: cherry, garnet rim. Nose: medium intensity, ripe fruit, red berry notes, wild herbs. Palate: fruity, correct.

TRILOGÍA 2009 T
monastrell, cabernet sauvignon, tempranillo

90 Colour: cherry, garnet rim. Nose: ripe fruit, sweet spices, creamy oak. Palate: flavourful, fruity, toasty, round tannins.

CELLER DEL ROURE

Ctra. de Les Alcusses, Km. 11,1
46640 Moixent (Valencia)
☎: +34 962 295 020
info@cellerdelroure.es

CULLEROT 2011 B
30% verdil, 30% pedro ximénez, 20% macabeo, 20% chardonnay

88 Colour: bright yellow. Nose: dried flowers, fragrant herbs, ripe fruit, dry stone. Palate: fresh, fruity, flavourful, spicy.

CULLEROT 2012 B
30% pedro ximénez, 30% verdil, 30% chardonnay, 10% macabeo

90 Colour: bright yellow. Nose: floral, citrus fruit, ripe fruit, wild herbs. Palate: powerful, flavourful, rich, fruity.

LES ALCUSSES 2009 T
40% monastrell, 10% garnacha tintorera, 10% cabernet sauvignon, 20% merlot, 10% syrah, 10% petit verdot

90 Colour: deep cherry, garnet rim. Nose: balanced, ripe fruit, scrubland. Palate: flavourful, balsamic, round tannins.

LES ALCUSSES 2010 T
monastrell, garnacha tintorera, cabernet sauvignon, merlot, syrah, petit verdot

91 Colour: cherry, garnet rim. Nose: ripe fruit, spicy, creamy oak, toasty. Palate: powerful, flavourful, toasty.

MADURESA 2009 T
35% mandó, 20% garnacha tintorera, 10% cabernet sauvignon, 5% monastrell, 15% syrah, 15% petit verdot

92 Colour: deep cherry, garnet rim. Nose: spicy, balsamic herbs, complex, ripe fruit. Palate: good structure, flavourful, spicy, round tannins.

PAROTET 2011 T
75% mando, 25% monastrell

89 Colour: deep cherry. Nose: candied fruit, warm, toasty. Palate: spicy, ripe fruit, fine tannins.

SETZE GALLETS 2011 T
30% garnacha tintorera, 30% monastrell, 15% mandó, 25% merlot

90 Colour: cherry, purple rim. Nose: expressive, fresh fruit, red berry notes, floral. Palate: flavourful, fruity, good acidity, round tannins.

SETZE GALLETS 2012 T
garnacha tintorera, monastrell, mando, merlot

88 Colour: bright cherry. Nose: ripe fruit, sweet spices, creamy oak, earthy notes. Palate: flavourful, fruity, toasty.

CHESTE AGRARIA COOP. V.

La Estación, 5
46380 Cheste (Valencia)
☎: +34 962 511 671 - Fax: +34 962 511 732
www.reymos.es
bodega@chesteagraria.com

REYMOS 1918 2012 ESP
moscatel

81

REYMOS SELECCIÓN 2012 ESP
moscatel

82

SOL DE REYMOS 2010 MISTELA
moscatel

85 Colour: old gold. Nose: powerfull, expressive, floral, pattiserie, candied fruit. Palate: flavourful, fine bitter notes, good finish.

VIÑA TENDIDA MOSCATO 2012 B
moscatel, garnacha

85 Colour: bright straw. Nose: white flowers, jasmine, varietal, medium intensity. Palate: fruity, sweet, easy to drink.

CLOS COR VÍ

Ruzafa 48-1
46006 (Valencia)
☎: +34 963 746 842 - Fax: +34 963 746 842
www.closcorvi.com
manager@closcorvi.com

CLOS COR VÍ 2012 B
riesling, viognier

89 Colour: bright yellow. Nose: powerfull, ripe fruit, sweet spices, creamy oak, fragrant herbs. Palate: rich, smoky aftertaste, flavourful, fresh, good acidity.

CLOS COR VÍ RIESLING 2012 B
riesling

90 Colour: bright yellow. Nose: powerfull, dried herbs, faded flowers, ripe fruit. Palate: flavourful, good acidity, long, balanced.

CLOS COR VÍ VIOGNIER 2012 B
viognier

88 Colour: bright yellow. Nose: candied fruit, faded flowers. Palate: ripe fruit, long, spicy, rich.

CLOS DE LA VALL

Pza. de la Hispanidad, 4
46640 Moixent (Valencia)
☎: +34 962 260 020
www.closdelavall.com
info@closdelavall.com

CLOS DE LA VALL 2009 TC
monastrell, cabernet sauvignon, tempranillo

88 Colour: cherry, garnet rim. Nose: toasty, cocoa bean, dried herbs. Palate: good structure, correct, toasty.

CLOS DE LA VALL 2011 B
macabeo, moscatel

88 Colour: bright yellow. Nose: expressive, balanced, white flowers, varietal, citrus fruit. Palate: balanced, long, good acidity.

CLOS DE LA VALL AUTOR 2008 T
90% mandó, 10% monastrell

89 Colour: cherry, garnet rim. Nose: spicy, creamy oak, toasty, complex, fruit preserve. Palate: powerful, flavourful, toasty, round tannins.

CLOS DE LA VALL NEGRE MOIXENT 2011 T
monastrell, cabernet sauvignon, tempranillo

85 Colour: cherry, garnet rim. Nose: medium intensity, spicy, wild herbs, tobacco. Palate: flavourful, correct, balsamic.

CLOS DE LA VALL PREMIUM 2008 T
tempranillo, monastrell, cabernet sauvignon

88 Colour: cherry, garnet rim. Nose: ripe fruit, spicy, creamy oak, toasty. Palate: powerful, flavourful, toasty.

CLOS DE LA VALL PX 2012 BFB
pedro ximénez

88 Colour: bright straw. Nose: roasted coffee, powerfull, sweet spices. Palate: flavourful, toasty, ripe fruit.

COOPERATIVA AGRÍCOLA EL VILLAR

Avda. del Agricultor, s/n
46170 Villar de Arzobispo (Valencia)
☎: +34 962 720 050 - Fax: +34 961 646 060
www.elvillar.com
info@elvillar.com

LADERAS 2012 B
macabeo, merseguera
83

LADERAS TEMPRANILLO 2012 T
tempranillo
83

LADERAS TEMPRANILLO BOBAL 2012 RD
bobal, tempranillo
84

TAPIAS 2007 TC
merlot
83

VIÑA NORA 2008 TC
tempranillo, garnacha
84

VIÑA VILLAR 2008 TC
tempranillo, merlot

86 Colour: cherry, garnet rim. Nose: ripe fruit, spicy, creamy oak, toasty. Palate: powerful, flavourful, spicy.

COOPERATIVA LA VIÑA (VINOS DE LA VIÑA)

Portal de Valencia, 52
46630 La Font de la Figuera (Valencia)
☎: +34 962 290 078 - Fax: +34 962 232 039
www.ventadelpuerto.com
info@vinosdelavina.com

CASA L'ANGEL CEPAS VIEJAS 2010 T
60% cabernet sauvignon, 40% tempranillo

88 Colour: cherry, garnet rim. Nose: ripe fruit, balsamic herbs, earthy notes, creamy oak. Palate: spicy, long, correct.

ICONO CABERNET SAUVIGNON 2012 T
cabernet sauvignon

85 Colour: cherry, garnet rim. Nose: ripe fruit, balanced, grassy. Palate: powerful, flavourful, balsamic.

ICONO CHARDONNAY 2012 B
chardonnay

87 Colour: bright straw. Nose: faded flowers, citrus fruit, tropical fruit. Palate: flavourful, fruity, balanced, fine bitter notes.

ICONO MERLOT 2012 T
merlot

87 Colour: cherry, garnet rim. Nose: red berry notes, ripe fruit, fragrant herbs. Palate: correct, powerful, flavourful.

ICONO SYRAH 2012 T
syrah

88 Colour: black cherry, purple rim. Nose: ripe fruit, medium intensity, fruit preserve, sweet spices. Palate: flavourful, ripe fruit.

JUAN DE JUANES VENDIMIA ORO 2010 T
45% syrah, 30% merlot, 12,5% cabernet sauvignon, 12,5% cabernet franc

89 Colour: bright cherry, garnet rim. Nose: creamy oak, dark chocolate, balsamic herbs, ripe fruit, fruit preserve. Palate: flavourful, powerful, long.

JUAN DE JUANES VENDIMIA ORO 2012 BFB
chardonnay

87 Colour: bright yellow. Nose: toasty, spicy, faded flowers. Palate: flavourful, fruity, good acidity, toasty.

VENTA DEL PUERTO Nº 12 2010 T
40% cabernet sauvignon, 40% tempranillo, 10% syrah, 10% merlot

90 Colour: cherry, garnet rim. Nose: ripe fruit, cocoa bean, sweet spices, creamy oak. Palate: powerful, flavourful, balsamic, long, spicy.

VENTA DEL PUERTO Nº 18 2009 T BARRICA
40% cabernet sauvignon, 40% tempranillo, 10% syrah, 10% merlot

91 Colour: very deep cherry, garnet rim. Nose: sweet spices, scrubland, ripe fruit. Palate: good structure, flavourful, long.

HERETAT DE TAVERNERS

Ctra. Fontanars - Moixent, Km. 1,8
46635 Fontanars dels Alforins (Valencia)
☎: +34 962 132 437 - Fax: +34 961 140 181
www.heretatdetaverners.com
info@heretatdetaverners.com

HERETAT DE TAVERNERS EL VERN 2010 TC
monastrell, tempranillo, cabernet sauvignon, merlot

85 Colour: cherry, garnet rim. Nose: ripe fruit, spicy, creamy oak, toasty. Palate: powerful, flavourful, toasty.

HERETAT DE TAVERNERS GRACIANO 2010 TC
100% graciano

91 Colour: cherry, garnet rim. Nose: ripe fruit, spicy, toasty, aromatic coffee. Palate: powerful, flavourful, toasty, round tannins.

HERETAT DE TAVERNERS MALLAURA 2008 TC
monastrell, tempranillo, cabernet sauvignon, garnacha

89 Colour: bright cherry, orangey edge. Nose: medium intensity, spicy, scrubland, ripe fruit. Palate: flavourful, fruity, good acidity.

HERETAT DE TAVERNERS REIXIU 2012 B
sauvignon blanc, chardonnay

88 Colour: straw. Nose: medium intensity, white flowers, faded flowers. Palate: fruity, balanced, flavourful, fine bitter notes.

PUNT DOLÇ T
monastrell, garnacha tintorera

90 Colour: bright cherry, orangey edge. Nose: candied fruit, honeyed notes, sweet spices, cocoa bean. Palate: flavourful, balanced.

LA BARONÍA DE TURIS

Ctra. Godelleta, 22
46359 Turis (Valencia)
☎: +34 962 526 011 - Fax: +34 962 527 282
www.baroniadeturis.es
baronia@baroniadeturis.es

1920 2009 T
cabernet sauvignon, merlot, tintorera, syrah

89 Colour: deep cherry, orangey edge. Nose: balanced, spicy, scrubland. Palate: good structure, flavourful, spicy, long.

LA LUNA DE MAR 2012 B
moscatel, semillon blanc

87 Colour: bright yellow. Nose: ripe fruit, tropical fruit, fragrant herbs. Palate: powerful, flavourful, balsamic.

MISTELA MOSCATEL TURÍS 2012 B
moscatel

87 Colour: golden. Nose: powerfull, floral, honeyed notes, candied fruit, fragrant herbs. Palate: flavourful, sweet, fresh, fruity, good acidity.

PAGO CASA GRAN

Ctra. Mogente Fontanares, km. 9,5
46640 Mogente (Valencia)
☎: +34 962 261 004 - Fax: +34 962 261 004
www.pagocasagran.com
comercial@pagocasagran.com

CASA BENASAL 2012 B
moscatel, gewürztraminer

90 Colour: bright straw. Nose: white flowers, fragrant herbs, ripe fruit, balanced. Palate: flavourful, fruity, long, good acidity.

CASA BENASAL 2012 RD
monastrell, syrah

89 Colour: raspberry rose. Nose: red berry notes, ripe fruit, balsamic herbs, dried flowers, spicy. Palate: powerful, flavourful, long.

CASA BENASAL 2012 T
garnacha tintorera, monastrell, syrah, cabernet sauvignon, merlot

88 Colour: cherry, purple rim. Nose: red berry notes, fruit liqueur notes, spicy, fragrant herbs. Palate: powerful, flavourful, easy to drink.

CASA BENASAL CRUX 2008 T
garnacha tintorera, monastrell, syrah

90 Colour: cherry, garnet rim. Nose: ripe fruit, spicy, creamy oak, fragrant herbs. Palate: fresh, fruity, flavourful, spicy, long.

CASA BENASAL ELEGANT 2008 T
garnacha tintorera, monastrell, syrah

91 Colour: cherry, garnet rim. Nose: ripe fruit, spicy, creamy oak, toasty, complex. Palate: powerful, flavourful, toasty, round tannins.

FALCATA ARENAL 2009 T
garnacha, monastrell

92 Colour: cherry, garnet rim. Nose: ripe fruit, spicy, creamy oak, toasty, complex, expressive. Palate: powerful, flavourful, toasty, round tannins, elegant.

FALCATA BIO 2012 B
moscatel, gewürztraminer

87 Colour: bright straw. Nose: fresh, fresh fruit, white flowers, expressive. Palate: flavourful, fruity, good acidity, balanced.

FALCATA BIO 2012 RD
monastrell, syrah

88 Colour: raspberry rose. Nose: elegant, candied fruit, dried flowers, fragrant herbs, red berry notes. Palate: light-bodied, flavourful, good acidity, long, spicy.

FALCATA BIO 2012 T
garnacha tintorera, monastrell, syrah, cabernet sauvignon, merlot

89 Colour: cherry, purple rim. Nose: red berry notes, ripe fruit, balsamic herbs, dry stone. Palate: fresh, fruity, flavourful, balanced.

FALCATA CASA GRAN 2009 T
garnacha tintorera, monastrell, syrah

90 Colour: cherry, garnet rim. Nose: red berry notes, ripe fruit, fragrant herbs, spicy. Palate: powerful, flavourful, long, spicy.

RAFAEL CAMBRA

Pza. Concepción, 13 - 19
46870 Ontinyent (Valencia)
☎: +34 626 309 327
www.rafaelcambra.es
rafael@rafaelcambra.es

EL BON HOMME 2012 T
monastrell, cabernet sauvignon

89 Colour: cherry, garnet rim. Nose: medium intensity, balanced, ripe fruit. Palate: balanced, balsamic.

RAFAEL CAMBRA DOS 2011 T
cabernet sauvignon, cabernet franc, monastrell

92 Colour: bright cherry. Nose: ripe fruit, sweet spices, creamy oak, expressive. Palate: flavourful, fruity, toasty, round tannins, balanced.

RAFAEL CAMBRA UNO 2011 T
monastrell

91 Colour: cherry, garnet rim. Nose: red berry notes, ripe fruit, balsamic herbs, creamy oak. Palate: balsamic, long, toasty.

VALSAN 1831

Ctra. Cheste - Godelleta, Km. 1
46370 Chiva (Valencia)
☎: +34 962 510 861 - Fax: +34 962 511 361
www.cherubino.es
cherubino@cherubino.es

CUVA VELLA MOSCATEL
moscatel

93 Colour: dark mahogany. Nose: complex, fruit liqueur notes, dried fruit, pattiserie, toasty, acetaldehyde, aromatic coffee. Palate: sweet, rich, unctuous, powerful, balanced, elegant.

DRASSANES 2011 T
syrah, bobal, tempranillo

89 Colour: cherry, garnet rim. Nose: sweet spices, red berry notes, ripe fruit. Palate: powerful, flavourful, fruity, toasty.

DRASSANES 2012 B
chardonnay, semillon, merseguera, moscatel

89 Colour: bright yellow. Nose: white flowers, ripe fruit, tropical fruit. Palate: flavourful, fruity, long.

EL NOVIO PERFECTO 2012 B
moscatel, viura

83

LES DUNES 2012 B
macabeo, moscatel

87 Colour: bright straw. Nose: dried flowers, fragrant herbs, candied fruit, ripe fruit. Palate: rich, powerful, flavourful.

LES DUNES 2012 RD
bobal

87 Colour: rose, purple rim. Nose: powerfull, ripe fruit, red berry notes, floral, expressive. Palate: powerful, fruity, fresh.

LES DUNES 2012 T
tempranillo

88 Colour: cherry, purple rim. Nose: red berry notes, ripe fruit, floral, lactic notes, mineral. Palate: powerful, flavourful, balanced.

MARQUÉS DE CARO 2008 TR
tempranillo, cabernet sauvignon

87 Colour: cherry, garnet rim. Nose: balanced, dark chocolate, scrubland. Palate: flavourful, spicy, round tannins, long.

MARQUÉS DE CARO 2009 TC
bobal, tempranillo, cabernet sauvignon

85 Colour: dark-red cherry, orangey edge. Nose: fruit liqueur notes, spicy, sweet spices. Palate: spicy, correct.

MARQUÉS DE CARO 2012 B
moscatel, macabeo

86 Colour: bright straw. Nose: medium intensity, floral, ripe fruit, tropical fruit. Palate: fruity, correct.

MARQUÉS DE CARO MOSCATEL 2012 B
moscatel

87 Colour: bright yellow. Nose: candied fruit, floral, citrus fruit, honeyed notes. Palate: rich, flavourful, full.

MARQUÉS DE CARO TEMPRANILLO 2012 T
tempranillo

88 Colour: cherry, purple rim. Nose: expressive, fresh fruit, red berry notes, floral. Palate: flavourful, fruity, good acidity.

VITTORE 2012 B
moscatel

88 Colour: golden. Nose: floral, honeyed notes, fragrant herbs, wild herbs, powerfull, complex. Palate: flavourful, sweet, fresh, fruity, good acidity.

VINÍCOLA ONTENIENSE COOP. V.

Avda. Almansa, 17
46870 Ontinyent (Valencia)
☎: +34 962 380 849 - Fax: +34 962 384 419
www.coopontinyent.com
info@coopontinyent.com

ONTINIUM TEMPRANILLO 2012 T
tempranillo

85 Colour: cherry, purple rim. Nose: ripe fruit, fruit preserve, balsamic herbs. Palate: correct, fruity.

ONTINIUM1 2011 T BARRICA
tempranillo

86 Colour: cherry, garnet rim. Nose: toasty, sweet spices, cocoa bean. Palate: flavourful, good acidity.

VIÑA UMBRIA 2012 T
monastrell
80

VINNICO

Muela, 16
3730 Jávea (Alicante)
☎: +34 965 791 967 - Fax: +34 966 461 471
www.vinnico.com
info@vinnico.com

BESITOS MOSCATO 2012 B

85 Colour: bright straw. Nose: fresh fruit, white flowers, dried herbs. Palate: flavourful, fruity, good acidity.

BESITOS MOSCATO 2012 RD

84

VIÑAS DEL PORTILLO S.L.

P.I. El Llano F2 P4
46360 Buñol (Valencia)
☎: +34 962 504 827 - Fax: +34 962 500 937
www.alturia.es
vinasdelportillo@vinasdelportillo.es

ALBUFERA 2010 T
tempranillo, monastrell

87 Colour: bright cherry. Nose: ripe fruit, sweet spices, creamy oak, wild herbs. Palate: flavourful, fruity, balsamic.

ALTURIA 2012 B
malvasía, moscatel, merseguera

87 Colour: bright straw. Nose: white flowers, fresh, citrus fruit, tropical fruit. Palate: fruity, easy to drink, correct, fine bitter notes.

VIÑEDOS Y BODEGAS VEGALFARO

Ctra. Pontón - Utiel, Km. 3
46430 Requena (Valencia)
☎: +34 962 320 680 - Fax: +34 962 321 126
www.vegalfaro.com
rodolfo@vegalfaro.com

PASAMONTE 2012 B
sauvignon blanc

88 Colour: bright straw. Nose: citrus fruit, floral, balsamic herbs, fruit expression, medium intensity. Palate: fresh, fruity, flavourful, easy to drink.

PASAMONTE TINTORERA 2011 T
garnacha tintorera

90 Colour: bright cherry. Nose: ripe fruit, creamy oak, expressive, varietal. Palate: flavourful, fruity, toasty, slightly dry, soft tannins.

ZAGROMONTE

Ctra. L'Ombria, Km. 1
46635 Fontanars dels Alforins (Valencia)
☎: +34 962 222 261 - Fax: +34 962 222 257
www.bodegas-torrevellisca.es
info@bodegas-torrevellisca.es

ARGENTUM 2009 TC
tempranillo, cabernet sauvignon

86 Colour: cherry, garnet rim. Nose: ripe fruit, spicy, creamy oak, toasty. Palate: powerful, flavourful, toasty, round tannins.

ARQUIS 2010 T
tempranillo

86 Colour: cherry, garnet rim. Nose: ripe fruit, creamy oak, fine reductive notes. Palate: powerful, flavourful, toasty.

AURUM 2010 TC
merlot, cabernet sauvignon

88 Colour: cherry, garnet rim. Nose: spicy, creamy oak, toasty, ripe fruit, fruit preserve. Palate: powerful, flavourful, toasty, round tannins.

BRUNDISIUM 2009 TC
tempranillo, cabernet sauvignon, cabernet franc

86 Colour: dark-red cherry, orangey edge. Nose: medium intensity, dried herbs, ripe fruit. Palate: correct, spicy, ripe fruit.

EMBRUJO NEGRO 2011 T
monastrell, syrah

83

EMBRUJO NEGRO 2012 T
tempranillo, cabernet sauvignon, merlot

80

EMBRUJO SECO 2012 B
verdejo

81

EMBRUJO SEMI SECO 2011 B
malvasía

82

DO VALLE DE GÜÍMAR / D.O.P.

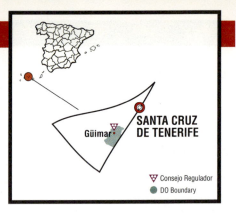

LOCATION:

On the island of Tenerife. It practically constitutes a prolongation of the Valle de la Orotava region to the southeast, forming a valley open to the sea, with the Las Dehesas region situated in the mountains and surrounded by pine forests where the vines grow in an almost Alpine environment. It covers the municipal districts of Arafo, Candelaria and Güímar.

CLIMATE:

Although the influence of the trade winds is more marked than in Abona, the significant difference in altitude in a much reduced space must be pointed out, which gives rise to different microclimates, and pronounced contrasts in day-night temperatures, which delays the harvest until 1st November.

SOIL:

Volcanic at high altitudes, there is a black tongue of lava crossing the area where the vines are cultivated on a hostile terrain with wooden frames to raise the long vine shoots.

GRAPE VARIETIES:

WHITE: *Gual, Listán Blanco, Malvasía, Moscatel, Verdello* and *Vijariego*.
RED: *Bastardo Negro, Listán Negro* (15% of total), *Malvasía Tinta, Moscatel Negro, Negramoll, Vijariego Negro, Cabernet Sauvignon, Merlot, Pinot Noir, Ruby Cabernet, Syrah* and *Tempranillo*.

FIGURES:

Vineyard surface: 276 – **Wine-Growers:** 551 – **Wineries:** 21– **2012 Harvest rating:** N/A – **Production:** 300.025 litres – **Market percentages:** 100% domestic

2008	2009	2010	2011	2012
VERY GOOD	AVERAGE	VERY GOOD	GOOD	S/C

CONSEJO REGULADOR
Tafetana, 14 - 38500 Güímar (Santa Cruz de Tenerife) ☎: +34 922 514 709 - Fax: +34 922 514 485
consejo@vinosvalleguimar.com   www.vinosvalleguimar.com

BODEGA COMARCAL
VALLE DE GÜIMAR

Subida a Los Loros, Km. 4
38550 Arafo (Santa Cruz de Tenerife)
☎: +34 922 510 437 - Fax: +34 922 510 437
www.bodegacomarcalguimar.com
info@bodegacomarcalguimar.com

BRUMAS DE AYOSA 2012 RD
listán negro

81

BRUMAS DE AYOSA 2012 B
listán blanco

84

BRUMAS DE AYOSA 2012 ESP
listán blanco

81

BRUMAS DE AYOSA 2012 ESP RESERVA
listán blanco

80

BRUMAS DE AYOSA 2012 T
listán negro, merlot, syrah

83

BRUMAS DE AYOSA AFRUTADO 2012 B
listán blanco, moscatel de alejandría, marmajuelo, malvasía

85 Colour: bright straw. Nose: medium intensity, dried herbs, wild herbs, faded flowers. Palate: flavourful, fruity, sweet.

BRUMAS DE AYOSA AFRUTADO 2012 ESP
listán blanco

81

BRUMAS DE AYOSA MALVASÍA
2012 BLANCO DULCE
malvasía

85 Colour: bright straw. Nose: balanced, white flowers, jasmine, ripe fruit, citrus fruit. Palate: flavourful, fruity, good acidity.

PICO CHO MARCIAL 2012 B
listán blanco

83

PICO CHO MARCIAL 2012 T
listán negro

83

BODEGA CONTIEMPO

Chinguaro, 26-B - San Francisco Javier
38500 Güímar (Santa Cruz de Tenerife)
☎: +34 922 512 552
www.vinocontiempo.com
bodega@vinocontiempo.com

CONTIEMPO 2012 RD
listán negro, tempranillo, verijadiego

82

CONTIEMPO MALVASÍA DULCE
2012 BLANCO DULCE
malvasía

86 Colour: bright yellow. Nose: medium intensity, white flowers, citrus fruit. Palate: rich, flavourful, fruity, easy to drink, good acidity.

CONTIEMPO MALVASÍA SECO 2012 B
malvasía

85 Colour: yellow. Nose: expressive, fresh fruit, white flowers, dried flowers. Palate: fruity, good acidity, balanced, fine bitter notes.

CONTIEMPO MOSCATEL AFRUTADO 2012 B
moscatel

87 Colour: bright yellow. Nose: white flowers, ripe fruit, expressive, jasmine. Palate: flavourful, fruity, sweet, rich.

CONTIEMPO TINTO DE POSTRE 2012 T
baboso negro

87 Colour: deep cherry, purple rim. Nose: ripe fruit, candied fruit, raspberry, powerfull. Palate: balanced, good acidity.

CONTIEMPO VENDIMIA SELECCIONADA 2012 T
syrah

87 Colour: black cherry, purple rim. Nose: spicy, ripe fruit, dried herbs. Palate: flavourful, full, balanced, round tannins.

CONTIEMPO VIDUEÑOS SECO 2012 B
marmajuelo, malvasía, moscatel, verdello, gual

88 Colour: bright yellow. Nose: fresh, fresh fruit, expressive, wild herbs. Palate: flavourful, fruity, good acidity, balanced.

ROSA DE RASA ESP
syrah

79

CÁNDIDO HERNÁNDEZ PÍO

Los Tomillos s/n
38530 Candelaria (Santa Cruz de Tenerife)
☎: +34 922 513 288 - Fax: +34 922 511 631
www.bodegaschp.es
almacenlahidalga@telefonica.net

CALIUS 2008 TR
vijariego negro, merlot, tempranillo

89 Colour: dark-red cherry, orangey edge. Nose: expressive, ripe fruit, fruit preserve, spicy, cocoa bean, balsamic herbs. Palate: flavourful, full.

CALIUS 2012 T
vijariego negro, merlot, tempranillo

85 Colour: cherry, purple rim. Nose: red berry notes, ripe fruit. Palate: flavourful, fruity, correct, good acidity.

CALIUS MARMAJUELO 2012 B
85% marmajuelo, 15% malvasía, verdejo, vijariego blanco

84

EL BORUJO

Subida Los Loros, km. 4,2
38550 Arafo (Santa Cruz de Tenerife)
☎: +34 636 824 919
www.elborujo.es
el_borujo@hotmail.com

EL BORUJO 2012 B
50% moscatel de alejandría, 50% listán blanco

86 Colour: bright straw. Nose: fresh, white flowers, ripe fruit, jasmine. Palate: flavourful, fruity, good acidity, balanced.

EL BORUJO 2012 B
50% listán blanco, 30% albillo, 10% moscatel, 10% vijariego blanco

89 Colour: bright straw. Nose: fresh, fresh fruit, white flowers. Palate: flavourful, fruity, good acidity, balanced.

EL BORUJO 2012 T
100% listán negro

80

LOS LOROS 2012 BFB
40% gual, 30% marmajuelo, 30% moscatel

92 Colour: bright yellow. Nose: powerfull, ripe fruit, sweet spices, creamy oak, fragrant herbs. Palate: rich, smoky aftertaste, flavourful, fresh, good acidity.

EL REBUSCO BODEGAS

La Punta, 75 Araya
38530 Candelaria (Santa Cruz de Tenerife)
☎: +34 608 014 944
www.elrebuscobodegas.es
elrebusco@gmail.com

DIS-TINTO 2012 T
100% merlot

86 Colour: cherry, purple rim. Nose: ripe fruit. Palate: flavourful, fruity, good acidity, round tannins, spicy, balsamic.

LA TENTACIÓN AFRUTADO 2012 B
listán blanco, moscatel de alejandría, malvasía

84

FERRERA

Calvo Sotelo, 44
38550 Arafo (Santa Cruz de Tenerife)
☎: +34 649 487 835 - Fax: +34 922 237 359
carmengloria@bodegaferrera.com

FERRERA 2012 B
albillo, listán blanco, moscatel

86 Colour: bright straw. Nose: balanced, medium intensity, dried herbs, fresh. Palate: fruity, correct, fine bitter notes.

FERRERA 2012 T

88 Colour: black cherry, purple rim. Nose: medium intensity, fragrant herbs, ripe fruit, red berry notes. Palate: good structure, round tannins.

FERRERA AFRUTADO 2012 B
listán blanco, moscatel

85 Colour: bright straw. Nose: ripe fruit, tropical fruit. Palate: sweet, fruity, flavourful, easy to drink.

MOMENTO DE FERRERA 2011 BFB
malvasía, albillo

88 Colour: bright yellow. Nose: ripe fruit, candied fruit, creamy oak, sweet spices. Palate: rich, fruity, flavourful.

LOS PELADOS

Hoya Cartaya, 32 - Chacona
38500 Güimar (Santa Cruz de Tenerife)
☎: +34 922 512 786 - Fax: +34 922 514 485
bodegaslospelados@hotmail.com

LOS PELADOS 2012 B
84

LOS PELADOS 2012 T
85 Colour: cherry, purple rim. Nose: red berry notes, ripe fruit, medium intensity. Palate: fruity, easy to drink.

SAT VIÑA LAS CAÑAS

Barranco Badajoz
38500 Güimar (Santa Cruz de Tenerife)
☎: +34 922 512 716
vegalascanas@hotmail.com

AMOR ALMA & ORIGEN 2012 RD
listán negro
83

GRAN VIRTUD 2010 T BARRICA
listán negro, syrah
90 Colour: bright cherry. Nose: ripe fruit, sweet spices, expressive, scrubland. Palate: flavourful, fruity, round tannins.

GRAN VIRTUD DULCE NATURAL 2008 B
listán blanco, malvasía, moscatel
92 Colour: light mahogany. Nose: balanced, elegant, candied fruit, balsamic herbs, spicy. Palate: flavourful, good acidity, sweet.

GRAN VIRTUD LISTÁN BLANCO 2012 B
listán blanco
89 Colour: bright straw. Nose: fresh, white flowers, expressive. Palate: flavourful, fruity, good acidity, balanced.

VEGA LAS CAÑAS AFRUTADO 2012 B
listán blanco, moscatel
84

VIÑA HERZAS

38004 Santa Cruz de Tenerife (Tenerife)
☎: +34 922 511 405 - Fax: +34 922 290 064
morraherza@yahoo.es

VIÑAS HERZAS 2012 B
86 Colour: bright straw. Nose: fresh fruit, white flowers, medium intensity. Palate: fruity, easy to drink, correct.

VIÑAS HERZAS 2012 T
83

DO VALLE DE LA OROTAVA / D.O.P.

LOCATION:

In the north of the island of Tenerife. It borders to the west with the DO Ycoden-Daute-Isora and to the east with the DO Tacoronte-Acentejo. It extends from the sea to the foot of the Teide, and comprises the municipal districts of La Orotava, Los Realejos and El Puerto de la Cruz.

CLIMATE:

As with the other regions on the islands, the weather is conditioned by the trade winds, which in this region result in wines with a moderate alcohol content and a truly Atlantic character. The influence of the Atlantic is also very important, in that it moderates the temperature of the costal areas and provides a lot of humidity. Lastly, the rainfall is rather low, but is generally more abundant on the north face and at higher altitudes.

SOIL:

Light, permeable, rich in mineral nutrients and with a slightly acidic pH due to the volcanic nature of the island. The vineyards are at an altitude of between 250 mm and 700 m.

GRAPE VARIETIES:

WHITE:
MAIN: *Güal, Malvasía, Verdello, Vijariego, Albillo, Forastera Blanca* o *Doradilla, Sabro, Breval* and *Burrablanca.*
AUTHORIZED: *Bastardo Blanco, Forastera Blanca* (*Gomera*), *Listán Blanco, Marmajuelo, Moscatel, Pedro Ximénez* and *Torrontés.*
RED:
MAIN: *Listán Negro, Malvasía Rosada, Negramoll, Castellana Negra, Mulata, Tintilla, Cabernet Sauvignon, Listán Prieto, Merlot, Pinot Noir, Ruby Cabernet, Syrah* and *Tempranillo.*
AUTHORIZED: *Bastardo Negro, Moscatel Negra, Tintilla* and *Vijariego Negra.*

FIGURES:

Vineyard surface: 365 – **Wine-Growers:** 614 – **Wineries:** 13 – **2012 Harvest rating:** Excellent – **Production:** 300.000 litres – **Market percentages:** 95% domestic. 5% export

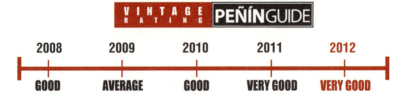

CONSEJO REGULADOR
Parque Recreativo El Bosquito, nº1 - Urb. La Marzagana II - La Perdona - 38315 La Orotava (Santa Cruz de Tenerife)
☎: +34 922 309 923 - Fax: +34 922 309 924 info@dovalleorotava.com www.dovalleorotava.com

BODEGA TAFURIASTE

Las Candias Altas, 11
38312 La Orotava (Santa Cruz de Tenerife)
☎: +34 922 336 027 - Fax: +34 922 336 027
www.bodegatafuriaste.com
vinos@bodegatafuriaste.com

TAFURIASTE 2012 RD
listán negro

83

TAFURIASTE 2012 T
listán negro

87 Colour: light cherry, garnet rim. Nose: medium intensity, varietal, red berry notes, ripe fruit, dried herbs. Palate: flavourful, round tannins.

TAFURIASTE AFRUTADO 2012 B
96% listán blanco, 4% moscatel

84

TAFURIASTE SECO 2012 B
97% listán blanco, 3% moscatel

84

BODEGA TAJINASTE

El Ratiño, 5 La Habanera
38315 La Orotava (Santa Cruz de Tenerife)
☎: +34 922 308 720 - Fax: +34 922 105 080
www.tajinaste.net
bodega@tajinaste.net

CAN 2011 T
listán negro, vijariego negro

93 Colour: very deep cherry, garnet rim. Nose: ripe fruit, complex, wild herbs, dried herbs, creamy oak. Palate: good structure, flavourful, round tannins.

TAJINASTE 2012 RD
listán negro

84

TAJINASTE 2012 T MACERACIÓN CARBÓNICA
100% listán negro

86 Colour: cherry, purple rim. Nose: medium intensity, red berry notes, ripe fruit. Palate: fruity, correct, fine bitter notes.

TAJINASTE 4 MESES EN BARRICA 2011 T BARRICA
100% listán negro

88 Colour: cherry, garnet rim. Nose: sweet spices, balanced, ripe fruit. Palate: flavourful, good structure, good acidity, round tannins.

TAJINASTE TRADICIONAL 2012 T
100% listán negro

87 Colour: bright cherry, purple rim. Nose: red berry notes, ripe fruit. Palate: flavourful, fruity, easy to drink.

TAJINASTE VENDIMIA SELECCIONADA 2011 T
100% listán negro

87 Colour: bright cherry. Nose: sweet spices, creamy oak, fruit preserve, ripe fruit. Palate: flavourful, fruity, toasty, round tannins.

BODEGA VALLEORO

Ctra. General La Oratova - Los Realejos, Km. 4,5
38315 La Orotava (Santa Cruz de Tenerife)
☎: +34 922 308 031 - Fax: +34 922 308 233
www.bodegavalleoro.com
info@bodegavalleoro.com

GRAN TEHYDA 2012 RD
listán negro

84

BODEGAS EL PENITENTE

Camino La Habanera, 286
38300 La Orotava (Santa Cruz de Tenerife)
☎: +34 922 309 024 - Fax: +34 922 309 024
www.bodegaselpenitentesl.es
bodegas@elpenitentesl.es

ARAUTAVA 2012 B
listán blanco

88 Colour: bright straw. Nose: balanced, expressive, fresh fruit, wild herbs, citrus fruit. Palate: flavourful, fruity, good acidity, balanced.

ARAUTAVA 2012 T
listán negro

89 Colour: bright cherry, purple rim. Nose: balanced, red berry notes, ripe fruit, wild herbs. Palate: flavourful, ripe fruit, spicy, good acidity, round tannins.

ARAUTAVA 2012 T FERMENTADO EN BARRICA
listán negro

88 Colour: deep cherry, purple rim. Nose: red berry notes, ripe fruit, balanced, expressive, dry stone. Palate: long, spicy.

ARAUTAVA FINCA LA HABANERA 2012 B
albillo

89 Colour: bright straw. Nose: expressive, white flowers, ripe fruit, sweet spices. Palate: rich, spicy, long, good acidity.

ARAUTAVA KRYOS 2012 T
MACERACIÓN CARBÓNICA
listán negro

89 Colour: light cherry. Nose: expressive, red berry notes. Palate: flavourful, fruity, good acidity, balanced, fine bitter notes.

BODEGAS DE MIRANDA 2012 RD
listán negro

83

LA HAYA

Calzadillas, s/n La Cruz Santa
38415 Los Realejos (Santa Cruz de Tenerife)
☎: +34 629 051 413 - Fax: +34 922 345 313
jaghcatire@telefonica.net

LA HAYA 2012 B BARRICA

86 Colour: yellow, pale. Nose: ripe fruit, faded flowers, spicy. Palate: fruity, correct, good acidity.

LA HAYA AFRUTADO 2011 B

81

LA SUERTITA

Real de la Cruz Santa, 35-A
38413 Los Realejos (Santa Cruz de Tenerife)
☎: +34 669 408 761
bodegalasuertita@yahoo.es

LA SUERTITA 2011 B BARRICA
listán blanco

88 Colour: bright straw. Nose: sweet spices, wild herbs, ripe fruit. Palate: fruity, flavourful, spicy.

LA SUERTITA 2012 B
listán blanco

86 Colour: bright straw. Nose: balanced, fragrant herbs, fresh fruit, citrus fruit. Palate: correct, easy to drink.

LA SUERTITA AFRUTADO 2012 B
listán blanco

85 Colour: bright straw. Nose: white flowers, faded flowers, ripe fruit. Palate: fruity, easy to drink, good finish.

LA SUERTITA ALBILLO 2011 B
albillo

83

LOS GÜINES

Pista Los Guines, s/n - El Horno
38410 Los Realejos (Santa Cruz de Tenerife)
☎: +34 922 343 320 - Fax: +34 922 353 855
www.bodegalosguines.com

LOS GÜINES 2012 B

84

LOS GÜINES 2012 T

82

PROPIEDAD VITÍCOLA
SUERTES DEL MARQUÉS

Ctra. General La Perdoma,
Las Suertes (Finca Esquilón)
38300 La Orotava (Santa Cruz de Tenerife)
☎: +34 922 501 300 - Fax: +34 922 503 462
www.suertesdelmarques.com
ventas@suertesdelmarques.com

7 FUENTES 2012 T
90% listán negro, 10% tintilla

91 Colour: cherry, purple rim. Nose: spicy, wild herbs, red berry notes, ripe fruit. Palate: flavourful, good structure, good acidity.

SUERTES DEL MARQUÉS CANDIO 2010 T
100% listán negro

92 Colour: cherry, garnet rim. Nose: expressive, ripe fruit, spicy, creamy oak, dried herbs. Palate: full, flavourful, round tannins.

SUERTES DEL MARQUÉS EL CIRUELO 2011 T
100% listán negro

92 Colour: dark-red cherry, garnet rim. Nose: medium intensity, ripe fruit, dried herbs, mineral. Palate: flavourful, good acidity, round tannins.

SUERTES DEL MARQUÉS EL ESQUILÓN 2011 T
70% listán negro, 30% tintilla

90 Colour: cherry, garnet rim. Nose: balanced, ripe fruit, grassy. Palate: good acidity, correct, round tannins, balsamic.

SUERTES DEL MARQUÉS LA SOLANA 2011 T
100% listán negro

93 Colour: cherry, garnet rim. Nose: wild herbs, medium intensity, spicy. Palate: flavourful, fruity, balanced.

SUERTES DEL MARQUÉS LOS PASITOS 2011 T
100% baboso negro

91 Colour: light cherry, garnet rim. Nose: balanced, grassy, spicy. Palate: ripe fruit, balanced, good acidity, round tannins.

SUERTES DEL MARQUÉS TRENZADO 2012 FI
75% listán blanco, 25% pedro ximénez, gual, marmajuelo, baboso blanco, otras.

92 Colour: bright yellow. Nose: complex, expressive, pungent, varnish, dry nuts, dried herbs, faded flowers. Palate: rich, powerful, fresh, fine bitter notes, elegant.

SUERTES DEL MARQUÉS VIDONIA 2011 B
90% listán blanco, 10% otras

90 Colour: bright yellow. Nose: powerfull, spicy, dried herbs, ripe fruit. Palate: correct, smoky aftertaste, fine bitter notes, balanced, elegant.

SECADERO

San Benito
38410 Los Realejos (Santa Cruz de Tenerife)
☎: +34 665 807 966
www.bodegasecadero.com
pab_estevez@hotmail.com

CUPRUM 2011 TC
75% tintilla, 25% listán negro

85 Colour: cherry, garnet rim. Nose: medium intensity, grassy, balanced, spicy. Palate: fruity, good acidity.

CUPRUM 2012 T
100% listán negro

88 Colour: cherry, purple rim. Nose: balanced, expressive, balsamic herbs, ripe fruit. Palate: full, flavourful, round tannins.

CUPRUM 2012 T BARRICA
75% tintilla, 25% listán negro

86 Colour: deep cherry, garnet rim. Nose: ripe fruit, violets, sweet spices. Palate: fruity, slightly dry, soft tannins.

CUPRUM SEMISECO 2012 B
75% listán blanco, 25% malvasía

84

DO VINOS DE MADRID / D.O.P.

LOCATION:

In the south of the province of Madrid, it covers three distinct sub-regions: Arganda, Navalcarnero and San Martín de Valdeiglesias.

CLIMATE:

Extreme continental, with cold winters and hot summers. The average annual rainfall ranges from 461 mm in Arganda to 658 mm in San Martín.

SOIL:

Rather unfertile soil and granite subsoil in the sub-region of San Martín de Valdeiglesias; in Navalcarnero the soil is brownish-grey, poor, with a subsoil of coarse sand and clay; in the sub-region of Arganda the soil is brownish-grey, with an acidic pH and granite subsoil.

GRAPE VARIETIES:

WHITE: *Malvar, Airén, Albillo, Parellada, Macabeo, Torrontés* and *Moscatel de Grano Menudo*.
RED: *Tinto Fino* (Tempranillo), *Garnacha, Merlot, Cabernet Sauvignon* and *Syrah*.

SUB-REGIONS:

San Martín. It comprises 9 municipal districts and has more than 3,821 Ha of vineyards, with mainly the Garnacha (red) and Albillo (white) varieties.
Navalcarnero. It comprises 19 municipal districts with a total of about 2,107 Ha. The most typical wines are reds and rosés based on the Garnacha variety.
Arganda. With 5,830 Ha and 26 municipal districts, it is the largest sub-region of the DO. The main varieties are the white Malvar and the red Tempranillo or Tinto Fino.

FIGURES:

Vineyard surface: 8,390 – **Wine-Growers:** 2,891 – **Wineries:** 44 – **2012 Harvest rating:** Good – **Production:** 8.919.287 litres – **Market percentages:** 77% domestic. 23% export

2008	2009	2010	2011	2012
VERY GOOD	GOOD	VERY GOOD	VERY GOOD	GOOD

CONSEJO REGULADOR
Ronda de Atocha, 7 - 28012 Madrid - ☎: +34 915 348 511 / Fax: +34 915 538 574
prensa@vinosdemadrid.es   www.vinosdemadrid.es

BERNABELEVA

Ctra. Avila Toledo (N-403), Km. 81,600
28680 San Martín de Valdeiglesias (Madrid)
☎: +34 915 091 909
www.bernabeleva.com
bodega@bernabeleva.com

BERNABELEVA "ARROYO DE TÓRTOLAS" 2011 T
garnacha

93 Colour: light cherry, garnet rim. Nose: elegant, ripe fruit, mineral, sweet spices. Palate: balanced, good acidity, round tannins.

BERNABELEVA "CARRIL DEL REY" 2011 T
garnacha

95 Colour: light cherry, garnet rim. Nose: medium intensity, ripe fruit, mineral. Palate: balanced, full, good acidity, round tannins, long, complex.

BERNABELEVA VIÑA BONITA 2011 T
garnacha

94 Colour: light cherry. Nose: balsamic herbs, wild herbs, floral, red berry notes, fruit liqueur notes, spicy, mineral. Palate: powerful, flavourful, round, spicy, balanced.

CANTOCUERDAS ALBILLO 2011 B
albillo

92 Colour: bright yellow. Nose: ripe fruit, dried flowers, fragrant herbs, sweet spices, dry stone. Palate: powerful, flavourful, rich, spicy, long.

CANTOCUERDAS MOSCATEL DE GRANO MENUDO 2011 B
moscatel grano menudo

94 Colour: golden. Nose: powerfull, floral, honeyed notes, candied fruit, fragrant herbs, earthy notes. Palate: flavourful, sweet, fresh, fruity, good acidity, long, elegant.

NAVAHERREROS BLANCO DE BERNABELEVA 2011 B
albillo, macabeo

91 Colour: bright yellow. Nose: ripe fruit, balanced, expressive, elegant. Palate: fruity, good acidity, ripe fruit, spicy, rich.

NAVAHERREROS GARNACHA DE BERNABELEVA 2011 T
garnacha

92 Colour: cherry, garnet rim. Nose: elegant, ripe fruit, dried flowers, sweet spices. Palate: flavourful, round tannins, fruity aftestaste.

BODEGA DE CARLOS III

Cortijo de San Isidro
28300 Aranjuez (Madrid)
☎: +34 915 357 735 - Fax: +34 915 547 027
www.realcortijo.com
clientes@realcortijo.com

HOMET 2006 TR
70% tempranillo, 10% cabernet sauvignon, 10% syrah, 10% merlot

86 Colour: pale ruby, brick rim edge. Nose: ripe fruit, balsamic herbs, spicy, tobacco, waxy notes, fine reductive notes. Palate: powerful, flavourful, spicy, long.

BODEGA ECOLÓGICA LUIS SAAVEDRA

Ctra. de Escalona, 5
28650 Cenicientos (Madrid)
☎: +34 914 606 053 - Fax: +34 914 606 053
www.bodegasaavedra.com
info@bodegasaavedra.com

CORUCHO 2010 TC
garnacha, tinto fino

88 Colour: cherry, garnet rim. Nose: powerfull, ripe fruit, spicy. Palate: flavourful, round tannins.

CORUCHO 2011 T ROBLE
garnacha, tinto fino, merlot

86 Colour: very deep cherry, purple rim. Nose: fruit preserve, ripe fruit, sweet spices. Palate: flavourful, long.

CORUCHO 2012 RD
100% garnacha

84

CORUCHO GARNACHA 2012 T
garnacha

88 Colour: cherry, purple rim. Nose: red berry notes, ripe fruit, balsamic herbs. Palate: flavourful, fruity, good acidity, balanced.

LUIS SAAVEDRA 2009 TC
garnacha, syrah

89 Colour: cherry, garnet rim. Nose: ripe fruit, spicy, creamy oak, toasty, complex. Palate: powerful, flavourful, toasty, round tannins.

LUIS SAAVEDRA 2010 T
garnacha

89 Colour: bright cherry, garnet rim. Nose: balanced, ripe fruit, wild herbs. Palate: good structure, flavourful, full.

SEFARDÍ HERITAGE KOSHER 2009 T ROBLE
garnacha

82

BODEGA MARAÑONES

Hilero, 7 - Nave 9
28696 Pelayos de la Presa (Madrid)
☎: +34 918 647 702
www.bodegamaranones.com
bodega@bodegamaranones.com

LABROS 2011 T
garnacha

92 Colour: light cherry. Nose: red berry notes, fruit liqueur notes, wild herbs, floral, dry stone, spicy. Palate: powerful, flavourful.

MARAÑONES 2011 T
garnacha

94 Colour: cherry, garnet rim. Nose: expressive, balanced, wild herbs, elegant, ripe fruit, mineral. Palate: long, balanced, good acidity, round tannins.

PEÑA CABALLERA 2011 T
garnacha

94 Colour: bright cherry, garnet rim. Nose: red berry notes, ripe fruit, balsamic herbs, elegant, spicy. Palate: balanced, round tannins, long.

PICARANA 2012 B
albillo

92 Colour: bright yellow. Nose: dried flowers, ripe fruit, wild herbs, spicy, expressive. Palate: flavourful, spicy, balanced, long, balsamic.

PIESDESCALZOS 2012 B
albillo

93 Colour: yellow. Nose: ripe fruit, fragrant herbs, dried flowers. Palate: balanced, fine bitter notes, spicy, long.

TREINTA MIL MARAVEDÍES 2011 T
garnacha, syrah, morenillo

91 Colour: cherry, garnet rim. Nose: red berry notes, ripe fruit, balsamic herbs, spicy, earthy notes. Palate: flavourful, complex, spicy, long, balanced.

BODEGA Y VIÑEDOS GOSÁLBEZ ORTI

Real, 14
28813 Pozuelo del Rey (Madrid)
☎: +34 918 725 804 - Fax: +34 918 725 804
www.qubel.com
bodega@qubel.com

MAYRIT 2010 TC
70% tempranillo, 30% syrah

85 Colour: cherry, garnet rim. Nose: ripe fruit, spicy, creamy oak, toasty. Palate: powerful, flavourful, toasty.

MAYRIT 2012 B
100% sauvignon blanc

80

QUBÉL NATURE 2005 T
80% tempranillo, 10% cabernet sauvignon, 10% garnacha

90 Colour: pale ruby, brick rim edge. Nose: elegant, spicy, fine reductive notes, wet leather, aged wood nuances, fruit liqueur notes. Palate: spicy, elegant, long.

QUBÉL REVELACIÓN 2011 T
70% tempranillo, 10% cabernet sauvignon, 20% syrah

87 Colour: cherry, purple rim. Nose: medium intensity, ripe fruit, wild herbs. Palate: fruity, round tannins.

BODEGAS EL REGAJAL

Antigua Ctra. Andalucía, Km. 50,5
28223 Aranjuez (Madrid)
☎: +34 913 078 903 - Fax: +34 913 576 312
www.elregajal.es
isabel@elregajal.es

EL REGAJAL SELECCIÓN ESPECIAL 2011 T
syrah, tempranillo, cabernet sauvignon, merlot

91 Colour: bright cherry. Nose: ripe fruit, sweet spices, creamy oak, expressive, balsamic herbs, earthy notes. Palate: flavourful, fruity, toasty.

LAS RETAMAS DEL REGAJAL 2011 T
syrah, tempranillo, cabernet sauvignon, merlot

90 Colour: cherry, purple rim. Nose: expressive, fresh fruit, red berry notes, floral, sweet spices, creamy oak. Palate: flavourful, fruity, good acidity.

BODEGAS ORUSCO

Alcalá, 54
28511 Valdilecha (Madrid)
☎: +34 918 738 006 - Fax: +34 918 738 336
www.bodegasorusco.com
esther@bodegasorusco.com

ARMONIUM 2010 T
merlot, cabernet sauvignon

89 Colour: very deep cherry, garnet rim. Nose: powerfull, ripe fruit, fruit preserve, balsamic herbs. Palate: good structure, flavourful.

MAÍN 2010 TC
tempranillo, cabernet sauvignon

85 Colour: deep cherry, garnet rim. Nose: ripe fruit, fruit preserve, wild herbs, spicy. Palate: fruity, correct.

VIÑA MAÍN 2012 T
tempranillo, syrah

84

COMANDO G VITICULTORES

Avda. Constitución, 23
28640 Cadalso de los Vidrios (Madrid)
☎: +34 918 640 602
www.comandog.es
info@comandog.es

LA BRUJA AVERÍA 2012 T
garnacha

93 Colour: deep cherry. Nose: balsamic herbs, scrubland, spicy. Palate: easy to drink, long.

LAS UMBRÍAS 2011 T
garnacha

94 Colour: deep cherry. Nose: fruit liqueur notes, fruit expression, spicy, balsamic herbs. Palate: light-bodied, fruity, spicy, balsamic.

COMERCIAL GRUPO FREIXENET S.A.

Joan Sala, 2
8770 Sant Sadurní D'Anoia (Barcelona)
☎: +34 938 917 000 - Fax: +34 938 183 095
www.freixenet.es
freixenet@freixenet.es

HEREDAD TORRESANO 2009 T ROBLE
tinto fino

86 Colour: cherry, garnet rim. Nose: spicy, creamy oak, toasty, fruit preserve. Palate: powerful, flavourful, toasty.

HEREDAD TORRESANO 2009 TC
tinto fino

86 Colour: very deep cherry, garnet rim. Nose: powerfull, fruit preserve, sweet spices, fruit liqueur notes. Palate: flavourful, round tannins.

FIGUEROA

Convento, 19
28380 Colmenar de Oreja (Madrid)
☎: +34 918 944 859 - Fax: +34 918 944 859
bodegasjesusfigueroa@hotmail.com

FIGUEROA 2010 TC
tempranillo

89 Colour: deep cherry, garnet rim. Nose: balanced, spicy, ripe fruit. Palate: full, flavourful, fruity, round tannins.

FIGUEROA 2012 B
malvar, macabeo, moscatel grano menudo

85 Colour: bright straw. Nose: fresh, fresh fruit, white flowers. Palate: flavourful, fruity, good acidity, balanced, easy to drink.

FIGUEROA 2012 RD
tempranillo

85 Colour: rose, purple rim. Nose: powerfull, ripe fruit, red berry notes, floral, expressive. Palate: powerful, fruity, fresh.

FIGUEROA 2012 T
tempranillo

85 Colour: cherry, purple rim. Nose: red berry notes, ripe fruit, floral. Palate: flavourful, fruity, good acidity.

FIGUEROA 2012 T ROBLE
tempranillo, merlot

89 Colour: bright cherry. Nose: sweet spices, creamy oak, red berry notes, ripe fruit. Palate: flavourful, fruity, toasty.

FIGUEROA SEMIDULCE B
macabeo, malvar

84

FIGUEROA SYRAH 2010 T
100% syrah

84

LAS MORADAS DE SAN MARTÍN

Pago de Los Castillejos Ctra. M-541, Km. 4,7
28680 San Martín de Valdeiglesias (Madrid)
☎: +34 691 676 570 - Fax: +34 974 300 046
www.lasmoradasdesanmartin.es

LAS MORADAS DE SAN MARTÍN INITIO 2008 T
garnacha

90 Colour: cherry, garnet rim. Nose: ripe fruit, wild herbs, balanced. Palate: flavourful, good structure, round tannins, spicy.

LAS MORADAS DE SAN MARTÍN SENDA 2009 T
garnacha

91 Colour: cherry, garnet rim. Nose: ripe fruit, spicy, creamy oak, toasty, earthy notes. Palate: powerful, flavourful, toasty, balanced, elegant.

LAS MORADAS DE SAN MARTÍN LIBRO SIETE LAS LUCES 2008 T
garnacha

91 Colour: cherry, garnet rim. Nose: ripe fruit, spicy, creamy oak, toasty, complex. Palate: powerful, flavourful, toasty, round tannins, round.

PAGOS DE FAMILIA
MARQUÉS DE GRIÑÓN

Finca Casa de Vacas - Ctra. CM-4015, Km. 23
45692 Malpica de Tajo (Toledo)
☎: +34 925 597 222 - Fax: +34 925 789 416
www.pagosdefamilia.com
service@pagosdefamilia.com

EL RINCÓN 2008 T
95% syrah, 5% garnacha

90 Colour: cherry, garnet rim. Nose: ripe fruit, fruit preserve, scrubland, earthy notes. Palate: powerful, flavourful, ripe fruit.

RICARDO BENITO

Las Eras, 1
28600 Navalcarnero (Madrid)
☎: +34 918 110 097 - Fax: +34 918 112 663
www.bodegasricardobenito.com
bodega@ricardobenito.com

ASIDO 2009 T
tempranillo, merlot, cabernet sauvignon

89 Colour: cherry, garnet rim. Nose: medium intensity, ripe fruit, fruit preserve, spicy, aromatic coffee. Palate: round tannins, full, good structure.

DIVIDIVO 2008 T
tinto fino, merlot, cabernet sauvignon, garnacha

91 Colour: dark-red cherry, orangey edge. Nose: balanced, old leather, ripe fruit, balsamic herbs. Palate: fruity, flavourful, good acidity.

DIVO 2007 T
tinto fino

93 Colour: pale ruby, brick rim edge. Nose: ripe fruit, balsamic herbs, mineral, cocoa bean, dark chocolate, sweet spices, creamy oak, fine reductive notes. Palate: balanced, elegant, flavourful, spicy, long.

DUÁN 2009 T
garnacha, syrah, tempranillo, merlot, cabernet sauvignon

87 Colour: cherry, garnet rim. Nose: red berry notes, ripe fruit, fragrant herbs. Palate: powerful, flavourful, spicy, long.

MADRILEÑO DE RICARDO BENITO 2010 T
tempranillo

84

SEÑORÍO DE MEDINA SIDONIA 2010 T
tempranillo

86 Colour: cherry, garnet rim. Nose: ripe fruit, balsamic herbs, spicy, creamy oak. Palate: powerful, flavourful, spicy, long.

TAPÓN DE ORO 2010 T
tempranillo, garnacha

88 Colour: cherry, garnet rim. Nose: medium intensity, ripe fruit, wild herbs. Palate: flavourful, correct, balanced.

TAPÓN DE ORO 2012 B
moscatel grano menudo, malvar

87 Colour: bright yellow. Nose: ripe fruit, floral, varietal, citrus fruit. Palate: fruity, good acidity, fine bitter notes.

S.A.T. 1431 SAN ESTEBAN
PROTOMÁRTIR

Pza. de los Caños, 30-46
28650 Cenicientos (Madrid)
☎: +34 918 642 487 - Fax: +34 918 642 487
sanesteban@918642487.e.telefonica.net

PIEDRA ESCRITA 2012 RD
garnacha

78

PIEDRA ESCRITA 2012 T
garnacha, tempranillo

82

SEÑORÍO DE VAL AZUL

Urb. Valgrande, 37
28370 Chinchón (Madrid)
☎: +34 616 005 565
www.senoriodevalazul.es
evaayuso@arrakis.es

FABIO 2008 T
cabernet sauvignon, syrah, merlot, tempranillo

83

VAL AZUL 2008 T
cabernet sauvignon, syrah, merlot, tempranillo

85 Colour: deep cherry, garnet rim. Nose: old leather, spicy, dried herbs, fruit preserve. Palate: flavourful, round tannins.

SOLERA BODEGAS

Arco, 14
28380 Colmenar de Oreja (Madrid)
☎: +34 918 943 407 - Fax: +34 918 943 407
www.solerabodegas.com
c.herrero@solerabodegas.com

MOURIZ 2008 T
tempranillo

84

MOURIZ 2009 T
tempranillo

85 Colour: cherry, garnet rim. Nose: ripe fruit, spicy, creamy oak, violet drops. Palate: powerful, flavourful, toasty.

MOURIZ 2010 B
malvar

85 Colour: bright yellow. Nose: dried flowers, balsamic herbs, ripe fruit, petrol notes. Palate: powerful, flavourful, spicy.

TAGONIUS

Ctra. Ambite, Km. 4,4
28550 Tielmes (Madrid)
☎: +34 918 737 505 - Fax: +34 918 746 161
www.tagonius.com
gerencia@tagonius.com

TAGOMIUS BLANC 2012 B

88 Colour: bright straw. Nose: ripe fruit, dry nuts, powerfull, toasty. Palate: flavourful, fruity, spicy, toasty, long, round, varietal.

TAGONIUS 2004 TR

91 Colour: cherry, garnet rim. Nose: balanced, ripe fruit, spicy. Palate: fruity, good acidity, balanced, round tannins.

TAGONIUS 2005 TR

91 Colour: pale ruby, brick rim edge. Nose: elegant, spicy, fine reductive notes, wet leather, aged wood nuances, fruit liqueur notes. Palate: spicy, fine tannins, elegant, long.

TAGONIUS 2006 TC

89 Colour: cherry, garnet rim. Nose: ripe fruit, spicy, creamy oak, toasty, fine reductive notes. Palate: powerful, flavourful, toasty, round tannins, elegant.

TAGONIUS 2006 TR

90 Colour: deep cherry, garnet rim. Nose: expressive, balanced, ripe fruit, spicy. Palate: flavourful, good structure, round tannins.

TAGONIUS 2007 TC

86 Colour: deep cherry, orangey edge. Nose: powerfull, macerated fruit, grassy. Palate: flavourful, round tannins.

TAGONIUS 2011 T
tempranillo, cabernet sauvignon, merlot, syrah

85 Colour: cherry, garnet rim. Nose: red berry notes, ripe fruit, balsamic herbs, spicy. Palate: powerful, flavourful, spicy.

TAGONIUS 2011 T ROBLE
tempranillo, cabernet sauvignon, merlot, syrah

88 Colour: deep cherry, garnet rim. Nose: powerfull, ripe fruit, sweet spices. Palate: good structure, round tannins.

TAGONIUS GRAN VINO 2004 TR

92 Colour: bright cherry, garnet rim. Nose: creamy oak, cocoa bean, ripe fruit, aromatic coffee. Palate: balanced, good acidity, round tannins.

TAGONIUS MARIAGE 2005 T

90 Colour: pale ruby, brick rim edge. Nose: fragrant herbs, balsamic herbs, ripe fruit, spicy, cocoa bean, waxy notes, cigar, wet leather. Palate: powerful, flavourful, spirituous, fine tannins.

UVAS FELICES

Agullers, 7
8003 Barcelona (Barcelona)
☎: +34 902 327 777
www.vilaviniteca.es

EL HOMBRE BALA 2011 T
100% garnacha

94 Colour: cherry, garnet rim. Nose: balsamic herbs, scrubland, red berry notes. Palate: flavourful, good acidity, spicy. Personality.

LA MUJER CAÑÓN 2011 T

92 Colour: light cherry, garnet rim. Nose: elegant, balanced, expressive, wild herbs. Palate: full, flavourful, fine tannins, good acidity.

VINÍCOLA DE ARGANDA SOCIEDAD COOPERATIVA MADRILEÑA

Camino de San Martín de la Vega, 16
28500 Arganda del Rey (Madrid)
☎: +34 918 710 201 - Fax: +34 918 710 201
www.vinicoladearganda.com
vinicola@cvarganda.e.telefonica.net

BALADÍ 2011 BFB
100% malvar

84

PAGO VILCHES 2012 B
100% malvar

81

PAGO VILCHES 2012 RD
100% tempranillo

84

PAGO VILCHES 2012 T
100% tempranillo

84

PERUCO 2008 TR
100% tempranillo

87 Colour: ruby red, orangey edge. Nose: ripe fruit, spicy, creamy oak, fine reductive notes. Palate: powerful, flavourful, toasty, round tannins.

VIÑA RENDERO 2009 TC
100% tempranillo

84

VIÑA RENDERO S/C T ROBLE
100% tempranillo

79

VIÑA RENDERO SELECCIÓN ESPECIAL 2010 T ROBLE
100% tempranillo

85 Colour: cherry, garnet rim. Nose: ripe fruit, fruit preserve, balsamic herbs, creamy oak. Palate: powerful, flavourful, fine bitter notes.

VINOS JEROMÍN

San José, 8
28590 Villarejo de Salvanés (Madrid)
☎: +34 918 742 030 - Fax: +34 918 744 139
www.vinosjeromin.com
comercial@vinosjeromin.com

DOS DE MAYO EDICIÓN LIMITADA 2009 TC
100% tempranillo

89 Colour: cherry, garnet rim. Nose: red berry notes, ripe fruit, balsamic herbs, creamy oak. Palate: powerful, flavourful, spicy, long.

FÉLIX MARTÍNEZ CEPAS VIEJAS 2009 TR
90% tempranillo, 10% syrah

91 Colour: cherry, garnet rim. Nose: ripe fruit, spicy, creamy oak, toasty, mineral. Palate: powerful, flavourful, toasty, round tannins, balanced.

GREGO 2009 TC
60% tempranillo, syrah, 10% garnacha

89 Colour: cherry, garnet rim. Nose: ripe fruit, spicy, scrubland. Palate: powerful, flavourful, toasty, balanced.

GREGO 2011 T ROBLE
65% tempranillo, 35% syrah

86 Colour: very deep cherry. Nose: spicy, wild herbs, ripe fruit. Palate: flavourful, round tannins.

GREGO GARNACHA CENTENARIAS 2010 T ROBLE
100% garnacha

86 Colour: cherry, garnet rim. Nose: balanced, ripe fruit, fruit preserve, sweet spices, warm. Palate: good acidity, round tannins.

GREGO MOSCATEL SECO 2010 B
100% moscatel grano menudo

86 Colour: bright golden. Nose: faded flowers, honeyed notes. Palate: balanced, good acidity, good finish.

MANU VINO DE AUTOR 2007 TC
tempranillo, syrah, garnacha, merlot, cabernet sauvignon

91 Colour: cherry, garnet rim. Nose: ripe fruit, fragrant herbs, spicy, cocoa bean, creamy oak, mineral. Palate: spicy, flavourful, balanced, round, round tannins.

PUERTA CERRADA 2012 B
malvar, airén

85 Colour: bright straw. Nose: dried herbs, dried flowers. Palate: correct, balanced, easy to drink.

PUERTA CERRADA 2012 RD
tempranillo, garnacha, malvar

84

PUERTA CERRADA 2012 T
tempranillo, garnacha

82

PUERTA DE ALCALÁ 2009 TR
100% tempranillo

88 Colour: cherry, garnet rim. Nose: ripe fruit, spicy, creamy oak, toasty. Palate: powerful, flavourful, toasty, round tannins.

PUERTA DE ALCALÁ 2010 TC
100% tempranillo

88 Colour: cherry, garnet rim. Nose: ripe fruit, spicy, toasty. Palate: powerful, flavourful, toasty, round tannins.

PUERTA DE ALCALÁ 2012 B
100% malvar

84

PUERTA DE ALCALÁ 2012 RD
tempranillo, garnacha

84

PUERTA DE ALCALÁ 2012 T
75% tempranillo, 25% syrah

84

PUERTA DEL SOL MALVAR Nº1 2012 B
100% malvar

85 Colour: bright yellow. Nose: white flowers, citrus fruit, balanced, ripe fruit, tropical fruit. Palate: flavourful, fruity.

PUERTA DEL SOL Nº2 2012 T JOVEN
70% tempranillo, 20% syrah, 10% merlot

85 Colour: cherry, purple rim. Nose: red berry notes, ripe fruit, balsamic herbs. Palate: powerful, flavourful, warm.

PUERTA DEL SOL Nº3 2011 BFB
100% malvar

86 Colour: bright yellow. Nose: powerfull, ripe fruit, sweet spices, creamy oak, roasted coffee. Palate: rich, smoky aftertaste, flavourful, fresh.

PUERTA DEL SOL Nº4 TEMPRANILLO 2010 TC
100% tempranillo

86 Colour: cherry, garnet rim. Nose: ripe fruit, balsamic herbs, warm. Palate: flavourful, round tannins, spicy.

PUERTA DEL SOL Nº5 VARIETALES 2009 TC
70% cabernet sauvignon, 30% merlot

88 Colour: deep cherry, garnet rim. Nose: powerfull, ripe fruit, spicy, wild herbs. Palate: flavourful, good structure, round tannins.

VEGA MADROÑO 2012 B
malvar, airén

84

VEGA MADROÑO 2012 RD
tempranillo, garnacha, syrah, merlot, malvar

83

VEGA MADROÑO 2012 T
tempranillo, merlot

83

VINOS Y ACEITES LAGUNA

Illescas, 5
28360 Villaconejos (Madrid)
☎: +34 918 938 196 - Fax: +34 918 938 344
www.lagunamadrid.com
vyalaguna@gmail.com

ALMA DE VALDEGUERRA 2012 B
malvar

84

ALMA DE VALDEGUERRA 2012 RD
tempranillo

86 Colour: rose, purple rim. Nose: powerfull, ripe fruit, red berry notes, floral, expressive. Palate: powerful, fruity, fresh, sweet, easy to drink.

ALMA DE VALDEGUERRA 2012 T
tempranillo

87 Colour: bright cherry, purple rim. Nose: balanced, fruit expression, lactic notes, violet drops. Palate: ripe fruit, easy to drink.

LOCATION:

Occupying the northeast of the island of Tenerife and comprising the municipal districts of San Juan de La Rambla, La Guancha, Icod de los Vinos, Los Silos, El Tanque, Garachico, Buenavista del Norte, Santiago del Teide and Guía de Isora.

CLIMATE:

Mediterranean, characterised by the multitude of microclimates depending on the altitude and other geographical conditions. The trade winds provide the humidity necessary for the development of the vines. The average annual temperature is 19°C and the average annual rainfall is around 540 mm.

SOIL:

Volcanic ash and rock on the higher grounds, and clayey lower down. The vines are cultivated at very different heights, ranging from 50 to 1,400 m.

GRAPE VARIETIES:

WHITE: *Bermejuela* (or *Marmajuelo*), *Güal, Malvasía, Moscatel, Pedro Ximénez, Verdello, Vijariego, Albillo, Bastardo Blanco, Forastera Blanca, Listán Blanco* (majority), *Sabro* and *Torrontés*.
RED: *Tintilla, Listán Negro* (majority), *Malvasía Rosada, Negramoll Castellana, Bastardo Negra, Moscatel Negra* and *Vijariego Negra*.

FIGURES:

Vineyard surface: 215 – **Wine-Growers:** 530 – **Wineries:** 15 – **2012 Harvest rating:** Excellent – **Production:** 405.950 litres – **Market percentages:** 99% domestic. 1% export

CONSEJO REGULADOR
La Palmita, 10 - 38440 La Guancha (Sta. Cruz de Tenerife) ☎: +34 922 130 246 - Fax: +34 922 828 159
ycoden@ycoden.com / promocion@ycoden.com   www.ycoden.com

BODEGA COMARCAL DE ICOD

Camino Cuevas del Rey, 1
38430 Icod de los Vinos (Santa Cruz de Tenerife)
☎: +34 922 122 395 - Fax: +34 922 814 688
www.bodegasinsularestenerife.es
icod@bodegasinsularestenerife.es

EL ANCÓN 2012 T
100% listán negro

88 Colour: cherry, purple rim. Nose: balanced, expressive, fruit expression. Palate: fruity, flavourful, round tannins.

EL ANCÓN 2012 T BARRICA
50% listán negro, 20% tintilla, 30% baboso negro

89 Colour: cherry, purple rim. Nose: expressive, red berry notes, ripe fruit, violets, sweet spices. Palate: balanced, ripe fruit, round tannins.

EL ANCÓN MALVASÍA 2009 B BARRICA
100% malvasía

93 Colour: bright yellow. Nose: candied fruit, sweet spices, balanced, citrus fruit. Palate: full, flavourful, good acidity, sweet, long.

EL ANCÓN TINTILLA 2011 T
100% tintilla

88 Colour: dark-red cherry, garnet rim. Nose: ripe fruit, dark chocolate. Palate: good structure, flavourful, spicy, ripe fruit, good acidity.

MIRADERO 2012 BLANCO AFRUTADO
100% listán blanco

85 Colour: straw, pale. Nose: medium intensity, fresh. Palate: fruity, easy to drink, correct.

MIRADERO 2012 ROSADO AFRUTADO
100% listán negro

83

TÁGARA 2012 B
100% listán blanco

86 Colour: bright straw. Nose: ripe fruit, floral, sweet spices. Palate: toasty, ripe fruit, good acidity.

TÁGARA AFRUTADO 2012 B
100% listán blanco

85 Colour: straw, pale. Nose: medium intensity, fresh, white flowers. Palate: fruity, light-bodied, good finish, correct.

TÁGARA MALVASÍA MARMAJUELO 2012 B
50% malvasía, 50% marmajuelo

87 Colour: bright straw, greenish rim. Nose: balanced, expressive, floral, ripe fruit. Palate: fruity, flavourful, easy to drink.

BODEGA VIÑA ENGRACIA

38430 Icod de los Vinos (Santa Cruz de Tenerife)
☎: +34 922 810 857 - Fax: +34 922 860 895
www.vinosengracia.com
vinosengracia@hotmail.com

VIÑA ENGRACIA 2012 B
listán blanco

86 Colour: bright straw. Nose: fresh, jasmine. Palate: flavourful, fruity, good acidity, balanced.

VIÑA ENGRACIA 2012 RD
listán negro, negramoll, listán blanco

80

VIÑA ENGRACIA 2012 T
listán negro, negramoll, tintilla

79

VIÑA ENGRACIA AFRUTADO 2012 B
listán blanco

84

VIÑA ENGRACIA SEMISECO 2012 B
listán blanco

83

BODEGA VIÑA ZANATA

El Sol, 3
38440 La Guancha (Santa Cruz de Tenerife)
☎: +34 922 828 166 - Fax: +34 922 828 166
www.zanata.net
zanata@zanata.net

TARA TINTILLA 2010 T
tintilla

85 Colour: cherry, garnet rim. Nose: medium intensity, dried herbs. Palate: fruity, flavourful, easy to drink.

VIÑA ZANATA 2012 B
listán blanco

85 Colour: bright straw. Nose: fresh fruit, dried flowers, medium intensity. Palate: fruity, easy to drink, fine bitter notes.

VIÑA ZANATA 2012 RD
listán negro

81

VIÑA ZANATA 2012 T
50% listán negro, 40% negramoll, 10% tintilla

84

VIÑA ZANATA AFRUTADO 2012 B
50% listán blanco, 40% moscatel, 10% vijariego blanco

85 Colour: bright straw. Nose: medium intensity, dried flowers, ripe fruit. Palate: fruity, correct.

VIÑA ZANATA MARMAJUELO 2012 B
marmajuelo

84

BODEGAS VIÑAMONTE

Avda. Villanueva, 34
38440 La Guancha (Santa Cruz de Tenerife)
☎: +34 922 130 037 - Fax: +34 922 130 037
www.bodegasvinamonte.com

VIÑAMONTE 2012 B
listán blanco

87 Colour: bright straw. Nose: fresh, fresh fruit, expressive, scrubland. Palate: flavourful, fruity, good acidity, balanced, spicy.

VIÑAMONTE 2012 T
listán negro

80

VIÑAMONTE AFRUTADO 2012 B
listán blanco

85 Colour: bright straw. Nose: expressive, grassy, citrus fruit, ripe fruit. Palate: fruity, flavourful.

VIÑAMONTE DULCE 2010 T
60% listán negro, negramoll, tintilla

86 Colour: dark-red cherry, orangey edge. Nose: grassy, scrubland, ripe fruit. Palate: flavourful, balsamic.

VIÑAMONTE DULCE 2011 B
listán blanco

85 Colour: bright straw. Nose: medium intensity, faded flowers, dried flowers, citrus fruit. Palate: fruity, easy to drink, good finish.

BODEGAS VIÑÁTIGO

Cabo Verde, s/n
38440 La Guancha (Santa Cruz de Tenerife)
☎: +34 922 828 768 - Fax: +34 922 829 936
www.vinatigo.com
vinatigo@vinatigo.com

VIÑÁTIGO GUAL 2012 B
100% gual

87 Colour: bright straw, greenish rim. Nose: fresh fruit, balanced, fragrant herbs. Palate: fruity, fine bitter notes, good acidity.

VIÑÁTIGO LISTÁN BLANCO 2012 B
listán blanco

85 Colour: bright straw. Nose: citrus fruit, dried herbs, balanced. Palate: fruity, easy to drink, good acidity.

VIÑÁTIGO LISTÁN NEGRO 2012 RD
100% listán negro

83

VIÑÁTIGO LISTÁN NEGRO 2012 T
100% listán negro

85 Colour: cherry, purple rim. Nose: ripe fruit, scrubland. Palate: flavourful, fruity, good acidity, round tannins.

VIÑÁTIGO MARMAJUELO 2012 B
100% marmajuelo

90 Colour: bright straw. Nose: fresh, fresh fruit, white flowers, scrubland. Palate: flavourful, fruity, good acidity, balanced.

VIÑÁTIGO VIJARIEGO 2011 BFB
100% vijariego blanco

86 Colour: bright yellow. Nose: faded flowers, spicy, balsamic herbs. Palate: fruity, rich, toasty, correct.

C.B. LUIS, ANTONIO Y
JAVIER LÓPEZ DE AYALA

El Majuelos, 2
38450 Garachico (Santa Cruz de Tenerife)
☎: +34 922 133 079 - Fax: +34 922 830 066
jlopezaz38@hotmail.es

HACIENDA SAN JUAN 2012 T
100% baboso negro

86 Colour: deep cherry, purple rim. Nose: powerfull, ripe fruit, dried herbs. Palate: fruity, flavourful, long.

HACIENDA SAN JUAN BN
100% malvasía

79

VIÑA SPINOLA

Camino Esparragal, s/n
38470 Los Silos (Santa Cruz de Tenerife)
☎: +34 922 840 977 - Fax: +34 922 840 977

VIÑA SPINOLA 2012 B
77

VIÑA SPINOLA 2012 T
80

VIÑA SPINOLA MALVASÍA SECO 2003 B
83

VIÑA SPINOLA MALVASÍA SECO 2004 B

85 Colour: bright golden. Nose: balsamic herbs, ripe fruit, candied fruit. Palate: fine bitter notes, toasty.

VIÑA SPINOLA MALVASÍA SECO 2008 B

86 Colour: bright golden. Nose: candied fruit, spicy, faded flowers. Palate: spirituous, flavourful, fruity, good acidity.

VIÑA SPINOLA MALVASÍA SECO 2009 B

87 Colour: bright golden. Nose: candied fruit, faded flowers, honeyed notes, medium intensity, expressive. Palate: fruity, easy to drink, fine bitter notes.

VIÑA SPINOLA MALVASÍA SECO 2010 B
79

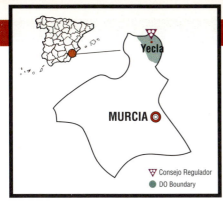

LOCATION:

In the northeast of the province of Murcia, within the plateau region, and comprising a single municipal district, Yecla.

CLIMATE:

Continental, with a slight Mediterranean influence, with hot summers and cold winters, and little rainfall, which is usually around 300 mm per annum.

SOIL:

Fundamentally deep limestone, with good permeability. The vineyards are on undulating terrain at a height of between 400 m and 800 m above sea level.

GRAPE VARIETIES:

WHITE: *Merseguera, Airén, Macabeo, Malvasía, Chardonnay.*
RED: *Monastrell* (majority 85% of total), *Garnacha Tinta, Cabernet Sauvignon, Cencibel* (*Tempranillo*), *Merlot, Tintorera, Syrah.*

SUB-REGIONS:

Yecla Campo Arriba, with Monastrell as the most common variety and alcohol contents of up to 14°, and **Yecla Campo Abajo,** whose grapes produce a lower alcohol content (around 12° for reds and 11.5° for whites).

FIGURES:

Vineyard surface: 5,900 – **Wine-Growers:** 520 – **Wineries:** 8 – **2012 Harvest rating:** Very Good – **Production:** 6.168.204 litres – **Market percentages:** 6% domestic. 94% export

2008	2009	2010	2011	2012
GOOD	GOOD	VERY GOOD	VERY GOOD	VERY GOOD

CONSEJO REGULADOR
Poeta Francisco A. Jiménez, s/n - P.I. Urbayecla II - 30510 Yecla (Murcia)
☎: +34 968 792 352 - Fax: +34 968 792 352   info@yeclavino.com   www.yeclavino.com

BODEGA TRENZA

Avda. Matías Saenz Tejada, s/n. Edif. Fuengirola
Center - Local 1
29640 Fuengirola (Málaga)
☎: +34 615 343 320 - Fax: +34 952 588 467
www.bodegatrenza.com
info@bodegatrenza.com

LA NYMPHINA 2012 T
100% monastrell

90 Colour: cherry, purple rim. Nose: ripe fruit, floral, sweet
spices, balsamic herbs. Palate: powerful, flavourful, long,
balanced, elegant.

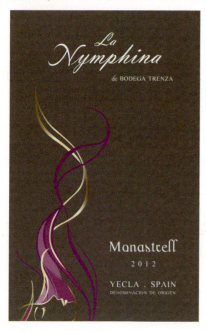

BODEGAS BARAHONDA

Ctra. de Pinoso, km. 3
30510 Yecla (Murcia)
☎: +34 968 718 696 - Fax: +34 968 790 928
www.barahonda.com
info@barahonda.com

BARAHONDA 2010 TC
monastrell, syrah, petit verdot

87 Colour: cherry, garnet rim. Nose: ripe fruit, creamy
oak, toasty, complex, powerfull. Palate: powerful, flavourful, toasty.

BARAHONDA 2012 B
macabeo, airén

85 Colour: bright straw. Nose: fresh, fresh fruit, white
flowers, dried herbs. Palate: flavourful, fruity, good acidity,
correct.

BARAHONDA 2012 RD
monastrell

85 Colour: rose, purple rim. Nose: powerfull, ripe fruit, red
berry notes, floral, expressive, lactic notes. Palate: powerful,
fruity, fresh.

BARAHONDA BARRICA 2011 T BARRICA
monastrell, syrah

89 Colour: bright cherry. Nose: ripe fruit, sweet spices,
creamy oak, cocoa bean, dark chocolate. Palate: flavourful,
fruity, toasty.

BARAHONDA MONASTRELL 2012 T
monastrell

88 Colour: cherry, purple rim. Nose: expressive, fresh fruit,
red berry notes, floral. Palate: flavourful, fruity, good acidity,
round tannins.

CARRO 2012 T
monastrell, syrah, merlot, tempranillo

85 Colour: cherry, garnet rim. Nose: ripe fruit, fragrant
herbs, sweet spices. Palate: powerful, flavourful, correct.

HC MONASTRELL 2011 T
monastrell

87 Colour: cherry, garnet rim. Nose: ripe fruit, spicy,
creamy oak, toasty, complex. Palate: powerful, flavourful,
toasty, round tannins.

HC PETIT VERDOT 2010 T
petit verdot

90 Colour: cherry, garnet rim. Nose: ripe fruit, spicy, creamy oak, toasty, complex, balsamic herbs. Palate: powerful, flavourful, toasty, balanced.

TRANCO 2010 T
monastrell, cabernet sauvignon

87 Colour: cherry, garnet rim. Nose: ripe fruit, spicy, toasty, cocoa bean. Palate: powerful, flavourful, toasty.

BODEGAS CASTAÑO

Ctra. Fuenteálamo, 3 - Apdo. 120
30510 Yecla (Murcia)
☎: +34 968 791 115 - Fax: +34 968 791 900
www.bodegascastano.com
info@bodegascastano.com

CASA CISCA 2011 T
100% monastrell

95 Colour: cherry, garnet rim. Nose: ripe fruit, spicy, creamy oak, toasty, complex, earthy notes, dark chocolate. Palate: powerful, flavourful, toasty, round tannins.

CASTAÑO MACABEO CHARDONNAY 2012 B
chardonnay

87 Colour: bright straw. Nose: fresh, fresh fruit, expressive, lactic notes. Palate: flavourful, fruity, good acidity, balanced.

CASTAÑO MONASTRELL 2012 RD JOVEN
100% monastrell

84

CASTAÑO MONASTRELL 2012 T
100% monastrell

90 Colour: cherry, purple rim. Nose: fresh fruit, red berry notes, floral. Palate: flavourful, fruity, good acidity, round tannins.

HÉCULA 2011 T
100% monastrell

90 Colour: bright cherry. Nose: ripe fruit, sweet spices, creamy oak, expressive, balsamic herbs. Palate: flavourful, fruity, toasty, round tannins.

VIÑA AL LADO DE LA CASA 2008 T

89 Colour: deep cherry, garnet rim. Nose: ripe fruit, warm, balanced, earthy notes. Palate: flavourful, round tannins, spicy.

VIÑA AL LADO DE LA CASA 2010 T
75% monastrell, 10% cabernet sauvignon, 10% syrah, 5% garnacha tintorera

88 Colour: cherry, garnet rim. Nose: toasty, overripe fruit, powerfull. Palate: powerful, flavourful, spicy.

VIÑA DETRÁS DE LA CASA SYRAH 2011 T
syrah

94 Colour: deep cherry, garnet rim. Nose: creamy oak, sweet spices, ripe fruit. Palate: rich, flavourful, good structure, round tannins, toasty.

BODEGAS LA PURÍSIMA

Ctra. de Pinoso, 3 Apdo. 27
30510 Yecla (Murcia)
☎: +34 968 751 257 - Fax: +34 968 795 116
www.bodegaslapurisima.com
info@bodegaslapurisima.com

ENESENCIA 2011 T
monastrell

79

ESTÍO 2012 RD
monastrell, syrah, merlot, cabernet sauvignon

85 Colour: rose, purple rim. Nose: ripe fruit, red berry notes, floral, expressive. Palate: powerful, fruity, fresh.

ESTÍO 2012 T
monastrell, syrah

85 Colour: cherry, purple rim. Nose: expressive, fresh fruit, red berry notes, floral. Palate: flavourful, fruity, good acidity, round tannins.

ESTÍO MACABEO 2012 B
macabeo

83

IGLESIA VIEJA 2008 TC
monastrell, syrah, cabernet sauvignon

84

IV EXPRESIÓN 2008 T
monastrell, syrah, garnacha

84

LA PURÍSIMA 2012 B
samsó blanc, macabeo, verdejo

87 Colour: bright straw. Nose: ripe fruit, floral, fragrant herbs. Palate: rich, powerful, flavourful.

LA PURÍSIMA 2012 RD
monastrell, syrah, merlot

88 Colour: rose, purple rim. Nose: powerfull, ripe fruit, red berry notes, floral, lactic notes. Palate: powerful, fruity, fresh.

LA PURÍSIMA 2012 T
monastrell

89 Colour: cherry, purple rim. Nose: red berry notes, ripe fruit, balsamic herbs, earthy notes, expressive. Palate: rich, powerful, flavourful.

LA PURÍSIMA OLD VINES EXPRESIÓN 2009 T
monastrell, syrah, garnacha

91 Colour: cherry, garnet rim. Nose: earthy notes, ripe fruit, spicy, creamy oak, expressive. Palate: balanced, elegant, long, flavourful.

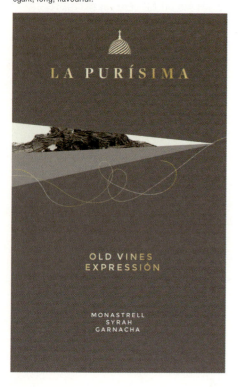

LA PURÍSIMA PREMIUM 2010 T
monastrell, garnacha

90 Colour: cherry, garnet rim. Nose: ripe fruit, spicy, creamy oak, balsamic herbs, mineral. Palate: powerful, flavourful, toasty.

LA PURÍSIMA SYRAH 2012 T
syrah

88 Colour: cherry, purple rim. Nose: floral, red berry notes, ripe fruit, warm, balanced. Palate: powerful, flavourful, fruity, rich.

TRAPÍO 2008 T
monastrell

84

TRAPÍO 2010 T
100% monastrell

87 Colour: cherry, garnet rim. Nose: ripe fruit, spicy, creamy oak. Palate: powerful, flavourful, toasty.

VALCORSO 2012 B
macabeo, sauvignon blanc

85 Colour: bright straw. Nose: fresh, fresh fruit, white flowers. Palate: flavourful, fruity, good acidity, balanced.

VALCORSO MONASTRELL 2012 T BARRICA
monastrell

86 Colour: bright cherry. Nose: ripe fruit, sweet spices, creamy oak. Palate: flavourful, fruity, toasty.

VALCORSO SYRAH 2012 T
syrah

88 Colour: cherry, purple rim. Nose: expressive, fresh fruit, red berry notes, floral. Palate: flavourful, fruity, good acidity, round tannins.

CÍA. DE VINOS DEL ATLÁNTICO

Girasol, 4
11500 El Puerto de Santa María (Cádiz)
☎: +34 956 874 770 - Fax: +34 911 850 945
www.vinosatlantico.com
veronica@vinosatlantico.com

BELLUM EL REMATE 2009 T
100% monastrell

88 Colour: pale ruby, brick rim edge. Nose: macerated fruit, aromatic coffee, cocoa bean, expressive. Palate: powerful, flavourful, sweet, toasty, balanced.

ELO 2010 T
100% monastrell

88 Colour: cherry, garnet rim. Nose: spicy, wild herbs, varietal, fruit preserve. Palate: powerful, flavourful, toasty, round tannins.

NABUCCO 2011 T
50% monastrell, 50% syrah

86 Colour: bright cherry. Nose: ripe fruit, sweet spices, creamy oak, cocoa bean. Palate: flavourful, fruity, toasty, balanced.

VINOS SIN LEY MONASTRELL 2011 T
100% monastrell

89 Colour: bright cherry. Nose: ripe fruit, sweet spices, creamy oak, expressive. Palate: flavourful, fruity, toasty, balanced.

DANIEL ALBA BODEGAS

Avda. Córdoba, 25
30510 Yecla (Murcia)
☎: +34 628 687 673
www.danielalbabodegas.com
info@danielalbabodegas.com

LA MÁQUINA 2010 T
85% monastrell, 8% syrah, 7% garnacha

89 Colour: bright cherry. Nose: sweet spices, creamy oak, macerated fruit. Palate: flavourful, fruity, toasty, round tannins.

VINNICO

Muela, 16
3730 Jávea (Alicante)
☎: +34 965 791 967 - Fax: +34 966 461 471
www.vinnico.com
info@vinnico.com

FLOR DEL MONTGÓ ORGANIC MONASTRELL 2012 T
monastrell

88 Colour: cherry, purple rim. Nose: expressive, fresh fruit, red berry notes, floral. Palate: flavourful, fruity, good acidity.

JALEA 2011 T
monastrell

88 Colour: bright cherry. Nose: ripe fruit, sweet spices, creamy oak, expressive. Palate: flavourful, fruity, toasty, round tannins.

MONTGÓ 2011 T
70% monastrell, 20% syrah, 10% cabernet sauvignon

85 Colour: bright cherry. Nose: ripe fruit, sweet spices, creamy oak. Palate: flavourful, fruity, toasty.

RED FISH 2011 T
cabernet sauvignon

88 Colour: bright cherry. Nose: ripe fruit, sweet spices, creamy oak, expressive, balsamic herbs. Palate: flavourful, fruity, toasty.

SUSPIROS MONASTRELL 2011 T
monastrell

89 Colour: cherry, garnet rim. Nose: ripe fruit, spicy, creamy oak, toasty, complex. Palate: powerful, flavourful, toasty, round tannins.

The "Vinos de Pago" are linked to a single winery, and it is a status given to that winery on the grounds of unique micro-climatic features and proven evidence of consistent high quality over the years, with the goal to produce wines of sheer singularity. So far, only 15 "Vinos de Pago" labels have been granted for different autonomous regions (Aragón, La Mancha, Comunidad Valenciana and Navarra). The "Vinos de Pago" category has the same status as a DO. This "pago" should not be confused with the other "pago" term used in the wine realm, which refers to a plot, a smaller vineyard within a bigger property. The "Pagos de España" association was formed in 2000 when a group of small producers of single estate wines got together to defend the singularity of their wines. In 2003, the association became Grandes Pagos de España, responding to the request of many colleagues in other parts of the country who wished to make the single-growth concept better known, and to seek excellence through the direct relationship between wines and their places of origin.

PAGO AYLÉS: Situated in the municipality of Mezalocha (Zaragoza), within the limits of the Cariñena appellation. The production area is located within the Ebro basin, principally around the depression produced by the River Huerva. The soils consist of limestone, marl and composites. The climate is temperate continental with low average annual rainfall figures of 350 to 550mm. The varieties authorized for the production of red and rosé wines are: garnacha, merlot, tempranillo and cabernet sauvignon.

PAGO CALZADILLA: Located in the Mayor river valley, in the part of the Alcarria region that belongs to the province of Cuenca, it enjoys altitude levels ranging between 845 and 1005 meters. The vines are mostly planted on limestone soils with pronounced slopes (with up to a 40% incline), so terraces and slant plots have become the most common feature, following the altitude gradients. The grape varieties planted are tempranillo, cabernet-sauvignon, garnacha and syrah.

PAGO CAMPO DE LA GUARDIA: The vineyards are in the town of La Guardia, to the northeast of the province of Toledo, on a high plateau known as Mesa de Ocaña. Soils are deep and with varying degrees of loam, clay and sand. The climate follows a continental pattern, with hot and dry summers and particularly dry and cold winters. The presence of the Tajo River to the north and the Montes de Toledo to the south promote lower rainfall levels than in neighbouring areas, and thus more concentration of aromas and phenolic compounds.

PAGO CASA DEL BLANCO: Its vineyards are located at an altitude of 617 metres in Campo de Calatrava, in the town of Manzanares, right in the centre of the province of Ciudad Real, and therefore with a mediterranean/continental climate. Soils have varying degrees of loam and sand, and are abundant in lithium, surely due to the ancient volcanic character of the region.

PAGO CHOZAS CARRASCAL: In San Antonio de Requena. This is the third Estate of the Community of Valencia, with just 31 hectares. Located at 720 metres above sea level. It has a continental climatology with Mediterranean influence. Low rainfall (and average of 350-400 litres annually), its soils are loam texture tending to clay and sandy. The varieties uses are: bobal, tempranillo, garnacha, cabernet sauvignon, merlot, syrah, cabernet franc and monastrell for red wines and chardonnay, sauvignon blanc and macabeo for white wines.

PAGO DEHESA DEL CARRIZAL: Property of Marcial Gómez Sequeira, Dehesa del Carrizal is located in the town of Retuerta de Bullaque, to the north of Ciudad Real. It enjoys a continental climate and high altitude (900 metres). The winemaker, Ignacio de Miguel, uses primarily foreign (French) varieties such as *cabernet sauvignon.*

PAGO DOMINIO DE VALDEPUSA: Located in the town of Malpica de Tajo (Toledo), its owner, Carlos Falcó (Marqués de Griñón) pioneered the introduction in Spain of foreign grape varieties such as *cabernet sauvignon*

PAGO EL TERRERAZO: El Terrerazo, property of Bodegas Mustiguilo, is the first "Vinos de Pago" label granted within the autonomous region of Valencia. It comprises 62 hectares at an altitude of 800 meters between Utiel and Sinarcas where an excellent clone of *bobal* –that yields small and loose berries– is grown. It enjoys a mediterranean-continental climate and the vineyard gets the influence of humid winds blowing from the sea, which is just 80 kilometres away from the property. Soils are characterized limestone and clay in nature, with abundant sand and stones.

PAGO FINCA ÉLEZ: It became the first of all Vino de Pago designations of origin. Its owner is Manuel Manzaneque, and it is located at an altitude of 1000 metres in El Bonillo, in the province of Albacete. The winery became renown by its splendid *chardonnay*, but today also make a single-varietal *syrah* and some other red renderings.

PAGO FLORENTINO: Located in the municipality of Malagón (Ciudad Real), between natural lagoons to the south and the Sierra de Malagón to the north, at an altitude of some 630-670 metres. Soils are mainly siliceous with limestone and stones on the surface and a subsoil of slate and limestone. The climate is milder and dryer than that of neighbouring towns.

PAGO GUIJOSO: Finca El Guijoso is property of Bodegas Sánchez Muliterno, located in El Bonillo, between the provinces of Albacete and Ciudad Real. Surrounded by bitch and juniper woods, the vines are planted on stone (guijo in Spanish, from which it takes its name) soils at an altitude of 1000 metres. Wines are all made from French varieties, and have a clear French lean also in terms of style.

PAGO LOS BALAGUESES: The "Pago de los Balagueses" is located to the south west of the Utiel-Requena wine region, just 20 kilometres away from Requena. At approximately 700 metres over the sea level, it enjoys a continental type of climate with mediterranean influence and an average annual rainfall of around 450 mm. The vines are planted on low hills –a feature that favours water drainage– surrounded by pines, almond and olive trees, thus giving shape to a unique landscape.

PAGO DE OTAZU: Its vineyards are located in Navarra, between two mountain ranges (Sierra del Perdón and Sierra de Echauri), and is probably the most northerly of all Spanish wine regions. It is a cool area with Atlantic climate and a high day-night temperature contrast. Soils in that part of the country, near the city of Pamplona, are limestone-based with abundant clay and stones, therefore with good drainage that allows vines to sink their roots deeper into the soil.

PAGO PRADO DE IRACHE: Its vineyard is located in the municipality of Ayegui (Navarra) at an altitude of 450 metres. Climate is continental with strong Atlantic influence and soils are mainly of a loamy nature.

PAGO SEÑORÍO DE ARÍNZANO: Located in the city of Estella, in Navarra, to the northeast of Spain, the vineyard is in a valley near the Pyrenees and crossed by the Ega river, which moderates the temperatures. Climate has here a strong Atlantic influence with high day-night temperature contrast. Soils are complex in nature, with varying levels of loam, marl, clay and highly degraded limestone rock.

PAGO AYLÉS
BODEGA PAGO AYLÉS

Finca Aylés. Ctra. A-1101, Km. 24
50152 Mezalocha (Zaragoza)
☎: +34 976 140 473 - Fax: +34 976 140 268
www.pagoayles.com
pagoayles@pagoayles.com

"A" DE AYLÉS 2011 T
tempranillo, merlot, garnacha, cabernet sauvignon

91 Colour: bright cherry. Nose: ripe fruit, sweet spices, creamy oak, cocoa bean, toasty, balsamic herbs. Palate: flavourful, fruity, toasty, round tannins.

"L" DE AYLÉS 2012 RD
garnacha, cabernet sauvignon

90 Colour: rose. Nose: powerfull, ripe fruit, red berry notes, floral, lactic notes, expressive. Palate: powerful, fruity, fresh, balanced.

"Y" DE AYLÉS 2011 T
tempranillo, merlot, garnacha, cabernet sauvignon

92 Colour: cherry, garnet rim. Nose: red berry notes, ripe fruit, sweet spices, toasty, wild herbs. Palate: powerful, flavourful, spicy, long, toasty, round tannins.

AYLÉS "TRES DE 3000" 2010 T
garnacha, cabernet sauvignon, tempranillo

91 Colour: cherry, garnet rim. Nose: ripe fruit, spicy, creamy oak, toasty, complex, balanced. Palate: powerful, flavourful, toasty, round tannins, elegant.

PAGO CALZADILLA
PAGO CALZADILLA

Ctra. Huete a Cuenca, Km. 3
16500 Huete (Cuenca)
☎: +34 969 143 020 - Fax: +34 969 147 047
www.pagodecalzadilla.net
info@pagodecalzadilla.com

CALZADILLA CLASSIC 2008 T
60% tempranillo, 20% cabernet sauvignon, 10% syrah, 10% garnacha

89 Colour: cherry, garnet rim. Nose: spicy, creamy oak, balsamic herbs, overripe fruit. Palate: concentrated, powerful, flavourful, balsamic, round tannins.

GRAN CALZADILLA 2007 T
70% tempranillo, 30% cabernet sauvignon

93 Colour: cherry, garnet rim. Nose: ripe fruit, spicy, creamy oak, toasty, fragrant herbs. Palate: powerful, flavourful, toasty, round tannins, balanced, elegant.

PAGO CAMPO DE LA GUARDIA
BODEGAS MARTÚE

Campo de la Guardia, s/n
45760 La Guardia (Toledo)
☎: +34 925 123 333 - Fax: +34 925 123 332
www.martue.com
bodegasenlaguardia@martue.com

MARTÚE 2009 TC
33% cabernet sauvignon, 22% merlot, 21% tempranillo, 13% petit verdot, 11% syrah

88 Colour: cherry, garnet rim. Nose: powerfull, ripe fruit, wild herbs, creamy oak. Palate: balanced, spicy, long.

MARTÚE CHARDONNAY 2011 B
100% chardonnay

86 Colour: bright yellow. Nose: ripe fruit, faded flowers, dried herbs, creamy oak. Palate: powerful, flavourful, warm.

MARTÚE ESPECIAL 2008 TR
50% merlot, 27% cabernet sauvignon, 21% syrah, 2% malbec

89 Colour: cherry, garnet rim. Nose: ripe fruit, balsamic herbs, spicy, cocoa bean, creamy oak. Palate: powerful, flavourful, long, toasty.

MARTÚE SYRAH 2009 T
100% syrah

87 Colour: cherry, garnet rim. Nose: fruit preserve, dried flowers, warm, sweet spices. Palate: powerful, flavourful, rich.

PAGO CASA DEL BLANCO
PAGO CASA DEL BLANCO

Ctra. Manzanares a Moral , Km. 23,2
13200 Manzanares (Ciudad Real)
☎: +34 917 480 606 - Fax: +34 913 290 266
www.pagocasadelblanco.com
quixote@pagocasadelblanco.com

QUIXOTE CABERNET SAUVIGNON SYRAH 2008 T
cabernet sauvignon, syrah

88 Colour: cherry, garnet rim. Nose: ripe fruit, spicy, toasty, balsamic herbs. Palate: powerful, flavourful, toasty.

QUIXOTE MALBEC CABERNET FRANC 2008 T
malbec, cabernet franc

86 Colour: cherry, garnet rim. Nose: ripe fruit, damp earth, wet leather, tobacco. Palate: powerful, flavourful, long, spicy.

QUIXOTE MERLOT TEMPRANILLO PETIT VERDOT 2008 T
merlot, tempranillo, petit verdot

88 Colour: cherry, garnet rim. Nose: ripe fruit, sweet spices, creamy oak, scrubland. Palate: flavourful, fruity, toasty.

QUIXOTE PETIT VERDOT 2008 T
petit verdot

88 Colour: cherry, garnet rim. Nose: ripe fruit, wild herbs, dried flowers, spicy. Palate: powerful, rich, long, harsh oak tannins.

PAGO CHOZAS CARRASCAL
CHOZAS CARRASCAL

Vereda Real de San Antonio s/n
46390 San Antonio de Requena (Valencia)
☎: +34 963 410 395
www.chozascarrascal.es
chozas@chozascarrascal.es

EL CF DE CHOZAS CARRASCAL 2012 T
cabernet franc

95 Colour: bright cherry. Nose: ripe fruit, sweet spices, fruit expression, red berry notes, spicy. Palate: flavourful, fruity, toasty, round tannins.

LAS OCHO 2010 T

93 Colour: cherry, garnet rim. Nose: ripe fruit, creamy oak, complex, earthy notes, mineral. Palate: powerful, flavourful, toasty, round tannins, long.

LAS TRES 2012 BFB
chardonnay, sauvignon blanc, macabeo

91 Colour: bright yellow. Nose: sweet spices, creamy oak, fragrant herbs, candied fruit, citrus fruit. Palate: rich, smoky aftertaste, flavourful, fresh, good acidity.

PAGO DEHESA DEL CARRIZAL
DEHESA DEL CARRIZAL

Carretera de Retuerta del Bullaque
a Navas de Estena Km 5
13194 Retuerta del Bullaque (Ciudad Real)
☎: +34 925 421 773 - Fax: +34 925 421 761
www.dehesadelcarrizal.com
bodega@dehesadelcarrizal.com

DEHESA DEL CARRIZAL CABERNET SAUVIGNON 2008 T
cabernet sauvignon

90 Colour: cherry, garnet rim. Nose: ripe fruit, fragrant herbs, sweet spices, creamy oak. Palate: powerful, balsamic, spicy, long.

DEHESA DEL CARRIZAL CHARDONNAY 2011 B
chardonnay

91 Colour: bright yellow. Nose: floral, ripe fruit, dried herbs, sweet spices, creamy oak. Palate: spicy, correct, long, toasty, balanced.

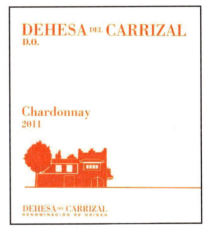

DEHESA DEL CARRIZAL COLECCIÓN PRIVADA 2009 T
cabernet sauvignon, syrah, petit verdot, merlot

92 Colour: cherry, garnet rim. Nose: ripe fruit, spicy, creamy oak, toasty, balsamic herbs. Palate: powerful, flavourful, toasty, round tannins.

DEHESA DEL CARRIZAL MV 2010 T
cabernet sauvignon, syrah, petit verdot

90 Colour: cherry, garnet rim. Nose: red berry notes, ripe fruit, balsamic herbs, spicy, creamy oak. Palate: powerful, flavourful, concentrated.

DEHESA DEL CARRIZAL PETIT VERDOT 2010 T
petit verdot

90 Colour: cherry, garnet rim. Nose: ripe fruit, spicy, complex, fragrant herbs. Palate: powerful, flavourful, toasty, balsamic.

FINCA CAÍZ CARRIZAL SYRAH 2009 T
syrah

92 Colour: cherry, garnet rim. Nose: ripe fruit, balsamic herbs, spicy, violet drops, toasty, mineral. Palate: powerful, flavourful, long, balanced.

PAGO DOMINIO DE VALDEPUSA
PAGOS DE FAMILIA MARQUÉS DE GRIÑÓN

Finca Casa de Vacas - Ctra. CM-4015, Km. 23
45692 Malpica de Tajo (Toledo)
☎: +34 925 597 222 - Fax: +34 925 789 416
www.pagosdefamilia.com
service@pagosdefamilia.com

CALIZA 2009 T
70% syrah, 30% petit verdot

89 Colour: cherry, garnet rim. Nose: red berry notes, ripe fruit, balsamic herbs, dry stone, fine reductive notes. Palate: balanced, flavourful, spicy, balsamic.

MARQUÉS DE GRIÑÓN CABERNET SAUVIGNON 2008 T
100% cabernet sauvignon

91 Colour: cherry, garnet rim. Nose: ripe fruit, spicy, balsamic herbs, earthy notes, balanced. Palate: powerful, spicy, long, round tannins.

MARQUÉS DE GRIÑÓN EMERITVS 2008 TR
63% cabernet sauvignon, 32% petit verdot, 5% syrah

93 Colour: cherry, garnet rim. Nose: expressive, ripe fruit, spicy, balsamic herbs, fine reductive notes, elegant. Palate: round tannins, long, spicy, flavourful.

MARQUÉS DE GRIÑÓN PETIT VERDOT 2008 T
100% petit verdot

91 Colour: cherry, garnet rim. Nose: ripe fruit, spicy, creamy oak, toasty, scrubland, balanced. Palate: powerful, flavourful, toasty, round tannins.

MARQUÉS DE GRIÑÓN SYRAH 2007 T
100% syrah

90 Colour: cherry, garnet rim. Nose: ripe fruit, fruit liqueur notes, balsamic herbs, dried flowers, sweet spices, creamy oak. Palate: round tannins, concentrated, powerful, flavourful.

SVMMA VARIETALIS 2008 T
70% syrah, 16% petit verdot, 14% cabernet sauvignon

91 Colour: cherry, garnet rim. Nose: ripe fruit, spicy, creamy oak, earthy notes. Palate: powerful, flavourful, toasty, round tannins.

PAGO EL TERRERAZO
MUSTIGUILLO VIÑEDOS Y BODEGA

Ctra. N-330, km 196,5 El Terrerazo
46300 Utiel (Valencia)
☎: +34 962 168 260 - Fax: +34 962 168 259
www.bodegamustiguillo.com
info@bodegamustiguillo.com

QUINCHA CORRAL 2009 T
100% bobal

94 Colour: cherry, garnet rim. Nose: spicy, creamy oak, toasty, complex, sweet spices, fruit expression. Palate: powerful, flavourful, toasty, round tannins.

QUINCHA CORRAL 2011 T
100% bobal

96 Colour: very deep cherry. Nose: powerfull, characterful, ripe fruit, fruit expression, sweet spices, creamy oak. Palate: powerful, concentrated, complex, ripe fruit, round.

PAGO FINCA ÉLEZ
VIÑEDOS Y BODEGA MANUEL MANZANEQUE

Ctra. Ossa de Montiel a El Bonillo, Km. 11,500
2610 El Bonillo (Albacete)
☎: +34 967 585 003 - Fax: +34 967 370 649
www.manuelmanzaneque.com
info@manuelmanzaneque.com

MANUEL MANZANEQUE CHARDONNAY 2009 BFB
chardonnay

90 Colour: bright golden. Nose: ripe fruit, dry nuts, powerfull, toasty, aged wood nuances, smoky. Palate: flavourful, fruity, spicy, toasty, long.

MANUEL MANZANEQUE CHARDONNAY 2012 B
chardonnay

85 Colour: bright golden. Nose: ripe fruit, macerated fruit, floral, fragrant herbs. Palate: powerful, flavourful, rich, warm.

MANUEL MANZANEQUE ESCENA 2007 T
tempranillo, cabernet sauvignon

92 Colour: cherry, garnet rim. Nose: ripe fruit, mineral, spicy, fine reductive notes, balanced. Palate: round tannins, long, flavourful, balanced.

MANUEL MANZANEQUE FINCA ÉLEZ 2007 TC
cabernet sauvignon, merlot, tempranillo

88 Colour: cherry, garnet rim. Nose: spicy, creamy oak, fruit preserve. Palate: powerful, flavourful, toasty, round tannins.

MANUEL MANZANEQUE NUESTRA SELECCIÓN 2007 T
cabernet sauvignon, merlot, tempranillo

91 Colour: cherry, garnet rim. Nose: ripe fruit, balsamic herbs, spicy, creamy oak, balanced. Palate: powerful, flavourful, spicy, long.

MANUEL MANZANEQUE SYRAH 2006 T
syrah

90 Colour: cherry, garnet rim. Nose: ripe fruit, sweet spices, aromatic coffee, dark chocolate, roasted coffee. Palate: rich, flavourful, long, spicy, balanced.

PAGO FLORENTINO
PAGO FLORENTINO

Ctra. Porzuna - Camino Cristo
del Humilladero km. 3
13420 Malagón (Ciudad Real)
☎: +34 983 681 146 - Fax: +34 983 681 147
www.pagoflorentino.com
bodega@pagoflorentino.com

PAGO FLORENTINO 2010 T
100% cencibel

90 Colour: cherry, garnet rim. Nose: red berry notes, ripe fruit, aromatic coffee, sweet spices. Palate: rich, powerful, flavourful, toasty, long.

PAGO GUIJOSO
BODEGAS Y VIÑEDOS SÁNCHEZ MULITERNO

Ctra. El Bonillo a Ossa de Montiel, km. 11
2610 El Bonillo (Albacete)
☎: +34 967 193 222 - Fax: +34 967 193 292
www.sanchez-muliterno.com
bodegas@sanchez-muliterno.com

DIVINUS 2008 BFB
100% chardonnay

84

FLOR DE DIVINUS 2012 B
chardonnay

88 Colour: bright yellow. Nose: citrus fruit, ripe fruit, fragrant herbs, expressive. Palate: powerful, flavourful, long, balanced.

MAGNIFICUS 2006 T
100% syrah

89 Colour: cherry, garnet rim. Nose: fruit preserve, scrubland, creamy oak, spicy, toasty, wet leather, tobacco. Palate: powerful, flavourful, toasty, balanced.

VEGA GUIJOSO 2009 T
63% merlot, 30% syrah, 7% cabernet sauvignon

86 Colour: cherry, garnet rim. Nose: fruit preserve, balsamic herbs, spicy, toasty. Palate: long, powerful, flavourful, spicy.

VIÑA CONSOLACIÓN 2004 TGR
cabernet sauvignon

89 Colour: ruby red, orangey edge. Nose: ripe fruit, fruit liqueur notes, balsamic herbs, aged wood nuances, toasty. Palate: spicy, long, flavourful, balanced.

VIÑA CONSOLACIÓN 2006 TR
cabernet sauvignon

87 Colour: pale ruby, brick rim edge. Nose: spicy, fine reductive notes, wet leather, aged wood nuances, fruit liqueur notes, acetaldehyde. Palate: spicy, long, balsamic.

PAGO LOS BALAGUESES
VIÑEDOS Y BODEGAS VEGALFARO

Ctra. Pontón - Utiel, Km. 3
46430 Requena (Valencia)
☎: +34 962 320 680 - Fax: +34 962 321 126
www.vegalfaro.com
rodolfo@vegalfaro.com

PAGO DE LOS BALAGUESES CHARDONNAY 2012 B
chardonnay

90 Colour: bright yellow. Nose: powerfull, ripe fruit, sweet spices, creamy oak, fragrant herbs. Palate: rich, smoky after-taste, flavourful, fresh, good acidity.

PAGO DE LOS BALAGUESES MERLOT 2011 T
merlot

92 Colour: cherry, garnet rim. Nose: ripe fruit, balsamic herbs, mineral, cocoa bean, creamy oak. Palate: powerful, flavourful, spicy, balsamic, balanced.

PAGO DE LOS BALAGUESES SYRAH 2011 TC
syrah

93 Colour: cherry, garnet rim. Nose: violet drops, red berry notes, ripe fruit, fragrant herbs, earthy notes. Palate: powerful, flavourful, good acidity, spicy, elegant.

PAGO PRADO DE IRACHE
BODEGAS IRACHE

Monasterio de Irache, 1
31240 Ayegui (Navarra)
☎: +34 948 551 932 - Fax: +34 948 554 954
www.irache.com
irache@irache.com

PRADO IRACHE VINO DE PAGO 2006 T
tempranillo, cabernet sauvignon, merlot

92 Colour: cherry, garnet rim. Nose: ripe fruit, spicy, creamy oak, toasty, mineral. Palate: powerful, flavourful, toasty, round tannins, balanced, elegant.

PAGO SEÑORÍO DE ARINZANO
PROPIEDAD DE ARÍNZANO

Crta. NA-132, km. 3,1
31292 Arinzano (Navarra)
☎: +34 948 555 285 - Fax: +34 948 555 415
www.bodegaschivite.com
info@arinzano.com

ARÍNZANO LA CASONA 2008 T
tempranillo, merlot

94 Colour: cherry, garnet rim. Nose: ripe fruit, spicy, creamy oak, toasty, mineral. Palate: powerful, flavourful, toasty, round tannins.

GRAN VINO DE ARÍNZANO 2008 T
tempranillo

96 Colour: deep cherry. Nose: powerfull, ripe fruit, sweet spices. Palate: flavourful, ripe fruit, good acidity, spicy, round tannins.

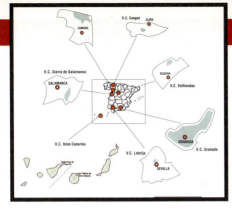

So far, there are only seven wine regions that have achieved the status "Vino de Calidad" ("Quality Wine Produced in Specified Regions"): Cangas, Lebrija, Valtiendas, Granada, Sierra de Salamanca, Valles de Benavente and Islas Canarias, regions that are allowed to label their wines with the VCPRD seal. This quality seal works as a sort of "training" session for the DO category, although it is still quite unknown for the average consumer.

VINO DE CALIDAD / D.O.P. DE CANGAS

Located to the south-eastern part of the province of Asturias, bordering with León, Cangas del Narcea has unique climatic conditions, completely different to the rest of the municipalities of Asturias; therefore, its wines have sheer singularity. With lower rainfall levels and more sunshine hours than the rest the province, vines are planted on slate, siliceous and sandy soils. The main varieties are albarín blanco and albillo (white), along with *garnacha tintorera*, *mencía* and *verdejo negro* (red).

VINO DE CALIDAD / D.O.P. GRANADA

Wines that come from anywhere within the provincial limits of Granada, it includes nearly 20 wineries and a hundred growers. It enjoys a mediterranean climate with Atlantic influence. Characterized by a rugged topography, the vineyards occupy mostly the highest areas, with an average altitude of around 1200 meters, a feature that provides this territory with an ample day-night temperature differential. The region is promoting white grape varieties such as *vijiriega*, *moscatel* and *pedro ximénez*, as well as red (*tempranillo*, *garnacha*, *monastrell*) and even some French ones, widely planted in the province. Soil structure, although diverse, is based mainly on clay and slate.

VINO DE CALIDAD / D.O.P. DE LEBRIJA

Recognized by the Junta de Andalucía on March the 11th 2009. The production area includes the towns of Lebrija and El Cuervo, in the province of Sevilla.
The wines ascribed to the "Vino de Calidad de Lebrija" designation of quality will be made solely from the following grape varieties:
– **White varieties:** *moscatel de Alejandría, palomino, palomino fino, sauvignon blanc* and that traditionally known as *vidueño* (*montúo de pilas, mollar cano, moscatel morisco, perruno*).
– **Red varieties:** *cabernet sauvignon, syrah, tempranillo, merlot* and *tintilla de Rota*.
Types of wines: white, red, generosos (fortified) and generosos de licor, naturally sweet and mistelas.

VINO DE CALIDAD / D.O.P. SIERRA DE SALAMANCA

The "Vino de Calidad" status was ratified to Sierra de Salamanca by the Junta de Castilla y León (Castilla y León autonomous government) in June 2010, becoming the third one to be granted within the region. Sierra de Salamanca lies in the south of the province of Salamanca, and includes 26 towns, all within the same province. Vines are planted mostly on terraces at the top of the hills and on clay soils based on limestone. Authorized varieties are *viura, moscatel de grano menudo* and *palomino* (white), as well as *rufete, garnacha* and *tempranillo* (red).

VINO DE CALIDAD / D.O.P. DE LOS VALLES DE BENAVENTE

Recognized by the Junta de Castilla y León in September 2000, the VCPRD comprises nowadays more than 50 municipalities and three wineries in Benavente, Santibáñez de Vidriales and San Pedro de Ceque. The production areas within the region are five (Valle Vidriales, Valle del Tera, Valle Valverde, La Vega and Tierra de Campos) around the city of Benavente, the core of the region. Four rivers (Tera, Esla, Órbigo and Valderadey, all of them tributary to the Duero river) give the region its natural borders.

VINO DE CALIDAD / D.O.P. VALTIENDAS

An area to the north of the province of Segovia relatively known thanks to the brand name Duratón, also the name of the river that crosses a region that has mainly *tempranillo* planted, a grape variety known there also as *tinta del país*. The wines are fruitier and more acidic than those from Ribera del Duero, thanks to an altitude of some 900 metres and clay soils with plenty of stones.

VINO DE CALIDAD / D.O.P. ISLAS CANARIAS

Approved in May 2011, the date of publication in the Boletín Oficial de Canarias (BOC), the constitution of its management board took place on 27 December, 2012. The production area covers the entire territory of the Canary Islands, allowing free movement of grapes in the Canary Islands. Its regulations cover broad grape varieties from the Canary Islands, as well as international ones.

VINO DE CALIDAD / D.O.P. CANGAS
ANTONIO ALVAREZ ALVAREZ (CHICOTE)

La Galiana, 88 Villarino de Limés
33817 Cangas de Narcea (Asturias)
☎: +34 985 810 934
www.bodegachicote.com
bodegachicote@hotmail.com

PENDERUYOS 2012 T
mencía, albarín tinto, carrasquín, verdejo negro

87 Colour: cherry, purple rim. Nose: fresh fruit, red berry notes, floral, balsamic herbs. Palate: flavourful, fruity, good acidity.

PENDERUYOS SELECCIÓN 2012 T
verdejo negro, albarín tinto, carrasquín, mencía

89 Colour: cherry, purple rim. Nose: expressive, fresh fruit, red berry notes, floral. Palate: flavourful, fruity, good acidity, round tannins.

BODEGA MONASTERIO DE CORIAS

Monasterio de Corias, s/n
33800 Cangas del Narcea (Asturias)
☎: +34 985 810 493
www.monasteriodecorias.com
bodega@monasteriodecorias.es

CORIAS GUILFA 2011 T
60% carrasquín, 40% verdejo negro

92 Colour: light cherry, garnet rim. Nose: red berry notes, ripe fruit, balsamic herbs, creamy oak. Palate: powerful, flavourful, spicy, long.

CORIAS GUILFA 2012 BFB
albariño

92 Colour: bright yellow. Nose: powerfull, ripe fruit, sweet spices, creamy oak, fragrant herbs. Palate: rich, smoky aftertaste, flavourful, fresh, good acidity.

MONASTERIO DE CORIAS SEIS OCTAVOS 2012 T BARRICA
60% albarín tinto, 40% mencía

89 Colour: cherry, purple rim. Nose: ripe fruit, scrubland, damp earth, creamy oak. Palate: powerful, flavourful, spicy.

MONASTERIO DE CORIAS VIÑA GRANDIELLA 2012 B
albarín

88 Colour: bright straw. Nose: fresh fruit, white flowers, fragrant herbs. Palate: flavourful, fruity, balanced.

BODEGAS OBANCA

Obanca, 12
33800 Cangas del Narcea (Asturias)
☎: +34 626 956 571 - Fax: +34 985 811 539
www.obanca.com
informacion@obanca.com

CASTRO DE LIMÉS OROCANTABRICO 2012 BFB
albarín

93 Colour: bright yellow. Nose: powerfull, ripe fruit, sweet spices, creamy oak, fragrant herbs. Palate: rich, flavourful, fresh, good acidity.

LLUMES 2010 T
verdejo negro

93 Colour: light cherry, garnet rim. Nose: red berry notes, fragrant herbs, dry stone, creamy oak. Palate: flavourful, spicy, balanced, elegant.

OBANCA 2012 T JOVEN
carrasquín

89 Colour: cherry, purple rim. Nose: fresh fruit, red berry notes, floral. Palate: flavourful, fruity, good acidity, round tannins.

VINO DE CALIDAD / D.O.P. DE GRANADA
BODEGAS AL ZAGAL

Paraje Las Cañaillas, s/n
18518 Cogollos de Guadix (Granada)
☎: +34 958 105 605
www.bodegasalzagal.es
bodegas@bodegasalzagal.es

REY ZAGAL 2009 TC
80% tempranillo, 20% cabernet sauvignon

85 Colour: cherry, garnet rim. Nose: ripe fruit, spicy, creamy oak, balsamic herbs. Palate: powerful, flavourful, toasty.

REY ZAGAL 2009 TR
50% tempranillo, 50% merlot

88 Colour: pale ruby, brick rim edge. Nose: spicy, fine reductive notes, aged wood nuances, fruit liqueur notes. Palate: spicy, long, round tannins.

REY ZAGAL 2010 T
tempranillo, merlot, cabernet sauvignon

87 Colour: cherry, garnet rim. Nose: ripe fruit, wild herbs, spicy, creamy oak. Palate: long, powerful, balanced.

REY ZAGAL SAUVIGNON BLANC 2012 B
sauvignon blanc

84

BODEGAS FONTEDEI

Doctor Horcajadas, 10
18570 Deifontes (Granada)
☎: +34 958 407 957
www.bodegasfontedei.com
bodegasfontedei@gmail.com

ALBAYDA 2012 B
chardonnay, otras

90 Colour: bright straw. Nose: ripe fruit, tropical fruit, white flowers, fragrant herbs, sweet spices. Palate: powerful, flavourful, spicy, long.

FONTEDEI LINDARAJA 2011 T
tempranillo, syrah

89 Colour: cherry, garnet rim. Nose: ripe fruit, spicy, creamy oak, toasty. Palate: powerful, flavourful, toasty, round tannins.

BODEGAS NAZARÍES

Calle Real, 23
18700 Albuñol (Granada)
☎: +34 680 912 928
www.bodegasnazaries.com
info@bodegasnazaries.com

TORRE DE COMARES 2010 T
100% tempranillo

84

BODEGAS SEÑORÍO DE NEVADA

Ctra. de Cónchar, s/n
18659 Villamena (Granada)
☎: +34 958 777 092 - Fax: +34 958 107 367
www.senoriodenevada.es
info@senoriodenevada.es

SEÑORÍO DE NEVADA BRONCE 2009 T
cabernet sauvignon, merlot

88 Colour: very deep cherry. Nose: candied fruit, spicy, scrubland. Palate: ripe fruit, spicy.

SEÑORÍO DE NEVADA ORO SELECCIÓN 2009 T
syrah, merlot, cabernet sauvignon

89 Colour: cherry, garnet rim. Nose: ripe fruit, spicy, creamy oak. Palate: powerful, flavourful, toasty, round tannins.

SEÑORÍO DE NEVADA PLATA 2009 T
syrah, merlot

87 Colour: deep cherry. Nose: ripe fruit, spicy, scrubland. Palate: fine bitter notes, good acidity.

VIÑA DAURO 2011 T
merlot, syrah

87 Colour: very deep cherry. Nose: ripe fruit, cocoa bean, scrubland. Palate: spicy, ripe fruit, fine bitter notes.

BODEGAS TIERRA HERMOSA

Avda. Ricardo Soriano, 1 3ºA
29601 Marbella (Málaga)
☎: +34 657 207 196 - Fax: +34 935 385 677
www.tierrahermosa.com
isabel@tierrahermosa.com

NEBLERÍO 2010 T
100% tempranillo

85 Colour: cherry, garnet rim. Nose: ripe fruit, spicy, creamy oak, toasty, warm, balsamic herbs, earthy notes. Palate: powerful, flavourful, toasty.

DOMINIO BUENAVISTA

Ctra. de Almería, s/n
18480 Ugíjar (Granada)
☎: +34 958 767 254 - Fax: +34 958 990 226
www.dominiobuenavista.com
info@dominiobuenavista.com

VELETA BLANCO ESP
80% vijariego blanco, 20% chardonnay

78

VELETA CABERNET SAUVIGNON 2009 T
100% cabernet sauvignon

87 Colour: cherry, garnet rim. Nose: ripe fruit, spicy, creamy oak, balsamic herbs, earthy notes. Palate: powerful, flavourful, toasty, round tannins.

VELETA ROSADO BLANC DE NOIR ESP
70% tempranillo, 30% garnacha

80

VELETA TEMPRANILLO 2009 T
100% tempranillo

89 Colour: cherry, garnet rim. Nose: red berry notes, ripe fruit, dry stone, wild herbs, sweet spices. Palate: powerful, long, balanced, correct.

VELETA TEMPRANILLO 2011 T
100% tempranillo

88 Colour: cherry, garnet rim. Nose: ripe fruit, balsamic herbs, damp earth, expressive. Palate: powerful, flavourful, spicy.

VELETA TEMPRANILLO ROSÉ 2012 RD
90% tempranillo, 10% chardonnay

83

VELETA VIJIRIEGA 2012 B
90% vijariego blanco, 10% chardonnay

85 Colour: bright straw. Nose: dried flowers, fragrant herbs, earthy notes, ripe fruit. Palate: rich, flavourful, correct.

IRVING

Finca el Duque Ctra. de Huéscar a Santiago de la Espada. km 13,500
18830 Huéscar (Granada)
☎: +34 653 527 560 - Fax: +34 917 150 632
www.irving.es
pedidos@irving.es

IRVING 2011 T

84

IRVING COLECCIÓN FAMILIAR 2010 T

88 Colour: deep cherry. Nose: powerfull, toasty, characterful. Palate: powerful, fruity, fine bitter notes, good acidity.

IRVING SHIRAZ 2010 T
syrah

91 Colour: bright cherry. Nose: sweet spices, creamy oak, candied fruit, powerfull. Palate: flavourful, fruity, toasty, round tannins.

LOS BARRANCOS

Ctra. Cádiar - Albuñol, km. 9,4
18449 Lobras (Granada)
☎: +34 958 343 218 - Fax: +34 958 343 412
www.losbarrancos.es
cesarortegar@gmail.com

CERRO DE LA RETAMA 2010 T
cabernet sauvignon, tempranillo, merlot

90 Colour: dark-red cherry, garnet rim. Nose: ripe fruit, wild herbs, spicy, earthy notes, creamy oak. Palate: powerful, flavourful, spicy, long, balanced.

LOMA DE LOS FELIPES 2011 T
tempranillo, cabernet sauvignon, merlot

88 Colour: cherry, garnet rim. Nose: ripe fruit, spicy, creamy oak, toasty, balsamic herbs. Palate: powerful, flavourful, toasty, round tannins.

MARQUÉS DE CASA PARDIÑAS C.B.

Finca San Torcuato
18540 Huélago (Granada)
☎: +34 630 901 094 - Fax: +34 958 252 297
www.marquesdecasapardiñas.com
info@spiracp.es

SPIRA VENDIMIA SELECCIONADA 2011 T
tempranillo, cabernet sauvignon

91 Colour: bright cherry. Nose: ripe fruit, creamy oak, fruit expression. Palate: flavourful, fruity, toasty, good acidity.

SPIRA VENDIMIA SELECCIONADA 2012 T
80% tempranillo, 20% cabernet sauvignon

92 Colour: deep cherry, purple rim. Nose: fresh fruit, red berry notes, balsamic herbs, spicy. Palate: fruity, fresh, ripe fruit, balsamic.

NESTARES RINCÓN WINES & FOODS, S.L.

Finca Juan de Reyes, s/n Contraviesa (GR-5204) del Haza del Lino a Cádiar, km-4
18430 Torvizcón (Granada)
☎: +34 655 959 500
www.alpujarride.com
info@alpujarride.com

NESTARES RINCÓN 1.0 2012
tempranillo, merlot, syrah

90 Colour: cherry, purple rim. Nose: red berry notes, ripe fruit, earthy notes, balsamic herbs, spicy. Palate: powerful, flavourful, balsamic.

PAGO DE ALMARAES

Ctra. Fonelas, Km. 1
18510 Benalúa (Granada)
☎: +34 958 348 752
www.bodegaspagodealmaraes.es
info@bodegaspagodealmaraes.es

MEMENTO 2009 T
tempranillo, merlot, cabernet sauvignon, syrah

89 Colour: cherry, garnet rim. Nose: powerfull, fruit preserve, scrubland, creamy oak. Palate: powerful, flavourful, spicy, long.

MENCAL 2012 B
moscatel, sauvignon blanc, chardonnay

85 Colour: bright straw. Nose: fresh, fresh fruit, white flowers. Palate: flavourful, fruity, good acidity, correct.

RIBERA DEL FARBES 2012 T
syrah, tempranillo

86 Colour: cherry, purple rim. Nose: expressive, red berry notes, floral, balsamic herbs. Palate: flavourful, fruity, good acidity.

VINO DE CALIDAD / D.O.P. ISLAS CANARIAS

VIÑEDOS Y BODEGAS AGUERE

38280 Tegueste (Santa Cruz de Tenerife)
☎: +34 637 372 458
www.vinosblessed.com
bodega@vinosblesses.com

BLESSED 2012 T
syrah

87 Colour: black cherry, purple rim. Nose: ripe fruit, medium intensity, spicy. Palate: flavourful, fruity, round tannins.

BLESSED CUVÉE DON TOMÁS 2012 T
syrah, tintilla

89 Colour: very deep cherry, cherry, purple rim. Nose: powerfull, ripe fruit, spicy, dried herbs. Palate: flavourful, round tannins, long.

BODEGA TAJINASTE

El Ratiño, 5 La Habanera
38315 La Orotava (Santa Cruz de Tenerife)
☎: +34 922 308 720 - Fax: +34 922 105 080
www.tajinaste.net
bodega@tajinaste.net

TAJINASTE 2012 B
listán blanco, albillo

85 Colour: yellow, pale. Nose: dried herbs, ripe fruit, balanced, citrus fruit. Palate: flavourful, good finish.

TAJINASTE AFRUTADO 2012 B
listán blanco, moscatel

84

VINO DE CALIDAD / D.O.P. DE LOS VALLES DE BENAVENTE

BODEGA EL TESORO

Camino Viñas, s/n
49622 Brime de Urz (Zamora)
☎: +34 636 982 233
bodega_el_tesoro@terra.com

PETAVONIUM 2009 TC
prieto picudo

87 Colour: cherry, garnet rim. Nose: fruit preserve, balsamic herbs, creamy oak. Palate: spicy, toasty, flavourful.

BODEGAS OTERO

Avda. El Ferial, 22
49600 Benavente (Zamora)
☎: +34 980 631 600 - Fax: +34 980 631 722
www.bodegasotero.es
info@bodegasotero.es

OTERO 2008 TR
prieto picudo

87 Colour: cherry, garnet rim. Nose: ripe fruit, spicy, creamy oak, balsamic herbs. Palate: powerful, flavourful, long, balanced.

OTERO 2009 TC
prieto picudo

86 Colour: cherry, garnet rim. Nose: ripe fruit, spicy, creamy oak. Palate: powerful, flavourful, toasty, round tannins.

VALLEOSCURO 2012 B
verdejo

86 Colour: bright straw, greenish rim. Nose: medium intensity, ripe fruit, dried herbs. Palate: flavourful, fruity, good finish.

VALLEOSCURO PRIETO PICUDO 2012 RD
prieto picudo

88 Colour: rose, purple rim. Nose: dried flowers, red berry notes. Palate: fruity, flavourful, long, balanced.

VALLEOSCURO PRIETO PICUDO TEMPRANILLO 2012 RD
prieto picudo, tempranillo

87 Colour: rose, bright. Nose: balanced, red berry notes, ripe fruit. Palate: fruity, correct, balanced.

VALLEOSCURO PRIETO PICUDO TEMPRANILLO 2012 T
prieto picudo, tempranillo

88 Colour: cherry, purple rim. Nose: expressive, fresh fruit, red berry notes, floral. Palate: flavourful, fruity, good acidity.

VINO DE CALIDAD / D.O.P. DE SIERRA DE SALAMANCA
CÁMBRICO

Paraje El Guijarral
37658 Villanueva del Conde (Salamanca)
☎: +34 923 281 006 - Fax: +34 923 213 605
www.cambrico.com
alberto@cambrico.com

575 UVAS DE CÁMBRICO 2009 T
58% tempranillo, 35% rufete, 7% garnacha

90 Colour: cherry, garnet rim. Nose: ripe fruit, spicy, creamy oak, toasty, complex. Palate: powerful, flavourful, toasty, round tannins.

VIÑAS DEL CÁMBRICO 2011 T
55% tempranillo, 36% rufete, 9% garnacha

91 Colour: cherry, garnet rim. Nose: red berry notes, ripe fruit, balsamic herbs, sweet spices, mineral. Palate: powerful, flavourful, spicy, balanced.

ROCHAL

Salas Pombo, 17
37670 Santibáñez de la Sierra (Salamanca)
☎: +34 923 435 260 - Fax: +34 923 435 260
www.bodegasrochal.com
info@bodegasrochal.com

ZAMAYÓN 2012 T
rufete

86 Colour: cherry, purple rim. Nose: fruit expression, violet drops, medium intensity, macerated fruit. Palate: fruity, correct.

ZAMAYÓN CALIXTO NIETO 2010 T
rufete, tempranillo

90 Colour: cherry, garnet rim. Nose: red berry notes, ripe fruit, wild herbs, dry stone, spicy, creamy oak. Palate: powerful, flavourful, fruity, spicy, long.

ZAMAYÓN OSIRIS 2010 T
rufete, tempranillo

88 Colour: cherry, garnet rim. Nose: ripe fruit, dried herbs. Palate: balanced, good acidity, round tannins.

VINOS LA ZORRA

San Pedro, s/n
37610 Mogarraz (Salamanca)
☎: +34 923 418 042 - Fax: +34 923 418 018
www.vinoslazorra.es
estanverdes@vinoslazorra.es

LA CABRAS PINTÁS 2012 T
rufete, tempranillo, garnacha

89 Colour: cherry, purple rim. Nose: red berry notes, ripe fruit, spicy, balsamic herbs, floral, earthy notes. Palate: rich, powerful, flavourful, balanced.

LA VIEJA ZORRA 2010 T ROBLE
rufete, tempranillo, garnacha

93 Colour: cherry, garnet rim. Nose: ripe fruit, spicy, creamy oak, toasty, balsamic herbs, mineral. Palate: powerful, flavourful, toasty, round tannins, elegant.

LA ZORRA 2012 T
rufete, tempranillo

90 Colour: bright cherry, purple rim. Nose: ripe fruit, sweet spices, creamy oak, dry stone. Palate: flavourful, fruity, toasty.

LA ZORRA BLANCA 2012 B
palomino, moscatel grano menudo

88 Colour: bright yellow. Nose: powerfull, ripe fruit, sweet spices, creamy oak, fragrant herbs. Palate: rich, flavourful, fresh.

VINO DE CALIDAD / D.O.P. VALTIENDAS
BODEGA VIÑA SANCHA

Coto de Cárdaba, s/n
40314 Valtiendas (Segovia)
☎: +34 947 500 428 - Fax: +34 947 502 866
www.fincacardaba.com
info@fincacardaba.com

VIÑA SANCHA FINCA CÁRDABA 2012 RD
100% tempranillo

87 Colour: raspberry rose. Nose: powerfull, ripe fruit, red berry notes, floral, expressive. Palate: powerful, fruity, fresh.

BODEGAS VAGAL

La Fuente, 19
40314 Valtiendas (Segovia)
☎: +34 921 527 331 - Fax: +34 921 527 332
www.vagal.com
jose.vagal@gmail.com

VAGAL CUVÉE JOANA 2012 T
100% tinta del país

89 Colour: bright cherry, purple rim. Nose: ripe fruit, sweet spices, creamy oak, expressive. Palate: flavourful, fruity, toasty, round tannins.

VAGAL FE 2012 RD
100% tinta del país

88 Colour: dark-red cherry. Nose: powerfull, ripe fruit, red berry notes, expressive, fragrant herbs. Palate: powerful, fruity, fresh, rich.

VAGAL PAGO ARDALEJOS 2010 T
100% tinta del país

92 Colour: cherry, garnet rim. Nose: ripe fruit, spicy, creamy oak, toasty, balsamic herbs, mineral. Palate: powerful, flavourful, toasty.

SANZ Y NÚÑEZ S.L.

Ctra. de Valladolid - Soria, 40 H
47300 Peñafiel (Valladolid)
☎: +34 689 432 081
dominiodeperoleja@hotmail.es

DOMINIO DE PEROLEJA 2011 T ROBLE
tempranillo

90 Colour: bright cherry. Nose: sweet spices, creamy oak, characterful, balsamic herbs. Palate: flavourful, fruity, toasty, round tannins.

The number of "Vino de la Tierra" categories granted so far, 45, means the status is growing in importance, given that growers are only required to specify geographical origin, grape variety and alcohol content. For some, it means an easy way forward for their more experimental projects, difficult to be contemplated by the stern regulations of the designations of origin, as it is the case of vast autonomous regions such as La Mancha, Castilla y León or Extremadura. For the great majority, it is a category able to fostering vineyards with high quality potential, a broader varietal catalogue and therefore the opportunity to come up with truly singular wines, a sort of sideway entrance to the DO status.

The different "Vino de la Tierra" designations have been listed in alphabetical order.

In theory, the "Vino de la Tierra" status is one step below that of the DO, and it is the Spanish equivalent to the French "Vins de Pays", which pioneered worldwide this sort of category. In Spain, however, it has some unique characteristics. For example, the fact that the designation "Vino de la Tierra" is not always the ultimate goal, but it is rather used as a springboard to achieve the highly desired DO category. In addition, as it has happened in other countries, many producers have opted for this type of association with less stringent regulations that allow them greater freedom to produce wine. Therefore, in this section there is a bit of everything: from great wines to more simple and ordinary examples, a broad catalogue that works as a sort of testing (and tasting!) field for singularity as well as for new flavours and styles derived from the use of local, autochthonous varieties.

The new Spanish Ley del Vino (Wine Law) maintains the former status of "Vino de la Tierra", but establishes an intermediate step between this and the DO one. They are the so-called 'Vinos de Calidad con Indicación Geográfica' (Quality Wines with Geographical Indication), under which the region in question must remain for a minimum of five years.

In the light of the tasting carried out for this section, there is a steady improvement in the quality of these wines, as well as fewer misgivings on the part of the wineries about the idea of joining these associations.

VT / I.G.P.3 RIBERAS
Granted by the administration at the end of 2008 for the wines produced and within the "3 Riberas" geographical indication. The different typologies are: rosé, white, red and noble wines.

VT / I.G.P.ABANILLA
This small wine region comprises the municipalities of Abanilla and Fortuna –in the eastern part of the province of Murcia– and some 1500 hectares, although most of its production is sold to the neighbouring DO Alicante. The region enjoys a hot, dry climate, limestone soils and low rainfall, features all that account for good quality prospects, although there are some differences to be found between the northern and the southern areas within it, given the different altitudes. The grape varieties allowed in the region for red winemaking are: *bonicaire, cabernet sauvignon, forcallat tinta, garnacha tintorera, merlot, petit verdot, crujidera* and *syrah*. For white wines, we find *chardonnay, malvasía, moravia dulce, moscatel de grano menudo* and *sauvignon blanc*.

VT / I.G.P.ALTIPLANO DE SIERRA NEVADA
With the goal to free Granada's geographical indication exclusively for the "Vino de Calidad" category, in 2009 the VT I.G.P.Norte de Granada changed its name to VT I.G.P.Altiplano de Sierra Nevada. The new geographical indication comprises 43 municipalities in the north of the province of Granada. The authorized grape varieties for white wine production in the region are *chardonnay, baladí verdejo, airen, torrontés, palomino, pedro ximénez, macabeo and sauvignon blanc*; also *tempranillo, monastrell, garnacha tinta, cabernet franc, cabernet sauvignon, pinot noir, merlot*, and *syrah* for red wines.

VT / I.G.P. BAILÉN

Bailén wine region comprises 350 hectares in some municipal districts within the province of Jaén but fairly close to La Mancha. Wines are made mainly from the grape variety known as "*molinera de Bailén*", that cannot be found anywhere else in the world, but also from other red grape varieties such as *garnacha tinta*, *tempranillo* and *cabernet sauvignon*, as well as the white *pedro ximénez*.

VT / I.G.P. BAJO ARAGÓN

The most "mediterranean" region within Aragón autonomous community, it borders three different provinces (Tarragona, Castellón and Teruel) and is divided in four areas: Campo de Belchite, Bajo Martín, Bajo Aragón and Matarraña. Soils are mainly clay and limestone in nature, very rich in minerals with high potash content. The climate is suitable for the right maturation of the grapes, with the added cooling effect of the 'Cierzo' (northerly wind), together with the day-night temperature contrast, just the perfect combination for the vines. The main varieties are *garnacha* (both red and white), although foreign grapes like *syrah*, *cabernet sauvignon*, *merlot* and *chardonnay* are also present, as well as *tempranillo* and *cariñena*.
www.vinodelatierradelbajoaragon.com

VT / I.G.P. BARBANZA E IRIA

The last geographical indication to be granted to the autonomous region of Galicia back in 2007, Barbanza e Iria is located within the Ribera de la Ría de Arosa wine region, in the north of the province of Pontevedra. They make both red an white wines from with varieties such as *albariño*, *caíño blanco*, *godello*, *loureiro blanco* (also known as *marqués*), *treixadura* and *torrontés* (white); and *brancellao*, *caíño tinto*, *espadeiro*, *loureiro tinto*, *mencía* and *susón* (red).

VT / I.G.P. BETANZOS

Betanzos, in the province of La Coruña, became the second VT I.G.P. designation to be granted in Galicia. The vineyards is planted with local white varieties like *blanco legítimo*, *Agudelo* (*godello*) and *jerez*, as well as red grapes like *garnacha*, *mencía* and *tempranillo*.

VT / I.G.P. CÁDIZ

Located in the south of the province of Cádiz, a vast region with a long history of wine production, the "Vinos de la Tierra de Cádiz" comprises 15 municipalities still under the regulations of the DO regarding grape production, but not

winemaking. The authorised white varieties are: *garrido*, *palomino*, *chardonnay*, *moscatel*, *mantúa*, *perruno*, *macabeo*, *sauvignon blanc* y *pedro ximénez*, as well as the red *tempranillo*, *syrah*, *cabernet sauvignon*, *garnacha tinta*, *monastrel*, *merlot*, *tintilla de rota*, *petit verdot* and *cabernet franc*.

VT / I.G.P. CAMPO DE CARTAGENA

Campo de Cartagena is a flatland region close to the Mediterranean Sea and surrounded by mountains of a moderate height. The vineyard surface ascribed to the VT I.G.P. is just 8 hectares. The climate is mediterranean bordering on an arid, desert type, with very hot summers, mild temperatures for the rest of the year, and low and occasional rainfall. The main varieties in the region are *bonicaire*, *forcallat tinta*, *petit verdot*, *tempranillo*, *garnacha tintorera*, *crujidera*, *merlot*, *syrah* and *cabernet sauvignon* (red); and *chardonnay*, *malvasía*, *moravia dulce*, *moscatel de grano menudo* and *sauvignon blanc* (white).

VT / I.G.P. CASTELLÓ

Located in the eastern part of Spain, on the Mediterranean coast, the geographical indication Vinos de la Tierra de Castelló is divided in two different areas: Alto Palancia –Alto Mijares, Sant Mateu and Les Useres–, and Vilafamés. The climatic conditions in this wine region are good to grow varieties such as *tempranillo*, *monastrell*, *garnacha*, *garnacha tintorera*, *cabernet sauvignon*, *merlot* and *syrah* (red), along with *macabeo* and *merseguera* (white).
www.vinosdecastellon.com

VT / I.G.P. CASTILLA Y LEÓN

Another one of the regional 'macro-designations' for the wines produced in up to 317 municipalities within the autonomous region of Castilla y León. A continental climate with little rainfall, together with diverse soil patterns, are the most distinctive features of a region that can be divided into the Duero basin (part of the Spanish central high plateau) and the mountainous perimeter that surrounds it.
www.asovintcal.com

VT / I.G.P. CASTILLA

Castilla-La Mancha, a region that has the largest vineyard surface in the planet (600.000 hectares, equivalent to 6% of the world's total vineyard surface, and to half of Spain's) has been using this Vino de la Tierra label since 1999 (the year the status was granted) for wines produced outside its designations of origin. The main grape varieties are *airén*, *albillo*, *chardonnay*, *macabeo* (*viura*), *malvar*, *sauvignon blanc*, *merseguera*, *moscatel de grano menudo*, *pardillo* (*marisancho*), *Pedro Ximénez* and *torrontés* (white);and *bobal*, *cabernet sauvignon*, *garnacha tinta*, *merlot*, *monastrell*, *petit verdot*, *syrah*, *tempranillo*, *cencibel* (*jacivera*), *coloraíllo*, *frasco*, *garnacha tintorera*, *moravia agria*, *moravia dulce* (*crujidera*), *negral* (tinto basto) and *tinto velasco* (red).

VT / I.G.P.CÓRDOBA
It includes the wines produced in the province of Córdoba, with the exception of those bottled within the DO Montilla-Moriles label. All in all, we are talking of some 300 hectares and red and rosé wines made from *cabernet sauvignon*, *merlot*, *syrah*, *tempranillo*, *pinot noir* and *tintilla de Rota* grape varieties.

VT / I.G.P.COSTA DE CANTABRIA
Wines produced in the Costa de Cantabria wine region as well as some inland valleys up to an altitude of 600 meters. The grape varieties used for white winemaking are *godello*, *albillo*, *chardonnay*, *malvasía*, *ondarribi zuri*, *picapoll blanco* and *verdejo blanco*; and just two for red wines: *ondarribi beltza* and *verdejo negro*. The region comprises some 8 hectares of vineyards.

VT / I.G.P.CUMBRES DE GUADALFEO
Formerly known as "Vino de la Tierra de Contraviesa-Alpujarra", this geographical indication is used for wines made in the wine region located in the western part of the Alpujarras, in a border territory between two provinces (Granada and Almería), two rivers (Guadalfeo and Andarax), and very close to the Mediterranean Sea. The grape varieties used for white wine production are *montúa*, *chardonnay*, *sauvignon blanc*, *moscatel*, *jaén blanca*, *Pedro Ximénez*, *vijirego* y *perruno*; for red wines, they have *garnacha tinta*, *tempranillo*, *cabernet sauvignon*, *cabernet franc*, *merlot*, *pinot noir* and *syrah*.

VT / I.G.P.DESIERTO DE ALMERÍA
Granted in the summer of 2003, the wine region comprises a diverse territory in the north of the province of Almería that includes the Tabernas Dessert as well as parts of the Sierra de Alhamilla, Sierra de Cabrera and the Cabo de Gata Natural Park. Harsh, climatic desert conditions follow a regular pattern of hot days and cooler nights that influence heavily the character of the resulting wines. The vineyard's average altitude is 525

meters. The varieties planted are *chardonnay*, *moscatel*, *macabeo* and *sauvignon blanc* (white); as well as *tempranillo*, *cabernet sauvignon*, *monastrell*, *merlot*, *syrah* and *garnacha tinta* (red). **www.vinosdealmeria.es/zonas-viticolas/desierto-de-almeria**

VT / I.G.P.EIVISSA
The production area includes the entire island of Ibiza (Eivissa), with the vineyards located in small valleys amongst the mountains –which are never higher than 500 meters– on clay-reddish soil covered by a thin limestone crust. Low rainfall levels and hot, humid summers are the most interesting climatic features. The authorized red varieties are *monastrell*, *tempranillo*, *cabernet sauvignon*, *merlot* and *syrah*; *macabeo*, *parellada*, *malvasía*, *chardonnay* and *moscatel* make up the white-grape catalogue.

VT/ I.G.P.EXTREMADURA
It comprises all the municipalities within the provinces of Cáceres and Badajoz, made up of six different wine regions. In December 1990, the regional government approved the regulations submitted by the Comisión Interprofesional de Vinos de la Tierra de Extremadura, and approved its creation. The varieties used for the production of white wines are *alarije*, *borba*, *cayetana blanca*, *chardonnay*, *chelva*, *malvar*, *viura*, *parellada*, *Pedro Ximénez* and *verdejo*; for red wines, they have *bobal*, *mazuela*, *monastrell*, *tempranillo*, *garnacha*, *graciano*, *merlot*, *syrah* and *cabernet sauvignon*.

VT / I.G.P.FORMENTERA
This geographical indication comprises the wines produced in the island of Formentera. The dry, subtropical mediterranean climate, characterised by abundant sunshine hours and summers with high temperatures and humidity levels but little rainfall, evidently requires grape varieties well adapted to this type of weather. Red varieties are *monastrell*, *fogoneu*, *tempranillo*, *cabernet sauvignon* and *merlot*; *malvasía*, *premsal blanco*, *chardonnay* and *viognier* make up its white-grape catalogue.

VT / I.G.P.GÁLVEZ
Gálvez wine region, located in the province of Toledo, comprises nine municipalities: Cuerva, Gálvez, Guadamur, Menasalvas, Mazambraz, Polán, Pulgar, San Martín de Montalbán and Totanes. The authorized grape varieties are *tempranillo* and *garnacha tinta*.

VT / I.G.P. ILLA DE MENORCA

The island of Menorca, a Biosphere Reserve, has a singular topography of gentle slopes; marl soils with a complex substratum of limestone, sandstone and slate, a mediterranean climate and northerly winter winds are the most significant features from a viticultural point of view. The wines produces in the island should be made exclusively from white grape varieties like *chardonnay*, *macabeo*, *malvasía*, *moscatel*, *parellada* or *moll*; as for the red renderings, *cabernet sauvignon*, *merlot*, *monastrell*, *tempranillo* and *syrah* get clearly the upper hand.

VT / I.G.P. LADERAS DE GENIL

Formerly known (up to 2009) as VT I.G.P. Granada Suroeste, the label includes some 53 municipalities in the province of Granada. The region enjoys a unique microclimate very suitable for grape growing, given its low rainfall and the softening effect of the Mediterranean Sea. The white grape varieties used for wine production are *vijiriego*, *macabeo*, Pedro Ximénez, *palomino*, *moscatel de Alejandría*, *chardonnay* and *sauvignon blanc*; as well as the red *garnacha tinta*, *perruna*, *tempranillo*, *cabernet sauvignon*, *merlot*, *syrah* and *pinot noir*, predominantly.

VT / I.G.P. LAUJAR-ALPUJARRA

This wine region is located at an altitude of 800 to 1500 meters between the Sierra de Gádor and the Sierra Nevada Natural Park. It has some 800 hectares of vines grown on terraces. Soils are chalk soils poor in organic matter, rocky and with little depth. The climate is moderately continental, given the sea influence and its high night-day temperature differential. The predominant grape varieties are *jaén blanco*, *macabeo*, *vijiriego*, Pedro Ximénez, *chardonay* and *moscatel de grano menudo* (white); and *cabernet sauvignon*, *merlot*, monastrell, *tempranillo*, *garnachas tinta* and *syrah* (red).
www.vinosdealmeria.es/bodegas/vino-de-la-tierra-laujar-alpujarra

VT / I.G.P. LIÉBANA

VT I.G.P. Liébana includes the municipalities of Potes, Pesagüero, Cabezón de Liébana, Camaleño, Castro Cillorigo y Vega de Liébana, all of them within the area of Liébana, located in the southwest of the Cantabria bordering with Asturias, León and Palencia. The authorized varieties are *mencía*, *tempranillo*, *garnacha*, *garciano*, *merlot*, *syrah*, *pinot noir*, *albarín negro* and *cabernet sauvignon* (red); and *palomino*, *godello*, *verdejo*, *albillo*, *chardonnay* and *albarín blanco* (white).

VT / I.G.P. LOS PALACIOS

Los Palacios is located in the south-western part of the province of Sevilla, by the lower area of the Guadalquivir river valley. The wines included in this VT I.G.P. are white wines made from *airén*, *chardonnay*, *colombard* and *sauvignon blanc*.

VT / I.G.P. MALLORCA

The production area of VT I.G.P. Mallorca includes all the municipalities within the island, which has predominantly limestone soils with abundant clay and sandstone, and a mediterranean climate with mild temperatures all-year-round. Red varieties present in the island are *callet*, *manto negro*, *cabernet sauvignon*, *fogoneu*, *merlot*, *monastrell*, *syrah*, *tempranillo* and *pinot noir*; along with the white *prensal* (*moll*), *chardonnay*, *macabeo*, *malvasía*, *moscatel de Alejandría*, *moscatel de grano menudo*, *parellada*, *riesling* and *sauvignon blanc*.

VT / I.G.P. NORTE DE ALMERÍA

The Vinos de la Tierra Norte de Almería label comprises four municipalities in the Norte de Almería area, right in the north of the province. They produce white, red and rosé wines from grape varieties such as *airén*, *chardonnay*, *macabeo* and *sauvignon blanc* (white); as well as *cabernet sauvignon*, *merlot*, *monastrell*, *tempranillo* and *syrah* for red winemaking and *tempranillo* and *monastrell* for rosé.

VT / I.G.P. POZOHONDO

The regulations for VT I.G.P. Pozoblanco were approved by the autonomous government of Castilla-La Mancha in the year 2000. It comprises the municipalities of Alcadozo, Peñas de San Pedro and Pozohondo, all of them in the province of Albacete.

VT / I.G.P. RIBERA DEL ANDARAX

The Ribera del Andarax wine region is located in the middle area of the Andarax river valley at an altitude of 700 to 900 meters. Soils are varied in structure, with abundant slate, clay and sand. It enjoys an extreme mediterranean climate, with low occasional rainfall and high average temperatures. The grape varieties present in the region are predominantly *macabeo*,

chardonnay and *sauvignon blanc* (white); and *cabernet sauvignon*, *merlot*, *syrah*, *garnacha*, *tempranillo*, *monastrell* and *pinot noir* (red).
www.vinosdealmeria.es/zonas-viticolas/ribera-de-andarax

VT / I.G.P. RIBERA DEL GÁLLEGO-CINCO VILLAS

Ribera del Gállego-Cinco Villas wine region is located in the territory along the Gállego river valley until it almost reaches the city of Zaragoza. Although small, its vineyards are shared between the provinces of Huesca and Zaragoza. Soils are mostly gravel in structure, which affords good drainage. The grape varieties used for wine production are *garnacha*, *tempranillo*, *carbernet sauvignon* and *merlot* (red), and mostly *macabeo* for white wines.
www.vinosdelatierradearagon.es

VT / I.G.P. RIBERA DEL JILOCA

Ribera del Jiloca, located in the south-eastern part of Aragón along the Jiloca river valley, is a wine region with a great winemaking potential, given its geo-climatic conditions. Vines are mostly planted on slate terraces perched on the slopes of the Sistema Ibérico mountain range, at high altitude, something that affords wines of great quality and singularity. Vines are planted mostly on alluvial limestone terraces of ancient river beds. *Garnacha* is the predominant grape, followed by *macabeo*. A dry climate, abundant sunlight hours and cold winters are the features that account for the excellent quality of the local grapes.
www.vinosdelatierradearagon.es/empresas/ribera_del_jiloca.php

VT / I.G.P. RIBERA DEL QUEILES

Up to sixteen municipalities from two different provinces (seven from Navarra and nine from Zaragoza) are part of the VT I.G.P. Ribera del Queiles. Wines are exclusively red, made from *cabernet sauvignon*, *graciano*, *garnacha tinta*, *merlot*, *tempranillo* and *syrah*. It has a regulating and controlling body (Comité Regulador de Control y Certificación) and so far just one winery.
www.vinosdelatierradearagon.es

VT / I.G.P. SERRA DE TRAMUNTANA-COSTA NORD

Currently, this VT I.G.P. comprises 41,14 hectares an up to eighteen municipal districts in the island of Mallorca, between the cape of Formentor and the southwest coast of Andratx, with mainly brownish-grey and limestone soils. Single-variety wines from *malvasía*, *moscatel*, *moll*, *parellada*, *macabeo*, *chardonnay* and *sauvignon blanc* (white), as well as *cabernet sauvignon*, *merlot*, *syrah*, *monastrell*, *tempranillo*, *callet* and *manto negro* (red) stand out.

VT / I.G.P. I.G.P. SIERRA DE ALCARAZ

The Sierra del Alcaraz wine region comprises the municipal districts of Alcaraz, El Ballestero, El Bonillo, Povedilla, Robledo, and Viveros, located in the western part of the province of Albacete, bordering with Ciudad Real. The VT I.G.P. status was granted by the autonomous government of Castilla-La Mancha in the year 2000. The red varieties planted in the region are *cabernet sauvignon*, *merlot*, *bobal*, *monastrell*, *garnacha tinta* and *garnacha tintorera*; along with white *moravia dulce*, *chardonnay*, *chelva*, *eva*, *alarije*, *malvar*, *borba*, *parellada*, *cayetana blanca* and *Pedro Ximénez*.

VT / I.G.P. SIERRA DE LAS ESTANCIAS Y LOS FILABRES

Located in the namesake mountain region in the province of Almería, this VT I.G.P. was approved along with its regulations in 2008. The grape varieties planted in the region are *airén*, *chardonnay*, *macabeo*, *sauvignon blanc* and *moscatel de grano menudo* –also known as morisco–, all of them white; and red *cabernet sauvignon*, *merlot*, *monastrell*, *tempranillo*, *syrah*, *garnacha tinta*, *pinot noir* and *petit verdot*.

VT / I.G.P. SIERRA NORTE DE SEVILLA

This region, located in the north of the province of Sevilla at the foothills of Sierra Morena, has a landscape of gentle hills and altitudes that range from 250 to almost 1000 metres. The climate in the region is mediterranean, with hot, dry summers, mild winters and a fairly high average rainfall. Since 1998, grape varieties such as *tempranillo*, *garnacha tinta*, *cabernet sauvignon*, *cabernet franc*, *merlot*, *pinot noir*, *petit verdot* and *syrah* (red); and *chardonnay*, *Pedro Ximénez*, *colombard*, *sauvignon blanc*, *palomino* and *moscatel de Alejandría* (white) have been planted in the region.

VT / I.G.P.SIERRA SUR DE JAÉN
In this VT I.G.P.there are some 400 hectares planted with vines, although a minor percentage are table grapes. The label includes wines made in the Sierra Sur de Jaén wine region. White wines are made from *jaén blanca* and *chardonnay*, and red from *garnacha tinta*, *tempranillo*, *cabernet sauvignon*, *merlot*, *syrah* and *pinot noir*.

VT / I.G.P.TORREPEROGIL
This geographical indication in the province of Jaén, whose regulations were approved in 2006, comprises 300 hectares in the area of La Loma, right in the centre of the province. The climate is mediterranean with continental influence, with cold winters and dry and hot summers. The wines are made mainly from *garnacha tinta*, *syrah*, *cabernet sauvignon* and *tempranillo* (red); and *jaén blanco* and *Pedro Ximénez* (white).

VT / I.G.P.VALDEJALÓN
Established in 1998, it comprises 36 municipal districts in the mid- and lower-Jalón river valley. The vines are planted on alluvial, brownish-grey limestone soils, with low annual average rainfall of some 350 mm. They grape varieties planted are white (*macabeo*, *garnacha blanca*, *moscatel* and *airén*) and red (*garnacha*, *tempranillo*, *cabernet sauvignon*, *syrah*, *monastrell* and *merlot*).
www.vinodelatierravaldejalon.com

VT / I.G.P.VALLE DEL CINCA
Located in the southeast of the province of Huesca, almost bordering with Catalunya, Valle del Cinca is a traditional wine region that enjoys favourable climatic and soil conditions for vine growing: soils are mainly limestone and clay, and the average annual rainfall barely reaches 300 mm (irrigation is usually required). Grape varieties predominantly planted in the region are *macabeo* and *chardonnay* (white), along with *garnacha tinta*, *tempranillo*, *cabernet sauvignon* and *merlot* (red).
www.vinosdelatierradearagon.es

VT / I.G.P.VALLE DEL MIÑO-OURENSE
This wine region is located in the north of the province of Ourense, along the Miño river valley. The authorized grape varieties are *treixadura*, *torrontés*, *godello*, *albariño*, *loureira* and *palomino* –also known as *xerez*– for white wines, and *mencía*, *brancellao*, *mouratón*, *sousón*, *caíño* and *garnacha* for reds.

VT / I.G.P.VALLES DE SADACIA
A designation created to include the wines made from the grape variety known as *moscatel riojana*, which was practically lost with the phylloxera bug and has been recuperated to produce both "vino de licor" and normal white *moscatel*. Depending on winemaking, the latter may either be dry, semi-dry or sweet. The vineyards that belong to this VT I.G.P.are mainly located in the south-western part of the region, in the Sadacia and Cidacos river valleys, overall a very suitable territory for vine growing purposes.

VT / I.G.P.VILLAVICIOSA DE CÓRDOBA
One of the most recent geographical indications granted by the autonomous government of Andalucía back in 2008, it includes white and sweet wines made in the Villaviciosa wine region. The authorized varieties are *baladí verdejo*, *moscatel de Alejandría*, *palomino fino*, *palomino*, *Pedro Ximénez*, *airén*, *calagraño Jaén*, *torrontés* and *verdejo*.

3 RIBERAS
BODEGA SAN MARTÍN S. COOP.

Ctra. de Sanguesa, s/n
31495 San Martín de Unx (Navarra)
☎: +34 948 738 294 - Fax: +34 948 738 297
www.bodegasanmartin.com
enologia@bodegasanmartin.com

FLOR DE UNX 2012 RD
100% garnacha

88 Colour: rose, purple rim. Nose: powerfull, ripe fruit, red berry notes, floral, expressive. Palate: powerful, fruity, fresh, sweetness.

ALTIPLANO DE SIERRA NEVADA
BODEGAS MUÑANA

Ctra. Graena a La Peza, s/n
18517 Cortes y Graena (Granada)
☎: +34 958 670 715 - Fax: +34 958 670 715
bodegasmunana.blogspot.com
munanaydelirio@gmail.com

MUÑANA 3 CEPAS 2009 T
syrah, cabernet sauvignon, merlot

88 Colour: cherry, garnet rim. Nose: ripe fruit, fruit preserve, scrubland, sweet spices. Palate: powerful, flavourful, long, spicy.

MUÑANA PETIT VERDOT 2009 T
100% petit verdot

87 Colour: cherry, garnet rim. Nose: ripe fruit, balsamic herbs, spicy, creamy oak, mineral. Palate: powerful, flavourful, balanced.

MUÑANA ROJO 2009 T
tempranillo, cabernet sauvignon, monastrell

89 Colour: cherry, garnet rim. Nose: ripe fruit, spicy, creamy oak, earthy notes. Palate: powerful, flavourful, toasty, round tannins.

BAJO ARAGÓN
AMPRIUS LAGAR

Los −Enebros, 74 − 2ª planta
44002 (Teruel)
☎: +34 978 623 077
www.ampriuslagar.es
pedrocasas@ampriuslagar.es

LAGAR D'AMPRIUS GARNACHA 2011 T
garnacha

88 Colour: cherry, garnet rim. Nose: spicy, creamy oak, toasty, fruit preserve. Palate: powerful, flavourful, toasty, round tannins.

LAGAR D'AMPRIUS GARNACHA SYRAH 2010 T
syrah, garnacha

87 Colour: very deep cherry. Nose: powerfull, overripe fruit, dark chocolate, toasty. Palate: powerful, ripe fruit, round tannins.

BODEGA COOP. NTRA. SRA. DEL OLIVAR

Avda. José Antonio, 18
50131 Lecera (Zaragoza)
☎: +34 976 835 016
www.valssira.es
valssira@bodegasvalssira.es

VALSSIRA 12 2010 T
garnacha

86 Colour: pale ruby, brick rim edge. Nose: fruit preserve, balsamic herbs, damp earth, spicy, fine reductive notes. Palate: powerful, flavourful, spicy, long.

VALSSIRA 2012 B

82

VALSSIRA 2012 RD
garnacha

88 Colour: rose, purple rim. Nose: powerfull, red berry notes, floral, expressive, ripe fruit. Palate: powerful, fruity, fresh.

VALSSIRA 2012 T
garnacha

88 Colour: cherry, garnet rim. Nose: scrubland, wild herbs, red berry notes, fruit liqueur notes. Palate: powerful, flavourful, balanced.

VALSSIRA 2012 T FERMENTADO EN BARRICA
garnacha

86 Colour: bright cherry. Nose: ripe fruit, sweet spices, creamy oak. Palate: flavourful, fruity, toasty.

VALSSIRA 24 MESES BARRICA 2009 T
garnacha

86 Colour: cherry, garnet rim. Nose: spicy, fine reductive notes, wet leather, aged wood nuances, fruit liqueur notes. Palate: spicy, long, ripe fruit.

BODEGAS CRIAL LLEDÓ

Arrabal de la Fuente, 23
44624 Lledó (Teruel)
☎: +34 978 891 909 - Fax: +34 978 891 995
www.crial.es
crial@bodegascrial.com

CRIAL 2012 B
garnacha blanca, macabeo

86 Colour: bright straw. Nose: fresh, fresh fruit, white flowers. Palate: flavourful, fruity, good acidity, balanced.

CRIAL 2012 RD
garnacha

84

CRIAL 2012 T
50% garnacha, 25% syrah, 25% cabernet sauvignon

86 Colour: cherry, purple rim. Nose: red berry notes, fruit liqueur notes, scrubland. Palate: powerful, flavourful, spicy.

CRIAL LLEDÓ 2009 TC
85% cabernet sauvignon, 15% garnacha

87 Colour: cherry, garnet rim. Nose: ripe fruit, spicy, creamy oak, toasty, complex. Palate: powerful, flavourful, toasty.

CELLER D'ALGARS

Cooperativa, 9
44622 Arenys De Lledó (Teruel)
☎: +34 978 853 147 - Fax: +34 978 853 147
www.enigmma.es
info@cellerdalgars.com

DOS TIERRAS 2010 T
garnacha, syrah, cabernet sauvignon

87 Colour: cherry, garnet rim. Nose: ripe fruit, spicy, creamy oak, toasty, fragrant herbs. Palate: powerful, flavourful, toasty, spicy.

MUSAS 2012 B
garnacha blanca, chenin blanc, macabeo

89 Colour: bright straw. Nose: fresh fruit, tropical fruit, white flowers, fragrant herbs. Palate: fresh, fruity, light-bodied, easy to drink.

PUNTA ESTE 2011 T
syrah, garnacha, cabernet sauvignon

86 Colour: bright cherry. Nose: ripe fruit, sweet spices, creamy oak. Palate: flavourful, fruity, toasty.

VIRTUTIS CAUSA 2007 T
syrah, garnacha, cabernet sauvignon

89 Colour: pale ruby, brick rim edge. Nose: spicy, fine reductive notes, wet leather, aged wood nuances, fruit liqueur notes. Palate: long, ripe fruit, balsamic.

DOMINIO MAESTRAZGO

Royal III, B12
44550 Alcorisa (Teruel)
☎: +34 978 840 642 - Fax: +34 978 840 642
www.dominiomaestrazgo.com
bodega@dominiomaestrazgo.com

DOMINIO MAESTRAZGO 2011 T ROBLE
garnacha, tempranillo, syrah

89 Colour: cherry, garnet rim. Nose: fruit preserve, wild herbs, sweet spices, creamy oak. Palate: rich, powerful, flavourful, long.

DOMINIO MAESTRAZGO GARNACHA BLANCA 2012 B
garnacha blanca

84

DOMINIO MAESTRAZGO SYRAH 2011 T BARRICA
syrah

88 Colour: cherry, garnet rim. Nose: sweet spices, creamy oak, violet drops. Palate: flavourful, fruity, toasty, round tannins.

REX DEUS 2010 T ROBLE
garnacha, syrah

92 Colour: cherry, garnet rim. Nose: ripe fruit, spicy, creamy oak, toasty, fine reductive notes, mineral. Palate: powerful, flavourful, toasty, round tannins.

SANTOLEA 2012 T
garnacha, tempranillo

86 Colour: cherry, purple rim. Nose: red berry notes, ripe fruit, floral, earthy notes. Palate: rich, flavourful, powerful.

EVOHE BODEGAS

Ignacio de Ara, 3 Local
50002 Zaragoza (Zaragoza)
☎: +34 976 461 056 - Fax: +34 976 461 558
www.evohegarnacha.com
nosotros@evohegarnacha.com

EVOHÉ GARNACHA VIÑAS VIEJAS 2012 T
garnacha

90 Colour: cherry, purple rim. Nose: red berry notes, ripe fruit, balsamic herbs. Palate: flavourful, fruity, good acidity.

MONTANER

Avda. Aragón 85
50710 Maella (Zaragoza)
☎: +34 976 638 384 - Fax: +34 976 638 384
vinosmontaner@telefonica.net

BARONO 2 2009 TC
garnacha, syrah, cabernet sauvignon

89 Colour: cherry, garnet rim. Nose: ripe fruit, spicy, creamy oak, toasty, complex. Palate: powerful, flavourful, toasty, round tannins.

BARONO 2010 T
garnacha, syrah, cabernet sauvignon

86 Colour: cherry, garnet rim. Nose: ripe fruit, spicy, creamy oak. Palate: powerful, flavourful, spicy.

BARONO 2011 TC
garnacha, syrah, cabernet sauvignon

83

FINCA MAS NOU DEL BARONO 2012 T
60% garnacha, 20% syrah, 20% cabernet sauvignon

87 Colour: cherry, purple rim. Nose: fresh fruit, red berry notes, floral. Palate: flavourful, fruity, good acidity.

VENTA D'AUBERT

Ctra. Valderrobres a Arnes, Km. 28
44623 Cretas (Teruel)
☎: +34 978 769 021 - Fax: +34 978 769 031
www.ventadaubert.com
ventadaubert@gmx.net

VENTA D'AUBERT 2005 T
merlot, syrah, cabernet sauvignon

89 Colour: pale ruby, brick rim edge. Nose: spicy, fine reductive notes, wet leather, aged wood nuances, fruit liqueur notes. Palate: spicy, elegant, long.

VENTA D'AUBERT 2012 B
chardonnay, viognier, garnacha blanca

92 Colour: bright straw. Nose: floral, fragrant herbs, fruit expression, citrus fruit, earthy notes, expressive. Palate: powerful, flavourful, long, spicy.

VENTA D'AUBERT CABERNET SAUVIGNON 2008 T
cabernet sauvignon

90 Colour: cherry, garnet rim. Nose: ripe fruit, spicy, creamy oak, balsamic herbs, dry stone. Palate: powerful, flavourful, toasty, round tannins.

VENTA D'AUBERT MERLOT 2007 T
100% merlot

86 Colour: cherry, garnet rim. Nose: fruit liqueur notes, scrubland, spicy, cigar, wet leather. Palate: flavourful, correct, spicy.

VENTA D'AUBERT VIOGNIER 2011 B
viognier

92 Colour: bright straw, greenish rim. Nose: dried flowers, ripe fruit, citrus fruit, fragrant herbs, expressive. Palate: rich, flavourful, balanced, elegant.

VENTUS 2009 TC
39% garnacha, 37% cabernet sauvignon, 8% cabernet franc, 8% merlot, 5% syrah, 3% monastrell

89 Colour: cherry, garnet rim. Nose: ripe fruit, spicy, creamy oak, dry stone, wild herbs. Palate: powerful, flavourful, toasty.

BODEGAS BARBADILLO

Luis de Eguilaz, 11
11540 Sanlúcar de Barrameda (Cádiz)
☎: +34 956 385 500 - Fax: +34 956 385 501
www.barbadillo.com
barbadillo@barbadillo.com

CASTILLO DE SAN DIEGO 2012 B
palomino

87 Colour: bright straw. Nose: fresh, fresh fruit, white flowers, medium intensity. Palate: flavourful, fruity, good acidity, balanced.

GIBALBÍN 2011 T
tempranillo, syrah, merlot, cabernet sauvignon, tintilla de rota

86 Colour: cherry, purple rim. Nose: fresh fruit, floral. Palate: flavourful, fruity, good acidity, round tannins.

GIBALBÍN 2011 TC
tempranillo, syrah, cabernet sauvignon, tintilla de rota

84

MAESTRANTE 2012 B
palomino

85 Colour: bright straw. Nose: candied fruit, citrus fruit, floral. Palate: flavourful, ripe fruit, good acidity.

BODEGAS OSBORNE

Fernán Caballero, 7
11500 El Puerto de Santa María (Cádiz)
☎: +34 956 869 000 - Fax: +34 925 869 026
www.osborne.es
carolina.cerrato@osborne.es

GADIR 2011 B
52% chardonnay, 48% palomino

82

ENTRECHUELOS

Finca Torrecera Ctra. Jerez - La Ina, Km. 14,5
11595 Torrecera (Cádiz)
☎: +34 856 030 073 - Fax: +34 856 030 033
www.entrechuelos.com
comercial@entrechuelos.com

ENTRECHUELOS 2011 T ROBLE
syrah, merlot, tempranillo, cabernet sauvignon

86 Colour: bright cherry. Nose: ripe fruit, sweet spices, creamy oak, expressive. Palate: flavourful, fruity, toasty, round tannins.

ENTRECHUELOS 2012 B
100% chardonnay

88 Colour: bright straw. Nose: fresh, fresh fruit, white flowers, expressive. Palate: flavourful, fruity, good acidity, balanced.

ENTRECHUELOS PREMIUM 2008 T
syrah, tempranillo, cabernet sauvignon, tempranillo

89 Colour: cherry, garnet rim. Nose: ripe fruit, spicy, creamy oak, toasty, complex. Palate: powerful, flavourful, toasty, round tannins.

FINCA MONCLOA

Manuel María González, 12
11403 Jerez de la Frontera (Cádiz)
☎: +34 956 357 000 - Fax: +34 956 357 043
www.gonzalezbyass.com
nacional@gonzalezbyass.com

FINCA MONCLOA 09 BARRICAS 2009 T
52,2% cabernet sauvignon, 28,3% syrah, 13% petit verdot, 6,5% tintilla de rota

93 Colour: cherry, garnet rim. Nose: ripe fruit, spicy, creamy oak, powerfull, sweet spices, roasted coffee. Palate: powerful, flavourful, toasty, round tannins.

FINCA MONCLOA 2009 T
51,9% syrah, 45,9% cabernet sauvignon, 1,6% tintilla de rota, petit verdot

92 Colour: cherry, garnet rim. Nose: spicy, creamy oak, toasty, complex, candied fruit. Palate: powerful, flavourful, toasty, round tannins.

HUERTA DE ALBALÁ

Ctra. CA - 6105, Km. 4
11630 Arcos de la Frontera (Cádiz)
☎: +34 956 101 300 - Fax: +34 856 023 053
www.huertadealbala.com
bodega@huertadealbala.com

BARBAZUL 2012 B
100% chardonnay

87 Colour: bright straw. Nose: fresh, fresh fruit, white flowers. Palate: flavourful, fruity, good acidity, balanced.

BARBAZUL 2012 RD
100% syrah

88 Colour: rose, purple rim. Nose: powerfull, ripe fruit, red berry notes, floral, expressive. Palate: powerful, fruity, fresh.

BARBAZUL 2012 T
60% syrah, 20% merlot, 15% cabernet sauvignon, 5% tintilla de rota

87 Colour: cherry, purple rim. Nose: fresh fruit, red berry notes, floral. Palate: flavourful, fruity, good acidity, round tannins.

TABERNER 2008 T
65% syrah, 25% merlot, 10% cabernet sauvignon

87 Colour: bright cherry. Nose: sweet spices, creamy oak, candied fruit, wet leather. Palate: flavourful, fruity, toasty, round tannins.

TABERNER Nº 1 2008 T
60% merlot, 40% syrah

89 Colour: cherry, garnet rim. Nose: ripe fruit, spicy, creamy oak, toasty. Palate: powerful, flavourful, toasty, round tannins.

MIGUEL DOMECQ

Finca Torrecera, Ctra. Jerez - La Ina, Km. 14,5
11595 Torrecera (Cádiz)
☎: +34 856 030 073 - Fax: +34 856 030 033
comercial@entrechuelos.com

ALHOCEN 2012 B
100% chardonnay

87 Colour: bright straw. Nose: fresh, fresh fruit, white flowers. Palate: flavourful, fruity, good acidity, balanced.

ALHOCEN SELECCIÓN PERSONAL 2008 TR
cabernet sauvignon, merlot, syrah, tempranillo

88 Colour: very deep cherry. Nose: creamy oak, dark chocolate, ripe fruit. Palate: powerful, flavourful, spicy.

ALHOCEN SYRAH MERLOT 2010 TR
merlot, syrah

89 Colour: bright cherry. Nose: ripe fruit, sweet spices, creamy oak, expressive. Palate: flavourful, fruity, toasty, round tannins.

PUERTA NUEVA S.L.

Medina, 79
11402 Jerez de la Frontera (Cádiz)
☎: +34 956 338 163 - Fax: +34 956 338 163
www.cortijodejara.com
puertanueva.sl@cortijodejara.es

CORTIJO DE JARA 2010 T
merlot, syrah, tempranillo

83

CORTIJO DE JARA 2011 T
merlot, syrah, tempranillo

83

CASTELLÓN
BODEGA LES USERES

Ctra. Vall d'AlbaLes - Les Useres, Km. 11
12118 Les Useres (Castellón)
☎: +34 964 388 525 - Fax: +34 964 338 526
www.bodegalesuseres.com
info@bodegalesuseres.es

86 WINEGROWERS 2008 TR
tempranillo, cabernet sauvignon

85 Colour: pale ruby, brick rim edge. Nose: spicy, fine reductive notes, wet leather, aged wood nuances, fruit liqueur notes. Palate: spicy, long, flavourful.

BODEGAS CASTILLO DE LA DUQUESA

Calle Mar, 116
12181 Benlloch (Castellón)
☎: +34 693 299 449 - Fax: +34 964 037 731
www.banus.eu
banuswine@gmail.com

BANÚS 2012 B
100% verdejo

86 Colour: bright yellow. Nose: ripe fruit, tropical fruit, white flowers, dried herbs. Palate: powerful, flavourful, rich.

BANÚS 2012 T
100% tempranillo

85 Colour: cherry, garnet rim. Nose: ripe fruit, fruit liqueur notes, wild herbs. Palate: powerful, rich, flavourful, easy to drink.

ILDVM CABERNET SAUVIGNON 2011 T
100% cabernet sauvignon

85 Colour: cherry, garnet rim. Nose: ripe fruit, spicy, creamy oak, green pepper. Palate: powerful, flavourful, toasty, balsamic.

ILDVM MERLOT VINO DE AUTOR 2011 T
100% merlot

89 Colour: cherry, garnet rim. Nose: ripe fruit, spicy, creamy oak, toasty, balsamic herbs, damp earth. Palate: powerful, flavourful, toasty, balanced.

ILDVM SAUVIGNON BLANC 2012 B
100% sauvignon blanc

87 Colour: bright yellow. Nose: citrus fruit, floral, wild herbs, ripe fruit. Palate: spicy, easy to drink, fresh, fruity.

ILDVM SYRAH 2011 T
100% syrah

86 Colour: bright cherry. Nose: ripe fruit, sweet spices, creamy oak, balsamic herbs. Palate: flavourful, fruity, toasty, round tannins.

ILDVM TEMPRANILLO 2011 T
100% tempranillo

87 Colour: cherry, garnet rim. Nose: ripe fruit, fruit liqueur notes, earthy notes, sweet spices, creamy oak. Palate: rich, flavourful, balsamic, spicy.

BODEGAS Y VIÑEDOS BARÓN D'ALBA

Partida Vilar la Call, 10
12118 Les Useres (Castellón)
☎: +34 608 032 884 - Fax: +34 964 313 455
www.barondalba.com
barondalba@gmail.com

CLOS D' ESGARRACORDES 2012 RD
50% monastrell, 35% garnacha, 5% syrah

81

CLOS D'ESGARRACORDES 2008 TC
40% tempranillo, 20% merlot, 30% cabernet sauvignon, 10% syrah

85 Colour: cherry, garnet rim. Nose: green pepper, grassy, toasty, fruit preserve. Palate: powerful, flavourful, balsamic.

CLOS D'ESGARRACORDES 2011 T BARRICA
50% tempranillo, 33% monastrell, 12% garnacha, 5% syrah

90 Colour: light cherry, garnet rim. Nose: red berry notes, ripe fruit, balsamic herbs, spicy, creamy oak. Palate: flavourful, balsamic, spicy, long.

CLOS D'ESGARRACORDES 2012 B
100% macabeo

85 Colour: bright straw. Nose: tropical fruit, ripe fruit, floral, dried herbs. Palate: light-bodied, fruity, easy to drink.

MASÍA DE LA HOYA

Avda. Navarro Reverter, 1
12400 Segorbe (Castellón)
☎: +34 964 710 050 - Fax: +34 964 713 484
www.masiadelahoya.com
masiadelahoya@masiadelahoya.com

MASÍA DE LA HOYA 2010 T
cabernet sauvignon, monastrell

83

MASÍA DE LA HOYA SYRAH 2009 T
syrah

84

CASTILLA
AGRÍCOLA CASA DE LA VIÑA

Ctra. de la Solana Vva de los Infantes, Km. 15,2
13248 Alhambra (Ciudad Real)
☎: +34 926 696 044
www.bodegascasadelavina.com
bodega@bodegascasadelavina.com

CASA DE LA VIÑA CHARDONNAY 2012 B
chardonnay

83

CASA DE LA VIÑA EDICIÓN LIMITADA 2009 T
tempranillo, syrah

89 Colour: cherry, purple rim. Nose: fresh fruit, red berry notes, floral, sweet spices. Palate: flavourful, fruity, good acidity, round tannins.

CASA DE LA VIÑA MERLOT 2012 RD
merlot

85 Colour: light cherry. Nose: floral, candied fruit, fragrant herbs. Palate: fresh, fruity, light-bodied, easy to drink.

CASA DE LA VIÑA SAUVIGNON BLANC 2012 B
sauvignon blanc

84

CASA DE LA VIÑA TEMPRANILLO 2008 T BARRICA
tempranillo

86 Colour: bright cherry. Nose: ripe fruit, creamy oak, lactic notes. Palate: flavourful, fruity, toasty.

CASA DE LA VIÑA TEMPRANILLO 2012 T
tempranillo

85 Colour: cherry, purple rim. Nose: floral, red berry notes, ripe fruit. Palate: flavourful, fruity, good acidity.

ALDONZA WINES

Ctra. Comarcal 313, Km. 1
2160 Lezuza (Albacete)
☎: +34 967 217 711 - Fax: +34 967 240 499
dcomercial@aldonzavinos.com

ALDONZA NAVAMARÍN 2008 TR
17% tempranillo, 35% cabernet sauvignon, 22% syrah, 26% merlot

90 Colour: cherry, garnet rim. Nose: ripe fruit, spicy, creamy oak, toasty. Palate: flavourful, spicy, toasty, round tannins.

ALDONZA SELECCIÓN 2008 T
23% tempranillo, 28% cabernet sauvignon, 24% syrah, 25% merlot

87 Colour: pale ruby, brick rim edge. Nose: fine reductive notes, wet leather, aged wood nuances, sweet spices. Palate: spicy, long, oaky.

ALENUR

Paseo de la Libertad 6 1º A
2001 Albacete (Albacete)
☎: +34 967 242 982 - Fax: +34 967 242 541
www.alenur.com
davidmolina@alenur.com

OLÉ ALENUR 2011 T
tempranillo

85 Colour: bright cherry. Nose: ripe fruit, sweet spices, creamy oak. Palate: flavourful, fruity, toasty, round tannins.

OLÉ ALENUR 2012 B
airén, sauvignon blanc

84

ALTOLANDÓN

Ctra. N-330, km. 242
16330 Landete (Cuenca)
☎: +34 962 300 662 - Fax: +34 962 300 662
www.altolandon.com
altolandon@altolandon.com

L´AME MALBEC 2010 T
100% malbec

88 Colour: cherry, garnet rim. Nose: fragrant herbs, spicy, creamy oak, overripe fruit. Palate: powerful, flavourful, spicy, balanced.

ARÚSPIDE S.L.

Ciriaco Cruz, 2
13300 Valdepeñas (Ciudad Real)
☎: +34 926 347 075 - Fax: +34 926 347 875
www.aruspide.com
info@aruspide.com

ÁGORA 2012 T MACERACIÓN CARBÓNICA
100% tempranillo

88 Colour: cherry, purple rim. Nose: expressive, fresh fruit, red berry notes, floral. Palate: flavourful, fruity, good acidity.

ÁGORA LÁGRIMA 2012 B
85% airén, 15% verdejo

84

ÁGORA VIOGNIER 2012 B
100% viognier

85 Colour: bright straw. Nose: white flowers, tropical fruit, balsamic herbs, earthy notes. Palate: fresh, fruity, easy to drink.

AUTOR DE ARÚSPIDE CHARDONNAY 2010 B
100% chardonnay

88 Colour: bright straw. Nose: floral, candied fruit, fragrant herbs, sweet spices, creamy oak. Palate: powerful, rich, fruity, flavourful.

AUTOR DE ARÚSPIDE TEMPRANILLO 2007 T
100% tempranillo

88 Colour: cherry, garnet rim. Nose: spicy, fine reductive notes, wet leather, aged wood nuances, fruit liqueur notes. Palate: spicy, long, toasty, correct.

EL LINZE 2008 T
85% syrah, 15% tinto velasco

89 Colour: cherry, garnet rim. Nose: ripe fruit, spicy, creamy oak, toasty, complex. Palate: powerful, flavourful, toasty, round tannins.

EL LINZE 2010 B
100% viognier

89 Colour: bright straw. Nose: fresh, fresh fruit, white flowers, expressive, creamy oak. Palate: flavourful, fruity, good acidity, balanced, spicy.

PURA SAVIA 2012 T
100% tempranillo

86 Colour: cherry, purple rim. Nose: ripe fruit, floral, balsamic herbs, medium intensity. Palate: powerful, flavourful, balsamic, ripe fruit.

BODEGA ABAXTERRA

CM 3200, Km. 27,5 (Ctra. de Castellar de Santiago a Torre de Juan Abad)
13343 Villamanrique (Ciudad Real)
☎: +34 635 295 098 - Fax: +34 916 925 426
www.bodegas-abaxterra.com
mcelices@gmail.com

ABAXTERRA 2011 T
tempranillo, syrah

88 Colour: cherry, garnet rim. Nose: ripe fruit, spicy, creamy oak. Palate: powerful, flavourful, toasty, round tannins.

BODEGA DEHESA DE LUNA

Ctra. CM-3106, km. 16
2630 La Roda (Albacete)
☎: +34 967 548 508 - Fax: +34 967 548 022
www.dehesadeluna.com
contacto@dehesadeluna.com

DEHESA DE LUNA 2011 T
tempranillo, cabernet sauvignon, syrah

89 Colour: cherry, garnet rim. Nose: ripe fruit, spicy, creamy oak, toasty, balsamic herbs, damp earth. Palate: powerful, flavourful, toasty.

DEHESA DE LUNA TEMPRANILLO 2011 T
tempranillo

88 Colour: cherry, garnet rim. Nose: earthy notes, powerfull, warm, overripe fruit, toasty. Palate: powerful, concentrated, fine bitter notes.

BODEGA HACIENDA LA PRINCESA

Ctra. San Carlos del Valle, km. 8 - Apdo. Correos 281
13300 Valdepeñas (Ciudad Real)
☎: +34 638 335 185
www.haciendalaprincesa.com
haciendalaprincesa@telefonica.net

HACIENDA LA PRINCESA DEBIR GALA 2008 T
100% tempranillo

88 Colour: cherry, garnet rim. Nose: fruit preserve, aged wood nuances, spicy, fine reductive notes. Palate: powerful, flavourful, balanced.

HACIENDA LA PRINCESA DEBIR SUCUNZA 2010 TC
50% merlot, 50% tempranillo

84

BODEGA LOS ALJIBES

Finca Los Aljibes
2520 Chinchilla de Montearagón (Albacete)
☎: +34 967 260 015 - Fax: +34 967 261 450
www.fincalosaljibes.com
info@fincalosaljibes.com

ALJIBES 2009 T
cabernet franc, cabernet sauvignon, merlot

90 Colour: dark-red cherry, orangey edge. Nose: ripe fruit, fragrant herbs, spicy, creamy oak, dry stone. Palate: powerful, flavourful, spicy, long.

ALJIBES CABERNET FRANC 2010 T
cabernet franc

91 Colour: cherry, garnet rim. Nose: ripe fruit, spicy, creamy oak, dry stone. Palate: powerful, flavourful, toasty, round tannins.

ALJIBES SYRAH 2010 T
syrah

90 Colour: cherry, garnet rim. Nose: ripe fruit, violet drops, balsamic herbs, earthy notes. Palate: powerful, flavourful, spicy, long, balanced.

LA GALANA 2011 TC
garnacha tintorera

89 Colour: cherry, garnet rim. Nose: ripe fruit, spicy, creamy oak, balsamic herbs. Palate: powerful, flavourful, toasty.

VIÑA ALJIBES 2011 T
cabernet sauvignon, merlot, petit verdot, garnacha tintorera

86 Colour: bright cherry. Nose: ripe fruit, sweet spices, creamy oak. Palate: flavourful, fruity, toasty.

VIÑA ALJIBES 2012 B
chardonnay, sauvignon blanc

86 Colour: bright straw. Nose: fresh, fresh fruit, white flowers, expressive. Palate: flavourful, fruity, good acidity.

VIÑA ALJIBES 2012 RD
syrah

88 Colour: rose, purple rim. Nose: powerfull, ripe fruit, red berry notes, floral, lactic notes. Palate: powerful, fruity, fresh.

BODEGA RODRÍGUEZ DE VERA

Ctra. de Pétrola, km. 3,2
2695 Chinchilla de Montearagón (Albacete)
☎: +34 696 168 873
www.rodriguezdevera.com
info@rodriguezdevera.com

RODRÍGUEZ DE VERA 2010 T
100% merlot

82

SORRASCA 2010 T
75% petit verdot, 25% merlot

85 Colour: cherry, garnet rim. Nose: ripe fruit, spicy, creamy oak, toasty, balsamic herbs. Palate: powerful, flavourful, toasty.

BODEGA ROMAILA

Ctra. Almonacid de Toledo a Nambroca s/n
45420 Almoncid de Toledo (Toledo)
☎: +34 915 416 561 - Fax: +34 915 416 562
www.romaila.es
administracion@romaila.es

FINCA ROMAILA 2008 T
syrah, tempranillo, cabernet sauvignon, graciano

88 Colour: cherry, garnet rim. Nose: ripe fruit, spicy, creamy oak, toasty, balsamic herbs. Palate: powerful, flavourful, toasty.

OH! DE ROMAILA 2011 T
syrah, tempranillo, cabernet sauvignon, graciano, petit verdot

87 Colour: bright cherry. Nose: ripe fruit, sweet spices, creamy oak, expressive. Palate: flavourful, fruity, toasty, round tannins.

BODEGAS ABANICO

Pol. Ind Ca l'Avellanet - Susany, 6
8553 Seva (Barcelona)
☎: +34 938 125 676 - Fax: +34 938 123 213
www.bodegasabanico.com
info@exportiberia.com

SINFONÍA TEMPRANILLO 2012 T
100% tempranillo

88 Colour: cherry, purple rim. Nose: expressive, fresh fruit, red berry notes, floral. Palate: flavourful, fruity, good acidity, round tannins.

BODEGAS ANHELO

Jabalón, 14
13350 Moral de Calatrava (Ciudad Real)
☎: +34 626 929 262
www.bodegasanhelo.com
j.sanchez@bodegasanhelo.com

ANHELO 2012 RD
100% tempranillo

86 Colour: rose, purple rim. Nose: powerfull, ripe fruit, red berry notes, floral, expressive. Palate: powerful, fruity, fresh.

ANHELO RIESLING 2012 B
100% riesling

87 Colour: bright straw. Nose: fresh fruit, white flowers, lactic notes, fragrant herbs. Palate: flavourful, fruity, good acidity.

ANHELO TEMPRANILLO 2011 T
100% tempranillo

83

BODEGAS BALMORAL

Mayor, 32 - 1º
2001 (Albacete)
☎: +34 967 508 382 - Fax: +34 967 235 301
www.vinedosbalmoral.com
info@vinedosbalmoral.com

EDONÉ 2010 ESP
83% chardonnay, 12% macabeo, 5% pinot noir

81

EDONÉ ROSÉ 2010 ESP
70% tempranillo, 25% syrah, 5% pinot noir

85 Colour: coppery red. Nose: ripe fruit, red berry notes. Palate: fine bitter notes, good acidity, fine bead.

MARAVIDES 2011 T
syrah, tempranillo, cabernet sauvignon, merlot

90 Colour: cherry, garnet rim. Nose: ripe fruit, spicy, creamy oak, toasty, complex. Palate: powerful, flavourful, toasty, round tannins, balanced.

BODEGAS BARREDA

Ramalazo, 2
45880 Corral de Almaguer (Toledo)
☎: +34 925 207 223 - Fax: +34 925 207 223
www.bodegas-barreda.com
nacional@bodegas-barreda.com

TORRE DE BARREDA AMIGOS 2009 T
65% tempranillo, 25% syrah, 10% cabernet sauvignon

90 Colour: cherry, garnet rim. Nose: red berry notes, ripe fruit, balsamic herbs, sweet spices, creamy oak. Palate: powerful, flavourful, long, toasty.

TORRE DE BARREDA PAÑOFINO 2008 T
100% tempranillo

92 Colour: cherry, garnet rim. Nose: ripe fruit, spicy, creamy oak, toasty, fragrant herbs, mineral. Palate: powerful, flavourful, toasty, round tannins.

TORRE DE BARREDA SYRAH 2011 T
100% syrah

87 Colour: cherry, garnet rim. Nose: red berry notes, fruit liqueur notes, spicy, toasty, floral. Palate: powerful, flavourful, long.

TORRE DE BARREDA TEMPRANILLO 2011 T
100% tempranillo

86 Colour: bright cherry. Nose: ripe fruit, sweet spices, creamy oak. Palate: flavourful, fruity, toasty.

BODEGAS CRIN ROJA

Paraje Mainetes
2651 Fuenteálamo (Albacete)
☎: +34 938 743 511 - Fax: +34 938 737 204
www.crinroja.es
info@crinroja.es

CRIN ROJA CABERNET SAUVIGNON SYRAH 2012 T
85% cabernet sauvignon, 15% syrah

85 Colour: cherry, purple rim. Nose: red berry notes, floral, balsamic herbs, spicy. Palate: flavourful, fruity, good acidity.

CRIN ROJA MACABEO 2012 B
100% macabeo

85 Colour: bright straw. Nose: fresh, fresh fruit, white flowers, expressive. Palate: flavourful, fruity, good acidity, balanced.

CRIN ROJA TEMPRANILLO 2012 T
100% tempranillo

83

MONTAL MACABEO AIREN 2012 B

86 Colour: bright straw. Nose: floral, fragrant herbs, candied fruit. Palate: fresh, fruity, flavourful.

MONTAL MONASTRELL 2010 T
85% monastrell, 15% syrah

86 Colour: cherry, garnet rim. Nose: fruit preserve, sweet spices, fine reductive notes, dark chocolate. Palate: powerful, flavourful, spicy.

BODEGAS DEL MUNI

Ctra. de Lillo, 48
45310 Villatobas (Toledo)
☎: +34 925 152 511 - Fax: +34 925 152 511
www.bodegasdelmuni.com
info@bodegasdelmuni.com

CORPUS DEL MUNI 2011 T ROBLE
tempranillo, syrah, garnacha, petit verdot

86 Colour: bright cherry. Nose: sweet spices, creamy oak, fruit preserve. Palate: flavourful, fruity, toasty.

CORPUS DEL MUNI BLANCA SELECCIÓN 2012 B
chardonnay, sauvignon blanc, verdejo

87 Colour: bright straw. Nose: citrus fruit, ripe fruit, floral, dried herbs. Palate: powerful, flavourful, long.

CORPUS DEL MUNI LUCÍA SELECCIÓN 2007 TC
tempranillo

89 Colour: cherry, garnet rim. Nose: ripe fruit, spicy, creamy oak, complex, balsamic herbs. Palate: powerful, flavourful, toasty, round tannins.

CORPUS DEL MUNI SELECCIÓN ESPECIAL" 2009 T
tempranillo

88 Colour: cherry, garnet rim. Nose: ripe fruit, spicy, creamy oak, toasty, complex. Palate: powerful, flavourful, toasty, round tannins.

CORPUS DEL MUNI VENDIMIA SELECCIONADA 2012 T JOVEN
tempranillo

90 Colour: cherry, purple rim. Nose: expressive, fresh fruit, red berry notes, floral. Palate: flavourful, fruity, good acidity, round tannins.

BODEGAS EL PROGRESO

Avda. de la Virgen, 89
13670 Villarubia de los Ojos (Ciudad Real)
☎: +34 926 896 135 - Fax: +34 926 896 135
www.bodegaselprogreso.com
laboratorio@bodegaselprogreso.com

MI CHUPITO 2012 B
100% airén

79

BODEGAS ESCUDERO

Ctra. de Arnedo, s/n
26587 Grávalos (La Rioja)
☎: +34 941 398 008 - Fax: +34 941 398 070
www.familiaescudero.com
info@familiaescudero.com

TUDEJEM 2010 T
100% cencibel

83

BODEGAS FINCA LA ESTACADA

Ctra. N-400, Km. 103
16400 Tarancón (Cuenca)
☎: +34 969 327 099 - Fax: +34 969 327 199
www.laestacada.com
laestacada@laestacada.es

**FINCA LA ESTACADA 12 MESES
BARRICA 2010 T BARRICA**
tempranillo

87 Colour: cherry, garnet rim. Nose: spicy, ripe fruit, dried herbs, medium intensity. Palate: fruity, flavourful, soft tannins.

FINCA LA ESTACADA VARIETALES 2008 TR
tempranillo, cabernet sauvignon, syrah, merlot

88 Colour: dark-red cherry, orangey edge. Nose: ripe fruit, spicy, creamy oak, toasty, fine reductive notes. Palate: powerful, flavourful, toasty.

SECUA CABERNET-SYRAH 2010 T
80% cabernet sauvignon, 20% syrah

88 Colour: cherry, garnet rim. Nose: ripe fruit, spicy, toasty, balsamic herbs, aromatic coffee, warm. Palate: powerful, flavourful, toasty.

SECUA CRIANZA EN LÍAS 2010 B
80% sauvignon blanc, 20% viognier

90 Colour: bright yellow. Nose: powerfull, ripe fruit, sweet spices, creamy oak, fragrant herbs. Palate: rich, smoky aftertaste, flavourful, fresh.

SECUA VENDIMIA TARDÍA 2011 B
100% chardonnay

88 Colour: golden. Nose: powerfull, floral, candied fruit, fragrant herbs. Palate: flavourful, sweet, fresh, fruity, good acidity, long.

BODEGAS KAME

Avda. del Cantábrico, s/n
1013 Vitoria (Álava)
☎: +34 945 282 844 - Fax: +34 945 271 319
www.egurenugarte.com
info@egurenugarte.com

KAME 2009 T
tempranillo, cabernet sauvignon, syrah, petit verdot

88 Colour: cherry, garnet rim. Nose: ripe fruit, spicy, creamy oak, balsamic herbs. Palate: powerful, flavourful, toasty.

KAME 2012 B
100% macabeo

87 Colour: bright straw. Nose: powerfull, fragrant herbs, fresh fruit, white flowers. Palate: flavourful, fresh, fruity.

KAME MUSCAT 2012 B
100% moscatel

85 Colour: bright straw. Nose: candied fruit, tropical fruit, floral. Palate: fresh, fruity, easy to drink.

**MERCEDES EGUNON CABERNET
SAUVIGNON 2011 T**
cabernet sauvignon

84

**MERCEDES EGUNON CABERNET
SAUVIGNON 2012 RD**
cabernet sauvignon

82

MERCEDES EGUNON SAUVIGNON BLANC 2012 B
sauvignon blanc

85 Colour: bright straw. Nose: fresh, fresh fruit, white flowers, expressive. Palate: flavourful, fruity, good acidity.

**MERCEDES EGUNON SHIRAZ
TEMPRANILLO 2011 T**
syrah, tempranillo

85 Colour: cherry, garnet rim. Nose: ripe fruit, toasty, spicy. Palate: long, spicy, toasty.

PAZOS DE EGUNON 2012 T
100% tempranillo

84

REINARES 2012 B
100% viura

82

REINARES 2012 RD
tempranillo

82

REINARES TEMPRANILLO 2012 T
tempranillo

83

BODEGAS LAHOZ

Ctra. N-310, km. 108,5
13630 Socuéllamos (Ciudad Real)
☎: +34 926 699 083 - Fax: +34 926 514 929
www.bodegaslahoz.com
info@bodegaslahoz.com

ABAD DE SOTO TEMPRANILLO 2009 T BARRICA
tempranillo

86 Colour: cherry, garnet rim. Nose: red berry notes, ripe fruit, sweet spices, creamy oak. Palate: powerful, flavourful, toasty.

RECATO SAUVIGNON BLANC 2010 BFB
sauvignon blanc

85 Colour: bright golden. Nose: ripe fruit, dry nuts, powerfull, toasty, aged wood nuances. Palate: flavourful, fruity, spicy, toasty, long.

RECATO TEMPRANILLO 9 MESES 2007 T BARRICA
tempranillo

88 Colour: bright cherry. Nose: ripe fruit, sweet spices, creamy oak, expressive. Palate: flavourful, fruity, toasty, round tannins.

BODEGAS LAZO

Finca La Zorrera, s/n
2436 Férez (Albacete)
☎: +34 622 766 900
www.lazotur.com
info@lazotur.com

CABEZA DEL HIERRO 2010 T
monastrell, bobal

85 Colour: pale ruby, brick rim edge. Nose: spicy, wet leather, aged wood nuances, fruit liqueur notes, damp earth, acetaldehyde. Palate: spicy, pruney, balsamic.

CABEZA DEL HIERRO 2011 T
34% monastrell, 17% bobal, 17% tempranillo, 17% syrah, 17% cabernet sauvignon, 17% petit verdot

89 Colour: cherry, garnet rim. Nose: ripe fruit, spicy, creamy oak, dry stone. Palate: powerful, flavourful, toasty, balanced.

FIANZA 2011 T
90% syrah, 10% monastrell

86 Colour: cherry, garnet rim. Nose: ripe fruit, spicy, creamy oak, toasty. Palate: powerful, flavourful, toasty.

FIANZA SELECCIÓN 2010 T
syrah

87 Colour: ruby red, orangey edge. Nose: fruit preserve, scrubland, damp earth, spicy. Palate: spicy, balsamic, correct.

FIANZA SELECCIÓN SYRAH 2011 T
syrah

88 Colour: cherry, garnet rim. Nose: ripe fruit, sweet spices, creamy oak. Palate: flavourful, fruity, toasty, spicy.

FIANZA SYRAH 2010 T
syrah

88 Colour: cherry, garnet rim. Nose: ripe fruit, spicy, creamy oak, toasty. Palate: powerful, flavourful, toasty, round tannins.

BODEGAS LÓPEZ PANACH

Finca El Calaverón, s/n
2600 Villarrobledo (Albacete)
☎: +34 967 573 140
www.lopezpanach.com
bodegas@lopezpanach.com

LÓPEZ PANACH COUPAGE 2011 T
tempranillo, merlot, syrah, cabernet sauvignon

80

BODEGAS MANO A MANO

Ctra. CM-412, Km. 100
13248 Alhambra (Ciudad Real)
☎: +34 926 694 317
www.bodegasmanoamano.com
info@bodegasmanoamano.com

MANO A MANO 2011 T
100% tempranillo

90 Colour: bright cherry. Nose: ripe fruit, new oak, spicy. Palate: flavourful, fruity, toasty, round tannins.

MANON 2011 T
100% tempranillo

89 Colour: very deep cherry. Nose: powerfull, ripe fruit, roasted coffee. Palate: powerful, ripe fruit, fine bitter notes.

RIBOTA 2011 T
tempranillo

89 Colour: very deep cherry. Nose: powerfull, ripe fruit, roasted coffee, dark chocolate. Palate: flavourful, ripe fruit, good acidity, fine bitter notes.

VENTA LA OSSA SYRAH 2010 T
100% syrah

93 Colour: cherry, garnet rim. Nose: ripe fruit, spicy, creamy oak, toasty, complex. Palate: powerful, flavourful, toasty, round tannins.

VENTA LA OSSA TEMPRANILLO 2010 TC
100% tempranillo

93 Colour: cherry, garnet rim. Nose: spicy, creamy oak, toasty, ripe fruit. Palate: powerful, flavourful, toasty, round tannins.

VENTA LA OSSA TNT 2011 T
touriga nacional, tempranillo

93 Colour: very deep cherry. Nose: scrubland, ripe fruit, violet drops. Palate: fruity, ripe fruit, long, fine bitter notes, round tannins.

BODEGAS MAS QUE VINOS

Camino de los Molinos, s/n
45312 Cabañas de Yepes (Toledo)
☎: +34 925 122 281 - Fax: +34 925 137 003
www.bodegasercavio.com
masquevinos@fer.es

EL SEÑORITO 2010 T
100% tempranillo

92 Colour: cherry, garnet rim. Nose: red berry notes, ripe fruit, sweet spices, mineral, balsamic herbs, expressive. Palate: powerful, flavourful, spicy, long, balanced.

ERCAVIO 2012 B
airén

88 Colour: bright straw. Nose: dried flowers, balsamic herbs, dried herbs, citrus fruit, ripe fruit. Palate: powerful, flavourful, warm.

ERCAVIO 2012 RD
tempranillo

88 Colour: raspberry rose. Nose: elegant, candied fruit, dried flowers, dried herbs. Palate: light-bodied, flavourful, good acidity, long, spicy.

ERCAVIO 31 NOVIEMBRE 2012 T
70% garnacha, 30% tempranillo

89 Colour: cherry, purple rim. Nose: red berry notes, fruit preserve, floral, fragrant herbs. Palate: fruity, flavourful, easy to drink.

ERCAVIO TEMPRANILLO 2011 T ROBLE
tempranillo

88 Colour: bright cherry. Nose: ripe fruit, sweet spices, creamy oak, balsamic herbs. Palate: flavourful, fruity, toasty, balanced.

ERCAVIO TEMPRANILLO 2012 T
tempranillo

90 Colour: cherry, purple rim. Nose: expressive, floral, red berry notes, ripe fruit. Palate: flavourful, fruity, good acidity.

LA BUENA VID 2009 T
tempranillo, graciano

90 Colour: cherry, garnet rim. Nose: ripe fruit, spicy, toasty, fine reductive notes. Palate: powerful, flavourful, toasty.

LA PLAZUELA 2007 T
tempranillo

93 Colour: cherry, garnet rim. Nose: wild herbs, ripe fruit, sweet spices, creamy oak, toasty, expressive. Palate: rich, powerful, flavourful, spicy, long, elegant.

BODEGAS MIGUEL ANGEL AGUADO ZAZO

Cantalejos, 2
45165 San Martín de Montalbán (Toledo)
☎: +34 653 821 659 - Fax: +34 925 417 206
www.bodegasmiguelaguado.com
info@bodegasmiguelaguado.com

SAN MARTINEÑO 2008 TR
cabernet sauvignon, garnacha
84

SAN MARTINEÑO 2012 B
macabeo
82

SAN MARTINEÑO 2012 RD
garnacha
84

SAN MARTINEÑO GARNACHA 2012 T
garnacha

85 Colour: cherry, purple rim. Nose: floral, red berry notes, ripe fruit. Palate: flavourful, fruity, good acidity.

SAN MARTINEÑO GARNACHA SEMI 2012 RD
garnacha
81

SAN MARTINEÑO TEMPRANILLO 2012 T
tempranillo
82

BODEGAS MIGUEL CALATAYUD

Postas, 20
13300 Valdepeñas (Ciudad Real)
☎: +34 926 348 070 - Fax: +34 926 322 150
www.vegaval.com
vegaval@vegaval.com

ÉCHAME UN CAPOTE 2011 T ROBLE
100% petit verdot
82

BODEGAS MONTALVO WILMOT

Ctra. Ruidera, km. 10,2 Finca Los Cerrillos
13710 Argamasilla de Alba (Ciudad Real)
☎: +34 926 699 069 - Fax: +34 926 699 069
www.montalvowilmot.com
nieveslucendo@montalvowilmot.com

MONTALVO WILMOT CABERNET DE FAMILIA 2006 T
100% cabernet sauvignon

88 Colour: cherry, garnet rim. Nose: ripe fruit, balsamic herbs, earthy notes, sweet spices, fine reductive notes. Palate: powerful, flavourful, spicy.

MONTALVO WILMOT COLECCIÓN PRIVADA 2008 T ROBLE
75% tempranillo, 25% cabernet sauvignon

88 Colour: cherry, garnet rim. Nose: ripe fruit, spicy, creamy oak, toasty. Palate: powerful, flavourful, toasty, round tannins.

MONTALVO WILMOT SYRAH 2011 T ROBLE
100% syrah

87 Colour: cherry, garnet rim. Nose: fruit preserve, toasty, sweet spices. Palate: powerful, classic aged character, long.

MONTALVO WILMOT TEMPRANILLO-CABERNET2010 T ROBLE
75% tempranillo, 25% cabernet sauvignon

89 Colour: cherry, garnet rim. Nose: red berry notes, candied fruit, balsamic herbs, floral, sweet spices. Palate: long, spicy, balsamic, correct.

BODEGAS MUREDA

Ctra. N-IV, Km. 184,1
13300 Valdepeñas (Ciudad Real)
☎: +34 926 318 058 - Fax: +34 926 318 058
www.mureda.es
bmoreno@mureda.es

MUREDA 100 2009 T
tempranillo

86 Colour: cherry, garnet rim. Nose: fruit preserve, balsamic herbs, sweet spices, toasty. Palate: flavourful, spicy, long.

MUREDA CHARDONNAY 2012 B
chardonnay

85 Colour: bright straw. Nose: citrus fruit, ripe fruit, floral, fragrant herbs. Palate: fresh, fruity, rich, flavourful.

MUREDA MERLOT 2011 T
merlot

84

MUREDA SAUVIGNON BLANC 2012 B
sauvignon blanc

84

MUREDA SYRAH 2011 T
syrah

89 Colour: cherry, garnet rim. Nose: red berry notes, ripe fruit, floral, sweet spices. Palate: powerful, fruity, good acidity.

BODEGAS NAVARRO LÓPEZ

Autovía Madrid - Cádiz, Km. 193
13210 Valdepeñas (Ciudad Real)
☎: +34 902 193 431 - Fax: +34 902 193 432
www.bodegasnavarrolopez.com
laboratorio2@navarrolopez.com

PARA CELSUS 2012 T
tempranillo

87 Colour: cherry, purple rim. Nose: fresh fruit, red berry notes, floral, balsamic herbs, lactic notes. Palate: flavourful, fruity, easy to drink.

PREMIUM 1904 2011 T
tempranillo, graciano

89 Colour: bright cherry. Nose: ripe fruit, sweet spices, creamy oak. Palate: flavourful, fruity, toasty, round tannins.

Premium1904

una equilibrada mezcla

de uvas de las variedades tempranillo

y graciano, cosechadas en 2011,

dan lugar a este excelente vino tinto

de la tierra de castilla.

ROJO GARNACHA 2012 T
garnacha

87 Colour: cherry, purple rim. Nose: red berry notes, floral, lactic notes. Palate: flavourful, fruity, correct.

ROJO TEMPRANILLO 2012 T
tempranillo

85 Colour: cherry, purple rim. Nose: red berry notes, ripe fruit, balsamic herbs. Palate: flavourful, fruity, good acidity.

ROJO TEMPRANILLO CABERNET 2012 T
tempranillo, cabernet sauvignon

84

ROJO TEMPRANILLO GARNACHA 2012 T
tempranillo, garnacha

86 Colour: cherry, purple rim. Nose: red berry notes, fragrant herbs, floral, lactic notes. Palate: fresh, fruity, flavourful.

TIERRA CALAR 2012 B
macabeo

83

TIERRA CALAR 2012 T
tempranillo

87 Colour: cherry, purple rim. Nose: expressive, fresh fruit, red berry notes, floral. Palate: flavourful, fruity, good acidity.

BODEGAS OLCAVIANA

Ctra. de Munera La Roda, Km. 31,8
2630 La Roda (Albacete)
☎: +34 967 570 081 - Fax: +34 967 548 695
www.bodegasolcaviana.com
info@bodegasolcaviana.com

1564 2012 B
viognier, chardonnay, riesling

87 Colour: bright straw. Nose: fresh, fresh fruit, white flowers, sweet spices. Palate: flavourful, fruity, good acidity.

1564 LAUDE 2010 T
cabernet sauvignon, petit verdot, tempranillo, merlot

88 Colour: cherry, garnet rim. Nose: ripe fruit, sweet spices, creamy oak, balsamic herbs. Palate: powerful, flavourful, complex.

1564 SYRAH 2011 T
syrah

86 Colour: cherry, garnet rim. Nose: ripe fruit, spicy, creamy oak, toasty. Palate: powerful, flavourful, toasty.

OLCAVIANA 2012 B
verdejo

83

OLCAVIANA 2012 T
tempranillo, syrah

86 Colour: cherry, purple rim. Nose: floral, ripe fruit, balsamic herbs. Palate: light-bodied, fresh, fruity.

VEGA PASION 2012 B
macabeo, sauvignon blanc

84

VEGA PASION 2012 RD
syrah, petit verdot

85 Colour: light cherry. Nose: fruit preserve, fruit expression, red berry notes. Palate: light-bodied, fruity, fresh.

VEGA PASION 2012 T
syrah, tempranillo

85 Colour: cherry, purple rim. Nose: red berry notes, floral, lactic notes. Palate: flavourful, fruity, good acidity.

BODEGAS ORDÓÑEZ

Bartolomé Esteban Murillo, 11
29700 Vélez- Málaga (Málaga)
☎: +34 952 504 706 - Fax: +34 951 284 796
www.grupojorgeordonez.com
info@jorgeordonez.es

TRITÓN 2011 T
mencía

89 Colour: cherry, purple rim. Nose: ripe fruit, spicy. Palate: flavourful, fruity, round tannins, balanced.

BODEGAS RASGÓN

Polig. Ind. Avda. Pricipal s/n
13200 Manzanares (Ciudad Real)
☎: +34 926 647 194 - Fax: +34 926 647 044
www.rasgon.com
bodegas@rasgon.com

RASGÓN BARRICA 2011 T
80% tempranillo, 20% graciano

84

BODEGAS REAL

Finca Marisánchez - Ctra. de Valdepeñas a Cózar, Km. 12,8
13300 Valdepeñas (Ciudad Real)
☎: +34 914 577 588 - Fax: +34 914 577 210
www.bodegas-real.com
comercial@bodegas-real.com

FINCA MARISÁNCHEZ 2009 T ROBLE
tempranillo, merlot, syrah

87 Colour: cherry, garnet rim. Nose: ripe fruit, spicy, creamy oak, balsamic herbs. Palate: powerful, flavourful, toasty, round tannins.

FINCA MARISÁNCHEZ CHARDONNAY 2012 B

85 Colour: bright yellow. Nose: ripe fruit, faded flowers, dried herbs. Palate: warm, powerful, flavourful.

VEGA IBOR TEMPRANILLO 2010 T BARRICA

88 Colour: cherry, garnet rim. Nose: red berry notes, ripe fruit, balsamic herbs, creamy oak. Palate: powerful, flavourful, spicy.

BODEGAS RÍO NEGRO

Ctra. CM 1001, Km. 37,400
19230 Cogolludo (Guadalajara)
☎: +34 639 301 817 - Fax: +34 913 026 750
www.fincarionegro.com
info@fincarionegro.es

FINCA RÍO NEGRO 2010 T
tempranillo, syrah, cabernet sauvignon, merlot

92 Colour: cherry, purple rim. Nose: new oak, toasty, sweet spices, red berry notes, ripe fruit, fruit expression, spicy, creamy oak.

BODEGAS ROMERO DE ÁVILA SALCEDO

Avda. Constitución, 4
13200 La Solana (Ciudad Real)
☎: +34 926 631 426
www.bodegasromerodeavila.com
administracion@bodegasromerodeavila.com

BONDAD 2010 T ROBLE
syrah, tempranillo

83

BONDAD 3 MESES EN BARRICA 2011 T
tempranillo, syrah

85 Colour: bright cherry. Nose: ripe fruit, sweet spices, creamy oak. Palate: flavourful, fruity, toasty.

BONDAD TEMPRANILLO 2011 T
tempranillo

86 Colour: bright cherry. Nose: ripe fruit, sweet spices, creamy oak, balsamic herbs. Palate: flavourful, fruity, toasty.

BODEGAS SAN ISIDRO DE PEDRO MUÑOZ

Ctra. El Toboso, 1
13620 Pedro Muñoz (Ciudad Real)
☎: +34 926 586 057 - Fax: +34 926 568 380
www.viacotos.com
administracion@viacotos.com

CARRIL DE COTOS 2010 TC
100% tempranillo

84

CARRIL DE COTOS AIRÉN 2012 B
100% airén

83

CARRIL DE COTOS CABERNET SAUVIGNON 2009 T BARRICA
100% cabernet sauvignon

85 Colour: cherry, garnet rim. Nose: ripe fruit, spicy, toasty, green pepper. Palate: powerful, flavourful, toasty.

CARRIL DE COTOS SEMIDULCE 2012 B
100% airén

83

CARRIL DE COTOS TEMPRANILLO 2011 T
100% tempranillo

88 Colour: cherry, garnet rim. Nose: red berry notes, ripe fruit, dried herbs. Palate: flavourful, fruity, good acidity.

BODEGAS TAVERA S.L.

Ctra. Valmojado - Toledo, Km. 22
45182 Arcicóllar (Toledo)
☎: +34 666 294 012
www.bodegastavera.com
info@bodegastavera.com

NEREO GARNACHA 2011 T
100% garnacha

84

NEREO SYRAH TEMPRANILLO 2011 T
syrah, tempranillo

83

NEREO TEMPRANILLO SYRAH GARNACHA 2009 T
tempranillo, syrah, garnacha

87 Colour: bright cherry. Nose: sweet spices, creamy oak, fruit preserve. Palate: flavourful, fruity, toasty, round tannins.

TAVERA ANTIGUOS VIÑEDOS 2011 T
100% garnacha

87 Colour: bright cherry. Nose: ripe fruit, expressive, medium intensity. Palate: flavourful, fruity, toasty, round tannins.

BODEGAS VENTA MORALES

Plaza de Grecia, 1 Local 1-B
(Toledo)
☎: +34 925 167 493
www.bodegasvolver.com
export@bodegasvolver.com

VENTA MORALES 2012 B
macabeo

84

VENTA MORALES 2012 T
tempranillo

88 Colour: very deep cherry, purple rim. Nose: ripe fruit, fruit expression, balanced. Palate: fruity, flavourful.

BODEGAS VERUM

Ctra. Argamasilla de Alba, km. 0,800
13700 Tomelloso (Ciudad Real)
☎: +34 926 511 404 - Fax: +34 926 515 047
www.bodegasverum.com
administracion@bodegasverum.com

VERUM 2009 T ROBLE
60% cabernet sauvignon, 20% tempranillo, 20% merlot

86 Colour: dark-red cherry, orangey edge. Nose: wet leather, cigar, scrubland, spicy. Palate: powerful, lacks fruit.

VERUM MERLOT TEMPRANILLO CABERNET SAUVIGNON 2010 TC
50% tempranillo, 30% merlot, 20% cabernet sauvignon

86 Colour: cherry, garnet rim. Nose: ripe fruit, spicy, grassy, fine reductive notes. Palate: powerful, flavourful, toasty.

VERUM SAUVIGNON BLANC GEWÜRZTRAMINER 2012 B
80% sauvignon blanc, 20% gewürztraminer

87 Colour: bright yellow. Nose: white flowers, fragrant herbs, tropical fruit. Palate: light-bodied, fresh, fruity, easy to drink.

VERUM TEMPRANILLO CABERNET FRANC 2012 RD
70% cabernet franc, 30% tempranillo

86 Colour: rose, purple rim. Nose: red berry notes, ripe fruit, balsamic herbs, floral. Palate: powerful, flavourful, fruity.

VERUM TEMPRANILLO V RESERVA DE FAMILIA 2009 T
100% tempranillo

88 Colour: cherry, garnet rim. Nose: red berry notes, ripe fruit, balsamic herbs, sweet spices, creamy oak. Palate: powerful, flavourful, rich.

VERUM TERRA AIREN DE PIE FRANCO 2010 B
100% airén

87 Colour: bright yellow. Nose: ripe fruit, balsamic herbs, faded flowers. Palate: rich, powerful, flavourful, long, spicy.

BODEGAS VILLAVID

Niño Jesús, 25
16280 Villarta (Cuenca)
☎: +34 962 189 006 - Fax: +34 962 189 125
www.villavid.com
info@villavid.com

GOLDEN BUBBLES OF VILLAVID ESP
verdejo, macabeo

86 Colour: bright straw. Nose: dried herbs, floral, tropical fruit. Palate: fresh, fruity, flavourful.

SECRET BUBBLES OF VILLAVID ROSADO 2011 ESP
bobal

88 Colour: rose. Nose: red berry notes, floral, lactic notes, expressive. Palate: fresh, fruity, flavourful, easy to drink.

WOMAN SOUL OF VILLAVID 2012 B
verdejo, macabeo

85 Colour: golden. Nose: powerfull, floral, candied fruit, fragrant herbs. Palate: flavourful, sweet, fresh, fruity.

BODEGAS VITIVINOS

Camino de Cabezuelas, s/n
2270 Villamalea (Albacete)
☎: +34 967 483 114 - Fax: +34 967 483 964
www.vitivinos.com
comercial@vitivinos.com

LLANOS DEL MARQUÉS BOBAL 2012 T
100% bobal

85 Colour: cherry, garnet rim. Nose: ripe fruit, balsamic herbs, damp earth. Palate: powerful, flavourful, correct.

BODEGAS Y VIÑEDOS ALCARREÑOS

Cº Viejo de las Navas, s/n
19162 Pioz (Guadalajara)
☎: +34 949 234 320 - Fax: +34 949 234 321
www.bovial.es
bovial@bovial.es

BOVIAL CAMINO BLANCO 2012 B

86 Colour: bright yellow. Nose: ripe fruit, tropical fruit, fragrant herbs, floral. Palate: fresh, fruity, flavourful.

BOVIAL CAMINO ROSADO 2012 RD

85 Colour: rose, purple rim. Nose: powerfull, ripe fruit, red berry notes, floral. Palate: powerful, fruity, fresh.

BOVIAL MONTE ALCARRIA 2009 T

85 Colour: cherry, garnet rim. Nose: ripe fruit, spicy, creamy oak, toasty. Palate: powerful, flavourful, toasty.

CASTILLO DE PIOZ 2009 T

87 Colour: cherry, garnet rim. Nose: ripe fruit, fruit liqueur notes, wild herbs, creamy oak. Palate: powerful, flavourful, toasty.

BODEGAS Y VIÑEDOS CASA DEL VALLE

Ctra. de Yepes - Añover de Tajo,
Km. 47,700 - Finca Valdelagua
45313 Yepes (Toledo)
☎: +34 925 155 533 - Fax: +34 925 147 019
www.bodegacasadelvalle.es
casadelvalle@bodegasolarra.es

FINCA VALDELAGUA 2008 T
40% cabernet sauvignon, 40% syrah, 20% merlot

89 Colour: cherry, garnet rim. Nose: spicy, creamy oak, fine reductive notes, ripe fruit. Palate: powerful, flavourful, spicy, long.

HACIENDA CASA DEL VALLE CABERNET SAUVIGNON 2010 T
100% cabernet sauvignon

87 Colour: deep cherry, garnet rim. Nose: ripe fruit, balsamic herbs, spicy, creamy oak. Palate: powerful, flavourful, spicy, long.

HACIENDA CASA DEL VALLE SYRAH 2010 T
100% syrah

86 Colour: cherry, garnet rim. Nose: ripe fruit, fruit preserve, balsamic herbs, creamy oak. Palate: powerful, flavourful, spicy, long.

BODEGAS Y VIÑEDOS CASTIBLANQUE

Isaac Peral, 19
13610 Campo de Criptana (Ciudad Real)
☎: +34 926 589 147 - Fax: +34 926 589 148
www.bodegascastiblanque.com
info@bodegascastiblanque.com

BALDOR OLD VINES 2009 T
100% cabernet sauvignon

85 Colour: cherry, garnet rim. Nose: ripe fruit, spicy, toasty. Palate: powerful, flavourful, toasty.

BALDOR TRADICIÓN CHARDONNAY 2010 BFB
100% chardonnay

87 Colour: bright golden. Nose: candied fruit, acetaldehyde, faded flowers, slightly evolved. Palate: rich, fruity, spicy, long.

BALDOR TRADICIÓN SYRAH 2009 T
100% syrah

86 Colour: cherry, garnet rim. Nose: fruit preserve, floral, sweet spices, creamy oak. Palate: powerful, flavourful, long.

BALDOR TRADICIÓN TEMPRANILLO 2011 T
100% tempranillo

85 Colour: cherry, garnet rim. Nose: ripe fruit, spicy, creamy oak, balsamic herbs. Palate: powerful, flavourful, toasty.

ILEX 2012 RD
100% syrah

84

ILEX 2012 T
80% tempranillo, 20% garnacha

84

ILEX AIRÉN 2012 B
100% airén

83

ILEX COUPAGE 2009 T
50% syrah, 10% garnacha, 30% tempranillo, 10% cabernet sauvignon

86 Colour: cherry, garnet rim. Nose: red berry notes, ripe fruit, balsamic herbs, dark chocolate, sweet spices. Palate: spicy, toasty, correct.

ILEX MOSCATEL 2012 B
100% moscatel

83

LA TRISTE FIGURA 2012 T
50% tempranillo, 50% cabernet sauvignon

83

BODEGAS Y VIÑEDOS CERRO DEL ÁGUILA

Avda. de Toledo, 23
45127 Ventas con Peña Aguilera (Toledo)
☎: +34 625 443 153
bodegascerrodelaguila@gmail.com

MALABRA 2011 T
syrah, garnacha

91 Colour: cherry, purple rim. Nose: red berry notes, ripe fruit, violet drops, sweet spices, creamy oak. Palate: rich, spicy, fruity.

PUERTO CARBONERO 2011 T
garnacha, syrah

89 Colour: cherry, garnet rim. Nose: ripe fruit, dry stone, spicy, balsamic herbs, balanced. Palate: powerful, flavourful, spicy, balanced.

BODEGAS Y VIÑEDOS JESÚS RECUERO. JESÚS Mª RECUERO MARTÍNEZ

La Puebla, 14
45810 Villanueva de Alcardete (Toledo)
☎: +34 925 166 396 - Fax: +34 925 167 278
www.bodegasrecuero.com
info@bodegasrecuero.com

RECUERO GUARDA FAMILIAR 2007 T
tempranillo

90 Colour: pale ruby, brick rim edge. Nose: spicy, fine reductive notes, aged wood nuances, fruit liqueur notes. Palate: spicy, fine tannins, elegant, long.

SIGILO MORAVIA 2010 T
100% moravia

84

SIGILO RED VINTAGE 2011 T
moravia, garnacha, velasco, tempranillo

86 Colour: cherry, garnet rim. Nose: red berry notes, ripe fruit, balsamic herbs, sweet spices, creamy oak. Palate: powerful, flavourful, toasty.

BODEGAS Y VIÑEDOS PINUAGA

Ctra. N-301 Km. 95,5
45880 Corral de Almaguer (Toledo)
☎: +34 914 577 117 - Fax: +34 914 577 117
www.bodegaspinuaga.com
info@bodegaspinuaga.com

PINUAGA 200 CEPAS 2010 T
tempranillo

88 Colour: cherry, garnet rim. Nose: ripe fruit, spicy, balsamic herbs, creamy oak. Palate: powerful, flavourful, long.

PINUAGA 2011 T
tempranillo

88 Colour: bright cherry. Nose: ripe fruit, sweet spices, creamy oak. Palate: flavourful, fruity, toasty, round tannins.

PINUAGA LA SENDA 2011 T
80% merlot, 20% tempranillo

87 Colour: cherry, garnet rim. Nose: red berry notes, ripe fruit, fragrant herbs, floral, creamy oak. Palate: powerful, flavourful, balsamic.

PINUAGA NATURE 3 MESES BARRICA 2012 T
tempranillo

87 Colour: bright cherry. Nose: ripe fruit, sweet spices, creamy oak, expressive. Palate: flavourful, fruity, toasty, round tannins.

BODEGAS Y VIÑEDOS SÁNCHEZ MULITERNO

Ctra. El Bonillo a Ossa de Montiel, km. 11
2610 El Bonillo (Albacete)
☎: +34 967 193 222 - Fax: +34 967 193 292
www.sanchez-muliterno.com
bodegas@sanchez-muliterno.com

FINCA LA SABINA 2010 T
100% tempranillo

88 Colour: cherry, garnet rim. Nose: ripe fruit, spicy, creamy oak, toasty. Palate: powerful, flavourful, toasty, round tannins.

FINCA LA SABINA 2011 T
tempranillo

87 Colour: cherry, garnet rim. Nose: fruit preserve, balsamic herbs, creamy oak, toasty. Palate: rich, powerful, flavourful.

BODEGAS ZIRIES

Menasalbas, 18
45120 San Pablo de los Montes (Toledo)
☎: +34 679 443 792
www.lobecasope.com
flequi@ziries.es

MELÉ 2011 T
100% garnacha

88 Colour: cherry, garnet rim. Nose: fruit preserve, cocoa bean, sweet spices. Palate: good structure, fruity, ripe fruit, fine bitter notes.

NAVALEGUA 2012 T BARRICA
garnacha

86 Colour: deep cherry, purple rim. Nose: powerfull, fruit preserve, slightly evolved. Palate: flavourful, fruity.

ZIRIES 2011 T
garnacha

90 Colour: cherry, garnet rim. Nose: balanced, scrubland, spicy, ripe fruit. Palate: balanced, round tannins, good acidity.

CAPILLA DEL FRAILE

Finca Capilla del Fraile, s/n
45600 San Bartolomé de las Abiertas (Toledo)
☎: +34 925 599 329
www.capilladelfraile.com
info@capilladelfraile.com

CAPILLA DEL FRAILE 2008 T
60% syrah, 40% petit verdot

88 Colour: dark-red cherry, garnet rim. Nose: ripe fruit, sweet spices, creamy oak. Palate: powerful, flavourful, long, spicy.

CASA CARRIL CRUZADO

Casa Carril Cruzado
16236 Villagarcía del Llano (Cuenca)
☎: +34 967 571 154 - Fax: +34 967 571 155
www.carrilcruzado.com
bodega@carrilcruzado.com

CASA CARRIL CRUZADO PETIT VERDOT 2011 T
petit verdot

82

CASA GUALDA

Casa Gualda
16708 Pozoamargo (Cuenca)
☎: +34 969 387 173 - Fax: +34 969 387 202
www.casagualda.com
info@casagualda.com

CASA GUALDA NATURA 2011 T
tempranillo, syrah

84

CASAQUEMADA

Ctra. Ruidera, Km. 5,5
13710 Argamasilla de Alba (Ciudad Real)
☎: +34 628 621 187
www.casaquemada.es
casaquemada@casaquemada.es

ALBA DE CASA QUEMADA 2010 T
100% syrah

89 Colour: bright cherry. Nose: ripe fruit, sweet spices, creamy oak, mineral. Palate: flavourful, fruity, toasty.

ANEA DE CASAQUEMADA 2007 T
100% syrah

88 Colour: cherry, garnet rim. Nose: fruit preserve, scrubland, spicy, wet leather, tobacco. Palate: powerful, balanced, toasty, long.

BRINCHO KOSHER 2007 T
100% tempranillo

88 Colour: cherry, garnet rim. Nose: ripe fruit, roasted coffee, aromatic coffee, expressive. Palate: rich, powerful, long, toasty.

HACIENDA CASAQUEMADA 2007 T
100% tempranillo

89 Colour: cherry, garnet rim. Nose: ripe fruit, spicy, creamy oak, toasty, mineral, fine reductive notes. Palate: powerful, flavourful, toasty, round tannins, elegant.

CONSTANTES VITALES

Plaza de Matute nº 12
28012 Madrid (Madrid)
☎: +34 609 119 248
www.miravinos.es
info@miravinos.es

LOS DUELISTAS 2012 T
tempranillo

91 Colour: bright cherry. Nose: sweet spices, creamy oak. Palate: flavourful, fruity, toasty, round tannins.

MALACABEZA 2012 T
88% tempranillo, 12% graciano

93 Colour: cherry, garnet rim. Nose: spicy, creamy oak, toasty. Palate: powerful, flavourful, toasty, fine tannins.

COSECHEROS Y CRIADORES

Diputación, s/n
1320 Oyón (Álava)
☎: +34 945 601 412 - Fax: +34 945 622 488
www.familiamartinezbujanda.com
nacional@cosecherosycriadores.com

INFINITUS CABERNET SAUVIGNON 2012 T
cabernet sauvignon

85 Colour: cherry, purple rim. Nose: ripe fruit, balsamic herbs, medium intensity. Palate: powerful, fresh, fruity.

INFINITUS GEWÜRZTRAMINER 2012 B
gewürztraminer

88 Colour: bright straw. Nose: white flowers, candied fruit, tropical fruit. Palate: flavourful, fruity, good acidity.

INFINITUS MALBEC 2012 T
malbec

86 Colour: cherry, purple rim. Nose: red berry notes, floral, balsamic herbs. Palate: flavourful, fruity, good acidity.

INFINITUS MERLOT 2012 T
merlot

85 Colour: cherry, purple rim. Nose: ripe fruit, fragrant herbs, medium intensity. Palate: powerful, fresh, fruity.

INFINITUS MOSCATEL 2012 B
moscatel

87 Colour: golden. Nose: powerfull, floral, honeyed notes, candied fruit, fragrant herbs. Palate: flavourful, sweet, fresh, fruity, good acidity, long.

INFINITUS SYRAH 2012 T
syrah

86 Colour: cherry, purple rim. Nose: red berry notes, fruit liqueur notes, balsamic herbs, floral. Palate: powerful, flavourful, correct.

INFINITUS TEMPRANILLO 2012 T
tempranillo

87 Colour: cherry, purple rim. Nose: fresh fruit, red berry notes, floral, balsamic herbs. Palate: flavourful, fruity, correct.

INFINITUS TEMPRANILLO CABERNET FRANC 2012 RD
tempranillo, cabernet franc

85 Colour: rose, purple rim. Nose: powerfull, ripe fruit, red berry notes, floral. Palate: powerful, fruity, fresh.

INFINITUS TEMPRANILLO CABERNET SAUVIGNON 2012 T
cabernet sauvignon, tempranillo

84

INFINITUS VIURA CHARDONNAY 2012 B
viura, chardonnay

85 Colour: bright straw. Nose: floral, fragrant herbs, ripe fruit. Palate: flavourful, powerful, rich.

DEHESA DE LOS LLANOS

Ctra. Peñas de San Pedro, Km. 5,5
2006 (Albacete)
☎: +34 967 243 100 - Fax: +34 967 243 093
www.dehesadelosllanos.com
info@dehesadelosllanos.es

MAZACRUZ 2011 T
syrah, tempranillo, merlot

88 Colour: cherry, garnet rim. Nose: ripe fruit, sweet spices, expressive, dark chocolate. Palate: flavourful, fruity, toasty.

MAZACRUZ 2012 B
verdejo, sauvignon blanc

88 Colour: bright straw. Nose: candied fruit, white flowers, fragrant herbs. Palate: powerful, flavourful, rich.

MAZACRUZ CIMA 2009 T
petit verdot, merlot, cabernet sauvignon, graciano

89 Colour: cherry, garnet rim. Nose: ripe fruit, spicy, creamy oak, toasty. Palate: powerful, flavourful, toasty.

MAZACRUZ CIMA 2011 B
verdejo

90 Colour: bright yellow. Nose: powerfull, ripe fruit, sweet spices, creamy oak, fragrant herbs. Palate: rich, smoky aftertaste, flavourful, fresh, good acidity.

DEHESA Y VIÑEDOS DE NAVAMARÍN

Ctra. Comarcal 313, Km. 1
2160 Lezuza (Albacete)
☎: +34 967 376 005 - Fax: +34 967 376 003
www.aldonzavinos.com
pedrojnavarro@aldonzavinos.com

ALDONZA ALBO 2012 B
69% sauvignon blanc, 31% macabeo

85 Colour: bright yellow. Nose: ripe fruit, faded flowers, dried herbs. Palate: correct, rich, flavourful.

ALDONZA PISCES 2008 T
tempranillo, cabernet sauvignon, syrah

84

DIONISOS

13300 Valdepeñas (Ciudad Real)
☎: +34 926 313 248
www.labodegadelasestrellas.com
dionisos@labodegadelasestrellas.com

DIONISOS 2012 B
50% airén, 50% viura

84

PAGOS DEL CONUCO 2011 T
100% tempranillo

88 Colour: cherry, purple rim. Nose: expressive, fresh fruit, red berry notes, floral, spicy, balsamic herbs. Palate: flavourful, fruity, good acidity, round tannins.

PRINCESA DE TEMPRANILLO 2012 RD
tempranillo

84

DOMINIO DE EGUREN

Camino de San Pedro, s/n
1309 Páganos (Álava)
☎: +34 945 600 117 - Fax: +34 945 600 590
www.eguren.com
info@eguren.com

CÓDICE 2011 T
100% tempranillo

91 Colour: bright cherry. Nose: ripe fruit, sweet spices, creamy oak, expressive. Palate: flavourful, fruity, toasty, round tannins, balanced.

DOMINIO DE PUNCTUM ORGANIC & BIODYNAMIC WINES

Finca Fabian, s/n - Aptdo. 71
16660 Las Pedroñeras (Cuenca)
☎: +34 912 959 997 - Fax: +34 912 959 998
www.dominiodepunctum.com
export@dominiodepunctum.com

FINCA FABIAN CHARDONNAY 2012 B
100% chardonnay

86 Colour: bright yellow. Nose: ripe fruit, dried herbs, floral. Palate: rich, powerful, spicy.

FINCA FABIAN TEMPRANILLO 2012 T
100% tempranillo

90 Colour: cherry, purple rim. Nose: fresh fruit, red berry notes, floral. Palate: flavourful, fruity, good acidity, round tannins.

PUNCTUM CABERNET SAUVIGNON MERLOT 2012 T
50% cabernet sauvignon, 50% merlot

88 Colour: cherry, garnet rim. Nose: balsamic herbs, earthy notes, red berry notes, ripe fruit. Palate: light-bodied, fruity, balsamic.

PUNCTUM TEMPRANILLO PETIT VERDOT 2011 T ROBLE
70% tempranillo, 30% petit verdot

87 Colour: cherry, garnet rim. Nose: ripe fruit, spicy, creamy oak, dried herbs. Palate: powerful, flavourful, toasty.

VIENTO ALISEO CABERNET SAUVIGNON GRACIANO 2011 T ROBLE
50% graciano, 50% cabernet sauvignon

88 Colour: cherry, garnet rim. Nose: earthy notes, red berry notes, ripe fruit, creamy oak. Palate: balsamic, spicy, toasty.

VIENTO ALISEO TEMPRANILLO PETIT VERDOT 2012 T
70% tempranillo, 30% petit verdot

90 Colour: cherry, purple rim. Nose: lactic notes, red berry notes, fragrant herbs, fresh, expressive. Palate: balanced, fruity, flavourful.

VIENTO ALISEO VIOGNIER 2012 B
100% viognier

84

ENCOMIENDA DE CERVERA

Arzobispo Cañizares, 1
13270 Almagro (Ciudad Real)
☎: +34 926 102 099 - Fax: +34 926 222 297
www.encomiendadecervera.com
info@ecervera.com

1758 SELECCIÓN CENCIBEL 2010 TC
cencibel

85 Colour: cherry, garnet rim. Nose: fruit liqueur notes, balsamic herbs, spicy, toasty. Palate: powerful, flavourful, long.

VULCANUS TEMPRANILLO 2010 TC
tempranillo

87 Colour: cherry, garnet rim. Nose: ripe fruit, spicy, toasty, dark chocolate. Palate: powerful, flavourful, toasty.

FÉLIX SOLÍS

Autovía del Sur, Km. 199
13300 Valdepeñas (Ciudad Real)
☎: +34 926 322 400 - Fax: +34 926 322 417
www.felixsolisavantis.com
fsa@felixsolisavantis.com

CONSIGNA 2012 RD
tempranillo

83

CONSIGNA CABERNET SAUVIGNON 2012 T
cabernet sauvignon

83

CONSIGNA CHARDONNAY 2012 B
chardonnay

83

CONSIGNA MERLOT 2012 T
merlot

85 Colour: black cherry, purple rim. Nose: fruit liqueur notes, lactic notes, fragrant herbs. Palate: powerful, flavourful, correct.

CONSIGNA SEMIDULCE AIRÉN 2012 B
airén

83

CONSIGNA SHIRAZ 2012 T
syrah

84

CONSIGNA TEMPRANILLO 2012 T
tempranillo

86 Colour: cherry, purple rim. Nose: expressive, fresh fruit, red berry notes, floral. Palate: flavourful, fruity, good acidity.

ORQUESTRA 2012 RD
tempranillo

83

ORQUESTRA CABERNET SAUVIGNON 2012 T
cabernet sauvignon

83

ORQUESTRA CHARDONNAY 2012 B
chardonnay

84

ORQUESTRA MERLOT 2012 T
merlot

86 Colour: cherry, purple rim. Nose: red berry notes, floral, fragrant herbs. Palate: fresh, fruity, flavourful.

ORQUESTRA TEMPRANILLO 2012 T
tempranillo

85 Colour: cherry, garnet rim. Nose: powerfull, fruit preserve, balsamic herbs. Palate: warm, powerful, flavourful.

FINCA CASA ALARCÓN

Ctra. Montealegre del Castillo, km 4,5
2660 Caudete (Albacete)
☎: +34 965 929 193 - Fax: +34 965 229 405
www.casalarcon.com
beatriz.andres@anara.es

BLAU 2009 T
monastrell, merlot

85 Colour: ruby red, garnet rim. Nose: grassy, wet leather, tobacco, slightly evolved. Palate: powerful, spicy, lacks balance.

CASA ALARCÓN 2012 RD
petit verdot, syrah

83

CASA ALARCÓN VIOGNIER 2012 B
100% viognier

85 Colour: bright yellow. Nose: ripe fruit, dried herbs, white flowers. Palate: fresh, fruity, easy to drink.

DON JAIME DE CASA ALARCÓN 2010 T
tempranillo, cabernet sauvignon, syrah

86 Colour: cherry, garnet rim. Nose: ripe fruit, spicy, creamy oak, toasty. Palate: powerful, flavourful, toasty.

NEA 2009 T
100% petit verdot

80

TRIA 2010 T
syrah

87 Colour: light cherry, cherry, garnet rim. Nose: red berry notes, floral, fragrant herbs, creamy oak. Palate: flavourful, spicy, correct.

FINCA CONSTANCIA

Camino del Bravo, s/n
45543 Otero (Toledo)
☎: +34 914 903 700 - Fax: +34 916 612 124
www.www.fincaconstancia.es
lslara@gonzalezbyass.es

ALTOS DE LA FINCA 2011 T
petit verdot, syrah

90 Colour: cherry, garnet rim. Nose: ripe fruit, spicy, creamy oak, toasty, complex. Palate: powerful, flavourful, spicy.

FINCA CONSTANCIA 2011 T
syrah, cabernet sauvignon, petit verdot, tempranillo, graciano, cabernet franc

89 Colour: bright cherry. Nose: ripe fruit, sweet spices, creamy oak, balsamic herbs. Palate: flavourful, fruity, toasty.

FINCA CONSTANCIA GRACIANO PARCELA 12 2011 T
graciano

88 Colour: bright cherry. Nose: ripe fruit, sweet spices, creamy oak, expressive. Palate: flavourful, fruity, toasty, slightly dry, soft tannins.

FINCA CONSTANCIA TEMPRANILLO PARCELA 23 2011 T
tempranillo

88 Colour: bright cherry. Nose: ripe fruit, sweet spices, creamy oak. Palate: flavourful, fruity, toasty.

FINCA CONSTANCIA VERDEJO PARCELA 52 2012 B
verdejo

90 Colour: bright yellow. Nose: powerfull, ripe fruit, sweet spices, creamy oak, fragrant herbs. Palate: rich, flavourful, fresh, good acidity.

FINCA EL CONVENTO

Ctra. Urda-Villarrubia De Los Ojos, Km. 6
45480 Urda (Toledo)
☎: +34 925 472 300 - Fax: +34 925 472 269
ergconvento@agropecuariaelconvento.com

FINCA EL CONVENTO 2009 T
cabernet sauvignon, syrah, merlot, petit verdot

85 Colour: cherry, garnet rim. Nose: spicy, creamy oak, fruit preserve. Palate: powerful, flavourful, toasty.

FINCA EL CONVENTO 2010 T
cabernet sauvignon, syrah

87 Colour: cherry, garnet rim. Nose: ripe fruit, spicy, creamy oak, toasty. Palate: powerful, flavourful, toasty.

VIRTUD DEL CONVENTO 2009 T
cabernet sauvignon

89 Colour: cherry, garnet rim. Nose: ripe fruit, toasty, grassy. Palate: powerful, flavourful, toasty.

FINCA EL REGAJO

Lope de Vega, 24
2651 Fuenteálamo (Albacete)
☎: +34 699 311 950
www.fincadelregajo.es
fincadelregajo@fincadelregajo.es

MACEDONIO 2012 T ROBLE
100% monastrell

86 Colour: black cherry, purple rim. Nose: ripe fruit, fruit preserve, balsamic herbs, sweet spices, creamy oak. Palate: rich, powerful, fruity.

MACEDONIO SELECCIÓN 2009 T
100% petit verdot

88 Colour: cherry, garnet rim. Nose: ripe fruit, spicy, creamy oak, toasty. Palate: powerful, flavourful, toasty.

PUERTO PINAR VIOGNIER 2012 B
100% viognier

85 Colour: bright straw. Nose: white flowers, ripe fruit, fragrant herbs. Palate: rich, powerful, flavourful.

FINCA LA LAGUNILLA - CASA CORREDOR

Casas de Corredor, s/n (Autovía Madrid/Alicante, salida 168, La Encina
2660 Caudete (Albacete)
☎: +34 966 842 064
www.casacorredor.es
jdminano@casacorredor.es

CASA CORREDOR CABERNET 2010 T
cabernet sauvignon

86 Colour: cherry, garnet rim. Nose: ripe fruit, spicy, toasty, balsamic herbs. Palate: powerful, flavourful, toasty.

CASA CORREDOR CABERNET TEMPRANILLO MERLOT 2009 T ROBLE

84

CASA CORREDOR CABERNET/TEMPRANILLO/MERLOT 2009 T
cabernet sauvignon, tempranillo, merlot

85 Colour: ruby red, orangey edge. Nose: ripe fruit, spicy, warm, fine reductive notes, grassy. Palate: spicy, long, flavourful.

CASA CORREDOR SYRAH 2010 T
syrah

85 Colour: cherry, garnet rim. Nose: red berry notes, ripe fruit, violet drops. Palate: powerful, flavourful, spicy.

SENSUM MACABEO 2012 B
macabeo

85 Colour: bright straw. Nose: fresh, fresh fruit, white flowers. Palate: flavourful, fruity, easy to drink.

FINCA LORANQUE

Finca Loranque
45593 Bargas (Toledo)
☎: +34 669 476 849
www.fincaloranque.com
fincaloranque@fincaloranque.com

LACRUZ DE FINCA LORANQUE CABERNET SAUVIGNON 2007 T
100% cabernet sauvignon

88 Colour: cherry, garnet rim. Nose: ripe fruit, spicy, creamy oak, toasty, fine reductive notes. Palate: powerful, flavourful, long.

LACRUZ DE FINCA LORANQUE SYRAH 2008 T
100% syrah

87 Colour: cherry, garnet rim. Nose: ripe fruit, spicy, creamy oak, dried flowers. Palate: powerful, flavourful, toasty, round tannins.

LACRUZ SYRAH 2012 T
syrah

85 Colour: cherry, purple rim. Nose: expressive, ripe fruit, sweet spices. Palate: flavourful, fine bitter notes, good acidity.

FINCA LOS ALIJARES

Avda. de la Paz, 5
45180 Camarena (Toledo)
☎: +34 918 174 364 - Fax: +34 918 174 364
www.fincalosalijares.com
gerencia@fincalosalijares.com

FINCA LOS ALIJARES GRACIANO 2010 TC
100% graciano

89 Colour: cherry, garnet rim. Nose: ripe fruit, spicy, creamy oak. Palate: powerful, flavourful, toasty, long.

FINCA LOS ALIJARES GRACIANO AUTOR 2010 T
100% graciano

86 Colour: cherry, garnet rim. Nose: ripe fruit, spicy, creamy oak, aged wood nuances. Palate: powerful, flavourful, toasty.

FINCA LOS ALIJARES MOSCATEL 2012 B
moscatel

83

FINCA LOS ALIJARES VIOGNIER 2012 B
100% viognier

86 Colour: bright straw. Nose: fresh, fresh fruit, white flowers, fragrant herbs. Palate: flavourful, fruity, good acidity.

FONTANA

Extramuros, s/n
16411 Fuente de Pedro Naharro (Cuenca)
☎: +34 969 125 433 - Fax: +34 969 125 387
www.bodegasfontana.com
gemag@bodegasfontana.com

DUETO DE FONTANA 2004 TC
50% merlot, 50% cabernet sauvignon

89 Colour: pale ruby, brick rim edge. Nose: fruit liqueur notes, fruit preserve, balsamic herbs, waxy notes, wet leather, cigar. Palate: round tannins, powerful, flavourful, long.

GRAN FONTAL 2008 T
100% tempranillo

91 Colour: cherry, garnet rim. Nose: ripe fruit, spicy, creamy oak, toasty, balsamic herbs. Palate: powerful, flavourful, toasty, round tannins, balanced.

MÁXIMO

Camino Viejo de Logroño, 26
1320 Oyón (Álava)
☎: +34 945 622 216 - Fax: +34 945 622 315
www.bodegasmaximo.com
maximo@bodegasmaximo.com

MÁXIMO GARNACHA 2012 T
100% garnacha

88 Colour: cherry, garnet rim. Nose: red berry notes, ripe fruit, sweet spices, balsamic herbs. Palate: powerful, flavourful, spicy, easy to drink.

MÁXIMO MERLOT 2011 T
merlot

80

MÁXIMO SYRAH 2012 T
syrah

85 Colour: bright cherry. Nose: ripe fruit, creamy oak, roasted coffee. Palate: flavourful, fruity, toasty.

MÁXIMO TEMPRANILLO 2011 T
100% tempranillo

89 Colour: bright cherry, garnet rim. Nose: ripe fruit, sweet spices, creamy oak, expressive. Palate: flavourful, fruity, toasty.

MÁXIMO TEMPRANILLO 2012 T
tempranillo

86 Colour: bright cherry. Nose: sweet spices, creamy oak, fruit expression. Palate: flavourful, toasty, round tannins.

MONTREAGA S.L.U.

Ctra. N-420, Km. 333,2
16649 Monreal del Llano (Cuenca)
☎: +34 647 492 424
www.mont-reaga.com
mont-reaga@mont-reaga.com

BLANCO DE MONTREAGA 2010 B
100% sauvignon blanc

87 Colour: bright yellow. Nose: powerfull, ripe fruit, sweet spices, creamy oak, fragrant herbs. Palate: rich, flavourful, fresh, good acidity.

FATA MORGANA 2008 TINTO DULCE
100% merlot

90 Colour: ruby red. Nose: acetaldehyde, varnish, sweet spices, aromatic coffee, expressive. Palate: powerful, flavourful, long, toasty, balanced, fine bitter notes.

ISOLA DE MONTREAGA 2012 T
50% tempranillo, 50% syrah

83

LAS LIRAS 2005 T
100% cabernet sauvignon

89 Colour: cherry, garnet rim. Nose: fruit preserve, scrubland, wet leather, waxy notes, tobacco. Palate: powerful, flavourful, spicy, balsamic.

MONTREAGA CLÁSICO 2005 T
100% syrah

89 Colour: pale ruby, brick rim edge. Nose: wet leather, aged wood nuances, fruit liqueur notes, fragrant herbs, earthy notes. Palate: spicy, fine tannins, long.

MONTREAGA EL SECRETO 2004 T
50% cabernet sauvignon, 50% syrah

90 Colour: ruby red, brick rim edge. Nose: ripe fruit, balsamic herbs, dark chocolate, sweet spices, fine reductive notes. Palate: powerful, flavourful, long, toasty.

MONTREAGA LA ESENCIA 2006 T
100% syrah

90 Colour: cherry, garnet rim. Nose: ripe fruit, spicy, creamy oak, toasty, earthy notes. Palate: powerful, flavourful, toasty, round tannins.

TEMPO DE MONTREAGA 2009 T
50% cabernet sauvignon, 50% merlot

85 Colour: cherry, garnet rim. Nose: fruit liqueur notes, damp earth, grassy. Palate: powerful, flavourful, spicy, toasty.

TEMPO LA ESPERA 2005 T
70% cabernet sauvignon, 30% merlot

88 Colour: pale ruby, brick rim edge. Nose: spicy, fine reductive notes, wet leather, aged wood nuances, fruit liqueur notes. Palate: spicy, fine tannins, long.

ORGANIC SIGNATURE WINES

Extramuros, s/n
2260 Fuentealbilla (Albacete)
☎: +34 967 472 503 - Fax: +34 967 472 516
info@franchete.com

FRANCHETE ASSEMBLAGE 2011 T
cabernet sauvignon, bobal, tempranillo, garnacha tintorera

84

FRANCHETE CABERNET SAUVIGNON ECOLÓGICO 2007 TC
100% cabernet sauvignon

80

FRANCHETE TINTO 2005 T BARRICA
cabernet sauvignon

78

OSBORNE MALPICA DE TAJO

Ctra. Malpica - Pueblanueva, km. 6
45692 Malpica del Tajo (Toledo)
☎: +34 925 860 990 - Fax: +34 925 860 905
www.osborne.es
carolina.cerrato@osborne.es

SOLAZ 2012 B
viura, verdejo

83

SOLAZ 2012 RD
syrah, mencía

85 Colour: rose, purple rim. Nose: powerfull, ripe fruit, red berry notes, floral. Palate: powerful, fruity, fresh.

SOLAZ COUPAGE 2010 T
syrah, tempranillo

85 Colour: cherry, garnet rim. Nose: ripe fruit, spicy, creamy oak, balsamic herbs. Palate: powerful, flavourful, toasty, correct.

SOLAZ TEMPRANILLO CABERNET SAUVIGNON 2011 T
tempranillo, cabernet sauvignon

84

PAGO DE VALLEGARCÍA

Finca Vallegarcía, s/n
13194 Retuerta del Bullaque (Ciudad Real)
☎: +34 925 421 407 - Fax: +34 925 421 822
www.vallegarcia.com
info@vallegarcia.com

HIPPERIA 2009 T
cabernet sauvignon, merlot, petit verdot

93 Colour: cherry, garnet rim. Nose: red berry notes, ripe fruit, cocoa bean, sweet spices, mineral, balsamic herbs. Palate: powerful, spicy, good acidity, balanced.

PETIT HIPPERIA 2011 T
cabernet sauvignon, merlot, cabernet franc, petit verdot, syrah

90 Colour: cherry, garnet rim. Nose: ripe fruit, sweet spices, creamy oak, earthy notes. Palate: flavourful, fruity, toasty, round tannins.

VALLEGARCÍA SYRAH 2009 T
syrah

93 Colour: bright cherry. Nose: ripe fruit, sweet spices, creamy oak, expressive, floral, balanced. Palate: flavourful, fruity, toasty, round tannins, elegant.

VALLEGARCÍA VIOGNIER 2011 BFB
viognier

92 Colour: bright yellow. Nose: ripe fruit, sweet spices, creamy oak. Palate: rich, smoky aftertaste, flavourful, fresh.

PAGO DEL VICARIO

Ctra. Ciudad Real - Porzuna, (CM-412) Km. 16
13196 Las casas (Ciudad Real)
☎: +34 926 666 027 - Fax: +34 670 099 520
www.pagodelvicario.com
info@pagodelvicario.com

PAGO DEL VICARIO 50-50 2008 T

87 Colour: cherry, garnet rim. Nose: ripe fruit, scrubland, spicy, toasty, fine reductive notes. Palate: powerful, flavourful, spicy, long.

PAGO DEL VICARIO AGIOS 2007 T

84

PAGO DEL VICARIO BLANCO DE TEMPRANILLO 2012 B

88 Colour: bright straw. Nose: fresh fruit, fragrant herbs, white flowers, violet drops. Palate: fresh, fruity, easy to drink.

PAGO DEL VICARIO CORTE DULCE B

83

PAGO DEL VICARIO MERLOT DULCE T

84

PAGO DEL VICARIO MONAGÓS 2007 T

85 Colour: cherry, garnet rim. Nose: spicy, aromatic coffee, waxy notes, cigar, ripe fruit. Palate: rich, powerful, flavourful.

PAGO DEL VICARIO PENTA 2010 T

88 Colour: cherry, garnet rim. Nose: toasty, aromatic coffee, sweet spices, ripe fruit. Palate: rich, flavourful, spicy.

PAGO DEL VICARIO PETIT VERDOT 2012 RD

87 Colour: rose, purple rim. Nose: powerfull, ripe fruit, red berry notes, floral, expressive. Palate: powerful, fruity, fresh.

TALVA 2007 BFB

85 Colour: bright golden. Nose: dry nuts, powerfull, toasty, aged wood nuances, citrus fruit, ripe fruit. Palate: flavourful, fruity, spicy, toasty, long.

QUINTA DE AVES

Ctra. CR-P-5222, Km. 11,200
13350 Moral de Calatrava (Ciudad Real)
☎: +34 915 716 514 - Fax: +34 915 711 151
www.quintadeaves.es
mortega@quintadeaves.es

QUINTA DE AVES ALAUDA CHARDONNAY 2012 B
100% chardonnay

87 Colour: bright yellow. Nose: ripe fruit, citrus fruit, floral, balsamic herbs. Palate: fruity, powerful, flavourful.

QUINTA DE AVES ALAUDA MOSCATEL & CHARDONNAY 2012 B
50% sauvignon blanc, 50% moscatel

86 Colour: bright straw. Nose: candied fruit, floral, tropical fruit. Palate: light-bodied, fruity, confected.

QUINTA DE AVES NOCTUA 2012 T
100% syrah

88 Colour: cherry, purple rim. Nose: expressive, fresh fruit, red berry notes, floral. Palate: flavourful, fruity, good acidity, round tannins.

QUINTA DE AVES NOCTUA 2012 T BARRICA
50% tempranillo, 20% merlot, 15% syrah, 15% graciano

87 Colour: cherry, purple rim. Nose: floral, ripe fruit, aged wood nuances. Palate: flavourful, fruity, spicy.

TINEDO

Ctra. CM 3102, Km. 30
13630 Socuéllamos (Ciudad Real)
☎: +34 926 118 999
www.tinedo.com
info@tinedo.com

CALA N 1 2010 T
88% tempranillo, 6% syrah, 4% cabernet sauvignon, 2% roussanne

87 Colour: cherry, garnet rim. Nose: ripe fruit, spicy, balsamic herbs, wild herbs. Palate: powerful, flavourful, balsamic, long.

CALA N 2 2010 T
83% tempranillo, 15% graciano, 2% roussanne

89 Colour: cherry, garnet rim. Nose: ripe fruit, balsamic herbs, earthy notes, spicy, expressive. Palate: spicy, good acidity, flavourful, balanced.

UVAS FELICES

Agullers, 7
8003 Barcelona (Barcelona)
☎: +34 902 327 777
www.vilaviniteca.es

SOSPECHOSO 2010 T
tempranillo, tinta de Toro

88 Colour: bright cherry. Nose: ripe fruit, sweet spices. Palate: flavourful, fruity, round tannins, balanced.

SOSPECHOSO 2012 B
airén, macabeo, verdejo

86 Colour: bright straw. Nose: ripe fruit, dried herbs. Palate: fruity, easy to drink, good acidity.

SOSPECHOSO 2012 RD

88 Colour: coppery red. Nose: floral, red berry notes, fruit expression. Palate: flavourful, light-bodied, fruity.

VINÍCOLA DE CASTILLA

Pol. Ind. Calle I, s/n
13200 Manzanares (Ciudad Real)
☎: +34 926 647 800 - Fax: +34 926 610 466
www.vinicoladecastilla.com
nacional@vinicoladecastilla.com

OLIMPO PRIVILEGIO 2010 T BARRICA
tempranillo, syrah, petit verdot

83

OLIMPO PRIVILEGIO 2011 B BARRICA
moscatel, chardonnay, sauvignon blanc

84

PAGO CASTILLA REAL T
tempranillo

86 Colour: cherry, garnet rim. Nose: ripe fruit, spicy, creamy oak, wet leather, tobacco. Palate: powerful, flavourful, long.

PAGO PEÑUELAS T
tempranillo

84

TIERRAS DEL QUIJOTE T ROBLE
tempranillo

83

VINNICO

Muela, 16
3730 Jávea (Alicante)
☎: +34 965 791 967 - Fax: +34 966 461 471
www.vinnico.com
info@vinnico.com

CAPA TEMPRANILLO 2011 T
90% tempranillo, 10% syrah

86 Colour: bright cherry. Nose: ripe fruit, sweet spices, creamy oak. Palate: flavourful, fruity, toasty.

EL PASO DEL LAZO 2012 T
90% tempranillo, 10% syrah

87 Colour: cherry, garnet rim. Nose: red berry notes, ripe fruit, creamy oak. Palate: powerful, spicy, long, flavourful.

LA NIÑA DE COLUMBUS 2012 B
100% sauvignon blanc

84

LA NIÑA DE COLUMBUS SHIRAZ 2012 T
100% syrah

85 Colour: cherry, purple rim. Nose: floral, red berry notes, fruit liqueur notes. Palate: fresh, fruity, flavourful, easy to drink.

VINOS COLOMAN S.A.T.

Goya, 17
13620 Pedro Muñoz (Ciudad Real)
☎: +34 926 586 410 - Fax: +34 926 586 656
www.satcoloman.com
coloman@satcoloman.com

PEDROTEÑO 2012 T
100% tempranillo

84

PEDROTEÑO AIRÉN 2012 B
100% airén

81

VIÑEDOS MEJORANTES S.L.

Ctra. de Villafranca, Km. 2
45860 Villacañas (Toledo)
☎: +34 925 200 023 - Fax: +34 925 200 023
www.portillejo.es
portillejo@portillejo.com

MONTE GUDELLO 2010 T
cabernet sauvignon, tempranillo

86 Colour: ruby red. Nose: fruit preserve, herbaceous, scrubland, fine reductive notes. Palate: powerful, flavourful.

VIÑEDOS Y BODEGAS MUÑOZ

Ctra. Villarrubia, 11
45350 Noblejas (Toledo)
☎: +34 925 140 070 - Fax: +34 925 141 334
www.bodegasmunoz.com
info@bodegasmunoz.com

FINCA MUÑOZ BARREL AGED 2009 T ROBLE
100% tempranillo

89 Colour: cherry, garnet rim. Nose: red berry notes, ripe fruit, creamy oak, toasty. Palate: balanced, flavourful, spicy.

FINCA MUÑOZ CEPAS VIEJAS 2009 T
100% tempranillo

90 Colour: cherry, garnet rim. Nose: ripe fruit, spicy, creamy oak, balsamic herbs, toasty. Palate: powerful, flavourful, toasty, round tannins.

LEGADO MUÑOZ CHARDONNAY 2012 B
100% chardonnay

88 Colour: bright yellow. Nose: powerfull, ripe fruit, sweet spices, creamy oak, fragrant herbs. Palate: rich, flavourful, fresh, good acidity.

LEGADO MUÑOZ GARNACHA 2011 T
100% garnacha

87 Colour: bright cherry. Nose: ripe fruit, sweet spices, creamy oak, expressive. Palate: flavourful, fruity, toasty, round tannins.

LEGADO MUÑOZ TEMPRANILLO 2012 T
100% tempranillo

84

CASTILLA-CAMPO DE CALATRAVA
AMANCIO MENCHERO MÁRQUEZ

Legión, 27
13260 Bolaños de Calatrava (Ciudad Real)
☎: +34 926 870 076 - Fax: +34 926 871 558
www.vinos-menchero.com
amanciomenchero@hotmail.com

CUBA 38 2012 T
tempranillo

84

CASTILLA Y LEÓN
A + WINES

Primavera, 7
28290 Las Matas (Madrid)
☎: +34 606 456 789
antoniomoralesp@yahoo.es

ALBANTO 2011 B
60% chardonnay, 20% godello, 20% dona blanca

90 Colour: bright yellow. Nose: ripe fruit, white flowers, faded flowers. Palate: rich, flavourful, good acidity, balanced.

ALBANTO MAGNUM 2011 BFB
chardonnay, godello, dona blanca

94 Colour: bright straw. Nose: balanced, expressive, mineral, spicy. Palate: good acidity, fine bitter notes, long, rich, flavourful.

ABADÍA RETUERTA

Ctra. N-122 Soria, km. 332,5
47340 Sardón de Duero (Valladolid)
☎: +34 983 680 314 - Fax: +34 983 680 286
www.abadia-retuerta.com
info@abadia-retuerta.es

ABADÍA RETUERTA LE DOMAINE 2012 B
80% sauvignon blanc, 20% verdejo, otras

91 Colour: bright straw. Nose: white flowers, fragrant herbs, citrus fruit, fruit expression. Palate: powerful, rich, fruity, flavourful.

ABADÍA RETUERTA PAGO GARDUÑA SYRAH 2010 T
100% syrah

94 Colour: cherry, garnet rim. Nose: red berry notes, ripe fruit, violet drops, aromatic coffee, dark chocolate. Palate: powerful, rich, flavourful, spicy, long, toasty.

ABADÍA RETUERTA PAGO NEGRALADA 2010 T
100% tempranillo

94 Colour: bright cherry, garnet rim. Nose: ripe fruit, sweet spices, creamy oak, mineral, balanced. Palate: flavourful, fruity, toasty, rich, elegant.

ABADÍA RETUERTA PAGO VALDEBELLÓN 2010 T
100% cabernet sauvignon

93 Colour: black cherry, garnet rim. Nose: ripe fruit, balsamic herbs, wild herbs, earthy notes, aromatic coffee, creamy oak. Palate: powerful, flavourful, spicy, long, balsamic.

ABADÍA RETUERTA PETIT VERDOT PV T
100% petit verdot

95 Colour: deep cherry, garnet rim. Nose: red berry notes, sweet spices, cocoa bean, dark chocolate, creamy oak, balanced, balsamic herbs. Palate: rich, flavourful, spicy, long, elegant.

ABADÍA RETUERTA SELECCIÓN ESPECIAL 2010 T
75% tempranillo, 15% cabernet sauvignon, 10% syrah

93 Colour: cherry, garnet rim. Nose: ripe fruit, spicy, creamy oak, toasty, earthy notes. Palate: powerful, flavourful, toasty, round tannins.

AGRÍCOLA CASTELLANA. BODEGA CUATRO RAYAS

Ctra. Rodilana, s/n
47491 La Seca (Valladolid)
☎: +34 983 816 320 - Fax: +34 983 816 562
www.cuatrorayas.org
info@cuatrorayas.org

CABALLERO DE CASTILLA 2012 B
100% verdejo

84

CABALLERO DE CASTILLA 2012 RD
100% tempranillo

82

CABALLERO DE CASTILLA TEMPRANILLO 2011 T ROBLE
100% tempranillo

85 Colour: bright cherry. Nose: ripe fruit, sweet spices, creamy oak. Palate: flavourful, fruity, toasty.

DOLCE BIANCO VERDEJO 2012 SEMIDULCE
100% verdejo

85 Colour: bright straw. Nose: medium intensity, floral, candied fruit. Palate: fresh, fruity, flavourful.

ARRIAGA Y MIMÉNDEZ COMPAÑÍA DE VINOS

Capitán Cortés, 6. Piso 4º Puerta 3
26003 Logroño (La Rioja)
☎: +34 941 210 448 - Fax: +34 941 287 072
www.arriagaymimendez.com

MITERNA CORTE UNO 2006 T BARRICA
prieto picudo

88 Colour: pale ruby, brick rim edge. Nose: spicy, wet leather, aged wood nuances, fruit liqueur notes. Palate: spicy, fine tannins, long.

AXIAL

Pla-za Calle Castillo de Capua, 10 Nave 7
50197 (Zaragoza)
☎: +34 976 780 136 - Fax: +34 976 303 035
www.axialvinos.com
info@axialvinos.com

LA GRANJA 360 VERDEJO VIURA 2012 B
70% verdejo, 30% viura

85 Colour: bright straw. Nose: fresh, fresh fruit, white flowers. Palate: flavourful, fruity, good acidity, easy to drink.

BELONDRADE

Quinta San Diego - Camino del Puerto, s/n
47491 La Seca (Valladolid)
☎: +34 983 481 001
www.belondrade.com
info@belondrade.com

QUINTA APOLONIA BELONDRADE 2012 B
verdejo

90 Colour: bright straw. Nose: white flowers, varietal, ripe fruit. Palate: flavourful, fruity, good acidity, balanced.

QUINTA CLARISA BELONDRADE 2012 RD
tempranillo

88 Colour: brilliant rose. Nose: candied fruit, dried flowers, fragrant herbs, red berry notes. Palate: flavourful, good acidity, long, spicy.

BLACKBOARD WINES

Conrado Albaladejo, 31 BW 61
3540 (Alicante)
☎: +34 686 097 742
www.blackboardwines.com
sales@blackboardwines.com

THE TAPAS WINE COLLECTION VERDEJO 2012 B
verdejo

86 Colour: bright straw. Nose: fresh, white flowers, dried herbs, tropical fruit. Palate: flavourful, fruity, good acidity.

BODEGA ALISTE

49520 Figueruela de Abajo (Zamora)
☎: +34 676 986 570
www.vinosdealiste.com
javier@hacedordevino.com

ALISTE 2011 T ROBLE
60% tempranillo, 30% garnacha, 10% syrah

88 Colour: cherry, garnet rim. Nose: red berry notes, ripe fruit, balsamic herbs, earthy notes. Palate: powerful, flavourful, thin.

GEIJO 2011 BFB
viura, verdejo, chardonnay

86 Colour: bright golden. Nose: ripe fruit, dry nuts, powerfull, toasty, aged wood nuances. Palate: flavourful, fruity, spicy, long.

MARINA DE ALISTE 2011 T
90% tempranillo, 10% syrah

90 Colour: cherry, garnet rim. Nose: ripe fruit, sweet spices, creamy oak, expressive, earthy notes. Palate: flavourful, fruity, toasty.

BODEGA DON JUAN DEL AGUILA

Real de Abajo, 100
5110 El Barraco (Ávila)
☎: +34 920 281 032
www.donjuandelaguila.es
bodegadonjuandelaguila@gmail.com

GAZNATA 2011 T
garnacha

87 Colour: cherry, garnet rim. Nose: ripe fruit, fruit preserve, balsamic herbs, spicy. Palate: flavourful, balsamic, correct.

GAZNATA 2012 RD
garnacha

82

GAZNATA FINCA MARIANO 2010 T
garnacha

89 Colour: dark-red cherry, orangey edge. Nose: ripe fruit, fruit liqueur notes, balsamic herbs, dry stone. Palate: powerful, flavourful, spicy, mineral.

GAZNATA GREDOS 2010 T
garnacha

88 Colour: cherry, garnet rim. Nose: ripe fruit, spicy, toasty, dry stone, scrubland. Palate: powerful, flavourful, toasty.

BODEGA EL ALBAR LURTON

Camino Magarin, s/n
47529 Villafranca del Duero (Valladolid)
☎: +34 983 034 030 - Fax: +34 983 034 040
www.francoislurton.es
bodega@francoislurton.es

EL ALBAR LURTON BARRICAS 2008 T

91 Colour: cherry, garnet rim. Nose: ripe fruit, creamy oak, sweet spices, balsamic herbs. Palate: powerful, flavourful, toasty, balanced, fine tannins.

BODEGA FINCA FUENTEGALANA

Ctra. M-501, Alcorcón - Plasencia, km. 65
5429 Navahondilla (Ávila)
☎: +34 646 843 231
www.fuentegalana.com
info@fuentegalana.com

TOROS DE GUISANDO COUPAGE 2009 T
merlot, syrah, tempranillo

86 Colour: cherry, garnet rim. Nose: ripe fruit, creamy oak, toasty, balsamic herbs. Palate: powerful, flavourful, toasty.

TOROS DE GUISANDO SYRAH 2009 T
syrah

87 Colour: cherry, garnet rim. Nose: ripe fruit, spicy, creamy oak, toasty. Palate: powerful, flavourful, toasty.

BODEGA MICROBIO WINES

Pza. La Iglesia, 7
40447 Nieva (Segovia)
microbiowines@gmail.com

ISSE 2 VIGNERONS 2011 B
50% verdejo, 50% treixadura, torrontés, godello, albariño, otras.

93 Colour: bright yellow. Nose: ripe fruit, citrus fruit, fragrant herbs, dried flowers, sweet spices. Palate: rich, flavourful, spicy, long.

LIVRE 2011 T
mencía

91 Colour: cherry, purple rim. Nose: red berry notes, fruit liqueur notes, fragrant herbs, spicy, creamy oak. Palate: fruity, powerful, flavourful.

SIETEJUNTOS MERLOT 2011 T
merlot

89 Colour: bright cherry. Nose: ripe fruit, sweet spices, creamy oak, balsamic herbs. Palate: flavourful, fruity, toasty, balanced.

SIETEJUNTOS SYRAH 2011 T
syrah

95 Colour: bright cherry. Nose: ripe fruit, sweet spices, creamy oak, expressive, balsamic herbs, violet drops. Palate: flavourful, fruity, toasty, round tannins.

SIETEJUNTOS TEMPRANILLO 2011 T
tempranillo

90 Colour: cherry, garnet rim. Nose: ripe fruit, spicy, creamy oak, toasty. Palate: powerful, flavourful, toasty.

BODEGA PAGO DE CALLEJO

Avda. Aranda, 3
9441 Sotillo de la Ribera (Burgos)
☎: +34 947 532 312 - Fax: +34 947 532 304
www.noecallejo.blogspot.com
callejo@bodegasfelixcallejo.com

FINCA VALDELROBLE 2010 T
60% tempranillo, 30% merlot, 10% syrah

90 Colour: cherry, garnet rim. Nose: damp earth, scrubland, spicy, ripe fruit, creamy oak. Palate: toasty, powerful, flavourful, long.

BODEGAS AGEJAS

Camino El Pavillo
40392 Cabañas de Polendos (Segovia)
☎: +34 921 120 008
www.bodegasagejas.com
info@bodegasagejas.com

RIBERA DE POLENDOS 2012 T ROBLE
tempranillo

89 Colour: cherry, purple rim. Nose: expressive, fresh fruit, red berry notes, floral, lactic notes. Palate: flavourful, fruity, good acidity.

BODEGAS ARRAYÁN

Finca La Verdosa, s/n
45513 Santa Cruz del Retamar (Toledo)
☎: +34 916 633 131 - Fax: +34 916 632 796
www.arrayan.es
comercial@arrayan.es

GARNACHA DE ARRAYÁN 2011 T
garnacha

93 Colour: cherry, garnet rim. Nose: ripe fruit, fruit liqueur notes, wild herbs, mineral, spicy, creamy oak. Palate: powerful, flavourful, balsamic, mineral.

BODEGAS CANOPY

Avda. Barber, 71
45004 (Toledo)
☎: +34 619 244 878 - Fax: +34 925 283 681
achacon@bodegascanopy.com

K OS 2009 T
100% garnacha

91 Colour: light cherry. Nose: ripe fruit, fragrant herbs, sweet spices, creamy oak, mineral. Palate: flavourful, balanced, spicy, long.

BODEGAS CASTELO DE MEDINA

Ctra. CL-602, Km. 48
47465 Villaverde de Medina (Valladolid)
☎: +34 983 831 884 - Fax: +34 983 831 857
www.castelodemedina.com
comunicacion@castelodemedina.com

VEGA BUSIEL 2009 T
60% syrah, 40% tempranillo

84

BODEGAS DE LOS HEREDEROS DEL MARQUÉS DE RISCAL

Ctra. N-VI, km. 172,600
47490 Rueda (Valladolid)
☎: +34 983 868 083 - Fax: +34 983 868 563
www.marquesderiscal.com
comunicacion@marquesderiscal.com

RISCAL 1860 2011 T ROBLE
90% tinta de Toro, 5% syrah, 5% merlot

87 Colour: cherry, purple rim. Nose: red berry notes, ripe fruit, scrubland, spicy, toasty. Palate: rich, powerful, flavourful.

BODEGAS ESCUDERO

Ctra. de Arnedo, s/n
26587 Grávalos (La Rioja)
☎: +34 941 398 008 - Fax: +34 941 398 070
www.familiaescudero.com
info@familiaescudero.com

CREPÚSCULO 2007 T
100% tinta del país

84

BODEGAS FRUTOS VILLAR

Ctra. Burgos-Portugal Km. 113,7
47270 Cigales (Valladolid)
☎: +34 983 586 868 - Fax: +34 983 580 180
www.bodegasfrutosvillar.com
bodegasfrutosvillar@bodegasfrutosvillar.com

DON FRUTOS VERDEJO 2012 B
100% verdejo

85 Colour: bright straw. Nose: ripe fruit, floral, fragrant herbs. Palate: powerful, fresh, fruity.

BODEGAS GODELIA

Antigua Ctra. N-VI, Pieros Cacabelos, Km. 403,5
24547 Cacabelos (León)
☎: +34 987 546 279 - Fax: +34 987 548 026
www.godelia.es
info@godelia.es

LIBAMUS 2011 T
100% mencía

91 Colour: cherry, garnet rim. Nose: raspberry, fruit preserve, balsamic herbs, cocoa bean, sweet spices, creamy oak. Palate: rich, powerful, flavourful, spicy, sweet.

BODEGAS LEDA

Mayor, 48
47320 Tudela de Duero (Valladolid)
☎: +34 983 520 682
www.bodegasleda.com
info@bodegasleda.com

LEDA VIÑAS VIEJAS 2009 T
100% tempranillo

93 Colour: cherry, garnet rim. Nose: red berry notes, ripe fruit, earthy notes, sweet spices, creamy oak. Palate: powerful, flavourful, long, spicy, balanced, elegant.

MÁS DE LEDA 2010 T
100% tempranillo

92 Colour: cherry, garnet rim. Nose: balsamic herbs, scrubland, earthy notes, ripe fruit, spicy, creamy oak. Palate: powerful, flavourful, long, balanced.

BODEGAS MAURO

Cervantes, 12
47320 Tudela de Duero (Valladolid)
☎: +34 983 521 972 - Fax: +349 835 219 973
www.bodegasmauro.com
comunicacion@bodegasmauro.com

MAURO 2011 T
tempranillo, syrah

91 Colour: cherry, garnet rim. Nose: spicy, creamy oak, toasty, ripe fruit. Palate: powerful, flavourful, toasty, round tannins.

MAURO VENDIMIA SELECCIONADA 2008 T
90% tinto fino, 10% syrah

93 Colour: cherry, garnet rim. Nose: ripe fruit, spicy, creamy oak, toasty, balanced, elegant. Palate: powerful, flavourful, toasty, round tannins, elegant.

TERREUS 2010 T
100% tempranillo

95 Colour: very deep cherry. Nose: sweet spices, cocoa bean, ripe fruit, fruit expression. Palate: powerful, full, fruity, good structure.

BODEGAS MOCEN

Arribas, 7-9
47490 Rueda (Valladolid)
☎: +34 983 868 533 - Fax: +34 983 868 514
www.bodegasantano.com
info@bodegasmocen.com

BRAVÍA 2011 T ROBLE
tempranillo

87 Colour: bright cherry. Nose: sweet spices, creamy oak, red berry notes, balsamic herbs. Palate: flavourful, fruity, toasty.

BRAVÍA 2012 RD
tempranillo

88 Colour: rose, purple rim. Nose: powerfull, ripe fruit, red berry notes, floral, expressive. Palate: powerful, fruity, fresh.

COBRANZA 2010 T
tempranillo

87 Colour: cherry, garnet rim. Nose: ripe fruit, spicy, creamy oak, toasty, complex. Palate: powerful, flavourful, toasty.

COBRANZA VENDIMIA SELECCIONADA 2005 T
tempranillo

88 Colour: dark-red cherry. Nose: fruit preserve, scrubland, wet leather, aged wood nuances, creamy oak. Palate: powerful, flavourful, toasty.

BODEGAS ORDÓÑEZ

Bartolomé Esteban Murillo, 11
29700 Vélez- Málaga (Málaga)
☎: +34 952 504 706 - Fax: +34 951 284 796
www.grupojorgeordonez.com
info@jorgeordonez.es

TINETA AVANTE 2010 T

90 Colour: cherry, garnet rim. Nose: ripe fruit, balanced, creamy oak. Palate: balanced, round tannins, good acidity.

BODEGAS PEÑASCAL

Ctra. Valladolid a Segovia (N-601)
km. 7,3 Pol. 2 Parcela 273
47140 Laguna de Duero (Valladolid)
☎: +34 983 546 080 - Fax: +34 983 546 081
www.penascal.es
rrpp@vina-mayor.es

CUERDA DEL AIRE 2012 B
85% sauvignon blanc, 15% verdejo

85 Colour: bright straw. Nose: floral, fragrant herbs, fruit expression. Palate: fresh, fruity, easy to drink.

CUERDA DEL AIRE 2012 RD
85% tempranillo, 15% syrah

84

CUESTA DEL AIRE TEMPRANILLO SHIRAZ 2012 T
85% tempranillo, 15% syrah

85 Colour: cherry, purple rim. Nose: floral, ripe fruit, fruit liqueur notes. Palate: flavourful, fruity, good acidity.

BODEGAS SANTA RUFINA

Pago Fuente La Teja. Pol. Ind. 3 - Parcela 102
47290 Cubillas de Santa Marta (Valladolid)
☎: +34 983 585 202 - Fax: +34 983 585 202
www.bodegassantarufina.com
info@bodegassantarufina.com

BOSQUE REAL TEMPRANILLO 2009 T
100% tempranillo

84

BOSQUE REAL VERDEJO 2012 B
100% verdejo

84

ULTIMATUM MERLOT 2009 T
100% merlot

85 Colour: ruby red. Nose: floral, fruit liqueur notes, fragrant herbs, spicy. Palate: fresh, fruity, balsamic.

BODEGAS TRITÓN

Pol.1 Parc. 146/148 Paraje Cantagrillos
49708 Villanueva de Campeán (Zamora)
☎: +34 968 435 022 - Fax: +34 968 716 051
www.orowines.com
info@orowines.com

ENTRESUELOS 2010 T
100% tempranillo

91 Colour: cherry, garnet rim. Nose: ripe fruit, spicy, complex, varietal. Palate: flavourful, toasty, round tannins, balsamic.

ENTRESUELOS 2011 T
100% tempranillo

90 Colour: very deep cherry. Nose: powerfull, sweet spices, dark chocolate, toasty. Palate: powerful, ripe fruit, harsh oak tannins.

REJÓN 2011 T
100% tempranillo

95 Colour: cherry, garnet rim. Nose: ripe fruit, spicy, creamy oak, toasty, characterful, powerfull. Palate: powerful, flavourful, toasty, round tannins.

TRIDENTE MENCÍA 2011 T
100% mencía

92 Colour: very deep cherry. Nose: balsamic herbs, ripe fruit, fruit expression, red berry notes. Palate: ripe fruit, spicy, good acidity.

TRIDENTE PRIETO PICUDO 2011 T
100% prieto picudo

91 Colour: very deep cherry. Nose: powerfull, complex, characterful, fruit liqueur notes, roasted coffee. Palate: spicy, fine bitter notes, good acidity.

TRIDENTE TEMPRANILLO 2010 T
100% tempranillo

93 Colour: cherry, garnet rim. Nose: ripe fruit, spicy, creamy oak, complex, varietal. Palate: powerful, flavourful, toasty, round tannins.

BODEGAS VINOS DE LEÓN - VILE, S.A.

La Vega, s/n
24009 Armunia (León)
☎: +34 987 209 712 - Fax: +34 987 209 800
www.bodegasvinosdeleon.es
info@bodegasvinosdeleon.es

PALACIO DE LEÓN CUVÉE 2010 T
100% tempranillo

85 Colour: bright cherry. Nose: ripe fruit, sweet spices, creamy oak. Palate: fruity, toasty, powerful.

PALACIO DE LEÓN TEMPRANILLO 2011 T
100% tempranillo

84

BODEGAS VIZAR

Ctra. N 122, Km. 341
47329 Villabáñez (Valladolid)
☎: +34 983 682 690 - Fax: +34 983 682 125
www.bodegasvizar.es
info@bodegasvizar.es

VIZAR SELECCIÓN ESPECIAL 2009 T
50% tempranillo, 50% syrah

93 Colour: cherry, garnet rim. Nose: ripe fruit, spicy, creamy oak, toasty, expressive, mineral. Palate: powerful, flavourful, toasty, round tannins, long, round.

VIZAR
AÑADA: 2009
PARCELA: El Redondal
UVA: 100% Syrah
CRIANZA: 14 meses Roble Francés
ALCOHOL: 13,5 %
PRODUCCIÓN: 3.000 botellas

VIZAR SYRAH 2009 T
100% syrah

91 Colour: cherry, garnet rim. Nose: damp earth, scrubland, red berry notes, ripe fruit, dried flowers. Palate: powerful, flavourful, spicy, long.

BODEGAS Y VIÑEDOS EL CODONAL

Pza. de la Constitución, 3
40462 Aldeanueva del Codonal (Segovia)
☎: +34 921 582 063
www.bodegaselcodonal.com
pedro.gomez@bodegaselcodonal.com

CODONAL VINUM NOBILE 2011 B
100% verdejo

90 Colour: bright yellow. Nose: powerfull, ripe fruit, sweet spices, creamy oak, fragrant herbs. Palate: rich, smoky aftertaste, flavourful, fresh, good acidity.

BODEGAS Y VIÑEDOS LA MEJORADA

Monasterio de La Mejorada
47410 Olmedo (Valladolid)
☎: +34 606 707 041
www.lamejorada.es
contacto@lamejorada.es

LA MEJORADA LAS CERCAS 2009 T
60% tempranillo, 40% syrah

93 Colour: cherry, garnet rim. Nose: red berry notes, ripe fruit, balsamic herbs, mineral, spicy, creamy oak. Palate: powerful, flavourful, balanced, elegant, round tannins.

LA MEJORADA LAS CERCAS 2010 T ROBLE
60% tempranillo, 40% syrah

93 Colour: cherry, garnet rim. Nose: red berry notes, balsamic herbs, violet drops, sweet spices, creamy oak. Palate: powerful, flavourful, balanced, elegant.

LA MEJORADA LAS NORIAS 2009 T ROBLE
tempranillo

91 Colour: bright cherry. Nose: ripe fruit, sweet spices, creamy oak, expressive. Palate: flavourful, fruity, toasty, round tannins.

LA MEJORADA LAS NORIAS 2010 T
tempranillo

92 Colour: cherry, garnet rim. Nose: red berry notes, ripe fruit, balsamic herbs, dry stone, sweet spices, creamy oak. Palate: powerful, flavourful, balanced, long.

LA MEJORADA TIENTO 2009 T

92 Colour: cherry, garnet rim. Nose: ripe fruit, spicy, creamy oak, toasty, characterful, earthy notes. Palate: powerful, flavourful, toasty, round tannins.

VILLALAR ORO 2009 T ROBLE
tempranillo

87 Colour: cherry, garnet rim. Nose: fruit preserve, scrubland, creamy oak, toasty. Palate: powerful, flavourful, long.

VILLALAR ORO 2010 T
tempranillo

88 Colour: cherry, garnet rim. Nose: red berry notes, ripe fruit, wild herbs, creamy oak. Palate: powerful, flavourful, spicy, long.

BODEGAS Y VIÑEDOS RIBERA DEL DURATÓN S.L.

Ctra. Valtiendas - Aranda, s/n
40314 Valtiendas (Segovia)
☎: +34 921 527 285 - Fax: +34 914 595 700
www.riberadelduraton.com
sofia@riberadelduraton.com

ALTOS DEL DURATÓN 2010 T
75% tempranillo, 25% syrah

88 Colour: cherry, garnet rim. Nose: ripe fruit, balsamic herbs, spicy, creamy oak. Palate: powerful, flavourful, spicy, long.

DURATÓN 2008 T
50% tempranillo, 50% syrah

89 Colour: cherry, garnet rim. Nose: ripe fruit, spicy, creamy oak, toasty. Palate: powerful, flavourful, toasty.

DURATÓN 2009 T
60% tempranillo, 40% syrah

90 Colour: cherry, garnet rim. Nose: ripe fruit, sweet spices, creamy oak. Palate: flavourful, fruity, toasty, round tannins.

DURATÓN SYRAH 2007 T
95% syrah, 5% tempranillo

87 Colour: bright cherry. Nose: ripe fruit, sweet spices, creamy oak, balsamic herbs. Palate: flavourful, fruity, toasty.

CLUNIA

Camino Torre, 1
9410 Coruña del Conde (Burgos)
☎: +34 607 185 951 - Fax: +34 948 818 574
ppavez@principedeviana.com

CLUNIA 2010 T
tempranillo

93 Colour: cherry, garnet rim. Nose: ripe fruit, sweet spices, creamy oak, expressive. Palate: flavourful, fruity, toasty, balanced, elegant.

CLUNIA SYRAH 2010 T
100% syrah

92 Colour: cherry, garnet rim. Nose: ripe fruit, creamy oak, toasty, complex. Palate: powerful, flavourful, toasty, round tannins.

CLUNIA SYRAH 2011 T
100% syrah

92 Colour: bright cherry. Nose: ripe fruit, sweet spices, creamy oak, expressive, powerfull. Palate: flavourful, fruity, toasty, round tannins.

CLUNIA TEMPRANILLO 2011 T
100% tempranillo

92 Colour: cherry, purple rim. Nose: floral, red berry notes, fruit expression, creamy oak. Palate: balanced, correct, fine bitter notes.

FINCA EL RINCÓN DE CLUNIA 2010 T
100% tempranillo

94 Colour: cherry, garnet rim. Nose: powerfull, expressive, characterful, toasty, new oak. Palate: fine bitter notes, balanced, toasty, powerful, good structure.

COMANDO G VITICULTORES

Avda. Constitución, 23
28640 Cadalso de los Vidrios (Madrid)
☎: +34 918 640 602
www.comandog.es
info@comandog.es

RUMBO AL NORTE 2011 T
garnacha

93 Colour: light cherry, garnet rim. Nose: elegant, expressive, ripe fruit, scrubland, spicy. Palate: balanced, good acidity, fine tannins.

COMPAÑÍA DE VINOS MIGUEL MARTÍN

Ctra. Burgos - Portugal, Km. 101
47290 Cubillas de Santa María (Valladolid)
☎: +34 983 250 319 - Fax: +34 983 250 329
www.ciadevinos.com
exportacion@ciadevinos.com

MARTÍN VERÁSTEGUI 2008 BFB
100% verdejo

88 Colour: bright golden. Nose: ripe fruit, dry nuts, powerfull, toasty, aged wood nuances, wet leather, cigar. Palate: flavourful, fruity, spicy, toasty, long.

MARTÍN VERÁSTEGUI 2012 RD
tempranillo, garnacha

87 Colour: rose. Nose: red berry notes, ripe fruit, floral, rose petals. Palate: powerful, flavourful, easy to drink.

MARTÍN VERÁSTEGUI P.X. B
100% pedro ximénez

89 Colour: dark mahogany. Nose: fruit liqueur notes, dried fruit, pattiserie, toasty. Palate: sweet, rich, unctuous, powerful.

MARTÍN VERÁSTEGUI VENDIMIA SELECCIONADA 2006 T
85% tempranillo, 15% garnacha

90 Colour: pale ruby, brick rim edge. Nose: elegant, spicy, fine reductive notes, wet leather, aged wood nuances, fruit liqueur notes. Palate: spicy, fine tannins, long.

RETOLA 12 MESES 2008 T
100% tempranillo

87 Colour: cherry, garnet rim. Nose: ripe fruit, spicy, creamy oak, toasty. Palate: powerful, flavourful, toasty.

RETOLA 6 MESES 2011 T
100% tempranillo

85 Colour: bright cherry. Nose: ripe fruit, sweet spices, creamy oak. Palate: flavourful, fruity, toasty, harsh oak tannins.

COMPAÑÍA DE VINOS TELMO RODRÍGUEZ

El Monte
1308 Lanciego (Álava)
☎: +34 945 628 315 - Fax: +34 945 628 314
www.telmorodriguez.com
contact@telmorodriguez.com

PEGASO "BARRANCOS DE PIZARRA" 2010 T
100% garnacha

93 Colour: deep cherry. Nose: fruit liqueur notes, fruit liqueur notes, spicy, scrubland. Palate: fruity, spicy, fine bitter notes, good acidity.

PEGASO "GRANITO" 2010 T
100% garnacha

96 Colour: deep cherry. Nose: floral, fruit expression, red berry notes, spicy. Palate: spicy, long, good acidity, elegant.

DANI LANDI

28640 Cadalso de los Vidrios (Madrid)
☎: +34 696 366 555
www.danilandi.com
daniel@danilandi.com

EL REVENTÓN 2011 T
100% garnacha

93 Colour: deep cherry. Nose: ripe fruit, expressive, elegant, scrubland. Palate: spicy, ripe fruit, good acidity.

LAS UVAS DE LA IRA 2012 B
100% albillo

90 Colour: bright yellow. Nose: powerfull, sweet spices, fragrant herbs, candied fruit. Palate: flavourful, good acidity.

DE ALBERTO

Ctra. de Valdestillas, 2
47231 Serrada (Valladolid)
☎: +34 983 559 107 - Fax: +34 983 559 084
www.dealberto.com
info@dealberto.com

CCCL 2007 T BARRICA
80% tempranillo, 20% cabernet sauvignon

85 Colour: cherry, garnet rim. Nose: ripe fruit, scrubland, aged wood nuances, toasty. Palate: powerful, flavourful, spicy.

FINCA VALDEMOYA 2007 T
80% tempranillo, 20% cabernet sauvignon

86 Colour: cherry, garnet rim. Nose: ripe fruit, spicy, creamy oak. Palate: powerful, flavourful, toasty.

FINCA VALDEMOYA 2012 RD
100% tempranillo

88 Colour: rose, purple rim. Nose: powerfull, ripe fruit, red berry notes, expressive, sweet spices. Palate: powerful, fruity, fresh.

DEHESA DE CADOZOS

Ctra. de Bermillo de Sayago a Almeida, km. 21
49211 Villamor de Cadozos (Zamora)
☎: +34 914 550 253 - Fax: +34 915 280 238
www.cadozos.com

CADOZOS 2005 T
tinto fino, pinot noir

90 Colour: pale ruby, brick rim edge. Nose: ripe fruit, balsamic herbs, damp earth, spicy, creamy oak. Palate: elegant, round, mineral, flavourful.

SAYAGO 830 2010 T
tinto fino, pinot noir

87 Colour: cherry, garnet rim. Nose: ripe fruit, spicy, complex, balsamic herbs, damp earth. Palate: powerful, flavourful, toasty, long.

DOMINIO DOSTARES

P.I. Bierzo Alto, Los Barredos, 4
24318 San Román de Bembibre (León)
☎: +34 987 514 550 - Fax: +34 987 514 570
www.dominiodostares.com
info@dominiodetares.com

CUMAL 2010 T

93 Colour: cherry, garnet rim. Nose: red berry notes, ripe fruit, balsamic herbs, sweet spices, creamy oak, mineral, elegant. Palate: flavourful, fruity, spicy, long, round tannins, balanced.

ESTAY 2010 T
100% prieto picudo

88 Colour: cherry, garnet rim. Nose: ripe fruit, creamy oak, toasty. Palate: powerful, flavourful, toasty.

LLANOS DE CUMAL 2010 T

90 Colour: cherry, garnet rim. Nose: ripe fruit, spicy, creamy oak, toasty, complex. Palate: powerful, flavourful, toasty, round tannins, balanced.

TOMBÚ 2012 RD
100% prieto picudo

87 Colour: rose, purple rim. Nose: red berry notes, candied fruit, balsamic herbs, lactic notes. Palate: fresh, fruity, easy to drink.

ENOLÓGICA WAMBA

El Puente, 7
9220 Pampliega (Burgos)
☎: +34 662 073 038 - Fax: +34 947 423 048
www.enologicawamba.es
contacto@enologicawamba.es

AMBISNA VERDEJO 2012 B
verdejo

88 Colour: bright straw. Nose: fresh, fresh fruit, white flowers. Palate: flavourful, fruity, good acidity, easy to drink.

ERMITA DEL CONDE

Camino de la Torre, 1
9410 Coruña del Conde (Burgos)
☎: +34 682 207 160
www.ermitadelconde.com
bodega@ermitadelconde.com

ERMITA DEL CONDE 2010 T
100% tinto fino

91 Colour: cherry, garnet rim. Nose: red berry notes, balsamic herbs, spicy, creamy oak, balanced. Palate: flavourful, spicy, long, elegant.

ERMITA DEL CONDE ALBILLO CENTENARIO 2011 B
100% albillo

88 Colour: bright yellow. Nose: powerfull, ripe fruit, sweet spices, creamy oak, fragrant herbs. Palate: rich, smoky aftertaste, flavourful, fresh, good acidity.

FINCA CÁRDABA

Coto de Cárdaba, s/n
40314 Valtiendas (Segovia)
☎: +34 921 527 470 - Fax: +34 921 527 470
www.fincacardaba.com
info@fincacardaba.com

FINCA CÁRDABA 2008 TC
100% tempranillo

89 Colour: cherry, garnet rim. Nose: ripe fruit, spicy, creamy oak, toasty, fine reductive notes. Palate: powerful, flavourful, toasty, round tannins.

FINCA CÁRDABA SELECCIÓN 2005 T
100% tempranillo

90 Colour: pale ruby, brick rim edge. Nose: elegant, spicy, fine reductive notes, wet leather, aged wood nuances, fruit liqueur notes. Palate: spicy, fine tannins, elegant, long.

FINCA LA RINCONADA

Castronuño
47520 Castronuño (Valladolid)
☎: +34 914 901 871 - Fax: +34 916 620 430
www.barcolobo.com
info@barcolobo.com

BARCOLOBO 12 MESES BARRICA 2010 T
75% tempranillo, 15% syrah, 10% cabernet sauvignon

92 Colour: cherry, garnet rim. Nose: ripe fruit, spicy, creamy oak, toasty, complex. Palate: powerful, flavourful, toasty, round tannins.

BARCOLOBO VERDEJO 2012 BFB
100% verdejo

89 Colour: bright yellow. Nose: powerfull, ripe fruit, sweet spices, creamy oak, fragrant herbs. Palate: rich, flavourful, fresh, good acidity.

FINCA TORREMILANOS

Finca Torremilanos, s/n
9400 Aranda de Duero (Burgos)
☎: +34 947 510 377 - Fax: +34 947 508 044
www.torremilanos.com
torremilanos@torremilanos.com

PEÑALBA-LÓPEZ 2011 B
40% tempranillo blanco, 40% sauvignon blanc, 10% chardonnay, 10% viura

90 Colour: bright yellow. Nose: powerfull, ripe fruit, sweet spices, creamy oak, fragrant herbs. Palate: rich, smoky after-taste, flavourful, fresh.

PEÑALBA-LÓPEZ GARNACHA 2010 T
garnacha

90 Colour: cherry, garnet rim. Nose: wild herbs, ripe fruit, mineral. Palate: good structure, balanced, round tannins.

FORTUNA WINES

Sanjurjo Badia, 22 - 3B
36207 Vigo (Pontevedra)
☎: +34 691 561 471
www.fortunawines.es
info@fortunawines.es

ALAIA VERDEJO 2012 B
verdejo

84

DEHESA DE RUBIALES ALAIA 2010 T ROBLE
prieto picudo, merlot, tempranillo

86 Colour: cherry, garnet rim. Nose: ripe fruit, fruit liqueur notes, spicy, creamy oak. Palate: powerful, flavourful, spicy.

MARILEN BELLO PRIETO PICUDO 2010 T ROBLE
prieto picudo, merlot, tempranillo

84

GARNACHA ALTO ALBERCHE

Camino del Pimpollar, s/n
5100 Navaluenga (Ávila)
☎: +34 616 416 542
www.bodegagarnachaaltoalberche.com
sietenavas@live.com

7 NAVAS 2010 T ROBLE
garnacha

90 Colour: bright cherry. Nose: ripe fruit, sweet spices, creamy oak, mineral. Palate: flavourful, fruity, toasty, round tannins.

7 NAVAS 2012 T
garnacha

90 Colour: cherry, purple rim. Nose: expressive, fresh fruit, red berry notes, floral, mineral. Palate: flavourful, fruity, good acidity, round tannins.

7 NAVAS FINCA FAUSTINA 2009 T
100% garnacha

92 Colour: cherry, garnet rim. Nose: ripe fruit, fruit preserve, scrubland, damp earth. Palate: powerful, spicy, long, balanced.

GRUPO YLLERA

A-6 Madrid - Coruña, Km. 173, 5
47490 Rueda (Valladolid)
☎: +34 983 868 097 - Fax: +34 983 868 177
www.grupoyllera.com
grupoyllera@grupoyllera.com

CUVI 2012 T ROBLE
100% tempranillo

88 Colour: cherry, purple rim. Nose: red berry notes, floral. Palate: flavourful, fruity, good acidity, round tannins.

YLLERA 2011 TC

88 Colour: cherry, garnet rim. Nose: spicy, creamy oak, roasted coffee. Palate: powerful, flavourful, toasty, round tannins.

YLLERA 30 ANIVERSARIO 2010 TC
100% tempranillo

90 Colour: bright cherry. Nose: ripe fruit, sweet spices, creamy oak, expressive. Palate: flavourful, fruity, toasty, round tannins.

YLLERA 5.5 ROSÉ FRIZZANTE ESP
verdejo, tempranillo

85 Colour: brilliant rose. Nose: candied fruit, raspberry. Palate: sweet, fresh, fruity.

YLLERA 5.5 VERDEJO FRIZZANTE ESP
100% verdejo

87 Colour: bright straw. Nose: medium intensity, fresh fruit, dried herbs, floral. Palate: fresh, fruity, flavourful, good acidity.

YLLERA DOMINUS GRAN SELECCIÓN VIÑEDOS VIEJOS 2006 T
100% tempranillo

90 Colour: very deep cherry. Nose: powerfull, warm, over-ripe fruit, toasty. Palate: powerful, spicy, ripe fruit.

HACIENDA ZORITA NATURAL RESERVE

Ctra. Zamora - fermoselle, km. 58
49220 Fermoselle (Zamora)
☎: +34 980 613 163 - Fax: +34 980 613 163
www.the-haciendas.com
agarcia@the-haciendas.com

HACIENDA ZORITA MAGISTER 2010 T
60% tempranillo, 30% syrah, 10% merlot

91 Colour: cherry, garnet rim. Nose: ripe fruit, toasty, sweet spices, balsamic herbs. Palate: powerful, flavourful, toasty, balanced.

HACIENDA ZORITA NATURAL RESERVE 2009 T
100% syrah

89 Colour: cherry, garnet rim. Nose: ripe fruit, spicy, toasty, wild herbs, damp earth. Palate: powerful, flavourful, spicy, long.

HEREDAD DE URUEÑA

Ctra. Toro a Medina de Rioseco, km 21,300
47862 Urueña (Valladolid)
☎: +34 915 610 920 - Fax: +34 915 634 131
www.heredaduruena.com
direccion@heredaduruena.com

FORUM ETIQUETA NEGRA 2011 T
tinta de Toro, tinta del país

91 Colour: cherry, garnet rim. Nose: red berry notes, ripe fruit, balsamic herbs, sweet spices, creamy oak, expressive. Palate: powerful, flavourful, long, balanced.

SANTOS MERLOT 2011 T
merlot, cabernet sauvignon

88 Colour: bright cherry. Nose: ripe fruit, sweet spices, creamy oak, fragrant herbs. Palate: flavourful, fruity, toasty.

SANTOS SYRAH 2011 T
syrah

89 Colour: cherry, garnet rim. Nose: fruit preserve, sweet spices, creamy oak, warm. Palate: powerful, rich, spicy.

SANTOS TEMPRANILLO 2011 T
tinta del país

90 Colour: cherry, garnet rim. Nose: powerfull, balsamic herbs, red berry notes, ripe fruit, mineral. Palate: flavourful, spicy, long, toasty.

LEYENDA DEL PÁRAMO

Ctra. de León s/n, Paraje El Cueto
24230 Valdevimbre (León)
☎: +34 662 401 435 - Fax: +34 987 424 844
www.leyendadelparamo.com
info@leyendadelparamo.com

FLOR DEL PÁRAMO 2011 T
100% prieto picudo

89 Colour: bright cherry. Nose: sweet spices, creamy oak, red berry notes, ripe fruit. Palate: flavourful, fruity, toasty.

FLOR DEL PÁRAMO 2012 B
100% albarín

88 Colour: bright straw. Nose: fresh, fresh fruit, white flowers, expressive. Palate: flavourful, fruity, good acidity, balanced.

FLOR DEL PÁRAMO 2012 RD
100% prieto picudo

87 Colour: rose, purple rim. Nose: ripe fruit, red berry notes, floral, expressive. Palate: powerful, fruity, fresh.

MALDIVINAS VIÑA Y VINO

Los Pinillas, 1
28032 (Madrid)
☎: +34 615 163 719
www.maldivinas.es
carlos@maldivinas.es

DOBLE PUNTA 2011 T
garnacha

87 Colour: deep cherry, garnet rim. Nose: varnish, cocoa bean, fruit liqueur notes. Palate: flavourful, astringent, round tannins.

LA MOVIDA 2011 T
garnacha

92 Colour: very deep cherry. Nose: powerfull, fruit preserve, dark chocolate, scrubland, mineral. Palate: balsamic, fruity, round tannins.

LA MOVIDA GRANITO 2011

93 Colour: cherry, garnet rim. Nose: wild herbs, red berry notes, ripe fruit, dry stone, spicy. Palate: balanced, powerful, flavourful, spicy, long.

LA MOVIDA LADERAS 2011 T
garnacha

92 Colour: cherry, garnet rim. Nose: ripe fruit, fruit liqueur notes, balsamic herbs, creamy oak. Palate: fresh, fruity, flavourful, spicy, correct.

MELGARAJO

Plaza Mayor, 9
47009 Melgar de Abajo (Valladolid)
☎: +34 983 786 012
www.melgarajo.es
melgarajo@melgarajo.es

MELGUS 2010 T
prieto picudo

90 Colour: cherry, purple rim. Nose: ripe fruit, fragrant herbs, spicy, creamy oak, earthy notes. Palate: flavourful, powerful, balanced.

VALDELEÑA 2010 T
prieto picudo

88 Colour: cherry, garnet rim. Nose: ripe fruit, spicy, creamy oak, toasty, complex. Palate: powerful, flavourful, toasty, round tannins.

VALDELEÑA 2011 T
prieto picudo

85 Colour: cherry, purple rim. Nose: red berry notes, ripe fruit, balsamic herbs. Palate: powerful, flavourful, easy to drink.

VALDELEÑA 2011 T ROBLE
prieto picudo

85 Colour: bright cherry. Nose: ripe fruit, creamy oak, aromatic coffee. Palate: flavourful, fruity, toasty, round tannins.

VALDELEÑA 2012 B
verdejo

85 Colour: bright straw. Nose: floral, ripe fruit, balsamic herbs, dried herbs, expressive. Palate: powerful, flavourful, balanced.

VALDELEÑA 2012 RD
prieto picudo

88 Colour: rose, purple rim. Nose: powerfull, ripe fruit, red berry notes, floral, lactic notes. Palate: powerful, fruity, fresh.

MENADE

Ctra. Rueda Nava del Rey, km. 1
47490 Rueda (Valladolid)
☎: +34 983 103 223 - Fax: +34 983 816 561
www.menade.es
info@menade.es

DOMINIO DE MORFEO "CEPAS VIEJAS" 2009 T
tempranillo, garnacha

88 Colour: cherry, garnet rim. Nose: red berry notes, ripe fruit, balsamic herbs, spicy. Palate: powerful, flavourful, spicy, long.

DOMINIO DE MORFEO "CEPAS VIEJAS" 2010 T
tempranillo, garnacha

89 Colour: cherry, garnet rim. Nose: red berry notes, mineral, balsamic herbs, spicy, creamy oak. Palate: powerful, flavourful, spicy, long.

OSSIAN VIDES Y VINOS

San Marcos, 5
40447 Nieva (Segovia)
☎: +34 696 159 121 - Fax: +34 921 594 207
www.ossian.es
ossian@ossian.es

CAPITEL 2011 BFB
100% verdejo

93 Colour: bright yellow. Nose: powerfull, ripe fruit, sweet spices, creamy oak, fragrant herbs. Palate: rich, smoky aftertaste, flavourful, fresh, good acidity.

OSSIAN 2011 BFB
100% verdejo

94 Colour: bright yellow. Nose: ripe fruit, dried herbs, mineral, spicy, creamy oak. Palate: powerful, flavourful, long, spicy, balsamic, balanced.

QUINTA SARDONIA

Casa, s/n - Granja Sardón
47340 Sardón de Duero (Valladolid)
☎: +34 650 498 353 - Fax: +34 983 032 884
www.quintasardonia.es
jbougnaud@quintasardonia.com

QUINTA SARDONIA QS 2008 T
57,7% tinto fino, 29,5% cabernet sauvignon, 4,5% syrah, 4% merlot, 2,5% petit verdot, 1,8% otras.

91 Colour: cherry, garnet rim. Nose: fruit preserve, spicy, creamy oak, mineral, toasty, balanced. Palate: powerful, flavourful, spicy, long.

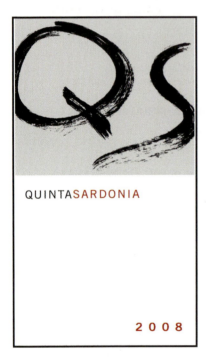

QUINTASARDONIA

2008

QUINTA SARDONIA QS 2009 T

93 Colour: cherry, garnet rim. Nose: ripe fruit, spicy, creamy oak, toasty, mineral. Palate: powerful, flavourful, toasty, round tannins, balanced.

RAUL PÉREZ BODEGAS Y VIÑEDOS

Bulevar Rey Juan Carlos 1º Rey de España, 11 B
24400 Ponferrada (León)
☎: +34 679 230 480
www.raulperezbodegas.es
raulperez@raulperezbodegas.es

VINO DE FAMILIA CEBREROS 2011 T
100% garnacha

94 Colour: cherry, garnet rim. Nose: ripe fruit, spicy, creamy oak, toasty, earthy notes, balsamic herbs. Palate: powerful, flavourful, toasty, round tannins.

RODRÍGUEZ SANZO

Manuel Azaña, 9
47014 (Valladolid)
☎: +34 983 150 150 - Fax: +34 983 150 151
www.rodriguezsanzo.com
comunicacion@valsanzo.com

PARAJES VERDEJO VIOGNIER 2011 B
50% verdejo, 50% viognier

91 Colour: bright yellow. Nose: powerfull, ripe fruit, sweet spices, creamy oak, fragrant herbs. Palate: rich, smoky aftertaste, flavourful, fresh, good acidity.

SANZO TEMPRANILLO FRIZZANTE 2012 RD
100% tempranillo

86 Colour: rose, purple rim. Nose: powerfull, ripe fruit, red berry notes, floral, lactic notes. Palate: powerful, fruity, fresh.

SANZO TEMPRANILLO FRIZZANTE 2012 T
100% tempranillo

87 Colour: cherry, purple rim. Nose: raspberry, balsamic herbs, red berry notes. Palate: fresh, fruity, easy to drink.

SANZO VERDEJO FRIZZANTE 2012 B
100% verdejo

89 Colour: bright straw. Nose: fresh, fresh fruit, white flowers, expressive. Palate: flavourful, fruity, good acidity, sweetness.

T H SANZO TEMPRANILLO 2009 T
100% tempranillo

88 Colour: bright cherry. Nose: ripe fruit, sweet spices, creamy oak, expressive. Palate: flavourful, fruity, toasty, round tannins.

RUBEN DIAZ VITICULTOR

Nueva, 26 - 1
5260 Cebreros (Ávila)
☎: +34 654 975 456 - Fax: +34 918 631 346
garnachasdegredos@gmail.com

AIRUN 2009 T
garnacha

91 Colour: cherry, garnet rim. Nose: ripe fruit, spicy, creamy oak, complex, mineral. Palate: flavourful, toasty, round tannins.

TONEL Nº 7 LA SORPRESA 2005 AM
albillo

88 Colour: iodine, amber rim. Nose: powerfull, complex, elegant, dry nuts, toasty. Palate: rich, fine bitter notes, fine solera notes, long, spicy.

RUDELES - TIERRAS EL GUIJARRAL

Trasterrera, 10
42345 Peñalba de San Esteban (Soria)
☎: +34 618 644 633 - Fax: +34 975 350 082
www.rudeles.com
jmartin@rudeles.com

VALDEBONITA ALBILLO 2012 B
100% albillo

87 Colour: bright straw. Nose: ripe fruit, dry nuts, powerfull, toasty, aged wood nuances, fragrant herbs. Palate: flavourful, fruity, spicy, toasty, long.

VALDEBONITA GARNACHA 2011 T
100% garnacha

90 Colour: cherry, garnet rim. Nose: red berry notes, fruit liqueur notes, balsamic herbs, spicy, expressive. Palate: rich, powerful, flavourful, balanced.

VINNICO

Muela, 16
3730 Jávea (Alicante)
☎: +34 965 791 967 - Fax: +34 966 461 471
www.vinnico.com
info@vinnico.com

AVENT 2012 T
tempranillo

87 Colour: cherry, purple rim. Nose: expressive, fresh fruit, red berry notes, floral, lactic notes. Palate: flavourful, fruity, good acidity, easy to drink.

VINOS DE ARGANZA

Río Ancares
24560 Toral de los Vados (León)
☎: +34 987 544 831 - Fax: +34 987 563 532
www.vinosdearganza.com
admon@vinosdearganza.com

LAGAR DE ROBLA PREMIUM 2009 T
mencía

88 Colour: cherry, garnet rim. Nose: ripe fruit, wild herbs, spicy, creamy oak. Palate: powerful.

LAGAR DE ROBLA PREMIUM 2010 T
mencía

90 Colour: cherry, garnet rim. Nose: red berry notes, ripe fruit, balsamic herbs, sweet spices, creamy oak. Palate: powerful, flavourful, spicy.

VINOS MALAPARTE

Avda. Camilo José Cela, 2
40200 Cuéllar (Segovia)
☎: +34 921 105 204
www.vinosmalaparte.es
info@vinosmalaparte.es

LAS LOMAS 2011 T
tinto fino

90 Colour: bright cherry. Nose: ripe fruit, sweet spices, creamy oak. Palate: flavourful, fruity, toasty, balanced.

OUI 2011 RD FERMENTADO EN BARRICA
100% tempranillo

88 Colour: rose, purple rim. Nose: powerfull, ripe fruit, floral, aged wood nuances, spicy, sweet spices. Palate: powerful, fruity, fresh.

VIÑA ALBARES

Camino Real, s/n
24310 Albares de la Ribera (León)
☎: +34 635 600 449
www.vinaalbareswine.com
info@vinaalbareswine.com

ALBARES EDICIÓN LIMITADA 2009 T BARRICA

89 Colour: cherry, garnet rim. Nose: ripe fruit, spicy, creamy oak, balsamic herbs. Palate: powerful, flavourful, toasty, harsh oak tannins.

QUINTA DEL OBISPO 2009 T ROBLE

87 Colour: cherry, garnet rim. Nose: ripe fruit, creamy oak, toasty, fine reductive notes. Palate: flavourful, toasty, round tannins.

VIÑAS DEL CÉNIT

Ctra. de Circunvalación, s/n
49708 Villanueva de Campeán (Zamora)
☎: +34 980 569 346
www.bodegascenit.com
info@bodegascenit.com

ALEO 2011 T ROBLE
tempranillo

91 Colour: bright cherry. Nose: ripe fruit, sweet spices, creamy oak, expressive. Palate: flavourful, fruity, toasty, round tannins.

VENTA MAZARRÓN 2011 T
100% tempranillo

93 Colour: bright cherry. Nose: ripe fruit, sweet spices, creamy oak, expressive. Palate: flavourful, fruity, toasty, round tannins.

VIÑEDOS DE VILLAESTER

49800 Toro (Zamora)
☎: +34 948 645 008 - Fax: +34 948 645 166
www.familiabelasco.com
info@familiabelasco.com

AVUTARDA 2010 T
tempranillo, cabernet sauvignon

89 Colour: cherry, garnet rim. Nose: red berry notes, ripe fruit, sweet spices, creamy oak. Palate: powerful, flavourful, spicy, long.

WEINWERK EL LAGARTO

Renteilichtung 1
45134 Essen
☎: +34 980 700 043 - Fax: +34 980 700 043
www.gourmet-lagarto.de
info@gourmet-lagarto.de

RUBY LUBY DE WEINWERK 2011 T
tinta de Toro, garnacha, prieto picudo

87 Colour: bright cherry. Nose: ripe fruit, sweet spices, creamy oak, expressive. Palate: flavourful, fruity, toasty.

CÓRDOBA
NAVISA

Avda. José Padillo Delgado, s/n
14550 Montilla (Córdoba)
☎: +34 957 650 450 - Fax: +34 957 651 747
www.navisa.es
navisa@navisa.es

VALPINA 2008 T
syrah, tempranillo, cabernet sauvignon

83

COSTA DE CANTABRIA
BODEGA NATES

Bº Llamosa, s/n
39761 Nates (Cantabria)
☎: +34 616 111 907
www.bodegasnates.net
comercial@bodegasnates.es

NATES 2012 B
95% albariño, 5% godello

87 Colour: bright straw. Nose: fresh, fresh fruit, white flowers, tropical fruit. Palate: flavourful, fruity, good acidity, balanced.

SEÑORÍO DEL PAS

Bº San Martín s/n
39638 Villafufre (Cantabria)
☎: +34 630 543 351
www.senoriodelpas.es
info@senoriodelpas.es

SEÑORÍO DEL PAS 2012 B
85% godello, 15% gewürztraminer

84

CUMBRES DEL GUADALFEO
BODEGA GARCÍA DE VERDEVIQUE

Cortijo Los García de Verdevique
18439 Castaras (Granada)
☎: +34 958 957 925
www.bodegasgarciadeverdevique.com
info@bodegasgarciadeverdevique.com

LOS GARCÍA DE VERDEVIQUE 2007 T
tempranillo, cabernet sauvignon, syrah

87 Colour: ruby red, orangey edge. Nose: fruit preserve, dried herbs, spicy, creamy oak, waxy notes, cigar. Palate: powerful, flavourful, spicy, long.

LOS GARCÍA DE VERDEVIQUE 2008 T
tempranillo, cabernet sauvignon, syrah

91 Colour: cherry, garnet rim. Nose: spicy, wild herbs, ripe fruit, creamy oak. Palate: powerful, flavourful, spicy, long.

LOS GARCÍA DE VERDEVIQUE 2009 T
tempranillo, cabernet sauvignon, syrah

86 Colour: cherry, garnet rim. Nose: ripe fruit, mineral, spicy, creamy oak. Palate: warm, powerful, harsh oak tannins.

DOMINIO BUENAVISTA

Ctra. de Almería, s/n
18480 Ugíjar (Granada)
☎: +34 958 767 254 - Fax: +34 958 990 226
www.dominiobuenavista.com
info@dominiobuenavista.com

DON MIGUEL 2010 T
cabernet sauvignon

85 Colour: deep cherry, garnet rim. Nose: powerfull, candied fruit, sweet spices. Palate: fruity, ripe fruit, flavourful.

NOLADOS 2009 T
40% cabernet franc, 40% cabernet sauvignon, 20% tempranillo

90 Colour: cherry, garnet rim. Nose: ripe fruit, spicy, dry stone, fragrant herbs. Palate: powerful, flavourful, toasty.

SIERRA SOL 2009 T
tempranillo

85 Colour: cherry, garnet rim. Nose: ripe fruit, spicy, creamy oak, toasty, earthy notes. Palate: powerful, flavourful, toasty.

SWEET MELODIES DULCE NATURAL 2012 B
viognier

85 Colour: old gold. Nose: ripe fruit, dried flowers, honeyed notes, fragrant herbs. Palate: rich, powerful, flavourful, balsamic.

EIVISSA
CAN RICH

Camí de Sa Vorera, s/n
7820 San Antonio (Illes Balears)
☎: +34 971 803 377 - Fax: +34 971 803 377
www.bodegascanrich.com
info@bodegascanrich.com

BES CAN RICH 2012 RD
monastrell

80

CAN RICH 2012 B
malvasía, chardonnay

88 Colour: bright straw. Nose: fresh fruit, closed, short, balanced, fresh, neat. Palate: correct, light-bodied, fresh, fruity, lacks expression.

CAN RICH 2012 RD
tempranillo, syrah

81

CAN RICH ERESO 2011 BFB
chardonnay

86 Colour: bright yellow. Nose: short, fresh, neat, fresh fruit. Palate: flavourful, light-bodied, fruity, fresh, lacks expression.

CAN RICH NEGRE 2009 T
tempranillo, merlot, cabernet sauvignon

88 Colour: cherry, garnet rim. Nose: fresh fruit, spicy, medium intensity, balanced. Palate: creamy, ripe fruit, flavourful, spirituous.

CAN RICH SELECCIÓN 2007 T
cabernet sauvignon, merlot, tempranillo

88 Colour: cherry, garnet rim. Nose: ripe fruit, medium intensity, balanced, cocoa bean. Palate: flavourful, fruity, spirituous, ripe fruit.

LAUSOS CABERNET SAUVIGNON 2007 T
cabernet sauvignon

90 Colour: cherry, garnet rim. Nose: ripe fruit, dark chocolate, aromatic coffee. Palate: ripe fruit, toasty, round tannins.

SA COVA

Sa Cova
7816 Sant Mateu D'Albarca (Illes Balears)
☎: +34 971 187 046 - Fax: +34 971 187 046
www.sacovaibiza.com
sacova-ibiza@telefonica.net

SA COVA 2012 RD
monastrell

88 Colour: onion pink. Nose: candied fruit, dried flowers, fragrant herbs. Palate: light-bodied, flavourful, good acidity, long, spicy.

SA COVA 9 2010 T
monastrell, syrah, merlot

87 Colour: cherry, garnet rim. Nose: ripe fruit, spicy, creamy oak, balsamic herbs. Palate: powerful, flavourful, toasty.

SA COVA BLANC DE BLANC 2012 B
malvasía, macabeo, moscatel

87 Colour: bright straw. Nose: fresh, fresh fruit, white flowers, expressive. Palate: flavourful, fruity, good acidity, balanced, fine bitter notes.

SA COVA CLOT D'ALBARCA 2009 T
syrah, merlot

90 Colour: cherry, garnet rim. Nose: ripe fruit, spicy, creamy oak, toasty, complex. Palate: powerful, flavourful, toasty, round tannins.

SA COVA PRIVAT 2009 T
syrah, monastrell

89 Colour: cherry, garnet rim. Nose: spicy, wild herbs, earthy notes, creamy oak, ripe fruit. Palate: powerful, flavourful, spicy, long.

TOTEM WINES

Camino viejo de San Mateu, s/n
7814 Santa gertrudis (Illes Balears)
☎: +34 654 507 809
www.totemwines.com
laurent@totemwines.com

IBIZKUS 2011 T
100% monastrell

88 Colour: deep cherry. Nose: fruit preserve, warm, toasty. Palate: fine bitter notes, good acidity.

IBIZKUS 2012 RD
monastrell, tempranillo, syrah

85 Colour: raspberry rose. Nose: raspberry, fresh fruit, varietal. Palate: correct, fruity, sweetness.

LA DEDICATORIA 2011 T
100% monastrell

85 Colour: deep cherry. Nose: overripe fruit, fruit preserve, warm. Palate: sweetness, spirituous.

LA SAVIA DIVINA 2012 T
syrah, monastrell

92 Colour: cherry, garnet rim. Nose: ripe fruit, spicy, creamy oak, toasty, complex. Palate: powerful, flavourful, toasty, round tannins.

TÓTEM 2009 T
100% monastrell

89 Colour: cherry, garnet rim. Nose: spicy, ripe fruit, short. Palate: ripe fruit, fruity, spicy.

VINOS CAN MAYMÓ

Can Maymó
7816 Sant Mateu d'Albarca (Illes Balears)
☎: +34 971 805 100 - Fax: +34 971 805 100
www.bodegascanmaymo.com
info@bodegascanmaymo.com

CAN MAYMÓ MERLOT 2010 T
merlot

87 Colour: cherry, garnet rim. Nose: cocoa bean, ripe fruit, short. Palate: spicy, ripe fruit, lacks expression, slightly acidic.

CAN MAYMÓ 2010 T BARRICA
syrah, merlot

86 Colour: light cherry. Nose: short, ripe fruit, spicy. Palate: fruity, correct, lacks expression, smoky aftertaste.

CAN MAYMÓ 2012 B
malvasía, moscatel

88 Colour: bright straw. Nose: fresh, white flowers. Palate: flavourful, fruity, good acidity, balanced.

CAN MAYMÓ 2012 RD
syrah

89 Colour: onion pink. Nose: elegant, candied fruit, dried flowers, fragrant herbs, red berry notes. Palate: light-bodied, flavourful, good acidity, long, spicy.

CAN MAYMÓ TRADICIÓN 2011 T
monastrell, tempranillo, merlot, syrah

85 Colour: cherry, garnet rim. Nose: short, neat, spicy. Palate: slightly acidic, spirituous, lacks expression.

EXTREMADURA
BODEGA DE MIRABEL

Buenavista, 31
10220 Pago de San Clemente (Cáceres)
☎: +34 927 323 154 - Fax: +34 927 323 154
info@fgoodwines.com

MIRABEL 2010 T
65% tempranillo, 35% cabernet sauvignon

91 Colour: cherry, garnet rim. Nose: ripe fruit, spicy, wild herbs, balanced. Palate: good structure, full, round tannins.

PAGO DE MIRABEL 2012 T
100% garnacha

92 Colour: cherry, garnet rim. Nose: medium intensity, ripe fruit, spicy. Palate: flavourful, fruity, sweet tannins, long, balanced.

TRIBEL DE MIRABEL 2010 T
60% tempranillo, 40% cabernet sauvignon

90 Colour: cherry, garnet rim. Nose: spicy, toasty, ripe fruit, wild herbs. Palate: flavourful, balanced, ripe fruit.

BODEGA MARQUÉS DE VALDUEZA

Fortuny, 19 1º Dcha
28010 (Madrid)
☎: +34 913 191 508 - Fax: +34 913 084 034
www.marquesdevaldueza.com
contact@marquesdevaldueza.com

MARQUÉS DE VALDUEZA ETIQUETA ROJA 2009 T
58% cabernet sauvignon, 42% syrah

90 Colour: bright cherry, garnet rim. Nose: wild herbs, ripe fruit, spicy. Palate: good structure, flavourful, round tannins.

MARQUÉS DE VALDUEZA GRAN VINO DE GUARDA 2008 T
syrah, merlot

92 Colour: cherry, garnet rim. Nose: balanced, elegant, spicy, earthy notes, balsamic herbs. Palate: balanced, fine bitter notes, round tannins.

VALDUEZA 2009 T
cabernet sauvignon, merlot, syrah

90 Colour: cherry, garnet rim. Nose: fruit preserve, powerfull, dark chocolate, dried herbs. Palate: flavourful, round tannins, spicy.

VALDUEZA 2010 T
merlot, syrah, cabernet sauvignon

84

BODEGA SAN MARCOS

Ctra. Aceuchal, s/n
6200 Almendralejo (Badajoz)
☎: +34 924 670 410 - Fax: +34 924 665 505
www.campobarro.com
ventas@bodegasanmarcos.com

CAMPOBRAVO 2012 B
cayetana blanca, moscatel

85 Colour: bright yellow. Nose: balanced, white flowers, citrus fruit. Palate: correct, good acidity, easy to drink.

CAMPOBRAVO 2012 RD
syrah

84

BODEGAS CAÑALVA

Coto, 54
10136 Cañamero (Cáceres)
☎: +34 927 369 405 - Fax: +34 927 369 405
www.bodegascanalva.com
info@bodegascanalva.com

CAÑALVA S/C T
tempranillo

84

CAÑALVA CABERNET SAUVIGNON MERLOT 2011 T
75% cabernet sauvignon, 25% merlot

89 Colour: cherry, garnet rim. Nose: ripe fruit, sweet spices, balanced. Palate: full, flavourful, round tannins, ripe fruit.

CAÑALVA COUPAGE ESPECIAL 2010 TC
25% tempranillo, 25% cabernet sauvignon, 25% syrah, 25% merlot

88 Colour: bright cherry. Nose: ripe fruit, sweet spices, creamy oak. Palate: flavourful, fruity, toasty, round tannins.

CAÑALVA SELECCIÓN 2010 T
85% tempranillo, 15% cabernet sauvignon

87 Colour: bright cherry. Nose: sweet spices, creamy oak, fruit preserve. Palate: flavourful, fruity, toasty, round tannins.

CAÑALVA TEMPRANILLO 2011 T
100% tempranillo

86 Colour: cherry, garnet rim. Nose: fruit preserve, sweet spices, cocoa bean. Palate: fruity, flavourful, easy to drink, good finish.

CAÑALVA TINTO FINO 2008 T
100% tempranillo

85 Colour: cherry, garnet rim. Nose: ripe fruit, toasty, sweet spices. Palate: correct, easy to drink.

LUZ 2012 RD
100% garnacha

83

LUZ 2012 SEMIDULCE
85% macabeo, 15% moscatel

84

BODEGAS CARLOS PLAZA

Sol s/n
6196 Cortegana (Badajoz)
☎: +34 924 687 932 - Fax: +34 924 667 569
www.bodegascarlosplaza.com
carlos@bodegascarlosplaza.com

CARLOS PLAZA 2010 T
70% tempranillo, 15% syrah, 15% merlot

86 Colour: cherry, garnet rim. Nose: ripe fruit, sweet spices. Palate: easy to drink, fruity, correct.

CARLOS PLAZA 2012 T
90% tempranillo, 10% syrah

89 Colour: cherry, garnet rim. Nose: red berry notes, ripe fruit, balanced. Palate: flavourful, fruity, balanced.

LA LLAVE ROJA 2010 T
70% tempranillo, 15% syrah, 15% merlot

87 Colour: cherry, garnet rim. Nose: ripe fruit, sweet spices, fruit preserve. Palate: flavourful, ripe fruit, spicy.

LA LLAVE ROJA 2012 T
90% tempranillo, 10% syrah

89 Colour: cherry, garnet rim. Nose: medium intensity, red berry notes, balanced. Palate: balanced, good acidity, fruity aftestaste.

BODEGAS DE OCCIDENTE

Granados, 1
6200 Almendralejo (Badajoz)
☎: +34 662 952 801
www.bodegasdeoccidente.es
info@bodegasdeoccidente.es

BUCHE 2011 T
tempranillo

87 Colour: bright cherry, garnet rim. Nose: dark chocolate, fruit preserve, spicy. Palate: flavourful, round tannins, good structure.

GRAN BUCHE 2010 T
tempranillo

90 Colour: bright cherry. Nose: ripe fruit, expressive, sweet spices. Palate: flavourful, fruity, toasty, round tannins.

BODEGAS ORAN

Hiedra, 21
6200 Almendralejo (Badajoz)
☎: +34 662 952 800
www.bodegasoran.com
info@bodegasoran.com

ENTREMARES 2012 B

85 Colour: bright straw. Nose: medium intensity, white flowers. Palate: fruity, flavourful, easy to drink.

BODEGAS RUIZ TORRES

Ctra. EX 116, km.33,8
10136 Cañamero (Cáceres)
☎: +34 927 369 027 - Fax: +34 927 369 383
www.ruiztorres.com
info@ruiztorres.com

ANTEROS 2012 B
100% pardina

79

RUIZ TORRES CABERNET SAUVIGNON 2008 T
100% cabernet sauvignon

86 Colour: cherry, garnet rim. Nose: toasty, spicy, ripe fruit, wild herbs. Palate: flavourful, round tannins.

RUIZ TORRES SYRAH 2008 T
100% syrah

88 Colour: cherry, garnet rim. Nose: ripe fruit, spicy, creamy oak, toasty. Palate: powerful, flavourful, toasty, round tannins.

TRAMPAL 2009 TC
tempranillo

79

BODEGAS TORIBIO VIÑA PUEBLA

Luis Chamizo, 12-21
6310 Puebla de Sancho Pérez (Badajoz)
☎: +34 924 551 449
www.bodegastoribio.com
info@bodegastoribio.com

ADN TORIVÍN 2010 T ROBLE
tempranillo

88 Colour: cherry, garnet rim. Nose: balanced, ripe fruit, sweet spices. Palate: fruity, flavourful, round tannins, easy to drink.

TORIBIO ECOLÓGICO 2012 T
tempranillo

89 Colour: cherry, purple rim. Nose: medium intensity, ripe fruit. Palate: fruity, flavourful, easy to drink, fruity aftertaste.

TORIVÍN 2012 B
macabeo, eva beba, verdejo

86 Colour: bright straw. Nose: fresh, white flowers, expressive. Palate: flavourful, fruity, good acidity, balanced.

TORIVÍN 2012 T
tempranillo, syrah, garnacha, graciano

87 Colour: light cherry, purple rim. Nose: medium intensity, red berry notes, ripe fruit. Palate: easy to drink, correct, good finish.

TORIVÍN 4X4 2011 T ROBLE
tempranillo, garnacha, cabernet sauvignon, syrah

87 Colour: cherry, garnet rim. Nose: sweet spices, candied fruit, dried herbs. Palate: flavourful, round tannins.

VIÑA PUEBLA 2009 TC
tempranillo, cabernet sauvignon, syrah

88 Colour: cherry, garnet rim. Nose: creamy oak, toasty, ripe fruit. Palate: powerful, flavourful, round tannins, long, good acidity.

VIÑA PUEBLA GOLOSINA 2012 RD
garnacha

86 Colour: rose, bright. Nose: medium intensity, red berry notes. Palate: fine bitter notes, correct, good acidity, fresh, fruity.

VIÑA PUEBLA GOLOSINA EVA 2012 B
eva beba, macabeo, verdejo

84

VIÑA PUEBLA MACABEO 2012 B
macabeo

85 Colour: bright straw. Nose: floral, fruit expression, medium intensity. Palate: flavourful, fruity, easy to drink.

VIÑA PUEBLA TEMPRANILLO 2012 T
tempranillo

88 Colour: light cherry, purple rim. Nose: red berry notes, ripe fruit, violets. Palate: fruity, flavourful, easy to drink, long.

BODEGAS VIÑA EXTREMEÑA

Lago de Alange, s/n
6200 Almendralejo (Badajoz)
☎: +34 924 670 158 - Fax: +34 924 670 159
www.vinexsa.com
info@vinexsa.com

CORTE REAL 2007 T
tempranillo, cabernet sauvignon

86 Colour: cherry, garnet rim. Nose: ripe fruit, spicy, toasty, wild herbs, tobacco. Palate: flavourful, good acidity.

TENTUDIA PREMIUM 2010 T
50% cabernet sauvignon, 50% syrah

86 Colour: cherry, garnet rim. Nose: medium intensity, ripe fruit. Palate: flavourful, fruity, easy to drink, good acidity, good finish.

TERRA MAGNA 2006 T
50% cabernet sauvignon, 50% merlot

86 Colour: light cherry, orangey edge. Nose: ripe fruit, spicy, tobacco. Palate: flavourful, good acidity, good finish.

CARREFOUR

Campezo, 16
28022 Madrid (Madrid)
☎: +34 902 202 000
www.carrefour.es

EL HAYEDO 2012 T
tempranillo, cabernet sauvignon

86 Colour: cherry, purple rim. Nose: balanced, fruit expression, violet drops. Palate: fruity, flavourful, good acidity.

COLOMA VIÑEDOS Y BODEGAS

Finca Torre Bermeja del Colmenar, Ctra. EX-363, km. 5,6
6170 Alvarado (Badajoz)
☎: +34 924 440 028 - Fax: +34 924 440 409
www.bodegascoloma.com
coloma@bodegascoloma.com

EVANDRIA MERLOT NOIR 2010 T
merlot

89 Colour: bright cherry, garnet rim. Nose: powerfull, ripe fruit, fruit preserve, toasty, spicy. Palate: flavourful, fruity, sweet tannins.

EVANDRIA PINOT NOIR 2012 RD
100% pinot noir

87 Colour: rose, bright. Nose: floral, red berry notes, balanced. Palate: fruity, good acidity, fine bitter notes.

CRASH WINES

Juan de la Cierva
6830 La Zarza (Badajoz)
☎: +34 916 295 841
www.pagolosbalancines.com
info@pagolosbalancines.com

CRASH CHARDONNAY 2012 B
chardonnay

86 Colour: bright yellow. Nose: ripe fruit, tropical fruit, white flowers. Palate: powerful, flavourful, fruity.

CRASH PINK 2012 RD
garnacha, tempranillo

86 Colour: rose, purple rim. Nose: powerfull, ripe fruit, red berry notes, floral. Palate: powerful, fruity, fresh, thin.

CRASH RED 2011 T
tempranillo, syrah, garnacha tintorera, garnacha

86 Colour: cherry, garnet rim. Nose: ripe fruit, balsamic herbs, medium intensity. Palate: powerful, flavourful, warm.

CRASH WHITE 2012 B
verdejo, chardonnay

84

HIJOS DE FRANCISCO ESCASO

Ctra. Villafranca, 15
6360 Fuente del Maestre (Badajoz)
☎: +34 924 530 012 - Fax: +34 924 531 703
franciscoescaso@infonegocio.com

VALLARCAL 2008 TR
tempranillo

81

VALLARCAL 2011 T ROBLE
tempranillo

85 Colour: cherry, garnet rim. Nose: sweet spices, overripe fruit. Palate: flavourful, spicy, correct.

VALLARCAL 2012 B
pardina

84

VALLARCAL ENVEJECIDO 2009 TC
tempranillo

82

LUIS GURPEGUI MUGA

Avda. Celso Muerza, 8
31560 San Adrián (Navarra)
☎: +34 948 670 050 - Fax: +34 948 670 259
www.gurpegui.es
bodegas@gurpegui.es

PINTORESCO 2012 T
tempranillo

87 Colour: bright cherry. Nose: red berry notes, ripe fruit, balsamic herbs. Palate: flavourful, fruity, round tannins, rich.

PAGO LOS BALANCINES

Paraje la Agraria, s/n
6475 Oliva de Mérida (Badajoz)
☎: +34 916 295 841
www.pagolosbalancines.com
info@pagolosbalancines.com

ALUNADO 2012 BFB
100% chardonnay

90 Colour: bright straw. Nose: floral, fragrant herbs, ripe fruit, sweet spices, creamy oak. Palate: powerful, rich, spicy, concentrated.

LOS BALANCINES HÚNICO 2012 T ROBLE
80% tempranillo, 20% syrah

89 Colour: bright cherry. Nose: ripe fruit, sweet spices, creamy oak, expressive. Palate: flavourful, fruity, toasty, round tannins.

SANTA MARTA VIRGEN

Cooperativa, s/n
6150 Santa Marta de los Barros (Badajoz)
☎: +34 924 690 218 - Fax: +34 924 690 043
www.bodegasantamarta.com
info@bodegasantamarta.com

CALAMÓN 2012 B
pardina

83

CALAMÓN 2012 RD

83

VIÑA PLACENTINA

Circunvalación Sur Urb. Haza del Obispo
Finca Pago de los Ángeles
10600 Plasencia (Cáceres)
☎: +34 927 116 250 - Fax: +34 927 418 102
www.vinaplacentina.com
info@vinaplacentina.com

VIÑA PLACENTINA ETIQUETA NEGRA 2007 T
cabernet sauvignon, merlot

85 Colour: light cherry, bright ochre rim. Nose: spicy, old leather. Palate: fruity, good acidity, correct, fine bitter notes.

VIÑA PLACENTINA ETIQUETA ROJA 2010 T ROBLE
cabernet sauvignon, merlot

82

VIÑA PLACENTINA PAGO DE LOS ÁNGELES 2005 T
cabernet sauvignon

86 Colour: deep cherry, orangey edge. Nose: powerfull, fruit preserve, fruit liqueur notes, old leather, tobacco. Palate: correct, spicy.

VIÑEDOS Y BODEGAS FUENTES

Ctra. Alange, Km. 17,700
6200 Almendralejo (Badajoz)
☎: +34 924 671 406

LENEUS 2012 TC
100% tempranillo

86 Colour: cherry, garnet rim. Nose: cocoa bean, ripe fruit, fruit preserve, roasted coffee. Palate: flavourful, round tannins.

FORMENTERA
CAP DE BARBARIA S.L.

Elisenda de Pinos, 1 Casa A
8034 (Barcelona)
☎: +34 609 855 556
www.capdebarbaria.com
info@capdebarbaria.com

PETIT CAP DE BARBARIA 2011 T

90 Colour: dark-red cherry, garnet rim. Nose: iodine notes, dried herbs, ripe fruit. Palate: flavourful, fine bitter notes.

TERRAMOLL

Ctra. de La Mola, Km. 15,5
7872 Formentera (Illes Balears)
☎: +34 971 327 293 - Fax: +34 971 327 293
www.terramoll.es
jabalde@terramoll.es

ES MONESTIR 2010 TC
monastrell

91 Colour: cherry, garnet rim. Nose: ripe fruit, spicy, creamy oak, toasty, complex, balsamic herbs. Palate: powerful, flavourful, toasty, round tannins.

ROSA DE MAR 2012 RD
merlot, cabernet sauvignon, monastrell

87 Colour: rose, purple rim. Nose: powerfull, ripe fruit, red berry notes, floral. Palate: powerful, fruity, fresh.

SAVINA 2012 B
garnacha, viognier, moscatel grano menudo, moll, malvasía

89 Colour: bright straw. Nose: scrubland, neat, fresh, ripe fruit, expressive, powerfull, varietal. Palate: good finish, fruity, flavourful.

TERRAMOLL PRIMUS 2006 TC
merlot, monastrell

88 Colour: dark-red cherry. Nose: complex, sweet spices, mineral, ripe fruit. Palate: warm, spirituous, powerful, spicy, roasted-coffee aftertaste.

TERRAMOLL PRIMUS 2012 BFB
viognier, malvasía

86 Colour: pale. Nose: closed, neat, fresh, fresh fruit. Palate: fruity, fresh, flavourful, lacks expression.

ILLA DE MENORCA
BODEGAS BINIFADET

Ses Barraques, s/n
7720 San Luis (Illes Balears)
☎: +34 971 150 715
www.binifadet.com
binifadet@binifadet.com

BINIFADET 2012 B
chardonnay

86 Colour: bright straw. Nose: fresh fruit, white flowers. Palate: flavourful, fruity, good acidity.

BINIFADET 2012 RD

87 Colour: coppery red. Nose: medium intensity, ripe fruit, warm. Palate: fruity, good acidity, flavourful.

BINIFADET 2012 T
syrah

88 Colour: cherry, purple rim. Nose: powerfull, warm, ripe fruit. Palate: powerful, concentrated, sweetness.

BODEGAS MENORQUINAS

Camí de Tramuntana, Km. 1
7740 Es Mercadal (Illes Balears)
☎: +34 651 906 934
www.fusioamenorca.wordpress.com
bodegasmenorquinas@msn.com

FUSIÓ BLANC 2012 B
macabeo, parellada

88 Colour: bright straw. Nose: powerfull, candied fruit, citrus fruit, honeyed notes. Palate: powerful, fruity, pruney.

FINCA SA MARJALETA

Camí D'Alpere, s/n
7760 Ciutadella de Menorca (Illes Balears)
☎: +34 971 382 740 - Fax: +34 971 385 737
www.marjaleta.com
marjaleta@telefonica.net

IAMONTANUM 2010 T
14,5% syrah

92 Colour: cherry, garnet rim. Nose: ripe fruit, spicy, creamy oak, toasty, mineral. Palate: powerful, flavourful, toasty, round tannins.

IAMONTANUM 2011 T
syrah

91 Colour: cherry, garnet rim. Nose: ripe fruit, spicy, creamy oak, toasty, complex. Palate: powerful, flavourful, toasty, round tannins.

IAMONTANUM 2012 B
viognier

90 Colour: bright straw. Nose: white flowers, fresh fruit, fruit expression, varietal, fresh. Palate: fruity, fresh, light-bodied, slightly acidic.

HORT

Cami de Sant Patrici, s/n
7750 Ferreries (Illes Balears)
☎: +34 971 373 702 - Fax: +34 971 155 193
www.santpatrici.com
info@santpatrici.com

HORT CAYETANA 2012 RD
syrah, merlot

83

HORT CUPATGE 2009 T
cabernet sauvignon, merlot, syrah

87 Colour: light cherry, orangey edge. Nose: toasty, sweet spices, ripe fruit. Palate: flavourful, rich, spirituous, sweetness.

HORT MERLOT 2010 T
merlot

87 Colour: light cherry, orangey edge. Nose: short, closed, earthy notes, spicy. Palate: astringent, fruity, lacks expression.

SA FORANA

Cugullonet Nou - Camí de Sa Forana
7712 Sant Climent - Mahón (Illes Balears)
☎: +34 607 242 510
www.saforana.com
saforana@saforana.com

600 METROS 2012 T
ull de llebre, syrah, merlot, cabernet sauvignon

92 Colour: cherry, garnet rim. Nose: ripe fruit, spicy, creamy oak, toasty, complex, characterful. Palate: powerful, flavourful, toasty, round tannins.

SA FORANA 2010 T
cabernet sauvignon, merlot, syrah

88 Colour: bright cherry. Nose: sweet spices, creamy oak, earthy notes. Palate: flavourful, fruity, toasty, round tannins.

VINYA SA CUDIA

Cos de Gracia, 7
7702 Mahón (Illes Balears)
☎: +34 686 361 445 - Fax: +34 971 353 607
www.vinyasacudia.com
amjdoctor@gmail.com

VINYA SA CUDÍA 2012 B
100% malvasía

83

VINYES BINITORD DE MENORCA

Santa Catarina, 1
7760 Ciutadella de Menorca (Illes Balears)
☎: +34 654 909 714
www.binitord.com
info@binitord.com

BINITORD BLANC 2012 B
chardonnay, merlot, macabeo, syrah

90 Colour: bright straw. Nose: fresh, fresh fruit, white flowers, expressive, spicy. Palate: flavourful, fruity, good acidity.

BINITORD NEGRE 2010 T
cabernet sauvignon, syrah, tempranillo, merlot

87 Colour: cherry, garnet rim. Nose: neat, ripe fruit, spicy. Palate: balanced, flavourful, ripe fruit.

BINITORD ROSAT 2012 RD
tempranillo, syrah

84

BINITORD ROURE 2009 T
tempranillo, cabernet sauvignon, syrah

87 Colour: cherry, garnet rim. Nose: medium intensity, short, neat, closed. Palate: correct, flavourful, fruity, ripe fruit.

LADERAS DEL GENIL
BODEGAS H. CALVENTE

Viñilla, 6
18699 Jete (Granada)
☎: +34 958 644 179 - Fax: +34 958 644 179
www.bodegashcalvente.com
info@bodegashcalvente.com

CALVENTE FINCA DE LA GUINDALERA 2010 T

84

XATE-O 2012 B

87 Colour: bright straw. Nose: fresh, fresh fruit, white flowers, honeyed notes. Palate: flavourful, fruity, good acidity, balanced.

BODEGAS TIERRA HERMOSA

Avda. Ricardo Soriano, 1 3ºA
29601 Marbella (Málaga)
☎: +34 657 207 196 - Fax: +34 935 385 677
www.tierrahermosa.com
isabel@tierrahermosa.com

VEINTE GRADOS 2010 T
tempranillo, garnacha, syrah

89 Colour: bright cherry. Nose: ripe fruit, sweet spices, creamy oak, earthy notes. Palate: flavourful, fruity, toasty, round tannins. Personality.

LAUJAR-ALPUJARRA
CORTIJO EL CURA

Paraje de Ojancos s/n
4470 Laujar de Andarax (Almería)
☎: +34 950 513 562 - Fax: +34 950 164 020
www.cortijoelcura.com
info@cortijoelcura.com

INFANTE FRANCISCO DOMINGO 2011 RD
garnacha

80

JÁNCOR 2007 T BARRICA
garnacha, cabernet sauvignon, syrah, merlot

84

ORO DEL LLANO 2012 B
jaen blanca, chardonnay

80

SÁNCHEZ VIZCAINO 2006 TR
garnacha, cabernet sauvignon, syrah, merlot

85 Colour: pale ruby, brick rim edge. Nose: spicy, fine reductive notes, wet leather, aged wood nuances, fruit liqueur notes, earthy notes. Palate: spicy, long, toasty.

SIERRA GÁDOR 2011 T
garnacha, cabernet sauvignon, merlot, syrah

83

SIERRA GÁDOR 2012 T
garnacha, merlot, cabernet sauvignon, syrah

85 Colour: deep cherry, purple rim. Nose: medium intensity, ripe fruit, balsamic herbs. Palate: fruity, flavourful, round tannins.

VALLE DE LAUJAR

Ctra. de Laujar a Berja, Km. 2,2
4470 Laujar de Andarax (Almería)
☎: +34 950 514 200 - Fax: +34 950 608 001

FINCA MATAGALLO 2010 T
80

VIÑA LAUJAR B
86 Colour: golden. Nose: powerfull, honeyed notes, candied fruit, fragrant herbs. Palate: flavourful, sweet, fresh, fruity, good acidity, long.

VIÑA LAUJAR COTA 950 2010 B
82

VIÑA LAUJAR SYRAH 2010 T
84

MALLORCA
4 KILOS VINÍCOLA

1ª Volta, 168 Puigverd
7200 Felanitx (Illes Balears)
☎: +34 660 226 641 - Fax: +34 971 580 523
www.4kilos.com
fgrimalt@4kilos.com

12 VOLTS 2011 T
syrah, merlot, cabernet sauvignon, callet, fogoneu

92 Colour: bright cherry. Nose: ripe fruit, sweet spices, creamy oak, scrubland. Palate: flavourful, fruity, toasty, round tannins.

4 KILOS 2011 T
93 Colour: cherry, garnet rim. Nose: balanced, fruit expression, scrubland, spicy. Palate: good structure, full, fruity, round tannins.

BINIGRAU

Fiol, 33
7143 Biniali (Illes Balears)
☎: +34 971 512 023 - Fax: +34 971 886 495
www.binigrau.es
info@binigrau.es

B - BINIGRAU 2010 T
80% manto negro, callet, 20% merlot

93 Colour: cherry, garnet rim. Nose: fruit liqueur notes, ripe fruit, complex, spicy. Palate: spirituous, elegant, warm, powerful, flavourful, full.

BINIGRAU CHARDONNAY 2012 BFB
chardonnay

90 Colour: bright yellow. Nose: powerfull, ripe fruit, sweet spices, creamy oak, fragrant herbs. Palate: rich, smoky aftertaste, flavourful, fresh, good acidity.

BINIGRAU DOLÇ 2010 T
manto negro, merlot

87 Colour: cherry, garnet rim. Nose: fruit liqueur notes, neat, fresh, medium intensity. Palate: pruney, powerful, flavourful, sweet.

E - BINIGRAU 2012 RD
50% manto negro, 50% merlot

88 Colour: light cherry. Nose: powerfull, ripe fruit, red berry notes, floral, expressive. Palate: powerful, fruity, fresh.

E - BINIGRAU 2012 T
50% manto negro, 50% merlot

90 Colour: cherry, garnet rim. Nose: medium intensity, expressive, spicy, ripe fruit. Palate: powerful, full, flavourful, sweetness, spicy.

NOU NAT 2012 B
60% prensal, 40% chardonnay

92 Colour: bright straw. Nose: fruit expression, fresh fruit, fine lees, powerfull, balanced. Palate: elegant, round, sweetness, complex, powerful, flavourful.

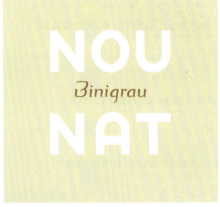

OBAC'11 2011 TC
manto negro, callet, merlot, cabernet sauvignon, syrah

90 Colour: light cherry. Nose: aromatic coffee, dried herbs, spicy, ripe fruit. Palate: ripe fruit, flavourful, spirituous, sweetness.

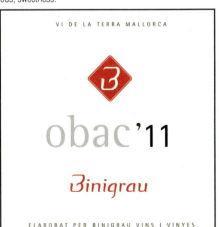

BODEGA BINIAGUAL

Llogaret de Biniagual, Cami de Muro s/n
7350 Binissalem (Mallorca)
☎: +34 678 079 148 - Fax: +34 971 886 108
www.bodegabiniagual.com
info@bodegabiniagual.com

FINCA BINIAGUAL VERÁN 2009 T
57% manto negro, 26% syrah, 17% cabernet sauvignon

88 Colour: cherry, garnet rim. Nose: ripe fruit, spicy, creamy oak, toasty. Palate: powerful, flavourful, toasty, round tannins.

BODEGA MESQUIDA MORA

Pas des Frare - Cantonada Cami de Sa
7260 Porreres (Illes Balears)
☎: +34 971 647 106 - Fax: +34 971 168 205
www.mesquidamora.com
info@mesquidamora.com

ACROLLAM BLANC 2012 B
prensal, chardonnay

88 Colour: bright straw. Nose: candied fruit, fruit preserve. Palate: sweetness, flavourful, full.

ACROLLAM ROSAT 2012 RD
merlot, cabernet sauvignon

85 Colour: rose, purple rim. Nose: powerfull, ripe fruit, red berry notes, floral. Palate: powerful, fruity, fresh.

SINCRONÍA BLANC ECOLOGIC 2012 B
prensal, parellada, chardonnay

88 Colour: bright straw. Nose: medium intensity, neat, fresh, fresh fruit. Palate: good acidity, full, fruity, flavourful.

SINCRONÍA NEGRE ECOLOGIC 2012 T
callet, manto negro, syrah, merlot

90 Colour: cherry, purple rim. Nose: expressive, fresh fruit, red berry notes, floral, earthy notes. Palate: flavourful, fruity, good acidity, round tannins.

SINCRONÍA ROSAT ECOLOGIC 2012 RD
callet, cabernet sauvignon, merlot

80

SOTIL NEGRE ECOLOGIC 2011 T
callet, manto negro

90 Colour: bright cherry. Nose: toasty, spicy, earthy notes, damp earth. Palate: flavourful, good acidity, fine tannins.

BODEGAS ÁNGEL

Ctra. Sta María - Sencelles, km. 4,8
7320 Santa María del Camí (Illes Balears)
☎: +34 971 621 638 - Fax: +34 971 621 638
www.bodegasangel.com
info@bodegasangel.com

ÁNGEL BLANC DE BLANCA 2012 B
prensal, chardonnay

89 Colour: bright straw. Nose: fresh, fresh fruit, white flowers. Palate: flavourful, fruity, good acidity, balanced.

ÁNGEL CABERNET SAUVIGNON 2010 T
cabernet sauvignon

88 Colour: deep cherry. Nose: short, balanced, ripe fruit. Palate: correct, round, flavourful, powerful.

ÁNGEL GRAN SELECCIÓ 2009 T ROBLE
cabernet sauvignon, merlot, callet, manto negro

91 Colour: cherry, garnet rim. Nose: ripe fruit, spicy, creamy oak, toasty, earthy notes, characterful. Palate: powerful, flavourful, toasty, round tannins.

ÁNGEL LAU ROSA 2012 RD
merlot, manto negro

85 Colour: rose, purple rim. Nose: powerfull, ripe fruit, red berry notes, floral. Palate: powerful, fruity, fresh.

ÁNGEL MANT BLANC 2011 B
manto negro

88 Colour: bright straw. Nose: fresh fruit, neat, fresh, medium intensity. Palate: correct, fruity, fresh, powerful.

ÁNGEL NEGRE 2010 T ROBLE
manto negro, cabernet sauvignon, merlot, syrah, callet

92 Colour: bright cherry. Nose: sweet spices, creamy oak, expressive, scrubland, earthy notes. Palate: flavourful, fruity, toasty, round tannins.

ÁNGEL SYRAH 2010 T
syrah

88 Colour: cherry, garnet rim. Nose: medium intensity, expressive, ripe fruit, spicy. Palate: powerful, flavourful, spicy, ripe fruit.

ÁNGEL VIOGNIER 2011 B
viognier

89 Colour: bright golden. Nose: neat, fresh, closed, candied fruit. Palate: full, flavourful, rich, sweetness.

BODEGAS CA'N VIDALET

Ctra. Alcudia - Pollença Ma 2201, Km. 4,85
7460 Pollença (Illes Balears)
☎: +34 971 531 719 - Fax: +34 971 535 395
www.canvidalet.com
info@canvidalet.com

CA'N VIDALET BLANC DE BLANCS 2012 B
chardonnay, moscatel, sauvignon blanc, prensal

89 Colour: bright straw. Nose: fresh, fresh fruit, characterful. Palate: flavourful, fruity, good acidity, balanced.

CA'N VIDALET BLANC DE NEGRES 2012 RD
merlot, cabernet sauvignon, syrah

87 Colour: coppery red. Nose: elegant, candied fruit, dried flowers, red berry notes. Palate: light-bodied, flavourful, good acidity, long, spicy.

CA'N VIDALET SES PEDRES 2011 B
chardonnay

90 Colour: bright straw. Nose: elegant, complex, fresh, neat.

CA'N VIDALET SO DEL XIPRER 2009 T
70% merlot, 30% cabernet sauvignon

88 Colour: dark-red cherry. Nose: spicy, roasted coffee, medium intensity, balanced. Palate: creamy, ripe fruit, grainy tannins.

BODEGAS JOSÉ LUIS FERRER

Conquistador, 103
7350 Binissalem (Illes Balears)
☎: +34 971 511 050 - Fax: +34 971 870 084
www.vinosferrer.com
secretaria@vinosferrer.com

JOSÉ L. FERRER DUES MANTONEGRO CABERNET 2011 T
cabernet sauvignon, manto negro

87 Colour: bright cherry. Nose: ripe fruit, sweet spices, creamy oak. Palate: flavourful, fruity, toasty, round tannins.

JOSÉ L. FERRER DUES MOLL CHARDONNAY MOLL 2012 B
moll, chardonnay

88 Colour: bright straw. Nose: fresh, fresh fruit, white flowers, expressive. Palate: flavourful, fruity, good acidity, balanced.

JOSÉ L. FERRER DUES SYRAH CALLET 2011 T
callet, syrah

90 Colour: light cherry, garnet rim. Nose: fruit expression, ripe fruit, neat, complex, varietal, aromatic coffee. Palate: creamy, ripe fruit, powerful, flavourful, spirituous.

BODEGAS SON PUIG S.L.

Finca Son Puig
7194 Puigpunyent (Illes Balears)
☎: +34 971 614 184 - Fax: +34 971 614 184
www.sonpuig.com
info@sonpuig.com

GRAN SONPUIG 2007 T
merlot, cabernet sauvignon

90 Colour: cherry, garnet rim. Nose: ripe fruit, spicy, creamy oak, toasty, complex. Palate: powerful, flavourful, toasty, round tannins.

SONPUIG 2011 BFB
chardonnay, prensal, sauvignon blanc

91 Colour: bright yellow. Nose: powerfull, ripe fruit, sweet spices, creamy oak. Palate: rich, smoky aftertaste, flavourful, fresh, good acidity.

SONPUIG 2010 T
merlot, cabernet sauvignon, tempranillo, callet

87 Colour: deep cherry. Nose: scrubland, wet leather. Palate: flavourful, fine bitter notes, good acidity.

SONPUIG BLANC D'ESTIU 2011 B
prensal, chardonnay, sauvignon blanc

87 Colour: bright straw. Nose: medium intensity, ripe fruit, citrus fruit. Palate: flavourful, good acidity.

SONPUIG ESTIU 2011 T
merlot, callet, tempranillo, cabernet sauvignon

86 Colour: very deep cherry. Nose: ripe fruit, spicy, toasty. Palate: flavourful, good acidity, fine bitter notes.

CELLER TIANNA NEGRE

Camí des Mitjans. Desvio a la izquierda en el km. 1,5 de la Ctra. Binissalem-Inca
7350 Binissalem (Illes Balears)
☎: +34 971 886 826 - Fax: +34 971 226 201
www.tiannanegre.com
info@tiannanegre.com

TIANNA BOCCHORIS BLANC 2012 B
sauvignon blanc, prensal, giró

91 Colour: bright yellow. Nose: powerfull, ripe fruit, sweet spices, creamy oak, fragrant herbs. Palate: rich, flavourful, fresh, good acidity.

COMERCIAL GRUPO FREIXENET S.A.

Joan Sala, 2
8770 Sant Sadurní D'Anoia (Barcelona)
☎: +34 938 917 000 - Fax: +34 938 183 095
www.freixenet.es
freixenet@freixenet.es

SUSANA SEMPRE 2012 B
47,5% chardonnay, 47,5% prensal, 5% manto negro

88 Colour: pale. Nose: closed, elegant, fresh fruit. Palate: good acidity, elegant, fruity, fresh.

SUSANA SEMPRE MAIOR NEGRE 2010 T
66% cabernet sauvignon, 17% manto negro, 12% merlot, 3% callet, 2% syrah

90 Colour: bright cherry. Nose: ripe fruit, sweet spices, expressive, balsamic herbs, toasty. Palate: flavourful, fruity, toasty, round tannins.

FINCA SON BORDILS

Ctra. Inca - Sineu, Km. 4,1
7300 Inca (Illes Balears)
☎: +34 971 182 200 - Fax: +34 971 182 202
www.sonbordils.es
info@sonbordils.es

BISBALS DE SON BORRDILS 2007 T
55% merlot, 23% cabernet sauvignon, 20% manto negro, 1% syrah, 1% callet

88 Colour: light cherry, orangey edge. Nose: characterful, neat, scrubland, ripe fruit. Palate: powerful, flavourful, spirituous, sweetness, sweet tannins.

FINCA SON BORDILS CABERNET SAUVIGNON 2006 T
99,2% cabernet sauvignon, callet

87 Colour: dark-red cherry, orangey edge. Nose: short, balanced, medium intensity. Palate: powerful, flavourful, sweetness, spirituous.

FINCA SON BORDILS CHARDONNAY 2012 B
93% chardonnay, 7% prensal

90 Colour: bright straw. Nose: fruit expression, elegant, complex. Palate: elegant, balanced, spirituous, round, flavourful, powerful.

FINCA SON BORDILS MERLOT 2006 T
93,1% merlot, 6,9% manto negro, cabernet sauvignon, callet, monastrell

90 Colour: light cherry, orangey edge. Nose: elegant, balanced, mineral, ripe fruit. Palate: powerful, flavourful, full, round, elegant, soft tannins.

FINCA SON BORDILS ROSAT DE MONASTRELL 2012 RD
100% monastrell

89 Colour: bright, rose. Nose: raspberry, red berry notes, varietal, neat, fresh. Palate: correct, powerful, light-bodied, fruity, easy to drink.

FINCA SON BORDILS SYRAH 2006 T
95% syrah, 5% cabernet sauvignon

87 Colour: dark-red cherry, orangey edge. Nose: red clay notes, macerated fruit, ripe fruit, spicy. Palate: soft tannins, rich, full, powerful.

FINCA SON BORDILS SYRAH MAGNUM 2007 T
100% syrah

90 Colour: cherry, garnet rim. Nose: spicy, ripe fruit, balanced, complex. Palate: round, spirituous, balanced, elegant.

SON BORDILS BLANC DE RAÏM BLANC 2012 B
93% prensal, 7% viognier

91 Colour: bright straw. Nose: fresh, fresh fruit, white flowers, expressive. Palate: flavourful, fruity, good acidity, balanced.

SON BORDILS BLANC DOLC 2012 B
76% prensal, 24% moscatel grano menudo

89 Colour: bright straw. Nose: complex, fresh, neat, medium intensity, fruit preserve. Palate: complex, full, powerful, flavourful.

SON BORDILS MUSCAT 2012 B
100% moscatel grano menudo

90 Colour: bright straw. Nose: fruit expression, varietal, neat, fresh, balanced. Palate: fruity, fresh, full, powerful, complex.

SON BORDILS NEGRE 2008 T
63% merlot, 33% cabernet sauvignon, 4% manto negro

88 Colour: deep cherry. Nose: caramel, sweet spices, ripe fruit. Palate: spirituous, round, powerful, flavourful, full, sweet tannins.

JAUME DE PUNTIRÓ

Pza. Nova 23
7320 Santa María del Camí (Illes Balears)
☎: +34 971 620 023
www.vinsjaumedepuntiro.com
pere@vinsjaumedepuntiro.com

PORPRAT 2009 T
merlot

87 Colour: very deep cherry. Nose: characterful, earthy notes. Palate: flavourful, good acidity, balanced.

OLIVER MARAGUES

Cami de ses vinyes s/n
7210 Algaida (Mallorca)
☎: +34 971 125 028 - Fax: +34 971 665 773
www.olivermoragues.com
info@olivermoragues.com

OM 2011 T

89 Colour: bright cherry. Nose: sweet spices, creamy oak, expressive, scrubland. Palate: flavourful, fruity, toasty, round tannins.

SON CAMPANER

Pou Bauza 19B
7350 Binissalem (Mallorca)
☎: +34 971 870 004
www.soncampaner.es
info@soncampaner.es

SON CAMPANER ATHOS 2011 T
syrah, cabernet sauvignon

91 Colour: cherry, garnet rim. Nose: ripe fruit, spicy, creamy oak, toasty, expressive. Palate: powerful, flavourful, toasty, round tannins.

SON CAMPANER BLANC DE BLANCS 2012 B
macabeo, prensal, chardonnay

89 Colour: bright straw. Nose: fresh, fresh fruit, white flowers, expressive. Palate: flavourful, fruity, good acidity, balanced.

SON CAMPANER BLANC DE NEGRES 2012 RD
syrah, merlot, manto negro

88 Colour: raspberry rose. Nose: fresh fruit, fruit expression, varietal. Palate: sweetness, fruity, fresh, powerful, flavourful.

SON CAMPANER MERLOT 2011 T
merlot

90 Colour: cherry, garnet rim. Nose: ripe fruit, spicy, creamy oak, toasty. Palate: powerful, flavourful, toasty, round tannins.

SON CAMPANER TERRA ROSSA 2011 T
callet, merlot, cabernet sauvignon, syrah

92 Colour: bright cherry. Nose: ripe fruit, sweet spices, creamy oak, balsamic herbs, scrubland. Palate: flavourful, fruity, toasty, round tannins.

SON PRIM PETIT

Ctra. Inca - Sencelles, Km. 4,9
7140 Sencelles (Mallorca)
☎: +34 971 872 758
www.sonprim.com
correo@sonprim.com

SON PRIM BLANC DE MERLOT 2012 B
merlot

83

SON PRIM ROSSAT 2012 RD
manto negro, merlot

88 Colour: raspberry rose. Nose: fresh fruit, neat, fresh, balanced. Palate: fruity, fresh, flavourful.

SON VIVES

Font de la Vila, 2
7191 Banyalbufar (Illes Ballears)
☎: +34 609 601 904 - Fax: +34 971 718 065
www.sonvives.com
toni@darder.com

FUSIÓ DE BLANCS 2012 B

87 Colour: bright straw. Nose: faded flowers, candied fruit, fruit preserve. Palate: sweetness, fine bitter notes.

JUXTA MARE MALVASÍA 2012 B

84

VINS NADAL

Ramón Llull, 2
7350 Binissalem (Illes Balears)
☎: +34 971 511 058 - Fax: +34 971 870 150
www.vinsnadal.com
albaflor@vinsnadal.com

COUPAGE 110 VINS NADAL 2010 T BARRICA
65% manto negro, 24% cabernet sauvignon, 8% merlot, 3% syrah

89 Colour: cherry, garnet rim. Nose: ripe fruit, spicy, creamy oak, toasty, complex. Palate: powerful, flavourful, toasty, round tannins.

MERLOT 110 VINS NADAL 2007 T BARRICA
merlot

87 Colour: pale ruby, brick rim edge. Nose: medium intensity, ripe fruit, spicy. Palate: flavourful, sweetness.

SYRAH 110 VINS NADAL 2007 T BARRICA
syrah

88 Colour: cherry, garnet rim. Nose: spicy, ripe fruit, short. Palate: spicy, slightly acidic, fruity.

VINYES MORTITX

Ctra. Pollença Lluc, Km. 10,9
7315 Escorca (Illes Balears)
☎: +34 971 182 339 - Fax: +34 871 100 053
www.vinyesmortitx.com
bodega@vinyesmortitx.com

FLAIRES DE MORTITX 2012 RD
monastrell, syrah, tempranillo, cabernet sauvignon

82

L'ERGULL DE MORTITX 2010 BFB
malvasía, moscatel, chardonnay, riesling

87 Colour: bright yellow. Nose: ripe fruit, sweet spices, creamy oak. Palate: rich, smoky aftertaste, flavourful, fresh, good acidity.

L'U BLANC 2011 B
malvasía

90 Colour: bright straw. Nose: fresh, fresh fruit, white flowers. Palate: flavourful, fruity, good acidity, balanced.

L'U NEGRE DE MORTITX 2009 TC
syrah, cabernet sauvignon, tempranillo

90 Colour: cherry, garnet rim. Nose: spicy, creamy oak, toasty, characterful. Palate: powerful, flavourful, toasty, round tannins.

MORTITX BLANC 2012 B
malvasía, moscatel, chardonnay, riesling

87 Colour: bright straw. Nose: closed, short, fresh. Palate: fruity, fresh, rich, flavourful.

MORTITX NEGRE 2011 T
syrah, merlot, cabernet sauvignon, monastrell, tempranillo

87 Colour: dark-red cherry, garnet rim. Nose: short, warm, medium intensity, ripe fruit, spicy. Palate: ripe fruit, flavourful, lacks expression.

MORTITX ROSAT 2012 RD
merlot, cabernet sauvignon, monastrell, syrah, tempranillo

85 Colour: light cherry. Nose: fruit expression, red berry notes. Palate: flavourful, light-bodied, good acidity.

MORTITX ROSAT SELECCIO 2011 RD
monastrell, syrah, cabernet sauvignon

79

MORTITX SYRAH 2008 T
syrah

88 Colour: cherry, garnet rim. Nose: spicy, creamy oak, toasty. Palate: powerful, flavourful, toasty, round tannins.

RODAL PLA DE MORTITX 2009 T
syrah, tempranillo, merlot, cabernet sauvignon

90 Colour: cherry, garnet rim. Nose: ripe fruit, spicy, creamy oak, toasty, complex. Palate: powerful, flavourful, toasty, round tannins.

RIBERA DEL ANDARAX
PAGOS DE INDALIA

Paseo de los Baños, 2
4458 Padules (Almería)
☎: +34 950 510 728
www.pagosdeindalia.com
juanma@pagosdeindalia.com

INDALIA PINOT NOIR 2011 T
pinot noir

90 Colour: light cherry. Nose: floral, earthy notes, dried herbs, dry stone, spicy. Palate: balanced, elegant, spicy, balsamic.

INDALIA SYRAH 2011 T
100% syrah

89 Colour: bright cherry. Nose: ripe fruit, sweet spices, creamy oak, expressive. Palate: flavourful, fruity, toasty, balanced.

INDALIA VENDIMIA SELECCIONADA 2011 T

90 Colour: cherry, garnet rim. Nose: ripe fruit, spicy, creamy oak, toasty, damp earth. Palate: powerful, flavourful, toasty.

RIBERA DEL GÁLLEGO - CINCO VILLAS
BODEGAS EJEANAS

Avda. Cosculluela, 23
50600 Ejea de los Caballeros (Zaragoza)
☎: +34 976 663 770 - Fax: +34 976 663 770
www.bodegasejeanas.com
info@bodegasejeanas.com

UVA NOCTURNA 2012 B
chardonnay, verdejo, moscatel

85 Colour: bright yellow. Nose: ripe fruit, dried herbs, citrus fruit. Palate: powerful, flavourful, correct.

UVA NOCTURNA GARNACHA 2011 T ROBLE
100% garnacha

87 Colour: cherry, garnet rim. Nose: ripe fruit, wild herbs, spicy. Palate: powerful, rich, flavourful.

UVA NOCTURNA GARNACHA PLUS 2007 T
100% garnacha

86 Colour: pale ruby, brick rim edge. Nose: spicy, fine reductive notes, wet leather, aged wood nuances. Palate: spicy, fine tannins, long.

UVA NOCTURNA MERLOT 2011 T
100% merlot

88 Colour: bright cherry. Nose: ripe fruit, creamy oak, fragrant herbs. Palate: flavourful, fruity, toasty.

UVA NOCTURNA TEMPRANILLO GARNACHA 2009 T ROBLE
tempranillo, garnacha

85 Colour: bright cherry. Nose: ripe fruit, sweet spices, balsamic herbs. Palate: flavourful, fruity, toasty, harsh oak tannins.

VEGA DE LUCHÁN 2009 T BARRICA
80% tempranillo, 20% cabernet sauvignon

88 Colour: cherry, garnet rim. Nose: ripe fruit, spicy, creamy oak, toasty, balsamic herbs. Palate: powerful, flavourful, toasty.

VEGA DE LUCHÁN 2012 RD
merlot, cabernet sauvignon

88 Colour: rose, purple rim. Nose: powerfull, ripe fruit, red berry notes, floral, lactic notes. Palate: powerful, fruity, fresh.

VEGA DE LUCHÁN MOSCATEL 2009 B
moscatel, verdejo

87 Colour: golden. Nose: powerfull, floral, honeyed notes, candied fruit, fragrant herbs. Palate: flavourful, sweet, fresh, fruity, good acidity, long.

EDRA

Ctra A - 132, km 26
22800 Ayerbe (Huesca)
☎: +34 679 420 455 - Fax: +34 974 380 829
www.bodega-edra.com
edra@bodega-edra.com

EDRA MERLOT SYRAH 2008 T
syrah, merlot

88 Colour: cherry, garnet rim. Nose: ripe fruit, grassy, dried flowers, creamy oak. Palate: balsamic, spicy, balanced.

EDRA XTRA SYRAH 2007 T
syrah

89 Colour: cherry, garnet rim. Nose: ripe fruit, fruit preserve, balsamic herbs, fine reductive notes, spicy. Palate: light-bodied, spicy, flavourful.

EVOHE BODEGAS

Ignacio de Ara, 3 Local
50002 Zaragoza (Zaragoza)
☎: +34 976 461 056 - Fax: +34 976 461 558
www.evohegarnacha.com
nosotros@evohegarnacha.com

EVOHÉ TEMPRANILLO VIÑAS VIEJAS 2012 T
tempranillo

84

RIBERA DEL QUEILES
BODEGA DEL JARDÍN

San Juan, 14
31520 Cascante (Navarra)
☎: +34 948 850 055 - Fax: +34 948 850 097
www.bodegadeljardin.es
info@bodegadeljardin.es

1 PULSO 2009 T
tempranillo, garnacha

87 Colour: cherry, garnet rim. Nose: balsamic herbs, wild herbs, spicy, creamy oak. Palate: powerful, flavourful, spicy.

2 PULSO 2009 T
tempranillo, merlot, cabernet sauvignon

90 Colour: cherry, garnet rim. Nose: ripe fruit, spicy, creamy oak, toasty, complex. Palate: powerful, flavourful, toasty, round tannins.

3 PULSO 2009 T
tempranillo, garnacha

89 Colour: bright cherry. Nose: ripe fruit, sweet spices, creamy oak, roasted coffee. Palate: flavourful, fruity, toasty, round tannins.

EDRA

Ctra A - 132, km 26
22800 Ayerbe (Huesca)
☎: +34 679 420 455 - Fax: +34 974 380 829
www.bodega-edra.com
edra@bodega-edra.com

EDRA GRULLAS DE PASO 2010 T
tempranillo, garnacha, merlot, cabernet sauvignon

88 Colour: cherry, garnet rim. Nose: ripe fruit, damp earth, scrubland, spicy. Palate: balsamic, balanced, long.

GUELBENZU

Paraje La Lombana s/n
50513 Vierlas (Zaragoza)
☎: +34 948 202 200 - Fax: +34 948 202 200
www.guelbenzu.com
info@taninia.com

GUELBENZU AZUL 2009 T
tempranillo

90 Colour: cherry, garnet rim. Nose: ripe fruit, spicy, creamy oak, toasty. Palate: powerful, flavourful, toasty, round tannins.

GUELBENZU EVO 2007 T
cabernet sauvignon

89 Colour: cherry, garnet rim. Nose: ripe fruit, fruit liqueur notes, aged wood nuances, tobacco, fine reductive notes, scrubland. Palate: powerful, spicy, long.

GUELBENZU LAUTUS 2005 T BARRICA

89 Colour: pale ruby, brick rim edge. Nose: spicy, fine reductive notes, wet leather, aged wood nuances, fruit liqueur notes. Palate: spicy, fine tannins, elegant, long.

GUELBENZU VIERLAS 2010 T
syrah

87 Colour: cherry, garnet rim. Nose: fruit preserve, aromatic coffee, sweet spices, roasted coffee. Palate: powerful, flavourful, toasty.

SIERRA NORTE DE SEVILLA
COLONIAS DE GALEÓN

Plazuela, 39
41370 Cazalla de la Sierra (Sevilla)
☎: +34 955 710 092 - Fax: +34 955 710 093
www.coloniasdegaleon.com
info@coloniasdegaleon.com

COLONIAS DE GALEÓN 2010 T ROBLE
40% cabernet franc, 30% tempranillo, 15% syrah, 15% merlot

82

COLONIAS DE GALEÓN 2012 T MACERACIÓN CARBÓNICA
50% cabernet franc, 30% tempranillo, 20% syrah

85 Colour: cherry, purple rim. Nose: expressive, fresh fruit, red berry notes, floral. Palate: flavourful, fruity, good acidity.

OCNOS 2011 BFB
80% chardonnay, 20% viognier

82

PETIT OCNOS 2011 RD
cabernet franc

78

PETIT OCNOS SOBRE LÍAS B
100% chardonnay

83

SILENTE SELECCIÓN 2007 T ROBLE
50% cabernet franc, 30% merlot, 10% tempranillo, 10% syrah

90 Colour: cherry, garnet rim. Nose: ripe fruit, spicy, creamy oak, toasty, complex. Palate: powerful, flavourful, toasty, round tannins, balanced, elegant.

VALDEJALÓN
LATIDOS DE VINO (EPILENSE DE VINOS Y VIÑEDOS)

La Quimera del oro, 30 - 3ºD
50019 (Zaragoza)
☎: +34 669 148 771
www.latidosdevino.com
fmora@latidosdevino.com

LATIDOS DE VINO "AMOR" 2009 TC
90% garnacha, 10% syrah

90 Colour: cherry, garnet rim. Nose: ripe fruit, spicy, creamy oak, toasty, complex. Palate: powerful, flavourful, toasty, round tannins.

LATIDOS DE VINO "BESO" 2012 RD
garnacha

87 Colour: rose, purple rim. Nose: powerfull, ripe fruit, red berry notes, floral, expressive. Palate: powerful, fruity, fresh.

LATIDOS DE VINO "DESEO" 2012 B
80% macabeo, 20% garnacha blanca

82

LATIDOS DE VINO "PASIÓN" 2012 T
garnacha

90 Colour: cherry, purple rim. Nose: red berry notes, ripe fruit, floral, balsamic herbs, expressive, lactic notes. Palate: powerful, flavourful, long.

LATIDOS DE VINO "PLACER" 2012 B
100% moscatel romano

88 Colour: golden. Nose: powerfull, floral, honeyed notes, candied fruit, fragrant herbs. Palate: flavourful, sweet, fresh, fruity, good acidity, long.

VALLE DEL CINCA
NUVIANA

Ctra. A-1241, km 11
22533 Belver de Cinca (Huesca)
☎: +34 974 478 800
www.nuviana.com
e.izquierdo@codorniu.com

VERANZA 2010 T
50% cabernet sauvignon, 25% syrah, 25% tempranillo

84

VERANZA 2012 B
100% chardonnay

85 Colour: bright straw. Nose: candied fruit, ripe fruit, dried herbs. Palate: powerful, flavourful.

VERANZA 2012 RD
72% cabernet sauvignon, 28% tempranillo

86 Colour: rose, purple rim. Nose: candied fruit, floral, fragrant herbs, expressive. Palate: fresh, fruity, easy to drink.

VALONGA, BODEGAS Y VIÑEDOS

Monte Valonga, s/n
22522 Belver de Cinca (Huesca)
☎: +34 974 435 127 - Fax: +34 974 339 101
www.valonga.com
bodegas@valonga.com

BUSARDO SELECCIÓN 2011 T ROBLE
garnacha, tempranillo, syrah

88 Colour: cherry, garnet rim. Nose: ripe fruit, spicy, creamy oak, toasty, earthy notes. Palate: powerful, flavourful, toasty, correct.

BUSARDO SYRAH 2010 T ROBLE
100% syrah

85 Colour: cherry, garnet rim. Nose: ripe fruit, creamy oak, scrubland. Palate: powerful, flavourful, toasty.

VALONGA SASO ALTO 2007 T
garnacha, syrah

89 Colour: cherry, garnet rim. Nose: ripe fruit, balsamic herbs, spicy, sweet spices, creamy oak. Palate: complex, spicy, flavourful, round tannins.

VIÑEDOS DE ESPAÑA
EL ESCOCÉS VOLANTE

Barrio La Rosa Bajo, 16
50300 Calatayud (Zaragoza)
☎: +34 637 511 133
www.escocesvolante.es
info@escocesvolante.es

EL PUÑO HA IDO AL GRANO 2011 BFB
viognier

90 Colour: bright straw. Nose: white flowers, dry stone, fragrant herbs, sweet spices, creamy oak. Palate: fresh, fruity, spicy, long.

FINCA LA LAGUNILLA - CASA CORREDOR

Casas de Corredor, s/n (Autovía Madrid/Alicante, salida 168, La Encina
2660 Caudete (Albacete)
☎: +34 966 842 064
www.casacorredor.es
jdminano@casacorredor.es

CASA CORREDOR TEMPRANILLO 2010 T
tempranillo

87 Colour: cherry, garnet rim. Nose: sweet spices, creamy oak, red berry notes, ripe fruit. Palate: flavourful, fruity, toasty.

VINYES MORTITX

Ctra. Pollença Lluc, Km. 10,9
7315 Escorca (Illes Balears)
☎: +34 971 182 339 - Fax: +34 871 100 053
www.vinyesmortitx.com
bodega@vinyesmortitx.com

DOLÇ DE GEL MORTITX 2010 B
moscatel, riesling

89 Colour: bright golden. Nose: closed, neat, white flowers, fruit preserve. Palate: unctuous, elegant, good acidity, fruity, powerful, sweet.

Just outside the "Vino de Calidad" status, we find the "Vino de Mesa" ("Table Wine") category, which are those not included in any of the other categories (not even in the "Vino de la Tierra" one, regarded as "Vino de Mesa" by the Ley del Vino ("Wine Law"). The present editions of our Guide has up to 41 table wines rated as excellent, something which is quite telling, and force us to a change of mind in regard to the popular prejudice against this category, traditionally related –almost exclusively– to bulk, cheap wines.

In this section we include wines made in geographical areas that do not belong to any designation of origin (DO as such) or association of Vino de la Tierra, although most of them come indeed from wines regions with some vine growing and winemaking tradition.

We do not pretend to come up with a comprehensive account of the usually overlooked vinos de mesa (table wines), but to enumerate here some Spanish wines that were bottled with no geographic label whatsoever.

The wineries are listed alphabetically within their Autonomous regions. The reader will discover some singular wines of –in some cases– excellent quality that could be of interest to those on the look out for novelties or alternative products to bring onto their tables.

ALEMANY I CORRIO

Melió, 78
8720 Vilafranca del Penedès (Barcelona)
☎: +34 938 922 746 - Fax: +34 938 172 587
sotlefriec@sotlefriec.com

NÚVOLS 2012 B
60% xarel.lo, 40% garnacha blanca

90 Colour: bright straw. Nose: floral, citrus fruit, dried herbs, dry stone, fruit expression. Palate: fresh, fruity, flavourful.

AVINYÓ CAVAS

Masia Can Fontanals
8793 Avinyonet del Penedès (Barcelona)
☎: +34 938 970 055 - Fax: +34 938 970 691
www.avinyo.com
avinyo@avinyo.com

PETILLANT BLANC 2012 B
xarel.lo, moscatel, macabeo

85 Colour: bright straw. Nose: fresh, fresh fruit, white flowers, expressive. Palate: flavourful, fruity, fine bead.

BODEGA ECOLÓGICA JOAQUÍN FERNÁNDEZ

Finca Los Frutales Paraje de los Frontones
29400 Ronda (Málaga)
☎: +34 665 899 200 - Fax: +34 951 166 043
www.bodegajf.com
info@bodegajf.es

BLANCO DE TINTA 2012 B BARRICA
merlot

85 Colour: raspberry rose. Nose: jasmine, expressive, balanced, sweet spices. Palate: rich, spicy, good finish.

BODEGA F. SCHATZ

Finca Sanguijuela, s/n Apdo. Correos 131
29400 Ronda (Málaga)
☎: +34 952 871 313 - Fax: +34 952 871 313
www.f-schatz.com
bodega@f-schatz.com

ACINIPO 2004 TC
lemberger

88 Colour: cherry, garnet rim. Nose: ripe fruit, spicy, tobacco, cocoa bean. Palate: flavourful, spicy, fine bitter notes.

SCHATZ ROSADO 2012 RD
muskattrolinger

88 Colour: rose, purple rim. Nose: powerfull, ripe fruit, red berry notes, floral, expressive, sweet spices. Palate: powerful, fruity, fresh.

BODEGA KIENINGER

Los Frontones, 67
29400 Ronda (Málaga)
☎: +34 952 879 554
www.bodegakieninger.com
martin@bodegakieninger.com

7 VIN BLAUFRAENKISCH 2011 T
100% blaufraenkisch

93 Colour: cherry, garnet rim. Nose: ripe fruit, balsamic herbs, sweet spices, creamy oak, tobacco. Palate: correct, flavourful, spicy, long, balanced. Personality.

7 VIN ZWEIGELT 2011 T
100% zweigelt

91 Colour: cherry, garnet rim. Nose: ripe fruit, spicy, creamy oak, scrubland, earthy notes. Palate: powerful, flavourful, toasty, round tannins.

BODEGA MAS L'ALTET

Mas L'Altet Partida de la Creu, s/n
3838 Alfafara (Alicante)
☎: +34 963 816 849
www.bodegamaslaltet.com
nina@bodegamaslaltet.com

AVI DE MAS L'ALTET 2010 T
58% syrah, 25% cabernet sauvignon, 13% garnacha, 4% merlot

90 Colour: cherry, garnet rim. Nose: ripe fruit, spicy, creamy oak, balsamic herbs. Palate: powerful, flavourful, toasty, round tannins, long.

LA NINETA 2011 T
86% garnacha, 7% syrah, 7% cabernet sauvignon

90 Colour: cherry, garnet rim. Nose: red berry notes, ripe fruit, balsamic herbs, mineral, creamy oak. Palate: powerful, flavourful, long, balanced.

BODEGA VICENTE FLORS

Pda. Pou D'encalbo, s/n
12118 Les Useres (Castellón)
☎: +34 671 618 851
www.bodegaflors.com
bodega@bodegaflors.com

CLOTÀS 2009 T
tempranillo, cabernet sauvignon

89 Colour: cherry, garnet rim. Nose: ripe fruit, spicy, creamy oak, toasty, scrubland, mineral. Palate: powerful, flavourful, toasty.

CLOTÀS MONASTRELL 2010 T
monastrell

88 Colour: cherry, garnet rim. Nose: red berry notes, ripe fruit, scrubland, spicy. Palate: long, powerful, flavourful, easy to drink.

FLOR DE CLOTÀS 2010 T
tempranillo

88 Colour: cherry, garnet rim. Nose: sweet spices, cocoa bean, red berry notes, ripe fruit, toasty. Palate: powerful, flavourful, rich.

FLOR DE CLOTÀS 2011 T
tempranillo

87 Colour: cherry, purple rim. Nose: red berry notes, ripe fruit, wild herbs, sweet spices. Palate: powerful, flavourful, long, toasty.

BODEGAS ARZUAGA NAVARRO

Ctra. N-122, Km. 325
47350 Quintanilla de Onésimo (Valladolid)
☎: +34 983 681 146 - Fax: +34 983 681 147
www.arzuaganavarro.com
bodeg@arzuaganavarro.com

FAN D. ORO 2011 BFB

90 Colour: bright golden. Nose: ripe fruit, dry nuts, powerfull, toasty, aged wood nuances, aromatic coffee. Palate: flavourful, spicy, toasty, long.

BODEGAS BENTOMIZ

Finca Almendro - Pago Cuesta Robano
29752 Sayalonga (Málaga)
☎: +34 952 115 939
www.bodegasbentomiz.com
info@bodegasbentomiz.com

ARIYANAS DAVID 2011 T
100% merlot

87 Colour: cherry, garnet rim. Nose: powerfull, fruit preserve, sweet spices, mineral. Palate: sweet, flavourful.

BODEGAS EL REGAJAL

Antigua Ctra. Andalucía, Km. 50,5
28223 Aranjuez (Madrid)
☎: +34 913 078 903 - Fax: +34 913 576 312
www.elregajal.es
isabel@elregajal.es

GALIA 2010 T
tempranillo, garnacha

93 Colour: cherry, garnet rim. Nose: red berry notes, ripe fruit, balsamic herbs, spicy, creamy oak, dry stone. Palate: rich, fruity, flavourful, long, balanced, elegant.

BODEGAS FONTEDEI

Doctor Horcajadas, 10
18570 Deifontes (Granada)
☎: +34 958 407 957
www.bodegasfontedei.com
bodegasfontedei@gmail.com

FONTEDEI TINTA FINA 2009 T ROBLE
tempranillo, garnacha

84

GARNATA 2009 T
syrah, merlot

85 Colour: cherry, garnet rim. Nose: ripe fruit, fruit preserve, scrubland, creamy oak. Palate: powerful, flavourful.

PRADO NEGRO 2010 T
tempranillo, cabernet sauvignon, garnacha

85 Colour: cherry, garnet rim. Nose: ripe fruit, spicy, creamy oak, toasty, earthy notes. Palate: powerful, flavourful, toasty.

PRADO NEGRO 2010 T
tempranillo, garnacha, cabernet sauvignon

88 Colour: cherry, garnet rim. Nose: spicy, creamy oak, toasty, fruit preserve. Palate: powerful, flavourful, toasty, balanced.

BODEGAS JOSÉ MOLINA

Fresca, 4
29170 Colmenar (Málaga)
☎: +34 952 730 956
www.bodegasjosemolina.es
contactar@bodegasjosemolina.es

PRIMERA INTENCIÓN "A MELADO" AROMATIZADO B
pedro ximénez

87 Colour: golden. Nose: powerfull, floral, honeyed notes, candied fruit, fragrant herbs. Palate: flavourful, sweet, fresh, fruity, good acidity, long.

PRIMERA INTENCIÓN "MOUNTAIN" NATURALMENTE DULCE B
pedro ximénez

85 Colour: old gold. Nose: faded flowers, varnish, candied fruit, sweet spices. Palate: ripe fruit, sweet, toasty.

PRIMERA INTENCIÓN 2008 T
tempranillo, syrah, otras

80

BODEGAS MARCOS MIÑAMBRES

Camino de Pobladura, s/n
24234 Villamañán (León)
☎: +34 987 767 038
satvined@picos.com

M. MIÑAMBRES 2009 T
tempranillo, prieto picudo

86 Colour: dark-red cherry, garnet rim. Nose: fruit liqueur notes, woody, spicy, ripe fruit, wild herbs. Palate: easy to drink, spicy, flavourful, powerful, fresh, fruity, lacks expression.

M. MIÑAMBRES 2012 RD
prieto picudo, tempranillo

78

M. MIÑAMBRES ALBARÍN 2012 B
albarín

88 Colour: bright straw. Nose: complex, characterful, varietal, grassy, balsamic herbs, fresh fruit. Palate: fruity, powerful, flavourful, good structure.

BODEGAS MARQUÉS DE VIZHOJA

Finca La Moreira s/n
36438 Cequeliños Arbo (Pontevedra)
☎: +34 986 665 825 - Fax: +34 986 665 960
www.marquesdevizhoja.com
marquesdevizhoja@marquesdevizhoja.com

MARQUÉS DE VIZHOJA 2012 B

86 Colour: bright straw. Nose: fresh, fresh fruit, white flowers, dried herbs. Palate: flavourful, fruity, good acidity.

BODEGAS MIGUEL CALATAYUD

Postas, 20
13300 Valdepeñas (Ciudad Real)
☎: +34 926 348 070 - Fax: +34 926 322 150
www.vegaval.com
vegaval@vegaval.com

TREBOLÉ 2012 B
sauvignon blanc, moscatel

85 Colour: golden. Nose: powerfull, floral, honeyed notes, candied fruit, fragrant herbs. Palate: flavourful, sweet, fresh, fruity, good acidity.

TREBOLÉ 2012 T
tempranillo, garnacha

83

BODEGAS OBANCA

Obanca, 12
33800 Cangas del Narcea (Asturias)
☎: +34 626 956 571 - Fax: +34 985 811 539
www.obanca.com
informacion@obanca.com

CASTRO DE LIMÉS 2011 T
carrasquin, albarín tinto, verdejo negro, mencía

92 Colour: cherry, garnet rim. Nose: red berry notes, ripe fruit, sweet spices, dry stone, creamy oak. Palate: powerful, flavourful, spicy, balsamic, balanced.

LA DESCARGA 2010 T
carrasquín, albarín tinto, verdejo negro, mencía

91 Colour: light cherry. Nose: ripe fruit, spicy, creamy oak, toasty. Palate: powerful, flavourful, toasty.

LA DESCARGA 2012 B
albarín, albillo

90 Colour: bright straw. Nose: fresh, fresh fruit, white flowers, fragrant herbs, mineral. Palate: flavourful, fruity, good acidity, balanced, elegant.

BODEGAS Y VIÑEDOS CASTIBLANQUE

Isaac Peral, 19
13610 Campo de Criptana (Ciudad Real)
☎: +34 926 589 147 - Fax: +34 926 589 148
www.bodegascastiblanque.com
info@bodegascastiblanque.com

LAGAR DE ENSANCHA T
48% tempranillo, 36% cabernet sauvignon, 16% syrah
84

SOLAMENTE 2012 T
tempranillo
82

SOLAMENTE S/C B
60% airén, 40% verdejo
83

SOLAMENTE S/C RD
100% syrah
84

ZUMO DE AMOR T
50% tempranillo, 50% syrah
82

BODEGAS Y VIÑEDOS SENTENCIA

Los Pedrones
46355 Requena (Valencia)
☎: +34 665 969 009
www.bodegassentencia.com
info@bodegassentencia.com

SENTENCIA 2009 T

89 Colour: cherry, garnet rim. Nose: spicy, creamy oak, toasty, complex, fruit preserve, candied fruit. Palate: powerful, flavourful, toasty, round tannins.

BRUNO MURCIANO & DAVID SAMPEDRO GIL

8 Avenida Banda De Musica El Angel
46315 Caudete de las Fuentes (Valencia)
☎: +34 962 319 096
bru.murciano@yahoo.es

EL SUEÑO DE BRUNO 2011 T
100% bobal

89 Colour: bright cherry. Nose: powerfull, warm, ripe fruit. Palate: flavourful, toasty, round tannins.

LA MALKERIDA 100% BOBAL 2012 T
100% bobal

91 Colour: bright cherry. Nose: ripe fruit, sweet spices, creamy oak, expressive. Palate: flavourful, fruity, toasty, round tannins.

CAN RICH

Camí de Sa Vorera, s/n
7820 San Antonio (Illes Balears)
☎: +34 971 803 377 - Fax: +34 971 803 377
www.bodegascanrich.com
info@bodegascanrich.com

CAN RICH BLANCO 2011 BN
malvasía

86 Colour: bright straw. Nose: medium intensity, dried herbs, fine lees, floral, fruit preserve. Palate: fresh, fruity, flavourful, good acidity.

CAN RICH ROSADO 2011 BN
syrah
83

CARREFOUR

Campezo, 16
28022 Madrid (Madrid)
☎: +34 902 202 000
www.carrefour.es

TENTADOR MISTELA
83

CARRIEL DELS VILARS

Mas Can Carriel
17753 Els Vilars (Girona)
☎: +34 972 563 335
carrieldelsvilars@hotmail.com

CARRIEL DELS VILARS 2007 TR
garnacha, syrah, cabernet sauvignon, samsó

84

CARRIEL DELS VILARS 2011 BN
macabeo, xarel.lo, parellada, garnacha blanca

88 Colour: bright golden. Nose: fine lees, dry nuts, complex, scrubland. Palate: powerful, flavourful, good acidity, fine bead, fine bitter notes.

CARRIEL DELS VILARS 2012 T
garnacha, syrah, cabernet sauvignon, samsó

89 Colour: cherry, garnet rim. Nose: ripe fruit, fruit preserve, scrubland, earthy notes, spicy. Palate: rich, powerful, spicy, long.

CAVAS DEL AMPURDÁN

Pza. del Carme, 1
17491 Perelada (Girona)
☎: +34 972 538 011 - Fax: +34 972 538 277
www.blancpescador.com
perelada@castilloperelada.com

BLANC PESCADOR PREMIUM BLANCO DE AGUJA
67% xarel.lo, 33% chardonnay

84

BLANC PESCADOR VINO DE AGUJA B
60% macabeo, 20% parellada, 20% xarel.lo

82

CRESTA AZUL B
60% moscatel, 20% macabeo, 10% xarel.lo, 10% parellada

84

CRESTA ROSA PREMIUM ROSADO DE AGUJA
85% pinot noir, 15% syrah

86 Colour: rose. Nose: floral, red berry notes, ripe fruit, fragrant herbs. Palate: light-bodied, fruity, fresh, flavourful, easy to drink.

CRESTA ROSA VINO DE AGUJA RD
40% tempranillo, 40% cariñena, 20% garnacha

84

PESCADOR ROSÉ ROSADO DE AGUJA
60% trepat, 20% garnacha, 20% merlot

84

CELLER LA MUNTANYA

Rotonda Quatrecamins, Cami I - Alquerieta, Nave B
3830 Muro de Alcoy (Alicante)
☎: +34 965 531 248 - Fax: +34 965 531 248
www.cellerlamuntanya.com
info@cellerlamuntanya.com

ALBIR 2011 B
50% malvasía, 30% merseguera, 20% verdil

89 Colour: bright yellow. Nose: ripe fruit, dried flowers, dried herbs, earthy notes, dry nuts, spicy. Palate: rich, powerful, flavourful.

ALMOROIG 2007 T
69% monastrell, 16% giró, 15% garnacha tintorera

90 Colour: cherry, garnet rim. Nose: spicy, fine reductive notes, aged wood nuances, fruit liqueur notes. Palate: spicy, long, powerful, flavourful.

CELLER LA MUNTANYA DOLÇ NATURAL 2010 B
100% malvasía

94 Colour: golden. Nose: powerfull, floral, honeyed notes, candied fruit, fragrant herbs, sweet spices, toasty, petrol notes. Palate: flavourful, sweet, fresh, fruity, good acidity, long, balanced.

CELLER LA MUNTANYA MURO VI NEGRE 2010 T
45% monastrell, 25% giró, 25% garnacha tintorera, 5% bonicaire

93 Colour: cherry, garnet rim. Nose: red berry notes, ripe fruit, scrubland, spicy, earthy notes, dry stone. Palate: powerful, flavourful, long, spicy.

LLIURE ALBIR 2010 B
50% malvasía, 35% garnacha blanca, 15% verdil

91 Colour: bright yellow. Nose: powerfull, ripe fruit, sweet spices, creamy oak, fragrant herbs. Palate: rich, flavourful, fresh, good acidity, elegant.

MINIFUNDI 2010 T
50% monastrell, 25% giró, 25% garnacha tintorera

90 Colour: cherry, garnet rim. Nose: ripe fruit, complex, damp earth, dark chocolate, cocoa bean, spicy, toasty. Palate: powerful, flavourful, toasty.

PAQUITO EL CHOCOLATERO 2009 T
monastrell, giró, garnacha

88 Colour: deep cherry. Nose: medium intensity, warm, ripe fruit, spicy. Palate: powerful, ripe fruit, spicy.

CELLER RAMÓN SADURNI

Can Sadurní
8799 Olerdola (Barcelona)
☎: +34 666 771 308
auladelvi@hotmail.com

RR SADURNÍ 2012 B
moscatel, otras

83

RR SADURNÍ 2012 B
xarel.lo

84

RR SADURNÍ 2012 RD
merlot

84

DANIEL V. RAMOS
(ZERBEROS FINCA)

San Pedro de Alcántara, 1
5170 El Tiemblo (Ávila)
☎: +34 687 410 952
winesdanielramosvinos.blogspot.com
dvrcru@gmail.com

ROSÉ 2011 RD
garnacha

90 Colour: onion pink. Nose: candied fruit, dried flowers, fragrant herbs, dry nuts. Palate: light-bodied, flavourful, good acidity, long, spicy.

WHITE 2012 B
sauvignon blanc

88 Colour: bright yellow. Nose: ripe fruit, dry nuts, floral, dried herbs, spicy. Palate: powerful, rich, flavourful.

ZERBEROS A + P 2010 T ROBLE
garnacha

91 Colour: bright cherry. Nose: sweet spices, creamy oak. Palate: flavourful, fruity, toasty, round tannins.

ZERBEROS ARENA 2010 T ROBLE
garnacha

92 Colour: bright cherry. Nose: candied fruit, warm, spicy. Palate: good acidity, fruity, sweetness.

ZERBEROS DELTIEMBLO 2011 T
garnacha

92 Colour: cherry, garnet rim. Nose: spicy, creamy oak, toasty. Palate: powerful, flavourful, toasty, round tannins.

ZERBEROS PIZARRA 2010 T ROBLE
garnacha

91 Colour: bright cherry. Nose: ripe fruit, sweet spices, creamy oak, expressive, scrubland. Palate: flavourful, fruity, toasty, round tannins.

ZERBEROS VIENTO ZEPHYROS 2011 B ROBLE
albillo, sauvignon blanc

90 Colour: bright golden. Nose: dry nuts, dried herbs, faded flowers, ripe fruit, mineral. Palate: powerful, rich, flavourful, spicy.

ZERBEROS VINO PRECIOSO 2011 B
albillo

91 Colour: bright golden. Nose: ripe fruit, dry nuts, powerfull, toasty, aged wood nuances, earthy notes. Palate: flavourful, fruity, spicy, toasty, long.

DESCALZOS VIEJOS

Finca Descalzos Viejos- Partido de los Molinos, s/n
29400 Ronda (Málaga)
☎: +34 952 874 696 - Fax: +34 952 874 696
www.descalzosviejos.com
info@descalzosviejos.com

DV MINIMA 2007 T
garnacha

88 Colour: light cherry, orangey edge. Nose: fruit preserve, fruit liqueur notes, toasty, dry nuts. Palate: flavourful, sweet, balanced.

DOMINIO DEL UROGALLO

El Carrascal, 7
33800 Cangas de Narcea (Asturias)
☎: +34 626 568 238
www.dominiodelurogallo.com
info@dominiodelurogallo.com

DOMINIO DEL UROGALLO LA ZORRINA 2011 T
70% carrasquín, 20% verdejo negro, 5% mencía, 5% garnacha

88 Colour: cherry, garnet rim. Nose: ripe fruit, fruit preserve, scrubland, damp earth. Palate: flavourful, spicy, balsamic, long.

DOMINIO DEL UROGALLO LAS YOLAS 2011 B
100% albillo

92 Colour: bright golden. Nose: ripe fruit, dry nuts, powerfull, toasty, aged wood nuances. Palate: flavourful, fruity, spicy, toasty, long.

DOMINIO DEL UROGALLO RETOITOIRO 2011 T
70% verdejo negro, 20% albarín tinto, 10% carrasquín

92 Colour: cherry, garnet rim. Nose: red berry notes, ripe fruit, balsamic herbs, mineral, sweet spices. Palate: rich, flavourful, spicy, long, round tannins, elegant.

PESICO 2011 B
100% albarín

93 Colour: bright yellow. Nose: ripe fruit, floral, dried herbs, sweet spices, toasty, mineral. Palate: powerful, flavourful, long, balsamic, spicy.

PESICO 2011 T
mencía, albarín tinto, carrasquín, verdejo negro

91 Colour: bright cherry. Nose: ripe fruit, sweet spices, creamy oak, aromatic coffee. Palate: flavourful, fruity, toasty, round tannins, balanced.

ECCOCIWINE

GIV 6701, km. 4
17462 San Martí Vell (Girona)
☎: +34 616 863 209
www.eccociwine.com
info@eccociwine.com

ECCOCI BLANCO 2011 B
roussanne, viognier, petit manseng

86 Colour: bright straw. Nose: faded flowers, ripe fruit, dried herbs. Palate: correct, fresh, fruity.

ECCOCI BLANCO 2012 B
roussanne, viognier, petit manseng

90 Colour: bright straw. Nose: fresh, fresh fruit, white flowers, expressive. Palate: flavourful, fruity, good acidity, balanced.

ECCOCI ROSADO 2012 RD
petit verdot

88 Colour: onion pink. Nose: elegant, candied fruit, dried flowers, fragrant herbs. Palate: light-bodied, flavourful, long, spicy.

ECCOCI TINTO PREMIUM 2011 T
petit verdot, cabernet franc, merlot

90 Colour: bright cherry. Nose: ripe fruit, sweet spices, creamy oak, mineral, balsamic herbs. Palate: flavourful, fruity, toasty, round tannins.

ECCOCI TINTO PREMIUM 2009 T
petit verdot, cabernet franc, merlot

91 Colour: cherry, garnet rim. Nose: red berry notes, ripe fruit, balsamic herbs, creamy oak. Palate: flavourful, long, spicy.

ECCOMI TINTO SUPER PREMIUM 2009 TC
marselan, cabernet franc, merlot

92 Colour: cherry, garnet rim. Nose: ripe fruit, wild herbs, earthy notes, spicy, creamy oak. Palate: balanced, elegant, flavourful, long, balsamic.

EDRA

Ctra A - 132, km 26
22800 Ayerbe (Huesca)
☎: +34 679 420 455 - Fax: +34 974 380 829
www.bodega-edra.com
edra@bodega-edra.com

EDRA BLANCOLUZ 2012 B
100% viognier

86 Colour: bright yellow, greenish rim. Nose: white flowers, citrus fruit, ripe fruit. Palate: flavourful, fruity, balanced.

ELÍAS MORA

Juan Mora, s/n
47530 San Román de Hornija (Valladolid)
☎: +34 983 784 029 - Fax: +34 983 784 190
www.bodegaseliasmora.com
info@bodegaseliasmora.com

DULCE BENAVIDES S/C
100% tinta de Toro

90 Colour: cherry, garnet rim. Nose: ripe fruit, fruit preserve, balsamic herbs, spicy, creamy oak. Palate: powerful, flavourful, spicy, long.

ENVINATE

Gran Vía, 2 1°C
27600 Sarría (Lugo)
☎: +34 682 207 160
asesoria@envinate.es

PUZZLE 2011 T
garnacha, touriga, tempranillo, monastrell

92 Colour: cherry, garnet rim. Nose: sweet spices, creamy oak, red berry notes, ripe fruit. Palate: flavourful, fruity, toasty.

TÁGANAN PARCELA AMOGOJE 2012 B
malvasía, forastera, marmajuelo, albillo, vijariego blanco, otras.

91 Colour: bright yellow. Nose: ripe fruit, wild herbs, dry stone, spicy, creamy oak. Palate: rich, flavourful, spicy, balanced.

TÁGANAN PARCELA MARGAELAGUA 2012 T
negramoll, listán negro, baboso, vijariego, malvasía negra, moscatel negro

93 Colour: bright cherry. Nose: ripe fruit, sweet spices, creamy oak, expressive. Palate: flavourful, fruity, toasty, round tannins.

TINTA AMARELA 2012 T
trincadeira preta

95 Colour: cherry, purple rim. Nose: red berry notes, floral, wild herbs, spicy, expressive, balanced. Palate: powerful, flavourful, spicy, fresh, fruity, elegant.

EQUIPO NAVAZOS

Cartuja, 1 - módulo 6
11401 Jerez de la Frontera (Cádiz)
www.equiponavazos.com
equipo@navazos.com

LA BOTA DE FLORPOWER Nº 44 2010 B
palomino

95 Colour: bright yellow. Nose: expressive, spicy, roasted almonds. Palate: powerful, sweetness, fine bitter notes, good acidity. Personality.

NAVAZOS NIEPOORT 2012 B
palomino

94 Colour: bright straw. Nose: flor yeasts, ripe fruit, white flowers. Palate: fruity, fresh, good acidity, long.

EVOHE BODEGAS

Ignacio de Ara, 3 Local
50002 Zaragoza (Zaragoza)
☎: +34 976 461 056 - Fax: +34 976 461 558
www.evohegarnacha.com
nosotros@evohegarnacha.com

EVOHÉ MAZUELA VIÑAS VIEJAS 2011 T
mazuelo

84

JORGE ORDÓÑEZ & CO

Bartolome Esteban Murillo, 11
29700 Velez-Málaga (Málaga)
☎: +34 952 504 706 - Fax: +34 951 284 796
www.jorgeordonez.es
info@jorgeordonez.es

BOTANI 2012 ESP
100% moscatel de alejandría

87 Colour: bright straw. Nose: candied fruit, citrus fruit, white flowers. Palate: flavourful, sweet, fine bead.

KAIROS

Dels Nostris, 26
8185 Lliçà de Vall (Barcelona)
☎: +34 938 437 036 - Fax: +34 938 439 671
www.kairosvino.com
kairos@vinodegaraje.com

KAIROS 2012 T
100% tempranillo

90 Colour: cherry, garnet rim. Nose: red berry notes, ripe fruit, balsamic herbs, sweet spices. Palate: powerful, flavourful, toasty, balanced.

LA CALANDRIA. PURA GARNACHA

Camino de Aspra, s/n
31521 Murchante (Navarra)
☎: +34 630 904 327
www.puragarnacha.com
luis@lacalandria.org

TIERGA 2010 T
garnacha

92 Colour: bright cherry. Nose: ripe fruit, sweet spices, creamy oak, balsamic herbs, mineral. Palate: flavourful, fruity, toasty, round tannins.

LIBERALIA ENOLÓGICA

Camino del Palo, s/n
49800 Toro (Zamora)
☎: +34 980 692 571 - Fax: +34 980 692 571
www.liberalia.es
liberalia@liberalia.es

ARIANE 2011 ESP
92% verdejo, 8% moscatel grano menudo

84

DURADERO 2010 T
50% tinta de Toro, 40% tinta roriz, 10% touriga nacional

90 Colour: bright cherry. Nose: ripe fruit, sweet spices, creamy oak, expressive. Palate: flavourful, fruity, toasty, round tannins.

MAS COMTAL

Mas Comtal, 1
8793 Avinyonet del Penedès (Barcelona)
☎: +34 938 970 052 - Fax: +34 938 970 591
www.mascomtal.com
mascomtal@mascomtal.com

ANTISTIANA 2011 B
incrocio manzoni

91 Colour: bright straw. Nose: citrus fruit, fragrant herbs, dry stone, floral, expressive. Palate: rich, flavourful, balanced, elegant.

GRAN ANGULAR CABERNET FRANC 2011 TC
cabernet franc

90 Colour: cherry, garnet rim. Nose: red berry notes, ripe fruit, spicy, creamy oak. Palate: powerful, flavourful, spicy, long, balanced.

MAS COMTAL PIZZICATO FRIZZANTE 2012 RD
muscato de Hamburgo

85 Colour: raspberry rose. Nose: candied fruit, dried flowers, fragrant herbs. Palate: light-bodied, flavourful, long.

MAS DE LA REAL DE SELLA

Calle Sella, 42 Local 3
3570 Villajoyosa (Alicante)
☎: +34 699 308 250 - Fax: +34 966 881 611
www.masdelarealdesella.es
info@masdelarealdesella.es

MAS DE SELLA CARRERÓ 2010 TR
cabernet franc, garnacha, marselan, syrah, cabernet sauvignon

93 Colour: cherry, garnet rim. Nose: powerfull, earthy notes, balsamic herbs, ripe fruit, spicy, creamy oak. Palate: balanced, powerful, flavourful, spicy, long.

MAS DE SELLA VENDIMIA SELECCIONADA 2011 T
cabernet franc, garnacha, marselan, syrah, cabernet sauvignon

92 Colour: bright cherry. Nose: ripe fruit, sweet spices, creamy oak, balsamic herbs, dry stone. Palate: flavourful, fruity, toasty, round tannins, elegant.

MAS DE TORUBIO

Plaza del Carmen, 4
44623 Cretas (Teruel)
☎: +34 669 214 845
www.masdetorubio.com
masdetorubio@hotmail.com

MAS DE TORUBIO 2012 T
60% garnacha, 40% merlot

82

XADO 2011 T ROBLE
60% garnacha, 40% cabernet sauvignon

82

XADO 2012 B
garnacha blanca

84

MUSTIGUILLO VIÑEDOS Y BODEGA

Ctra. N-330, km 196,5 El Terrerazo
46300 Utiel (Valencia)
☎: +34 962 168 260 - Fax: +34 962 168 259
www.bodegamustiguillo.com
info@bodegamustiguillo.com

FINCA CALVESTRA 2012 B
100% merseguera

94 Colour: bright straw. Nose: ripe fruit, sweet spices, mineral. Palate: fruity, fresh, complex, good acidity, long.

MESTIZAJE 2012 B
75% merseguera, 10% viognier, malvasía

93 Colour: bright yellow. Nose: powerfull, ripe fruit, sweet spices, fragrant herbs. Palate: rich, flavourful, fresh, good acidity.

MESTIZAJE 2012 T
85% bobal, garnacha, syrah, tempranillo

92 Colour: very deep cherry. Nose: ripe fruit, fruit expression, scrubland. Palate: fruity, flavourful, complex, round.

NESTARES RINCÓN WINES & FOODS, S.L.

Finca Juan de Reyes, s/n Contraviesa (GR-5204) del Haza del Lino a Cádiar, km-4
18430 Torvizcón (Granada)
☎: +34 655 959 500
www.alpujarride.com
info@alpujarride.com

NESTARES RINCÓN VITIS VINÍFERA 2012 T
tempranillo, merlot, syrah

86 Colour: cherry, purple rim. Nose: red berry notes, ripe fruit, balsamic herbs, earthy notes. Palate: spicy, balsamic, flavourful.

PAGO DE LA ROGATIVA

Pedro Antonio de Alarcón 40, p 1, 5ºD
18002 Granada (Granada)
www.pagodelarogativa.es
info@pagodelarogativa.es

PAGO DE LA ROGATIVA 2011 T ROBLE
tempranillo, cabernet sauvignon

87 Colour: bright cherry. Nose: medium intensity, fresh, red berry notes. Palate: flavourful, easy to drink.

PAGO DE LA ROGATIVA 2011 TC
tempranillo, cabernet sauvignon

89 Colour: bright cherry. Nose: ripe fruit, sweet spices, expressive, fresh fruit, red berry notes, fruit expression. Palate: flavourful, fruity, round tannins.

PAGO DE THARSYS

Ctra. Nacional III, km. 274
46340 Requena (Valencia)
☎: +34 962 303 354 - Fax: +34 962 329 000
www.pagodetharsys.com
pagodetharsys@pagodetharsys.com

PAGO DE THARSYS MERLOT 2008 T
merlot

89 Colour: pale ruby, brick rim edge. Nose: red berry notes, ripe fruit, fragrant herbs, spicy, fine reductive notes. Palate: flavourful, spicy, long, balanced.

PAGO DE THARSYS VENDIMIA NOCTURNA 2012 B
albariño, godello

87 Colour: bright straw. Nose: white flowers, fragrant herbs, candied fruit. Palate: powerful, long, flavourful.

PAGO DEL MARENOSTRUM

Ctra. A-348, Km. 85-86
4460 Fondón (Almería)
☎: +34 926 666 027 - Fax: +34 670 099 520
www.pagodelvicario.com
info@pagodelvicario.com

1500 H 2007 T
pinot noir, tempranillo, merlot, cabernet sauvignon

86 Colour: cherry, garnet rim. Nose: ripe fruit, fruit preserve, wild herbs, spicy, slightly evolved. Palate: powerful, flavourful, spicy, long.

1500 H PINOT NOIR 2007 T
100% pinot noir

88 Colour: pale ruby, brick rim edge. Nose: scrubland, fruit liqueur notes, spicy, wet leather, tobacco, damp earth. Palate: flavourful, spicy, long, slightly evolved.

PARDAS

Finca Can Comas, s/n
8775 Torrelavit (Barcelona)
☎: +34 938 995 005
www.pardas.net
pardas@cancomas.com

PARDAS SUMOLL ROSAT 2012 RD
100% sumoll

86 Colour: light cherry, bright. Nose: balanced, balsamic herbs. Palate: flavourful, fruity, slightly acidic.

PÉREZ CARAMÉS

Peña Picón, s/n
24500 Villafranca del Bierzo (León)
☎: +34 987 540 197 - Fax: +34 987 540 314
www.perezcarames.com
enoturismo@perezcarames.com

CASAR DE SANTA INÉS 2011 T
80% merlot, 20% pinot noir

83

PRÍNCIPE ALFONSO DE HOHENLOHE

Estación de Parchite, 104
29400 Ronda (Málaga)
☎: +34 914 365 900
www.haciendas-espana.com
gromero@arcoinvest-group.com

ÁNDALUS PETIT VERDOT (MARQUÉS DE LA CONCORDIA FAMILY OF WINES) 2005 T

91 Colour: pale ruby, brick rim edge. Nose: spicy, fine reductive notes, wet leather, aged wood nuances, fruit liqueur notes. Palate: spicy, fine tannins, elegant, long.

PUERTA NUEVA S.L.

Medina, 79
11402 Jerez de la Frontera (Cádiz)
☎: +34 956 338 163 - Fax: +34 956 338 163
www.cortijodejara.com
puertanueva.sl@cortijodejara.es

CORTIJO DE JARA 2012 B
gewürztraminer, sauvignon blanc

84

SEÑORÍO DE VALDESNEROS

Avda. La Paz, 4
34230 Torquemada (Palencia)
☎: +34 979 800 545 - Fax: +34 979 800 545
www.bodegasvaldesneros.com
sv@bodegasvaldesneros.com

AMANTIA 2011 T
tempranillo

87 Colour: onion pink. Nose: candied fruit, floral, fragrant herbs, sweet spices. Palate: powerful, fruity, flavourful, balanced.

TRESGE WINERY

Ctra. de Picanya, 18 Puerta 10
46200 Paiporta (Valencia)
☎: +34 961 182 737
www.gratiaswines.com
info@3gwineconsulting.com

GRATIAS MÁXIMAS 2011 T
100% bobal

86 Colour: cherry, garnet rim. Nose: ripe fruit, spicy, creamy oak, toasty. Palate: powerful, flavourful, toasty.

GRATIAS ROSÉ 2012 RD
100% bobal

85 Colour: rose, purple rim. Nose: powerfull, ripe fruit, red berry notes, floral, lactic notes. Palate: powerful, fresh, fine bitter notes.

VALQUEJIGOSO

Ctra, Villamanta - Méntrida, s/n
28610 Villamanta (Madrid)
☎: +34 650 492 390
www.valquejigoso.com
aureliogarcia@valquejigoso.com

VALQUEJIGOSO V2 2008 T
57% cabernet sauvignon, 16% petit verdot, 11% tempranillo, 9% cabernet franc, 7% negral

94 Colour: very deep cherry. Nose: mineral, ripe fruit, dark chocolate, cocoa bean, toasty. Palate: fruity, fine bitter notes, good acidity, spicy, fine tannins.

VINOS COLOMAN S.A.T.

Goya, 17
13620 Pedro Muñoz (Ciudad Real)
☎: +34 926 586 410 - Fax: +34 926 586 656
www.satcoloman.com
coloman@satcoloman.com

MANCHEGAL 2012 T
tempranillo

79

MANCHEGAL ROSADO AGUJA RD
tempranillo

85 Colour: raspberry rose. Nose: lactic notes, candied fruit, rose petals. Palate: fresh, fruity, flavourful, easy to drink.

VINS DE TALLER

Sant Jordi, 4 B
17469 Vilamalla (Girona)
☎: +34 972 525 578 - Fax: +34 972 525 578
www.vinsdetaller.com
info@vinsdetaller.com

VINS DE TALLER BASEIA 2012 B
100% viognier

91 Colour: bright straw. Nose: ripe fruit, wild herbs, dried herbs, floral, mineral, creamy oak. Palate: powerful, flavourful, spicy, long, balanced.

VINS DE TALLER GEUM 2012 T
100% merlot

90 Colour: bright cherry. Nose: ripe fruit, sweet spices, creamy oak, balsamic herbs, mineral. Palate: flavourful, fruity, toasty.

VINS DE TALLER GRIS 2012 RD
100% marselan

89 Colour: onion pink. Nose: candied fruit, dried flowers, fragrant herbs, red berry notes. Palate: light-bodied, flavourful, good acidity, long, spicy.

VINS DE TALLER MM 2009 TC
38% marselan, 47% merlot, 15% cot

91 Colour: cherry, garnet rim. Nose: ripe fruit, spicy, creamy oak, toasty, complex, damp earth. Palate: powerful, flavourful, toasty, balanced.

VINS DE TALLER PHLOX 2012 B
49% roussanne, 43% marsanne, 8% chardonnay

89 Colour: bright straw. Nose: floral, citrus fruit, fresh fruit, dried herbs, mineral. Palate: fresh, balsamic, balanced, flavourful.

VINS DE TALLER SIURA 2010 T
44% marselan, 44% merlot, 12% cot

84

VINS DE TALLER VRMC 2010 BFB
30% viognier, 40% roussanne, 17% marselan, 13% cortese

90 Colour: bright yellow. Nose: ripe fruit, dried herbs, sweet spices, creamy oak, mineral. Palate: powerful, flavourful, long, toasty.

VINS DEL COMTAT

Turballos, 1
3820 Cocentaina (Alicante)
☎: +34 667 669 287 - Fax: +34 965 593 194
www.vinsdelcomtat.com
vinsdelcomtat@gmail.com

VIOGNIER DE VINS DEL COMTAT 2012 B
100% viognier

87 Colour: bright straw. Nose: fresh, fresh fruit, white flowers, expressive. Palate: flavourful, fruity, good acidity, balanced.

VINS DEL TROS

Major, 13
43782 Vilalba dels Arcs (Tarragona)
☎: +34 605 096 447 - Fax: +34 977 438 042
www.vinsdeltros.com
info@vinsdeltros.com

LO MORENILLO 2011 T
100% morenillo

88 Colour: cherry, garnet rim. Nose: ripe fruit, wild herbs, spicy, tobacco. Palate: complex, powerful, flavourful, spicy.

VINS TONI GELABERT

Camí dels Horts de Llodrá Km. 1,3
7500 Manacor (Illes Balears)
☎: +34 610 789 531
www.vinstonigelabert.com
info@vinstonigelabert.com

TORRE DES CANONGE BLANC B
giró

91 Colour: bright yellow. Nose: powerfull, ripe fruit, sweet spices, creamy oak, fragrant herbs. Palate: rich, smoky aftertaste, flavourful, fresh, good acidity, balanced, elegant.

VIÑEDO Y BODEGA HERETAT DE CESILIA

Paraje Alcaydias, 4
3660 Novelda (Alicante)
☎: +34 965 605 385 - Fax: +34 965 604 763
www.heretatdecesilia.com
administracion@heretatdecesilia.com

AD GAUDE 2007 T

88 Colour: cherry, garnet rim. Nose: spicy, creamy oak, toasty, fruit preserve. Palate: powerful, flavourful, toasty, round tannins.

AD GAUDE HERETAT 2007 T
monastrell, syrah, cabernet sauvignon, petit verdot

85 Colour: cherry, garnet rim. Nose: ripe fruit, spicy, creamy oak. Palate: powerful, flavourful, toasty.

AZAL 2012 B
albariño, sauvignon blanc, macabeo

85 Colour: bright straw. Nose: ripe fruit, citrus fruit, faded flowers. Palate: good acidity, fine bitter notes.

CARDENAL ÁLVAREZ TINTO

92 Colour: dark mahogany. Nose: acetaldehyde, fruit preserve, dark chocolate, sweet spices, creamy oak, expressive. Palate: balanced, unctuous, powerful, flavourful.

SPARKLING WINES-TRADITIONAL METHOD

All the wines included in this section are made by the so-called traditional method of a second fermentation in the bottle, the same one used in Cava –and Champagne– production, but in areas outside those ascribed to Cava or any other Spanish DO. They represent a tiny part of all the sparkling wines made in Spain and their figures and quality are understandably far away from those of Cava.

BODEGAS BARBADILLO

Luis de Eguilaz, 11
11540 Sanlúcar de Barrameda (Cádiz)
☎: +34 956 385 500 - Fax: +34 956 385 501
www.barbadillo.com
barbadillo@barbadillo.com

BARBADILLO BETA BR
palomino, chardonnay

85 Colour: bright straw. Nose: medium intensity, dried herbs, fine lees, floral, ripe fruit. Palate: fresh, fruity, flavourful.

CARREFOUR

Campezo, 16
28022 Madrid (Madrid)
☎: +34 902 202 000
www.carrefour.es

BASIUM VINO DE AGUJA RD
tempranillo, cabernet sauvignon, merlot, bobal

83

BASIUM VINO DE AGUJA S/C B
airén, verdejo

83

CELLER MANYÉ FORTUNY

Dr. Gaspà, 17 La Secuita
43765 El Masroig
☎: +34 977 611 206
cellermanye@gmail.com

MEDVSA BN GRAN RESERVA
40% cartoixà, 30% parellada, 30% macabeo

88 Colour: bright straw. Nose: spicy, dry nuts, balanced, ripe fruit. Palate: flavourful, good acidity, balanced, fine bitter notes.

JOSEP Mª RAVENTÓS I BLANC

Plaça del Roure, s/n
8770 Sant Sadurní D'Anoia (Barcelona)
☎: +34 938 183 262 - Fax: +34 938 912 500
www.raventos.com
raventos@raventos.com

L'HEREU 2011 BR
macabeo, xarel.lo, parellada

90 Colour: bright straw. Nose: fine lees, floral, fragrant herbs, expressive. Palate: powerful, flavourful, good acidity, fine bead, balanced.

RAVENTÓS I BLANC DE NIT 2011 BR
macabeo, xarel.lo, parellada, monastrell

90 Colour: raspberry rose. Nose: dried flowers, candied fruit, dried herbs, fine lees. Palate: fresh, fruity, powerful, fine bead.

RAVENTÓS I BLANC GRAN RESERVA PERSONAL M.R.N. 1998 BN
30% macabeo, 25% xarel.lo, 40% parellada, 5% chardonnay

96 Colour: bright golden. Nose: dry nuts, fragrant herbs, complex, smoky, lees reduction notes. Palate: powerful, flavourful, good acidity, fine bead, fine bitter notes.

RAVENTÓS I BLANC GRAN RESERVA PERSONAL M.R.N. 2000 BN GRAN RESERVA
40% macabeo, 25% xarel.lo, 27% parellada, 8% chardonnay

95 Colour: bright golden. Nose: fine lees, fragrant herbs, complex. Palate: powerful, flavourful, good acidity, fine bead, fine bitter notes.

RAVENTÓS I BLANC LA FINCA 2010 BN GRAN RESERVA
xarel.lo, macabeo, parellada, chardonnay

91 Colour: bright golden. Nose: fine lees, dry nuts, fragrant herbs, complex. Palate: powerful, flavourful, good acidity, fine bead, fine bitter notes.

LOBBAN WINES

Creueta, 24
8784 St. Jaume Sesoliveres (Barcelona)
☎: +34 667 551 695
www.lapamelita.com
info@lapamelita.com

LA PAMELITA 2006 TINTO ESPUMOSO
95% syrah, 5% garnacha

80

LA ROSITA 2009 ESP
95% garnacha, 5% syrah

83

PRADA A TOPE

La Iglesia, s/n
24546 Canedo (León)
☎: +34 987 563 366 - Fax: +34 987 567 000
www.pradaatope.es
info@pradaatope.es

XAMPRADA 2009 ESP RESERVA
mencía

81

XAMPRADA ECÓLOGICO SECO 2010 ESP
godello, chardonnay

83

XAMPRADA EXTRA BRUT 2010 ESP
godello, chardonnay

83

XAMPRADA EXTRA BRUT ROSADO 2010 ESP
mencía, godello

80

XAMPRADA ROSADO SECO 2010 ESP
mencía, godello

82

ESPUMOSOS-CUEVA
BODEGAS ALCARDET

Mayor, 130
45810 Villanueva de Alcardete (Toledo)
☎: +34 925 166 375 - Fax: +34 925 166 611
www.alcardet.com
alcardet@alcardet.com

ALCARDET 2006 ESP
airén, macabeo

84

VIN DORÉ 24 K BRUT IMPERIAL BR
airén, sauvignon blanc, macabeo

91 Colour: bright yellow. Nose: balanced, ripe fruit, spicy, fine lees. Palate: flavourful, good acidity, balanced, fine bitter notes.

VIÑEDOS Y RESERVAS

Ctra. Quintanar, Km. 2
45810 Villanueva de Alcardete (Toledo)
☎: +34 925 167 536 - Fax: +34 925 167 265
www.cuevassantoyo.com
vr@cuevassantoyo.com

**CAROLUS RESERVA IMPERIAL 2010
BN FERMENTADO EN BARRICA**
50% chardonnay, 50% airén

84

CUEVAS SANTOYO 2010 BR
macabeo, airén

80

CUEVAS SANTOYO 2010 BRUT NATURE
macabeo, airén

83

GLOSARY and INDEXES

TERMINOLOGY RELATED TO COLOUR

AMBER. The first step in the oxidative ageing of sherry generoso wines, brandies, whiskies and rum, somewhere between yellow and coppery red.

BEADS. The slow rising string of bubbles in a sparkling wine.

BRICK RED. An orangey hue, similar to that of a brick, used to describe reds aged in bottle for more than 10 years or in barrel for longer than six.

BRILLIANT. Related to a young and neat wine.

CANDY CHERRY. This is used to define a colour lighter than a red but darker than a rosé.

CLEAN. Utterly clean, immaculate.

CLOUDY. Lacking clarity.

COPPERY. A reddish nuance that can be appreciated in whites aged in wood for a long period, generally amontillados and some palo cortados.

CHERRY. Commonly used to express red colour. It can take all sort of degrees from 'light' all the way to 'very dark' or almost 'black cherry'.

DARK. This often refers to a tone slightly lighter than 'deep' and synonymous to "medium-intensity".

DEEP. A red with a very dark colour, which hardly lets us see the bottom of the glass.

DULL. A wine lacking in liveliness, usually with an ochre hue.

GARNET RED. A common nuance in medium to light reds. If the wine is an intense cherry red it could have a garnet rim only if it comes from cooler regions; if it is more luminous and open than the violet rim of a dark wine, it generally would be a young wine.

GOLDEN. Gold in colour with yellow –predominantly– to reddish tones.

GLIMMER. A vague brilliance.

IODINE. A tone similar to iodine tincture stains (old gold and brownish) displayed by rancio and generoso wines have after their long oxidative ageing.

LIVELY. A reflection of the youth of a wine through bright, brilliant colours.

MAHOGANY. Describes the second stage of ageing in brandies, rum and generoso sherry (fortified) wines. A hue between brown and yellow displayed by wines when long aged.

OCHRE. Yellow-orangey hue, the last colour phase of a table wine, generally found in wines with a long oxidative ageing; it is a sign of their decline.

OILY. A wine that appears dense to the eye, usually sweet and with high alcohol content.

OLD GOLD. Gold colour with the brownish tones found in amontillados and a bit lighter than the mahogany nuance predominant in oloroso sherry.

ONION SKIN. A touch lighter than salmon colour.

OPAQUE. A wine with such depth of colour we cannot see the bottom of the glass. Generally found in very old pedro ximénez and therefore akin to caramelised notes.

OPEN. Very pale, not at all intense.

ORANGEY EDGE. Intermediate phase between a deep red and brick red found towards the rim in red wines of a medium age. It generally appears sooner in wines with higher alcohol content and it is also typical of wines made from pinot noir.

RASPBERRY. Sort of pinkish colour with a bluish rim, it is the optimal colour for rosé wines since it denotes freshness, youth and a good acidity.

RIM. Also known as 'edge', it refers to the lighter colour the wine displays at the edge of the oval when we hold the glass at 45°, as opposed to the 'core' or main body of colour right in the centre. If it is a young red, it will show normally violet or raspberry nuances; when slightly older, it will be a deeper red or garnet, and if has been in the bottle for more than five years it might be anything from ruby to tawny through brick red and orangey.

RUBY. Slightly orangey hue with a yellow nuance found in old wines that have lost part of their original cherry colour.

SALMON. A tone slightly redder than pink found in rosé wines with less acidity and more alcohol.

STEELY. Pale colour with metallic reflections (reminiscent of those from steel) found in some whites.

STRAW-COLOURED. This term should be understood as straw yellow, the colour found in the majority of young white wines, halfway between yellow and green. It can also be described as "lemony".

TERMINOLOGY RELATED TO AROMA

ACETONE. Very close notes to those of nail varnish, typical of very old eau de vie.

ALCOHOL. It is not a pejorative term for an excess of alcohol –in which case we would refer to it as burning–, but just a predominant, non-aggressive note.

ALDEHYDE. A sensory note of oxidized, slightly rancid alcohol, typical of old wines with high alcohol content that have undergone oxidative ageing.

ANIMAL. Not a positive note, generally the result of long storage in bottle, also referred to as 'wet dog' or 'wet hide' and normally associated with a lack of hygiene. If it is found in younger vintages, then it could be a symptom of "brett" (see brett).

ATTIC. An aroma associated with that of old dry wood and dust typical of attics, mainly found in fortified wines aged in wood and in very old wines aged for a long period in old barrels which happen to have also been bottled for more than ten years.

BALSAMIC. A trait usually associated to wood-aged wines in hot regions, where high temperatures accelerate their evolution. It also refers to the aroma of dry herbs such as eucalyptus and bay leaf, as well as incense and tar.

BLACK FRUIT. It refers to the sort of toasted aromas of very ripe grapes, those almost 'burnt skin' notes found in reds that have undergone a long vatting period in contact with the skins.

"BRETT". This is the abbreviation for a new term (brettanomyces) to describe an old problem: the aroma of stables, henhouse, and wet new leather generally found along with reductive off-odours in wines that have been in the bottle for more than ten years. These aromas were considered part of the sensory complexity of old wines and therefore tolerated. Nowadays, due to better olfactory research and more hygienic working conditions in the wineries, they are easily detected and considered more a defect. In addition, today brett is often found in younger wines as this particular bacteria or yeast usually develops better in wines with higher ph levels. The increase in the ph of wines is quite common these days due to global warming, riper grapes and the use of fertilizers over the past thirty-five years.

BROOM. An aroma reminiscent of Mediterranean shrubs, only a bit dryer.

CANDIED FRUIT. This is a sweet nuance, somewhere between toasted and jammy, which is found in whites with a long oxidative ageing and in some sweet white wines.

CAROB. Anybody who has chewed or smelt one of those beans cannot would easily recall its typical blend of sweetness and toasted notes, as well as the slightly rustic nuance. It is usually found in old brandy aged in soleras of pedro ximénez and in deep, concentrated wines made from very ripe grapes.

CEDAR. The somewhat perfumed aroma of cedar, a soft wood commonly found in Morocco.

CHARACTERFUL. Used to express the singularity of a wine above the rest. It may refer to winemaking, terroir or the peculiarities of its ageing.

CITRUS. An aroma reminiscent of lemon, orange and grapefruit.

CLASSIC RIOJA. A note named after the more traditional and popular style of Rioja, with predominantly woody notes (normally from very old wood) along with a typical character of sweet spices and occasionally candle wax nuances instead of fruit, given the oxidative character provided by long ageing periods.

CLEAR. A wine with no defects, neither in the nose nor in the palate.

CLOSED. A term to describe a faint or not properly developed nose. Almost always found in concentrated wines from a good vintage, which evolve very slowly in the bottle, but it can also be found in wines recently bottled.

COCOA. Delicate, slightly toasted aroma found in wines aged in wood for a moderately long time that have evolved very well in the bottle.

COMPLEX. A wine abundant in aromas and flavours related either to grape variety, soil or ageing, although none of those features is particularly prominent.

CREAMY. Aroma of finely toasted oak (usually French) with notes of caramelised vanilla.

DATES. A sweet aroma with hints of dates and a raisiny nuance.

EARTHY. An aroma somewhere between clay and dust typical of red wines made from ripe grapes and with high alcohol content. It can also refer in some wines to a mineral nuance.

ELEGANT. A harmonious combination of fine, somewhat restrained aromatic notes related to perfumed wood, and a light, pleasantly balanced richness or complexity (see complex).

ETHEREAL. This is used to describe spirits, fortified wines and wines with a certain intensity of alcohol in their oxidative evolution; the strength of the alcohol reveals the rancid-type aromas. It has a lot to do with age.

EVOLUTION NOTES. Generally used to describe wines aged prematurely by either oxygen or heat, e.g., a wine that has been left in a glass for several hours.

FINE. A synonym for elegant.

FINE LEES. This is an aroma between herbaceous and slightly toasty that is produced by the contact of the wine with the lees (dead yeasts cells) after the fermentation has taken place, a process called autolysis that helps to make the wine more complex and to give it a richer aroma.

FLOR. This is a pungent, saline aroma typically found in sherry wines, particularly fino, manzanilla and, to a lesser degree, amontillado. It is caused by a film-forming yeast known as 'flor' in Spanish (literally flower), which transfers to the wine its singular smell and flavour.

FLORAL. Reminiscent of the petals of certain flowers –such as roses and jasmine–noticeable in certain northern withes or in quality reds after a bottle-ageing spell that also delivers some spicy notes.

FRAGRANT HERBS. An aroma similar to soaps and perfumes made from lavender, rosemary, lemon, orange blossom or jasmine. It is found in white wines that undergo pre-fermentative cold skin maceration.

FRESH. A wine with lively aroma and hardly any alcohol expression.

FRESH FRUIT. These are fruity notes produced by a slow grape-ripening cycle typical of mild climates.

FRUIT EXPRESSION. Related to different flavours and aromas reminiscent of various fruits and fine herbs.

FRUITY. Fruit notes with a fine herbal character and even hints of green grass.

HERBACEOUS. A vague note of vine shoots, scrub and geranium leaf caused by an incomplete maturation of the grape skin.

INTENSE. A powerful aroma that can be immediately referred to as such when first nosing the wine.

IODINE. This refers to iodine tincture, a combination of the sweetish smell of alcohol, toasted notes, liniment and varnish or lacquer.

JAM. Typical notes of very ripe black fruit slightly caramelised by a slow oxidative ageing in oak barrels. Very similar to forest fruit jam (prunes, blackberries, blueberries, redcurrants, cherries…). Found in red wines –generally from southern regions– with a high concentration of fruit notes giving that they are made resorting to long vatting periods, which provide longer contact with the skins.

MACERATION. These are aromas similar to those produced during fermentation and that –logically– found in young wines.

MEDITERRANEAN. An aroma where various prominent notes (sweetness, alcohol, burning and raisiny notes, caramel…) produced by grapes grown in hot regions blend in to characterize the wines.

MINERAL NOTES. Used to describe wines that have a subtle nose with plenty of notes reminiscent of flint, slate, hot stones or dry sand.

MUSK. A term to describe the sweet and grapey notes typical of highly aromatic varieties such as moscatel, riesling and gewürztraminer.

ROASTED COFFEE. (See terms of taste).

SUBDUED FRUIT. It generally refers to aromas produced by a fast ripening of the grapes typical of warm climates.

NUTS. Notes generally found in white wines with oxidative ageing; the oxygen in the air gives rise to aromas and flavours reminiscent of nuts (bitter almond, hazelnut, walnut…). When ageing spells are longer and –most importantly– take place in older casks, there will appear notes that are closer to fruits like figs, dates and raisins.

ORANGE PEEL. Typical fruity aroma found in certain white wines with, above all, a vibrant spicy character.

ORGANIC NOTES. A way to define the fermentative aromas –essentially related to yeast– and typical of young white wines and also fortified generoso wines from the sherry region.

OVERRIPE FRUIT. An aroma typical of young wines that are already slightly oxidized and reminiscent of grape bunches with some signs of rot –noble or not–, or simply bruised or recently pressed grapes.

OXIDATIVE EVOLUTION. Notes related to the tendency of a wine to age by the action of oxygen that passes through the pores of the cask or barrel (micro-oxidation), or during racking.

PATISSERIE. An aroma between sweet and toasted with hints of caramelised sugar and vanilla typical of freshly baked cakes. It is found in wines –generally sweet– that have been aged in oak for a long time and it is caused by both oxidative evolution and the aromatic elements (mainly vanillin) found in oak.

PEAT. A slightly burnt aroma that occurs when the notes of ripe grapes blend in with the toasted aromas of new oak in wines with a high alcohol content.

PHENOLIC. A short and derivative way to describe polyphenols (a combination of the tannins and anthocyanins, vegetal elements of the grape), it describes aromas of grape skins macerated for a long time that yield notes somewhere between ink and a pressed bunch of grapes.

PORT. This is the sweet aroma of wine made from somewhat raisiny or overripe grapes and reminiscent of the vintage Ports made with a short oxidative ageing.

PUNGENT. A prominent aromatic note produced by the combination of alcohol, wood and flor notes and typical of –particularly– fino sherry wines.

RANCIO. This is not a defect but a note better known as "sherryfied" and brought about by oxidative ageing.

RED FRUIT. An aromatic note that refers to forest red fruits (blackberries, redcurrants, mulberries) as well as slightly unripe cherries and plums.

REDUCTION. A wine aroma caused by the lack of oxygen during long bottle ageing, which gives rise to notes like tobacco, old leather, vanilla, cinnamon, cocoa, attic, dust, etc.

REDUCTION OFF-ODOURS. This is a negative set of aromas, halfway between boiled cabbage and boiled eggs, produced by the lees in wines that have not been properly aerated or racked.

REDUCTIVE TANK OFF-ODOURS. A smell between metal and boiled fruit typical of wines stored in large vats at high temperatures. The sulphur added –probably in excess– combines with the wine and reduces its freshness and the expression of fruit notes. This phenomenon is largely found in the production of bulk wines.

RIPE GRAPE SKIN. The aroma that a very ripe grape gives off when squeezed, similar to that of ink or of ripe grape bunches just pressed.

SALINE. This is the note acquired by a fino that has aged in soleras under flor yeast.

SEASONED WOOD. It refers to notes that may appear in wines aged in barrel for a long period –more than four or five years– which have lost the fine toasted aromas and flavours of new oak.

SHRUB. An aroma typically herbal found in Mediterranean regions, a mixture of rosemary, thyme and other typically semi-arid herbs. It refers to the dry, herbaceous note found generally in white and red wines from warmer regions.

SOLERA. An aroma close to the damp, seasoned, aged aroma of an old bodega for oloroso wines.

SPICY. It refers to the most common household spices (pepper, cloves, cinnamon) that appear in wines that undergo long and slow oxidative ageing in oak casks or barrels.

SPIRITUOUS. Both a flavour and an olfactory feature related to high alcohol content but without burning sensations. It is an almost 'intellectual' term to define alcohol, since that product is nothing else but the "spirit of wine".

STEWED FRUIT. Notes of stewed or 'cooked' fruit appear in wines made from well-ripened –not overripe– grapes and are similar to those of jam.

TAR. The pitchy, petrolly aromas of very toasted wood, associated with concentrated red wines with lots of colour, structure and alcohol.

TERROIR. An aromatic note determined by the soil and climate and therefore with various nuances: mountain herbs, minerals, stones, etc.

TOASTED SUGAR. Sweet caramelised aromas.

TOFFEE. A note typical of the milk coffee creams (lactic and toasted nuances mixed together) and present in some crianza red wines.

TROPICAL NOTES. The sweet white fruit aromas present in white wines made from grapes that have ripened very quickly and lack acidity.

TRUFFLE. Similar note to that of a mixture of damp earth and mushrooms.

UNDERGROWTH. This is the aromatic nuance between damp earth, grass and fallen leaves found in well-assembled, wood-aged reds that have a certain fruity expression and good phenolic concentration.

VANILLA. A typical trait of wines –also fortified– aged in oak, thanks to the vanillin, an element contained in that type of wood.

VARIETAL EXPRESSION. This is the taste and aroma of the variety or varieties used to make the wine.

VARNISH. A typical smell found in very old or fortified wines due to the oxidation of the alcohol after a long wood-ageing period. The varnished-wood note is similar to the aroma of eau de vie or spirits aged in wood.

VARNISHED WOOD. A sharp note typical of wines aged in wood for a long period, during which the alcohol oxidises and gives off an aroma of acetone, wood or nail varnish.

VISCOUS. The sweet taste and aromatic expression of wines with high alcohol content.

VOLATILE. A note characteristic of wines with high volatile acidity, i.e., just the first sign of them turning into vinegar. It is typical of poorly stabilized young wines or aged wines either with a high alcohol content or that have taken on this note during the slow oxidative wood-ageing phase, although we should remember it is a positive trait in the case of generoso wines.

WINE PRESS. The aroma of the vegetal parts of the grape after fermentation, vaguely reminiscent of pomace brandy, grapeskins and ink.

WITHERED FLOWERS. This is a sort of 'toasty' nuance typical of good champagnes made with a high percentage of pinot noir and some cavas which have aged perfectly in the bottle and on their lees for a long time.

WOODY. It describes an excess of notes of wood in a wine. The reason could be either a too long ageing period or the wine's lack of structure.

YEASTY. The dry aroma of bread yeast that can be perceived in young cavas or champagnes, or wines that have just been bottled.

TERMINOLOGY RELATED TO THE PALATE

ALCOHOL. A gentle, even sweet note of fine spirits; it is not a defect.

ALCOHOLIC EDGES. A slight excess of alcohol perceived on the tongue, but which does not affect the overall appreciation of the wine.

AMPLE. A term used to describe richness. It is a sensation generally experienced on the attack.

BITTER. A slight, non-aggressive note of bitterness, often found in some sherry wines (finos, amontillados) and the white wines from Rueda; it should not be regarded as a negative feature, quite on the contrary, it helps to counterbalance soft or slightly sweet notes.

CARAMELISED. A very sweet and toasted note typical of some unctuous wines aged in oloroso or pedro ximénez casks.

DENSE. This is related to the body of the wine, a thick sensation on the palate.

FATNESS. "Gordo" (fat) is the adjective used in Jerez to describe a wine with good body; it is the antonym of "fino" (light).

FLABBY. Used to describe a wine low in acidity that lacks freshness.

FLAVOURFUL. A pronounced and pleasant sensation on the palate produced by the combination of various sweet nuances.

FULL. A term used to describe volume, richness, some sweetness and round tannins; that is, a wine with a fleshy character and an almost fat palate.

LIGHT. The opposite of meaty, dense or concentrated; i.e., a wine with little body.

LONG. This refers to the persistence of the flavour after the wine has been swallowed.

MEATY. A wine that has body, structure and which can almost literally be "chewed".

NOTES OF WOOD. Well-defined notes somewhere between woody and resin generally found in wines matured in younger casks.

OILY. This is the supple, pleasantly fat sensation produced by glycerine. It is more prominent in older wines –thanks to the decrease in acidity– or in certain varieties such as riesling, gewürztraminer, chardonnay, albariño and godello.

OXIDATIVE AGEING. It refers to the influence of the air in the evolution of wine. Depending on the level of oxygen in the air, oxidation will take place in wine to a greater or lesser extent. Oxidative ageing happens when the air comes in contact with the wine either during racking –which ages the wine faster– or through the pores of the wood.

PASTY. This is not a pejorative term, simply a very sweet and dense taste.

ROASTED COFFEE. The sweet and toasted note of caramelised sugar typically found in wines aged in oak barrels –generally burnt inside–, or else the taste of very ripe (sometimes even overripe) grapes.

ROUGH TANNINS. Just unripe tannins either from the wood or the grape skins.

ROUND. This is an expression commonly used to describe a wine without edges, supple, with volume and body.

SWEETENED. Related to sweetness, only with an artificial nuance.

SWEETNESS. A slightly sweet note that stands out in a wine with an overall dry or tannic character.

SOFT TANNINS. Both alcohol and adequately ripened grapes help to balance out the natural bitter character of the tannins. They are also referred to as fat or oily tannins.

TANNIC. This is term derived from tannin, a substance generally found in the skin of the grape and in the wood that yields a somewhat harsh, vegetal note. In wines, it displays a slightly harsh, sometimes even grainy texture.

UNCTUOUS. This refers to the fat, pleasant note found in sweet wines along with their somewhat sticky sweetness.

VELVETY. A smooth, pleasant note on the palate typical of great wines where the tannins and the alcohol have softened down during ageing.

VIGOROUS. A wine with high alcohol content.

WARM. The term speaks of alcohol in a more positive way.

WELL-BALANCED. A term that helps to define a good wine: none of the elements that are part of it (alcohol, acidity, dry extract, oak) is more prominent than the other, just pure balance.

WINERIES

WINERIES

WINERIES

WINERIES

WINES

WINES

WINES

WINES

WINES

WINES

WINES

WINES

WINES

WINES

WINES

WINES

WINES

WINES

MAP OF THE DO´S IN SPAIN AND VINOS DE PAGO

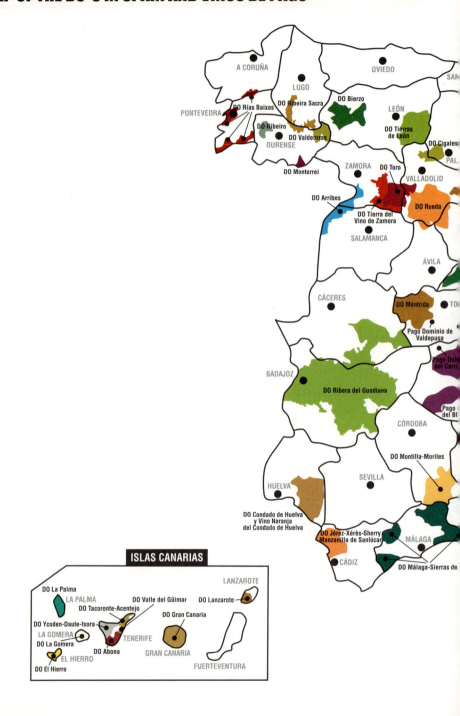

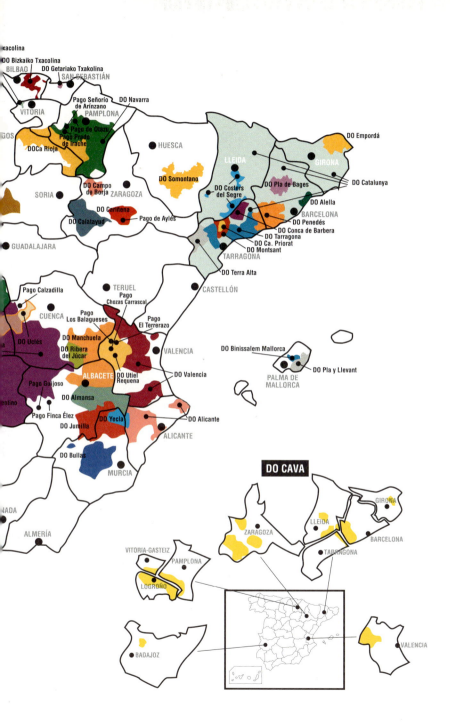

Txacolina
DO Bizkaiko Txacolina
DO Getariako Txakolina
BILBAO
SAN SEBASTIÁN
VITORIA
Pago Señorío
de Arínzano
DO Navarra
PAMPLONA
Pago de Otazu
Pago Prado
de Irache
DOCa Rioja
DO Campo
de Borja
ZARAGOZA
SORIA
DO Cariñena
DO Calatayud
Pago de Aylés
GUADALAJARA
HUESCA
DO Somontano
LLEIDA
DO Costers
del Segre
DO Pla de Bages
DO Empordá
GIRONA
DO Catalunya
DO Alella
BARCELONA
DO Penedés
DO Conca de Barbera
DO Tarragona
DO Ca. Priorat
DO Montsant
TARRAGONA
DO Terra Alta

Pago Calzadilla
Pago
Chozas Carrascal
TERUEL
CUENCA
Pago
Los Balagueses
Pago
El Terrerazo
DO Uclés
DO Manchuela
DO Ribera
del Júcar
ALBACETE
DO Utiel
Requena
Pago Guijoso
ntino
DO Almansa
Pago Finca Élez
DO Yecla
DO Jumilla
DO Bullas
MURCIA
CASTELLÓN
VALENCIA
DO Valencia
DO Alicante
ALICANTE
DO Binissalem Mallorca
DO Pla y Llevant
PALMA DE
MALLORCA

NADA
ALMERÍA

DO CAVA

VITORIA-GASTEIZ
PAMPLONA
LOGROÑO
ZARAGOZA
LLEIDA
GIRONA
TARRAGONA
BARCELONA

BADAJOZ
VALENCIA

MAP OF VINOS DE LA TIERRA AND VINOS DE CALIDAD

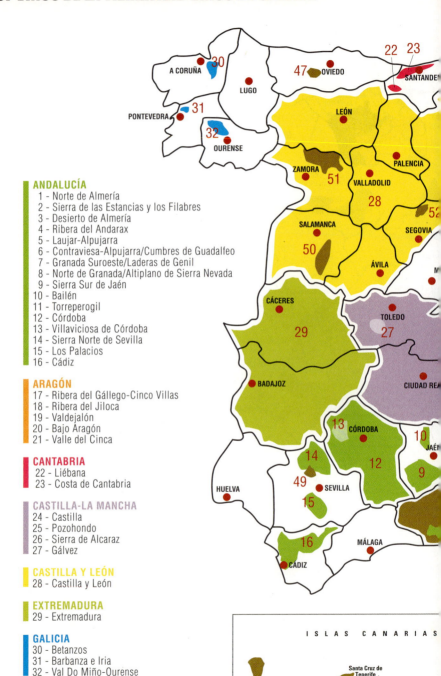

ANDALUCÍA
1 - Norte de Almería
2 - Sierra de las Estancias y los Filabres
3 - Desierto de Almería
4 - Ribera del Andarax
5 - Laujar-Alpujarra
6 - Contraviesa-Alpujarra/Cumbres de Guadalfeo
7 - Granada Suroeste/Laderas de Genil
8 - Norte de Granada/Altiplano de Sierra Nevada
9 - Sierra Sur de Jaén
10 - Bailén
11 - Torreperogil
12 - Córdoba
13 - Villaviciosa de Córdoba
14 - Sierra Norte de Sevilla
15 - Los Palacios
16 - Cádiz

ARAGÓN
17 - Ribera del Gállego-Cinco Villas
18 - Ribera del Jiloca
19 - Valdejalón
20 - Bajo Aragón
21 - Valle del Cinca

CANTABRIA
22 - Liébana
23 - Costa de Cantabria

CASTILLA-LA MANCHA
24 - Castilla
25 - Pozohondo
26 - Sierra de Alcaraz
27 - Gálvez

CASTILLA Y LEÓN
28 - Castilla y León

EXTREMADURA
29 - Extremadura

GALICIA
30 - Betanzos
31 - Barbanza e Iria
32 - Val Do Miño-Ourense

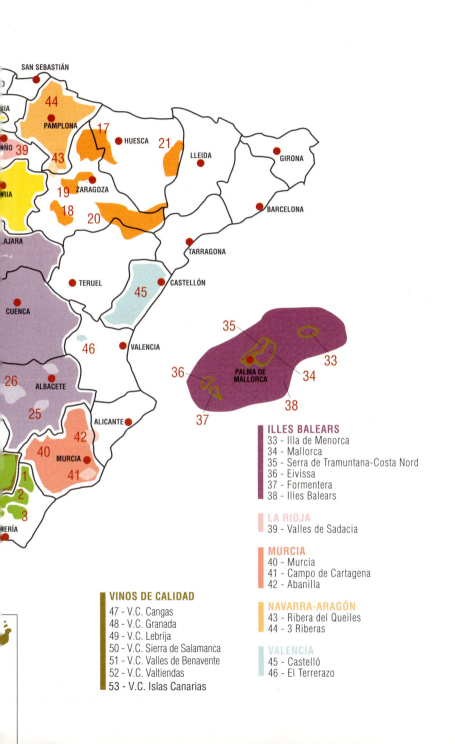

ILLES BALEARS
33 - Illa de Menorca
34 - Mallorca
35 - Serra de Tramuntana-Costa Nord
36 - Eivissa
37 - Formentera
38 - Illes Balears

LA RIOJA
39 - Valles de Sadacia

MURCIA
40 - Murcia
41 - Campo de Cartagena
42 - Abanilla

NAVARRA-ARAGÓN
43 - Ribera del Queiles
44 - 3 Riberas

VALENCIA
45 - Castelló
46 - El Terrerazo

VINOS DE CALIDAD
47 - V.C. Cangas
48 - V.C. Granada
49 - V.C. Lebrija
50 - V.C. Sierra de Salamanca
51 - V.C. Valles de Benavente
52 - V.C. Valtiendas
53 - V.C. Islas Canarias